Code of Federal Regulations

REGULATIONS

Title 12
Banks and Banking

Part 1100 to End

Revised as of January 1, 2012

Containing a codification of documents
of general applicability and future effect

As of January 1, 2012

Published by the Office of the Federal Register
National Archives and Records Administration
as a Special Edition of the Federal Register

As of January 1, 2012

Title 12, Part 900 to End

Revised as of January 1, 2011

Is Replaced by

Title 12, Parts 900 to 1099

and

Title 12, Part 1100 to End

Table of Contents

Cite this Code: CFR

To cite the regulations in this volume use title, part and section number. Thus, 12 CFR 1101.1 *refers to title 12, part 1101, section 1.*

Explanation

The Code of Federal Regulations is a codification of the general and permanent rules published in the Federal Register by the Executive departments and agencies of the Federal Government. The Code is divided into 50 titles which represent broad areas subject to Federal regulation. Each title is divided into chapters which usually bear the name of the issuing agency. Each chapter is further subdivided into parts covering specific regulatory areas.

Each volume of the Code is revised at least once each calendar year and issued on a quarterly basis approximately as follows:

Title 1 through Title 16..........as of January 1
Title 17 through Title 27..........as of April 1
Title 28 through Title 41..........as of July 1
Title 42 through Title 50..........as of October 1

The appropriate revision date is printed on the cover of each volume.

LEGAL STATUS

The contents of the Federal Register are required to be judicially noticed (44 U.S.C. 1507). The Code of Federal Regulations is prima facie evidence of the text of the original documents (44 U.S.C. 1510).

HOW TO USE THE CODE OF FEDERAL REGULATIONS

The Code of Federal Regulations is kept up to date by the individual issues of the Federal Register. These two publications must be used together to determine the latest version of any given rule.

To determine whether a Code volume has been amended since its revision date (in this case, January 1, 2012), consult the "List of CFR Sections Affected (LSA)," which is issued monthly, and the "Cumulative List of Parts Affected," which appears in the Reader Aids section of the daily Federal Register. These two lists will identify the Federal Register page number of the latest amendment of any given rule.

EFFECTIVE AND EXPIRATION DATES

Each volume of the Code contains amendments published in the Federal Register since the last revision of that volume of the Code. Source citations for the regulations are referred to by volume number and page number of the Federal Register and date of publication. Publication dates and effective dates are usually not the same and care must be exercised by the user in determining the actual effective date. In instances where the effective date is beyond the cutoff date for the Code a note has been inserted to reflect the future effective date. In those instances where a regulation published in the Federal Register states a date certain for expiration, an appropriate note will be inserted following the text.

OMB CONTROL NUMBERS

The Paperwork Reduction Act of 1980 (Pub. L. 96–511) requires Federal agencies to display an OMB control number with their information collection request.

Many agencies have begun publishing numerous OMB control numbers as amendments to existing regulations in the CFR. These OMB numbers are placed as close as possible to the applicable recordkeeping or reporting requirements.

OBSOLETE PROVISIONS

Provisions that become obsolete before the revision date stated on the cover of each volume are not carried. Code users may find the text of provisions in effect on a given date in the past by using the appropriate numerical list of sections affected. For the period before April 1, 2001, consult either the List of CFR Sections Affected, 1949–1963, 1964–1972, 1973–1985, or 1986–2000, published in eleven separate volumes. For the period beginning April 1, 2001, a "List of CFR Sections Affected" is published at the end of each CFR volume.

"[RESERVED]" TERMINOLOGY

The term "[Reserved]" is used as a place holder within the Code of Federal Regulations. An agency may add regulatory information at a "[Reserved]" location at any time. Occasionally "[Reserved]" is used editorially to indicate that a portion of the CFR was left vacant and not accidentally dropped due to a printing or computer error.

INCORPORATION BY REFERENCE

What is incorporation by reference? Incorporation by reference was established by statute and allows Federal agencies to meet the requirement to publish regulations in the Federal Register by referring to materials already published elsewhere. For an incorporation to be valid, the Director of the Federal Register must approve it. The legal effect of incorporation by reference is that the material is treated as if it were published in full in the Federal Register (5 U.S.C. 552(a)). This material, like any other properly issued regulation, has the force of law.

What is a proper incorporation by reference? The Director of the Federal Register will approve an incorporation by reference only when the requirements of 1 CFR part 51 are met. Some of the elements on which approval is based are:

(a) The incorporation will substantially reduce the volume of material published in the Federal Register.

(b) The matter incorporated is in fact available to the extent necessary to afford fairness and uniformity in the administrative process.

(c) The incorporating document is drafted and submitted for publication in accordance with 1 CFR part 51.

What if the material incorporated by reference cannot be found? If you have any problem locating or obtaining a copy of material listed as an approved incorporation by reference, please contact the agency that issued the regulation containing that incorporation. If, after contacting the agency, you find the material is not available, please notify the Director of the Federal Register, National Archives and Records Administration, 8601 Adelphi Road, College Park, MD 20740-6001, or call 202-741-6010.

CFR INDEXES AND TABULAR GUIDES

A subject index to the Code of Federal Regulations is contained in a separate volume, revised annually as of January 1, entitled CFR INDEX AND FINDING AIDS. This volume contains the Parallel Table of Authorities and Rules. A list of CFR titles, chapters, subchapters, and parts and an alphabetical list of agencies publishing in the CFR are also included in this volume.

An index to the text of "Title 3—The President" is carried within that volume.

The Federal Register Index is issued monthly in cumulative form. This index is based on a consolidation of the "Contents" entries in the daily Federal Register.

A List of CFR Sections Affected (LSA) is published monthly, keyed to the revision dates of the 50 CFR titles.

REPUBLICATION OF MATERIAL

There are no restrictions on the republication of material appearing in the Code of Federal Regulations.

INQUIRIES

For a legal interpretation or explanation of any regulation in this volume, contact the issuing agency. The issuing agency's name appears at the top of odd-numbered pages.

For inquiries concerning CFR reference assistance, call 202–741–6000 or write to the Director, Office of the Federal Register, National Archives and Records Administration, 8601 Adelphi Road, College Park, MD 20740-6001 or e-mail fedreg.info@nara.gov.

THIS TITLE

Title 12—BANKS AND BANKING is composed of nine volumes. The parts in these volumes are arranged in the following order: Parts 1–199, 200–219, 220–229, 230–299, 300–499, 500–599, 600–899, 900–1099, and 1100–end. The first volume containing parts 1–199 is comprised of chapter I—Comptroller of the Currency, Department of the Treasury. The second, third and fourth volumes containing parts 200–299 are comprised of chapter II—Federal Reserve System. The fifth volume containing parts 300–499 is comprised of chapter III—Federal Deposit Insurance Corporation and chapter IV—Export-Import Bank of the United States. The sixth volume containing parts 500–599 is comprised of chapter V—Office of Thrift Supervision, Department of the Treasury. The seventh volume containing parts 600–899 is comprised of chapter VI—Farm Credit Administration, chapter VII—National Credit Union Administration, chapter VIII—Federal Financing Bank. The eighth volume containing parts 900–1099 is comprised of chapter IX—Federal Housing Finance Board and Chapter X—Bureau of Consumer Financial Protection. The ninth volume containing parts 1100 to end is comprised of chapter XI—Federal Financial Institutions Examination Council, chapter XIV—Farm Credit System Insurance Corporation, chapter XV—Department of the Treasury, chapter XVII—Office of Federal Housing Enterprise Oversight, Department of Housing and Urban Development and chapter XVIII—Community Development Financial Institutions Fund, Department of the Treasury. The contents of these volumes represent all of the current regulations codified under this title of the CFR as of January 1, 2012.

For this volume, Jonn V. Lilyea was Chief Editor. The Code of Federal Regulations publication program is under the direction of Michael L. White, assisted by Ann Worley.

Title 12—Banks and Banking

(This book contains part 1100 to end)

CHAPTER XI—FEDERAL FINANCIAL INSTITUTIONS EXAMINATION COUNCIL

PART 1101—DESCRIPTION OF OFFICE, PROCEDURES, PUBLIC INFORMATION

AUTHORITY: 5 U.S.C. 552; 12 U.S.C. 3307.

SOURCE: 45 FR 46794, July 11, 1980, unless otherwise noted.

§ 1101.1 Scope and purpose.

This part implements the Freedom of Information Act (FOIA), 5 U.S.C. 552, with respect to the Federal Financial Institutions Examination Council (Council), and establishes related information disclosure procedures.

§ 1101.2 Authority and functions.

(a) The Council was established by the Federal Financial Institutions Examination Council Act of 1978 (Act), 12 U.S.C. 3301–3308. It is composed of the Comptroller of the Currency; the Chairman of the Federal Deposit Insurance Corporation; a Governor of the Board of Governors of the Federal Reserve System; the Chairman of the Federal Home Loan Bank Board; and the Chairman of the National Credit Union Administration Board.

(b) The statutory functions of the Council are set out at 12 U.S.C. 3305. In summary, the mission of the Council is to promote consistency and progress in federal examination and supervision of financial institutions and their affiliates. The Council is empowered to prescribe uniform principles, standards, and reporting forms and systems; make recommendations in the interest of uniformity; and conduct examiner schools open to personnel of the agencies represented on the Council and employees of state financial institutions supervisory agencies.

§ 1101.3 Organization and methods of operation.

(a) Statutory requirements relating to the Council's organization are stated in 12 U.S.C. 3303.

(b) *Council staff.* Administrative support and substantive coordination for Council activities are provided by a small staff detailed on a full-time basis from the five member agencies. The Executive Secretary and Deputy Executive Secretary of the Council supervise this staff.

(c) *Agency Liaison Group, Task Forces and Legal Advisory Group.* Most staff support in the substantive areas of the Council's duties is provided by interagency task forces and the Council's Legal Advisory Group (LAG). These task forces and the LAG are responsible for securing the services, as needed, of staff experts from the five agencies; supervising research and other investigative work for the Council; and preparing reports and recommendations for the Council. The Agency Liaison Group (ALG) is responsible for the overall coordination of the respective agencies' staff contributions to Council business. The ALG, the task forces, and the LAG are each composed of Council member agency staff serving the Council on a part-time basis.

(d) *State Liaison Committee.* Under 12 U.S.C. 3306, the Council has established a State Liaison Committee, composed of five representatives of state financial institutions supervisory agencies.

(e) *Council address.* Council offices are located at 3501 Fairfax Drive, Room B–7081a, Arlington, VA, 22226–3550.

[45 FR 46794, July 11, 1980, as amended at 53 FR 7341, Mar. 8, 1988; 75 FR 71014, Nov. 22, 2010]

§ 1101.4 Disclosure of information, policies, and records.

(a) *Statements of policy published in the Federal Register or available for public inspection and copying; indices.* Under 5 U.S.C. 552(a)(1), the Council publishes general rules, policies and interpretations in the FEDERAL REGISTER. Under 5 U.S.C. 552(a)(2), policies and interpretations adopted by the Council, including instructions to Council staff affecting members of the public, and an index to the same, are available for public inspection and copying at the office of the Executive Secretary of the Council, 3501 Fairfax Drive, Room B–7081a, Arlington, VA, 22226–3550, during regular business hours. Policies and interpretations of the Council may be withheld from disclosure under the principles stated in paragraph (b)(1) of this section.

(b) *Other records of the Council available to the public upon request; procedures*—(1) *General rule and exemptions.* Under 5 U.S.C. 552(a)(3), all other records of the Council are available to the public upon request, except to the extent exempted from disclosure as provided in this paragraph (b). Except as specifically authorized by the Council, the following records, and portions thereof, are not available to the public:

(i) A record, or portion thereof, which is specifically authorized under criteria established by an Executive Order to be kept secret in the interest of national defense or foreign policy and which is, in fact, properly classified pursuant to such Executive Order.

(ii) A record, or portion thereof, relating solely to the internal personnel rules and practices of an agency.

(iii) A record, or portion thereof, specifically exempted from disclosure by statute (other than 5 U.S.C. 552b), provided that such statute (A) requires that the matters be withheld from the public in such a manner as to leave no discretion on the issue, or (B) establishes particular criteria for withholding or refers to particular types of matters to be withheld.

(iv) A record, or portion thereof, containing trade secrets and commercial or financial information obtained from a person and privileged or confidential.

(v) An intra-agency or interagency memorandum or letter that would not be routinely available by law to a private party in litigation, including, but not limited to, memoranda, reports, and other documents prepared by the personnel of the Council or its constituent agencies, and records of deliberations of the Council and discussions of meetings of the Council, any Council Committee, or Council staff, that are not subject to 5 U.S.C. 552b (the Government in the Sunshine Act).

(vi) A personnel, medical, or similar record, including a financial record, or any portion thereof, the disclosure of which would constitute a clearly unwarranted invasion of personal privacy.

(vii) Records or information compiled for law enforcement purposes, to the extent permitted under 5 U.S.C. 552(b)(7), including records relating to a proceeding by a financial institution's state or federal regulatory agency for the issuance of a cease-and-desist order, or order of suspension or removal, or assessment of a civil money penalty and the granting, withholding, or revocation of any approval, permission, or authority.

(viii) A record, or portion thereof, containing, relating to, or derived from an examination, operating, or condition report prepared by, or on behalf of, or for the use of any state or federal agency directly or indirectly responsible for the regulation or supervision of financial institutions.

(ix) A record, or portion thereof, which contains or is related to geological and geophysical information and data, including maps, concerning wells.

(2) *Discretionary release of exempt information.* Notwithstanding the applicability of an exemption, the Council or the Council's designee may elect, under the circumstances of a particular request, to disclose all or a portion of any requested record where permitted by law. Such disclosure has no precedential significance.

(3) *Procedure for records request*—(i) *Initial request.* Requests for records shall be submitted in writing to the Executive Secretary of the Council:

(A) By sending a letter to: FFIEC, Attn: Executive Secretary, 3501 Fairfax Drive, Room B–7081a, Arlington, VA 22226–3550. Both the mailing envelope and the request should be marked "Freedom of Information Request," "FOIA Request," or the like; or

(B) By facsimile clearly marked "Freedom of Information Act Request," "FOIA Request," or the like to the Executive Secretary at (703) 562–6446; or

(C) By e-mail to the address provided on the FFIEC's World Wide Web page, found at: *http://www.ffiec.gov.* Requests must reasonably describe the records sought.

(ii) *Contents of request.* All requests should contain the following information:

(A) The name and mailing address of the requester, an electronic mail address, if available, and the telephone number at which the requester may be reached during normal business hours;

(B) A statement as to whether the information is intended for commercial use, and whether the requester is an educational or noncommercial scientific institution, or news media representative;

(C) A statement agreeing to pay all applicable fees, or a statement identifying any desired fee limitation, or a request for a waiver or reduction of fees that satisfies paragraph (b)(5)(ii)(H) of this section.

(iii) *Defective requests.* The Council need not accept or process a request that does not reasonably describe the records requested or that does not otherwise comply with the requirements of this section. The Executive Secretary may return a defective request specifying the deficiency. The requester may submit a corrected request, which will be treated as an initial request.

(iv) *Expedited processing.* (A) Where a person requesting expedited access to records has demonstrated a compelling need for the records, or where the Executive Secretary has determined to expedite the response, the Executive Secretary shall process the request as soon as practicable. To show a compelling need for expedited processing, the requester shall provide a statement demonstrating that:

(*1*) Failure to obtain the records on an expedited basis could reasonably be expected to pose an imminent threat to the life or physical safety of an individual; or

(*2*) The requester is primarily engaged in information dissemination as a main professional occupation or activity, and there is urgency to inform the public of the government activity involved in the request.

(B) The requester's statement must be certified to be true and correct to the best of the person's knowledge and belief and explain in detail the basis for requesting expedited processing.

(C) The formality of the certification required to obtain expedited treatment may be waived by the Executive Secretary as a matter of administrative discretion.

(v) *Response to initial requests.* (A) Except where the Executive Secretary has determined to expedite the processing of a request, the Executive Secretary will respond by mail or electronic mail to all properly submitted initial requests within 20 working days of receipt. The time for response may be extended up to 10 additional working days, as provided in 5 U.S.C. 552(a)(6)(B), or for other periods by agreement between the requester and the Executive Secretary.

(B) In response to a request that reasonably describes the records sought and otherwise satisfies the requirements of this section, a search shall be conducted of records in existence and maintained by the Council on the date of receipt of the request, and a review made of any responsive information located. The Executive Secretary shall notify the requester of:

(*1*) The Executive Secretary's determination of the response to the request;

(*2*) The reasons for the determination;

(*3*) If the response is a denial of an initial request or if any information is withheld, the Executive Secretary will advise the requester in writing:

(*i*) If the denial is in part or in whole;

(*ii*) The name and title of each person responsible for the denial (when other than the person signing the notification);

(*iii*) The exemptions relied on for the denial; and

(*iv*) The right of the requester to appeal the denial to the Chairman of the Council within 10 working days following the date of issuance of the notification, as specified in paragraph (b)(3)(vi) of this section.

(vi) *Appeals of responses to initial requests.* If a request is denied in whole or in part, the requester may appeal in writing, within 10 working days of the date of issuance of a denial determination. Appeals shall be submitted to the Chairman of the Council: (A) By sending a letter to: FFIEC, Attn: Executive Secretary, 3501 Fairfax Drive, Room B-

7081a, Arlington, VA, 22226–3550. Both the mailing envelope and the request should be marked "Freedom of Information Act Appeal," "FOIA Appeal," or the like; or (B) By facsimile clearly marked "Freedom of Information Act Appeal," "FOIA Appeal," or the like to the Executive Secretary at (703) 562–6446. Appeals should refer to the date and tracking number of the original request and the date of the Council's initial ruling. Appeals should include an explanation of the basis for the appeal.

(vii) *Council response to appeals.* The Chairman of the Council, or another member designated by the Chairman, will respond to all properly submitted appeals within 20 working days of actual receipt of the appeal by the Executive Secretary. The time for response may be extended up to 10 additional working days, as provided in 5 U.S.C. 552(a)(6)(B), or for other periods by agreement between the requester and the Chairman or the Chairman's designee.

(4) *Procedure for access to records if request is granted.* (i) When a request for access to records is granted, in whole or in part, a copy of the records to be disclosed will be promptly delivered to the requester or made available for inspection, whichever was requested. Inspection of records, or duplication and delivery of copies of records will be arranged so as not to interfere with their use by the Council and other users of the records.

(ii) When delivery to the requester is to be made, copies of requested records shall be sent to the requester by regular U.S. mail to the address indicated in the request, unless the Executive Secretary deems it appropriate to send the documents by another means.

(iii) The Council shall provide a copy of the record in any form or format requested if the record is readily reproducible by the Council in that form or format, but the Council need not provide more than one copy of any record to a requester.

(iv) By arrangement with the requester, the Executive Secretary may elect to send the responsive records electronically if a substantial portion of the records is in electronic format. If the information requested is subject to disclosure under the Privacy Act of 1974, 5 U.S.C. 552a, it will not be sent by electronic means unless reasonable security measures can be established.

(5) *Fees for document search, review, and duplication; waiver and reduction of fees*—(i) *Definitions*—(A) *Direct costs* means those expenditures which the Council actually incurs in searching for, duplicating, and reviewing documents to respond to a FOIA request.

(B) *Search* means all time spent looking for material that is responsive to a request, including page-by-page or line-by-line identification of material within documents. Searches may be done manually or by computer using existing programming.

(C) *Duplication* means the process of making a copy of a document necessary to respond to a FOIA request. Such copies can take the form of paper copy, microfilm, audiovisual records, or machine readable records (*e.g.*, magnetic tape or computer disk).

(D) *Review* means the process of examining documents located in response to a request that is for a commercial use (*see* paragraph (b)(5)(i)(E) of this section) to determine whether any portion of any document located is permitted to be withheld and processing such documents for disclosure.

(E) *Commercial use request* means a request from or on behalf of one who seeks information for a use or purpose that furthers the commercial, trade, or profit interests of the requester or the person on whose behalf the request is made. In determining whether a request falls within this category, the Executive Secretary will determine the use to which a requester will put the records requested and seek additional information as the Executive Secretary deems necessary.

(F) *Educational institution* means a preschool, an elementary or secondary school, an institution of undergraduate higher education, an institution of graduate higher education, an institution of professional education, and an institution of vocational education, which operates a program or programs of scholarly research.

(G) *Noncommercial scientific institution* means an institution that is not operated on a "commercial" basis as that term is referenced in paragraph (b)(5)(i)(E) of this section, and which is operated solely for the purposes of conducting scientific research, the results of which are not intended to promote any particular product or industry.

(H) *Representative of the news media* means any person or entity that gathers information of potential interest to a segment of the public, uses its editorial skills to turn the raw materials into a distinct work, and distributes that work to an audience. In this clause, the term "news" means information that is about current events or that would be of current interest to the public. Examples of news-media entities are television or radio stations broadcasting to the public at large and publishers of periodicals (but only if such entities qualify as disseminators of "news") who make their products available for purchase by or subscription by or free distribution to the general public. These examples are not all-inclusive. Moreover, as methods of news delivery evolve (for example, the adoption of the electronic dissemination of newspapers through telecommunications services), such alternative media shall be considered to be news-media entities. A freelance journalist shall be regarded as working for a news-media entity if the journalist can demonstrate a solid basis for expecting publication through that entity, whether or not the journalist is actually employed by the entity. A publication contract would present a solid basis for such an expectation; the Council may also consider the past publication record of the requester in making such a determination.

(ii) *Fees to be charged.* The Council will charge fees that recoup the full allowable direct costs it incurs. The Council may contract with the private sector to locate, reproduce, and/or disseminate records. Provided, however, that the Council has ensured that the ultimate cost to the requester is no greater than it would be if the Council performed these tasks. Fees are subject to change as costs change. In no case will the Council contract out responsibilities which the FOIA provides that it alone may discharge, such as determining the applicability of an exemption, or determining whether to waive or reduce fees.

(A) *Manual searches and review.* The Council will charge fees at the following rates for manual searches for and review of records:

(*1*) If search/review is done by clerical staff, the hourly rate for GS–7, step 5, plus 16 percent of the rate to cover benefits;

(*2*) If search/review is done by professional staff, the hourly rate for GS–13, step 5, plus 16 percent of the rate to cover benefits.

(B) *Computer searches.* The Council will charge fees at the hourly rate for GS–13, step 5, plus 16 percent of the rate to cover benefits, plus the hourly cost of operating the computer for computer searches for records.

(C) *Duplication of records.* (*1*) The per-page fee for paper copy reproduction of a document is $.25;

(*2*) The fee for documents generated by computer is the hourly rate for the computer operator (at GS 7, step 5, plus 16 percent for benefits if clerical staff, and GS 13, step 5, plus 16 percent for benefits if professional staff) plus the cost of materials (computer paper, tapes, disks, labels, etc.).

(*3*) If any other method of duplication is used, the Council will charge the actual direct cost of duplicating the documents.

(D) If search, duplication and/or review is provided by personnel of member agencies of the Council, fees will reflect their actual hourly rates, plus 16 percent for benefits.

(E) *Fees to exceed $25.* If the Council estimates that duplication and/or search fees are likely to exceed $25, it will notify the requester of the estimated amount of fees, unless the requester has indicated in advance his/her willingness to pay fees as high as those anticipated. In the case of such notification by the Council, the requester will then have the opportunity to confer with Council personnel with the object of reformulating the request to meet his/her needs at a lower cost.

(F) *Other services.* Complying with requests for special services such as certifying records as true copies or mailing records by express mail is entirely at the discretion of the Council. The Council will recover the full costs of providing such services to the extent it elects to provide them.

(G) *Restriction on assessing fees.* The Council will not charge fees to any requester, including commercial use requesters, if the cost of collecting a fee would be equal to or greater than the fee itself.

(H) *Waiving or reducing fees.* As part of the initial request for records, a requester may ask that the Council waive or reduce fees if disclosure of the records is in the public interest because it is likely to contribute significantly to public understanding of the operations or activities of the Council and is not primarily in the commercial interest of the requester. The initial request for records must also state the justification for a waiver or reduction of fees. Determinations as to a waiver or reduction of fees will be made by the Executive Secretary of the Council and the requester will be notified in writing of his/her determination. A determination not to grant a request for a waiver or reduction of fees under this paragraph may be appealed to the Chairman of the Council pursuant to the procedure set forth in paragraph (b)(3)(vi) of this section.

(iii) *Categories of requesters.* (A) Commercial use requesters. The Council will assess fees for commercial use requesters sufficient to recover the full direct costs of searching for, reviewing for release, the duplicating the records sought.

(iii) *Categories of requesters.* (A) Commercial use requesters. The Council will assess fees for commercial use requesters which recover the full direct costs of searching for, reviewing for release, the duplicating the records sought. Commercial use requesters are not entitled to two hours of free search time nor 100 free pages of reproduction of documents.

(B) Requesters who are representatives of the news media, educational and noncommercial scientific institution requesters. The Council shall provide documents to requesters in these categories for the cost of reproduction alone, excluding fees for the first 100 pages.

(C) All other requesters. The Council shall charge requesters who do not fit into any of the categories above fees which recover the full reasonable direct cost of searching for and reproducing records that are responsive to the request, except that the first 100 pages of reproduction and the first two hours of search time shall be furnished without a fee.

(D) All requesters must specifically describe records sought.

(iv) *Interest on unpaid fees.* The Council may begin assessing interest charges on an unpaid bill starting on the 31st day following the day on which the bill was sent. Interest will be at the rate prescribed in section 3717 of title 31 U.S.C. and will accrue from the date of the billing.

(iv) *Interest on unpaid fees.* The Council may begin assessing interest charges on an unpaid bill starting on the 31st day following the day on which the bill was sent. Interest will be at the rate prescribed in 31 U.S.C. 3717 and will accrue from the date of the billing.

(vi) *Aggregating requests.* A requester(s) may not file multiple requests each seeking portions of a document or documents, solely in order to avoid payment of fees. If this is done, the Council may aggregate any such requests and charge accordingly. In no case will the Council aggregate multiple requests on unrelated subjects from the same requester.

(vii) *Advance payment of fees.* The Council will not require a requester to make an assurance of payment or an advance payment unless:

(A) The Council estimates or determines that allowable charges that a requester may be required to pay are likely to exceed $250. The Council will notify the requester of the likely cost and obtain satisfactory assurance of full payment where the requester has a history of prompt payment of FOIA fees, or require an advance payment of an amount up to the full estimated charges in the case of requesters with no history of payment; or

(B) A requester has previously failed to pay a fee charged in a timely fashion. The Council may require the requester to pay the full amount owed plus any applicable interest as provided in paragraph (b)(5)(iv) of this section or demonstrate that he/she has, in fact, paid the fee, and to make an advance payment of the full amount of the estimated fee before the Council begins to process a new request or a pending request from that requester.

(C) When the Council acts under paragraph (b)(5)(vii) (A) or (B) of this section, the administrative time limits prescribed in subsection (a)(6) of the FOIA (*i.e.*, 20 working days from receipt of initial requests, plus permissible extensions of these time limits) will begin only after the Council has received the fee payments described.

(6) *Records of another agency.* If a requested record originated with or incorporates the information of another state or federal agency or department, upon receipt of a request for the record the Council will promptly inform the requester of this circumstance and immediately shall forward the request to the originating agency or department either for processing in accordance with the latter's regulations or for guidance with respect to disposition.

[45 FR 46794, July 11, 1980, as amended at 53 FR 7341, Mar. 8, 1988; 75 FR 71014, ≤Nov. 22, 2010]

§ 1101.5 Testimony and production of documents in response to subpoena, order, etc.

No person shall testify, in court or otherwise, as a result of activities on behalf of the Council without prior written authorization from the Council. This section shall not restrict the authority of a Council member to testify before Congress on matters within his or her official responsibilities as a Council member. No person shall furnish documents reflecting information of the Council in compliance with a subpoena, order, or otherwise, without prior written authorization from the Council. The Council may authorize testimony or production of documents after the litigant (or the litigant's attorney) submits an affidavit to the Council setting forth the interest of the litigant and the testimony or documents desired. Authorization to testify or produce documents is limited to authority expressly granted by the Council. When the Council has not authorized testimony or production of documents, the individual to whom the subpoena or order has been directed will appear in court and respectfully state that he or she is unable to comply further with the subpoena or order by reason of this section.

PART 1102—APPRAISER REGULATION

Subpart A—Temporary Waiver Requests

Subpart B—Rules of Practice for Proceedings

Subpart C—Rules Pertaining to the Privacy of Individuals and Systems of Records Maintained by the Appraisal Subcommittee

Subpart D—Description of Office, Procedures, Public Information

Subpart A—Temporary Waiver Requests

AUTHORITY: 12 U.S.C. 3348(b).

SOURCE: 57 FR 10982, Apr. 1, 1992, unless otherwise noted.

§ 1102.1 Authority, purpose and scope.

(a) *Authority.* This subpart is issued under section 1119(b) of Title XI of the Financial Institutions Reform, Recovery, and Enforcement Act of 1989 ("FIRREA") (12 U.S.C. § 3348(b)).

(b) *Purpose and scope.* This subpart prescribes rules of practice and procedure governing temporary waiver proceedings under Section 1119(b) of Title XI of FIRREA (12 U.S.C. 3348(b)). These procedures apply whenever a State appraiser regulatory agency requests the Appraisal Subcommittee of the Federal Financial Institutions Examination Council ("ASC") for a waiver of any requirement relating to certification or licensing of a person to perform appraisals under Title XI of FIRREA. They also apply whenever the ASC, based on sufficient, credible information or requests received from other persons or entities, initiates a temporary waiver proceeding.

§ 1102.2 Requirements for requests.

A request will not be deemed received by the ASC unless it fully and accurately sets out:

(a) If the requester is a State Appraiser Regulatory Agency, a written, duly authorized determination by the State Appraiser Regulatory Agency that there is a scarcity of State licensed or State certified appraisers leading to significant delays in obtaining appraisals in federally related transactions. The scarcity can relate to the entire State or to particular geographical or political subdivisions. In the absence of such a written determination, a State Appraiser Regulatory Agency must ask the ASC for such a determination;

(b) The requirement or requirements of State law from which relief is being sought;

(c) A description of all significant problems currently being encountered in efforts to comply with Title XI;

(d) The nature of the scarcity of certified or licensed appraisers (including supporting documentation);

(e) The extent of the delays anticipated or experienced in obtaining the services of certified or licensed appraisers (including supporting documentation);

(f) The reasons why the requester believes that the requirement or requirements are causing the scarcity of certified or licensed appraisers and the service delays; and

(g) A specific plan for expeditiously alleviating the scarcity and the service delays.

§ 1102.3 Other requests and information submissions.

The federal financial institutions regulatory agencies and the Resolution Trust Corporation, their respective regulated financial institutions, and other persons or institutions with a demonstrable interest in appraiser regulation, may ask the ASC for a determination under § 1102.2(a) of this subpart, and may ask that the ASC exercise its discretionary authority to initiate a temporary waiver proceeding. Such regulated financial institutions and other persons or institutions do not need to comply with § 1102.2(g) of this subpart, but are strongly encouraged to include meaningful suggestions and recommendations for remedying the situation. A copy of the request or informational submission shall be forwarded promptly to the State Appraiser Regulatory Agency. The ASC shall consider these submissions and requests in exercising its authority to initiate a temporary waiver procedure. When the ASC initiates a temporary waiver proceeding, these documents shall correspond to a received request under § 1102.4 of this subpart.

§ 1102.4 Notice and comment.

The ASC shall publish promptly in the FEDERAL REGISTER a notice respecting:

(a) The received request; or

(b) The ASC order initiating a temporary waiver proceeding. The notice or initiation order shall contain a concise general statement of the nature and basis for the action and shall give interested persons 30 calendar days from its publication in which to submit written data, views and arguments.

§ 1102.5 Subcommittee determination.

Within 45 calendar days of the date of the publication of the notice or initiation order in the FEDERAL REGISTER, the ASC, by order, shall either grant or deny a waiver in whole, in part, and upon specified terms and conditions, including provisions for waiver termination. Such order shall respond to comments received from interested members of the public and shall provide the reasons for the ASC's finding. The order shall be published promptly in the FEDERAL REGISTER, which, in the case of an approval order, shall be after Federal Financial Institution Examination Council concurrence. Upon the ASC's determination that an emergency exists, the ASC may issue an interim approval order simultaneously with its action under § 1120.4 of this subpart. Any ASC approval order shall be effective only upon Federal Financial Institution Examination Council concurrence.

§ 1102.6 Waiver extension.

The ASC may initiate an extension of temporary waiver relief and shall follow §§ 1102.4, 1102.5 and 1102.7 of this subpart. A State Appraiser Regulatory Agency also may request an extension of temporary waiver relief by forwarding an additional written request to the ASC. A request for an extension from State Appraiser Regulatory Agency shall be subject to all the requirements of this subpart.

§ 1102.7 Waiver termination.

The ASC at any time may terminate a waiver order on the finding that:

(a) The significant delays in obtaining the services of certified or licensed appraisers no longer exist; or

(b) The terms and conditions of the waiver order are not being satisfied. The ASC shall publish a finding of waiver termination promptly in the FEDERAL REGISTER, giving interested persons no less than 30 calendar days from publication in which to submit written data, views and arguments. In the absence of further ASC action to the contrary, the finding of waiver termination automatically shall become final 21 calendar days after the close of the comment period.

Subpart B—Rules of Practice for Proceedings

AUTHORITY: 12 U.S.C. 3332, 3335, 3347, and 3348(c).

SOURCE: 57 FR 31650, July 17, 1992, unless otherwise noted.

§ 1102.20 Authority, purpose, and scope.

(a) *Authority.* This subpart is issued under sections 1103, 1106, 1118 and 1119(c) of Title XI of the Financial Institutions Reform, Recovery, and Enforcement Act of 1989 (FIRREA) (12 U.S.C. 3332, 3335, 3347, and 3348(c)).

(b) *Purpose and scope.* This subpart prescribes rules of practice and procedure governing non-recognition proceedings under section 1118 of Title XI (12 U.S.C. 3347); and other proceedings necessary to carry out the purposes of Title XI under section 1119(c) of Title XI (12 U.S.C. 3348(c)).

[57 FR 31650, July 17, 1992, as amended at 57 FR 35004, Aug. 7, 1992]

§ 1102.21 Definitions.

As used in this subpart:

(a) *Subcommittee* or *ASC* means the Appraisal Subcommittee of the Federal Financial Institutions Examination

Council, as established under section 1011 of Title XI (12 U.S.C. 3310).

(b) *Party* means the ASC or a person, agency or other entity named as a party, including, when appropriate, persons appearing in the proceeding under § 1102.22 of this subpart.

(c) *Respondent* means any party other than the ASC.

(d) *Secretary* means the Secretary of the ASC under its Rules of Operation.

§ 1102.22 Appearance and practice before the Subcommittee.

(a) *By attorneys and notice of appearance.* Any person who is a member in good standing of the bar of the highest court of any State or of the District of Columbia, or of any possession, territory, or commonwealth of the United States, may represent parties before the ASC upon filing with the Secretary a written notice of appearance stating that he or she is currently qualified as provided in this paragraph and is authorized to represent the particular party on whose behalf he or she acts.

(b) *By non-attorneys.* An individual may appear on his or her own behalf. A member of a partnership may represent the partnership, and an officer, director or employee of any government unit, agency, institution, corporation or authority may represent that unit, agency, institution, corporation or authority. The partner, officer, director or employee must file with the Secretary a written statement that he or she has been duly authorized by the partnership, government unit, agency, institution, corporation or authority to act on its behalf. The ASC may require the representative to attach to the statement appropriate supporting documentation, such as a corporate resolution.

(c) *Conduct during proceedings.* All participants in a proceeding shall conduct themselves with dignity and in an orderly and ethical manner. The attorney or other representative of a party shall make every effort to restrain a client from improper conduct in connection with a proceeding. Improper language or conduct, refusal to comply with directions, use of dilatory tactics, or refusal to adhere to reasonable standards of orderly and ethical conduct constitute grounds for immediate exclusion from the proceeding at the direction of the ASC.

§ 1102.23 Formal requirements as to papers filed.

(a) *Form.* All papers filed under this subpart must be double-spaced and printed or typewritten on 8½″×11″ paper. All copies shall be clear and legible.

(b) *Caption.* All papers filed must include at the head thereof, or on a title page, the name of the ASC and of the filing party, the title and/or docket number of the proceeding and the subject of the particular paper.

(c) *Party names, signatures, certificates of service.* All papers filed must set forth the name, address and telephone number of the attorney or party making the filing, must be signed by the attorney or party, and must be accompanied by a certification setting forth when and how service has been made on all other parties.

(d) *Copies.* Unless otherwise specifically provided in the notice of proceeding or by the ASC during the proceeding, an original and one copy of all documents and papers shall be furnished to the Secretary.

§ 1102.24 Filing requirements.

(a) *Filing.* All papers filed with the ASC in any proceeding shall be filed with the Secretary, Appraisal Subcommittee, 2000 K Street, NW., Suite 310, Washington, DC 20006.

(b) *Manner of filing.* Unless otherwise specified by the ASC, filing may be accomplished by:

(1) Personal service;

(2) Delivering the papers to a reliable commercial courier service, overnight delivery service, or to the U.S. Post Office for Express Mail delivery; and

(3) Mailing the papers by first class, registered, or certified mail.

[57 FR 31650, July 17, 1992, as amended at 69 FR 2501, Jan. 16, 2004]

§ 1102.25 Service.

(a) *Methods; appearing party.* A serving party, who has made an appearance under § 1102.22 of this subpart, shall use one or more of the following methods of service:

(1) Personal service;

(2) Delivering the papers to a reliable commercial courier service, overnight delivery service, or to the U.S. Post Office for Express Mail delivery; and

(3) Mailing the papers by first class, registered, or certified mail.

(b) *Methods; non-appearing party.* If a party has not appeared in the proceeding in accordance with § 1102.22 of this subpart, the ASC or any other party shall make service by any of the following methods:

(1) By personal service;

(2) By delivery to a person of suitable age and discretion at the party's last known address;

(3) By registered or certified mail addressed to the party's last known address; or

(4) By any other manner reasonably calculated to give actual notice.

(c) *By the Subcommittee.* All papers required to be served by the ASC shall be served by the Secretary unless some other person shall be designated for such purpose by the ASC.

(d) *By the respondent.* All papers filed in a proceeding under this subpart shall be served by a respondent on the Secretary and each party's attorney, or, if any party is not so represented, then upon such party. Such service may be made by any of the appropriate methods specified in paragraphs (a) and (b) of this section.

§ 1102.26 When papers are deemed filed or served.

(a) *Effectiveness.* Filing and service are deemed effective:

(1) For personal service or same-day commercial courier delivery, upon actual delivery; and

(2) For overnight commercial delivery service, U.S. Express Mail delivery, or first class, registered, or certified mail, upon deposit in, or delivery to, an appropriate point of collection.

(b) *Modification.* The effective times for filing and service in paragraph (a) of this section may be modified by the ASC in the case of filing or by agreement of the parties in the case of service.

§ 1102.27 Computing time.

(a) *General rule.* In computing any period of time prescribed or allowed by this subpart, the date of the act, event or default from which the designated period of time begins to run is not included. The last day so computed is included, unless it is a Saturday, Sunday, or Federal holiday, in which event the period runs until the end of the next day which is not a Saturday, Sunday or Federal holiday. Intermediate Saturdays, Sundays, and Federal holidays shall not be included in the computation.

(b) *For service and filing responsive papers.* Whenever a time limit is measured by a prescribed period from the service of any notice or paper, the applicable time periods are calculated as follows:

(1) If service is made by first class, registered or certified mail, add three days to the prescribed period; and

(2) If service is made by express mail or overnight delivery service, add one day to the prescribed period.

§ 1102.28 Documents and exhibits in proceedings public.

Unless and until otherwise ordered by the ASC or unless otherwise provided by statute or by ASC regulation, all documents, papers and exhibits filed in connection with any proceeding, other than those that may be withheld from disclosure under applicable law, shall be placed by the Secretary in the proceeding's public file and will be available for public inspection and copying at the address set out in § 1102.24 of this subpart.

§ 1102.29 Conduct of proceedings.

(a) *In general.* Unless otherwise provided in the notice of proceedings, all proceedings under this subpart shall be conducted as hereinafter provided.

(b) *Written submissions.* All aspects of the proceeding shall be conducted by written submissions only, with the exception of oral presentations allowed under § 1102.36 of this subpart.

(c) *Disqualification.* A Subcommittee member who deems himself or herself disqualified may at any time withdraw. Upon receipt of a timely and sufficient affidavit of personal bias or disqualification of such member, the ASC will rule on the matter as a part of the record and decision in the case.

(d) *User of ASC staff.* Appropriate members of the ASC's staff who are not engaged in the performance of investigative or prosecuting functions in the proceeding may advise and assist the ASC in the consideration of the case and in the preparation of appropriate documents for its disposition.

(e) *Authority of Subcommittee Chairperson.* The Chairperson of the ASC, in consultation with other members of the ASC whenever appropriate, shall have complete charge of the proceeding and shall have the duty to conduct it in a fair and impartial manner and to take all necessary action to avoid delay in the disposition of proceedings in accordance with this subpart.

(f) *Conferences.* (1) The ASC may on its own initiative or at the request of any party, direct all parties or counsel to meet with one or more duly authorized ASC members or staff at a specified time and place, or to submit to the ASC or its designee, suggestions in writing for the purpose of considering any or all of the following:

(i) Scheduling of matters, including a timetable for the information-gathering phase of the proceeding;

(ii) Simplification and clarification of the issues;

(iii) Stipulations and admissions of fact and of the content and authenticity of documents;

(iv) Matters of which official notice will be taken; and

(v) Such other matters as may aid in the orderly disposition of the proceeding, including disclosure of the names of persons submitting affidavits or other documents and exhibits which may be introduced into the public file of the proceeding.

(2) Such conferences will not be recorded, but the Secretary shall place in the proceeding's public file a memorandum summarizing the results of the conference and shall provide a copy of the memorandum to each party. The memorandum shall control the subsequent course of the proceedings, unless the ASC for good cause shown by one or more parties to the conference, modifies those results and instructs the Secretary to place an amendatory memorandum to that effect in the public file.

(g) *Changes or extensions of time and changes of place of proceeding.* The ASC, in connection with initiating a specific proceedings under §1102.32 of this subpart, may instruct the Secretary to publish in the FEDERAL REGISTER time limits different from those specified in this subpart, and may, on its own initiative or for good cause shown, issue an exemption changing the place of the proceeding or extending any time limit prescribed by this subpart, including the date for ending the information-gathering phase of the proceeding.

(h) *Call for further briefs, memoranda, statements; reopening of matters.* The ASC may call for the production of further information upon any issue, the submission of briefs, memoranda and statements (together with written responses), and, upon appropriate notice, may reopen any aspect of the proceeding at any time prior to a decision on the matter.

[57 FR 31650, July 17, 1992, as amended at 57 FR 35004, Aug. 7, 1992]

§ 1102.30 Rules of evidence.

(a) *In general.* (1) Except as is otherwise set forth in this section, relevant, material and reliable evidence that is not unduly repetitive is admissible to the fullest extent authorized by the Administrative Procedure Act (5 U.S.C. 551 *et seq.*) and other applicable law.

(2) Evidence that would be admissible under the Federal Rules of Evidence is admissible in a proceeding conducted under this subpart.

(3) Evidence that would be inadmissible under the Federal Rules of Evidence may be deemed or ruled admissible in a proceeding conducted under this subpart if such evidence is relevant, material, reliable and not unduly repetitive.

(b) *Stipulations.* Any party may stipulate in writing as to any relevant matters of fact, law, or the authenticity of any relevant documents. The Secretary shall place such stipulations in the public file, and they shall be binding on the parties.

(c) *Official notice.* Every matter officially noticed by the ASC shall appear in the public file, unless the ASC determines that the matter must be withheld from public disclosure under applicable Federal law.

§ 1102.31 Burden of proof.

The ultimate burden of proof shall be on the respondent. The burden of going forward with a *prima facie* case shall be on the ASC.

§ 1102.32 Notice of Intention to Commence a Proceeding.

The ASC shall instruct the Secretary or other designated officer acting for the ASC to publish in the FEDERAL REGISTER a Notice of Intention To Commence A Proceeding (Notice of Intention). The Notice of Intention shall be served upon the party or parties to the proceeding and shall commence at the time of service. The Notice of Intention shall state the legal authority and jurisdiction under which the proceeding is to be held; shall contain, or incorporate by appropriate reference, a specific statement of the matters of fact or law constituting the grounds for the proceeding; and shall state a date no sooner than 25 days after service of the Notice of Intention is made for termination of the information-gathering phase of the proceeding. The Notice of Intention also must contain a bold-faced warning respecting the effect of a failure to file a Rebuttal or Notice Not To Contest under § 1102.33(d) of this subpart. The ASC may amend a Notice of Intention in any manner and to the extent consistent with provisions of applicable law.

§ 1102.33 Rebuttal or Notice Not To Contest.

(a) *When required.* A party to the proceeding may file either a Rebuttal or a Notice Not to Contest the statements contained in the Notice of Intention or any amendment thereto with the Secretary within 15 days after being served with the Notice of Intention or an amendment to such Notice. The Secretary shall place the Rebuttal or the Notice Not To Contest in the public file.

(b) *Requirements of Rebuttal; effect of failure to deny.* A Rebuttal filed under this section shall specifically admit, deny or state that the party does not have sufficient information to admit or deny each statement in the Notice of Intention. A statement of lack of information shall have the effect of a denial. Any statement not denied shall be deemed to be admitted. When a party intends to deny only a part or a qualification of a statement, the party shall admit so much of it as is true and shall deny only the remainder.

(c) *Notice Not To Contest.* A party filing a Notice Not To Contest the statement of fact set forth in the Notice of Intention shall constitute a waiver of the party's opportunity to rebut the facts alleged, and together with the Notice of Intention and any referenced documents, will provide a record basis on which the ASC shall decide the matter. The filing of a Notice Not To Contest shall not constitute a waiver of the right of such party to a judicial review of the ASC's decision, findings and conclusions.

(d) *Effect of failure to file Rebuttal or Notice Not To Contest.* Failure of a party to file a response required by this section within the time provided shall constitute a waiver of the party's opportunity to rebut and to contest the statements in the Notice of Intention and shall constitute authorization for the ASC to find the facts to be as presented in the Notice of Intention and to file with the Secretary a decision containing such findings and appropriate conclusions. The ASC, for good cause shown, will permit the filing of a Rebuttal after the prescribed time.

§ 1102.34 Briefs, memoranda and statements.

(a) *By the parties.* Until the end of the information-gathering phase of the proceeding, any party may file with the Secretary a written brief, memorandum or other statement providing factual data and policy and legal arguments regarding the matters set out in the Notice of Intention. The filing party shall simultaneously serve other parties to the proceeding with a copy of the document. No later than ten days after such service, any party may file with the Secretary a written response to the document and must simultaneously serve a copy thereof on the other parties to the proceeding. The Secretary will receive documents and responses and will place them in the public file.

(b) *By interested persons, in non-recognition proceedings.* Until the end of the information-gathering phase of a proceeding under section 1118 of FIRREA (12 U.S.C. 3347), any person with a demonstrable, direct interest in the outcome of the proceeding may file with the Secretary a written brief, memorandum or other statement providing factual data and policy and legal arguments regarding the matters set out in the Notice of Intention. The ASC's Chairperson or his or her designee may not accept any such written brief, memorandum or other statement if the submitting person cannot demonstrate a direct interest in the outcome of the proceeding. Upon acceptance of the written brief, memorandum or other statement, the Secretary shall make copies of the document and forward one copy thereof to each party to the proceeding. No later than ten days after such service, any party may file with the Secretary a written response to the document and must simultaneously serve one copy thereof on the other parties to the proceeding. The Secretary will place a copy of such briefs, memoranda, statements and responses in the public file.

§ 1102.35 Opportunity for informal settlement.

Any party may at any time submit to the Secretary, for consideration by the Subcommittee, written offers or proposals for settlement of a proceeding, without prejudice to the rights of the parties. No offer or proposal shall be included in the proceeding's public file over the objection of any party to such proceeding. This paragraph shall not preclude settlement of any proceeding by the filing of a Notice Not To Contest as provided in § 1102.33(c) or by the submission of the case to the ASC on a stipulation of facts.

§ 1102.36 Oral presentations.

(a) *In general.* A party does not have a right to an oral presentation. Under this section, a party's request to make an oral presentation may be denied if such a denial is appropriate and reasonable under the circumstances. An oral presentation shall be considered as an opportunity to offer, emphasize and clarify the facts, policies and laws concerning the proceeding.

(b) *Method and time of request.* Between the commencement of the proceeding and ten days before the end of the information-gathering phase, any party to the proceeding may file with the Secretary a letter requesting that the Secretary schedule an opportunity for the party to give an oral presentation to the ASC. That letter shall include the reasons why an oral presentation is necessary.

(c) *ASC processing.* The Secretary must promptly forward the letter request to the Chairman of the ASC. The Chairman, after informally contacting other ASC members and the ASC's senior staff for their views, will instruct the Secretary to forward a letter to the party either: Scheduling a date and time for the oral presentation and specifying the allowable duration of the presentation; or declining the request and providing the reasons therefor. The party's letter request and the ASC's response will be included in the proceeding's public file.

(d) *Procedure on presentation day.* On the appropriate date and time, the party or his or her attorney (if any) will make the oral presentation before the ASC. Any ASC member may ask the party or the attorney, as the case may be, pertinent questions relating to the content of the oral presentation. Oral presentations will not be recorded or otherwise transcribed. The Secretary must enter promptly into the proceeding's public file a memorandum summarizing the subjects discussed during the oral presentation.

§ 1102.37 Decision of the Subcommittee and judicial review.

At a reasonable time after the end of the information-gathering phase of the proceeding, but not exceeding 35 days, the ASC shall issue a final decision, containing specified terms and conditions as it deems appropriate, in the matter and shall cause the decision to be published promptly in the FEDERAL REGISTER. The final decision shall be effective on issuance. The Secretary shall serve the decision upon the parties promptly, shall place it in the proceeding's public file and shall furnish it to such other persons as the ASC may direct. Pursuant to the provisions of chapter 7 of title 5 of the U.S. Code and section 1118(c)(3) of title XI of FIRREA (12 U.S.C. 3348(c)(3)), a final decision of the ASC is a prerequisite to seeking judicial review.

§1102.38 Compliance activities.

(a) Where, from complaints received from members of the public, communications from Federal or State agencies, examination of information by the ASC, or otherwise, it appears that a person has violated, is violating or is about to violate title XI of FIRREA or the rules or regulations thereunder, the ASC staff may commence an informal, preliminary inquiry into the matter. If, upon such inquiry, it appears that one or more allegations relate to possible violations of regulations administered by another agency or instrumentality of the Federal Government, then the matter shall be referred to that agency or instrumentality for appropriate action. The ASC, pursuant to its responsibilities under section 1103(a)(2) of title XI (12 U.S.C. 3332(a)(2)) and section 1119(c) of title XI (12 U.S.C. 3348)), shall monitor the matter. If, upon inquiry, it appears that one or more allegations are within the ASC's jurisdiction, then the ASC, in its discretion, may determine to commence a formal investigation respecting the matter and shall instruct the Secretary to create a public file for the formal investigation. The Secretary shall place in that file a memorandum naming the person or persons subject to the investigation and the statutory basis for the investigation.

(b) Unless otherwise instructed by the ASC or required by law, the Secretary shall ensure that all other papers, documents and materials gathered or submitted in connection with the investigation are non-public and for ASC use only.

(c) Persons who become involved in preliminary inquiries or formal investigations may, on their own initiative, submit a written statement to the Secretary setting forth their interests, positions or views regarding the subject matter of the investigation. Upon request, the staff, in its discretion, may advise such persons of the general nature of the investigation, including the indicated violations as they pertain to them and the amount of time that may be available for preparing and submitting such a statement prior to the presentation of a staff recommendation to the ASC. Upon the commencement of a formal investigation or a proceeding under this subpart, the Secretary shall place any such statement in the appropriate public file.

(d) In instances where the staff has concluded its inquiry of a particular matter and has determined that it will not recommend the commencement of a formal investigation or a proceeding under this subpart against a person, the staff shall advise the person that its inquiry has been terminated. Such advice, if given, must in no way be construed as indicating that the person has been exonerated or that no action may ultimately result from the staff's inquiry into the particular matter.

§1102.39 Duty to cooperate.

In the course of the investigations and proceedings, the ASC (and its staff, with appropriate authorization) must provide parties or persons ample opportunity to work out problems by consent, by settlement, or in some other manner.

Subpart C—Rules Pertaining to the Privacy of Individuals and Systems of Records Maintained by the Appraisal Subcommittee

AUTHORITY: Privacy Act of 1974, Pub. L. 93–579, 88 Stat. 1896; 12 U.S.C. 552a, as amended.

SOURCE: 57 FR 36357, Aug. 13, 1992, unless otherwise noted.

§1102.100 Authority, purpose and scope.

(a) This subpart is issued under the Privacy Act of 1974, Public Law 93–579, 88 Stat. 1896; 12 U.S.C. 552a, as amended.

(b) The Privacy Act of 1974 is based, in part, on the finding by Congress that "in order to protect the privacy of individuals identified in information systems maintained by Federal agencies, it is necessary and proper for the Congress to regulate the collection, maintenance, use, and dissemination of information by such agencies." To achieve this objective, the Act generally provides that Federal agencies must advise an individual upon request whether records maintained by the agency in a system of records pertain to the individual and must grant the individual access to such records. The Act further provides that individuals may request amendments to records pertaining to them that are maintained by the agency, and that the agency shall either grant the requested amendments or set forth fully its reasons for refusing to do so.

(c) The Appraisal Subcommittee of the Federal Financial Institutions Examination Council (ASC), pursuant to subsection (f) of the Privacy Act, adopts the following rules and procedures to implement the provisions of the Act summarized above and other provisions of the Act. These rules and procedures are applicable to all requests for information and access or amendment to records pertaining to an individual that are contained in any system of records that is maintained by the ASC.

§ 1102.101 Definitions.

The following definitions shall apply for purposes of this subpart:

(a) The terms *individual, maintain, record, system of records*, and *routine use* are defined for purposes of these rules as they are defined in 5 U.S.C. 552a(a)(2), (a)(3), (a)(4), (a)(5) and (a)(7).

(b) *ASC* or *Subcommittee* means the Appraisal Subcommittee of the Federal Financial Institutions Examination Council.

(c) *Privacy Act Officer* means the ASC's Associate Director for Administration or such other ASC staff officer, other than the Executive Director, duly designated by the ASC's Executive Director.

§ 1102.102 Times, places and requirements for requests pertaining to individual records in a record system and for the identification of individuals making requests for access to records pertaining to them.

(a) *Place to make request.* Any request by an individual to be advised whether any system of records maintained by the ASC and named by the individual contains a record pertaining to him or her, or any request by an individual for access to a record pertaining to him or her that is contained in a system of records maintained by the ASC, shall be submitted in person at the ASC between 9 a.m. and 4:30 p.m., Monday through Friday, which is located at 1401 H Street, NW., Suite 760,Washington, DC 20005, or by mail addressed to: Privacy Act Officer, ASC, 1401 H Street, NW., Suite 760,Washington, DC 20005. All requests will be required to be put in writing and signed by the individual making the request. In the case of requests for access that are made by mail, the envelope should be clearly marked "Privacy Act Request."

(1) *Information to be included in requests.* Each request by an individual concerning whether the ASC maintains in a system of records a record that pertains to the individual, or for access to any record pertaining to the individual that is maintained by the ASC in a system of records, shall include such information as will assist the ASC in identifying those records as to which the individual is seeking information or access. Where practicable, the individual should identify the system of records that is the subject of his or her request by reference to the ASC's notices of systems of records, which are published in the FEDERAL REGISTER, as required by section (e)(4) of the Privacy Act, 5 U.S.C. 552a(e)(4). Where a system of records is compiled on the basis of a specific identification scheme, the individual should include in his or her request the identification number or other identifier assigned to the individual. In the event the individual does not know that number or identifier, the individual shall provide other information, including his or her full name, address, date of birth and subject matter of the record, to aid in processing his or her request. If additional information is required before a request can be processed, the individual shall be so advised.

(2) *Verification of identity.* When the fact of the existence of a record is not required to be disclosed under the Freedom of Information Act, 5 U.S.C. 552, as amended, or when a record as to which access has been requested is not required to be disclosed under that Act, the individual seeking the information or requesting access to the record shall be required to verify his or her identity

before access will be granted or information given. For this purpose, individuals shall appear at the ASC located at 1401 H Street, NW., Suite 760,Washington, DC 20005, between 9 a.m. to 4:30 p.m., Monday through Friday. The ASC's Office is not open on Saturdays, Sundays or Federal holidays.

(3) *Methods for verifying identity—appearance in person.* For the purpose of verifying identity, an individual seeking information regarding pertinent records or access to those records shall furnish documentation that may reasonably be relied on to establish the individual's identity. Such documentation might include a valid birth certificate, driver's license, employee or military identification card, and medicare card.

(4) *Method for verifying identity—by mail.* Where an individual cannot appear at the ASC's Office for the purpose of verifying identity, the individual shall submit, along with the request for information or access, a signed and notarized statement attesting to his or her identity. Where access is being sought, the sworn statement shall include a representation that the records being sought pertain to the individual and a stipulation that the individual is aware that knowingly and willfully requesting or obtaining records pertaining to an individual from the ASC under false pretenses is a criminal offense.

(5) *Additional procedures for verifying identity.* When it appears appropriate to the Privacy Act Officer, other arrangements may be made for the verification of identity as are reasonable under the circumstances and appear to be effective to prevent unauthorized disclosure of, or access to, individual records.

(b) *Acknowledgement of requests for information pertaining to individual records in a record system or for access to individual records.* (1) Except where an immediate acknowledgement is given for requests made in person, the receipt of a request for information pertaining to individual records in a record system will be acknowledged within 10 days, excluding Saturdays, Sundays and Federal holidays. Requests will be processed as promptly as possible and a response to such requests will be given within 30 days (excluding Saturdays, Sundays, and Federal holidays) unless, within the 30 day period and for cause shown, the individual making the request is notified in writing that a longer period is necessary.

[57 FR 36357, Aug. 13, 1992, as amended at 69 FR 2501, Jan. 16, 2004; 75 FR 36270, June 25, 2010]

§1102.103 Disclosure of requested records.

(a) *Initial review.* Requests by individuals for access to records pertaining to them will be referred to the ASC's Privacy Act Officer, who initially will determine whether access will be granted.

(b) *Grant of request for access.* (1) If it is determined that a request for access to records pertaining to an individual will be granted, the individual will be advised by mail that access will be given at the ASC or a copy of the requested record will be provided by mail if the individual shall so indicate. Where the individual requests that copies of the record be mailed to or her or requests copies of a record upon reviewing it at the ASC, the individual shall pay the cost of making requested copies, as set forth in §1102.109 of this subpart.

(2) In granting access to an individual to a record pertaining to him or her, the ASC staff shall take steps to prevent the unauthorized disclosure of information pertaining to other individuals.

(c) *Denial of request for access.* If it is determined that access will not be granted, the individual making the request will be notified of that fact and given the reasons why access is being denied. The individual also will be advised of his or her right to seek review by the Executive Director of the initial decision to deny access, in accordance with the procedures set forth in §1102.107 of this subpart.

(d) *Time for acting on requests for access.* Access to a record pertaining to an individual normally will be granted or denied within 30 days (excluding Saturdays, Sundays, and Federal holidays) after the receipt of the request for access, unless the individual making the request is notified in writing within the 30 day period that, for good cause shown, a longer time is required. In such cases, the individual making the request shall be informed in writing of the difficulties encountered and an indication shall be given as to when it is anticipated that access may be granted or denied.

(e) *Authorization to allow designated person to review and discuss records pertaining to another individual.* An individual, who is granted access to records pertaining to him or her and who appears at the ASC Office to review the records, may be accompanied by another person of his or her choosing. Where the records as to which access has been granted are not required to be disclosed under provisions of the Freedom of Information Act, 5 U.S.C. 552, as amended, the individual requesting the records, before being granted access, shall execute a written statement, signed by him or her, specifically authorizing the latter individual to review and discuss the records. If such authorization has not been given as described, the person who has accompanied the individual making the request will be excluded from any review or discussion of the records.

(f) *Exclusion for certain records.* Nothing contained in these rules shall allow an individual access to any information compiled in reasonable anticipation of an administrative judicial or civil action or proceeding.

§ 1102.104 Special procedure: Medical records.

(a) *Statement of physician or mental health professional.* When an individual requests access to records pertaining to the individual that include medical and/or psychological information, the ASC, if it deems it necessary under the particular circumstances, may require the individual to submit with the request a signed statement by the individual's physician or a mental health professional indicating that, in his or her opinion, disclosure of the requested records or information directly to the individual will not have an adverse effect on the individual.

(b) *Designation of physician or mental health professional to receive records.* If the ASC believes, in good faith, that disclosure of medical and/or psychological information, directly to an individual could have an adverse effect on that individual, the individual may be asked to designate in writing a physician or mental health professional to whom the individual would like the records to be disclosed, and disclosure that otherwise would be made to the individual will instead be made to the designated physician or mental health professional.

§ 1102.105 Requests for amendment of records.

(a) *Place to make requests.* A request by an individual to amend records pertaining to him or her may be made in person during normal business hours at the ASC located at 2000 K Street, NW., Suite 310, Washington, DC , or by mail addressed to the Privacy Act Officer, ASC, 1401 H Street, NW., Suite 760,Washington, DC 20005.

(1) *Information to be included in requests.* Each request to amend an ASC record shall reasonably describe the record sought to be amended. Such description should include, for example, relevant names, dates and subject matter to permit the record to be located among the records maintained by the ASC. An individual who has requested that a record pertaining to the individual be amended will be advised promptly if the record cannot be located on the basis of the description given and that further identifying information is necessary before the request can be processed. An initial evaluation of a request presented in person will be made immediately to ensure that the request is complete and to indicate what, if any, additional information will be required. Verification of the individual's identity as set forth in § 1102.102(a) (2), (3), (4) and (5) may also be required.

(2) *Basis for amendment.* An individual requesting an amendment to a record pertaining to the individual shall specify the substance of the amendment and set forth facts and provide such materials that would support his or her contention that the record as maintained by the ASC is not accurate, timely or complete, or that the record is not necessary and relevant to accomplish a statutory purpose of the ASC as authorized by law or by Executive Order of the President.

(b) *Acknowledgement of requests for amendment.* Receipt of a request to amend a record pertaining to an individual normally will be acknowledged in writing within 10 days after such request has been received, excluding Saturdays, Sundays and Federal holidays. When a request to amend is made in person, the individual making the request will be given a written acknowledgement when the request is presented. The acknowledgement will describe the request received and indicate when it is anticipated that action will be taken on the request. No acknowledgement will be sent when the request for amendment will be reviewed, and an initial decision made, within the 10 day period after such request has been received.

[57 FR 36357, Aug. 13, 1992, as amended at 69 FR 2501, Jan. 16, 2004; 75 FR 36270, June 25, 2010]

§ 1102.106 Review of requests for amendment.

(a) *Initial review.* As in the case of requests for access, requests by individuals for amendment to records pertaining to them will be referred to the ASC's Privacy Act Officer for an initial determination.

(b) *Standards to be applied in reviewing requests.* In reviewing requests to amend records, the Privacy Act Officer will be guided by the criteria set forth in 5 U.S.C. 552(e) (1) and (5), *i.e.*, that records maintained by the ASC shall contain only such information as is necessary and relevant to accomplish a statutory purpose of the ASC as required by statute or Executive Order of the President and that such information also be accurate, timely, relevant and complete. These criteria will be applied whether the request is to add material to a record or to delete information from a record.

(c) *Time for acting on requests.* Initial review of a request by an individual to amend a record shall be completed as promptly as is reasonably possible and normally within 30 days (excluding Saturdays, Sundays, and Federal holidays) from the date the request was received, unless unusual circumstances preclude completion of review within that time. If the anticipated completion date indicated in the acknowledgement cannot be met, the individual requesting the amendment will be advised in writing of the delay and the reasons therefor, and also advised when action is expected to be completed.

(d) *Grant of requests to amend records.* If a request to amend a record is granted in whole or in part, the Privacy Act Officer will:

(1) Advise the individual making the request in writing of the extent to which it has been granted;

(2) Amend the record accordingly; and

(3) Where an accounting of disclosures of the record has been kept pursuant to 5 U.S.C. 552a(c), advise all previous recipients of the record of the fact that the record has been amended and the substance of the amendment.

(e) *Denial of requests to amend records.* If an individual's request to amend a record pertaining to him is denied in whole or in part, the Privacy Act Officer will:

(1) Promptly advise the individual making the request in writing of the extent to which the request has been denied;

(2) State the reasons for the denial of the request;

(3) Describe the procedures established by the ASC to obtain further review within the ASC of the request to amend, including the name and address of the person to whom the appeal is to be addressed; and

(4) Inform the individual that the Privacy Act Officer will provide information and assistance to the individual in perfecting an appeal of the initial decision.

§ 1102.107 Appeal of initial adverse agency determination regarding access or amendment.

(a) *Administrative review.* Any person who has been notified pursuant to § 1102.103(c) that a request for access to records pertaining to him or her has been denied in whole or in part, or pursuant to § 1102.106(e) of this subpart that a request for amendment has been denied in whole or in part, or who has received no response to a request for access or to amend within 30 days (excluding Saturdays, Sundays and Federal holidays) after the request was received by the ASC's staff (or within such extended period as may be permitted in accordance with §§ 1102.103(d) and 1102.106(c) of this subpart), may appeal the adverse determination or failure to respond by applying for an order of the Executive Director determining and directing that access to the record be granted or that the record be amended in accordance with his or her request.

(1) The application shall be in writing and shall describe the record in issue and set forth the proposed amendment and the reasons therefor.

(2) The application shall be delivered to the ASC, 2000 K Street, NW., Suite 310, Washington, DC, or by mail addressed to the Privacy Act Officer, ASC, 1401 H Street, NW., Suite 760,Washington, DC 20005.

(3) The applicant may state such facts and cite such legal or other authorities in support of the application.

(4) The Executive Director will make a determination with respect to any appeal within 30 days after the receipt of such appeal (excluding Saturdays, Sundays, and Federal holidays), unless for good cause shown, the Executive Director shall extend that period. If such an extension is made, the individual who is appealing shall be advised in writing of the extension, the reasons therefor, and the anticipated date when the appeal will be decided.

(5) In considering an appeal from a denial of a request to amend a record, the Executive Director shall apply the same standards as set forth in § 1102.106(b).

(6) If the Executive Director concludes that access should be granted, the Executive Director shall issue an order granting access and instructing the Privacy Act Officer to comply with § 1102.103(b).

(7) If the Executive Director concludes that the request to amend the record should be granted in whole or in part, the Executive Director shall issue an order granting the requested amendment in whole or in part and instructing the Privacy Act Officer to comply with the requirements of § 1102.106(d) of this subpart, to the extent applicable.

(8) If the Executive Director affirms the initial decision denying access, the Executive Director shall issue an order denying access and advising the individual seeking access of:

(i) The order;

(ii) The reasons for denying access; and

(iii) The individual's right to obtain judicial review of the decision pursuant to 5 U.S.C. 552a(g)(1)(B).

(9) If the Executive Director determines that the decision of the Privacy Act Officer denying a request to amend a record should be upheld, the Executive Director shall issue an order denying the request and the individual shall be advised of:

(i) The order refusing to amend the record and the reasons therefor;

(ii) The individual's right to file a concise statement setting forth his or her disagreement with the Executive Director's decision not to amend the record;

(iii) The procedures for filing such a statement of disagreement with the Executive Director;

(iv) The fact that any such statement of disagreement will be made available to anyone to whom the record is disclosed, together with, if the Executive Director deems it appropriate, a brief statement setting forth the Executive Director's reasons for refusing to amend;

(v) The fact that prior recipients of the record in issue will be provided with the statement of disagreement and the Executive Director's statement, if any, to the extent that an accounting of such disclosures has been maintained pursuant to 5 U.S.C. 552a(c); and

(vi) The individual's right to seek judicial review of the Executive Director's refusal to amend, pursuant to 5 U.S.C. 552a(g)(1)(A).

(b) *Statement of disagreement.* As noted in paragraph (a)(9)(ii) of this section, an individual may file with the Executive Director a statement setting forth his or her disagreement with the Executive Director's denial of his or her request to amend a record.

(1) Such statement of disagreement shall be delivered to the ASC, 1401 H Street, NW., Suite 760,Washington, DC 20005, within 30 days after receipt by

the individual of the Executive Director's order denying the amendment, excluding Saturdays, Sundays and Federal holidays. For good cause shown, this period can be extended for a reasonable time.

(2) Such statement of disagreement shall concisely state the basis for the individual's disagreement. Unduly lengthy or irrelevant materials will be returned to the individual by the Executive Director for appropriate revisions before they become a permanent part of the individual's record.

(3) The record about which a statement of disagreement has been filed will clearly note which part of the record is disputed and the Executive Director will provide copies of the statement of disagreement and, if the Executive Director deems it appropriate, provide a concise statement of his or her reasons for refusing to amend the record, to persons or other agencies to whom the record has been or will be disclosed.

[57 FR 36357, Aug. 13, 1992, as amended at 69 FR 2501, Jan. 16, 2004; 75 FR 36270, June 25, 2010]

§ 1102.108 General provisions.

(a) *Extensions of time.* Pursuant to §§ 1102.103(b), 1102.104(d), 1102.109(c) and 1102.109(a)(4) of this subpart, the time within which a request for information, access or amendment by an individual with respect to records maintained by the ASC that pertain to him or her normally would be processed may be extended for good cause shown or because of unusual circumstances. As used in these rules, *good cause* and *unusual circumstances* shall include, but only to the extent reasonably necessary to the proper processing of a particular request:

(1) The need to search for and collect the requested records from establishments that are separate from the ASC. Some records of the ASC may be stored in Federal Records Centers in accordance with law—including many of the documents that have been on file with the ASC for more than 2 years—and cannot be made available promptly. Any person who has requested for personal examination a record stored at the Federal Records Center will be notified when the record will be made available.

(2) The need to search for, collect, and appropriately examine a voluminous amount of separate and distinct records which may be demanded in a single request. While every reasonable effort will be made to comply fully with each request as promptly as possible on a first-come, first-served basis, work done to search for, collect and appropriately examine records in response to a request for a large number of records will be contingent upon the availability of processing personnel in accordance with an equitable allocation of time to all members of the public who have requested or wish to request records.

(3) The need for consultation, which shall be conducted with all practicable speed, with another agency having a substantial interest in the determination of the request, or among two or more components within the ASC having substantial subject-matter interest herein.

(b) *Effective date of action.* Whenever it is provided in this subpart that an acknowledgement or response to a request will be given by specific times, deposit in the mails of such acknowledgement or response by that time, addressed to the person making the request, will be deemed full compliance.

(c) *Records in use by a member of the ASC or its staff.* Although every effort will be made to make a record in use by a member of the ASC or its staff available when requested, it may occasionally be necessary to delay making such a record available when doing so at the time the request is made would seriously interfere with the work of the ASC or its staff.

(d) *Missing or lost records.* Any person who has requested a record or a copy of a record pertaining to him or her will be notified if the record sought cannot be found. If the person so requests, he or she will be notified if the record subsequently is found.

(e) *Oral requests; misdirected written requests*—(1) *Telephone and other oral requests.* Before responding to any request by an individual for information concerning whether records maintained by the ASC in a system of records pertain to the individual or to any request for access to records by an individual, such request must be in writing and signed by the individual making the request. The Executive Director will not entertain any appeal from an alleged denial of failure to comply with an oral request. Any person who has made an oral request for information or access to records who believes that the request has been improperly denied should resubmit the request in appropriate written form to obtain proper consideration and, if need be, administrative review.

(2) *Misdirected written requests.* The ASC cannot assure that a timely or satisfactory response will be given to written requests for information, access or amendment by an individual with respect to records pertaining to him or her that are directed to the ASC other than in a manner prescribed in §§ 1102.103(a), 1102.106(a), 1102.108(a)(2), and 1102.110 of this subpart. Any staff member who receives a written request for information, access or amendment should promptly forward the request to the Privacy Act Officer. Misdirected requests for records will be considered to have been received by the ASC only when they have been actually received by the Privacy Act Officer in cases under § 1102.108(a)(2). The Executive Director will not entertain any appeal from an alleged denial or failure to comply with a misdirected request, unless it is clearly shown that the request was in fact received by the Privacy Act Officer.

§ 1102.109 Fees.

(a) There will be no charge assessed to the individual for the ASC's expense involved in searching for or reviewing the record. Copies of the ASC's records will be provided by a commercial copier at rates established by a contract between the copier and the ASC or by the ASC at the rates in § 1101.4(b)(5)(ii) of 12 CFR part 1101.

(b) *Waiver or reduction of fees.* Whenever the Executive Director of the ASC determines that good cause exists to grant a request for reduction or waiver of fees for copying documents, he or she may reduce or waive any such fees.

§ 1102.110 Penalties.

Title 18 U.S.C. 1001 makes it a criminal offense, subject to a maximum fine of $10,000, or imprisonment for not more than 5 years or both, to knowingly and willingly make or cause to be made any false or fraudulent statements or representations in any matter within the jurisdiction of any agency of the United States. 5 U.S.C. 552a(i) makes it a misdemeanor punishable by a fine of not more than $5,000 for any person knowingly and willfully to request or obtain any record concerning an individual from the ASC under false pretenses. 5 U.S.C. 552a(i) (1) and (2) provide criminal penalties for certain violations of the Privacy Act by officers and employees of the ASC.

Subpart D—Description of Office, Procedures, Public Information

AUTHORITY: 5 U.S.C. 552, 553(e); and Executive Order 12600, 52 FR 23781 (3 CFR, 1987 Comp., p. 235).

SOURCE: 57 FR 60724, Dec. 22, 1992, unless otherwise noted.

§ 1102.300 Purpose and scope.

This part sets forth the basic policies of the Appraisal Subcommittee of the Federal Financial Institutions Examination Council ("ASC") regarding information it maintains and the procedures for obtaining access to such information. This part does not apply to the Federal Financial Institutions Examination Council. Section 1102.301 sets forth definitions applicable to this part 1102, subpart D. Section 1102.302 describes the ASC's statutory authority and functions. Section 1102.303 describes the ASC's organization and methods of operation. Section 1102.304 describes the types of information and documents typically published in the FEDERAL REGISTER. Section 1102.305 explains how to access public records maintained on the ASC's World Wide Web site and at the ASC's office and describes the categories of records generally found there. Section 1102.306 implements the Freedom of Information Act ("FOIA") (5 U.S.C. 552). Section 1102.307 authorizes the discretionary disclosure of exempt records under certain limited circumstances. Section

1102.308 provides anyone with the right to petition the ASC to issue, amend, and repeal rules of general application. Section 1102.309 sets out the ASC's confidential treatment procedures. Section 1102.310 outlines procedures for serving a subpoena or other legal process to obtain information maintained by the ASC.

[64 FR 72496, Dec. 28, 1999]

§ 1102.301 Definitions.

For purposes of this subpart:

(a) *ASC* means the Appraisal Subcommittee of the Federal Financial Institutions Examination Council.

(b) *Commercial use request* means a request from, or on behalf of, a requester who seeks records for a use or purpose that furthers the commercial, trade, or profit interests of the requester or the person on whose behalf the request is made. In determining whether a request falls within this category, the ASC will determine the use to which a requester will put the records requested and seek additional information as it deems necessary.

(c) *Direct costs* means those expenditures the ASC actually incurs in searching for, duplicating, and, in the case of commercial requesters, reviewing records in response to a request for records.

(d) *Disclose or disclosure* mean to give access to a record, whether by producing the written record or by oral discussion of its contents. Where the ASC member or employee authorized to release ASC documents makes a determination that furnishing copies of the documents is necessary, these words include the furnishing of copies of documents or records.

(e) *Duplication* means the process of making a copy of a record necessary to respond to a request for records or for inspection of original records that contain exempt material or that cannot otherwise be directly inspected. Such copies can take the form of paper copy, microfilm, audiovisual records, or machine readable records (*e.g.*, magnetic tape or computer disk).

(f) *Educational institution* means a preschool, a public or private elementary or secondary school, an institution of undergraduate or graduate higher education, an institution of professional education, and an institution of vocational education, which operates a program or programs of scholarly research.

(g) *Field review* includes, but is not limited to, formal and informal investigations of potential irregularities occurring at State appraiser regulatory agencies involving suspected violations of Federal or State civil or criminal laws, as well as such other investigations as may conducted pursuant to law.

(h) *Non-commercial scientific institution* means an institution that is not operated on a commercial basis as that term is defined in paragraph (b) of this section, and which is operated solely for the purpose of conducting scientific research, the results of which are not intended to promote any particular product or industry.

(i) *Record* includes records, files, documents, reports correspondence, books, and accounts, or any portion thereof, in any form the ASC regularly maintains them.

(j) *Representative of the news media* means any person primarily engaged in gathering news for, or a free-lance journalist who can demonstrate a reasonable expectation of having his or her work product published or broadcast by, an entity that is organized and operated to publish or broadcast news to the public. The term news means information that is about current events or that would be of current interest to the general public.

(k) *Review* means the process of examining documents located in a response to a request that is for a commercial use to determine whether any portion of any document located is permitted to be withheld. It also includes processing any documents for disclosure, *e.g*, doing all that is necessary to excise them and otherwise prepare them for release. Review does not include time spent resolving general legal or policy issues regarding the application of exemptions.

(l) *Search* includes all time spent looking for material that is responsive to a request, including page-by-page or line-by-line identification of material within records. Searches may be done manually and/or by computer using existing programming.

(m) *State appraiser regulatory agency* includes, but is not limited to, any board, commission, individual or other entity that is authorized by State law to license, certify, and supervise the activities or persons authorized to perform appraisals in connections with federally related transactions and real estate related financial transactions that require the services of a State licensed or certified appraiser.

[64 FR 72496, Dec. 28, 1999]

§ 1102.302 ASC authority and functions.

(a) *Authority.* The ASC was established on August 9, 1989, pursuant to title XI of the Financial Institutions Reform, Recovery, and Enforcement Act of 1989, as amended ("FIRREA"), 12 U.S.C. 3331 and 3310 through 3351. Title XI is intended "to provide that Federal financial and public policy interests in real estate related transactions will be protected by requiring that real estate appraisals utilized in connection with federally related transactions are performed in writing, in accordance with uniform standards, by individuals whose competency has been demonstrated and whose professional conduct will be subject to effective supervision." 12 U.S.C. 3331.

(b) *Functions.* The ASC's statutory functions are generally set out in 12 U.S.C. 3332. In summary, the ASC must:

(1) Monitor the requirements established by the States for the certification and licensing of individuals who are qualified to perform appraisals in connection with federally related transactions, including a code of professional responsibility;

(2) Monitor the requirements of the Federal financial institutions regulatory agency and Resolution Trust Corporation with respect to appraisal standards for federally related transactions and determinations as to which federally related transactions require the services of a State certified appraiser and which require the services of a State licensed appraiser;

(3) Monitor and review the practices, procedures, activities and organizational structure of the Appraisal Foundation; and

(4) Maintain a national registry of State certified and licensed appraisers eligible to perform appraisals in federally related transactions.

§ 1102.303 Organization and methods of operation.

(a) *Statutory and other guidelines.* Statutory requirements relating to the ASC's organization are stated in 12 U.S.C. 3310, 3333 and 3334. The ASC has adopted and published Rules of Operation guiding its administration, meetings and procedures. These Rules of Operation were published at 56 FR 28561 (June 21, 1991) and 56 FR 33451 (July 22, 1991).

(b) *ASC members and staff.* The ASC is composed of six members, each being designated by the head of their respective agencies: the Board of Governors of the Federal Reserve System, Federal Deposit Insurance Corporation, Office of the Comptroller of the Currency, National Credit Union Administration, Office of Thrift Supervision, and the Department of Housing and Urban Development. Administrative support and substantive program, policy, and legal guidance for ASC activities are provided by a small, full-time, professional staff supervised by an Executive Director.

(c) *FFIEC.* Title XI placed the ASC within FFIEC as a separate, appropriated agency of the United States Government with specific statutory responsibilities under Federal law.

(d) *ASD Address* ASC offices are located at 2000 K Street, NW., Suite 310; Washington, DC 20006.

[57 FR 60724, Dec. 22, 1992, as amended at 64 FR 72497, Dec. 28, 1999]

§ 1102.304 Federal Register publication.

The ASC publishes the following information in the FEDERAL REGISTER for the guidance of the public:

(a) Description of its organization and the established places at which, the officers from whom, and the methods whereby, the public may secure information, make submittals or re nests, or obtain decisions;

(b) Statements of the general course and method by which its functions are channeled and determined, including the nature and requirements of all formal and informal procedures available;

(c) Rules of procedure, descriptions of forms available or the places at which forms may be obtained, and instructions as to the scope and contents of all papers, reports or examinations;

(d) Substantive rules of general applicability adopted as authorized by law, and statements of general policy or interpretations of general applicability formulated and adopted by the ASC;

(e) Every amendment, revision or repeal of the foregoing; and

(f) General notices of proposed rulemaking.

[64 FR 72497, Dec. 28, 1999]

§ 1102.305 Publicly available records.

(a) *Records available on the ASCs World Wide Web site*—(1) Discretionary release of documents. The ASC encourages the public to explore the wealth of resources available on the ASC's Internet World Wide Web site, located at: *http://www.asc.gov*. The ASC has elected to publish a broad range to materials on its Web site.

(2) *Documents required to be made available via computer telecommunications.* (i) The following types of documents created on or after November 1, 1996, and required to be made available through computer telecommunications, may be found on the ASC's Internet World Wide Web site located at: *http://www.asc.gov:*

(A) Final opinions, including concurring and dissenting opinions, as well as final orders, made in the adjudication of cases;

(B) Statements of policy and interpretations adopted by the ASC that are not published in the FEDERAL REGISTER;

(C) Administrative staff manuals and instructions to staff that affect a member of the public;

(D) Copies of all records (regardless of form or format), such as correspondence relating to field reviews or other regulatory subjects, released to any person under § 1102.306 that, because of the nature of their subject matter, the ASC has determined are likely to be the subject of subsequent requests;

(E) A general index of the records referred to in paragraph (a)(2)(i)(D) of this section.

(ii) To the extent permitted by law, the ASC may delete identifying details when it makes available or publishes any records. If reduction is necessary, the ASC will, to the extent technically feasible, indicate the amount of material deleted at the place in the record where such deletion is made unless that indication in and of itself will jeopardize the purpose for the redaction.

(b) *Types of written communications.* The following types of written communications shall be subject to paragraph (a) of this section:

(1) The ASC's annual report to Congress;

(2) All final opinions and orders made in the adjudication of cases;

(3) All statements of general policy not published in the FEDERAL REGISTER.

(4) Requests for the ASC or its staff to provide interpretive advice with respect to the meaning or application of any statute administered by the ASC or any rule or regulation adopted thereunder and any ASC responses thereto;

(5) Requests for a statement that, on the basis of the facts presented in such a request, the ASC would not take any enforcement action pertaining to the facts as represented and any ASC responses thereto: and

(6) Correspondence between the ASC and a State appraiser regulatory agency arising out of the ASC's field review of the State agency's appraiser regulatory program.

(c) *Applicable fees.* (1) If applicable, fees for furnishing records under this section are as set forth in § 1102.306(e).

(2) Information on the ASC's World Wide Web site is available to the public without charge. If, however, information available on the ASC's World Wide Web site is provided pursuant to a Freedom of Information Act request processed under g 1102.306 then fees apply and will be assessed pursuant to § 1102.306(e).

[59 FR 1902, Jan. 13, 1994, as amended at 64 FR 72497, Dec. 28, 1999]

§ 1102.306 Procedures for requesting records.

(a) *Making a request for records.* (1) The request shall be submitted in writing to the Executive Director:

(i) By facsimile clearly marked "Freedom of Information Act Request" to (202) 293–6251;

(ii) By letter to the Executive Director marked "Freedom of Information Act Request"; 2000 K Street, NW., Suite 301; Washington, DC 20006; or

(iii) By sending Internet e-mail to the Executive Director marked "Freedom of Information Act Request" at his or her e-mail address listed on the ASC's World Wide Web site.

(2) The request shall contain the following information:

(i) The name and address of the requester, an electronic mail address, if available, and the telephone number at which the requester may be reached during normal business hours;

(ii) Whether the requester is an educational institution, non-commercial scientific institution, or news media representative;

(iii) A statement agreeing to pay the applicable fees, or a statement identifying a maximum fee that is acceptable to the requester, or a request for a waiver or reduction of fees that satisfies paragraph (e)(1)(x) of this section; and

(iv) The preferred form and format of any responsive information requested, if other than paper copies.

(3) A request for identifiable records shall reasonably describe the records in a way that enables the ASC's staff to identify and produce the records with reasonable effort and without unduly burdening or significantly interfering with any ASC operations.

(b) *Defective requests.* The ASC need not accept or process a request that does not reasonably describe the records requested or that does not otherwise comply with the requirements of this subpart. The ASC may return a defective request, specifying the deficiency. The requester may submit a corrected request, which will be treated as a new request.

(c) *Processing requests*—(1) *Receipt of requests.* Upon receipt of any request that satisfies paragraph (a) of this section, the Executive Director shall assign the request to the appropriate processing track pursuant to this section. The date of receipt for any request, including one that is addressed incorrectly or that is referred by another agency, is the date the Executive Director actually receives the request.

(2) *Expedited processing.* (i) Where a person requesting expedited access to records has demonstrated a compelling need for the records, or where the ASC has determined to expedite the response, the ASC shall process the request as soon as practicable. To show a compelling need for expedited processing, the requester shall provide a statement demonstrating that:

(A) The failure to obtain the records on an expedited basis could reasonably be expected to pose an imminent threat to the life or physical safety of an individual; or

(B) The requester can establish that it is primarily engaged in information dissemination as its main professional occupation or activity, and there is urgency to inform the public of the government activity involved in the re request; and

(C) The requester's statement must be certified to be true and correct to the best of the person's knowledge and belief and explain in detail the basis for requesting expedited processing.

(ii) The formality of the certification required to obtain expedited treatment may be waived by the Executive Director as a matter of administrative discretion.

(3) A requester seeking expedited processing will be notified whether expedited processing has been granted within ten (10) working days of the receipt of the request. If the request for expedited processing is denied, the requester may file an appeal pursuant to the procedures set forth in paragraph (g) of this section, and the ASC shall respond to the appeal within ten (10) working days after receipt of the appeal.

(4) *Priority of responses.* Consistent with sound administrative process, the ASC processes requests in the order they are received. However, in the ASC's discretion, or upon a court order in a matter to which the ASC is a party, a particular request may be processed out of turn.

(5) *Notification.* (i) The time for response to requests will be twenty (20) working days except:

(A) In the case of expedited treatment under paragraph (c)(2) of this section;

(B) Where the running of such time is suspended for the calculation of a cost estimate for the requester if the ASC determines that the processing of the request may exceed the requester's maximum fee provision or if the charges are likely to exceed $250 as provided for in paragraph (e)(1)(iv) of this section;

(C) Where the running of such time is suspended for the payment of fees pursuant to the paragraph (c)(5)(i)(B) and (e)(1) of this section; or

(D) In unusual circumstances, as defined in 5 U.S.C. 552(a)(6)(B) and further described in paragraph (c)(5)(iii) of this section.

(ii) In unusual circumstances as referred to in paragraph (c)(5)(i)(D) of this section, the time limit may be extended for a period of:

(A) Ten (10) working days as provided by written notice to the requester, setting forth the reasons for the extension and the date on which a determination is expected to be dispatched; or

(B) Such alternative time period as agreed to by the requester or as reasonably determined by the ASC when the ASC notifies the requester that the request cannot be processed in the specified time limit.

(iii) Unusual circumstances may arise when:

(A) The records are in facilities that are not located at the ASC's Washington office;

(B) The records requested are voluminous or are not in close proximity to one another; or

(C) There is a need to consult with another agency or among two or more components of the ASC having a substantial interest in the determination.

(6) *Response to request.* In response to a request that satisfies the requirements of paragraph (a) of this section, a search shall be conducted of records maintained by the ASC in existence on the date of receipt of the request, and a review made of any responsive information located. To the extent permitted by law, the ASC may redact identifying details when it makes available or publishes any records. If redaction is appropriate, the ASC will, to the extent technically feasible, indicate the amount of material deleted at the place in the record where such deletion is made unless that indication in and of itself will jeopardize the purpose for the redaction. The ASC shall notify the requester of:

(i) The ASC's determination of the request;

(ii) The reasons for the determination;

(iii) If the response is a denial of an initial request or if any information is withheld, the ASC will advise the requester in writing:

(A) If the denial is in part or in whole;

(B) The name and title of each person responsible for the denial (when other than the person signing the notification);

(C) The exemptions relied on for the denial; and

(D) The right of the requester to appeal the denial to the Chairman of the ASC within 30 business days following receipt of the notification, as specified in paragraph (h) of this section.

(d) *Providing responsive records.* (1) Copies of requested records shall be sent to the requester by regular U.S. mail to the address indicated in the request, unless the requester elects to take delivery of the documents at the ASC or makes other acceptable arrangements, or the ASC deems it appropriate to send the documents by another means.

(2) The ASC shall provide a copy of the record in any form or format requested if the record is readily reproducible by the ASC in that form or format, but the ASC need not provide more than one copy of any record to a requester.

(3) By arrangement with the requester, the ASC may elect to send the responsive records electronically if a substantial portion of the request is in electronic format. If the information requested is made pursuant to the Privacy Act of 1974, 5 U.S.C. 552a, it will not be sent by electronic means unless reasonable security measures can be provided.

(e) *Fees*—(1) *General rules.* (i) Persons requesting records of the ASC shall be charged for the direct costs of search, duplication, and review as set forth in paragraphs (e)(2) and (e)(3) of this section, unless such costs are less than the ASC's cost of processing the requester's remittance.

(ii) Requesters will be charged for search and review costs even if responsive records are not located or, if located, are determined to be exempt from disclosure.

(iii) Multiple requests seeking similar or related records from the same requester or group of requesters will be aggregated for the purposes of this section.

(iv) If the ASC determines that the estimated costs of search, duplication, or review of requested records will exceed the dollar amount specified in the request, or if no dollar amount is specified, the ASC will advise the requester of the estimated costs. The requester must agree in writing to pay the costs of search, duplication, and review prior to the ASC initiating any records search.

(v) If the ASC estimates that its search, duplication, and review costs will exceed $250, the requester must pay an amount equal to 20 percent of the estimated costs prior to the ASC initiating any records search.

(vi) The ASC ordinarily will collect all applicable fees under the final invoice before releasing copies of requested records to the requester.

(vii) The ASC may require any requester who has previously failed to pay charges under this section within 30 calendar days of mailing of the invoice to pay in advance the total estimated costs of search, duplication, and review. The ASC also may require a requester who has any charges outstanding in excess of 30 calendar days following mailing of the invoice to pay the full amount due, or demonstrate that the fee has been paid in full, prior to the ASC initiating any additional records search.

(viii) The ASC may begin assessing interest charges on unpaid bills on the 31st day following the day on which the invoice was sent. Interest will be at the rate prescribed in § 3717 of title 31 of the United States Code and will accrue from the date of the invoice.

(ix) The time limit for the ASC to respond to a request will not begin to run until the ASC has received the requester's written agreement under paragraph (e)(1)(iv) of this section, and advance payment under paragraph (e)(1)(v) or (vii) of this section, or payment of outstanding charges under paragraph (e)(1)(vii) or (viii) of this section.

(x) As part of the initial request, a requester may ask that the ASC waive or reduce fees if disclosure of the records is in the public interest because it is likely to contribute significantly to public understanding of the operations or activities of the government and is not primarily in the commercial interest of the requester. Determinations as to a waiver or reduction of fees will be made by the Executive Director (or designee), and the requester will be notified in writing of his or her determination. A determination not to grant a request for a waiver or reduction of fees under this paragraph may be appealed to the ASC's Chairman pursuant to the procedure set forth in paragraph (g) of this section.

(2) *Chargeable fees by category of requester.* (i) Commercial use requesters shall be charged search, duplication, and review costs.

(ii) Educational institutions, noncommercial scientific institutions, and news media representatives shall be charged duplication costs, except for the first 100 pages.

(iii) Requesters not described in paragraph (e)(2)(i) or (ii) of this section shall be charged the full reasonable direct cost of search and duplication, except for the first two hours of search time and first 100 pages of duplication.

(3) *Fee schedule.* The dollar amount of fees which the ASC may charge to records requesters will be established by the Executive Director. The ASC may charge fees that recoup the full allowable direct costs it incurs. Fees are subject to change as costs change. The fee schedule will be published periodically on the ASC's Internet World Wide Web site (*http://www.asc.gov*) and will be effective on the date of publication.

Copies of the fee schedule may be obtained by request at no charge by contacting the Executive Director by letter, Internet email or facsimile.

(i) *Manual searches for records.* The ASC will charge for manual searches for records at the basic rate of pay of the employee making the search plus 16 percent to cover employee benefit costs.

(ii) *Computer searches for records.* The fee for searches of computerized records is the actual direct cost of the search, including computer time, computer runs, and the operator's time apportioned to the search multiplied by the operator's basic rate of pay plus 16 percent to cover employee benefit costs.

(iii) *Duplication of records.* (A) The per-page fee for paper copy reproduction of documents is $.25.

(B) For other methods of reproduction or duplication, the ASC will charge the actual direct costs of reproducing or duplicating the documents, including each involved employee's basic rate of pay plus 16 percent to cover employee benefit costs.

(iv) *Review of records.* The ASC will charge commercial use requesters for the review of records at the time of processing the initial request to determine whether they are exempt from mandatory disclosure at the basic rate of pay of the employee making the search plus 16 percent to cover employee benefit costs. The ASC will not charge at the administrative appeal level for review of an exemption already applied. When records or portions of records are withheld in full under an exemption which is subsequently determined not to apply, the ASC may charge for a subsequent review to determine the applicability of other exemptions not previously considered.

(v) *Other services.* Complying with requests for special services, other than a readily produced electronic form or format, is at the ASC's discretion. The ASC may recover the full costs of providing such services to the requester.

(4) *Use of contractors.* The ASC may contact with independent contractors to locate, reproduce, and/or disseminate records; provided, however, that the ASC has determined that the ultimate cost to the requester will be no greater than it would be if the ASC performed these tasks itself. In no case will the ASC contract our responsibilities which FOIA provides that the ASC alone may discharge, such as determining the applicability of an exemption or whether to waive or reduce fees.

(f) *Exempt information.* A request for records may be denied if the requested record contains information that falls into one or more of the following categories.[1] If the requested record contains both exempt and nonexempt information, the nonexempt portions, which may reasonable be segregated from the exempt portions, will be released to the requester. If redaction is necessary, the ASC will, to the extent technically feasible, indicate the amount of material deleted at the place in the record where such deletion is made unless that indication in and of itself will jeopardize the purpose for the redaction. The categories of exempt records are as follows:

(1) Records that are specifically authorized under criteria established by an Executive Order to be kept secret in the interest of national defense or foreign policy and are in fact properly classified pursuant to such Executive Order;

(2) Records related solely to the internal personnel rules and practices of the ASC;

(3) Records specifically exempted from disclosure by statute, provided that such statute:

(i) Requires that the matters be withheld from the public in such a manner as to leave no discretion on the issue; or

(ii) Establishes particular criteria for withholding or refers to particular types of matters to be withheld;

(4) Trade secrets and commercial or financial information obtained from a

[1] Classification of a record as exempt from disclosure under the provisions of this paragraph (f) shall not be construed as authority to withhold the record if it is otherwise subject to disclosure under the Privacy Act of 1974 (5 U.S.C. 552a) or other Federal statute, any applicable regulation of ASC or any other Federal agency having jurisdiction thereof, or any directive or order of any court of competent jurisdiction.

person that is privileged or confidential;

(5) Interagency or intra-agency memoranda or letters that would not be available by law to a private party in litigation with the ASC;

(6) Personnel, medical, and similar files (including financial files) the disclosure of which would constitute a clearly unwarranted invasion of personal privacy;

(7) Records compiled for law enforcement purposes, but only to the extent that the production of such law enforcement records:

(i) Could reasonably be expected to interfere with enforcement proceedings;

(ii) Would deprive a person of a right to a fair trail or an impartial adjudication;

(ii) Could reasonably be expected to constitute an unwarranted invasion of personal privacy;

(iv) Could reasonably be expected to disclose the identity of a confidential source, including a State, local, or foreign agency or authority or any private institution which furnished records on a confidential basis;

(v) Would disclose techniques and procedures for law enforcement investigations or prosecutions, or would disclose guidelines for law enforcement investigations or prosecutions if such disclosure could reasonably be expected to risk circumvention of the law; or

(vi) Could reasonably be expected to endanger the life or physical safety of any individual;

(8) Records that are contained in or related to examination, operating, or condition reports prepared by, on behalf of, or for the use of the ASC or any agency responsible for the regulation or supervision of financial institutions; or

(9) Geological and geophysical information and data, including maps, concerning wells.

(g) *Appeals.* (1) Appeals should be addressed to the Executive Director; ASC; 2000 K Street, NW., Suite 310; Washington, DC 20006.

(2) A person whose initial request for records under this section, or whose request for a waiver of fees under paragraph (e)(1)(x) of this section, has been denied, either in part or in whole, has the right to appeal the denial to the ASC's Chairman (or designee) within 30 business days after receipt of notification of the denial. Appeals of denials of initial requests or for a waiver of fees must be in writing and include any additional information relevant to consideration of the appeal.

(3) Except in the case of an appeal for expedited treatment under paragraph (c)(3) of this section, the ASC will notify the appellant in writing within 20 business days after receipt of the appeal and will state:

(i) Whether it is granted or denied in whole or in part;

(ii) The name and title of each person responsible for the denial (if other than the person signing the notification);

(iii) The exemptions relied upon for the denial in the case of initial requests for records; and

(iv) The right to judicial review of the denial under the FOIA.

(4) If a requester is appealing for denial of expedited treatment, the ASC will notify the appellant within ten business days after receipt of the appeal of the ASC's disposition.

(5) Complete payment of any outstanding fee invoice will be required before an appeal is processed.

(h) *Records of another agency.* If a requested record is the property of another Federal agency or department, and that agency or department, either in writing or by regulation, expressly retains ownership of such record, upon receipt of a request for the record the ASC will promptly inform the requester of this ownership and immediately shall forward the request to the proprietary agency or department either for processing in accordance with the latter's regulations or for guidance with respect to disposition.

[64 FR 72497, Dec. 28, 1999; 65 FR 31960, May 19, 2000, as amended at 69 FR 2501, Jan. 16, 2004]

§ 1102.307 Disclosure of exempt records.

(a) *Disclosure prohibited.* Except as provided in paragraph (b) of this section or by 12 CFR part 1102, subpart C, no person shall disclose or permit the disclosure of any exempt records, or information contained therein, to any persons other than those officers, directors, employees, or agents of the ASC or a State appraiser regulatory agency who has a need for such records in the performance of their official duties. In any instance in which any person has possession, custody or control of ASC exempt records or information contained therein, all copies of such records shall remain the property of the ASC and under no circumstances shall any person, entity or agency disclose or make public in any manner the exempt records or information without written authorization from the Executive Director, after consultation with the ASC General Counsel.

(b) *Disclosure authorized.* Exempt records or information of the ASC may be disclosed only in accordance with the conditions and requirements set forth in this paragraph (b). Requests for discretionary disclosure of exempt records of information pursuant to this paragraph (b) may be submitted directly to the Executive Director. Such administrative request must clearly state that it seeks discretionary disclosure of exempt records, clearly identify the records sought, provide sufficient information for the ASC to evaluate whether there is good cause for disclosure, and meet all other conditions set forth in paragraph (b)(1) through (3) of this section. Authority to disclose or authorize disclosure of exempt records of the ASC is delegated to the Executive Director, after consultation with the ASC General Counsel.

(1) *Disclosure by Executive Director.* (i) The Executive Director, or designee, may disclose or authorize the disclosure of any exempt record in response to a valid judicial subpoena, court order, or other legal process, and authorize any current or former member, officer, employee, agent of the ASC, or third party, to appear and testify regarding an exempt record or any information obtained in the performance of such person's official duties, at any administrative or judicial hearing or proceeding where such person has been served with a valid subpoena, court order, or other legal process requiring him or her to testify. The Executive Director shall consider the relevancy of such exempt records or testimony to the ligation, and the interests of justice, in determining whether to disclose such records or testimony. Third parties seeking disclosure of exempt records or testimony in litigation to which the ASC is not a party shall submit a request for discretionary disclosure directly to the Executive Director. Such requests shall specify the information sought with reasonable particularity and shall be accompanied by a statement with supporting documentation showing in detail the relevance of such exempt information to the litigation, justifying good cause for disclosure, and a commitment to be bound by a protective order. Failure to exhaust such administration request prior to service of a subpoena or other legal process may, in the Executive Director's discretion, serve as a basis for objection to such subpoena or legal process.

(ii) The Executive Director, or designee, may in his or her discretion and for good cause, disclose or authorize disclosure of any exempt record or testimony by a current or former member, officer, employee, agent of the ASC, or third party, sought in connection with any civil or criminal hearing, proceeding or investigation without the service of a judicial subpoena, or other legal process requiring such disclosure or testimony. If he or she determines that the records or testimony are relevant to the hearing, proceeding or investigation and that disclosure is in the best interests of justice and not otherwise prohibited by Federal statute. Where the Executive Director or designee authorizes a current or former member, officer, director, empl9oyee or agent of the ASC to testify or disclose exempt records pursuant to this paragraph (b)(1), he or she may, in his or her discretion, limit the authorization to so much of the record or testimony as is relevant to the issues at such hearing, proceeding or investigation, and he or she shall give authorization only upon fulfillment of such conditions as he or she deems necessary and practicable to protect the confidential nature of such records or testimony.

(2) *Authorization for disclosure by the Chairman of the ASC.* Except where expressly prohibited by law, the Chairman of the ASC may, in his or her discretion, authorize the disclosure of any

ASC records. Except where disclosure is required by law, the Chairman may direct any current or former member, officer, director, employee or agent of the ASC to refuse to disclose any record or to give testimony if the Chairman determines, in his or her discretion, that refusal to permit such disclosure is in the public interest.

(3) *Limitations on disclosure.* All steps practicable shall be taken to protect the confidentiality of exempt records and information. Any disclosure permitted by paragraph (b) of this section is discretionary and nothing in paragraph (b) of this section shall be construed as requiring the disclosure of information. Further, nothing in paragrah (b) of this section shall be construed as restricting, in any manner, the authority of the ASC, the Chairman of the ASC, the Executive Director, the ASC General Counsel, or their designees, in their discretion and in light of the facts and circumstances attendant in any given case, to require conditions upon, and to limit, the form, manner, and extent of any disclosure permitted by this section. Wherever practicable, disclosure of exempt records shall be made pursuant to a protective order and redacted to exclude all irrelevant or non-responsive exempt information.

[64 FR 72500, Dec. 28, 1999]

§ 1102.308 Right to petition for issuance, amendment and repeal of rules of general application.

Any person desiring the issuance, amendment or repeal of a rule of general application may file a petition for those purposes with the Executive Director of the ASC. The petition shall include a statement setting forth the text or substance of any proposed rule or amendment desired or shall specify the rule for which repeal is desired. The petitioner also shall state the nature of his or her interest and the reasons for seeking ASC action. The Executive Director shall acknowledge receipt of the petition within ten business days of receipt. As soon as reasonably practicable, the ASC shall consider the petition and related staff recommendations and shall take such action as it deems appropriate. The Executive Director shall notify the petitioner in writing of the ASC action within ten business days of the action.

[59 FR 1902, Jan. 13, 1994. Redesignated at 64 FR 72497, Dec. 28, 1999]

§ 1102.309 Confidential treatment procedures.

(a) *In general.* Any submitter of written information to the ASC who desires that some or all of his or her submission be afforded confidential treatment under 5 U.S.C. 552(b)(4) (*i.e.*, trade secrets and commercial or financial information obtained from a person and privileged or confidential) shall file a request for confidential treatment with the Executive Director of the ASC at the time the written information is submitted to the ASC or within ten business days thereafter. Nothing in this section limits the authority of the ASC and its staff to make determinations regarding access to documents under this subpart.

(b) *Form of request.* A request for confidential treatment shall be submitted in a separate letter or memorandum conspicuously entitled, "Request for Confidential Treatment." Each request shall state in reasonable detail the facts and arguments supporting the request and its legal justification. If the submitter had been required by the ASC to provide the particular information, conclusory statements that the information would be useful to competitors or would impair sales or similar statements generally will not be considered sufficient to justify confidential treatment. When the submitter had voluntarily provided the particular information to the ASC, the submitter must specifically identify the documents or information which are of a kind the submitter would not customarily make available to the public.

(c) *Designation and separation of confidential material.* Submitters shall clearly designate all information considered confidential and shall clearly separate such information from other non-confidential information, whenever possible.

(d) *ASC action on request.* A request for confidential treatment of information will be considered only in connection with a request for access to the information under FOIA as implemented by this subpart. Upon the receipt of a request for access, the Executive Director or his or her designee ("ASC Officer") as soon as possible shall provide the submitter with a written notice describing the request and shall provide the submitter with a reasonable opportunity, no longer than ten business days, to submit written objections to disclosure of the information. Notice may be given orally, and such notice shall be promptly confirmed in writing. The ASC Officer may provide a submitter with a notice if the submitter did not request confidential treatment of the requested information. If the ASC required the submitter to provide the requested information, the ASC Officer would need substantial reason to believe that disclosure of the requested information would result in substantial competitive harm to the submitter. If the submitter provided the information voluntarily to the ASC, the ASC officer would need to believe that the information is of a kind the submitter would not customarily make available to the public. The ASC Officer similarly shall notify the person seeking disclosure of the information under FOIA of the existence of a request for confidential treatment. These notice requirements need not be followed if the ASC Officer determines under this subpart that the information should not be disclosed; the information has been published or has been officially made available to the public; disclosure of the information is required by law (other than FOIA); or the submitter's request for confidential treatment appears obviously frivolous, in such instance the submitter shall be given written notice of the determination to disclose the information at least five business days prior to release. The ASC Officer shall carefully consider the issues involved, and if disclosure of the requested information is warranted, a written notice, containing a brief description of why the submitter's objections were not sustained, must be forwarded to the submitter within ten business days. The time for response may be extended up to ten additional business days, as provided in 5 U.S.C. 552(a)(6)(B), or for other periods by agreement between the requester and the ASC Officer. This notice shall be provided to the submitter at least five business days prior to release of the requested information.

(e) *Notice of lawsuit.* The ASC Officer shall notify a submitter of any filing of any suit against the ASC pursuant to 5 U.S.C. 552 to compel disclosure of documents or information covered by the submitter's request for confidential treatment within ten business days of service of the suit. The ASC Officer also shall notify the requester of the documents or information of any suit filed by the submitter against the ASC to enjoin their disclosure within ten business days of service of the suit.

[59 FR 1902, Jan. 13, 1994. Redesignated at 64 FR 72497, Dec. 28, 1999]

§1102.310 Service of process.

(a) *Service.* Any subpoena or other legal process to obtain information maintained by the ASC shall be duly issued by a court having jurisdiction over the ASC, and served upon the Chairman ASC; 2000 K Street, NW., Suite 310; Washington, DC 20006. Where the ASC is named as a party, service of process shall be made pursuant to the Federal Rules of Civil Procedure upon the Chairman at the above address. The Chairman shall immediately forward any subpoena, court order or legal process to the General Counsel. If consistent with the terms of the subpoena, court order or legal process, the ASC may require the payment of fees, in accordance with the fee schedule referred to in §1102.306(e) prior to the release of any records requested pursuant to any subpoena or other legal process.

(b) *Notification by person served.* If any current or former member, officer, employee or agent of the ASC, or any other person who has custody of records belonging to the ASC, is served with a subpoena, court order, or other process requiring that person's attendance as a witness concerning any matter related to official duties, or the production of any exempt record of the ASC, such person shall promptly advise the Executive Director of such service, the testimony and records described in the subpoena, and all relevant facts that may assist the Executive Director, in consultation with the ASC General Counsel, in determining whether the individual in question should be authorized to testify or the records should be produced. Such person also should inform the court or tribunal that issued the process and the attorney for the party upon whose application the process was issued, if known, of the substance of this section.

(c) *Appearance by person served.* Absent the written authorization of the Executive Director or designee to disclose the requested information, any current or former member, officer, employee, or agent of the ASC, and any other person having custody of records of the ASC, who is required to respond to a subpoena or other legal process, shall attend at the time and place therein specified and respectfully decline to produce any such record or give any testimony with respect thereto, basing such refusal on this section.

[64 FR 72501, Dec. 28, 1999]

CHAPTER XII—FEDERAL HOUSING FINANCE AGENCY

SUBCHAPTER A—ORGANIZATION AND OPERATIONS

SUBCHAPTER B—ENTITY REGULATIONS

SUBCHAPTER C—ENTERPRISES

SUBCHAPTER D—FEDERAL HOME LOAN BANKS

SUBCHAPTER A—ORGANIZATION AND OPERATIONS

PART 1202—FREEDOM OF INFORMATION ACT

AUTHORITY: Pub. L. 110–289, 122 Stat. 2654; 5 U.S.C. 301, 552; 12 U.S.C. 4526; E.O. 12600, 52 FR 23781, 3 CFR, 1987 Comp., p. 235; E.O. 13392, 70 FR 75373–75377, 3 CFR, 2006 Comp., p. 216–200.

SOURCE: 76 FR 29634, May 23, 2011, unless otherwise noted.

§ 1202.1 Why did FHFA issue this regulation?

(a) The Freedom of Information Act (FOIA) (5 U.S.C. 552), is a federal law that requires FHFA and other Federal Government agencies to disclose certain Federal Government records to the public.

(b) This regulation explains the rules that FHFA and the FHFA Office of Inspector General (FHFA–OIG) both follow when processing and responding to requests for records under FOIA. It also explains what you must do to request records from FHFA or FHFA–OIG under FOIA. You should read this regulation together with FOIA, which explains in more detail your rights and the records FHFA or FHFA–OIG may release to you.

(c) If you want to request information about yourself under the Privacy Act (5 U.S.C. 552a), you should file your request using FHFA's Privacy Act regulations at part 1204 of this title. If you file a FOIA request for information about yourself, FHFA or FHFA–OIG will process it as a request under the Privacy Act regulation.

(d) FHFA and FHFA–OIG may make public information that they routinely publish or disclose when performing their activities without following these procedures.

(e) This regulation applies to both FHFA and FHFA–OIG.

§ 1202.2 What do the terms in this regulation mean?

Some of the terms you need to understand while reading this regulation are—

Appeals Officer or FOIA Appeals Officer means a person designated by the FHFA Director to process appeals of denials of requests for FHFA records under FOIA. For appeals pertaining to FHFA–OIG records, *Appeals Officer or FOIA Appeals Officer* means a person designated by the FHFA Inspector General to process appeals of denials of requests for FHFA–OIG records under FOIA.

Confidential commercial information means records provided to the Federal Government by a submitter that contain material exempt from release under Exemption 4 of FOIA, 5 U.S.C. 552(b)(4), because disclosure could reasonably be expected to cause substantial competitive harm.

Days, unless stated as "calendar days," are working days and do not include Saturdays, Sundays, and federal holidays. If the last day of any period prescribed herein falls on a Saturday, Sunday, or federal holiday, the last day of the period will be the next working day that is not a Saturday, Sunday, or federal holiday.

Direct costs means the expenses, including contract services, incurred by FHFA or FHFA–OIG, in searching for, reviewing and/or duplicating records to respond to a request for information.

In the case of a commercial use request, the term also means those expenditures FHFA or FHFA–OIG actually incurs in reviewing records to respond to the request. Direct costs include the cost of the time of the employee performing the work, the cost of any computer searches, and the cost of operating duplication equipment. Direct costs do not include overhead expenses such as costs of space, and heating or lighting the facility in which the records are stored.

Employee, for the purposes of this regulation, means any person holding an appointment to a position of employment with FHFA or FHFA–OIG, or any person who formerly held such an appointment; any conservator appointed by FHFA; or any agent or independent contractor acting on behalf of FHFA or FHFA–OIG, even though the appointment or contract has terminated.

FHFA means the Federal Housing Finance Agency and includes its predecessor agencies, the Office of Federal Housing Enterprise Oversight (OFHEO) and the Federal Housing Finance Board (FHFB).

FHFA–OIG means the Office of Inspector General for FHFA.

FOIA Officer and Chief FOIA Officer are persons designated by the FHFA Director to process and respond to requests for FHFA records under FOIA.

FOIA Official is a person designated by the FHFA Inspector General to process requests for FHFA–OIG records under FOIA.

Office of Finance means the Office of Finance of the Federal Home Loan Bank System or any successor thereto.

Readily reproducible means that the requested record or records exist in electronic format and can be downloaded or transferred intact to a computer disk, tape, or another electronic medium with equipment and software currently in use by FHFA or FHFA–OIG.

Record means information or documentary material FHFA or FHFA–OIG maintains in any form or format, including electronic, which FHFA or FHFA–OIG—

(1) Created or received under federal law or in connection with the transaction of public business;

(2) Preserved or determined is appropriate for preservation as evidence of operations or activities of FHFA or FHFA–OIG, or because of the value of the information it contains; and

(3) Controls at the time it receives a request for disclosure.

Regulated entities means the Federal Home Loan Mortgage Corporation and any affiliate thereof, the Federal National Mortgage Association and any affiliate thereof, and the Federal Home Loan Banks.

Requester means any person seeking access to FHFA or FHFA–OIG records under FOIA.

Search time means the amount of time spent by or on behalf of FHFA or FHFA–OIG in attempting to locate records responsive to a request, whether manually or by electronic means, including but not limited to page-by-page or line-by-line identification of responsive material within a record or extraction of electronic information from electronic storage media.

Submitter means any person or entity providing confidential information to the Federal Government. The term "submitter" includes, but is not limited to corporations, state governments, and foreign governments.

Unusual circumstances means the need to—

(1) Search for and/or collect records from agencies, offices, facilities, or locations that are separate from the office processing the request;

(2) Search, review, and/or duplicate a voluminous amount of separate and distinct records in order to process a single request; or

(3) Consult with another agency or among two or more components of FHFA or FHFA–OIG that have a substantial interest in the determination of a request.

§ 1202.3 What information can I obtain through FOIA?

(a) *General*. FHFA and FHFA–OIG prohibit employees from releasing or disclosing confidential or otherwise non-public information that FHFA or FHFA–OIG possesses, except as authorized by this regulation, by the Director of FHFA for FHFA records, or by the FHFA Inspector General for FHFA–OIG records, when the disclosure is necessary for the performance of official duties.

(b) *Records.* You may request that FHFA or FHFA–OIG disclose to you its records on a subject of interest to you. FOIA only requires the disclosure of records. It does not require FHFA or FHFA–OIG to create compilations of information or to provide narrative responses to questions or queries. Some information is exempt from disclosure.

(c) *Reading rooms.* (1) FHFA maintains electronic and physical reading rooms. FHFA's physical reading room is located at 1700 G Street, NW., Fourth Floor, Washington, DC 20552, and is open to the public by appointment from 9 a.m. to 3 p.m. each business day. For an appointment, contact the FOIA Officer by calling (202) 414–6425 or by e-mail at *foia@fhfa.gov.* The electronic reading room is part of the FHFA Web site at *http://www.fhfa.gov.* FHFA–OIG also maintains electronic and physical reading rooms. FHFA–OIG's physical reading room is located at 1625 Eye Street, NW., Washington, DC 20006, and is open to the public by appointment from 9 a.m. to 3 p.m. each business day. For an appointment, contact FHFA–OIG by calling (202) 408–2577 or by e-mail at *bryan.saddler@fhfa.gov.* The electronic reading room is part of the FHFA–OIG Web site at *http://www.fhfaoig.gov.*

(2) Each reading room has the following records created after November 1, 1996, by FHFA or its predecessor agencies, or by FHFA–OIG, and current indices to the following records created by FHFA or its predecessor agencies or FHFA–OIG before or after November 1, 1996:

(i) Final opinions or orders issued in adjudication;

(ii) Statements of policy and interpretation that are not published in the FEDERAL REGISTER;

(iii) Administrative staff manuals and instructions to staff that affect a member of the public and are not exempt from disclosure under FOIA; and

(iv) Copies of records released under FOIA that FHFA or FHFA–OIG determines have become or are likely to become the subject of subsequent requests for substantially similar records.

§ 1202.4 What information is exempt from disclosure?

(a) *General.* Unless the Director of FHFA or his or her designee for FHFA records, the FHFA Inspector General or his or her designee for FHFA–OIG records, or any regulation or statute specifically authorizes disclosure, neither FHFA nor FHFA–OIG will release records that are—

(1) Specifically authorized under criteria established by an Executive Order to be kept secret in the interest of national defense or foreign policy, and in fact is properly classified pursuant to such Executive Order;

(2) Related solely to FHFA's or FHFA–OIG's internal personnel rules and practices;

(3) Specifically exempted from disclosure by statute (other than 5 U.S.C. 552a), provided that such statute—

(i) Requires that the matters be withheld from the public in such a manner as to leave no discretion on the issue, or

(ii) Establishes particular criteria for withholding or refers to particular types of matters to be withheld;

(4) Trade secrets and commercial or financial information obtained from a person and privileged or confidential;

(5) Contained in inter-agency or intra-agency memoranda or letters that would not be available by law to a private party in litigation with FHFA or FHFA–OIG;

(6) Contained in personnel, medical or similar files (including financial files) the disclosure of which would constitute a clearly unwarranted invasion of personal privacy;

(7) Compiled for law enforcement purposes, but only to the extent that the production of such law enforcement records or information—

(i) Could reasonably be expected to interfere with enforcement proceedings;

(ii) Would deprive a person of a right to fair trial or an impartial adjudication;

(iii) Could reasonably be expected to constitute an unwarranted invasion of personal privacy;

(iv) Could reasonably be expected to disclose the identity of a confidential source, including a state, local, or foreign agency or authority or any private institution or an entity that is regulated and examined by FHFA that furnished information on a confidential basis, and, in the case of a record compiled by FHFA–OIG or a criminal law enforcement authority in the course of a criminal investigation or by an agency conducting a lawful national security intelligence investigation, information furnished by a confidential source;

(v) Would disclose techniques and procedures for law enforcement investigations or prosecutions, or would disclose guidelines for law enforcement investigations or prosecutions if such disclosure could reasonably be expected to risk circumvention of the law; or

(vi) Could reasonably be expected to endanger the life or physical safety of any individual.

(8) Contained in or related to examination, operating, or condition reports that are prepared by, on behalf of, or for the use of an agency responsible for the regulation or supervision of financial institutions; or

(9) Geological and geophysical information and data, including maps, concerning wells.

(b) *Discretion to apply exemptions.* Although records or parts of them may be exempt from disclosure, FHFA or FHFA–OIG may elect under the circumstances of any particular request not to apply an exemption. This election does not generally waive the exemption and it does not have precedential effect. FHFA or FHFA–OIG may still apply an exemption to any other records or portions of records, regardless of when the request is received.

(c) *Redacted portion.* If a requested record contains exempt information and information that can be disclosed and the portions can reasonably be segregated from each other, the disclosable portion of the record will be released to the requester after FHFA or FHFA–OIG deletes the exempt portions. If it is technically feasible, FHFA or FHFA–OIG will indicate the amount of the information deleted at the place in the record where the deletion is made and include a notation identifying the exemption that was applied, unless including that indication would harm an interest protected by an exemption.

(d) *Exempt and redacted material.* FHFA and FHFA–OIG are not required to provide an itemized index correlating each withheld document (or redacted portion) with a specific exemption justification.

(e) *Disclosure to Congress.* This section does not allow FHFA or FHFA–OIG to withhold any information from, or to prohibit the disclosure of any information to, Congress or any Congressional committee or subcommittee.

§ 1202.5 How do I request information from FHFA or FHFA–OIG under FOIA?

(a) *Where to send your request.* FOIA requests must be in writing. You may make a request for FHFA or FHFA–OIG records by writing directly to FHFA's FOIA Office through electronic mail, mail, delivery service, or facsimile. The electronic mail address is: *foia@fhfa.gov.* For mail or delivery service, the mailing address is: FOIA Officer, Federal Housing Finance Agency, 1700 G Street, NW., Washington, DC 20552. The facsimile number is: (202) 414–8917. Requests for FHFA–OIG records will be forwarded to FHFA–OIG for processing and direct response. You can help FHFA and FHFA–OIG process your request by marking electronic mail, letters, or facsimiles and the subject line, envelope, or facsimile cover sheet with "FOIA Request." FHFA's "Freedom of Information Act Reference Guide," which is available on FHFA's Web site, *http://www.fhfa.gov,* provides additional information to assist you in making your request.

(b) *Provide your name and address.* Your request must include your full name, your address and, if different, the address at which FHFA or FHFA–OIG is to notify you about your request, a telephone number at which you can be reached during normal business hours, and an electronic mail address, if any.

(c) *Request is under FOIA.* Your request must have a statement identifying it as being made under FOIA.

(d) *Your FOIA status.* If you are submitting your request as a "commercial use" requester, an "educational institution" requester, a "non-commercial scientific institution" requester, or a "representative of the news media" for the purposes of the fee provisions of FOIA, your request must include a statement specifically identifying your status.

(e) *Describing the records you request.* You must describe the records that you seek in enough detail to enable FHFA or FHFA–OIG personnel to locate them with a reasonable amount of effort. Your request should include as much specific information as possible that you know about each record you request, such as the date, title, name, author, recipient, subject matter, or file designations, or the description of the record.

(f) *How you want the records produced to you.* Your request must tell FHFA or FHFA–OIG whether you will inspect the records before duplication or want them duplicated and furnished without inspection.

(g) *Agreement to pay fees.* In your FOIA request you must agree to pay all applicable fees charged under § 1202.11, up to $100.00, unless you seek a fee waiver. When making a request, you may specify a higher or lower amount you will pay without consultation. Your inability to pay a fee does not justify granting a fee waiver.

(h) *Valid requests.* FHFA and FHFA–OIG will only process valid requests. A valid request must meet all the requirements of this part.

§ 1202.6 What if my request does not have all the information FHFA or FHFA–OIG requires?

If FHFA or FHFA–OIG determines that your request does not reasonably describe the records you seek, is overly broad, cannot yet be processed for reasons related to fees, or lacks required information, you will be informed in writing why your request cannot be processed. You will be given 15 calendar days to modify your request to meet all requirements. This request for additional information tolls the time period for FHFA or FHFA–OIG to respond to your request under § 1202.7.

(a) If you respond with the necessary information, FHFA or FHFA–OIG will process that response as a new request and the time period for FHFA or FHFA–OIG to respond to your request will start from the date the additional information is actually received by FHFA or FHFA–OIG.

(b) If you do not respond or provide additional information within the time allowed, or if the additional information you provide is still incomplete or insufficient, FHFA and FHFA–OIG will consider your request withdrawn and will notify you that it will not be processed.

§ 1202.7 How will FHFA and FHFA–OIG respond to my FOIA request?

(a) *Authority to grant or deny requests.* The FOIA Officer and the Chief FOIA Officer are authorized to grant or deny any request for FHFA records. For FHFA–OIG records, the designated FHFA–OIG FOIA Official is authorized to grant or deny any request for FHFA–OIG records.

(b) *Multi-Track request processing.* FHFA and FHFA–OIG use a multi-track system to process FOIA requests. This means that a FOIA request is processed based on its complexity. When FHFA or FHFA–OIG receives your request, it is assigned to a Standard Track or Complex Track. FHFA or FHFA–OIG will notify you if your request is assigned to the Complex Track as described in paragraph (f) of this section.

(1) *Standard Track.* FHFA and FHFA–OIG assign FOIA requests that are routine and require little or no search time, review, or analysis to the Standard Track. FHFA and FHFA–OIG respond to these requests within 20 days after receipt, in the order in which they are received. If FHFA or FHFA–OIG determines while processing your Standard Track request, that it is more appropriately a Complex Track request, it will be reassigned to the Complex Track and you will be notified as described in paragraph (f) of this section.

(2) *Complex Track.* (i) FHFA and FHFA–OIG assign requests that are non-routine to the Complex Track. Complex Track requests are those to which FHFA or FHFA–OIG determines that the request and/or response may—

(A) Be voluminous;

(B) Involve two or more FHFA or FHFA–OIG units;

(C) Require consultation with other agencies or entities;

(D) Require searches of archived documents;

(E) Seek confidential commercial information as described in § 1202.8;

(F) Require an unusually high level of effort to search for, review and/or duplicate records;

(G) Cause undue disruption to the day-to-day activities of FHFA in regulating and supervising the regulated entities; or

(H) Cause undue disruption to the day-to-day activities of FHFA–OIG in carrying out its statutory responsibilities.

(ii) FHFA or FHFA–OIG will respond to Complex Track requests as soon as reasonably possible, regardless of the date of receipt.

(c) *Referrals to other agencies.* When FHFA or FHFA–OIG receives a request seeking records that originated in another Federal Government agency, FHFA or FHFA–OIG will refer the request to the other agency for response. You will be notified if your request is referred to another agency.

(d) *Responses to FOIA requests.* FHFA or FHFA–OIG will respond to your request by granting or denying it in full, or by granting and denying it in part. The response will be in writing. In determining which records are responsive to your request, FHFA and FHFA–OIG will conduct searches for records FHFA or FHFA–OIG possesses as of the date of your request.

(1) *Requests that FHFA or FHFA–OIG grants.* If FHFA or FHFA–OIG grants your request, the response will include the requested records or details about how FHFA or FHFA–OIG will provide them to you and the amount of any fees charged.

(2) *Requests that FHFA or FHFA–OIG denies, or grants and denies in part.* If FHFA or FHFA–OIG denies your request in whole or in part because a requested record does not exist or cannot be located, is not readily reproducible in the form or format you sought, is not subject to FOIA, or is exempt from disclosure, the written response will include the requested releasable records, if any, the amount of any fees charged, the reasons for denial, and a notice and description of your right to file an administrative appeal under § 1202.9.

(e) *Format and delivery of disclosed records.* If FHFA or FHFA–OIG grants, in whole or in part, your request for disclosure of records under FOIA, the records may be made available to you in the form or format you requested, if they are readily reproducible in that form or format. The records will be sent to the address you provided by regular U.S. Mail or by electronic mail unless alternate arrangements are made by mutual agreement, such as your agreement to pay express or expedited delivery service fees or to pick up records at FHFA or FHFA–OIG offices.

(f) *Extensions of time.* (1) In unusual circumstances, FHFA or FHFA–OIG may extend the Standard Track time limit in paragraph (b)(1) of this section for no more than 10 days and notify you of—

(i) The reason for the extension; and

(ii) The date on which the determination is expected.

(2) For requests in the Complex Track, FHFA or FHFA–OIG will provide you with an opportunity to modify or reformulate your request so that it may be processed on the Standard Track. If the request cannot be modified or reformulated to permit processing on the Standard Track, FHFA or FHFA–OIG will notify you regarding an alternative time period for processing the request.

§ 1202.8 If the requested records contain confidential commercial information, what procedures will FHFA or FHFA–OIG follow?

(a) *General.* FHFA or FHFA–OIG will not disclose confidential commercial information in response to your FOIA request except as described in this section.

(b) *Designation of confidential commercial information.* Submitters of commercial information must use good-faith efforts to designate, by appropriate markings, either at the time of submission or at a reasonable time thereafter, those portions of the information they deem to be protected under 5 U.S.C. 552(b)(4) and § 1202.4(a)(4). Any such designation will expire 10 years after the records are submitted to the Federal

Government, unless the submitter requests, and provides reasonable justification for, a designation period of longer duration.

(c) *Pre-disclosure notification.* Except as provided in paragraph (e) of this section, if your FOIA request encompasses confidential commercial information, FHFA or FHFA–OIG will, prior to disclosure of the information and to the extent permitted by law, provide prompt written notice to a submitter that confidential commercial information was requested when—

(1) The submitter has in good faith designated the information as confidential commercial information protected from disclosure under 5 U.S.C. 552(b)(4) and § 1202.4(a)(4); or

(2) FHFA or FHFA–OIG has reason to believe that the request seeks confidential commercial information, the disclosure of which may result in substantial competitive harm to the submitter.

(d) *Content of pre-disclosure notification.* When FHFA or FHFA–OIG sends a pre-disclosure notification to a submitter, it will contain—

(1) A description of the confidential commercial information requested or copies of the records or portions thereof containing the confidential business information; and

(2) An opportunity to object to disclosure within 10 days or such other time period that FHFA or FHFA–OIG may allow, by providing to FHFA or FHFA–OIG a detailed written statement demonstrating all reasons the submitter opposes disclosure.

(e) *Exceptions to pre-disclosure notification.* FHFA or FHFA–OIG is not required to send a pre-disclosure notification if—

(1) FHFA or FHFA–OIG determines that information should not be disclosed;

(2) The information has been published lawfully or has been made officially available to the public;

(3) Disclosure of the information is required by law, other than FOIA;

(4) The information requested is not designated by the submitter as confidential commercial information pursuant to this section; or

(5) The submitter's designation, under paragraph (b) of this section, appears on its face to be frivolous; except that FHFA or FHFA–OIG will provide the submitter with written notice of any final decision to disclose the designated confidential commercial information within a reasonable number of days prior to a specified disclosure date.

(f) *Submitter's objection to disclosure.* A submitter may object to disclosure within 10 days after date of the Pre-disclosure Notification, or such other time period that FHFA or FHFA–OIG may allow, by delivering to FHFA or FHFA–OIG a statement demonstrating all grounds on which it opposes disclosure, and all reasons supporting its contention that the information should not be disclosed. The submitter's objection must contain a certification by the submitter, or an officer or authorized representative of the submitter, that the grounds and reasons presented are true and correct to the best of the submitter's knowledge. The submitter's objection may itself be subject to disclosure under FOIA.

(g) *Notice of intent to disclose information.* FHFA or FHFA–OIG will carefully consider all grounds and reasons provided by a submitter objecting to disclosure. If FHFA or FHFA–OIG decides to disclose the information over the submitter's objection, the submitter will be provided with a written notice of intent to disclose at least 10 days before the date of disclosure. The written notice will contain—

(1) A statement of the reasons why the information will be disclosed;

(2) A description of the information to be disclosed; and

(3) A specific disclosure date.

(h) *Notice to requester.* FHFA or FHFA–OIG will give a requester whose request encompasses confidential commercial information—

(1) A written notice that the request encompasses confidential commercial information that may be exempt from disclosure under 5 U.S.C. 552(b)(4) and § 1202.4(a)(4) and that the submitter of the information has been given a pre-disclosure notification with the opportunity to comment on the proposed disclosure of the information; and

(2) A written notice that a notice of intent to disclose has been provided to the submitter, and that the submitter

has 10 days, or such other time period that FHFA or FHFA–OIG may allow, to respond.

(i) *Notice of FOIA lawsuit.* FHFA or FHFA–OIG will promptly notify the submitter whenever a requester files suit seeking to compel disclosure of the submitter's confidential commercial information. FHFA or FHFA–OIG will promptly notify the requester whenever a submitter files suit seeking to prevent disclosure of information.

§ 1202.9 How do I appeal a response denying my FOIA request?

(a) *Right of appeal.* If FHFA or FHFA–OIG denied your request in whole or in part, you may appeal the denial by writing directly to the FOIA Appeals Officer through electronic mail, mail, delivery service, or facsimile. The electronic mail address is: *foia@fhfa.gov.* For mail or delivery service, the mailing address is: FOIA Appeals Officer, Federal Housing Finance Agency, 1700 G Street, NW., Washington, DC 20552. The facsimile number is: (202) 414–8917. You can help FHFA and FHFA–OIG process your appeal by marking electronic mail, letters, or facsimiles and the subject line, envelope, or facsimile cover sheet with "FOIA Appeal." For appeals of denials, whether in whole or in part, made by FHFA–OIG, the appeal must be clearly marked by adding "FHFA–OIG" after "FOIA Appeal." All appeals from denials, in whole or in part, made by FHFA–OIG will be forwarded to the FHFA–OIG FOIA Appeals Officer for processing and direct response. FHFA's "Freedom of Information Act Reference Guide," which is available on FHFA's Web site, *http://www.fhfa.gov,* provides additional information to assist you in making your appeal.

(b) *Timing, form, content, and receipt of an appeal.* Your appeal must be written and submitted within 30 calendar days of the date of the decision by FHFA or FHFA–OIG denying, in whole or in part, your request. Your appeal must include a copy of the initial request, a copy of the letter denying the request in whole or in part, and a statement of the circumstances, reasons, or arguments you believe support disclosure of the requested record(s). FHFA and FHFA–OIG will not consider an improperly addressed appeal to have been received for the purposes of the 20-day time period of paragraph (d) of this section until it is actually received by FHFA.

(c) *Extensions of time to appeal.* If you need more time to file your appeal, you may request, in writing, an extension of time of no more than 10 calendar days in which to file your appeal, but only if your request is made within the original 30-calendar day time period for filing the appeal. Granting such an extension is in the sole discretion of the FHFA or FHFA–OIG FOIA Appeals Officer.

(d) *Final action on appeal.* FHFA's or FHFA–OIG's determination on your appeal will be in writing, signed by the FHFA or FHFA–OIG FOIA Appeals Officer, and sent to you within 20 days after the appeal is received, or by the last day of the last extension under paragraph (e) of this section. The determination of an appeal is the final action of FHFA or FHFA–OIG on a FOIA request. A determination may—

(1) Affirm, in whole or in part, the initial denial of the request and may include a brief statement of the reason or reasons for the decision, including each FOIA exemption relied upon;

(2) Reverse, in whole or in part, the denial of a request in whole or in part, and require the request to be processed promptly in accordance with the decision; or

(3) Remand a request to FHFA or FHFA–OIG, as appropriate, for re-processing, stating the time limits for responding to the remanded request.

(e) *Notice of delayed determinations on appeal.* If FHFA or FHFA–OIG cannot send a determination on your appeal within the 20-day time limit, the designated Appeals Officer will continue to process the appeal and upon expiration of the time limit, will inform you of the reason(s) for the delay and the date on which a determination may be expected. In this notice of delay, the FHFA or FHFA–OIG FOIA Appeals Officer may request that you forebear seeking judicial review until a final determination is made.

(f) *Judicial review.* If the denial of your request for records is upheld in whole or in part, or if a determination on your appeal has not been sent at the end of the 20-day period in paragraph (d) of this section, or the last extension thereof, you may seek judicial review under 5 U.S.C. 552(a)(4).

§ 1202.10 Will FHFA or FHFA–OIG expedite my request or appeal?

(a) *Request for expedited processing.* You may request, in writing, expedited processing of an initial request or of an appeal. FHFA or FHFA–OIG may grant expedited processing, and give your request or appeal priority if your request for expedited processing demonstrates a compelling need by establishing one or more of the following—

(1) Circumstances in which the lack of expedited treatment could reasonably be expected to pose an imminent threat to the life or physical safety of an individual;

(2) An urgency to inform the public about an actual or alleged Federal Government activity if you are a person primarily engaged in disseminating information;

(3) The loss of substantial due process or rights;

(4) A matter of widespread and exceptional media interest in which there exists possible questions about the Federal Government's integrity, affecting public confidence; or

(5) Humanitarian need.

(b) *Certification of compelling need.* Your request for expedited processing must include a statement certifying that the reason(s) you present demonstrate a compelling need are true and correct to the best of your knowledge.

(c) *Determination on request.* FHFA or FHFA–OIG will notify you within 10 days of receipt of your request whether expedited processing has been granted. If a request for expedited treatment is granted, the request will be given priority and will be processed as soon as practicable. If a request for expedited processing is denied, any appeal under § 1202.9 of that decision will be acted on expeditiously.

§ 1202.11 What will it cost to get the records I requested?

(a) *Assessment of fees, generally.* FHFA or FHFA–OIG will assess you for fees covering the direct costs of responding to your request and costs for duplicating records, except as otherwise provided in a statute with respect to the determination of fees that may be assessed for disclosure, search time, or review of particular records.

(b) *Assessment of fees, categories of requesters.* The fees that FHFA or FHFA–OIG may assess vary depending on the type of request or the type of requester you are—

(1) *Commercial use.* If you request records for a commercial use, the fees that FHFA or FHFA–OIG may assess are limited to FHFA's or FHFA–OIG's operating costs incurred for document search, review, and duplication.

(2) *Educational institution, noncommercial scientific institution, or representative of the news media.* If you are not requesting records for commercial use and you are an educational institution or a noncommercial scientific institution, whose purpose is scholarly or scientific research, or a representative of the news media, the fees that may be assessed are limited to standard reasonable charges for duplication in excess of 100 pages or an electronic equivalent of 100 pages.

(3) *Other.* If neither paragraph (b)(1) nor paragraph (b)(2) of this section applies, the fees assessed are limited to the costs for document searching in excess of two hours and duplication in excess of 100 pages, or an electronic equivalent of 100 pages.

(c) *Fee schedule.* The current schedule of fees is maintained on FHFA's Web site at: *http://www.fhfa.gov.*

(d) *Notice of anticipated fees in excess of $100.00.* When FHFA or FHFA–OIG determines or estimates that the fees chargeable to you will exceed $100.00, you will be notified of the actual or estimated amount of fees you will incur, unless you earlier indicated your willingness to pay fees as high as those anticipated. When you are notified that the actual or estimated fees exceed $100.00, your FOIA request will not be considered received by FHFA or FHFA–OIG until you agree to pay the anticipated total fee.

(e) *Advance payment of fees.* FHFA or FHFA–OIG may request that you pay estimated fees or a deposit in advance of responding to your request. If FHFA or FHFA–OIG requests advance payment or a deposit, your request will not be considered received by FHFA or FHFA–OIG until the advance payment or deposit is received. FHFA or FHFA–OIG will request advance payment or a deposit if—

(1) The fees are likely to exceed $500.00. FHFA or FHFA–OIG will notify you of the likely cost and obtain from you satisfactory assurance of full payment if you have a history of prompt payment of FOIA fees to FHFA or FHFA–OIG;

(2) You do not have a history of payment, or if the estimate of fees exceeds $1,000.00, FHFA or FHFA–OIG may require an advance payment of fees in an amount up to the full estimated charge that will be incurred;

(3) You previously failed to pay a fee to FHFA or FHFA–OIG in a timely fashion, *i.e.*, within 30 calendar days of the date of a billing, FHFA or FHFA–OIG may require you to make advance payment of the full amount of the fees anticipated before processing a new request or finishing processing of a pending request; or

(4) You have an outstanding balance due from a prior request. FHFA or FHFA–OIG may require you to pay the full amount owed plus any applicable interest, as provided in paragraph (f) of this section, or demonstrate that the fee owed has been paid, as well as payment of the full amount of anticipated fees before processing your request.

(f) *Interest.* FHFA or FHFA–OIG may charge you interest on an unpaid bill starting on the 31st calendar day following the day on which the bill was sent. Once a fee payment has been received by FHFA or FHFA–OIG, even if not processed, FHFA or FHFA–OIG will stay the accrual of interest. Interest charges will be assessed at the rate prescribed by 31 U.S.C. 3717 and will accrue from the date of the billing.

(g) *FHFA or FHFA–OIG assistance to reduce costs.* If FHFA or FHFA–OIG notifies you of estimated fees exceeding $100.00 or requests advance payment or a deposit, you will have an opportunity to consult with FHFA or FHFA–OIG FOIA staff to modify or reformulate your request to meet your needs at a lower cost.

(h) *Fee waiver requests.* You may request a fee waiver in accordance with FOIA and this regulation. FHFA or FHFA–OIG may grant your fee waiver request if disclosure of the information is in the public interest because it is likely to contribute significantly to public understanding of the operations or activities of the Federal Government and is not primarily in the commercial interest of the requester. In submitting a fee waiver request, you must address the following six factors—

(1) Whether the subject of the requested records concerns the operations or activities of the Federal Government;

(2) Whether the disclosure is likely to contribute to an understanding of Federal Government operations or activities;

(3) Whether disclosure of the requested information will contribute to public understanding;

(4) Whether the disclosure is likely to contribute significantly to public understanding of Federal Government operations or activities;

(5) Whether the requester has a commercial interest that would be furthered by the requested disclosure; and

(6) Whether the magnitude of the identified commercial interest of the requester is sufficiently large, in comparison with the public interest in disclosure, that disclosure is primarily in the commercial interest of the requester.

(i) *Determination on request.* FHFA or FHFA–OIG will notify you within 20 days of receipt of your request whether the fee waiver has been granted. A request for fee waiver that is denied may only be appealed when a final decision has been made on the initial FOIA request.

§ 1202.12 Is there anything else I need to know about FOIA procedures?

This FOIA regulation does not and shall not be construed to create any right or to entitle any person, as of right, to any service or to the disclosure of any record to which such person is not entitled under FOIA. This regulation only provides procedures for requesting records under FOIA.

PART 1203—EQUAL ACCESS TO JUSTICE ACT

Subpart A—General Provisions

Subpart B—Information Required From Applicants

Subpart C—Procedures for Filing and Consideration of the Application for Award

AUTHORITY: 12 U.S.C. 4526, 5 U.S.C. 504.

SOURCE: 75 FR 65219, Oct. 22, 2010, unless otherwise noted..

Subpart A—General Provisions

§ 1203.1 Purpose and scope.

(a) This part implements the Equal Access to Justice Act, 5 U.S.C. 504, by establishing procedures for the filing and consideration of applications for awards of fees and other expenses to eligible individuals and entities who are parties to adversary adjudications before FHFA.

(b) This part applies to the award of fees and other expenses in connection with adversary adjudications before FHFA. However, if a court reviews the underlying decision of the adversary adjudication, an award for fees and other expenses may be made only pursuant to 28 U.S.C. 2412(d)(3).

§ 1203.2 Definitions.

As used in this part:

Adjudicative officer means the official who presided at the underlying adversary adjudication, without regard to whether the official is designated as a hearing examiner, administrative law judge, administrative judge, or otherwise.

Adversary adjudication means an administrative proceeding conducted by FHFA under 5 U.S.C. 554 in which the position of FHFA or any other agency of the United States is represented by counsel or otherwise, including but not limited to an adjudication conducted under the Safety and Soundness Act, as amended, and any implementing regulations. Any issue as to whether an administrative proceeding is an adversary adjudication for purposes of this part will be an issue for resolution in the proceeding on the application for award.

Affiliate means an individual, corporation, or other entity that directly or indirectly controls or owns a majority of the voting shares or other interests of the party, or any corporation or other entity of which the party directly or indirectly owns or controls a majority of the voting shares or other interest, unless the adjudicative officer determines that it would be unjust and contrary to the purpose of the Equal Access to Justice Act in light of the actual relationship between the affiliated entities to consider them to be affiliates for purposes of this part.

Agency counsel means the attorney or attorneys designated by the General Counsel of FHFA to represent FHFA in an adversary adjudication covered by this part.

Demand of FHFA means the express demand of FHFA that led to the adversary adjudication, but does not include a recitation by FHFA of the maximum statutory penalty when accompanied by an express demand for a lesser amount.

Director means the Director of the Federal Housing Finance Agency.

Fees and other expenses means reasonable attorney or agent fees, the reasonable expenses of expert witnesses, and the reasonable cost of any study, analysis, engineering report, or test, which the agency finds necessary for the preparation of the eligible party's case.

FHFA means the Federal Housing Finance Agency.

Final disposition date means the date on which a decision or order disposing of the merits of the adversary adjudication or any other complete resolution of the adversary adjudication, such as a settlement or voluntary dismissal, becomes final and unappealable, both within the agency and to the courts.

Party means an individual, partnership, corporation, association, or public or private organization that is named or admitted as a party, that is admitted as a party for limited purposes, or that is properly seeking and entitled as of right to be admitted as a party in an adversary adjudication.

Position of FHFA means the position taken by FHFA in the adversary adjudication, including the action or failure to act by FHFA upon which the adversary adjudication was based.

§ 1203.3 Eligible parties.

(a) To be eligible for an award of fees and other expenses under the Equal Access to Justice Act, the applicant must show that it meets all conditions of eligibility set out in this paragraph and has complied with all the requirements in Subpart B of this part. The applicant must also be a party to the adversary adjudication for which it seeks an award.

(b) To be eligible for an award of fees and other expenses for prevailing parties, a party must be one of the following:

(1) An individual who has a net worth of not more than $2 million;

(2) The sole owner of an unincorporated business who has a net worth of not more than $7 million, including both personal and business interest, and not more than 500 employees; however, a party who owns an unincorporated business will be considered to be an "individual" rather than the "sole owner of an unincorporated business" if the issues on which the party prevails are related primarily to personal interests rather than to business interests;

(3) A charitable or other tax-exempt organization described in section 501(c)(3) of the Internal Revenue Code, 26 U.S.C. 501(c)(3), with not more than 500 employees;

(4) A cooperative association as defined in section 15(a) of the Agricultural Marketing Act, 12 U.S.C. 1141j(a), with not more than 500 employees;

(5) Any other partnership, corporation, association, unit of local government, or organization that has a net worth of not more than $7 million and not more than 500 employees; or

(6) For the purposes of an application filed pursuant to 5 U.S.C. 504(a)(4), a small entity as defined in 5 U.S.C. 601.

(c) For purposes of eligibility under this section:

(1) The employees of a party must include all persons who regularly perform services for remuneration for the party, under the party's direction and control. Part-time employees must be included on a proportional basis.

(2) The net worth and number of employees of the party and its affiliates must be aggregated to determine eligibility.

(3) The net worth and number of employees of a party will be determined as of the date the underlying adversary adjudication was initiated.

(4) A party that participates in an adversary adjudication primarily on behalf of one or more entities that would be ineligible for an award is not itself eligible for an award.

§ 1203.4 Standards for awards.

(a) An eligible party that files an application for award of fees and other expenses in accordance with this part will receive an award of fees and other expenses related to defending against a demand of FHFA if the demand was in excess of the decision in the underlying adversary adjudication and was unreasonable when compared with the decision under the facts and circumstances of the case, unless the party has committed a willful violation of law or otherwise acted in bad faith, or unless special circumstances make an award unjust. The burden of proof that the demand of FHFA was substantially in excess of the decision and is unreasonable when compared with the decision is on the eligible party.

(b) An eligible party that submits an application for award in accordance with this part will receive an award of fees and other expenses incurred in connection with an adversary adjudication in which it prevailed or in a significant and discrete substantive portion of the adversary adjudication in which it prevailed, unless the position of FHFA in the adversary adjudication was substantially justified or special circumstances make an award unjust. FHFA has the burden of proof to show that its position was substantially justified and may do so by showing that its position was reasonable in law and in fact.

§ 1203.5 Allowable fees and expenses.

(a) Awards of fees and other expenses will be based on rates customarily charged by persons engaged in the business of acting as attorneys, agents, and expert witnesses, even if the services were made available without charge or at a reduced rate to the party. However, except as provided in § 1203.6, an award for the fee of an attorney or agent may not exceed $125 per hour and an award to compensate an expert witness may not exceed the highest rate at which FHFA pays expert witnesses. However, an award may also include the reasonable expenses of the attorney, agent, or expert witness as a separate item if he or she ordinarily charges clients separately for such expenses.

(b) In determining the reasonableness of the fee sought for an attorney, agent, or expert witness, the adjudicative officer will consider the following:

(1) If the attorney, agent, or expert witness is in private practice, his or her customary fees for similar services; or, if the attorney, agent, or expert witness is an employee of the eligible party, the fully allocated costs of the services;

(2) The prevailing rate for similar services in the community in which the attorney, agent, or expert witness ordinarily performs services;

(3) The time actually spent in the representation of the eligible party;

(4) The time reasonably spent in light of the difficulty or complexity of the issues in the adversary adjudication; and

(5) Such other factors as may bear on the value of the services provided.

(c) In determining the reasonable cost of any study, analysis, engineering report, test, project, or similar matter prepared on behalf of a party, the adjudicative officer will consider the prevailing rate for similar services in the community in which the services were performed.

(d) Fees and other expenses incurred before the date on which an adversary adjudication was initiated will be awarded only if the eligible party can demonstrate that they were reasonably incurred in preparation for the adversary adjudication.

§ 1203.6 Rulemaking on maximum rate for fees.

If warranted by an increase in the cost of living or by special circumstances, FHFA may adopt regulations providing for an award of attorney or agent fees at a rate higher than $125 per hour in adversary adjudications covered by this part. Special circumstances include the limited availability of attorneys or agents who are qualified to handle certain types of adversary adjudications. FHFA will conduct any rulemaking proceedings for this purpose under the informal rulemaking procedures of the Administrative Procedure Act, 5 U.S.C. 553.

§ 1203.7 Awards against other agencies.

If another agency of the United States participates in an adversary adjudication before FHFA and takes a position that was not substantially justified, the award or appropriate portion of the award to an eligible party that prevailed over that agency will be made against that agency.

§§ 1203.8–1203.9 [Reserved]

Subpart B—Information Required From Applicants

§ 1203.10 Contents of the application for award.

(a) An application for award of fees and other expenses under either § 1203.4(a) and § 1203.4(b) must:

(1) Identify the applicant and the adversary adjudication for which an award is sought;

(2) State the amount of fees and other expenses for which an award is sought;

(3) Provide the statements and documentation required by paragraph (b) or (c) of this section and § 1203.12 and any additional information required by the adjudicative officer; and

(4) Be signed by the applicant or an authorized officer or attorney of the applicant and contain or be accompanied by a written verification under oath or under penalty of perjury that the information provided in the application is true and correct.

(b) An application for award under § 1203.4(a) must show that the demand of FHFA was substantially in excess of, and was unreasonable when compared to, the decision in the underlying adversary adjudication under the facts and circumstances of the case. It must also show that the applicant is a small entity as defined in 5 U.S.C. 601.

(c) An application for award under § 1203.4(b) must:

(1) Show that the applicant has prevailed in a significant and discrete substantive portion of the underlying adversary adjudication and identify the position of FHFA in the adversary adjudication that the applicant alleges was not substantially justified;

(2) State the number of employees of the applicant and describe briefly the type and purposes of its organization or business (if the applicant is not an individual);

(3) State that the net worth of the applicant does not exceed $2 million, if the applicant is an individual; or for all other applicants, state that the net worth of the applicant and its affiliates, if any, does not exceed $7 million; and

(4) Include one of the following:

(i) A detailed exhibit showing the net worth (net worth exhibit) of the applicant and its affiliates, if any, when the underlying adversary adjudication was initiated. The net worth exhibit may be in any form convenient to the applicant as long as the net worth exhibit provides full disclosure of the assets and liabilities of the applicant and its affiliates, if any, and is sufficient to determine whether the applicant qualifies as an eligible party;

(ii) A copy of a ruling by the Internal Revenue Service that shows that the applicant qualifies as an organization described in section 501(c)(3) of the Internal Revenue Code, 26 U.S.C. 501(c)(3); or in the case of a tax-exempt organization not required to obtain a ruling from the Internal Revenue Service on its exempt status, a statement that describes the basis for the belief that the applicant qualifies under such section; or

(iii) A statement that the applicant is a cooperative association as defined in section 15(a) of the Agricultural Marketing Act, 12 U.S.C. 1141j(a).

§ 1203.11 Confidentiality of net worth exhibit.

Unless otherwise ordered by the Director, or required by law, the statement of net worth will be for the confidential use of the adjudicative officer, the Director, and agency counsel.

§ 1203.12 Documentation for fees and expenses.

(a) The application for award must be accompanied by full and itemized documentation of the fees and other expenses for which an award is sought. The adjudicative officer may require the applicant to provide vouchers, receipts, logs, or other documentation for any fees or expenses claimed.

(b) A separate itemized statement must be submitted for each entity or individual whose services are covered by the application. Each itemized statement must include:

(1) The hours spent by each entity or individual;

(2) A description of the specific services performed and the rates at which each fee has been computed; and

(3) Any expenses for which reimbursement is sought, the total amount claimed, and the total amount paid or payable by the applicant or by any other person or entity.

§§ 1203.13–1203.19 [Reserved]

Subpart C—Procedures for Filing and Consideration of the Application for Award

§ 1203.20 Filing and service of the application for award and related papers.

(a) An application for an award of fees and other expenses must be filed no later than 30 days after the final disposition of the underlying adversary adjudication.

(b) An application for award and other papers related to the proceedings on the application for award must be filed and served on all parties in the same manner as papers are filed and served in the underlying adversary adjudication, except as otherwise provided in this part.

(c) The computation of time for filing and service of the application of award and other papers must be computed in the same manner as in the underlying adversary adjudication.

§ 1203.21 Response to the application for award.

(a) Agency counsel must file a response within 30 days after service of an application for award of fees and other expenses except as provided in paragraphs (b) and (c) of this section. In the response, agency counsel must explain any objections to the award requested and identify the facts relied upon to support the objections. If any of the alleged facts are not already in the record of the underlying adversary adjudication, agency counsel must include with the response either supporting affidavits or a request for further proceedings under § 1203.25.

(b) If agency counsel and the applicant believe that the issues in the application for award can be settled, they may jointly file a statement of their intent to negotiate a settlement. The filing of this statement will extend the time for filing a response for an additional 30 days. Upon request by agency counsel and the applicant, the adjudicative officer may grant for good cause further time extensions.

(c) Agency counsel may request that the adjudicative officer extend the time period for filing a response. If agency counsel does not respond or otherwise does not contest or settle the application for award within the 30-day period or the extended time period, the adjudicative officer may make an award of fees and other expenses upon a satisfactory showing of entitlement by the applicant.

§ 1203.22 Reply to the response.

Within 15 days after service of a response, the applicant may file a reply. If the reply is based on any alleged facts not already in the record of the underlying adversary adjudication, the applicant must include with the reply either supporting affidavits or a request for further proceedings under § 1203.25.

§ 1203.23 Comments by other parties.

Any party to the underlying adversary adjudication other than the applicant and agency counsel may file comments on an application for award within 30 calendar days after it is served, or on a response within 15 calendar days after it is served. A commenting party may not participate further in proceedings on the application unless the adjudicative officer determines that the public interest requires such participation in order to permit full exploration of matters raised in the comments.

§ 1203.24 Settlement.

The applicant and agency counsel may agree on a proposed settlement of an award before the final decision on the application for award is made, either in connection with a settlement of the underlying adversary adjudication or after the underlying adversary adjudication has been concluded. If the eligible party and agency counsel agree on a proposed settlement of an award before an application for award has been filed, the application must be filed with the proposed settlement.

§ 1203.25 Further proceedings on the application for award.

(a) On request of either the applicant or agency counsel, on the adjudicative officer's own initiative, or as requested by the Director under § 1203.27, the adjudicative officer may order further proceedings, such as an informal conference, oral argument, additional written submissions, or, as to issues other than substantial justification (such as the applicant's eligibility or substantiation of fees and expenses), pertinent discovery or an evidential hearing. Such further proceedings will be held only when necessary for full and fair resolution of the issues arising from the application for award and will be conducted as promptly as possible. The issue as to whether the position of FHFA in the underlying adversary adjudication was substantially justified will be determined on the basis of the whole administrative record that was made in the underlying adversary adjudication.

(b) A request that the adjudicative officer order further proceedings under this section must specifically identify the information sought on the disputed issues and must explain why the additional proceedings are necessary to resolve the issues.

§ 1203.26 Decision of the adjudicative officer.

(a) The adjudicative officer must make the initial decision on the basis of the written record, except if further proceedings are ordered under § 1203.25.

(b) The adjudicative officer must issue a written initial decision on the application for award within 30 days after completion of proceedings on the application. The initial decision will become the final decision of FHFA after 30 days from the day it was issued, unless review is ordered under § 1203.27.

(c) In all initial decisions, the adjudicative officer must include findings and conclusions with respect to the applicant's eligibility and an explanation of the reasons for any difference between the amount requested by the applicant and the amount awarded. If the applicant has sought an award against more than one agency, the adjudicative officer must also include findings and conclusions with respect to the allocation of payment of any award made.

(d) In initial decisions on applications filed pursuant to § 1203.4(a), the adjudicative officer must include findings and conclusions as to whether FHFA made a demand that was substantially in excess of the decision in the underlying adversary adjudication and that was unreasonable when compared with that decision; and, if at issue, whether the applicant has committed a willful violation of the law or otherwise acted in bad faith, or whether special circumstances would make the award unjust.

(e) In decisions on applications filed pursuant to § 1203.4(b), the adjudicative officer must include written findings and conclusions as to whether the applicant is a prevailing party and whether the position of FHFA was substantially justified; and, if at issue, whether the applicant unduly protracted or delayed the underlying adversary adjudication or whether special circumstance make the award unjust.

§ 1203.27 Review by FHFA.

Within 30 days after the adjudicative officer issues an initial decision under § 1203.26, either the applicant or agency counsel may request the Director to review the initial decision of the adjudicative officer. The Director may also decide, at his or her discretion, to review the initial decision. If review is ordered, the Director must issue a final decision on the application for award or remand the application for award to the adjudicative officer for further proceedings under § 1203.25.

§ 1203.28 Judicial review.

Any party, other than the United States, that is dissatisfied with the final decision on an application for award of fees and expenses under this part may seek judicial review as provided in 5 U.S.C. 504(c)(2).

§ 1203.29 Payment of award.

To receive payment of an award of fees and other expenses granted under this part, the applicant must submit a copy of the final decision that grants the award and a certification that the applicant will not seek review of the decision in the United States courts to the Director, Federal Housing Finance Agency, 1700 G Street, NW., Washington, DC 20552. FHFA must pay the amount awarded to the applicant within 60 days of receipt of the submission of the copy of the final decision and the certification, unless judicial review of the award has been sought by any party to the proceedings.

PART 1204—PRIVACY ACT IMPLEMENTATION

Sec.

AUTHORITY: 5 U.S.C. 552a.

SOURCE: 76 FR 51871, Aug. 19, 2011, unless otherwise noted.

§ 1204.1 Why did FHFA issue this part?

The Federal Housing Finance Agency (FHFA) issued this part to—

(a) Implement the Privacy Act, a Federal law that helps protect private information about individuals that Federal agencies collect or maintain. You should read this part together with the Privacy Act, which provides additional information about records maintained on individuals;

(b) Establish rules that apply to all FHFA and FHFA Office of Inspector General (FHFA–OIG) maintained systems of records retrievable by an individual's name or other personal identifier;

(c) Describe procedures through which you may request access to records, request amendment or correction of those records, or request an accounting of disclosures of those records by FHFA or FHFA–OIG;

(d) Inform you, that when it is appropriate to do so, FHFA or FHFA–OIG automatically processes a Privacy Act request for access to records under both the Privacy Act and FOIA, following the rules contained in this part and in FHFA's Freedom of Information Act regulation at part 1202 of this title so that you will receive the maximum amount of information available to you by law;

(e) Notify you that this part does not entitle you to any service or to the disclosure of any record to which you are not entitled under the Privacy Act. It also does not, and may not be relied upon, to create any substantive or procedural right or benefit enforceable against FHFA or FHFA–OIG; and

(f) Notify you that this part applies to both FHFA and FHFA–OIG.

§ 1204.2 What do the terms in this part mean?

The following definitions apply to the terms used in this part—

Access means making a record available to a subject individual.

Amendment means any correction of, addition to, or deletion from a record.

Court means any entity conducting a legal proceeding.

Days, unless stated as "calendar days," are working days and do not include Saturdays, Sundays, and federal holidays. If the last day of any period prescribed herein falls on a Saturday, Sunday, or federal holiday, the last day of the period will be the next working day that is not a Saturday, Sunday, or federal holiday.

FHFA means the Federal Housing Finance Agency and includes its predecessor agencies, the Office of Federal Housing Enterprise Oversight (OFHEO) and the Federal Housing Finance Board (FHFB).

FHFA–OIG means the Office of Inspector General for FHFA.

FOIA means the Freedom of Information Act, as amended (5 U.S.C. 552).

Individual means a natural person who is either a citizen of the United States of America or an alien lawfully admitted for permanent residence.

Maintain includes collect, use, disseminate, or control.

Privacy Act means the Privacy Act of 1974, as amended (5 U.S.C. 552a).

Privacy Act Appeals Officer means a person designated by the FHFA Director to process appeals of denials of requests for or seeking amendment of records maintained by FHFA under the Privacy Act. For appeals pertaining to records maintained by FHFA–OIG, *Privacy Act Appeals Officer* means a person designated by the FHFA Inspector General to process appeals of denials of requests for or seeking amendment of records maintained by FHFA–OIG under the Privacy Act.

Privacy Act Officer means a person designated by the FHFA Director who has primary responsibility for privacy and data protection policy and is authorized to process requests for or amendment of records maintained by FHFA under the Privacy Act. For requests pertaining to records maintained by FHFA–OIG, *Privacy Act Officer* means a person designated by the FHFA Inspector General to process requests for or amendment of records maintained by FHFA–OIG under the Privacy Act.

Record means any item, collection, or grouping of information about an individual that FHFA or FHFA–OIG maintains within a system of records, including, but not limited to, the individual's name, an identifying number, symbol, or other identifying particular assigned to the individual, such as a finger or voice print, or photograph.

Routine use means the purposes for which records and information contained in a system of records may be disclosed by FHFA or FHFA–OIG without the consent of the subject of the record. Routine uses for records are identified in each system of records notice. Routine use does not include disclosure that subsection (b) of the Privacy Act (5 U.S.C. 552a(b)) otherwise permits.

Senior Agency Official for Privacy means a person designated by the FHFA Director who has the authority and responsibility to oversee and supervise the FHFA privacy program and implementation of the Privacy Act.

System of Records means a group of records FHFA or FHFA–OIG maintains or controls from which information is retrieved by the name of an individual or by some identifying number, symbol, or other identifying particular assigned to the individual. Single records or groups of records that are not retrieved by a personal identifier are not part of a system of records.

System of Records Notice means a notice published in the FEDERAL REGISTER which announces the creation, deletion, or amendment of one or more system of records. System of records notices are also used to identify a system of records' routine uses.

§ 1204.3 How do I make a Privacy Act request?

(a) *What is a valid request?* In general, a Privacy Act request can be made on your own behalf for records or information about you. You can make a Privacy Act request on behalf of another individual as the parent or guardian of a minor, or as the guardian of someone determined by a court to be incompetent. You also may request access to another individual's record or information if you have that individual's written consent, unless other conditions of disclosure apply.

(b) *How and where do I make a request?* Your request must be in writing. Regardless of whether your request seeks records from FHFA, FHFA–OIG, or both, you may appear in person to submit your written request to the FHFA Privacy Act Officer, or send your written request to the FHFA Privacy Act Officer by electronic mail, mail, delivery service, or facsimile. The electronic mail address is: *privacy@fhfa.gov*. For mail or delivery service, the address is: FHFA Privacy Act Officer, Federal Housing Finance Agency, 1700 G Street, NW., Washington, DC 20552. The facsimile number is (202) 414–6425. Requests for FHFA–OIG maintained records will be forwarded to FHFA–OIG for processing and direct response. You can help FHFA and FHFA–OIG process your request by marking electronic mail, letters, or facsimiles and the subject line, envelope, or facsimile cover sheet with "Privacy Act Request." FHFA's "Privacy Act Reference Guide," which is available on FHFA's Web site, *http://www.fhfa.gov*, provides additional information to assist you in making your request.

(c) *What must the request include?* You must describe the record that you want in enough detail to enable either the FHFA or FHFA–OIG Privacy Act Officer to locate the system of records containing it with a reasonable amount of effort. Include specific information about each record sought, such as the time period in which you believe it was compiled, the name or identifying number of each system of records in which you believe it is kept, and the date, title or name, author, recipient, or subject matter of the record. As a general rule, the more specific you are about the record that you want, the more likely FHFA or FHFA–OIG will be able to locate it in response to your request.

(d) *How do I request amendment or correction of a record?* If you are requesting an amendment or correction of any FHFA or FHFA–OIG record, identify each particular record in question and the system of records in which the record is located, describe the amendment or correction that you want, and state why you believe that the record is not accurate, relevant, timely, or complete. You may submit any documentation that you think would be helpful, including an annotated copy of the record.

(e) *How do I request for an accounting of disclosures?* If you are requesting an accounting of disclosures by FHFA or FHFA–OIG of a record to another person, organization, or Federal agency, you must identify each particular record in question. An accounting generally includes the date, nature, and purpose of each disclosure, as well as the name and address of the person, organization, or Federal agency to which the disclosure was made, subject to §1204.7.

(f) *Must I verify my identity?* Yes. When making requests under the Privacy Act, your request must verify your identity to protect your privacy or the privacy of the individual on whose behalf you are acting. If you make a Privacy Act request and you do not follow these identity verification procedures, FHFA or FHFA–OIG cannot and will not process your request.

(1) *How do I verify my identity?* To verify your identity, you must state your full name, current address, and date and place of birth. In order to help identify and locate the records you request, you also may, at your option, include your Social Security number. If you make your request in person and your identity is not known to either the FHFA or FHFA–OIG Privacy Act Officer, you must provide either two forms of unexpired identification with photographs issued by a federal, state, or local government agency or entity (*i.e.* passport, passport card, driver's license, ID card, etc.), or one form of unexpired identification with a photograph issued by a federal, state, or local government agency or entity (*i.e.* passport, passport card, driver's license, ID card, etc.) and a properly authenticated birth certificate. If you make your request by mail, your signature either must be notarized or submitted under 28 U.S.C. 1746, a law that permits statements to be made under penalty of perjury as a substitute for notarization. You may fulfill this requirement by having your signature on your request letter witnessed by a notary or by including the following statement just before the signature on your request letter: "I declare (or certify, verify, or state) under penalty of perjury that the foregoing is true and correct. Executed on [date]. [Signature]."

(2) *How do I verify parentage or guardianship?* If you make a Privacy Act request as the parent or guardian of a minor, or as the guardian of someone determined by a court to be incompetent, with respect to records or information about that individual, you must establish—

(i) The identity of the individual who is the subject of the record, by stating the individual's name, current address, date and place of birth, and, at your option, the Social Security number of the individual;

(ii) Your own identity, as required in paragraph (f)(1) of this section;

(iii) That you are the parent or guardian of the individual, which you may prove by providing a properly authenticated copy of the individual's birth certificate showing your parentage or a properly authenticated court order establishing your guardianship; and

(iv) That you are acting on behalf of the individual in making the request.

§ 1204.4 How will FHFA or FHFA–OIG respond to my Privacy Act request?

(a) *How will FHFA or FHFA–OIG locate the requested records?* FHFA or FHFA–OIG will search to determine if requested records exist in the system of records it owns or controls. You can find FHFA and FHFA–OIG system of records notices on our Web site at *http://www.fhfa.gov*. You can also find descriptions of OFHEO and FHFB system of records that have not yet been superseded on the FHFA Web site. A description of the system of records also is available in the "Privacy Act Issuances" compilation published by the Office of the Federal Register of the National Archives and Records Administration. You can access the "Privacy Act Issuances" compilation in most large reference and university libraries or electronically at the Government Printing Office Web site at: *http://www.gpoaccess.gov/privacyact/index.html*. You also can request a copy of FHFA or FHFA–OIG system of records from the Privacy Act Officer.

(b) *How long does FHFA or FHFA–OIG have to respond?* Either the FHFA or FHFA–OIG Privacy Act Officer generally will respond to your request in writing within 20 days after receiving it, if it meets the § 1204.3 requirements. For requests to amend a record, either the FHFA or FHFA–OIG Privacy Act Officer will respond within 10 days after receipt of the request to amend. FHFA or FHFA–OIG may extend the response time in unusual circumstances, such as when consultation is needed with another Federal agency (if that agency is subject to the Privacy Act) about a record or to retrieve a record shipped offsite for storage. If you submit your written request in person, either the FHFA or FHFA–OIG Privacy Act Officer may disclose records or information to you directly and create a written record of the grant of the request. If you are to be accompanied by another person when accessing your record or any information pertaining to you, FHFA or FHFA–OIG may require your written authorization before permitting access or discussing the record in the presence of the other person.

(c) *What will the FHFA or FHFA–OIG response include?* The written response will include a determination to grant or deny your request in whole or in part, a brief explanation of the reasons for the determination, and the amount of the fee charged, if any, under § 1204.6. If you are granted a request to access a record, FHFA or FHFA–OIG will make the record available to you. If you are granted a request to amend or correct a record, the response will describe any amendments or corrections made and advise you of your right to obtain a copy of the amended or corrected record.

(d) *What is an adverse determination?* An adverse determination is a determination on a Privacy Act request that—

(1) Withholds any requested record in whole or in part;

(2) Denies a request for an amendment or correction of a record in whole or in part;

(3) Declines to provide a requested accounting of disclosures;

(4) Advises that a requested record does not exist or cannot be located; or

(5) Finds what has been requested is not a record subject to the Privacy Act.

(e) *What will be stated in a response that includes an adverse determination?* If an adverse determination is made with respect to your request, either the FHFA or FHFA–OIG Privacy Act Officer's written response under this section will identify the person responsible for the adverse determination, state that the adverse determination is not a final action of FHFA or FHFA–OIG, and state that you may appeal the adverse determination under § 1204.5.

§ 1204.5 What if I am dissatisfied with the response to my Privacy Act request?

(a) *May I appeal the response?* You may appeal any adverse determination made in response to your Privacy Act request. If you wish to seek review by a court of any adverse determination or denial of a request, you must first appeal it under this section.

(b) *How do I appeal the response?*—(1) You may appeal by submitting in writing, a statement of the reasons you believe the adverse determination should be overturned. FHFA or FHFA–OIG must receive your written appeal within 30 calendar days of the date of the adverse determination under § 1204.4. Your written appeal may include as much or as little related information as you wish, as long as it clearly identifies the determination (including the request number, if known) that you are appealing.

(2) If FHFA or FHFA–OIG denied your request in whole or in part, you may appeal the denial by writing directly to the FHFA Privacy Act Appeals Officer through electronic mail, mail, delivery service, or facsimile. The electronic mail address is: *privacy@fhfa.gov*. For mail or express mail, the address is: FHFA Privacy Act Appeals Officer, Federal Housing Finance Agency, 1700 G Street, NW., Washington, DC 20552. The facsimile number is: (202) 414–8917. For appeals of FHFA–OIG denials, whether in whole or in part, the appeal must be clearly marked by adding "FHFA–OIG" after "Privacy Act Appeal." All appeals from denials, in whole or part, made by FHFA–OIG will be forwarded to the FHFA–OIG Privacy Act Appeals Officer for processing and direct response. You can help FHFA and FHFA–OIG process your appeal by marking electronic mail, letters, or facsimiles and the subject line, envelope, or facsimile cover sheet with "Privacy Act Appeal." FHFA's "Privacy Act Reference Guide," which is available on FHFA's Web site, *http://www.fhfa.gov*, provides additional information to assist you in making your appeal. FHFA or FHFA–OIG ordinarily will not act on an appeal if the Privacy Act request becomes a matter of litigation.

(3) If you need more time to file your appeal, you may request an extension of time of no more than ten (10) calendar days in which to file your appeal, but only if your request is made within the original 30-calendar day time period for filing the appeal. Granting an extension is in the sole discretion of either the FHFA or FHFA–OIG Privacy Act Appeals Officer.

(c) *Who has the authority to grant or deny appeals?* For appeals from the FHFA Privacy Act Officer, the FHFA Privacy Act Appeals Officer is authorized to act on your appeal. For appeals from the FHFA–OIG Privacy Act Officer, the FHFA–OIG Privacy Act Appeals Officer is authorized to act on your appeal.

(d) *When will FHFA or FHFA–OIG respond to my appeal?* FHFA or FHFA–OIG generally will respond to you in writing within 30 days of receipt of an appeal that meets the requirements of paragraph (b) of this section, unless for good cause shown, the FHFA or FHFA–OIG Privacy Act Appeals Officer extends the response time.

(e) *What will the FHFA or FHFA–OIG response include?* The written response will include the determination of either the FHFA or FHFA–OIG Privacy Act Appeals Officer, whether to grant or deny your appeal in whole or in part, a brief explanation of the reasons for the determination, and information about the Privacy Act provisions for court review of the determination.

(1) If your appeal concerns a request for access to records or information and the appeal determination grants your access, the records or information, if any, will be made available to you.

(2)(i) If your appeal concerns an amendment or correction of a record and the appeal determination grants your request for an amendment or correction, the response will describe any amendment or correction made to the record and advise you of your right to obtain a copy of the amended or corrected record under this part. FHFA or FHFA–OIG will notify all persons, organizations, or Federal agencies to which it previously disclosed the record, if an accounting of that disclosure was made, that the record has been amended or corrected. Whenever the record is subsequently disclosed, the record will be disclosed as amended or corrected.

(ii) If the response to your appeal denies your request for an amendment or correction to a record, the response will advise you of your right to file a Statement of Disagreement under paragraph (f) of this section.

(f) *What is a Statement of Disagreement?*—(1) A Statement of Disagreement is a concise written statement in which you clearly identify each part of any record that you dispute and explain your reason(s) for disagreeing with either the FHFA or FHFA–OIG Privacy Act Appeals Officer's denial, in whole or in part, of your appeal requesting amendment or correction. Your Statement of Disagreement must be received by either the FHFA or FHFA–OIG Privacy Act Officer within 30 calendar days of either the FHFA or

FHFA–OIG Privacy Act Appeals Officer's denial, in whole or in part, of your appeal concerning amendment or correction of a record. FHFA and FHFA–OIG will place your Statement of Disagreement in the system of records in which the disputed record is maintained. FHFA and FHFA–OIG may also append a concise statement of its reason(s) for denying the request for an amendment or correction of the record.

(2) FHFA and FHFA–OIG will notify all persons, organizations, and Federal agencies to which it previously disclosed the disputed record, if an accounting of that disclosure was made, that the record is disputed and provide your Statement of Disagreement and the FHFA or FHFA–OIG concise statement, if any. Whenever the disputed record is subsequently disclosed, a copy of your Statement of Disagreement and the FHFA or FHFA–OIG concise statement, if any, will also be disclosed.

§ 1204.6 What does it cost to get records under the Privacy Act?

(a) *Must I agree to pay fees?* Your Privacy Act request is your agreement to pay all applicable fees, unless you specify a limit on the amount of fees you agree to pay. FHFA or FHFA–OIG will not exceed the specified limit without your written agreement.

(b) *How does FHFA or FHFA–OIG calculate fees?* FHFA and FHFA–OIG will charge a fee for duplication of a record under the Privacy Act in the same way it charges for duplication of records under FOIA in 12 CFR 1202.11. There are no fees to search for or review records.

§ 1204.7 Are there any exemptions from the Privacy Act?

(a) *What is a Privacy Act exemption?* The Privacy Act authorizes the Director and the FHFA Inspector General to exempt records or information in a system of records from some of the Privacy Act requirements, if the Director or the FHFA Inspector General, as appropriate, determines that the exemption is necessary.

(b) *How do I know if the records or information I want are exempt?*—(1) Each system of records notice will advise you if the Director or the FHFA Inspector General has determined records or information in records are exempt from Privacy Act requirements. If the Director or the FHFA Inspector General has claimed an exemption for a system of records, the system of records notice will identify the exemption and the provisions of the Privacy Act from which the system is exempt.

(2) Until superseded by FHFA or FHFA–OIG systems of records, the following OFHEO and FHFB systems of records are, under 5 U.S.C. 552a(k)(2) or (k)(5), exempt from the Privacy Act requirements of 5 U.S.C. 552a(c)(3), (d), (e)(1), (e)(4)(G), (e)(4)(H), (e)(4)(I), and (f)—

(i) OFHEO–11 Litigation and Enforcement Information System; and

(ii) FHFB–5 Agency Personnel Investigative Records.

(c) *What exemptions potentially apply to FHFA–OIG records?* Unless the FHFA Inspector General, his or her designee, or a statute specifically authorizes disclosure, FHFA–OIG will not release records of matters that are subject to the following exemptions—

(1) To the extent that the systems of records entitled "FHFA–OIG Audit Files Database," "FHFA–OIG Investigative & Evaluative Files Database," "FHFA–OIG Investigative & Evaluative MIS Database," "FHFA–OIG Hotline Database," and "FHFA–OIG Correspondence Database" contain any information compiled by FHFA–OIG for the purpose of criminal law enforcement investigations, such information falls within the scope of exemption (j)(2) of the Privacy Act, 5 U.S.C. 552a(j)(2), and therefore these systems of records are exempt from the requirements of the following subsections of the Privacy Act to that extent, for the reasons stated in paragraphs (1)(i) through (vi) of this section.

(i) From 5 U.S.C. 552a(c)(3), because release of an accounting of disclosures to an individual who is the subject of an investigation or evaluation could reveal the nature and scope of the investigation or evaluation and could result in the altering or destruction of evidence, improper influencing of witnesses, and other evasive actions that could impede or compromise the investigation or evaluation.

(ii) From 5 U.S.C. 552a(d)(1), because release of investigative or evaluative records to an individual who is the subject of an investigation or evaluation could interfere with pending or prospective law enforcement proceedings, constitute an unwarranted invasion of the personal privacy of third parties, reveal the identity of confidential sources, or reveal sensitive investigative or evaluative techniques and procedures.

(iii) From 5 U.S.C. 552a(d)(2), because amendment or correction of investigative or evaluative records could interfere with pending or prospective law enforcement proceedings, or could impose an impossible administrative and investigative or evaluative burden by requiring FHFA–OIG to continuously retrograde its investigations or evaluations attempting to resolve questions of accuracy, relevance, timeliness, and completeness.

(iv) From 5 U.S.C. 552a(e)(1), because it is often impossible to determine relevance or necessity of information in the early stages of an investigation or evaluation. The value of such information is a question of judgment and timing; what appears relevant and necessary when collected may ultimately be evaluated and viewed as irrelevant and unnecessary to an investigation or evaluation. In addition, FHFA–OIG may obtain information concerning the violation of laws other than those within the scope of its jurisdiction. In the interest of effective law enforcement, FHFA–OIG should retain this information because it may aid in establishing patterns of unlawful activity and provide leads for other law enforcement agencies. Further, in obtaining evidence during an investigation or evaluation, information may be provided to FHFA–OIG that relates to matters incidental to the main purpose of the investigation or evaluation, but which may be pertinent to the investigative or evaluative jurisdiction of another agency. Such information cannot readily be identified.

(v) From 5 U.S.C. 552a(e)(2), because in a law enforcement investigation or an evaluation it is usually counterproductive to collect information to the greatest extent practicable directly from the subject thereof. It is not always feasible to rely upon the subject of an investigation or evaluation as a source for information which may implicate him or her in illegal activities. In addition, collecting information directly from the subject could seriously compromise an investigation or evaluation by prematurely revealing its nature and scope, or could provide the subject with an opportunity to conceal criminal activities, or intimidate potential sources, in order to avoid apprehension.

(vi) From 5 U.S.C. 552a(e)(3), because providing such notice to the subject of an investigation or evaluation, or to other individual sources, could seriously compromise the investigation or evaluation by prematurely revealing its nature and scope, or could inhibit cooperation, permit the subject to evade apprehension, or cause interference with undercover activities.

(2) To the extent that the systems of records entitled "FHFA–OIG Audit Files Database," "FHFA–OIG Investigative & Evaluative Files Database," "FHFA–OIG Investigative & Evaluative MIS Database," "FHFA–OIG Hotline Database," and "FHFA–OIG Correspondence Database," contain information compiled by FHFA–OIG for the purpose of criminal law enforcement investigations, such information falls within the scope of exemption (k)(2) of the Privacy Act, 5 U.S.C. 552a(k)(2), and therefore these systems of records are exempt from the requirements of the following subsections of the Privacy Act to that extent, for the reasons stated in paragraphs (c)(2)(i) through (iv) of this section.

(i) From 5 U.S.C. 552a(c)(3), because release of an accounting of disclosures to an individual who is the subject of an investigation or evaluation could reveal the nature and scope of the investigation or evaluation and could result in the altering or destruction of evidence, improper influencing of witnesses, and other evasive actions that could impede or compromise the investigation or evaluation.

(ii) From 5 U.S.C. 552a(d)(1), because release of investigative or evaluative records to an individual who is the subject of an investigation or evaluation could interfere with pending or prospective law enforcement proceedings, constitute an unwarranted invasion of the personal privacy of third parties, reveal the identity of confidential sources, or reveal sensitive investigative or evaluative techniques and procedures.

(iii) From 5 U.S.C. 552a(d)(2), because amendment or correction of investigative or evaluative records could interfere with pending or prospective law enforcement proceedings, or could impose an impossible administrative and investigative or evaluative burden by requiring FHFA–OIG to continuously retrograde its investigations or evaluations attempting to resolve questions of accuracy, relevance, timeliness, and completeness.

(iv) From 5 U.S.C. 552a(e)(1), because it is often impossible to determine relevance or necessity of information in the early stages of an investigation or evaluation. The value of such information is a question of judgment and timing; what appears relevant and necessary when collected may ultimately be evaluated and viewed as irrelevant and unnecessary to an investigation or evaluation. In addition, FHFA–OIG may obtain information concerning the violation of laws other than those within the scope of its jurisdiction. In the interest of effective law enforcement, FHFA–OIG should retain this information because it may aid in establishing patterns of unlawful activity and provide leads for other law enforcement agencies. Further, in obtaining evidence during an investigation or evaluation, information may be provided to FHFA–OIG that relates to matters incidental to the main purpose of the investigation or evaluation but which may be pertinent to the investigative or evaluative jurisdiction of another agency. Such information cannot readily be identified.

(3) To the extent that the systems of records entitled "FHFA–OIG Audit Files Database," "FHFA–OIG Investigative & Evaluative Files Database," "FHFA–OIG Investigative & Evaluative MIS Database," "FHFA–OIG Hotline Database," and "FHFA–OIG Correspondence Database" contain any investigatory material compiled by FHFA–OIG for the purpose of determining suitability, eligibility, or qualifications for Federal civilian employment or Federal contracts, the release of which would reveal the identity of a source who furnished information to the Government under an express promise that the identity of the source would be held in confidence, such information falls within the scope of exemption (k)(5) of the Privacy Act, 5 U.S.C. 552a(k)(5), and therefore these systems of records are exempt from the requirements of subsection (d)(1) of the Privacy Act to that extent, because release would reveal the identity of a source who furnished information to the Government under an express promise of confidentiality. Revealing the identity of a confidential source could impede future cooperation by sources, and could result in harassment or harm to such sources.

§ 1204.8 How are records secured?

(a) *What controls must FHFA and FHFA–OIG have in place?* FHFA and FHFA–OIG must establish administrative and physical controls to prevent unauthorized access to their systems of records, unauthorized or inadvertent disclosure of records,. and physical damage to or destruction of records. The stringency of these controls corresponds to the sensitivity of the records that the controls protect. At a minimum, the administrative and physical controls must ensure that—

(1) Records are protected from public view;

(2) The area in which records are kept is supervised during business hours to prevent unauthorized persons from having access to them;

(3) Records are inaccessible to unauthorized persons outside of business hours; and

(4) Records are not disclosed to unauthorized persons or under unauthorized circumstances in either oral or written form.

(b) *Is access to records restricted?* Access to records is restricted to authorized employees who require access in order to perform their official duties.

§ 1204.9 Does FHFA or FHFA–OIG collect and use Social Security numbers?

FHFA and FHFA–OIG collect Social Security numbers only when it is necessary and authorized. At least annually, the FHFA Privacy Act Officer or the Senior Agency Official for Privacy will inform employees who are authorized to collect information that—

(a) Individuals may not be denied any right, benefit, or privilege as a result of refusing to provide their Social Security numbers, unless the collection is authorized either by a statute or by a regulation issued prior to 1975; and

(b) They must inform individuals who are asked to provide their Social Security numbers—

(1) If providing a Social Security number is mandatory or voluntary;

(2) If any statutory or regulatory authority authorizes collection of a Social Security number; and

(3) The uses that will be made of the Social Security number.

§ 1204.10 What are FHFA and FHFA-OIG employee responsibilities under the Privacy Act?

At least annually, the FHFA Privacy Act Officer or the Senior Agency Official for Privacy will inform employees about the provisions of the Privacy Act, including the Privacy Act's civil liability and criminal penalty provisions. Unless otherwise permitted by law, an authorized FHFA or FHFA-OIG employee shall—

(a) Collect from individuals only information that is relevant and necessary to discharge FHFA or FHFA-OIG responsibilities;

(b) Collect information about an individual directly from that individual whenever practicable;

(c) Inform each individual from whom information is collected of—

(1) The legal authority to collect the information and whether providing it is mandatory or voluntary;

(2) The principal purpose for which FHFA or FHFA-OIG intends to use the information;

(3) The routine uses FHFA or FHFA-OIG may make of the information; and

(4) The effects on the individual, if any, of not providing the information.

(d) Ensure that the employee's office does not maintain a system of records without public notice and notify appropriate officials of the existence or development of any system of records that is not the subject of a current or planned public notice;

(e) Maintain all records that are used in making any determination about an individual with such accuracy, relevance, timeliness, and completeness as is reasonably necessary to ensure fairness to the individual in the determination;

(f) Except for disclosures made under FOIA, make reasonable efforts, prior to disseminating any record about an individual, to ensure that the record is accurate, relevant, timely, and complete;

(g) When required by the Privacy Act, maintain an accounting in the specified form of all disclosures of records by FHFA or FHFA-OIG to persons, organizations, or Federal agencies;

(h) Maintain and use records with care to prevent the unauthorized or inadvertent disclosure of a record to anyone; and

(i) Notify the appropriate official of any record that contains information that the Privacy Act does not permit FHFA or FHFA-OIG to maintain.

§ 1204.11 May FHFA-OIG obtain Privacy Act records from other Federal agencies for law enforcement purposes?

(a) The FHFA Inspector General is authorized under the Inspector General Act of 1978, as amended, to make written requests under 5 U.S.C. 552a(b)(7) for transfer of records maintained by other Federal agencies which are necessary to carry out an authorized law enforcement activity under the Inspector General Act of 1978, as amended.

(b) The FHFA Inspector General delegates the authority under paragraph (a) of this section to the following FHFA-OIG officials—

(1) Principal Deputy Inspector General;

(2) Deputy Inspector General for Audits;

(3) Deputy Inspector General for Investigations;

(4) Deputy Inspector General for Evaluations; and

(5) Deputy Inspector General for Administration.

(c) The officials listed in paragraph (b) of this section may not further delegate or re-delegate the authority described in paragraph (a) of this section.

PART 1206—ASSESSMENTS

AUTHORITY: 12 U.S.C. 4516.

SOURCE: 73 FR 56713, Sept. 30, 2008, unless otherwise noted.

§ 1206.1 Purpose.

This part sets forth the policy and procedures of the FHFA with respect to the establishment and collection of the assessments of the Regulated Entities under 12 U.S.C. 4516.

§ 1206.2 Definitions.

As used in this part:

Act means the Federal Housing Finance Regulatory Reform Act of 2008.

Adequately capitalized means the adequately capitalized capital classification under 12 U.S.C. 1364 and related regulations.

Director means the Director of the Federal Housing Finance Agency or his or her designee.

Enterprise means the Federal National Mortgage Association or the Federal Home Loan Mortgage Corporation; and "Enterprises" means, collectively, the Federal National Mortgage Association and the Federal Home Loan Mortgage Corporation.

Federal Home Loan Bank, or *Bank,* means a Federal Home Loan Bank established under section 12 of the Federal Home Loan Bank Act (12 U.S.C. 1432).

FHFA means the Federal Housing Finance Agency.

Minimum required regulatory capital means the highest amount of capital necessary for a Bank to comply with any of the capital requirements established by the Director and applicable to it.

Regulated Entity means the Federal National Mortgage Association, the Federal Home Loan Mortgage Corporation, or any of the Federal Home Loan Banks.

Surplus funds means any amounts that are not obligated as of September 30 of the fiscal year for which the assessment was made.

Total exposure means the sum, as of the most recent June quarterly minimum capital report of the Enterprise, of the amounts of the following assets and off-balance sheet obligations that are used to calculate the quarterly minimum capital requirement of the Enterprise under 12 CFR part 1750:

(1) On-balance sheet assets;

(2) Guaranteed mortgage-backed securities; and

(3) Other off-balance sheet obligations as determined by the Director.

Working capital fund means an account for amounts collected from the Regulated Entities to establish an operating reserve that is intended to provide for the payment of large or multiyear capital and operating expenditures, as well as unanticipated expenses.

§ 1206.3 Annual assessments.

(a) *Establishing assessments.* The Director shall establish annual assessments on the Regulated Entities in an amount sufficient to maintain a working capital fund and provide for the payment of the FHFA's costs and expenses, including, but not limited to:

(1) Expenses of any examinations under 12 U.S.C. 4517 and section 20 of the Federal Home Loan Bank Act (12 U.S.C. 1440);

(2) Expenses of obtaining any reviews and credit assessments under 12 U.S.C. 4519;

(3) Expenses of any enforcement activities under 12 U.S.C. 3645;

(4) Expenses of other FHFA litigation under 12 U.S.C. 4513;

(5) Expenses relating to the maintenance of the FHFA records relating to examinations and other reviews of the Regulated Entities;

(6) Such amounts in excess of actual expenses for any given year deemed necessary to maintain a working capital fund;

(7) Expenses relating to monitoring and ensuring compliance with housing goals;

(8) Expenses relating to conducting reviews of new products;

(9) Expenses related to affordable housing and community programs;

(10) Other administrative expenses of the FHFA;

(11) Expenses related to preparing reports and studies;

(12) Expenses relating to the collection of data and development of systems to calculate the House Price Index (HPI) and the conforming loan limit;

(13) Amounts deemed necessary by the Director to wind up the affairs of the Office of Federal Housing Enterprise Oversight and the Federal Housing Finance Board; and

(14) Expenses relating to other responsibilities of the FHFA under the Safety and Soundness Act, the Federal Home Loan Bank Act and the Act.

(b) *Allocating assessments.* The Director shall allocate the annual assessments as follows:

(1) *Enterprises.* Assessments collected from the Enterprises shall not exceed amounts sufficient to provide for payment of the costs and expenses relating to the Enterprises as determined by the Director. Each Enterprise shall pay a proportional share that bears the same ratio to the total portion of the annual assessment allocated to the Enterprises that the total exposure of each Enterprise bears to the total exposure of both Enterprises.

(2) *Federal Home Loan Banks.* Assessments collected from the Banks shall not exceed amounts sufficient to provide for payment of the costs and expenses relating to the Banks as determined by the Director. Each Bank shall pay a *pro rata* share of the annual assessments based on the ratio between its minimum required regulatory capital and the aggregate minimum required regulatory capital of every Bank.

(c) *Timing and amount of semiannual payment.* Each Regulated Entity shall pay on or before October 1 and April 1 an amount equal to one-half of its annual assessment.

(d) *Surplus funds.* Surplus funds shall be credited to the annual assessment by reducing the amount collected in the following semiannual period by the amount of the surplus funds. Surplus funds shall be allocated to all Regulated Entities in the same proportion in which they were collected, except as determined by the Director.

§ 1206.4 Increased costs of regulation.

(a) *Increase for inadequate capitalization.* The Director may, at his or her discretion, increase the amount of a semiannual payment allocated to a Regulated Entity that is not classified as adequately capitalized to pay additional estimated costs of regulation of that Regulated Entity.

(b) *Increase for enforcement activities.* The Director may, at his or her discretion, adjust the amount of a semiannual payment allocated to a Regulated Entity to ensure that the Regulated Entity bears the estimated costs of enforcement activities under the Act related to that Regulated Entity.

(c) *Additional assessment for deficiencies.* At any time, the Director may make and collect from any Regulated Entity an assessment, payable immediately or through increased semiannual payments, to cover the estimated amount of any deficiency for the semiannual period as a result of increased costs of regulation of a Regulated Entity due to its classification as other than adequately capitalized, or as a result of enforcement activities related to that Regulated Entity. Any amount remaining from such additional assessment and the semiannual payments at the end of any semiannual period during which such an additional assessment is made shall be deducted *pro rata* (based upon the amount of the additional assessments) from the assessment for the following semiannual period for that Regulated Entity.

§ 1206.5 Working capital fund.

(a) *Assessments.* The Director shall establish and collect from the Regulated Entities such assessments he or she deems necessary to maintain a working capital fund.

(b) *Purposes.* Assessments collected to maintain the working capital fund shall be used to establish an operating reserve and to provide for the payment of large or multiyear capital and operating expenditures as well as unanticipated expenses.

(c) *Remittance of excess assessed funds.* At the end of each year for which an assessment under this section is made, the Director shall remit to each Regulated Entity any amount of assessed and collected funds in excess of the amount the Director deems necessary to maintain a working capital fund in the same proportions as paid under the most recent annual assessment.

§ 1206.6 Notice and review.

(a) *Written notice of budget.* The Director shall provide to each Regulated Entity written notice of the projected budget for the Agency for the upcoming fiscal year. Such notice shall be provided at least 30 days before the beginning of the applicable fiscal year.

(b) *Written notice of assessments.* The Director shall provide each Regulated Entity with written notice of assessments as follows:

(1) *Annual assessments.* The Director shall provide each Regulated Entity with written notice of the annual assessment and the semiannual payments to be collected under this part. Notice of the annual assessment and semiannual payments shall be provided before the start of the new fiscal year.

(2) *Immediate assessments.* The Director shall provide each Regulated Entity with written notice of any immediate assessments to be collected under § 1206.4 of this chapter. Notice of any immediate assessment and the required payments shall be provided at such reasonable time as determined by the Director.

(3) *Changes to assessments.* The Director shall provide each Regulated Entity with written notice of any changes in the assessment procedures that the Director, in his or her sole discretion, deems necessary under the circumstances.

(c) *Request for review.* At the written request of a Regulated Entity, the Director, in his or her discretion, may review the calculation of the proportional share of the annual assessment, the semiannual payments, and any partial payments to be collected under this part. The determination of the Director upon such review is final. Except as provided by the Director, review by the Director does not suspend the requirement that the Regulated Entity make the semiannual payment or partial payment on or before the date it is due. Any adjustments determined appropriate shall be credited or otherwise addressed by the following year's assessment for that entity.

§ 1206.7 Delinquent payment.

The Director may assess interest and penalties on any delinquent semiannual payment or other payment assessed under this part in accordance with 31 U.S.C. 3717 (interest and penalty on claims) and part 1704 of this title (debt collection).

§ 1206.8 Enforcement of payment.

The Director may enforce the payment of any assessment under 12 U.S.C. 4631 (cease-and-desist proceedings), 12 U.S.C. 4632 (temporary cease-and-desist orders), and 12 U.S.C. 4626 (civil money penalties).

PART 1207—MINORITY AND WOMEN INCLUSION

Subpart A—General

Subpart B—Minority and Women Inclusion and Diversity at the Federal Housing Finance Agency

Subpart C—Minority and Women Inclusion and Diversity at Regulated Entities and the Office of Finance

AUTHORITY: 12 U.S.C. 4520 and 4526; 12 U.S.C. 1833e; E.O. 11478.

SOURCE: 75 FR 81402, Dec. 28, 2010, unless otherwise noted.

Subpart A—General

§ 1207.1 Definitions.

The following definitions apply to the terms used in this part:

Business and activities means operational, commercial, and economic endeavors of any kind, whether for profit or not for profit and whether regularly or irregularly engaged in by a regulated entity or the Office of Finance, and includes, but is not limited to, management of the regulated entity or the Office of Finance, employment, procurement, insurance, and all types of contracts, including contracts for the issuance or guarantee of any debt, equity, or mortgage-related securities, the management of mortgage and securities portfolios, the making of equity investments, the purchase, sale and servicing of single- and multi-family mortgage loans, and the implementation of affordable housing or community investment programs and initiatives.

Director means the Director of FHFA or his or her designee.

Disability has the same meaning as defined in 29 CFR 1630.2(g) and 1630.3 and Appendix to Part 1630—Interpretive Guidance on Title I of the Americans with Disabilities Act.

Disabled-owned business means a business, and includes financial institutions, mortgage banking firms, investment banking firms, investment consultants or advisors, financial services entities, asset management entities, underwriters, accountants, brokers, brokers-dealers, and providers of legal services—

(1) Qualified as a Service-Disabled Veteran-Owned Small Business Concern as defined in 13 CFR 125.8 through 125.13; or

(2) More than fifty percent (50%) of the ownership or control of which is held by one or more persons with a disability; and

(3) More than fifty percent (50%) of the net profit or loss of which accrues to one or more persons with a disability.

FHFA means the Federal Housing Finance Agency.

Minority means any Black (or African) American, Native American (or American Indian), Hispanic (or Latino) American, or Asian American.

Minority-owned business means a business, and includes financial institutions, mortgage banking firms, investment banking firms, investment consultants or advisors, financial services entities, asset management entities, underwriters, accountants, brokers, brokers-dealers and providers of legal services—

(1) More than fifty percent (50%) of the ownership or control of which is held by one or more minority individuals; and

(2) More than fifty percent (50%) of the net profit or loss of which accrues to one or more minority individuals.

Office of Finance means the Office of Finance of the Federal Home Loan Bank System.

Reasonable accommodation has the same meaning as defined in 29 CFR 1630.2(o) and Appendix to Part 1630—Interpretive Guidance on Title I of the Americans with Disabilities Act.

Regulated entity means the Federal Home Loan Mortgage Corporation, the Federal National Mortgage Association, any Federal Home Loan Bank and/or any affiliate thereof that is subject to the regulatory authority of FHFA. The term "*regulated entities*" means (collectively) the Federal Home Loan Mortgage Corporation, the Federal National Mortgage Association, and/or any affiliate Federal Home Loan Bank and/or any affiliate thereof that is subject to the regulatory authority of FHFA.

Women-owned business means a business, and includes financial institutions, mortgage banking firms, investment banking firms, investment consultants or advisors, financial services entities, asset management entities, underwriters, accountants, brokers, brokers-dealers and providers of legal services—

(1) More than fifty percent (50%) of the ownership or control of which is held by one or more women;

(2) More than fifty percent (50%) of the net profit or loss of which accrues to one or more women; and

(3) A significant percentage of senior management positions of which are held by women.

§ 1207.2 Policy, purpose, and scope.

(a) *General policy.* FHFA's policy is to promote non-discrimination, diversity and, at a minimum, the inclusion of women, minorities, and individuals with disabilities in its own activities and in the business and activities of the regulated entities and the Office of Finance.

(b) *Purpose.* This part establishes minimum standards and requirements for the regulated entities and the Office of Finance to promote diversity and ensure, to the maximum extent possible in balance with financially safe and sound business practices, the inclusion and utilization of minorities, women, individuals with disabilities, and minority-, women-, and disabled-owned businesses at all levels, in management and employment, in all business and activities, and in all contracts for services of any kind, including services that require the services of investment banking, asset management entities, broker-dealers, financial services entities, underwriters, accountants, investment consultants, and providers of legal services.

(c) *Scope.* This part applies to each regulated entity's and the Office of Finance's implementation of and adherence to diversity, inclusion and nondiscrimination policies, practices and principles.

§ 1207.3 Limitations.

(a) Except as expressly provided herein for enforcement by FHFA, the regulations in this part do not, are not intended to, and should not be construed to create any right or benefit, substantive or procedural, enforceable at law, in equity, or through administrative proceeding, by any party against the United States, its departments, agencies, or entities, its officers, employees, or agents, a regulated entity or the Office of Finance, their officers, employees or agents, or any other person.

(b) The contract clause required by section 1207.21(b)(6) and the itemized data reporting on numbers of contracts and amounts involved required under §§ 1207.22 and 1207.23(b)(11) through § 1207.23(b)(13) apply only to contracts for services in any amount and to contracts for goods that equal or exceed $10,000 in annual value, whether in a single contract, multiple contracts, a series of contracts or renewals of contracts, with a single vendor.

§§ 1207.4 through 1207.9 [Reserved]

Subpart B—Minority and Women Inclusion and Diversity at the Federal Housing Finance Agency

§ 1207.10 through 1207.19 [Reserved]

Subpart C—Minority and Women Inclusion and Diversity at Regulated Entities and the Office of Finance

§ 1207.20 Office of Minority and Women Inclusion.

(a) *Establishment.* Each regulated entity and the Office of Finance shall establish and maintain an Office of Minority and Women Inclusion, or designate and maintain an office to perform the responsibilities of this part, under the direction of an officer of the regulated entity or the Office of Finance who reports directly to either the Chief Executive Officer or the Chief Operating Officer, or the equivalent. Each regulated entity and the Office of Finance shall notify the Director within thirty (30) days after any change in the designation of the office performing the responsibilities of this part.

(b) *Adequate resources.* Each regulated entity and the Office of Finance will ensure that its Office of Minority and Women Inclusion, or the office designated to perform the responsibilities of this part, is provided human, technological, and financial resources sufficient to fulfill the requirements of this part.

(c) *Responsibilities.* Each Office of Minority and Women Inclusion, or the office designated to perform the responsibilities of this part, is responsible for fulfilling the requirements of this part, 12 U.S.C. 1833e(b) and 4520, and such standards and requirements as the Director may issue hereunder.

§ 1207.21 Equal opportunity in employment and contracting.

(a) *Equal opportunity notice.* Each regulated entity and the Office of Finance shall publish a statement, endorsed by its Chief Executive Officer and approved by its Board of Directors, confirming its commitment to the principles of equal opportunity in employment and in contracting, at a minimum regardless of color, national origin, sex, religion, age, disability status, or genetic information. The notice also shall confirm commitment against retaliation or reprisal. Publication shall include, at a minimum, conspicuous posting in all regulated entity and Office of Finance physical facilities, including through alternative media formats, as necessary, and accessible posting on the regulated entity's and the Office of Finance's Web site. The notice shall be updated and re-published, reendorsed by the Chief Executive Officer and re-approved by the Board of Directors annually.

(b) *Policies and procedures.* Each regulated entity and the Office of Finance shall develop, implement, and maintain policies and procedures to ensure, to the maximum extent possible in balance with financially safe and sound business practices, the inclusion and utilization of minorities, women, individuals with disabilities, and minority-, women-, and disabled-owned businesses in all business and activities and at all levels of the regulated entity and the Office of Finance, including in management, employment, procurement, insurance, and all types of contracts. The policies and procedures of each regulated entity and the Office of Finance at a minimum shall:

(1) Confirm its adherence to the principles of equal opportunity and nondiscrimination in employment and in contracting;

(2) Describe its policy against discrimination in employment and contracting;

(3) Establish internal procedures to receive and attempt to resolve complaints of discrimination in employment and in contracting. Publication will include at a minimum making the procedure conspicuously accessible to employees and applicants through print, electronic, or alternative media formats, as necessary, and through the regulated entity's or the Office of Finance's Web site;

(4) Establish an effective procedure for accepting, reviewing and granting or denying requests for reasonable accommodations of disabilities from employees or applicants for employment;

(5) Encourage the consideration of diversity in nominating or soliciting nominees for positions on boards of directors and engage in recruiting and outreach directed at encouraging individuals who are minorities, women and individuals with disabilities to seek or apply for employment with the regulated entity or the Office of Finance;

(6) Except as limited by §1207.3(b), require that each contract it enters contains a material clause committing the contractor to practice the principles of equal employment opportunity and non-discrimination in all its business activities and requiring each such contractor to include the clause in each subcontract it enters for services or goods provided to the regulated entity or the Office of Finance;

(7) Identify the types of contracts the regulated entity considers exempt under §1207.3(b) and any commercially reasonable thresholds, exceptions, and limitations the regulated entity establishes for the implementation of §1207.21(c)(2). The policies and procedures must address the rationale and need for implementing the thresholds, exceptions, or limitations;

(8) Be published and accessible to employees, applicants for employment, contractors, potential contractors, and members of the public through print, electronic, or alternative media formats, as necessary, and through the regulated entity's or the Office of Finance's Web site; and

(9) Be reviewed at the direction of the officer immediately responsible for directing the Office of Minority and Women Inclusion, or other office designated to perform the responsibilities of this part, at least annually to assess their effectiveness and to incorporate appropriate changes.

(c) *Outreach for contracting.* Each regulated entity and the Office of Finance shall establish a program for outreach designed to ensure to the maximum extent possible the inclusion in contracting opportunities of minorities, women, individuals with disabilities, and minority-, women-, and disabled-owned businesses. The program at a minimum shall:

(1) Apply to all contracts entered into by the regulated entity or the Office of Finance, including contracts with financial institutions, investment banking firms, investment consultants or advisors, financial services entities, mortgage banking firms, asset management entities, underwriters, accountants, brokers, brokers-dealers, and providers of legal services;

(2) Establish policies, procedures and standards requiring the publication of contracting opportunities designed to encourage contractors that are minorities, women, individuals with disabilities, and minority-, women-, and disabled-owned businesses to submit offers or bid for the award of such contracts; and

(3) Ensure the consideration of the diversity of a contractor when the regulated entity or the Office of Finance reviews and evaluates offers from contractors.

§ 1207.22 Regulated entity and Office of Finance reports.

(a) *General.* Each regulated entity and the Office of Finance, through its Office of Minority and Women Inclusion, or other office designated to perform the responsibilities of this part, shall report in writing, in such format as the Director may require, to the Director describing its efforts to promote diversity and ensure the inclusion and utilization of minorities, women, individuals with disabilities, and minority-, women-, and disabled-owned businesses at all levels, in management and employment, in all business and activities, and in all contracts for services and the results of such efforts.

(1) Within 180 days after the effective date of this regulation each regulated entity and the Office of Finance shall submit to the Director or his or her designee a preliminary status report describing actions taken, plans for and progress toward implementing the provisions of 12 U.S.C. 4520 and this part; and including to the extent available the data and information required by this part to be included in an annual report.

(2) FHFA intends to use the preliminary status report solely for the purpose of examining the submitting regulated entity or the Office of Finance and reporting to the institution on its operations and the condition of its program.

(b) *FHFA use of reports.* The data and information reported to FHFA under this part (except for the initial report under paragraph (a)(1) of this section) are intended to be used for any permissible supervisory and regulatory purpose, including examinations, enforcement actions, identification of matters requiring attention, and production of FHFA examination, operating and condition reports related to one or more of the regulated entities and the Office of Finance. FHFA may use the information and data submitted to issue aggregate reports and data summaries that each regulated entity and the Office of Finance may use to assess its own progress and accomplishments, or to the public as it deems necessary. FHFA is not requiring, and does not desire, that reports under this part contain personally identifiable information.

(c) *Frequency of reports.* Each regulated entity and the Office of Finance shall submit an annual report on or before March 1 of each year, beginning in 2012, reporting on the period of January 1 through December 31 of the preceding year, and such other reports as the Director may require. If the date for submission falls on a Saturday, Sunday, or Federal holiday, the report is due no later than the next day that is not a Saturday, Sunday, or Federal holiday.

(d) *Annual summary.* Each regulated entity and the Office of Finance shall include in its annual report to the Director (pursuant to 12 U.S.C. 1723a(k), 1456(c), or 1440, with respect to the regulated entities) a summary of its activities under this part during the previous year, including at a minimum, detailed information describing the actions taken by the regulated entity or the Office of Finance pursuant to 12 U.S.C. 4520 and a statement of the total amounts paid by the regulated entity or the Office of Finance to contractors during the previous year and the percentage of such amounts paid to contractors that are minorities or minority-owned businesses, women or women-owned businesses, and individuals with disabilities and disabled-owned businesses respectively, as limited by § 1207.3(b).

§ 1207.23 Annual reports—format and contents.

(a) *Format.* Each annual report shall consist of a detailed summary of the regulated entity's or the Office of Finance's activities during the reporting year to carry out the requirements of this part, which report may also be made a part of the regulated entity's or the Office of Finance's annual report to the Director. The report shall contain a table of contents and conclude with a certification by the regulated entity's or the Office of Finance's officer responsible for the annual report that the data and information presented in the report are accurate, and are approved for submission.

(b) *Contents.* The annual report shall contain the information provided in the regulated entity's or the Office of Finance's annual summary pursuant to § 1207.22(d) and, in addition to any other information or data the Director may require, shall include:

(1) The EEO–1 Employer Information Report (Form EEO–1 used by the Equal Employment Opportunity Commission (EEOC) and the Office of Federal Contract Compliance Programs (OFCCP) to collect certain demographic information) or similar reports filed by the regulated entity or the Office of Finance during the reporting year. If the regulated entity or the Office of Finance does not file Form EEO–1 or similar reports, the regulated entity or the Office of Finance shall submit to FHFA a completed Form EEO–1;

(2) All other reports or plans the regulated entity or the Office of Finance submitted to the EEOC, the Department of Labor, OFCCP or Congress ("reports or plans" is not intended to include separate complaints or charges of discrimination or responses thereto) during the reporting year;

(3) Data showing by minority and gender the number of individuals applying for employment with the regulated entity or the Office of Finance in each occupational or job category identified on the Form EEO–1 during the reporting year;

(4) Data showing by minority and gender the number of individuals hired for employment with the regulated entity or the Office of Finance in each occupational or job category identified on the Form EEO–1 during the reporting year;

(5) Data showing by minority, gender and disability classification, and categorized as voluntary or involuntary, the number of separations from employment with the regulated entity or the Office of Finance in each occupational or job category identified on the Form EEO–1 during the reporting year;

(6) Data showing the number of requests for reasonable accommodation received from employees and applicants for employment, the number of requests granted, and the disabilities accommodated and the types of accommodation granted during the reporting year;

(7) Data showing for the reporting year by minority, gender, and disability classification the number of individuals applying for promotion at the regulated entity or the Office of Finance—

(i) Within each occupational or job category identified on the Form EEO–1; and

(ii) From one such occupational or job category to another;

(8) Data showing by minority, gender, and disability classification the number of individuals—

(i) Promoted at the regulated entity or the Office of Finance within each occupational or job category identified on the Form EEO–1, after applying for such a promotion;

(ii) Promoted at the regulated entity or the Office of Finance within each occupational or job category identified on the Form EEO–1, without applying for such a promotion; and

(iii) Promoted at the regulated entity or the Office of Finance from one occupational or job category identified on the Form EEO–1 to another such category, after applying for such a promotion;

(9) A comparison of the data reported under paragraphs (b)(1) through (b)(8) of this section to such data as reported in the previous year together with a narrative analysis;

(10) Descriptions of all regulated entity or Office of Finance outreach activity during the reporting year to recruit individuals who are minorities, women, or persons with disabilities for employment, to solicit or advertise for minority or minority-owned, women or women-owned, and disabled-owned contractors or contractors who are individuals with disabilities to offer proposals or bids to enter into business with the regulated entity or Office of Finance, or to inform such contractors of the regulated entity's or Office of Finance's contracting process, including the identification of any partners, organizations, or government offices with which the regulated entity or the Office of Finance participated in such outreach activity;

(11) Cumulative data separately showing the number of contracts entered with minorities or minority-owned businesses, women or women-owned businesses and individuals with disabilities or disabled-owned businesses during the reporting year;

(12) Cumulative data separately showing for the reporting year the total amount the regulated entity or the Office of Finance paid to contractors that are minorities or minority-owned businesses, women or women-owned and individuals with disabilities or disabled-owned businesses;

(13) The annual total of amounts paid to contractors and the percentage of which was paid separately to minorities or minority-owned businesses, women or women-owned businesses and individuals with disabilities or disabled-owned businesses during the reporting year;

(14) Certification of compliance with §§ 1207.20 and 1207.21, together with sufficient documentation to verify compliance;

(15) Data for the reporting year showing, separately, the number of equal opportunity complaints (including administrative agency charges or complaints, arbitral or judicial claims) against the regulated entity or the Office of Finance that—

(i) Claim employment discrimination, by basis or kind of the alleged discrimination (race, sex, disability, *etc.*) and by result (settlement, favorable, or unfavorable outcome);

(ii) Claim discrimination in any aspect of the contracting process or administration of contracts, by basis of the alleged discrimination and by result; and

(iii) Were resolved through the regulated entity's or the Office of Finance's internal processes;

(16) Data showing for the reporting year amounts paid to claimants by the regulated entity or the Office of Finance for settlements or judgments on discrimination complaints—

(i) In employment, by basis of the alleged discrimination; and

(ii) In any aspect of the contracting process or in the administration of contracts, by basis of the alleged discrimination;

(17) A comparison of the data reported under paragraphs (b)(12) and (b)(13) of this section with the same information reported for the previous year;

(18) A narrative identification and analysis of the reporting year's activities the regulated entity or the Office of Finance considers successful and unsuccessful in achieving the purpose and policy of regulations in this part and a description of progress made from the previous year; and

(19) A narrative identification and analysis of business activities, levels, and areas in which the regulated entity's or the Office of Finance's efforts need to improve with respect to achieving the purpose and policy of regulations in this part, together with a description of anticipated efforts and results the regulated entity or the Office of Finance expects in the succeeding year.

§ 1207.24 Enforcement.

The Director may enforce this regulation and standards issued under it in any manner and through any means within his or her authority, including through identifying matters requiring attention, corrective action orders, directives, or enforcement actions under 12 U.S.C. 4513b and 4514. The Director may conduct examinations of a regulated entity's or the Office of Finance's activities under and in compliance with this part pursuant to 12 U.S.C. 4517.

PART 1208—DEBT COLLECTION

Subpart A—General

Subpart B—Salary Offset

Subpart C—Administrative Offset

Subpart D—Tax Refund Offset

Subpart E—Administrative Wage Garnishment

AUTHORITY: 5 U.S.C. 5514; 12 U.S.C. 4526; 26 U.S.C. 6402(d); 31 U.S.C. 3701–3720D; 31 CFR 285.2; 31 CFR Chapter IX.

Subpart A—General

SOURCE: 75 FR 68958, Nov. 10, 2010, unless otherwise noted.

§ 1208.1 Authority and scope.

(a) *Authority.* FHFA issues this part 1208 under the authority of 5 U.S.C. 5514 and 31 U.S.C. 3701–3720D, and in conformity with the Federal Claims Collection Standards (FCCS) at 31 CFR chapter IX; the regulations on salary offset issued by the Office of Personnel Management (OPM) at 5 CFR part 550, subpart K; the regulations on tax refund offset issued by the United States Department of the Treasury (Treasury) at 31 CFR 285.2; and the regulations on administrative wage garnishment issued by Treasury at 31 CFR 285.11.

(b) *Scope.*—(1) This part applies to debts that are owed to the Federal Government by Federal employees; other persons, organizations, or entities that are indebted to FHFA; and by Federal employees of FHFA who are indebted to other agencies, except for those debts listed in paragraph (b)(2) of this section.

(2) Subparts B and C of this part 1208 do not apply to—

(i) Debts or claims arising under the Internal Revenue Code (26 U.S.C. 1 *et seq.*), the Social Security Act (42 U.S.C. 301 *et seq.*) or the tariff laws of the United States;

(ii) Any case to which the Contract Disputes Act (41 U.S.C. 601 *et seq.*) applies;

(iii) Any case where collection of a debt is explicitly provided for or provided by another statute, *e.g.* travel advances under 5 U.S.C. 5705 and employee training expenses under 5 U.S.C. 4108, or, as provided for by title 11 of the United States Code, when the claims involve bankruptcy;

(iv) Any debt based in whole or in part on conduct in violation of the antitrust laws or involving fraud, the presentation of a false claim, or misrepresentation on the part of the debtor or any party having an interest in the claim, unless the Department of Justice authorizes FHFA to handle the collection; or

(v) Claims between agencies.

(3) Nothing in this part precludes the compromise, suspension, or termination of collection actions, where appropriate, under standards implementing the Debt Collection Improvement Act (DCIA) (31 U.S.C. 3701 *et seq.*), the FCCS (31 CFR chapter IX) or the use of alternative dispute resolution methods if they are not inconsistent with applicable law and regulations.

(4) Nothing in this part precludes an employee from requesting waiver of an erroneous payment under 5 U.S.C. 5584, 10 U.S.C. 2774, or 32 U.S.C. 716, or from questioning the amount or validity of a debt, in the manner set forth in this part.

§ 1208.2 Definitions.

The following terms apply to this part, unless defined otherwise elsewhere–

Administrative offset means an action, pursuant to 31 U.S.C. 3716, in which the Federal Government withholds funds payable to, or held by the Federal Government for a person, organization, or other entity in order to collect a debt from that person, organization, or other entity. Such funds include funds payable by the Federal Government on behalf of a State Government.

Agency means an executive department or agency; a military department; the United States Postal Service; the Postal Regulatory Commission; any nonappropriated fund instrumentality described in 5 U.S.C. 2105(c); the United States Senate; the United States House of Representatives; any court, court administrative office, or instrumentality in the judicial or legislative branches of the Government; or a Government corporation. If an agency under this definition is a component of an agency, the broader definition of agency may be used in applying the provisions of 5 U.S.C. 5514(b) (concerning the authority to prescribe regulations).

Centralized administrative offset means the mandatory referral to the Secretary of the Treasury by a creditor agency of a past due debt which is more than 180 days delinquent, for the purpose of collection under the Treasury's centralized offset program.

Certification means a written statement received by a paying agency from a creditor agency that requests the paying agency to institute salary offset of an employee, to the Financial Management Service (FMS) for offset or to the Secretary of the Treasury for centralized administrative offset, and specifies that required procedural protections have been afforded the debtor. Where the debtor requests a hearing on a claimed debt, the decision by a hearing official or administrative law judge constitutes a certification.

Claim or debt (used interchangeably in this part) means any amount of funds or property that has been determined by an agency official to be due the Federal Government by a person, organization, or entity, except another agency. It also means any amount of money, funds, or property owed by a person to a State, the District of Columbia, American Samoa, Guam, the United States Virgin Islands, the Commonwealth of the Northern Mariana Islands, or the Commonwealth of Puerto Rico. For purposes of this part, a debt owed to FHFA constitutes a debt owed to the Federal Government. A claim or debt includes:

(1) Funds owed on account of loans made, insured, or guaranteed by the Federal Government, including any deficiency or any difference between the price obtained by the Federal Government in the sale of a property and the amount owed to the Federal Government on a mortgage on the property;

(2) Unauthorized expenditures of agency funds;

(3) Overpayments, including payments disallowed by audits performed by the Inspector General of the agency administering the program;

(4) Any amount the Federal Government is authorized by statute to collect for the benefit of any person;

(5) The unpaid share of any non-Federal partner in a program involving a Federal payment, and a matching or cost-sharing payment by the non-Federal partner;

(6) Any fine or penalty assessed by an agency; and

(7) Other amounts of money or property owed to the Federal Government.

Compromise means the settlement or forgiveness of a debt under 31 U.S.C. 3711, in accordance with standards set forth in the FCCS and applicable Federal law.

Creditor agency means the agency to which the debt is owed, including a debt collection center when acting on behalf of a creditor agency in matters pertaining to the collection of a debt.

Debt See the definition of the terms "Claim or debt" of this section.

Debt collection center means the Department of the Treasury or any other agency or division designated by the Secretary of the Treasury with authority to collect debts on behalf of creditor agencies in accordance with 31 U.S.C. 3711(g).

Debtor means the person, organization, or entity owing money to the Federal Government.

Delinquent debt means a debt that has not been paid by the date specified in the agency's initial written demand for payment or applicable agreement or instrument (including a post-delinquency payment agreement) unless other satisfactory payment arrangements have been made.

Director means the Director of FHFA or Director's designee.

Disposable pay means that part of current basic pay, special pay, incentive pay, retired pay, or retainer pay (or in the case of an employee not entitled to basic pay, other authorized pay) remaining after the deduction of any amount required by law to be withheld (other than deductions to execute garnishment orders in accordance with 5 CFR parts 581 and 582). FHFA will apply the order of precedence contained in OPM guidance (PPM–2008–01; Order Of Precedence When Gross Pay Is Not Sufficient To Permit All Deductions), as follows—

(1) Retirement deductions for defined benefit plan (including Civil Service Retirement System, Federal Employees Retirement System, or other similar defined benefit plan);

(2) Social security (OASDI) tax;

(3) Medicare tax;

(4) Federal income tax;

(5) Basic health insurance premium (including Federal Employees Health Benefits premium, pre-tax or post-tax, or premium for similar benefit under another authority but not including amounts deducted for supplementary coverage);

(6) Basic life insurance premium (including Federal Employees' Group Life Insurance—FEGLI—Basic premium or premium for similar benefit under another authority);

(7) State income tax;

(8) Local income tax;

(9) Collection of debts owed to the U.S. Government (e.g., tax debt, salary overpayment, failure to withhold proper amount of deductions, advance of salary or travel expenses, etc.; debts which may or may not be delinquent; debts which may be collected through the Treasury's Financial Management Services Treasury Offset Program, an automated centralized debt collection program for collecting Federal debt from Federal payments):

(i) Continuous levy under the Federal Payment Levy Program (tax debt); and

(ii) Salary offsets (whether involuntary under 5 U.S.C. 5514 or similar authority or required by a voluntarily signed written agreement; if multiple debts are subject to salary offset, the order is based on when each offset commenced—with earliest commencing offset at the top of the order—unless there are special circumstances, as determined by the paying agency).

(10) Court-Ordered collection/debt:

(i) Child support (may include attorney and other fees as provided for in 5 CFR 581.102(d)). If there are multiple child support orders, the priority of orders is governed by 42 U.S.C. 666(b) and implementing regulations, as required by 42 U.S.C. 659(d)(2);

(ii) Alimony (may include attorney and other fees as provided for in 5 CFR 581.102(d)). If there are multiple alimony orders, they are prioritized on a first-come, first-served basis, as required by 42 U.S.C. 659(d)(3);

(iii) Bankruptcy; and

(iv) Commercial garnishments.

(11) Optional benefits:

(i) Health care/limited-expense health care flexible spending accounts (pre-tax benefit under FedFlex or equivalent cafeteria plan);

(ii) Dental (pre-tax benefit under FedFlex or equivalent cafeteria plan);

(iii) Vision (pre-tax benefit under FedFlex or equivalent cafeteria plan);

(iv) Health Savings Account (pre-tax benefit under FedFlex or equivalent cafeteria plan);

(v) Optional life insurance premiums (FEGLI optional benefits or similar benefits under other authority);

(vi) Long-term care insurance premiums;

(vii) Dependent-care flexible spending accounts (pre-tax benefit under FedFlex or equivalent cafeteria plan);

(viii) Thrift Savings Plan (TSP):

(A) Loan payments;

(B) Basic contributions; and

(C) Catch-up contributions; and

(ix) Other optional benefits.

(12) Other voluntary deductions/allotments:

(i) Military service deposits;

(ii) Professional associations;

(iii) Union dues;

(iv) Charities;

(v) Bonds;

(vi) Personal account allotments (*e.g.*, to savings or checking account); and

(vii) Additional voluntary deductions (on first-come, first-served basis); and

(13) IRS paper levies.

Employee means a current employee of FHFA or other agency, including a current member of the Armed Forces or a Reserve of the Armed Forces of the United States.

Federal Claims Collection Standards (FCCS) means standards published at 31 CFR chapter IX.

FHFA means the Federal Housing Finance Agency.

Garnishment means the process of withholding amounts from the disposable pay of a person employed outside the Federal Government, and the paying of those amounts to a creditor in satisfaction of a withholding order.

Hearing official means an individual who is responsible for conducting any hearing with respect to the existence or amount of a debt claimed and for rendering a final decision on the basis of such hearing. A hearing official may not be under the supervision or control of the Director of FHFA when FHFA is the creditor agency but may be an administrative law judge.

Notice of intent means a written notice of a creditor agency to a debtor that states that the debtor owes a debt to the creditor agency and apprises the debtor of the applicable procedural rights.

Notice of salary offset means a written notice from the paying agency to an employee after a certification has been issued by a creditor agency that informs the employee that salary offset will begin at the next officially established pay interval.

Paying agency means an agency of the Federal Government that employs the individual who owes a debt to an agency of the Federal Government and transmits payment requests in the form of certified payment vouchers, or other similar forms, to a disbursing official for disbursement. The same agency may be both the creditor agency and the paying agency.

Salary offset means an administrative offset to collect a debt under 5 U.S.C. 5514 by deductions at one or more officially established pay intervals from the current pay account of an employee without his or her consent.

Waiver means the cancellation, remission, forgiveness, or non-recovery of a debt allegedly owed by an employee to FHFA or another agency as permitted or required by 5 U.S.C. 5584 or 8346(b), 10 U.S.C. 2774, 32 U.S.C. 716, or any other law.

Withholding order means any order for withholding or garnishment of pay issued by an agency, or judicial, or administrative body. For purposes of administrative wage garnishment, the terms "wage garnishment order" and "garnishment order" have the same meaning as "withholding order."

§ 1208.3 Referrals to the Department of the Treasury, collection services, and use of credit bureaus.

(a) *Referral of delinquent debts.*—(1) FHFA shall transfer to the Secretary of the Department of the Treasury any past due, legally enforceable nontax debt that has been delinquent for a period of 180 days or more so that the Secretary may take appropriate action to collect the debt or terminate collection action in accordance with 31 U.S.C. 3716, 5 U.S.C. 5514, 5 CFR 550.1108, 31 CFR part 285, and the FCCS.

(2) FHFA may transfer any past due, legally enforceable nontax debt that has been delinquent for less than a period of 180 days to a debt collection center for collection in accordance with 31 U.S.C. 3716, 5 U.S.C. 5514, 5 CFR 550.1108, 31 CFR part 285, and the FCCS.

(b) *Collection Services.* Section 13 of the Debt Collection Act (31 U.S.C. 3718) authorizes agencies to enter into contracts for collection services to recover debts owed the Federal Government. The Debt Collection Act requires that certain provisions be contained in such contracts, including:

(1) The agency retains the authority to resolve a dispute, including the authority to terminate a collection action or refer the matter to the Attorney General for civil remedies; and

(2) The contractor is subject to the Privacy Act of 1974, as it applies to private contractors, as well as subject to State and Federal laws governing debt collection practices.

(c) *Referrals to collection agencies.*—(1) FHFA has authority to contract for collection services to recover delinquent debts in accordance with 31 U.S.C. 3718(a) and the FCCS (31 CFR 901.5).

(2) FHFA may use private collection agencies where it determines that their use is in the best interest of the Federal Government. Where FHFA determines that there is a need to contract for collection services, the contract will provide that:

(i) The authority to resolve disputes, compromise claims, suspend or terminate collection action, or refer the matter to the Department of Justice for litigation or to take any other action under this part will be retained by FHFA;

(ii) Contractors are subject to the Privacy Act of 1974, as amended, to the extent specified in 5 U.S.C. 552a(m) and to applicable Federal and State laws and regulations pertaining to debt collection practices, such as the Fair Debt Collection Practices Act, 15 U.S.C. 1692;

(iii) The contractor is required to strictly account for all amounts collected;

(iv) The contractor must agree that uncollectible accounts shall be returned with appropriate documentation to enable FHFA to determine whether to pursue collection through litigation or to terminate collection; and

(v) The contractor must agree to provide any data in its files requested by FHFA upon returning the account to FHFA for subsequent referral to the Department of Justice for litigation.

§ 1208.4 Reporting delinquent debts to credit bureaus.

(a) FHFA may report delinquent debts to consumer reporting agencies (31 U.S.C. 3701(a)(3), 3711). Sixty calendar days prior to release of information to a consumer reporting agency, the debtor shall be notified, in writing, of the intent to disclose the existence of the debt to a consumer reporting agency. Such notice of intent may be a separate correspondence or included in correspondence demanding direct payment. The notice shall be in conformance with 31 U.S.C. 3711(e) and the FCCS. In the notice, FHFA shall provide the debtor with:

(1) An opportunity to inspect and copy agency records pertaining to the debt;

(2) An opportunity for an administrative review of the legal enforceability or past due status of the debt;

(3) An opportunity to enter into a repayment agreement on terms satisfactory to FHFA to prevent FHFA from

reporting the debt as overdue to consumer reporting agencies, and provide deadlines and method for requesting this relief;

(4) An explanation of the rate of interest that will accrue on the debt, that all costs incurred to collect the debt will be charged to the debtor, the authority for assessing these costs, and the manner in which FHFA will calculate the amount of these costs;

(5) An explanation that FHFA will report the debt to the consumer reporting agencies to the detriment of the debtor's credit rating; and

(6) A description of the collection actions that the agency may take in the future if those presently proposed actions do not result in repayment of the debt, including the filing of a lawsuit against the borrower by the agency and assignment of the debt for collection by offset against Federal income tax refunds or the filing of a lawsuit against the debtor by the Federal Government.

(b) The information that may be disclosed to the consumer reporting agency is limited to:

(1) The debtor's name, address, social security number or taxpayer identification number, and any other information necessary to establish the identity of the individual;

(2) The amount, status, and history of the claim; and

(3) FHFA program or activity under which the claim arose.

(c) *Subsequent reports.* FHFA may update its report to the credit bureau whenever it has knowledge of events that substantially change the status of the amount of liability.

(d) *Subsequent reports of delinquent debts.* Pursuant to 31 CFR 901.4, FHFA will report delinquent debt to the Department of Housing and Urban Development's Credit Alert Interactive Voice Response System (CAIVRS).

(e) *Privacy Act considerations.* A delinquent debt may not be reported under this section unless a notice issued pursuant to the Privacy Act, 5 U.S.C. 552a(e)(4), authorizes the disclosure of information about the debtor to a credit bureau or CAIVRS.

§§ 1208.5–1208.19 [Reserved]

Subpart B—Salary Offset

§ 1208.20 Authority and scope.

(a) *Authority.* FHFA may collect debts owed by employees to the Federal Government by means of salary offset under the authority of 5 U.S.C. 5514; 5 CFR part 550, subpart K; and this subpart B.

(b) *Scope.*—(1) The procedures set forth in this subpart B apply to situations where FHFA is attempting to collect a debt by salary offset that is owed to it by an individual employed by FHFA or by another agency; or where FHFA employs an individual who owes a debt to another agency.

(2) The procedures set forth in this subpart B do not apply to:

(i) Any routine intra-agency adjustment of pay that is attributable to clerical or administrative error or delay in processing pay documents that have occurred within the four pay periods preceding the adjustment, or any adjustment to collect a debt amounting to $50 or less. However, at the time of any such adjustment, or as soon thereafter as possible, FHFA or its designated payroll agent shall provide the employee with a written notice of the nature and the amount of the adjustment and a point of contact for contesting such adjustment.

(ii) Any negative adjustment to pay that arises from an employee's election of coverage or a change in coverage under a Federal benefits program that requires periodic deductions from pay, if the amount to be recovered was accumulated over four pay periods or less. However, at the time such adjustment is made, FHFA or its payroll agent shall provide in the employee's earnings statement a clear and concise statement that informs the employee of the previous overpayment.

§ 1208.21 Notice requirements before salary offset where FHFA is the creditor agency.

(a) *Notice of Intent.* Deductions from an employee's salary may not be made unless FHFA provides the employee with a Notice of Intent at least 30 calendar days before the salary offset is initiated.

(b) *Contents of Notice of Intent.* The Notice of Intent shall advise the employee of the following:

(1) That FHFA has reviewed the records relating to the claim and has determined that the employee owes the debt;

(2) That FHFA intends to collect the debt by deductions from the employee's current disposable pay account;

(3) The amount of the debt and the facts giving rise to the debt;

(4) The frequency and amount of the intended deduction (stated as a fixed dollar amount or as a percentage of pay not to exceed 15 percent of disposable pay), and the intention to continue the deductions until the debt and all accumulated interest are paid in full or otherwise resolved;

(5) The name, address, and telephone number of the person to whom the employee may propose a written alternative schedule for voluntary repayment, in lieu of salary offset. The employee shall include a justification for the alternative schedule in his or her proposal. If the terms of the alternative schedule are agreed upon by the employee and FHFA, the alternative written schedule shall be signed by both the employee and FHFA;

(6) An explanation of FHFA's policy concerning interest, penalties, and administrative costs, the date by which payment should be made to avoid such costs, and a statement that such assessments must be made unless excused in accordance with the FCCS;

(7) The employee's right to inspect and copy all records of FHFA pertaining to his or her debt that are not exempt from disclosure or to receive copies of such records if he or she is unable personally to inspect the records as the result of geographical or other constraints;

(8) The name, address, and telephone number of the FHFA employee to whom requests for access to records relating to the debt must be sent;

(9) The employee's right to a hearing conducted by an impartial hearing official with respect to the existence and amount of the debt claimed or the repayment schedule *i.e.*, the percentage of disposable pay to be deducted each pay period, so long as a request is filed by the employee as prescribed in §1208.23; the name and address of the office to which the request for a hearing should be sent; and the name, address, and telephone number of a person whom the employee may contact concerning procedures for requesting a hearing;

(10) The filing of a request for a hearing on or before the 30th calendar day following receipt of the Notice of Intent will stay the commencement of collection proceedings and a final decision on whether a hearing will be held (if a hearing is requested) or will be issued at the earliest practical date, but not later than 60 calendar days after the request for the hearing;

(11) FHFA shall initiate certification procedures to implement a salary offset unless the employee files a request for a hearing on or before the 30th calendar day following receipt of the Notice of Intent;

(12) Any knowingly false or frivolous statement, representations, or evidence may subject the employee to:

(i) Disciplinary procedures appropriate under 5 U.S.C. chapter 75, 5 CFR part 752, or any other applicable statutes or regulations;

(ii) Penalties under the False Claims Act, 31 U.S.C. 3729 through 3731, or under any other applicable statutory authority; or

(iii) Criminal penalties under 18 U.S.C. 286, 287, 1001, and 1002, or under any other applicable statutory authority;

(13) That the employee also has the right to request waiver of overpayment pursuant to 5 U.S.C. 5584 and may exercise any other rights and remedies available to the employee under statutes or regulations governing the program for which the collection is being made;

(14) Unless there are applicable contractual or statutory provisions to the contrary, amounts paid on or deducted from debts that are later waived or found not to be owed to the Federal Government shall be promptly refunded to the employee; and

(15) Proceedings with respect to the debt are governed by 5 U.S.C. 5514.

§ 1208.22 Review of FHFA records related to the debt.

(a) *Request for review.* An employee who desires to inspect or copy FHFA records related to a debt owed by the employee to FHFA must send a letter to the individual designated in the Notice of Intent requesting access to the relevant records. The letter must be received in the office of that individual within 15 calendar days after the employee's receipt of the Notice of Intent.

(b) *Review location and time.* In response to a timely request submitted by the employee, the employee shall be notified of the location and time when the employee may inspect and copy records related to his or her debt that are not exempt from disclosure. If the employee is unable personally to inspect such records as the result of geographical or other constraints, FHFA shall arrange to send copies of such records to the employee. The debtor shall pay copying costs unless they are waived by FHFA. Copying costs shall be assessed pursuant to FHFA's Freedom of Information Act Regulation, 12 CFR part 1202.

§ 1208.23 Opportunity for a hearing where FHFA is the creditor agency.

(a) *Request for a hearing.*—(1) *Time-period for submission.* An employee who requests a hearing on the existence or amount of the debt held by FHFA or on the salary-offset schedule proposed by FHFA, must send a written request to FHFA. The request for a hearing must be received by FHFA on or before the 30th calendar day following receipt by the employee of the Notice of Intent.

(2) *Failure to submit timely.* If the employee files a request for a hearing after the expiration of the 30th calendar day, the employee shall not be entitled to a hearing. However, FHFA may accept the request if the employee can show that the delay was the result of circumstances beyond his or her control or that he or she failed to receive actual notice of the filing deadline.

(3) *Contents of request.* The request for a hearing must be signed by the employee and must fully identify and explain with reasonable specificity all the facts, evidence, and witnesses, if any, that the employee believes support his or her position. The employee must also specify whether he or she requests an oral hearing. If an oral hearing is requested, the employee should explain why a hearing by examination of the documents without an oral hearing would not resolve the matter.

(4) *Failure to request a hearing.* The failure of an employee to request a hearing will be considered an admission by the employee that the debt exists in the amount specified in the Notice of Intent that was provided to the employee under § 1208.21(b).

(b) *Obtaining the services of a hearing official.*—(1) *Debtor is not an FHFA employee.* When the debtor is not an FHFA employee and FHFA cannot provide a prompt and appropriate hearing before an administrative law judge or other hearing official, FHFA may request a hearing official from an agent of the paying agency, as designated in 5 CFR part 581, appendix A, or as otherwise designated by the paying agency. The paying agency must cooperate with FHFA to provide a hearing official, as required by the FCCS.

(2) *Debtor is an FHFA employee.* When the debtor is an FHFA employee, FHFA may contact any agent of another agency, as designated in 5 CFR part 581, appendix A, or as otherwise designated by the agency, to request a hearing official.

(c) *Procedure.*—(1) *Notice of hearing.* After the employee requests a hearing, the hearing official shall notify the employee of the form of the hearing to be provided. If the hearing will be oral, the notice shall set forth the date, time, and location of the hearing, which must occur no more than 30 calendar days after the request is received, unless the employee requests that the hearing be delayed. If the hearing will be conducted by an examination of documents, the employee shall be notified within 30 calendar days that he or she should submit evidence and arguments in writing to the hearing official within 30 calendar days.

(2) *Oral hearing.*—(i) An employee who requests an oral hearing shall be provided an oral hearing if the hearing official determines that the matter cannot be resolved by an examination of the documents alone, as for example, when an issue of credibility or veracity

is involved. The oral hearing need not be an adversarial adjudication; and rules of evidence need not apply. Witnesses who testify in an oral hearing shall do so under oath or affirmation.

(ii) Oral hearings may take the form of, but are not limited to:

(A) Informal conferences with the hearing official in which the employee and agency representative are given full opportunity to present evidence, witnesses, and argument;

(B) Informal meetings in which the hearing examiner interviews the employee; or

(C) Formal written submissions followed by an opportunity for oral presentation.

(3) *Hearing by examination of documents.* If the hearing official determines that an oral hearing is not necessary, he or she shall make the determination based upon an examination of the documents.

(d) *Record.* The hearing official shall maintain a summary record of any hearing conducted under this section.

(e) *Decision.*—(1) The hearing official shall issue a written opinion stating his or her decision, based upon all evidence and information developed during the hearing, as soon as practicable after the hearing, but not later than 60 calendar days after the date on which the request was received by FHFA, unless the hearing was delayed at the request of the employee, in which case the 60-day decision period shall be extended by the number of days by which the hearing was postponed.

(2) The decision of the hearing official shall be final and is considered to be an official certification regarding the existence and the amount of the debt for purposes of executing salary offset under 5 U.S.C. 5514. If the hearing official determines that a debt may not be collected by salary offset, but FHFA finds that the debt is still valid, FHFA may seek collection of the debt through other means in accordance with applicable law and regulations.

(f) *Content of decision.* The written decision shall include:

(1) A summary of the facts concerning the origin, nature, and amount of the debt;

(2) The hearing official's findings, analysis, and conclusions; and

(3) The terms of any repayment schedules, if applicable.

(g) *Failure to appear.* If, in the absence of good cause shown, such as illness, the employee or the representative of FHFA fails to appear, the hearing official shall proceed with the hearing as scheduled, and make his or her decision based upon the oral testimony presented and the documentation submitted by both parties. At the request of both parties, the hearing official may schedule a new hearing date. Both parties shall be given reasonable notice of the time and place of the new hearing.

§ 1208.24 Certification where FHFA is the creditor agency.

(a) *Issuance.* FHFA shall issue a certification in all cases where the hearing official determines that a debt exists or the employee admits the existence and amount of the debt, as for example, by failing to request a hearing.

(b) *Contents.* The certification must be in writing and state:

(1) That the employee owes the debt;

(2) The amount and basis of the debt;

(3) The date the Federal Government's right to collect the debt first accrued;

(4) The date the employee was notified of the debt, the action(s) taken pursuant to FHFA's regulations, and the dates such actions were taken;

(5) If the collection is to be made by lump-sum payment, the amount and date such payment will be collected;

(6) If the collection is to be made in installments through salary offset, the amount or percentage of disposable pay to be collected in each installment and, if FHFA wishes, the desired commencing date of the first installment, if a date other than the next officially established pay period; and

(7) A statement that FHFA's regulation on salary offset has been approved by OPM pursuant to 5 CFR part 550, subpart K.

§ 1208.25 Voluntary repayment agreements as alternative to salary offset where FHFA is the creditor agency.

(a) *Proposed repayment schedule.* In response to a Notice of Intent, an employee may propose to repay the debt voluntarily in lieu of salary offset by submitting a written proposed repayment schedule to FHFA. Any proposal under this section must be received by FHFA within 30 calendar days after receipt of the Notice of Intent.

(b) *Notification of decision.* In response to a timely proposal by the employee, FHFA shall notify the employee whether the employee's proposed repayment schedule is acceptable. FHFA has the discretion to accept, reject, or propose to the employee a modification of the proposed repayment schedule.

(1) If FHFA decides that the proposed repayment schedule is unacceptable, the employee shall have 30 calendar days from the date he or she received notice of the decision in which to file a request for a hearing.

(2) If FHFA decides that the proposed repayment schedule is acceptable or the employee agrees to a modification proposed by FHFA, an agreement shall be put in writing and signed by both the employee and FHFA.

§ 1208.26 Special review where FHFA is the creditor agency.

(a) *Request for review.*—(1) An employee subject to salary offset or a voluntary repayment agreement may, at any time, request a special review by FHFA of the amount of the salary offset or voluntary repayment, based on materially changed circumstances, including, but not limited to, catastrophic illness, divorce, death, or disability.

(2) The request for special review must include an alternative proposed offset or payment schedule and a detailed statement, with supporting documents, that shows why the current salary offset or payments result in extreme financial hardship to the employee and his or her spouse and dependents. The detailed statement must indicate:

(i) Income from all sources;

(ii) Assets;

(iii) Liabilities;

(iv) Number of dependents;

(v) Expenses for food, housing, clothing, and transportation;

(vi) Medical expenses; and

(vii) Exceptional expenses, if any.

(b) *Evaluation of request.* FHFA shall evaluate the statement and supporting documents and determine whether the original offset or repayment schedule imposes extreme financial hardship on the employee, for example, by preventing the employee from meeting essential subsistence expenses such as food, housing, clothing, transportation, and medical care. FHFA shall notify the employee in writing within 30 calendar days of such determination, including, if appropriate, a revised offset or payment schedule. If the special review results in a revised offset or repayment schedule, FHFA shall provide a new certification to the paying agency.

§ 1208.27 Notice of salary offset where FHFA is the paying agency.

(a) *Notice.* Upon issuance of a proper certification by FHFA (for debts owed to FHFA) or upon receipt of a proper certification from another creditor agency, FHFA shall send the employee a written notice of salary offset.

(b) *Content of notice.* Such written notice of salary offset shall advise the employee of the:

(1) Certification that has been issued by FHFA or received from another creditor agency;

(2) Amount of the debt and of the deductions to be made; and

(3) Date and pay period when the salary offset will begin.

(c) If FHFA is not the creditor agency, FHFA shall provide a copy of the notice of salary offset to the creditor agency and advise the creditor agency of the dollar amount to be offset and the pay period when the offset will begin.

§ 1208.28 Procedures for salary offset where FHFA is the paying agency.

(a) *Generally.* FHFA shall coordinate salary deductions under this section and shall determine the amount of an employee's disposable pay and the amount of the salary offset subject to the requirements in this section. Deductions shall begin the pay period following the issuance of the certification by FHFA or the receipt by FHFA of the certification from another agency, or as soon thereafter as possible.

(b) Upon issuance of a proper certification by FHFA for debts owed to FHFA, or upon receipt of a proper certification from a creditor agency,

FHFA shall send the employee a written notice of salary offset. Such notice shall advise the employee:

(1) That certification has been issued by FHFA or received from another creditor agency;

(2) Of the amount of the debt and of the deductions to be made; and provided for in the certification, and

(3) Of the initiation of salary offset at the next officially established pay interval or as otherwise provided for in the certification.

(c) Where appropriate, FHFA shall provide a copy of the notice to the creditor agency and advise such agency of the dollar amount to be offset and the pay period when the offset will begin.

(d) *Types of collection.*—(1) *Lump-sum payment.* If the amount of the debt is equal to or less than 15 percent of the employee's disposable pay, such debt ordinarily will be collected in one lump-sum payment.

(2) *Installment deductions.* Installment deductions will be made over a period not greater than the anticipated period of employment. The size and frequency of installment deductions will bear a reasonable relation to the size of the debt and the employee's ability to pay. However, the amount deducted for any pay period will not exceed 15 percent of the disposable pay from which the deduction is made unless the employee has agreed in writing to the deduction of a greater amount. The installment payment should normally be sufficient in size and frequency to liquidate the debt in no more than three years. Installment payments of less than $50 should be accepted only in the most unusual circumstances.

(3) *Lump-sum deductions from final check.* In order to liquidate a debt, a lump-sum deduction exceeding 15 percent of disposable pay may be made pursuant to 31 U.S.C. 3716 from any final salary payment due a former employee, whether the former employee was separated voluntarily or involuntarily.

(4) *Lump-sum deductions from other sources.* Whenever an employee subject to salary offset is separated from FHFA, and the balance of the debt cannot be liquidated by offset of the final salary check, FHFA may offset any later payments of any kind to the former employee to collect the balance of the debt pursuant to 31 U.S.C. 3716.

(e) *Multiple debts.*—(1) Where two or more creditor agencies are seeking salary offset, or where two or more debts are owed to a single creditor agency, FHFA may, at its discretion, determine whether one or more debts should be offset simultaneously within the 15 percent limitation.

(2) In the event that a debt owed FHFA is certified while an employee is subject to salary offset to repay another agency, FHFA may, at its discretion, determine whether the debt to FHFA should be repaid before the debt to the other agency is repaid, repaid simultaneously with the other debt, or repaid after the debt to the other agency.

(3) A levy pursuant to the Internal Revenue Code of 1986 shall take precedence over other deductions under this section, as provided in 5 U.S.C. 5514(d).

§ 1208.29 Coordinating salary offset with other agencies.

(a) *Responsibility of FHFA as the creditor agency.*—(1) FHFA shall be responsible for:

(i) Arranging for a hearing upon proper request by a Federal employee;

(ii) Preparing the Notice of Intent consistent with the requirements of § 1208.21;

(iii) Obtaining hearing officials from other agencies pursuant to § 1208.23(b); and

(iv) Ensuring that each certification of debt pursuant to § 1208.24(b) is sent to a paying agency.

(2) Upon completion of the procedures set forth in §§ 1208.24 through 1208.26, FHFA shall submit to the employee's paying agency, if applicable, a certified debt claim and an installment agreement or other instruction on the payment schedule.

(i) If the employee is in the process of separating from the Federal Government, FHFA shall submit its debt claim to the employee's paying agency for collection by lump-sum deduction from the employee's final check. The paying agency shall certify the total amount of its collection and furnish a copy of the certification to FHFA and to the employee.

(ii) If the employee is already separated and all payments due from his or her former paying agency have been paid, FHFA may, unless otherwise prohibited, request that money due and payable to the employee from the Federal Government, including payments from the Civil Service Retirement and Disability Fund (5 CFR 831.1801) or other similar funds, be administratively offset to collect the debt.

(iii) When an employee transfers to another paying agency, FHFA shall not repeat the procedures described in §§ 1208.24 through 1208.26. Upon receiving notice of the employee's transfer, FHFA shall review the debt to ensure that collection is resumed by the new paying agency.

(b) *Responsibility of FHFA as the paying agency.*—(1) *Complete claim.* When FHFA receives a certified claim from a creditor agency, the employee shall be given written notice of the certification, the date salary offset will begin, and the amount of the periodic deductions. Deductions shall be scheduled to begin at the next officially established pay interval or as otherwise provided for in the certification.

(2) *Incomplete claim.* When FHFA receives an incomplete certification of debt from a creditor agency, FHFA shall return the claim with notice that procedures under 5 U.S.C. 5514 and 5 CFR 550.1104 must be followed, and that a properly certified claim must be received before FHFA will take action to collect the debt from the employee's current pay account.

(3) *Review.* FHFA is not authorized to review the merits of the creditor agency's determination with respect to the amount or validity of the debt certified by the creditor agency.

(4) *Employees who transfer from one paying agency to another agency.* If, after the creditor agency has submitted the debt claim to FHFA, the employee transfers to another agency before the debt is collected in full, FHFA must certify the total amount collected on the debt as required by 5 CFR 550.1109. One copy of the certification shall be furnished to the employee and one copy shall be sent to the creditor agency along with notice of the employee's transfer. If FHFA is aware that the employee is entitled to payments from the Civil Service Retirement and Disability Fund or other similar payments, it must provide written notification to the agency responsible for making such payments that the debtor owes a debt (including the amount) and that the requirements set forth herein and in 5 CFR part 550, subpart K, have been met. FHFA must submit a properly certified claim to the new payment agency before a collection can be made.

§ 1208.30 Interest, penalties, and administrative costs.

Where FHFA is the creditor agency, FHFA shall assess interest, penalties, and administrative costs pursuant to 31 U.S.C. 3717 and the FCCS, 31 CFR chapter IX.

§ 1208.31 Refunds.

(a) Where FHFA is the creditor agency, FHFA shall promptly refund any amount deducted under the authority of 5 U.S.C. 5514 when:

(1) FHFA receives notice that the debt has been waived or otherwise found not to be owing to the Federal Government; or

(2) An administrative or judicial order directs FHFA to make a refund.

(b) Unless required by law or contract, refunds under this section shall not bear interest.

§ 1208.32 Request from a creditor agency for the services of a hearing official.

(a) FHFA may provide qualified personnel to serve as hearing officials upon request of a creditor agency when:

(1) The debtor is employed by FHFA and the creditor agency cannot provide a prompt and appropriate hearing before a hearing official furnished pursuant to another lawful arrangement; or

(2) The debtor is employed by the creditor agency and that agency cannot arrange for a hearing official.

(b) Services provided by FHFA to creditor agencies under this section shall be provided on a fully reimbursable basis pursuant to 31 U.S.C. 1535, or other applicable authority.

§ 1208.33 Non-waiver of rights by payments.

A debtor's payment, whether voluntary or involuntary, of all or any portion of a debt being collected pursuant to this subpart B shall not be construed as a waiver of any rights that the debtor may have under any statute, regulation, or contract, except as otherwise provided by law or contract.

Subpart C—Administrative Offset

§ 1208.40 Authority and scope.

(a) The provisions of this subpart C apply to the collection of debts owed to the Federal Government arising from transactions with FHFA. Administrative offset is authorized under the Debt Collection Improvement Act of 1996 (DCIA). This subpart C is consistent with the Federal Claims Collection Standards (FCCS) on administrative offset issued by the Department of Justice.

(b) FHFA may collect a debt owed to the Federal Government from a person, organization, or other entity by administrative offset, pursuant to 31 U.S.C. 3716, where:

(1) The debt is certain in amount;

(2) Administrative offset is feasible, desirable, and not otherwise prohibited;

(3) The applicable statute of limitations has not expired; and

(4) Administrative offset is in the best interest of the Federal Government.

§ 1208.41 Collection.

(a) FHFA may collect a claim from a person, organization, or other entity by administrative offset of monies payable by the Federal Government only after:

(1) Providing the debtor with due process required under this part; and

(2) Providing the paying agency with written certification that the debtor owes the debt in the amount stated and that FHFA, as creditor agency, has complied with this part.

(b) Prior to initiating collection by administrative offset, FHFA should determine that the proposed offset is within the scope of this remedy, as set forth in 31 CFR 901.3(a). Administrative offset under 31 U.S.C. 3716 may not be used to collect debts more than 10 years after the Federal Government's right to collect the debt first accrued, except as otherwise provided by law. In addition, administrative offset may not be used when a statute explicitly prohibits its use to collect the claim or type of claim involved.

(c) Unless otherwise provided, debts or payments not subject to administrative offset under 31 U.S.C. 3716 may be collected by administrative offset under common law, or any other applicable statutory authority.

§ 1208.42 Administrative offset prior to completion of procedures.

FHFA shall not be required to follow the procedures described in § 1208.43 where:

(a) Prior to the completion of the procedures described in § 1208.43, FHFA may effect administrative offset if failure to offset would substantially prejudice its ability to collect the debt, and if the time before the payment is to be made does not reasonably permit completion of the procedures described in § 1208.43. Such prior administrative offset shall be followed promptly by the completion of the procedures described in § 1208.43. Amounts recovered by administrative offset but later found not to be owed to FHFA shall be promptly refunded. This section applies only to administrative offset pursuant to 31 CFR 901.3(c), and does not apply when debts are referred to the Department of the Treasury for mandatory centralized administrative offset under 31 CFR 901.3(b)(1).

(b) The administrative offset is in the nature of a recoupment (*i.e.*, FHFA may offset a payment due to the debtor when both the payment due to the debtor and the debt owed to FHFA arose from the same transaction); or

(c) In the case of non-centralized administrative offsets, FHFA first learns of the existence of a debt due when there would be insufficient time to afford the debtor due process under these procedures before the paying agency makes payment to the debtor; in such cases, the Director shall give the debtor notice and an opportunity for review as soon as practical and shall refund any money ultimately found not to be due to the Federal Government.

§ 1208.43 Procedures.

Unless the procedures described in § 1208.42 are used, prior to collecting any debt by administrative offset or referring such claim to another agency for collection through administrative offset, FHFA shall provide the debtor with the following:

(a) Written notification of the nature and amount of the debt, the intention of FHFA to collect the debt through administrative offset, and a statement of the rights of the debtor under this section;

(b) An opportunity to inspect and copy the records of FHFA related to the debt that are not exempt from disclosure;

(c) An opportunity for review within FHFA of the determination of indebtedness. Any request for review by the debtor shall be in writing and shall be submitted to FHFA within 30 calendar days of the date of the notice of the offset. FHFA may waive the time limits for requesting review for good cause shown by the debtor. FHFA shall provide the debtor with a reasonable opportunity for an oral hearing when:

(1) An applicable statute authorizes or requires FHFA to consider waiver of the indebtedness involved, the debtor requests waiver of the indebtedness, and the waiver determination turns on an issue of credibility or veracity; or

(2) The debtor requests reconsideration of the debt and FHFA determines that the question of the indebtedness cannot be resolved by review of the documentary evidence, as for example, when the validity of the debt turns on an issue of credibility or veracity. Unless otherwise required by law, an oral hearing under this subpart C is not required to be a formal evidentiary hearing, although FHFA shall document all significant matters discussed at the hearing. In those cases where an oral hearing is not required by this subpart C, FHFA shall make its determination on the request for waiver or reconsideration based upon a review of the written record; and

(d) An opportunity to enter into a written agreement for the voluntary repayment of the amount of the claim at the discretion of FHFA.

§ 1208.44 Interest, penalties, and administrative costs.

FHFA shall assess interest, penalties, and administrative costs on debts owed to the Federal Government, in accordance with 31 U.S.C. 3717 and the FCCS. FHFA may also assess interest and related charges on debts that are not subject to 31 U.S.C. 3717 and the FCCS to the extent authorized under the common law or other applicable statutory authority.

§ 1208.45 Refunds.

FHFA shall refund promptly those amounts recovered by administrative offset but later found not to be owed to the Federal Government. Unless required by law or contract, such refunds shall not bear interest.

§ 1208.46 No requirement for duplicate notice.

Where FHFA has previously given a debtor any of the required notice and review opportunities with respect to a particular debt, FHFA is not required to duplicate such notice and review opportunities prior to initiating administrative offset.

§ 1208.47 Requests for administrative offset to other Federal agencies.

(a) FHFA may request that a debt owed to FHFA be collected by administrative offset against funds due and payable to a debtor by another agency.

(b) In requesting administrative offset, FHFA, as creditor, shall certify in writing to the agency holding funds of the debtor:

(1) That the debtor owes the debt;

(2) The amount and basis of the debt; and

(3) That FHFA has complied with the requirements of its own administrative offset regulations and the applicable provisions of the FCCS with respect to providing the debtor with due process, unless otherwise provided.

§ 1208.48 Requests for administrative offset from other Federal agencies.

(a) Any agency may request that funds due and payable to a debtor by FHFA be administratively offset in order to collect a debt owed to such agency by the debtor.

(b) FHFA shall initiate the requested administrative offset only upon:

(1) Receipt of written certification from the creditor agency that:

(i) The debtor owes the debt, including the amount and basis of the debt;

(ii) The agency has prescribed regulations for the exercise of administrative offset; and

(iii) The agency has complied with its own administrative offset regulations and with the applicable provisions of the FCCS, including providing any required hearing or review.

(2) A determination by FHFA that collection by administrative offset against funds payable by FHFA would be in the best interest of the Federal Government as determined by the facts and circumstances of the particular case and that such administrative offset would not otherwise be contrary to law.

§ 1208.49 Administrative offset against amounts payable from Civil Service Retirement and Disability Fund.

(a) *Request for administrative offset.* Unless otherwise prohibited by law, FHFA may request that monies that are due and payable to a debtor from the Civil Service Retirement and Disability Fund (Fund) be offset administratively in reasonable amounts in order to collect in one full payment or in a minimal number of payments debt owed to FHFA by the debtor. Such requests shall be made to the appropriate officials of OPM in accordance with such regulations as may be prescribed by FHFA or OPM.

(b) *Contents of certification.* When making a request for administrative offset under paragraph (a) of this section, FHFA shall provide OPM with a written certification that:

(1) The debtor owes FHFA a debt, including the amount of the debt;

(2) FHFA has complied with the applicable statutes, regulations, and procedures of OPM; and

(3) FHFA has complied with the requirements of the FCCS, including any required hearing or review.

(c) If FHFA decides to request administrative offset under paragraph (a) of this section, it shall make the request as soon as practicable after completion of the applicable procedures. This will satisfy any requirement that administrative offset be initiated prior to the expiration of the applicable statute of limitations. At such time as the debtor makes a claim for payments from the Fund, if at least one year has elapsed since the administrative offset request was originally made, the debtor shall be permitted to offer a satisfactory repayment plan in lieu of administrative offset if he or she establishes that changed financial circumstances would render the administrative offset unjust.

(d) If FHFA collects part or all of the debt by other means before deductions are made or completed pursuant to paragraph (a) of this section, FHFA shall act promptly to modify or terminate its request for administrative offset under paragraph (a) of this section.

Subpart D—Tax Refund Offset

§ 1208.50 Authority and scope.

The provisions of 26 U.S.C. 6402(d) and 31 U.S.C. 3720A authorize the Secretary of the Treasury to offset a delinquent debt owed the Federal Government from the tax refund due a taxpayer when other collection efforts have failed to recover the amount due. In addition, FHFA is authorized to collect debts by means of administrative offset under 31 U.S.C. 3716 and, as part of the debt collection process, to notify the United States Department of Treasury's Financial Management Service of the amount of such debt for collection by tax refund offset.

§ 1208.51 Definitions.

The following terms apply to this subpart D—

Debt or claim means an amount of money, funds or property which has been determined by FHFA to be due to the Federal Government from any person, organization, or entity, except another Federal agency.

(1) A debt becomes eligible for tax refund offset procedures if:

(i) It cannot currently be collected pursuant to the salary offset procedures of 5 U.S.C. 5514(a)(1);

(ii) The debt is ineligible for administrative offset or cannot be collected currently by administrative offset; and

(iii) The requirements of this section are otherwise satisfied.

(2) All judgment debts are past due for purposes of this subpart D. Judgment debts remain past due until paid in full.

Debtor means a person who owes a debt or a claim. The term "person" includes any individual, organization or entity, except another Federal agency.

Dispute means a written statement supported by documentation or other evidence that all or part of an alleged debt is not past due or legally enforceable, that the amount is not the amount currently owed, that the outstanding debt has been satisfied, or in the case of a debt reduced to judgment, that the judgment has been satisfied or stayed.

Notice means the information sent to the debtor pursuant to § 1208.53. The date of the notice is that date shown on the notice letter as its date of issuance.

Tax refund offset means withholding or reducing a tax refund payment by an amount necessary to satisfy a debt owed by the payee(s) of a tax refund payment.

Tax refund payment means any overpayment of Federal taxes to be refunded to the person making the overpayment after the Internal Revenue Service (IRS) makes the appropriate credits.

§ 1208.52 Procedures.

(a) *Referral to the Department of the Treasury*.—(1) FHFA may refer any past due, legally enforceable nonjudgment debt of an individual, organization, or entity to the Department of the Treasury for tax refund offset if FHFA's or the referring agency's rights of action accrued more than three months but less than 10 years before the offset is made.

(2) Debts reduced to judgment may be referred at any time.

(3) Debts in amounts lower than $25 are not subject to referral.

(4) In the event that more than one debt is owed, the tax refund offset procedures shall be applied in the order in which the debts became past due.

(5) FHFA shall notify the Department of the Treasury of any change in the amount due promptly after receipt of payment or notice of other reductions.

(b) *Notice*. FHFA shall provide the debtor with written notice of its intent to offset before initiating the offset. Notice shall be mailed to the debtor at the current address of the debtor, as determined from information obtained from the Internal Revenue Service pursuant to 26 U.S.C. 6103(m)(2), (4), (5) or maintained by FHFA. The notice sent to the debtor shall state the amount of the debt and inform the debtor that:

(1) The debt is past due;

(2) FHFA intends to refer the debt to the Department of the Treasury for offset from tax refunds that may be due to the taxpayer;

(3) FHFA intends to provide information concerning the delinquent debt exceeding $100 to a consumer reporting bureau unless such debt has already been disclosed; and

(4) Before the debt is reported to a consumer reporting agency, if applicable, and referred to the Department of the Treasury for offset from tax refunds, the debtor has 65 calendar days from the date of notice to request a review under paragraph (d) of this section.

(c) *Report to consumer reporting agency*. If the debtor neither pays the amount due nor presents evidence that the amount is not past due or is satisfied or stayed, FHFA will report the debt to a consumer reporting agency at the end of the notice period, if applicable, and refer the debt to the Department of the Treasury for offset from the taxpayer's Federal tax refund. FHFA shall certify to the Department of the Treasury that reasonable efforts have been made by FHFA to obtain payment of such debt.

(d) *Request for review*. A debtor may request a review by FHFA if he or she believes that all or part of the debt is not past due or is not legally enforceable, or in the case of a judgment debt, that the debt has been stayed or the amount satisfied, as follows:

(1) The debtor must send a written request for review to FHFA at the address provided in the notice.

(2) The request must state the amount disputed and reasons why the debtor believes that the debt is not past due, is not legally enforceable, has been satisfied, or if a judgment debt, has been satisfied or stayed.

(3) The request must include any documents that the debtor wishes to be considered or state that additional information will be submitted within the time permitted.

(4) If the debtor wishes to inspect records establishing the nature and amount of the debt, the debtor must make a written request to FHFA for an opportunity for such an inspection. The office holding the relevant records not exempt from disclosure shall make them available for inspection during normal business hours within one week from the date of receipt of the request.

(5) The request for review and any additional information submitted pursuant to the request must be received by FHFA at the address stated in the notice within 65 calendar days of the date of issuance of the notice.

(6) In reaching its decision, FHFA shall review the dispute and shall consider its records and any documentation and arguments submitted by the debtor. FHFA shall send a written notice of its decision to the debtor. There is no administrative appeal of this decision.

(7) If the evidence presented by the debtor is considered by a non-FHFA agent or other entities or persons acting on behalf of FHFA, the debtor shall be accorded at least 30 calendar days from the date the agent or other entity or person determines that all or part of the debt is past due and legally enforceable to request review by FHFA of any unresolved dispute.

(8) Any debt that previously has been reviewed pursuant to this section or any other section of this part, or that has been reduced to a judgment, may not be disputed except on the grounds of payments made or events occurring subsequent to the previous review or judgment.

(9) To the extent that a debt owed has not been established by judicial or administrative order, a debtor may dispute the existence or amount of the debt or the terms of repayment. With respect to debts established by a judicial or administrative order, FHFA review will be limited to issues concerning the payment or other discharge of the debt.

§ 1208.53 No requirement for duplicate notice.

Where FHFA has previously given a debtor any of the required notice and review opportunities with respect to a particular debt, FHFA is not required to duplicate such notice and review opportunities prior to initiating tax refund offset.

§ 1208.54–1208.59 [Reserved]

Subpart E—Administrative Wage Garnishment

§ 1208.60 Scope and purpose.

These administrative wage garnishment procedures are issued in compliance with 31 U.S.C. 3720D and 31 CFR 285.11(f). This subpart E provides procedures for FHFA to collect money from a debtor's disposable pay by means of administrative wage garnishment. The receipt of payments pursuant to this subpart E does not preclude FHFA from pursuing other debt collection remedies, including the offset of Federal payments. FHFA may pursue such debt collection remedies separately or in conjunction with administrative wage garnishment. This subpart E does not apply to the collection of delinquent debts from the wages of Federal employees from their Federal employment. Federal pay is subject to the Federal salary offset procedures set forth in 5 U.S.C. 5514 and other applicable laws.

§ 1208.61 Notice.

At least 30 days before the initiation of garnishment proceedings, FHFA will send, by first class mail to the debtor's last known address, a written notice informing the debtor of:

(a) The nature and amount of the debt;

(b) FHFA's intention to initiate proceedings to collect the debt through deductions from the debtor's pay until the debt and all accumulated interest penalties and administrative costs are paid in full;

(c) An explanation of the debtor's rights as set forth in § 1208.62(c); and

(d) The time frame within which the debtor may exercise these rights. FHFA shall retain a stamped copy of the notice indicating the date the notice was mailed.

§ 1208.62 Debtor's rights.

FHFA shall afford the debtor the opportunity:

(a) To inspect and copy records related to the debt;

(b) To enter into a written repayment agreement with FHFA, under terms agreeable to FHFA; and

(c) To the extent that a debt owed has not been established by judicial or administrative order, to request a hearing concerning the existence or amount of the debt or the terms of the repayment schedule. With respect to debts established by a judicial or administrative order, a debtor may request a hearing concerning the payment or other discharge of the debt. The debtor is not entitled to a hearing concerning the terms of the proposed repayment schedule if these terms have been established by written agreement.

§ 1208.63 Form of hearing.

(a) If the debtor submits a timely written request for a hearing as provided in § 1208.62(c), FHFA will afford the debtor a hearing, which at FHFA's option may be oral or written. FHFA will provide the debtor with a reasonable opportunity for an oral hearing when FHFA determines that the issues in dispute cannot be resolved by review of the documentary evidence, for example, when the validity of the claim turns on the issue of credibility or veracity.

(b) If FHFA determines that an oral hearing is appropriate, the time and location of the hearing shall be established by FHFA. An oral hearing may, at the debtor's option, be conducted either in person or by telephone conference. All travel expenses incurred by the debtor in connection with an in-person hearing will be borne by the debtor. All telephonic charges incurred during the hearing will be the responsibility of the agency.

(c) In cases when it is determined that an oral hearing is not required by this section, FHFA will accord the debtor a "paper hearing," that is, FHFA will decide the issues in dispute based upon a review of the written record.

§ 1208.64 Effect of timely request.

If FHFA receives a debtor's written request for a hearing within 15 business days of the date FHFA mailed its notice of intent to seek garnishment, FHFA shall not issue a withholding order until the debtor has been provided the requested hearing, and a decision in accordance with § 1208.68 and § 1208.69 has been rendered.

§ 1208.65 Failure to timely request a hearing.

If FHFA receives a debtor's written request for a hearing after 15 business days of the date FHFA mailed its notice of intent to seek garnishment, FHFA shall provide a hearing to the debtor. However, FHFA will not delay issuance of a withholding order unless it determines that the untimely filing of the request was caused by factors over which the debtor had no control, or FHFA receives information that FHFA believes justifies a delay or cancellation of the withholding order.

§ 1208.66 Hearing official.

A hearing official may be any qualified individual, as determined by FHFA, including an administrative law judge.

§ 1208.67 Procedure.

After the debtor requests a hearing, the hearing official shall notify the debtor of:

(a) The date and time of a telephonic hearing;

(b) The date, time, and location of an in-person oral hearing; or

(c) The deadline for the submission of evidence for a written hearing.

§ 1208.68 Format of hearing.

FHFA will have the burden of proof to establish the existence or amount of the debt. Thereafter, if the debtor disputes the existence or amount of the debt, the debtor must prove by a preponderance of the evidence that no debt exists, or that the amount of the debt is incorrect. In addition, the debtor may present evidence that the terms of the repayment schedule are unlawful, would cause a financial hardship to the debtor, or that collection of the debt may not be pursued due to operation of law. The hearing official shall maintain a record of any hearing held under this section. Hearings are not required to be formal, and evidence may be offered without regard to formal rules of evidence. Witnesses who testify in oral hearings shall do so under oath or affirmation.

§ 1208.69 Date of decision.

The hearing official shall issue a written opinion stating his or her decision as soon as practicable, but not later than 60 days after the date on which the request for such hearing was received by FHFA. If FHFA is unable to provide the debtor with a hearing and decision within 60 days after the receipt of the request for such hearing:

(a) FHFA may not issue a withholding order until the hearing is held and a decision rendered; or

(b) If FHFA had previously issued a withholding order to the debtor's employer, the withholding order will be suspended beginning on the 61st day after the date FHFA received the hearing request and continuing until a hearing is held and a decision is rendered.

§ 1208.70 Content of decision.

The written decision shall include:

(a) A summary of the facts presented;

(b) The hearing official's findings, analysis and conclusions; and

(c) The terms of any repayment schedule, if applicable.

§ 1208.71 Finality of agency action.

A decision by a hearing official shall become the final decision of FHFA for the purpose of judicial review under the Administrative Procedure Act.

§ 1208.72 Failure to appear.

In the absence of good cause shown, a debtor who fails to appear at a scheduled hearing will be deemed as not having timely filed a request for a hearing.

§ 1208.73 Wage garnishment order.

(a) Unless FHFA receives information that it believes justifies a delay or cancellation of the withholding order, FHFA will send by first class mail a withholding order to the debtor's employer within 30 calendar days after the debtor fails to make a timely request for a hearing (*i.e.*, within 15 business days after the mailing of the notice of FHFA's intent to seek garnishment) or, if a timely request for a hearing is made by the debtor, within 30 calendar days after a decision to issue a withholding order becomes final.

(b) The withholding order sent to the employer will be in the form prescribed by the Secretary of the Treasury, on FHFA's letterhead, and signed by the head of the agency or delegate. The order will contain all information necessary for the employer to comply with the withholding order, including the debtor's name, address, and social security number, as well as instructions for withholding and information as to where payments should be sent.

(c) FHFA will keep a stamped copy of the order indicating the date it was mailed.

§ 1208.74 Certification by employer.

Along with the withholding order, FHFA will send to the employer a certification in a form prescribed by the Secretary of the Treasury. The employer shall complete and return the certification to FHFA within the time frame prescribed in the instructions to the form. The certification will address matters such as information about the debtor's employment status and disposable pay available for withholding.

§ 1208.75 Amounts withheld.

(a) Upon receipt of the garnishment order issued under this section, the employer shall deduct from all disposable pay paid to the debtor during each pay period the amount of garnishment described in paragraphs (b) through (d) of this section.

(b) Subject to the provisions of paragraphs (c) and (d) of this section, the amount of garnishment shall be the lesser of:

(1) The amount indicated on the garnishment order up to 15 percent of the debtor's disposable pay; or

(2) The amount set forth in 15 U.S.C. 1673(a)(2). The amount set forth at 15 U.S.C. 1673(a)(2) is the amount by which the debtor's disposable pay exceeds an amount equivalent to thirty times the minimum wage.

(c) When a debtor's pay is subject to withholding orders with priority, the following shall apply:

(1) Unless otherwise provided by Federal law, withholding orders issued under this section shall be paid in the amounts set forth under paragraph (b) of this section and shall have priority over other withholding orders which are served later in time. However, withholding orders for family support shall have priority over withholding orders issued under this section.

(2) If amounts are being withheld from a debtor's pay pursuant to a withholding order served on an employer before a withholding order issued pursuant to this section, or if a withholding order for family support is served on an employer at any time, the amounts withheld pursuant to the withholding order issued under this section shall be the lesser of:

(i) The amount calculated under paragraph (b) of this section; or

(ii) An amount equal to 25 percent of the debtor's disposable pay less the amount(s) withheld under the withholding order(s) with priority.

(3) If a debtor owes more than one debt to FHFA, FHFA may issue multiple withholding orders. The total amount garnished from the debtor's pay for such orders will not exceed the amount set forth in paragraph (b) of this section.

(d) An amount greater than that set forth in paragraphs (b) and (c) of this section may be withheld upon the written consent of the debtor.

(e) The employer shall promptly pay to FHFA all amounts withheld in accordance with the withholding order issued pursuant to this section.

(f) An employer shall not be required to vary its normal pay and disbursement cycles in order to comply with the withholding order.

(g) Any assignment or allotment by the employee of the employee's earnings shall be void to the extent it interferes with or prohibits execution of the withholding order under this section, except for any assignment or allotment made pursuant to a family support judgment or order.

(h) The employer shall withhold the appropriate amount from the debtor's wages for each pay period until the employer receives notification from FHFA to discontinue wage withholding. The garnishment order shall indicate a reasonable period of time within which the employer is required to commence wage withholding.

§ 1208.76 Exclusions from garnishment.

FHFA will not garnish the wages of a debtor it knows has been involuntarily separated from employment until the debtor has been re-employed continuously for at least 12 months. The debtor has the burden of informing FHFA of the circumstances surrounding an involuntary separation from employment.

§ 1208.77 Financial hardship.

(a) A debtor whose wages are subject to a wage withholding order under this section, may, at any time, request a review by FHFA of the amount garnished, based on materially changed circumstances such as disability, divorce, or catastrophic illness which result in financial hardship.

(b) A debtor requesting a review under this section shall submit the basis for claiming that the current amount of garnishment results in a financial hardship to the debtor, along with supporting documentation.

(c) If a financial hardship is found, FHFA will downwardly adjust, by an amount and for a period of time agreeable to FHFA, the amount garnished to reflect the debtor's financial condition. FHFA will notify the employer of any adjustments to the amounts to be withheld.

§ 1208.78 Ending garnishment.

(a) Once FHFA has fully recovered the amounts owed by the debtor, including interest, penalties, and administrative costs consistent with the Federal Claims Collection Standards, FHFA will send the debtor's employer notification to discontinue wage withholding.

(b) At least annually, FHFA will review its debtors' accounts to ensure that garnishment has been terminated for accounts that have been paid in full.

§ 1208.79 Prohibited actions by employer.

The Debt Collection Improvement Act of 1996 prohibits an employer from discharging, refusing to employ, or taking disciplinary action against the debtor due to the issuance of a withholding order under this subpart E.

§ 1208.80 Refunds.

(a) If a hearing official determines that a debt is not legally due and owing to the United States, FHFA shall promptly refund any amount collected by means of administrative wage garnishment.

(b) Unless required by Federal law or contract, refunds under this section shall not bear interest.

§ 1208.81 Right of action.

FHFA may sue any employer for any amount that the employer fails to withhold from wages owed and payable to its employee in accordance with this subpart E. However, a suit will not be filed before the termination of the collection action involving a particular debtor, unless earlier filing is necessary to avoid expiration of any applicable statute of limitations. For purposes of this subpart E, "termination of the collection action" occurs when the agency has terminated collection action in accordance with the FCCS or other applicable standards. In any event, termination of the collection action will have been deemed to occur if FHFA has not received any payments to satisfy the debt from the particular debtor whose wages were subject to garnishment, in whole or in part, for a period of one (1) year.

PART 1209—RULES OF PRACTICE AND PROCEDURE

Subpart A—Scope and Authority

Sec.

Subpart B—Enforcement Proceedings Under Sections 1371 Through 1379D of the Safety and Soundness Act

Subpart C—Rules of Practice and Procedure

Subpart D—Parties and Representational Practice Before the Federal Housing Finance Agency; Standards of Conduct

Subpart E—Civil Money Penalty Inflation Adjustments

Subpart F—Suspension or Removal of an Entity-Affiliated Party Charged With Felony

AUTHORITY: 5 U.S.C. 554, 556, 557, and 701 *et seq.;* 12 U.S.C. 4501, 4503, 4511, 4513, 4513b, 4517, 4526, 4531, 4535, 4536, 4581, 4585, 4631–4641; and 28 U.S.C. 2461 note.

SOURCE: 76 FR 53607, Aug. 26, 2011, unless otherwise noted.

Subpart A—Scope and Authority

§ 1209.1 Scope.

(a) *Authority.* This part sets forth the Rules of Practice and Procedure for hearings on the record in administrative enforcement proceedings in accordance with the Federal Housing Enterprises Financial Safety and Soundness Act of 1992, Title XIII of the Housing and Community Development Act of 1992, Public Law 102–550, sections 1301 *et seq.*, codified at 12 U.S.C. 4501 *et seq.*, as amended (the "Safety and Soundness Act"), as stated in § 1209.4 of this part.[1]

(b) *Enforcement Proceedings.* Subpart B of this part (Enforcement Proceedings Under sections 1371 through 1379D of the Safety and Soundness Act) sets forth the statutory authority for enforcement proceedings under sections 1371 through 1379D of the Safety and Soundness Act (12 U.S.C. 4631 through 4641) (Enforcement Proceedings).

(c) *Rules of Practice and Procedure.* Subpart C of this part (Rules of Practice and Procedure) prescribes the general rules of practice and procedure applicable to adjudicatory proceedings that the Director is required by statute to conduct on the record after opportunity for a hearing under the Administrative Procedure Act, 5 U.S.C. 554, 556, and 557, under the following statutory provisions:

(1) Enforcement proceedings under sections 1371 through 1379D of the Safety and Soundness Act, as amended (12 U.S.C. 4631 through 4641);

(2) Removal, prohibition, and civil money penalty proceedings for violations of post-employment restrictions imposed by applicable law; and

(3) Proceedings under section 102 of the Flood Disaster Protection Act of 1973, as amended (42 U.S.C. 4012a) to assess civil money penalties.

(d) *Representation and conduct.* Subpart D of this part (Parties and Representational Practice before the Federal Housing Finance Agency; Standards of Conduct) sets out the rules of representation and conduct that shall govern any appearance by any person, party, or representative of any person or party, before a presiding officer, the Director of FHFA, or a designated representative of the Director or FHFA staff, in any proceeding or matter pending before the Director.

(e) *Civil money penalty inflation adjustments.* Subpart E of this part (Civil Money Penalty Inflation Adjustments) sets out the requirements for the periodic adjustment of maximum civil money penalty amounts under the Federal Civil Penalties Inflation Adjustment Act of 1990, as amended (Inflation

[1] As used in this part, the "Safety and Soundness Act" means the Federal Housing Enterprise Financial Safety and Soundness Act of 1992, as amended. *See* § 1209.3. The Safety and Soundness Act was amended by the Housing and Economic Recovery Act of 2008, Public Law No. 110–289, sections 1101 *et seq.*, 122 Stat. 2654 (July 30, 2008) (HERA). Specifically, sections 1151 through 1158 of HERA amended sections 1371 through 1379D of the Safety and Soundness Act, (codified at 12 U.S.C. 4631 through 4641) (hereafter, "Enforcement Proceedings").

Adjustment Act) on a recurring four-year cycle.[2]

(f) *Informal proceedings.* Subpart F of this part (Suspension or Removal of an Entity-Affiliated Party Charged with Felony) sets out the scope and procedures for the suspension or removal of an entity-affiliated party charged with a felony under section 1377(h) of the Safety and Soundness Act (12 U.S.C. 4636a(h)), which provides for an informal hearing before the Director.

§ 1209.2 Rules of construction.

For purposes of this part:

(a) Any term in the singular includes the plural and the plural includes the singular, if such use would be appropriate;

(b) Any use of a masculine, feminine, or neuter gender encompasses all three, if such use would be appropriate; and

(c) Unless the context requires otherwise, a party's representative of record, if any, on behalf of that party, may take any action required to be taken by the party.

§ 1209.3 Definitions.

For purposes of this part, unless explicitly stated to the contrary:

Adjudicatory proceeding means a proceeding conducted pursuant to these rules, on the record, and leading to the formulation of a final order other than a regulation.

Agency has the meaning defined in section 1303(2) of the Safety and Soundness Act (12 U.S.C. 4502(2)).

Associated with the regulated entity means, for purposes of section 1379 of the Safety and Soundness Act (12 U.S.C. 4637), any direct or indirect involvement or participation in the conduct of operations or business affairs of a regulated entity, including engaging in activities related to the operations or management of, providing advice or services to, consulting or contracting with, serving as agent for, or in any other way affecting the operations or business affairs of a regulated entity—with or without regard to—any direct or indirect payment, promise to make payment, or receipt of any compensation or thing of value, such as money, notes, stock, stock options, or other securities, or other benefit or remuneration of any kind, by or on behalf of the regulated entity, except any payment made pursuant to a retirement plan or deferred compensation plan, which is determined by the Director to be permissible under section 1318(e) of the Safety and Soundness Act (12 U.S.C. 4518(e)), or by reason of the death or disability of the party, in the form and manner commonly paid or provided to retirees of the regulated entity, unless such payment, compensation, or such benefit is promised or provided to or for the benefit of said party for the provision of services or other benefit to the regulated entity.

Authorizing statutes has the meaning defined in section 1303(3) of the Safety and Soundness Act (12 U.S.C. 4502(3)).

Bank Act means the Federal Home Loan Bank Act, as amended (12 U.S.C. 1421 *et seq.*).

Board or Board of Directors means the board of directors of any Enterprise or Federal Home Loan Bank (Bank), as provided for in the respective authorizing statutes.

Decisional employee means any member of the Director's or the presiding officer's staff who has not engaged in an investigative or prosecutorial role in a proceeding and who may assist the Director or the presiding officer, respectively, in preparing orders, recommended decisions, decisions, and other documents under subpart C of this part.

Director has the meaning defined in section 1303(9) of the Safety and Soundness Act (12 U.S.C. 4502(9)); except, as the context requires in this part, "director" may refer to a member of the Board of Directors or any Board committee of an Enterprise, a Federal Home Loan Bank, or the Office of Finance.

Enterprise has the meaning defined in section 1303(10) of the Safety and Soundness Act (12 U.S.C. 4502(10)).

Entity-affiliated party has the meaning defined in section 1303(11) of the Safety and Soundness Act (12 U.S.C. 4502(11)), and may include an executive

[2] Public Law 101–410, 104 Stat. 890, as amended by the Debt Collection Improvement Act of 1996, Public Law 104–134, Title III, sec. 31001(s)(1), Apr. 26, 1996, 110 Stat. 1321–373; Public Law 105–362, Title XIII, sec. 1301(a), Nov. 10, 1998, 112 Stat. 3293 (28 U.S.C. 2461 note).

officer, any director, or management of the Office of Finance, as applicable under relevant provisions of the Safety and Soundness Act or FHFA regulations.

Executive officer has the meaning defined in section 1303(12) of the Safety and Soundness Act (12 U.S.C. 4502(12)), and may include an executive officer of the Office of Finance, as applicable under relevant provisions of the Safety and Soundness Act or FHFA regulations.

FHFA means the Federal Housing Finance Agency as defined in section 1303(2) of the Safety and Soundness Act (12 U.S.C. 4502(2)).

Notice of charges means the charging document served by FHFA to commence an enforcement proceeding under this part for the issuance of a cease and desist order; removal, suspension, or prohibition order; or an order to assess a civil money penalty, under 12 U.S.C. 4631 through 4641 and § 1209.23. A "notice of charges," as used or referred to as such in this part, is not an "effective notice" under section 1375(a) of the Safety and Soundness Act (12 U.S.C. 4635(a)).

Office of Finance has the meaning defined in section 1303(19) of the Safety and Soundness Act (12 U.S.C. 4502(19)).

Party means any person named as a respondent in any notice of charges, or FHFA, as the context requires in this part.

Person means an individual, sole proprietor, partnership, corporation, unincorporated association, trust, joint venture, pool, syndicate, organization, regulated entity, entity-affiliated party, or other entity.

Presiding officer means an administrative law judge or any other person appointed by or at the request of the Director under applicable law to conduct an adjudicatory proceeding under this part.

Regulated entity has the meaning defined in section 1303(20) of the Safety and Soundness Act (12 U.S.C. 4502(20)).

Representative of record means an individual who is authorized to represent a person or is representing himself and who has filed a notice of appearance and otherwise has complied with the requirements under § 1209.72. FHFA's representative of record may be referred to as FHFA counsel of record, agency counsel or enforcement counsel.

Respondent means any party that is the subject of a notice of charges under this part.

Safety and Soundness Act means Title XIII of the Housing and Community Development Act of 1992, Public Law 102–550, known as the Federal Housing Enterprises Financial Safety and Soundness Act of 1992, as amended (12 U.S.C. 4501 *et seq.*)

Violation has the meaning defined in section 1303(25) of the Safety and Soundness Act (12 U.S.C. 4502(25)).

Subpart B—Enforcement Proceedings Under Sections 1371 Through 1379D of the Safety and Soundness Act

§ 1209.4 Scope and authority.

The rules of practice and procedure set forth in Subpart C (Rules of Practice and Procedure) of this part shall be applicable to any hearing on the record conducted by FHFA in accordance with sections 1371 through 1379D of the Safety and Soundness Act (12 U.S.C. 4631 through 4641), as follows:

(a) Cease-and-desist proceedings under sections 1371 and 1373 of the Safety and Soundness Act, (12 U.S.C. 4631, 4633);

(b) Civil money penalty assessment proceedings under sections 1373 and 1376 of the Safety and Soundness Act, (12 U.S.C. 4633, 4636); and

(c) Removal and prohibition proceedings under sections 1373 and 1377 of the Safety and Soundness Act, (12 U.S.C. 4633, 4636a), except removal proceedings under section 1377(h) of the Safety and Soundness Act, (12 U.S.C. 4636a(h)).

§ 1209.5 Cease and desist proceedings.

(a) *Cease and desist proceedings*—(1) *Authority*—(i) *In general.* As prescribed by section 1371(a) of the Safety and Soundness Act (12 U.S.C. 4631(a)), if in the opinion of the Director, a regulated entity or any entity-affiliated party is engaging or has engaged, or the Director has reasonable cause to believe that the regulated entity or any entity-affiliated party is about to engage, in an unsafe or unsound practice in conducting the business of the regulated entity or the Office of Finance, or is violating or has violated, or the Director has reasonable cause to believe is about to violate, a law, rule, regulation, or order, or any condition imposed in writing by the Director in connection with the granting of any application or other request by the regulated entity or the Office of Finance or any written agreement entered into with the Director, the Director may issue and serve upon the regulated entity or entity-affiliated party a notice of charges (as described in §1209.23) to institute cease and desist proceedings, except with regard to the enforcement of any housing goal that must be addressed under sections 1341 and 1345 of the Safety and Soundness Act (12 U.S.C. 4581, 4585).

(ii) *Hearing on the record.* In accordance with section 1373 of the Safety and Soundness Act (12 U.S.C. 4633), a hearing on the record shall be held in the District of Columbia. Subpart C of this part shall govern the hearing procedures.

(iii) *Consent to order.* Unless the party served with a notice of charges shall appear at the hearing personally or through an authorized representative of record, the party shall be deemed to have consented to the issuance of the cease and desist order.

(2) *Unsatisfactory rating.* In accordance with section 1371(b) of the Safety and Soundness Act (12 U.S.C. 4631(b)), if a regulated entity receives, in its most recent report of examination, a less-than-satisfactory rating for asset quality, management, earnings, or liquidity, the Director may deem the regulated entity to be engaging in an unsafe or unsound practice within the meaning of section 1371(a) of the Safety and Soundness Act (12 U.S.C. 4631(a)), if any such deficiency has not been corrected.

(3) *Order.* As provided by section 1371(c)(2) of the Safety and Soundness Act (12 U.S.C. 4631(c)(2)), if the Director finds on the record made at a hearing in accordance with section 1373 of the Safety and Soundness Act (12 U.S.C. 4633) that any practice or violation specified in the notice of charges has been established (or the regulated entity or entity-affiliated party consents pursuant to section 1373(a)(4) of the Safety and Soundness Act (12 U.S.C. 4633(a)(4)), the Director may issue and serve upon the regulated entity, executive officer, director, or entity-affiliated party, an order (as set forth in §1209.55) requiring such party to cease and desist from any such practice or violation and to take affirmative action to correct or remedy the conditions resulting from any such practice or violation.

(b) *Affirmative action to correct conditions resulting from violations or activities.* The authority to issue a cease and desist order or a temporary cease and desist order requiring a regulated entity, executive officer, director, or entity-affiliated party to take affirmative action to correct or remedy any condition resulting from any practice or violation with respect to which such cease and desist order or temporary cease and desist order is set forth in section 1371(a), (c)(2), and (d) of the Safety and Soundness Act (12 U.S.C. 4631(a), (c)(2), and (d)), and includes the authority to:

(1) Require the regulated entity or entity-affiliated party to make restitution, or to provide reimbursement, indemnification, or guarantee against loss, if—

(i) Such entity or party or finance facility was unjustly enriched in connection with such practice or violation, or

(ii) The violation or practice involved a reckless disregard for the law or any applicable regulations, or prior order of the Director;

(2) Require the regulated entity to seek restitution, or to obtain reimbursement, indemnification, or guarantee against loss; as

(3) Restrict asset or liability growth of the regulated entity;

(4) Require the regulated entity to obtain new capital;

(5) Require the regulated entity to dispose of any loan or asset involved;

(6) Require the regulated entity to rescind agreements or contracts;

(7) Require the regulated entity to employ qualified officers or employees (who may be subject to approval by the Director at the direction of the Director); and

(8) Require the regulated entity to take such other action, as the Director

determines appropriate, including limiting activities.

(c) *Authority to limit activities.* As provided by section 1371(e) of the Safety and Soundness Act (12 U.S.C. 4631(e)), the authority of the Director to issue a cease and desist order under section 1371 of the Safety and Soundness Act (12 U.S.C. 4631) or a temporary cease and desist order under section 1372 of the Safety and Soundness Act (12 U.S.C. 4632), includes the authority to place limitations on the activities or functions of the regulated entity or entity-affiliated party or any executive officer or director of the regulated entity or entity-affiliated party.

(d) *Effective date of order; judicial review—(1) Effective date.* The effective date of an order is as set forth in section 1371(f) of the Safety and Soundness Act (12 U.S.C. 4631(f)).

(2) *Judicial review.* Judicial review is governed by section 1374 of the Safety and Soundness Act (12 U.S.C. 4634).

§ 1209.6 Temporary cease and desist orders.

(a) *Temporary cease and desist orders*—(1) *Grounds for issuance.* The grounds for issuance of a temporary cease and desist order are set forth in section 1372(a) of the Safety and Soundness Act (12 U.S.C. 4632(a)). In accordance with section 1372(a) of the Safety and Soundness Act (12 U.S.C. 4632(a)), the Director may:

(i) Issue a temporary order requiring that regulated entity or entity-affiliated party to cease and desist from any violation or practice specified in the notice of charges; and

(ii) Require that regulated entity or entity-affiliated party to take affirmative action to prevent or remedy any insolvency, dissipation, condition, or prejudice, pending completion of the proceedings.

(2) *Additional requirements.* As provided by section 1372(a)(2) of the Safety and Soundness Act (12 U.S.C. 4632(a)(2)), an order issued under section 1372(a)(1) of the Safety and Soundness Act (12 U.S.C. 4632(a)(1)) may include any requirement authorized under section 1371(d) of the Safety and Soundness Act (12 U.S.C. 4631(d)).

(b) *Effective date of temporary order.* The effective date of a temporary order is as provided by section 1372(b) of the Safety and Soundness Act (12 U.S.C. 4632(b)). And, unless set aside, limited, or suspended by a court in proceedings pursuant to the judicial review provisions of section 1372(d) of the Safety and Soundness Act (12 U.S.C. 4632(d)), shall remain in effect and enforceable pending the completion of the proceedings pursuant to such notice of charges, and shall remain effective until the Director dismisses the charges specified in the notice or until superseded by a cease-and-desist order issued pursuant to section 1371 of the Safety and Soundness Act (12 U.S.C. 4631).

(c) *Incomplete or inaccurate records*—(1) *Temporary order.* As provided by section 1372(c) of the Safety and Soundness Act (12 U.S.C. 4632(c)), if a notice of charges served under section 1371(a) or (b) of the Safety and Soundness Act (12 U.S.C. 4631(a), (b)), specifies on the basis of particular facts and circumstances that the books and records of the regulated entity served are so incomplete or inaccurate that the Director is unable, through the normal supervisory process, to determine the financial condition of the regulated entity or the details or the purpose of any transaction or transactions that may have a material effect on the financial condition of that regulated entity, the Director may issue a temporary order requiring:

(i) The cessation of any activity or practice that gave rise, whether in whole or in part, to the incomplete or inaccurate state of the books or records; or

(ii) Affirmative action to restore the books or records to a complete and accurate state.

(2) *Effective period.* Any temporary order issued under section 1372(c)(1) of the Safety and Soundness Act (12 U.S.C. 4632(c)(1)) shall become effective upon service, and remain in effect and enforceable unless set aside, limited, or suspended in accordance with section 1372(d) of the Safety and Soundness Act (12 U.S.C. 4632(d)), as provided by section 1372(c)(2) of the Safety and Soundness Act (12 U.S.C. 4632(c)(2)).

(d) *Judicial review.* Section 1372(d) of the Safety and Soundness Act (12 U.S.C. 4632(d)), authorizes a regulated entity, executive officer, director, or entity-affiliated party that has been served with a temporary order pursuant to section 1372(a) or (b) of the Safety and Soundness Act (12 U.S.C. 4632(a), (b)) to apply to the United States District Court for the District of Columbia within 10 days after service of the temporary order for an injunction setting aside, limiting, or suspending the enforcement, operation, or effectiveness of the temporary order, pending the completion of the administrative enforcement proceeding. The district court has jurisdiction to issue such injunction.

(e) *Enforcement of temporary order.* As provided by section 1372(e) of the Safety and Soundness Act (12 U.S.C. 4632(e)), in the case of any violation, threatened violation, or failure to obey a temporary order issued pursuant to this section, the Director may bring an action in the United States District Court for the District of Columbia for an injunction to enforce a temporary order, and the district court is to issue such injunction upon a finding made in accordance with section 1372(e) of the Safety and Soundness Act (12 U.S.C. 4632(e)).

§ 1209.7 Civil money penalties.

(a) *Civil money penalty proceedings*—(1) *In general.* Section 1376 of the Safety and Soundness Act (12 U.S.C. 4636) governs the imposition of civil money penalties. Upon written notice, which shall conform to the requirements of § 1209.23 of this part, and a hearing on the record to be conducted in accordance with subpart C of this part, the Director may impose a civil money penalty on any regulated entity or any entity-affiliated party as provided by section 1376 of the Safety and Soundness Act for any violation, practice, or breach addressed under sections 1371, 1372, or 1376 of the Safety and Soundness Act (12 U.S.C. 4631, 4632, 4636), except with regard to the enforcement of housing goals that are addressed separately under sections 1341 and 1345 of the Safety and Soundness Act (12 U.S.C. 4581, 4585).

(2) *Amount of penalty*—(i) *First Tier.* Section 1376(b)(1) of the Safety and Soundness Act (12 U.S.C. 4636(b)(1)) prescribes the civil penalty for violations as stated therein, in the amount of $10,000 for each day during which a violation continues.

(ii) *Second Tier.* Section 1376(b)(2) of the Safety and Soundness Act (12 U.S.C. 4636(b)(2)) provides that notwithstanding paragraph (b)(1) thereof, a regulated entity or entity-affiliated party shall forfeit and pay a civil penalty of not more than $50,000 for each day during which a violation, practice, or breach continues, if the regulated entity or entity-affiliated party commits any violation described in (b)(1) thereof, recklessly engages in an unsafe or unsound practice, or breaches any fiduciary duty, and the violation, practice, or breach is part of a pattern of misconduct; causes or is likely to cause more than a minimal loss to the regulated entity; or results in pecuniary gain or other benefit to such party.

(iii) *Third Tier.* Section 1376(b)(3) of the Safety and Soundness Act (12 U.S.C. 4636(b)(3)) provides that, notwithstanding paragraphs (b)(1) and (b)(2) thereof, any regulated entity or entity-affiliated party shall forfeit and pay a civil penalty, in accordance with section 1376(b)(4) of the Safety and Soundness Act (12 U.S.C. 4636(b)(4)), for each day during which such violation, practice, or breach continues, if such regulated entity or entity-affiliated party:

(A) Knowingly—

(*1*) Commits any violation described in any subparagraph of section 1376(b)(1) of the Safety and Soundness Act;

(*2*) Engages in any unsafe or unsound practice in conducting the affairs of the regulated entity; or

(*3*) Breaches any fiduciary duty; and

(B) Knowingly or recklessly causes a substantial loss to the regulated entity or a substantial pecuniary gain or other benefit to such party by reason of such violation, practice, or breach.

(b) *Maximum amounts*—(1) *Maximum daily penalty.* Section 1376(b)(4) of the Safety and Soundness Act (12 U.S.C. 4636(b)(4)), prescribes the maximum daily amount of a civil penalty that may be assessed for any violation, practice, or breach pursuant to section 1376(b)(3) of the Safety and Soundness Act (12 U.S.C. 4636(b)(3)), in the case of any entity-affiliated party (not to exceed $2,000,000.00), and in the case of any regulated entity ($2,000,000.00).

(2) *Inflation Adjustment Act.* The maximum civil penalty amounts are subject to periodic adjustment under the Federal Civil Penalties Inflation Adjustment Act of 1990, as amended (28 U.S.C. 2461 note), as provided in subpart E of this part.

(c) *Factors in determining amount of penalty.* In accordance with section 1376(c)(2) of the Safety and Soundness Act (12 U.S.C. 4636(c)(2)), in assessing civil money penalties on a regulated entity or an entity-affiliated party in amounts as provided in section 1376(b) of the Safety and Soundness Act (12 U.S.C. 4636(b)), the Director shall give consideration to such factors as:

(1) The gravity of the violation, practice, or breach;

(2) Any history of prior violations or supervisory actions, or any attempts at concealment;

(3) The effect of the penalty on the safety and soundness of the regulated entity or the Office of Finance;

(4) Any loss or risk of loss to the regulated entity or to the Office of Finance;

(5) Any benefits received or derived, whether directly or indirectly, by the respondent(s);

(6) Any injury to the public;

(7) Any deterrent effect on future violations, practices, or breaches;

(8) The financial capacity of the respondent(s), or any unusual circumstance(s) of hardship upon an executive officer, director, or other individual;

(9) The promptness, cost, and effectiveness of any effort to remedy or ameliorate the consequences of the violation, practice, or breach;

(10) The candor and cooperation, if any, of the respondent(s); and

(11) Any other factors the Director may determine by regulation to be appropriate.

(d) *Review of imposition of penalty.* Section 1376(c)(3) of the Safety and Soundness Act (12 U.S.C. 4636(c)(3)) governs judicial review of a penalty order under section 1374 of the Safety and Soundness Act (12 U.S.C. 4634).

§ 1209.8 Removal and prohibition proceedings.

(a) *Removal and prohibition proceedings*—(1) *Authority to issue order.* As provided by section 1377(a)(1) of the Safety and Soundness Act (12 U.S.C. 4636a(a)(1)), the Director may serve upon a party described in paragraph (a)(2) of this section, or any officer, director, or management of the Office of Finance, a notice of the intention of the Director to suspend or remove such party from office, or to prohibit any further participation by such party in any manner in the conduct of the affairs of the regulated entity or the Office of Finance.

(2) *Applicability.* As provided by section 1377(a)(2) of the Safety and Soundness Act (12 U.S.C. 4636a(a)(2)), a party described in this paragraph is an entity-affiliated party or any officer, director, or management of the Office of Finance, if the Director determines that:

(i) That party, officer, or director has, directly or indirectly—

(A) Violated—

(*1*) Any law or regulation;

(*2*) Any cease and desist order that has become final;

(*3*) Any condition imposed in writing by the Director in connection with an application, notice, or other request by a regulated entity; or

(*4*) Any written agreement between such regulated entity and the Director;

(B) Engaged or participated in any unsafe or unsound practice in connection with any regulated entity or business institution; or

(C) Committed or engaged in any act, omission, or practice which constitutes a breach of such party's fiduciary duty;

(ii) By reason of such violation, practice, or breach—

(A) Such regulated entity or business institution has suffered or likely will suffer financial loss or other damage; or

(B) Such party directly or indirectly received financial gain or other benefit; and

(iii) The violation, practice, or breach described in subparagraph (i) of this section—

(A) Involves personal dishonesty on the part of such party; or

(B) Demonstrates willful or continuing disregard by such party for the safety or soundness of such regulated entity or business institution.

(3) *Applicability to business entities.* Under section 1377(f) of the Safety and Soundness Act (12 U.S.C. 4636a(f)), this remedy applies only to a person who is an individual, unless the Director specifically finds that it should apply to a corporation, firm, or other business entity.

(b) *Suspension order*—(1) *Suspension or prohibition authorized.* If the Director serves written notice under section 1377(a) of the Safety and Soundness Act (12 U.S.C. 4636a(a)) upon a party subject to that section, the Director may, by order, suspend or remove such party from office, or prohibit such party from further participation in any manner in the conduct of the affairs of the regulated entity or the Office of Finance, if the Director:

(i) Determines that such action is necessary for the protection of the regulated entity or the Office of Finance; and

(ii) Serves such party with written notice of the order.

(2) *Effective period.* The effective period of any order under section 1377(b)(1) of the Safety and Soundness Act (12 U.S.C. 4636a(b)(1)) is specified in section 1377(b)(2) of the Safety and Soundness Act (12 U.S.C. 4636a(b)(2)). An order of suspension shall become effective upon service and, absent a court-ordered stay, remains effective and enforceable until the date the Director dismisses the charges or the effective date of an order issued by the Director under section 1377(c)(4) of the Safety and Soundness Act (12 U.S.C. 4636a(c)(4),(5)).

(3) *Copy of order to be served on regulated entity.* In accordance with section 1377(b)(3) of the Safety and Soundness Act (12 U.S.C. 4636a(b)(3)), the Director will serve a copy of any order to suspend, remove, or prohibit participation in the conduct of the affairs on the Office of Finance or any regulated entity with which such party is affiliated at the time such order is issued.

(c) *Notice; hearing and order*—(1) *Written notice.* A notice of the intention of the Director to issue an order under sections 1377(a) and (c) of the Safety and Soundness Act, (12 U.S.C. 4636a(a), (c)), shall conform with § 1209.23, and may include any such additional information as the Director may require.

(2) *Hearing.* A hearing on the record shall be held in the District of Columbia in accordance with sections 1373(a)(1) and 1377(c)(2) of the Safety and Soundness Act. *See* 12 U.S.C. 4633(a)(1), 4636a(c)(2).

(3) *Consent.* As provided by section 1377(c)(3) of the Safety and Soundness Act (12 U.S.C. 4636a(c)(3)), unless the party that is the subject of a notice delivered under paragraph (a) of this section appears in person or by a duly authorized representative of record, in the adjudicatory proceeding, such party shall be deemed to have consented to the issuance of an order under this section.

(4) *Issuance of order of suspension or removal.* As provided by section 1377(c)(4) of the Safety and Soundness Act (12 U.S.C. 4636a(c)(4)), the Director may issue an order under this part, as the Director may deem appropriate, if:

(i) A party is deemed to have consented to the issuance of an order under paragraph (d); or

(ii) Upon the record made at the hearing, the Director finds that any of the grounds specified in the notice have been established.

(5) *Effectiveness of order.* As provided by section 1377(c)(5) of the Safety and Soundness Act (12 U.S.C. 4636a(c)(5)), any order issued and served upon a party in accordance with this section shall become effective at the expiration of 30 days after the date of service upon such party and any regulated entity or entity-affiliated party. An order issued upon consent under paragraph (c)(3) of this section, however, shall become effective at the time specified therein. Any such order shall remain effective and enforceable except to such extent as it is stayed, modified, terminated, or set aside by action of the Director or a reviewing court.

(d) *Prohibition of certain activities and industry-wide prohibition*—(1) *Prohibition of certain activities.* As provided by section 1377(d) of the Safety and Soundness Act (12 U.S.C. 4636a(d)), any person subject to an order issued under subpart B of this part shall not—

(i) Participate in any manner in the conduct of the affairs of any regulated entity or the Office of Finance;

(ii) Solicit, procure, transfer, attempt to transfer, vote, or attempt to vote any proxy, consent, or authorization with respect to any voting rights in any regulated entity;

(iii) Violate any voting agreement previously approved by the Director; or

(iv) Vote for a director, or serve or act as an entity-affiliated party of a regulated entity or as an officer or director of the Office of Finance.

(2) *Industry-wide prohibition.* As provided by section 1377(e)(1) of the Safety and Soundness Act (12 U.S.C. 4636a(e)(1)), except as provided in section 1377(e)(2) of the Safety and Soundness Act (12 U.S.C. 4636a(e)(2)), any person who, pursuant to an order issued under section 1377 of the Safety and Soundness Act (12 U.S.C. 4636a), has been removed or suspended from office in a regulated entity or the Office of Finance, or prohibited from participating in the conduct of the affairs of a regulated entity or the Office of Finance, may not, while such order is in effect, continue or commence to hold any office in, or participate in any manner in the conduct of the affairs of, any regulated entity or the Office of Finance.

(3) *Relief from industry-wide prohibition at the discretion of the Director*—(i) *Relief from order.* As provided by section 1377(e)(2) of the Safety and Soundness Act (12 U.S.C. 4636a(e)(2)), if, on or after the date on which an order has been issued under section 1377 of the Safety and Soundness Act (12 U.S.C. 4636a) that removes or suspends from office any party, or prohibits such party from participating in the conduct of the affairs of a regulated entity or the Office of Finance, such party receives the written consent of the Director, the order shall cease to apply to such party with respect to the regulated entity or the Office of Finance to the extent described in the written consent. Such written consent shall be on such terms and conditions as the Director therein may specify in his discretion. Any such consent shall be publicly disclosed.

(ii) *No private right of action; no final agency action.* Nothing in this paragraph shall be construed to require the Director to entertain or to provide such written consent, or to confer any rights to such consideration or consent upon any party, regulated entity, entity-affiliated party, or the Office of Finance. Additionally, whether the Director consents to relief from an outstanding order under this part is committed wholly to the discretion of the Director, and such determination shall not be a final agency action for purposes of seeking judicial review.

(4) *Violation of industry-wide prohibition.* As provided by section 1377(e)(3) of the Safety and Soundness Act (12 U.S.C. 4636a(e)(3)), any violation of section 1377(e)(1) of the Safety and Soundness Act (12 U.S.C. 4636a(e)(1)) by any person who is subject to an order issued under section 1377(h) of the Safety and Soundness Act (12 U.S.C. 4636a(h)) (suspension or removal of entity-affiliated party charged with felony) shall be treated as a violation of the order.

(e) *Stay of suspension or prohibition of entity-affiliated party.* As provided by section 1377(g) of the Safety and Soundness Act (12 U.S.C. 4636a(g)), not later than 10 days after the date on which any entity-affiliated party has been suspended from office or prohibited from participation in the conduct of the affairs of a regulated entity, such party may apply to the United States District Court for the District of Columbia, or the United States district court for the judicial district in which the headquarters of the regulated entity is located, for a stay of such suspension or prohibition pending the completion of the administrative enforcement proceeding pursuant to section 1377(c) of the Safety and Soundness Act (12 U.S.C. 4636a(c)). The court shall have jurisdiction to stay such suspension or prohibition, but such jurisdiction does not extend to the administrative enforcement proceeding.

§ 1209.9 Supervisory actions not affected.

As provided by section 1311(c) of the Safety and Soundness Act (12 U.S.C. 4511(c)), the authority of the Director to take action under subtitle A of the Safety and Soundness Act (12 U.S.C. 4611 *et seq.*) (*e.g.*, the appointment of a conservator or receiver for a regulated entity; entering into a written agreement or pursuing an informal agreement with a regulated entity as the Director deems appropriate; and undertaking other such actions as may be applicable to undercapitalized, significantly undercapitalized or critically undercapitalized regulated entities), or to initiate enforcement proceedings under subtitle C of the Safety and Soundness Act (12 U.S.C. 4631 *et seq.*), shall not in any way limit the general supervisory or regulatory authority granted the Director under section 1311(b) of the Safety and Soundness Act (12 U.S.C. 4511(b)). The selection and form of regulatory or supervisory action under the Safety and Soundness Act is committed to the discretion of the Director, and the selection of one form of action or a combination of actions does not foreclose the Director from pursuing any other supervisory action authorized by law.

Subpart C—Rules of Practice and Procedure

§ 1209.10 Authority of the Director.

The Director may, at any time during the pendency of a proceeding, perform, direct the performance of, or waive performance of any act that could be done or ordered by the presiding officer.

§ 1209.11 Authority of the Presiding Officer.

(a) *General rule.* All proceedings governed by subpart C of this part shall be conducted consistent with the provisions of chapter 5 of Title 5 of the United States Code. The presiding officer shall have complete charge of the adjudicative proceeding, conduct a fair and impartial hearing, avoid unnecessary delay, and assure that a complete record of the proceeding is made.

(b) *Powers.* The presiding officer shall have all powers necessary to conduct the proceeding in accordance with paragraph (a) of this section and 5 U.S.C. 556(c). The presiding officer is authorized to:

(1) *Control the proceedings.* (i) Upon reasonable notice to the parties, not earlier than 30 days or later than 60 days after service of a notice of charges under the Safety and Soundness Act, set a date, time, and place for an evidentiary hearing on the record, within the District of Columbia, as provided in section 1373 of the Safety and Soundness Act (12 U.S.C. 4633), in a scheduling order that may be issued in conjunction with the initial scheduling conference set under § 1209.36, or otherwise as the presiding officer finds in the best interest of justice, in accordance with this part; and

(ii) Upon reasonable notice to the parties, reset or change the date, time, or place (within the District of Columbia) of an evidentiary hearing;

(2) Continue or recess the hearing in whole or in part for a reasonable period of time;

(3) Hold conferences to address legal or factual issues, or evidentiary matters materially relevant to the charges or allowable defenses; to regulate the timing and scope of discovery and rule on discovery plans; or otherwise to consider matters that may facilitate an effective, fair, and expeditious disposition of the proceeding;

(4) Administer oaths and affirmations;

(5) Issue and enforce subpoenas, subpoenas *duces tecum*, discovery and protective orders, as authorized by this part, and to revoke, quash, or modify such subpoenas issued by the presiding officer;

(6) Take and preserve testimony under oath;

(7) Rule on motions and other procedural matters appropriate in an adjudicatory proceeding, except that only the Director shall have the power to grant summary disposition or any motion to dismiss the proceeding or to make a final determination of the merits of the proceeding;

(8) Take all actions authorized under this part to regulate the scope, timing, and completion of discovery of any non-privileged documents that are materially relevant to the charges or allowable defenses;

(9) Regulate the course of the hearing and the conduct of representatives and parties;

(10) Examine witnesses;

(11) Receive materially relevant evidence, and rule upon the admissibility of evidence or exclude, limit, or otherwise rule on offers of proof;

(12) Upon motion of a party, take official notice of facts;

(13) Recuse himself upon his own motion or upon motion made by a party;

(14) Prepare and present to the Director a recommended decision as provided in this part;

(15) Establish time, place, and manner limitations on the attendance of the public and the media for any public hearing; and

(16) Do all other things necessary or appropriate to discharge the duties of a presiding officer.

§ 1209.12 Public hearings; closed hearings.

(a) *General rule.* As provided in section 1379B(b) of the Safety and Soundness Act (12 U.S.C. 4639(b)), all hearings shall be open to the public, except that the Director, in his discretion, may determine that holding an open hearing would be contrary to the public interest. The Director may make such determination *sua sponte* at any time by written notice to all parties, or as provided in paragraphs (b) and (c) of this section.

(b) *Motion for closed hearing.* Within 20 days of service of the notice of charges, any party may file with the presiding officer a motion for a private hearing and any party may file a pleading in reply to the motion. The presiding officer shall forward the motion and any reply, together with a recommended decision on the motion, to the Director, who shall make a final determination. Such motions and replies are governed by § 1209.28 of this part. A determination under this section is committed to the discretion of the Director and is not a reviewable final agency action.

(c) *Filing documents under seal.* FHFA counsel of record, in his discretion, may file or require the filing of any document or part of a document under seal, if such counsel makes a written determination that disclosure of the document would be contrary to the public interest. The presiding officer shall issue an order to govern confidential information, and take all appropriate steps to preserve the confidentiality of such documents in whole or in part, including closing any portion of a hearing to the public or issuing a protective order under such terms as may be acceptable to FHFA counsel of record.

(d) *Procedures for closed hearing.* An evidentiary hearing, or any part thereof, that is closed for the purpose of offering into evidence testimony or documents filed under seal as provided in paragraph (c) of this section shall be conducted under procedures that may include: prior notification to the submitter of confidential information; provisions for sealing portions of the record, briefs, and decisions; *in camera* arguments, offers of proof, and testimony; and limitations on representatives of record or other participants, as the presiding officer may designate. Additionally, at such proceedings the presiding officer may make an opening statement as to the confidentiality and limitations and deliver an oath to the parties, representatives of record, or other approved participants as to the confidentiality of the proceedings.

§ 1209.13 Good faith certification.

(a) *General requirement.* Every filing or submission of record following the issuance of a notice of charges by the Director shall be signed by at least one representative of record in his individual name and shall state that representative's business contact information, which shall include his address, electronic mail address, and telephone number; and the names, addresses and telephone numbers of all other representatives of record for the person making the filing or submission.

(b) *Effect of signature.* (1) By signing a document, a representative of record or party appearing *pro se* certifies that:

(i) The representative of record or party has read the filing or submission of record;

(ii) To the best of his knowledge, information and belief formed after reasonable inquiry, the filing or submission of record is well-grounded in fact and is warranted by existing law or a good faith, non-frivolous argument for the extension, modification, or reversal of existing law, regulation, or FHFA order or policy; and

(iii) The filing or submission of record is not made for any improper purpose, such as to harass or to cause unnecessary delay or needless increase in the cost of litigation.

(2) If a filing or submission of record is not signed, the presiding officer shall strike the filing or submission of record, unless it is signed promptly after the omission is called to the attention of the pleader or movant.

(c) *Effect of making oral motion or argument.* The act of making any oral motion or oral argument by any representative or party shall constitute a certification that to the best of his knowledge, information, and belief, formed after reasonable inquiry, his statements are well-grounded in fact and are warranted by existing law or a good faith, non-frivolous argument for the extension, modification, or reversal of existing law, regulation, or FHFA order or policy, and are not made for any improper purpose, such as to harass or to cause unnecessary delay or to needlessly increase litigation-related costs.

§ 1209.14 Ex parte communications.

(a) *Definition.* (1) *Ex parte* communication means any material oral or written communication relevant to an adjudication of the merits of any proceeding under this subpart that was neither on the record nor on reasonable prior notice to all parties that takes place between:

(i) An interested person outside FHFA (including the person's representative of record); and

(ii) The presiding officer handling that proceeding, the Director, a decisional employee assigned to that proceeding, or any other person who is or may be reasonably expected to be involved in the decisional process.

(2) A communication that is procedural in that it does not concern the merits of an adjudicatory proceeding, such as a request for status of the proceeding, does not constitute an *ex parte* communication.

(b) *Prohibition of ex parte communications.* From the time a notice of charges commencing a proceeding under this part is issued by the Director until the date that the Director issues his final decision pursuant to § 1209.55 of this part, no person referred to in paragraph (a)(1)(i) of this section shall knowingly make or cause to be made an *ex parte* communication with the Director or the presiding officer. The Director, presiding officer, or a decisional employee shall not knowingly make or cause to be made an *ex parte* communication.

(c) *Procedure upon occurrence of ex parte communication.* If an *ex parte* communication is received by any person identified in paragraph (a) of this section, that person shall cause all such written communications (or, if the communication is oral, a memorandum stating the substance of the communication) to be placed on the record of the proceeding and served on all parties. All parties to the proceeding shall have an opportunity within 10 days of receipt of service of the *ex parte* communication to file responses thereto, and to recommend sanctions that they believe to be appropriate under the circumstances, in accordance with paragraph (d) of this section.

(d) *Sanctions.* Any party or representative for a party who makes an *ex parte* communication, or who encourages or solicits another to make an *ex parte* communication, may be subject to any appropriate sanction or sanctions imposed by the Director or the presiding officer, including, but not limited to, exclusion from the proceedings, an adverse ruling on the issue that is the subject of the prohibited communication, or other appropriate and commensurate action(s).

(e) *Consultations by presiding officer.* Except to the extent required for the disposition of *ex parte* matters as authorized by law, the presiding officer may not consult a person or party on any matter relevant to the merits of the adjudication, unless upon notice to and opportunity for all parties to participate.

(f) *Separation of functions.* An employee or agent engaged in the performance of any investigative or prosecuting function for FHFA in a case may not, in that or in a factually related case, participate or advise in the recommended decision, the Director's review under § 1209.55 of the recommended decision, or the Director's final determination on the merits based upon his review of the recommended decision, except as a witness or counsel in the adjudicatory proceedings. This section shall not prohibit FHFA counsel of record from providing necessary and appropriate legal advice to the Director on supervisory (including information or legal advice as to settlement issues) or regulatory matters.

§ 1209.15 Filing of papers.

(a) *Filing.* All pleadings, motions, memoranda, and any other submissions or papers required to be filed in the proceeding shall be addressed to the presiding officer and filed with FHFA, 1700 G Street, NW., Fourth Floor, Washington, DC 20552, in accordance with paragraphs (b) and (c) of this section.

(b) *Manner of filing.* Unless otherwise specified by the Director or the presiding officer, filing shall be accomplished by:

(1) *Overnight delivery.* Overnight U.S. Postal Service delivery or delivery by a reliable commercial delivery service for same day or overnight delivery to the address stated above; or

(2) *U.S. Mail.* First class, registered, or certified mail via the U.S. Postal Service; and

(3) *Electronic media.* Transmission by electronic media shall be required by and upon any conditions specified by the Director or the presiding officer. FHFA shall provide a designated site for the electronic filing of all papers in a proceeding in accordance with any conditions specified by the presiding officer. All papers filed by electronic media shall be filed concurrently in a manner set out above and in accordance with paragraph (c) of this section.

(c) *Formal requirements as to papers filed*—(1) *Form.* To be filed, all papers must set forth the name, address, telephone number, and electronic mail address of the representative or party seeking to make the filing. Additionally, all such papers must be accompanied by a certification setting forth when and how service has been made on all other parties. All papers filed must be double-spaced on 8½ x 11-inch paper and must be clear, legible, and formatted as required by paragraph (c)(5) of this section.

(2) *Signature.* All papers filed must be dated and signed as provided in § 1209.13.

(3) *Caption.* All papers filed must include at the head thereof, or on a title page, the FHFA caption, title and docket number of the proceeding, the name of the filing party, and the subject of the particular paper.

(4) *Number of copies.* Unless otherwise specified by the Director or the presiding officer, an original and one copy of all pleadings, motions and memoranda, or other such papers shall be filed, except that only one copy of transcripts of testimony and exhibits shall be filed.

(5) *Content format.* All papers filed shall be formatted in such program(s) (*e.g.*, MS WORD©, MS Excel©, or WordPerfect©) as the presiding officer or Director shall specify.

§ 1209.16 Service of papers.

(a) Except as otherwise provided, a party filing papers or serving a subpoena shall serve a copy upon the representative of record for each party to the proceeding so represented, and upon any party who is not so represented, in accordance with the requirements of this section.

(b) Except as provided in paragraphs (c)(2) and (d) of this section, a serving party shall use one or more of the following methods of service:

(1) Personal service;

(2) Overnight U.S. Postal Service delivery or delivery by a reliable commercial delivery service for same day or overnight delivery to the parties' respective street addresses; or

(3) First class, registered, or certified mail via the U.S. Postal Service; and

(4) For transmission by electronic media, each party shall promptly provide the presiding officer and all parties, in writing, an active electronic mail address where service will be accepted on behalf of such party. Any document transmitted via electronic mail for service on a party shall comply in all respects with the requirements of § 1209.15(c).

(5) Service of pleadings or other papers made by facsimile may not exceed a total page count of 30 pages. Any paper served by facsimile transmission

shall meet the requirements of § 1209.15(c).

(6) Any party serving a pleading or other paper by electronic media under paragraph (4) of this section also shall concurrently serve that pleading or paper by one of the methods specified in paragraphs (1) through (5) of this section.

(c) *By the Director or the presiding officer.* (1) All papers required to be served by the Director or the presiding officer upon a party who has appeared in the proceeding in accordance with § 1209.72 shall be served by the means specified in paragraph (b) of this section.

(2) If a notice of appearance has not been filed in the proceeding for a party in accordance with § 1209.72, the Director or the presiding officer shall make service upon the party by any of the following methods:

(i) By personal service;

(ii) If the person to be served is an individual, by delivery to a person of suitable age and discretion at the physical location where the individual resides or works;

(iii) If the person to be served is a corporation or other association, by delivery to an officer, managing or general agent, or to any other agent authorized by appointment or by law to receive service and, if the agent is one authorized by statute to receive service and the statute so requires, by also mailing a copy to the party;

(iv) By registered or certified mail addressed to the person's last known address; or

(v) By any other method reasonably calculated to give actual notice.

(d) *Subpoenas.* Service of a subpoena may be made:

(1) By personal service;

(2) If the person to be served is an individual, by delivery to a person of suitable age and discretion at the physical location where the individual resides or works;

(3) If the person to be served is a corporation or other association, by delivery to an officer, managing or general agent, or to any other agent authorized by appointment or by law to receive service and, if the agent is one authorized by statute to receive service and the statute so requires, by also mailing a copy to the party;

(4) By registered or certified mail addressed to the person's last known address; or

(5) By any other method reasonably calculated to give actual notice.

(e) *Area of service.* Service in any State or the District of Columbia, or any commonwealth, possession, territory or other place subject to the jurisdiction of the United States, or on any person doing business in any State or the District of Columbia, or any commonwealth, possession, territory or other place subject to the jurisdiction of the United States, or on any person as otherwise permitted by law, is effective without regard to the place where the hearing is held.

(f) *Proof of service.* Proof of service of papers filed by a party shall be filed before action is taken thereon. The proof of service, which shall serve as prima facie evidence of the fact and date of service, shall show the date and manner of service and may be by written acknowledgment of service, by declaration of the person making service, or by certificate of a representative of record. However, failure to file proof of service contemporaneously with the papers shall not affect the validity of actual service. The presiding officer may allow the proof to be amended or supplied, unless to do so would result in material prejudice to a party.

§ 1209.17 Time computations.

(a) *General rule.* In computing any period of time prescribed or allowed under this part, the date of the act or event that commences the designated period of time is not included. Computations shall include the last day of the time period, unless the day falls on a Saturday, Sunday, or Federal holiday. When the last day is a Saturday, Sunday or Federal holiday, the period of time shall run until the end of the next day that is not a Saturday, Sunday, or Federal holiday. Intermediate Saturdays, Sundays and Federal holidays are included in the computation of time. However, when the time period within which an act is to be performed is 10 days or less, not including any additional time allowed for in paragraph (c) of this section, intermediate Saturdays, Sundays and Federal holidays are not included.

(b) *When papers are deemed to be filed or served.* (1) Filing or service are deemed to be effective:

(i) In the case of personal service or same day reliable commercial delivery service, upon actual service;

(ii) In the case of U.S. Postal Service or reliable commercial overnight delivery service, or first class, registered, or certified mail, upon deposit in or delivery to an appropriate point of collection;

(iii) In the case of transmission by electronic media, as specified by the authority receiving the filing, in the case of filing; or

(iv) In the case of transmission by electronic media or facsimile, when the device through which the document was sent provides a reliable indicator that the document has been received by the opposing party, in the case of service.

(2) The effective filing and service dates specified in paragraph (b)(1) of this section may be modified by the Director or the presiding officer, or by agreement of the parties in the case of service.

(c) *Calculation of time for service and filing of responsive papers.* Whenever a time limit is measured by a prescribed period from the service of any notice, pleading or paper, the applicable time limits shall be calculated as follows:

(1) If service was made by delivery to the U.S. Postal Service for longer than overnight delivery service by first class, registered, or certified mail, add three calendar days to the prescribed period for the responsive pleading or other filing.

(2) If service was personal, or was made by delivery to the U.S. Postal Service or any reliable commercial delivery service for overnight delivery, add one calendar-day to the prescribed period for the responsive pleading or other filing.

(3) If service was made by electronic media transmission or facsimile, add one calendar-day to the prescribed period for the responsive pleading or other filing—unless otherwise determined by the Director or the presiding officer *sua sponte,* or upon motion of a party in the case of filing or by prior agreement among the parties in the case of service.

§ 1209.18 Change of time limits.

Except as otherwise by law required, the presiding officer may extend any time limit that is prescribed above or in any notice or order issued in the proceedings. After the referral of the case to the Director pursuant to § 1209.53, the Director may grant extensions of the time limits for good cause shown. Extensions may be granted on the motion of a party after notice and opportunity to respond is afforded all nonmoving parties, or on the Director's or the presiding officer's own motion.

§ 1209.19 Witness fees and expenses.

Witnesses (other than parties) subpoenaed for testimony (or for a deposition in lieu of personal appearance at a hearing) shall be paid the same fees for attendance and mileage as are paid in the United States district courts in proceedings in which the United States is a party, provided that, in the case of a discovery subpoena addressed to a party, no witness fees or mileage shall be paid. Fees for witnesses shall be tendered in advance by the party requesting the subpoena, except that fees and mileage need not be tendered in advance where FHFA is the party requesting the subpoena. FHFA shall not be required to pay any fees to or expenses of any witness who was not subpoenaed by FHFA.

§ 1209.20 Opportunity for informal settlement.

Any respondent may, at any time in the proceeding, unilaterally submit to FHFA's counsel of record written offers or proposals for settlement of a proceeding without prejudice to the rights of any of the parties. No such offer or proposal shall be made to any FHFA representative other than FHFA counsel of record. Submission of a written settlement offer does not provide a basis for adjourning, deferring or otherwise delaying all or any portion of a proceeding under this part. No settlement offer or proposal, or any subsequent negotiation or resolution, is admissible as evidence in any proceeding.

§ 1209.21 Conduct of examination.

Nothing in this part limits or constrains in any manner any duty, authority, or right of FHFA to conduct or to continue any examination, investigation, inspection, or visitation of any regulated entity or entity-affiliated party.

§ 1209.22 Collateral attacks on adjudicatory proceeding.

If an interlocutory appeal or collateral attack is brought in any court concerning all or any part of an adjudicatory proceeding, the challenged adjudicatory proceeding shall continue without regard to the pendency of that court proceeding. No default or other failure to act as directed in the adjudicatory proceeding within the times prescribed in subpart C of this part shall be excused based on the pendency before any court of any interlocutory appeal or collateral attack.

§ 1209.23 Commencement of proceeding and contents of notice of charges.

Proceedings under subpart C of this part are commenced by the Director by the issuance of a notice of charges, as defined in § 1209.3(p), that must be served upon a respondent. A notice of charges shall state all of the following:

(a) The legal authority for the proceeding and for FHFA's jurisdiction over the proceeding;

(b) A statement of the matters of fact or law showing that FHFA is entitled to relief;

(c) A proposed order or prayer for an order granting the requested relief;

(d) Information concerning the nature of the proceeding and pertinent procedural matters, including: the requirement that the hearing shall be held in the District of Columbia; the presiding officer will set the date and location for an evidentiary hearing in a scheduling order to be issued not less than 30 days or more than 60 days after service of the notice of charges; contact information for FHFA enforcement counsel and the presiding officer, if known; submission information for filings and appearances, the time within which to request a hearing, and citation to FHFA Rules of Practice and Procedure; and

(e) Information concerning proper filing of the answer, including the time within which to file the answer as required by law or regulation, a statement that the answer shall be filed with the presiding officer or with FHFA as specified therein, and the address for filing the answer (and request for a hearing, if applicable).

§ 1209.24 Answer.

(a) *Filing deadline.* Unless otherwise specified by the Director in the notice, respondent shall file an answer within 20 days of service of the notice of charges initiating the enforcement action.

(b) *Content of answer.* An answer must respond specifically to each paragraph or allegation of fact contained in the notice of charges and must admit, deny, or state that the party lacks sufficient information to admit or deny each allegation of fact. A statement of lack of information has the effect of a denial. Denials must fairly meet the substance of each allegation of fact denied; general denials are not permitted. When a respondent denies part of an allegation, that part must be denied and the remainder specifically admitted. Any allegation of fact in the notice that is not denied in the answer is deemed admitted for purposes of the proceeding. A respondent is not required to respond to the portion of a notice that constitutes the prayer for relief or proposed order. The answer must set forth affirmative defenses, if any, asserted by the respondent.

(c) *Default.* Failure of a respondent to file an answer required by this section within the time provided constitutes a waiver of such respondent's right to appear and contest the allegations in the notice. If no timely answer is filed, FHFA counsel of record may file a motion for entry of an order of default. Upon a finding that no good cause has been shown for the failure to file a timely answer, the presiding officer shall file with the Director a recommended decision containing the findings and the relief sought in the notice. Any final order issued by the Director based upon a respondent's failure to answer is deemed to be an order issued upon consent.

§ 1209.25 Amended pleadings.

(a) *Amendments.* The notice or answer may be amended or supplemented at any stage of the proceeding. The respondent must answer an amended notice within the time remaining for the respondent's answer to the original notice, or within 10 days after service of the amended notice, whichever period is longer, unless the Director or presiding officer orders otherwise for good cause shown.

(b) *Amendments to conform to the evidence.* When issues not raised in the notice or answer are tried at the hearing by express or implied consent of the parties, or as the presiding officer may allow for good cause shown, such issues will be treated in all respects as if they had been raised in the notice or answer, and no formal amendments are required. If evidence is objected to at the hearing on the ground that it is not within the issues raised by the notice or answer, the presiding officer may admit the evidence when admission is likely to assist in adjudicating the merits of the action. The presiding officer will do so freely when the determination of the merits of the action is served thereby and the objecting party fails to satisfy the presiding officer that the admission of such evidence would unfairly prejudice that party's action or defense upon the merits. The presiding officer may grant a continuance to enable the objecting party to meet such evidence.

§ 1209.26 Failure to appear.

Failure of a respondent to appear in person at the hearing or by a duly authorized representative of record constitutes a waiver of respondent's right to a hearing and is deemed an admission of the facts as alleged and consent to the relief sought in the notice. Without further proceedings or notice to the respondent, the presiding officer shall file with the Director a recommended decision containing the Agency's findings and the relief sought in the notice.

§ 1209.27 Consolidation and severance of actions.

(a) *Consolidation.* On the motion of any party, or on the presiding officer's own motion, the presiding officer may consolidate, for some or all purposes, any two or more proceedings, if each such proceeding involves or arises out of the same transaction, occurrence or series of transactions or occurrences, or involves at least one common respondent or a material common question of law or fact, unless such consolidation would cause unreasonable delay or injustice. In the event of consolidation under this section, appropriate adjustment to the pre-hearing schedule must be made to avoid unnecessary expense, inconvenience, or delay.

(b) *Severance.* The presiding officer may, upon the motion of any party, sever the proceeding for separate resolution of the matter as to any respondent only if the presiding officer finds that undue prejudice or injustice to the moving party would result from not severing the proceeding and such undue prejudice or injustice would outweigh the interests of judicial economy and expedition in the complete and final resolution of the proceeding.

§ 1209.28 Motions.

(a) *In writing.* (1) Except as otherwise provided herein, an application or request for an order or ruling must be made by written motion.

(2) All written motions must state with particularity the relief sought and must be accompanied by a proposed order.

(3) No oral argument may be held on written motions except as otherwise directed by the presiding officer. Written memoranda, briefs, affidavits, or other relevant material or documents may be filed in support of or in opposition to a motion.

(b) *Oral motions.* A motion may be made orally on the record, unless the presiding officer directs that such motion be reduced to writing, in which case the motion will be subject to the requirements of this section.

(c) *Filing of motions.* Motions must be filed with the presiding officer and served on all parties; except that following the filing of a recommended decision, motions must be filed with the Director. Motions for pre-trial relief such as motions *in limine* or objections to offers of proof or experts shall be filed not less than 10 days prior to the date of the evidentiary hearing, except as provided with the consent of the presiding officer for good cause shown.

(d) *Responses and replies.* (1) Except as otherwise provided herein, any party may file a written response to a non-dispositive motion within 10 days after service of any written motion, or within such other period of time as may be established by the presiding officer or the Director; and the moving party may file a written reply to a written response to a non-dispositive motion within five days after the service of the response, unless some other period is ordered by the presiding officer or the Director. The presiding officer shall not rule on any oral or written motion before each party with an interest in the motion has had an opportunity to respond as provided in this section.

(2) The failure of a party to oppose a written motion or an oral motion made on the record is deemed as consent by that party to the entry of an order substantially in the form of the order accompanying the motion.

(e) *Dilatory motions.* Frivolous, dilatory, or substantively repetitive motions are prohibited. The filing of such motions may form the basis for sanctions.

(f) *Dispositive motions.* Dispositive motions are governed by §§ 1209.34 and 1209.35 of this part.

§ 1209.29 Discovery.

(a) *General rule*—(1) *Limits on discovery.* Subject to the limitations set out in paragraphs (a)(2), (b), (d), and (e) of this section, a party to a proceeding under this part may obtain document discovery by serving upon any other party in the proceeding a written request to produce documents. For purposes of such requests, the term "documents" may be defined to include records, drawings, graphs, charts, photographs, recordings, or data stored in electronic form or other data compilations from which information can be obtained or translated, if necessary, by the parties through detection devices into reasonably usable form (*e.g.*, electronically stored information), as well as written material of all kinds.

(2) *Discovery plan.* (i) In the initial scheduling conference held in accordance with § 1209.36, or otherwise at the earliest practicable time, the presiding officer shall require the parties to confer in good faith to develop and submit a joint discovery plan for the timely, cost-effective management of document discovery (including, if applicable, electronically stored information). The discovery plan should provide for the coordination of similar discovery requests by multiple parties, if any, and specify how costs are to be apportioned among those parties. The discovery plan shall specify the form of electronic productions, if any. Documents are to be produced in accordance with the technical specifications described in the discovery plan.

(ii) Discovery in the proceeding may commence upon the approval of the discovery plan by the presiding officer. Thereafter, the presiding officer may interpret or modify the discovery plan for good cause shown or in his or her discretion due to changed circumstances.

(iii) Nothing in paragraph (a)(2) of this section shall be interpreted or deemed to require the production of documents that are privileged or not reasonably accessible because of undue burden or cost, or to require any document production otherwise inconsistent with the limitations on discovery set forth in this part.

(b) *Relevance and scope.* (1) A party may obtain document discovery regarding any matter not privileged that is materially relevant to the charges or allowable defenses raised in the pending proceeding.

(2) The scope of available discovery shall be limited in accordance with subpart C of this part. Any request for the production of documents that seeks to obtain privileged information or documents not materially relevant under paragraph (b)(1) of this section, or that is unreasonable, oppressive, excessive in scope, unduly burdensome, cumulative, or repetitive of any prior discovery requests, shall be denied or modified.

(3) A request for document discovery is unreasonable, oppressive, excessive in scope, or unduly burdensome—and shall be denied or modified—if, among other things, the request:

(i) Fails to specify justifiable limitations on the relevant subject matter, time period covered, search parameters, or the geographic location(s) or data repositories to be searched;

(ii) Fails to identify documents with sufficient specificity;

(iii) Seeks material that is duplicative, cumulative, or obtainable from another source that is more accessible, cost-effective, or less burdensome;

(iv) Calls for the production of documents to be delivered to the requesting party or his or her designee and fails to provide a written agreement by the requestor to pay in advance for the costs of production in accordance with § 1209.30, or otherwise fails to take into account costs associated with processing electronically stored information or any cost-sharing agreements between the parties;

(v) Fails to afford the responding party adequate time to respond; or

(vi) Fails to take into account retention policies or security protocols with respect to Federal information systems.

(c) *Forms of discovery.* Discovery shall be limited to requests for production of documents for inspection and copying. No other form of discovery shall be allowed. Discovery by use of interrogatories is not permitted. This paragraph shall not be interpreted to require the creation of a document.

(d) *Privileged matter*—(1) *Privileged documents are not discoverable.* (i) Privileges include the attorney-client privilege, work-product privilege, any government's or government agency's deliberative process privilege, and any other privileges provided by the Constitution, any applicable act of Congress, or the principles of common law.

(ii) The parties may enter into a written agreement to permit a producing party to assert applicable privileges of a document even after its production and to request the return or destruction of privileged matter (claw back agreement). The parties shall file the claw back agreement with the presiding officer. To ensure the enforceability of the terms of any such claw back agreement, the presiding officer shall enter an order. Any party may petition the presiding officer for an order specifying claw back procedures for good cause shown.

(2) *No effect on examination authority.* The limitations on discoverable matter provided for in this part are not intended and shall not be construed to limit or otherwise affect the examination, regulatory or supervisory authority of FHFA.

(e) *Time limits.* All discovery matters, including all responses to discovery requests, shall be completed at least 20 days prior to the date scheduled for the commencement of the testimonial phase of the hearing. No exception to this discovery time limit shall be permitted, unless the presiding officer finds on the record that good cause exists for waiving the 20-day requirement of this paragraph.

(f) *Production.* Documents must be produced as they are kept in the usual course of business, or labeled and organized to correspond with the categories in the request, or otherwise produced in a manner determined by mutual agreement between the requesting party and the party or non-party to whom the request is directed in accordance with this part.

§ 1209.30 Request for document discovery from parties.

(a) *General rule.* Each request for the production of documents must conform to the requirements of this part.

(1) *Limitations.* Subject to applicable limitations on discovery in this part, a party may serve (requesting party) a request on another party (responding party) for the production of any non-privileged, discoverable documents in the possession, custody, or control of the responding party. A requesting party shall serve a copy of any such document request on all other parties. Each request for the production of documents must, with reasonable particularity, identify or describe the documents to be produced, either by individual item or by category, with sufficient specificity to enable the responding party to respond consistent with the requirements of this part.

(2) *Discovery plan.* Document discovery under subpart C of this part shall be consistent with any discovery plan approved by the presiding officer under § 1209.29.

(b) *Production and costs*—(1) *General rule.* Subject to the applicable limitations on discovery in this part and the discovery plan, the requesting party shall specify a reasonable time, place, and manner for the production of documents and the performance of any related acts. The responding party shall produce documents to the requesting party in a manner consistent with the discovery plan.

(2) *Costs.* All costs associated with document productions—including, without limitation, photocopying (as specified in paragraph (b)(4) of this section) or electronic processing (as specified in paragraph (b)(5) of this section)—shall be born by the requesting party, or otherwise in accordance with any discovery plan approved by the presiding officer that may require such costs be apportioned between parties, or as otherwise ordered by the presiding officer. If consistent with the discovery plan approved by the presiding officer, the responding party may require receipt of payment of any such document production costs in advance before any such production of responsive documents.

(3) *Organization.* Unless otherwise provided for in any discovery plan approved by the presiding officer under §1209.29 of this part, or by order of the presiding officer, documents must be produced as they are kept in the usual course of business or they shall be labeled and organized to correspond with the categories in the document request.

(4) *Photocopying charges.* Photocopying charges are to be set at the current rate per page imposed by FHFA under the fee schedule pursuant to §1202.11(c) of this part for requests for documents filed under the Freedom of Information Act, 5 U.S.C. 552.

(5) *Electronic processing.* In the event that any party seeks the production of electronically stored information (*i.e.*, information created, stored, communicated, or used in digital format requiring the use of computer hardware and software), the parties shall confer in good faith to resolve common discovery issues related to electronically stored information, such as preservation, search methodology, collection, and need for such information; the suitability of alternative means to obtain it; and the format of production. Consistent with the discovery plan approved by the presiding officer under §1209.29, costs associated with the processing of such electronic information (*i.e.*, imaging; scanning; conversion of "native" files to images that are viewable and searchable; indexing; coding; database or Web-based hosting; searches; branding of endorsements, such as "confidential" or document control numbering; privilege reviews; and copies of production discs) and delivery of any such document production, shall be born by the requesting party, apportioned among the parties, or as otherwise ordered by the presiding officer. Nothing in this part shall be deemed to require FHFA to produce privileged documents or any electronic records in violation of applicable Federal law or security protocols.

(c) *Obligation to update responses.* A party who has responded to a discovery request is not required to supplement the response, unless:

(1) The responding party learns that in some material respect the information disclosed is incomplete or incorrect, and

(2) The additional or corrective information has not otherwise been made known to the other parties during the discovery process or in writing.

(d) *Motions to strike or limit discovery requests.* (1) Any party served with a document discovery request may object within 30 days of service of the request by filing a motion to strike or limit the request in accordance with the provisions of §1209.28 of this part. No other party may file an objection. If an objection is made only to a portion of an item or category in a request, the objection shall specify that portion. Any objections not made in accordance with this paragraph and §1209.28 are waived.

(2) The party who served the request that is the subject of a motion to strike or limit may file a written response in accordance with the provisions of §1209.28. A reply by the moving party, if any, shall be governed by §1209.28. No other party may file a response.

(e) *Privilege.* At the time other documents are produced, all documents withheld on a claim of privilege must be reasonably identified, together with a statement of the basis for the assertion of privilege on a privilege log.

When similar documents that are protected by the government's deliberative process, investigative or examination privilege, the attorney work-product doctrine, or the attorney-client privilege are voluminous, such documents may be identified on the log by category instead of by individual document. The presiding officer has discretion to permit submission of a privilege log subsequent to the document production(s), which may occur on a rolling basis if agreed to by the parties in the discovery plan, and to determine whether an identification by category is sufficient to provide notice of withheld documents.

(f) *Motions to compel production.* (1) If a party withholds any document as privileged or fails to comply fully with a document discovery request, the requesting party may, within 10 days of the assertion of privilege or of the time the failure to comply becomes known to the requesting party, file a motion in accordance with the provisions of §1209.28 for the issuance of a subpoena compelling the production of any such document.

(2) The party who asserted the privilege or failed to comply with the request may, within five days of service of a motion for the issuance of a subpoena compelling production, file a written response to the motion. No other party may file a response.

(g) *Ruling on motions*—(1) *Appropriate protective orders.* After the time for filing a response to a motion to compel pursuant to this section has expired, the presiding officer shall rule promptly on any such motion. The presiding officer may deny, grant in part, or otherwise modify any request for the production of documents, if he determines that a discovery request, or any one or more of its terms, seeks to obtain the production of documents that are privileged or otherwise not within the scope of permissible discovery under §1209.29(b), and may issue appropriate protective orders, upon such conditions as justice may require.

(2) *No stay.* The pendency of a motion to strike or limit discovery, or to compel the production of any document, shall not stay or continue the proceeding, unless otherwise ordered by the presiding officer. Notwithstanding any other provision in this part, the presiding officer may not release, or order any party to produce, any document withheld on the basis of privilege, if the withholding party has stated to the presiding officer its intention to file with the Director a timely motion for interlocutory review of the presiding officer's privilege determination or order to produce the documents, until the Director has rendered a decision on the motion for interlocutory review.

(3) *Interlocutory review by the Director.* Interlocutory review of a privilege determination or document discovery subpoena of the presiding officer shall be in accordance with §1209.33. To the extent necessary to rule promptly on such matters, the Director may request that the presiding officer provide additional information from the record. As provided by §1209.33 of this part, a pending interlocutory review of a privilege determination or document discovery subpoena shall not stay the proceedings, unless otherwise ordered by the presiding officer or the Director.

(h) *Enforcement of document discovery subpoenas*—(1) *Authority.* If the presiding officer or Director issues a subpoena compelling production of documents by a party in a proceeding under this part, in the event of noncompliance with the subpoena and to the extent authorized by section 1379D(c)(1) of the Safety and Soundness Act (12 U.S.C. 4641(c)(1)), the Director or the subpoenaing party may apply to the appropriate United States district court for an order requiring compliance with the subpoena.

(2) *United States district court jurisdiction.* As provided by section 1379D(c)(2) of the Safety and Soundness Act (12 U.S.C. 4641(c)(2)), the appropriate United States district court has the jurisdiction and power to order and to require compliance with any discovery subpoena issued under this part.

(3) *No stay; sanctions.* The judicial enforcement of a discovery subpoena shall not operate as a stay of the proceedings, unless the presiding officer or the Director orders a stay of such duration as the presiding officer or Director may find reasonable and in the best interest of the parties or as justice may require. A party's right to seek judicial

enforcement of a subpoena shall not in any manner limit the sanctions that may be imposed by the presiding officer or Director against a party who fails to produce or induces another to fail to produce subpoenaed documents.

§ 1209.31 Document discovery subpoenas to non-parties.

(a) *General rules*—(1) *Application for subpoena.* As provided under this part, any party may apply to the presiding officer for the issuance of a document discovery subpoena addressed to any person who is not a party to the proceeding. The application must contain the proposed document subpoena, and a brief statement of facts demonstrating that the documents are materially relevant to the charges and issues presented in the proceeding and the reasonableness of the scope of the document request. The subpoenaing party shall specify a reasonable time, place, and manner for production in response to the subpoena, and state its unequivocal intention to pay for the production of the documents as provided in this part.

(2) *Service of subpoena.* A party shall apply for a document subpoena under this section only within the time period during which such party could serve a discovery request under § 1209.30 of this part. The party obtaining the document subpoena is responsible for serving it on the subpoenaed person and for serving copies on all other parties. Document subpoenas may be served in the District of Columbia, or any State, Territory, possession, or other place subject to the jurisdiction of the United States, or as otherwise provided by law.

(3) *Presiding officer's discretion.* The presiding officer shall issue promptly any document subpoena applied for under this section subject to the application conditions set forth in this section and his or her discretion. If the presiding officer determines that the application does not set forth a valid basis for the issuance of the requested document subpoena, or that any of its terms are unreasonable, oppressive, excessive in scope, unduly burdensome, or otherwise objectionable under § 1209.29(b), he may refuse to issue the requested document subpoena or may issue it in a modified form upon such additional conditions as may be determined by the presiding officer.

(b) *Motion to quash or modify*—(1) *Limited appearance.* Any non-party to a pending proceeding to whom a document subpoena is directed may enter a limited appearance, through a representative or on his or her own behalf, before the presiding officer to file with the presiding officer a motion to quash or modify such subpoena, accompanied by a statement of the basis for quashing or modifying the subpoena.

(2) *Objections.* Any motion to quash or modify a document subpoena must be filed on the same basis, including the assertion of any privileges, upon which a party could object to a discovery document request under § 1209.30 and during the same time limits during which such an objection could be filed.

(3) *Responses and replies.* The party who obtained the subpoena may respond to such motion within 10 days of service of the motion; the response shall be served on the non-party in accordance with this part. Absent express leave of the presiding officer, no other party may respond to the non-party's motion. The non-party may file a reply within five days of service of a response.

(4) *No stay.* A non-party's right to seek to quash or modify a document subpoena shall not stay the proceeding, or limit in any manner the sanctions that may be imposed by the presiding officer against a party who induces another to fail to produce any such subpoenaed documents. No party may rely upon the pendency of a non-party's motion to quash or modify a document subpoena to excuse performance of any action required of that party under this part.

(c) *Enforcing document subpoenas to non-parties*—(1) *Application for enforcement of subpoena.* If a non-party fails to comply with any subpoena issued pursuant to this section or with any order of the presiding officer that directs compliance with all or any portion of a document subpoena issued pursuant to this section, the subpoenaing party or any other aggrieved party to the proceeding may, to the extent authorized by section 1379D(c) of the Safety and Soundness Act (12 U.S.C. 4641(c)), apply to an appropriate United States district court for an order requiring compliance with the subpoena.

(2) *No stay.* A party's right to seek district court enforcement of a non-party document production subpoena under this section shall not automatically stay an enforcement proceeding under of the Safety and Soundness Act.

(3) *Sanctions.* A party's right to seek district court enforcement of a non-party document subpoena shall in no way limit the sanctions that may be imposed by the presiding officer on a party who induces another to fail to comply with any subpoena issued under this section.

§ 1209.32 Deposition of witness unavailable for hearing.

(a) *General rules.* (1) If a witness will not be available for the hearing, a party desiring to preserve that witness's testimony for the record may apply to the presiding officer in accordance with the procedures set forth in paragraph (a)(2) of this section for the issuance of a subpoena or subpoena *duces tecum* requiring attendance of the witness at a deposition for the purpose of preserving that witness's testimony. The presiding officer may issue a deposition subpoena under this section upon a showing that:

(i) The witness will be unable to attend or may be prevented from attending the testimonial phase of the hearing because of age, sickness, or infirmity, or will be otherwise unavailable;

(ii) The subpoenaing party did not cause or contribute to the unavailability of the witness for the hearing;

(iii) The witness has personal knowledge and the testimony is reasonably expected to be materially relevant to claims, defenses, or matters determined to be at issue in the proceeding; and

(iv) Taking the deposition will not result in any undue burden to any other party and will not cause undue delay of the proceeding.

(2) The application must contain a proposed deposition subpoena and a brief statement of the reasons for the issuance of the subpoena. The subpoena must name the witness whose deposition is to be taken and specify the time and place for taking the deposition. A deposition subpoena may require the witness to be deposed anywhere within the United States, or its Territories and possessions, in which that witness resides or has a regular place of employment or such other convenient place as the presiding officer shall fix.

(3) Subpoenas must be issued promptly upon request, unless the presiding officer determines that the request fails to set forth a valid basis under this section for its issuance. Before making a determination that there is no valid basis for issuing the subpoena, the presiding officer shall require a written response from the party requesting the subpoena or require attendance at a conference to determine whether there is a valid basis upon which to issue the requested subpoena.

(4) The party obtaining a deposition subpoena is responsible for serving it on the witness and for serving copies on all parties. Unless the presiding officer orders otherwise, no deposition under this section shall be taken on fewer than 10 days' notice to the witness and all parties. Deposition subpoenas may be served anywhere within the United States or its Territories and possessions, or on any person doing business anywhere within the United States or its Territories and possessions, or as otherwise permitted by law.

(b) *Objections to deposition subpoenas.* (1) The witness and any party who has not had an opportunity to oppose a deposition subpoena issued under this section may file a motion with the presiding officer under § 1209.28 of this part to quash or modify the subpoena prior to the time for compliance specified in the subpoena, but not more than 10 days after service of the subpoena.

(2) A statement of the basis for the motion to quash or modify a subpoena issued under this section must accompany the motion. The motion must be served on all parties.

(c) *Procedure upon deposition.* (1) Each witness testifying pursuant to a deposition subpoena must be duly sworn and each party shall have the right to examine the witness. Objections to questions or documents must be in short form, stating the grounds for the objection. Failure to object to questions or documents is not deemed a waiver except where the ground for objection might have been avoided if the objection had been presented timely. All questions, answers, and objections must be recorded and transcribed. Videotaped depositions must be transcribed for the record; copies and transcriptions must be supplied to each party.

(2) Any party may move before the presiding officer for an order compelling the witness to answer any questions the witness has refused to answer or submit any evidence that, during the deposition, the witness has refused to submit.

(3) The deposition transcript must be subscribed by the witness, unless the parties and the witness, by stipulation, have waived the signing, or the witness is ill, cannot be found, or has refused to sign. If the deposition is not subscribed by the witness, the court reporter taking the deposition shall certify that the transcript is a true and complete transcript of the deposition.

(d) *Enforcing subpoenas.* If a subpoenaed person fails to comply with any subpoena issued pursuant to this section or with any order of the presiding officer made upon motion under paragraph (c)(2) of this section, the subpoenaing party or other aggrieved party may, to the extent authorized by section 1379D(c) of the Safety and Soundness Act (12 U.S.C. 4641(c)), apply to an appropriate United States district court for an order requiring compliance with the portions of the subpoena that the presiding officer has ordered enforced. A party's right to seek court enforcement of a deposition subpoena in no way limits the sanctions that may be imposed by the presiding officer on a party who fails to comply with or induces a failure to comply with a subpoena issued under this section.

§ 1209.33 Interlocutory review.

(a) *General rule.* The Director may review a ruling of the presiding officer prior to the certification of the record to the Director only in accordance with the procedures set forth in this section.

(b) *Scope of review.* The Director may exercise interlocutory review of a ruling of the presiding officer if the Director finds that:

(1) The ruling involves a controlling question of law or policy as to which substantial grounds exist for a difference of opinion;

(2) Immediate review of the ruling may materially advance the ultimate termination of the proceeding;

(3) Subsequent modification of the ruling at the conclusion of the proceeding would be an inadequate remedy; or

(4) Subsequent modification of the ruling would cause unusual delay or expense.

(c) *Procedure.* Any motion for interlocutory review shall be filed by a party with the presiding officer within 10 days of his or her ruling. Upon the expiration of the time for filing all responses, the presiding officer shall refer the matter to the Director for final disposition. In referring the matter to the Director, the presiding officer may indicate agreement or disagreement with the asserted grounds for interlocutory review of the ruling in question.

(d) *Suspension of proceeding.* Neither a request for interlocutory review nor any disposition of such a request by the Director under this section suspends or stays the proceeding unless otherwise ordered by the presiding officer or the Director.

§ 1209.34 Summary disposition.

(a) *In general.* The presiding officer shall recommend that the Director issue a final order granting a motion for summary disposition if the undisputed pleaded facts, admissions, affidavits, stipulations, documentary evidence, matters as to which official notice may be taken, and any other evidentiary materials properly submitted in connection with a motion for summary disposition show that:

(1) There is no genuine issue as to any material fact; and

(2) The movant is entitled to a decision in its favor as a matter of law.

(b) *Filing of motions and responses.* (1) Any party who believes there is no genuine issue of material fact to be determined and that such party is entitled to a decision as a matter of law may move at any time for summary disposition in its favor of all or any part of the proceeding. Any party, within 30 days after service of such motion or within such time period as allowed by the presiding officer, may file a response to such motion.

(2) A motion for summary disposition must be accompanied by a statement of material facts as to which the movant contends there is no genuine issue. Such motion must be supported by documentary evidence, which may take the form of admissions in pleadings, stipulations, depositions, investigatory depositions, transcripts, affidavits, and any other evidentiary materials that the movant contends support its position. The motion must also be accompanied by a brief containing the points and authorities in support of the contention of the movant. Any party opposing a motion for summary disposition must file a statement setting forth those material facts as to which the party contends a genuine dispute exists. Such opposition must be supported by evidence of the same type as that submitted with the motion for summary disposition and a brief containing the points and authorities in support of the contention that summary disposition would be inappropriate.

(c) *Hearing on motion.* At the request of any party or on his or her own motion, the presiding officer may hear oral argument on the motion for summary disposition.

(d) *Decision on motion.* Following receipt of a motion for summary disposition and all responses thereto, the presiding officer shall determine whether the movant is entitled to summary disposition. If the presiding officer determines that summary disposition is warranted, the presiding officer shall submit a recommended decision to that effect to the Director, under § 1209.53. If the presiding officer finds that the moving party is not entitled to summary disposition, the presiding officer shall make a ruling denying the motion.

§ 1209.35 Partial summary disposition.

If the presiding officer determines that a party is entitled to summary disposition as to certain claims only, he shall defer submitting a recommended decision to the Director as to those claims. A hearing on the remaining issues must be ordered. Those claims for which the presiding officer has determined that summary disposition is warranted will be addressed in the recommended decision filed at the conclusion of the hearing.

§ 1209.36 Scheduling and pre-hearing conferences.

(a) *Scheduling conference.* After service of a notice of charges commencing a proceeding under this part, the presiding officer shall order the representative(s) of record for each party, and any party not so represented who is appearing *pro se*, to meet in person or to confer by telephone at a specified time within 30 days of service of such notice for the purpose of setting the time and place of the testimonial hearing on the record to be held within the District of Columbia and scheduling the course and conduct of the proceeding (the "scheduling conference"). The identification of potential witnesses, the time for and manner of discovery, and the exchange of any pre-hearing materials including witness lists, statements of issues, stipulations, exhibits, and any other materials also may be determined at the scheduling conference.

(b) *Pre-hearing conferences.* The presiding officer may, in addition to the scheduling conference, on his or her own motion or at the request of any party, direct representatives for the parties to meet with (in person or by telephone) at a pre-hearing conference to address any or all of the following:

(1) Simplification and clarification of the issues;

(2) Stipulations, admissions of fact and the contents, authenticity and admissibility into evidence of documents;

(3) Matters of which official notice may be taken;

(4) Limitation of the number of witnesses;

(5) Summary disposition of any or all issues;

(6) Resolution of discovery issues or disputes;

(7) Amendments to pleadings; and

(8) Such other matters as may aid in the orderly disposition of the proceeding.

(c) *Transcript.* The presiding officer, in his or her discretion, may require that a scheduling or pre-hearing conference be recorded by a court reporter. Any transcript of the conference and any materials filed, including orders, become part of the record of the proceeding. A party may obtain a copy of a transcript at such party's expense.

(d) *Scheduling or pre-hearing orders.* Within a reasonable time following the conclusion of the scheduling conference or any pre-hearing conference, the presiding officer shall serve on each party an order setting forth any agreements reached and any procedural determinations made.

§ 1209.37 Pre-hearing submissions.

(a) *General.* Within the time set by the presiding officer, but in no case later than 10 days before the start of the hearing, each party shall serve on every other party the serving party's:

(1) Pre-hearing statement;

(2) Final list of witnesses to be called to testify at the hearing, including name and address of each witness, and a short summary of the expected testimony of each witness;

(3) List of the exhibits to be introduced at the hearing along with a copy of each exhibit; and

(4) Stipulations of fact, if any.

(b) *Effect of failure to comply.* No witness may testify and no exhibit may be introduced at the hearing that is not listed in the pre-hearing submissions pursuant to paragraph (a) of this section, except for good cause shown.

§ 1209.38 Hearing subpoenas.

(a) *Issuance.* (1) Upon application of a party to the presiding officer showing relevance and reasonableness of scope of the testimony or other evidence sought, the presiding officer may issue a subpoena or a subpoena *duces tecum* requiring the attendance of a witness at the hearing or the production of documentary or physical evidence at such hearing. The application for a hearing subpoena must also contain a proposed subpoena specifying the attendance of a witness or the production of evidence from any place within the United States or its territories and possessions, or as otherwise provided by law, at the designated place where the hearing is being conducted. The party making the application shall serve a copy of the application and the proposed subpoena on every other party.

(2) A party may apply for a hearing subpoena at any time before the commencement of or during a hearing. During a hearing, a party may make an application for a subpoena orally on the record before the presiding officer.

(3) The presiding officer shall promptly issue any hearing subpoena applied for under this section; except that, if the presiding officer determines that the application does not set forth a valid basis for the issuance of the subpoena, or that any of its terms are unreasonable, oppressive, excessive in scope, or unduly burdensome, he may refuse to issue the subpoena or may issue the subpoena in a modified form upon any conditions consistent with subpart C of this part. Upon issuance by the presiding officer, the party making the application shall serve the subpoena on the person named in the subpoena and on each party.

(b) *Motion to quash or modify.* (1) Any person to whom a hearing subpoena is directed or any party may file a motion to quash or modify such subpoena, accompanied by a statement of the basis for quashing or modifying the subpoena. The movant must serve the motion on each party and on the person named in the subpoena. Any party may respond to the motion within 10 days of service of the motion.

(2) Any motion to quash or modify a hearing subpoena must be filed prior to the time specified in the subpoena for compliance, but no more than 10 days after the date of service of the subpoena upon the movant.

(c) *Enforcing subpoenas.* If a subpoenaed person fails to comply with any subpoena issued pursuant to this section or any order of the presiding officer that directs compliance with all or any portion of a hearing subpoena, the subpoenaing party or any other aggrieved party may seek enforcement of the subpoena pursuant to § 1209.31. A party's right to seek court enforcement of a hearing subpoena shall in no way limit the sanctions that may be imposed by the presiding officer on a party who induces a failure to comply with subpoenas issued under this section.

§§ 1209.39—1209.49 [Reserved]

§ 1209.50 Conduct of hearings.

(a) *General rules*—(1) *Conduct.* Hearings shall be conducted in accordance with chapter 5 of Title 5 and other applicable law and so as to provide a fair and expeditious presentation of the relevant disputed issues. Except as limited by this subpart, each party has the right to present its case or defense by oral and documentary evidence and to conduct such cross examination as may be required for full disclosure of the facts.

(2) *Order of hearing.* FHFA counsel of record shall present its case-in-chief first, unless otherwise ordered by the presiding officer or unless otherwise expressly specified by law or regulation. FHFA counsel of record shall be the first party to present an opening statement and a closing statement and may make a rebuttal statement after the respondent's closing statement. If there are multiple respondents, respondents may agree among themselves as to the order of presentation of their cases, but if they do not agree, the presiding officer shall fix the order.

(3) *Examination of witnesses.* Only one representative for each party may conduct an examination of a witness, except that in the case of extensive direct examination, the presiding officer may permit more than one representative for the party presenting the witness to conduct the examination. A party may have one representative conduct the direct examination and another representative conduct re-direct examination of a witness, or may have one representative conduct the cross examination of a witness and another representative conduct the re-cross examination of a witness.

(4) *Stipulations.* Unless the presiding officer directs otherwise, all documents that the parties have stipulated as admissible shall be admitted into evidence upon commencement of the hearing.

(b) *Transcript.* The hearing shall be recorded and transcribed. The transcript shall be made available to any party upon payment of the cost thereof. The presiding officer shall have authority to order the record corrected, either upon motion to correct, upon stipulation of the parties, or following notice to the parties upon the presiding officer's own motion.

§ 1209.51 Evidence.

(a) *Admissibility.* (1) Except as is otherwise set forth in this section, relevant, material, and reliable evidence that is not unduly repetitive is admissible to the fullest extent authorized by the Administrative Procedure Act (5 U.S.C. 552 *et seq.*) and other applicable law.

(2) Evidence that would be admissible under the Federal Rules of Evidence is admissible in a proceeding conducted pursuant to subpart C of this part.

(3) Evidence that would be inadmissible under the Federal Rules of Evidence may not be deemed or ruled to be inadmissible in a proceeding conducted pursuant to subpart C of this part if such evidence is relevant, material, probative and reliable, and not unduly repetitive.

(b) *Official notice.* (1) Official notice may be taken of any material fact that may be judicially noticed by a United States district court and of any materially relevant information in the official public records of any Federal or State government agency.

(2) All matters officially noticed by the presiding officer or the Director shall appear on the record.

(3) If official notice is requested of any material fact, the parties, upon timely request, shall be afforded an opportunity to object.

(c) *Documents.* (1) A duplicate copy of a document is admissible to the same extent as the original, unless a genuine issue is raised as to whether the copy is in some material respect not a true and legible copy of the original.

(2) Subject to the requirements of paragraph (a)(1) of this section, any document, including a report of examination, oversight activity, inspection, or visitation prepared by FHFA or by

another Federal or State financial institution's regulatory agency, is admissible either with or without a sponsoring witness.

(3) Witnesses may use existing or newly created charts, exhibits, calendars, calculations, outlines, or other graphic material to summarize, illustrate, or simplify the presentation of testimony. Such materials may, subject to the presiding officer's discretion, be used with or without being admitted into evidence.

(d) *Objections.* (1) Objections to the admissibility of evidence must be timely made and rulings on all objections must appear in the record.

(2) When an objection to a question or line of questioning is sustained, the examining representative of record may make a specific proffer on the record of what he or she expected to prove by the expected testimony of the witness. The proffer may be by representation of the representative or by direct interrogation of the witness.

(3) The presiding officer shall retain rejected exhibits, adequately marked for identification, for the record and transmit such exhibits to the Director.

(4) Failure to object to admission of evidence or to any ruling constitutes a waiver of the objection.

(e) *Stipulations.* The parties may stipulate as to any relevant matters of fact or the authentication of any document to be admitted into evidence. Such stipulations must be received in evidence at a hearing, are binding on the parties with respect to the matters stipulated, and shall be made part of the record.

(f) *Depositions of unavailable witnesses.* (1) If a witness is unavailable to testify at a hearing and that witness has testified in a deposition in accordance with § 1209.32, a party may offer as evidence all or any part of the transcript of the deposition, including deposition exhibits, if any.

(2) Such deposition transcript is admissible to the same extent that testimony would have been admissible had that person testified at the hearing, provided that if a witness refused to answer proper questions during the deposition the presiding officer may, on that basis, limit the admissibility of the deposition in any manner that justice requires.

(3) Only those portions of a deposition or related exhibits received in evidence at the hearing in accordance with this section shall constitute a part of the record.

§ 1209.52 Post-hearing filings.

(a) *Proposed findings and conclusions and supporting briefs.* (1) Using the same method of service for each party, the presiding officer shall serve notice upon each party that the certified transcript, together with all hearing exhibits and exhibits introduced but not admitted into evidence at the hearing, has been filed with the presiding officer. Any party may file with the presiding officer proposed findings of fact, proposed conclusions of law, and a proposed order within 30 days after the parties have received notice that the transcript has been filed with the presiding officer, unless otherwise ordered by the presiding officer.

(2) Proposed findings and conclusions must be supported by citation to any relevant authorities and by page and line references to any relevant portions of the record. A post-hearing brief may be filed in support of proposed findings and conclusions, either as part of the same document or in a separate document.

(3) A party is deemed to have waived any issue not raised in proposed findings or conclusions timely filed by that party.

(b) *Reply briefs.* Reply briefs may be filed within 15 days after the date on which the parties' proposed findings and conclusions and proposed order are due. Reply briefs shall be limited strictly to responding to new matters, issues, or arguments raised by another party in papers filed in the proceeding. A party who has not filed proposed findings of fact and conclusions of law or a post-hearing brief may not file a reply brief.

(c) *Simultaneous filing required.* The presiding officer shall not order the filing by any party of any brief or reply brief supporting proposed findings and conclusions in advance of the other party's filing of its brief.

§ 1209.53 Recommended decision and filing of record.

(a) *Filing of recommended decision and record.* Within 45 days after expiration of the time allowed for filing reply briefs under § 1209.52(b), the presiding officer shall file with and certify to the Director, for decision, the record of the proceeding. The record must include the presiding officer's recommended decision, recommended findings of fact and conclusions of law, and proposed order; all pre-hearing and hearing transcripts, exhibits and rulings; and the motions, briefs, memoranda, and other supporting papers filed in connection with the hearing. The presiding officer shall serve upon each party the recommended decision, recommended findings and conclusions, and proposed order.

(b) *Filing of index.* At the same time the presiding officer files with and certifies to the Director, for final determination, the record of the proceeding, the presiding officer shall furnish to the Director a certified index of the entire record of the proceeding. The certified index shall include, at a minimum, an entry for each paper, document or motion filed with the presiding officer in the proceeding, the date of the filing, and the identity of the filer. The certified index shall also include an exhibit index containing, at a minimum, an entry consisting of exhibit number and title or description for: each exhibit introduced and admitted into evidence at the hearing; each exhibit introduced but not admitted into evidence at the hearing; each exhibit introduced and admitted into evidence after the completion of the hearing; and each exhibit introduced but not admitted into evidence after the completion of the hearing.

§ 1209.54 Exceptions to recommended decision.

(a) *Filing exceptions.* Within 30 days after service of the recommended decision, recommended findings and conclusions, and proposed order under § 1209.53, a party may file with the Director written exceptions to the presiding officer's recommended decision, recommended findings and conclusions, and proposed order; to the admission or exclusion of evidence; or to the failure of the presiding officer to make a ruling proposed by a party. A supporting brief may be filed at the time the exceptions are filed, either as part of the same document or in a separate document.

(b) *Effect of failure to file or raise exceptions.* (1) Failure of a party to file exceptions to those matters specified in paragraph (a) of this section within the time prescribed is deemed a waiver of objection thereto.

(2) No exception need be considered by the Director if the party taking exception had an opportunity to raise the same objection, issue, or argument before the presiding officer and failed to do so.

(c) *Contents.* (1) All exceptions and briefs in support of such exceptions must be confined to the particular matters in or omissions from the presiding officer's recommendations to which that party takes exception.

(2) All exceptions and briefs in support of exceptions must set forth page or paragraph references to the specific parts of the presiding officer's recommendations to which exception is taken, the page or paragraph references to those portions of the record relied upon to support each exception, and the legal authority relied upon to support each exception. Exceptions and briefs in support shall not exceed a total of 30 pages, except by leave of the Director on motion.

(3) One reply brief may be submitted by each party opposing the exceptions within 10 days of service of exceptions and briefs in support of exceptions. Reply briefs shall not exceed 15 pages, except by leave of the Director on motion.

§ 1209.55 Review by Director.

(a) *Notice of submission to the Director.* When the Director determines that the record in the proceeding is complete, the Director shall serve notice upon the parties that the case has been submitted to the Director for final decision.

(b) *Oral argument before the Director.* Upon the initiative of the Director or on the written request of any party filed with the Director within the time for filing exceptions, the Director may order and hear oral argument on the recommended findings, conclusions, decision and order of the presiding officer. A written request by a party must show good cause for oral argument and state reasons why arguments cannot be presented adequately in writing. A denial of a request for oral argument may be set forth in the Director's final decision. Oral argument before the Director must be transcribed.

(c) *Director's final decision and order.* (1) Decisional employees may advise and assist the Director in the consideration and disposition of the case. The final decision of the Director will be based upon review of the entire record of the proceeding, except that the Director may limit the issues to be reviewed to those findings and conclusions to which opposing arguments or exceptions have been filed by the parties.

(2) The Director shall render a final decision and issue an appropriate order within 90 days after notification to the parties that the case has been submitted for final decision, unless the Director orders that the action or any aspect thereof be remanded to the presiding officer for further proceedings. Copies of the final decision including findings of fact and an appropriate order of the Director shall be served upon each party to the proceeding and as otherwise required by statute.

(3) The Director may modify, terminate, or set aside an order in accordance with section 1373(b)(2) of the Safety and Soundness Act (12 U.S.C. 4633(b)(2)).

§ 1209.56 Exhaustion of administrative remedies.

To exhaust administrative remedies as to any issue on which a party disagrees with the presiding officer's recommendations, a party must file exceptions with the Director under § 1209.54 of this part. A party must exhaust administrative remedies as a precondition to seeking judicial review of any final decision and order issued under this part.

§ 1209.57 Judicial review; no automatic stay.

(a) *Judicial review.* Judicial review of any final order of the Director shall be exclusively as provided by section 1374 of the Safety and Soundness Act (12 U.S.C. 4634).

(b) *No automatic stay.* Commencement of proceedings for judicial review of a final decision and order of the Director may not, unless specifically ordered by the Director or a reviewing court, operate as a stay of any order issued by the Director. The Director may, in his or her discretion and on such terms as he finds just, stay the effectiveness of all or any part of an order of the Director pending a final decision on a petition for review of that order.

§§ 1209.58—1209.69 [Reserved]

Subpart D—Parties and Representational Practice Before the Federal Housing Finance Agency; Standards of Conduct

§ 1209.70 Scope.

Subpart D of this part contains rules governing practice by parties or their representatives before FHFA. This subpart addresses the imposition of sanctions by the presiding officer or the Director against parties or their representatives in an adjudicatory proceeding under this part. This subpart also covers other disciplinary sanctions—censure, suspension, or disbarment—against individuals who appear before FHFA in a representational capacity either in an adjudicatory proceeding under this part or in any other matters connected with presentations to FHFA relating to a client's or other principal's rights, privileges, or liabilities. This representation includes, but is not limited to, the practice of attorneys and accountants. Employees of FHFA are not subject to disciplinary proceedings under this subpart.

§ 1209.71 Definitions.

Practice before FHFA for the purposes of subpart D of this part, includes, but is not limited to, transacting any business with FHFA as counsel of record, representative, or agent for any other person, unless the Director orders otherwise. Practice before FHFA also includes the preparation of any statement, opinion, or other paper by a counsel, representative or agent that is filed with FHFA in any certification, notification, application, report, or other document, with the consent of such counsel, representative, or agent. Practice before FHFA does not include work prepared for a regulated entity or entity-affiliated party solely at the request of such party for use in the ordinary course of its business.

§ 1209.72 Appearance and practice in adjudicatory proceedings.

(a) *Appearance before FHFA or a presiding officer*—(1) *By attorneys.* A party may be represented by an attorney who is a member in good standing of the bar of the highest court of any State, commonwealth, possession or territory of the United States, or the District of Columbia, and who is not currently suspended or disbarred from practice before FHFA.

(2) *By non-attorneys.* An individual may appear on his or her own behalf, *pro se.* A member of a partnership may represent the partnership and a duly authorized officer, director, employee, or other agent of any corporation or other entity not specifically listed herein may represent such corporation or other entity; provided that such officer, director, employee, or other agent is not currently suspended or disbarred from practice before FHFA. A duly authorized officer or employee of any Government unit, agency, or authority may represent that unit, agency, or authority.

(b) *Notice of appearance.* Any person appearing in a representative capacity on behalf of a party, including FHFA, shall execute and file a notice of appearance with the presiding officer at or before the time such person submits papers or otherwise appears on behalf of a party in the adjudicatory proceeding. Such notice of appearance shall include a written declaration that the individual is currently qualified as provided in paragraph (a)(1) or (a)(2) of this section and is authorized to represent the particular party. By filing a notice of appearance on behalf of a party in an adjudicatory proceeding, the representative thereby agrees and represents that he is authorized to accept service on behalf of the represented party and that, in the event of withdrawal from representation, he or she will, if required by the presiding officer, continue to accept service until a new representative has filed a notice of appearance or until the represented party indicates that he or she will proceed on a *pro se* basis. Unless the representative filing the notice is an attorney, the notice of appearance shall also be executed by the person represented or, if the person is not an individual, by the chief executive officer, or duly authorized officer of that person.

§ 1209.73 Conflicts of interest.

(a) *Conflict of interest in representation.* No representative shall represent another person in an adjudicatory proceeding if it reasonably appears that such representation may be limited materially by that representative's responsibilities to a third person or by that representative's own interests. The presiding officer may take corrective measures at any stage of a proceeding to cure a conflict of interest in representation, including the issuance of an order limiting the scope of representation or disqualifying an individual from appearing in a representative capacity for the duration of the proceeding.

(b) *Certification and waiver.* If any person appearing as counsel or other representative represents two or more parties to an adjudicatory proceeding, or also represents a non-party on a matter relevant to an issue in the proceeding, that representative must certify in writing at the time of filing the notice of appearance required by § 1209.72 of this part as follows:

(1) That the representative has personally and fully discussed the possibility of conflicts of interest with each affected party and non-party; and

(2) That each affected party and non-party waives any right it might otherwise have had to assert any known conflicts of interest or to assert any non-material conflicts of interest during the course of the proceeding.

§ 1209.74 Sanctions.

(a) *General rule.* Appropriate sanctions may be imposed during the course of any proceeding when any party or representative of record has acted or failed to act in a manner required by applicable statute, regulation, or order, and that act or failure to act:

(1) Constitutes contemptuous conduct, which includes dilatory, obstructionist, egregious, contumacious, unethical, or other improper conduct at any phase of any proceeding, hearing, or appearance before a presiding officer or the Director;

(2) Has caused some other party material and substantive injury, including, but not limited to, incurring expenses including attorney's fees or experiencing prejudicial delay;

(3) Is a clear and unexcused violation of an applicable statute, regulation, or order; or

(4) Has delayed the proceeding unduly.

(b) *Sanctions.* Sanctions that may be imposed include, but are not limited to, any one or more of the following:

(1) Issuing an order against a party;

(2) Rejecting or striking any testimony or documentary evidence offered, or other papers filed, by the party;

(3) Precluding the party from contesting specific issues or findings;

(4) Precluding the party from offering certain evidence or from challenging or contesting certain evidence offered by another party;

(5) Precluding the party from making a late filing or conditioning a late filing on any terms that may be just; or

(6) Assessing reasonable expenses, including attorney's fees, incurred by any other party as a result of the improper action or failure to act.

(c) *Procedure for imposition of sanctions.* (1) The presiding officer, on the motion of any party, or on his or her own motion, and after such notice and responses as may be directed by the presiding officer, may impose any sanction authorized by this section. The presiding officer shall submit to the Director for final ruling any sanction that would result in a final order that terminates the case on the merits or is otherwise dispositive of the case.

(2) Except as provided in paragraph (d) of this section, no sanction authorized by this section, other than refusing to accept late papers, shall be imposed without prior notice to all parties and an opportunity for any representative or party against whom sanctions may be imposed to be heard. The presiding officer shall determine and direct the appropriate notice and form for such opportunity to be heard. The opportunity to be heard may be limited to an opportunity to respond verbally immediately after the act or inaction in question is noted by the presiding officer.

(3) For purposes of interlocutory review, motions for the imposition of sanctions by any party and the imposition of sanctions shall be treated the same as motions for any other ruling by the presiding officer.

(4) Nothing in this section shall be read to preclude the presiding officer or the Director from taking any other action or imposing any other restriction or sanction authorized by any applicable statute or regulation.

(d) *Sanctions for contemptuous conduct.* If, during the course of any proceeding, a presiding officer finds any representative or any individual representing themself to have engaged in contemptuous conduct, the presiding officer may summarily suspend that individual from participating in that or any related proceeding or impose any other appropriate sanction.

§ 1209.75 Censure, suspension, disbarment, and reinstatement.

(a) *Discretionary censure, suspension, and disbarment.* (1) The Director may censure any individual who practices or attempts to practice before FHFA or suspend or revoke the privilege to appear or practice before FHFA of such individual if, after notice of and opportunity for hearing in the matter, that individual is found by the Director—

(i) Not to possess the requisite qualifications or competence to represent others;

(ii) To be seriously lacking in character or integrity or to have engaged in material unethical or improper professional conduct;

(iii) To have caused unfair and material injury or prejudice to another party, such as prejudicial delay or unnecessary expenses including attorney's fees;

(iv) To have engaged in, or aided and abetted, a material and knowing violation of the Safety and Soundness Act, the Federal Home Loan Mortgage Corporation Act, the Federal National Mortgage Association Charter Act, or the rules or regulations issued under those statutes, or any other applicable law or regulation;

(v) To have engaged in contemptuous conduct before FHFA;

(vi) With intent to defraud in any manner, to have willfully and knowingly deceived, misled, or threatened any client or prospective client; or

(vii) Within the last 10 years, to have been convicted of an offense involving moral turpitude, dishonesty, or breach of trust, if the conviction has not been reversed on appeal. A conviction within the meaning of this paragraph shall be deemed to have occurred when the convicting court enters its judgment or order, regardless of whether an appeal is pending or could be taken and includes a judgment or an order on a plea of *nolo contendere* or on consent, regardless of whether a violation is admitted in the consent.

(2) Suspension or revocation on the grounds set forth in paragraphs (a)(1)(ii) through (vii) of this section shall only be ordered upon a further finding that the individual's conduct or character was sufficiently egregious as to justify suspension or revocation. Suspension or disbarment under this paragraph shall continue until the applicant has been reinstated by the Director for good cause shown or until, in the case of a suspension, the suspension period has expired.

(3) If the final order against the respondent is for censure, the individual may be permitted to practice before FHFA, but such individual's future representations may be subject to conditions designed to promote high standards of conduct. If a written letter of censure is issued, a copy will be maintained in FHFA's files.

(b) *Mandatory suspension and disbarment.* (1) Any counsel who has been and remains suspended or disbarred by a court of the United States or of any State, commonwealth, possession or territory of the United States, or the District of Columbia; any accountant or other licensed expert whose license to practice has been revoked in any State, commonwealth, possession or territory of the United States, or the District of Columbia; any person who has been and remains suspended or barred from practice by or before the Department of Housing and Urban Development, the Office of the Comptroller of the Currency, the Board of Governors of the Federal Reserve System, the Office of Thrift Supervision, the Federal Deposit Insurance Corporation, the National Credit Union Administration, the Federal Housing Finance Board, the Farm Credit Administration, the Securities and Exchange Commission, or the Commodity Futures Trading Commission is also suspended automatically from appearing or practicing before FHFA. A disbarment or suspension within the meaning of this paragraph shall be deemed to have occurred when the disbarring or suspending agency or tribunal enters its judgment or order, regardless of whether an appeal is pending or could be taken and regardless of whether a violation is admitted in the consent.

(2) A suspension or disbarment from practice before FHFA under paragraph (b)(1) of this section shall continue until the person suspended or disbarred is reinstated under paragraph (d)(2) of this section.

(c) *Notices to be filed.* (1) Any individual appearing or practicing before FHFA who is the subject of an order, judgment, decree, or finding of the types set forth in paragraph (b)(1) of this section shall file promptly with the Director a copy thereof, together with any related opinion or statement of the agency or tribunal involved.

(2) Any individual appearing or practicing before FHFA who is or within the last 10 years has been convicted of a felony or of a misdemeanor that resulted in a sentence of prison term or in a fine or restitution order totaling more than $5,000 promptly shall file a notice with the Director. The notice shall include a copy of the order imposing the sentence or fine, together with any related opinion or statement of the court involved.

(d) *Reinstatement.* (1) Unless otherwise ordered by the Director, an application for reinstatement for good cause may be made in writing by a person suspended or disbarred under paragraph (a)(1) of this section at any time more than three years after the effective date of the suspension or disbarment and, thereafter, at any time more than one year after the person's most recent application for reinstatement. An applicant for reinstatement hereunder may, in the Director's sole discretion, be afforded a hearing.

(2) An application for reinstatement for good cause by any person suspended or disbarred under paragraph (b)(1) of this section may be filed at any time, but not less than one year after the applicant's most recent application. An applicant for reinstatement for good cause hereunder may, in the Director's sole discretion, be afforded a hearing. If, however, all the grounds for suspension or disbarment under paragraph (b)(1) of this section have been removed by a reversal of the order of suspension or disbarment or by termination of the underlying suspension or disbarment, any person suspended or disbarred under paragraph (b)(1) of this section may apply immediately for reinstatement and shall be reinstated by FHFA upon written application notifying FHFA that the grounds have been removed.

(e) *Conferences*—(1) *General rule.* The FHFA counsel of record may confer with a proposed respondent concerning allegations of misconduct or other grounds for censure, disbarment, or suspension, regardless of whether a proceeding for censure, disbarment or suspension has been commenced. If a conference results in a stipulation in connection with a proceeding in which the individual is the respondent, the stipulation may be entered in the record at the request of either party to the proceeding.

(2) *Resignation or voluntary suspension.* In order to avoid the institution of or a decision in a disbarment or suspension proceeding, a person who practices before FHFA may consent to censure, suspension, or disbarment from practice. At the discretion of the Director, the individual may be censured, suspended, or disbarred in accordance with the consent offered.

(f) *Hearings under this section.* Hearings conducted under this section shall be conducted in substantially the same manner as other hearings under this part, except that in proceedings to terminate an existing FHFA suspension or disbarment order, the person seeking the termination of the order shall bear the burden of going forward with an application and with proof and that the Director may, in the Director's sole discretion, direct that any proceeding to terminate an existing suspension or disbarment by FHFA be limited to written submissions. All hearings held under this section shall be closed to the public unless the Director, on the Director's own motion or upon the request of a party, otherwise directs.

§§ 1209.76—1209.79 [Reserved]

Subpart E—Civil Money Penalty Inflation Adjustments

§ 1209.80 Inflation adjustments.

The maximum amount of each civil money penalty within FHFA's jurisdiction, as set by the Safety and Soundness Act and thereafter adjusted in accordance with the Inflation Adjustment Act, on a recurring four-year cycle, is as follows:

U.S. Code citation	Description	Adjusted maximum penalty amount
12 U.S.C. 4636(b)(1)	First Tier	$10,000
12 U.S.C. 4636(b)(2)	Second Tier	50,000
12 U.S.C. 4636(b)(4)	Third Tier (Entity-Affiliated party)	2,000,000
12 U.S.C. 4636(b)(4)	Third Tier (Regulated entity)	2,000,000

§ 1209.81 Applicability.

The inflation adjustments set out in § 1209.80 shall apply to civil money penalties assessed in accordance with the provisions of the Safety and Soundness Act, 12 U.S.C. 4636, and subparts B and C of this part, for violations occurring after the effective date of July 30, 2008.

§§ 1209.82—1209.99 [Reserved]

Subpart F—Suspension or Removal of an Entity-Affiliated Party Charged With Felony

§ 1209.100 Scope.

Subpart F of this part applies to informal hearings afforded to any entity-affiliated party who has been suspended, removed, or prohibited from further participation in the business affairs of a regulated entity by a notice or order issued by the Director under section 1377(h) of the Safety and Soundness Act (12 U.S.C. 4636a(h)).

§ 1209.101 Suspension, removal, or prohibition.

(a) *Notice of suspension or prohibition.* (1) As provided by section 1377(h)(1) of the Safety and Soundness Act (12 U.S.C. 4636a(h)(1)), if an entity-affiliated party is charged in any information, indictment, or complaint, with the commission of or participation in a crime that involves dishonesty or breach of trust that is punishable by imprisonment for more than one year under State or Federal law, the Director may, if continued service or participation by such party may pose a threat to the regulated entity or impair public confidence in the regulated entity, by written notice served upon such party, suspend such party from office or prohibit such party from further participation in any manner in the conduct of the affairs of any regulated entity.

(2) In accordance with section 1377(h)(1) of the Safety and Soundness Act (12 U.S.C. 4636a(h)(1)), the notice of suspension or prohibition is effective upon service. A copy of such notice will be served on the relevant regulated entity. The notice will state the basis for the suspension and the right of the party to request an informal hearing as provided in § 1209.102. The suspension or prohibition is to remain in effect until the information, indictment, or complaint is finally disposed of, or until terminated by the Director, or otherwise as provided in paragraph (c) of this section.

(b) *Order of removal or prohibition.* As provided by section 1377(h)(2) of the Safety and Soundness Act (12 U.S.C. 4636a(h)(2)), at such time as a judgment of conviction is entered (or pretrial diversion or other plea bargain is agreed to) in connection with a crime as referred to above in paragraph (a) (the "conviction"), and the conviction is no longer subject to appellate review, the Director may, if continued service or participation by such party may pose a threat to the regulated entity or impair public confidence in the regulated entity, issue an order removing such party from office or prohibiting such party from further participation in any manner in the conduct of the affairs of the regulated entity without the prior written consent of the Director. A copy of such order will be served on the relevant regulated entity, at which time the entity-affiliated party shall immediately cease to be a director or officer of the regulated entity. The notice will state the basis for the removal or prohibition and the right of the party to request a hearing as provided in § 1209.102.

(c) *Effective period.* Unless terminated by the Director, a notice of suspension or order of removal issued under section 1377(h)(1) or (2) of the Safety and Soundness Act (12 U.S.C. 4636a(h)(1), (2)) shall remain effective and outstanding until the completion of any informal hearing or appeal provided under section 1377(h)(4) of the Safety and Soundness Act (12 U.S.C. 4636a(h)(4)). The pendency of an informal hearing, if any, does not stay any notice of suspension or prohibition or order of removal or prohibition under subpart F of this part.

(d) *Effect of acquittal.* As provided by section 1377(h)(2)(B)(ii) of the Safety and Soundness Act (12 U.S.C. 4636a(h)(2)(B)(ii)), a finding of not guilty or other disposition of the charge does not preclude the Director from instituting removal, suspension, or prohibition proceedings under section 1377(a) or (b) of the Safety and Soundness Act (12 U.S.C. 4636a(a), (b)).

(e) *Preservation of authority.* Action by the Director under section 1377(h) of the Safety and Soundness Act (12 U.S.C. 4636a(h)), shall not be deemed as a predicate or a bar to any other regulatory, supervisory, or enforcement action under the Safety and Soundness Act.

§ 1209.102 Hearing on removal or suspension.

(a) *Hearing requests*—(1) *Deadline.* An entity-affiliated party served with a notice of suspension or prohibition or an order of removal or prohibition, within 30 days of service of such notice or order, may submit to the Director a written request to appear before the Director to show that his or her continued service or participation in the affairs of the regulated entity will not pose a threat to the interests of, or threaten to impair public confidence in, the Enterprises or the Banks. The request must be addressed to the Director and sent to the Federal Housing Finance Agency at 1700 G Street, NW., Washington, DC 20552, by:

(i) Overnight U.S. Postal Service delivery or delivery by a reliable commercial delivery service for same day or overnight delivery to the address stated above; or

(ii) First class, registered, or certified mail via the U.S. Postal Service.

(2) *Waiver of appearance.* An entity-affiliated party may elect in writing to waive his or her right to appear to make a statement in person or through counsel and have the matter determined solely on the basis of his or her written submission.

(b) *Form and timing of hearing*—(1) *Informal hearing.* Hearings under subpart F of this part are not subject to the formal adjudication provisions of the Administrative Procedure Act (5 U.S.C. 554 through 557), and are not conducted under subpart C of this part.

(2) *Setting of the hearing.* Upon receipt of a timely request for a hearing, the Director will give written notice and set a date within 30 days for the entity-affiliated party to appear, personally, or through counsel, before the Director or his or her designee(s) to submit written materials (or, at the discretion of the Director, oral testimony and oral argument) to make the necessary showing under paragraph (a) of this section. The entity-affiliated party may submit a written request for additional time for the hearing to commence, without undue delay, and the Director may extend the hearing date for a specified time.

(3) *Oral testimony.* The Director or his or her designee, in his or her discretion, may deny, permit, or limit oral testimony in the hearing.

(c) *Conduct of the hearing*—(1) *Hearing officer.* A hearing under this section may be presided over by the Director or one or more designated FHFA employees, except that an officer designated by the Director (hearing officer) to conduct the hearing may not have been involved in an underlying criminal proceeding, a factually related proceeding, or an enforcement proceeding in a prosecutorial or investigative role. This provision does not preclude the Director otherwise from seeking information on the matters at issue from appropriate FHFA staff on an as needed basis consistent with § 1209.101(d)(2).

(2) *Submissions.* All submissions of the requestor and FHFA's counsel of record must be received by the Director or his or her designee no later than 10 days prior to the date set for the hearing. FHFA may respond in writing to the requestor's submission and serve the requestor (and any other interested party such as the regulated entity) not later than the date fixed by the hearing officer for submissions or other time period as the hearing officer may require.

(3) *Procedures*—(i) *Fact finding authority of the hearing officer.* The hearing officer shall determine all procedural matters under subpart F of this part, permit or limit the appearance of witnesses in accordance with paragraph (b)(3) of this section, and impose time limits as he or she deems reasonable. All oral statements, witness testimony, if permitted, and documents submitted that are found by the hearing officer to be materially relevant to the proceeding and not unduly repetitious may be considered. The hearing officer may question any person appearing in the proceeding, and may make any ruling reasonably necessary to ensure the full and fair presentation of evidence and to facilitate the efficient and effective operation of the proceeding.

(ii) *Statements to an officer.* Any oral or written statement made to the Director, a hearing officer, or any FHFA employee under subpart F of this part is deemed to be a statement made to a

Federal officer or agency within the meaning of 18 U.S.C. 1006.

(iii) *Oral testimony.* If either the requestor or FHFA counsel of record desires to present oral testimony to supplement the party's written submission he or she must make a request in writing to the hearing officer not later than 10 days prior to the hearing, as provided in paragraph (c)(2) of this section, or within a shorter time period as permitted by the hearing officer for good cause shown. The request should include the name of the individual(s), a statement generally descriptive of the expected testimony, and the reasons why such oral testimony is warranted. The hearing officer generally will not admit witnesses, absent a strong showing of specific and compelling need. Witnesses, if admitted, shall be sworn.

(iv) *Written materials.* Each party must file a copy of any affidavit, memorandum, or other written material to be presented at the hearing with the hearing officer and serve copies on any other interested party (such as the affected regulated entity) not later than 10 days prior to commencement of the informal hearing, as provided in paragraph (c)(2), or within a shorter time period as permitted by the hearing officer for good cause shown.

(v) *Relief.* The purpose of the hearing is to determine whether the suspension or prohibition from participation in any manner in the conduct of the affairs of the regulated entity will be continued, terminated, or otherwise modified, or whether the order removing such party from office or prohibiting the party from further participation in any manner in the conduct of the affairs of the regulated entity will be rescinded or otherwise modified.

(vi) *Ultimate question.* In deciding on any request for relief from a notice of suspension or prohibition, the hearing officer shall not consider the ultimate question of guilt or innocence with respect to the outstanding criminal charge(s). In deciding on a request for relief from a removal order, the hearing officer shall not consider challenges to or efforts to impeach the validity of the conviction. In either case, the hearing officer may consider facts that show the nature of the events on which the conviction or charges were based.

(4) *Record.* If warranted under the circumstances of the matter, the hearing officer may require that a transcript of the proceedings be prepared at the expense of the requesting party. The hearing officer may order the record be kept open for a reasonable time following the hearing, not to exceed five business days, to permit the filing of additional pertinent submissions for the record. Thereafter, no further submissions are to be admitted to the record, absent good cause shown.

§ 1209.103 Recommended and final decisions.

(a) *Recommended decision*—(1) *Written recommended decision of the hearing officer.* Not later than 20 days following the close of the hearing (or if the requestor waived a hearing, from the deadline for submission of the written materials), the hearing officer will serve a copy of the recommended decision on the parties to the proceeding. The recommended decision must include a summary of the findings, the parties' respective arguments, and support for the determination.

(2) *Five-day comment period.* Not later than five business days after receipt of the recommended decision, the parties shall submit written comments in response to the recommended decision, if any, to the hearing officer. The hearing officer shall not grant any extension of the stated time for responses to a recommended decision.

(3) *Recommended decision to be transmitted to the Director.* The hearing officer shall promptly forward the recommended decision, and written comments, if any, and the record to the Director for final determination.

(b) *Decision of the Director.* Within 60 days of the date of the hearing, or if the requestor waived a hearing the date fixed for the hearing, the Director will notify the entity-affiliated party in writing by registered mail of the disposition of his or her request for relief from the notice of suspension or prohibition or the order of removal or prohibition. The decision will state whether the suspension or prohibition will be continued, terminated, or otherwise modified, or whether the order removing such party from any participation in the affairs of the regulated entity will be rescinded or otherwise modified. The decision will contain a brief statement of the basis for an adverse determination. The Director's decision is a final and non-appealable order.

(c) *Effect of notice or order.* A removal or prohibition by order shall remain in effect until terminated by the Director. A suspension or prohibition by notice remains in effect until the criminal charge is disposed of or until terminated by the Director.

(d) *Reconsideration.* A suspended or removed entity-affiliated party subsequently may petition the Director to reconsider the final decision any time after the expiration of a 12-month period from the date of the decision, but no such request may be made within 12 months of a previous petition for reconsideration. An entity-affiliated party must submit a petition for reconsideration in writing; the petition shall state the specific grounds for relief from the notice of suspension or order or removal and be supported by a memorandum and any other documentation materially relevant to the request for reconsideration. No hearing will be held on a petition for reconsideration, and the Director will inform the requestor of the disposition of the reconsideration request in a timely manner. A decision on a request for reconsideration shall not constitute an appealable order.

PART 1212—POST-EMPLOYMENT RESTRICTION FOR SENIOR EXAMINERS

Subpart A [Reserved]

Subpart B—Post-Employment Restriction for Senior Examiners

AUTHORITY: 12 U.S.C. 4526, 12 U.S.C. 4517(e).

SOURCE: 74 FR 51075, Oct. 5, 2009, unless otherwise noted.

Subpart A [Reserved]

Subpart B—Post-Employment Restriction for Senior Examiners

§1212.1 Purpose and scope.

This subpart sets forth a one-year post-employment restriction applicable to senior examiners of the Federal Housing Finance Agency (FHFA). This restriction is in addition to the post-employment restriction applicable to employees of FHFA under 12 U.S.C. 4523.

§1212.2 Definitions.

For purposes of subpart B of this part, the term:

Consultant means a person who works directly on matters for, or on behalf of, a regulated entity or the Office of Finance.

Director means the Director of FHFA or his or her designee.

Employee means an officer or employee of FHFA, including a special Government employee.

Federal Home Loan Bank or *Bank* means a Bank established under the Federal Home Loan Bank Act; the term "Federal Home Loan Banks" means, collectively, all the Federal Home Loan Banks.

Office of Finance means the Office of Finance of the Federal Home Loan Bank System, or any successor thereto.

Regulated entity means the Federal National Mortgage Association and any affiliate thereof, the Federal Home Loan Mortgage Corporation and any affiliate thereof, any Federal Home Loan Bank; the term "regulated entities" means, collectively, the Federal National Mortgage Association and any affiliate thereof, the Federal Home Loan Mortgage Corporation and any affiliate thereof, and the Federal Home Loan Banks.

Safety and Soundness Act means the Federal Housing Enterprises Financial Safety and Soundness Act of 1992, as amended by the Federal Housing Finance Regulatory Reform Act of 2008, Division A of the Housing and Economic Recovery Act of 2008, Public Law No. 110–289, 122 Stat. 2654 (2008).

Senior examiner means an employee of FHFA who has been:

(1) Authorized by FHFA to conduct examinations or inspections on behalf of FHFA;

(2) Assigned continuing, broad and lead responsibility for examining a regulated entity or the Office of Finance; and

(3) Assigned responsibilities for examining, inspecting and supervising the regulated entity or the Office of Finance that—

(i) Represents a substantial portion of the employee's assigned responsibilities; and

(ii) Requires the employee to interact routinely with officers or employees of the regulated entity or the Office of Finance.

§ 1212.3 Post-employment restriction for senior examiners.

(a) *Prohibition.* An employee of FHFA who serves as the senior examiner of a regulated entity or the Office of Finance for two or more months during the last 12 months of his or her employment with FHFA may not, within one year after leaving the employment of FHFA, knowingly accept compensation as an employee, officer, director, or consultant from a regulated entity or the Office of Finance unless the Director grants a waiver pursuant to § 1212.4.

(b) *Effective date.* The post-employment restriction in paragraph (a) of this section shall not apply to any officer or employee of FHFA or any former officer or employee of FHFA who ceased to be an officer or employee of FHFA before November 4, 2009.

§ 1212.4 Waiver.

At the written request of a senior examiner or former senior examiner, the Director may waive the post-employment restriction in § 1212.3 if he or she certifies, in writing, and on a case-by-case basis, that granting a waiver of such restriction does not affect the integrity of the supervisory program of FHFA.

§ 1212.5 Penalties.

(a) *General.* A senior examiner who, after leaving the employment of FHFA, violates the restriction set forth in § 1212.3 shall be subject to one or both of the following penalties—

(1) An order:

(i) Removing the individual from office at the regulated entity or the Office of Finance or prohibiting the individual from further participation in the affairs of the relevant regulated entity or the Office of Finance for a period of up to five years; and

(ii) Prohibiting the individual from participating in the affairs of any regulated entity or the Office of Finance for a period of up to five years; and/or

(2) A civil money penalty of not more than $250,000.

(b) *Other penalties.* The penalties set forth in paragraph (a) of this section are not exclusive, and a senior examiner who violates the restrictions in § 1212.3 also may be subject to other administrative, civil, or criminal remedies or penalties as provided in law.

(c) *Procedural rights.* The procedures applicable to actions under paragraph (a) of this section are those provided in the Safety and Soundness Act under section 1376, in connection with the imposition of a civil money penalty; under section 1377, in connection with a removal and prohibition order (12 U.S.C. 4636 and 4636a, respectively); and under any regulations issued by FHFA implementing such procedures.

PART 1213—OFFICE OF THE OMBUDSMAN

Sec.

AUTHORITY: 12 U.S.C. 4511(b)(2), 4517(i), and 4526.

SOURCE: 76 FR 7481, Feb. 10, 2011, unless otherwise noted.

§ 1213.1 Purpose and scope.

(a) *Purpose.* The purpose of this part is to establish within FHFA the Office of the Ombudsman (Office) under section 1317(i) of the Federal Housing Enterprises Financial Safety and Soundness Act of 1992 (12 U.S.C. 4517(i)), as amended, and to set forth the authorities and duties of the Ombudsman.

(b) *Scope.* (1) This part applies to complaints and appeals from any regulated entity and any person that has a business relationship with a regulated entity regarding any matter relating to the regulation and supervision of such regulated entity or the Office of Finance by FHFA.

(2) The establishment of the Office does not alter or limit any other right or procedure associated with appeals, complaints, or administrative matters submitted by a person regarding any matter relating to the regulation and supervision of a regulated entity or the Office of Finance under any other law or regulation.

§1213.2 Definitions.

For purposes of this part, the term:

Business relationship means any existing or potential interaction between a person and a regulated entity or the Office of Finance for the provision of goods or services. The term *business relationship* does not include any interaction between a mortgagor and a regulated entity that directly or indirectly owns, purchased, guarantees, or sold the mortgage.

Director means the Director of FHFA or his or her designee.

FHFA means the Federal Housing Finance Agency.

Office of Finance means the Office of Finance of the Federal Home Loan Bank System.

Person means an organization, business entity, or individual that has a business relationship with a regulated entity or the Office of Finance, or that represents the interests of a person that has a business relationship with a regulated entity or the Office of Finance. The term *person* does not include an individual borrower.

Regulated entity means the Federal National Mortgage Association and any affiliate, the Federal Home Loan Mortgage Corporation and any affiliate, and any Federal Home Loan Bank.

§1213.3 Authorities and duties of the Ombudsman.

(a) *General.* The Office shall be headed by an Ombudsman, who shall consider complaints and appeals from any regulated entity, the Office of Finance, and any person that has a business relationship with a regulated entity or the Office of Finance regarding any matter relating to the regulation and supervision of such regulated entity or the Office of Finance by FHFA. In considering any complaint or appeal under this part, the Ombudsman shall:

(1) Conduct inquiries and submit findings of fact and recommendations to the Director concerning resolution of the complaint or appeal, and

(2) Act as a facilitator or mediator to advance the resolution of the complaint or appeal.

(b) *Other duties.* The Ombudsman shall:

(1) Establish procedures for carrying out the functions of the Office,

(2) Establish and publish procedures for receiving and considering complaints and appeals, and

(3) Report annually to the Director on the activities of the Office, or more frequently, as determined by the Director.

§1213.4 Complaints and appeals from a regulated entity or the Office of Finance.

(a) *Complaints*—(1) *General.* Any regulated entity or the Office of Finance may submit a complaint in accordance with procedures established by the Ombudsman.

(2) *Matters subject to complaint.* A regulated entity or the Office of Finance may submit a complaint regarding any matter relating to the regulation and supervision of a regulated entity or the Office of Finance by FHFA that is not subject to appeal or in litigation, arbitration, or mediation. The Ombudsman may further define what matters are subject to complaint.

(b) *Appeals*—(1) *General.* Any regulated entity or the Office of Finance may submit an appeal in accordance with procedures established by the Ombudsman.

(2) *Matters subject to appeal.* A regulated entity or the Office of Finance may submit an appeal regarding any

final, written regulatory or supervisory conclusion, decision, or examination rating by FHFA. The Ombudsman may further define what matters are subject to appeal.

(3) *Matters not subject to appeal.* Matters for which there is an existing avenue of appeal or for which there is another forum for appeal; non-final decisions or conclusions; and matters in ongoing litigation, arbitration, or mediation, unless there has been a breakdown in the process, may not be appealed. Matters not subject to appeal include, but are not limited to, appointments of conservators or receivers, preliminary examination conclusions, formal enforcement decisions, formal and informal rulemakings, Freedom of Information Act appeals, final FHFA decisions subject to judicial review, and matters within the jurisdiction of the FHFA Inspector General. The Ombudsman may further define what matters are not subject to appeal.

(4) *Effect of filing an appeal.* An appeal under this section does not excuse a regulated entity or the Office of Finance from complying with any regulatory or supervisory decision while the appeal is pending. However, the Director, upon consideration of a written request, may waive compliance with a regulatory or supervisory decision during the pendency of the appeal.

§ 1213.5 Complaints from a person.

(a) *General.* Any person that has a business relationship with a regulated entity or the Office of Finance may submit a complaint in accordance with procedures established by the Ombudsman.

(b) *Matters subject to complaint.* A person may submit a complaint regarding any matter relating to the regulation and supervision of a regulated entity or the Office of Finance by FHFA that is not a matter in litigation, arbitration, or mediation. The Ombudsman may further define what matters are subject to complaints.

§ 1213.6 No retaliation.

Neither FHFA nor any FHFA employee may retaliate against a regulated entity, the Office of Finance, or a person for submitting a complaint or appeal under this part. The Ombudsman shall receive and address claims of retaliation. Upon receiving a complaint, the Ombudsman, in coordination with the Inspector General, shall examine the basis of the alleged retaliation. Upon completion of the examination, the Ombudsman shall report the findings to the Director with recommendations, including a recommendation to take disciplinary action against any FHFA employee found to have retaliated.

§ 1213.7 Confidentiality.

The Ombudsman shall ensure that safeguards exist to preserve confidentiality. If a party requests that information and materials remain confidential, the Ombudsman shall not disclose the information or materials, without approval of the party, except to appropriate reviewing or investigating officials, such as the Inspector General, or as required by law. However, the resolution of certain complaints (such as complaints of retaliation against a regulated entity or the Office of Finance) may not be possible if the identity of the party remains confidential. In such cases, the Ombudsman shall discuss with the party the circumstances limiting confidentiality.

SUBCHAPTER B—ENTITY REGULATIONS

PART 1225—MINIMUM CAPITAL—TEMPORARY INCREASE

AUTHORITY: 12 U.S.C. 4513, 4526 and 4612.

SOURCE: 76 FR 11674, Mar. 3, 2011, unless otherwise noted.

§ 1225.1 Purpose.

FHFA is responsible for ensuring the safe and sound operation of regulated entities. In furtherance of that responsibility, this part sets forth standards and procedures FHFA will employ to determine whether to require or rescind a temporary increase in the minimum capital levels for a regulated entity or entities pursuant to 12 U.S.C. 4612(d).

§ 1225.2 Definitions.

For purposes of this part, the term:

Enterprise means the Federal National Mortgage Association or the Federal Home Loan Mortgage Corporation; and the term *Enterprises* means, collectively, the Federal National Mortgage Association and the Federal Home Loan Mortgage Corporation.

Minimum capital level means the lowest amount of capital meeting any regulation or orders issued pursuant to 12 U.S.C. 1426(a)(2) and 12 U.S.C. 4612, or any similar requirement established for a Federal Home Loan Bank by regulation, order or other action.

Regulated entity means—

(1) The Federal National Mortgage Association and any affiliate thereof;

(2) The Federal Home Loan Mortgage Corporation and any affiliate thereof; and

(3) Any Federal Home Loan Bank.

Rescission means a removal in whole or in part of an increase in the temporary minimum capital level.

§ 1225.3 Procedures.

(a) *Information*—(1) *Information to the regulated entity or entities.* If the Director determines, based on standards enunciated in this part, that a temporary increase in the minimum capital level is necessary, the Director will provide notice to the affected regulated entity or entities 30 days in advance of the date that the temporary minimum capital requirement becomes effective, unless the Director determines that an exigency exists that does not permit such notice or the Director determines a longer time period would be appropriate.

(2) *Information to the Government.* The Director shall inform the Secretary of the Treasury, the Secretary of Housing and Urban Development, and the Chairman of the Securities and Exchange Commission of a temporary increase in the minimum capital level contemporaneously with informing the affected regulated entity or entities.

(b) *Comments.* The affected regulated entity or entities may provide comments regarding or objections to the temporary increase to FHFA within 15 days or such other period as the Director determines appropriate under the circumstances. The Director may determine to modify, delay, or rescind the announced temporary increase in response to such comments or objection, but no further notice is required for the temporary increase to become effective upon the date originally determined by the Director.

(c) *Communication.* The Director shall transmit notice of a temporary increase or rescission of a temporary increase in the minimum capital level in writing, using electronic or such other means as appropriate. Such communication shall set forth, at a minimum, the bases for the Director's determination, the amount of increase or decrease in the minimum capital level, the anticipated duration of such increase, and a description of the procedures for requesting a rescission of the temporary increase in the minimum capital level.

(d) *Written plan.* In making a finding under this part, the Director may require a written plan to augment capital to be submitted on a timely basis to address the methods by which such temporary increase may be attained and the time period for reaching the new temporary minimum capital level.

(e) *Time frame for review of temporary increase for purpose of rescission.* (1) Absent an earlier determination to rescind in whole or in part a temporary increase in the minimum capital level for a regulated entity or entities, the Director shall no less than every 12 months, consider the need to maintain, modify, or rescind such increase.

(2) A regulated entity or regulated entities may at any time request in writing such review by the Director.

§ 1225.4 Standards and factors.

(a) *Standard for imposing a temporary increase.* In making a determination to increase temporarily a minimum capital requirement for a regulated entity or entities, the Director will consider the necessity and consistency of such an increase with the prudential regulation and the safe and sound operations of a regulated entity. The Director may impose a temporary minimum-capital increase if consideration of one or more of the following factors leads the Director to the judgment that the current minimum capital requirement for a regulated entity is insufficient to address the entity's risks:

(1) Current or anticipated declines in the value of assets held by a regulated entity; the amounts of mortgage-backed securities issued or guaranteed by the regulated entity; and, its ability to access liquidity and funding;

(2) Credit (including counterparty), market, operational and other risks facing a regulated entity, especially where an increase in risks is foreseeable and consequential;

(3) Current or projected declines in the capital held by a regulated entity;

(4) A regulated entity's material noncompliance with regulations, written orders, or agreements;

(5) Housing finance market conditions;

(6) Level of reserves or retained earnings;

(7) Initiatives, operations, products, or practices that entail heightened risk;

(8) With respect to a Bank, the ratio of the market value of its equity to par value of its capital stock where the market value of equity is the value calculated and reported by the Bank as "market value of total capital" under 12 CFR 932.5(a)(1)(ii)(A); or

(9) Other conditions as detailed by the Director in the notice provided under § 1225.3.

(b) *Standard for rescission of a temporary increase.* In making a determination to rescind a temporary increase in the minimum capital level for a regulated entity or entities, whether in full or in part, the Director will consider the consistency of such a rescission with the prudential regulation and safe and sound operations of a regulated entity. The Director will rescind, in full or in part, a temporary minimum capital increase if consideration of one or more of the following factors leads the Director to the judgment that rescission of a temporary minimum-capital increase for a regulated entity is appropriate considering the entity's risks:

(1) Changes to the circumstances or facts that led to the imposition of a temporary increase in the minimum capital levels;

(2) The meeting of targets set for a regulated entity in advance of any capital or capital-related plan agreed to by the Director;

(3) Changed circumstances or facts based on new developments occurring since the imposition of the temporary increase in the minimum capital level, particularly where the original problems or concerns have been successfully addressed or alleviated in whole or in part; or

(4) Such other standard as the Director may consider as detailed by the Director in the notice provided under § 1225.3.

§ 1225.5 Guidances.

The Director may determine, from time to time, issue guidance to elaborate, to refine or to provide new information regarding standards or procedures contained herein.

PART 1229—CAPITAL CLASSIFICATIONS AND PROMPT CORRECTIVE ACTION

Subpart A—Federal Home Loan Banks

Subpart B—Enterprises

AUTHORITY: 12 U.S.C. 1426, 4513, 4526, 4613, 4614, 4615, 4616, 4617, 4618, 4622, 4623.

SOURCE: 74 FR 5604, Jan. 30, 2009, unless otherwise noted.

Subpart A—Federal Home Loan Banks

§ 1229.1 Definitions.

For purposes of this subpart:

Bank written in title case, means a Federal Home Loan Bank established under section 12 of the Bank Act (12 U.S.C. 1432).

Bank Act means the Federal Home Loan Bank Act, as amended (12 U.S.C. 1421 through 1449).

Capital distribution means any payment by the Bank, whether in cash or stock, of a dividend, any return of capital or retained earnings by the Bank to its shareholders, any transaction in which the Bank redeems or repurchases capital stock, or any transaction in which the Bank redeems, repurchases or retires any other instrument which is included in the calculation of its total capital.

Class A stock means capital stock issued by a Bank, including subclasses, that has the characteristics specified in section 6(a)(4)(A)(i) of the Bank Act (12 U.S.C. 1426(a)(4)(A)(i)) and related regulations.

Class B stock means capital stock issued by a Bank, including subclasses, that has the characteristics specified in section 6(a)(4)(A)(ii) of the Bank Act (12 U.S.C. 1426(a)(4)(A)(ii)) and related regulations.

Consolidated obligations means any bond, debenture or note on which the Banks are jointly and severally liable and which was issued under section 11 of the Bank Act (12 U.S.C. 1431) and any implementing regulations, whether or not such instrument was originally issued jointly by the Banks or by the Federal Housing Finance Board on behalf of the Banks.

Critical capital level for a Bank means an amount equal to 2 percent of the Bank's total assets.

Director means the Director of the Federal Housing Finance Agency or his or her designee.

Executive officer means for a Bank any of the following persons, provided that the Director may from time to time add or remove persons, positions, or functions to or from the list (individually for one or more Banks or jointly for all the Banks) by communication to the affected Banks:

(1) Executive officers about whom the Banks must publicly disclose detailed compensation information under Regulation S–K, 17 CFR part 229, issued by the Securities and Exchange Commission;

(2) Any other executive who occupies one of the following positions or is in charge of one of the following subject areas:

(i) Overall Bank operations, such as the Chief Operating Officer or an equivalent employee;

(ii) Chief Financial Officer or an equivalent employee;

(iii) Chief Administrative Officer or an equivalent employee;

(iv) Chief Risk Officer or an equivalent employee;

(v) Asset and Liability Management officer, or an equivalent employee;

(vi) Chief Accounting Officer or an equivalent employee;

(vii) General Counsel or an equivalent employee;

(viii) Strategic Planning officer or an equivalent employee;

(ix) Internal Audit officer or an equivalent employee; or

(x) Chief Information Officer or an equivalent employee; or

(3) Any other individual, without regard to title:

(i) Who is in charge of a principal business unit, division or function; or

(ii) Who reports directly to the Bank's chairman of the board of directors, vice chairman of the board of directors, president or chief operating officer.

FHFA means the Federal Housing Finance Agency.

Minimum capital requirement means the leverage and total capital requirements established for a Bank under section 6(a)(2) of the Bank Act (12 U.S.C. 1426(a)(2)) and related regulations, as such requirements may be revised by the Director, or any similar requirement established for a Bank by regulation, order, written agreement or other action.

New business activity means any activity undertaken by a Bank that requires approval from the FHFA under part 980 of this title.

Permanent capital means the retained earnings of a Bank, determined in accordance with generally accepted accounting principles in the United States (GAAP), plus the amount paid-in for the Bank's Class B stock.

Risk-based capital requirement means any capital requirement established for a Bank under section 6(a)(3) of the Bank Act (12 U.S.C. 1426(a)(3)) and related regulations that ensures a Bank will hold sufficient permanent capital and reserves to support the risks that arise from its operations.

Safety and Soundness Act means the Federal Housing Enterprises Financial Safety and Soundness Act of 1992 (12 U.S.C. 4501 *et seq.*) as amended.

Tangible equity means, for a Bank, the paid-in value of its outstanding capital stock plus its retained earnings calculated in accordance with generally accepted accounting principles in the United States (GAAP) less the amount of any assets that would be intangible assets under GAAP.

Total capital means the sum of the Bank's permanent capital, the amount paid-in for its Class A stock, the amount of any general allowances for losses, and the amount of any other instruments indentified in a Bank's capital plan that the Director has determined to be available to absorb losses incurred by such Bank. For a Bank that has issued neither Class A nor Class B stock, the Bank's total capital shall be the measure of capital used to determine compliance with its minimum capital requirement.

§ 1229.2 Determination of a Bank's capital classification.

(a) *Quarterly determination.* The Director shall determine the capital classification for each Bank no less often than once a quarter based on the capital classifications in § 1229.3 of this subpart. The Director may make a determination with regard to a capital classification for a Bank more often than the minimum required under this paragraph or make a determination for one or more Banks without making a determination for all the Banks.

(b) *Notification to a Bank.* Before finalizing any action to classify a Bank under this section, the Director shall provide a Bank written notice describing the proposed action and an opportunity to submit information that the Bank considers relevant to the proposed action in accordance with § 1229.12 of this subpart.

(c) *Notification to the FHFA.* A Bank shall provide written notification within ten calendar days of any event or development that has caused or is likely to cause its permanent or total capital to fall below the level necessary to maintain its capital classification at the level assigned in the most recent capital classification or reclassification determination by the Director or that is contained in the most recent notice of a proposed capital classification or reclassification provided under § 1229.12(a) of this subpart.

§ 1229.3 Criteria for a Bank's capital classification.

(a) *Adequately capitalized.* Except where the Director has exercised authority to reclassify a Bank, a Bank shall be considered adequately capitalized if, at the time of the determination under § 1229.2(a) of this subpart, the Bank has sufficient permanent and total capital, as applicable, to meet or exceed its risk-based and minimum capital requirements.

(b) *Undercapitalized.* Except where the Director has exercised authority to reclassify a Bank, a Bank shall be considered undercapitalized if, at the time of the determination under § 1229.2(a) of this subpart, the Bank does not have sufficient permanent or total capital, as applicable, to meet any one or more of its risk-based or minimum capital requirements but such deficiency is not of a magnitude to classify the Bank as significantly undercapitalized or critically undercapitalized.

(c) *Significantly undercapitalized.* Except where the Director has exercised authority to reclassify a Bank, a Bank shall be considered significantly undercapitalized if, at the time of the determination under § 1229.2(a) of this subpart, the amount of permanent or total capital held by the Bank is less than 75 percent of what is required to meet any one of its risk-based or minimum capital requirements but the magnitude of the Bank's deficiency in total capital is not sufficient to classify it as critically undercapitalized.

(d) *Critically undercapitalized.* Except where the Director has exercised authority to reclassify a Bank, a Bank shall be considered critically undercapitalized if, at the time of the determination under § 1229.2(a) of this subpart, the total capital held by the Bank is less than or equal to the critical capital level for a Bank as defined under § 1229.1 of this subpart.

§ 1229.4 Reclassification by the Director.

(a) *Discretionary reclassification.* Where the Director determines that any of the grounds described in paragraph (b) of this section exist, the Director may reclassify a Bank as:

(1) Undercapitalized, if it is otherwise classified as adequately capitalized;

(2) Significantly undercapitalized, if it is otherwise classified as undercapitalized; or

(3) Critically undercapitalized if it is otherwise classified as significantly undercapitalized.

(b) *Grounds for discretionary reclassification.* Notwithstanding any other provision of this subpart, the Director may at any time reclassify a Bank under this section if:

(1) The Director determines in writing that:

(i) The Bank is engaging in conduct that could result in the rapid depletion of permanent or total capital;

(ii) The value of collateral pledged to the Bank has decreased significantly; or

(iii) The value of property subject to mortgages owned by the Bank has decreased significantly.

(2) The Director determines, after notice to the Bank and opportunity for an informal hearing before the Director, that a Bank is in an unsafe and unsound condition; or

(3) The Director finds, under § 1371(b) of Safety and Soundness Act (12 U.S.C. 4631(b)), that the Bank is engaging in an unsafe and unsound practice because the Bank's asset quality, management, earnings or liquidity were found to be less than satisfactory during the most recent examination, and any deficiency has not been corrected.

(c) *Procedures.* Before finalizing any action to reclassify a Bank under this section, the Director shall provide a Bank written notice describing the proposed action and an opportunity to submit information that the Bank considers relevant to the Director's proposed action in accordance with § 1229.12 of this subpart.

(d) *Duration.* Any condition, action or inaction by a Bank that is the basis for a decision to reclassify a Bank under this section or under any other authority provided the Director may be considered by the Director and form the basis of further, subsequent actions to reclassify the Bank until such time as the Bank remedies such condition or takes necessary action to correct such situation to the satisfaction of the Director.

(e) *Reservation of authority.* Nothing in this section shall prevent the Director from exercising any other authority under the Safety and Soundness Act, the Bank Act or any regulation to reclassify a Bank for reasons not set forth in paragraph (b) of this section or to take any other action against a Bank.

§ 1229.5 Capital distributions for adequately capitalized Banks.

(a) *Restriction.* An adequately capitalized Bank may not make a capital distribution if after doing so the Bank's capital would be insufficient to maintain a classification of adequately capitalized. A Bank may not make a capital distribution if such distribution would violate any restriction on the redemption or repurchase of capital stock or the payment of a dividend set forth in section 6 of the Bank Act (12 U.S.C. 1426) and any other applicable regulation.

(b) *Exception.* Notwithstanding the restriction in paragraph (a) of this section, the Director may permit a Bank to repurchase or redeem its shares of stock if the transaction is made in connection with the issuance of additional Bank shares or obligations in at least an equivalent amount to the shares that are redeemed or repurchased and will reduce the Bank's financial obligations or otherwise improve its financial condition. Any transaction under this paragraph also must conform with any restriction on the redemption or repurchase of Bank stock set forth in section 6 of the Bank Act (12 U.S.C. 1426) and in any other applicable regulation.

§ 1229.6 Mandatory actions applicable to undercapitalized Banks.

(a) *Mandatory Actions by the Bank.* A Bank that is classified as undercapitalized shall:

(1) Submit to the Director for approval a capital restoration plan that complies with the the requirements and procedures established by § 1229.11 of this part and receive approval from the Director for such plan;

(2) Fulfill all terms, conditions and obligations contained in the capital restoration plan as approved by the Director;

(3) Not make any capital distribution that would result in the Bank being reclassified as significantly undercapitalized or critically undercapitalized, nor make a capital distribution if such distribution would violate any restriction on the redemption or repurchase of capital stock or the declaration or payment of a dividend set forth in section 6 of the Bank Act (12 U.S.C. 1426) or in any other applicable regulation;

(4) Not permit its average total assets in any calendar quarter to exceed its average total assets during the preceding calendar quarter, where such average is calculated based on the total amount of assets held by the Bank for each day in a quarter, unless:

(i) The Director has approved the Bank's capital restoration plan; and

(ii) The Director determines that:

(A) The increase in total assets is consistent with the approved capital restoration plan; and

(B) The ratio of tangible equity to the Bank's total assets is increasing at a rate sufficient to enable the Bank to become adequately capitalized within a reasonable time and consistent with any schedule established in the capital restoration plan; and

(5) Not acquire, directly or indirectly, an equity interest in any operating entity (other than as necessary to enforce a security interest granted to the Bank) nor engage in any new business activity unless:

(i) The Director has approved the Bank's capital restoration plan, the Bank is implementing the capital restoration plan and the Director determines that proposed acquisition or activity will further achievement of the goals set forth in that plan; or

(ii) The Director determines that the proposed acquisition or activity will be consistent with the safe and sound operation of the Bank and will further the Bank's compliance with its risk-based and minimum capital requirements in a reasonable period of time.

(b) *Mandatory reclassification by the Director.* The Director shall reclassify an undercapitalized Bank as significantly undercapitalized if:

(1) The Bank does not submit a capital restoration plan that is substantially in compliance with § 1229.11 of this subpart and within the time frame required.

(2) The Director does not approve the capital restoration plan submitted by the Bank; or

(3) The Director determines that the Bank has failed in any material respect to comply with its approved capital restoration plan or fulfill any schedule for action established by that plan.

(c) *Monitoring.* The Director shall monitor the condition of any undercapitalized Bank and monitor the Bank's compliance with the capital restoration plan and any restrictions imposed under this section or § 1229.7 of this subpart. As part of this process, the Director shall review the capital restoration plan and any restrictions or requirements imposed on the undercapitalized Bank to determine whether such plan, restrictions or requirements are consistent with the safe and sound operation of the Bank and will further the Bank's compliance with its risk-based and minimum capital requirements in a reasonable period of time.

[74 FR 5604, Jan. 30, 2009, as amended at 74 FR 38513, Aug. 4, 2009]

§ 1229.7 Discretionary actions applicable to undercapitalized Banks.

(a) *Discretionary safeguards.* The Director may take any action with regard to an undercapitalized Bank that may be taken with regard to a significantly undercapitalized Bank under section 1366 of the Safety and Soundness Act (12 U.S.C. 4616) or § 1229.7 or § 1229.8 of this subpart if the Director determines that such action is necessary to assure the safe and sound operation of the Bank and the Bank's compliance with its risk-based and minimum capital requirements in a reasonable period of time.

(b) *Procedures.* Before finalizing any action under this section, the Director shall provide a Bank written notice describing the proposed action or actions and an opportunity to submit information that the Bank considers relevant to the Director's decision to take such action in accordance with § 1229.12 of this subpart.

§ 1229.8 Mandatory actions applicable to significantly undercapitalized Banks.

A Bank that is classified as significantly undercapitalized:

(a) Shall submit to the Director for approval a capital restoration plan that complies with the requirements and procedures established by § 1229.11 of this part and receive approval from the Director for such plan;

(b) Fulfill all terms, conditions and obligations contained in the capital restoration plan once the plan is approved by the Director;

(c) Shall not make any capital distribution that would result in the Bank being reclassified as critically undercapitalized or that would violate any restriction on the redemption or repurchase of capital stock or the payment of a dividend set forth in section 6 of the Bank Act (12 U.S.C. 1426) or any applicable regulation;

(d) Shall not make any capital distribution not otherwise prohibited under paragraph (c) of this section absent the prior written approval of the Director, provided that the Director may approve such distribution only if the Director determines that:

(1) The capital distribution will enhance the ability of the Bank to meet its risk-based and minimum capital requirements promptly;

(2) The capital distribution will contribute to the long-term financial safety and soundness of the Bank; or

(3) The capital distribution is otherwise in the public interest;

(e) Shall not without prior written approval of the Director pay a bonus to any executive officer, provided that for purposes of this paragraph a bonus shall include any amount paid or accruing to an executive officer under a profit sharing arrangement;

(f) Shall not without the prior written approval of the Director compensate an executive officer at a rate exceeding the average rate of compensation of that officer during the 12 months preceding the calendar month in which the Bank became significantly undercapitalized, provided however, that for purposes of calculating the executive officer's average rate of compensation, such compensation shall not include any bonus or profit sharing paid or accruing to the officer during the 12 month period;

(g) Comply with § 1229.6(a)(4) and (a)(5) of this subpart; and

(h) Comply with any on-going restrictions or obligations that were imposed on the Bank by the Director under § 1229.7 of this subpart.

[74 FR 5604, Jan. 30, 2009, as amended at 74 FR 38513, Aug. 4, 2009]

§ 1229.9 Discretionary actions applicable to significantly undercapitalized Banks.

(a) *Actions by the Director.* The Director shall carry out this section by taking, at any time, one or more of the following actions with respect to a significantly undercapitalized Bank:

(1) Limit the increase in any obligations or class of obligations of the Bank, including any off-balance sheet obligations. Such limitation may be stated in an absolute dollar amount, as a percentage of current obligations or in any other form chosen by the Director;

(2) Reduce the amount of any obligations or class of obligations held by the Bank, including any off-balance sheet obligations. Such reduction may be stated in an absolute dollar amount, as a percentage of current obligations or in any other form chosen by the Director;

(3) Limit the increase in, or prohibit the growth of any asset or class of assets held by the Bank. Such limitation may be stated in an absolute dollar amount, as a percentage of current assets or in any other form chosen by the Director;

(4) Reduce the amount of any asset or class of asset held by the Bank. Such reduction may be stated in an absolute dollar amount, as a percentage of current obligations or in any other form chosen by the Director;

(5) Acquire new capital in the form and amount determined by the Director, which specifically may include requiring a Bank to increase its level of retained earnings;

(6) Modify, limit or terminate any activity of the Bank that the Director determines creates excessive risk;

(7) Take steps to improve the management at the Bank by:

(i) Ordering a new election for the Bank's board of directors in accordance with procedures established by the Director;

(ii) Dismissing particular directors or executive officers, in accordance with section 1366(b)(5)(B) of the Safety and Soundness Act (12 U.S.C. 4616(b)(5)(B)), who held office for more than 180 days immediately prior to the date on which the Bank became undercapitalized, provided further that such dismissals shall not be considered removal pursuant to an enforcement action under section 1377 of the Safety and Soundness Act (12 U.S.C. 4636a) and shall not be subject to the requirements necessary to remove an officer or director under that section; or

(iii) Ordering the Bank to hire qualified executive officers, the hiring of whom, prior to employment by the Bank and at of the option of the Director, may be subject to review and approval by the Director; or

(8)(i) Reclassify a significantly undercapitalized Bank as critically undercapitalized if:

(A) The Bank does not submit a capital restoration plan that is substantially in compliance with § 1229.11 of this part and within the time frame required;

(B) The Director does not approve the capital restoration plan submitted by the Bank; or

(C) The Director determines that the Bank has failed to make reasonable, good faith efforts to comply with its approved capital restoration plan and fulfill any schedule established by that plan.

(ii) Subject to paragraph (c) of this section, the Director may reclassify a significantly undercapitalized Bank under paragraph (a)(8)(i) of this section at any time the grounds for such action exist, notwithstanding the fact that such grounds had formed the basis on which the Director reclassified a Bank from undercapitalized to significantly undercapitalized.

(b) *Additional safeguards.* The Director may require a significantly undercapitalized Bank to take any other action not specifically listed in this section if the Director determines such action will help ensure the safe and sound operation of the Bank and the Bank's compliance with its risk-based and minimum capital requirements in a reasonable period of time more than any action specifically authorized under paragraph (a) of this section.

(c) *Procedures.* Before finalizing any action under this section, the Director shall provide a Bank written notice describing the proposed action or actions and an opportunity to submit information that the Bank considers relevant to the Director's decision to take such action in accordance with § 1229.12 of this subpart.

§ 1229.10 Actions applicable to critically undercapitalized Banks.

(a) *Appointment of conservator or receiver.* Notwithstanding any other provision of federal or state law, the Director may appoint the FHFA as conservator or receiver of any Bank at any time after the Director determines that the Bank is, or the Director otherwise exercises authority to reclassify the Bank as, critically undercapitalized.

(b) *Periodic determination*—(1) *Determination.* Not later than 30 calendar days after the Director first determines that a Bank is, or the Director otherwise exercises authority to reclassify the Bank as, critically undercapitalized, and a least once during each succeeding 30-day calendar period, the Director make a determination in writing as to whether:

(i) The assets of the Bank are, and during the preceding 60 calendar days have been, less than its obligations to its creditors and others, provided that the Director shall consider as an obligation only that amount of outstanding consolidated obligations for which the Bank is primary obligor or for which the Bank has been ordered to make payments of principal or interest on behalf of another Bank, or is actually making payments of principal or interest on behalf of another Bank; or

(ii) The Bank is not, and during the previous 60 calendar days has not been paying its debts on a regular basis as such debts become due, provided that this provision does not apply to any unpaid debts that are the subject of a *bona fide* dispute.

(2) *Mandatory receivership.* If the Director determines that the conditions described in either paragraph (b)(1)(i) or (b)(1)(ii) of this section applies to a Bank, the Director shall appoint the FHFA as receiver for the Bank. The appointment of the FHFA as receiver under this paragraph shall immediately terminate any conservatorship established for the Bank.

(3) *Determination not required.* A determination under paragraph (b)(1) of this section shall not be required during any period in which the FHFA serves as receiver for a Bank.

(c) *Judicial review.* If the Director appoints the FHFA as conservator or receiver of a Bank under paragraph (a) or (b)(2) of this section, the Bank may within 30 days of such appointment bring an action in the United States district court for the judicial district in which the Bank was established pursuant to section 3 of the Bank Act (12 U.S.C. 1423) or in the United States District Court for the District of Columbia, for an order requiring the FHFA to remove itself as conservator or receiver.

(d) *Other applicable actions.* Until such time as FHFA is appointed as conservator or receiver for a critically undercapitalized Bank, a critically undercapitalized Bank shall be subject to all mandatory restrictions or obligations applicable to a significantly undercapitalized Bank under § 1229.8 of this subpart and will remain subject to any on-going restrictions or obligations that the Director imposed on the Bank under § 1229.7 or § 1229.9 of this subpart, or any restrictions or obligations that are applicable to the Bank under the terms of an approved capital restoration plan.

[74 FR 5604, Jan. 30, 2009, as amended at 74 FR 38513, Aug. 4, 2009]

§ 1229.11 Capital restoration plans.

(a) *Contents.* Each capital restoration plan submitted by a Bank shall set forth a plan to restore its permanent and total capital to levels sufficient to fulfill its risk-based and minimum capital requirements within a reasonable period of time. Such plan must be feasible given general market conditions and the conditions of the Bank and, at a minimum, shall:

(1) Describe the actions the Bank will take, including any changes that the Bank will make to member stock purchase requirements, to assure that it will become adequately capitalized within the meaning of § 1229.3(a) of this subpart and, if appropriate, to resolve any structural or long term causes for the capital deficiency;

(2) Specify the level of permanent and total capital the Bank will achieve and maintain and provide quarterly

projections indicating how each component of total and permanent capital and the major components of income, assets and liabilities are expected to change over the term of the plan;

(3) Specify the types and levels of activities in which the Bank will engage during the term of the plan, including any new business activities that it intends to begin during such term;

(4) Describe any other actions the Bank intends to take to comply with any other requirements imposed on it under this subpart A of part 1229;

(5) Provide a schedule which sets forth dates for meeting specific goals and benchmarks and taking other actions described in the proposed capital restoration plan, including setting forth a schedule for it to restore its permanent and total capital to levels necessary for meeting its risk-based and minimum capital requirements; and

(6) Address such other items that the Director shall provide in writing in advance of such submission.

(b) *Deadline for submission.* A Bank must submit a proposed capital restoration plan no later than 15 business-days after it receives written notification that such a plan is required either because the notice specifically states that the Director has required the submission of a plan or the notice indicates that the Bank's capital classification or reclassification is to a category for which a capital restoration plan is a mandatory action required of the Bank. The Director may extend this deadline if the Director determines that such extension is necessary. Any such extension shall be in writing and provide a specific date by which the Bank must submit its proposed capital restoration plan.

(c) *Review of the plan by the Director.* The Director shall have 30 calendar days from the date the Bank submits a proposed capital restoration plan to approve or disapprove the plan. The Director may extend the period for consideration of a capital restoration plan for a single 30 calendar day period by providing the Bank with written notification that the decision deadline has been extended. The Director shall provide the Bank with written notification of the decision to approve or not approve a proposed capital restoration plan. If the Director does not approve the capital restoration plan, the written notification of such decision shall provide the reasons for the disapproval.

(d) *Resubmission.* If the Director does not approve the Bank's proposed capital restoration plan, the Bank shall submit a new capital restoration plan acceptable to the Director within 30 calendar days of the date that the Bank was notified of the disapproval. The Director may extend the period for the Bank's submission of a new acceptable capital restoration plan upon a determination that such extension is in the public interest. The Director shall provide the Bank written notice of the extension and include in such notice the date by which the Bank must submit an acceptable plan.

(e) *Amendments.* The Director, in his or her sole discretion, may approve amendments to an approved capital restoration plan if, after consideration of changes in conditions of the Bank, changes in market conditions and other relevant factors, the Director determines that such amendments are consistent with the restoration of the Bank's capital to levels necessary to meet its risk-based and minimum capital requirements in a reasonable period of time and with the safe and sound operations of the Bank.

(f) *Effectiveness of provisions.* A Bank is obligated to implement and fulfill all provisions of an approved capital restoration plan. Unless expressly addressed by the terms of the capital restoration plan, a Bank remains bound by each and every obligation and requirement set forth in the approved capital restoration plan until such requirement or obligation is amended under paragraph (e) of this section or terminated in writing by the Director.

(g) *Appointment of conservator or receiver.* Notwithstanding any other provision of federal or state law, the Director may appoint the FHFA as conservator or receiver of any Bank that is classified as undercapitalized or significantly undercapitalized if the Bank fails to submit a capital restoration plan acceptable to the Director within the time frames established by this section or if the Bank materially fails to implement any capital restoration plan that has been approved by the Director. A Bank may within 30 days of such appointment bring an action in the United States district court for the judicial district in which the Bank is established pursuant to section 3 of the Bank Act (12 U.S.C. 1423) or in the United States District Court for the District of Columbia, for an order requiring the FHFA to remove itself as conservator or receiver.

[74 FR 5604, Jan. 30, 2009, as amended at 74 FR 38513, Aug. 4, 2009]

§ 1229.12 Procedures related to capital classification and other actions.

(a) *Classification or reclassification of a Bank.* Before finalizing any decision to classify a Bank under § 1229.2(a) of this subpart or reclassify the Bank under § 1229.4(a) of this subpart, the Director shall provide the Bank with written notification of the proposed action that states the reasons for the proposed action and describes the information on which the proposed action is based. The notice required under this paragraph may be combined with the notice of a proposed supervisory action required under paragraph (b) of this section. The Director also may combine a notice informing the Bank of its capital classification and simultaneously informing the Bank that the Director intends to reclassify a Bank to a lower capital classification category.

(b) *Notice of a supervisory action.* Before finalizing any action or actions authorized under § 1229.7 or § 1229.9 of this subpart, the Director shall provide the Bank with written notification of the proposed action that states the reasons for the proposed action and describes the information on which the proposed action is based. The notice required under this paragraph may be combined with the notice of a proposed action to classify or reclassify the Bank required under paragraph (a) of this section.

(c) *Bank response.* During the 30 calendar day period beginning on the date that the Bank is provided notice under paragraph (a) or (b) of this section of a proposed action or actions, a Bank may submit to the Director any information that the Bank considers relevant or appropriate for the Director to consider in determining whether to finalize the proposed action. The Director may, in his or her sole discretion, convene an informal hearing with representatives of the Bank to receive or discuss any such information. The Director, in his or her sole discretion, also may extend the period in which the Bank may respond to a notice for an additional 30 calendar days for good cause, or shorten such comment period if the Director determines the condition of the Bank requires faster action or a shorter comment period or if the Bank consents to a shorter comment period. The Director shall inform the Bank in writing, which may be provided as part of the notice required under paragraphs (a) or (b) of this section, of any decision to extend or shorten the comment period. The failure of a Bank to provide information during the allotted comment period will waive any right of the Bank to comment on the proposed action.

(d) *Final action.* At the earlier of the completion of the comment period established under paragraph (c) or the receipt of information provided by the Bank during such period, the Director shall determine whether to take the proposed action or actions that were the subject of the notice under paragraphs (a) or (b) of this section, after taking into consideration any information provided by the Bank. Such notice shall respond to any information submitted by the Bank. Any final order that the Bank take action, refrain from action or comply with any other requirement that was the subject of a notice under paragraph (b) of this section shall take effect upon the Bank's receipt of the notice required under this paragraph, unless a different effective date is set forth in this notice, and shall remain in effect and binding on the Bank until terminated in writing by the Director or until any terms and conditions for termination, as set forth in the notice, have been met.

(e) *Final actions under this section.* Any final decision that the Bank take action, refrain from action or comply with any other requirement that was the subject of a notice under paragraph (b) of this section shall constitute an order under the Safety and Soundness Act. The Director in his or her discretion may apply to the United States

District Court for the District of Columbia or to the United States district court for the judicial district in which the Bank in question is established pursuant to section 3 of the Bank Act (12 U.S.C. 1423) for the enforcement of such order, as allowed under § 1375 of the Safety and Soundness Act (12 U.S.C. 4635) . In addition, a Bank or any executive officer or director of a Bank can be subject to enforcement action, including the imposition of civil monetary penalties, under § 1371, § 1372 or § 1376 of the Safety and Soundness Act (12 U.S.C. 4631, 4632, or 4636) for failure to comply with such an order.

(f) *Judicial review.* A Bank that is not classified as critically undercapitalized may obtain judicial review of any final capital classification decision or of any final decision to take supervisory action made by the Director under § 1229.2, § 1229.4, § 1229.7 or § 1229.9 in accordance with the requirements and procedures set forth in § 1369D of the Safety and Soundness Act (12 U.S.C. 4623).

Subpart B—Enterprises

AUTHORITY: 12 U.S.C. 4513b, 4526, 4613, 4614, 4615, 4616, 4617.

SOURCE: 76 FR 35733, June 20, 2011, unless otherwise noted.

§ 1229.13 Definitions.

For purposes of this subpart:

Capital distribution means—

(1) Any dividend or other distribution in cash or in kind made with respect to any shares of, or other ownership interest in, an Enterprise, except a dividend consisting only of shares of the Enterprise;

(2) Any payment made by an Enterprise to repurchase, redeem, retire, or otherwise acquire any of its shares or other ownership interests, including any extension of credit made to finance an acquisition by the Enterprise of such shares or other ownership interests, except to the extent the Enterprise makes a payment to repurchase its shares for the purpose of fulfilling an obligation of the Enterprise under an employee stock ownership plan that is qualified under the Internal Revenue Code of 1986 (26 U.S.C. 401 *et seq.*) or any substantially equivalent plan as determined by the Director of FHFA in writing in advance; and

(3) Any payment of any claim, whether or not reduced to judgment, liquidated or unliquidated, fixed, contingent, matured or unmatured, disputed or undisputed, legal, equitable, secured or unsecured, arising from rescission of a purchase or sale of an equity security of an Enterprise or for damages arising from the purchase, sale, or retention of such a security.

PART 1231—GOLDEN PARACHUTE PAYMENTS

AUTHORITY: 12 U.S.C. 4518(e).

SOURCE: 73 FR 53357, Sept. 16, 2008, unless otherwise noted.

§ 1231.1 Purpose.

The purpose of this part is to implement section 1318(e) of the Act by setting forth the standards that the Director will take into consideration in determining whether to limit or prohibit golden parachute payments to entity-affiliated parties.

[73 FR 54673, Sept. 23, 2008]

§ 1231.2 Definitions.

The following definitions apply to the terms used in this part:

(a) *Act* means the Federal Housing Enterprises Financial Safety and Soundness Act of 1992 (12 U.S.C. 4501 *et seq.*), as amended by the Federal Housing Finance Regulatory Reform Act of 2008, enacted under Division A of the HERA.

(b) *Director* means the Director of FHFA or his or her designee.

(c) *Enterprise* means the Federal National Mortgage Association and the Federal Home Loan Mortgage Corporation (collectively, Enterprises) and, except as provided by the Director, any affiliate thereof.

(d) *Entity-affiliated party* means—

(1) Any director, officer, employee, or controlling stockholder of, or agent for, a regulated entity;

(2) Any shareholder, affiliate, consultant, or joint venture partner of a regulated entity, and any other person, as determined by the Director (by regulation or on a case-by-case basis) that participates in the conduct of the affairs of a regulated entity, provided that a member of a Bank shall not be deemed to have participated in the affairs of that Bank solely by virtue of being a shareholder of, and obtaining advances from, that Bank;

(3) Any independent contractor for a regulated entity (including any attorney, appraiser, or accountant), if—

(i) The independent contractor knowingly or recklessly participates in—

(A) Any violation of any law or regulation;

(B) Any breach of fiduciary duty; or

(C) Any unsafe or unsound practice; and

(ii) Such violation, breach, or practice caused, or is likely to cause, more than a minimal financial loss to, or a significant adverse effect on, the regulated entity;

(4) Any not-for-profit corporation that receives its principal funding, on an ongoing basis, from any regulated entity; and

(5) The Office of Finance.

(e) *Federal Home Loan Bank* means a bank established under the Federal Home Loan Act; the term "Federal Home Loan Banks" means, collectively, all the Federal Home Loan Banks.

(f)(1) *Golden parachute payment* means any payment (or any agreement to make any payment) in the nature of compensation by any regulated entity for the benefit of any current entity-affiliated party pursuant to an obligation of such regulated entity that—

(i) Is contingent on, or by its terms is payable on or after, the termination of such party's primary employment or affiliation with the regulated entity; and

(ii) Is received on or after the date on which—

(A) The regulated entity became insolvent;

(B) Any conservator or receiver is appointed for such regulated entity; or

(C) The Director determines that the regulated entity is in a troubled condition.

(2) The term "golden parachute payment" shall not include:

(i) Any payment made pursuant to a pension or retirement plan which is qualified (or is intended within a reasonable period of time to be qualified) under section 401 of the Internal Revenue Code of 1986 (26 U.S.C. 401) or pursuant to a pension or other retirement plan which is governed by the laws of any foreign country;

(ii) Any payment made pursuant to a bona fide deferred compensation plan or arrangement which the Director determines, by regulation or order, to be permissible; or

(iii) Any payment made by reason of death or by reason of termination caused by the disability of an entity-affiliated party.

(3) Any payment which would be a golden parachute payment but for the fact that such payment was made before the date referred to in paragraph (f)(1)(ii) shall be treated as a golden parachute payment if the payment was made in contemplation of the occurrence of an event described that paragraph.

(g) *FHFA* means the Federal Housing Finance Agency.

(h) *HERA* means the Housing and Economic Recovery Act of 2008, Public Law No. 110–289, 122 Stat. 2654 (July 30, 2008).

(i) *Office of Finance* means the Office of Finance of the Federal Home Loan Bank System (or any successor thereto).

(j) *Regulated entity* means the Federal National Mortgage Association and any affiliate thereof; the Federal Home Loan Mortgage Corporation and any affiliate thereof; or any Federal Home Loan Bank; the term "regulated entities" means, collectively, the Federal National Mortgage Association and any affiliate thereof; the Federal Home Loan Mortgage Corporation and any affiliate thereof; and any Federal Home Loan Bank.

(k) *Troubled condition* means a regulated entity that—

(1) Is subject to a cease-and-desist order or written agreement issued by the FHFA that requires action to improve the financial condition of the regulated entity or is subject to a proceeding initiated by the Director,

which contemplates the issuance of an order that requires action to improve the financial condition of the regulated entity, unless otherwise informed in writing by the FHFA; or

(2) Is informed in writing by the Director that it is in a troubled condition for purposes of the requirements of this part on the basis of the regulated entity's most recent report of examination or other information available to the FHFA.

(l)–(n) [Reserved]

§§ 1231.3—1231.4 [Reserved]

§ 1231.5 Factors to be taken into account.

In determining whether to prohibit or limit any golden parachute payment, the Director shall consider the following factors—

(a) Whether there is a reasonable basis to believe that the entity-affiliated party has committed any fraudulent act or omission, breach of trust or fiduciary duty, or insider abuse with regard to the regulated entity that has had a material effect on the financial condition of the regulated entity;

(b) Whether there is a reasonable basis to believe that the entity-affiliated party is substantially responsible for the insolvency of the regulated entity, the appointment of a conservator or receiver for the regulated entity, or the troubled condition of the regulated entity (as defined in regulations prescribed by the Director);

(c) Whether there is a reasonable basis to believe that the entity-affiliated party has materially violated any applicable provision of Federal or State law or regulation that has had a material effect on the financial condition of the regulated entity;

(d) Whether the entity-affiliated party was in a position of managerial or fiduciary responsibility;

(e) The length of time that the party was affiliated with the regulated entity, and the degree to which the payment reasonably reflects compensation earned over the period of employment and the compensation involved represents a reasonable payment for services rendered; and

(f) Any other factor the Director determines relevant to the facts and circumstances surrounding the golden parachute payment, including any fraudulent act or omission, breach of fiduciary duty, violation of law, rule, regulation, order, or written agreement, and the level of willful misconduct, breach of fiduciary duty, and malfeasance on the part of an entity-affiliated party.

[73 FR 53357, Sept. 16, 2008, as amended at 73 FR 54673, Sept. 23, 2008; 74 FR 5102, Jan. 29, 2009]

PART 1233—REPORTING OF FRAUDULENT FINANCIAL INSTRUMENTS

Sec.

AUTHORITY: 12 U.S.C. 4511, 4513, 4514, 4526, 4642.

SOURCE: 75 FR 4258, Jan. 27, 2010, unless otherwise noted.

§ 1233.1 Purpose.

The purpose of this part is to implement the Safety and Soundness Act by requiring each regulated entity to report to FHFA upon discovery that it has purchased or sold a fraudulent loan or financial instrument, or suspects a possible fraud relating to the purchase or sale of any loan or financial instrument. In addition, each regulated entity must establish and maintain internal controls, policies, procedures, and operational training to discover such transactions.

§ 1233.2 Definitions.

The following definitions apply to the terms used in this part:

Bank or *Federal Home Loan Bank* means a Bank established under the Federal Home Loan Bank Act; the term "Federal Home Loan Banks" means, collectively, all the Federal Home Loan Banks.

Director means the Director of FHFA or his or her designee.

Enterprise means the Federal National Mortgage Association, the Federal Home Loan Mortgage Corporation (collectively, Enterprises), and any affiliate thereof.

Entity-affiliated party means—

(1) Any director, officer, employee, or controlling stockholder of, or agent for, a regulated entity;

(2) Any shareholder, affiliate, consultant, or joint venture partner of a regulated entity, and any other person, as determined by the Director (by regulation or on a case-by-case basis) that participates in the conduct of the affairs of a regulated entity, provided that a member of a Federal Home Loan Bank shall not be deemed to have participated in the affairs of that Federal Home Loan Bank solely by virtue of being a shareholder of, and obtaining advances from, that Federal Home Loan Bank;

(3) Any independent contractor for a regulated entity (including any attorney, appraiser, or accountant);

(4) Any not-for-profit corporation that receives its principal funding, on an ongoing basis, from any regulated entity; and

(5) The Office of Finance.

Financial instrument means any legally enforceable agreement, certificate, or other writing, in hardcopy or electronic form, having monetary value including, but not limited to, any agreement, certificate, or other writing evidencing an asset pledged as collateral to a Bank by a member to secure an advance by the Bank to that member.

Fraud means a misstatement, misrepresentation, or omission that cannot be corrected and that was relied upon by a regulated entity to purchase or sell a loan or financial instrument.

Possible fraud means that a regulated entity has a reasonable belief, based upon a review of information available to the regulated entity, that fraud may be occurring or has occurred.

Purchased or sold or relating to the purchase or sale means any transaction involving a financial instrument including, but not limited to, any purchase, sale, other acquisition, or creation of a financial instrument by the member of a Bank to be pledged as collateral to the Bank to secure an advance by the Bank to that member, the pledging by a member to a Bank of such financial instrument to secure such an advance, the making of a grant by a Bank under its affordable housing program or community investment program, and the effecting of a wire transfer or other form of electronic payments transaction by the Bank.

Regulated entity means the Federal National Mortgage Association and any affiliate thereof, the Federal Home Loan Mortgage Corporation and any affiliate thereof, and any Federal Home Loan Bank; the term "regulated entities" means, collectively, the Federal National Mortgage Association and any affiliate thereof, the Federal Home Loan Mortgage Corporation and any affiliate thereof, and the Federal Home Loan Banks.

Safety and Soundness Act means the Federal Housing Enterprises Financial Safety and Soundness Act of 1992, as amended by the Federal Housing Finance Regulatory Reform Act of 2008, Division A of the Housing and Economic Recovery Act of 2008, Public Law 110–289, 122 Stat. 2654 (2008).

§ 1233.3 Reporting.

(a) *Timeframe for reporting.* (1) A regulated entity shall submit to the Director a timely written report upon discovery by the regulated entity that it has purchased or sold a fraudulent loan or financial instrument, or suspects a possible fraud relating to the purchase or sale of any loan or financial instrument.

(2) In addition to submitting a report in accordance with paragraph (a)(1) of this section, in any situation that would have a significant impact on the regulated entity, the regulated entity shall immediately report any fraud or possible fraud to the Director by telephone or electronic communication.

(b) *Format for reporting.* (1) The report shall be in such format and shall be filed in accordance with such procedures that the Director may prescribe.

(2) The Director may require a regulated entity to provide such additional or continuing information relating to such fraud or possible fraud that the Director deems appropriate.

(3) A regulated entity may satisfy the reporting requirements of this section by submitting the required information on a form or in another format used by any other regulatory agency,

provided it has first obtained the prior written approval of the Director.

(c) *Retention of records.* A regulated entity or entity-affiliated party shall maintain a copy of any report submitted to the Director and the original or business record equivalent of any supporting documentation for a period of five years from the date of submission.

(d) *Nondisclosure.* (1) A regulated entity or entity-affiliated party may not disclose to any person that it has submitted a report to the Director pursuant to this section, unless it has first obtained the prior written approval of the Director.

(2) The restriction in paragraph (d)(1) of this section does not prohibit a regulated entity from—

(i) Disclosing or reporting such fraud or possible fraud pursuant to legal requirements, including reporting to appropriate law enforcement or other governmental authorities; or

(ii) Taking any legal or business action it may deem appropriate, including any action involving the party or parties connected with the fraud or possible fraud.

(e) *No waiver of privilege.* A regulated entity does not waive any privilege it may possess under any applicable law as a consequence of reporting fraud or possible fraud under this part.

§ 1233.4 Internal controls, policies, procedures, and training.

(a) *In general.* Each regulated entity shall establish and maintain adequate and efficient internal controls, policies, procedures, and an operational training program to discover and report fraud or possible fraud in connection with the purchase or sale of any loan or financial instrument.

(b) *Examination.* The examination by FHFA of fraud reporting programs of each regulated entity includes an evaluation of the effectiveness of the internal controls, policies, procedures, and operational training program in place to minimize risks from fraud and to report fraud or possible fraud to FHFA in accordance with this regulation.

§ 1233.5 Protection from liability for reports.

As provided by section 1379E of the Safety and Soundness Act (12 U.S.C. 4642(b)), a regulated entity that, in good faith, submits a report pursuant to this part, and any entity-affiliated party, that, in good faith, submits or requires a person to submit a report pursuant to this part, shall not be liable to any person under any provision of law or regulation, any constitution, law, or regulation of any State or political subdivision of any State, or under any contract or other legally enforceable agreement (including any arbitration agreement) for such report, or for any failure to provide notice of such report to the person who is the subject of such report, or any other persons identified in the report.

§ 1233.6 Supervisory action.

Failure by a regulated entity to comply with this part may subject the regulated entity or the board members, officers, or employees thereof to supervisory action by FHFA, including but not limited to, cease-and-desist proceedings and civil money penalties.

PART 1235—RECORD RETENTION FOR REGULATED ENTITIES AND OFFICE OF FINANCE

Sec.

AUTHORITY: 12 U.S.C. 4511(b), 4513(a), 4513b(a)(10) and (11), 4526.

SOURCE: 76 FR 33127, June 8, 2011, unless otherwise noted.

§ 1235.1 Purpose and scope.

The purpose of this part is to set forth minimum requirements for a record retention program for each regulated entity and the Office of Finance. The requirements are intended to further prudent management as well as to ensure that complete and accurate records of each regulated entity and the Office of Finance are readily accessible to FHFA.

§ 1235.2 Definitions.

For purposes of this part, the term—

Director means the Director of FHFA, or his or her designee.

Electronic record means a record created, generated, communicated, or stored by electronic means.

E-mail means a document created or received on a computer network for transmitting messages electronically, and any attachments which may be transmitted with the document.

Employee means any officer or employee of a regulated entity or the Office of Finance.

Federal Home Loan Bank means a Bank established under the Federal Home Loan Bank Act; the term "Federal Home Loan Banks" means, collectively, all the Federal Home Loan Banks.

FHFA means the Federal Housing Finance Agency.

Financing Corporation means the entity established by the Competitive Equality Banking Act of 1987, as a mixed-ownership government corporation whose purpose is to function as a financing vehicle for the Federal Savings & Loan Insurance Corporation. The Financing Corporation has a board of directors consisting of the managing director of the Office of Finance and two Federal Home Loan Bank presidents.

Office of Finance means the Office of Finance of the Federal Home Loan Bank System.

Record means any information, whether generated internally or received from outside sources by a regulated entity or the Office of Finance, related to the conduct of the business of a regulated entity or the Office of Finance (which business, in the case of the Office of Finance, shall include any functions performed with respect to the Financing Corporation) or to legal or regulatory requirements, regardless of the following—

(1) Form or format, including hard copy documents (*e.g.*, files, logs, and reports), electronic documents (*e.g.*, e-mail, databases, spreadsheets, PowerPoint presentations, electronic reporting systems, electronic tapes and back-up tapes, optical discs, CD–ROMS, and DVDs), and voicemail or recorded telephone line records;

(2) Where the information is stored or located, including network servers, desktop or laptop computers and handheld computers, other wireless devices with text messaging capabilities, and on-site or off-site at a storage facility;

(3) Whether the information is maintained or used on regulated entity or Office of Finance equipment, or on personal or home computer systems of an employee; or

(4) Whether the information is active or inactive.

Record hold means a requirement, an order, or a directive from a regulated entity, the Office of Finance, or FHFA that the regulated entity or the Office of Finance is to retain records relating to a particular issue in connection with an actual or a potential FHFA examination, investigation, enforcement proceeding, or litigation of which the regulated entity or the Office of Finance has received notice from FHFA or otherwise has knowledge.

Record retention schedule means a schedule that details the categories of records a regulated entity or the Office of Finance is required to retain and the corresponding retention periods. The record retention schedule includes all media, such as microfilm and machine-readable computer records, for each record category.

Regulated entity means the Federal National Mortgage Association and any affiliate thereof, the Federal Home Loan Mortgage Corporation and any affiliate thereof, or any Federal Home Loan Bank; the term "regulated entities" means, collectively, the Federal National Mortgage Association and any affiliate thereof, the Federal Home Loan Mortgage Corporation and any affiliate thereof, and the Federal Home Loan Banks.

Retention period means the length of time that records must be kept before they are destroyed, as determined by the organization's record retention schedule. Records not authorized for destruction have a retention period of "permanent."

Safety and Soundness Act means the Federal Housing Enterprises Financial

Safety and Soundness Act of 1992 (12 U.S.C. 4501 *et seq.*), as amended.

§ 1235.3 Establishment and evaluation of a record retention program.

(a) *Establishment.* Each regulated entity and the Office of Finance shall establish and maintain a written record retention program and provide a copy of such program to the Deputy Director of the Division of Enterprise Regulation, or his or her designee, or the Deputy Director for the Division of Federal Home Loan Bank Regulation, or his or her designee, as appropriate, within 180 days of the effective date of this part, and annually thereafter, and whenever a significant revision to the program has been made.

(b) *Evaluation.* Management of each regulated entity and the Office of Finance shall evaluate in writing the adequacy and effectiveness of the record retention program at least every two years and provide a copy of the evaluation to the board of directors and the Director.

§ 1235.4 Minimum requirements of a record retention program.

(a) *General minimum requirements.* The record retention program established and maintained by each regulated entity and the Office of Finance under § 1235.3 shall:

(1) Assure that retained records are complete and accurate;

(2) Assure that the form of retained records and the retention period—

(i) Are appropriate to support administrative, business, external and internal audit functions, and litigation of the regulated entity or the Office of Finance; and

(ii) Comply with requirements of applicable laws and regulations, including this part;

(3) Assign in writing the authorities and responsibilities for record retention activities for employees, including line managers and corporate management;

(4) Include policies and procedures concerning record holds, consistent with § 1235.5, and, as appropriate, integrate them with policies and procedures throughout the organization;

(5) Include an accurate, current, and comprehensive record retention schedule that lists records by major categories, subcategories, record type, and retention period, which retention period is appropriate to the specific record and consistent with applicable legal, regulatory, fiscal, operational, and business requirements;

(6) Include appropriate security and internal controls to protect records from unauthorized access and data alteration;

(7) Provide for appropriate back-up and recovery of electronic records to ensure the same accuracy as the primary records;

(8) Provide for a periodic testing of the ability to access records; and

(9) Provide for the proper disposition of records.

(b) *Minimum storage requirements for electronic records.* Electronic records, preferably searchable, must be maintained on immutable, non-rewritable storage in a manner that provides for both ready access by any person who is entitled to access the records, including staff of FHFA, and accurate reproduction for later reference by transmission, printing or other means.

(c) *Communication and training.* (1) The record retention program established and maintained by each regulated entity and the Office of Finance under § 1235.3 shall provide for periodic training and communication throughout the organization.

(2) The record retention program shall:

(i) Provide for communication throughout the organization on record retention policies, procedures, and record retention schedule updates; and

(ii) Provide for training of and notice to all employees on a periodic basis on their record retention responsibilities, including instruction regarding penalties provided by law for the unlawful removal or destruction of records. The record retention program also shall provide for training for the agents or independent contractors of a regulated entity or the Office of Finance, as appropriate, consistent with their respective roles and responsibilities to the regulated entity or the Office of Finance.

§ 1235.5 Record hold.

(a) *Notification by FHFA.* In the event that FHFA is requiring a record hold, FHFA shall notify the chief executive officer of the regulated entity or the Office of Finance. Regulated entities and the Office of Finance must have a written policy for handling notice of a record hold.

(b) *Notification by a regulated entity or the Office of Finance.* The record retention program of a regulated entity and the Office of Finance shall—

(1) Address how employees and, as appropriate, how agents or independent contractors consistent with their respective roles and responsibilities to the regulated entity or the Office of Finance, will receive prompt notification of a record hold;

(2) Designate an individual to communicate specific requirements and instructions, including, when necessary, the instruction to cease immediately any otherwise permissible destruction of records; and

(3) Provide that any employee and, as appropriate, any agent or independent contractor consistent with his or her respective role and responsibility to the regulated entity or Office of Finance, who has received notice of a potential investigation, enforcement proceeding, or litigation by FHFA involving the regulated entity or the Office of Finance or an employee, or otherwise has actual knowledge that an issue is subject to such an investigation, enforcement proceeding or litigation, shall notify immediately the legal department or the individual providing legal services as well as senior management of the regulated entity or the Office of Finance and shall retain any records that may be relevant in any way to such investigation, enforcement proceeding, or litigation.

(c) *Method of record retention during a record hold.* The record retention program of each regulated entity and the Office of Finance shall address the method by which the regulated entity or the Office of Finance will retain records during a record hold. Specifically, the program shall describe the method for the continued preservation of electronic records, including e-mail, and, as applicable, the conversion of records from paper to electronic form as well as any alternative storage method.

(d) *Access to and retrieval of records during a record hold.* The record retention program of each regulated entity or the Office of Finance shall ensure access to and retrieval of records by the regulated entity and the Office of Finance, and access, upon request, by FHFA, during a record hold. Such access shall be by reasonable means, consistent with the nature and availability of the records and existing information technology.

§ 1235.6 Access to records.

Each regulated entity and the Office of Finance shall make its records available promptly upon request by FHFA, at a location and in a form and manner acceptable to FHFA.

§ 1235.7 Supervisory action.

(a) *Supervisory action.* Failure by a regulated entity or the Office of Finance to comply with this part may subject the regulated entity or the Office of Finance or the board members, officers, or employees thereof to supervisory action by FHFA under the Safety and Soundness Act, including but not limited to cease-and-desist proceedings, temporary cease-and-desist proceedings, and civil money penalties.

(b) *No limitation of authority.* This part does not limit or restrict the authority of FHFA to act under its safety and soundness mandate, in accordance with the Safety and Soundness Act. Such authority includes, but is not limited to, conducting examinations, requiring reports and disclosures, and enforcing compliance with applicable laws, rules, and regulations.

PART 1237—CONSERVATORSHIP AND RECEIVERSHIP

Sec.

Subpart A—Powers

AUTHORITY: 12 U.S.C. 4513b, 4526, 4617.

SOURCE: 76 FR 35733, June 20, 2011, unless otherwise noted.

§ 1237.1 Purpose and applicability.

The provisions of this part shall apply to the appointment and operations of the Federal Housing Finance Agency ("Agency") as conservator or receiver of a regulated entity. These provisions implement and supplement the procedures and process set forth in the Federal Housing Enterprises Financial Safety and Soundness Act of 1992, as amended, by the Housing and Economic Recovery Act of 2008 (HERA), Public Law 110–289 for conduct of a conservatorship or receivership of such entity.

§ 1237.2 Definitions.

For the purposes of this part the following definitions shall apply:

Agency means the Federal Housing Finance Agency ("FHFA") established under 12 U.S.C. 4511, as amended.

Authorizing statutes mean—

(1) The Federal National Mortgage Association Charter Act,

(2) The Federal Home Loan Mortgage Corporation Act, and

(3) The Federal Home Loan Bank Act.

Capital distribution has, with respect to a Bank, the definition stated in § 1229.1 of this chapter, and with respect to an Enterprise, the definition stated in § 1229.13 of this chapter.

Compensation means any payment of money or the provision of any other thing of current or potential value in connection with employment.

Conservator means the Agency as appointed by the Director as conservator for a regulated entity.

Default; in danger of default:

(1) *Default* means, with respect to a regulated entity, any official determination by the Director, pursuant to which a conservator or receiver is appointed for a regulated entity.

(2) *In danger of default* means, with respect to a regulated entity, the definition under section 1303(8)(B) of the Safety and Soundness Act or applicable FHFA regulations.

Director means the Director of the Federal Housing Finance Agency.

Enterprise means the Federal National Mortgage Association and any affiliate thereof or the Federal Home Loan Mortgage Corporation and any affiliate thereof.

Entity-affiliated party means any party meeting the definition of an entity-affiliated party under section 1303(11) of the Safety and Soundness Act or applicable FHFA regulations.

Equity security of any person shall mean any and all shares, interests, rights to purchase or otherwise acquire, warrants, options, participations or other equivalents of or interests (however designated) in equity, ownership or profits of such person, including any preferred stock, any limited or general partnership interest and any limited liability company membership interest, and any securities or other rights or interests convertible into or exchangeable for any of the foregoing.

Executive officer means, with respect to an Enterprise, any person meeting the definition of executive officer under section 1303(12) of the Safety and Soundness Act and applicable FHFA regulations under that section, and, with respect to a Bank, an executive officer as defined in applicable FHFA regulations.

Golden parachute payment means, with respect to a regulated entity, the definition under 12 CFR part 1231 or other applicable FHFA regulations.

Limited-life regulated entity means an entity established by the Agency under section 1367(i) of the Safety and Soundness Act with respect to a Federal Home Loan Bank in default or in danger of default, or with respect to an Enterprise in default or in danger of default.

Receiver means the Agency as appointed by the Director to act as receiver for a regulated entity.

Regulated entity means:

(1) The Federal National Mortgage Association and any affiliate thereof;

(2) The Federal Home Loan Mortgage Corporation and any affiliate thereof; and

(3) Any Federal Home Loan Bank.

Securities litigation claim means any claim, whether or not reduced to judgment, liquidated or unliquidated, fixed, contingent, matured or unmatured, disputed or undisputed, legal, equitable, secured or unsecured, arising from rescission of a purchase or sale of an equity security of a regulated entity or for damages arising from the purchase, sale, or retention of such a security.

Transfer means every mode, direct or indirect, absolute or conditional, voluntary or involuntary, of disposing of or parting with property or with an interest in property, including retention of title as a security interest and foreclosure of the equity of redemption of the regulated entity.

Subpart A—Powers

§ 1237.3 Powers of the Agency as conservator or receiver.

(a) *Operation of the regulated entity*. The Agency, as it determines appropriate to its operations as either conservator or receiver, may:

(1) Take over the assets of and operate the regulated entity with all the powers of the shareholders (including the authority to vote shares of any and all classes of voting stock), the directors, and the officers of the regulated entity and conduct all business of the regulated entity;

(2) Continue the missions of the regulated entity;

(3) Ensure that the operations and activities of each regulated entity foster liquid, efficient, competitive, and resilient national housing finance markets;

(4) Ensure that each regulated entity operates in a safe and sound manner;

(5) Collect all obligations and money due the regulated entity;

(6) Perform all functions of the regulated entity in the name of the regulated entity that are consistent with the appointment as conservator or receiver;

(7) Preserve and conserve the assets and property of the regulated entity (including the exclusive authority to investigate and prosecute claims of any type on behalf of the regulated entity, or to delegate to management of the regulated entity the authority to investigate and prosecute claims); and

(8) Provide by contract for assistance in fulfilling any function, activity, action, or duty of the Agency as conservator or receiver.

(b) *Agency as receiver*. The Agency, as receiver, shall place the regulated entity in liquidation, employing the additional powers expressed in 12 U.S.C. 4617(b)(2)(E).

(c) *Powers as conservator or receiver*. The Agency, as conservator or receiver, shall have all powers and authorities specifically provided by section 1367 of the Safety and Soundness Act and paragraph (a) of this section, including incidental powers, which include the authority to suspend capital classifications under section 1364(e)(1) of the Safety and Soundness Act during the duration of the conservatorship or receivership of that regulated entity.

(d) *Transfer or sale of assets and liabilities*. The Agency may, as conservator or receiver, transfer or sell any asset or liability of the regulated entity in default, and may do so without any approval, assignment, or consent with respect to such transfer or sale. Exercise of this authority by the Agency as conservator will nullify any restraints on sales or transfers in any agreement not entered into by the Agency as conservator. Exercise of this authority by the Agency as receiver will nullify any restraints on sales or transfers in any agreement not entered into by the Agency as receiver.

§ 1237.4 Receivership following conservatorship; administrative expenses.

If a receivership immediately succeeds a conservatorship, the administrative expenses of the conservatorship shall also be deemed to be administrative expenses of the subsequent receivership.

§ 1237.5 Contracts entered into before appointment of a conservator or receiver.

(a) The conservator or receiver for any regulated entity may disaffirm or repudiate any contract or lease to which such regulated entity is a party pursuant to section 1367(d) of the Safety and Soundness Act.

(b) For purposes of section 1367(d)(2) of the Safety and Soundness Act, a reasonable period shall be defined as a period of 18 months following the appointment of a conservator or receiver.

§ 1237.6 Authority to enforce contracts.

The conservator or receiver may enforce any contract entered into by the regulated entity pursuant to the provisions and subject to the restrictions of section 1367(d)(13) of the Safety and Soundness Act.

Subpart B—Claims

§ 1237.7 Period for determination of claims.

Before the end of the 180-day period beginning on the date on which any claim against a regulated entity is filed with the Agency as receiver, the Agency shall determine whether to allow or disallow the claim and shall notify the claimant of any determination with respect to such claim. This period may be extended by a written agreement between the claimant and the Agency as receiver, which may include an agreement to toll any applicable statute of limitations.

§ 1237.8 Alternate procedures for determination of claims.

Claimants seeking a review of the determination of claims may seek alternative dispute resolution from the Agency as receiver in lieu of a judicial determination. The Director may by order, policy statement, or directive establish alternative dispute resolution procedures for this purpose.

§ 1237.9 Priority of expenses and unsecured claims.

(a) *General.* The receiver will grant priority to unsecured claims against a regulated entity or the receiver for that regulated entity that are proven to the satisfaction of the receiver in the following order:

(1) Administrative expenses of the receiver (or an immediately preceding conservator).

(2) Any other general or senior liability of the regulated entity (that is not a liability described under paragraph (a)(3) or (a)(4) of this section).

(3) Any obligation subordinated to general creditors (that is not an obligation described under paragraph (a)(4) of this section).

(4) Any claim by current or former shareholders or members arising as a result of their current or former status as shareholders or members, including, without limitation, any securities litigation claim. Within this priority level, the receiver shall recognize the priorities of shareholder claims *inter se*, such as that preferred shareholder claims are prior to common shareholder claims. This subparagraph (a)(4) shall not apply to any claim by a current or former member of a Federal Home Loan Bank that arises from transactions or relationships distinct from the current or former member's ownership, purchase, sale, or retention of an equity security of the Federal Home Loan Bank.

(b) *Similarly situated creditors.* All claimants that are similarly situated shall be treated in a similar manner, except that the receiver may take any action (including making payments) that does not comply with this section, if:

(1) The Director determines that such action is necessary to maximize the value of the assets of the regulated entity, to maximize the present value return from the sale or other disposition of the assets of the regulated entity, or to minimize the amount of any loss realized upon the sale or other disposition of the assets of the regulated entity; and

(2) All claimants that are similarly situated under paragraph (a) of this section receive not less than the amount such claimants would have received if the receiver liquidated the assets and liabilities of the regulated entity in receivership and such action had not been taken.

(c) *Priority determined at default.* The receiver will determine priority based on a claim's status at the time of default, such default having occurred at the time of entry into the receivership, or if a conservatorship immediately preceded the receivership, at the time of entry into the conservatorship provided the claim then existed.

Subpart C—Limited-Life Regulated Entities

§ 1237.10 Limited-life regulated entities.

(a) *Status.* The United States Government shall be considered a person for purposes of section 1367(i)(6)(C)(i) of the Safety and Soundness Act.

(b) *Investment authority.* The requirements of section 1367(i)(4) shall apply only to the liquidity portfolio of a limited-life regulated entity.

(c) *Policies and procedures.* The Agency may draft such policies and procedures with respect to limited-life regulated entities as it determines to be necessary and appropriate, including policies and procedures regarding the timing of the creation of limited-life regulated entities.

§ 1237.11 Authority of limited-life regulated entities to obtain credit.

(a) *Ability to obtain credit.* A limited-life regulated entity may obtain unsecured credit and issue unsecured debt.

(b) *Inability to obtain credit.* If a limited-life regulated entity is unable to obtain unsecured credit or issue unsecured debt, the Director may authorize the obtaining of credit or the issuance of debt by the limited-life regulated entity with priority over any and all of the obligations of the limited-life regulated entity, secured by a lien on property of the limited-life regulated entity that is not otherwise subject to a lien, or secured by a junior lien on property of the limited-life regulated entity that is subject to a lien.

(c) *Limitations.* The Director, after notice and a hearing, may authorize a limited-life regulated entity to obtain credit or issue debt that is secured by a senior or equal lien on property of the limited-life regulated entity that is already subject to a lien (other than mortgages that collateralize the mortgage-backed securities issued or guaranteed by an Enterprise) only if the limited-life regulated entity is unable to obtain such credit or issue such debt otherwise on commercially reasonable terms and there is adequate protection of the interest of the holder of the earlier lien on the property with respect to which such senior or equal lien is proposed to be granted.

(d) *Adequate protection.* The adequate protection referred to in paragraph (c) of this section may be provided by:

(1) Requiring the limited-life regulated entity to make a cash payment or periodic cash payments to the holder of the earlier lien, to the extent that there is likely to be a decrease in the value of such holder's interest in the property subject to the lien;

(2) Providing to the holder of the earlier lien an additional or replacement lien to the extent that there is likely to be a decrease in the value of such holder's interest in the property subject to the lien; or

(3) Granting the holder of the earlier lien such other relief, other than entitling such holder to compensation allowable as an administrative expense under section 1367(c) of the Safety and Soundness Act, as will result in the realization by such holder of the equivalent of such holder's interest in such property.

Subpart D—Other

§ 1237.12 Capital distributions while in conservatorship.

(a) Except as provided in paragraph (b) of this section, a regulated entity shall make no capital distribution while in conservatorship.

(b) The Director may authorize, or may delegate the authority to authorize, a capital distribution that would otherwise be prohibited by paragraph (a) of this section if he or she determines that such capital distribution:

(1) Will enhance the ability of the regulated entity to meet the risk-based capital level and the minimum capital level for the regulated entity;

(2) Will contribute to the long-term financial safety and soundness of the regulated entity;

(3) Is otherwise in the interest of the regulated entity; or

(4) Is otherwise in the public interest.

(c) This section is intended to supplement and shall not replace or affect any other restriction on capital distributions imposed by statute or regulation.

§ 1237.13 Payment of Securities Litigation Claims while in conservatorship.

(a) *Payment of Securities Litigation Claims while in conservatorship.* The Agency, as conservator, will not pay a Securities Litigation Claim against a regulated entity, except to the extent the Director determines is in the interest of the conservatorship.

(b) *Claims against limited-life regulated entities.* A limited-life regulated entity shall not assume, acquire, or succeed to any obligation that a regulated entity for which a receiver has been appointed may have to any shareholder of the regulated entity that arises as a result of the status of that person as a shareholder of the regulated entity, including any Securities Litigation Claim. No creditor of the regulated entity shall have a claim against a limited-life regulated entity unless the receiver has transferred that liability to the limited-life regulated entity. The charter of the regulated entity, or of the limited-life regulated entity, is not an asset against which any claim can be made by any creditor or shareholder of the regulated entity.

§ 1237.14 Golden parachute payments. [Reserved]

SUBCHAPTER C—ENTERPRISES

PART 1249—BOOK-ENTRY PROCEDURES

AUTHORITY: 12 U.S.C. 4501, 4502, 4511, 4513, 4526.

SOURCE: 75 FR 55928, Sept. 14, 2010, unless otherwise noted.

§ 1249.10 Definitions.

(a) *General.* Unless the context requires otherwise, terms used in this part that are not defined in this part, have the meanings as set forth in 31 CFR 357.2 and in 12 CFR 1282.1. Definitions and terms used in 31 CFR part 357 should read as though modified to effectuate their application to the Enterprises.

(b) *Other terms.* As used in this part, the term:

Book-entry Enterprise Security means an Enterprise Security issued or maintained in the Book-entry System. Book-entry Enterprise Security also means the separate interest and principal components of a Book-entry Enterprise Security if such security has been designated by the Enterprise as eligible for division into such components and the components are maintained separately on the books of one or more Federal Reserve Banks.

Book-entry System means the automated book-entry system operated by the Federal Reserve Banks acting as the fiscal agent for the Enterprises, on which Book-entry Enterprise Securities are issued, recorded, transferred and maintained in book-entry form.

Definitive Enterprise Security means an Enterprise Security in engraved or printed form, or that is otherwise represented by a certificate.

Eligible Book-entry Enterprise Security means a Book-entry Enterprise Security issued or maintained in the Book-entry System which by the terms of its Securities Documentation is eligible to be converted from book-entry form into definitive form.

Enterprise Security means any security or obligation of Fannie Mae or Freddie Mac issued under its respective Charter Act in the form of a Definitive Enterprise Security or a Book-entry Enterprise Security.

Entitlement Holder means a Person or an Enterprise to whose account an interest in a Book-entry Enterprise Security is credited on the records of a Securities Intermediary.

Federal Reserve Bank Operating Circular means the publication issued by each Federal Reserve Bank that sets forth the terms and conditions under which the Reserve Bank maintains Book-entry Securities accounts (including Book-entry Enterprise Securities) and transfers Book-entry Securities (including Book-entry Enterprise Securities).

Participant means a Person or Enterprise that maintains a Participant's Securities Account with a Federal Reserve Bank.

Person, as used in this part, means and includes an individual, corporation, company, governmental entity, association, firm, partnership, trust, estate, representative, and any other similar organization, but does not mean or include the United States, an Enterprise, or a Federal Reserve Bank.

Revised Article 8 has the same meaning as in 31 CFR 357.2.

Securities Documentation means the applicable statement of terms, trust indenture, securities agreement or other documents establishing the terms of a Book-entry Enterprise Security.

Security means any mortgage participation certificate, note, bond, debenture, evidence of indebtedness, collateral-trust certificate, transferable share, certificate of deposit for a security, or, in general, any interest or instrument commonly known as a "security".

Transfer message means an instruction of a Participant to a Federal Reserve Bank to effect a transfer of a Book-entry Security (including a Book-entry Enterprise Security) maintained in the Book-entry System, as set forth in Federal Reserve Bank Operating Circulars.

§ 1249.11 Maintenance of Enterprise Securities.

An Enterprise Security may be maintained in the form of a Definitive Enterprise Security or a Book-entry Enterprise Security. A Book-entry Enterprise Security shall be maintained in the Book-entry System.

§ 1249.12 Law governing rights and obligations of United States, Federal Reserve Banks, and Enterprises; rights of any person against United States, Federal Reserve Banks, and Enterprises; law governing other interests.

(a) Except as provided in paragraph (b) of this section, the following rights and obligations are governed solely by the book-entry regulations contained in this part, the Securities Documentation, and Federal Reserve Bank Operating Circulars (but not including any choice of law provisions in the Securities Documentation to the extent such provisions conflict with the Book-entry regulations contained in this part):

(1) The rights and obligations of an Enterprise and the Federal Reserve Banks with respect to:

(i) A Book-entry Enterprise Security or Security Entitlement; and

(ii) The operation of the Book-entry System as it applies to Enterprise Securities; and

(2) The rights of any Person, including a Participant, against an Enterprise and the Federal Reserve Banks with respect to:

(i) A Book-entry Enterprise Security or Security Entitlement; and

(ii) The operation of the Book-entry System as it applies to Enterprise Securities;

(b) A security interest in a Security Entitlement that is in favor of a Federal Reserve Bank from a Participant and that is not recorded on the books of a Federal Reserve Bank pursuant to §1249.13(c)(1), is governed by the law (not including the conflict-of-law rules) of the jurisdiction where the head office of the Federal Reserve Bank maintaining the Participant's Securities Account is located. A security interest in a Security Entitlement that is in favor of a Federal Reserve Bank from a Person that is not a Participant, and that is not recorded on the books of a Federal Reserve Bank pursuant to §1249.13(c)(1), is governed by the law determined in the manner specified in paragraph (d) of this section.

(c) If the jurisdiction specified in the first sentence of paragraph (b) of this section is a State that has not adopted Revised Article 8, then the law specified in paragraph (b) of this section shall be the law of that State as though Revised Article 8 had been adopted by that State.

(d) To the extent not otherwise inconsistent with this part, and notwithstanding any provision in the Securities Documentation setting forth a choice of law, the provisions set forth in 31 CFR 357.11 regarding law governing other interests apply and shall be read as though modified to effectuate the application of 31 CFR 357.11 to the Enterprises.

§ 1249.13 Creation of Participant's Security Entitlement; security interests.

(a) A Participant's Security Entitlement is created when a Federal Reserve Bank indicates by book-entry that a Book-entry Enterprise Security has been credited to a Participant's Securities Account.

(b) A security interest in a Security Entitlement of a Participant in favor of the United States to secure deposits of public money, including without limitation deposits to the Treasury tax and loan accounts, or other security interest in favor of the United States that is required by Federal statute, regulation, or agreement, and that is marked on the books of a Federal Reserve Bank is thereby effected and perfected, and has priority over any other interest in the securities. Where a security interest in favor of the United States in a Security Entitlement of a Participant is marked on the books of a Federal Reserve Bank, such Federal Reserve Bank may rely, and is protected in relying, exclusively on the order of an authorized representative of the United States directing the transfer of the security. For purposes of this paragraph, an "authorized representative of the United States" is the official designated in the applicable regulations or agreement to which a Federal Reserve Bank is a party, governing the security interest.

(c)(1) An Enterprise and the Federal Reserve Banks have no obligation to agree to act on behalf of any Person or to recognize the interest of any transferee of a security interest or other limited interest in favor of any Person except to the extent of any specific requirement of Federal law or regulation or to the extent set forth in any specific agreement with the Federal Reserve Bank on whose books the interest of the Participant is recorded. To the extent required by such law or regulation or set forth in an agreement with a Federal Reserve Bank, or the Federal Reserve Bank Operating Circular, a security interest in a Security Entitlement that is in favor of a Federal Reserve Bank, an Enterprise, or a Person may be created and perfected by a Federal Reserve Bank marking its books to record the security interest. Except as provided in paragraph (b) of this section, a security interest in a Security Entitlement marked on the books of a Federal Reserve Bank shall have priority over any other interest in the securities.

(2) In addition to the method provided in paragraph (c)(1) of this section, a security interest, including a security interest in favor of a Federal Reserve Bank, may be perfected by any method by which a security interest may be perfected under applicable law as described in § 1249.12(b) or (d). The perfection, effect of perfection or nonperfection and priority of a security interest are governed by such applicable law. A security interest in favor of a Federal Reserve Bank shall be treated as a security interest in favor of a clearing corporation in all respects under such law, including with respect to the effect of perfection and priority of such security interest. A Federal Reserve Bank Operating Circular shall be treated as a rule adopted by a clearing corporation for such purposes.

§ 1249.14 Obligations of Enterprises; no adverse claims.

(a) Except in the case of a security interest in favor of the United States or a Federal Reserve Bank or otherwise as provided in § 1249.13(c)(1), for the purposes of this part, each Enterprise and the Federal Reserve Banks shall treat the Participant to whose Securities Account an interest in a Book-entry Enterprise Security has been credited as the person exclusively entitled to issue a Transfer Message, to receive interest and other payments with respect thereof and otherwise to exercise all the rights and powers with respect to such Security, notwithstanding any information or notice to the contrary. Neither the Federal Reserve Banks nor an Enterprise shall be liable to a Person asserting or having an adverse claim to a Security Entitlement or to a Book-entry Enterprise Security in a Participant's Securities Account, including any such claim arising as a result of the transfer or disposition of a Book-entry Enterprise Security by a Federal Reserve Bank pursuant to a Transfer Message that the Federal Reserve Bank reasonably believes to be genuine.

(b) The obligation of the Enterprise to make payments (including payments of interest and principal) with respect to Book-entry Enterprise Securities is discharged at the time payment in the appropriate amount is made as follows:

(1) Interest or other payments on Book-entry Enterprise Securities is either credited by a Federal Reserve Bank to a Funds Account maintained at such Federal Reserve Bank or otherwise paid as directed by the Participant.

(2) Book-entry Enterprise Securities are redeemed in accordance with their terms by a Federal Reserve Bank withdrawing the securities from the Participant's Securities Account in which

they are maintained and by either crediting the amount of the redemption proceeds, including both redemption proceeds, where applicable, to a Funds Account at such Federal Reserve Bank or otherwise paying such redemption proceeds as directed by the Participant. No action by the Participant ordinarily is required in connection with the redemption of a Book-entry Enterprise Security.

§ 1249.15 Authority of Federal Reserve Banks.

(a) Each Federal Reserve Bank is hereby authorized as fiscal agent of the Enterprises to perform the following functions with respect to the issuance of Book-entry Enterprise Securities offered and sold by an Enterprise to which this part applies, in accordance with the Securities Documentation, Federal Reserve Bank Operating Circulars, this part, and any procedures established by the Director consistent with these authorities:

(1) To service and maintain Book-entry Enterprise Securities in accounts established for such purposes;

(2) To make payments with respect to such securities, as directed by the Enterprise;

(3) To effect transfer of Book-entry Enterprise Securities between Participants' Securities Accounts as directed by the Participants;

(4) To effect conversions between Book-entry Enterprise Securities and Definitive Enterprise Securities with respect to those securities as to which conversion rights are available pursuant to the applicable Securities Documentation; and

(5) To perform such other duties as fiscal agent as may be requested by the Enterprise.

(b) Each Federal Reserve Bank may issue Federal Reserve Bank Operating Circulars not inconsistent with this part, governing the details of its handling of Book-entry Enterprise Securities, Security Entitlements, and the operation of the Book-entry System under this part.

§ 1249.16 Withdrawal of Eligible Book-entry Enterprise Securities for conversion to definitive form.

(a) Eligible Book-entry Enterprise Securities may be withdrawn from the Book-entry System by requesting delivery of like Definitive Enterprise Securities.

(b) A Federal Reserve Bank shall, upon receipt of appropriate instructions to withdraw Eligible Book-entry Enterprise Securities from book-entry in the Book-entry System, convert such securities into Definitive Enterprise Securities and deliver them in accordance with such instructions. No such conversion shall affect existing interests in such Enterprise Securities.

(c) All requests for withdrawal of Eligible Book-entry Enterprise Securities must be made prior to the maturity or date of call of the securities.

(d) Enterprise Securities which are to be delivered upon withdrawal may be issued in either registered or bearer form, to the extent permitted by the applicable Securities Documentation.

§ 1249.17 Waiver of regulations.

The Director reserves the right, in the Director's discretion, to waive any provision(s) of this part in any case or class of cases for the convenience of an Enterprise, the United States, or in order to relieve any person(s) of unnecessary hardship, if such action is not inconsistent with law, does not adversely affect any substantial existing rights, and the Director is satisfied that such action will not subject an Enterprise or the United States to any substantial expense or liability.

§ 1249.18 Liability of Enterprises and Federal Reserve Banks.

An Enterprise and the Federal Reserve Banks may rely on the information provided in a Transfer Message, and are not required to verify the information. An Enterprise and the Federal Reserve Banks shall not be liable for any action taken in accordance with the information set out in a Transfer Message, or evidence submitted in support thereof.

§ 1249.19 Additional provisions.

(a) *Additional requirements.* In any case or any class of cases arising under this part, an Enterprise may require such additional evidence and a bond of indemnity, with or without surety, as may in the judgment of the Enterprise be necessary for the protection of the interests of the Enterprise.

(b) *Notice of attachment for Enterprise Securities in Book-entry System.* The interest of a debtor in a Security Entitlement may be reached by a creditor only by legal process upon the Securities Intermediary with whom the debtor's securities account is maintained, except where a Security Entitlement is maintained in the name of a secured party, in which case the debtor's interest may be reached by legal process upon the secured party. These regulations do not purport to establish whether a Federal Reserve Bank is required to honor an order or other notice of attachment in any particular case or class of cases.

PART 1250—FLOOD INSURANCE

Sec.

AUTHORITY: 12 U.S.C. 4521(a)(4) and 4526; 28 U.S.C. 2461 note; 42 U.S.C. 4001 note; 42 U.S.C. 4012a(f)(3), (4), (5), (8), (9), and (10).

SOURCE: 74 FR 2349, Jan. 15, 2009, unless otherwise noted.

§ 1250.1 Purpose.

The purpose of this part is to set forth the responsibilities of the Federal National Mortgage Association and the Federal Home Loan Mortgage Corporation (collectively, Enterprises) under the Flood Disaster Protection Act of 1973 (FDPA), as amended (42 U.S.C. 4002 *et seq.*) and the procedures to be used by the Federal Housing Finance Agency (FHFA) in any proceeding to assess civil money penalties against an Enterprise.

§ 1250.2 Procedural requirements.

(a) *Procedures.* An Enterprise shall implement procedures reasonably designed to ensure for any loan that is secured by improved real estate or a mobile home located in an area that has been identified, at the time of the origination of the loan or at any time during the term of the loan, by the Director of the Federal Emergency Management Agency as an area having special flood hazards and in which flood insurance is available under the National Flood Insurance Act of 1968 (42 U.S.C. 4001 *et seq.*), as amended and purchased by the Enterprise, the building or mobile home and any personal property securing the loan is covered for the term of the loan by flood insurance in an amount at least equal to the lesser of the outstanding principal balance of the loan or the maximum limit of coverage made available with respect to the particular type of property under the National Flood Insurance Act of 1968, as amended.

(b) *Applicability.* (1) Paragraph (a) of this section shall apply only with respect to any loan made, increased, extended, or renewed after September 22, 1995.

(2) Paragraph (a) of this section shall not apply to any loan having an original outstanding balance of $5,000 or less and a repayment term of one year or less.

§ 1250.3 Civil money penalties.

(a) *In general.* If an Enterprise is determined by the Director of FHFA, or his or her designee, to have a pattern or practice of purchasing loans in violation of the procedures established pursuant to § 1250.2, the Director of FHFA, or his or her designee, may assess civil money penalties against such Enterprise in such amount or amounts as deemed to be appropriate under paragraph (c) of this section.

(b) *Notice and hearing.* A civil money penalty under this section may be assessed only after notice and an opportunity for a hearing on the record has been provided to the Enterprise.

(c) *Amount.* The maximum civil money penalty amount is $385 for each violation that occurs before the effective date of this part, with total penalties not to exceed $110,000. For violations that occur on or after the effective date of this part, the civil money penalty under this section may not exceed $485 for each violation, with total penalties assessed under this section against an Enterprise during any calendar year not to exceed $140,000.

(d) *Deposit of penalties.* Any penalties under this section shall be paid into the National Flood Mitigation Fund in accordance with section 1367 of the National Flood Insurance Act of 1968 (42 U.S.C. 4104d.), as amended.

(e) *Additional penalties.* Any penalty under this section shall be in addition to, and shall not preclude, any civil remedy, or criminal penalty otherwise available.

(f) *Statute of limitations.* No civil money penalty may be imposed under this section after the expiration of the four-year period beginning on the date of the occurrence of the violation for which the penalty is authorized under this section.

PART 1252—PORTFOLIO HOLDINGS

Sec.

AUTHORITY: 12 U.S.C. 4624.

SOURCE: 74 FR 5618, Jan. 30, 2009, unless otherwise noted.

§ 1252.1 Enterprise portfolio holding criteria.

The Enterprises are required to comply with the portfolio holdings criteria set forth in their respective Senior Preferred Stock Purchase Agreements with the Department of the Treasury, as they may be amended from time to time.

§ 1252.2 Effective duration.

This part shall be in effect for each Enterprise so long as—

(a) This part has not been superseded through amendment, and

(b) The Enterprise remains subject to the terms and obligations of the respective Senior Preferred Stock Purchase Agreement.

PART 1253—PRIOR APPROVAL FOR ENTERPRISE PRODUCTS

Sec.

AUTHORITY: 12 U.S.C. 4526; 12 U.S.C. 4541.

SOURCE: 74 FR 31604, July 2, 2009, unless otherwise noted.

§ 1253.1 Purpose and authority.

The purpose of this part is to establish policies and procedures implementing the prior approval authority for enterprise products, in accordance with section 1321 of the Federal Housing Enterprises Financial Safety and Soundness Act of 1992 (Safety and Soundness Act) (12 U.S.C. 4541), as amended.

§ 1253.2 Definitions.

For purposes of this part:

Authorizing statute means, in the case of Fannie Mae, the Federal National Mortgage Association Charter Act (12 U.S.C. 1716 *et seq.*) and, in the case of Freddie Mac, the Federal Home Loan Mortgage Corporation Act (12 U.S.C. 1451 *et seq.*).

Director means the Director of the Federal Housing Finance Agency or his or her designee.

Enterprise means the Federal National Mortgage Association (Fannie Mae) or the Federal Home Loan Mortgage Corporation (Freddie Mac).

FHFA means the Federal Housing Finance Agency.

New activity means with respect to an Enterprise, any business line, business practice, or service, including guarantee, financial instrument, consulting, or marketing, that is proposed to be undertaken by the Enterprise either on a standalone basis or as an incident to providing one or more Enterprise products to the market, and which was—

(a) Not initially engaged in prior to July 30, 2008;

(b) Commenced by the Enterprise prior to July 30, 2008, but which, after July 30, 2008, the Enterprise ceased to engage in, and presently intends to resume; or

(c) Offered or engaged in by the Enterprise after July 30, 2008, at a significantly different level, or in a significantly different manner, in terms of the activity's effect on public interest or risk to the Enterprise or the mortgage finance or financial system.

The term "new activity" does not include—

(1) Any Enterprise business practice, transactions, or conduct performed solely as an incident to the administration of the Enterprise's internal affairs to conduct its business; or

(2) Any business practice or service undertaken by an Enterprise that is *de minimis* in scope, volume, risk, or duration.

New product means any activity that the Director determines merits public notice and comment on matters of compliance with the applicable authorizing statute, safety and soundness, or public interest. "New product" does not include—

(a) The automated loan underwriting system of an Enterprise in existence as of July 30, 2008, including any upgrade to the technology, operating system, or software to operate the underwriting system;

(b) Any modification to the mortgage terms and conditions or mortgage underwriting criteria relating to the mortgages that are purchased or guaranteed by the Enterprise, provided that such modifications do not alter the underlying transaction so as to include services or financing, other than residential mortgage financing;

(c) Any activity that is substantially similar to the activities described in paragraphs (a) or (b) of this section;

(d) Any activity that is substantially similar to an activity or product that has been approved in accordance with this part for either Enterprise; or

(e) Any activity that is substantially similar to an activity or product continuously undertaken by the other Enterprise since prior to July 30, 2008.

Substantially similar. In considering whether an activity is "substantially similar" to any activity described in section 1321(e)(1)(A) and (B) of the Safety and Soundness Act, 12 U.S.C. 4541(e)(1)(A) and in paragraphs (a) or (b) of this section under the definition of new product, or to any activity approved in accordance with this part, or continuously engaged in by the other Enterprise as referenced in paragraphs (d) and (e) of this section under the definition of new product, the Director may consider if the activity in question—

(1) Is a product;

(2) Is authorized under the applicable authorizing statute;

(3) Represents an upgrade to the way an approved product is delivered;

(4) Poses a significant change in risk to the Enterprise or the mortgage finance system from a previously approved product or activity;

(5) Involves a significant change in terms, conditions, or limitations expressly contained in any prior approval granted under this part;

(6) Poses a significant change in its effect on the public interest compared to a previously approved product or activity;

(7) Poses a significant change from a previously approved product or activity and if so, does a tradeoff exist in the composite of risk, public interest, and safety and soundness elements in the proposed new activity;

(8) Is likely to have significantly more enterprise resources dedicated to it;

(9) Requires approval by regulators other than FHFA, including Federal, State, or local regulators;

(10) Involves new classes or types of borrowers, investors, or counterparties;

(11) Involves new classes or types of collateral; or

(12) Such other factor as the Director determines to be appropriate.

§ 1253.3 Notice of new activity.

(a) Before commencing a new activity, an Enterprise must submit a Notice of New Activity (Notice) to the FHFA, and either receive a determination that the new activity is not a new product, await passage of the 15 business-day period as described in paragraph (d) of this section, or, where FHFA determines the new activity to be a new product, await approval of the new product under § 1253.4. In addition, for any new activity that an Enterprise seeks to engage in which FHFA had previously approved in accordance with this part for the other Enterprise, or in which the other Enterprise had engaged continuously since prior to July 30, 2008, the Enterprise must submit a Notice to FHFA. In support of its Notice, the Enterprise shall submit information sufficient to allow the Director to make a determination on the Notice pursuant to section 1321 of the Safety and Soundness Act (12 U.S.C. 4541), as amended, including any information required by FHFA by regulation or otherwise. The Enterprise shall provide a thorough, meaningful, complete and specific description of the new activity such that the public will be able to provide fully informed comment on the new activity if FHFA determines the new activity to be a new product. Such information shall include that contained in the FHFA Notice Form and the Instructions for the FHFA Notice of New Activity Form (Notice Form Instructions) that appear in the appendix of this part. The Notice Form and Notice Form Instructions may be amended from time to time by written direction of the Director. Requests for confidential treatment for any portion of an Enterprise's submission must be made consistent with §1253.5.

(b) FHFA will evaluate a Notice to establish whether the submission contains sufficient information for FHFA to make a determination whether the new activity is a new product subject to prior approval. Upon establishing that the Notice contains sufficient information, FHFA shall deem the submission complete and "received" for purposes of section 1321(e)(2)(B) of the Safety and Soundness Act (12 U.S.C. 4541(e)(2)(B)), and shall notify the Enterprise accordingly.

(c) No later than 15 business-days after the Notice is deemed completed and "received" for purposes of section 1321(e)(2)(B) of the Safety and Soundness Act (12 U.S.C. 4541(e)(2)(B)), the Director will make a written determination on the Notice, and shall notify the Enterprise accordingly. The Director may also approve the new activity subject to such terms, conditions, or limitations on the Enterprise's engagement in the new activity as the Director determines to be appropriate.

(d) If the Director fails to make a determination within the 15 business-day period specified in paragraph (c) of this section, the Enterprise may commence the new activity. The Director's failure to make a determination within the 15-day period does not limit or restrict the Director's safety and soundness authority or the authority of the Director to review the new activity to determine whether the activity is consistent with the statutory mission of the Enterprise.

§ 1253.4 New product approval.

(a) *Public notice.* If the Director determines that the new activity is a new product, FHFA shall publish a public notice soliciting comments on the proposed product for a 30 calendar-day period.

(1) The public notice will describe the new product and state the closing date of the public comment period. The public notice will provide instructions for submission of public comment.

(2) The Director will consider all public comments received by the closing date of the comment period.

(3) In computing the 30 calendar-day public comment period, FHFA excludes the day on which the public notice is published in the FEDERAL REGISTER, from which the period begins to run, and includes the last day of the period, regardless of whether it is a Saturday, Sunday, or legal holiday.

(b) *Director's determination.* (1) No later than 30 calendar-days after the end of the public comment period, the Director will provide the Enterprise with a written determination on whether it may proceed with the new product. The written determination will specify the grounds for the Director's determination.

(2) The Director will approve the new product if the Director determines that the new product complies with the applicable authorizing statute, is in the public interest, and is consistent with the safety and soundness of the Enterprise and the mortgage finance and financial system. The Enterprise may then offer the new product subject to any terms, conditions, or limitations as may be established by the Director.

(3) Among the factors that the Director may consider when determining whether a new product is in the public interest are—

(i) The degree to which the new product might reasonably be expected to advance any of the purposes of the Enterprise under the applicable authorizing statute;

(ii) The degree to which the new product serves underserved markets as set forth in section 1335 of the Safety and Soundness Act (12 U.S.C. 4565);

(iii) The degree to which the new product is being supplied or could be supplied by non-government-sponsored-enterprise firms;

(iv) Other alternatives for providing the new product;

(v) The degree to which the new product promotes competition in the marketplace or, to the contrary, would result in less competition and greater concentration of economic activity or risk;

(vi) The degree to which Enterprise provision of the new product overcomes natural market barriers or inefficiencies;

(vii) The degree to which Enterprise provision of the new product might raise or mitigate systemic risks to the mortgage, mortgage finance or other financial markets;

(viii) The degree to which the new product furthers fair housing; and

(ix) Such other factors determined appropriate by the Director.

(4) The Director will disapprove the new product if the Director determines that approval is inconsistent with applicable law, regulation, or FHFA policy thereunder, or contrary to public interest or the safety and soundness of the Enterprise or the mortgage finance or financial system. If the Director disapproves the new product, the Enterprise may not offer the new product.

(5) The Director may establish terms, conditions, or limitations on the Enterprise's offering of the new product to ensure that the product offering is consistent with applicable statutory and regulatory standards, FHFA policies, public interest, or the safety and soundness of the Enterprise or the mortgage finance or financial system.

(6) If the Director fails to make a determination within the 30 calendar-day period that begins on the day after the end of the public comment period, the Enterprise may offer the new product. The Director's failure to make a determination within such 30-day period does not limit or restrict the Director's safety and soundness authority or the authority of the Director to review the new product to determine that the product is consistent with the statutory mission of the Enterprise.

(c) *Temporary approval.* (1) FHFA may approve a new product without first seeking public comments as described in § 1253.4(c) if—

(i) The Enterprise submits a specific request for Temporary Approval that describes the exigent circumstances that make the delay associated with the 30-day public comment period contrary to the public interest and the Director determines that exigent circumstances exist and that delay associated with first seeking public comment would be contrary to the public interest; or

(ii) Notwithstanding the absence of a request by the Enterprise for Temporary Approval, the Director determines on his or her own initiative that there are exigent circumstances that make the delay associated with first seeking public comment contrary to the public interest.

(2) The Director may impose terms, conditions, or limitations on the Temporary Approval to ensure that the new product offering is consistent with applicable statutory and regulatory standards, FHFA policies, public interest, and the safety and soundness of the Enterprise or the mortgage finance system.

(3) If the Director grants Temporary Approval, the Director will notify the Enterprise in writing of the Director's decision, and include the period for which it is effective and any terms, conditions or limitations. Upon granting of Temporary Approval, FHFA will also publish the request for public comment to begin the process for permanent approval.

(4) If the Director denies a request for Temporary Approval, the Director will notify the Enterprise in writing of the Director's decision, and will evaluate the new product in accordance with paragraphs (a) through (c) of this section.

(d) *Additional information.* The Director may request any information in addition to that supplied in the completed Notice if, as a result of public comment or otherwise in the course of considering the Notice, the Director believes that the information is necessary for his or her decision. The Director may disapprove a new product if he or she does not receive the information requested from the Enterprise in sufficient time to permit adequate evaluation of the information within the time periods set forth in paragraph (c) of this section.

§ 1253.5 Confidential information.

(a) *Information presumed public.* FHFA will treat all information an Enterprise submits in a Notice as public information, except as provided in paragraphs (b) through (d) of this section. FHFA will also treat information provided by a commenter, in response to a notice requesting comment on an Enterprise new product, as public information, except as provided in paragraphs (b) through (d) of this section.

(b) *Confidential treatment request.* An Enterprise or commenter may designate specific information as confidential and request that it not be made publicly available. For any information that an Enterprise or commenter seeks confidential treatment, the Enterprise or commenter is required to submit a complete copy of the Notice or comment, with a specific request for confidential treatment. Simultaneously, the Enterprise or commenter is required to submit a copy of the Notice or comment containing only those portions for which no request for confidential treatment is made, and from which those portions for which confidential treatment is requested have been redacted. The Enterprise or commenter must specify the bases for designated information not being made public as set forth in paragraph (c) of this section.

(c) *Required information.* The Enterprise or commenter is required to provide the following information in support of its request for confidential treatment of the designated information—

(1) Identification of the specific information for which confidential treatment is sought, and the specific Notice for which the information is being submitted;

(2) Explanation of the bases for the proposed confidential treatment including, but not limited to, why the information is "commercial or financial information obtained from a person and privileged or confidential" as that phrase is used in Exemption 4 of the Freedom of Information Act (FOIA), 5 U.S.C. 552(b)(4), and § 1202.4(a)(4) of this chapter;

(3) Explanation of the relevance and necessity of the information to whether the Notice should be approved or denied;

(4) Explanation of how disclosure of the information would result in substantial harm to the competitive position of the Enterprise or commenter;

(5) Explanation of whether the information is available to the public and the extent of any previous disclosure to third parties;

(6) Justification of the time period during which the Enterprise or commenter asserts that the material should not be available for public disclosure; and

(7) Any other information that the Enterprise or commenter seeking confidential treatment believes may be useful in assessing whether its request for confidentiality should be granted.

(d) *FHFA determination.* FHFA will determine whether the designated information may be withheld from public disclosure and will notify the Enterprise or commenter of the determination. In the event that FHFA determines the information may not be withheld from public disclosure, the Enterprise or commenter may withdraw the information or consent to public disclosure. Requests for confidential treatment that do not comply with paragraphs (b) and (c) of this section will not be considered.

§ 1253.6 Certifying and nullifying an approval.

(a) An Enterprise shall certify, through an executive officer, as that term is defined by § 1770.3(g) of this title, that any filing or supporting material submitted to FHFA pursuant to regulations in this part contains no material misrepresentations or omissions. FHFA may review and verify any information filed in connection with a Notice. If FHFA discovers a material misrepresentation or omission after the Director has rendered a decision on the filing, FHFA may nullify any approval or modify the terms, conditions, and limitations to such approval. For purposes of this paragraph, an Enterprise's authority to offer a new product or engage in a new activity by reason of the Director's not having made an explicit determination within the statutory time period constitutes an approval.

(b) Any person responsible for any material misrepresentation or omission in a submission or supporting materials may be subject to enforcement action and other penalties, including criminal penalties provided in 18 U.S.C. 1001.

§ 1253.7 Failure to comply.

(a) Unless the Director otherwise informs the Enterprise in writing, an Enterprise must cease offering a new product or engaging in a new activity immediately upon discovering or receiving notice from the Director that the Enterprise has—

(1) Offered a new product or commenced a new activity without submitting a Notice;

(2) Offered a new product or commenced a new activity after submitting a Notice but before approval is granted, and before the expiration of the time provided for the Director to make a determination under §§ 1253.3 and 1253.4;

(3) Offered a new product after the Director disapproved it; or

(4) Failed to adhere to any terms, conditions or limitations established by the Director in his or her approval of a new product or activity.

(b) Within five (5) business-days of the discovery or notice of any of the events described in paragraph (a) of this section, the Enterprise must provide the Director a written description of the failure or failures of controls that resulted in the offering of the new product or commencement of the new activity in contravention of this regulation, and the steps that the Enterprise has taken or will take to remediate the control failures. The Enterprise must provide the board of directors of the Enterprise and chief risk officer, internal audit, and compliance officer of the Enterprise with a copy of the written description on the same date the description is provided to the Director of FHFA.

(c) In the event that the Enterprise elects to resubmit the Notice of a new product or new activity that was undertaken in contravention of this regulation, the resubmission must provide sufficient documentation of the effectiveness of the remediation efforts described in paragraph (b) of this section.

(d) Failure to comply with paragraphs (a) or (b) of this section above may result in FHFA's taking enforcement action, including pursuant to 12 U.S.C. 4631 (orders to cease and desist), 12 U.S.C. 4632 (temporary orders to cease and desist), and 12 U.S.C. 4636 (civil money penalties).

§ 1253.8 Availability of new product to an Enterprise after it has been approved for the other Enterprise.

(a) If the Director approves a new product for one Enterprise or the new product is otherwise available to that Enterprise under § 1253.4, the other Enterprise may also undertake that new product, subject to submitting a request to the Director in the form of a Notice under § 1253.3 and approval by the Director.

(b) The Director may require such further information from the requesting Enterprise as he or she deems necessary to approve or deny the request. Approving the request does not require public notice and comment.

§ 1253.9 Preservation of authority.

(a) The Director's exercise of his or her authority pursuant to the prior approval authority for products under section 1321 of the Safety and Soundness Act (12 U.S.C. 4541), and this regulation and other issuances in no way restricts—

(1) The safety and soundness authority of the Director over all new and existing products or activities; or

(2) The authority of the Director to review all new and existing products or activities to determine that such products or activities are consistent with the statutory mission of an Enterprise.

APPENDIX TO PART 1253—PRIOR APPROVAL FOR ENTERPRISE PRODUCTS—INSTRUCTIONS AND NOTICE OF NEW ACTIVITY FORM

Appendix to Part 1253

PRIOR APPROVAL FOR ENTERPRISE PRODUCTS

INSTRUCTIONS for the NOTICE of NEW ACTIVITY FORM

INSTRUCTIONS FOR NNA SUBMISSION

GENERAL INSTRUCTIONS

The Notice of New Activity (NNA) submission addresses two functions of the Federal Housing Finance Agency—it provides information on activities that may constitute a new product or new activity under the Housing and Economic Recovery Act of 2008 (12 USC 4541) and on activities that do not constitute a new product subject to the approval provisions of the law, but represent an activity that merits safety and soundness review under multiple provisions of the Federal Housing Enterprises Financial Safety and Soundness Act (12 USC 4501 *et seq.*)

Once the submission is made, FHFA will first determine if the activity is a new product and will direct consideration of such product under the provisions of the statute and regulation, which may involve public comment. If the new activity is determined not to be a new product, then the information contained in the submission will be employed by FHFA for a review of safety and soundness matters as part of its routine supervisory program.

A. Notice of New Activity (NNA) Submission

1. *New Activity.* A new activity for purposes of this submission includes the planned deployment of a new activity that constitutes a new product under the approval provision of FHEFSSA as amended by HERA or a significant expansion or alteration of an existing activity or product that does not require approval under HERA amendments of 2008 but is to be reviewed under safety and soundness provisions of the Act. A new activity may include alteration of an existing activity in such a manner as to affect significantly the risk, management, capital effect, operational controls, legal effect, anticipated business impact on the Enterprise (dollar effect), and accounting or taxation for such activity. This will include a pilot program.

A new activity does not include a minor, non-substantive transaction or activity that does not involve significant credit, interest rate, operational (including internal control and accounting) or reputation risk separate and apart from an existing activity. In general, a new activity would not include an increase in an existing product or activity of less than a 25% investment increase. For example, if an existing multi-family mortgage purchase activity will be altered to require collection and analysis of additional loan data to facilitate Enterprise purchases, even though the change may be labeled as "new" by the Enterprise in its communications, the Enterprise may inform FHFA that it does not constitute a new activity but rather an activity or product addition or enhancement. The Enterprises will work with examiners to assure clarity regarding whether an activity is new and fits within the Notice of New Activity (NNA) submission requirement.

2. *New Product.* A new product is determined by the Director of the Federal Housing Finance Agency (FHFA) in line with the Federal Housing Enterprises Financial Safety and Soundness Act of 1992 and the FHFA new product regulation at 12 CFR part 1253.

A new product does not include: (a) the automated loan underwriting system of an Enterprise in existence as of July 30, 2008, including any upgrade to the technology, operating system, or software to operate the underwriting system; and (b) any modification to the mortgage terms and conditions or mortgage underwriting criteria relating to the mortgages that are purchased or guaranteed by the Enterprise, provided that such modifications do not alter the underlying transaction so as to include services or financing, other than residential mortgage financing; or (c) any activity that is substantially similar to the activities described in (a) and (b).

3. *Expanded activity or product.* In general, a significant expansion of an activity or product constitutes an expanded existing activity or product, subject to a submission requirement for a safety and soundness review, if it fits one or more of the following criteria:

-- expanded scope of an activity or product, including a significant increase in size, in risk levels (credit, interest rate, market or operational) or a significant change in activity or product limits or marketing;

-- movement from a pilot program or product test to a fully deployed activity or product; or

-- such other criteria as provided in writing by the Director.

4. *Consultation with FHFA.* Prior to submitting a NNA, an Enterprise may seek clarification that while an initiative meets one or more of the criteria for an expanded activity or product, the change does not meet a level of significance to justify filing a NNA or presents timing concerns that are not addressed under procedures set forth below.

B. Exemptions

The exemptions from submitting a NNA included in the definitions provided above do not exempt reporting or other communications to examiners or other offices under separate requests by or reporting requirements of FHFA.

C. Procedures and Content

1. *Submission to FHFA*

(a) *Normal Submission.* Completed notices of new business activities or products, or expansion or alteration of an existing activity or product, should be provided on a NNA to FHFA. If a determination is made that an activity represents a new product and that a public comment period is required, the Director shall so inform the Enterprise as soon as practicable. Unless notified otherwise in writing by FHFA, an Enterprise may not undertake a new activity until more than fifteen (15) business days after a completed notice was submitted to FHFA, or a new product until more than sixty (60) days after a determination that an activity represents a new product.

(b) *Temporary Approval.* An Enterprise may request temporary approval for a new product pursuant to 12 CFR 1253.4(c) upon exigent circumstances that make the delay associated with the 30-day public comment period contrary to the public interest. If an Enterprise requests temporary approval, it shall indicate such request on the NNA along with any supporting information. An Enterprise may request temporary approval for an expanded product or activity where circumstances exist meriting such temporary approval, such as a compelling business need, public interest, judicial order, regulatory directive from another federal agency or other emergency situation. Such request should be made at the time of submitting a NNA.

(c) *Confidentiality.* Information labeled confidential or proprietary contained in a NNA will be considered for such treatment by FHFA pursuant to 12 CFR 1253.5.

(d) *Completing NNA Form.*

(i) Provide a response or comment on every item in the Form. If an item on the Form is not applicable or relevant, state so and briefly explain why.

(ii) Responses or comments should be comprehensive; address all issues contained in an item.

(iii) Provide appropriate supporting documentation. Indicate on the form the number of the supporting item(s) and on the attached item(s) to which requirement the documentation refers.

(iv) If all items are not addressed, or if the information does not provide FHFA with sufficient bases upon which to make a determination, FHFA will not consider the Form received and will not process the Form.

(e) *Submitting the Form*

(i) Submit an electronic copy of the Form and supporting documents to: newproducts@fhfa.gov. Be sure to clearly label supporting documents and reference the item(s) to which they relate; and,

(ii) Submit hard copy of the Form and supporting documents to: Senior Associate Director for Housing Mission and Goals, Office of Housing Mission and Goals, Federal Housing Finance Agency, 1700 G Street, NW., Fourth Floor, Washington, DC 20552.

D. Supplemental Instructions

Name of Proposed Activity/New Product	Insert the name by which the Enterprise refers to the proposed new activity/new product.
Item 1	The indication that a new activity is or is not a new product should include detailed information in support of such a determination. Reference should be made to the Federal Housing Enterprises Financial Safety and Soundness Act of 1992, as amended, and to FHFA regulation on new products. Such supporting information should include a legal analysis and supporting historical information. Even if a new product determination has been previously made by FHFA, the Enterprise should note such determination and why the new activity does or does not fit within such prior determination as well as whether there are safety and soundness or charter matters that require additional consideration for the Enterprise to offer such activity or product. The description should address the factors the Director may consider when determining whether a new activity is "substantially similar" to the activities described in 12 USC 4541(e)(1)(A) and (B) or other activities that have been previously approved in accordance with 12 USC 4541 which include: (1) if the activity in question is a product; (2) whether the new activity is authorized under the Charter Act (Fannie Mae) or Corporation Act (Freddie Mac); (3) whether the activity in question represents an upgrade to the way an approved product is delivered; (4) whether the activity in question poses a significant change in risk to the Enterprise or mortgage finance system from a previously approved product or activity; (5) whether the activity in question involves a significant change in terms, conditions, or limitations expressly contained in any prior approval granted under this part; (6) whether the activity in question poses a significant change in its effect on the public interest compared to a previously approved product or activity; (7) the tradeoff between any combinations of changes in risk, public interest, and safety and soundness; (8) whether the activity in question is likely to require the dedication of significantly more Enterprise resources; (9) whether the activity in question requires approval by regulators other than FHFA; (10) whether the activity in question involves new classes or types of borrowers, investors, or counterparties or new classes or types of collateral; or (12) such other factors as FHFA determines appropriate.

Item 5	Information about the management structure should include names and titles. Organizational charts should be attached. Staffing plans should indicate authorized and on-board levels as of a stated date.
Item 6	The description should address the factors the Director may consider when determining whether the proposed new activity is in the public interest. These factors include: (1) the degree to which the proposed new activity might reasonably be expected to advance any of the four charter purposes of Fannie Mae or Freddie Mac; (2) the degree to which the activity serves underserved markets as set forth at 12 USC 4565; (3) the degree to which the activity is being supplied or could be supplied by non-government-sponsored-enterprise firms; (4) other alternatives for providing the service to the market; (5) the degree to which the new activity promotes competition in the marketplace or, to the contrary, would result in less competition and greater concentration of economic activity or risk; (6) the degree to which Enterprise provision of the service overcomes natural market barriers or inefficiencies; (7) the degree to which Enterprise provision of the activity might raise or mitigate systemic risks to mortgage and financial markets; (8) the degree to which the activity furthers fair housing; and (9) such other factor determined appropriate by FHFA.
Item 8	This includes applications for patents, and requires copies of correspondence FROM the Enterprise TO other regulators or foreign governments. "Foreign governments" includes agencies and regulatory bodies of foreign governments.
Item 15	The description should indicate whether and the extent to which the proposed new activity increases or decreases risk for each risk component (credit, market, model, governance (including reputation), and operational risk).

The instructions provided here and the information required by the FHFA Notice of New Activity Form may be modified by FHFA from time to time, and written notice will be provided in advance to the Enterprises of any such modification.

	*FEDERAL HOUSING FINANCE AGENCY*	**NNA NUMBER ASSIGNED** NNA-F[illegible]-200 ☐ – ☐ ☐ ☐

12 CFR Part 1253 – Appendix
NOTICE OF NEW ACTIVITY FORM
SEE INSTRUCTIONS FOR INFORMATION REQUIRED TO BE SUPPLIED ON THIS FORM

Enterprise: ______________________________

Purpose of the Proposed New Activity/New Product/Expanded Activity Submission

The Notice of New Activity (NNA) submission addresses two functions of the Federal Housing Finance Agency—it provides information on activities that may constitute a new product or new activity under the Housing and Economic Recovery Act of 2008 (12 USC 4541) and on activities that do not constitute a new product subject to the approval provisions of the law, but represent an activity that merits safety and soundness review under multiple provisions of the Federal Housing Enterprises Financial Safety and Soundness Act (12 USC 4501 et seq.)

Once the submission is made, FHFA will first determine if the activity is a new product and will direct consideration of such product under the provisions of the statute and regulation, which may involve public comment. If the new activity is determined not to be a new product, then the information contained in the submission will be employed by FHFA for a review of safety and soundness matters as part of its routine supervisory program.

Enterprise Contact Information:

Name:
Title:
Telephone Number:
Email Address:

Name of the Proposed New Activity/New Product/Expanded Activity:

Description of the Proposed New Activity/New Product/Expanded Activity:

1. *Description of Activity/New Product.* Provide a complete and specific description of the proposed new activity, and provide the Enterprise's view of why this proposed new activity should or should not be considered a new product.

FHFA Form # 071 (06/2009) (Notice of New Activity Form)

1 of 4

(For example, explain why an activity relates to an upgrade of the automated underwriting system in existence as of July 30, 2008, relates to a modification to mortgage terms and conditions without altering the underlying transaction or relates to any activity substantially similar to any existing activity, as provided under 12 USC 4541(e) and 12 CFR Part 1253).

[If the activity is considered a new product, insure that any information the Enterprise feels should not be made public is so designated with an explanation for such designation. Also, if the activity is considered a new product, please provide the Enterprise's view on whether the new product should be considered for temporary approval.]

NOTE: the term "new activity" as employed here, encompasses "new product." Also see definition of "new activity" in 12 CFR 1253.2.

2. *Business Rationale and intended market.* Describe the business rationale for the proposed new activity. If the proposed new activity represents a business line for the Enterprise, describe the business line, and the rationale for the business line, and what products are being offered or proposed to be offered under such business line. Also describe the intended market for the proposed activity, including any market research performed relating to the proposed activity.

3. *Unusual or Unique Characteristics.* Describe any unusual or unique characteristics of the activity, including those involving reputation risks.

4. *Projected Size and Start Date of the New Activity.* State the anticipated commencement date for the proposed new activity. Describe and provide analysis, including assumptions, development expenses, expectations for the impact of and projections for the projected quarterly size (for example, in terms of cost, personnel, volume of activity, or risk metrics) of the proposed new activity for the first 12 quarterly periods of deployment and projected profit and loss..

5. *Units and Personnel with Responsibility over the New Activity.* Describe the Enterprise business units(s) involved in conducting the proposed new activity, including any non-Enterprise affiliation or subsidiary relationships, and the roles of each. Describe the management structure, including proposed manager(s) of the proposed new activity; reporting lines, planned oversight, and review of the activity; and proposed staffing for the activity.

6. *Impact on Public Interest.* Describe the impact of the proposed new activity on the public interest compared to a previously approved activity. Provide sufficient information to address the factors the Director may consider when determining whether the proposed activity is in the public interest, including: (1) the degree to which the proposed product might reasonably be expected to advance any of the four charter purposes of Fannie Mae or Freddie Mac; (2) the degree to which the proposed product serves underserved markets

---

as set forth at 12 USC 4565; (3) the degree to which the proposed product is being supplied or could be supplied by non-government-sponsored-enterprise firms; (4) other alternatives for providing the service to the market; (5) the degree to which Enterprise provision of the service overcomes natural market barriers or inefficiencies; (6) the degree to which Enterprise provision of the proposed product might raise or mitigate systemic risks to mortgage and financial markets; and (7) the degree to which the proposed product furthers fair housing.

7. *Legal Analysis.* Provide a legal opinion on whether the proposed activity complies with the Enterprise's authorizing statute, does or does not constitute a new product and other legal matters relating to the deployment and offering of the new product.. Provide copies of legal opinions from in-house or outside counsel relating to the Enterprise's proposed activity. If the Enterprise is relying on the "necessary and incidental" authority, describe in detail how the proposed new activity is necessary and incidental to one or more specific charter authorities. Legal analysis should include other non-charter compliance matters. If legal analysis was provided for a similar activity such analysis may be appended with such additional analysis as is appropriate.

8. *Other Regulatory Applications.* Provide copies of all notice and/or application documents— including any application for patents– the Enterprise has submitted to other regulators (federal, state or local) or to foreign governments relating to the proposed new activity. Include all presentation documents, correspondence with the regulator or government pertaining to the application or notice, and all decisional documents issued by the regulator or foreign government.

9. *Relationships with non-secondary market participants.* Describe the extent to which the proposed new activity includes relationships with non-secondary market participants, including, but not limited to: borrowers, real estate brokers, housing counselors, mortgage brokers and government officials.

10. *Business Requirements.* Describe any business requirements for the proposed new activity, including for example, data processing systems, accounting systems, performance tracking systems, and interface capacity with other Enterprise systems and departments.

11. *Acquisition.* If an acquisition is involved, describe the financial features of the transaction and provide pro forma financials of the acquiree.

12. *Accounting Treatment.* Explain whether the proposed new activity is expected to have an accounting effect; explain any accounting treatment proposed for the new activity.

13. *Tax Implications.* Describe the anticipated tax impact of the proposed new activity, and provide analysis, including assumptions, expectations for the impact of, and projections for tax liabilities (credits) associated with the proposed new activity on a quarterly basis for the first 12 quarterly periods of the new activity's commencement.

FHFA Form # 071 (06/2009) (Notice of New Activity Form)

3 of 4

14. *Earnings and Capital Implications.* Describe, explain and provide analysis, including assumptions, expectations for the impact of, and projections for the anticipated impact to earnings and capital of the proposed new activity on a quarterly basis for the first 12 quarterly periods of the new activity's commencement.

15. *Risk Implications.* Describe the impact of the proposed new activity on the risk profile of the Enterprise and on the mortgage finance system from a previously approved activity. Provide sufficient information to document whether the impact represents a material change to the Enterprise's risk profile.

16. *Performance reports and Risk Controls.* Describe the type of information that will be contained in the routine reports that will be generated to capture the performance of the proposed activity, and include prototype of such performance reports. Describe any and all routine and special controls in place or planned to be put in place for the proposed new activity. Include in the description: operational risk controls; credit risk controls; market risk controls; model risk controls; and governance (including reputation) risk controls. To the extent possible, quantify the risks associated with the proposed activity.

17. *Other Safety and Soundness Implications.* Describe how the proposed new activity is consistent with the safety and soundness of the Enterprise and the mortgage finance and financial system. Include information about the process the Enterprise went through to develop the proposed new activity and to obtain necessary internal approvals (including at the executive level, the executive committee level and/or Board of Directors level). Provide copies of any: presentations made to executives, executive committees or Board of Directors; minutes of meetings at which such presentations were made; and decision documents. FHFA will automatically consider such Board presentations, minutes, and decisions documents for confidential treatment under 12 CFR 1253.5.

CERTIFICATION:

To the best of my knowledge and belief, the information contained in this filing, including any supporting materials, contains no material misrepresentations or omissions, is true, correct and complete.

Signed: ______________________________

Print Name: ___________________________

Title: ________________________________

Date: ______________________

FHFA Form # 071 (06/2009) (Notice of New Activity Form)

SUBCHAPTER D—FEDERAL HOME LOAN BANKS

PART 1261—FEDERAL HOME LOAN BANK DIRECTORS

Subpart A—Definitions

Subpart B—Federal Home Loan Bank Boards of Directors: Eligibility and Elections

Subpart C—Federal Home Loan Bank Directors' Compensation and Expenses

Subpart D [Reserved]

AUTHORITY: 12 U.S.C. 1426, 1427, 1432, 4511 and 4526.

SOURCE: 73 FR 55715, Sept. 26, 2008, unless otherwise noted.

Subpart A—Definitions

SOURCE: 75 FR 17039, May 5, 2010, unless otherwise noted.

§ 1261.1 Definitions.

As used in this part:

Bank written in title case means a Federal Home Loan Bank established under section 12 of the Bank Act (12 U.S.C. 1432).

Bank Act means the Federal Home Loan Bank Act, as amended (12 U.S.C. 1421 through 1449).

Director means the Director of the Federal Housing Finance Agency.

FHFA means Federal Housing Finance Agency.

Subpart B—Federal Home Loan Bank Boards of Directors: Eligibility and Elections

§ 1261.2 Definitions.

As used in this Subpart B:

Bona fide resident of a Bank district means an individual who:

(1) Maintains a principal residence in the Bank district; or

(2) If serving as an independent director, owns or leases in his or her own name a residence in the Bank district and is employed in a voting state in the Bank district.

FHFA ID number means the number assigned to a member by FHFA and used by FHFA and the Banks to identify a particular member.

Independent directorship means a directorship, as defined by section 7(a)(4)(A) of the Bank Act, 12 U.S.C. 1427(a)(4)(A), that is filled by a plurality vote of the members at large by an individual having the qualifications specified by section 7(a)(3)(B)(i) or (ii), 12 U.S.C. 1427(a)(3)(B)(i) or (ii).

Member directorship means a directorship, as defined by section 7(a)(4)(A) of the Bank Act, 12 U.S.C. 1427(a)(4)(A), that is filled by a plurality vote of the members located in a particular State by an individual who is an officer or director of a member located in that State, and includes guaranteed directorships and stock directorships.

Method of equal proportions means the mathematical formula used by FHFA to allocate member directorships among the States in a Bank's district based on the relative amounts of Bank stock required to be held as of the record date by members located in each State.

Public interest director means an individual serving in a public interest directorship.

Public interest directorship means an independent directorship filled by an individual with more than four years experience representing consumer or community interests in banking services, credit needs, housing or consumer financial protections.

Record date means December 31 of the calendar year immediately preceding the election year.

Stock directorship means a member directorship that is designated by FHFA as representing the members located in a particular voting State based on the amount of Bank stock required to be held by the members in that State as of the record date, other than a guaranteed directorship.

Voting State means the District of Columbia, Puerto Rico, or the State of the United States in which a member's principal place of business, as determined in accordance with 12 CFR part 1263, or any successor provision, is located as of the record date. The voting State of a member with a principal place of business located in the U.S. Virgin Islands as of the record date is Puerto Rico, and the voting State of a member with a principal place of business located in American Samoa, Guam, or the Commonwealth of the Northern Mariana Islands as of the record date is Hawaii.

[73 FR 55715, Sept. 26, 2008, as amended at 74 FR 51460, Oct. 7, 2009. Redesignated and amended at 75 FR 17039, 17040, Apr. 5, 2010]

§ 1261.3 General provisions.

(a) *Board size and composition.* Annually, the FHFA Director will determine the size of the board of directors for each Bank and will designate at least a majority, but no more than 60 percent, of the directorships as member directorships and the remainder as independent directorships. Annually, the board of directors of each Bank shall determine how many, if any, of the independent directorships with terms beginning the following January 1 shall be public interest directorships, ensuring that at all times the Bank will have at least two public interest independent directorships.

(b) *Term of directorships.* The term of office of each directorship commencing on or after January 1, 2009 shall be four years, except as adjusted pursuant to section 7(d) of the Bank Act (12 U.S.C 1427(d)) to achieve a staggered board, and shall commence on January 1 of the calendar year so designated by FHFA.

(c) *Annual elections.* Each Bank annually shall conduct an election the purpose of which is to fill all directorships designated by FHFA as commencing on January 1 of the calendar year immediately following the year in which such election is commenced. Subject to the provisions of the Bank Act and in accordance with the requirements of this subpart, the disinterested members of the board of directors of each Bank, or a committee of disinterested directors, shall administer and conduct the annual election of directors. In so doing, the disinterested directors may use Bank staff or independent contractors to perform ministerial and administrative functions concerning the elections process.

(d) *Location of members.* In accordance with section 7(c) of the Bank Act (12 U.S.C 1427(c)), for purposes of the election of member directors, a member is deemed to be located in its voting state, unless otherwise designated by the Director.

(e) *Dates.* If any date specified in this part for action by a Bank, or specified by a Bank pursuant to this part, falls on a Saturday, Sunday, or Federal holiday, the relevant time period is deemed to be extended to the next calendar day that is not a Saturday, Sunday, or Federal holiday.

[73 FR 55715, Sept. 26, 2008, as amended at 74 FR 51460, Oct. 7, 2009. Redesignated at 75 FR 17039, Apr. 5, 2010]

§ 1261.4 Designation of member directorships.

(a) *Determination of voting stock.* (1) On or before April 10 of each year, each Bank shall deliver to FHFA a capital stock report that indicates, as of the record date, the number of members located in each voting State in the Bank's district, the number of shares of Bank stock that each member (identified by its FHFA ID number) was required to hold, and the number of shares of Bank stock that all members located in each voting State were required to hold. If a Bank has issued more than one class of stock, it shall report the total shares of stock of all classes required to be held by the members. The Bank shall certify to FHFA that, to the best of its knowledge, the information provided in the capital stock report is accurate and complete, and that it has notified each member of its minimum capital stock holding requirement as of the record date.

(2) If a Bank's capital plan was not in effect as of the record date, the number of shares of Bank stock that any member was required to hold as of the record date shall be determined in accordance with §§1263.20 and 1263.22 of this chapter. If a Bank's capital plan was in effect as of the record date, the number of shares of Bank stock that any member was required to hold as of the record date shall be determined in accordance with the minimum investment established by the capital plan for that Bank; however, for any member whose Bank stock is less than the minimum investment during a transition period, the amount of Bank stock to be reported shall be the number of shares of Bank stock actually owned by the member as of the record date.

(b) *Designation of member directorships as stock directorships.* Using the method of equal proportions, the Director annually will conduct a designation of member directorships for each Bank based on the number of shares of Bank stock required to be held by the members in each State as of December 31 of the preceding calendar year. If a Bank has issued more than one class of stock, the Director will designate the directorships for each State in that Bank district based on the combined number of shares required to be held by the members in that State. For purposes of conducting the designation, if a Bank's capital plan was not in effect on the immediately preceding December 31, the number of shares of Bank stock required to be held by members as of that date shall be determined in accordance with §§1263.20 and 1263.22 of this chapter. If a Bank's capital plan was in effect on the immediately preceding December 31, the number of shares of Bank stock required to be held by members as of that date shall be determined in accordance with the minimum investment established by such capital plan; however, for any members whose Bank stock is less than the minimum investment during a transition period, the amount of stock to be used in the designation of directorships shall be the number of shares of Bank stock actually owned by those members as of that December 31. In all cases, the Director will designate the directorships by using the information provided by each Bank in its capital stock report required by paragraph (a)(1) of this section.

(c) *Allocation of directorships.* The member directorships designated by the Director will be allocated among the States by the Director in accordance with section 7(b) and (c) of the Bank Act.

(d) *Notification.* On or before June 1 of each year, FHFA will notify each Bank in writing of the total number of directorships established for the Bank and the number of member directorships designated as representing the members in each voting state in the Bank district.

(e) *Change of state.* If the annual designation of member directorships results in an existing directorship being redesignated as representing members in a different State, that directorship shall be deemed to terminate in the previous State as of December 31 of that year, and a new directorship to begin in the succeeding State as of January 1 of the next year. The new directorship shall be filled by vote of the members in the succeeding State and, in order to maintain the staggered terms of directorships, shall be adjusted to a term equal to the remaining term of the previous directorship if it had not been redesignated to another State.

[74 FR 51460, Oct. 7, 2009. Redesignated and amended at 75 FR 17039, 17040, Apr. 5, 2010]

§1261.5 Director eligibility.

(a) *Eligibility requirements for member directors.* Each member director, and each nominee to a member directorship, shall be:

(1) A citizen of the United States; and

(2) An officer or director of a member that is located in the district in which the Bank is located and that meets all

minimum capital requirements established by its appropriate Federal banking agency or appropriate State regulator. In the case of a director elected by the members, the institution of which the director is an officer or director must have been a member as of the record date. In the case of a director elected by a Bank's board of directors to fill a vacancy, the institution of which the director is an officer or director must be a member at the time the board acts.

(b) *State designation for member directors.* Each member director, and each nominee to a member directorship, shall be an officer or director of a member that is located in the State to which the Director has allocated such directorship under § 1261.4(c)..

(c) *Eligibility requirements for independent directors.* Each independent director, and each nominee to an independent directorship, shall be:

(1) A citizen of the United States; and

(2) A bona fide resident of the district in which the Bank is located.

(d) *Restrictions.* (1) A nominee is not eligible if he or she:

(i) Is an incumbent director, unless:

(A) The incumbent director's term of office would expire before the new term of office would begin; and

(B) The new term of office would not be barred by the term limit provision of section 7(d) of the Bank Act (12 U.S.C. 1427(d)); or

(ii) Is a former director whose service would be barred by the term limit provision of section 7(d) of the Bank Act.

(2) For purposes of applying the term limit provision of section 7(d) of the Bank Act (12 U.S.C. 1427(d)):

(i) A term of office that is adjusted after July 30, 2008 to a period of fewer than four years shall not be deemed to be a full term;

(ii) Any member director's election and service to a directorship with a three year term of office prior to July 30, 2008 shall be deemed to be a full term;

(iii) Any three-year term of office that ends immediately before a term of office that is adjusted after July 30, 2008 to a period of fewer than four years, and any term of office commencing immediately following such adjusted term of office, shall constitute consecutive full terms of office; and

(iv) Any period of time served by a director who has been elected by the board of directors to fill a vacancy shall not be deemed to constitute a full term.

(e) *Loss of eligibility.* A director shall become ineligible to remain in office if, during his or her term of office, the directorship to which he or she has been elected is eliminated. The incumbent director shall become ineligible after the close of business on December 31 of the year in which the directorship is eliminated.

(2) In the case of a redesignation to another State, the redesignated directorship shall be filled by a majority vote of the remaining Bank directors, in accordance with § 1261.14(a).

[73 FR 55715, Sept. 26, 2008, as amended at 74 FR 51461, Oct. 7, 2009; 75 FR 17039, 17040, Apr. 5, 2010.]

§ 1261.6 Determination of member votes.

(a) *In general.* Each Bank shall determine, in accordance with this section, the number of votes that each member of the Bank may cast for each directorship that is to be filled by the vote of the members.

(b) *Number of votes.* For each member directorship and each independent directorship that is to be filled in an election, each member shall be entitled to cast one vote for each share of Bank stock that the member was required to hold as of the record date. Notwithstanding the preceding sentence, the number of votes that any member may cast for any one directorship shall not exceed the average number of shares of Bank stock required to be held as of the record date by all members located in the same State as of the record date. If a Bank has issued more than one class of stock, it shall calculate the average number of shares separately for each class of stock, using the total number of members in a State as the denominator, and shall apply those limits separately in determining the maximum number of votes that any member owning that class of stock may cast in the election. If a Bank's capital plan was not in effect as of the record date, the number of shares of

Bank stock that a member was required to hold as of the record date shall be determined in accordance with §§1263.20 and 1263.22 of this chapter. If a Bank's capital plan was in effect as of the record date, the number of shares of Bank stock that a member was required to hold as of the record date shall be determined in accordance with the minimum investment requirement established by the Bank's capital plan; however, for any member whose Bank stock is less than the minimum investment during a transition period, the amount of Bank stock to be used shall be the number of shares of Bank stock actually owned by the member as of the record date.

(c) *Voting preferences.* If the board of directors of a Bank includes any voting preferences as part of its approved capital plan, those preferences shall supersede the provisions of paragraph (b) of this section that otherwise would allow a member to cast one vote for each share of Bank stock it was required to hold as of the record date. If a Bank establishes a voting preference for a class of stock, the members with voting rights shall remain subject to the provisions of section 7(b) of the Bank Act (12 U.S.C. 1427(b)) that prohibit any member from casting any vote in excess of the average number of shares of stock required to be held by all members in its state.

[73 FR 55715, Sept. 26, 2008, as amended at 74 FR 51461, Oct. 7, 2009. Redesignated and amended at 75 FR 17039, Apr. 5, 2010]

§ 1261.7 Nominations for member and independent directorships.

(a) *Election announcement.* (1) Within a reasonable time in advance of an election, a Bank shall notify each member in its district of the commencement of the election process. Such notice shall include:

(1) The number of member directorships designated for each voting state in the Bank district and the number of independent directorships for the Bank;

(2) The name of each incumbent Bank director, the name and location of the member at which each member director serves, and the name and location of the organization with which each independent director is affiliated, if any, and the expiration date of each Bank director's term of office;

(3) A brief statement describing the skills and experience the Bank believes are most likely to add strength to the board of directors, provided that the Bank previously has conducted the annual assessment permitted by §1261.9 and the Bank has elected to provide the results of the assessment to the members;

(4) An attachment indicating the name, location, and FHFA ID number of every member in the member's voting state, and the number of votes each such member may cast for each directorship to be filled by such members, as determined in accordance with §1261.6; and

(5) If a member directorship is to be filled by members in a State, a nominating certificate for those members.

(b) *Member directorship nominations.* (1) Any member that is entitled to vote in the election may nominate an eligible individual to fill each available member directorship for its voting state by delivering to its Bank, prior to a deadline to be established by the Bank and set forth in the notice required in paragraph (a) of this section, a nominating certificate duly adopted by the member's governing body or by an individual authorized by the member's governing body to act on its behalf.

(2) The nominating certificate shall include the name of the nominee and the name, location, and FHFA ID number of the member the nominee serves as an officer or director.

(3) The Bank shall establish a deadline for delivery of nominating certificates, which shall be no earlier than 30 calendar days after the date on which the Bank delivers the notice required by paragraph (a) of this section, and the Bank shall not accept certificates received after that deadline. The Bank shall retain all accepted nominating certificates for at least two years after the date of the election.

(c) *Accepting member directorship nominations.* Promptly after receipt of any nominating certificate, a Bank shall notify in writing any individual nominated for a member directorship. An individual may accept the nomination only by delivering to the Bank, prior to a deadline established by the Bank and set forth in its notice, an executed director eligibility certification form prescribed by FHFA. A Bank shall allow each nominee at least 30 calendar days after the date the Bank delivered the notice of nomination within which to deliver the executed form. A nominee may decline the nomination by so advising the Bank in writing, or by failing to deliver a properly executed director eligibility certification form prior to the deadline. Each Bank shall retain all information received under this paragraph for at least two years after the date of the election.

(d) *Independent directorship nominations.* (1) Any individual who seeks to be an independent director of the board of directors of a Bank may deliver to the Bank, on or before the deadline set by the Bank for delivery of nominating certificates, an executed independent director application form prescribed by FHFA that demonstrates that the individual both is eligible and has either of the following qualifications:

(i) More than four years experience representing consumer or community interests in banking services, credit needs, housing, or consumer financial protections; or

(ii) Knowledge of or experience in one or more of the areas set forth in paragraph (e) of this section.

(2) Any other interested party may recommend to the Bank that it consider a particular individual as a nominee for an independent directorship, but the Bank shall not nominate any individual unless the individual has delivered to the Bank, on or before the date the Bank has set for delivery of nominating certificates, an executed independent director application form prescribed by FHFA. The application form prescribed by FHFA will provide a means by which an individual can indicate an intent to be considered for a public interest directorship. The board of directors of the Bank may consider any individual for any independent directorship nomination, provided it has determined that the individual is eligible and qualified, but the board shall nominate for a public interest directorship only an individual who indicates on the application form a desire to be considered for a public interest directorship. The board of directors of the Bank shall consult with the Bank's Advisory Council before nominating any individual for any independent directorship. Each Bank shall include in its bylaws the procedures it intends to use for the nomination and election of the independent directors, and shall retain all information received under this paragraph for at least two years after the date of the election.

(3) Each Bank shall determine the number of public interest directorships to be included among its authorized independent directorships, provided that each Bank shall at all times have at least two such directorships, and shall announce that number to its members in the notice required by paragraph (a) of this section. In submitting nominations to its members, each Bank shall nominate at least as many individuals as there are independent directorships to be filled in that year's election.

(e) *Independent director qualifications.* (1) Each independent director and each nominee for an independent directorship, other than a public interest directorship, shall have experience in, or knowledge of, one or more of the following areas: auditing and accounting, derivatives, financial management, organizational management, project development, risk management practices, and the law. Before nominating any individual for an independent directorship, other than a public interest directorship, the board of directors of a Bank shall determine that such knowledge or experience of the nominee is commensurate with that needed to oversee a financial institution with a size and complexity that is comparable to that of the Bank.

(2) Each public interest independent director and each nominee for a public interest directorship shall have more than four years experience representing consumer or community interests in banking services, credit needs, housing or consumer financial protection.

(f) *Eligibility verification.* Using the information provided on member director eligibility forms prescribed by FHFA, each Bank shall verify that each nominee for each member directorship meets all the eligibility requirements for such directorship. Using the information provided on independent director application forms prescribed by FHFA, each Bank shall verify that each nominee for each public interest independent directorship and each other independent directorship meets all eligibility requirements and any knowledge or experience qualifications for such directorship, as set forth in the Bank Act and this subpart. Before announcing any independent director nominee, the Bank shall deliver to FHFA, for the Director's review, a copy of the independent director application forms executed by the individuals nominated for independent directorships. If within two weeks of such delivery FHFA provides comments to the Bank on any independent director nominee, the board of directors of the Bank shall consider the FHFA's comments in determining whether to proceed with those nominees or to reopen the nomination.

[73 FR 55715, Sept. 26, 2008, as amended at 74 FR 51461, Oct. 7, 2009. Redesignated and amended at 75 FR 17039, Apr. 5, 2010]

§ 1261.8 Election process.

(a) *Ballots.* Promptly after fulfilling the requirements of § 1261.7(f), each Bank shall prepare and deliver a ballot to each member that was a member as of the record date. The Bank shall include with each ballot a closing date for the Bank's receipt of voted ballots, which date shall be no earlier than 30 calendar days after the date such ballot is delivered to the member.

(i) For states in which one or more member directorships are to be filled in the election, an alphabetical listing of the names of each nominee for such directorship, the name, location, and FHFA ID number of the member each nominee serves, the nominee's title or position with the member, and the number of member directorships to be filled by the members in that voting state in the election;

(ii) An alphabetical listing of the names of each nominee for a public interest independent directorship and a brief description of each nominee's experience representing consumer and community interests;

(iii) An alphabetical listing of the names nominee for the other independent directorships and a brief description of each nominee's qualifications, including his or her knowledge or experience in the areas of financial management, auditing and accounting, risk management practices, derivatives, project development, organizational management and any other area of knowledge or experience set forth in § 1261.7(e);

(iv) A statement that write-in candidates are not permitted; and

(v) A confidentiality statement prohibiting the Bank from disclosing how any member voted.

(2) At the election of the Bank, a ballot also may include, in the body or as an attachment, a brief description of the skills and experience of each nominee for a member directorship.

(b) *Statement on skills and experience.* If a Bank has conducted an annual assessment permitted by § 1261.9 and has included the results of the assessment as part of the notice to members required in § 1261.7(a), it may include with each ballot a statement of the results of that assessment or any subsequent assessment. If the statement differs from the statement provided under § 1261.7(a)(3), the Bank also shall include an explanation of why the statements differ.

(c) *Lack of member directorship nominees.* If, for any voting State, the number of nominees for the member directorships for that State is equal to or fewer than the number of such directorships to be filled in that year's election, the Bank shall deliver a notice to the members in the affected voting State (in lieu of including any member directorship nominees on the ballot for that State) that such nominees shall be deemed elected without further action, due to an insufficient number of nominees to warrant balloting. Thereafter, the Bank shall declare elected all such eligible nominees and in doing so shall designate particular nominees to guaranteed directorships or stock directorships, respectively, if necessary. The nominees declared elected shall be included as directors-elect in the report of election required under paragraph (g) of this section. Any member directorship that is not filled due to a lack of nominees shall be deemed vacant as of January 1 of the following year and shall be filled by the Bank's board of directors in accordance with § 1261.14(a).

(d) *Voting.* For each directorship to be filled, a member may cast the number of votes determined by the Bank pursuant to § 1261.6. A member may not split its votes among multiple nominees for a single directorship, and, where there are multiple directorships to be filled, either within the member's voting state or at large, in the case of independent directorships, a member may not cumulatively vote for a single nominee. If any member votes, it shall by resolution of its governing body either authorize the voting for specific nominees or delegate to an individual the authority to vote for specific nominees. To vote, a member shall:

(1) Mark on the ballot the name of not more than one of the nominees for each directorship to be filled. Each nominee so selected shall receive all of the votes that the member is entitled to cast.

(2) Execute and deliver the ballot to the Bank on or before the closing date. A Bank shall not allow a member to change a ballot after it has been delivered to the Bank.

(e) *Counting ballots.* A Bank shall not review any ballot until after the closing date, and shall not include in the election results any ballot received after the closing date. Promptly after the closing date, each Bank shall tabulate the votes cast in the election: for the member directorships, the Bank shall tabulate votes by each voting state; for the independent directorships, the Bank shall tabulate votes for the district at-large. Any ballots cast in violation of paragraph (d) of this section shall be void.

(f) *Declaring results.* (1) *For member directorships.* The Bank shall declare elected the nominee receiving the highest number of votes. If more than one member directorship is to be filled for a particular State, the Bank shall declare elected each successive nominee receiving the next highest number of votes until all such open directorships are filled.

(2) *For independent directorships.* (i) The bank shall tabulate separately the votes received for public interest independent director nominees and those received for other independent director nominees, in each case in accordance with paragraph (f)(2)(ii) of this section.

(ii) If the number of nominees exceeds the number of directorships to be filled, the Bank shall declare elected the nominee receiving the highest number of votes. If more than one directorship is to be filled, the Bank shall declare elected each successive nominee receiving the next highest number of votes for such directorship until all such open directorships are filled.

(iii) If the number of nominees is no more than the number of directorships to be filled, the Bank shall declare elected each nominee receiving at least 20 percent of the number of votes eligible to be cast in the election. If any directorship is not filled due to any nominee's failure to receive at least 20 percent of the votes eligible to be cast, the Bank shall continue the election process for that directorship under the procedures in paragraph (h) of this section.

(3) *Tie votes.* In the event of a tie for the last available directorship, the disinterested incumbent members of the board of directors of the Bank, by a majority vote, shall declare elected one of the nominees for whom the number of votes cast was tied.

(4) *Eligibility.* A Bank shall not declare elected a nominee that it has reason to know is ineligible to serve, nor shall it seat a director-elect that it has reason to know is ineligible to serve.

(5) *Record retention.* The Bank shall retain all ballots it receives for at least two years after the date of the election, and shall not disclose how any member voted.

(g) *Report of election.* Promptly following the election, each Bank shall deliver a notice to its members, to each nominee, and to FHFA that contains the following information:

(1) For each member directorship, the name of the director-elect, the name and location of the member at which he or she serves, his or her title or position at the member, the voting State represented, and the expiration date of the term of office;

(2) For each independent directorship, the name of the director-elect, whether the director-elect will fill a

public interest directorship and, if so, the consumer or community interest represented by such directorship, any qualifications under § 1261.7(e), and the expiration date of the term of office;

(3) For member directorships, the total number of eligible votes, the number of members voting in the election, and the total number of votes cast for each nominee, which shall be reported by State; and

(4) For independent directorships, the total number of eligible votes, the number of members voting in the election, and the total number of votes cast for each nominee, which shall be reported for the district at large.

(h) *Failure to fill all independent directorships.* If any independent directorship is not filled due to the failure of any nominee to receive at least 20 percent of the eligible vote, the Bank shall continue the election process for that directorship under the following procedures:

(1) The Bank's board of directors, after again consulting with the Bank's Advisory Council, shall nominate at least as many individuals as there are independent directorships to be filled. It may nominate individuals who failed to be elected in the initial vote. The Bank thereafter shall deliver to FHFA a copy of the independent director application form executed by each nominee.

(2) The Bank then shall follow the provisions in this section that are applicable to the election process for independent directors, except for the following:

(i) The Bank shall not place the name of any nominee on a ballot without prior approval of FHFA; and

(ii) The Bank may adopt a closing date that is earlier than 30 calendar days after delivery of the ballots to the eligible voting members, provided the Bank determines that an earlier closing date provides a reasonable amount of time to vote the ballots.

[73 FR 55715, Sept. 26, 2008, as amended at 74 FR 51462, Oct. 7, 2009. Redesignated and amended at 75 FR 17039, 17040, Apr. 5, 2010]

§ 1261.9 Actions affecting director elections.

(a) *Banks.* Each Bank, acting through its board of directors, may conduct an annual assessment of the skills and experience possessed by the members of its board of directors as a whole and may determine whether the capabilities of the board would be enhanced through the addition of individuals with particular skills and experience. If the board of directors determines that the Bank could benefit by the addition to the board of directors of individuals with particular qualifications, such as auditing and accounting, derivatives, financial management, organizational management, project development, risk management practices, or the law , it may identify those qualifications and so inform the members as part of its announcement of elections pursuant to § 1261.7(a).

(b) *Support for nomination or election.* (1) A Bank director, officer, attorney, employee, or agent, acting in his or her personal capacity, may support the nomination or election of any individual for a member directorship, provided that no such individual shall purport to represent the views of the Bank or its board of directors in doing so.

(2) A Bank director, officer, attorney, employee or agent and the board of directors and Advisory Council (including members of the Council) of a Bank may support the candidacy of any individual nominated by the board of directors for election to an independent directorship.

(c) *Prohibition.* Except as provided in paragraphs (a) and (b) of this section, no director, officer, attorney, employee, or agent of a Bank shall:

(1) Communicate in any manner that a director, officer, attorney, employee, or agent of a Bank, directly or indirectly, supports or opposes the nomination or election of a particular individual for a directorship; or

(2) Take any other action to influence the voting with respect to any particular individual.

[73 FR 55715, Sept. 26, 2008, as amended at 74 FR 51463, Oct. 7, 2009]

§ 1261.10 Independent director conflict of interests.

(a) *Employment interests.* During any independent director's term of service, such director shall not serve as an officer, employee, or director of any member of the Bank on whose board the individual sits, or of any recipient of advances from such Bank, and shall not serve as an officer of any Bank. An independent director or nominee for any independent directorship shall disclose all such interests to the Bank on whose board of directors the individual serves or which is considering the individual for nomination to its board of directors.

(b) *Holding companies.* Service as an officer, employee, or director of a holding company that controls one or more members of, or one or more recipients of advances from, the Bank on whose board an independent director serves is not deemed to be service as an officer, employee or director of a member or recipient of advances if the assets of all such members or all such recipients of advances constitute less than 35 percent of the assets of the holding company, on a consolidated basis.

(c) *Attribution.* For purposes of determining compliance with this section, a Bank shall attribute to the independent director any officer position, employee position, or directorship of the director's spouse.

[73 FR 55715, Sept. 26, 2008, as amended at 74 FR 51463, Oct. 7, 2009]

§ 1261.11 Conflict-of-interests policy for Bank directors.

(a) *Adoption of conflict-of-interests policy.* Each Bank shall adopt a written conflict-of-interests policy that applies to all members of its board of directors. At a minimum, the conflict-of-interests policy of each Bank shall:

(1) Require the directors to administer the affairs of the Bank fairly and impartially and without discrimination in favor of or against any member;

(2) Require independent directors to comply with § 1261.10(a);

(3) Prohibit the use of a director's official position for personal gain;

(4) Require directors to disclose actual or apparent conflicts of interests and establish procedures for addressing such conflicts;

(5) Require the establishment of internal controls to ensure that conflict-of-interests reports are made and filed and that conflict-of-interests issues are disclosed and resolved; and

(6) Establish procedures to monitor compliance with the conflict-of-interests policy.

(b) *Disclosure and recusal.* A director shall disclose to the Bank's board of directors any financial interests he or she has, as well as any financial interests known to the director of any immediate family member or business associate of the director, in any matter to be considered by the Bank's board of directors and in any other business matter or proposed business matter involving the Bank and any other person or entity. A director shall disclose fully the nature of his or her interests in the matter and shall provide to the Bank's board of directors any information requested to aid in its consideration of the director's interest. A director shall refrain from considering or voting on any issue in which the director, any immediate family member, or any business associate has any financial interest.

(c) *Confidential Information.* Directors shall not disclose or use confidential information they receive solely by reason of their position with the Bank to obtain any benefit for themselves or for any other individual or entity.

(d) *Gifts.* No Bank director shall accept, and each Bank director shall discourage the director's immediate family members from accepting, any gift that the director believes or has reason to believe is given with the intent to influence the director's actions as a member of the Bank's board of directors, or where acceptance of such gift would have the appearance of intending to influence the director's actions as a member of the board. Any insubstantial gift would not be expected to trigger this prohibition.

(e) *Compensation.* Directors shall not accept compensation for services performed for the Bank from any source other than the Bank for which the services are performed.

(f) *Definitions.* For purposes of this section:

(1) *Immediate family member* means parent, sibling, spouse, child, or dependent, or any relative sharing the same residence as the director.

(2) *Financial interest* means a direct or indirect financial interest in any activity, transaction, property, or relationship that involves receiving or providing something of monetary value, and includes, but is not limited to any right, contractual or otherwise, to the payment of money, whether contingent or fixed. It does not include a deposit or savings account maintained with a member, nor does it include a loan or extension of credit obtained from a member in the normal course of business on terms that are available generally to the public.

(3) *Business associate* means any individual or entity with whom a director has a business relationship, including, but not limited to:

(i) Any corporation or organization of which the director is an officer or partner, or in which the director beneficially owns ten percent or more of any class of equity security, including subordinated debt;

(ii) Any other partner, officer, or beneficial owner of ten percent or more of any class of equity security, including subordinated debt, of any such corporation or organization; and

(iii) Any trust or other estate in which a director has a substantial beneficial interest or as to which the director serves as trustee or in a similar fiduciary capacity.

[73 FR 55715, Sept. 26, 2008, as amended at 74 FR 51463, Oct. 7, 2009]

§ 1261.12 Reporting requirements for Bank directors.

(a) *Annual reporting.* Annually, each Bank shall require each of its directors to execute and deliver to the Bank the appropriate director eligibility certification form prescribed by FHFA for the type of directorship held by such director. The Bank promptly shall deliver to FHFA a copy of the certification form delivered to it by each director.

(b) *Report of noncompliance.* At any time that any director believes or has reason to believe that he or she no longer meets the eligibility requirements set forth in the Bank Act or this subpart, the director promptly shall so notify the Bank and FHFA in writing. At any time that a Bank believes or has reason to believe that any director no longer meets the eligibility requirements set forth in the Bank Act or this subpart, the Bank promptly shall notify FHFA in writing.

[74 FR 51463, Oct. 7, 2009]

§ 1261.13 Ineligible Bank directors.

Upon a determination by FHFA or a Bank that any director of the Bank no longer satisfies the eligibility requirements set forth in the Bank Act or this part, or has failed to comply with the reporting requirements of § 1261.12, the directorship shall immediately become vacant. Any director that is determined to have failed to comply with any of these requirements shall not continue to serve as a Bank director. Whenever a Bank makes such a determination, the Bank promptly shall notify the Bank director and FHFA in writing.

[74 FR 51464, Oct. 7, 2009]

§ 1261.14 Vacant Bank directorships.

(a) *Filling unexpired terms.* (1) When a vacancy occurs on the board of directors of any Bank, the board of directors of the Bank shall elect, by a majority vote of the remaining Bank directors sitting as a board, an individual to fill the unexpired term of office of the vacant directorship, regardless of whether the remaining Bank directors constitute a quorum of the Bank's board of directors.

(2) The board of directors of the Bank may fill an anticipated vacancy prior to the effective date of the vacancy, provided the board does so no sooner than the date of the regularly scheduled board meeting that occurs immediately prior to the effective date of the vacancy.

(3) The board of directors shall elect only an individual who satisfies all the eligibility requirements in the Bank Act and in this subpart that applied to his or her predecessor and, for independent directorships, also satisfies any of the qualifications in the Bank Act or this subpart. If a Bank does not have at least two sitting public interest independent directors, the board of directors of the Bank shall designate the directorship as a public interest directorship and shall elect an individual

who satisfies a public interest independent directorship qualification in the Bank Act or in this subpart.

(b) *Verifying eligibility.* Prior to any election by the board of directors, the Bank shall obtain an executed member director eligibility certification form prescribed by FHFA from each individual being considered to fill a member directorship and an executed independent director application form prescribed by FHFA from each individual being considered to fill an independent directorship. Using the executed forms, each Bank shall verify each individual's eligibility and, as to independent directors, also shall verify the individual's qualifications. Before any independent director is elected by the board of directors of a Bank, the Bank shall deliver to FHFA for its review a copy of the application form of each individual being considered by the board. The Bank shall retain the information it receives in accordance with § 1261.7(c) and (d).

(c) *Notification.* Promptly after allowing the individual to assume the directorship, as provided in paragraph (b) of this section, a Bank shall notify FHFA and each member located in the Bank's district in writing of the following:

(1) For each member directorship filled by the board of a Bank, the name of the director, the name, location, and FHFA ID number of the member the director serves, the director's title or position with the member, the voting State that the director represents, and the expiration date of the director's term of office; and

(2) For each independent directorship filled by the board of a Bank, the name of the director, the name and location of the organization with which the director is affiliated, if any, the director's title or position with such organization, and the expiration date of the director's term of office.

[74 FR 51464, Oct. 7, 2009, as amended at 75 FR 17039, Apr. 5, 2010]

§ 1261.15 Minimum number of member directorships.

Except with respect to member directorships of a Bank resulting from the merger of any two or more Banks, the number of member directorships allocated to each state shall not be less than the number of directorships allocated to that state on December 31, 1960. The following list sets forth the states whose members held more than one directorship on December 31, 1960:

State	Number of elective directorships on December 31, 1960
California	3
Colorado	2
Illinois	4
Indiana	5
Iowa	2
Kansas	3
Kentucky	2
Louisiana	2
Massachusetts	3
Michigan	3
Minnesota	2
Missouri	2
New Jersey	4
New York	4
Ohio	4
Oklahoma	2
Pennsylvania	6
Tennessee	2
Texas	3
Wisconsin	4

§ 1261.16 [Reserved]

Subpart C—Federal Home Loan Bank Directors' Compensation and Expenses

SOURCE: 75 FR 17040, Apr. 5, 2010, unless otherwise noted.

§ 1261.20 Definitions.

As used in this subpart C:

Compensation means any payment of money or the provision of any other thing of current or potential value in connection with service as a director. Compensation includes all direct and indirect payments of benefits, both cash and non-cash, granted to or for the benefit of any director.

Expenses means necessary and reasonable travel, subsistence and other related expenses incurred in connection with the performance of official duties as are payable to senior officers of the Bank under the Bank's travel policy, except gift or entertainment expenses.

§ 1261.21 General.

(a) *Standard.* Each Bank may pay its directors reasonable compensation for the time required of them, and their necessary expenses, in the performance of their duties, as determined by a resolution adopted by the board of directors of the Bank and subject to the provisions of this subpart.

(b) *Reporting.* (1) *Following calendar year.* By December 31 of each calendar year, each Bank shall report to the Director the compensation it anticipates paying to its directors for the following calendar year.

(2) *Preceding calendar year.* No later than the tenth business day of each calendar year, each Bank shall report to the Director the following information relating to director compensation, expenses and meeting attendance for the immediately preceding calendar year:

(i) The total compensation paid to each director;

(ii) The total expenses paid to each director;

(iii) The total compensation paid to all directors;

(iv) The total expenses paid to all directors;

(v) The total of all expenses incurred at group functions that are not reimbursed to individual directors, such as the cost of group meals in connection with board and committee meetings;

(vi) The total number of meetings held by the board and its designated committees; and

(vii) The number of board and designated committee meetings each director attended in-person or through electronic means such as video or teleconferencing.

§ 1261.22 Directors' compensation policy.

(a) *General.* Each Bank's board of directors annually shall adopt a written compensation policy to provide for the payment of reasonable compensation and expenses to the directors for the time required of them in performing their duties as directors. Payments under the directors' compensation policy may be based on any factors that the board of directors determines reasonably to be appropriate, subject to the requirements in this subpart.

(b) *Minimum contents.* The compensation policy shall address the activities or functions for which director attendance or participation is necessary and which may be compensated, and shall explain and justify the methodology used to determine the amount of compensation to be paid to the Bank directors. The compensation policy shall require that any compensation paid to a director reflect the amount of time the director has spent on official Bank business, and shall require that compensation be reduced, as necessary to reflect lesser attendance or performance at board or committee meetings during a given year.

(c) *Prohibited payments.* A Bank shall not pay a director who regularly fails to attend board or committee meetings, and shall not pay fees to a director that do not reflect the director's performance of official Bank business conducted prior to the payment of such fees.

(d) *Submission requirements.* No later than the tenth business day after adopting its annual policy for director compensation and expenses, and at least 30 days prior to disbursing the first payment to any director, each Bank shall submit to the Director a copy of the policy, along with all studies or other supporting materials upon which the board relied in determining the level of compensation and expenses to pay to its directors.

§ 1261.23 Director disapproval.

The Director may determine, based upon his or her review of a Bank's director compensation policy, methodology and/or other related materials, that the compensation and/or expenses to be paid to the directors are not reasonable. In such case, the Director may order the Bank to refrain from making any further payments under that compensation policy. Any such order shall apply prospectively only and will not affect either compensation or expenses that have been earned but not yet paid or reimbursed or payments that had been made prior to the date of the Director's determination and order.

§ 1261.24 Board meetings.

(a) *Number of meetings.* The board of directors of each Bank shall hold as many meetings each year as necessary and appropriate to carry out its fiduciary responsibilities with respect to the effective oversight of Bank management and such other duties and obligations as may be imposed by applicable laws, provided the board of directors of a Bank must hold a minimum of six in-person meetings in any year.

(b) *Site of meetings.* The bank usually should hold board of director and committee meetings within the district served by the Bank. The Bank shall not hold board of director or committee meetings in any location that is not within the United States, including its possessions and territories.

Subpart D [Reserved]

PART 1263—MEMBERS OF THE BANKS

Subpart A—Definitions

Sec.

Subpart B—Membership Application Process

Subpart C—Eligibility Requirements

Subpart D—Stock Requirements

Subpart E—Consolidations Involving Members

Subpart F—Withdrawal and Removal from Membership

Subpart G—Orderly Liquidation of Advances and Redemption of Stock

Subpart H—Reacquisition of Membership

Subpart I—Bank Access to Information

Subpart J—Membership Insignia

AUTHORITY: 12 U.S.C. 1422, 1423, 1424, 1426, 1430, 1442, 4511, 4513.

SOURCE: 75 FR 690, Jan. 5, 2010, unless otherwise noted.

Subpart A—Definitions

§ 1263.1 Definitions.

For purposes of this part:

Adjusted net income means net income, excluding extraordinary items such as income received from, or expense incurred in, sales of securities or fixed assets, reported on a regulatory financial report.

Aggregate unpaid loan principal means the aggregate unpaid principal of a subscriber's or member's home mortgage loans, home-purchase contracts and similar obligations.

Allowance for loan and lease losses means a specified balance-sheet account held to fund potential losses on loans or leases, which is reported on a regulatory financial report.

Appropriate regulator means:

(1) In the case of an insured depository institution or CDFI credit union,

the Federal Deposit Insurance Corporation, Board of Governors of the Federal Reserve System, National Credit Union Administration, Office of the Comptroller of the Currency, Office of Thrift Supervision, or appropriate State regulator that has regulatory authority over, or is empowered to institute enforcement action against, the institution, as applicable, and

(2) In the case of an insurance company, an appropriate State regulator accredited by the National Association of Insurance Commissioners.

Bank Act means the Federal Home Loan Bank Act, as amended (12 U.S.C. 1421 through 1449).

CDFI credit union means a State-chartered credit union that has been certified as a CDFI by the CDFI Fund and that does not have Federal share insurance.

CDFI Fund means the Community Development Financial Institutions Fund established under section 104(a) of the Community Development Banking and Financial Institutions Act of 1994 (12 U.S.C. 4703(a)).

CFI asset cap means $1 billion, as adjusted annually by FHFA, beginning in 2009, to reflect any percentage increase in the preceding year's Consumer Price Index (CPI) for all urban consumers, as published by the U.S. Department of Labor.

Class A stock means capital stock issued by a Bank, including subclasses, that has the characteristics specified in section 6(a)(4)(A)(i) of the Bank Act (12 U.S.C. 1426(a)(4)(A)(i)) and applicable FHFA regulations.

Class B stock means capital stock issued by a Bank, including subclasses, that has the characteristics specified in section 6(a)(4)(A)(ii) of the Bank Act (12 U.S.C. 1426(a)(4)(A)(ii)) and applicable FHFA regulations.

Combination business or farm property means real property for which the total appraised value is attributable to residential, and business or farm uses.

Community development financial institution or CDFI means an institution that is certified as a community development financial institution by the CDFI Fund under the Community Development Banking and Financial Institutions Act of 1994 (12 U.S.C. 4701 *et seq.*), other than a bank or savings association insured under the Federal Deposit Insurance Act (12 U.S.C. 1811 *et seq.*), a holding company for such a bank or savings association, or a credit union insured under the Federal Credit Union Act (12 U.S.C. 1751 *et seq.*).

Community financial institution or CFI means an institution:

(1) The deposits of which are insured under the Federal Deposit Insurance Act (12 U.S.C. 1811 *et seq.*); and

(2) The total assets of which, as of the date of a particular transaction, are less than the CFI asset cap, with total assets being calculated as an average of total assets over three years, with such average being based on the institution's regulatory financial reports filed with its appropriate regulator for the most recent calendar quarter and the immediately preceding 11 calendar quarters.

Composite regulatory examination rating means a composite rating assigned to an institution following the guidelines of the Uniform Financial Institutions Rating System (issued by the Federal Financial Institutions Examination Council), including a CAMELS rating or other similar rating, contained in a written regulatory examination report.

Consolidation includes a consolidation, a merger, or a purchase of all of the assets and assumption of all of the liabilities of an entity by another entity.

Director means the Director of FHFA or his or her designee.

Dwelling unit means a single room or a unified combination of rooms designed for residential use.

Enforcement action means any written notice, directive, order, or agreement initiated by an applicant for Bank membership or by its appropriate regulator to address any operational, financial, managerial or other deficiencies of the applicant identified by such regulator. An "enforcement action" does not include a board of directors' resolution adopted by the applicant in response to examination weaknesses identified by such regulator.

Funded residential construction loan means the portion of a loan secured by real property made to finance the on-site construction of dwelling units on one-to-four family property or multifamily property disbursed to the borrower.

Gross revenues means, in the case of a CDFI applicant, total revenues received from all sources, including grants and other donor contributions and earnings from operations.

Home mortgage loan means:

(1) A loan, whether or not fully amortizing, or an interest in such a loan, which is secured by a mortgage, deed of trust, or other security agreement that creates a first lien on one of the following interests in property:

(i) One-to-four family property or multifamily property, in fee simple;

(ii) A leasehold on one-to-four family property or multifamily property under a lease of not less than 99 years that is renewable, or under a lease having a period of not less than 50 years to run from the date the mortgage was executed; or

(iii) Combination business or farm property where at least 50 percent of the total appraised value of the combined property is attributable to the residential portion of the property, or in the case of any community financial institution, combination business or farm property, on which is located a permanent structure actually used as a residence (other than for temporary or seasonal housing), where the residence constitutes an integral part of the property; or

(2) A mortgage pass-through security that represents an undivided ownership interest in:

(i) Long-term loans, provided that, at the time of issuance of the security, all of the loans meet the requirements of paragraph (1) of this definition; or

(ii) A security that represents an undivided ownership interest in long-term loans, provided that, at the time of issuance of the security, all of the loans meet the requirements of paragraph (1) of this definition.

Insured depository institution means an insured depository institution as defined in section 2(9) of the Bank Act, as amended (12 U.S.C. 1422(9)).

Long-term means a term to maturity of five years or greater.

Manufactured housing means a manufactured home as defined in section 603(6) of the National Manufactured Housing Construction and Safety Standards Act of 1974, as amended (42 U.S.C. 5402(6)).

Multifamily property means:

(1) Real property that is solely residential and includes five or more dwelling units;

(2) Real property that includes five or more dwelling units combined with commercial units, provided that the property is primarily residential; or

(3) Nursing homes, dormitories, or homes for the elderly.

Nonperforming loans and leases means the sum of the following, reported on a regulatory financial report:

(1) Loans and leases that have been past due for 90 days (60 days, in the case of credit union applicants) or longer but are still accruing;

(2) Loans and leases on a nonaccrual basis; and

(3) Restructured loans and leases (not already reported as nonperforming).

Nonresidential real property means real property that is not used for residential purposes, including business or industrial property, hotels, motels, churches, hospitals, educational and charitable institution buildings or facilities, clubs, lodges, association buildings, golf courses, recreational facilities, farm property not containing a dwelling unit, or similar types of property.

One-to-four family property means:

(1) Real property that is solely residential, including one-to-four family dwelling units or more than four family dwelling units if each dwelling unit is separated from the other dwelling units by dividing walls that extend from ground to roof, such as row houses, townhouses or similar types of property;

(2) Manufactured housing if applicable State law defines the purchase or holding of manufactured housing as the purchase or holding of real property;

(3) Individual condominium dwelling units or interests in individual cooperative housing dwelling units that are part of a condominium or cooperative building without regard to the number of total dwelling units therein; or

(4) Real property which includes one-to-four family dwelling units combined with commercial units, provided the property is primarily residential.

Operating expenses means, in the case of a CDFI applicant, expenses for business operations, including, but not limited to, staff salaries and benefits, professional fees, interest, loan loss provision, and depreciation, contained in the applicant's audited financial statements.

Other real estate owned means all other real estate owned (*i.e.*, foreclosed and repossessed real estate), reported on a regulatory financial report, and does not include direct and indirect investments in real estate ventures.

Regulatory examination report means a written report of examination prepared by the applicant's appropriate regulator, containing, in the case of insured depository institution applicants, a composite rating assigned to the institution following the guidelines of the Uniform Financial Institutions Rating System, including a CAMELS rating or other similar rating.

Regulatory financial report means a financial report that an applicant is required to file with its appropriate regulator on a specific periodic basis, including the quarterly call report for commercial banks, thrift financial report for savings associations, quarterly or semi-annual call report for credit unions, the National Association of Insurance Commissioners' annual or quarterly report for insurance companies, or other similar report, including such report maintained by the appropriate regulator on a computer on-line database.

Residential mortgage loan means any one of the following types of loans, whether or not fully amortizing:

(1) Home mortgage loans;

(2) Funded residential construction loans;

(3) Loans secured by manufactured housing whether or not defined by State law as secured by an interest in real property;

(4) Loans secured by junior liens on one-to-four family property or multifamily property;

(5) Mortgage pass-through securities representing an undivided ownership interest in

(i) Loans that meet the requirements of paragraphs (1) through (4) of this definition at the time of issuance of the security;

(ii) Securities representing an undivided ownership interest in loans, provided that, at the time of issuance of the security, all of the loans meet the requirements of paragraphs (1) through (4) of this definition; or

(iii) Mortgage debt securities as defined in paragraph (6) of this definition;

(6) Mortgage debt securities secured by

(i) Loans, provided that, at the time of issuance of the security, substantially all of the loans meet the requirements of paragraphs (1) through (4) of this definition;

(ii) Securities that meet the requirements of paragraph (5) of this definition; or

(iii) Securities secured by assets, provided that, at the time of issuance of the security, all of the assets meet the requirements of paragraphs (1) through (5) of this definition;

(7) Home mortgage loans secured by a leasehold interest, as defined in paragraph (1)(ii) of the definition of "home mortgage loan," except that the period of the lease term may be for any duration; or

(8) Loans that finance properties or activities that, if made by a member, would satisfy the statutory requirements for the Community Investment Program established under section 10(i) of the Bank Act (12 U.S.C. 1430(i)), or the regulatory requirements established for any CICA program.

Restricted assets means both permanently restricted assets and temporarily restricted assets, as those terms are used in Financial Accounting Standard No. 117, or any successor publication.

Total assets means the total assets reported on a regulatory financial report or, in the case of a CDFI applicant, the total assets contained in the applicant's audited financial statements.

Unrestricted cash and cash equivalents means, in the case of a CDFI applicant, cash and highly liquid assets that can be easily converted into cash that are not restricted in a manner that prevents their use in paying expenses, as contained in the applicant's audited financial statements.

Subpart B—Membership Application Process

§ 1263.2 Membership application requirements.

(a) *Application.* An applicant for membership in a Bank shall submit to that Bank an application that satisfies the requirements of this part. The application shall include a written resolution or certification duly adopted by the applicant's board of directors, or by an individual with authority to act on behalf of the applicant's board of directors, of the following:

(1) *Applicant review.* Applicant has reviewed the requirements of this part and, as required by this part, has provided to the best of applicant's knowledge the most recent, accurate, and complete information available; and

(2) *Duty to supplement.* Applicant will promptly supplement the application with any relevant information that comes to applicant's attention prior to the Bank's decision on whether to approve or deny the application, and if the Bank's decision is appealed pursuant to § 1263.5, prior to resolution of any appeal by FHFA.

(b) *Digest.* The Bank shall prepare a written digest for each applicant stating whether or not the applicant meets each of the requirements in §§ 1263.6 to 1263.18, the Bank's findings, and the reasons therefor.

(c) *File.* The Bank shall maintain a membership file for each applicant for at least three years after the Bank decides whether to approve or deny membership or, in the case of an appeal to FHFA, for three years after the resolution of the appeal. The membership file shall contain at a minimum:

(1) *Digest.* The digest required by paragraph (b) of this section.

(2) *Required documents.* All documents required by §§ 1263.6 to 1263.18, including those documents required to establish or rebut a presumption under this part, shall be described in and attached to the digest. The Bank may retain in the file only the relevant portions of the regulatory financial reports required by this part. If an applicant's appropriate regulator requires return or destruction of a regulatory examination report, the date that the report is returned or destroyed shall be noted in the file.

(3) *Additional documents.* Any additional document submitted by the applicant, or otherwise obtained or generated by the Bank, concerning the applicant.

(4) *Decision resolution.* The decision resolution described in § 1263.3(b).

§ 1263.3 Decision on application.

(a) *Authority.* FHFA hereby authorizes the Banks to approve or deny all applications for membership, subject to the requirements of this part. The authority to approve membership applications may be exercised only by a committee of the Bank's board of directors, the Bank president, or a senior officer who reports directly to the Bank president, other than an officer with responsibility for business development.

(b) *Decision resolution.* For each applicant, the Bank shall prepare a written resolution duly adopted by the Bank's board of directors, by a committee of the board of directors, or by an officer with delegated authority to approve membership applications. The decision resolution shall state:

(1) That the statements in the digest are accurate to the best of the Bank's knowledge, and are based on a diligent and comprehensive review of all available information identified in the digest; and

(2) The Bank's decision and the reasons therefor. Decisions to approve an application should state specifically that:

(i) The applicant is authorized under the laws of the United States and the laws of the appropriate State to become a member of, purchase stock in, do business with, and maintain deposits in, the Bank to which the applicant has applied; and

(ii) The applicant meets all of the membership eligibility criteria of the Bank Act and this part.

(c) *Action on applications.* The Bank shall act on an application within 60 calendar days of the date the Bank deems the application to be complete. An application is "complete" when a Bank has obtained all the information required by this part, and any other information the Bank deems necessary, to process the application. If an application that was deemed complete subsequently is deemed incomplete because the Bank determines during the review process that additional information is necessary to process the application, the Bank may stop the 60-day clock until the application again is deemed complete, and then resume the clock where it left off. The Bank shall notify an applicant in writing when its application is deemed by the Bank to be complete, and shall maintain a copy of such letter in the applicant's membership file. The Bank shall notify an applicant if the 60-day clock is stopped, and when the clock is resumed, and shall maintain a written record of such notifications in the applicant's membership file. Within three business days of a Bank's decision on an application, the Bank shall provide the applicant and FHFA with a copy of the Bank's decision resolution.

§ 1263.4 Automatic membership.

(a) *Automatic membership for certain charter conversions.* An insured depository institution member that converts from one charter type to another automatically shall become a member of the Bank of which the converting institution was a member on the effective date of such conversion, provided that the converting institution continues to be an insured depository institution and the assets of the institution immediately before and immediately after the conversion are not materially different. In such case, all relationships existing between the member and the Bank at the time of such conversion may continue.

(b) *Automatic membership for transfers.* Any member whose membership is transferred pursuant to § 1263.18(d) automatically shall become a member of the Bank to which it transfers.

(c) *Automatic membership, in the Bank's discretion, for certain consolidations.*—(1) If a member institution (or institutions) and a nonmember institution are consolidated, and the consolidated institution has its principal place of business in a State in the same Bank district as the disappearing institution (or institutions), and the consolidated institution will operate under the charter of the nonmember institution, on the effective date of the consolidation, the consolidated institution may, in the discretion of the Bank of which the disappearing institution (or institutions) was a member immediately prior to the effective date of the consolidation, automatically become a member of such Bank upon the purchase of the minimum amount of Bank stock required for membership in that Bank, as required by § 1263.20, provided that:

(i) 90 percent or more of the consolidated institution's total assets are derived from the total assets of the disappearing member institution (or institutions); and

(ii) The consolidated institution provides written notice to such Bank, within 60 calendar days after the effective date of the consolidation, that it desires to be a member of the Bank.

(2) The provisions of § 1263.24(b)(4)(i) shall apply, and upon approval of automatic membership by the Bank, the provisions of § 1263.24(c) and (d) shall apply.

§ 1263.5 Appeals.

(a) *Appeals by applicants.*—(1) *Filing procedure.* Within 90 calendar days of the date of a Bank's decision to deny an application for membership, the applicant may file a written appeal of the decision with FHFA.

(2) *Documents.* The applicant's appeal shall be addressed to the Deputy Director for Federal Home Loan Bank Regulation, Federal Housing Finance Agency, 1625 Eye Street, NW., Washington, DC 20006, with a copy to the Bank, and shall include the following documents:

(i) *Bank's decision resolution.* A copy of the Bank's decision resolution; and

(ii) *Basis for appeal.* An applicant must provide a statement of the basis for the appeal with sufficient facts, information, analysis, and explanation to rebut any applicable presumptions, or otherwise to support the applicant's position.

(b) *Record for appeal.*—(1) *Copy of membership file.* Upon receiving a copy of an appeal, the Bank whose action has been appealed (appellee Bank) shall provide FHFA with a copy of the applicant's complete membership file. Until FHFA resolves the appeal, the appellee Bank shall supplement the materials provided to FHFA as any new materials are received.

(2) *Additional information.* FHFA may request additional information or further supporting arguments from the appellant, the appellee Bank, or any other party that FHFA deems appropriate.

(c) *Deciding appeals.* FHFA shall consider the record for appeal described in paragraph (b) of this section and shall resolve the appeal based on the requirements of the Bank Act and this part within 90 calendar days of the date the appeal is filed with FHFA. In deciding the appeal, FHFA shall apply the presumptions in this part, unless the appellant or appellee Bank presents evidence to rebut a presumption as provided in § 1263.17.

Subpart C—Eligibility Requirements

§ 1263.6 General eligibility requirements.

(a) *Requirements.* Any building and loan association, savings and loan association, cooperative bank, homestead association, insurance company, savings bank, community development financial institution (including a CDFI credit union), or insured depository institution, upon submission of an application satisfying all of the requirements of the Bank Act and this part, shall be eligible to become a member of a Bank if:

(1) It is duly organized under Tribal law, or under the laws of any State or of the United States;

(2) It is subject to inspection and regulation under the banking laws, or under similar laws, of any State or of the United States or, in the case of a CDFI, is certified by the CDFI Fund;

(3) It makes long-term home mortgage loans;

(4) Its financial condition is such that advances may be safely made to it;

(5) The character of its management is consistent with sound and economical home financing; and

(6) Its home financing policy is consistent with sound and economical home financing.

(b) *Additional eligibility requirement for insured depository institutions other than community financial institutions.* In order to be eligible to become a member of a Bank, an insured depository institution applicant other than a community financial institution also must have at least 10 percent of its total assets in residential mortgage loans.

(c) *Additional eligibility requirement for applicants that are not insured depository institutions.* In order to be eligible to become a member of a Bank, an applicant that is not an insured depository institution also must have mortgage-related assets that reflect a commitment to housing finance, as determined by the Bank in its discretion.

(d) *Ineligibility.* Except as otherwise provided in this part, if an applicant does not satisfy the requirements of this part, the applicant is ineligible for membership.

§ 1263.7 Duly organized requirement.

An applicant shall be deemed to be duly organized, as required by section 4(a)(1)(A) of the Bank Act (12 U.S.C. 1424(a)(1)(A)) and § 1263.6(a)(1), if it is chartered by a State or Federal agency as a building and loan association, savings and loan association, cooperative bank, homestead association, insurance company, savings bank, or insured depository institution or, in the case of a CDFI applicant, is incorporated under State or Tribal law.

§ 1263.8 Subject to inspection and regulation requirement.

An applicant shall be deemed to be subject to inspection and regulation, as required by section 4(a)(1)(B) of the Bank Act (12 U.S.C. 1424 (a)(1)(B)) and § 1263.6(a)(2) if, in the case of an insured depository institution or insurance company applicant, it is subject to inspection and regulation by its appropriate regulator. A CDFI applicant that is certified by the CDFI Fund is not subject to this requirement.

§ 1263.9 Makes long-term home mortgage loans requirement.

An applicant shall be deemed to make long-term home mortgage loans, as required by section 4(a)(1)(C) of the Bank Act (12 U.S.C. 1424(a)(1)(C)) and § 1263.6(a)(3), if, based on the applicant's most recent regulatory financial report filed with its appropriate regulator, or other documentation provided to the Bank, in the case of a CDFI applicant that does not file such reports, the applicant originates or purchases long-term home mortgage loans.

§ 1263.10 Ten percent requirement for certain insured depository institution applicants.

An insured depository institution applicant that is subject to the 10 percent requirement of section 4(a)(2)(A) of the Bank Act (12 U.S.C. 1424(a)(2)(A)) and § 1263.6(b) shall be deemed to be in compliance with such requirement if, based on the applicant's most recent regulatory financial report filed with its appropriate regulator, the applicant has at least 10 percent of its total assets in residential mortgage loans, except that any assets used to secure mortgage debt securities as described in paragraph (6) of the definition of "residential mortgage loan" set forth in § 1263.1 shall not be used to meet this requirement.

§ 1263.11 Financial condition requirement for depository institutions and CDFI credit unions.

(a) *Review requirement.* In determining whether a building and loan association, savings and loan association, cooperative bank, homestead association, savings bank, insured depository institution, or CDFI credit union has complied with the financial condition requirements of section 4(a)(2)(B) of the Bank Act (12 U.S.C. 1424(a)(2)(B)) and § 1263.6(a)(4), the Bank shall obtain as a part of the membership application and review each of the following documents:

(1) *Regulatory financial reports.* The regulatory financial reports filed by the applicant with its appropriate regulator for the last six calendar quarters and three year-ends preceding the date the Bank receives the application;

(2) *Financial statement.* In order of preference—

(i) The most recent independent audit of the applicant conducted in accordance with generally accepted auditing standards by a certified public accounting firm which submits a report on the applicant;

(ii) The most recent independent audit of the applicant's parent holding company conducted in accordance with generally accepted auditing standards by a certified public accounting firm which submits a report on the consolidated holding company but not on the applicant separately;

(iii) The most recent directors' examination of the applicant conducted in accordance with generally accepted auditing standards by a certified public accounting firm;

(iv) The most recent directors' examination of the applicant performed by other external auditors;

(v) The most recent review of the applicant's financial statements by external auditors;

(vi) The most recent compilation of the applicant's financial statements by external auditors; or

(vii) The most recent audit of other procedures of the applicant.

(3) *Regulatory examination report.* The applicant's most recent available regulatory examination report prepared by its appropriate regulator, a summary prepared by the Bank of the applicant's strengths and weaknesses as cited in the regulatory examination report, and a summary prepared by the Bank or applicant of actions taken by the applicant to respond to examination weaknesses;

(4) *Enforcement actions.* A description prepared by the Bank or applicant of any outstanding enforcement actions against the applicant, responses by the applicant, reports as required by the enforcement action, and verbal or written indications, if available, from the appropriate regulator of how the applicant is complying with the terms of the enforcement action; and

(5) *Additional information.* Any other relevant document or information concerning the applicant that comes to the Bank's attention in reviewing the applicant's financial condition.

(b) *Standards.* An applicant of the type described in paragraph (a) of this section shall be deemed to be in compliance with the financial condition requirement of section 4(a)(2)(B) of the Bank Act (12 U.S.C. 1424(a)(2)(B)) and § 1263.6(a)(4), if:

(1) *Recent composite regulatory examination rating.* The applicant has received a composite regulatory examination rating from its appropriate regulator within two years preceding the date the Bank receives the application;

(2) *Capital requirement.* The applicant meets all of its minimum statutory and regulatory capital requirements as reported in its most recent quarter-end regulatory financial report filed with its appropriate regulator; and

(3) *Minimum performance standard*—(i) Except as provided in paragraph (b)(3)(iii) of this section, the applicant's most recent composite regulatory examination rating from its appropriate regulator within the past two years was "1", or the most recent rating was "2" or "3" and, based on the applicant's most recent regulatory financial report filed with its appropriate regulator, the applicant satisfied all of the following performance trend criteria—

(A) *Earnings.* The applicant's adjusted net income was positive in four of the six most recent calendar quarters;

(B) *Nonperforming assets.* The applicant's nonperforming loans and leases plus other real estate owned, did not exceed 10 percent of its total loans and leases plus other real estate owned, in the most recent calendar quarter; and

(C) *Allowance for loan and lease losses.* The applicant's ratio of its allowance for loan and lease losses plus the allocated transfer risk reserve to nonperforming loans and leases was 60 percent or greater during four of the six most recent calendar quarters.

(ii) For applicants that are not required to report financial data to their appropriate regulator on a quarterly basis, the information required in paragraph (b)(3)(i) of this section may be reported on a semi-annual basis.

(iii) A CDFI credit union applicant must meet the performance trend criteria in paragraph (b)(3)(i) of this section irrespective of its composite regulatory examination rating.

(c) *Eligible collateral not considered.* The availability of sufficient eligible collateral to secure advances to the applicant is presumed and shall not be considered in determining whether an applicant is in the financial condition required by section 4(a)(2)(B) of the Bank Act (12 U.S.C. 1424(a)(2)(B)) and § 1263.6(a)(4).

§ 1263.12 Character of management requirement.

(a) *General.* A building and loan association, savings and loan association, cooperative bank, homestead association, savings bank, insured depository institution, insurance company, and CDFI credit union shall be deemed to be in compliance with the character of management requirements of section 4(a)(2)(C) of the Bank Act (12 U.S.C. 1424(a)(2)(C)) and § 1263.6(a)(5) if the applicant provides to the Bank an unqualified written certification duly adopted by the applicant's board of directors, or by an individual with authority to act on behalf of the applicant's board of directors, that:

(1) *Enforcement actions.* Neither the applicant nor any of its directors or senior officers is subject to, or operating under, any enforcement action instituted by its appropriate regulator;

(2) *Criminal, civil or administrative proceedings.* Neither the applicant nor any of its directors or senior officers has been the subject of any criminal, civil or administrative proceedings reflecting upon creditworthiness, business judgment, or moral turpitude since the most recent regulatory examination report; and

(3) *Criminal, civil or administrative monetary liabilities, lawsuits or judgments.* There are no known potential criminal, civil or administrative monetary liabilities, material pending lawsuits, or unsatisfied judgments against the applicant or any of its directors or senior officers since the most recent regulatory examination report, that are significant to the applicant's operations.

(b) *CDFIs other than CDFI credit unions.* A CDFI applicant, other than a CDFI credit union, shall be deemed to be in compliance with the character of management requirement of § 1263.6(a)(5), if the applicant provides an unqualified written certification duly adopted by the applicant's board of directors, or by an individual with authority to act on behalf of the applicant's board of directors, that:

(1) *Criminal, civil or administrative proceedings.* Neither the applicant nor any of its directors or senior officers has been the subject of any criminal, civil or administrative proceedings reflecting upon creditworthiness, business judgment, or moral turpitude in the past three years; and

(2) *Criminal, civil or administrative monetary liabilities, lawsuits or judgments.* There are no known potential criminal, civil or administrative monetary liabilities, material pending lawsuits, or unsatisfied judgments against the applicant or any of its directors or senior officers arising within the past three years that are significant to the applicant's operations.

§ 1263.13 Home financing policy requirement.

(a) *Standard.* An applicant shall be deemed to be in compliance with the home financing policy requirements of section 4(a)(2)(C) of the Bank Act (12 U.S.C. 1424(a)(2)(C)) and § 1263.6(a)(6), if the applicant has received a Community Reinvestment Act (CRA) rating of "Satisfactory" or better on its most recent formal, or if unavailable, informal or preliminary, CRA performance evaluation.

(b) *Written justification required.* An applicant that is not subject to the CRA shall file, as part of its application for membership, a written justification acceptable to the Bank of how and why the applicant's home financing policy is consistent with the Bank System's housing finance mission.

§ 1263.14 De novo insured depository institution applicants.

(a) *Duly organized, subject to inspection and regulation, financial condition and character of management requirements.* An insured depository institution applicant whose date of charter approval is within three years prior to the date the Bank receives the applicant's application for membership in the Bank (*de novo* applicant) is deemed to meet the requirements of §§ 1263.7, 1263.8, 1263.11 and 1263.12.

(b) *Makes long-term home mortgage loans requirement.* A de novo applicant shall be deemed to make long-term home mortgage loans as required by § 1263.9, if it has filed as part of its application for membership, a written justification acceptable to the Bank of how its home financing credit policy and lending practices will include originating or purchasing long-term home mortgage loans.

(c) *10 percent requirement*—(1) *One-year requirement.* A de novo applicant subject to the 10 percent requirement of section 4(a)(2)(A) of the Bank Act (12 U.S.C. 1424(a)(2)(A)) and § 1263.6(b) shall have until one year after commencing its initial business operations to meet the 10 percent requirement of § 1263.10.

(2) *Conditional approval.* A de novo applicant shall be conditionally deemed to be in compliance with the 10 percent requirement of section 4(a)(2)(A) of the Bank Act (12 U.S.C. 1424(a)(2)(A)) and § 1263.6(b). A de novo applicant that receives such conditional membership approval is subject to the stock purchase requirements established by FHFA regulation or the Bank's capital plan, as applicable, as well as FHFA regulations governing advances to members.

(3) *Approval.* A de novo applicant shall be deemed to be in compliance with the 10 percent requirement of section 4(a)(2)(A) of the Bank Act (12 U.S.C. 1424(a)(2)(A)) and § 1263.6(b) upon receipt by the Bank from the applicant, within one year after commencement of the applicant's initial business operations, of evidence acceptable to the Bank that the applicant satisfies the 10 percent requirement.

(4) *Conditional approval deemed null and void.* If the requirements of paragraph (c)(3) of this section are not satisfied, a de novo applicant shall be deemed to be in noncompliance with the 10 percent requirement of section 4(a)(2)(A) of the Bank Act (12 U.S.C. 1424(a)(2)(A)) and § 1263.6(b), and its conditional membership approval is deemed null and void.

(5) *Treatment of outstanding advances and Bank stock.* If a de novo applicant's conditional membership approval is deemed null and void pursuant to paragraph (c)(4) of this section, the liquidation of any outstanding indebtedness owed by the applicant to the Bank and redemption of stock of such Bank shall be carried out in accordance with § 1263.29.

(d) *Home financing policy requirement*—(1) *Conditional approval.* A de novo applicant that has not received its first formal, or, if unavailable, informal or preliminary, CRA performance evaluation, shall be conditionally deemed to be in compliance with the home financing policy requirement of section 4(a)(2)(C) of the Bank Act (12 U.S.C. 1424(a)(2)(C)) and § 1263.6(a)(6), if the applicant has filed, as part of its application for membership, a written justification acceptable to the Bank of how and why its home financing credit policy and lending practices will meet the credit needs of its community. An applicant that receives such conditional membership approval is subject to the stock purchase requirements established by FHFA regulation or the Bank's capital plan, as applicable, as well as FHFA regulations governing advances to members.

(2) *Approval.* A de novo applicant that has been granted conditional approval under paragraph (d)(1) of this section shall be deemed to be in compliance with the home financing policy requirement of section 4(a)(2)(C) of the Bank Act (12 U.S.C. 1424(a)(2)(C)) and § 1263.6(a)(6) upon receipt by the Bank of evidence from the applicant that it received a CRA rating of "Satisfactory" or better on its first formal, or if unavailable, informal or preliminary, CRA performance evaluation.

(3) *Conditional approval deemed null and void.* If the de novo applicant's first such CRA rating is "Needs to Improve" or "Substantial Non-Compliance," the applicant shall be deemed to be in noncompliance with the home financing policy requirement of section 4(a)(2)(C) of the Bank Act (12 U.S.C. 1424(a)(2)(C)) and § 1263.6(a)(6), subject to rebuttal by the applicant under § 1263.17(f), and its conditional membership approval is deemed null and void.

(4) *Treatment of outstanding advances and Bank stock.* If the applicant's conditional membership approval is deemed null and void pursuant to paragraph (d)(3) of this section, the liquidation of any outstanding indebtedness owed by the applicant to the Bank and redemption of stock of such Bank shall be carried out in accordance with § 1263.29.

§ 1263.15 Recent merger or acquisition applicants.

An applicant that merged with or acquired another institution prior to the date the Bank receives its application for membership is subject to the requirements of §§ 1263.7 to 1263.13 except as provided in this section.

(a) *Financial condition requirement*—(1) *Regulatory financial reports.* For purposes of § 1263.11(a)(1), an applicant that, as a result of a merger or acquisition preceding the date the Bank receives its application for membership, has not yet filed regulatory financial reports with its appropriate regulator for the last six calendar quarters and three year-ends preceding such date, shall provide any regulatory financial reports that the applicant has filed with its appropriate regulator.

(2) *Performance trend criteria.* For purposes of § 1263.11(b)(3)(i)(A) to (C), an applicant that, as a result of a merger or acquisition preceding the date the Bank receives its application for membership, has not yet filed combined regulatory financial reports with its appropriate regulator for the last six calendar quarters preceding such date, shall provide pro forma combined financial statements for those calendar quarters in which actual combined regulatory financial reports are unavailable.

(b) *Home financing policy requirement.* For purposes of § 1263.13, an applicant that, as a result of a merger or acquisition preceding the date the Bank receives its application for membership, has not received its first formal, or if unavailable, informal or preliminary, CRA performance evaluation, shall file as part of its application, a written justification acceptable to the Bank of how and why the applicant's home financing credit policy and lending practices will meet the credit needs of its community.

(c) *Makes long-term home mortgage loans requirement; 10 percent requirement.* For purposes of determining compliance with §§ 1263.9 and 1263.10, a Bank may, in its discretion, permit an applicant that, as a result of a merger or acquisition preceding the date the Bank receives its application for membership, has not yet filed a consolidated regulatory financial report as a combined entity with its appropriate regulator, to provide the combined pro forma financial statement for the combined entity filed with the regulator that approved the merger or acquisition.

§ 1263.16 Financial condition requirement for insurance company and certain CDFI applicants.

(a) *Insurance companies.* An insurance company applicant shall be deemed to meet the financial condition requirement of § 1263.6(a)(4) if, based on the information contained in the applicant's most recent regulatory financial report filed with its appropriate regulator, the applicant meets all of its minimum statutory and regulatory capital requirements and the capital standards established by the National Association of Insurance Commissioners.

(b) *CDFIs other than CDFI credit unions*—(1) *Review requirement.* In order for a Bank to determine whether a CDFI applicant, other than a CDFI credit union, has complied with the financial condition requirement of § 1263.6(a)(4), the applicant shall submit, as a part of its membership application, each of the following documents, and the Bank shall consider all such information prior to acting on the application for membership:

(i) *Financial statements.* An independent audit conducted within the prior year in accordance with generally accepted auditing standards by a certified public accounting firm, plus more recent quarterly statements, if available, and financial statements for the two years prior to the most recent audited financial statement. At a minimum, all such financial statements must include income and expense statements, statements of activities, statements of financial position, and statements of cash flows. The financial statement for the most recent year must include separate schedules or disclosures of the financial position of each of the applicant's affiliates, descriptions of their lines of business, detailed financial disclosures of the relationship between the applicant and its affiliates (such as indebtedness or subordinate debt obligations), disclosures of interlocking directorships with each affiliate, and identification of temporary and permanently restricted funds and the requirements of these restrictions;

(ii) *CDFI Fund certification.* The certification that the applicant has received from the CDFI Fund. If the certification is more than three years old, the applicant must also submit a written statement attesting that there have been no material events or occurrences since the date of certification that would adversely affect its strategic direction, mission, or business operations; and

(iii) *Additional information.* Any other relevant document or information a Bank requests concerning the applicant's financial condition that is not contained in the applicant's financial statements, as well as any other information that the applicant believes demonstrates that it satisfies the financial condition requirement of § 1263.6(a)(4), notwithstanding its failure to meet any of the financial condition standards of paragraph (b)(2) of this section.

(2) *Standards.* A CDFI applicant, other than a CDFI credit union, shall be deemed to be in compliance with the financial condition requirement of § 1263.6(a)(4) if it meets all of the following minimum financial standards—

(i) *Net asset ratio.* The applicant's ratio of net assets to total assets is at least 20 percent, with net and total assets including restricted assets, where net assets is calculated as the residual value of assets over liabilities and is based on information derived from the applicant's most recent financial statements;

(ii) *Earnings.* The applicant has shown positive net income, where net income is calculated as gross revenues less total expenses, is based on information derived from the applicant's most recent financial statements, and is measured as a rolling three-year average;

(iii) *Loan loss reserves.* The applicant's ratio of loan loss reserves to loans and leases 90 days or more delinquent (including loans sold with full recourse) is at least 30 percent, where loan loss reserves are a specified balance sheet account that reflects the amount reserved for loans expected to be uncollectible and are based on information derived from the applicant's most recent financial statements;

(iv) *Liquidity*. The applicant has an operating liquidity ratio of at least 1.0 for the four most recent quarters, and for one or both of the two preceding years, where the numerator of the ratio includes unrestricted cash and cash equivalents and the denominator of the ratio is the average quarterly operating expense.

§ 1263.17 Rebuttable presumptions.

(a) *Rebutting presumptive compliance*. The presumption that an applicant meeting the requirements of §§ 1263.7 to 1263.16 is in compliance with section 4(a) of the Bank Act (12 U.S.C. 1424(a)) and § 1263.6(a) and (b), may be rebutted, and the Bank may deny membership to the applicant, if the Bank obtains substantial evidence to overcome the presumption of compliance.

(b) *Rebutting presumptive noncompliance*. The presumption that an applicant not meeting a particular requirement of §§ 1263.8, 1263.11, 1263.12, 1263.13, or 1263.16, is in noncompliance with section 4(a) of the Bank Act (12 U.S.C. 1424(a)), and § 1263.6(a)(2), (4), (5), or (6) may be rebutted. The applicant shall be deemed to meet such requirement, if the applicable requirements in this section are satisfied.

(c) *Presumptive noncompliance by insurance company applicant with "subject to inspection and regulation" requirement of § 1263.8*. If an insurance company applicant is not subject to inspection and regulation by an appropriate State regulator accredited by the National Association of Insurance Commissioners (NAIC), as required by § 1263.8, the applicant or the Bank shall prepare a written justification that provides substantial evidence acceptable to the Bank that the applicant is subject to inspection and regulation as required by § 1263.6(a)(2), notwithstanding the lack of NAIC accreditation.

(d) *Presumptive noncompliance with financial condition requirements of §§ 1263.11 and 1263.16*—(1) *Applicants subject to § 1263.11*. For applicants subject to § 1263.11, in the case of an applicant's lack of a composite regulatory examination rating within the two-year period required by § 1263.11(b)(1), a variance from the rating required by § 1263.11(b)(3)(i), or a variance from a performance trend criterion required by § 1263.11(b)(3)(i), the applicant or the Bank shall prepare a written justification pertaining to such requirement that provides substantial evidence acceptable to the Bank that the applicant is in the financial condition required by § 1263.6(a)(4), notwithstanding the lack of rating or variance.

(2) *Applicants subject to § 1263.16*. For applicants subject to § 1263.16, in the case of an insurance company applicant's variance from a capital requirement or standard of § 1263.16(a) or, in the case of a CDFI applicant's variance from the standards of § 1263.16(b), the applicant or the Bank shall prepare a written justification pertaining to such requirement or standard that provides substantial evidence acceptable to the Bank that the applicant is in the financial condition required by § 1263.6(a)(4), notwithstanding the variance.

(e) *Presumptive noncompliance with character of management requirement of § 1263.12*—(1) *Enforcement actions*. If an applicant or any of its directors or senior officers is subject to, or operating under, any enforcement action instituted by its appropriate regulator, the applicant shall provide or the Bank shall obtain:

(i) *Regulator confirmation*. Written or verbal confirmation from the applicant's appropriate regulator that the applicant or its directors or senior officers are in substantial compliance with all aspects of the enforcement action; or

(ii) *Written analysis*. A written analysis acceptable to the Bank indicating that the applicant or its directors or senior officers are in substantial compliance with all aspects of the enforcement action. The written analysis shall state each action the applicant or its directors or senior officers are required to take by the enforcement action, the actions actually taken by the applicant or its directors or senior officers, and whether the applicant regards this as substantial compliance with all aspects of the enforcement action.

(2) *Criminal, civil or administrative proceedings*. If an applicant or any of its directors or senior officers has been the

subject of any criminal, civil or administrative proceedings reflecting upon creditworthiness, business judgment, or moral turpitude since the most recent regulatory examination report or, in the case of a CDFI applicant, during the past three years, the applicant shall provide or the Bank shall obtain—

(i) *Regulator confirmation.* Written or verbal confirmation from the applicant's appropriate regulator that the proceedings will not likely result in enforcement action; or

(ii) *Written analysis.* A written analysis acceptable to the Bank indicating that the proceedings will not likely result in enforcement action or, in the case of a CDFI applicant, that the proceedings will not likely have a significantly deleterious effect on the applicant's operations. The written analysis shall state the severity of the charges, and any mitigating action taken by the applicant or its directors or senior officers.

(3) *Criminal, civil or administrative monetary liabilities, lawsuits or judgments.* If there are any known potential criminal, civil or administrative monetary liabilities, material pending lawsuits, or unsatisfied judgments against the applicant or any of its directors or senior officers since the most recent regulatory examination report or, in the case of a CDFI applicant, occurring within the past three years, that are significant to the applicant's operations, the applicant shall provide or the Bank shall obtain—

(i) *Regulator confirmation.* Written or verbal confirmation from the applicant's appropriate regulator that the liabilities, lawsuits or judgments will not likely cause the applicant to fall below its applicable capital requirements set forth in §§ 1263.11(b)(2) and 1263.16(a); or

(ii) *Written analysis.* A written analysis acceptable to the Bank indicating that the liabilities, lawsuits or judgments will not likely cause the applicant to fall below its applicable capital requirements set forth in § 1263.11(b)(2) or § 1263.16(a), or the net asset ratio set forth in § 1263.16(b)(2)(i). The written analysis shall state the likelihood of the applicant or its directors or senior officers prevailing, and the financial consequences if the applicant or its directors or senior officers do not prevail.

(f) *Presumptive noncompliance with home financing policy requirements of §§ 1263.13 and 1263.14(d).* If an applicant received a "Substantial Non-Compliance" rating on its most recent formal, or if unavailable, informal or preliminary, CRA performance evaluation, or a "Needs to Improve" CRA rating on its most recent formal, or if unavailable, informal or preliminary, CRA performance evaluation and a CRA rating of "Needs to Improve" or better on any immediately preceding CRA performance evaluation, the applicant shall provide or the Bank shall obtain:

(1) *Regulator confirmation.* Written or verbal confirmation from the applicant's appropriate regulator of the applicant's recent satisfactory CRA performance, including any corrective action that substantially improved upon the deficiencies cited in the most recent CRA performance evaluation(s); or

(2) *Written analysis.* A written analysis acceptable to the Bank demonstrating that the CRA rating is unrelated to home financing, and providing substantial evidence of how and why the applicant's home financing credit policy and lending practices meet the credit needs of its community.

§ 1263.18 Determination of appropriate Bank district for membership.

(a) *Eligibility.* (1) An institution eligible to become a member of a Bank under the Bank Act and this part may become a member only of the Bank of the district in which the institution's principal place of business is located, except as provided in paragraph (a)(2) of this section. A member shall promptly notify its Bank in writing whenever it relocates its principal place of business to another State and the Bank shall inform FHFA in writing of any such relocation.

(2) An institution eligible to become a member of a Bank under the Bank Act and this part may become a member of the Bank of a district adjoining the district in which the institution's principal place of business is located, if demanded by convenience and then only with the approval of FHFA.

(b) *Principal place of business.* Except as otherwise designated in accordance with this section, the principal place of business of an institution is the State in which the institution maintains its home office established as such in conformity with the laws under which the institution is organized.

(c) *Designation of principal place of business.* (1) A member or an applicant for membership may request in writing to the Bank in the district where the institution maintains its home office that a State other than the State in which it maintains its home office be designated as its principal place of business. Within 90 calendar days of receipt of such written request, the board of directors of the Bank in the district where the institution maintains its home office shall designate a State other than the State where the institution maintains its home office as the institution's principal place of business, provided that all of the following criteria are satisfied:

(i) At least 80 percent of the institution's accounting books, records, and ledgers are maintained, located or held in such designated State;

(ii) A majority of meetings of the institution's board of directors and constituent committees are conducted in such designated State; and

(iii) A majority of the institution's five highest paid officers have their place of employment located in such designated State.

(2) Written notice of a designation made pursuant to paragraph (c)(1) of this section shall be sent to the Bank in the district containing the designated State, FHFA, and the institution.

(3) The notice of designation made pursuant to paragraph (c)(1) of this section shall include the State designated as the principal place of business and the resulting Bank to which membership will be transferred.

(4) If the board of directors of the Bank in the district where the institution maintains its home office fails to make the designation requested by the member or applicant pursuant to paragraph (c)(1) of this section, then the member or applicant may request in writing that FHFA make the designation.

(d) *Transfer of membership.* (1) No transfer of membership from one Bank to another Bank shall take effect until the Banks involved reach an agreement on a method of orderly transfer.

(2) In the event that the Banks involved fail to agree on a method of orderly transfer, FHFA shall determine the conditions under which the transfer shall take place.

(e) *Effect of transfer.* A transfer of membership pursuant to this section shall be effective for all purposes, but shall not affect voting rights in the year of the transfer and shall not be subject to the provisions on termination of membership set forth in section 6 of the Bank Act (12 U.S.C. 1426) or §§ 1263.26 and 1263.27, nor the restriction on reacquiring Bank membership set forth in § 1263.30.

Subpart D—Stock Requirements

§ 1263.19 Par value and price of stock.

The capital stock of each Bank shall be sold at par, unless the Director has fixed a higher price.

§ 1263.20 Stock purchase.

(a) *Minimum stock purchase.* Each member shall purchase stock in the Bank of which it is a member in an amount specified by the Bank's capital plan, except that each member of a Bank that has not converted to the capital structure authorized by the Gramm-Leach-Bliley Act (GLB Act) shall purchase stock in the Bank in an amount equal to the greater of:

(1) $500;

(2) 1 percent of the member's aggregate unpaid loan principal; or

(3) 5 percent of the member's aggregate amount of outstanding advances.

(b) *Timing of minimum stock purchase.* (1) Within 60 calendar days after an institution is approved for membership in a Bank, the institution shall purchase its minimum stock requirement as set forth in paragraph (a) of this section.

(2) In the case of a Bank that has not converted to the capital structure authorized by the GLB Act, an institution that has been approved for membership may elect to purchase its minimum stock requirement in installments, provided that not less than one-

fourth of the total amount shall be purchased within 60 calendar days of the date of approval of membership, and that a further sum of not less than one-fourth of such total shall be purchased at the end of each succeeding period of four months from the date of approval of membership.

(c) *Commencement of membership.* An institution that has been approved for membership shall become a member at the time it purchases its minimum stock requirement or the first installment thereof pursuant to this section.

(d) *Failure to purchase minimum stock requirement.* If an institution that has submitted an application and been approved for membership fails to purchase its minimum stock requirement or its first installment within 60 calendar days of the date of its approval for membership, such approval shall be null and void and the institution, if it wants to become a member, shall be required to submit a new application for membership.

(e) *Reports.* The Bank shall make reports to FHFA setting forth purchases by institutions approved for membership of their minimum stock requirement pursuant to this section and in accordance with the instructions provided in the Data Reporting Manual issued by FHFA, as amended from time to time.

§ 1263.21 Issuance and form of stock.

(a) A Bank shall issue to each new member, as of the effective date of membership, stock in the member's name for the amount of stock purchased and paid for in full.

(b) If the member purchases stock in installments, the stock shall be issued in installments with the appropriate number of shares issued after each payment is made.

(c) A Bank that has not converted to the capital structure authorized by the GLB Act may issue stock in certificated or uncertificated form at the discretion of the Bank.

(d) A Bank that has not converted to the capital structure authorized by the GLB Act may convert all outstanding certificated stock to uncertificated form at its discretion.

§ 1263.22 Adjustments in stock holdings.

(a) *Adjustment in general.* A Bank may from time to time increase or decrease the amount of stock any member is required to hold.

(b)(1) *Annual adjustment.* A Bank shall calculate annually, in the manner set forth in § 1263.20(a), each member's required minimum holdings of stock in the Bank in which it is a member using calendar year-end financial data provided by the member to the Bank, pursuant to § 1263.31(d), and shall notify each member of the adjustment. The notice shall clearly state that the Bank's calculation of each member's minimum stock holdings is to be used to determine the number of votes that the member may cast in that year's election of directors and shall identify the State within the district in which the member will vote. A member that does not agree with the Bank's calculation of the minimum stock requirement or with the identification of its voting State may request FHFA to review the Bank's determination. FHFA shall promptly determine the member's minimum required holdings and its proper voting State, which determination shall be final.

(2) *Redemption of excess shares.* If, in the case of a Bank that has not converted to the capital structure authorized by the GLB Act and after the annual adjustment required by paragraph (b)(1) of this section is made, the amount of stock that a member is required to hold is decreased, the Bank may, in its discretion and upon proper application of the member, retire such excess stock, and the Bank shall pay for each share upon surrender of the stock an amount equal to the par value thereof (except that if at any time FHFA finds that the paid-in capital of a Bank is or is likely to be impaired as a result of losses in or depreciation of the assets held, the Bank shall on the order of FHFA withhold from the amount to be paid in retirement of the stock a *pro rata* share of the amount of such impairment as determined by FHFA) or, at its election, the Bank may credit any part of such payment against the member's debt to the Bank. The Bank's authority to retire such excess stock shall be further subject to

the limitations of section 6(f) of the Bank Act (12 U.S.C. 1426(f)).

(c) A member's stock holdings shall not be reduced under this section to an amount less than required by sections 6(b) and 10(c) of the Bank Act (12 U.S.C. 1426(b), 1430(c)).

§ 1263.23 Excess stock.

(a) *Sale of excess stock.* Subject to the restriction in paragraph (b) of this section, a member may purchase excess stock as long as the purchase is approved by the member's Bank and is permitted by the laws under which the member operates.

(b) *Restriction.* Any Bank with excess stock greater than 1 percent of its total assets shall not declare or pay any dividends in the form of additional shares of Bank stock or otherwise issue any excess stock. A Bank shall not issue excess stock, as a dividend or otherwise, if after the issuance, the outstanding excess stock at the Bank would be greater than 1 percent of its total assets.

Subpart E—Consolidations Involving Members

§ 1263.24 Consolidations involving members.

(a) *Consolidation of members.* Upon the consolidation of two or more institutions that are members of the same Bank into one institution operating under the charter of one of the consolidating institutions, the membership of the surviving institution shall continue and the membership of each disappearing institution shall terminate on the cancellation of its charter. Upon the consolidation of two or more institutions, at least two of which are members of different Banks, into one institution operating under the charter of one of the consolidating institutions, the membership of the surviving institution shall continue and the membership of each disappearing institution shall terminate upon cancellation of its charter, provided, however, that if more than 80 percent of the assets of the consolidated institution are derived from the assets of a disappearing institution, then the consolidated institution shall continue to be a member of the Bank of which that disappearing institution was a member prior to the consolidation, and the membership of the other institutions shall terminate upon the effective date of the consolidation.

(b) *Consolidation into nonmember*—(1) *In general.* Upon the consolidation of a member into an institution that is not a member of a Bank, where the consolidated institution operates under the charter of the nonmember institution, the membership of the disappearing institution shall terminate upon the cancellation of its charter.

(2) *Notification.* If a member has consolidated into a nonmember that has its principal place of business in a State in the same Bank district as the former member, the consolidated institution shall have 60 calendar days after the cancellation of the charter of the former member within which to notify the Bank of the former member that the consolidated institution intends to apply for membership in such Bank. If the consolidated institution does not so notify the Bank by the end of the period, the Bank shall require the liquidation of any outstanding indebtedness owed by the former member, shall settle all outstanding business transactions with the former member, and shall redeem or repurchase the Bank stock owned by the former member in accordance with § 1263.29.

(3) *Application.* If such a consolidated institution has notified the appropriate Bank of its intent to apply for membership, the consolidated institution shall submit an application for membership within 60 calendar days of so notifying the Bank. If the consolidated institution does not submit an application for membership by the end of the period, the Bank shall require the liquidation of any outstanding indebtedness owed by the former member, shall settle all outstanding business transactions with the former member, and shall redeem or repurchase the Bank stock owned by the former member in accordance with § 1263.29.

(4) *Outstanding indebtedness.* If a member has consolidated into a nonmember institution, the Bank need not

require the former member or its successor to liquidate any outstanding indebtedness owed to the Bank or to redeem its Bank stock, as otherwise may be required under § 1263.29, during:

(i) The initial 60 calendar-day notification period;

(ii) The 60 calendar-day period following receipt of a notification that the consolidated institution intends to apply for membership; and

(iii) The period of time during which the Bank processes the application for membership.

(5) *Approval of membership.* If the application of such a consolidated institution is approved, the consolidated institution shall become a member of that Bank upon the purchase of the amount of Bank stock required by section 6 of the Bank Act (12 U.S.C. 1426). If a Bank's capital plan has not taken effect, the amount of stock that the consolidated institution is required to own shall be as provided in §§ 1263.20 and 1263.22. If the capital plan for the Bank has taken effect, the amount of stock that the consolidated institution is required to own shall be equal to the minimum investment established by the capital plan for that Bank.

(6) *Disapproval of membership.* If the Bank disapproves the application for membership of the consolidated institution, the Bank shall require the liquidation of any outstanding indebtedness owed by, and the settlement of all other outstanding business transactions with, the former member, and shall redeem or repurchase the Bank stock owned by the former member in accordance with § 1263.29.

(c) *Dividends on acquired Bank stock.* A consolidated institution shall be entitled to receive dividends on the Bank stock that it acquires as a result of a consolidation with a member in accordance with applicable FHFA regulations.

(d) *Stock transfers.* With regard to any transfer of Bank stock from a disappearing member to the surviving or consolidated member, as appropriate, for which the approval of FHFA is required pursuant to section 6(f) of the Bank Act (12 U.S.C. 1426(f)), as in effect prior to November 12, 1999, such transfer shall be deemed to be approved by FHFA by compliance in all applicable respects with the requirements of this section.

Subpart F—Withdrawal and Removal From Membership

§ 1263.25 [Reserved]

§ 1263.26 Voluntary withdrawal from membership.

(a) *In general.* (1) Any institution may withdraw from membership by providing to the Bank written notice of its intent to withdraw from membership. A member that has so notified its Bank shall be entitled to have continued access to the benefits of membership until the effective date of its withdrawal. The Bank need not commit to providing any further services, including advances, to a withdrawing member that would mature or otherwise terminate subsequent to the effective date of the withdrawal. A member may cancel its notice of withdrawal at any time prior to its effective date by providing a written cancellation notice to the Bank. A Bank may impose a fee on a member that cancels a notice of withdrawal, provided that the fee or the manner of its calculation is specified in the Bank's capital plan.

(2) A Bank shall notify FHFA within 10 calendar days of receipt of any notice of withdrawal or notice of cancellation of withdrawal from membership.

(b) *Effective date of withdrawal.* The membership of an institution that has submitted a notice of withdrawal shall terminate as of the date on which the last of the applicable stock redemption periods ends for the stock that the member is required to hold, as of the date that the notice of withdrawal is submitted, under the terms of a Bank's capital plan as a condition of membership, unless the institution has cancelled its notice of withdrawal prior to the effective date of the termination of its membership.

(c) *Stock redemption periods.* The receipt by a Bank of a notice of withdrawal shall commence the applicable 6-month and 5-year stock redemption periods, respectively, for all of the Class A and Class B stock held by that member that is not already subject to a pending request for redemption. In the case of an institution, the membership of which has been terminated as a result of a merger or other consolidation into a nonmember or into a member of another Bank, the applicable stock redemption periods for any stock that is not subject to a pending notice of redemption shall be deemed to commence on the date on which the charter of the former member is cancelled.

(d) *Certification*. No institution may withdraw from membership unless, on the date that the membership is to terminate, there is in effect a certification from FHFA that the withdrawal of a member will not cause the Bank System to fail to satisfy its requirements under section 21B(f)(2)(C) of the Bank Act (12 U.S.C. 1441b(f)(2)(C)) to contribute toward the interest payments owed on obligations issued by the Resolution Funding Corporation.

§ 1263.27 Involuntary termination of membership.

(a) *Grounds*. The board of directors of a Bank may terminate the membership of any institution that:

(1) Fails to comply with any requirement of the Bank Act, any regulation adopted by FHFA, or any requirement of the Bank's capital plan;

(2) Becomes insolvent or otherwise subject to the appointment of a conservator, receiver, or other legal custodian under Federal or State law; or

(3) Would jeopardize the safety or soundness of the Bank if it were to remain a member.

(b) *Stock redemption periods*. The applicable 6-month and 5-year stock redemption periods, respectively, for all of the Class A and Class B stock owned by a member and not already subject to a pending request for redemption, shall commence on the date that the Bank terminates the institution's membership.

(c) *Membership rights*. An institution whose membership is terminated involuntarily under this section shall cease being a member as of the date on which the board of directors of the Bank acts to terminate the membership, and the institution shall have no right to obtain any of the benefits of membership after that date, but shall be entitled to receive any dividends declared on its stock until the stock is redeemed or repurchased by the Bank.

§ 1263.28 [Reserved]

Subpart G—Orderly Liquidation of Advances and Redemption of Stock

§ 1263.29 Disposition of claims.

(a) *In general*. If an institution withdraws from membership or its membership is otherwise terminated, the Bank shall determine an orderly manner for liquidating all outstanding indebtedness owed by that member to the Bank and for settling all other claims against the member. After all such obligations and claims have been extinguished or settled, the Bank shall return to the member all collateral pledged by the member to the Bank to secure its obligations to the Bank.

(b) *Bank stock*. If an institution that has withdrawn from membership or that otherwise has had its membership terminated remains indebted to the Bank or has outstanding any business transactions with the Bank after the effective date of its termination of membership, the Bank shall not redeem or repurchase any Bank stock that is required to support the indebtedness or the business transactions until after all such indebtedness and business transactions have been extinguished or settled.

Subpart H—Reacquisition of Membership

§ 1263.30 Readmission to membership.

(a) *In general*. An institution that has withdrawn from membership or otherwise has had its membership terminated and which has divested all of its shares of Bank stock, may not be readmitted to membership in any Bank, or acquire any capital stock of any Bank, for a period of 5 years from the date on which its membership terminated and it divested all of its shares of Bank stock.

(b) *Exceptions*. An institution that transfers membership between two Banks without interruption shall not be deemed to have withdrawn from

Bank membership or had its membership terminated.

Subpart I—Bank Access to Information

§ 1263.31 Reports and examinations.

As a condition precedent to Bank membership, each member:

(a) Consents to such examinations as the Bank or FHFA may require for purposes of the Bank Act;

(b) Agrees that reports of examinations by local, State or Federal agencies or institutions may be furnished by such authorities to the Bank or FHFA upon request;

(c) Agrees to give the Bank or the appropriate Federal banking agency, upon request, such information as the Bank or the appropriate Federal banking agency may need to compile and publish cost of funds indices and to publish other reports or statistical summaries pertaining to the activities of Bank members;

(d) Agrees to provide the Bank with calendar year-end financial data each year, for purposes of making the calculation described in § 1263.22(b)(1); and

(e) Agrees to provide the Bank with copies of reports of condition and operations required to be filed with the member's appropriate Federal banking agency, if applicable, within 20 calendar days of filing, as well as copies of any annual report of condition and operations required to be filed.

Subpart J—Membership Insignia

§ 1263.32 Official membership insignia.

Members may display the approved insignia of membership on their documents, advertising and quarters, and likewise use the words "Member Federal Home Loan Bank System."

PART 1264—FEDERAL HOME LOAN BANK HOUSING ASSOCIATES

AUTHORITY: 12 U.S.C. 1430b, 4511, 4513 and 4526.

SOURCE: 65 FR 44426, July 18, 2000, unless otherwise noted. Redesignated at 75 FR 8240, Feb. 24, 2010.

§ 1264.1 Definitions.

As used in this part:

Act means the Federal Home Loan Bank Act as amended (12 U.S.C. 1421 through 1449).

Bank written in title case means a Federal Home Loan Bank established under section 12 of the Act (12 U.S.C. 1432).

FHFA means the Federal Housing Finance Agency.

Governmental agency means the governor, legislature, and any other component of a federal, state, local, tribal, or Alaskan native village government with authority to act for or on behalf of that government.

State housing finance agency or *SHFA* means:

(1) A public agency, authority, or publicly sponsored corporation that serves as an instrumentality of any state or political subdivision of any state, and functions as a source of residential mortgage loan financing in that state; or

(2) A legally established agency, authority, corporation, or organization that serves as an instrumentality of any Indian tribe, band, group, nation, community, or Alaskan Native village recognized by the United States or any state, and functions as a source of residential mortgage loan financing for the Indian or Alaskan Native community.

[65 FR 44426, July 18, 2000, as amended at 67 FR 12849, Mar. 20, 2002; 75 FR 8240, Feb. 24, 2010]

§ 1264.2 Bank authority to make advances to housing associates.

Subject to the provisions of the Act and part 950 of this title, a Bank may make advances to an entity that is not a member of the Bank if the Bank has certified the entity as a housing associate under the provisions of this part.

[65 FR 44426, July 18, 2000, as amended at 75 FR 8240, Feb. 24, 2010]

§ 1264.3 Housing associate eligibility requirements.

(a) *General.* A Bank may certify as a housing associate any applicant that meets the following requirements, as determined using the criteria set forth in § 1264.4:

(1) The applicant is approved under title II of the National Housing Act (12 U.S.C. 1707, *et seq.*);

(2) The applicant is a chartered institution having succession;

(3) The applicant is subject to the inspection and supervision of some governmental agency;

(4) The principal activity of the applicant in the mortgage field consists of lending its own funds; and

(5) The financial condition of the applicant is such that advances may be safely made to it.

(b) *State housing finance agencies.* In addition to meeting the requirements in paragraph (a) of this section, any applicant seeking access to advances as a SHFA pursuant to § 1266.17(b)(2) of this chapter shall provide evidence satisfactory to the Bank, such as a copy of, or a citation to, the statutes and/or regulations describing the applicant's structure and responsibilities, that the applicant is a state housing finance agency as defined in § 1264.1.

[65 FR 44426, July 18, 2000, as amended at 75 FR 8240, Feb. 24, 2010; 75 FR 76622, Dec. 9, 2010]

§ 1264.4 Satisfaction of eligibility requirements.

(a) *HUD approval requirement.* An applicant shall be deemed to meet the requirement in section 10b(a) of the Act (12 U.S.C. 1430b(a)) and § 1264.3(a)(1) that it be approved under title II of the National Housing Act if it submits a current HUD Yearly Verification Report or other documentation issued by HUD stating that the Federal Housing Administration of HUD has approved the applicant as a mortgagee.

(b) *Charter requirement.* An applicant shall be deemed to meet the requirement in section 10b(a) of the Act and § 1264.3(a)(2) that it be a chartered institution having succession if it provides evidence satisfactory to the Bank, such as a copy of, or a citation to, the statutes and/or regulations under which the applicant was created, that:

(1) The applicant is a government agency; or

(2) The applicant is chartered under state, federal, local, tribal, or Alaskan Native village law as a corporation or other entity that has rights, characteristics, and powers under applicable law similar to those granted a corporation.

(c) *Inspection and supervision requirement.* (1) An applicant shall be deemed to meet the inspection and supervision requirement in section 10b(a) of the Act (12 U.S.C. 1430b(a)) and § 1264.3(a)(3) if it provides evidence satisfactory to the Bank, such as a copy of, or a citation to, relevant statutes and/or regulations, that, pursuant to statute or regulation, the applicant is subject to the inspection and supervision of a federal, state, local, tribal, or Alaskan native village governmental agency.

(2) An applicant shall be deemed to meet the inspection requirement if there is a statutory or regulatory requirement that the applicant be audited or examined periodically by a governmental agency or by an external auditor.

(3) An applicant shall be deemed to meet the supervision requirement if the governmental agency has statutory or regulatory authority to remove an applicant's officers or directors for cause or otherwise exercise enforcement or administrative control over actions of the applicant.

(d) *Mortgage activity requirement.* An applicant shall be deemed to meet the mortgage activity requirement in section 10b(a) of the Act (12 U.S.C. 1430b(a)) and § 1264.3(a)(4) if it provides documentary evidence satisfactory to the Bank, such as a financial statement or other financial documents that include the applicant's mortgage loan assets and their funding liabilities, that it lends its own funds as its principal activity in the mortgage field. For purposes of this paragraph, lending funds includes, but is not limited to, the purchase of whole mortgage loans. In the case of a federal, state, local, tribal, or Alaskan Native village government agency, appropriated funds shall be considered an applicant's own funds. An applicant shall be deemed to satisfy this requirement notwithstanding that the majority of its operations are unrelated to mortgage lending if its mortgage activity conforms to this requirement. An applicant that acts principally as a broker for others making mortgage loans, or whose principal activity is to make mortgage loans for the account of others, does not meet this requirement.

(e) *Financial condition requirement.* An applicant shall be deemed to meet the financial condition requirement in §1264.3(a)(5) if the Bank determines that advances may be safely made to the applicant. The applicant shall submit to the Bank copies of its most recent regulatory audit or examination report, or external audit report, and any other documentary evidence, such as financial or other information, that the Bank may require to make the determination.

[65 FR 44426, July 18, 2000, as amended at 67 FR 12849, Mar. 20, 2002; 70 FR 9510, Feb. 28, 2005; 75 FR 8240, Feb. 24, 2010]

§ 1264.5 Housing associate application process.

(a) *Authority.* The Banks are authorized to approve or deny all applications for certification as a housing associate, subject to the requirements of the Act and this part. A Bank may delegate the authority to approve applications for certification as a housing associate only to a committee of the Bank's board of directors, the Bank president, or a senior officer who reports directly to the Bank president other than an officer with responsibility for business development.

(b) *Application requirements.* An applicant for certification as a housing associate shall submit an application that satisfies the requirements of the Act and this part to the Bank of the district in which the applicant's principal place of business, as determined in accordance with part 925 of this title, is located.

(c) *Bank decision process*—(1) *Action on applications.* A Bank shall approve or deny an application for certification as a housing associate within 60 calendar days of the date the Bank deems the application to be complete. A Bank shall deem an application complete, and so notify the applicant in writing, when it has obtained all of the information required by this part and any other information it deems necessary to process the application. If a Bank determines during the review process that additional information is necessary to process the application, the Bank may deem the application incomplete and stop the 60-day time period by providing written notice to the applicant. When the Bank receives the additional information, it shall again deem the application complete, so notify the applicant in writing, and resume the 60-day time period where it stopped.

(2) *Decision on applications.* The Bank or a duly delegated committee of the Bank's board of directors, the Bank president, or a senior officer who reports directly to the Bank president other than an officer with responsibility for business development shall approve, or the board of directors of a Bank shall deny, each application for certification as a housing associate by a written decision resolution stating the grounds for the decision. Within three business days of a Bank's decision on an application, the Bank shall provide the applicant and the FHFA with a copy of the Bank's decision resolution.

(3) *File.* The Bank shall maintain a certification file for each applicant for at least three years after the date the Bank decides whether to approve or deny certification or the date the FHFA resolves any appeal, whichever is later. At a minimum, the certification file shall include all documents submitted by the applicant or otherwise obtained or generated by the Bank concerning the applicant, all documents the Bank relied upon in making its determination regarding certification, including copies of statutes and regulations, and the decision resolution.

[65 FR 44426, July 18, 2000, as amended at 70 FR 9510, Feb. 28, 2005; 75 FR 8240, Feb. 24, 2010]

§ 1264.6 Appeals.

(a) *General.* Within 90 calendar days of the date of a Bank's decision to deny an application for certification as a housing associate, the applicant may submit a written appeal to FHFA that includes the Bank's decision resolution and a statement of the basis for the appeal with sufficient facts, information, analysis and explanation to support the applicant's position. Send appeals to the Deputy Director for Federal Home Loan Bank Regulation, Federal Housing Finance Agency, 1625 Eye Street NW., Washington DC 20006, with a copy to the Bank.

(b) *Record for appeal.* Upon receiving a copy of an appeal, the Bank whose action has been appealed shall provide to the FHFA a complete copy of the applicant's certification file maintained by the Bank under §1264.5(c)(3). Until the FHFA resolves the appeal, the Bank shall promptly provide to the FHFA any relevant new materials it receives. The FHFA may request additional information or further supporting arguments from the applicant, the Bank, or any other party that the FHFA deems appropriate.

(c) *Deciding appeals.* Within 90 calendar days of the date an applicant files an appeal with the FHFA, the FHFA shall consider the record for appeal described in paragraph (b) of this section and resolve the appeal based on the requirements of the Act and this part.

[65 FR 44426, July 18, 2000, as amended at 70 FR 9510, Feb. 28, 2005; 75 FR 8240, Feb. 24, 2010]

PART 1265—CORE MISSION ACTIVITIES

Sec.

AUTHORITY: 12 U.S.C. 1430, 1430b, 1431, 4511, 4513 and 4526.

SOURCE: 65 FR 25278, May 1, 2000, unless otherwise noted. Redesignated at 75 FR 8240, Feb. 24, 2010.

§1265.1 Definitions.

As used in this part:

Acquired member assets or *AMA* means those assets that may be acquired by a Bank under part 955 of this title.

Advance means a loan from a Bank that is:

(1) Provided pursuant to a written agreement;

(2) Supported by a note or other written evidence of the borrower's obligations; and

(3) Fully secured by collateral in accordance with the Federal Home Loan Bank Act (12 U.S.C. 1421 through 1449) and applicable regulations.

Bank written in title case means a Federal Home Loan Bank established under section 12 of the Federal Home Loan Bank Act (12 U.S.C. 1432).

SBIC means a small business investment company formed pursuant to section 301 of the Small Business Investment Act (15 U.S.C. 681).

Targeted income level means:

(1) For rural areas, incomes at or below 115 percent of the median income for the area, as adjusted for family size in accordance with the methodology of the applicable area median income standard or, at the option of the Bank, for a family of four; and

(2) For urban areas, incomes at or below 100 percent of the median income for the area, as adjusted for family size in accordance with the methodology of the applicable area median income standard or, at the option of the Bank, for a family of four.

[75 FR 8240, Feb. 24, 2010]

§1265.2 Mission of the Banks.

The mission of the Banks is to provide to their members' and housing associates financial products and services, including but not limited to advances, that assist and enhance such members' and housing associates financing:

(a) Financing of housing, including single-family and multi-family housing serving consumers at all income levels; and

(b) Community lending.

[65 FR 25278, May 1, 2000, as amended at 67 FR 12850, Mar. 20, 2002; 67 FR 39791, June 10, 2002]

§1265.3 Core mission activities.

The following Bank activities qualify as core mission activities:

(a) Advances;

(b) Acquired member assets (AMA), except that United States government-insured or guaranteed whole single-family residential mortgage loans acquired under a commitment entered into after April 12, 2000 shall qualify only in a cumulative dollar amount up to 33 percent of: The cumulative total dollar amount of AMA acquired by a Bank after April 12, 2000, less the cumulative dollar amount of United States government-insured or guaranteed whole single-family residential mortgage loans acquired after April 12, 2000 under commitments entered into on or before April 12, 2000 (which calculation, at the discretion of two or more Banks, may be made based on aggregate transactions among those Banks);

(c) Standby letters of credit;

(d) Intermediary derivative contracts;

(e) Debt or equity investments:

(1) That primarily benefit households having a targeted income level, a significant proportion of which must benefit households with incomes at or below 80 percent of area median income, or areas targeted for redevelopment by local, state, tribal or Federal government (including Federal Empowerment Zones and Enterprise and Champion Communities), by providing or supporting one or more of the following activities:

(i) Housing;

(ii) Economic development;

(iii) Community services;

(iv) Permanent jobs; or

(v) Area revitalization or stabilization;

(2) In the case of mortgage- or asset-backed securities, the acquisition of which would expand liquidity for loans that are not otherwise adequately provided by the private sector and do not have a readily available or well established secondary market; and

(3) That involve one or more members or housing associates in a manner, financial or otherwise, and to a degree to be determined by the Bank;

(f) Investments in SBICs, where one or more members or housing associates of the Bank also make a material investment in the same activity;

(g) SBIC debentures, the short term tranche of SBIC securities, ore other debentures that are guaranteed by the Small Business Administration under title III of the Small Business Investment Act of 1958, as amended (15 U.S.C. 681 *et seq.*);

(h) Section 108 Interim Notes and Participation Certificates guaranteed by the Department of Housing and Urban Development under section 108 of the Housing and Community Development Act of 1974, as amended (42 U.S.C. 5308); and

(i) Investments and obligations issued or guaranteed under the Native American Housing Assistance and Self-Determination Act of 1996 (25 U.S.C. 4101 *et seq.*).

[65 FR 43981, July 17, 2000]

PART 1266—ADVANCES

Subpart A—Advances to Members

Subpart B—Advances to Housing Associates

Subpart C—Advances to Out-of-District Members and Housing Associates

AUTHORITY: 12 U.S.C. 1426, 1429, 1430, 1430b, 1431, 4511(b), 4513, 4526(a).

SOURCE: 58 FR 29469, May 20, 1993, unless otherwise noted. Redesignated at 65 FR 8256, Feb. 18, 2000 and 75 FR 76622, Dec. 9, 2010.

EDITORIAL NOTE: Nomenclature changes to part 1266 appear at 75 FR 76622, Dec. 9, 2010.

Subpart A—Advances to Members

§ 1266.1 Definitions.

As used in this part:

Advance means a loan from a Bank that is:

(1) Provided pursuant to a written agreement;

(2) Supported by a note or other written evidence of the borrower's obligation; and

(3) Fully secured by collateral in accordance with the Bank Act and this part.

Affiliate means any business entity that controls, is controlled by, or is under common control with, a member.

Bank, written in title case, means a Federal Home Loan Bank established under section 12 of the Bank Act, as amended (12 U.S.C. 1432).

Bank Act means the Federal Home Loan Bank Act, as amended (12 U.S.C. 1421 through 1449).

Capital deficient member means a member that fails to meet its minimum regulatory capital requirements as defined or otherwise required by the member's appropriate federal banking agency, insurer or, in the case of members that are not federally insured depository institutions, state regulator.

Cash equivalents means investments that—

(1) Are readily convertible into known amounts of cash;

(2) Have a remaining maturity of 90 days or less at the acquisition date; and

(3) Are held for liquidity purposes.

CFI member means a member that is a Community Financial Institution, as defined in §1263.1 of this chapter, except that, for purposes of this part, the member's average of total assets over three years shall be calculated by the Bank:

(1) Based on the average of total assets drawn from the institution's regulatory financial reports (as defined in §1263.1 of this chapter) filed with its appropriate regulator (as defined in §1263.1 of this chapter) for the three most recent calendar year-ends; and

(2) Annually, and shall be effective April 1 of each year.

Community development has the same meaning as under the definition set forth in the Community Reinvestment rule for the Federal Reserve System (12 CFR part 228), Federal Deposit Insurance Corporation (12 CFR part 345), the Office of Thrift Supervision (12 CFR part 563e) or the Office of the Comptroller of the Currency (12 CFR part 25), whichever is the CFI member's primary Federal regulator.

Community development loan means a loan, or a participation interest in such loan, that has as its primary purpose community development, but such loans shall not include:

(1) Any loan or instrument that qualifies as eligible security for an advance under §1266.7(a) of this part;

(2) Any loan that qualifies as a small agri-business loan, small business loan or small farm loan, under definitions set forth in this section; or

(3) Consumer loans or credit extended to one or more individuals for household, family or other personal expenditures.

Credit union means a credit union as defined in section 101 of the Federal Credit Union Act (12 U.S.C. 1752).

Depository institution means a bank, savings association, or credit union.

Dwelling unit means a single room or a unified combination of rooms designed for residential use by one household.

FHFA means the Federal Housing Finance Agency.

Improved residential real property means residential real property excluding real property to be improved, or in the process of being improved, by the construction of dwelling units.

Insurer means the FDIC for insured depository institutions, as defined section 3(c)(2) of the Federal Deposit Insurance Act (12 U.S.C. 1813(c)(2)), and the NCUA for federally-insured credit unions.

Long-term advance means an advance with an original term to maturity greater than five years.

Manufactured housing means a manufactured home as defined in section 603(6) of the Manufactured Home Construction and Safety Standards Act of 1974, as amended (42 U.S.C. 5402(6)).

Mortgage-backed security means:

(1) An equity security representing an ownership interest in:

(i) Fully disbursed, whole first mortgage loans on improved residential real property; or

(ii) Mortgage pass-through or participation securities which are themselves backed entirely by fully disbursed, whole first mortgage loans on improved residential real property; or

(2) An obligation, bond, or other debt security backed entirely by the assets described in paragraph (1)(i) or (ii) of this definition.

Multifamily property means:

(1)(i) Real property that is solely residential and which includes five or more dwelling units; or

(ii) Real property which includes five or more dwelling units with commercial units combined, provided the property is primarily residential.

(2) Multifamily property as defined in this section includes nursing homes, dormitories and homes for the elderly.

Nonresidential real property means real property not used for residential purposes, including business or industrial property, hotels, motels, churches, hospitals, educational and charitable institutions, clubs, lodges, association buildings, golf courses, recreational facilities, farm property not containing a dwelling unit, or similar types of property, except as otherwise determined by the FHFA in its discretion.

One-to-four family property means any of the following:

(1) Real property containing:

(i) One-to-four dwelling units; or

(ii) More than four dwelling units if each unit is separated from the other units by dividing walls that extend from ground to roof, including row houses, townhouses or similar types of property;

(2) Manufactured housing if:

(i) Applicable state law defines the purchase or holding of manufactured housing as the purchase or holding of real property; and

(ii) The loan to purchase the manufactured housing is secured by that manufactured housing;

(3) Individual condominium dwelling units or interests in individual cooperative housing dwelling units that are part of a condominium or cooperative building without regard to the number of total dwelling units therein; or

(4) Real property containing one-to-four dwelling units with commercial units combined, provided the property is primarily residential.

Residential housing finance assets means any of the following:

(1) Loans secured by residential real property;

(2) Mortgage-backed securities;

(3) Participations in loans secured by residential real property;

(4) Loans or investments providing financing for economic development projects for targeted beneficiaries;

(5) Loans secured by manufactured housing, regardless of whether such housing qualifies as residential real property;

(6) Any loans or investments which FHFA, in its discretion, otherwise determines to be residential housing finance assets; and

(7) For CFI members, and to the extent not already included in categories (1) through (6), small business loans, small farm loans, small agri-business loans, or community development loans.

Residential real property means:

(1) Any of the following:

(i) One-to-four family property;

(ii) Multifamily property;

(iii) Real property to be improved by the construction of dwelling units;

(iv) Real property in the process of being improved by the construction of dwelling units;

(2) The term residential real property does not include nonresidential real property as defined in this section.

Savings association means a savings association as defined in section 3(b) of the Federal Deposit Insurance Act, as amended (12 U.S.C. 1813(b)).

Small agri-business loans means loans to finance agricultural production and other loans to farmers that are within the legal lending limit of the reporting CFI member, and that are reported on either: Schedule RC-C, Part I, item 3 of the Report of Condition and Income filed by insured commercial banks and FDIC-supervised savings banks; or Schedule SC300, SC303 or SC306 of the Thrift Financial Report filed by savings associations (or equivalent successor schedules).

Small business loans means commercial and industrial loans that are within the legal lending limit of the reporting CFI member and that are reported on either: Schedule RC-C, Part I, item 1.e or Schedule RC-C, Part I, item 4 of the Report of Condition and Income filed by insured commercial banks and FDIC-supervised savings banks; or Schedule SC300, SC303 or SC306 of the Thrift Financial Report filed by savings associations (or equivalent successor schedules).

Small farm loans means loans secured primarily by farmland that are within the legal lending limit of the reporting CFI member, and that are reported on either: Schedule RC-C, Part I, item 1.a. or 1.b. of the Report of Condition and Income filed by insured commercial banks and FDIC-supervised savings banks; or Schedule SC260 of the Thrift Financial Report filed by savings associations (or equivalent successor schedules).

State housing finance agency or *SHFA* has the meaning set forth in §1264.1 of this chapter.

State regulator means a state insurance commissioner or state regulatory entity with primary responsibility for supervising a member borrower that is not a federally insured depository institution.

Tangible capital means:

(1) Capital, calculated according to GAAP, less "intangible assets" except for purchased mortgage servicing rights to the extent such assets are included in a member's core or Tier 1 capital, as reported in the member's Thrift Financial Report for members whose primary federal regulator is the OTS, or as reported in the Report of Condition and Income for members whose primary federal regulator is the FDIC, the OCC, or the FRB.

(2) Capital calculated according to GAAP, less intangible assets, as defined by a Bank for members that are not regulated by the OTS, the FDIC, the OCC, or the FRB; provided that a Bank shall include a member's purchased mortgage servicing rights to the extent such assets are included for the purpose of meeting regulatory capital requirements.

Targeted beneficiaries has the meaning set forth in §952.1 of this title.

[58 FR 29469, May 20, 1993, as amended at 58 FR 29477, May 20, 1993; 59 FR 2949, Jan. 20, 1994; 62 FR 8871, Feb. 27, 1997; 62 FR 12079, Mar. 14, 1997; 63 FR 35128, June 29, 1998; 63 FR 65545, Nov. 27, 1998; 64 FR 16621, Apr. 6, 1999; 65 FR 8262, Feb. 18, 2000; 65 FR 44428, July 18, 2000; 66 FR 50295, Oct. 3, 2001; 67 FR 12850, Mar. 20, 2002; 75 FR 76622, Dec. 9, 2010]

§ 1266.2 Authorization and application for advances; obligation to repay advances.

(a) *Application for advances.* A Bank may accept oral or written applications for advances from its members.

(b) *Obligation to repay advances.* (1) A Bank shall require any member to which an advance is made to enter into a primary and unconditional obligation to repay such advance and all other indebtedness to the Bank, together with interest and any unpaid costs and expenses in connection therewith, according to the terms under which such advance was made or other indebtedness incurred.

(2) Such obligations shall be evidenced by a written advances agreement that shall be reviewed by the Bank's legal counsel to ensure such agreement is in compliance with applicable law.

(c) *Secured advances.* (1) Each Bank shall make only fully secured advances to its members as set forth in the Bank Act, the provisions of this part and policy guidelines established by the FHFA.

(2) The Bank shall execute a written security agreement with each borrowing member which establishes the Bank's security interest in collateral securing advances.

(3) Such written security agreement shall, at a minimum, describe the type of collateral securing the advances and give the Bank a perfectible security interest in the collateral.

(d) *Form of applications and agreements.* Applications for advances, advances agreements and security agreements shall be in substantially such form as approved by the Bank's board of directors, or a committee thereof specifically authorized by the board of directors to approve such forms.

(e) *Status of secured lending.* All secured transactions, regardless of the form of the transaction, for money borrowed from a Bank by a member of any Bank shall be considered an advance subject to the requirements of this part.

[58 FR 29469, May 20, 1993, as amended at 64 FR 71278, Dec. 21, 1999; 65 FR 8262, Feb. 18, 2000. Redesignated at 65 FR 44429, July 18, 2000; 67 FR 12851, Mar. 20, 2002; 75 FR 76623, Dec. 9, 2010]

§ 1266.3 Purpose of long-term advances; Proxy test.

(a) A Bank shall make long-term advances only for the purpose of enabling any member to purchase or fund new or existing residential housing finance assets.

(b)(1) Prior to approving an application for a long-term advance, a Bank shall determine that the principal amount of all long-term advances currently held by the member does not exceed the total book value of residential housing finance assets held by such member. The Bank shall determine the total book value of such residential housing finance assets, using the most recent Thrift Financial Report, Report of Condition and Income, financial statement or other reliable documentation made available by the member.

(2) Applications for CICA advances are exempt from the requirements of paragraph (b)(1) of this section.

[75 FR 76623, Dec. 9, 2010]

§ 1266.4 Limitations on access to advances.

(a) *Credit underwriting.* A Bank, in its discretion, may:

(1) Limit or deny a member's application for an advance if, in the Bank's judgment, such member:

(i) Is engaging or has engaged in any unsafe or unsound banking practices;

(ii) Has inadequate capital;

(iii) Is sustaining operating losses;

(iv) Has financial or managerial deficiencies, as determined by the Bank, that bear upon the member's creditworthiness; or

(v) Has any other deficiencies, as determined by the Bank; or

(2) Make advances and renewals only if the Bank determines that it may safely make such advance or renewal to the member, including advances and renewals made pursuant to this section.

(b) *New advances to members without positive tangible capital.* (1) A Bank shall not make a new advance to a member without positive tangible capital unless the member's appropriate federal banking agency or insurer requests in writing that the Bank make such advance. The Bank shall promptly provide the FHFA with a copy of any such request.

(2) A Bank shall use the most recently available Thrift Financial Report, Report of Condition, and Income or other regulatory report of financial condition to determine whether a member has positive tangible capital.

(c) *Renewals of advances to members without positive tangible capital*—(1) *Renewal for 30-day terms.* A Bank may renew outstanding advances, for successive terms of up to 30 days each, to a member without positive tangible capital; provided, however, that a Bank shall honor any written request of the appropriate federal banking agency or insurer that the Bank not renew such advances.

(2) *Renewal for longer than 30-day terms.* A Bank may renew outstanding advances to a member without positive tangible capital for a term greater than 30 days at the written request of the appropriate federal banking agency or insurer.

(d) *Advances to capital deficient but solvent members.* (1) Except as provided in paragraph (d)(2)(i) of this section, a Bank may make a new advance or renew an outstanding advance to a capital deficient member that has positive tangible capital.

(2)(i) A Bank shall not lend to a capital deficient member that has positive tangible capital if it receives written notice from the appropriate federal banking agency or insurer that the member's use of Bank advances has been prohibited. The Bank shall promptly provide the FHFA with a copy of any such notice.

(ii) A Bank may resume lending to such a capital deficient member if the Bank receives a written statement from the appropriate federal banking agency or insurer which re-establishes the member's ability to use advances.

(e) *Reporting.* (1) Each Bank shall provide the FHFA with a report of the advances and commitments outstanding to each of its members in accordance with the instructions provided in the Data Reporting Manual issued by the FHFA, as amended from time to time.

(2) Each Bank shall, upon written request from a member's appropriate federal banking agency or insurer, provide to such entity information on advances and commitments outstanding to the member.

(f) *Members without federal regulators.* In the case of members that are not federally insured depository institutions, the references in paragraphs (b), (c), (d) and (e) of this section to "appropriate federal banking agency or insurer" shall mean the member's state regulator acting in a capacity similar to an appropriate federal banking agency or insurer.

(g) *Advance commitments.* (1) In the event that a member's access to advances from a Bank is restricted pursuant to this section, the Bank shall not fund outstanding commitments for advances not exercised prior to the imposition of the restriction. This requirement shall apply to all advance commitments made by a Bank after August 25, 1993.

(2) Each Bank shall include the stipulation contained in paragraph (g)(1) of this section as a clause in either:

(i) The written advances agreement required by § 1266.2(b)(2) of this part; or

(ii) The written advances application required by § 1266.2(a) of this part.

[58 FR 29469, May 20, 1993, as amended at 59 FR 2949, Jan. 20, 1994; 64 FR 71278, Dec. 21, 1999; 65 FR 8263, Feb. 18, 2000. Redesignated at 65 FR 44429, July 18, 2000, as amended at 67 FR 12851, Mar. 20, 2002; 71 FR 35500, June 21, 2006]

§ 1266.5 Terms and conditions for advances.

(a) *Advance maturities.* Each Bank shall offer advances with maturities of up to ten years, and may offer advances with longer maturities consistent with the safe and sound operation of the Bank.

(b) *Advance pricing*—(1) *General.* A Bank shall not price its advances to members below:

(i) The marginal cost to the Bank of raising matching term and maturity funds in the marketplace, including embedded options; and

(ii) The administrative and operating costs associated with making such advances to members.

(2) *Differential pricing.* (i) Each Bank may, in pricing its advances, distinguish among members based upon its assessment of:

(A) The credit and other risks to the Bank of lending to any particular member; or

(B) Other reasonable criteria that may be applied equally to all members.

(ii) Each Bank shall include in its member products policy required by § 917.4 of this title, standards and criteria for such differential pricing and shall apply such standards and criteria consistently and without discrimination to all members applying for advances.

(3) *Exceptions.* The advance pricing policies contained in paragraph (b)(1) of this section shall not apply in the case of:

(i) A Bank's CICA programs; and

(ii) Any other advances programs that are volume limited and specifically approved by the Bank's board of directors.

(c) *Authorization for pricing advances.* (1) A Bank's board of directors, a committee thereof, or the Bank's president, if so authorized by the Bank's board of directors, shall set the rates of interest on advances consistent with paragraph (b) of this section.

(2) A Bank president authorized to set interest rates on advances pursuant to this paragraph (c) may delegate any part of such authority to any officer or employee of the Bank.

(d) *Putable or convertible advances*—(1) *Disclosure.* A Bank that offers a putable or convertible advance to a member shall disclose in writing to such member the type and nature of the risks associated with putable or convertible advance funding. The disclosure should include detail sufficient to describe such risks.

(2) *Replacement funding for putable advances.* If a Bank terminates a putable advance prior to the stated maturity date of such advance, the Bank shall offer to provide replacement funding to

the member, provided the member is able to satisfy the normal credit and collateral requirements of the Bank for the replacement funding requested.

(3) *Definition.* For purposes of this paragraph (d), the term *putable advance* means an advance that a Bank may, at its discretion, terminate and require the member to repay prior to the stated maturity date of the advance.

[58 FR 29469, May 20, 1993, as amended at 61 FR 52687, Oct. 8, 1996; 65 FR 8263, Feb. 18, 2000. Redesignated and amended at 65 FR 44429, July 18, 2000]

§ 1266.6 Fees.

(a) *Fees in member products policy.* All fees charged by each Bank and any schedules or formulas pertaining to such fees shall be included in the Bank's member products policy required by § 917.4 of this title. Any such fee schedules or formulas shall be applied consistently and without discrimination to all members.

(b) *Prepayment fees.* (1) Except where an advance product contains a prepayment option, each Bank shall establish and charge a prepayment fee pursuant to a specified formula which makes the Bank financially indifferent to the borrower's decision to repay the advance prior to its maturity date.

(2) Prepayment fees are not required for:

(i) Advances with original terms to maturity or repricing periods of six months or less;

(ii) Advances funded by callable debt; or

(iii) Advances which are otherwise appropriately hedged so that the Bank is financially indifferent to their prepayment.

(3) The board of directors of each Bank, a designated committee thereof, or officers specifically authorized by the board of directors, may waive a prepayment fee only if such prepayment will not result in an economic loss to the Bank. Any such waiver must subsequently be ratified by the board of directors.

(4) A Bank, in determining whether or not to waive a prepayment fee, shall apply consistent standards to all of its members.

(c) *Commitment fees.* Each Bank may charge a fee for its commitment to fund an advance.

(d) *Other fees.* Each Bank is authorized to charge other fees as it deems necessary and appropriate.

[58 FR 29469, May 20, 1993; 65 FR 8263, Feb. 18, 2000. Redesignated and amended at 65 FR 44429, July 18, 2000]

§ 1266.7 Collateral.

(a) *Eligible security for advances to all members.* At the time of origination or renewal of an advance, each Bank shall obtain from the borrowing member or, in accordance with paragraph (g) of this section, an affiliate of the borrowing member, and thereafter maintain, a security interest in collateral that meets the requirements of one or more of the following categories:

(1) *Mortgage loans and privately issued securities.* (i) Fully disbursed, whole first mortgage loans on improved residential real property not more than 90 days delinquent; or

(ii) Privately issued mortgage-backed securities, excluding the following:

(A) Securities that represent a share of only the interest payments or only the principal payments from the underlying mortgage loans;

(B) Securities that represent a subordinate interest in the cash flows from the underlying mortgage loans;

(C) Securities that represent an interest in any residual payments from the underlying pool of mortgage loans; or

(D) Such other high-risk securities as the FHFA in its discretion may determine.

(2) *Agency securities.* Securities issued, insured or guaranteed by the United States Government, or any agency thereof, including without limitation:

(i) Mortgage-backed securities issued or guaranteed by Freddie Mac, Fannie Mae, Ginnie Mae, or any other agency of the United States Government;

(ii) Mortgages or other loans, regardless of delinquency status, to the extent that the mortgage or loan is insured or guaranteed by the United States or any agency thereof, or otherwise is backed by the full faith and credit of the United States, and such insurance, guarantee or other backing is for the direct benefit of the holder of the mortgage or loan; and

(iii) Securities backed by, or representing an equity interest in, mortgages or other loans referred to in paragraph (a)(2)(ii) of this section.

(3) *Cash or deposits.* Cash or deposits in a Bank.

(4) *Other real estate-related collateral.* (i) Other real estate-related collateral provided that:

(A) Such collateral has a readily ascertainable value, can be reliably discounted to account for liquidation and other risks, and can be liquidated in due course; and

(B) The Bank can perfect a security interest in such collateral.

(ii) Eligible other real estate-related collateral may include, but is not limited to:

(A) Privately issued mortgage-backed securities not otherwise eligible under paragraph (a)(1)(ii) of this section;

(B) Second mortgage loans, including home equity loans;

(C) Commercial real estate loans; and

(D) Mortgage loan participations.

(5) *Securities representing equity interests in eligible advances collateral.* Any security the ownership of which represents an undivided equity interest in underlying assets, all of which qualify either as:

(i) Eligible collateral under paragraphs (a)(1), (2), (3) or (4) of this section; or

(ii) Cash equivalents.

(b) *Additional collateral eligible as security for advances to CFI members or their affiliates*—(1) *General.* Subject to the requirements set forth in part 1272 of this chapter, a Bank is authorized to accept from CFI members or their affiliates as security for advances small business loans, small farm loans, small agri-business loans, or community development loans, in each case fully secured by collateral other than real estate, or securities representing a whole interest in such secured loans, provided that:

(i) Such collateral has a readily ascertainable value, can be reliably discounted to account for liquidation and other risks, and can be liquidated in due course; and

(ii) The Bank can perfect a security interest in such collateral.

(2) *Change in CFI status.* If a Bank determines, as of April 1 of each year, that a member that has previously qualified as a CFI no longer qualifies as a CFI, and the member has total advances outstanding that exceed the amount that can be fully secured by collateral under paragraph (a) of this section, the Bank may:

(i) Permit the advances of such member to run to their stated maturities; and

(ii) Renew such member's advances to mature no later than March 31 of the following year; provided that the total of the member's advances under paragraphs (b)(2)(i) and (ii) of this section shall be fully secured by collateral set forth in paragraphs (a) and (b) of this section.

(c) *Bank restrictions on eligible advances collateral.* A Bank at its discretion may further restrict the types of eligible collateral acceptable to the Bank as security for an advance, based upon the creditworthiness or operations of the borrower, the quality of the collateral, or other reasonable criteria.

(d) *Additional advances collateral.* The provisions of paragraph (a) of this section shall not affect the ability of any Bank to take such steps as it deems necessary to protect its secured position on outstanding advances, including requiring additional collateral, whether or not such additional collateral conforms to the requirements for eligible collateral in paragraphs (a) or (b) of this section or section 10 of the Bank Act (12 U.S.C. 1430).

(e) *Bank stock as collateral.* (1) Pursuant to section 10(c) of the Bank Act (12 U.S.C. 1430(c)), a Bank shall have a lien upon, and shall hold, the stock of a member in the Bank as further collateral security for all indebtedness of the member to the Bank.

(2) The written security agreement used by the Bank shall provide that the borrowing member's Bank stock is assigned as additional security by the member to the Bank.

(3) The security interest of the Bank in such member's Bank stock shall be entitled to the priority provided for in section 10(e) of the Bank Act (12 U.S.C. 1430(e)).

(f) *Advances collateral security requiring formal approval.* No home mortgage loan otherwise eligible to be accepted as collateral for an advance by a Bank under this section shall be accepted as collateral for an advance if any director, officer, employee, attorney or agent of the Bank or of the borrowing member is personally liable thereon, unless the board of directors of the Bank has specifically approved such acceptance by formal resolution, and the FHFA has endorsed such resolution.

(g) *Pledge of advances collateral by affiliates.* Assets held by an affiliate of a member that are eligible as collateral under paragraphs (a) or (b) of this section may be used to secure advances to that member only if:

(1) The collateral is pledged to secure either:

(i) The member's obligation to repay advances; or

(ii) A surety or other agreement under which the affiliate has assumed, along with the member, a primary obligation to repay advances made to the member; and

(2) The Bank obtains and maintains a legally enforceable security interest pursuant to which the Bank's legal rights and privileges with respect to the collateral are functionally equivalent in all material respects to those that the Bank would possess if the member were to pledge the same collateral directly, and such functional equivalence is supported by adequate documentation.

[58 FR 29469, May 20, 1993, as amended at 64 FR 16621, Apr. 6, 1999; 65 FR 8262, Feb. 18, 2000. Redesignated and amended at 65 FR 44429, July 18, 2000; 67 FR 12851, Mar. 20, 2002; 75 FR 76623, Dec. 9, 2010]

§ 1266.8 Banks as secured creditors.

(a) Except as provided in paragraph (b) of this section, notwithstanding any other provision of law, any security interest granted to a Bank by a member, or by an affiliate of a member, shall be entitled to priority over the claims and rights of any party, including any receiver, conservator, trustee or similar party having rights of a lien creditor, to such collateral.

(b) A Bank's security interest as described in paragraph (a) of this section shall not be entitled to priority over the claims and rights of a party that:

(1) Would be entitled to priority under otherwise applicable law; and

(2) Is an actual bona fide purchaser for value of such collateral or is an actual secured party whose security interest in such collateral is perfected in accordance with applicable state law.

[58 FR 29469, May 20, 1993. Redesignated at 65 FR 8256, Feb. 18, 2000 and further redesignated at 65 FR 44429, July 18, 2000, as amended at 67 FR 12851, Mar. 20, 2002]

§ 1266.9 Pledged collateral; verification.

(a) *Collateral safekeeping.* (1) A Bank may permit a member that is a depository institution to retain documents evidencing collateral pledged to the Bank, provided that the Bank and such member have executed a written security agreement pursuant to § 1266.2(c) of this part whereby such collateral is retained solely for the Bank's benefit and subject to the Bank's control and direction.

(2) A Bank shall take any steps necessary to ensure that its security interest in all collateral pledged by non-depository institutions for an advance is as secure as its security interest in collateral pledged by depository institutions.

(3) A Bank may at any time perfect its security interest in collateral securing an advance to a member.

(b) *Collateral verification.* Each Bank shall establish written procedures and standards for verifying the existence of collateral securing the Bank's advances, and shall regularly verify the existence of the collateral securing its advances in accordance with such procedures and standards.

[58 FR 29469, May 20, 1993, as amended at 64 FR 16621, Apr. 6, 1999; 65 FR 8263, Feb. 18, 2000. Redesignated at 65 FR 44430, July 18, 2000; 67 FR 12851, Mar. 20, 2002]

§ 1266.10 Collateral valuation; appraisals.

(a) *Collateral valuation.* Each Bank shall determine the value of collateral securing the Bank's advances in accordance with the collateral valuation procedures set forth in the Bank's member products policy established pursuant to § 917.4 of this title.

(b) *Fair application of procedures.* Each Bank shall apply the collateral valuation procedures consistently and fairly to all borrowing members, and the valuation ascribed to any item of collateral by the Bank shall be conclusive as between the Bank and the member.

(c) *Appraisals.* A Bank may require a member to obtain an appraisal of any item of collateral, and to perform such other investigations of collateral as the Bank deems necessary and proper.

[65 FR 44430, July 18, 2000]

§ 1266.11 Capital stock requirements; redemption of excess stock.

(a) *Capital stock requirement for advances.* For a Bank that has not converted to the capital structure authorized by the Gramm-Leach-Bliley Act, the aggregate amount of outstanding advance made by the Bank to a member shall not exceed 20 times the amount paid in by such member for capital stock in the Bank.

(b) *Unilateral Redemption of excess stock.* A Bank that has not converted to the capital structure authorized by the Gramm-Leach-Bliley Act:

(1) May, after providing 15 calendar days advance written notice to a member, require the redemption of that amount of the member's Bank capital stock that exceeds the applicable capital stock requirements in paragraph (a) of this section, provided that the member continues to comply with the minimum stock purchase requirement set forth in § 1263.20(a) of this chapter; and

(2) May not impose on, or accept from, a member a fee in lieu of redeeming a member's excess stock.

[75 FR 76623, Dec. 9, 2010]

§ 1266.12 Intradistrict transfer of advances.

(a) *Advances held by members.* A Bank may allow one of its members to assume an advance extended by the Bank to another of its members, provided the assumption complies with the requirements of this part governing the issuance of new advances. A Bank may charge an appropriate fee for processing the transfer.

(b) *Advances held by nonmembers.* A Bank may allow one of its members to assume an advance held by a nonmember, provided the advance was originated by the Bank and provided the assumption complies with the requirements of this part governing the issuance of new advances. A Bank may charge an appropriate fee for processing the transfer.

[59 FR 2950, Jan. 20, 1994. Redesignated at 65 FR 44430, July 18, 2000]

§ 1266.13 Special advances to savings associations.

(a) *Eligible institutions.* (1) A Bank, upon receipt of a written request from the Director of the OTS, may make short-term advances to a savings association member.

(2) Such request must certify that the member:

(i) Is solvent but presents a supervisory concern to the OTS because of the member's financial condition; and

(ii) Has reasonable and demonstrable prospects of returning to a satisfactory financial condition.

(b) *Terms and conditions.* Advances made by a Bank to a member savings association under this section shall:

(1) Be subject to all applicable collateral requirements of the Bank, this part and section 10(a) of the Bank Act (12 U.S.C. 1430(a)); and

(2) Be at the interest rate applicable to advances of similar type and maturity that are made available to other members that do not pose such a supervisory concern.

[58 FR 29469, May 20, 1993. Redesignated at 65 FR 8256, Feb. 18, 2000 and further redesignated at 65 FR 44430, July 18, 2000]

§ 1266.14 Advances to the Savings Association Insurance Fund.

(a) *Authority.* Upon receipt of a written request from the FDIC, a Bank may make advances to the FDIC for the use of the Savings Association Insurance Fund. The Bank shall provide a copy of such request to the FHFA.

(b) *Requirements.* Advances to the FDIC for the use of the Savings Association Insurance Fund shall:

(1) Bear a rate of interest not less than the Bank's marginal cost of funds, taking into account the maturities involved and reasonable administrative costs;

(2) Have a maturity acceptable to the Bank;

(3) Be subject to any prepayment, commitment, or other appropriate fees of the Bank; and

(4) Be adequately secured by collateral acceptable to the Bank.

[58 FR 29469, May 20, 1993, as amended at 65 FR 8262, Feb. 18, 2000. Redesignated at 65 FR 44430, July 18, 2000]

§ 1266.15 Liquidation of advances upon termination of membership.

If an institution's membership in a Bank is terminated, the Bank shall determine an orderly schedule for liquidating any indebtedness of such member to the Bank; this section shall not require a Bank to call any such indebtedness prior to maturity of the advance. The Bank shall deem any such liquidation a prepayment of the member's indebtedness, and the member shall be subject to any fees applicable to such prepayment.

[58 FR 29469, May 20, 1993. Redesignated at 65 FR 8256, Feb. 18, 2000 and further redesignated at 65 FR 44430, July 18, 2000]

Subpart B—Advances to Housing Associates

SOURCE: 62 FR 12079, Mar. 14, 1997, unless otherwise noted.

§ 1266.16 Scope.

Except as otherwise provided in §§ 1266.14 and 1266.17, the requirements of subpart A apply to this subpart.

[58 FR 29469, May 20, 1993. Redesignated at 65 FR 44430, July 18, 2000]

§ 1266.17 Advances to housing associates.

(a) *Authority.* Subject to the provisions of the Bank Act and this subpart, a Bank may make advances only to a housing associate whose principal place of business, as determined in accordance with part 1263 of this chapter, is located in the Bank's district.

(b) *Collateral requirements*—(1) *Advances to housing associates.* A Bank may make an advance to any housing associate upon the security of the following collateral:

(i) Mortgage loans insured by the Federal Housing Administration of HUD under title II of the National Housing Act; or

(ii) Securities representing a whole interest in the principal and interest payments due on a pool of mortgage loans insured by the Federal Housing Administration of HUD under title II of the National Housing Act. A Bank may only accept as collateral the securities described in this paragraph (b)(1)(ii) if the housing associate provides evidence that such securities are backed solely by mortgages of the type described in paragraph (b)(1)(i) of this section.

(2) *Certain advances to SHFAs.* (i) In addition to the collateral described in paragraph (b)(1) of this section, a Bank may make an advance to a housing associate that has satisfied the requirements of § 1264.3(b) for the purpose of facilitating residential or commercial mortgage lending that benefits individuals or families meeting the income requirements in section 142(d) or 143(f) of the Internal Revenue Code (26 U.S.C. 142(d) or 143(f)) upon the security of the following collateral:

(A) The collateral described in § 1266.7(a)(1) or (2).

(B) The collateral described in § 1266.7(a)(3). Solely for the purpose of facilitating acceptance of such collateral, a Bank may establish a cash collateral account for a housing associate that has satisfied the requirements of § 1264.3(b).

(C) The other real estate-related collateral described in § 1266.7(a)(4), provided that such collateral comprises mortgage loans on one-to-four family or multifamily residential property.

(ii) Prior to making an advance pursuant to this paragraph (b)(2), a Bank shall obtain a written certification from the housing associate that it shall use the proceeds of the advance for the purposes described in paragraph (b)(2)(i) of this section.

(c) *Terms and conditions*—(1) *General.* Subject to the provisions of this paragraph (c), a Bank, in its discretion, shall determine whether, and on what terms, it will make advances to a housing associate.

(2) *Advance pricing.* (i) A Bank shall price advances to housing associates in accordance with the requirements for pricing advances to members set forth

in § 1266.3(b). Wherever the term "member" appears in § 1266.3(b), the term shall be construed also to mean "housing associate."

(ii) A Bank shall apply the pricing criteria identified in § 1266.5(b)(2) equally to all of its member and housing associate borrowers.

(3) *Limit on advances.* The principal amount of any advance made to a housing associate may not exceed 90 percent of the unpaid principal of the mortgage loans or securities pledged as security for the advance. This limit does not apply to an advance made to a housing associate under paragraph (b)(2) of this section.

(d) *Transaction accounts.* Solely for the purpose of facilitating the making of advances to a housing associate, a Bank may establish a transaction account for each housing associate.

(e) *Loss of eligibility*—(1) *Notification of status changes.* A Bank shall require a housing associate that applies for an advance to agree in writing that it will promptly inform the Bank of any change in its status as a housing associate.

(2) *Verification of eligibility.* A Bank may, from time to time, require a housing associate to provide evidence that it continues to satisfy all of the eligibility requirements of the Bank Act, this subpart and part 1264 of this chapter.

(3) *Loss of eligibility.* A Bank shall not extend a new advance or renew an existing advance to a housing associate that no longer meets the eligibility requirements of the Bank Act, this subpart and part 1264 of this chapter until the entity has provided evidence satisfactory to the Bank that it is in compliance with such requirements.

[58 FR 29469, May 20, 1993, as amended by 65 FR 203, Jan. 4, 2000; 65 FR 8263, Feb. 18, 2000. Redesignated and amended at 65 FR 44430, July 18, 2000; 67 FR 12851, Mar. 20, 2002; 70 FR 9510, Feb. 28, 2005]

Subpart C—Advances to Out-of-District Members and Housing Associates

§ 1266.25 Advances to out-of-district members and housing associates.

(a) *Establishment of creditor/debtor relationship.* Any Bank may become a creditor to a member or housing associate of another Bank through the purchase of an outstanding advance, or a participation interest therein, from the other Bank, or through an arrangement with the other Bank that provides for the establishment of such a creditor/debtor relationship at the time an advance is made.

(b) *Applicability of advances requirements.* Any creditor/debtor relationship established pursuant to paragraph (a) of this section shall be subject to all of the provisions of this part that would apply to an advance made by a Bank to its own members or housing associates.

[65 FR 43981, July 17, 2000; 65 FR 46049, July 26, 2000, as amended at 67 FR 12852, Mar. 20, 2002]

PART 1267—FEDERAL HOME LOAN BANK INVESTMENTS

AUTHORITY: 12 U.S.C. 1429, 1430, 1430b, 1431, 1436, 4511, 4513, 4526.

SOURCE: 76 FR 29151, May 20, 2011, unless otherwise noted.

§ 1267.1 Definitions.

As used in this part:

Asset-backed security means a debt instrument backed by loans, but does not include debt instruments that meet the definition of a mortgage-backed security.

Bank, written in title case, means a Federal Home Loan Bank established under section 12 of the Bank Act, as amended (12 U.S.C. 1432).

Bank Act means the Federal Home Loan Bank Act, as amended (12 U.S.C. 1421 through 1449).

Consolidated obligation means any bond, debenture or note on which the Banks are jointly and severally liable and which was issued under section 11 of the Bank Act (12 U.S.C. 1431) and in accordance with any implementing regulations, whether or not such instrument was originally issued jointly by the Banks or by the Federal Housing Finance Board on behalf of the Banks.

Deposits in banks or trust companies means:

(1) A deposit in another Bank;

(2) A demand account in a Federal Reserve Bank;

(3) A deposit in or sale of Federal funds to:

(i) An insured depository institution, as defined in section 2(9) of the Bank Act, that is designated by the Bank's board of directors;

(ii) A trust company that is a member of the Federal Reserve System or insured by the Federal Deposit Insurance Corporation and is designated by the Bank's board of directors; or

(iii) A U.S. branch or agency of a foreign Bank as defined in the International Banking Act of 1978, as amended, (12 U.S.C. 3101 *et seq.*) that is subject to supervision of the Board of Governors of the Federal Reserve System and is designated by the Bank's board of directors.

Derivative contract means generally a financial contract the value of which is derived from the values of one or more referenced assets, rates, or indices of asset values, or credit-related events. Derivative contracts include interest rate derivative contracts, foreign exchange rate derivative contracts, equity derivative contracts, precious metals derivative contracts, commodity derivative contracts and credit derivatives, and any other instruments that pose similar risks.

GAAP means the United States generally accepted accounting principles.

Indexed principal swap means an interest rate swap agreement in which the notional principal balance amortizes based upon the prepayment experience of a specified group of mortgage-backed securities or asset-backed securities or the behavior of an interest rate index.

Interest-only stripped security means a class of mortgage-backed or asset-backed security that is allocated only the interest payments made on the underlying mortgages or loans and receives no principal payments.

Investment grade means:

(1) A credit quality rating in one of the four highest credit rating categories by an NRSRO and not below the fourth highest credit rating category by any NRSRO; or

(2) If there is no credit quality rating by an NRSRO, a determination by a Bank that the issuer, asset or instrument is the credit equivalent of investment grade using credit rating standards available from an NRSRO or similar standards.

Mortgage-backed security means a security or instrument, including collateralized mortgage obligations (CMOs), and Real Estate Mortgage Investment Trusts (REMICS), that represents an interest in, or is secured by, one or more pools of mortgage loans.

NRSRO means a credit rating organization registered with the Securities and Exchange Commission as a nationally recognized statistical rating organization.

Principal-only stripped security means a class of mortgage-backed or asset-backed security that is allocated only the principal payments made on the underlying mortgages or loans and receives no interest payments.

Total capital shall have the meaning set forth in § 1229.1 of this chapter.

§ 1267.2 Authorized investments and transactions.

(a) In addition to assets enumerated in parts 1266 and 955 of this title and subject to the applicable limitations set forth in this part, and in part 1272 of this chapter, each Bank may invest in:

(1) Obligations of the United States;

(2) Deposits in banks or trust companies;

(3) Obligations, participations or other instruments of, or issued by, the Federal National Mortgage Association or the Government National Mortgage Association;

(4) Mortgages, obligations, or other securities that are, or ever have been, sold by the Federal Home Loan Mortgage Corporation pursuant to section 305 or 306 of the Federal Home Loan Mortgage Corporation Act (12 U.S.C. 1454 or 1455);

(5) Stock, obligations, or other securities of any small business investment company formed pursuant to 15 U.S.C.

681, to the extent such investment is made for purposes of aiding members of the Bank; and

(6) Instruments that the Bank has determined are permissible investments for fiduciary or trust funds under the laws of the state in which the Bank is located.

(b) Subject to any applicable limitations set forth in this part and in part 1272 of this chapter, a Bank also may enter into the following types of transactions:

(1) Derivative contracts;

(2) Standby letters of credit, pursuant to the requirements of part 1269 of this title;

(3) Forward asset purchases and sales;

(4) Commitments to make advances; and

(5) Commitments to make or purchase other loans.

§ 1267.3 Prohibited investments and prudential rules.

(a) *Prohibited investments.* A Bank may not invest in:

(1) Instruments that provide an ownership interest in an entity, except for investments described in § 1265.3(e) and (f) of this chapter;

(2) Instruments issued by non-United States entities, except United States branches and agency offices of foreign commercial banks;

(3) Debt instruments that are not rated as investment grade, except:

(i) Investments described in § 1265.3(e) of this chapter; and

(ii) Debt instruments that were downgraded to a below investment grade rating after acquisition by the Bank;

(4) Whole mortgages or other whole loans, or interests in mortgages or loans, except:

(i) Acquired member assets;

(ii) Investments described in § 1265.3(e) of this title;

(iii) Marketable direct obligations of state, local, or Tribal government units or agencies, having at least the second highest credit rating from an NRSRO, where the purchase of such obligations by the Bank provides to the issuer the customized terms, necessary liquidity, or favorable pricing required to generate needed funding for housing or community lending;

(iv) Mortgage-backed securities, or asset-backed securities collateralized by manufactured housing loans or home equity loans, that meet the definition of the term "securities" under 15 U.S.C. 77b(a)(1) and are not otherwise prohibited under paragraphs (a)(5) through (a)(7) of this section, and

(v) Loans held or acquired pursuant to section 12(b) of the Bank Act (12 U.S.C. 1432(b)).

(5) Residual interest and interest accrual classes of securities;

(6) Interest-only and principal-only stripped securities; and

(7) Fixed rate mortgage-backed securities or eligible asset-backed securities or floating rate mortgage-backed securities or eligible asset-backed securities that on the trade date are at rates equal to their contractual cap, with average lives that vary more than six years under an assumed instantaneous interest rate change of 300 basis points, unless the instrument qualifies as an acquired member asset under part 955 of this title.

(b) *Foreign currency or commodity positions prohibited.* A Bank may not take a position in any commodity or foreign currency. The Banks may issue consolidated obligations denominated in a currency other than U.S. Dollars or linked to equity or commodity prices, provided that the Banks meet the requirements of § 1270.9(d) of this chapter, and all other applicable requirements related to issuing consolidated obligations.

(c) *Limits on certain investments.* (1) A purchase, otherwise authorized under this part, of mortgage-backed securities or asset-backed securities, may not cause the aggregate value of all such securities held by the Bank to exceed 300 percent of the Bank's total capital. For purposes of this limitation, such aggregate value will be measured as of the transaction trade date for such purchase, and total capital will be the most recent amount reported by a Bank to FHFA. A Bank will not be required to divest securities solely to bring the level of its holdings into compliance with the limits of this paragraph, provided that the original purchase of the securities complied with the limits in this paragraph.

(2) A Bank's purchase of any mortgage-backed or asset-backed security may not cause the value of its total holdings of mortgage-backed and asset-backed securities, measured as of the transaction trade date for such purchase, to increase in any calendar quarter by more than 50 percent of its total capital as of the beginning of such quarter.

(3) For purposes of applying the limits under this paragraph (c), the value of relevant mortgage-backed or asset-backed securities shall be calculated based on amortized historical costs for securities classified as held-to-maturity or available-for-sale and on fair value for trading securities.

§ 1267.4 Limitations and prudential requirements on use of derivative instruments.

(a) *Non-speculative use.* Derivative instruments that do not qualify as hedging instruments pursuant to GAAP may be used only if a non-speculative use is documented by the Bank.

(b) *Additional Prohibitions.* (1) A Bank may not enter into interest rate swaps that amortize according to behavior of instruments described in § 1267.3(a)(5) or (6) of this part.

(2) A Bank may not enter into indexed principal swaps that have average lives that vary by more than six years under an assumed instantaneous change in interest rates of 300 basis points, unless they are entered into in conjunction with the issuance of consolidated obligations or the purchase of permissible investments or entry into a permissible transaction in which all interest rate risk is passed through to the investor or counterparty.

(c) *Documentation requirements.* (1) Derivative transactions with a single counterparty shall be governed by a single master agreement when practicable.

(2) A Bank's agreement with the counterparty for over-the-counter derivative contracts shall include:

(i) A requirement that market value determinations and subsequent adjustments of collateral be made at least on a monthly basis;

(ii) A statement that failure of a counterparty to meet a collateral call will result in an early termination event;

(iii) A description of early termination pricing and methodology, with the methodology reflecting a reasonable estimate of the market value of the over-the-counter derivative contract at termination (standard International Swaps and Derivatives Association, Inc. language relative to early termination pricing and methodology may be used to satisfy this requirement); and

(iv) A requirement that the Bank's consent be obtained prior to the transfer of an agreement or contract by a counterparty.

§ 1267.5 Risk-based capital requirements for investments.

Any Bank which is not subject to the capital requirements set forth in part 932 of this title shall hold retained earnings plus general allowance for losses as support for the credit risk of all investments that are not rated by an NRSRO, or are rated or have a putative rating below the second highest credit rating, in an amount equal to or greater than the outstanding balance of the investments multiplied by:

(a) A factor associated with the credit rating of the investments as determined by FHFA on a case-by-case basis for rated assets to be sufficient to raise the credit quality of the asset to the second highest credit rating category; and

(b) 0.08 for assets having neither a putative nor actual rating.

PART 1269—STANDBY LETTERS OF CREDIT

Sec.

AUTHORITY: 12 U.S.C. 1429, 1430, 1430b, 1431, 4511, 4513 and 4526.

SOURCE: 63 FR 65699, Nov. 30, 1998, unless otherwise noted. Redesignated at 65 FR 8256,

Feb. 18, 2000, and further redesignated at 67 FR 12853, Mar. 20, 2002 and 75 FR 8240, Feb. 24, 2010.

§ 1269.1 Definitions.

As used in this part:

Act means the Federal Home Loan Bank Act as amended (12 U.S.C. 1421 through 1449).

Applicant means a person or entity at whose request or for whose account a standby letter of credit is issued.

Bank written in title case means a Federal Home Loan Bank established under section 12 of the Act (12 U.S.C. 1432).

Beneficiary means a person or entity who, under the terms of a standby letter of credit, is entitled to have its complying presentation honored.

Community lending means providing financing for economic development projects for targeted beneficiaries, and, for community financial institutions (as defined in § 1263.1 of this title), purchasing or funding small business loans, small farm loans or small agri-business loans (as defined in § 1266.1 of this chapter).

Confirm means to undertake, at the request or with the consent of the issuer, to honor a presentation under a standby letter of credit issued by a member or housing associate.

Document means a draft or other demand, document of title, investment security, certificate, invoice, or other record, statement, or representation of fact, law, right, or opinion that is presented under the terms of a standby letter of credit.

Investment grade means:

(1) A credit quality rating in one of the four highest credit rating categories by an NRSRO and not below the fourth highest credit rating category by any NRSRO; or

(2) If there is no credit quality rating by an NRSRO, a determination by a Bank that the issuer, asset or instrument is the credit equivalent of investment grade using credit rating standards available from an NRSRO or other similar standards.

Issuer means a person or entity that issues a standby letter of credit.

NRSRO means a credit rating organization registered with the Securities and Exchange Commission as a nationally recognized statistical rating organization.

Presentation means delivery of a document to an issuer, or an entity that has undertaken a confirmation at the request or with the consent of the issuer, for the giving of value under a standby letter of credit.

Residential housing finance means:

(1) The purchase or funding of "residential housing finance assets," as that term is defined in § 1266.1 of this chapter; or

(2) Other activities that support the development or construction of residential housing.

SHFA associate means a housing associate that is a "state housing finance agency," as that term is defined in § 1264.1 of this chapter, and that has met the requirements of § 1269.3(b) of this chapter.

Standby letter of credit means a definite undertaking by an issuer on behalf of an applicant that represents an obligation to the beneficiary, pursuant to a complying presentation: to repay money borrowed by, advanced to, or for the account of the applicant; to make payment on account of any indebtedness undertaken by the applicant; or to make payment on account of any default by the applicant in the performance of an obligation. The term *standby letter of credit* does not include a commercial letter of credit, or any short-term self-liquidating instrument used to finance the movement of goods.

[63 FR 65699, Nov. 30, 1998, as amended at 65 FR 8265, Feb. 18, 2000; 65 FR 44431, July 18, 2000. Redesignated and amended at 67 FR 12853, Mar. 20, 2002; 75 FR 8240, Feb. 24, 2010; 75 FR 76623, Dec. 9, 2010]

§ 1269.2 Standby letters of credit on behalf of members.

(a) *Authority and purposes.* Each Bank is authorized to issue or confirm on behalf of members standby letters of credit that comply with the requirements of this part, for any of the following purposes:

(1) To assist members in facilitating residential housing finance;

(2) To assist members in facilitating community lending;

(3) To assist members with asset/liability management; or

(4) To provide members with liquidity or other funding.

(b) *Fully secured.* A Bank, at the time it issues or confirms a standby letter of credit on behalf of a member, shall obtain and maintain a security interest in collateral that is sufficient to secure fully the member's unconditional obligation described in §1269.4(a)(2) of this part, and that complies with the requirements set forth in paragraph (c) of this section.

(c) *Eligible collateral.* (1) Any standby letter of credit issued or confirmed on behalf of a member may be secured in accordance with the requirements for advances under §1266.7 of this chapter.

(2) A standby letter of credit issued or confirmed on behalf of a member for a purpose described in paragraphs (a)(1) or (a)(2) of this section may, in addition to the collateral described in paragraph (c)(1) of this section, be secured by obligations of state or local government units or agencies rated as investment grade by an NRSRO.

[63 FR 65699, Nov. 30, 1998, as amended at 65 FR 8265, Feb. 18, 2000; 65 FR 44431, July 18, 2000. Redesignated and amended at 67 FR 12853, Mar. 20, 2002; 75 FR 8240, Feb. 24, 2010; 75 FR 76623, Dec. 9, 2010]

§1269.3 Standby letters of credit on behalf of housing associates.

(a) *Housing associates.* Each Bank is authorized to issue or confirm on behalf of housing associates standby letters of credit that are fully secured by collateral described in §1266.17(b)(1)(i) or (ii) of this chapter, and that otherwise comply with the requirements of this part, for any of the following purposes:

(1) To assist housing associates in facilitating residential housing finance;

(2) To assist housing associates in facilitating community lending;

(3) To assist housing associates with asset/liability management; or

(4) To provide housing associates with liquidity or other funding.

(b) *SHFA associates.* Each Bank is authorized to issue or confirm on behalf of SHFA associates standby letters of credit that are fully secured by collateral described in §1266.17(b)(2)(i)(A), (B) or (C) of this chapter, and that otherwise comply with the requirements of this part, for the purpose of facilitating residential or commercial mortgage lending that benefits individuals or families meeting the income requirements in section 142(d) or 143(f) of the Internal Revenue Code (26 U.S.C. 142(d) or 143(f)).

[63 FR 65699, Nov. 30, 1998, as amended at 65 FR 8265, Feb. 18, 2000; 65 FR 44431, July 18, 2000; 75 FR 8240, Feb. 24, 2010; 75 FR 76623, Dec. 9, 2010]

§1269.4 Obligation to Bank under all standby letters of credit.

(a) *Obligation to reimburse.* A Bank may issue or confirm a standby letter of credit only on behalf of a member or housing associate that has:

(1) Established with the Bank a cash account pursuant to §§1266.17(b)(2)(i)(B), 1266.17(d), or 969.2 of this title; and

(2) Assumed an unconditional obligation to reimburse the Bank for value given by the Bank to the beneficiary under the terms of the standby letter of credit by depositing immediately available funds into the account described in paragraph (a)(1) of this section not later than the date of the Bank's payment of funds to the beneficiary.

(b) *Prompt action to recover funds.* If a member or housing associate fails to fulfill the obligation described in paragraph (a)(2) of this section, the Bank shall take action promptly to recover the funds that such member or housing associate is obligated to repay.

(c) *Obligation financed by advance.* Notwithstanding the obligations and duties of the Bank and its member or housing associate under paragraphs (a) and (b) of this section, the Bank may, at its discretion, permit such member or housing associate to finance repayment of the obligation described in paragraph (a)(2) of this section by receiving an advance that complies with sections 10 or 10b of the Act (12 U.S.C. 1430, 1430(b)) and part 1266 of this title.

[63 FR 65699, Nov. 30, 1998, as amended at 65 FR 8265, Feb. 18, 2000; 65 FR 44431, July 18, 2000. Redesignated and amended at 67 FR 12853, Mar. 20, 2002; 75 FR 8240, Feb. 24, 2010; 75 FR 76623, Dec. 9, 2010]

§ 1269.5 Additional provisions applying to all standby letters of credit.

(a) *Requirements.* Each standby letter of credit issued or confirmed by a Bank shall:

(1) Contain a specific expiration date, or be for a specific term; and

(2) Require approval in advance by the Bank of any transfer of the standby letter of credit from the original beneficiary to another person or entity.

(b) *Additional collateral provisions.* (1) A Bank may take such steps as it deems necessary to protect its secured position on standby letters of credit, including requiring additional collateral, whether or not such additional collateral conforms to the requirements of § 1269.2 or § 1269.3 of this part.

(2) Collateral pledged by a member or housing associate to secure a letter of credit issued or confirmed on its behalf by a Bank shall be subject to the provisions of §§ 1266.7(d), 1266.7(e), 1266.8, 1266.9 and 1266.10 of this chapter.

[63 FR 65699, Nov. 30, 1998, as amended at 65 FR 8265, Feb. 18, 2000; 65 FR 44431, July 18, 2000. Redesignated and amended at 67 FR 12853, Mar. 20, 2002; 75 FR 8240, Feb. 24, 2010; 75 FR 76623, Dec. 9, 2010]

PART 1270—LIABILITIES

AUTHORITY: 12 U.S.C. 1431, 1432, 1435, 4511, 4512, 4513, and 4526.

SOURCE: 76 FR 18369, Apr. 4, 2011, unless otherwise noted.

Subpart A—Definitions

§ 1270.1 Definitions.

As used in this part, unless the context otherwise requires or indicates:

Adverse Claim means a claim that a claimant has a property interest in a Book-entry consolidated obligation and that it is a violation of the rights of the claimant for another Person to hold, transfer, or deal with the Security.

Bank, written in title case, means a Federal Home Loan Bank established under section 12 of the Bank Act.

Bank Act means the Federal Home Loan Bank Act, as amended (12 U.S.C. 1421 through 1449).

Book-entry consolidated obligation means a consolidated obligation maintained in the book-entry system of the Federal Reserve Banks.

Consolidated obligation means any bond, debenture or note on which the Banks are jointly and severally liable and which was issued under section 11 of the Bank Act (12 U.S.C. 1431) and in accordance with any implementing regulations, whether or not such instrument was originally issued jointly by the Banks or by the Federal Housing Finance Board on behalf of the Banks.

Deposits in banks or trust companies means:

(1) A deposit in another Bank;

(2) A demand account in a Federal Reserve Bank;

(3) A deposit in, or a sale of Federal funds to:

(i) An insured depository institution, as defined in section 2(9)(A) of the Bank Act (12 U.S.C. 1422(9)(A)), that is designated by a Bank's board of directors;

(ii) A trust company that is a member of the Federal Reserve System or insured by the FDIC, and is designated by a Bank's board of directors; or

(iii) A U.S. branch or agency of a foreign bank, as defined in the International Banking Act of 1978, as amended (12 U.S.C. 3101 *et seq.*), that is subject to the supervision of the Federal Reserve Board, and is designated by a Bank's board of directors.

Director, written in title case, means the Director of FHFA or his or her designee.

Entitlement Holder means a Person or a Bank to whose account an interest in a Book-entry consolidated obligation is credited on the records of a Securities Intermediary.

Federal Reserve Bank means a Federal Reserve Bank or branch, acting as fiscal agent for the Office of Finance, unless otherwise indicated.

Federal Reserve Bank Operating Circular means the publication issued by each Federal Reserve Bank that sets forth the terms and conditions under which the Federal Reserve Bank maintains Book-entry Securities accounts and transfers Book-entry Securities.

Federal Reserve Board means the Board of Governors of the Federal Reserve System.

FHFA means the Federal Housing Finance Agency.

Funds account means a reserve and/or clearing account at a Federal Reserve Bank to which debits or credits are posted for transfers against payment, Book-entry Securities transaction fees, or principal and interest payments.

Non-complying Bank means a Bank that has failed to provide the liquidity certification as required under § 1270.10(b)(1).

NRSRO means a credit rating organization registered with the Securities and Exchange Commission as a nationally recognized statistical rating organization.

Office of Finance means the Office of Finance, a joint office of the Banks established under part 1273 of this chapter and referenced in the Bank Act and the Safety and Soundness Act, including the Office of Finance acting as agent of the Banks in all matters relating to the issuance of Book-entry consolidated obligations and in the performance of all other necessary and proper functions relating to Book-entry consolidated obligations, including the payment of principal and interest due thereon.

Participant means a Person or a Bank that maintains a Participant's Securities Account with a Federal Reserve Bank.

Participant's Securities Account means an account in the name of a Participant at a Federal Reserve Bank to which Book-entry consolidated obligations held for a Participant are or may be credited.

Person means and includes an individual, corporation, company, governmental entity, association, firm, partnership, trust, estate, representative, and any other similar organization, but does not mean or include a Bank, the Director, FHFA, the Office of Finance, the United States, or a Federal Reserve Bank.

Repurchase agreement means an agreement in which a Bank sells securities and simultaneously agrees to repurchase those securities or similar securities at an agreed upon price, with or without a stated time for repurchase.

Revised Article 8 means Uniform Commercial Code, Revised Article 8, Investment Securities (with Conforming and Miscellaneous Amendments to Articles 1, 3, 4, 5, 9, and 10) 1994 Official Text. Copies of this publication are available from the Executive Office of the American Law Institute, 4025 Chestnut Street, Philadelphia, PA 19104, and the National Conference of Commissioners on Uniform State Laws, 676 North St. Clair Street, Suite 1700, Chicago, IL 60611.

Safety and Soundness Act means the Federal Housing Enterprises Financial Safety and Soundness Act of 1992 (12 U.S.C. 4501 *et seq.*) as amended.

SBIC means a small business investment company formed pursuant to section 301 of the Small Business Investment Act (15 U.S.C. 681).

Securities Intermediary means:

(1) A Person that is registered as a "clearing agency" under the Federal securities laws; a Federal Reserve Bank; any other person that provides clearance or settlement services with respect to a Book-entry consolidated obligation that would require it to register as a clearing agency under the Federal securities laws but for an exclusion or exemption from the registration requirement, if its activities as a clearing corporation, including promulgation of rules, are subject to regulation by a Federal or State governmental authority; or

(2) A Person (other than an individual, unless such individual is registered as a broker or dealer under the Federal securities laws), including a bank or broker, that in the ordinary course of its business maintains securities accounts for others and is acting in that capacity.

Security Entitlement means the rights and property interest of an Entitlement Holder with respect to a Book-entry consolidated obligation.

Transfer Message means an instruction of a Participant to a Federal Reserve Bank to effect a transfer of a Book-entry consolidated obligation, as set forth in Federal Reserve Bank Operating Circulars.

Subpart B—Sources of Funds

§ 1270.2 Authorized liabilities.

As a source of funds for business operations, each Bank is authorized to incur liabilities by:

(a) Accepting proceeds from the issuance of consolidated obligations issued in accordance with this part;

(b) Accepting time or demand deposits from members, other Banks or instrumentalities of the United States, and cash accounts from associates or members pursuant to §§ 1266.17(b)(2)(i)(B), 1266.17(d) and 1269.4(a)(1) of this chapter, or § 1270.3 of this part, or from other institutions for which the Bank is providing correspondent services pursuant to section 11(e) of the Bank Act (12 U.S.C. 1431(e));

(c) Purchasing Federal funds; and

(d) Entering into repurchase agreements.

§ 1270.3 Deposits from members.

(a) Banks may accept demand and time deposits from members, reserving the right to require notice of intention to withdraw any part of time deposits. Rates of interest paid on all deposits shall be set by the Bank's board of directors (or, between regular meetings thereof, by a committee of directors selected by the board) or by the Bank President, if so authorized by the board. Unless otherwise specified by the board, a Bank President may delegate to any officer or employee of the Bank any authority he possesses under this section.

(b) Each Bank shall at all times have at least an amount equal to the current deposits received from its members invested in:

(1) Obligations of the United States;

(2) Deposits in banks or trust companies; or

(3) Advances with a remaining maturity not to exceed five years that are made to members in conformity with part 1266 of this chapter.

Subpart C—Consolidated Obligations

§ 1270.4 Issuance of consolidated obligations.

(a) *Consolidated obligations issued by the Banks.* (1) Subject to the provisions of this part and such other rules, regulations, terms, and conditions as the Director may prescribe, the Banks may issue joint debt under section 11(c) of the Bank Act (12 U.S.C. 1431(c)), which shall be consolidated obligations, on which the Banks shall be jointly and severally liable in accordance with § 1270.10 of this part.

(2) Consolidated obligations shall be issued only through the Office of Finance, as agent of the Banks pursuant to this part and part 1273 of this chapter.

(3) All consolidated obligations shall be issued in *pari passu*.

(b) *Negative pledge requirement.* Each Bank shall at all times maintain assets described in paragraphs (b)(1) through (b)(6) of this section free from any lien or pledge, in an amount at least equal to a *pro rata* share of the total amount of currently outstanding consolidated obligations and equal to such Bank's participation in all such consolidated obligations outstanding, provided that any assets that are subject to a lien or pledge for the benefit of the holders of any issue of consolidated obligations shall be treated as if they were assets free from any lien or pledge for purposes of compliance with this paragraph (b). Eligible assets are:

(1) Cash;

(2) Obligations of or fully guaranteed by the United States;

(3) Secured advances;

(4) Mortgages as to which one or more Banks have any guaranty or insurance, or commitment therefor, by the United States or any agency thereof;

(5) Investments described in section 16(a) of the Bank Act (12 U.S.C. 1436(a)); and

(6) Other securities that have been assigned a rating or assessment by an NRSRO that is equivalent to or higher than the rating or assessment assigned by that NRSRO to consolidated obligations outstanding.

§ 1270.5 Leverage limit and credit rating requirements.

(a) *Bank leverage.* (1) Except as provided in paragraph (a)(2) of this section, the total assets of any Bank that is not subject to the capital requirements set forth in part 932 of this title shall not exceed 21 times the total of paid-in capital stock, retained earnings, and reserves (excluding loss reserves and liquidity reserves for deposits pursuant to section 11(g) of the Bank Act (12 U.S.C. 1431(g)) of that Bank.

(2) The aggregate amount of assets of any Bank that is not subject to the capital requirements set forth in part 932 of this title may be up to 25 times the total paid-in capital stock, retained earnings, and reserves of that Bank, provided that non-mortgage assets, after deducting the amount of deposits and capital, do not exceed 11 percent of such total assets. For the purposes of this section, the amount of non-mortgage assets equals total assets after deduction of:

(i) Advances;

(ii) Acquired member assets, including all United States government-insured or guaranteed whole single-family or multi-family residential mortgage loans;

(iii) Standby letters of credit;

(iv) Intermediary derivative contracts;

(v) Debt or equity investments:

(A) That primarily benefit households having a targeted income level, a significant proportion of which must benefit households with incomes at or below 80 percent of area median income, or areas targeted for redevelopment by local, state, tribal or Federal government (including Federal Empowerment Zones and Enterprise and Champion Communities), by providing or supporting one or more of the following activities:

(*1*) Housing;

(*2*) Economic development;

(*3*) Community services;

(*4*) Permanent jobs; or

(*5*) Area revitalization or stabilization;

(B) In the case of mortgage- or asset-backed securities, the acquisition of which would expand liquidity for loans that are not otherwise adequately provided by the private sector and do not have a readily available or well established secondary market; and

(C) That involve one or more members or housing associates in a manner, financial or otherwise, and to a degree to be determined by the Bank;

(vi) Investments in SBICs, where one or more members or housing associates of the Bank also make a material investment in the same activity;

(vii) SBIC debentures, the short term tranche of SBIC securities, or other debentures that are guaranteed by the Small Business Administration under title III of the Small Business Investment Act of 1958, as amended (15 U.S.C. 681 *et seq.*);

(viii) Section 108 Interim Notes and Participation Certificates guaranteed by the Department of Housing and Urban Development under section 108 of the Housing and Community Development Act of 1974, as amended (42 U.S.C. 5308);

(ix) Investments and obligations issued or guaranteed under the Native

American Housing Assistance and Self-Determination Act of 1996 (25 U.S.C. 4101 *et seq.*).

(x) Securities representing an interest in pools of mortgages (MBS) issued, guaranteed, or fully insured by the Government National Mortgage Association (Ginnie Mae), the Federal Home Loan Mortgage Corporation (Freddie Mac), or the Federal National Mortgage Association (Fannie Mae), or Collateralized Mortgage Obligations (CMOs), including Real Estate Mortgage Investment Conduits (REMICs), backed by such securities;

(xi) Other MBS, CMOs, and REMICs rated in the highest rating category by an NRSRO;

(xii) Asset-backed securities collateralized by manufactured housing loans or home equity loans and rated in the highest rating category by an NRSRO; and

(xiii) Marketable direct obligations of state or local government units or agencies, rated in one of the two highest rating categories by an NRSRO, where the purchase of such obligations by a Bank provides to the issuer the customized terms, necessary liquidity, or favorable pricing required to generate needed funding for housing or community development.

(b) *Credit ratings.* (1) The Banks, collectively, shall obtain from an NRSRO and, at all times, maintain a current credit rating on the Banks' consolidated obligations.

(2) Each Bank shall operate in such a manner and take any actions necessary, including without limitation reducing Bank leverage, to ensure that the Banks' consolidated obligations receive and continue to receive the highest credit rating from any NRSRO by which the consolidated obligations have then been rated.

(c) *Individual Bank credit rating.* Each Bank shall operate in such a manner and take any actions necessary to ensure that the Bank has and maintains an individual issuer credit rating of at least the second highest credit rating from any NRSRO providing a rating, where such rating is a meaningful measure of the individual Bank's financial strength and stability, and is updated at least annually by an NRSRO, or more frequently as required by FHFA, to reflect any material changes in the condition of the Bank.

§ 1270.6 Transactions in consolidated obligations.

The general regulations of the Department of the Treasury now or hereafter in force governing transactions in United States securities, except 31 CFR part 357 regarding book-entry procedure, are hereby incorporated into this subpart C of this part, so far as applicable and as necessarily modified to relate to consolidated obligations, as the regulations of FHFA for similar transactions on consolidated obligations. The book-entry procedure for consolidated obligations is contained in subpart D of this part.

§ 1270.7 Lost, stolen, destroyed, mutilated or defaced consolidated obligations.

United States statutes and regulations of the Department of the Treasury now or hereafter in force governing relief on account of the loss, theft, destruction, mutilation or defacement of United States securities, so far as applicable and as necessarily modified to relate to consolidated obligations, are hereby adopted as the regulations of FHFA for the issuance of substitute consolidated obligations or the payment of lost, stolen, destroyed, mutilated or defaced consolidated obligations.

§ 1270.8 Administrative provision.

The Secretary of the Treasury or the Acting Secretary of the Treasury is hereby authorized and empowered, as the agent of FHFA and the Banks, to administer §§ 1270.6 and 1270.7, and to delegate such authority at their discretion to other officers, employees, and agents of the Department of the Treasury. Any such regulations may be waived on behalf of FHFA and the Banks by the Secretary of the Treasury, the Acting Secretary of the Treasury, or by an officer of the Department of the Treasury authorized to waive similar regulations with respect to United States securities, but only in any particular case in which a similar regulation with respect to United States securities would be waived. The terms "securities" and "bonds" as used in this section shall, unless the context otherwise requires, include and apply to coupons and interim certificates.

§ 1270.9 Conditions for issuance of consolidated obligations.

(a) The Office of Finance board of directors shall authorize the offering for current and forward settlement (up to 12 months) or the reopening of consolidated obligations, as necessary, and authorize the maturities, rates of interest, terms and conditions thereof, subject to the provisions of 31 U.S.C. 9108.

(b) Consolidated obligations may be offered for sale only to the extent that Banks are committed to take the proceeds.

(c) Consolidated obligations shall not be purchased by any Bank as part of an initial issuance whether such consolidated obligation is purchased directly from the Office of Finance or indirectly from an underwriter.

(d) If the Banks issue consolidated obligations denominated in a currency other than U.S. Dollars or linked to equity or commodity prices, then any Bank accepting proceeds from those consolidated obligations shall meet the following requirements with regard to such consolidated obligations:

(1) The relevant foreign exchange, equity price or commodity price risks associated with the consolidated obligation must be hedged in accordance with § 956.6 of this title;

(2) If there is a default on the part of a counterparty to a contract hedging the foreign exchange, equity or commodity price risk associated with a consolidated obligation, the Bank shall enter into a replacement contract in a timely manner and as soon as market conditions permit.

§ 1270.10 Joint and several liability.

(a) *In general.* (1) Each and every Bank, individually and collectively, has an obligation to make full and timely payment of all principal and interest on consolidated obligations when due.

(2) Each and every Bank, individually and collectively, shall ensure that the timely payment of principal and interest on all consolidated obligations is given priority over, and is paid in full in advance of, any payment to or redemption of shares from any shareholder.

(3) The provisions of this part shall not limit, restrict or otherwise diminish, in any manner, the joint and several liability of all of the Banks on any consolidated obligation.

(b) *Certification and reporting.* (1) Before the end of each calendar quarter, and before declaring or paying any dividend for that quarter, the President of each Bank shall certify in writing to FHFA that, based on known current facts and financial information, the Bank will remain in compliance with the liquidity requirements set forth in section 11(g) of the Act (12 U.S.C. 1431(g)), and any regulations (as the same may be amended, modified or replaced), and will remain capable of making full and timely payment of all of its current obligations, including direct obligations, coming due during the next quarter.

(2) A Bank shall immediately provide written notice to FHFA if at any time the Bank:

(i) Is unable to provide the certification required by paragraph (b)(1) of this section;

(ii) Projects at any time that it will fail to comply with statutory or regulatory liquidity requirements, or will be unable to timely and fully meet all of its current obligations, including direct obligations, due during the quarter;

(iii) Actually fails to comply with statutory or regulatory liquidity requirements or to timely and fully meet all of its current obligations, including direct obligations, due during the quarter; or

(iv) Negotiates to enter or enters into an agreement with one or more other Banks to obtain financial assistance to meet its current obligations, including direct obligations, due during the quarter; the notice of which shall be accompanied by a copy of the agreement, which shall be subject to the approval of FHFA.

(c) *Consolidated obligation payment plans.* (1) A Bank promptly shall file a consolidated obligation payment plan for FHFA approval:

(i) If the Bank becomes a non-complying Bank as a result of failing to provide the certification required in paragraph (b)(1) of this section;

(ii) If the Bank becomes a non-complying Bank as a result of being required to provide the notice required pursuant to paragraph (b)(2) of this section, except in the event that a failure to make a principal or interest payment on a consolidated obligation when due was caused solely by a temporary interruption in the Bank's debt servicing operations resulting from an external event such as a natural disaster or a power failure; or

(iii) If FHFA determines that the Bank will cease to be in compliance with the statutory or regulatory liquidity requirements, or will lack the capacity to timely and fully meet all of its current obligations, including direct obligations, due during the quarter.

(2) A consolidated obligation payment plan shall specify the measures the non-complying Bank will undertake to make full and timely payments of all of its current obligations, including direct obligations, due during the applicable quarter.

(3) A non-complying Bank may continue to incur and pay normal operating expenses incurred in the regular course of business (including salaries, benefits, or costs of office space, equipment and related expenses), but shall not incur or pay any extraordinary expenses, or declare, or pay dividends, or redeem any capital stock, until such time as FHFA has approved the Bank's consolidated obligation payment plan or inter-Bank assistance agreement, or ordered another remedy, and all of the non-complying Bank's direct obligations have been paid.

(d) *FHFA payment orders; Obligation to reimburse.* (1) FHFA, in its discretion and notwithstanding any other provision in this section, may at any time order any Bank to make any principal or interest payment due on any consolidated obligation.

(2) To the extent that a Bank makes any payment on any consolidated obligation on behalf of another Bank, the paying Bank shall be entitled to reimbursement from the non-complying Bank, which shall have a corresponding obligation to reimburse the Bank providing assistance, to the extent of such payment and other associated costs (including interest to be determined by FHFA).

(e) *Adjustment of equities.* (1) Any non-complying Bank shall apply its assets to fulfill its direct obligations.

(2) If a Bank is required to meet, or otherwise meets, the direct obligations of another Bank due to a temporary interruption in the latter Bank's debt servicing operations (*e.g.*, in the event of a natural disaster or power failure), the assisting Bank shall have the same right to reimbursement set forth in paragraph (d)(2) of this section.

(3) If FHFA determines that the assets of a non-complying Bank are insufficient to satisfy all of its direct obligations as set forth in paragraph (e)(1) of this section, then FHFA may allocate the outstanding liability among the remaining Banks on a *pro rata* basis in proportion to each Bank's participation in all consolidated obligations outstanding as of the end of the most recent month for which FHFA has data, or otherwise as FHFA may prescribe.

(f) *Reservation of authority.* Nothing in this section shall affect the Director's authority to adjust equities between the Banks in a manner different than the manner described in paragraph (e) of this section, or to take enforcement or other action against any Bank pursuant to the Director's authority under the Safety and Soundness Act or the Bank Act, or otherwise to supervise the Banks and ensure that they are operated in a safe and sound manner.

(g) *No rights created.* (1) Nothing in this part shall create or be deemed to create any rights in any third party.

(2) Payments made by a Bank toward the direct obligations of another Bank are made for the sole purpose of discharging the joint and several liability of the Banks on consolidated obligations.

(3) Compliance, or the failure to comply, with any provision in this section shall not be deemed a default under the terms and conditions of the consolidated obligations.

§ 1270.11 Savings clause.

Any agreements or other instruments entered into in connection with the issuance of consolidated obligations prior to the amendments made to this part shall continue in effect with respect to all consolidated obligations issued under the authority of section 11 of the Bank Act (12 U.S.C. 1431) and pursuant to this part. References to consolidated obligations in such agreements and instruments shall be deemed to refer to all joint and several obligations of the Banks.

Subpart D—Book-Entry Procedure for Consolidated Obligations

§ 1270.12 Law governing rights and obligations of Banks, FHFA, Office of Finance, United States and Federal Reserve Banks; rights of any Person against Banks, FHFA, Office of Finance, United States and Federal Reserve Banks.

(a) Except as provided in paragraph (b) of this section, the rights and obligations of the Banks, FHFA, the Director, the Office of Finance, the United States and the Federal Reserve Banks with respect to: A Book-entry consolidated obligation or Security Entitlement and the operation of the Book-entry system, as it applies to consolidated obligations; and the rights of any Person, including a Participant, against the Banks, FHFA, the Director, the Office of Finance, the United States and the Federal Reserve Banks with respect to: A Book-entry consolidated obligation or Security Entitlement and the operation of the Book-entry system, as it applies to consolidated obligations; are governed solely by regulations of FHFA, including the regulations of this part 1270, the applicable offering notice, applicable procedures established by the Office of Finance, and Federal Reserve Bank Operating Circulars.

(b) A security interest in a Security Entitlement that is in favor of a Federal Reserve Bank from a Participant and that is not recorded on the books of a Federal Reserve Bank pursuant to §1270.14(c)(1), is governed by the law (not including the conflict-of-law rules) of the jurisdiction where the head office of the Federal Reserve Bank maintaining the Participant's Securities Account is located. A security interest in a Security Entitlement that is in favor of a Federal Reserve Bank from a Person that is not a Participant, and that is not recorded on the books of a Federal Reserve Bank pursuant to §1270.14(c)(1), is governed by the law determined in the manner specified in §1270.13.

(c) If the jurisdiction specified in the first sentence of paragraph (b) of this section is a State that has not adopted Revised Article 8, then the law specified in the first sentence of paragraph (b) of this section shall be the law of that State as though Revised Article 8 had been adopted by that State.

§ 1270.13 Law governing other interests.

(a) To the extent not inconsistent with this part 1270, the law (not including the conflict-of-law rules) of a Securities Intermediary's jurisdiction governs:

(1) The acquisition of a Security Entitlement from the Securities Intermediary;

(2) The rights and duties of the Securities Intermediary and Entitlement Holder arising out of a Security Entitlement;

(3) Whether the Securities Intermediary owes any duties to an adverse claimant to a Security Entitlement;

(4) Whether an Adverse Claim can be asserted against a Person who acquires a Security Entitlement from the Securities Intermediary or a Person who purchases a Security Entitlement or interest therein from an Entitlement Holder; and

(5) Except as otherwise provided in paragraph (c) of this section, the perfection, effect of perfection or non-perfection, and priority of a security interest in a Security Entitlement.

(b) The following rules determine a "Securities Intermediary's jurisdiction" for purposes of this section:

(1) If an agreement between the Securities Intermediary and its Entitlement Holder specifies that it is governed by the law of a particular jurisdiction, that jurisdiction is the Securities Intermediary's jurisdiction.

(2) If an agreement between the Securities Intermediary and its Entitlement Holder does not specify the governing law as provided in paragraph (b)(1) of this section, but expressly

specifies that the securities account is maintained at an office in a particular jurisdiction, that jurisdiction is the Securities Intermediary's jurisdiction.

(3) If an agreement between the Securities Intermediary and its Entitlement Holder does not specify a jurisdiction as provided in paragraphs (b)(1) or (b)(2) of this section, the Securities Intermediary's jurisdiction is the jurisdiction in which is located the office identified in an account statement as the office serving the Entitlement Holder's account.

(4) If an agreement between the Securities Intermediary and its Entitlement Holder does not specify a jurisdiction as provided in paragraphs (b)(1) or (b)(2) of this section and an account statement does not identify an office serving the Entitlement Holder's account as provided in paragraph (b)(3) of this section, the Securities Intermediary's jurisdiction is the jurisdiction in which is located the chief executive office of the Securities Intermediary.

(c) Notwithstanding the general rule in paragraph (a)(5) of this section, the law (but not the conflict-of-law rules) of the jurisdiction in which the Person creating a security interest is located governs whether and how the security interest may be perfected automatically or by filing a financing statement.

(d) If the jurisdiction specified in paragraph (b) of this section is a State that has not adopted Revised Article 8, then the law for the matters specified in paragraph (a) of this section shall be the law of that State as though Revised Article 8 had been adopted by that State. For purposes of the application of the matters specified in paragraph (a) of this section, the Federal Reserve Bank maintaining the Securities Account is a clearing corporation, and the Participant's interest in a Bank Book-entry Security is a Security Entitlement.

§ 1270.14 Creation of Participant's Security Entitlement; security interests.

(a) A Participant's Security Entitlement is created when a Federal Reserve Bank indicates by book entry that a Book-entry consolidated obligation has been credited to a Participant's Securities Account.

(b) A security interest in a Security Entitlement of a Participant in favor of the United States to secure deposits of public money, including, without limitation, deposits to the Treasury tax and loan accounts, or other security interest in favor of the United States that is required by Federal statute, regulation, or agreement, and that is marked on the books of a Federal Reserve Bank is thereby effected and perfected, and has priority over any other interest in the Securities. Where a security interest in favor of the United States in a Security Entitlement of a Participant is marked on the books of a Federal Reserve Bank, such Federal Reserve Bank may rely, and is protected in relying, exclusively on the order of an authorized representative of the United States directing the transfer of the Security. For purposes of this paragraph (b), an "authorized representative of the United States" is the official designated in the applicable regulations or agreement to which a Federal Reserve Bank is a party, governing the security interest.

(c)(1) The Banks, FHFA, the Director, the Office of Finance, the United States and the Federal Reserve Banks have no obligation to agree to act on behalf of any Person or to recognize the interest of any transferee of a security interest or other limited interest in a Security Entitlement in favor of any Person except to the extent of any specific requirement of Federal law or regulation or to the extent set forth in any specific agreement with the Federal Reserve Bank on whose books the interest of the Participant is recorded. To the extent required by such law or regulation or set forth in an agreement with a Federal Reserve Bank, or the Federal Reserve Bank Operating Circular, a security interest in a Security Entitlement that is in favor of a Federal Reserve Bank or a Person may be created and perfected by a Federal Reserve Bank marking its books to record the security interest. Except as provided in paragraph (b) of this section, a security interest in a Security Entitlement marked on the books of a Federal Reserve Bank shall have priority over any other interest in the Securities.

(2) In addition to the method provided in paragraph (c)(1) of this section, a security interest in a Security Entitlement, including a security interest in favor of a Federal Reserve Bank, may be perfected by any method by which a security interest may be perfected under applicable law as described in § 1270.12(b) or § 1270.13. The perfection, effect of perfection or nonperfection, and priority of a security interest are governed by that applicable law. A security interest in favor of a Federal Reserve Bank shall be treated as a security interest in favor of a clearing corporation in all respects under that law, including with respect to the effect of perfection and priority of the security interest. A Federal Reserve Bank Operating Circular shall be treated as a rule adopted by a clearing corporation for such purposes.

§ 1270.15 Obligations of the Banks and the Office of Finance; no Adverse Claims.

(a) Except in the case of a security interest in favor of the United States or a Federal Reserve Bank or otherwise as provided in § 1270.14(c)(1), for the purposes of this part 1270, the Banks, the Office of Finance and the Federal Reserve Banks shall treat the Participant to whose Securities Account an interest in a Book-entry consolidated obligations has been credited as the person exclusively entitled to issue a Transfer Message, to receive interest and other payments with respect thereof and otherwise to exercise all the rights and powers with respect to the Security, notwithstanding any information or notice to the contrary. Neither the Banks, FHFA, the Director, the Office of Finance, the United States, nor the Federal Reserve Banks are liable to a Person asserting or having an Adverse Claim to a Security Entitlement or to Book-entry consolidated obligations in a Participant's Securities Account, including any such claim arising as a result of the transfer or disposition of a Book-entry consolidated obligation by a Federal Reserve Bank pursuant to a Transfer Message that the Federal Reserve Bank reasonably believes to be genuine.

(b) The obligation of the Banks and the Office of Finance to make payments of interest and principal with respect to Book-entry consolidated obligations is discharged at the time payment in the appropriate amount is made as follows:

(1) Interest on Book-entry consolidated obligations is either credited by a Federal Reserve Bank to a Funds Account maintained at the Federal Reserve Bank or otherwise paid as directed by the Participant.

(2) Book-entry consolidated obligations are paid, either at maturity or upon redemption, in accordance with their terms by a Federal Reserve Bank withdrawing the securities from the Participant's Securities Account in which they are maintained and by either crediting the amount of the proceeds, including both principal and interest, where applicable, to a Funds Account at the Federal Reserve Bank or otherwise paying such principal and interest as directed by the Participant. No action by the Participant is required in connection with the payment of a Book-entry consolidated obligation, unless otherwise expressly required.

§ 1270.16 Authority of Federal Reserve Banks.

(a) Each Federal Reserve Bank is hereby authorized as fiscal agent of the Office of Finance: To perform functions with respect to the issuance of Book-entry consolidated obligations, in accordance with the terms of the applicable offering notice and with procedures established by the Office of Finance; to service and maintain Book-entry consolidated obligations in accounts established for such purposes; to make payments of principal, interest and redemption premium (if any), as directed by the Office of Finance; to effect transfer of Book-entry consolidated obligations between Participants' Securities Accounts as directed by the Participants; and to perform such other duties as fiscal agent as may be requested by the Office of Finance.

(b) Each Federal Reserve Bank may issue Operating Circulars not inconsistent with this part 1270, governing the details of its handling of Book-entry consolidated obligations, Security Entitlements, and the operation of the Book-entry system under this part 1270.

§ 1270.17 Liability of Banks, FHFA, Office of Finance and Federal Reserve Banks.

The Banks, FHFA, the Director, the Office of Finance and the Federal Reserve Banks may rely on the information provided in a tender, transaction request form, other transaction documentation, or Transfer Message, and are not required to verify the information. Neither the Banks, FHFA, the Director, the Office of Finance, the United States, nor the Federal Reserve Banks shall be liable for any action taken in accordance with the information set out in a tender, transaction request form, other transaction documentation, or Transfer Message, or evidence submitted in support thereof.

§ 1270.18 Additional requirements; notice of attachment for Book-entry consolidated obligations.

(a) *Additional requirements.* In any case or any class of cases arising under the regulations in this part 1270, the Office of Finance may require such additional evidence and a bond of indemnity, with or without surety, as may in its judgment, or in the judgment of the Banks or FHFA, be necessary for the protection of the interests of the Banks, FHFA, the Office of Finance or the United States.

(b) *Notice of attachment.* The interest of a debtor in a Security Entitlement may be reached by a creditor only by legal process upon the Securities Intermediary with whom the debtor's securities account is maintained, except where a Security Entitlement is maintained in the name of a secured party, in which case the debtor's interest may be reached by legal process upon the secured party. The regulations in this part 1270 do not purport to establish whether a Federal Reserve Bank is required to honor an order or other notice of attachment in any particular case or class of cases.

§ 1270.19 Reference to certain Department of Treasury commentary and determinations.

Notwithstanding provisions in § 1270.6 regarding Department of Treasury regulations set forth in 31 CFR part 357:

(a) The Department of Treasury TRADES Commentary (31 CFR part 357, appendix B) addressing the Department of Treasury regulations governing book-entry procedure for Treasury Securities is hereby referenced, so far as applicable and as necessarily modified to relate to Book-entry consolidated obligations, as an interpretive aid to this subpart D of this part.

(b) Determinations of the Department of Treasury regarding whether a State shall be considered to have adopted Revised Article 8 for purposes of 31 CFR part 357, as published in the FEDERAL REGISTER or otherwise, shall also apply to this subpart D of this part.

§ 1270.20 Consolidated obligations are not obligations of the United States or guaranteed by the United States.

Consolidated obligations are not obligations of the United States and are not guaranteed by the United States.

PART 1272—NEW BUSINESS ACTIVITIES

AUTHORITY: 12 U.S.C. 1431(a), 1432(a), 4511(b), 4513, 4526(a).

SOURCE: 65 FR 44431, July 18, 2000, unless otherwise noted. Redesignated at 75 FR 76622, Dec. 9, 2010.

EDITORIAL NOTE: Nomenclature changes to part appear at 75 FR 76624, Dec. 9, 2010.

§ 1272.1 Definitions.

As used in this part:

Bank, written in title case, means a Federal Home Loan Bank established under section 12 of the Bank Act, as amended (12 U.S.C. 1432).

Bank Act means the Federal Home Loan Bank Act, as amended (12 U.S.C. 1421 through 1449).

FHFA means the Federal Housing Finance Agency.

New business activity means any business activity undertaken, transacted, conducted, or engaged in by a Bank that has not been previously undertaken, transacted, conducted, or engaged in by that Bank, or was previously undertaken, transacted, conducted, or engaged in under materially different terms and conditions, such that it:

(1) Involves the acceptance of collateral enumerated under § 1266.7(a)(4) of this chapter;

(2) Involves the acceptance of classes of collateral enumerated under § 1266.7(b) of this chapter for the first time;

(3) Entails risks not previously and regularly managed by that Bank, its members, or both, as appropriate; or

(4) Involves operations not previously undertaken by that Bank.

[65 FR 44431, July 18, 2000. Redesignated and amended at 75 FR 76622, 76624, Dec. 9, 2010]

§ 1272.2 Limitation on Bank authority to undertake new business activities.

No Bank shall undertake any new business activity except in accordance with the procedures set forth in this part.

§ 1272.3 New business activity notice requirement.

At least sixty days prior to undertaking a new business activity, except as provided in § 1272.4(b), a Bank shall submit to the FHFA a written notice containing the following information:

(a) *General requirements.* Except as provided in paragraph (b) of this section, a Bank's notice of new business activity shall include:

(1) An opinion of counsel citing the statutory, regulatory, or other legal authority for the new business activity;

(2) A good faith estimate of the anticipated dollar volume of the activity over the short-and long-term;

(3) A full description of:

(i) The purpose and operation of the proposed activity;

(ii) The market targeted by the activity;

(iii) The delivery system for the activity; and

(iv) The effect of the activity on the housing, or relevant community lending, market;

(4) A demonstration of the Bank's capacity, through staff, or contractors employed by the Bank, sufficiency of experience and expertise, to safely administer and manage the risks associated with the new activity;

(5) An assessment of the risks associated with the activity, including the Bank's ability to manage these risks and the Bank's ability to manage the risks associated with increasing volumes of the new activity; and

(6) The criteria that the Bank will use to determine the eligibility of its members or housing associates to participate in the new activity.

(b) *New collateral activities.* If a proposed new business activity relates to the acceptance of collateral under § 1266.7 of this chapter, a Bank's notice of new business activity shall include:

(1) A description of the classes or amounts of collateral proposed to be accepted by the Bank;

(2) A copy of the Bank's member products policy, adopted pursuant to § 917.4 of this title;

(3) A copy of the Bank's procedures for determining the value of the collateral in question, established pursuant to § 1266.10 of this chapter; and

(4) A demonstration of the Bank's capacity, personnel, technology, experience and expertise to value, discount and manage the risks associated with the collateral in question.

[65 FR 44431, July 18, 2000, as amended at 67 FR 12854, Mar. 20, 2002]

§ 1272.4 Commencement of new business activities.

A Bank may commence a new business activity:

(a) Sixty days after receipt by the FHFA of the notice of new business activity under § 1272.3, if the FHFA has not issued to the Bank a notice as described in § 1272.5(a)(1) through (4);

(b) In the case of the acceptance of collateral enumerated under § 1266.7(a)(4) of this chapter, immediately upon receipt by the FHFA of a notice of new business activity under § 1272.3; or

(c) Immediately upon issuance by the FHFA of a letter of approval under § 1272.6.

§ 1272.5 Notice by the FHFA.

(a) *Issuance.* Within sixty days after receipt of a notice of new business activity under § 1272.3, the FHFA may issue to a Bank a notice that:

(1) Disapproves the new business activity;

(2) Instructs the Bank not to commence the new business pending further consideration by the FHFA;

(3) Declares an intent to examine the Bank;

(4) Requests additional information including but not limited to the requests listed in § 1272.7;

(5) Establishes conditions for the FHFA's approval of the new business activity, including but not limited to the conditions listed in § 1272.7; or

(6) Contains other instructions or information that the FHFA deems appropriate under the circumstances.

(b) *Effect.* Following receipt of a notice issued pursuant to paragraph (a) of this section, a Bank may not undertake any new business activity that is the subject of the notice until the Bank has received the FHFA's consent pursuant to § 1272.6.

§ 1272.6 FHFA consent.

The FHFA may at any time provide consent for a Bank to undertake a particular new business activity and setting forth the terms and conditions that apply to the activity, with which the Bank shall comply if the Bank undertakes the activity in question.

§ 1272.7 Examinations; requests for additional information.

(a) *General.* Nothing in this part shall limit in any manner the right of the FHFA to conduct any examination of any Bank.

(b) *Requests for additional information and conditions for approval.* With respect to a new business activity, nothing in this part shall limit the right of the FHFA at any time to:

(1) Request further information from a Bank concerning a new business activity; and

(2) Require a Bank to comply with certain conditions in order to undertake, or continue to undertake, the new business activity in question, including but not limited to:

(i) Successful completion of pre- or post-implementation safety and soundness examinations;

(ii) Demonstration by the Bank of adequate operational capacity, including the existence of appropriate policies, procedures and controls;

(iii) Demonstration by the Bank of its ability to manage the risks associated with accepting increasing volumes of particular collateral, or holding increasing volumes of particular assets, including the Bank's capacity reliably to value, discount and market the collateral or assets for liquidation;

(iv) Demonstration by the Bank that the new business activity is consistent with the housing finance and community lending mission of the Banks and the cooperative nature of the Bank System; and

(v) FHFA review of any contracts or agreements between the Bank and its members or housing associates.

PART 1273—OFFICE OF FINANCE

AUTHORITY: 12 U.S.C. 1431, 1440, 4511(b), 4513, 4514(a), 4526(a).

SOURCE: 75 FR 23161, May 3, 2010, unless otherwise noted.

§ 1273.1 Definitions.

For purposes of this part:

Audit Committee means the OF Independent Directors acting as the committee established in accordance with § 1273.9 of this part.

Bank written in title case, means a Federal Home Loan Bank established under section 12 of the Bank Act (12 U.S.C. 1432).

Bank Act means the Federal Home Loan Bank Act, as amended (12 U.S.C. 1421 through 1449).

Bank System means the Federal Home Loan Bank System, consisting of the twelve Banks and the Office of Finance.

Chair means the chairperson of the board of directors of the Office of Finance.

Chief Executive Officer or *CEO* means the chief executive officer of the Office of Finance.

Consolidated obligations means any bond, debenture or note on which the Banks are jointly and severally liable and which was issued under section 11 of the Bank Act (12 U.S.C. 1431) and any implementing regulations, whether or not such instrument was originally issued jointly by the Banks or by the Federal Housing Finance Board on behalf of the Banks.

FHFA means the Federal Housing Finance Agency.

Financing Corporation or *FICO* means the Financing Corporation established and supervised by FHFA under section 21 of the Bank Act (12 U.S.C. 1441).

Generally accepted accounting principles or *GAAP* means accounting principles generally accepted in the United States.

Independent Director means a member of the OF board of directors who meets the qualifications set forth in §1273.7(a)(2) of this part.

NRSRO means a credit rating organization registered as a Nationally Recognized Statistical Rating Organization with the Securities and Exchange Commission.

Office of Finance or *OF* means the Office of Finance, a joint office of the Banks established under this part 1273 and referenced in the Bank Act and the Safety and Soundness Act.

Resolution Funding Corporation or *REFCORP* means the Resolution Funding Corporation established by section 21B of the Bank Act (12 U.S.C. 1441b).

Safety and Soundness Act means the Federal Housing Enterprises Financial Safety and Soundness Act of 1992 (12 U.S.C. 4501 *et seq.*), as amended.

§ 1273.2 Authority of the OF.

(a) *General.* The OF shall enjoy such incidental powers under section 12(a) of the Bank Act (12 U.S.C. 1432(a)), as are necessary, convenient and proper to accomplish the efficient execution of its duties and functions pursuant to this part, including the authority to contract with a Bank or Banks for the use of Bank facilities or personnel in order to perform its functions or duties.

(b) *Agent.* The OF, in the performance of its duties, shall have the power to act on behalf of the Banks in issuing consolidated obligations and in paying principal and interest due on the consolidated obligations, or other obligations of the Banks.

(c) *Assessments.* The OF shall have authority to assess the Banks for the funding of its operations in accordance with §1273.5 of this part.

§ 1273.3 Functions of the OF.

(a) *Joint debt issuance.* Subject to parts 965 and 966 of this title, and this part, the OF, as agent for the Banks, shall offer, issue, and service (including making timely payments on principal and interest due) consolidated obligations.

(b) *Preparation of combined financial reports.* The OF shall prepare and issue the combined annual and quarterly financial reports for the Bank System in accordance with the requirements of §1273.6(b) and Appendix A of this part, using consistent accounting policies and procedures as provided in §1273.9(b) of this part.

(c) *Fiscal agent.* The OF shall function as the fiscal agent of the Banks.

(d) *Financing Corporation and Resolution Funding Corporation.* The OF shall perform such duties and responsibilities for FICO as may be required under part 995 of this title, or for REFCORP as may be required under part 996 of this title or authorized by FHFA pursuant to section 21B(c)(6)(B) of the Bank Act (12 U.S.C. 1441b(c)(6)(B)).

§ 1273.4 FHFA oversight.

(a) *Oversight and enforcement actions.* FHFA shall have such oversight authority over the OF, the OF board of directors, the officers, employees, agents, attorneys, accountants, or other OF staff as set forth in the Bank Act, the Safety and Soundness Act, and FHFA regulations issued thereunder.

(b) *Examinations.* Pursuant to section 20 of the Bank Act (12 U.S.C. 1440), FHFA shall examine the OF, all funds and accounts that may be established pursuant to this part 1273, and the operations and activities of the OF, as provided for in the Bank Act, the Safety and Soundness Act, or any regulations promulgated pursuant thereto.

(c) *Combined financial reports.* FHFA shall determine whether a combined Bank System annual or quarterly financial report complies with the standards of this part.

§ 1273.5 Funding of the OF.

(a) *Generally.* The Banks are responsible for jointly funding all the expenses of the OF, including the costs of indemnifying the members of the OF board of directors, the Chief Executive Officer, and other officers and employees of the OF, as provided for in this part.

(b) *Funding policies.*—(1) At the direction of and pursuant to policies and procedures adopted by the OF board of directors, the Banks shall periodically reimburse the OF in order to maintain sufficient operating funds under the budget approved by the OF board of directors. The OF operating funds shall be:

(i) Available for expenses of the OF and the OF board of directors, according to their approved budgets; and

(ii) Subject to withdrawal by check, wire transfer or draft signed by the Chief Executive Officer or other persons designated by the OF board of directors.

(2) Each Bank's respective *pro rata* share of the reimbursement described in paragraph (b)(1) of this section shall be based on a reasonable formula approved by the OF board of directors. Such formula shall be subject to the review of FHFA, and the OF board of directors shall make any changes to the formula as may be ordered by FHFA from time to time.

(c) *Alternative funding method.* With the prior approval of FHFA, the OF board of directors may, by contract with a Bank or Banks, choose to be reimbursed through a fee structure, in lieu of or in addition to assessment, for services provided to the Bank or Banks.

(d) *Prompt reimbursement.* Each Bank from time to time shall promptly forward funds to the OF in an amount representing its share of the reimbursement described in paragraph (b) of this section when directed to do so by the Chief Executive Officer pursuant to the procedures of the OF board of directors.

(e) *Indemnification expenses.* All expenses incident to indemnification of the members of the OF board of directors, the Chief Executive Officer, and other officers and employees of the OF shall be treated as an expense of the OF to be reimbursed by the Banks under the provisions of this part.

(f) *Operating funds segregated.* Any funds received by the OF from the Banks pursuant to this section for OF operating expenses promptly shall be deposited into one or more accounts and shall not be commingled with any proceeds from the sale of consolidated obligations in any manner.

§ 1273.6 Debt management duties of the OF.

(a) *Issuing and servicing of consolidated obligations.* The OF, as agent for the Banks, shall issue and service (including making timely payments on principal and interest due, subject to §§ 966.8 and 966.9 of this title) consolidated obligations pursuant to and in accordance with the policies and procedures established by the OF board of directors under this part.

(b) *Combined financial reports requirements.* The OF, under the oversight of the Audit Committee, shall prepare and distribute the combined annual and quarterly financial reports for the Bank System in accordance with the following requirements:

(1) The scope, form, and content of the disclosure generally shall be consistent with the requirements of the Securities and Exchange Commission Regulations S–K and S–X (17 CFR parts 229 and 210).

(2) Information about each Bank shall be presented as a segment of the Bank System as if generally accepted accounting principles regarding business segment disclosure applied to the combined annual and quarterly financial reports of the Bank System, and

shall be presented using consistent accounting policies and procedures as provided in §1273.9(b) of this part.

(3) The standards set forth in paragraphs (b)(1) and (b)(2) of this section are subject to the exceptions set forth in Appendix A to this part.

(4) The combined Bank System annual financial reports shall be filed with FHFA and distributed to each Bank and Bank member within 90 days after the end of the fiscal year. The combined Bank System quarterly financial reports shall be filed with FHFA and distributed to each Bank and Bank member within 45 days after the end of the of the first three fiscal quarters of each year.

(5) The Audit Committee shall ensure that the combined Bank System annual or quarterly financial reports comply with the standards of this part.

(6) The OF and the OF board of directors, including the Audit Committee, shall comply promptly with any directive of FHFA regarding the preparation, filing, amendment, or distribution of the combined Bank System annual or quarterly financial reports.

(7) Nothing in this section shall create or be deemed to create any rights in any third party.

(c) *Capital markets data.* The OF shall provide capital markets information concerning debt to the Banks.

(d) *NRSROs.* The OF shall manage the relationships with NRSROs in connection with their rating of consolidated obligations.

(e) *Research.* The OF shall conduct research reasonably related to the issuance or servicing of consolidated obligations.

(f) *Monitor Banks' credit exposure.* The OF shall timely monitor, and compile relevant data on, each Bank's and the Bank System's unsecured credit exposure to individual counterparties.

§ 1273.7 Structure of the OF board of directors.

(a) *Membership.* The OF board of directors shall consist of seventeen part-time members as follows:

(1) The twelve Bank presidents, *ex officio*, provided that if the presidency of any Bank becomes vacant, the person designated by the Bank's board of directors to temporarily fulfill the duties of president of that Bank shall serve on the OF board of directors until the presidency is filled permanently; and

(2) Five Independent Directors who—

(i) Each shall be a citizen of the United States;

(ii) As a group, shall have substantial experience in financial and accounting matters; and

(iii) Shall not have any material relationship with a Bank, or the OF (directly or as a partner, shareholder or officer of an organization), as determined under criteria set forth in a policy adopted by the OF board of directors. At a minimum, such policy shall provide that an Independent Director may not:

(A) Be an officer, director, or employee of any Bank or member of a Bank, or have been an officer director or employee of a Bank or member of a Bank during the previous three years;

(B) Be an officer or employee of the OF, or have been an officer or employee of the OF during the previous three years; or

(C) Be affiliated with any consolidated obligations selling or dealer group under contract with OF, or hold shares or any other financial interest in any entity that is part of a consolidated obligations seller or dealer group in an amount greater than the lesser of $250,000 or 0.01% of the market capitalization of the seller or dealer group; or in an amount that exceeds $1,000,000 for all entities that are part of any consolidated obligations seller dealer group, combined. For purposes of this paragraph (a)(2)(iii)(C), a holding company of an entity that is part of a consolidated obligations seller or dealer group shall be deemed to be part of the consolidated obligations selling or dealer group if the assets of the holding company's subsidiaries that are part of a consolidated obligation seller or dealer group constitute 35% or more of the consolidated assets of the holding company.

(b) *Terms.* (1) Except as provided in paragraphs (b)(2) and (c)(1) of this section, each Independent Director shall serve for five-year terms (which shall be staggered so that no more than one Independent Director seat would be scheduled to become vacant in any one year), and shall be subject to removal or suspension in accordance with § 1273.4(a) of this part. An Independent Director may not serve more than two full, consecutive terms, provided that any partial term served by an Independent Director pursuant to paragraph (b)(2) of this section, or time served by a private citizen member of the OF Board pursuant to an appointment made prior to the effective date of this part, shall not count as a term for purposes of this restriction.

(2) The OF board of directors shall fill any vacancy among the Independent Directors occurring prior to the scheduled end of a term by majority vote, subject to FHFA's review of, and non-objection to, the new Independent Director. The OF board of directors shall provide FHFA with the same biographic and background information about the new Independent Director required under paragraph (d) of this section, and FHFA shall have the same rights of non-objection to the Independent Director (and to appoint a different Independent Director) as set forth in paragraph (d) of this section. A person shall be elected (or otherwise appointed by FHFA) under this paragraph to serve only for the remainder of the term associated with the vacant directorship.

(c) *Initial selection of Independent Directors.* (1) As soon as practicable after the effective date of this regulation, FHFA shall fill the initial Independent Director positions by appointment. The Independent Directors shall be appointed for such periods of time, not to exceed five years, to assure the terms are staggered in accordance with paragraph (b)(1) of this section.

(2) The two Bank presidents and the private citizen member who constituted the OF board of directors immediately prior to the effective date of this rule shall, in consultation with the Banks, agree on a slate of at least five persons and nominate such persons for consideration for appointment as Independent Directors by FHFA under this paragraph (c). The nominations shall be submitted to FHFA on or before June 17, 2010. FHFA may appoint persons nominated under this paragraph or other persons identified by it and meeting the requirements of paragraph (a)(2) of this section, or some combination.

(d) *Election of Independent Directors after the initial terms.* Once the terms of the Independent Directors initially appointed by FHFA expire or the positions otherwise become vacant, the Independent Directors subsequently shall be elected by majority vote of the OF board of directors, subject to FHFA's review of, and non-objection to, each Independent Director. The OF board of directors shall provide FHFA with relevant biographic and background information, including information demonstrating that the new Independent Director meets the requirements of paragraph (a)(2) of this section, at least 20 business days before the person assumes any duties as a member of the OF board of directors. If the OF board of directors, in FHFA's judgment, fails to elect a suitably qualified person, FHFA may appoint some other person who meets the requirements of paragraph (a)(2) of this section. FHFA will provide notice of its objection to a particular Independent Director prior to the date that such Director is to assume duties as a member of the OF board of directors. Such notice shall indicate whether, given FHFA's objection, FHFA intends to fill the seat through appointment or a new election should be held by the OF board of directors.

(e) *Initial Selection of Chair and Vice-Chair.* The first Chair and Vice-Chair of the OF board of directors after the effective date of this regulation shall be appointed by FHFA. The Chair shall be selected from among the Independent Directors appointed under paragraph (c)(1) of this section. The Vice-Chair shall be selected from among all OF board directors.

(f) *Subsequent Election of Chair and Vice-Chair.* After the terms of the persons selected under paragraph (e) of this section expire or the positions otherwise become vacant:

(1) Subsequent Chairs shall be elected by majority vote of the OF board of directors from among the Independent Directors then serving on the OF board of directors; and

(2) Subsequent Vice-Chairs shall be elected by majority vote of the OF

board of directors from among all directors.

(3) The OF board of directors shall promptly inform FHFA of the election of a Chair or Vice-Chair. If FHFA objects to any Chair or Vice-Chair elected by the OF board of directors, FHFA shall provide written notice of its objection within 20 business days of the date that FHFA first receives the notice of the election of the Chair and or Vice-Chair, and the OF board of directors must then promptly elect a new Chair or Vice-Chair, as appropriate.

(g) *By-laws and Committees.* (1) The OF board of directors shall adopt by-laws governing the manner in which the board conducts its affairs, which shall be consistent with the requirements of this part and other applicable laws and regulations as administered by FHFA. The by-laws of the board of directors shall be subject to review and approval by FHFA.

(2) In addition to the Audit Committee required under § 1273.9 of this part, the OF board of directors may establish other committees, including an Executive Committee. The duties and powers of such committee, including any powers delegated by the OF board of directors, shall be specified in the by-laws of the board of directors or the charter of the committee.

(h) *Compensation.* (1) The Bank presidents shall not receive any additional compensation or reimbursement as a result of their service as a director of the OF board.

(2) The OF shall pay reasonable compensation and expenses to the Independent Directors in accordance with the requirements for payment of compensation and expenses to Bank directors as set forth in part 1261 of this title.

(i) *Corporate Governance and Indemnification.* (1) *General.* The corporate governance practices and procedures of the OF, and practices and procedures related to indemnification (including advancement of expenses) shall comply with applicable Federal law rules and regulations.

(2) *Election and designation of body of law.* To the extent not inconsistent with paragraph (i)(1) of this section, the OF shall elect to follow the corporate governance and indemnification practices and procedures set forth in one of the following: (i) The law of the jurisdiction in which the principal office of the OF is located, as amended; (ii) the Delaware General Corporation Law (Del. Code Ann. Title 8, as amended); or (iii) the Revised Model Business Corporation Act, as amended. The OF board of directors, as constituted under this part, shall designate in its by-laws the body of law elected pursuant to this paragraph (i)(2) within 90 calendar days from the date that it holds the organizational meeting required under § 1273.10(a) of this part.

(3) *Indemnification.* Subject to paragraphs (i)(1) and (i)(2) of this section, to the extent applicable, the OF shall indemnify (and advance the expenses of) its directors, officers and employees under such terms and conditions as are determined by the OF board of directors. The OF shall be authorized to maintain insurance for its directors, the CEO, and any other officer or employee of the OF. Nothing in this paragraph shall affect any rights to indemnification (including the advancement of expenses) that a director, the CEO, or any other officer or employee of the OF had with respect to any actions, omissions, transactions, or facts occurring prior to the effective date of this paragraph (i).

(j) *Delegation.* In addition to any delegation to a committee allowed under paragraph (g) of this section, the OF board of directors may delegate any of its authority or duties to any employee of the OF in order to enable OF to carry out its functions.

(k) *Outside staff and consultants.* In carrying out its duties and responsibilities, the OF board of directors, or any committee thereof, shall have authority to retain staff and outside counsel, independent accountants, or other outside consultants at the expense of the OF.

§ 1273.8 General duties of the OF board of directors.

(a) *General.* Each director shall have the duty to:

(1) Carry out his or her duties as director in good faith, in a manner such director believes to be in the best interests of the OF and the Bank System,

and with such care, including reasonable inquiry, as an ordinarily prudent person in a like position would use under similar circumstances;

(2) Administer the affairs of the OF fairly and impartially and without discrimination in favor of or against any Bank;

(3) At the time of appointment or election, or within a reasonable time thereafter, have a working familiarity with basic finance and accounting practices, including the ability to read and understand the Banks' combined balance sheets and income statements and the relevant financial statements of the OF and to ask substantive questions of management and the internal and external auditors with regard to both the combined financial statements of the Bank System and the operations and financial statements of the OF, as appropriate; and

(4) Direct the operations of the OF in conformity with the requirements set forth in the Bank Act, Safety and Soundness Act, and this chapter.

(b) *Meetings and quorum.* The OF board of directors shall conduct its business by majority vote of its members at meetings convened in accordance with its by-laws, and shall hold no fewer than six in-person meetings annually. Due notice shall be given to FHFA by the Chair prior to each meeting. A quorum, for purposes of meetings of the OF board of directors, shall require a majority of sitting board members, which must include a majority of sitting Independent Directors.

(c) *Duties regarding COs.* The OF board of directors shall oversee the establishment of policies regarding COs that shall:

(1) Govern the frequency and timing of issuance, issue size, minimum denomination, CO concessions, underwriter qualifications, currency of issuance, interest-rate change or conversion features, call features, principal indexing features, selection and retention of outside counsel, selection of clearing organizations, and the selection and compensation of underwriters for consolidated obligations, which shall be in accordance with the requirements and limitations set forth in paragraph (c)(4) of this section;

(2) Prohibit the issuance of COs intended to be privately placed with or sold without the participation of an underwriter to retail investors, or issued with a concession structure designed to facilitate the placement of the COs in retail accounts, unless the OF has given notice to the board of directors of each Bank describing a policy permitting such issuances, soliciting comments from each Bank's board of directors, and considering the comments received before adopting a policy permitting such issuance activities;

(3) Require all broker-dealers or underwriters under contract to the OF to have and maintain adequate suitability sales practices and policies, which shall be acceptable to, and subject to review by, the OF;

(4) Require that COs shall be issued efficiently and at the lowest all-in funding costs over time, consistent with—

(i) Prudent risk-management practices, prudential debt parameters, short and long-term market conditions, and the Banks' role as GSEs;

(ii) Maintaining reliable access to the short-term and long-term capital markets; and

(iii) Positioning the issuance of debt to take advantage of current and future capital market opportunities.

(d) *Other duties.* The OF board of directors shall:

(1) Set policies for management and operation of the OF;

(2) Approve a strategic business plan for the OF in accordance with the provisions of § 917.5 of this title, as appropriate;

(3) Review, adopt and monitor annual operating and capital budgets of the OF in accordance with the provisions of § 917.8 of this title, as appropriate;

(4) Select, employ, determine the compensation for, and assign the duties and functions of a Chief Executive Officer of the OF who shall—

(i) Be head of the OF and direct the implementation of the OF board of directors' policies;

(ii) Serve as a member of the Directorate of the FICO, pursuant to section 21(b)(1)(A) of the Bank Act (12 U.S.C. 1441(b)(1)(A)); and

(iii) Serve as a member of the Directorate of the REFCORP, pursuant to section 21B(c)(1)(A) of the Bank Act (12 U.S.C. 1441b(c)(1)(A)).

(5) Review and approve all contracts of the OF, except for contracts for which exclusive authority is provided to the Audit Committee by paragraphs (b)(5) and (b)(6) of § 1273.9; and

(6) Assume any other responsibilities that may from time to time be assigned to it by FHFA.

(e) *No rights created.* Nothing in this part shall create or be deemed to create any rights in any third party.

§ 1273.9 Audit Committee.

(a) *Composition.* The Independent Directors shall serve as the Audit Committee. The Audit Committee shall elect its chairperson from among its members. The Chairperson of the OF may also serve as chairperson of the Audit Committee, if the Audit Committee members so decide.

(b) *Responsibilities.*—(1) The Audit Committee shall be responsible for overseeing the audit function of the OF and the preparation and the accurate and meaningful combination of information submitted by the Banks in the Bank System's combined financial reports.

(2) For purposes of the combined financial reports, the Audit Committee shall ensure that the Banks adopt consistent accounting policies and procedures to the extent necessary for information submitted by the Banks to the OF to be combined to create accurate and meaningful combined financial reports.

(3) The Audit Committee, in consultation with FHFA, may establish common accounting policies and procedures for the information submitted by the Banks to the OF for the combined financial reports where the Committee determines such information provided by the several Banks is inconsistent and that consistent policies and procedures regarding that information are necessary to create accurate and meaningful combined financial reports.

(4) To the extent possible the Audit Committee shall operate consistent with the requirements pertaining to audit committee reports set forth in Item 407(d)(3) of Regulation S–K promulgated by the Securities and Exchange Commission.

(5) The Audit Committee shall oversee internal audit activities, including the selection, evaluation, compensation and, where appropriate, replacement of the internal auditor. The internal auditor shall report directly to the Audit Committee and administratively to executive management.

(6) The Audit Committee shall have the exclusive authority to employ and contract for the services of an independent, external auditor for the Banks' annual and quarterly combined financial statements and of an independent, external auditor for OF.

(7) The Audit Committee shall direct senior management to maintain the reliability and integrity of the accounting policies and financial reporting of the OF.

(8) The Audit Committee shall review the basis for the OF's financial statements and the external auditor's opinion rendered with respect to such financial statements.

(9) The Audit Committee shall ensure that senior management has established and is maintaining an adequate internal control system within the OF by:

(i) Reviewing the OF's internal control system and the resolution of identified material weaknesses and reportable conditions in the internal control system, including the prevention or detection of management override or compromise of the internal control system; and

(ii) Reviewing the programs and policies of the OF designed to ensure compliance with applicable laws, regulations, and policies and monitoring the results of these compliance efforts.

(10) The Audit Committee shall review the policies and procedures established by senior management to assess and monitor implementation of the OF strategic business plan and the operating goals and objectives contained therein.

(11) The Audit Committee shall provide an independent, direct channel of communication between the OF's board of directors and the internal and external auditors.

(12) The Audit Committee shall conduct or authorize investigations into

any matters within the Audit Committee's scope of responsibilities.

(13) The Audit Committee shall report periodically its findings to the OF's board of directors.

(14) The Audit Committee shall prepare written minutes of each Audit Committee meeting.

(c) *Charter.*—(1) The Audit Committee shall adopt, and the OF board of directors shall approve, a formal written charter, consistent with the duties and authority set forth in this section, that specifies the scope of the Audit Committee's powers and responsibilities. The Audit Committee and the OF board of directors shall:

(i) Review, and assess the adequacy of and, where appropriate, amend the Audit Committee charter on an annual basis; and

(ii) Re-adopt and re-approve, respectively, the Audit Committee charter not less often than every three years.

(2) The charter of the Audit Committee shall be subject to review and approval by FHFA.

(d) *No delegation.* The Audit Committee may not delegate the responsibilities assigned to it under this section to any person, or to any other committee or sub-committee of the OF board of directors.

§ 1273.10 Transition.

(a) Within 45 calendar days of the date on which FHFA first appoints an Independent Director pursuant to § 1273.7(c) of this part, the OF board of directors as structured under this part shall hold an organizational meeting. At the time of such meeting, the OF board of directors and its Audit Committee shall be deemed to be reconstituted in accordance with this part, and, except as set forth in paragraph (c) of this section, shall thereafter operate in accordance with this part. The date of this organizational meeting shall be set by the Independent Director that has been appointed as Chairman of the OF board of directors by FHFA pursuant to § 1273.7(e) of this part.

(b) Until the date of the organizational meeting required by paragraph (a) of this section, the board of directors of OF, and audit committee thereof, as in existence immediately prior to the effective date of this rule, shall continue to have power and authority to act as the OF board of directors or audit committee thereof, as applicable. Further, the board members who served as Chair and Vice-Chair of the OF board immediately prior to the effective date of this rule shall continue also to serve in these capacities until the date of the organizational meeting required under paragraph (a).

(c) Further, the audit committee as in existence immediately prior to the effective date of this rule shall continue to have responsibility and oversight authority with regard to the preparation and publication of the combined financial report for any reporting period that ends prior to July 1, 2010, unless the board of directors established under this part determines that the Audit Committee as established under this part should be given such responsibility.

Appendix A to Part 1273—Exceptions to the General Disclosure Standards

A. Related-party transactions. Item 404 of Regulation S–K, 17 CFR 229.404, requires the disclosure of certain relationships and related party transactions. In light of the cooperative nature of the Bank System, related-party transactions are to be expected, and a disclosure of all related-party transactions that meet the threshold would not be meaningful. Instead, the combined annual report will disclose the percent of advances to members an officer of which serves as a Bank director, and list the top ten holders of advances in the Bank System and the top five holders of advances by Bank, with a further disclosure indicating which of these members had an officer that served as a Bank director. The combined financial report will also disclose the top ten holders of advances in the Bank System by holding company, where the advances of all affiliates within a holding company are aggregated.

B. Biographical information. The biographical information required by Items 401 and 405 of Regulation S–K, 17 CFR 229.401 and 405, will be provided only for members of the OF board of directors, including the Bank presidents, the Chair and Vice-Chair of the board of directors of each Bank, and the Chief Executive Officer of OF.

C. Compensation. The information on compensation required by Item 402 of Regulation S–K, 17 CFR 229.402, will be provided only for Bank presidents and the CEO of the OF. Since stock in each Bank trades at par, the OF will not include the performance graph specified in Item 402(1) of Regulation S–K, 17 CFR 229.402(1).

D. Submission of matters to a vote of stockholders. No information will be presented on matters submitted to shareholders for a vote, as otherwise required by Item 4 of the SEC's form 10–K, 17 CFR 249.310. The only item shareholders vote upon is the annual election of directors.

E. Exhibits. The exhibits required by Item 601 of Regulation S–K, 17 CFR 229.601, are not applicable and will not be provided.

F. Per share information. The statement of financial information required by Items 301 and 302 of Rule S–K, 17 CFR 229.301 and 302, is inapplicable because the shares of the Banks are subscription capital that trades at par, and the shares expand or contract with changes in member assets or advance levels.

G. Beneficial ownership. Item 403 of Rule S–K, 17 CFR 229.403, requires the disclosure of security ownership of certain beneficial owners and management. The combined financial report will provide a listing of the ten largest holders of capital stock in the Bank System and a listing of the five largest holders of capital stock by Bank. This listing will also indicate which members had an officer that served as a director of a Bank. The combined financial report will also disclose the top ten holders of Bank stock in the Bank System by holding company, where the Bank stock of all affiliates within a holding company is aggregated.

PART 1274—FINANCIAL STATEMENTS OF THE BANKS

Sec.

AUTHORITY: 12 U.S.C. 1426, 1431, 4511(b), 4513, 4526(a).

SOURCE: 75 FR 23166, May 3, 2010, unless otherwise noted.

§ 1274.1 Definitions.

For purposes of this part:

Audit means an examination of the financial statements by an independent accountant in accordance with generally accepted auditing standards for the purpose of expressing an opinion thereon.

Audit report means a document in which an independent accountant indicates the scope the audit made and sets forth an opinion regarding the financial statement taken as a whole, or an assertion to the effect that an overall opinion cannot be expressed. When an overall opinion cannot be expressed, the reasons therefor shall be stated.

Bank written in title case, means a Federal Home Loan Bank established under section 12 of the Bank Act (12 U.S.C. 1432).

Bank System means the Federal Home Loan Bank System, consisting of the twelve Banks and the Office of Finance.

FHFA means the Federal Housing Finance Agency.

Financing Corporation or *FICO* means the Financing Corporation established and supervised by FHFA under section 21 of the Bank Act (12 U.S.C. 1441).

Office of Finance or *OF* has the same meaning as set forth in § 1273.1 of this chapter.

§ 1274.2 Audit requirements.

(a) Each Bank, the OF, and the FICO shall obtain annually an independent external audit of and an audit report on its individual financial statement.

(b) The OF audit committee shall obtain an audit and an audit report on the combined annual financial statements for the Bank System.

(c) All audits must be conducted in accordance with generally accepted auditing standards and in accordance with the most current government auditing standards issued by the Office of the Comptroller General of the United States.

(d) An independent, external auditor must meet at least twice each year with the audit committee of each Bank, the audit committee of OF, and the FICO Directorate.

(e) FHFA examiners shall have unrestricted access to all auditors' work papers and to the auditors to address substantive accounting issues that may arise during the course of any audit.

§ 1274.3 Requirements to provide financial and other information to FHFA and the OF.

In order to facilitate the preparation by the OF of combined Bank System annual and quarterly reports, each Bank shall provide to the OF in such form and within such timeframes as FHFA or the OF shall specify, all financial and other information and assistance that the OF shall request for that purpose. Nothing in this section shall contravene or be deemed to circumscribe in any manner the authority of FHFA to obtain any information from any Bank related to the preparation or review of any financial report.

PART 1278—VOLUNTARY MERGERS OF FEDERAL HOME LOAN BANKS

AUTHORITY: 12 U.S.C. 1432(a), 1446, 4511.

SOURCE: 76 FR 72833, Nov. 28, 2011, unless otherwise noted.

§ 1278.1 Definitions.

Bank, written in title case, means a Federal Home Loan Bank established under section 12 of the Bank Act (12 U.S.C. 1432).

Bank Act means the Federal Home Loan Bank Act, as amended (12 U.S.C. 1421 through 1449).

Constituent Bank means a Bank that is proposing to merge with one or more other Banks. Each Bank entering into a merger is a Constituent Bank, regardless of whether it is also a Continuing Bank.

Continuing Bank means a Bank that will exist as the result of a merger of two or more Constituent Banks, and when used in the singular shall include the plural.

Director, written in title case, means the Director of FHFA or his or her designee.

Disclosure Statement means a written document that contains, to the extent applicable, all of the items that a Bank would be required to include in a Form S–4 Registration Statement under the Securities Act of 1933 (or any successor form promulgated by the United States Securities and Exchange Commission governing disclosure required for securities issued in business combination transactions) when prepared as a prospectus as directed in Part I of the form, if the Bank were required to provide such a prospectus to its shareholders in connection with a merger.

Effective Date means the date on which the organization certificate of the Continuing Bank becomes effective as provided under § 1278.7.

FHFA means the Federal Housing Finance Agency.

Financial Statements means statements of condition, income, capital, and cash flows, with explanatory notes, in such form as the Banks are required to include in their filings made under the Securities and Exchange Act of 1934.

GAAP means accounting principles generally accepted in the United States as in effect from time to time.

Merge or *Merger* means:

(1) A merger of one or more Banks into another Bank;

(2) A consolidation of two or more Banks resulting in a new Bank;

(3) A purchase of substantially all of the assets, and assumption of substantially all of the liabilities, of one or more Banks by another Bank or Banks; or

(4) Any other business combination of two or more Banks into one or more resulting Banks.

Office of Finance means the Office of Finance, a joint office of the Banks established under part 1273 of this chapter.

Record Date means the date established by a Bank's board of directors for determining the members that are entitled to vote on the ratification of the merger agreement and the number of ballots that may be cast by each in the election.

§ 1278.2 Authority.

Any two or more Banks may merge voluntarily under authority of section 26(b) of the Bank Act, provided that each of the following requirements has been satisfied:

(a) The Constituent Banks have executed a written merger agreement that satisfies all requirements of § 1278.3;

(b) The Constituent Banks have jointly filed a merger application with FHFA that satisfies all requirements of § 1278.4;

(c) The Director has approved the merger application in accordance with the requirements of § 1278.5;

(d) The members of each Constituent Bank have ratified the merger agreement as provided under § 1278.6; and

(e) The Director has determined that the Constituent Banks have satisfied all conditions imposed in connection with the approval of the merger application, and has accepted the properly executed organization certificate of the Continuing Bank, as provided under § 1278.7.

§ 1278.3 Merger agreement.

A merger of Banks under the authority of § 1278.2 shall require a written merger agreement that:

(a) Has been authorized by the affirmative vote of a majority of a quorum of the board of directors of each Constituent Bank at a meeting on the record and has been executed by authorized signing officers of each Constituent Bank; and

(b) Sets forth all material terms and conditions of the merger, including, without limitation, provisions addressing each of the following matters—

(1) The proposed Effective Date and the proposed acquisition date for purposes of accounting for the transaction under GAAP, if that date is to be different from the Effective Date;

(2) The proposed organization certificate and bylaws of the Continuing Bank;

(3) The proposed capital structure plan for the Continuing Bank;

(4) The proposed size and structure of the board of directors for the Continuing Bank;

(5) The formula to be used to exchange the stock of the Constituent Banks for the stock of the Continuing Bank, and a provision prohibiting the issuance of fractional shares of stock;

(6) Any conditions that must be satisfied prior to the Effective Date, which must include approval by the Director and ratification by the members of the Constituent Banks;

(7) A statement of the representations or warranties, if any, made or to be made by any Constituent Bank;

(8) A description of the legal or accounting opinions or rulings, if any, that are required to be obtained or furnished by any party in connection with the proposed merger; and

(9) A statement that the board of directors of a Constituent Bank may terminate the merger agreement before the Effective Date upon a determination that:

(i) The information disclosed to members contained material errors or omissions;

(ii) Material misrepresentations were made to members regarding the impact of the merger;

(iii) Fraudulent activities were used to obtain members' approval; or

(iv) An event occurred subsequent to the members' vote that would have a significant adverse impact on the future viability of the Continuing Bank.

§ 1278.4 Merger application.

(a) *Contents of application.* Any two or more Banks that wish to merge shall submit to FHFA a merger application that addresses all material aspects of the proposed merger. As provided in § 1202.8 of this chapter, a Bank may submit separately any portions of the application that it believes contain confidential or privileged trade secrets or commercial or financial information, which portions will be handled in accordance with FHFA's Freedom of Information Act regulations set forth in part 1202 of this chapter. The application shall include, at a minimum, the following:

(1) A written statement that includes—

(i) A summary of the material features of the proposed merger;

(ii) The reasons for the proposed merger;

(iii) The effect of the proposed merger on the Constituent Banks and their members;

(iv) The proposed Effective Date, the proposed acquisition date for purposes of accounting for the transaction under GAAP, if that date is to be different from the Effective Date (including the reasons for designating a different acquisition date), and the Record Date established by each Constituent Bank's board of directors;

(v) If the Constituent Banks contemplate that the proposed merger will be one of two or more related transactions, a summary of the material features of any related transactions and the bearing that the consummation of, or failure to consummate, the related transactions is expected to have upon the proposed merger;

(vi) If not addressed by the merger agreement, the Banks' proposal for the ultimate size and composition of the board of directors for the Continuing Bank and their plan for reducing the board to its ultimate size and composition, as well as the names of the persons proposed to serve as directors and senior executive officers of the Continuing Bank immediately after the merger;

(vii) A description of all proposed material operational changes including, but not limited to, reductions in the existing staffs of the Constituent Banks (to the extent such information is known), whether and how Bank operations will be combined, and whether any Constituent Bank will continue to operate as a branch of the Continuing Bank;

(viii) Information demonstrating that the Continuing Bank will comply with all applicable capital requirements after the Effective Date;

(ix) A statement explaining all officer and director indemnification provisions; and

(x) An undertaking that the Constituent Banks will continue to disclose all material information, and update all items of the application, as appropriate;

(2) A copy of the executed merger agreement and a certified copy of the resolution of the board of directors of each Constituent Bank authorizing the merger agreement;

(3) A copy of the proposed organization certificate of the Continuing Bank;

(4) A copy of the proposed bylaws of the Continuing Bank;

(5) A copy of the proposed capital structure plan of the Continuing Bank;

(6) The most recent annual audited Financial Statements, and any interim quarterly financial statements for the year-to-date, for each Constituent Bank; and

(7) Pro forma Financial Statements for the Continuing Bank as of the date of the most recent statement of condition supplied under paragraph (a)(6) of this section, and forecasted pro forma Financial Statements for each of at least two years following such date.

(b) *Additional information.* FHFA may require the Constituent Banks to submit any additional information FHFA deems necessary to evaluate the proposed merger. If FHFA has determined a merger application to be complete as provided in paragraph (c) of this section, FHFA may require the Constituent Banks to submit additional information only with respect to matters derived from or prompted by the materials already submitted, or matters of a material nature that were not reasonably apparent previously, including matters concealed by the Constituent Banks or relating to developments that arose after the determination of completeness. If the Constituent Banks fail to provide the additional information in a timely manner, the Director may deem the failure to provide the required information as grounds to deny the application.

(c) *Completion of application.* Within 30 days of the receipt of a merger application, FHFA shall determine whether the application is complete and whether FHFA has all information necessary for the Director to evaluate the proposed merger.

(1) If FHFA determines that the application is complete and that it has all information necessary to evaluate the proposed merger, it shall so inform the Constituent Banks in writing.

(2) If FHFA determines that the application is incomplete, or that it requires additional information in order to evaluate the application, it shall so inform the Constituent Banks in writing, and shall specify the number of days within which the Constituent Banks must provide any additional information or materials. Within 15 days of receipt of the additional information or materials, FHFA shall inform the Constituent Banks in writing whether the merger application is complete.

§ 1278.5 Approval by Director.

(a) *Standards.* In determining whether to approve a merger of Banks under the authority of § 1278.2, the Director shall take into consideration the financial and managerial resources of the Constituent Banks, the future prospects of the Continuing Bank, and the effect of the proposed merger on the safety and soundness of the Continuing Bank and the Bank system.

(b) *Determination by Director.* After FHFA determines that a merger application is complete, as provided in §1278.4(c), the Director shall, within 30 days, either approve or deny the merger application. An approval of a merger application may include any conditions the Director determines to be appropriate, and shall in all cases be conditioned on each Constituent Bank demonstrating that it has obtained its members' ratification of the merger agreement in accordance with the requirements of §1278.6 by submitting to FHFA:

(1) A certified copy of the members' resolution ratifying the merger agreement, on which the members cast their votes; and

(2) A certification of the member vote from the Bank's corporate secretary or from an independent third party.

(c) *Notice.* If the Director approves the merger application, FHFA shall provide written notice of the approval and any conditions to each Constituent Bank, as well as to each other Bank and the Office of Finance. If the Director denies the merger application, FHFA shall provide written notice of the denial to each Constituent Bank, as well as to each other Bank and the Office of Finance, and the notice to the Constituent Banks shall include a statement of the reasons for the denial.

§ 1278.6 Ratification by Bank members.

(a) *Requirements for member vote.* No merger of Banks under the authority of §1278.2 may be consummated unless a merger agreement meeting the requirements of §1278.3 has been ratified by the affirmative vote of the members of each Constituent Bank in a voting process that meets the following requirements:

(1) *Notice of vote.* Each Constituent Bank shall submit the authorized merger agreement to its members for ratification by delivering to each institution that was a member as of the Record Date—

(i) A ballot that permits the member to vote for or against the ratification of the merger agreement, or to abstain from such vote; and

(ii) A Disclosure Statement that establishes a closing date for the Bank's receipt of completed ballots that is no earlier than 30 days after the date that the ballot and Disclosure Statement are delivered to its members.

(2) *Voting rights and requirements.* In the vote to ratify the merger agreement, each member of each Constituent Bank shall be entitled to cast one vote for each share of Bank stock that the member was required to own as of the Record Date, provided that the number of votes that any member may cast shall not exceed the average number of shares of Bank stock required to be held by all members of that Bank, calculated on a district-wide basis, as of the Record Date. A member must cast all of its votes either for or against the ratification of the merger agreement, or may abstain with respect to all of its votes. Each member's vote shall be made by resolution of its governing body, either authorizing the specific vote, or delegating to an individual the authority to vote.

(3) *Determination of result.* No Constituent Bank shall review any ballot until after the closing date established in the Disclosure Statement or include in the tabulation any ballot received after the closing date. A Constituent Bank shall tabulate the votes cast immediately after the closing date. The members of a Constituent Bank shall be considered to have ratified a merger agreement if a majority of votes cast in the election have been cast in favor of the ratification of the merger agreement. The Constituent Bank, or the Continuing Bank, as appropriate, shall retain all ballots received for at least two years after the date of the election, and shall not disclose how any member voted.

(4) *Notice of result.* Within 10 days of the closing date, a Constituent Bank shall deliver to its members, to each Constituent Bank with which it proposes to merge, and to FHFA a statement of—

(i) The total number of eligible votes;

(ii) The number of members voting in the election; and

(iii) The total number of votes cast both for and against ratification of the merger agreement, as well as those that were eligible to be cast by members that abstained and by members who failed to return completed ballots.

(b) *False and misleading statements.* In connection with a proposed merger, no Bank, nor any director, officer, or employee thereof, shall make any statement, written or oral, which, at the time and in the light of the circumstances under which it is made, is false or misleading with respect to any material fact, or which omits to state any material fact necessary in order to make the statement not false or misleading, or necessary to correct any earlier statement that has become false or misleading.

§ 1278.7 Consummation of the merger.

(a) *Post-approval submissions.* After the members of each Constituent Bank have voted to ratify the merger agreement, the Constituent Banks shall submit to FHFA:

(1) Evidence acceptable to the Director that all conditions imposed in connection with the approval of the merger application under § 1278.5 have been satisfied, including the items specified in §§ 1278.5(b)(1) and (2); and

(2) An organization certificate for the Continuing Bank, in such form as FHFA may specify, that has been executed by the individuals who will constitute the board of directors of the Continuing Bank.

(b) *Acceptance of organization certificate.* Upon determining that all conditions have been satisfied and that the organization certificate meets the requirements of § 1278.7(a)(2), the Director shall accept the organization certificate of the Continuing Bank by endorsing thereon the date of acceptance and the Effective Date, which date shall be:

(1) The proposed Effective Date set forth in the merger agreement or, if the merger agreement expresses the proposed Effective Date in terms of a range of dates, a date within the applicable range of dates; or

(2) If the proposed Effective Date set forth in the merger agreement has passed, the earlier of:

(i) The 10th business day following the date of acceptance of the organization certificate by the Director; or

(ii) The last business day preceding any date specified in the merger agreement by which the merger agreement will terminate if the merger has not become effective.

(c) *Effectiveness of merger.* After the Director has accepted the organization certificate of the Continuing Bank as provided in § 1278.7(b), and as of the commencement of the Effective Date specified on such organization certificate:

(1) The Continuing Bank shall become or remain a body corporate (depending on the type of transaction) operating under such organization certificate with all powers granted to a Bank under the Bank Act;

(2) The Continuing Bank shall succeed to all rights, titles, powers, privileges, books, records, assets, and liabilities of the Constituent Banks, as provided in the merger agreement; and

(3) The corporate existence of any Constituent Bank that is not a Continuing Bank shall cease, unless otherwise provided in the merger agreement.

(d) *Notice.* After accepting the organization certificate for the Continuing Bank, the Director shall provide to the Constituent Banks, and to each other Bank and the Office of Finance, prompt written notice of that fact, which shall include the date of acceptance and the Effective Date of the organization certificate.

SUBCHAPTER E—HOUSING GOALS AND MISSION

PART 1281—FEDERAL HOME LOAN BANK HOUSING GOALS

Subpart A—General

Subpart B—Housing Goals

Subpart C—Reporting Requirements

AUTHORITY: 12 U.S.C. 1430c.

SOURCE: 75 FR 81105, Dec. 27, 2010, unless otherwise noted.

Subpart A—General

§ 1281.1 Definitions.

As used in this part:

Acquired Member Assets (AMA) program means a program that authorizes a Bank to hold assets acquired from or through Bank members or housing associates by means of either a purchase or a funding transaction, subject to the requirements of 12 CFR parts 955 and 980, or successor regulations.

AMA-approved mortgage means a mortgage that meets the requirements of the AMA program at 12 CFR part 955, and is approved to be implemented under 12 CFR part 980, or successor regulations.

Balloon mortgage means a mortgage providing for payments at regular intervals, with a final payment (balloon payment) that is at least 5 percent more than the periodic payments. The periodic payments may cover some or all of the periodic principal or interest. Typically, the periodic payments are level monthly payments that would fully amortize the mortgage over a stated term and the balloon payment is a single payment due after a specific period (but before the mortgage would fully amortize) and pays off or satisfies the outstanding balance of the mortgage.

Bank means a Federal Home Loan Bank established under section 12 of the Bank Act (12 U.S.C. 1432).

Bank Act means the Federal Home Loan Bank Act, as amended (12 U.S.C. 1421 *et seq.*).

Bank System means the Federal Home Loan Bank System, consisting of the 12 Banks and the Office of Finance.

Borrower income means the total gross income relied on in making the credit decision.

Conforming mortgage means, with respect to a Bank, a conventional AMA-approved single-family mortgage having an original principal obligation that does not exceed the dollar limitation in effect at the time of such origination and applicable to such mortgage under 12 CFR 955.2(a)(1)(i) and 12 U.S.C. 1717(b)(2), as these sections may be amended.

Conventional mortgage means a mortgage other than a mortgage as to which a Bank has the benefit of any guaranty, insurance or other obligation by the United States or any of its agencies or instrumentalities.

Data Reporting Manual (DRM) means the manual prepared by FHFA in connection with the Banks' reporting requirements, as may be supplemented from time to time, including reporting requirements under this part.

Day means a calendar day.

Designated disaster area means any census tract that is located in a county designated by the federal government as adversely affected by a declared major disaster administered by FEMA, where individual assistance payments were authorized by FEMA. A census tract shall be treated as a "designated disaster area" for purposes of this part beginning on the January 1 after the FEMA designation of the county, or such earlier date as determined by FHFA, and continuing through December 31 of the third full calendar year following the FEMA designation. This time period may be adjusted for a particular disaster area by notice from FHFA to the Banks.

Director means the Director of FHFA, or his or her designee.

Dwelling unit means a room or unified combination of rooms intended for use, in whole or in part, as a dwelling by one or more persons, and includes a dwelling unit in a single-family property, multifamily property, or other residential or mixed-use property.

Families in low-income areas means:

(1) Any family that resides in a census tract or block numbering area in which the median income does not exceed 80 percent of the area median income;

(2) Any family with an income that does not exceed area median income that resides in a minority census tract; and

(3) Any family with an income that does not exceed area median income that resides in a designated disaster area.

Family means one or more individuals who occupy the same dwelling unit.

FEMA means the Federal Emergency Management Agency.

FHFA means the Federal Housing Finance Agency.

HMDA means the Home Mortgage Disclosure Act of 1975 (12 U.S.C. 2801, *et seq.*), as amended.

HOEPA mortgage means a mortgage covered by section 103(aa) of the Truth in Lending Act (15 U.S.C. 1602(aa)), as amended by the Home Ownership Equity Protection Act (HOEPA), as implemented by the Board of Governors of the Federal Reserve System.

HUD means the United States Department of Housing and Urban Development.

Low-income means income not in excess of 80 percent of area median income.

Median income means, with respect to an area, the unadjusted median family income for the area as most recently determined by HUD. FHFA will provide the Banks annually with information specifying how the median family income estimates for metropolitan areas are to be applied for the purposes of determining median family income.

Member means an institution that has been approved for membership in a Bank and has purchased capital stock in the Bank in accordance with 12 CFR 1263.20 or 1263.24(b), or successor regulation(s).

Metropolitan area means a metropolitan statistical area (MSA), or a portion of such an area, including Metropolitan Divisions, for which median family income estimates are determined by HUD.

Minority means any individual who is included within any one or more of the following racial and ethnic categories:

(1) American Indian or Alaskan Native—a person having origins in any of the original peoples of North and South America (including Central America), and who maintains tribal affiliation or community attachment;

(2) Asian—a person having origins in any of the original peoples of the Far East, Southeast Asia, or the Indian subcontinent, including, for example, Cambodia, China, India, Japan, Korea, Malaysia, Pakistan, the Philippine Islands, Thailand, and Vietnam;

(3) Black or African American—a person having origins in any of the black racial groups of Africa;

(4) Hispanic or Latino—a person of Cuban, Mexican, Puerto Rican, South or Central American, or other Spanish culture or origin, regardless of race; and

(5) Native Hawaiian or Other Pacific Islander—a person having origins in any of the original peoples of Hawaii, Guam, Samoa, or other Pacific Islands.

Minority census tract means a census tract that has a minority population of at least 30 percent and a median income of less than 100 percent of the area median income.

Moderate-income means income not in excess of area median income.

Mortgage means a member of such classes of liens, including subordinate liens, as are commonly given or are legally effective to secure advances on, or the unpaid purchase price of, real estate under the laws of the State in which the real estate is located, together with the credit instruments, if any, secured thereby, and includes interests in mortgages. "Mortgage" includes a mortgage, lien, including a subordinate lien, or other security interest on the stock or membership certificate issued to a tenant-stockholder or resident-member by a cooperative housing corporation, as defined in section 216 of the Internal Revenue Code of 1986, and on the proprietary lease, occupancy agreement, or right of tenancy in the dwelling unit of the tenant-stockholder or resident-member in such cooperative housing corporation.

Mortgage data means data obtained by the Director from the Bank or Banks under this part and/or the Data Reporting Manual.

Mortgage purchase means a transaction in which a Bank bought or otherwise acquired a mortgage.

Mortgage with unacceptable terms or conditions means a single-family mortgage, including a reverse mortgage, or a group or category of such mortgages, with one or more of the following terms or conditions:

(1) Excessive fees, where the total points and fees charged to a borrower exceed the greater of 5 percent of the loan amount or a maximum dollar amount of $1,000, or an alternative amount requested by a Bank and determined by the Director as appropriate for small mortgages;

(i) For purposes of this definition, points and fees include:

(A) Origination fees;

(B) Underwriting fees;

(C) Broker fees;

(D) Finder's fees; and

(E) Charges that the member imposes as a condition of making the loan, whether they are paid to the member or a third party;

(ii) For purposes of this definition, points and fees do not include:

(A) Bona fide discount points;

(B) Fees paid for actual services rendered in connection with the origination of the mortgage, such as attorneys' fees, notary's fees, and fees paid for property appraisals, credit reports, surveys, title examinations and extracts, flood and tax certifications, and home inspections;

(C) The cost of mortgage insurance or credit-risk price adjustments;

(D) The costs of title, hazard, and flood insurance policies;

(E) State and local transfer taxes or fees;

(F) Escrow deposits for the future payment of taxes and insurance premiums; and

(G) Other miscellaneous fees and charges that, in total, do not exceed 0.25 percent of the loan amount;

(2) An annual percentage rate that exceeds by more than 8 percentage points the yield on Treasury securities with comparable maturities as of the fifteenth day of the month immediately preceding the month in which the application for the extension of credit was received;

(3) Prepayment penalties, except where:

(i) The mortgage provides some benefit to the borrower in exchange for the prepayment penalty (*e.g.*, a rate or fee reduction for accepting the prepayment premium);

(ii) The borrower is offered the choice of another mortgage that does not contain payment of such a premium;

(iii) The terms of the mortgage provision containing the prepayment penalty are adequately disclosed to the borrower; and

(iv) The prepayment penalty is not charged when the mortgage debt is accelerated as the result of the borrower's default in making his or her mortgage payments;

(4) The sale or financing of prepaid single-premium credit life insurance products in connection with the origination of the mortgage;

(5) Underwriting practices contrary to the Interagency Guidance on Nontraditional Mortgage Product Risks (71 FR 58609) (Oct. 4, 2006), the Interagency Statement on Subprime Mortgage Lending (72 FR 37569) (July 10, 2007), or similar guidance subsequently issued by federal banking agencies;

(6) Failure to comply with fair lending requirements; or

(7) Other terms or conditions that are determined by the Director to be an unacceptable term or condition of a mortgage.

Non-metropolitan area means a county, or a portion of a county, including those counties that comprise Micropolitan Statistical Areas, located outside any metropolitan area for which median family income estimates are published annually by HUD.

Owner-occupied housing means single-family housing in which a mortgagor resides, including two- to four-unit owner-occupied properties where one or more units are used for rental purposes.

Purchase money mortgage means a mortgage given to secure a loan used for the purchase of a single-family residential property.

Refinancing mortgage means a mortgage undertaken by a borrower that satisfies or replaces an existing mortgage of such borrower. The term does not include:

(1) A renewal of a single payment obligation with no change in the original terms;

(2) A reduction in the annual percentage rate of the mortgage as computed under the Truth in Lending Act, with a corresponding change in the payment schedule;

(3) An agreement involving a court proceeding;

(4) A workout agreement, in which a change in the payment schedule or collateral requirements is agreed to as a result of the mortgagor's default or delinquency, unless the rate is increased or the new amount financed exceeds the unpaid balance plus earned finance charges and premiums for the continuation of insurance;

(5) The renewal of optional insurance purchased by the mortgagor and added to an existing mortgage; or

(6) A conversion of a balloon mortgage note on a single-family property to a fully amortizing mortgage note where the Bank already owns or has an interest in the balloon note at the time of the conversion.

Residence means a property where one or more families reside.

Residential mortgage means a mortgage on single-family housing.

Seasoned mortgage means a mortgage on which the date of the mortgage note is more than one year before the Bank purchased the mortgage.

Second mortgage means any mortgage that has a lien position subordinate only to the lien of the first mortgage.

Secondary residence means a dwelling where the mortgagor maintains (or will maintain) a part-time place of abode and typically spends (or will spend) less than the majority of the calendar year. A person may have more than one secondary residence at a time.

Single-family housing means a residence consisting of one to four dwelling units. Single-family housing includes condominium dwelling units and dwelling units in cooperative housing projects.

Very low-income means income not in excess of 50 percent of area median income.

Subpart B—Housing Goals

§ 1281.10 General.

Pursuant to the requirements of the Bank Act, as amended (12 U.S.C. 1430c), this subpart establishes:

(a) Three single-family owner-occupied purchase money mortgage housing goals, and one single-family refinancing mortgage housing goal;

(b) A volume threshold for the application of the housing goals to a Bank;

(c) Requirements for measuring performance under the housing goals; and

(d) Procedures for monitoring and enforcing the housing goals.

§ 1281.11 Bank housing goals.

(a) *Volume threshold.* The housing goals established in this section shall apply to a Bank for a calendar year only if the unpaid principal balance (UPB) of the Bank's purchases of AMA-approved mortgages in that year exceeds $2.5 billion.

(b) *Market-based housing goals.* A Bank that is subject to the housing goals shall be in compliance with a housing goal if its performance under the housing goal meets or exceeds the share of the market that qualifies for the housing goal. The size of the market for each housing goal shall be established annually by FHFA for each Bank district based on data reported pursuant to the Home Mortgage Disclosure Act for a given year. Unless otherwise adjusted by FHFA, the size of the market for each Bank district shall be determined based on the following criteria:

(1) Only owner-occupied, conventional loans secured by property located in that Bank district shall be considered;

(2) Purchase money mortgages and refinancing mortgages shall be counted only for the applicable housing goal or goals;

(3) All mortgages flagged as HOEPA loans or subordinate lien loans shall be excluded;

(4) All mortgages with original principal balances above the conforming loan limits for single unit properties for the year being evaluated (rounded to the nearest $1,000) shall be excluded;

(5) All mortgages with rate spreads of 150 basis points or more above the applicable average prime offer rate as reported in the Home Mortgage Disclosure Act data shall be excluded; and

(6) All mortgages that are missing information necessary to determine appropriate counting under the housing goals shall be excluded.

(c) *Low-income families housing goal.* For a Bank that is subject to the housing goals, the percentage share of such Bank's total purchases of purchase money AMA-approved mortgages on owner-occupied single-family housing that consists of mortgages for low-income families shall meet or exceed the share of such mortgages in the market as defined in paragraph (b) of this section.

(d) *Low-income areas housing goal.* For a Bank that is subject to the housing goals, the percentage share of such Bank's total purchases of purchase money AMA-approved mortgages on owner-occupied single-family housing that consists of mortgages for families in low-income areas shall meet or exceed the share of such mortgages in the market as defined in paragraph (b) of this section.

(e) *Very low-income families housing goal.* For a Bank that is subject to the housing goals, the percentage share of such Bank's total purchases of purchase money AMA-approved mortgages on owner-occupied single-family housing that consists of mortgages for very low-income families shall meet or exceed the share of such mortgages in the market as defined in paragraph (b) of this section.

(f) *Refinancing housing goal.* For a Bank that is subject to the housing goals, the percentage share of such Bank's total purchases of refinancing AMA-approved mortgages on owner-occupied single-family housing that consists of refinancing mortgages for low-income families shall meet or exceed the share of such mortgages in the market as defined in paragraph (b) of this section.

§ 1281.12 General counting requirements.

(a) *Calculating the numerator and denominator for the housing goals.* Performance under each of the housing goals shall be measured using a fraction that is converted into a percentage. Neither the numerator nor the denominator shall include Bank transactions or activities that are not AMA-approved mortgage purchases as defined by FHFA or that are specifically excluded as ineligible under § 1281.13(b).

(1) *The numerator.* The numerator of each fraction is the number of AMA-approved mortgage purchases of a Bank in a particular year that finance owner-occupied single-family properties that count toward achievement of a particular housing goal.

(2) *The denominator.* The denominator of each fraction is the total number of AMA-approved mortgage purchases of a Bank in a particular year that finance owner-occupied, single-family properties. A separate denominator shall be calculated for purchase money mortgages and for refinancing mortgages.

(b) *Missing data or information for the housing goals.*—(1) When a Bank lacks sufficient data or information to determine whether the purchase of a mortgage originated after 1992 counts toward achievement of a particular housing goal, that mortgage purchase shall be included in the denominator for that housing goal and shall not be included in the numerator for that housing goal.

(2) Mortgage purchases financing owner-occupied single-family properties shall be evaluated based on the income of the mortgagors and the area median income at the time the mortgage was originated. To determine whether mortgages may be counted under a particular family income level (*i.e.*, low- or very low-income), the income of the mortgagors is compared to the median income for the area at the time of the mortgage application, using the appropriate percentage factor provided under § 1281.1.

(c) *Credit toward multiple goals.* A mortgage purchase by a Bank in a particular year shall count toward the achievement of each housing goal for which such purchase qualifies in that year.

(d) *Application of median income.* For purposes of determining an area's median income under § 1281.1, the area is:

(1) The metropolitan area, if the property which is the subject of the mortgage is in a metropolitan area; and

(2) In all other areas, the county in which the property is located, except that where the State nonmetropolitan median income is higher than the county's median income, the area is the State nonmetropolitan area.

(e) *Sampling not permitted.* Performance under the housing goals for each year shall be based on a complete tabulation of mortgage purchases for that year; a sampling of such purchases is not acceptable.

(f) *Newly available data.* When a Bank uses data to determine whether a mortgage purchase counts toward achievement of any housing goal, and new data is released after the start of a calendar quarter, the Bank need not use the new data until the start of the following quarter.

§ 1281.13 Special counting requirements.

(a) *General.* FHFA shall determine whether a Bank shall receive full, partial, or no credit toward achievement of any of the housing goals for a transaction that otherwise qualifies under this part.

(b) *Not counted.* The following transactions or activities shall not be counted for purposes of the housing goals and shall not be included in the numerator or the denominator in calculating a Bank's performance under the housing goals, even if the transaction or activity would otherwise be counted under paragraph (c) of this section:

(1) Purchases of non-conventional single-family mortgages;

(2) Commitments to buy mortgages at a later date or time;

(3) Options to acquire mortgages;

(4) Rights of first refusal to acquire mortgages;

(5) Any interests in mortgages that the Director determines, in writing, shall not be treated as interests in mortgages;

(6) Mortgage purchases to the extent they finance any dwelling units that are secondary residences;

(7) Single-family refinancing mortgages that result from conversion of balloon notes to fully amortizing notes, if a Bank already owns, or has an interest in, the balloon note at the time conversion occurs;

(8) Purchases of subordinate lien mortgages (second mortgages);

(9) Purchases of mortgages that were previously counted by a Bank under any current or previous housing goal within the five years immediately preceding the current performance year;

(10) Purchases of mortgages where the property has not been approved for occupancy; and

(11) Any combination of factors in paragraphs (b)(1) through (b)(10) of this section.

(c) *Other special rules.* Subject to FHFA's determination of whether a Bank shall receive full, partial, or no credit for a transaction toward achievement of any of the housing goals as provided in paragraph (a) of this section, the transactions and activities identified in this paragraph (c) shall be treated as mortgage purchases as described. A transaction or activity that is covered by more than one paragraph below must satisfy the requirements of each such paragraph. The mortgages from each such transaction or activity shall be included in the denominator in calculating a Bank's performance under the housing goals, and shall be included in the numerator, as appropriate.

(1) *Cooperative housing and condominiums.* The purchase by a Bank of a mortgage on a cooperative housing unit ("a share loan") or a mortgage on a condominium unit shall be treated as a mortgage purchase for purposes of the housing goals.

(2) *Seasoned mortgages.* The purchase of a seasoned mortgage by a Bank shall be treated as a mortgage purchase for purposes of the housing goals, except where the Bank has already counted the mortgage under any current or previous housing goal within the five years immediately preceding the current performance year.

(3) *Purchase of refinancing mortgages.* The purchase of a refinancing mortgage by a Bank shall be treated as a mortgage purchase for purposes of the housing goals only if the refinancing is an arms-length transaction that is borrower-driven.

(d) *HOEPA mortgages and mortgages with unacceptable terms or conditions.* The purchase by a Bank of HOEPA mortgages and mortgages with unacceptable terms or conditions, as defined in §1281.1, shall be treated as mortgage purchases for purposes of the housing goals and shall be included in the denominator for each applicable housing goal, but such mortgages shall not be counted in the numerator for any housing goal.

(e) *FHFA review of transactions.* FHFA may determine whether and how any transaction or class of transactions shall be counted for purposes of the housing goals. FHFA will notify each Bank in writing of any determination regarding the treatment of any transaction or class of transactions under the housing goals.

§1281.14 Determination of compliance with housing goals; notice of determination.

(a) *Determination of compliance with housing goals.* On an annual basis, the Director shall determine whether each Bank has exceeded the volume threshold. For each Bank that has exceeded the volume threshold in a year, the Director shall determine the Bank's performance under each housing goal.

(b) *Failure to meet a housing goal.* If the Director determines that a Bank has failed to meet any housing goal, the Director shall notify the Bank in writing of such preliminary determination. Any notification to a Bank of a preliminary determination under this section shall provide the Bank with an opportunity to respond in writing in accordance with the following procedures:

(1) *Notice.* The Director shall provide written notice to a Bank of a preliminary determination under this section, the reasons for such determination, and the information on which the Director based the determination.

(2) *Response period.*—(i) *In general.* During the 30-day period beginning on the date on which notice is provided under paragraph (b)(1) of this section, the Bank may submit to the Director any written information that the Bank considers appropriate for consideration by the Director in finally determining whether such failure has occurred or whether the achievement of such goal was feasible.

(ii) *Extended period.* The Director may extend the period under paragraph (b)(2)(i) of this section for good cause for not more than 30 additional days.

(iii) *Shortened period.* The Director may shorten the period under paragraph (b)(2)(i) of this section for good cause.

(iv) *Failure to respond.* The failure of a Bank to provide information during the 30-day period under this paragraph (b)(2), as extended or shortened, shall waive any right of the Bank to comment on the proposed determination or action of the Director.

(3) *Consideration of information and final determination.* (i) *In general.* After the expiration of the response period under paragraph (b)(2) of this section or receipt of information provided during such period by a Bank, the Director shall issue a final determination on:

(A) Whether the Bank has failed to meet the housing goal; and

(B) Whether, taking into consideration market and economic conditions and the financial condition of the Bank, the achievement of the housing goal was feasible.

(ii) *Considerations.* In making a final determination under paragraph (b)(3)(i) of this section, the Director shall take into consideration any relevant information submitted by a Bank during the response period.

§1281.15 Housing plans.

(a) *Housing plan requirement.* If the Director determines that a Bank has failed to meet any housing goal and that the achievement of the housing goal was feasible, the Director may require the Bank to submit a housing plan for approval by the Director.

(b) *Nature of plan.* If the Director requires a housing plan, the housing plan shall:

(1) Be feasible;

(2) Be sufficiently specific to enable the Director to monitor compliance periodically;

(3) Describe the specific actions that the Bank will take to achieve the housing goal for the next calendar year; and

(4) Address any additional matters relevant to the plan as required, in writing, by the Director.

(c) *Deadline for submission.* The Bank shall submit the housing plan to the Director within 45 days after issuance of a notice requiring the Bank to submit a housing plan. The Director may extend the deadline for submission of a plan, in writing and for a time certain, to the extent the Director determines an extension is necessary.

(d) *Review of housing plan.* The Director shall review and approve or disapprove a housing plan as follows:

(1) *Approval.* The Director shall review each submission by a Bank, including a housing plan submitted under this section and, not later than 30 days after submission, approve or disapprove the plan or other action. The Director may extend the period for approval or disapproval for a single additional 30-day period if the Director determines it necessary. The Director shall approve any plan that the Director determines is likely to succeed, and conforms with the Bank Act, this part, and any other applicable provision of law.

(2) *Notice of approval and disapproval.* The Director shall provide written notice to a Bank submitting a housing plan of the approval or disapproval of the plan, which shall include the reasons for any disapproval of the plan, and of any extension of the period for approval or disapproval.

(e) *Resubmission.* If the Director disapproves an initial housing plan submitted by a Bank, the Bank shall submit an amended plan acceptable to the Director not later than 15 days after the Director's disapproval of the initial plan; the Director may extend the deadline if the Director determines an extension is in the public interest. If the amended plan is not acceptable to the Director, the Director may afford the Bank 15 days to submit a new plan.

(f) *Enforcement of housing plan.* If the Director finds that a Bank has failed to meet any housing goal, and that the achievement of the housing goal was feasible, and has required the Bank to submit a housing plan under this section, the Director may issue a cease and desist order, or impose civil money penalties, if the Bank refuses to submit such a plan, fails to submit an acceptable plan, or fails to comply with the approved plan. In taking such action, the Director shall follow procedures consistent with those provided in 12 U.S.C. 4581 through 4588 with respect to actions to enforce the housing goals.

Subpart C—Reporting Requirements

§ 1281.20 General.

This subpart establishes data submission and reporting requirements to provide the Director with mortgage and other information relating to the Banks' performance in connection with the housing goals, as supplemented from time to time in the Banks' Data Reporting Manual (DRM).

§ 1281.21 Mortgage Reports.

(a) *Loan-level data elements.* To implement the data collection and submission requirements for mortgage data, and to assist the Director in monitoring the Banks' housing goal activities, each Bank shall collect and compile computerized loan-level data on each AMA-approved mortgage purchase, as described in the DRM. The Director may, from time to time, issue a list in the DRM specifying the loan-level data elements to be collected and maintained by the Banks and provided to the Director. The Director may revise the DRM list by written notice to the Banks.

(b) *Semi-annual Mortgage Reports.* Each Bank shall submit to the Director, on a semi-annual basis, a Mortgage Report. The second semi-annual Mortgage Report each year shall serve as the annual Mortgage Report and shall be designated as such. Each Mortgage Report shall include:

(1) Aggregations of the loan-level mortgage data compiled by each Bank under paragraph (a) of this section for year-to-date AMA-approved mortgage purchases, in the format specified in writing by the Director;

(2) Year-to-date dollar volume, number of units, and number of AMA-approved mortgages on owner-occupied properties purchased by each Bank that do, and do not, qualify under each housing goal as set forth in this part; and

(3) Year-to-date computerized loan-level data consisting of the data elements required under paragraph (a) of this section.

(c) *Timing of Reports.* Each Bank shall submit its first semi-annual Mortgage Report within 45 days of the end of the second quarter. Each Bank shall submit its annual Mortgage Report within 60 days after the end of the calendar year.

(d) *Revisions to Reports.* At any time before submission of its annual Mortgage Report, a Bank may revise its first semi-annual Mortgage Report for that year.

(e) *Format.* The Banks shall submit to the Director computerized loan-level data with the Mortgage Report, in the format specified in writing by the Director.

[75 FR 81105, Dec. 27, 2010]

EFFECTIVE DATE NOTE: At 76 FR 79051, Dec. 21, 2011, §1281.21 was amended by revising paragraph (c); and removing paragraph (d) and redesignating paragraph (e) as new paragraph (d), effective Jan. 20, 2012. For the convenience of the user, the revised text is set forth as follows:

§1281.21 Mortgage Reports.

* * * * *

(c) *Timing of Reports.* Each Bank shall submit its first semi-annual Mortgage Report within two calendar months of the end of the second quarter. Each Bank shall submit its annual Mortgage Report within two calendar months of the end of the calendar year.

* * * * *

§1281.22 Periodic reports.

Each Bank shall provide to the Director such reports, information and data as the Director may request from time to time, or as may be supplemented in the DRM.

§1281.23 Bank data integrity.

(a) *Certification.* (1) The senior officer of each Bank who is responsible for submitting the annual Mortgage Report, or for submitting any other report(s), data or other information for which certification is requested in writing by the Director, shall certify such report(s), data or information.

(2) The certification shall state as follows: "To the best of my knowledge and belief, the information provided herein is true, correct and complete."

(b) *Adjustment to correct errors, omissions or discrepancies.* FHFA shall determine on an annual basis the official housing goals performance figures for a Bank that is subject to the housing goals. FHFA may resolve any error, omission or discrepancy by adjusting the Bank's official housing goals performance figure. If the Director determines that the year-end data reported by a Bank for a year preceding the latest year for which data on housing goals performance was reported to FHFA contained a material error, omission or discrepancy, the Director may increase the corresponding housing goal for the current year by the number of mortgages that the Director determines were overstated in the prior year's goal performance.

PART 1282—ENTERPRISE HOUSING GOALS AND MISSION

Sec.

Subpart A—General

Subpart B—Housing Goals

Subpart C [Reserved]

Subpart D—Reporting Requirements

AUTHORITY: 12 U.S.C. 4501, 4502, 4511, 4513, 4526, 4561–4566, 4603.

SOURCE: 75 FR 55930, Sept. 14, 2010., unless otherwise noted.

Subpart A—General

§ 1282.1 Definitions.

(a) *Statutory terms.* All terms defined in the Safety and Soundness Act are used in accordance with their statutory meaning unless otherwise defined in paragraph (b) of this section.

(b) *Other terms.* As used in this part, the term:

AHAR means the Annual Housing Activities Report that an Enterprise submits to the Director under section 309(n) of the Fannie Mae Charter Act or section 307(f) of the Freddie Mac Act.

AHAR information means data or information contained in the AHAR.

AHS means the American Housing Survey published by HUD and the Department of Commerce.

Balloon mortgage means a mortgage providing for payments at regular intervals, with a final payment ("balloon payment") that is at least 5 percent more than the periodic payments. The periodic payments may cover some or all of the periodic principal or interest. Typically, the periodic payments are level monthly payments that would fully amortize the mortgage over a stated term and the balloon payment is a single payment due after a specified period (but before the mortgage would fully amortize) and pays off or satisfies the outstanding balance of the mortgage.

Borrower income means the total gross income relied on in making the credit decision.

Charter Act means the Fannie Mae Charter Act, as amended, or the Freddie Mac Act, as amended.

Contract rent means the total rent that is, or is anticipated to be, specified in the rental contract as payable by the tenant to the owner for rental of a dwelling unit, including fees or charges for management and maintenance services and those utility charges that are included in the rental contract. In determining contract rent, rent concessions shall not be considered, *i.e.*, contract rent is not decreased by any rent concessions. Contract rent is rent net of rental subsidies. Anticipated rent for unoccupied units may be the market rent for similar units in the neighborhood as determined by the lender or appraiser for underwriting purposes.

Conventional mortgage means a mortgage other than a mortgage as to which an Enterprise has the benefit of any guaranty, insurance or other obligation by the United States or any of its agencies or instrumentalities.

Day means a calendar day.

Designated disaster area means any census tract that is located in a county designated by the federal government as adversely affected by a declared major disaster administered by FEMA, where individual assistance payments were authorized by FEMA. A census tract shall be treated as a "designated disaster area" for purposes of this part beginning on the January 1 after the FEMA designation of the county, or such earlier date as determined by FHFA, and continuing through December 31 of the third full calendar year following the FEMA designation. This time period may be adjusted for a particular disaster area by notice from FHFA to the Enterprises.

Director means the Director of FHFA or his or her designee.

Dwelling unit means a room or unified combination of rooms intended for use, in whole or in part, as a dwelling by one or more persons, and includes a dwelling unit in a single-family property, multifamily property, or other residential or mixed-use property.

Enterprise means Fannie Mae or Freddie Mac (*Enterprises* means, collectively, Fannie Mae and Freddie Mac).

Extremely low-income means:

(i) In the case of owner-occupied units, income not in excess of 30 percent of area median income; and

(ii) In the case of rental units, income not in excess of 30 percent of area median income, with adjustments for smaller and larger families in accordance with this part.

Families in low-income areas means:

(i) Any family that resides in a census tract or block numbering area in which the median income does not exceed 80 percent of the area median income;

(ii) Any family with an income that does not exceed area median income that resides in a minority census tract; and

(iii) Any family with an income that does not exceed area median income that resides in a designated disaster area.

Family means one or more individuals who occupy the same dwelling unit.

Fannie Mae means the Federal National Mortgage Association and any affiliate thereof.

Fannie Mae Charter Act means the Federal National Mortgage Association Charter Act, as amended (12 U.S.C. 1715 *et seq.*).

FEMA means the Federal Emergency Management Agency.

FHFA means the Federal Housing Finance Agency.

FOIA means the Freedom of Information Act, as amended (5 U.S.C. 552).

Freddie Mac means the Federal Home Loan Mortgage Corporation and any affiliate thereof.

Freddie Mac Act means the Federal Home Loan Mortgage Corporation Act, as amended (12 U.S.C. 1451 *et seq.*).

Ginnie Mae means the Government National Mortgage Association.

HMDA means the Home Mortgage Disclosure Act (12 U.S.C. 2801 *et seq.*).

HOEPA mortgage means a mortgage covered by section 103(aa) of the Home Ownership and Equity Protection Act (HOEPA) (15 U.S.C. 1602(aa)), as implemented by the Board of Governors of the Federal Reserve System.

HUD means the United States Department of Housing and Urban Development.

Lender means any entity that makes, originates, sells, or services mortgages, and includes the secured creditors named in the debt obligation and document creating the mortgage.

Low-income means:

(i) In the case of owner-occupied units, income not in excess of 80 percent of area median income; and

(ii) In the case of rental units, income not in excess of 80 percent of area median income, with adjustments for smaller and larger families in accordance with this part.

Median income means, with respect to an area, the unadjusted median family income for the area as most recently determined by HUD. FHFA will provide the Enterprises annually with information specifying how the median family income estimates for metropolitan areas are to be applied for the purposes of determining median family income.

Metropolitan area means a metropolitan statistical area (MSA), or a portion of such an area, including Metropolitan Divisions, for which median family income estimates are determined by HUD.

Minority means any individual who is included within any one or more of the following racial and ethnic categories:

(i) American Indian or Alaskan Native—a person having origins in any of the original peoples of North and South America (including Central America), and who maintains Tribal affiliation or community attachment;

(ii) Asian—a person having origins in any of the original peoples of the Far East, Southeast Asia, or the Indian subcontinent, including, for example, Cambodia, China, India, Japan, Korea, Malaysia, Pakistan, the Philippine Islands, Thailand, and Vietnam;

(iii) Black or African American—a person having origins in any of the black racial groups of Africa;

(iv) Hispanic or Latino—a person of Cuban, Mexican, Puerto Rican, South or Central American, or other Spanish culture or origin, regardless of race; and

(v) Native Hawaiian or Other Pacific Islander—a person having origins in any of the original peoples of Hawaii, Guam, Samoa, or other Pacific Islands.

Minority census tract means a census tract that has a minority population of at least 30 percent and a median income of less than 100 percent of the area median income.

Moderate-income means:

(i) In the case of owner-occupied units, income not in excess of area median income; and

(ii) In the case of rental units, income not in excess of area median income, with adjustments for smaller and larger families in accordance with this part.

Mortgage means a member of such classes of liens, including subordinate liens, as are commonly given or are legally effective to secure advances on, or the unpaid purchase price of, real estate under the laws of the State in which the real estate is located, together with the credit instruments, if any, secured thereby, and includes interests in mortgages. "Mortgage" includes a mortgage, lien, including a subordinate lien, or other security interest on the stock or membership certificate issued to a tenant-stockholder or resident-member by a cooperative housing corporation, as defined in section 216 of the Internal Revenue Code of 1986, and on the proprietary lease, occupancy agreement, or right of tenancy in the dwelling unit of the tenant-stockholder or resident-member in such cooperative housing corporation.

Mortgage data means data obtained by the Director from the Enterprises under section 309(m) of the Fannie Mae Charter Act and section 307(e) of the Freddie Mac Act.

Mortgage purchase means a transaction in which an Enterprise bought or otherwise acquired a mortgage or an interest in a mortgage for portfolio, resale, or securitization.

Mortgage revenue bond means a tax-exempt bond or taxable bond issued by a State or local government or agency where the proceeds from the bond issue are used to finance residential housing.

Mortgage with unacceptable terms or conditions means a single-family mortgage, including a reverse mortgage, or a group or category of such mortgages, with one or more of the following terms or conditions:

(i) Excessive fees, where the total points and fees charged to a borrower exceed the greater of 5 percent of the loan amount or a maximum dollar amount of $1000, or an alternative amount requested by an Enterprise and determined by the Director as appropriate for small mortgages.

(A) For purposes of this definition, points and fees include:

(*1*) Origination fees;

(*2*) Underwriting fees;

(*3*) Broker fees;

(*4*) Finder's fees; and

(*5*) Charges that the lender imposes as a condition of making the loan, whether they are paid to the lender or a third party;

(B) For purposes of this definition, points and fees do not include:

(*1*) Bona fide discount points;

(*2*) Fees paid for actual services rendered in connection with the origination of the mortgage, such as attorneys' fees, notary's fees, and fees paid for property appraisals, credit reports, surveys, title examinations and extracts, flood and tax certifications, and home inspections;

(*3*) The cost of mortgage insurance or credit-risk price adjustments;

(*4*) The costs of title, hazard, and flood insurance policies;

(*5*) State and local transfer taxes or fees;

(*6*) Escrow deposits for the future payment of taxes and insurance premiums; and

(*7*) Other miscellaneous fees and charges that, in total, do not exceed 0.25 percent of the loan amount;

(ii) An annual percentage rate that exceeds by more than 8 percentage points the yield on Treasury securities with comparable maturities as of the fifteenth day of the month immediately preceding the month in which the application for the extension of credit was received;

(iii) Prepayment penalties, except where:

(A) The mortgage provides some benefit to the borrower (*e.g.*, a rate or fee reduction for accepting the prepayment premium);

(B) The borrower is offered the choice of another mortgage that does not contain payment of such a premium;

(C) The terms of the mortgage provision containing the prepayment penalty are adequately disclosed to the borrower; and

(D) The prepayment penalty is not charged when the mortgage debt is accelerated as the result of the borrower's default in making his or her mortgage payments;

(iv) The sale or financing of prepaid single-premium credit life insurance products in connection with the origination of the mortgage;

(v) Underwriting practices contrary to the Interagency Guidance on Nontraditional Mortgage Product Risks (71 FR 58609) (Oct. 4, 2006), the Interagency Statement on Subprime Mortgage Lending (72 FR 37569) (July 10, 2007), or similar guidance subsequently issued by Federal banking agencies;

(vi) Failure to comply with fair lending requirements; or

(vii) Other terms or conditions that are determined by the Director to be an unacceptable term or condition of a mortgage.

Multifamily housing means a residence consisting of more than four dwelling units. The term includes cooperative buildings and condominium projects.

Non-metropolitan area means a county, or a portion of a county, including those counties that comprise Micropolitan Statistical Areas, located outside any metropolitan area for which median family income estimates are published annually by HUD.

Owner-occupied housing means single-family housing in which a mortgagor resides, including two- to four-unit owner-occupied properties where one or more units are used for rental purposes.

Participation means a fractional interest in the principal amount of a mortgage.

Private label security means any mortgage-backed security that is neither issued nor guaranteed by Fannie Mae, Freddie Mac, Ginnie Mae, or any other government agency.

Proprietary information means all mortgage data and all AHAR information that the Enterprises submit to the Director in the AHARs that contain trade secrets or privileged or confidential, commercial, or financial information that, if released, would be likely to cause substantial competitive harm.

Public data means all mortgage data and all AHAR information that the Enterprises submit to the Director in the AHARs that the Director determines are not proprietary and may appropriately be disclosed consistent with other applicable laws and regulations.

Purchase money mortgage means a mortgage given to secure a loan used for the purchase of a single-family residential property.

Refinancing mortgage means a mortgage undertaken by a borrower that satisfies or replaces an existing mortgage of such borrower. The term does not include:

(i) A renewal of a single payment obligation with no change in the original terms;

(ii) A reduction in the annual percentage rate of the mortgage as computed under the Truth in Lending Act (15 U.S.C. 1601 *et seq.*), with a corresponding change in the payment schedule;

(iii) An agreement involving a court proceeding;

(iv) A workout agreement, in which a change in the payment schedule or collateral requirements is agreed to as a result of the mortgagor's default or delinquency, unless the rate is increased or the new amount financed exceeds the unpaid balance plus earned finance charges and premiums for the continuation of insurance;

(v) The renewal of optional insurance purchased by the mortgagor and added to an existing mortgage;

(vi) A renegotiated balloon mortgage on a multifamily property where the balloon payment was due within 1 year after the date of the closing of the renegotiated mortgage; and

(vii) A conversion of a balloon mortgage note on a single-family property to a fully amortizing mortgage note where the Enterprise already owns or has an interest in the balloon note at the time of the conversion.

Rent means, for a dwelling unit:

(i) When the contract rent includes all utilities, the contract rent; or

(ii) When the contract rent does not include all utilities, the contract rent plus:

(A) The actual cost of utilities not included in the contract rent; or

(B) A utility allowance.

Rental housing means dwelling units in multifamily housing and dwelling units that are not owner-occupied in single-family housing.

Rental unit means a dwelling unit that is not owner-occupied and is rented or available to rent.

Residence means a property where one or more families reside.

Residential mortgage means a mortgage on single-family or multifamily housing.

Safety and Soundness Act means the Federal Housing Enterprises Financial Safety and Soundness Act of 1992, as amended (12 U.S.C. 4501 *et seq.*).

Seasoned mortgage means a mortgage on which the date of the mortgage note is more than 1 year before the Enterprise purchased the mortgage.

Second mortgage means any mortgage that has a lien position subordinate only to the lien of the first mortgage.

Secondary residence means a dwelling where the mortgagor maintains (or will maintain) a part-time place of abode and typically spends (or will spend) less than the majority of the calendar year. A person may have more than one secondary residence at a time.

Single-family housing means a residence consisting of one to four dwelling units. Single-family housing includes condominium dwelling units and dwelling units in cooperative housing projects.

Utilities means charges for electricity, piped or bottled gas, water, sewage disposal, fuel (oil, coal, kerosene, wood, solar energy, or other), and garbage and trash collection. Utilities do not include charges for cable or telephone service.

Utility allowance means either:

(i) The amount to be added to contract rent when utilities are not included in contract rent (also referred to as the "AHS-derived utility allowance"), as issued periodically by FHFA; or

(ii) The utility allowance established under the HUD Section 8 Program (42 U.S.C. 1437f) for the area where the property is located.

Very low-income means:

(i) In the case of owner-occupied units, income not in excess of 50 percent of area median income; and

(ii) In the case of rental units, income not in excess of 50 percent of area median income, with adjustments for smaller and larger families in accordance with this part.

Working day means a day when FHFA is officially open for business.

Subpart B—Housing Goals

§ 1282.11 General.

(a) *General.* Pursuant to the requirements of the Safety and Soundness Act (12 U.S.C. 4561–4564, 4566), this subpart establishes:

(1) Three single-family owner-occupied purchase money mortgage housing goals, a single-family owner-occupied purchase money mortgage housing subgoal, a single-family refinancing mortgage housing goal, a multifamily special affordable housing goal and a multifamily special affordable housing subgoal;

(2) Requirements for measuring performance under the goals; and

(3) Procedures for monitoring and enforcing the goals.

(b) *Annual goals.* Each housing goal shall be established by regulation no later than December 1 of the preceding year, except that any housing goal may be adjusted by regulation to reflect subsequent available data and market developments.

§ 1282.12 Single-family housing goals.

(a) *Single-family housing goals.* An Enterprise shall be in compliance with a single-family housing goal if its performance under the housing goal meets or exceeds either:

(1) The share of the market that qualifies for the goal; or

(2) The benchmark level for the goal.

(b) *Size of market.* The size of the market for each goal shall be established annually by FHFA based on data reported pursuant to the Home Mortgage Disclosure Act for a given year. Unless otherwise adjusted by FHFA, the size of the market shall be determined based on the following criteria:

(1) Only owner-occupied, conventional loans shall be considered;

(2) Purchase money mortgages and refinancing mortgages shall only be counted for the applicable goal or goals;

(3) All mortgages flagged as HOEPA loans or subordinate lien loans shall be excluded;

(4) All mortgages with original principal balances above the conforming loan limits for single unit properties for the year being evaluated (rounded to the nearest $1,000) shall be excluded;

(5) All mortgages with rate spreads of 150 basis points or more above the applicable average prime offer rate as reported in the Home Mortgage Disclosure Act data shall be excluded; and

(6) All mortgages that are missing information necessary to determine appropriate counting under the housing goals shall be excluded.

(c) *Low-income families housing goal.* The percentage share of each Enterprise's total purchases of purchase money mortgages on owner-occupied single-family housing that consists of mortgages for low-income families shall meet or exceed either:

(1) The share of such mortgages in the market as defined in paragraph (b) of this section in each year; or

(2) The benchmark level, which for 2010 and 2011 shall be 27 percent of the total number of purchase money mortgages purchased by that Enterprise in each year that finance owner-occupied single-family properties.

(d) *Very low-income families housing goal.* The percentage share of each Enterprise's total purchases of purchase money mortgages on owner-occupied single-family housing that consists of mortgages for very low-income families shall meet or exceed either:

(1) The share of such mortgages in the market as defined in paragraph (b) of this section in each year; or

(2) The benchmark level, which for 2010 and 2011 shall be 8 percent of the total number of purchase money mortgages purchased by that Enterprise in each year that finance owner-occupied single-family properties.

(e) *Low-income areas housing goal.* The percentage share of each Enterprise's total purchases of purchase money mortgages on owner-occupied single-family housing that consists of mortgages for families in low-income areas shall meet or exceed either:

(1) The share of such mortgages in the market as defined in paragraph (b) of this section in each year; or

(2) A benchmark level which shall be set annually by FHFA notice based on the benchmark level for the low-income areas housing subgoal, plus an adjustment factor reflecting the additional incremental share of mortgages for moderate-income families in designated disaster areas in the most recent year for which such data is available.

(f) *Low-income areas housing subgoal.* The percentage share of each Enterprise's total purchases of purchase money mortgages on owner-occupied single-family housing that consists of mortgages for families in low-income census tracts or for moderate-income families in minority census tracts shall meet or exceed either:

(1) The share of such mortgages in the market as defined in paragraph (b) of this section in each year; or

(2) The benchmark level, which for 2010 and 2011 shall be 13 percent of the total number of purchase money mortgages purchased by that Enterprise in each year that finance owner-occupied single-family properties.

(g) *Refinancing housing goal.* The percentage share of each Enterprise's total purchases of refinancing mortgages on owner-occupied single-family housing that consists of refinancing mortgages for low-income families shall meet or exceed either:

(1) The share of such mortgages in the market as defined in paragraph (b) of this section in each year; or

(2) The benchmark level, which for 2010 and 2011 shall be 21 percent of the total number of refinancing mortgages purchased by that Enterprise in each year that finance owner-occupied single-family properties.

§ 1282.13 Multifamily special affordable housing goal and subgoal.

(a) *Multifamily housing goal and subgoal.* An Enterprise shall be in compliance with a multifamily housing goal or subgoal if its performance under the housing goal or subgoal meets or exceeds the benchmark level for the goal.

(b) *Multifamily low-income housing goal.* For the years 2010 and 2011, the goal for each Enterprise's purchases of mortgages on multifamily residential housing affordable to low-income families shall be, for Fannie Mae, at least 177,750 dwelling units affordable to low-income families in multifamily residential housing financed by mortgages purchased by that Enterprise in each year, and for Freddie Mac, at least 161,250 such dwelling units in each year.

(c) *Multifamily very low-income housing subgoal.* For the years 2010 and 2011, the subgoal for each Enterprise's purchases of mortgages on multifamily residential housing affordable to very low-income families shall be, for Fannie Mae, at least 42,750 dwelling units affordable to very low-income families in multifamily residential housing financed by mortgages purchased by that Enterprise in each year, and for Freddie Mac, at least 21,000 such dwelling units in each year.

§ 1282.14 Discretionary adjustment of housing goals.

(a) An Enterprise may petition the Director in writing during any year to reduce any goal or subgoal for that year.

(b) The Director shall seek public comment on any such petition for a period of 30 days.

(c) The Director shall make a determination regarding the petition within 30 days after the end of the public comment period. If the Director requests additional information from the Enterprise after the end of the public comment period, the Director may extend the period for a final determination for a single additional 15-day period.

(d) The Director may reduce a goal or subgoal pursuant to a petition for reduction only if:

(1) Market and economic conditions or the financial condition of the Enterprise require such a reduction; or

(2) Efforts to meet the goal or subgoal would result in the constraint of liquidity, over-investment in certain market segments, or other consequences contrary to the intent of the Safety and Soundness Act or the purposes of the Charter Acts (12 U.S.C. 1716; 12 U.S.C. 1451 note).

§ 1282.15 General counting requirements.

(a) *Calculating the numerator and denominator for single-family housing goals.* Performance under each of the single-family housing goals shall be measured using a fraction that is converted into a percentage. Neither the numerator nor the denominator shall include Enterprise transactions or activities that are not mortgage purchases as defined by FHFA or that are specifically excluded as ineligible under § 1282.16(b).

(1) *The numerator.* The numerator of each fraction is the number of mortgage purchases of an Enterprise in a particular year that finance owner-occupied single-family properties that count toward achievement of a particular single-family housing goal.

(2) *The denominator.* The denominator of each fraction is the total number of mortgage purchases of an Enterprise in a particular year that finance owner-occupied single-family properties. A separate denominator shall be calculated for purchase money mortgages and for refinancing mortgages.

(b) *Missing data or information for single-family housing goals.* When an Enterprise lacks sufficient data or information to determine whether the purchase of a mortgage originated after 1992 counts toward achievement of a particular single-family housing goal, that mortgage purchase shall be included in the denominator for that housing goal, except under the circumstances described in this paragraph (b).

(1) Mortgage purchases financing owner-occupied single-family properties shall be evaluated based on the income of the mortgagors and the area median income at the time the mortgage was originated. To determine whether mortgages may be counted under a particular family income level, *i.e.*, low- or very low-income, the income of the mortgagors is compared to the median income for the area at the time of the mortgage application, using the appropriate percentage factor provided under § 1282.17.

(2) When the income of the mortgagor(s) is not available to determine whether a mortgage purchase counts toward achievement of a particular single-family housing goal, an Enterprise's performance with respect to such mortgage purchase may be evaluated using estimated affordability information by multiplying the number of mortgage purchases with missing borrower income information in each census tract by the percentage of all single-family owner-occupied mortgage originations in the respective tracts that would count toward achievement of each goal, as determined by FHFA

based on the most recent Home Mortgage Disclosure Act data available.

(3) The estimation methodology in paragraph (b)(2) of this section may be used up to a nationwide maximum that shall be calculated by multiplying, for each census tract, the percentage of all single-family owner-occupied mortgage originations with missing borrower incomes (as determined by FHFA based on the most recent Home Mortgage Disclosure Act data available for home purchase and refinance mortgages, respectively) by the number of Enterprise mortgage purchases secured by single-family owner-occupied properties for each census tract, summed up over all census tracts. Separate nationwide maximums shall be calculated for purchase money mortgages and for refinancing mortgages. If the nationwide maximum is exceeded, then the estimated number of goal-qualifying mortgages will be adjusted by the ratio of the applicable nationwide maximum to the total number of mortgage purchases secured by single-family owner-occupied properties for the Enterprise in that year. Mortgage purchases in excess of the nationwide maximum, and any units for which estimation information is not available, shall remain in the denominator of the respective goal calculation.

(c) *Counting dwelling units for multifamily housing goal and subgoal.* Performance under the multifamily housing goal and subgoal shall be measured by counting the number of dwelling units that count toward achievement of a particular housing goal or subgoal in all multifamily properties financed by mortgages purchased by an Enterprise in a particular year. Only dwelling units that are financed by mortgage purchases, as defined by FHFA, and that are not specifically excluded as ineligible under § 1282.16(b), may be counted for purposes of the multifamily housing goal and subgoal.

(d) *Counting rental units.* For purposes of counting rental units toward achievement of the multifamily housing goal and subgoal, mortgage purchases financing such units shall be evaluated based on the income of actual or prospective tenants where such data is available, *i.e.*, known to a lender, and the area median income at the time the mortgage was acquired.

(1) *Use of income.* Each Enterprise shall require lenders to provide to the Enterprise tenant income information, but only when such information is known to the lender. When the income of actual tenants is available, the income of the tenant shall be compared to the median income for the area, adjusted for family size as provided in § 1282.17, or as provided in § 1282.18 if family size is not known.

(i) When such tenant income information is available for all occupied units, the Enterprise's performance shall be based on the income of the tenants in the occupied units. For unoccupied units that are vacant and available for rent and for unoccupied units that are under repair or renovation and not available for rent, the Enterprise shall use rent levels for comparable units in the property to determine affordability, except as provided in paragraph (d)(1)(ii) of this section.

(ii) When income for tenants is available to a lender because a project is subject to a Federal housing program that establishes the maximum income for a tenant or a prospective tenant in rental units, the income of prospective tenants may be counted at the maximum income level established under such housing program for that unit. In determining the income of prospective tenants, the income shall be projected based on the types of units and market area involved. Where the income of prospective tenants is projected, each Enterprise must determine that the income figures are reasonable considering the rents (if any) on the same units in the past and considering current rents on comparable units in the same market area.

(2) *Use of rent.* When the income of the prospective or actual tenants of a dwelling unit is not available, performance under the multifamily housing goal and subgoal will be evaluated based on rent and whether the rent is affordable to the income group targeted by the housing goal and subgoal. A rent is affordable if the rent does not exceed the maximum income levels as provided in § 1282.19. In determining contract rent for a dwelling unit, the

actual rent or average rent by unit type shall be used.

(3) *Model units and rental offices.* A model unit or rental office in a multifamily property may be counted for purposes of the multifamily housing goal and subgoal only if an Enterprise determines that the number of such units is reasonable and minimal considering the size of the multifamily property.

(4) *Timeliness of information.* In evaluating affordability under the multifamily housing goal and subgoal, each Enterprise shall use tenant and rental information as of the time of mortgage acquisition.

(e) *Missing data or information for multifamily housing goal and subgoal.*—(1) When an Enterprise lacks sufficient information to determine whether a rental unit in a property securing a multifamily mortgage purchased by an Enterprise counts toward achievement of the multifamily housing goal or subgoal because neither the income of prospective or actual tenants, nor the actual or average rental data, are available, an Enterprise's performance with respect to such unit may be evaluated using estimated affordability information by multiplying the number of rental units with missing affordability information in properties securing multifamily mortgages purchased by the Enterprise in each census tract by the percentage of all rental dwelling units in the respective tracts that would count toward achievement of each goal and subgoal, as determined by FHFA based on the most recent decennial census.

(2) The estimation methodology in paragraph (e)(1) of this section may be used up to a nationwide maximum of ten percent of the total number of rental units in properties securing multifamily mortgages purchased by the Enterprise in the current year. Multifamily rental units in excess of this maximum, and any units for which estimation information is not available, shall not be counted for purposes of the multifamily housing goal and subgoal.

(f) *Credit toward multiple goals.* A mortgage purchase (or dwelling unit financed by such purchase) by an Enterprise in a particular year shall count toward the achievement of each housing goal for which such purchase (or dwelling unit) qualifies in that year.

(g) *Application of median income.*—(1) For purposes of determining an area's median income under §§ 1282.17 through 1282.19 and the definitions in § 1282.1, the area is:

(i) The metropolitan area, if the property which is the subject of the mortgage is in a metropolitan area; and

(ii) In all other areas, the county in which the property is located, except that where the State non-metropolitan median income is higher than the county's median income, the area is the State non-metropolitan area.

(2) When an Enterprise cannot precisely determine whether a mortgage is on dwelling unit(s) located in one area, the Enterprise shall determine the median income for the split area in the manner prescribed by the Federal Financial Institutions Examination Council for reporting under the Home Mortgage Disclosure Act, if the Enterprise can determine that the mortgage is on dwelling unit(s) located in:

(i) A census tract;

(ii) A census place code;

(iii) A block-group enumeration district;

(iv) A nine-digit zip code; or

(v) Another appropriate geographic segment that is partially located in more than one area ("split area").

(h) *Sampling not permitted.* Performance under the housing goals for each year shall be based on a complete tabulation of mortgage purchases (or dwelling units) for that year; a sampling of such purchases (or dwelling units) is not acceptable.

(i) *Newly available data.* When an Enterprise uses data to determine whether a mortgage purchase (or dwelling unit) counts toward achievement of any goal and new data is released after the start of a calendar quarter, the Enterprise need not use the new data until the start of the following quarter.

§ 1282.16 Special counting requirements.

(a) *General.* FHFA shall determine whether an Enterprise shall receive full, partial, or no credit toward achievement of any of the housing goals for a transaction that otherwise qualifies under this part. In this determination, FHFA will consider whether a transaction or activity of the Enterprise is substantially equivalent to a mortgage purchase and either creates a new market or adds liquidity to an existing market, provided however that such mortgage purchase actually fulfills the Enterprise's purposes and is in accordance with its Charter Act.

(b) *Not counted.* The following transactions or activities shall not be counted for purposes of the housing goals and shall not be included in the numerator or the denominator in calculating either Enterprise's performance under the housing goals, even if the transaction or activity would otherwise be counted pursuant to paragraph (c) of this section:

(1) Equity investments in low-income housing tax credits;

(2) Purchases of State and local government housing bonds except as provided in paragraph (c)(8) of this section;

(3) Purchases of single-family non-conventional mortgages and multifamily non-conventional mortgages, except:

(i) Multifamily mortgages acquired under a risk-sharing arrangement with a Federal agency;

(ii) Multifamily mortgages under other multifamily mortgage programs involving Federal guarantees, insurance or other Federal obligation where FHFA determines in writing that the financing needs addressed by the particular mortgage program are not well served and that the mortgage purchases under such program should count under the housing goals;

(4) Commitments to buy mortgages at a later date or time;

(5) Options to acquire mortgages;

(6) Rights of first refusal to acquire mortgages;

(7) Any interests in mortgages that the Director determines, in writing, shall not be treated as interests in mortgages;

(8) Mortgage purchases to the extent they finance any dwelling units that are secondary residences;

(9) Single-family refinancing mortgages that result from conversion of balloon notes to fully amortizing notes, if the Enterprise already owns or has an interest in the balloon note at the time conversion occurs;

(10) Purchases of subordinate lien mortgages (second mortgages);

(11) Purchases of mortgages or interests in mortgages that were previously counted by the Enterprise under any current or previous housing goal within the five years immediately preceding the current performance year;

(12) Purchases of mortgages where the property, or any units within the property, have not been approved for occupancy;

(13) Purchases of private label securities;

(14) Enterprise contributions to the Housing Trust Fund (12 U.S.C. 4568) or the Capital Magnet Fund (12 U.S.C. 4569), and mortgage purchases funded with such grant amounts; and

(15) Any combination of factors in paragraphs (b)(1) through (b)(14) of this section.

(c) *Other special rules.* Subject to FHFA's determination of whether an Enterprise shall receive full, partial, or no credit for a transaction toward achievement of any of the housing goals as provided in paragraph (a) of this section, the transactions and activities identified in this paragraph (c) shall be treated as mortgage purchases as described. A transaction or activity that is covered by more than one paragraph below must satisfy the requirements of each such paragraph. The mortgages (or dwelling units, for the multifamily housing goals) from each such transaction or activity shall be included in the denominator in calculating the Enterprise's performance under the housing goals, and shall be included in the numerator, as appropriate.

(1) *Credit enhancements.*—(i) Mortgages (or dwelling units) financed under a credit enhancement entered into by an Enterprise shall be treated as mortgage purchases for purposes of the housing goals only when:

(A) The Enterprise provides a specific contractual obligation to ensure timely payment of amounts due under a mortgage or mortgages financed by the issuance of housing bonds (such bonds may be issued by any entity, including a State or local housing finance agency); and

(B) The Enterprise assumes a credit risk in the transaction substantially equivalent to the risk that would have been assumed by the Enterprise if it had securitized the mortgages financed by such bonds.

(ii) When an Enterprise provides a specific contractual obligation to ensure timely payment of amounts due under any mortgage originally insured by a public purpose mortgage insurance entity or fund, the Enterprise may, on a case-by-case basis, seek approval from the Director for such activities to count toward achievement of the housing goals.

(2) [Reserved]

(3) *Risk-sharing.* Mortgages purchased under risk-sharing arrangements between an Enterprise and any Federal agency under which the Enterprise is responsible for a substantial amount of the risk shall be treated as mortgage purchases for purposes of the housing goals.

(4) *Participations.* Participations purchased by an Enterprise shall be treated as mortgage purchases for purposes of the housing goals only when the Enterprise's participation in the mortgage is 50 percent or more.

(5) *Cooperative housing and condominiums.*—(i) The purchase of a mortgage on a cooperative housing unit ("a share loan") or a mortgage on a condominium unit shall be treated as a mortgage purchase for purposes of the housing goals. Such a purchase shall be counted in the same manner as a mortgage purchase of single-family owner-occupied units.

(ii) The purchase of a mortgage on a cooperative building ("a blanket loan") or a mortgage on a condominium project shall be treated as a mortgage purchase for purposes of the housing goals. The purchase of a blanket loan or a condominium project mortgage shall be counted in the same manner as a mortgage purchase of a multifamily rental property.

(iii) Where an Enterprise purchases both a blanket loan on a cooperative building and share loans for units in the same building, both the blanket loan and the share loan(s) shall be treated as mortgage purchases for purposes of the housing goals. Where an Enterprise purchases both a condominium project mortgage and mortgages on condominium dwelling units in the same project, both the condominium project mortgages and the mortgages on condominium dwelling units shall be treated as mortgage purchases for purposes of the housing goals.

(6) *Seasoned mortgages.* An Enterprise's purchase of a seasoned mortgage shall be treated as a mortgage purchase for purposes of the housing goals, except where the Enterprise has already counted the mortgage under any current or previous housing goal within the five years immediately preceding the current performance year.

(7) *Purchase of refinancing mortgages.* The purchase of a refinancing mortgage by an Enterprise shall be treated as a mortgage purchase for purposes of the housing goals only if the refinancing is an arms-length transaction that is borrower-driven.

(8) *Mortgage revenue bonds.* The purchase or guarantee by an Enterprise of a mortgage revenue bond issued by a State or local housing finance agency shall be treated as a purchase of the underlying mortgages for purposes of the housing goals only to the extent the Enterprise has sufficient information to determine whether the underlying mortgages or mortgage-backed securities qualify for inclusion in the numerator for one or more housing goal.

(9) [Reserved]

(10) *Loan modifications.* An Enterprise's permanent modification, in accordance with the Making Home Affordable program announced on March 4, 2009, of a loan that is held in the Enterprise's portfolio or that is in a pool backing a security guaranteed by the Enterprise, shall be treated as a mortgage purchase for purposes of the housing goals. Each such permanent loan modification shall be counted in the same manner as a purchase of a refinancing mortgage.

(11) [Reserved]

(12) [Reserved]

(13) [Reserved]

(14) *Seller dissolution option.*—(i) Mortgages acquired through transactions involving seller dissolution options shall be treated as mortgage purchases

for purposes of the housing goals, only when:

(A) The terms of the transaction provide for a lockout period that prohibits the exercise of the dissolution option for at least one year from the date on which the transaction was entered into by the Enterprise and the seller of the mortgages; and

(B) The transaction is not dissolved during the one-year minimum lockout period.

(ii) The Director may grant an exception to the one-year minimum lockout period described in paragraphs (c)(14)(i)(A) and (B) of this section, in response to a written request from an Enterprise, if the Director determines that the transaction furthers the purposes of the Safety and Soundness Act and the Enterprise's Charter Act.

(iii) For purposes of this paragraph (c)(14), "seller dissolution option" means an option for a seller of mortgages to the Enterprises to dissolve or otherwise cancel a mortgage purchase agreement or loan sale.

(d) *HOEPA mortgages and mortgages with unacceptable terms or conditions.* HOEPA mortgages and mortgages with unacceptable terms or conditions, as defined in § 1282.1, shall be treated as mortgage purchases for purposes of the housing goals and shall be included in the denominator for each applicable single-family housing goal, but such mortgages shall not be counted in the numerator for any housing goal.

(e) *FHFA review of transactions.* FHFA may determine whether and how any transaction or class of transactions shall be counted for purposes of the housing goals, including treatment of missing data. FHFA will notify each Enterprise in writing of any determination regarding the treatment of any transaction or class of transactions under the housing goals.

§ 1282.17 Affordability—Income level definitions—family size and income known (owner-occupied units, actual tenants, and prospective tenants).

In determining whether a dwelling unit is affordable where income information (and family size, for rental housing) is known to the Enterprise, the affordability of the unit shall be determined as follows:

(a) *Moderate-income* means:

(1) In the case of owner-occupied units, income not in excess of 100 percent of area median income; and

(2) In the case of rental units, where the income of actual or prospective tenants is available, income not in excess of the following percentages of area median income corresponding to the following family sizes:

Number of persons in family	Percentage of area median income
1	70
2	80
3	90
4	100
5 or more	*

*100% plus (8% multiplied by the number of persons in excess of 4).

(b) *Low-income (80%)* means:

(1) In the case of owner-occupied units, income not in excess of 80 percent of area median income; and

(2) In the case of rental units, where the income of actual or prospective tenants is available, income not in excess of the following percentages of area median income corresponding to the following family sizes:

Number of persons in family	Percentage of area median income
1	56
2	64
3	72
4	80
5 or more	*

*80% plus (6.4% multiplied by the number of persons in excess of 4).

(c) *Low-income (60%)* means:

(1) In the case of owner-occupied units, income not in excess of 60 percent of area median income; and

(2) In the case of rental units, where the income of actual or prospective tenants is available, income not in excess of the following percentages of area median income corresponding to the following family sizes:

Number of persons in family	Percentage of area median income
1	42
2	48
3	54
4	60

Number of persons in family	Percentage of area median income
5 or more	*

*60% plus (4.8% multiplied by the number of persons in excess of 4).

(d) *Very low-income* means:

(1) In the case of owner-occupied units, income not in excess of 50 percent of area median income; and

(2) In the case of rental units, where the income of actual or prospective tenants is available, income not in excess of the following percentages of area median income corresponding to the following family sizes:

Number of persons in family	Percentage of area median income
1	35
2	40
3	45
4	50
5 or more	*

*50% plus (4.0% multiplied by the number of persons in excess of 4).

(e) *Extremely low-income* means:

(1) In the case of owner-occupied units, income not in excess of 30 percent of area median income; and

(2) In the case of rental units, where the income of actual or prospective tenants is available, income not in excess of the following percentages of area median income corresponding to the following family sizes:

Number of persons in family	Percentage of area median income
1	21
2	24
3	27
4	30
5 or more	*

*30% plus (2.4% multiplied by the number of persons in excess of 4).

§ 1282.18 Affordability—Income level definitions—family size not known (actual or prospective tenants).

In determining whether a rental unit is affordable where family size is not known to the Enterprise, income will be adjusted using unit size, and affordability determined as follows:

(a) *For moderate-income*, the income of prospective tenants shall not exceed the following percentages of area median income with adjustments, depending on unit size:

Unit size	Percentage of area median income
Efficiency	70
1 bedroom	75
2 bedrooms	90
3 bedrooms or more	*

*104% plus (12% multiplied by the number of bedrooms in excess of 3).

(b) *For low-income (80%)*, income of prospective tenants shall not exceed the following percentages of area median income with adjustments, depending on unit size:

Unit size	Percentage of area median income
Efficiency	56
1 bedroom	60
2 bedrooms	72
3 bedrooms or more	*

*83.2% plus (9.6% multiplied by the number of bedrooms in excess of 3).

(c) *For low-income (60%)*, income of prospective tenants shall not exceed the following percentages of area median income with adjustments, depending on unit size:

Unit size	Percentage of area median income
Efficiency	42
1 bedroom	45
2 bedrooms	54
3 bedrooms or more	*

*62.4% plus (7.2% multiplied by the number of bedrooms in excess of 3).

(d) *For very low-income*, income of prospective tenants shall not exceed the following percentages of area median income with adjustments, depending on unit size:

Unit size	Percentage of area median income
Efficiency	35
1 bedroom	37.5
2 bedrooms	45
3 bedrooms or more	*

*52% plus (6.0% multiplied by the number of bedrooms in excess of 3).

(e) *For extremely low-income*, income of prospective tenants shall not exceed the following percentages of area median income with adjustments, depending on unit size:

Unit size	Percentage of area median income
Efficiency	21
1 bedroom	22.5
2 bedrooms	27
3 bedrooms or more	*

*31.2% plus (3.6% multiplied by the number of bedrooms in excess of 3).

§ 1282.19 Affordability—Rent level definitions—tenant income is not known.

For purposes of determining whether a rental unit is affordable where the income of the family in the dwelling unit is not known to the Enterprise, the affordability of the unit is determined based on unit size as follows:

(a) *For moderate-income,* maximum affordable rents to count as housing for moderate-income families shall not exceed the following percentages of area median income with adjustments, depending on unit size:

Unit size	Percentage of area median income
Efficiency	21
1 bedroom	22.5
2 bedrooms	27
3 bedrooms or more	*

*31.2% plus (3.6% multiplied by the number of bedrooms in excess of 3).

(b) *For low-income (80%),* maximum affordable rents to count as housing for low-income (80%) families shall not exceed the following percentages of area median income with adjustments, depending on unit size:

Unit size	Percentage of area median income
Efficiency	16.8
1 bedroom	18
2 bedrooms	21.6
3 bedrooms or more	*

*24.96% plus (2.88% multiplied by the number of bedrooms in excess of 3).

(c) *For low-income (60%),* maximum affordable rents to count as housing for low-income (60%) families shall not exceed the following percentages of area median income with adjustments, depending on unit size:

Unit size	Percentage of area median income
Efficiency	12.6
1 bedroom	13.5
2 bedrooms	16.2
3 bedrooms or more	*

*18.72% plus (2.16% multiplied by the number of bedrooms in excess of 3).

(d) *For very low-income,* maximum affordable rents to count as housing for very low-income families shall not exceed the following percentages of area median income with adjustments, depending on unit size:

Unit size	Percentage of area median income
Efficiency	10.5
1 bedroom	11.25
2 bedrooms	13.5
3 bedrooms or more	*

*15.6% plus (1.8% multiplied by the number of bedrooms in excess of 3).

(e) *For extremely low-income,* maximum affordable rents to count as housing for extremely low-income families shall not exceed the following percentages of area median income with adjustments, depending on unit size:

Unit size	Percentage of area median income
Efficiency	6.3
1 bedroom	6.75
2 bedrooms	8.1
3 bedrooms or more	*

*9.36% plus (1.08% multiplied by the number of bedrooms in excess of 3).

(f) *Missing Information.* Each Enterprise shall make every effort to obtain the information necessary to make the calculations in this section. If an Enterprise makes such efforts but cannot obtain data on the number of bedrooms in particular units, in making the calculations on such units, the units shall be assumed to be efficiencies except as provided in § 1282.15(e)(1).

§ 1282.20 Determination of compliance with housing goals; notice of determination.

(a) *Single-family housing goals.* The Director shall evaluate each Enterprise's performance under the low-income families housing goal, the very low-income families housing goal, the low-income areas housing goal, the low-income areas housing subgoal, and the refinancing mortgages housing goal on an annual basis. If the Director determines that an Enterprise has failed, or there is a substantial probability that an Enterprise will fail, to meet a single-family housing goal established by this subpart, the Director shall notify the Enterprise in writing of such preliminary determination.

(b) *Multifamily housing goal and subgoal.* The Director shall evaluate each Enterprise's performance under the multifamily low-income housing goal and the multifamily very low-income housing subgoal on an annual basis. If the Director determines that an Enterprise has failed, or there is a substantial probability that an Enterprise will fail, to meet a multifamily housing goal or subgoal established by this subpart, the Director shall notify the Enterprise in writing of such preliminary determination.

(c) Any notification to an Enterprise of a preliminary determination under this section shall provide the Enterprise with an opportunity to respond in writing in accordance with the procedures at 12 U.S.C. 4566(b).

§ 1282.21 Housing plans.

(a) *General.* If the Director determines that an Enterprise has failed, or there is a substantial probability that an Enterprise will fail, to meet any housing goal and that the achievement of the housing goal was or is feasible, the Director may require the Enterprise to submit a housing plan for approval by the Director.

(b) *Nature of plan.* If the Director requires a housing plan, the housing plan shall:

(1) Be feasible;

(2) Be sufficiently specific to enable the Director to monitor compliance periodically;

(3) Describe the specific actions that the Enterprise will take:

(i) To achieve the goal for the next calendar year; and

(ii) If the Director determines that there is a substantial probability that the Enterprise will fail to meet a housing goal in the current year, to make such improvements and changes in its operations as are reasonable in the remainder of the year; and

(4) Address any additional matters relevant to the plan as required, in writing, by the Director.

(c) *Deadline for submission.* The Enterprise shall submit the housing plan to the Director within 45 days after issuance of a notice requiring the Enterprise to submit a housing plan. The Director may extend the deadline for submission of a plan, in writing and for a time certain, to the extent the Director determines an extension is necessary.

(d) *Review of housing plans.* The Director shall review and approve or disapprove housing plans in accordance with 12 U.S.C. 4566(c)(4) and (c)(5).

(e) *Resubmission.* If the Director disapproves an initial housing plan submitted by an Enterprise, the Enterprise shall submit an amended plan acceptable to the Director not later than 15 days after the Director's disapproval of the initial plan; the Director may extend the deadline if the Director determines an extension is in the public interest. If the amended plan is not acceptable to the Director, the Director may afford the Enterprise 15 days to submit a new plan.

Subpart C [Reserved]

Subpart D—Reporting Requirements

§ 1282.61 General.

This subpart establishes data submission and reporting requirements to carry out the requirements of the Enterprises' Charter Acts and the Safety and Soundness Act.

§ 1282.62 Mortgage reports.

(a) *Loan-level data elements.* To implement the data collection and submission requirements for mortgage data, and to assist the Director in monitoring the Enterprises' housing goal activities, each Enterprise shall collect and compile computerized loan-level data on each mortgage purchased in accordance with 12 U.S.C. 1456(e) and 1723a(m). The Director may, from time to time, issue a list entitled "Required Loan-level Data Elements" specifying the loan-level data elements to be collected and maintained by the Enterprises and provided to the Director. The Director may revise the list by written notice to the Enterprises.

(b) *Quarterly Mortgage Reports.* Each Enterprise shall submit to the Director a quarterly Mortgage Report. The fourth quarter Mortgage Report shall serve as the Annual Mortgage Report and shall be designated as such. Each Mortgage Report shall include:

(1) Aggregations of the loan-level mortgage data compiled by the Enterprise under paragraph (a) of this section for year-to-date mortgage purchases, in the format specified in writing by the Director;

(2) Year-to-date dollar volume, number of units, and number of mortgages on owner-occupied and rental properties purchased by the Enterprise that do, and do not, qualify under each housing goal as set forth in this part; and

(3) Year-to-date computerized loan-level data consisting of the data elements required under paragraph (a) of this section.

(c) *Timing of Reports.* The Enterprises shall submit the Mortgage Report for each of the first 3 quarters of each year within 60 days of the end of the quarter. Each Enterprise shall submit its Annual Mortgage Report within 75 days after the end of the calendar year.

(d) *Revisions to Reports.* At any time before submission of its Annual Mortgage Report, an Enterprise may revise any of its quarterly reports for that year.

(e) *Format.* The Enterprises shall submit to the Director computerized loan-level data with the Mortgage Report, in the format specified in writing by the Director.

§ 1282.63 Annual Housing Activities Report.

To comply with the requirements in sections 309(n) of the Fannie Mae Charter Act and 307(f) of the Freddie Mac Act and assist the Director in preparing the Director's Annual Report to Congress, each Enterprise shall submit to the Director an AHAR including the information listed in those sections of the Charter Acts. Each Enterprise shall submit such report within 75 days after the end of each calendar year, to the Director, the Committee on Financial Services of the House of Representatives, and the Committee on Banking, Housing, and Urban Affairs of the Senate. Each Enterprise shall make its AHAR available to the public online and at its principal and regional offices. Before making any such report available to the public, the Enterprise may exclude from the report any information that the Director has deemed proprietary.

§ 1282.64 Periodic reports.

Each Enterprise shall provide to the Director such reports, information and data as the Director may request from time to time.

§ 1282.65 Enterprise data integrity.

(a) *Certification.* (1) The senior officer of each Enterprise who is responsible for submitting the fourth quarter Annual Mortgage Report and the AHAR under sections 309(m) and (n) of the Fannie Mae Charter Act or sections 307(e) and (f) of the Freddie Mac Act, as applicable, or for submitting any other report(s), data or information for which certification is requested in writing by the Director, shall certify such report(s), data or information.

(2) The certification shall state as follows: "To the best of my knowledge and belief, the information provided herein is true, correct and complete."

(b) *Adjustment to correct errors, omissions or discrepancies in AHAR data.* FHFA shall determine the official housing goal performance figure for each Enterprise under the housing goals on an annual basis. FHFA may resolve any error, omission or discrepancy by adjusting the Enterprise's official housing goal performance figure. If the Director determines that the year-end data reported by an Enterprise for a year preceding the latest year for which data on housing goals performance was reported to FHFA contained a material error, omission or discrepancy, the Director may increase the corresponding housing goal for the current year by the number of mortgages (or dwelling units) that the Director determines were overstated in the prior year's goal performance.

PART 1290—COMMUNITY SUPPORT REQUIREMENTS

AUTHORITY: 12 U.S.C. 1430(g), 4511, 4513.

SOURCE: 75 FR 701, Jan. 5, 2010, unless otherwise noted.

§ 1290.1 Definitions.

For purposes of this part:

Advisory Council means the Advisory Council each Bank is required to establish pursuant to section 10(j)(11) of the Federal Home Loan Bank Act (12 U.S.C. 1430(j)(11)) and part 1291 of this chapter.

Appropriate Federal banking agency has the meaning set forth in section 3(q) of the Federal Deposit Insurance Act (12 U.S.C. 1813(q)) and, for federally insured credit unions, means the National Credit Union Administration.

Appropriate State regulator means any State officer, agency, supervisor, or other entity that has regulatory authority over, or is empowered to institute enforcement action against, a particular institution.

Bank means a Federal Home Loan Bank established under section 12 of the Federal Home Loan Bank Act (12 U.S.C. 1432).

CDFI Fund means the Community Development Financial Institutions Fund established under section 104(a) of the Community Development Banking and Financial Institutions Act of 1994 (12 U.S.C. 4703(a)).

Community development financial institution or CDFI means an institution that is certified as a community development financial institution by the CDFI Fund under the Community Development Banking and Financial Institutions Act of 1994 (12 U.S.C. 4701 *et seq.*).

CRA means the Community Reinvestment Act of 1977, as amended (12 U.S.C. 2901, *et seq.*).

CRA evaluation means the public disclosure portion of the CRA performance evaluation provided by a member's appropriate Federal banking agency.

Displaced homemaker means an adult who has not worked full-time, full-year in the labor force for a number of years, and during that period, worked primarily without remuneration to care for a home and family, and currently is unemployed or underemployed and is experiencing difficulty in obtaining or upgrading employment.

FHFA means Federal Housing Finance Agency.

First-time homebuyer means:

(1) An individual and his or her spouse, if any, who has had no present ownership interest in a principal residence during the three-year period prior to purchase of a principal residence.

(2) A displaced homemaker who, except for owning a residence with his or her spouse or residing in a residence owned by his or her spouse, meets the requirements of paragraph (1) of this definition.

(3) A single parent who, except for owning a residence with his or her spouse or residing in a residence owned by his or her spouse, meets the requirements of paragraph (1) of this definition.

Long-term advance means an advance with a term to maturity greater than one year.

Restriction on access to long-term advances means a member may not borrow long-term advances or renew any maturing advance for a term to maturity greater than one year.

Single parent means an individual who is unmarried or legally separated from a spouse and has custody or joint custody of one or more minor children or is pregnant.

Targeted community lending means providing financing for economic development projects for targeted beneficiaries.

§ 1290.2 Community support requirement.

(a) *Selection for community support review.* Except as otherwise provided in this section, FHFA shall select a member for community support review approximately once every two years.

(b) *Notice*—(1) *By the FHFA*. FHFA concurrently shall:

(i) Notify each Bank of the members within its district that have to submit community support statements during the calendar quarter; and

(ii) Publish a notice in the FEDERAL REGISTER that includes the name and address of each member required to submit a community support statement during the calendar quarter, and the deadline for submission of the community support statement to FHFA. The deadline for submission of a community support statement shall be no earlier than 45 calendar days after the date of publication of the notice in the FEDERAL REGISTER.

(2) *By the Banks*. Within 15 calendar days of the date of publication in the FEDERAL REGISTER of the notice required by paragraph (b)(1)(ii) of this section, a Bank shall provide written notice to—

(i) Each member within its district that is named in the FEDERAL REGISTER notice, that the member has to submit a community support statement to FHFA by the deadline stated in the FEDERAL REGISTER notice; and

(ii) Its Advisory Council and nonprofit housing developers, community groups, and other interested parties in its district of the name and address of each member within its district that has to submit a community support statement during the calendar quarter.

(c) *Required documents*. Each member selected for community support review must submit a completed Community Support Statement Form executed by an appropriate senior officer to FHFA and any other information FHFA may require to determine whether a member meets the community support standards.

(d) *Public comments*. In reviewing a member for compliance with the community support requirement, FHFA shall take into consideration any public comments it has received concerning the member.

(e) *Community Development Financial Institutions*. A member that has been certified as a community development financial institution by the CDFI Fund, other than a member that also is an insured depository institution or a CDFI credit union (as defined in §1263.1), shall be deemed to be in compliance with the community support requirements of section 10(g) of the Federal Home Loan Bank Act (Bank Act), 12 U.S.C. 1430(g), by virtue of that certification and is not subject to periodic review under paragraph (a) of this section.

§ 1290.3 Community support standards.

(a) *In general*. In reviewing a community support statement, FHFA shall take into account a member's performance under the CRA if the member is subject to the requirements of the CRA, and the member's record of lending to first-time homebuyers.

(b) *CRA standard*—(1) *Adequate performance*. A member that is subject to the requirements of the CRA shall be deemed to meet the CRA standard if the rating in the member's most recent CRA evaluation is "outstanding" or "satisfactory."

(2) *Probationary performance*. A member that is subject to the requirements of the CRA shall be subject to a probationary period if the rating in the member's most recent CRA evaluation is "Needs to Improve." The probationary period shall extend until the member's appropriate Federal banking agency completes its next CRA evaluation and issues a rating. The member will be eligible to receive long-term advances during the probationary period. If the member does not meet the CRA standard at the end of the probationary period, FHFA will restrict the member's access to long-term advances in accordance with §1290.5.

(3) *Inadequate performance*. FHFA will restrict a member's access to long-term advances in accordance with §1290.5 if the rating in the member's most recent CRA evaluation is "Substantial Non-Compliance."

(c) *First-time homebuyer standard*—(1) *Adequate performance*. In the absence of public comments or other information to the contrary, FHFA will presume that a member meets the first-time homebuyer standard if the member is subject to the requirements of the CRA and the rating in the member's most recent CRA evaluation is "outstanding." In determining whether other members meet the first-time homebuyer standard, FHFA will consider a member's description of its efforts to assist first-time or potential first-time homebuyers or its explanation of factors that affect its ability to assist first-time or potential first-time homebuyers. A member shall be deemed to meet the first-time homebuyer standard if the member otherwise demonstrates to the satisfaction of FHFA that it:

(i) Has an established record of lending to first-time homebuyers;

(ii) Has a program whereby it actively seeks to lend or support lending to first-time homebuyers, including, but not limited to, the following—

(A) Providing special credit products with flexible underwriting standards for first-time homebuyers;

(B) Participating in Federal, State, or local government, or nationwide homeownership lending programs that benefit, serve, or are targeted to, first-time homebuyers; or

(C) Participating in loan consortia for first-time homebuyer loans or loans that serve predominantly low- or moderate-income borrowers;

(iii) Has a program whereby it actively seeks to assist or support organizations that assist potential first-time homebuyers to qualify for mortgage loans, including, but not limited to, the following—

(A) Providing, participating in, or supporting special counseling programs or other homeownership education activities that benefit, serve, or are targeted to, first-time homebuyers;

(B) Providing or participating in marketing plans and related outreach programs targeted to first-time homebuyers;

(C) Providing technical assistance of financial support to organizations that assist first-time homebuyers;

(D) Participating with or financially supporting community or nonprofit groups that assist first-time homebuyers;

(E) Holding investments or making loans that support first-time homebuyer programs;

(F) Holding mortgage-backed securities that may include a pool of loans to low- and moderate-income homebuyers;

(G) Participating or investing in service organizations that assist credit unions in providing mortgages; or

(H) Participating in Bank targeted community lending programs; or

(iv) Has any combination of the elements described in paragraphs (c)(1)(i), (ii), or (iii) of this section.

(2) *Probationary performance.* If FHFA deems the evidence of first-time homebuyer performance to be unsatisfactory, the member will be subject to a one-year probationary period. The member will be eligible to receive long-term advances during the probationary period. If the member does not demonstrate compliance with the first-time homebuyer standard before the probationary period ends, FHFA will restrict the member's access to long-term advances in accordance with §1290.5.

(3) *Inadequate performance.* FHFA will restrict a member's access to long-term advances in accordance with §1290.5 if the member provides no evidence of first-time homebuyer performance.

§ 1290.4 Decision on community support statements.

(a) *Action on community support statements.* FHFA will act on each community support statement in accordance with the requirements of §1290.3 within 75 calendar days of the date FHFA deems the community support statement to be complete. FHFA will deem a community support statement complete when it has obtained all of the information required by this part and any other information it deems necessary to process the community support statement. If FHFA determines during the review process that additional information is necessary to process the community support statement, FHFA may deem the community support statement incomplete and stop the 75-day time period by providing written notice to the member. When FHFA receives the additional information, it shall again deem the community support statement complete and resume the 75-day time period where it stopped. FHFA will have 10 calendar days in addition to the 75-day time period to act on a community support statement if FHFA receives the additional information on or after the seventieth day of the 75-day time period.

(b) *Decision on community support statements.* FHFA will provide written notice to the member and the member's Bank of its determination regarding the community support statement submitted by the member. The notice will identify the reasons for FHFA's determination.

§ 1290.5 Restrictions on access to long-term advances.

(a) *Requirement.* FHFA will restrict a member's access to long-term advances if the member:

(1) Failed to comply with the requirements of this part;

(2) Submitted a community support statement that was not approved by FHFA;

(3) Did not receive a rating in a CRA evaluation of "outstanding" or "satisfactory" at the end of the probationary period described in § 1290.3(b)(2); or

(4) Failed to provide evidence satisfactory to FHFA of its first-time homebuyer performance before the end of the probationary period described in § 1290.3(c)(2).

(b) *Notice.* FHFA will provide written notice to a member and the member's Bank of its determination to restrict the member's access to long-term advances.

(c) *Effective date.* Restrictions on access to long-term advances will take effect 30 days after the date the notices required under paragraph (b) of this section are sent unless the member complies with the requirements of this part before the end of the 30-day period.

(d) *Removing restrictions.* (1) FHFA may remove restrictions on a member's access to long-term advances imposed under this section:

(i) If FHFA determines that application of the restriction may adversely affect the safety and soundness of the member. A member may submit a written request to FHFA to remove a restriction on access to long-term advances under this paragraph (d)(1)(i). The written request must include a clear and concise statement of the basis for the request, and a statement that application of the restriction may adversely affect the safety and soundness of the member from the member's appropriate Federal banking agency, or the member's appropriate State regulator for a member that is not subject to regulation or supervision by a Federal regulator. FHFA will consider each written request within 30 calendar days of receipt.

(ii) If FHFA determines that the member subsequently has complied with the requirements of this part. A member may submit a written request to FHFA to remove a restriction on access to long-term advances under this paragraph (d)(1)(ii). The written request must state with specificity how the member has complied with the requirements of this part. FHFA will consider each written request within 30 calendar days of receipt.

(2) FHFA will place a member on probation in accordance with § 1290.3(b)(2), if—

(i) The member's access to long-term advances was restricted on the basis of the member's inadequate performance under the CRA standard, as described in § 1290.3(b)(3);

(ii) The rating in the member's subsequent CRA evaluation is "Needs to Improve;" and

(iii) The member did not receive either a "Substantial Non-Compliance" CRA rating or a "Needs to Improve" CRA rating immediately preceding the CRA rating on which the member's inadequate performance under the CRA standard was based.

(3) FHFA will provide written notice to the member and the member's Bank of its determination under this paragraph (d). FHFA's determination takes effect on the date the notices are sent.

(e) *Community Investment Cash Advance (CICA) Programs.* A member that is subject to a restriction on access to long-term advances under this part is not eligible to participate in a CICA program offered under part 952 of this title and 1291 of this chapter. The restriction in this paragraph (e), does not apply to CICA applications or funding approved before the date the restriction is imposed.

§ 1290.6 Bank community support programs.

(a) *Requirement.* Consistent with the safe and sound operation of the Bank, each Bank shall establish and maintain a community support program. A Bank's community support program shall:

(1) Provide technical assistance to members;

(2) Promote and expand affordable housing finance;

(3) Identify opportunities for members to expand financial and credit services in underserved neighborhoods and communities;

(4) Encourage members to increase their targeted community lending and affordable housing finance activities by providing incentives such as awards or technical assistance to nonprofit housing developers or community groups with outstanding records of participation in targeted community lending or affordable housing finance partnerships with members; and

(5) Include an annual Targeted Community Lending Plan, approved by the Bank's board of directors and subject to modification, which shall require the Bank to—(i) Conduct market research in the Bank's district;

(ii) Describe how the Bank will address identified credit needs and market opportunities in the Bank's district for targeted community lending;

(iii) Consult with its Advisory Council and with members, housing associates, and public and private economic development organizations in the Bank's district in developing and implementing its Targeted Community Lending Plan; and

(iv) Establish quantitative targeted community lending performance goals.

(b) *Notice.* A Bank shall provide annually to each of its members a written notice:

(1) Identifying CICA programs and other Bank activities that may provide opportunities for a member to meet the community support requirements and to engage in targeted community lending; and

(2) Summarizing targeted community lending and affordable housing activities undertaken by members, housing associates, nonprofit housing developers, community groups, or other entities in the Bank's district, that may provide opportunities for a member to meet the community support requirements and to engage in targeted community lending.

§ 1290.7 Reports.

Each Advisory Council annual report submitted to FHFA pursuant to section 10(j)(11) of the Bank Act (12 U.S.C. 1430(j)(11)) must include an analysis of the Bank's targeted community lending and affordable housing activities.

PART 1291—FEDERAL HOME LOAN BANKS' AFFORDABLE HOUSING PROGRAM

Sec.

AUTHORITY: 12 U.S.C. 1430(j).

SOURCE: 71 FR 59286, Oct. 6, 2006, unless otherwise noted. Redesignated at 73 FR 61664, Oct. 17, 2008.

§ 1291.1 Definitions.

As used in this part:

Affordable means that:

(1) The rent charged to a household for a unit that is to be reserved for occupancy by a household with an income at or below 80 percent of the median income for the area, does not exceed 30 percent of the income of a household of the maximum income and size expected, under the commitment made in the AHP application, to occupy the unit (assuming occupancy of 1.5 persons per bedroom or 1.0 persons per unit without a separate bedroom); or

(2) The rent charged to a household, for rental units subsidized with Section 8 assistance under 42 U.S.C. 1437f or subsidized under another assistance program where the rents are charged in the same way as under the Section 8

program, if the rent complied with this §1291.1 of this part at the time of the household's initial occupancy and the household continues to be assisted through the Section 8 or another assistance program, respectively.

AHP project means a single-family or multifamily housing project for owner-occupied or rental housing that has been awarded or has received AHP subsidy under the competitive application program.

Competitive application program means a program established by a Bank under which the Bank awards and disburses AHP subsidy through a competitive application scoring process pursuant to the requirements of §1291.5 of this part.

Cost of funds means, for purposes of a subsidized advance, the estimated cost of issuing Bank System consolidated obligations with maturities comparable to that of the subsidized advance.

Direct subsidy means an AHP subsidy in the form of a direct cash payment.

Director means the Director of the Federal Housing Finance Agency, or his or her designate.

Eligible household means a household that meets the income limits and other requirements specified by a Bank for its competitive application program and homeownership set-aside programs, provided that:

(1) In the case of owner-occupied housing, the household's income may not exceed 80 percent of the median income for the area; and

(2) In the case of rental housing, the household's income in at least 20 percent of the units may not exceed 50 percent of the median income for the area.

Eligible project means a project eligible to receive AHP subsidy pursuant to the requirements of this part.

Eligible targeted refinancing program means a program offered by the U.S. Department of Housing and Urban Development (HUD), the U.S. Department of Agriculture (USDA), the Federal National Mortgage Association (Fannie Mae), the Federal Home Loan Mortgage Corporation (Freddie Mac), a State or local government, or a State or local housing finance agency for the limited purpose of refinancing (*i.e.*, paying off) first mortgages on primary residences for households that cannot afford or are at risk of not being able to afford their monthly payments, as defined by the program, in order to prevent foreclosure.

Family member means any individual related to a person by blood, marriage, or adoption.

FHFA means the Federal Housing Finance Agency.

Funding period means a time period, as determined by a Bank, during which the Bank accepts AHP applications for subsidy.

Homeownership set-aside program means a program established by a Bank under which the Bank disburses AHP direct subsidy pursuant to the requirements of §1291.6 of this part.

Loan pool means a group of mortgage or other loans meeting the requirements of this part that are purchased, pooled, and held in trust.

Low- or moderate-income household means a household that has an income of 80 percent or less of the median income for the area, with the income limit adjusted for household size in accordance with the methodology of the applicable median income standard, unless such median income standard has no household size adjustment methodology.

Low- or moderate-income neighborhood means any neighborhood in which 51 percent or more of the households have incomes at or below 80 percent of the median income for the area.

Median income for the area means one or more of the following median income standards as determined by a Bank, after consultation with its Advisory Council, in its AHP Implementation Plan:

(1) The median income for the area, as published annually by HUD;

(2) The median income for the area obtained from the Federal Financial Institutions Examination Council;

(3) The applicable median family income, as determined under 26 U.S.C. 143(f) (Mortgage Revenue Bonds) and published by a state agency or instrumentality;

(4) The median income for the area, as published by the United States Department of Agriculture; or

(5) The median income for an applicable definable geographic area, as published by a federal, state, or local government entity, and approved by the FHFA, at the request of a Bank, for use under the AHP.

Multifamily building means a structure with 5 or more dwelling units.

Net earnings of a Bank means the net earnings of a Bank for a calendar year after deducting the Bank's annual contribution to the Resolution Funding Corporation required under section 21B of the Act (12 U.S.C. 1441b), and before declaring or paying any dividend under section 16 of the Act (12 U.S.C. 1436). For purposes of this part, "dividend" includes any dividends on capital stock subject to a redemption request even if under GAAP those dividends are treated as an "interest expense."

Owner-occupied project means, for purposes of the competitive application program, one or more owner-occupied units in a single-family or multifamily building, including condominiums, cooperative housing, and manufactured housing.

Owner-occupied unit means a dwelling unit occupied by the owner of the unit. Housing with 2 to 4 dwelling units consisting of one owner-occupied unit and one or more rental units is considered a single owner-occupied unit.

Program means the Affordable Housing Program established pursuant to this part.

Rental project means, for purposes of the competitive application program, one or more dwelling units for occupancy by households that are not owner-occupants, including overnight and emergency shelters, transitional housing for homeless households, mutual housing, single-room occupancy housing, and manufactured housing.

Retention period means:

(1) Five years from closing for an AHP-assisted owner-occupied unit, or in the case of rehabilitation of a unit currently occupied by the owner where there is no closing, 5 years from the date established by the Bank in its AHP Implementation Plan; and

(2) Fifteen years from the date of project completion for a rental project.

Revolving loan fund means a capital fund established to make mortgage or other loans whereby loan principal is repaid into the fund and re-lent to other borrowers.

Single-family building means a structure with 1 to 4 dwelling units.

Sponsor means a not-for-profit or for-profit organization or public entity that:

(1) Has an ownership interest (including any partnership interest), as defined by the Bank in its AHP Implementation Plan, in a rental project;

(2) Is integrally involved, as defined by the Bank in its AHP Implementation Plan, in an owner-occupied project, such as by exercising control over the planning, development, or management of the project, or by qualifying borrowers and providing or arranging financing for the owners of the units;

(3) Operates a loan pool; or

(4) Is a revolving loan fund.

Subsidized advance means an advance to a member at an interest rate reduced below the Bank's cost of funds by use of a subsidy.

Subsidy means:

(1) A direct subsidy, provided that if a direct subsidy is used to write down the interest rate on a loan extended by a member, sponsor, or other party to a project, the subsidy must equal the net present value of the interest foregone from making the loan below the lender's market interest rate; or

(2) The net present value of the interest revenue foregone from making a subsidized advance at a rate below the Bank's cost of funds.

Very low-income household means a household that has an income at or below 50 percent of the median income for the area, with the income limit adjusted for household size in accordance with the methodology of the applicable median income standard, unless such median income standard has no household size adjustment methodology.

Visitable means, in either owner-occupied or rental housing, at least one entrance is at-grade (no steps) and approached by an accessible route such as a sidewalk, and the entrance door and all interior passage doors are at least 2 feet, 10 inches wide, offering 32 inches of clear passage space.

[71 FR 59286, Oct. 6, 2006, as amended at 73 FR 61664, Oct. 17, 2008; 74 FR 38521, Aug. 4, 2009]

§ 1291.2 Required annual AHP contributions; allocation of contributions.

(a) *Annual AHP contributions.* Each Bank shall contribute annually to its Program the greater of:

(1) 10 percent of the Bank's net earnings for the previous year; or

(2) That Bank's pro rata share of an aggregate of $100 million to be contributed in total by the Banks, such proration being made on the basis of the net earnings of the Banks for the previous year, except that the required annual AHP contribution for a Bank shall not exceed its net earnings in the previous year.

(b) *Allocation of contributions.* Each Bank, after consultation with its Advisory Council and pursuant to written policies adopted by the Bank's board of directors, shall allocate its annual required AHP contribution as follows:

(1) *Competitive application program.* Each Bank shall allocate annually that portion of its annual required AHP contribution that is not set aside to fund homeownership set-aside programs under paragraph (b)(2) of this section, to provide funds to members through a competitive application program, pursuant to the requirements of this part.

(2) *Homeownership set-aside programs*—(i) *Allocation amount; first-time homebuyers.* A Bank, in its discretion, may set aside annually, in the aggregate, up to the greater of $4.5 million or 35% of the Bank's annual required AHP contribution to provide funds to members participating in homeownership set-aside programs, including a mortgage refinancing set-aside program established under § 1291.6(f), provided that at least one-third of the Bank's aggregate annual set-aside allocation to such programs shall be to assist first-time homebuyers, pursuant to the requirements of this part.

(ii) *No delegation.* A Bank's board of directors shall not delegate to Bank officers or other Bank employees the responsibility for adopting its homeownership set-aside program policies.

(3) *Additional funding.* A Bank may accelerate to its current year's program from future annual required AHP contributions an amount up to the greater of $5 million or 20% of its annual required AHP contribution for the current year. The Bank may credit the amount of the accelerated contribution against required AHP contributions under this part 1291 over one or more of the subsequent five years.

[71 FR 59286, Oct. 6, 2006 as amended at 73 FR 61664, Oct. 17, 2008; 74 FR 38521, Aug. 4, 2009; 75 FR 29883, May 28, 2010]

§ 1291.3 AHP Implementation Plan.

(a) *Adoption; no delegation.* Each Bank, after consultation with its Advisory Council, shall adopt a written AHP Implementation Plan, and shall not amend the AHP Implementation Plan without first consulting its Advisory Council. The Bank's board of directors shall not delegate to Bank officers or other Bank employees the responsibility to consult with the Advisory Council prior to adopting or amending the AHP Implementation Plan. The AHP Implementation Plan shall set forth, at a minimum:

(1) The applicable median income standard or standards adopted by the Bank consistent with the definition of median income for the area in § 1291.1 of this part;

(2) The Bank's requirements for its competitive application program established pursuant to § 1291.5 of this part;

(3) The Bank's requirements for its homeownership set-aside programs, if adopted by the Bank pursuant to § 1291.6 of this part;

(4) The Bank's requirements for funding revolving loan funds, if adopted by the Bank pursuant to § 1291.5(c)(13) of this part;

(5) The Bank's requirements for funding loan pools, if adopted by the Bank pursuant to § 1291.5(c)(14) of this part;

(6) The Bank's requirements for monitoring under its competitive application program and any Bank homeownership set-aside programs, pursuant to § 1291.7 of this part;

(7) The Bank's requirements, including time limits, for re-use of repaid AHP direct subsidy, if adopted by the Bank pursuant to § 1291.8(f)(2) of this part; and

(8) The retention agreement requirements for projects and households under the competitive application program and any Bank homeownership

set-aside programs, pursuant to §1291.9(a)(7) and (a)(8) of this part.

(b) *Advisory Council review.* Prior to the amendment of a Bank's AHP Implementation Plan, the Bank shall provide its Advisory Council an opportunity to review the document, and the Advisory Council shall provide its recommendations to the Bank's board of directors for its consideration.

(c) *Notification of Plan amendments to the FHFA.* A Bank shall notify the FHFA of any amendments made to its AHP Implementation Plan within 30 days after the date of their adoption by the Bank's board of directors.

(d) *Public access.* A Bank shall publish its current AHP Implementation Plan on its publicly available Web site, and shall publish any amendments to the AHP Implementation Plan on the Web site within 30 days after the date of their adoption by the Bank's board of directors.

§ 1291.4 Advisory Councils.

(a) *Appointment.* (1) Each Bank's board of directors shall appoint an Advisory Council of 7 to 15 persons who reside in the Bank's District and are drawn from community and not-for-profit organizations that are actively involved in providing or promoting low- and moderate-income housing, and community and not-for-profit organizations that are actively involved in providing or promoting community lending, in the District.

(2) Each Bank shall solicit nominations for membership on the Advisory Council from community and not-for-profit organizations pursuant to a nomination process that is as broad and as participatory as possible, allowing sufficient time for responses.

(3) The Bank's board of directors shall appoint Advisory Council members from a diverse range of organizations so that representatives of no one group constitute an undue proportion of the membership of the Advisory Council, giving consideration to the size of the Bank's District and the diversity of low- and moderate-income housing and community lending needs and activities within the District.

(b) *Terms of Advisory Council members.* Pursuant to policies adopted by the Bank's board of directors, Advisory Council members shall be appointed by the Bank's board of directors to serve for terms of 3 years, which shall be staggered to provide continuity in experience and service to the Advisory Council, except that Advisory Council members may be appointed to serve for terms of 1 or 2 years solely for purposes of reconfiguring the staggering of the 3-year terms. No Advisory Council member may be appointed to serve for more than 3 full consecutive terms. An Advisory Council member appointed to fill a vacancy shall be appointed for the unexpired term of his or her predecessor in office.

(c) *Election of officers.* Each Advisory Council shall elect from among its members a chairperson, a vice chairperson, and any other officers the Advisory Council deems appropriate.

(d) *Duties*—(1) *Meetings with the Banks.* (i) The Advisory Council shall meet with representatives of the Bank's board of directors at least quarterly to provide advice on ways in which the Bank can better carry out its housing finance and community lending mission, including, but not limited to, advice on the low- and moderate-income housing and community lending programs and needs in the Bank's District, and on the use of AHP subsidies, Bank advances, and other Bank credit products for these purposes.

(ii) The Advisory Council's advice shall include recommendations on:

(A) The amount of AHP subsidies to be allocated to the Bank's competitive application program and any Bank homeownership set-aside programs;

(B) The AHP Implementation Plan and any subsequent amendments thereto;

(C) The scoring criteria, related definitions, and any additional optional District eligibility requirements for the competitive application program; and

(D) The eligibility requirements and any priority criteria for any Bank homeownership set-aside programs.

(2) *Summary of AHP applications.* The Bank shall comply with requests from the Advisory Council for summary information regarding AHP applications from prior funding periods.

(3) *Annual analysis; public access.* (i) Each Advisory Council annually shall submit to the FHFA by May 1 its analysis of the low- and moderate-income housing and community lending activity of the Bank by which it is appointed.

(ii) Within 30 days after the date the Advisory Council's annual analysis is submitted to the FHFA, the Bank shall publish the analysis on its publicly available Web site.

(e) *Expenses.* The Bank shall pay Advisory Council members' travel expenses, including transportation and subsistence, for each day devoted to attending meetings with representatives of the board of directors of the Bank and meetings requested by the FHFA.

(f) *No delegation.* A Bank's board of directors shall not delegate to Bank officers or other Bank employees the responsibility to appoint persons as members of the Advisory Council, or to meet with the Advisory Council at the quarterly meetings required by the Act (12 U.S.C. 1430(j)(11)).

§1291.5 Competitive application program.

(a) *Establishment of program.* A Bank shall establish a competitive application program pursuant to the requirements of this part.

(b) *Funding periods and application process*—(1) *Funding periods.* A Bank may accept applications for AHP subsidy under its competitive application program during a specified number of funding periods each year, as determined by the Bank.

(2) *Eligible applicants.* A Bank shall accept applications for AHP subsidy under its competitive application program only from institutions that are members of the Bank at the time the application is submitted to the Bank.

(3) *Submission of applications.* Except as provided in paragraph (c)(13)(i) of this section, a Bank shall require applications for AHP subsidy to contain information sufficient for the Bank to:

(i) Determine that the proposed AHP project meets the eligibility requirements of paragraph (c) of this section; and

(ii) Evaluate the application pursuant to the scoring guidelines adopted by the Bank pursuant to paragraph (d) of this section.

(4) *Review of applications submitted.* Except as provided in paragraph (c)(13)(ii) of this section, a Bank shall review the applications for AHP subsidy to determine that the proposed AHP project meets the eligibility requirements of paragraph (c) of this section, and shall evaluate the applications pursuant to the Bank's scoring guidelines adopted pursuant to paragraph (d) of this section.

(c) *Minimum eligibility requirements.* Projects receiving AHP subsidies pursuant to a Bank's competitive application program must meet the following eligibility requirements:

(1) *Owner-occupied or rental housing.* The AHP subsidy shall be used exclusively for:

(i) *Owner-occupied housing.* The purchase, construction, or rehabilitation of an owner-occupied project by or for very low-income or low- or moderate-income households. A household must have an income meeting the income targeting commitments in the approved AHP application at the time it is qualified by the project sponsor for participation in the project.

(ii) *Rental housing.* The purchase, construction, or rehabilitation of a rental project, where at least 20 percent of the units in the project are occupied by and affordable for very low-income households. A household must have an income meeting the income targeting commitments in the approved AHP application upon initial occupancy of the rental unit, or for projects involving the purchase or rehabilitation of rental housing that already is occupied, at the time the application for AHP subsidy is submitted to the Bank for approval.

(2) *Need for subsidy.* (i) The project's estimated sources of funds shall equal its estimated uses of funds, as reflected in the project's development budget. The difference between the project's sources of funds and uses of funds is the project's need for AHP subsidy, which is the maximum amount of AHP subsidy the project may receive. A Bank, in its discretion, may permit a project's sources of funds to include or exclude the estimated market value of

in-kind donations and voluntary professional labor or services (excluding the value of sweat equity), provided that the project's uses of funds also include or exclude, respectively, the value of such estimates.

(ii) A project's cash sources of funds shall include any cash contributions by the sponsor, any cash from sources other than the sponsor, and estimates of funds the project sponsor intends to obtain from other sources but which have not yet been committed to the project. In the case of homeownership projects where the sponsor extends permanent financing to the homebuyer, the sponsor's cash contribution shall include the present value of any payments the sponsor is to receive from the buyer, which shall include any cash down payment from the buyer, plus the present value of any purchase note the sponsor holds on the unit. If the note carries a market interest rate commensurate with the credit quality of the buyer, the present value of the note equals the face value of the note. If the note carries an interest rate below the market rate, the present value of the note shall be determined using the market rate to discount the cash flows.

(iii) A project's cash uses are the actual outlay of cash needed to pay for materials, labor, and acquisition or other costs of completing the project. Cash costs do not include in-kind donations, voluntary professional labor or services, or sweat equity.

(3) *Project costs*—(i) *In general.* (A) Taking into consideration the geographic location of the project, development conditions, and other non-financial household or project characteristics, a Bank shall determine that a project's costs, as reflected in the project's development budget, are reasonable, in accordance with the Bank's project cost guidelines.

(B) For purposes of determining the reasonableness of a developer's fee for a project as a percentage of total development costs, a Bank may, in its discretion, include estimates of the market value of in-kind donations and volunteer professional labor or services (excluding the value of sweat equity) committed to the project as part of the total development costs.

(ii) *Cost of property and services provided by a member.* The purchase price of property or services, as reflected in the project's development budget, sold to the project by a member providing AHP subsidy to the project, or, in the case of property, upon which such member holds a mortgage or lien, may not exceed the market value of such property or services as of the date the purchase price was agreed upon. In the case of real estate owned property sold to a project by a member providing AHP subsidy to the project, or property sold to the project upon which the member holds a mortgage or lien, the market value of such property is deemed to be the "as-is" or "as-rehabilitated" value of the property, whichever is appropriate. That value shall be reflected in an independent appraisal of the property performed by a state certified or licensed appraiser, as defined in 12 CFR 564.2(j) and (k), within 6 months prior to the date the Bank disburses AHP subsidy to the project.

(4) *Project feasibility*—(i) *Developmental feasibility.* The project must be likely to be completed and occupied, based on relevant factors contained in the Bank's project feasibility guidelines, including, but not limited to, the development budget, market analysis, and project sponsor's experience in providing the requested assistance to households.

(ii) *Operational feasibility of rental projects.* A rental project must be able to operate in a financially sound manner, in accordance with the Bank's project feasibility guidelines, as projected in the project's operating *pro forma.*

(5) *Financing costs.* The rate of interest, points, fees, and any other charges for all loans that are made for the project in conjunction with the AHP subsidy shall not exceed a reasonable market rate of interest, points, fees, and other charges for loans of similar maturity, terms, and risk.

(6) *Timing of AHP subsidy use.* Some or all of the AHP subsidy must be likely to be drawn down by the project or used by the project to procure other financing commitments within 12 months of the date of approval of the application for AHP subsidy funding the project.

(7) *Counseling costs.* AHP subsidies may be used to pay for counseling costs only where:

(i) Such costs are incurred in connection with counseling of homebuyers who actually purchase an AHP-assisted unit; and

(ii) The cost of the counseling has not been covered by another funding source, including the member.

(8) *Refinancing.* The project may use AHP subsidies to refinance an existing single-family or multi-family mortgage loan, provided that the refinancing produces equity proceeds and such equity proceeds up to the amount of the AHP subsidy in the project shall be used only for the purchase, construction, or rehabilitation of housing units meeting the eligibility requirements of this paragraph (c).

(9) *Retention*—(i) *Owner-occupied projects.* Each AHP-assisted unit in an owner-occupied project is, or is committed to be, subject to a 5-year retention agreement described in § 1291.9(a)(7) of this part.

(ii) *Rental projects.* AHP-assisted rental projects are, or are committed to be, subject to a 15-year retention agreement described in § 1291.9(a)(8) of this part.

(10) *Project sponsor qualifications*—(i) *In general.* A project's sponsor must be qualified and able to perform its responsibilities as committed to in the application for AHP subsidy funding the project.

(ii) *Revolving loan fund.* Pursuant to written policies adopted by a Bank's board of directors, a revolving loan fund sponsor that intends to use AHP direct subsidy in accordance with § 1291.5(c)(13) of this part shall:

(A) Provide audited financial statements that its operations are consistent with sound business practices; and

(B) Demonstrate the ability to re-lend AHP subsidy repayments on a timely basis and track the use of the AHP subsidy.

(iii) *Loan pool.* Pursuant to written policies adopted by a Bank's board of directors, a loan pool sponsor that intends to use AHP subsidy in accordance with § 1291.5(c)(14) of this part shall:

(A) Provide evidence of sound asset/liability management practices;

(B) Provide audited financial statements that its operations are consistent with sound business practices; and

(C) Demonstrate the ability to track the use of the AHP subsidy.

(11) *Fair housing.* The project, as proposed, must comply with applicable federal and state laws on fair housing and housing accessibility, including, but not limited to, the Fair Housing Act, the Rehabilitation Act of 1973, the Americans with Disabilities Act of 1990, and the Architectural Barriers Act of 1969, and must demonstrate how the project will be affirmatively marketed.

(12) *Calculation of AHP subsidy.* (i) Where an AHP direct subsidy is provided to a project to write down the interest rate on a loan extended by a member, sponsor, or other party to a project, the net present value of the interest foregone from making the loan below the lender's market interest rate shall be calculated as of the date the application for AHP subsidy is submitted to the Bank, and subject to adjustment under paragraph (g)(4) of this section.

(ii) Where an AHP subsidized advance is provided to a project, the net present value of the interest revenue foregone from making a subsidized advance at a rate below the Bank's cost of funds shall be determined as of the earlier of the date of disbursement of the subsidized advance or the date prior to disbursement on which the Bank first manages the funding to support the subsidized advance through its asset/liability management system, or otherwise.

(13) *Lending and re-lending of AHP direct subsidy by revolving loan funds.* Pursuant to written policies established by a Bank's board of directors after consultation with its Advisory Council, a Bank, in its discretion, may provide AHP direct subsidy under its competitive application program for eligible projects and households involving both the lending of the subsidy and subsequent lending of subsidy principal and interest repayments by a revolving loan fund, provided the following requirements are met:

(i) *Submission of application.* (A) An application for AHP subsidy under this paragraph (c)(13) shall include the revolving loan fund's criteria for the initial lending of the subsidy, identification of and information on a specific proposed AHP project if required in the Bank's discretion, the revolving loan fund's criteria for subsequent lending of subsidy principal and interest repayments, and any other information required by the Bank.

(B) The information in the application shall be sufficient for the Bank to:

(*1*) Determine that the criteria for the initial lending of the subsidy, the specific proposed project if applicable, and the criteria for subsequent lending of subsidy principal and interest repayments, meet the eligibility requirements of paragraph (c) of this section; and

(*2*) Evaluate the criteria for the initial lending of the subsidy, and the specific proposed project if applicable, pursuant to the scoring guidelines established by the Bank pursuant to paragraph (d) of this section.

(ii) *Review of application.* A Bank shall review the application for AHP subsidy to determine that the criteria for the initial lending of the subsidy, the specific proposed project if applicable, and the criteria for subsequent lending of subsidy principal and interest repayments, meet the eligibility requirements of paragraph (c) of this section, and shall evaluate the criteria for the initial lending of the subsidy and the specific proposed project, if applicable, pursuant to the scoring guidelines established by the Bank pursuant to paragraph (d) of this section.

(iii) *Initial lending of subsidy.* (A) The revolving loan fund's initial lending of the AHP subsidy shall meet the eligibility requirements of this paragraph (c), shall be to projects or households meeting the commitments in the approved application for AHP subsidy, and shall be subject to the requirements of §§1291.7(a) and 951.9 of this part, respectively.

(B) If a project or owner-occupied unit funded under this paragraph (c)(13)(iii) is in noncompliance with the commitments in the approved AHP application, or is sold or refinanced prior to the end of the applicable AHP retention period, the required amount of AHP subsidy shall be repaid to the revolving loan fund in accordance with §§1291.8 and 951.9 of this part, and the revolving loan fund shall re-lend such repaid subsidy, excluding the amounts of AHP subsidy principal already repaid to the revolving loan fund, to another project or owner-occupied unit meeting the initial lending requirements of this paragraph (c)(13)(iii) for the remainder of the retention period.

(iv) *Subsequent lending of AHP subsidy principal and interest repayments.* (A) AHP subsidy principal and interest repayments received by the revolving loan fund from the initial lending of the AHP direct subsidy shall be re-lent by the revolving loan fund in accordance with the requirements of this paragraph (c)(13)(iv), except that the revolving loan fund, in its discretion, may provide part or all of such repayments as nonrepayable grants to eligible projects in accordance with the requirements of this paragraph (c)(13)(iv).

(B) The revolving loan fund's subsequent lending of AHP subsidy principal and interest repayments shall be for the purchase, construction, or rehabilitation of owner-occupied projects for households with incomes at or below 80 percent of the median income for the area, or of rental projects where at least 20 percent of the units are occupied by and affordable for households with incomes at or below 50 percent of the median income for the area, and shall meet all other eligibility requirements of this paragraph (c).

(C) A Bank may, in its discretion, require the revolving loan fund's subsequent lending of subsidy principal and interest repayments to be subject to retention period, monitoring, and recapture requirements as defined by the Bank in its AHP Implementation Plan.

(v) *Return of unused AHP subsidy.* The revolving loan fund shall return to the Bank any AHP subsidy that will not be used according to the requirements in this paragraph (c)(13).

(14) *Use of AHP subsidy in loan pools.* Pursuant to written policies established by a Bank's board of directors after consultation with its Advisory Council, a Bank, in its discretion, may

provide AHP subsidy under its competitive application program for the origination of first mortgage or rehabilitation loans with subsidized interest rates to AHP-eligible households through a purchase commitment by an entity that will purchase and pool the loans, provided the following requirements are met:

(i) *Eligibility requirements.* The loan pool sponsor's use of the AHP subsidies shall meet the requirements under this paragraph (c)(14), and shall not be used for the purpose of providing liquidity to the originator or holder of the loans, or paying the loan pool's operating or secondary market transaction costs.

(ii) *Forward commitment.* (A) The loan pool sponsor shall purchase the loans pursuant to a forward commitment that identifies the loans to be originated with interest-rate reductions as specified in the approved application for AHP subsidy to households with incomes at or below 80 percent of the median income for the area. Both initial purchases of loans for the AHP loan pool and subsequent purchases of loans to substitute for repaid loans in the pool shall be made pursuant to the terms of such forward commitment and subject to time limits on the use of the AHP subsidy as specified by the Bank in its AHP Implementation Plan and the Bank's agreement with the loan pool sponsor, which shall not exceed 1 year from the date of approval of the AHP application.

(B) As an alternative to using a forward commitment, the loan pool sponsor may purchase an initial round of loans that were not originated pursuant to an AHP-specific forward commitment, provided that the entities from which the loans were purchased are required to use the proceeds from the initial loan purchases within time limits on the use of the AHP subsidy as specified by the Bank in its AHP Implementation Plan and the Bank's agreement with the loan pool sponsor, which shall not exceed 1 year from the date of approval of the AHP application. The proceeds shall be used by such entities to assist households that are income-eligible under the approved AHP application during subsequent rounds of lending, and such assistance shall be provided in the form of a below-market AHP-subsidized interest rate as specified in the approved AHP application.

(iii) Each AHP-assisted owner-occupied unit and rental project receiving AHP direct subsidy or a subsidized advance shall be subject to the requirements of §1291.7(a), 951.8, and 951.9, respectively, of this part.

(iv) Where AHP direct subsidy is being used to buy down the interest rate of a loan or loans from a member or other party, the loan pool sponsor shall use the full amount of the AHP direct subsidy to buy down the interest rate on a permanent basis at the time of closing on such loan or loans.

(15) *Optional District eligibility requirements.* A Bank may require a project receiving AHP subsidies to meet one or more of the following additional eligibility requirements adopted by the Bank's board of directors and included in its AHP Implementation Plan after consultation with its Advisory Council:

(i) *AHP subsidy limits.* A requirement that the amount of AHP subsidy requested for the project does not exceed limits established by the Bank as to the maximum amount of AHP subsidy available per member each year, or per member, per project, or per project unit in a single funding period; or

(ii) *Homebuyer or homeowner counseling.* A requirement that a household must complete a homebuyer or homeowner counseling program provided by, or based on one provided by, an organization recognized as experienced in homebuyer or homeowner counseling, respectively.

(16) *Prohibited uses of AHP subsidies.* The project shall not use AHP subsidies to pay for:

(i) *Certain prepayment fees.* Prepayment fees imposed by a Bank on a member for a subsidized advance that is prepaid, unless:

(A) The project is in financial distress that cannot be remedied through a project modification pursuant to §1291.5(f) of this part;

(B) The prepayment of the subsidized advance is necessary to retain the project's affordability and income targeting commitments;

(C) Subsequent to such prepayment, the project will continue to comply with the terms of the approved AHP application and the requirements of this part for the duration of the original retention period;

(D) Any unused AHP subsidy is returned to the Bank and made available for other AHP projects; and

(E) The amount of AHP subsidy used for the prepayment fee may not exceed the amount of the member's prepayment fee to the Bank.

(ii) *Cancellation fees.* Cancellation fees and penalties imposed by a Bank on a member for a subsidized advance commitment that is canceled.

(iii) *Processing fees.* Processing fees charged by members for providing AHP direct subsidies to a project.

(d) *Scoring of applications*—(1) *In general.* A Bank shall establish written scoring guidelines setting forth the Bank's AHP competitive application program scoring criteria and related definitions and point allocations, and implementing other applicable requirements pursuant to this paragraph (d). A Bank shall not adopt additional scoring criteria or point allocations, except as specifically authorized under this paragraph (d).

(2) *Point allocations.* (i) A Bank shall allocate 100 points among the 9 scoring criteria identified in paragraph (d)(5) of this section.

(ii) The scoring criterion for targeting identified in paragraph (d)(5)(iii) of this section shall be allocated at least 20 points.

(iii) The remaining scoring criteria shall be allocated at least 5 points each.

(3) *Fixed point and variable point scoring criteria.* A Bank shall designate each scoring criterion as either a fixed-point or a variable-point criterion, defined as follows:

(i) Fixed-point scoring criteria are those which cannot be satisfied in varying degrees and are either satisfied or not, with the total number of points allocated to the criterion awarded by the Bank to an application meeting the criterion; and

(ii) Variable-point criteria are those where there are varying degrees to which an application can satisfy the criteria, with the number of points that may be awarded to an application for meeting the criterion varying, depending on the extent to which the application satisfies the criterion, based on a fixed scale or on a scale relative to the other applications being scored. A Bank shall designate the targeting and subsidy-per-unit scoring criteria identified in paragraphs (d)(5)(iii) and (d)(5)(viii), respectively, of this section, as variable-point criteria.

(4) *Satisfaction of scoring criteria.* A Bank shall award scoring points to applications for proposed projects based on satisfaction of the scoring criteria adopted by the Bank pursuant to paragraph (d)(5) of this section.

(5) *Scoring criteria.* An application for a proposed project may receive scoring points based on satisfaction of the following 9 scoring criteria:

(i) *Use of donated or conveyed government-owned or other properties.* The financing of housing using a significant proportion, as defined by the Bank in its AHP Implementation Plan, of:

(A) Land or units donated or conveyed by the federal government or any agency or instrumentality thereof; or

(B) Land or units donated or conveyed by any other party for an amount significantly below the fair market value of the property, as defined by the Bank in its AHP Implementation Plan.

(ii) *Sponsorship by a not-for-profit organization or government entity.* Project sponsorship by a not-for-profit organization, a state or political subdivision of a state, a state housing agency, a local housing authority, a Native American Tribe, an Alaskan Native Village, or the government entity for Native Hawaiian Home Lands.

(iii) *Targeting.* The extent to which a project provides housing for very low- and low- or moderate-income households, as follows:

(A) *Rental projects.* An application for a rental project shall be awarded the maximum number of points available under this scoring criterion if 60 percent or more of the units in the project are reserved for occupancy by households with incomes at or below 50 percent of the median income for the area. Applications for projects with less than 60 percent of the units reserved for occupancy by households with incomes at or below 50 percent of the median income for the area shall be awarded points on a declining scale based on the percentage of units in a project that are reserved for households with incomes at or below 50 percent of the median income for the area, and on the percentage of the remaining units reserved for households with incomes at or below 80 percent of the median income for the area.

(B) *Owner-occupied projects.* Applications for owner-occupied projects shall be awarded points based on a declining scale to be determined by the Bank in its AHP Implementation Plan, taking into consideration percentages of units and targeted income levels.

(C) *Separate scoring.* For purposes of this scoring criterion, applications for owner-occupied projects and rental projects may be scored separately.

(iv) *Housing for homeless households.* The financing of rental housing, excluding overnight shelters, reserving at least 20 percent of the units for homeless households, the creation of transitional housing for homeless households permitting a minimum of 6 months occupancy, or the creation of permanent owner-occupied housing reserving at least 20 percent of the units for homeless households, with the term "homeless households" as defined by the Bank in its AHP Implementation Plan.

(v) *Promotion of empowerment.* The provision of housing in combination with a program offering: employment; education; training; homebuyer, homeownership, or tenant counseling; daycare services; resident involvement in decision making affecting the creation or operation of the project; or other services that assist residents to move toward better economic opportunities, such as welfare to work initiatives.

(vi) *First District priority.* The satisfaction of one of the following criteria, or one of a number of the following criteria, adopted by the Bank and set forth in the Bank's AHP Implementation Plan, as long as the total points available for meeting the criterion or criteria adopted under this category do not exceed the total points allocated to this category:

(A) *Special needs.* The financing of housing in which at least 20 percent of the units are reserved for occupancy by households with special needs, such as the elderly, mentally or physically disabled persons, persons recovering from physical abuse or alcohol or drug abuse, or persons with AIDS; or the financing of housing that is visitable by persons with physical disabilities who are not occupants of such housing;

(B) *Community development.* The financing of housing meeting housing needs documented as part of a community revitalization or economic development strategy approved by a unit of a state or local government;

(C) *First-time homebuyers.* The financing of housing for first-time homebuyers;

(D) *Member financial participation.* Member financial participation (excluding the pass-through of AHP subsidy) in the project, such as providing market rate or concessionary financing, fee waivers, or donations;

(E) *Disaster areas and displaced households.* The financing of housing located in federally declared disaster areas, or for households displaced from federally declared disaster areas due to a disaster;

(F) *Rural.* The financing of housing located in rural areas;

(G) *Urban.* The financing of urban infill or urban rehabilitation housing;

(H) *Economic diversity.* The financing of housing that is part of a strategy to end isolation of very low-income households by providing economic diversity through mixed-income housing in low- or moderate-income neighborhoods, or providing very low- or low- or moderate-income households with housing opportunities in neighborhoods or cities where the median income equals or exceeds the median income for the larger surrounding area, such as the city, county, or Primary Metropolitan Statistical Area, in which the neighborhood or city is located;

(I) *Fair housing remedy.* The financing of housing as part of a remedy undertaken by a jurisdiction adjudicated by a Federal, State, or local court to be in violation of title VI of the Civil Rights Act of 1964 (42 U.S.C. 2000d *et seq.*), the Fair Housing Act (42 U.S.C. 3601 *et seq.*), or any other Federal, State, or local fair housing law, or as part of a settlement of such claims;

(J) *Community involvement.* Demonstrated support for the project by local government, other than as a project sponsor, in the form of property tax deferment or abatement, zoning changes or variances, infrastructure improvements, fee waivers, or other similar forms of non-cash assistance, or demonstrated support for the project by community organizations or individuals, other than as project sponsors, through the commitment by such entities or individuals of donated goods and services, or volunteer labor;

(K) *Lender consortia.* The involvement of financing by a consortium of at least 2 financial institutions; or

(L) *In-District projects.* The financing of housing located in the Bank's District.

(vii) *Second District priority: Defined housing needs in the District.* The satisfaction of one or more housing needs in the Bank's District, as defined by the Bank in its AHP Implementation Plan. The Bank may, but is not required to, use one of the criteria listed in paragraph (d)(5)(vi) of this section, provided it is different from the criterion or criteria adopted by the Bank under such paragraph.

(viii) *AHP subsidy per unit*—(A) *Amount of subsidy.* The extent to which a project proposes to use the least amount of AHP subsidy per AHP-targeted unit. In the case of an application for a project financed by a subsidized advance, the total amount of AHP subsidy used by the project shall be estimated based on the Bank's cost of funds as of the date on which all applications are due for the funding period in which the application is submitted.

(B) *Separate scoring.* For purposes of this scoring criterion, applications for owner-occupied projects and rental projects may be scored separately.

(ix) *Community stability.* The promotion of community stability, such as by rehabilitating vacant or abandoned properties, being an integral part of a neighborhood stabilization plan approved by a unit of state or local government, and not displacing low- or moderate-income households, or if such displacement will occur, assuring that such households will be assisted to minimize the impact of such displacement.

(e) *Approval of AHP applications.* (1) A Bank shall approve applications for AHP subsidy in descending order starting with the highest scoring application until the total funding amount for the particular funding period, except for any amount insufficient to fund the next highest scoring application, has been allocated.

(2) The Bank also shall approve at least the next 4 highest scoring applications as alternates and, within 1 year of approval, may fund such alternates if any previously committed AHP subsidies become available.

(f) *Modifications of approved AHP applications*—(1) *Modification procedure.* If, prior to or after final disbursement of funds to a project from all funding sources, there is or will be a change in the project that would change the score that the project application received in the funding period in which it was originally scored and approved, had the changed facts been operative at that time, a Bank, in its discretion, may approve in writing a modification to the terms of the approved application, provided that:

(i) The project, incorporating any such changes, would meet the eligibility requirements of paragraph (c) of this section;

(ii) The application, as reflective of such changes, continues to score high enough to have been approved in the funding period in which it was originally scored and approved by the Bank; and

(iii) There is good cause for the modification, and the analysis and justification for the modification are documented by the Bank in writing.

(2) *AHP subsidy increases; no delegation.* Modifications involving an increase in AHP subsidy shall be approved or disapproved by a Bank's board of directors. The authority to approve or disapprove such requests shall not be delegated to Bank officers or other Bank employees.

(g) *Procedure for funding*—(1) *Disbursement of AHP subsidies to members.* (i) A Bank may disburse AHP subsidies only to institutions that are members of the Bank at the time they request a drawdown of the subsidies.

(ii) If an institution with an approved application for AHP subsidy loses its membership in a Bank, the Bank may disburse AHP subsidies to a member of such Bank to which the institution has transferred its obligations under the approved AHP application, or the Bank may disburse AHP subsidies through another Bank to a member of that Bank that has assumed the institution's obligations under the approved AHP application.

(2) *Progress towards use of AHP subsidy.* A Bank shall establish and implement policies, including time limits, for determining whether progress is being made towards draw-down and use of AHP subsidies by approved projects, and whether to cancel AHP application approvals for lack of such progress. If a Bank cancels any AHP application approvals due to lack of such progress, the Bank shall make the AHP subsidies available for other AHP-eligible projects.

(3) *Compliance upon disbursement of AHP subsidies.* A Bank shall establish and implement policies for determining, prior to its initial disbursement of AHP subsidies for an approved project, and prior to each subsequent disbursement if the need for AHP subsidy has changed, that the project meets the eligibility requirements of paragraph (c) of this section and all obligations committed to in the approved AHP application. If a Bank cancels any AHP application approvals due to noncompliance with eligibility requirements of paragraph (c) of this section, the Bank shall make the AHP subsidies available for other AHP-eligible projects.

(4) *Changes in approved AHP subsidy amount where a direct subsidy is used to write down prior to closing the principal amount or interest rate on a loan.* If a member is approved to receive AHP direct subsidy to write down prior to closing the principal amount or the interest rate on a loan to a project, and the amount of AHP subsidy required to maintain the debt service cost for the loan decreases from the amount of AHP subsidy initially approved by the Bank due to a decrease in market interest rates between the time of approval and the time the lender commits to the interest rate to finance the project, the Bank shall reduce the AHP subsidy amount accordingly. If market interest rates rise between the time of approval and the time the lender commits to the interest rate to finance the project, the Bank, in its discretion, may increase the AHP subsidy amount accordingly.

(5) *AHP outlay adjustment.* If a Bank reduces the amount of AHP subsidy approved for a project, the amount of such reduction shall be returned to the Bank's AHP fund. If a Bank increases the amount of AHP subsidy approved for a project, the amount of such increase shall be drawn first from any currently uncommitted or repaid AHP subsidies and then from the Bank's required AHP contribution for the next year.

(6) *Project sponsor notification of reuse of repaid AHP direct subsidy.* Prior to disbursement by a project sponsor of AHP direct subsidy repaid to and retained by such project sponsor pursuant to a subsidy re-use program authorized by the Bank under § 1291.8(f)(2) of this part, the project sponsor shall provide written notice to the member and the Bank of its intent to disburse the repaid AHP subsidy to a household satisfying the requirements of this part and the commitments made in the approved AHP application.

(h) *Bank board duties and delegation*—(1) *Duties.* A Bank's board of directors, after consultation with its Advisory Council, shall be responsible for:

(i) Adoption of the AHP Implementation Plan required pursuant to § 1291.3 of this part; and

(ii) Approving or disapproving the applications for AHP subsidy pursuant to § 1291.5(e) of this part.

(2) *No delegation.* The Bank's board of directors shall not delegate to Bank officers or other Bank employees the responsibilities set forth in paragraph (h)(1) of this section.

[71 FR 59286, Oct. 6, 2006, as amended at 74 FR 38522, Aug. 4, 2009]

§ 1291.6 Homeownership set-aside programs.

(a) *Establishment of program.* A Bank may establish one or more homeownership set-aside programs pursuant to the requirements of this part.

(b) *Eligible applicants.* A Bank shall accept applications for AHP direct subsidy under its homeownership set-aside programs only from institutions that are members of the Bank at the time the application is submitted to the Bank.

(c) *Minimum eligibility requirements.* A Bank's homeownership set-aside programs shall meet the following eligibility requirements:

(1) *Member allocation criteria.* AHP direct subsidies shall be provided to members pursuant to allocation criteria established by the Bank in its AHP Implementation Plan.

(2) *Eligible households.* Members shall provide AHP direct subsidies only to households that:

(i) Have incomes at or below 80 percent of the median income for the area at the time the household is accepted for enrollment by the member in the Bank's homeownership set-aside program, with such time of enrollment by the member defined by the Bank in its AHP Implementation Plan;

(ii) Complete a homebuyer or homeowner counseling program provided by, or based on one provided by, an organization experienced in homebuyer or homeowner counseling, in the case of households that are first-time homebuyers; and

(iii) Are first-time homebuyers, in the case of households receiving funds pursuant to the first-time homebuyer requirement in § 1291.2(b)(2) of this part, and meet such other eligibility criteria that may be established by the Bank in its AHP Implementation Plan, such as a matching funds requirement, homebuyer or homeowner counseling requirement for households that are not first-time homebuyers, or criteria that give priority for the purchase or rehabilitation of housing in particular areas or as part of a disaster relief effort.

(3) *Maximum grant amount.* Members shall provide AHP direct subsidies to households as a grant, in an amount up to a maximum of $15,000 per household, as established by the Bank in its AHP Implementation Plan, which limit shall apply to all households.

(4) *Eligible uses of AHP direct subsidy.* Households shall use the AHP direct subsidies to pay for down payment, closing cost, counseling, or rehabilitation assistance in connection with the household's purchase or rehabilitation of an owner-occupied unit, including a condominium or cooperative housing unit or manufactured housing, to be used as the household's primary residence.

(5) *Retention agreement.* An owner-occupied unit purchased or rehabilitated using AHP direct subsidy shall be subject to a 5-year retention agreement described in § 1291.9(a)(7) of this part.

(6) *Financial or other concessions.* The Bank may, in its discretion, require members and other lenders to provide financial or other concessions, as defined by the Bank in its AHP Implementation Plan, to households in connection with providing the AHP direct subsidy or financing to the household.

(7) *Financing costs.* The rate of interest, points, fees, and any other charges for all loans made in conjunction with the AHP direct subsidy shall not exceed a reasonable market rate of interest, points, fees, and other charges for loans of similar maturity, terms, and risk.

(8) *Counseling costs.* The AHP direct subsidies may be used to pay for counseling costs only where:

(i) Such costs are incurred in connection with counseling of homebuyers who actually purchase an AHP-assisted unit; and

(ii) The cost of the counseling has not been covered by another funding source, including the member.

(9) *Cash back to household.* A member may provide cash back to a household at closing on the mortgage loan in an amount not exceeding $250, as determined by the Bank in its AHP Implementation Plan, and a member shall use any AHP direct subsidy exceeding such amount that is beyond what is needed at closing for closing costs and the approved mortgage amount as a credit to reduce the principal of the mortgage loan or as a credit toward the household's monthly payments on the mortgage loan.

(d) *Approval of AHP applications.* A Bank shall approve applications for AHP direct subsidy in accordance with the Bank's criteria governing the allocation of funds.

(e) *Procedure for funding*—(1) *Disbursement of AHP direct subsidies to members.* (i) A Bank may disburse AHP direct subsidies only to institutions that are members of the Bank at the time they request a draw-down of the subsidies.

(ii) If an institution with an approved application for AHP direct subsidy loses its membership in a Bank, the Bank may disburse AHP direct subsidies to a member of such Bank to which the institution has transferred its obligations under the approved AHP application, or the Bank may disburse AHP direct subsidies through another Bank to a member of that Bank that has assumed the institution's obligations under the approved AHP application.

(2) *Reservation of homeownership set-aside subsidies.* A Bank shall establish and implement policies for reservation of homeownership set-aside subsidies for households enrolled in the Bank's homeownership set-aside program. The policies shall provide that set-aside subsidies be reserved no more than 2 years in advance of the Bank's time limit in its AHP Implementation Plan for draw-down and use of the subsidies by the household and the reservation of subsidies be made from the set-aside allocation of the year in which the Bank makes the reservation.

(3) *Progress towards use of AHP direct subsidy.* A Bank shall establish and implement policies, including time limits, for determining whether progress is being made towards draw-down and use of the AHP direct subsidies by eligible households, and whether to cancel AHP application approvals for lack of such progress. If a Bank cancels any AHP application approvals due to lack of such progress, it shall make the AHP direct subsidies available for other applicants for AHP direct subsidies under the homeownership set-aside program or for other AHP-eligible projects.

(f) *Mortgage refinancing program*—(1) *General.* A Bank may establish a homeownership set-aside program for the use of AHP direct subsidy by its members to assist in the refinancing of a household's mortgage loan, provided such program meets the requirements of this paragraph (f) and otherwise meets the requirements of regulations in this part. The provisions of paragraphs (c)(2)(ii), (c)(2)(iii), (c)(4), (c)(6) and (c)(8) of this section, shall not apply to such program.

(2) *Eligible loans.* A loan is eligible to be refinanced with AHP direct subsidy if the loan is secured by a first mortgage on an owner-occupied unit that is the primary residence of the household, and the loan is refinanced under an eligible targeted refinancing program.

(3) *Eligible uses of AHP direct subsidy.* Members may provide the AHP direct subsidy to:

(i) Reduce the outstanding principal balance of the loan by no more than the amount necessary for the new loan to qualify under both the maximum loan-to-value ratio and the maximum household mortgage debt-to-income ratio required by the eligible targeted refinancing program;

(ii) Pay loan closing costs; or

(iii) Pay for counseling costs only where:

(A) Such costs, including the cost of the homeowner's credit report, are incurred in connection with counseling of homeowners that actually refinance their homes with AHP assistance under the AHP set-aside refinancing program; and

(B) The cost of the counseling has not been covered by another source including the counseling organization, a funding source, or the member.

(4) *Eligible lender participants.* A Bank, in its discretion, may require that a household obtain its refinancing loan through a member participating in an eligible targeted refinancing program.

(5) *Counseling.*—(i) Except as provided in paragraph (f)(5)(ii) of this section, prior to enrollment in an AHP set-aside refinancing program established under this paragraph (f), a household must obtain counseling through the National Foreclosure Mitigation Counseling program or other counseling program used by a state or local government or housing finance agency, for foreclosure mitigation including counseling on whether the household qualifies, in conjunction with AHP subsidy, for refinancing under an eligible targeted refinancing program.

(ii) *Optional requirements.* A Bank, in its discretion, may permit its members, prior to such counseling, to take any of the following actions in paragraphs (f)(5)(ii)(A) through (C) of this section, provided that, in all cases, the household obtains such counseling prior to disbursement of the AHP subsidy on behalf of the household:

(A) Enroll households in the AHP set-aside refinancing program;

(B) Refer households directly to an eligible targeted refinancing program to determine eligibility for refinancing under the eligible targeted refinancing program; or

(C) Determine whether a household could qualify, in conjunction with AHP subsidy, for refinancing under an eligible targeted refinancing program.

(6) *Sunset.*—(i) This paragraph (f) shall expire on July 30, 2010.

(ii) A Bank may commit AHP subsidy to members or households under its AHP set-aside refinancing program until July 30, 2010.

(iii) A member may use the AHP subsidy committed by a Bank pursuant to paragraph (f)(6)(ii) of this section for a loan submitted to an eligible targeted refinancing program on or before December 31, 2010 that is subsequently approved for refinancing under such program.

[71 FR 59286, Oct. 6, 2006, as amended at 73 FR 61664, Oct. 17, 2008; 74 FR 38522, Aug. 4, 2009; 75 FR 29883, May 28, 2010]

§ 1291.7 Monitoring.

(a) *Competitive application program*—(1) *Initial monitoring policies for owner-occupied and rental projects*—(i)—*Adoption and implementation.* Pursuant to written policies established by a Bank, the Bank shall monitor each AHP owner-occupied and rental project under its competitive application program prior to, and within a reasonable period of time after, project completion to determine, at a minimum, whether:

(A) The project is making satisfactory progress towards completion, in compliance with the commitments made in the approved AHP application, Bank policies, and the requirements of this part;

(B) Following completion of the project, satisfactory progress is being made towards occupancy of the project by eligible households; and

(C) Within a reasonable period of time after project completion, the project meets the following requirements, at a minimum:

(*1*) The AHP subsidies were used for eligible purposes according to the commitments made in the approved AHP application;

(*2*) The household incomes and rents comply with the income targeting and rent commitments made in the approved AHP application;

(*3*) The project's actual costs were reasonable in accordance with the Bank's project cost guidelines, and the AHP subsidies were necessary for the completion of the project as currently structured;

(*4*) Each AHP-assisted unit of an owner-occupied project and rental project is subject to AHP retention agreements that meet the requirements of § 1291.9(a)(7) or (a)(8), respectively, of this part; and

(*5*) The services and activities committed to in the approved AHP application have been provided in connection with the project.

(ii) *Back-up and other project documentation.* The Bank's written monitoring policies shall include requirements for:

(A) Bank review of back-up project documentation regarding household incomes and rents maintained by the project sponsor or owner; and

(B) Maintenance and Bank review of other project documentation in the Bank's discretion.

(iii) *Sampling plan.* The Bank shall not use a sampling plan to select the projects to be monitored under this paragraph (a)(1), but may use a reasonable risk-based sampling plan to review the back-up project documentation.

(2) *Reliance on long-term tax credit monitoring for rental projects.* For completed AHP rental projects that have been allocated federal Low-Income Housing Tax Credits (tax credits), a Bank may, in its discretion, for purposes of long-term AHP monitoring under its competitive application program, rely on the monitoring by the state-designated housing credit agency administering the tax credits of the income targeting and rent requirements applicable under the Low-Income Housing Tax Credit Program, and the Bank need not obtain and review reports from such agency or otherwise monitor the projects' long-term AHP compliance.

(3) *Reliance on other long-term governmental monitoring for rental projects.* For completed AHP rental projects that received funds other than tax credits from federal, state, or local government entities, a Bank may, in its discretion, for purposes of long-term AHP monitoring under its competitive application program, rely on the monitoring by such entities of the income targeting and rent requirements applicable under their programs, provided that the Bank can show that:

(i) The compliance profiles regarding income targeting, rent, and retention period requirements of the AHP and the other programs are substantively equivalent;

(ii) The entity has demonstrated and continues to demonstrate its ability to monitor the project;

(iii) The entity agrees to provide reports to the Bank on the project's incomes and rents for the full 15-year AHP retention period; and

(iv) The Bank reviews the reports from the monitoring entity to confirm that they comply with the Bank's monitoring policies.

(4) *Long-term monitoring policies for rental projects*—(i) *Adoption and implementation.* In cases where a Bank does not rely on monitoring by a federal, state, or local government entity pursuant to paragraphs (a)(2) or (a)(3) of this section, pursuant to written policies established by the Bank, the Bank shall monitor completed AHP rental projects under its competitive application program, commencing in the second year after project completion to determine, at a minimum, whether during the full 15-year retention period, the household incomes and rents comply with the income targeting and rent commitments, respectively, made in the approved AHP applications.

(ii) *Annual project owner certifications; backup and other project documentation.* A Bank's written monitoring policies shall include requirements for:

(A) Bank review of annual certifications by project owners to the Bank that household incomes and rents are in compliance with the commitments made in the approved AHP application;

(B) Bank review of back-up project documentation regarding household incomes and rents maintained by the project owner; and

(C) Maintenance and Bank review of other project documentation in the Banks' discretion.

(iii) *Risk factors and other monitoring*—(A) *Risk factors; other monitoring.* A Bank's written monitoring policies shall take into account risk factors such as the amount of AHP subsidy in the project, type of project, size of project, location of project, sponsor experience, and any monitoring of the project provided by a federal, state, or local government entity.

(B) *Risk-based sampling plan.* A Bank may use a reasonable, risk-based sampling plan to select the rental projects to be monitored under this paragraph (a)(4), and to review the annual project owner certifications, back-up, and any other project documentation. The risk-based sampling plan and its basis shall be in writing.

(5) *Annual adjustment of targeting commitments.* For purposes of determining compliance with the targeting commitments in an approved AHP application for both initial and long-term AHP monitoring purposes under a Bank's competitive application program, such commitments shall be considered to adjust annually according to the current applicable median income data. A rental unit may continue to count toward meeting the targeting commitment of an approved AHP application as long as the rent charged to a household remains affordable, as defined in §1291.1 of this part, for the household occupying the unit.

(b) *Homeownership set-aside programs: Monitoring policies*—(1) *Adoption and implementation.* Pursuant to written policies adopted by a Bank, the Bank shall monitor compliance with the requirements of its homeownership set-aside programs, including monitoring to determine, at a minimum, whether:

(i) The AHP subsidy was provided to households meeting all applicable eligibility requirements in §1291.6(c)(2) of this part and the Bank's homeownership set-aside program policies; and

(ii) All other applicable eligibility requirements in §1291.6(c) and §1291.6(f) of this part and the Bank's homeownership set-aside program policies are met, including that the AHP-assisted units are subject to retention agreements required under § 1291.6(c)(5) of this part.

(2) *Member certifications; back-up and other documentation.* The Bank's written monitoring policies shall include requirements for:

(i) Bank review of certifications by members to the Bank, prior to disbursement of the AHP subsidy, that the subsidy will be provided in compliance with all applicable eligibility requirements in § 1291.6(c) and § 1291.6(f) of this part;

(ii) Bank review of back-up documentation regarding household incomes maintained by the member; and

(iii) Maintenance and Bank review of other documentation in the Bank's discretion.

(3) *Sampling plan.* The Bank may use a reasonable sampling plan to select the households to be monitored, and to review the back-up and any other documentation received by the Bank, but not the member certifications required in paragraph (b)(2) of this section. The sampling plan and its basis shall be in writing.

[71 FR 59286, Oct. 6, 2006, as amended at 73 FR 61664, Oct. 17, 2008]

§ 1291.8 Remedial actions for noncompliance.

(a) *Recovery of AHP subsidies.* A Bank shall recover the amount of any AHP subsidies (plus interest, if appropriate) that are not used in compliance with the commitments made in the approved application for AHP subsidy and the requirements of this part, if the misuse is the result of the actions or omissions of the member, the project sponsor, or the project owner.

(b) *Responsible party for repayment of AHP subsidies.* Except as provided in paragraph (c) of this section:

(1) If the member causes the AHP subsidies to be misused through its actions or omissions, the member shall repay the AHP subsidies to the Bank.

(2) If the project sponsor or owner causes the AHP subsidies to be misused through its actions or omissions, the following shall apply, as determined by the Bank in its discretion:

(i) The member shall recover the AHP subsidies from the project sponsor or owner and repay them to the Bank; or

(ii) The project sponsor or owner shall repay the AHP subsidies directly to the Bank.

(c) *Recovery not required.* Recovery of the AHP subsidies is not required if:

(1) The member, project sponsor, or project owner cures the noncompliance within a reasonable period of time;

(2) The circumstances of noncompliance are eliminated through a modification of the terms of the approved application for AHP subsidy pursuant to § 1291.5(f) of this part; or

(3) The member is unable to collect the AHP subsidy after making reasonable efforts to collect it.

(d) *Settlements.* A Bank may settle a claim for AHP subsidies that it has against a member, project sponsor, or project owner for less than the full amount due. If a Bank enters into such a settlement, the FHFA may require the Bank to reimburse its AHP fund in the amount of any shortfall under paragraph (e)(2) of this section, unless:

(1) The Bank has sufficient documentation showing that the sum agreed to be repaid under the settlement is reasonably justified, based on the facts and circumstances of the noncompliance (including the degree of culpability of the non-complying parties and the extent of the Bank's recovery efforts); or

(2) The Bank obtains a determination from the FHFA that the sum agreed to be repaid under the settlement is reasonably justified, based on the facts and circumstances of the noncompliance (including the degree of culpability of the non-complying parties and the extent of the Bank's recovery efforts).

(e) *Reimbursement of AHP fund*—(1) *By the Bank.* A Bank shall reimburse its AHP fund in the amount of any AHP subsidies (plus interest, if appropriate) misused as a result of the actions or omissions of the Bank.

(2) *By FHFA order.* The FHFA may order a Bank to reimburse its AHP fund in an appropriate amount upon determining that:

(i) The Bank has failed to reimburse its AHP fund as required under paragraph (e)(1) of this section; or

(ii) The Bank has failed to recover AHP subsidy from a member, project sponsor, or project owner pursuant to the requirements of paragraph (a) of this section, and has not shown that such failure is reasonably justified, considering factors such as the extent of the Bank's recovery efforts.

(f) *Use of repaid AHP subsidies*—(1) *Use of repaid AHP subsidies in other AHP-eligible projects.* Except as provided in paragraph (f)(2) of this section, amounts of AHP subsidy, including any interest, repaid to a Bank pursuant to this part shall be made available by the Bank for other AHP-eligible projects.

(2) *Re-use of repaid AHP direct subsidies in same project*—(i) *Requirements.* AHP direct subsidy, including any interest, repaid to a member or project sponsor under a homeownership set-aside program or the competitive application program, respectively, may be repaid by such parties to the Bank for subsequent disbursement to and re-use by such parties, or retained by such parties for subsequent re-use, as authorized by the Bank, in its discretion, after consultation with its Advisory Council, in its AHP Implementation Plan, provided all of the following requirements are satisfied:

(A) The member or the project sponsor originally provided the AHP direct subsidy as down payment, closing cost, rehabilitation, or interest rate buy down assistance to an eligible household to purchase or rehabilitate an owner-occupied unit pursuant to an approved AHP application;

(B) The AHP direct subsidy, including any interest, was repaid to the member or project sponsor as a result of a sale by the household of the unit prior to the end of the retention period to a purchaser that is not a low-or moderate-income household; and

(C) The repaid AHP direct subsidy is made available by the member or project sponsor, within the period of time specified by the Bank in its AHP Implementation Plan, to another AHP-eligible household to purchase or rehabilitate an owner-occupied unit in the same project in accordance with the terms of the approved AHP application.

(ii) *No delegation.* A Bank's board of directors shall not delegate to Bank officers or other Bank employees the responsibility to adopt any Bank policies on re-use of repaid AHP direct subsidies in the same project pursuant to paragraph (f)(2)(i) of this section.

(g) *Suspension and debarment*—(1) *At a Bank's initiative.* A Bank may suspend or debar a member, project sponsor, or project owner from participation in the Program if such party shows a pattern of noncompliance, or engages in a single instance of flagrant noncompliance, with the terms of an approved application for AHP subsidy or the requirements of this part.

(2) *At the FHFA's initiative.* The FHFA may order a Bank to suspend or debar a member, project sponsor, or project owner from participation in the Program if such party shows a pattern of noncompliance, or engages in a single instance of flagrant noncompliance, with the terms of an approved application for AHP subsidy or the requirements of this part.

(h) *Transfer of Program administration.* Without limitation on other remedies, the FHFA, upon determining that a Bank has engaged in mismanagement of its Program, may designate another Bank to administer all or a portion of the first Bank's annual AHP contribution, for the benefit of the first Bank's members, under such terms and conditions as the FHFA may prescribe.

(i) *FHFA actions under this section.* Except as provided in paragraph (d)(2) of this section, actions taken by the FHFA under this section are reviewable under § 907.9 of this chapter.

§ 1291.9 Agreements.

(a) *Agreements between Banks and members.* A Bank shall have in place with each member receiving an AHP subsidized advance or AHP direct subsidy an agreement or agreements containing, at a minimum, the following provisions, where applicable:

(1) *Notification of member.* The member has been notified of the requirements of this part as they may be amended from time to time, and all Bank policies relevant to the member's approved application for AHP subsidy.

(2) *AHP subsidy pass-through.* The member shall pass on the full amount of the AHP subsidy to the project or household, as applicable, for which the subsidy was approved.

(3) *Use of AHP subsidy*—(i) *Use of AHP subsidy by the member.* The member shall use the AHP subsidy in accordance with the terms of the member's approved application for the subsidy and the requirements of this part.

(ii) *Use of AHP subsidy by the project sponsor or owner.* The member shall have in place an agreement with each project sponsor or project owner in which the project sponsor or project owner agrees to use the AHP subsidy in accordance with the terms of the member's approved application for the subsidy and the requirements of this part.

(4) *Repayment of AHP subsidies in case of noncompliance*—(i) *Noncompliance by the member.* The member shall repay AHP subsidies to the Bank in accordance with the requirements of § 1291.8(b)(1) of this part.

(ii) *Noncompliance by a project sponsor or owner*—(A) *Agreement.* The member shall have in place an agreement with each project sponsor or project owner in which the project sponsor or project owner agrees to repay AHP subsidies to the member or the Bank in accordance with the requirements of § 1291.8(b)(2)(i) or (b)(2)(ii) of this part, respectively (as applicable).

(B) *Recovery of AHP subsidies.* The member shall recover from the project sponsor or project owner and repay to the Bank any AHP subsidy in accordance with the requirements of § 1291.8(b)(2)(i) of this part (if applicable).

(5) *Project monitoring*—(i) *Monitoring by the member.* The member shall comply with the monitoring requirements applicable to it, as established by the Bank in its monitoring policies pursuant to § 1291.7 of this part.

(ii) *Agreement.* The member shall have in place an agreement with each project sponsor and project owner, in which the project sponsor and project owner agree to comply with the monitoring requirements applicable to such parties, as established by the Bank in its monitoring policies pursuant to § 1291.7 of this part.

(6) *Transfer of AHP obligations*—(i) *To another member.* The member shall make best efforts to transfer its obligations under the approved application for AHP subsidy to another member in the event of its loss of membership in the Bank prior to the Bank's final disbursement of AHP subsidies.

(ii) *To a nonmember.* If, after final disbursement of AHP subsidies to the member, the member undergoes an acquisition or a consolidation resulting in a successor organization that is not a member of the Bank, the nonmember successor organization assumes the member's obligations under its approved application for AHP subsidy, and where the member received an AHP subsidized advance, the nonmember assumes such obligations until prepayment or orderly liquidation by the nonmember of the subsidized advance.

(7) *Retention agreements for owner-occupied units.* The member shall ensure that an AHP-assisted owner-occupied unit is subject to a deed restriction or other legally enforceable retention agreement or mechanism requiring that:

(i) The Bank or its designee is to be given notice of any sale or refinancing of the unit occurring prior to the end of the retention period;

(ii) In the case of a sale or refinancing of the unit prior to the end of the retention period, an amount equal to a pro rata share of the AHP subsidy that financed the purchase, construction, or rehabilitation of the unit, reduced for every year the seller owned the unit, shall be repaid to the Bank from any net gain realized upon the sale or refinancing, unless:

(A) The unit was assisted with a permanent mortgage loan funded by an AHP subsidized advance;

(B) The unit is sold to a very low-, or low- or moderate-income household; or

(C) Following a refinancing, the unit continues to be subject to a deed restriction or other legally enforceable retention agreement or mechanism described in this paragraph (a)(7); and

(iii) In the case of a direct subsidy, such repayment of AHP subsidy shall be made:

(A) *To the Bank.* If the Bank has not authorized re-use of the repaid AHP subsidy or has authorized re-use of the repaid subsidy but not retention of such repaid subsidy by the member or project sponsor pursuant to § 1291.8(f)(2) of this part, or has authorized retention and re-use of such repaid subsidy by the member or project sponsor pursuant to such section and the repaid subsidy is not re-used in accordance with the requirements of the Bank and such section; or

(B) *To the member or project sponsor.* To the member or project sponsor for reuse by such member or project sponsor, if the Bank has authorized retention and re-use of such subsidy by the member or project sponsor pursuant to § 1291.8(f)(2); and

(iv) The obligation to repay AHP subsidy to the Bank shall terminate after any foreclosure.

(8) *Retention agreements for rental projects.* The member shall ensure that an AHP-assisted rental project is subject to a deed restriction or other legally enforceable retention agreement or mechanism requiring that:

(i) The project's rental units, or applicable portion thereof, must remain occupied by and affordable for households with incomes at or below the levels committed to be served in the approved AHP application for the duration of the retention period;

(ii) The Bank or its designee is to be given notice of any sale or refinancing of the project occurring prior to the end of the retention period;

(iii) In the case of a sale or refinancing of the project prior to the end of the retention period, the full amount of the AHP subsidy received by the owner shall be repaid to the Bank, unless:

(A) The project continues to be subject to a deed restriction or other legally enforceable retention agreement or mechanism incorporating the income-eligibility and affordability restrictions committed to in the approved AHP application for the duration of the retention period; or

(B) If authorized by the Bank, in its discretion, the households are relocated, due to the exercise of eminent domain, or for expansion of housing or services, to another property that is made subject to a deed restriction or other legally enforceable retention agreement or mechanism incorporating the income-eligibility and affordability restrictions committed to in the approved AHP application for the remainder of the retention period; and

(iv) The income-eligibility and affordability restrictions applicable to the project shall terminate after any foreclosure.

(9) *Lending of AHP direct subsidies.* If a member or a project sponsor lends AHP direct subsidy to a project, any repayments of principal and payments of interest received by the member or the project sponsor must be paid forthwith to the Bank, unless the direct subsidy is being both lent and re-lent by a revolving loan fund pursuant to § 1291.5(c)(13) of this part.

(10) *Special provisions where members obtain AHP subsidized advances*—(i) *Repayment schedule.* The term of an AHP subsidized advance shall be no longer than the term of the member's loan to the project funded by the advance, and at least once in every 12-month period, the member shall be scheduled to make a principal repayment to the Bank equal to the amount scheduled to be repaid to the member on its loan to the project in that period.

(ii) *Prepayment fees.* Upon a prepayment of an AHP subsidized advance, the Bank shall charge a prepayment fee only to the extent the Bank suffers an economic loss from the prepayment.

(iii) *Treatment of loan prepayment by project.* If all or a portion of the loan or loans financed by an AHP subsidized advance are prepaid by the project to the member, the member may, at its option, either:

(A) Repay to the Bank that portion of the advance used to make the loan or loans to the project, and be subject to a fee imposed by the Bank sufficient to compensate the Bank for any economic loss the Bank experiences in reinvesting the repaid amount at a rate of return below the cost of funds originally used by the Bank to calculate the interest rate subsidy incorporated in the advance; or

(B) Continue to maintain the advance outstanding, subject to the Bank resetting the interest rate on that portion of the advance used to make the loan or loans to the project to a rate equal to the cost of funds originally used by the Bank to calculate the interest rate subsidy incorporated in the advance.

(b) *Agreements between Banks and project sponsors or owners.* A Bank shall have in place an agreement with each project sponsor or project owner, in which the project sponsor or project owner agrees to repay AHP subsidies directly to the Bank in accordance with the requirements of § 1291.8(b)(2)(ii) of this part (if applicable).

(c) *Application to existing AHP projects and units.* The requirements of section 10(j) of the Act (12 U.S.C. 1430(j)) and the provisions of this part, as amended, are incorporated into all agreements between Banks, members, project sponsors, and project owners receiving AHP subsidies under the competitive application program, and between Banks, members and unit owners under the homeownership set-aside program. To the extent the requirements of this part are amended from time to time, such agreements are deemed to incorporate the amendments to conform to any new requirements of this part. No amendment to this part shall affect the legality of actions taken prior to the effective date of such amendment.

§ 1291.10 Conflicts of interest.

(a) *Bank directors and employees.* (1) Each Bank's board of directors shall adopt a written policy providing that if a Bank director or employee, or such person's family member, has a financial interest in, or is a director, officer, or employee of an organization involved in, a project that is the subject of a pending or approved AHP application, the Bank director or employee shall not participate in or attempt to influence decisions by the Bank regarding the evaluation, approval, funding, monitoring, or any remedial process for such project.

(2) If a Bank director or employee, or such person's family member, has a financial interest in, or is a director, officer, or employee of an organization involved in, an AHP project such that he or she is subject to the requirements in paragraph (a)(1) of this section, such person shall not participate in or attempt to influence decisions by the Bank regarding the evaluation, approval, funding, monitoring, or any remedial process for such project.

(b) *Advisory Council members.* (1) Each Bank's board of directors shall adopt a written policy providing that if an Advisory Council member, or such person's family member, has a financial interest in, or is a director, officer, or employee of an organization involved in, a project that is the subject of a pending or approved AHP application, the Advisory Council member shall not participate in or attempt to influence decisions by the Bank regarding the approval for such project.

(2) If an Advisory Council member, or such person's family member, has a financial interest in, or is a director, officer, or employee of an organization involved in, an AHP project such that he or she is subject to the requirements in paragraph (b)(1) of this section, such person shall not participate in or attempt to influence decisions by the Bank regarding the approval for such project.

(c) *No delegation.* A Bank's board of directors shall not delegate to Bank officers or other Bank employees the responsibility to adopt the conflict of interest policies required by this section.

§ 1291.11 Temporary suspension of AHP contributions.

(a) *Request to FHFA.* If a Bank finds that the contributions required pursuant to § 1291.2(a) of this part are contributing to the financial instability of the Bank, the Bank may apply in writing to the FHFA for a temporary suspension of such contributions.

(b) *Director review.* (1) In determining the financial instability of a Bank, the Director shall consider such factors as:

(i) Severely depressed Bank earnings;

(ii) A substantial decline in Bank membership capital; and

(iii) A substantial reduction in Bank advances outstanding.

(2) *Limitations on grounds for suspension.* The Director shall not suspend a Bank's annual AHP contributions if it determines that the Bank's reduction in earnings is due to:

(i) A change in the terms of advances to members that is not justified by market conditions;

(ii) Inordinate operating and administrative expenses; or

(iii) Mismanagement.

[71 FR 59286, Oct. 6, 2006, as amended at 73 FR 61664, Oct. 17, 2008]

§ 1291.12 Affordable Housing Reserve Fund.

(a) *Deposits.* If a Bank fails to use or commit the full amount it is required to contribute to the Program in any year pursuant to § 1291.2(a) of this part, 90 percent of the unused or uncommitted amount shall be deposited by the Bank in an Affordable Housing Reserve Fund established and administered by the FHFA. The remaining 10 percent of the unused and uncommitted amount retained by the Bank should be fully used or committed by the Bank during the following year, and any remaining portion shall be deposited in the Affordable Housing Reserve Fund.

(b) *Use or commitment of funds.* Approval of applications for AHP subsidies from members sufficient to exhaust the amount a Bank is required to contribute pursuant to § 1291.2(a) of this part shall constitute use or commitment of funds. Amounts remaining unused or uncommitted at year-end are deemed to be used or committed if, in combination with AHP subsidies that have been returned to the Bank or decommitted from canceled projects, they are insufficient to fund:

(1) The next highest scoring AHP application in the Bank's final funding period of the year for its competitive application program;

(2) Pending applications for funds under the Bank's homeownership set-aside programs; and

(3) Project modifications approved by the Bank pursuant to the requirements of this part.

(c) *Carryover of insufficient amounts.* Such insufficient amounts as described in paragraph (b) of this section shall be carried over for use or commitment in the following year in the Bank's competitive application program or homeownership set-aside programs.

CHAPTER XIII—FINANCIAL STABILITY OVERSIGHT COUNCIL

PART 1320—DESIGNATION OF FINANCIAL MARKET UTILITIES

AUTHORITY: 12 U.S.C. 5321; 12 U.S.C. 5322; 12 U.S.C. 5463; 12 U.S.C. 5468; 12 U.S.C. 5469

SOURCE: 76 FR 44773, July 27, 2011, unless otherwise noted.

Subpart A—General

§ 1320.1 Authority and purpose.

(a) *Authority.* This part is issued by the Financial Stability Oversight Council under sections 111, 112, 804, 809, and 810 of the Dodd-Frank Wall Street Reform and Consumer Protection Act ("Dodd-Frank Act") (12 U.S.C. 5321, 5322, 5463, 5468, and 5469).

(b) *Purpose.* The purpose of this part is to set forth the standards and procedures governing the Council's designation of a financial market utility that the Council determines is, or is likely to become, systemically important.

§ 1320.2 Definitions.

The terms used in this part have the following meanings:

Appropriate Federal banking agency. The term "*appropriate Federal banking agency*" has the same meaning as in section 3(q) of the Federal Deposit Insurance Act (12 U.S.C. 1813(q)), as amended.

Board of Governors. The term "*Board of Governors*" means the Board of Governors of the Federal Reserve System.

Council. The term "*Council*" means the Financial Stability Oversight Council.

Designated clearing entity. The term "*designated clearing entity*" means a designated financial market utility that is a derivatives clearing organization registered under section 5b of the Commodity Exchange Act (7 U.S.C. 7a–1) or a clearing agency registered with the Securities and Exchange Commission under section 17A of the Securities Exchange Act of 1934 (15 U.S.C. 78q–1).

Designated financial market utility. The term "*designated financial market utility*" means a financial market utility that the Council has designated as systemically important under § 1320.13.

Financial institution. The term "*financial institution*"—

(1) Means—

(i) A depository institution as defined in section 3 of the Federal Deposit Insurance Act (12 U.S.C. 1813);

(ii) A branch or agency of a foreign bank, as defined in section 1(b) of the International Banking Act of 1978 (12 U.S.C. 3101);

(iii) An organization operating under section 25 or 25A of the Federal Reserve Act (12 U.S.C. 601–604a and 611 through 631);

(iv) A credit union, as defined in section 101 of the Federal Credit Union Act (12 U.S.C. 1752);

(v) A broker or dealer, as defined in section 3 of the Securities Exchange Act of 1934 (15 U.S.C. 78c);

(vi) An investment company, as defined in section 3 of the Investment Company Act of 1940 (15 U.S.C. 80a–3);

(vii) An insurance company, as defined in section 2 of the Investment Company Act of 1940 (15 U.S.C. 80a–2);

(viii) An investment adviser, as defined in section 202 of the Investment Advisers Act of 1940 (15 U.S.C. 80b–2);

(ix) A futures commission merchant, commodity trading advisor, or commodity pool operator, as defined in section 1a of the Commodity Exchange Act (7 U.S.C. 1a); and

(x) Any company engaged in activities that are financial in nature or incidental to a financial activity, as described in section 4 of the Bank Holding Company Act of 1956 (12 U.S.C. 1843(k)).

(2) Does not include designated contract markets, registered futures associations, swap data repositories, and swap execution facilities registered under the Commodity Exchange Act (7 U.S.C. 1 *et seq.*), or national securities exchanges, national securities associations, alternative trading systems, securities information processors solely with respect to the activities of the entity as a securities information processor, security-based swap data repositories, and swap execution facilities registered under the Securities Exchange Act of 1934 (15 U.S.C. 78a *et seq.*), or designated clearing entities, provided that the exclusions in this paragraph apply only with respect to the activities that require the entity to be so registered.

Financial market utility. The term "financial market utility"—

(1) Means any person that manages or operates a multilateral system for the purpose of transferring, clearing, or settling payments, securities, or other financial transactions among financial institutions or between financial institutions and the person; and

(2) Does not include—

(i) Designated contract markets, registered futures associations, swap data repositories, and swap execution facilities registered under the Commodity Exchange Act (7 U.S.C. 1 *et seq.*), or national securities exchanges, national securities associations, alternative trading systems, security-based swap data repositories, and swap data execution facilities registered under the Securities Exchange Act of 1934 (15 U.S.C. 78a *et seq.*), solely by reason of their providing facilities for comparison of data respecting the terms of settlement of securities or futures transactions effected on such exchange or by means of any electronic system operated or controlled by such entities, provided that the exclusions in this clause apply only with respect to the activities that require the entity to be so registered; and

(ii) Any broker, dealer, transfer agent, or investment company, or any futures commission merchant, introducing broker, commodity trading advisor, or commodity pool operator, solely by reason of functions performed by such institution as part of brokerage, dealing, transfer agency, or investment company activities, or solely by reason of acting on behalf of a financial market utility or a participant therein in connection with the furnishing by the financial market utility of services to its participants or the use of services of the financial market utility by its participants, provided that services performed by such institution do not constitute critical risk management or processing functions of the financial market utility.

Hearing date. The term "hearing date" means the later of—

(1) The date on which the Council receives all of the written materials timely submitted by the financial market utility for a hearing that is conducted without oral testimony; or

(2) The final date on which the Council convenes for the financial market utility to present oral testimony.

Payment, clearing, or settlement activity.

(1) The term "payment, clearing, or settlement activity" means an activity carried out by 1 or more financial institutions to facilitate the completion of financial transactions, but shall not include any offer or sale of a security under the Securities Act of 1933 (15 U.S.C. 77a *et seq.*), or any quotation, order entry, negotiation, or other pretrade activity or execution activity.

(2) For purposes of paragraph (1) of this definition, the term "financial transaction" includes—

(i) Funds transfers;

(ii) Securities contracts;

(iii) Contracts of sale of a commodity for future delivery;

(iv) Forward contracts;

(v) Repurchase agreements;

(vi) Swaps;

(vii) Security-based swaps;

(viii) Swap agreements;

(ix) Security-based swap agreements;

(x) Foreign exchange contracts;

(xi) Financial derivatives contracts; and

(xii) Any similar transaction that the Council determines to be a financial transaction for purposes of this part.

(3) When conducted with respect to a financial transaction, payment, clearing, and settlement activities may include—

(i) The calculation and communication of unsettled financial transactions between counterparties;

(ii) The netting of transactions;

(iii) Provision and maintenance of trade, contract, or instrument information;

(iv) The management of risks and activities associated with continuing financial transactions;

(v) Transmittal and storage of payment instructions;

(vi) The movement of funds;

(vii) The final settlement of financial transactions; and

(viii) Other similar functions that the Council may determine.

(4) Payment, clearing, and settlement activities shall not include public reporting of swap transactions under section 727 or 763(i) of the Dodd-Frank Act.

Supervisory Agency. (1) The term "Supervisory Agency" means the Federal agency that—

(i) Has primary jurisdiction over a designated financial market utility under Federal banking, securities, or commodity futures laws as follows—

(A) The Securities and Exchange Commission, with respect to a designated financial market utility that is a clearing agency registered with the Securities and Exchange Commission;

(B) The Commodity Futures Trading Commission, with respect to a designated financial market utility that is a derivatives clearing organization registered with the Commodity Futures Trading Commission;

(C) The appropriate Federal banking agency, with respect to a designated financial market utility that is an institution described in section 3(q) of the Federal Deposit Insurance Act;

(D) The Board of Governors, with respect to a designated financial market utility that is otherwise not subject to the jurisdiction of any agency listed in paragraphs (1)(i), (ii), and (iii) of this definition; or

(ii) Would have primary jurisdiction over a financial market utility if the financial market utility were a designated financial market utility under paragraph (1) of this definition.

(2) If a financial market utility is subject to the jurisdictional supervision of more than one agency listed in paragraph (1) of this definition, then such agencies should agree on one agency to act as the Supervisory Agency, and if such agencies cannot agree on which agency has primary jurisdiction, the Council shall decide which is the Supervisory Agency for purposes of this part.

Systemically important and systemic importance. The terms "systemically important" and "systemic importance" mean a situation where the failure of or a disruption to the functioning of a financial market utility could create, or increase, the risk of significant liquidity or credit problems spreading among financial institutions or markets and thereby threaten the stability of the financial system of the United States.

Subpart B—Consultations, Determinations and Hearings

§ 1320.10 Factors for consideration in designations.

In making any proposed or final determination with respect to whether a financial market utility is, or is likely to become, systemically important under this part, the Council shall take into consideration:

(a) The aggregate monetary value of transactions processed by the financial market utility, including without limitation—

(1) The number of transactions processed, cleared or settled;

(2) The value of transactions processed, cleared or settled; and

(3) The value of other financial flows.

(b) The aggregate exposure of the financial market utility to its counterparties, including without limitation—

(1) Credit exposures, which includes but is not limited to potential future exposures; and

(2) Liquidity exposures.

(c) The relationship, interdependencies, or other interactions of the financial market utility with other financial market utilities or payment, clearing, or settlement activities, including without limitation interactions with different types of participants in those utilities or activities.

(d) The effect that the failure of or a disruption to the financial market utility would have on critical markets, financial institutions, or the broader financial system, including without limitation—

(1) Role of the financial market utility in the market served;

(2) Availability of substitutes;

(3) Concentration of participants;

(4) Concentration by product type;

(5) Degree of tiering; and

(6) Potential impact or spillover in the event of a failure or disruption.

(e) Any other factors that the Council deems appropriate.

§ 1320.11 Consultation with financial market utility.

Before providing a financial market utility notice of a proposed determination under § 1320.12, the Council shall provide the financial market utility with—

(a) Written notice that the Council is considering whether to make a proposed determination with respect to the financial market utility under § 1320.13; and

(b) An opportunity to submit written materials to the Council, within such time as the Council determines to be appropriate, concerning—

(1) Whether the financial market utility is systemically important taking into consideration the factors set out in § 1320.10; and

(2) Proposed changes by the financial market utility that could—

(i) Reduce or increase the inherent systemic risk the financial market utility poses and the need for designation under § 1320.13; or

(ii) Reduce or increase the appropriateness of rescission under § 1320.13.

(3) The Council shall consider any written materials timely submitted by the financial market utility under this section before making a proposed determination under section 1320.13.

§ 1320.12 Advance notice of proposed determination.

(a) *Notice of proposed determination and opportunity for hearing.* Before making any final determination on designation or rescission under § 1320.13, the Council shall propose a determination and provide the financial market utility with advance notice of the proposed determination, and proposed findings of fact supporting that determination. A proposed determination shall be made by a vote of the Council in the manner described in § 1320.13(c).

(b) *Request for hearing.* Within 30 calendar days from the date of any provision of notice of the proposed determination of the Council, the financial market utility may request, in writing, an opportunity for a written or oral hearing before the Council to demonstrate that the proposed designation or rescission of designation is not supported by substantial evidence.

(c) *Written submissions.* Upon receipt of a timely request, the Council shall fix a time, not more than 30 calendar days after receipt of the request, unless extended by the Council at the request of the financial market utility, and place at which the financial market utility may appear, personally or through counsel, to submit written materials, or, at the sole discretion of the Council, oral testimony and oral argument.

§ 1320.13 Council determination regarding systemic importance.

(a) *Designation determination.* The Council shall designate a financial market utility if the Council determines that the financial market utility is, or is likely to become, systemically important.

(b) *Rescission determination.* The Council shall rescind a designation of systemic importance for a designated financial market utility if the Council determines that the financial market utility no longer meets the standards for systemic importance.

(c) *Vote required.* Any determination under paragraph (a) or (b) of this section and any proposed determination under § 1320.12 shall—

(1) Be made by the Council and must not be delegated by the Council; and

(2) Require the vote of not fewer than two-thirds of the members of the Council then serving, including the affirmative vote of the Chairperson of the Council.

(d) *Consultations.* Before making any determination under paragraph (a) or (b) of this section or any proposed determination under § 1320.12, the Council shall consult with the relevant Supervisory Agency and the Board of Governors.

§ 1320.14 Emergency exception.

(a) *Emergency exception.* Notwithstanding §§ 1320.11 and 1320.12, the Council may waive or modify any or all of the notice, hearing, and other requirements of §§ 1320.11 and 1320.12 with respect to a financial market utility if—

(1) The Council determines that the waiver or modification is necessary to prevent or mitigate an immediate threat to the financial system posed by the financial market utility; and

(2) The Council provides notice of the waiver or modification, and an explanation of the basis for the waiver or modification, to the financial market utility concerned, as soon as practicable, but not later than 24 hours after the waiver or modification.

(b) *Vote required.* Any determination by the Council under paragraph (a) to waive or modify any of the requirements of §§ 1320.11 and 1320.12 shall—

(1) Be made by the Council; and

(2) Require the affirmative vote of not fewer than two-thirds of members then serving, including the affirmative vote of the Chairperson of Council.

(c) *Request for hearing.* Within 10 calendar days from the date of any provision of notice of waiver or modification of the Council, the financial market utility may request, in writing, an opportunity for a written or oral hearing before the Council to demonstrate that the basis for the waiver or modification is not supported by substantial evidence.

(d) *Written submissions.* Upon receipt of a timely request, the Council shall fix a time, not more than 30 calendar days after receipt of the request, and place at which the financial market utility may appear, personally or through counsel, to submit written materials, or, at the sole discretion of the Counsel, oral testimony and oral argument.

(e) *Notification of hearing determination.* If a financial market utility makes a timely request for a hearing under paragraph (c) of this section, the Council shall, not later than 30 calendar days after the hearing date, notify the financial market utility of the determination of the Council, which shall include a statement of the basis for the determination of the Council.

§ 1320.15 Notification of final determination regarding systemic importance.

(a) *Notification of final determination after a hearing.* Within 60 calendar days of the hearing date, the Council shall provide to the financial market utility written notification of the final determination of the Council under § 1320.13, which shall include findings of fact upon which the determination of the Council is based.

(b) *Notification of final determination if no hearing.* If the Council does not receive a timely request for a hearing under § 1320.12, the Council shall provide the financial market utility written notification of the final determination of the Council under § 1320.13 not later than 30 calendar days after the expiration of the date by which a financial market utility could have requested a hearing.

§ 1320.16 Extension of time periods.

The Council may extend any time period established in§ 1320.12, § 1320.14, or § 1320.15 as the Council determines to be necessary or appropriate.

Subpart C—Information Collection

§ 1320.20 Council information collection and coordination.

(a) *Information collection to assess systemic importance.* The Council may require any financial market utility to submit such information to the Council as the Council may require for the sole purpose of assessing whether the financial market utility is systemically important.

(b) *Prerequisites to information collection.* Before requiring any financial market utility to submit information to the Council under paragraph (a) of this section, the Council shall—

(1) Determine that it has reasonable cause to believe that the financial market utility is, or is likely to become, systemically important, considering the standards set out in § 1320.10; or

(2) Determine that it has reasonable cause to believe that the designated financial market utility is no longer, or is no longer likely to become, systemically important, considering the standards set out in § 1320.10; and

(3) Coordinate with the Supervisory Agency for the financial market utility to determine if the information is available from, or may be obtained by, the Supervisory Agency in the form, format, or detail required by the Council.

(c) *Timing of response from the appropriate Supervisory Agency.* If the information, reports, records, or data requested by the Council under paragraph (b)(3) of this section are not provided in full by the Supervisory Agency in less than 15 calendar days after the date on which the material is requested, the Council may request the information directly from the financial market utility with notice to the Supervisory Agency.

(d) *Notice to financial market utility of information collection requirement.* In requiring a financial market utility to submit information to the Council, the Council shall provide to the financial market utility the following—

(1) Written notice that the Council is considering whether to make a proposed determination under § 1320.12; and

(2) A description of the basis for the Council's belief under paragraphs (b)(1) or (b)(2) of this section.

CHAPTER XIV—FARM CREDIT SYSTEM INSURANCE CORPORATION

PART 1400—ORGANIZATION AND FUNCTIONS

Subpart A—Organization and Functions

Subpart B [Reserved]

AUTHORITY: 12 U.S.C. 2277a-5; 12 U.S.C. 2277a-7.

SOURCE: 55 FR 36610, Sept. 6, 1990, unless otherwise noted.

Subpart A—Organization and Functions

§ 1400.1 Farm Credit System Insurance Corporation.

The Farm Credit System Insurance Corporation (Corporation) was created by sections 5.52 and 5.58 of the Farm Credit Act of 1971 (Act) to carry out the responsibilities set out in part E of title V of the Act, including insuring the timely payment of principal and interest on notes, bonds, debentures, and other obligations issued under subsection (c) or (d) of section 4.2 of the Farm Credit Act on behalf of one or more Farm Credit System banks.

§ 1400.2 Board of Directors of the Farm Credit System Insurance Corporation.

The Board of Directors of the Farm Credit System Insurance Corporation is entrusted with the responsibility to manage the Corporation. The Board of Directors consists of the members of the Farm Credit Administration Board. The Chairman of the Corporation is elected by the members of the Board.

§ 1400.3 Organization of the Farm Credit System Insurance Corporation.

Officers of the Corporation shall be appointed by the Board of Directors of the Corporation. Current information on the organization of the Corporation may be obtained from the Corporation, 1501 Farm Credit Drive, McLean, Virginia 22102–0826.

Subpart B [Reserved]

PART 1401—EMPLOYEE RESPONSIBILITIES AND CONDUCT

AUTHORITY: 5 U.S.C. 7301; 12 U.S.C. 2277a-7.

§ 1401.1 Cross-references to employee ethical conduct standards and financial disclosure regulations.

Board members, officers, and other employees of the Farm Credit System Insurance Corporation are subject to the Standards of Ethical Conduct for Employees of the Executive Branch at 5 CFR part 2635, the Farm Credit System Insurance Corporation regulation at 5 CFR part 4001, which supplements the Executive Branch-wide Standards, and the executive branch-wide financial disclosure regulations at 5 CFR part 2634.

[60 FR 30778, June 12, 1995]

PART 1402—RELEASING INFORMATION

Subpart A [Reserved]

Subpart B—Availability of Records of the Farm Credit System Insurance Corporation

Subpart C—Fees for Provision of Information

AUTHORITY: Secs. 5.58, 5.59 of the Farm Credit Act (12 U.S.C. 2277a-7, 2277a-8); 5 U.S.C. 552; 52 FR 10012; E.O. 12600, 52 FR 23781, 3 CFR, 1987 Comp., p. 235.

SOURCE: 59 FR 24638, May 12, 1994, unless otherwise noted.

Subpart A [Reserved]

Subpart B—Availability of Records of the Farm Credit System Insurance Corporation

§ 1402.10 Official records of the Farm Credit System Insurance Corporation.

(a) The Farm Credit System Insurance Corporation shall, upon any request for records which reasonably describes them and is made in accordance with the provisions of this subpart, make the records available as promptly as practicable to any person, except exempt records, which include the following:

(1) Records specifically authorized under criteria established by an Executive order to be kept secret in the interest of national defense or foreign policy and are in fact properly classified pursuant to such Executive order;

(2) Records related solely to the internal personnel rules and practices of the Farm Credit System Insurance Corporation, including matters which are for the guidance of agency personnel;

(3) Records which are specifically exempted from disclosure by statute;

(4) Trade secret, commercial, proprietary, or financial information obtained from any person or organization and privileged or confidential;

(5) Inter-agency or intra-agency memorandums or letters which would not be available by law to a private party in litigation with the Farm Credit System Insurance Corporation or in litigation in which the United States, as a real party in interest on behalf of the Farm Credit System Insurance Corporation, is a party;

(6) Personnel and similar files, the disclosure of which would constitute a clearly unwarranted invasion of personal privacy;

(7) Records or information compiled for law enforcement purposes, but only to the extent that the production of such law enforcement records or information:

(i) Could reasonably be expected to interfere with enforcement proceedings;

(ii) Would deprive a person of a right to a fair trial or an impartial adjudication;

(iii) Could reasonably be expected to constitute an unwarranted invasion of personal privacy;

(iv) Could reasonably be expected to disclose the identity of a confidential source, including a State, local, or foreign agency or authority or any private institution which furnished information on a confidential basis, and, in the case of a record or information compiled by criminal law enforcement authority in the course of a criminal investigation or by an agency conducting a lawful national security intelligence investigation, information furnished by a confidential source;

(v) Would disclose techniques and procedures for law enforcement investigations or prosecutions, or would disclose guidelines for law enforcement investigations or prosecutions if such disclosure could reasonably be expected to risk circumvention of the law; or

(vi) Could reasonably be expected to endanger the life or physical safety of any individual; and

(8) Records of or related to examination, operation, reports of condition and performance, or reports of or related to Farm Credit System institutions and that are prepared by, on behalf of, or for the use of the Farm Credit System Insurance Corporation.

(b) Any reasonably segregable portion of a record shall be provided to any person requesting such record after deletion of the portions which are exempt under this section.

(c) This section does not authorize withholding of information or limit the availability of records to the public, except as specifically stated in this section. This section is not authority to withhold information from Congress.

§ 1402.11 Current index.

The Farm Credit System Insurance Corporation will make available for public inspection and copying a current index to provide identifying information as to any matter required by 5 U.S.C. 552(a)(2)(C) to be made available or published in the FEDERAL REGISTER. Because of the anticipated infrequency of requests for material required to be indexed, it is determined that the publication of the index in the FEDERAL

REGISTER is unnecessary and impracticable. However, the Farm Credit System Insurance Corporation will provide a copy of such index to a member of the public upon request therefor at a cost not in excess of the direct cost of duplication.

§ 1402.12 Identification of records requested.

A member of the public who requests records from the Farm Credit System Insurance Corporation shall provide a reasonable description of the records sought including, where possible, specific information as to dates, titles, and subject matter, so that such records may be located without undue search or inquiry. If a record is not identified by a reasonable description, the request therefor may be denied.

§ 1402.13 Request for records.

Requests for records shall be in writing and addressed to the attention of the Freedom of Information Officer, Farm Credit System Insurance Corporation, McLean, Virginia 22102. A request improperly addressed will be deemed not to have been received for purposes of the 20-day time period set forth in § 1402.14(a) of this part until it is received, or would have been received, by the Freedom of Information Officer, with the exercise of due diligence by Corporation personnel. Records requested in conformance with this subpart and which are not exempt records may be received in person or by mail as specified in the request. Records to be received in person will be available for inspection or copying during business hours on a regular business day in the office of the Farm Credit System Insurance Corporation, 1501 Farm Credit Drive, McLean, Virginia, 22102.

[62 FR 49593, Sept. 23, 1997]

§ 1402.14 Response to requests for records.

(a) Within 20 days (excluding Saturdays, Sundays, and legal public holidays), or any extensions thereof as provided in paragraph (d) of this section, of the receipt of a request by the Freedom of Information Officer, the Freedom of Information Officer shall determine whether to comply with or deny such a request and transmit a written notice thereof to the requester.

(b) Within 30 days of the receipt of a notice denying, in whole or in part, a request for records, the requester may appeal the denial. The appeal shall be in writing addressed to the Chief Financial Officer, Farm Credit System Insurance Corporation, and both the letter and envelope shall be clearly marked "FOIA Appeal." An appeal improperly addressed shall be deemed not to have been received for purposes of the 20-day time period set forth in paragraph (c) of this section until it is received, or would have been received with the exercise of due diligence by Farm Credit System Insurance Corporation personnel.

(c) Within 20 days (excluding Saturdays, Sundays, and legal public holidays), or any extension thereof as provided in paragraph (d) of this section, of the receipt of an appeal, the Farm Credit System Insurance Corporation shall act upon the appeal and place a notice of the determination thereof in writing in the mail addressed to the requester. If the determination on the appeal upholds in whole or in part the denial of the request for records, or, if a determination on the appeal has not been mailed at the end of the 20-day period or the last extension thereof, the requester is deemed to have exhausted that person's administrative remedies, giving rise to a right of review in a district court of the United States as specified in 5 U.S.C. 552(a)(4). When a determination cannot be mailed within the applicable time limit, the appeal will nevertheless be processed. In such case, upon the expiration of the time limit, the requester will be informed of the reason for the delay, of the date on which a determination may be expected to be mailed, and of that person's right to seek judicial review. The requester may be asked to forego judicial review until determination of the appeal.

(d) In "unusual circumstances," the 20-day time limit prescribed in paragraphs (a) and (c) of this section, or both, may be extended by the Freedom of Information Officer or, in the case of an appeal, by the General Counsel, provided that the total of all extensions does not exceed 10 days (excluding Saturdays, Sundays, and legal public holidays). Extensions shall be made by written notice to the requester setting forth the reason for the extension and the date on which a determination is expected to be dispatched. As used in this paragraph, "*unusual circumstances*" means, but only to the extent reasonably necessary to the proper processing of the request:

(1) The need to search for and collect the requested records from facilities or other establishments that are separate from the office processing the request;

(2) The need to search for, collect, and appropriately examine a voluminous amount of separate and distinct records which are demanded in a single request; or

(3) The need for consultation, which shall be conducted with all practicable speed, with another agency having a substantial interest in the determination of the request or among two or more components of the agency having a substantial subject matter interest therein.

(e) A requester may obtain, upon request, expedited processing of a request for records when the requester demonstrates a "compelling need" for the information. The Freedom of Information Officer will notify the requester within 10 calendar days after receipt of such a request whether the Corporation granted expedited processing. If expedited processing was granted, the request will be processed as soon as practicable.

(1) For the purposes of this paragraph, "*compelling need*" means:

(i) That a failure to obtain requested records on an expedited basis could reasonably be expected to pose an imminent threat to the life or physical safety of an individual; or

(ii) With respect to a request made by a person primarily engaged in disseminating information, urgency to inform the public concerning actual or alleged Federal Government activity.

(2) A requester shall demonstrate a compelling need by a statement certified by the requester to be true and correct to the best of such person's knowledge and belief.

(3) The procedures of this paragraph (e) for expedited processing apply to both requests for information and to administrative appeals.

[59 FR 24638, May 12, 1994, as amended at 62 FR 49593, Sept. 23, 1997]

§ 1402.15 Business information.

(a) Business information provided to the Farm Credit System Insurance Corporation by a business submitter shall not be disclosed pursuant to a Freedom of Information Act request except in accordance with this section. The requirements of this section shall not apply if:

(1) The Farm Credit System Insurance Corporation determines that the information should not be disclosed;

(2) The information lawfully has been published or otherwise made available to the public; or

(3) Disclosure of the information is required by law (other than 5 U.S.C. 552).

(b) For the purpose of this section, the following definitions shall apply.

(1) *Business information* means trade secrets or other commercial or financial information.

(2) *Business submitter* means any person or entity which provides business information to the government.

(3) *Requester* means the person or entity making the Freedom of Information Act request.

(c)(1) The Freedom of Information Officer shall, to the extent permitted by law, provide a business submitter with prompt written notice of a request encompassing its business information whenever required under paragraph (d) of this section. Such notice shall either describe the exact nature of the business information requested or provide copies of the records or portions thereof containing the business information.

(2) Whenever the Freedom of Information Officer provides a business submitter with the notice set forth in paragraph (c)(1) of this section, the Freedom of Information Officer shall notify the requester that the request includes information that may arguably be exempt from disclosure under 5 U.S.C. 552(b)(4) and that the person or entity who submitted the information to the Farm Credit System Insurance Corporation has been given the opportunity to comment on the proposed disclosure of information.

(d)(1) The Farm Credit System Insurance Corporation shall provide a business submitter with notice of a request whenever:

(i) The business submitter has in good faith designated the information as commercially or financially sensitive information; or

(ii) The Farm Credit System Insurance Corporation has reason to believe that the disclosure of the information may result in commercial or financial injury to the business submitter.

(2) Notice of a request for business information falling within paragraph (d)(1)(i) of this section shall be required for a period of not more than 10 years after the date of submission unless the business submitter requests and provides acceptable justification for a specific notice period of greater duration.

(3) Whenever possible, the business submitter's claim of confidentiality should be supported by a statement or certification by an officer or authorized representative of the business submitter that the information in question is in fact a trade secret or commercial or financial information that is privileged or confidential.

(e) Through the notice described in paragraph (c) of this section, the Farm Credit System Insurance Corporation shall, to the extent permitted by law, afford a business submitter a reasonable period within which it can provide the Farm Credit System Insurance Corporation with a detailed statement of any objection to disclosure. Such statement shall specify all grounds for withholding any of the information under any exemption of the Freedom of Information Act and, in the case of the exemption provided by 5 U.S.C. 552(b)(4), shall demonstrate why the information is contended to be a trade secret or commercial or financial information that is privileged or confidential. Information provided by a business submitter pursuant to this paragraph may itself be subject to disclosure under the Freedom of Information Act.

(f)(1) The Farm Credit System Insurance Corporation shall consider carefully a business submitter's objections and specific grounds for nondisclosure prior to determining whether to disclose business information. Whenever the Farm Credit System Insurance Corporation decides to disclose business information over the objection of a business submitter, the Freedom of Information Officer shall forward to the business submitter a written notice which shall include:

(i) A statement of the reasons for which the business submitter's disclosure objections were not sustained;

(ii) A description of the business information to be disclosed; and

(iii) A specified disclosure date.

(2) The notice of intent to disclose required by this paragraph shall be sent, to the extent permitted by law, within a reasonable number of days prior to the specified date upon which disclosure is intended.

(3) The Freedom of Information Officer shall send a copy of such disclosure notice to the requester at the same time the notice is sent to the business submitter.

(g) Whenever a requester brings suit seeking to compel disclosure of business information covered by paragraph (d) of this section, the Farm Credit System Insurance Corporation shall promptly notify the business submitter of such action.

Subpart C—Fees for Provision of Information

§ 1402.20 Definitions.

For the purpose of this subpart, the following definitions shall apply:

(a) *Commercial use request* means a request for information that is from or on behalf of an individual or entity seeking information for a use or purpose that furthers the commercial, trade, or profit interests of the requester or on whose behalf the request is being made. To determine whether a request is properly classified as a commercial use request, the Farm Credit System Insurance Corporation shall determine the purpose for which the documents requested will be used. If the Farm Credit System Insurance Corporation has reasonable cause to doubt the purpose specified in the request, for which a requester will use the records sought, or where the purpose is not clear from the request itself, the Farm Credit System Insurance Corporation shall seek additional clarification before assigning the request to a specified category.

(b) *Direct costs* means those expenditures the Farm Credit System Insurance Corporation actually incurs in searching for and reproducing documents to respond to a request for information. In the case of a commercial use request, the term also means those expenditures the Farm Credit System Insurance Corporation actually incurs in reviewing documents to respond to the request. The direct cost shall include the salary of the employee performing work (the basic rate of pay for the employee plus 16 percent of that rate to cover benefits) and the cost of operating reproduction equipment. Not included in direct costs are overhead expenses such as costs of space, and heating or lighting the facility in which the records are stored.

(c) *Educational institution* means a preschool, a public or private elementary or secondary school, an institution of undergraduate higher education, an institution of graduate higher education, an institution of professional education, and an institution of vocational education that operates a program or programs of scholarly research.

(d) *Noncommercial scientific institution* refers to an institution that is not operated on a commercial, trade, or profit basis and that is operated solely for the purpose of conducting scientific research, the results of which are not intended to promote any particular product or industry.

(e) *Representative of the news media* means any person actively gathering news for an entity that is organized and operated to publish or broadcast news to the public. The term *news* means information that is about current events or that would be of current interest to the public. Examples of news media entities include television or radio stations broadcasting to the public at large, and publishers of periodicals (but only in those instances when the periodicals can qualify as disseminators of "news") who make their products available for purchase or subscription by the general public. These examples are not intended to be all-inclusive. As traditional methods of news delivery evolve (e.g., electronic dissemination of newspapers through telecommunication services), such alternative media would be included in this category. "Freelance" journalists may be regarded as working for a news organization if they can demonstrate a solid basis for expecting publication through that organization even though they are not actually employed by the organization. A publication contract would be the clearest proof that a journalist is working for a news organization, but the Farm Credit System Insurance Corporation may look to a requester's past publication record to determine whether a journalist is working for a news organization.

(f) *Reproduce* and *reproduction* mean the process of making a copy of a document necessary to respond to a request for information. Such copies take the form of paper copy, microfilm, audiovisual materials, or machine readable documentation (e.g., magnetic tape or disk), among others. The copy provided shall be in a form that is reasonably usable by requesters.

(g) *Review* means the process of examining documents located in response to a request for information to determine whether any portion of any document located is permitted to be withheld. It also includes processing any documents for disclosure (e.g., doing all that is necessary to prepare the documents for release). The term review does not include the time spent resolving general legal or policy issues regarding the application of exemptions. The Farm Credit System Insurance Corporation shall only charge fees for reviewing documents in response to a commercial use request.

(h) *Search* includes all time spent looking for material that is responsive to a request for information, including page-by-page or line-by-line identification of material within documents. Searching for material shall be done in the most efficient and least expensive manner so as to minimize the costs of the Farm Credit System Insurance Corporation and the requester. For example, a line-by-line search for responsive material should not be performed when merely reproducing an entire document would be the less expensive and the faster method of complying with a request for information. Searches may be done manually or by computer using existing programming. A "search" for material that is responsive to a request should be distinguished from a "review" of material to determine whether the material is exempt from disclosure.

§ 1402.21 Categories of requesters—fees.

There are four categories of requesters: Commercial use requesters; educational and noncommercial scientific institutions; representatives of the news media; and all other requesters.

(a) The Farm Credit System Insurance Corporation shall charge fees for records requested by or on behalf of educational institutions and noncommercial scientific institutions in an amount which equals the cost of reproducing the documents responsive to the request, excluding the costs of reproducing the first 100 pages. For a request to be included in this category, requesters must show that the request being made is authorized by and under the auspices of a qualifying institution and that the records are not sought for a commercial use but are sought in furtherance of scholarly research (if the request is from an educational institution) or scientific research (if the request is from a noncommercial scientific institution).

(b) The Farm Credit System Insurance Corporation shall charge fees for records requested by representatives of the news media in an amount which equals the cost of reproducing the documents responsive to the request, excluding the costs of reproducing the first 100 pages. For a request to be included in this category, the requester must qualify as a representative of the news media and the request must not be made for a commercial use. A request for records supporting the news dissemination function of the requester shall not be considered to be a request that is for a commercial use.

(c) The Farm Credit System Insurance Corporation shall charge fees for records requested by persons or entities making a commercial use request in an amount that equals the full direct costs for searching for, reviewing for release, and reproducing the records sought. Commercial use requesters are not entitled to 2 hours of free search time nor 100 free pages of reproduction of documents. In accordance with §1402.26, commercial use requesters may be charged the costs of searching for and reviewing records even if there is ultimately no disclosure of records.

(d) The Farm Credit System Insurance Corporation shall charge fees for records requested by persons or entities that are not classified in any of the categories listed in paragraphs (a), (b), or (c) of this section in an amount that equals the full reasonable direct cost of searching for and reproducing records that are responsive to the request, excluding the first 2 hours of search time and the cost of reproducing the first 100 pages of records. In accordance with §1402.26, requesters in this category may be charged the cost of searching for records even if there is ultimately no disclosure of records, excluding the first 2 hours of search time.

(e) For purposes of the exceptions contained in this section on assessment of fees, the word *pages* refers to paper copies of "8½ × 11" or "11 × 14." Thus, requesters are not entitled to 100 microfiche or 100 computer disks, for example. A microfiche containing the equivalent of 100 pages or a computer disk containing the equivalent of 100 pages of computer printout meets the terms of the exception.

(f) For purposes of paragraph (d) of this section, the term *search time* has as its basis, manual search. To apply this term to searches made by computer, the Farm Credit System Insurance Corporation will determine the hourly cost of operating the central processing unit and the operator's hourly salary plus 16 percent of that rate. When the cost of search (including the operator time and the cost of operating the computer to process a request) equals the equivalent dollar amount of 2 hours of the salary of the person performing the search, i.e., the operator, the Farm Credit System Insurance Corporation will begin assessing charges for computer search.

§ 1402.22 Fees to be charged.

(a) Generally, the fees charged for requests for records shall cover the full allowable direct costs of searching for, reproducing, and reviewing documents that are responsive to a request for information.

(b) Manual searches for records will be charged at the salary rate(s) (i.e., basic pay plus 16 percent of that rate) of the employee(s) making the search.

(c) Computer searches for records will be charged at the actual direct cost of providing the service. This will include the cost of operating the central processing unit for that portion of operating time that is directly attributable to searching for records and the operator/programmer salary apportionable to the search. A charge shall also be made for any substantial amounts of special supplies or materials used to contain, present, or make available the output of computers, based upon the prevailing levels of costs to the Farm Credit System Insurance Corporation for the type and amount of such supplies of materials that are used. Nothing in this paragraph shall be construed to entitle any person or entity, as a right, to any services in connection with computerized records, other than services to which such person or entity may be entitled under the provisions of this subpart.

(d) Only requesters who are seeking documents for commercial use may be charged for time spent reviewing records to determine whether they are exempt from mandatory disclosure. Charges may be assessed only for the initial review; i.e., the review undertaken the first time the Farm Credit System Insurance Corporation analyzes the applicability of a specific exemption to a particular record or portion of a record. Records or portions of records withheld in full under an exemption that is subsequently determined not to apply may be reviewed again to determine the applicability of other exemptions not previously considered. The costs for such a subsequent review is assessable.

(e) Records will be reproduced at a rate of $.15 per page. For copies prepared by computer, such as tapes or printouts, the requester shall be charged the actual cost, including operator time, of production of the tape or printout. For other methods of reproduction, the actual direct costs of producing the document(s) shall be charged.

(f) The Farm Credit System Insurance Corporation will recover the full costs of providing services such as those enumerated below when it elects to provide them:

(1) Certifying that records are true copies; or

(2) Sending records by special methods such as express mail.

(g) Remittances shall be in the form either of a personal check or bank draft drawn on a bank in the United States, or a postal money order. Remittances shall be made payable to the order of the Farm Credit System Insurance Corporation.

(h) A receipt for fees paid will be given upon request.

§ 1402.23 Waiver or reduction of fees.

(a) The Farm Credit System Insurance Corporation may grant a waiver or reduction of fees if the Farm Credit System Insurance Corporation determines that the disclosure of the information is in the public interest because it is likely to contribute significantly to public understanding of the operations or activities of the Government, and the disclosure of the information is not primarily in the commercial interest of the requester.

(b) The Farm Credit System Insurance Corporation will not charge fees to any requester, including commercial use requesters, if the cost of collecting a fee would be equal to or greater than the fee itself. The elements to be considered in determining the "cost of collecting a fee" are the administrative costs of receiving and recording a requester's remittance and processing the fee.

§ 1402.24 Advance payments—notice.

(a) Where it is anticipated that the fees chargeable will amount to more than $25 and the requester has not indicated in advance a willingness to pay fees as high as are anticipated, the requester shall be promptly notified of the amount of the anticipated fee or such portion thereof that can be readily estimated.

(b) If the anticipated fees exceed $250 and if the requester has a history of promptly paying fees charged in connection with information requests, the Farm Credit System Insurance Corporation may obtain satisfactory assurances that the requester will fully pay the fees anticipated.

(c) If the anticipated fees exceed $250 and if the requester has no history of paying fees charged in connection with information requests, the Farm Credit System Insurance Corporation may require an advance payment of fees in an amount up to the full amount anticipated.

(d) If the requester has previously failed to pay a fee charged within 30 days of the date of a billing for fees charged in connection with information requests, the Farm Credit System Insurance Corporation may require the requester to pay the fees owed, plus interest, or demonstrate that the full amount owed has been paid, and require the requester to make an advance payment of the full amount of the fees anticipated before processing a new request or a pending request from that requester.

(e) The notice of the amount of an anticipated fee or a request for an advance deposit shall include an offer to the requester to confer with identified Farm Credit System Insurance Corporation personnel to attempt to reformulate the request in a manner which will meet the needs of the requester at a lower cost.

§ 1402.25 Interest.

The Farm Credit System Insurance Corporation may begin charging interest on unpaid fees, starting on the 31st day following the day on which the bill for such fees was sent. Interest will not accrue if payment of the fees has been received by the Farm Credit System Insurance Corporation, even if said payment has not been processed. Interest will accrue at the rate prescribed in section 3717 of title 31, United States Code, and will accrue from the day on which the bill for such fees was sent.

§ 1402.26 Charges for unsuccessful searches or reviews.

The Farm Credit System Insurance Corporation may assess charges for time spent searching for records on behalf of requesters in the categories provided for in § 1402.21 (c) and (d), even if there are no records that are responsive to the request or there is ultimately no disclosure of records. The Farm Credit System Insurance Corporation may assess charges for time spent reviewing records for requesters in the category provided for in § 1402.21(c) even if the records located are determined to be exempt from disclosure.

§ 1402.27 Aggregating requests.

A requester may not file multiple requests at the same time, each seeking portions of a document or documents, solely in order to avoid payment of fees. When the Farm Credit System Insurance Corporation reasonably believes that a requester, or a group of requesters acting in concert, is attempting to break a request down into a series of requests for the purpose of evading the assessment of fees, the Farm Credit System Insurance Corporation may aggregate any such requests and charge accordingly. One element to be considered in determining whether a belief would be reasonable is the time period over which the requests have occurred.

PART 1403—PRIVACY ACT REGULATIONS

Sec.

AUTHORITY: Secs. 5.58, 5.59 of the Farm Credit Act (12 U.S.C. 2277a–7, 2277a–8); 5 U.S.C. app. 3, 5 U.S.C. 552a.

SOURCE: 59 FR 53084, Oct. 21, 1994, unless otherwise noted.

§ 1403.1 Purpose and scope.

(a) This part is published by the Farm Credit System Insurance Corporation pursuant to the Privacy Act of 1974 (Pub. L. 93–579, 5 U.S.C. 552a) which requires each Federal agency to promulgate rules to establish procedures for notification and disclosure to an individual of agency records pertaining to that person, and for review of such records.

(b) The records covered by this part include:

(1) Personnel and employment records maintained by the Farm Credit System Insurance Corporation not covered by §§ 293.101 through 293.108 of the regulations of the Office of Personnel Management (5 CFR 293.101 through 293.108); and

(2) Other records contained in record systems maintained by the Farm Credit System Insurance Corporation.

(c) This part does not apply to any records maintained by the Farm Credit System Insurance Corporation in its capacity as a receiver or conservator.

§ 1403.2 Definitions.

For the purposes of this part:

(a) *Agency* means the Farm Credit System Insurance Corporation. It does not include the Farm Credit System Insurance Corporation when it is acting as a receiver or a conservator;

(b) *Individual* means a citizen of the United States or an alien lawfully admitted for permanent residence;

(c) *Maintain* includes maintain, collect, use, or disseminate;

(d) *Record* means any item, collection, or grouping of information about an individual that is maintained by an agency including, but not limited to, that person's education, financial transactions, medical history, and criminal or employment history, and that contains that person's name, or the identifying number, symbol, or other identifying particular assigned to the individual, such as a finger or voice print or photograph;

(e) *Routine use* means, with respect to the disclosure of a record, the use of such record for a purpose that is compatible with the purpose for which it was collected;

(f) *Statistical record* means a record in a system of records maintained for statistical research or reporting purposes only and not used in whole or in part in making any determination about an identifiable individual, except as provided by 13 U.S.C. 8;

(g) *System of records* means a group of any records under the control of any agency from which information is retrieved by the name of an individual or by some identifying number, symbol, or other identifying particular assigned to the individual.

§ 1403.3 Procedures for requests pertaining to individual records in a record system.

(a) Any present or former employee of the Farm Credit System Insurance Corporation seeking access to that person's official civil service records maintained by the Farm Credit System Insurance Corporation shall submit a request in such manner as is prescribed by the Office of Personnel Management.

(b) Individuals shall submit their requests in writing to the Privacy Act Officer, Farm Credit System Insurance Corporation, McLean, Virginia 22102–0826, when seeking to obtain the following information from the Farm Credit System Insurance Corporation:

(1) Notification of whether the agency maintains a record pertaining to that person in a system of records;

(2) Notification of whether the agency has disclosed a record for which an accounting of disclosure is required to be maintained and made available to that person;

(3) A copy of a record pertaining to that person or the accounting of its disclosure; or

(4) The review of a record pertaining to that person or the accounting of its disclosure.

The request shall state the full name and address of the individual, and identify the system or systems of records believed to contain the information or record sought.

§ 1403.4 Times, places, and requirements for identification of individuals making requests.

The individual making written requests for information or records ordinarily will not be required to verify that person's identity. The signature upon such requests shall be deemed to be a certification by the requester that he or she is the individual to whom the record pertains, or the parent of a minor, or the duly appointed legal guardian of the individual to whom the record pertains. The Privacy Act Officer, however, may require such additional verification of identity in any instance in which the Privacy Act Officer deems it advisable.

§ 1403.5 Disclosure of requested information to individuals.

(a) The Privacy Act Officer shall, within a reasonable period of time after the date of receipt of a request for information of records:

(1) Determine whether or not such request shall be granted;

(2) Notify the requester of the determination, and, if the request is denied, of the reasons therefor; and

(3) Notify the requester that fees for reproducing copies of records may be charged as provided in § 1403.10.

(b) If access to a record is denied because the information therein has been compiled by the Farm Credit System Insurance Corporation in reasonable anticipation of a civil or criminal action proceeding, the Privacy Act Officer shall notify the requester of that person's right to judicial appeal under 5 U.S.C. 552a(g).

(c)(1) If access to a record is granted, the requester shall notify the Privacy Act Officer whether the requested record is to be copied and mailed to the requester or whether the record is to be made available for personal inspection.

(2) A requester who is an individual may be accompanied by an individual selected by the requester when the record is disclosed, in which case the requester may be required to furnish a written statement authorizing the discussion of the record in the presence of the accompanying person.

(d) If the record is to be made available for personal inspection, the requester shall arrange with the Privacy Act Officer a mutually agreeable time in the offices of the Farm Credit System Insurance Corporation for inspection of the record.

§ 1403.6 Special procedures for medical records.

Medical records in the custody of the Farm Credit System Insurance Corporation which are not subject to Office of Personnel Management regulations shall be disclosed either to the individual to whom they pertain or that person's authorized or legal representative or to a licensed physician named by the individual.

§ 1403.7 Request for amendment to record.

(a) If, after disclosure of the requested information, an individual believes that the record is not accurate, relevant, timely, or complete, that person may request in writing that the record be amended. Such a request shall be submitted to the Privacy Act Officer and shall identify the system of records and the record or information therein, a brief description of the material requested to be changed, the requested change or changes, and the reason for such change or changes.

(b) The Privacy Act Officer shall acknowledge receipt of the request within 10 days (excluding Saturdays, Sundays, and legal holidays) and, if a determination has not been made, advise the individual when that person may expect to be advised of action taken on the request. The acknowledgment may contain a request for additional information needed to make a determination.

§ 1403.8 Agency review of request for amendment of record.

Upon receipt of a request for amendment of a record, the Privacy Act Officer shall:

(a) Correct any portion of a record which the individual making the request believes is not accurate, relevant, timely, or complete and thereafter inform the individual in writing of such correction, or

(b) Inform the individual in writing of the refusal to amend the record and of the reasons therefor, and advise that the individual may appeal such determination as provided in § 1403.9.

§ 1403.9 Appeal of an initial adverse determination of a request to amend a record.

(a) Not more than 10 days (excluding Saturdays, Sundays, and legal holidays) after receipt by an individual of an adverse determination on the individual's request to amend a record or otherwise, the individual may appeal to the Chief Operating Officer, Farm Credit System Insurance Corporation, McLean, Virginia 22102–0826.

(b) The appeal shall be by letter, mailed or delivered to the Chief Operating Officer, Farm Credit System Insurance Corporation, McLean, Virginia 22102–0826. The letter shall identify the records involved in the same manner they were identified to the Privacy Act Officer, shall specify the dates of the request and adverse determination, and shall indicate the expressed basis for that determination. Also, the letter shall state briefly and succinctly the reasons why the adverse determination should be reversed.

(c) The review shall be completed and a final determination made by the Chief Operating Officer not later than 30 days (excluding Saturdays, Sundays, and legal holidays) from receipt of the request for such review, unless the Chief Operating Officer extends such 30-day period for good cause. If the 30-day period is extended, the individual shall be notified of the reasons therefor.

(d) If the Chief Operating Officer refuses to amend the record in accordance with the request, the individual shall be notified of the right to file a concise statement setting forth that person's disagreement with the final determination and that person's right under 5 U.S.C. 552a(g)(1)(A) to a judicial review of the final determination.

(e) If the refusal to amend a record as requested is confirmed, there shall be included in the disputed portion of the record a copy of the concise statement filed by the individual together with a concise statement of the reasons for not amending the record as requested. Such statements will be included when disclosure of the disputed record is made to persons and agencies as authorized under 5 U.S.C. 552a.

§ 1403.10 Fees for providing copies of records.

Fees for providing copies of records shall be charged in accordance with §§ 1402.22 and 1402.24 of this chapter.

§ 1403.11 Criminal penalties.

Section 552a(i)(3) of the Privacy Act (5 U.S.C. 552a(i)(3)) makes it a misdemeanor, subject to a maximum fine of $5,000, to knowingly and willfully request or obtain any record concerning any individual from an agency under false pretenses. Sections 552a(i) (1) and (2) of the Act (5 U.S.C. 552a(i) (1), (2)) provide penalties for violation by agency employees of the Act or regulations established thereunder.

§ 1403.12 Exemptions.

Specific. Pursuant to 5 U.S.C. 552a(k)(5), the investigatory material compiled for law enforcement purposes in the following system of records is exempt from subsections (c)(3), (d), (e)(1), (e)(4) (G), (H), and (I), and (f) of 5 U.S.C. 552a and from the provisions of this part:

Personnel Security Files—FCSIC.

PART 1408—COLLECTION OF CLAIMS OWED THE UNITED STATES

Subpart A—Administrative Collection of Claims

Sec.

Subpart B—Administrative Offset

Subpart C—Offset Against Salary

AUTHORITY: Sec. 5.58 of the Farm Credit Act (12 U.S.C. 2277a-7); 31 U.S.C. 3701–3719; 5 U.S.C. 5514; 4 CFR parts 101–105; 5 CFR part 550.

SOURCE: 59 FR 24899, May 13, 1994, unless otherwise noted.

Subpart A—Administrative Collection of Claims

§ 1408.1 Authority.

The regulations of this part are issued under the Federal Claims Collection Act of 1966, as amended by the Debt Collection Act of 1982, 31 U.S.C. 3701–3719 and 5 U.S.C. 5514, and in conformity with the joint regulations issued under that Act by the General Accounting Office and the Department of Justice (joint regulations) prescribing standards for administrative collection, compromise, suspension, and termination of agency collection actions, and referral to the General Accounting Office and to the Department of Justice for litigation of civil claims for money or property owed to the United States (4 CFR parts 101–105).

§ 1408.2 Applicability.

This part applies to all claims of indebtedness due and owing to the United States and collectible under procedures authorized by the Federal Claims Collection Act of 1966, as amended by the Debt Collection Act of 1982. The joint regulations and this part do not apply to conduct in violation of antitrust laws, tax claims, claims between Federal agencies, or to any claim which appears to involve fraud, presentation of a false claim, or misrepresentation on the part of the debtor or any other party having an interest in the claim, unless the Justice Department authorizes the Farm Credit System Insurance Corporation, pursuant to 4 CFR 101.3, to handle the claim in accordance with the provisions of 4 CFR parts 101 through 105. Additionally, this part does not apply to Farm Credit System Insurance Corporation's premiums regulations under part 1410 of this chapter.

§ 1408.3 Definitions.

In this part (except where the term is defined elsewhere in this part), the following definitions shall apply:

(a) *Administrative offset* or *offset*, as defined in 31 U.S.C. 3701(a)(1), means withholding money payable by the United States Government to, or held by the Government for, a person to satisfy a debt the person owes the Government.

(b) *Agency* means a department, agency, or instrumentality in the executive or legislative branch of the Government.

(c) *Claim* or *debt* means money or property owed by a person or entity to an agency of the Federal Government. A "claim" or "debt" includes amounts due the Government from loans insured by or guaranteed by the United States and all other amounts due from fees, leases, rents, royalties, services, sales of real or personal property, overpayment, penalties, damages, interest, and fines.

(d) *Claim certification* means a creditor agency's written request to a paying agency to effect an administrative offset.

(e) *Corporation* means the Farm Credit System Insurance Corporation.

(f) *Creditor agency* means an agency to which a claim or debt is owed.

(g) *Debtor* means the person or entity owing money to the Federal Government.

(h) *Hearing official* means an individual who is responsible for reviewing a claim under § 1408.10.

(i) *Paying agency* means an agency of the Federal Government owing money to a debtor against which an administrative or salary offset can be effected.

(j) *Salary offset* means an administrative offset to collect a debt under 5 U.S.C. 5514 by deductions at one or more officially established pay intervals from the current pay account of a debtor.

§ 1408.4 Delegation of authority.

The Corporation official(s) designated by the Chairman of the Farm Credit System Insurance Corporation are authorized to perform all duties which the Chairman is authorized to perform under these regulations, the Federal Claims Collection Act of 1966, as amended, and the joint regulations issued under that Act.

§ 1408.5 Responsibility for collection.

(a) The collection of claims shall be aggressively pursued in accordance with the provisions of the Federal Claims Collection Act of 1966, as amended, the joint regulations issued under that Act, and these regulations. Debts owed to the United States, together with charges for interest, penalties, and administrative costs, should be collected in one lump sum unless otherwise provided by law. If a debtor requests installment payments, the debtor, as requested by the Corporation, shall provide sufficient information to demonstrate that the debtor is unable to pay the debt in one lump sum. When appropriate, the Corporation shall arrange an installment payment schedule. Claims which cannot be collected directly or by administrative offset shall be either written off as administratively uncollectible or referred to the General Counsel for further consideration.

(b) The Chairman, or designee of the Chairman, may compromise claims for money or property arising out of the activities of the Corporation, where the claim (exclusive of charges for interest, penalties, and administrative costs) does not exceed $100,000. When the claim exceeds $100,000 (exclusive of charges for interest, penalties, and administrative costs), the authority to accept a compromise rests solely with the Department of Justice. The standards governing the compromise of claims are set forth in 4 CFR part 103.

(c) The Chairman, or designee of the Chairman, may suspend or terminate the collection of claims which do not exceed $100,000 (exclusive of charges for interest, penalties, and administrative costs) after deducting the amount of any partial payments or collections. If, after deducting the amount of any partial payments or collections, a claim exceeds $100,000 (exclusive of charges for interest, penalties, and administrative costs), the authority to suspend or terminate rests solely with the Department of Justice. The standards governing the suspension or termination of claim collections are set forth in 4 CFR part 104.

(d) The Corporation shall refer claims to the Department of Justice for litigation or to the General Accounting Office (GAO) for claims arising from audit exceptions taken by the GAO to payments made by the Corporation in accordance with 4 CFR part 105.

§ 1408.6 Demand for payment.

(a) A total of three progressively stronger written demands at not more than 30-day intervals should normally be made upon a debtor, unless a response or other information indicates that additional written demands would either be unnecessary or futile. When necessary to protect the Government's interest, written demands may be preceded by other appropriate actions under Federal law, including immediate referral for litigation and/or administrative offset.

(b) The initial demand for payment shall be in writing and shall inform the debtor of the following:

(1) The amount of the debt, the date it was incurred, and the facts upon which the determination of indebtedness was made;

(2) The payment due date, which shall be 30 calendar days from the date of mailing or hand delivery of the initial demand for payment;

(3) The right of the debtor to inspect and copy the records of the agency related to the claim or to receive copies if personal inspection is impractical. The debtor shall be informed that the debtor may be assessed for the cost of copying the documents in accordance with § 1408.7;

(4) The right of the debtor to obtain a review of the Corporation's determination of indebtedness;

(5) The right of the debtor to offer to enter into a written agreement with the agency to repay the amount of the claim. The debtor shall be informed that the acceptance of such an agreement is discretionary with the agency;

(6) That charges for interest, penalties, and administrative costs will be assessed against the debtor, in accordance with 31 U.S.C. 3717, if payment is not received by the payment due date;

(7) That if the debtor has not entered into an agreement with the Corporation to pay the debt, has not requested the Corporation to review the debt, or has not paid the debt by the payment due date, the Corporation intends to collect the debt by all legally available means, which may include initiating legal action against the debtor, referring the debt to a collection agency for collection, collecting the debt by offset, or asking other Federal agencies for assistance in collecting the debt by offset;

(8) The name and address of the Corporation official to whom the debtor shall send all correspondence relating to the debt; and

(9) Other information, as may be appropriate.

(c) If, prior to, during, or after completion of the demand cycle, the Corporation determines to collect the debt by either administrative or salary offset, the Corporation shall follow, as applicable, the requirements for a Notice of Intent to Collect by Administrative Offset or a Notice of Intent to Collect by Salary Offset set forth in § 1408.22.

(d) If no response to the initial demand for payment is received by the payment due date, the Corporation shall take further action under this part, under the Federal Claims Collection Act of 1966, as amended, under the joint regulations (4 CFR parts 101–105), or under any other applicable State or Federal law. These actions may include reports to credit bureaus, referrals to collection agencies, termination of contracts, debarment, and salary or administrative offset.

§ 1408.7 Right to inspect and copy records.

The debtor may inspect and copy the Corporation records related to the claim. The debtor shall give the Corporation reasonable advanced notice that he/she intends to inspect and copy the records involved. The debtor shall pay copying costs unless they are waived by the Corporation. Copying costs shall be assessed pursuant to § 1402.22 of this chapter.

§ 1408.8 Right to offer to repay claim.

(a) The debtor may offer to enter into a written agreement with the Corporation to repay the amount of the claim. The acceptance of such an offer and the decision to enter into such a written agreement is at the discretion of the Corporation.

(b) If the debtor requests a repayment arrangement because payment of the amount due would create a financial hardship, the Corporation shall analyze the debtor's financial condition. The Corporation may enter into a written agreement with the debtor permitting the debtor to repay the debt in installments if the Corporation determines, in its sole discretion, that payment of the amount due would create an undue financial hardship for the debtor. The written agreement shall set forth the amount and frequency of installment payments and shall, in accordance with § 1408.12, provide for the imposition of charges for interest, penalties, and administrative costs unless waived by the Corporation.

(c) The written agreement may require the debtor to execute a confess-judgment note when the total amount of the deferred installments will exceed $750. The Corporation shall provide the debtor with a written explanation of the consequences of signing a confess-judgment note. The debtor shall sign a statement acknowledging receipt of the written explanation. The statement shall recite that the written explanation was read and understood before execution of the note and that the debtor signed the note knowingly and voluntarily. Documentation of these procedures will be maintained in the Corporation's file on the debtor.

§ 1408.9 Right to agency review.

(a) If the debtor disputes the claim, the debtor may request a review of the Corporation's determination of the existence of the debt or of the amount of the debt. If only part of the claim is disputed, the undisputed portion should be paid by the payment due date.

(b) To obtain a review, the debtor shall submit a written request for review to the Corporation official named in the initial demand letter, within 15 calendar days after receipt of the letter. The debtor's request for review shall state the basis on which the claim is disputed.

(c) The Corporation shall promptly notify the debtor, in writing, that the Corporation has received the request for review. The Corporation shall conduct its review of the claim in accordance with § 1408.10.

(d) Upon completion of its review of the claim, the Corporation shall notify the debtor whether the Corporation's determination of the existence or amount of the debt has been sustained, amended, or canceled. The notification shall include a copy of the written decision issued by the hearing official pursuant to § 1408.10(e). If the Corporation's determination is sustained, this notification shall contain a provision which states that the Corporation intends to collect the debt by all legally available means, which may include initiating legal action against the debtor, referring the debt to a collection agency for collection, collecting the debt by offset, or asking other Federal agencies for assistance in collecting the debt by offset.

§ 1408.10 Review procedures.

(a) Unless an oral hearing is required by § 1408.23(d), the Corporation's review shall be a review of the written record of the claim.

(b) If an oral hearing is required under § 1408.23(d) the Corporation shall provide the debtor with a reasonable opportunity for such a hearing. The oral hearing, however, shall not be an adversarial adjudication and need not take the form of a formal evidentiary hearing. All significant matters discussed at the hearing, however, will be carefully documented.

(c) Any review required by this part, whether a review of the written record or an oral hearing, shall be conducted by a hearing official. In the case of a salary offset, the hearing official shall not be under the supervision or control of the Chairman of the Farm Credit System Insurance Corporation.

(d) The Corporation may be represented by legal counsel. The debtor may represent himself or herself or may be represented by an individual of the debtor's choice and at the debtor's expense.

(e) The hearing official shall issue a final written decision based on documentary evidence and, if applicable, information developed at an oral hearing. The written decision shall be issued as soon as practicable after the review but not later than 60 days after the date on which the request for review was received by the Corporation, unless the debtor requests a delay in the proceedings. A delay in the proceedings shall be granted if the hearing official determines, in his or her sole discretion, that there is good cause to grant the delay. If a delay is granted, the 60-day decision period shall be extended by the number of days by which the review was postponed.

(f) Upon issuance of the written opinion, the Corporation shall promptly notify the debtor of the hearing official's decision. Said notification shall include a copy of the written decision issued by the hearing official pursuant to paragraph (e) of this section.

§ 1408.11 Special review.

(a) An employee subject to salary offset, under subpart C of this part, or a voluntary repayment agreement, may, at any time, request a special review by the Corporation of the amount of the salary offset or voluntary repayment, based on materially changed circumstances such as, but not limited to, catastrophic illness, divorce, death, or disability.

(b) To determine whether an offset would prevent the employee from meeting essential subsistence expenses (costs incurred for food, housing, clothing, transportation, and medical care), the employee shall submit a detailed statement and supporting documents for the employee, his or her spouse, and dependents indicating:

(1) Income from all sources;

(2) Assets;

(3) Liabilities;

(4) Number of dependents;

(5) Expenses for food, housing, clothing, and transportation;

(6) Medical expenses; and

(7) Exceptional expenses, if any.

(c) If the employee requests a special review under this section, the employee shall file an alternative proposed offset or payment schedule and a statement, with supporting documents, showing why the current salary offset or payments result in an extreme financial hardship to the employee.

(d) The Corporation shall evaluate the statement and supporting documents, and determine whether the original offset or repayment schedule imposes an undue financial hardship on the employee. The Corporation shall notify the employee in writing of such determination, including, if appropriate, a revised offset or payment schedule.

§ 1408.12 Charges for interest, administrative costs, and penalties.

(a) Except as provided in paragraph (d) of this section, the Corporation shall:

(1) Assess interest on unpaid claims;

(2) Assess administrative costs incurred in processing and handling overdue claims; and

(3) Assess penalty charges not to exceed 6 percent a year on any part of a debt more than 90 days past due.

The imposition of charges for interest, administrative costs, and penalties shall be made in accordance with 31 U.S.C. 3717.

(b)(1) Interest shall accrue from the date of mailing or hand delivery of the initial demand for payment or the Notice of Intent to Collect by either Administrative or Salary Offset if the amount of the claim is not paid within 30 days from the date of mailing or hand delivery of the initial demand or notice.

(2) The 30-day period may be extended on a case-by-case basis if the Corporation reasonably determines that such action is appropriate. Interest shall only accrue on the principal of the claim and the interest rate shall remain fixed for the duration of the indebtedness, except, as provided in paragraph (c) of this section, in cases where a debtor has defaulted on a repayment agreement and seeks to enter into a new agreement, or if the Corporation reasonably determines that a higher rate is necessary to protect the interests of the United States.

(c) If a debtor defaults on a repayment agreement and seeks to enter into a new agreement, the Corporation may assess a new interest rate on the unpaid claim. In addition, charges for interest, administrative costs, and penalties which accrued but were not collected under the original repayment agreement shall be added to the principal of the claim to be paid under the new repayment agreement. Interest shall accrue on the entire principal balance of the claim, as adjusted to reflect any increase resulting from the addition of these charges.

(d) The Corporation may waive charges for interest, administrative costs, and/or penalties if it determines that:

(1) The debtor is unable to pay any significant sum toward the claim within a reasonable period of time;

(2) Collection of charges for interest, administrative costs, and/or penalties would jeopardize collection of the principal of the claim;

(3) Collection of charges for interest, administrative costs, or penalties would be against equity and good conscience; or

(4) It is otherwise in the best interest of the United States, including the situation where an installment payment agreement or offset is in effect.

§ 1408.13 Contracting for collection services.

The Chairman, or designee of the Chairman, may contract for collection services in accordance with 31 U.S.C. 3718 and 4 CFR 102.6 to recover debts.

§ 1408.14 Reporting of credit information.

The Chairman, or designee of the Chairman, may disclose to a consumer reporting agency information that an individual is responsible for a debt owed to the United States. Information will be disclosed to reporting agencies in accordance with the terms and conditions of agreements entered into between the Corporation and the reporting agencies. The terms and conditions of such agreements shall specify that all of the rights and protection afforded to the debtor under 31 U.S.C. 3711(f) have been fulfilled. The Corporation shall notify each consumer reporting agency, to which a claim was disclosed, when the debt has been satisfied.

§ 1408.15 Credit report.

In order to aid the Corporation in making appropriate determinations regarding the collection and compromise of claims; the collection of charges for interest, administrative costs, and penalties; the use of administrative offset; the use of other collection methods; and the likelihood of collecting the claim, the Corporation may institute, consistent with the provisions of the Fair Credit Reporting Act (15 U.S.C. 1681, et seq.), a credit investigation of the debtor immediately following a determination that the claim exists.

Subpart B—Administrative Offset

§ 1408.20 Applicability.

(a) The provisions of this subpart shall apply to the collection of debts by administrative [or salary] offset under 31 U.S.C. 3716, 5 U.S.C. 5514, or other statutory or common law.

(b) Offset shall not be used to collect a debt more than 10 years after the Government's right to collect the debt first accrued, unless facts material to the Government's right to collect the debt were not known and could not reasonably have been known by the official or officials of the Government who were charged with the responsibility of discovering and collecting such debt.

(c) Offset shall not be used with respect to:

(1) Debts owed by other agencies of the United States or by any State or local government;

(2) Debts arising under or payments made under the Social Security Act, the Internal Revenue Code of 1986, as amended, or tariff laws of the United States; or

(3) Any case in which collection by offset of the type of debt involved is explicitly provided for or prohibited by another statute.

(d) Unless otherwise provided by contract or law, debts or payments which are not subject to offset under 31 U.S.C. 3716 or 5 U.S.C. 5514 may be collected by offset if such collection is authorized under common law or other applicable statutory authority.

§ 1408.21 Collection by offset.

(a) Collection of a debt by administrative [or salary] offset shall be accomplished in accordance with the provisions of these regulations, 4 CFR 102.3, and 5 CFR part 550, subpart K. It is not necessary for the debt to be reduced to judgment or to be undisputed for offset to be used.

(b) The Chairman, or designee of the Chairman, may determine that it is feasible to collect a debt to the United States by offset against funds payable to the debtor.

(c) The feasibility of collecting a debt by offset will be determined on a case-by-case basis. This determination shall be made by considering all relevant factors, including the following: (1) The degree to which the offset can be accomplished in accordance with law. This determination should take into consideration relevant statutory, regulatory, and contractual requirements;

(2) The degree to which the Corporation is certain that its determination of the existence and amount of the debt is correct;

(3) The practicality of collecting the debt by offset. The cost, in time and money, of collecting the debt by offset and the amount of money which can reasonably be expected to be recovered through offset will be relevant to this determination; and

(4) Whether the use of offset will substantially interfere with or defeat the purpose of a program authorizing payments against which the offset is contemplated. For example, under a grant program in which payments are made in advance of the grantee's performance, the imposition of offset against such a payment may be inappropriate.

(d) The collection of a debt by offset may not be feasible when there are circumstances which would indicate that the likelihood of collection by offset is less than probable.

(e) The offset will be effected 31 days after the debtor receives a Notice of Intent to Collect by Administrative Offset (or Notice of Intent to Collect by Salary Offset if the offset is a salary offset), or upon the expiration of a stay of offset, unless the Corporation determines under § 1408.24 that immediate action is necessary.

(f) If the debtor owes more than one debt, amounts recovered through offset may be applied to them in any order. Applicable statutes of limitation would be considered before applying the amounts recovered to any debts owed.

§ 1408.22 Notice requirements before offset.

(a) Except as provided in § 1408.24, the Corporation will provide the debtor with 30 calendar days' written notice that unpaid debt amounts shall be collected by administrative [or salary] offset (Notice of Intent to Collect by Administrative [or Salary] Offset) before the Corporation imposes offset against any money that is to be paid to the debtor.

(b) The Notice of Intent to Collect by Administrative [or Salary] Offset shall be delivered to the debtor by hand or by mail and shall provide the following information:

(1) The amount of the debt, the date it was incurred, and the facts upon which the determination of indebtedness was made;

(2) In the case of an administrative offset, the payment due date, which shall be 30 calendar days from the date of mailing or hand delivery of the Notice;

(3) In the case of a salary offset:

(i) The Corporation's intention to collect the debt by means of deduction from the employee's current disposable pay account until the debt and all accumulated interest is paid in full; and

(ii) The amount, frequency, proposed beginning date, and duration of the intended deductions;

(4) The right of the debtor to inspect and copy the records of the Corporation related to the claim or to receive copies if personal inspection is impractical. The debtor shall be informed that he/she shall be assessed for the cost of copying the documents in accordance with § 1408.7 of this part;

(5) The right of the debtor to obtain a review of, and to request a hearing, on the Corporation's determination of indebtedness, the propriety of collecting the debt by offset, and, in the case of salary offset, the propriety of the proposed repayment schedule (i.e., the percentage of disposable pay to be deducted each pay period). The debtor shall be informed that to obtain a review, the debtor shall deliver a written request for a review to the Corporation official named in the Notice, within 15 calendar days after the debtor's receipt of the Notice. In the case of a salary offset, the debtor shall also be informed that the review shall be conducted by an official arranged for by the Corporation who shall be a hearing official not under the control of the Chairman of the Farm Credit System Insurance Corporation, or an administrative law judge;

(6) That the filing of a petition for hearing within 15 calendar days after receipt of the Notice will stay the commencement of collection proceedings;

(7) That a final decision on the hearing (if one is requested) will be issued at the earliest practical date, but not later than 60 days after the filing of the written request for review unless the employee requests, and the hearing official grants, a delay in the proceedings;

(8) The right of the debtor to offer to enter into a written agreement with the Corporation to repay the amount of the claim. The debtor shall be informed that the acceptance of such an agreement is discretionary with the Corporation;

(9) That charges for interest, penalties, and administrative costs shall be assessed against the debtor, in accordance with 31 U.S.C. 3717, if payment is not received by the payment due date. The debtor shall be informed that such assessments must be made unless excused in accordance with the Federal Claims Collection Standards (4 CFR parts 103 and 104);

(10) The amount of accrued interest and the amount of any other penalties or administrative costs which may have been added to the principal debt;

(11) That if the debtor has not entered into an agreement with the Corporation to pay the debt, has not requested the Corporation to review the debt, or has not paid the debt prior to the date on which the offset is to be imposed, the Corporation intends to collect the debt by administrative [or salary] offset or by requesting other Federal agencies for assistance in collecting the debt by offset. The debtor shall be informed that the offset shall be imposed against any funds that might become available to the debtor, until the principal debt and all accumulated interest and other charges are paid in full;

(12) The date on which the offset will be imposed, which shall be 31 calendar days from the date of mailing or hand delivery of the Notice. The debtor shall be informed that the Corporation reserves the right to impose an offset prior to this date if the Corporation determines that immediate action is necessary;

(13) That any knowingly false or frivolous statements, representations, or evidence may subject the debtor to:

(i) Penalties under the False Claims Act, 31 U.S.C. 3729 through 3731, or any other applicable statutory authority;

(ii) Criminal penalties under 18 U.S.C. 286, 287, 1001, and 1002, or any other applicable statutory authority; and, with regard to employees,

(iii) Disciplinary procedures appropriate under 5 U.S.C. chapter 75; 5 CFR part 752, or any other applicable statute or regulation;

(14) The name and address of the Corporation official to whom the debtor shall send all correspondence relating to the debt or the offset;

(15) Any other rights and remedies available to the debtor under statutes or regulations governing the program for which the collection is being made;

(16) That unless there are applicable contractual or statutory provisions to the contrary, amounts paid on or deducted for the debt, which are later waived or found not owed to the United States, will be promptly refunded to the employee; and

(17) Other information, as may be appropriate.

(c) When the procedural requirements of this section have been provided to the debtor in connection with the same debt or under some other statutory or regulatory authority, the Corporation is not required to duplicate those requirements before effecting offset.

§ 1408.23 Right to review of claim.

(a) If the debtor disputes the claim, the debtor may request a review of the Corporation's determination of the existence of the debt, the amount of the debt, the propriety of collecting the debt by offset, and in the case of salary offset, the propriety of the proposed repayment schedule. If only part of the claim is disputed, the undisputed portion should be paid by the payment due date.

(b) To obtain a review, the debtor shall submit a written request for review to the Corporation official named in the Notice of Intent to Collect by Administrative [or Salary] Offset within 15 calendar days after receipt of the notice. The debtor's written request for review shall state the basis on which the claim is disputed and shall specify whether the debtor requests an oral hearing or a review of the written record of the claim. If an oral hearing is requested, the debtor shall explain in the request why the matter cannot be resolved by a review of the documentary evidence alone.

(c) The Corporation shall promptly notify the debtor, in writing, that the Corporation has received the request for review. The Corporation shall conduct its review of the claim in accordance with § 1408.10.

(d) The Corporation's review of the claim, under this section, shall include providing the debtor with a reasonable opportunity for an oral hearing if:

(1) An applicable statute authorizes or requires the Corporation to consider waiver of the indebtedness, the debtor requests waiver of the indebtedness, and the waiver determination turns on an issue of credibility or veracity; or

(2) The debtor requests reconsideration of the debt and the Corporation determines that the question of the indebtedness cannot be resolved by reviewing the documentary evidence; for example, when the validity of the debt turns on an issue of credibility or veracity.

(e) A debtor waives the right to a hearing and will have his or her debt offset in accordance with the proposed offset schedule if the debtor:

(1) Fails to file a written request for review within the timeframe set forth in paragraph (b) of this section, unless the Corporation determines that the delay was the result of circumstances beyond his or her control; or

(2) Fails to appear at an oral hearing of which he or she was notified unless the hearing official determines that the failure to appear was due to circumstances beyond the employee's control.

(f) Upon completion of its review of the claim, the Corporation shall notify the debtor whether the Corporation's determination of the existence or amount of the debt has been sustained, amended, or canceled. The notification shall include a copy of the written decision issued by the hearing official, pursuant to § 1408.10(e). If the Corporation's determination is sustained, this notification shall contain a provision which states that the Corporation intends to collect the debt by offset or by requesting other Federal agencies for assistance in collecting the debt.

(g) When the procedural requirements of this section have been provided to the debtor in connection with the same debt or under some other statutory or regulatory authority, the Corporation is not required to duplicate those requirements before effecting offset.

§ 1408.24 Waiver of procedural requirements.

(a) The Corporation may impose offset against a payment to be made to a debtor prior to the completion of the procedures required by this part, if:

(1) Failure to impose the offset would substantially prejudice the Government's ability to collect the debt; and

(2) The timing of the payment against which the offset will be imposed does not reasonably permit the completion of those procedures.

(b) The procedures required by this part shall be complied with promptly after the offset is imposed. Amounts recovered by offset, which are later found not to be owed to the Government, shall be promptly refunded to the debtor.

§ 1408.25 Coordinating offset with other Federal agencies.

(a)(1) Any creditor agency which requests the Corporation to impose an offset against amounts owed to the debtor shall submit to the Corporation a claim certification which meets the requirements of this paragraph. The Corporation shall submit the same certification to any agency that the Corporation requests to effect an offset.

(2) The claim certification shall be in writing. It shall certify the debtor owes the debt and that all of the applicable requirements of 31 U.S.C. 3716 and 4 CFR part 102 have been met. If the intended offset is to be a salary offset, a claim certification shall instead certify that the debtor owes the debt and that the applicable requirements of 5 U.S.C. 5514 and 5 CFR part 550, subpart K, have been met.

(3) A certification that the debtor owes the debt shall state the amount of the debt, the factual basis supporting the determination of indebtedness, and the date on which payment of the debt was due. A certification that the requirements of 31 U.S.C. 3716 and 4 CFR part 102 have been met shall include a statement that the debtor has been sent a Notice of Intent to Collect by Administrative Offset at least 31 calendar days prior to the date of the intended offset or a statement that pursuant to 4 CFR 102.3(b)(5) said Notice was not required to be sent. A certification that the requirements of 5 U.S.C. 5514 and 5 CFR part 550, subpart K, have been met shall include a statement that the debtor has been sent a Notice of Intent to Collect by Salary Offset at least 31 calendar days prior to the date of the intended offset or a statement that pursuant to 4 CFR 102.3(b)(5) said Notice was not required to be sent.

(b)(1) The Corporation shall not effect an offset requested by another Federal agency without first obtaining the claim certification required by paragraph (a) of this section. If the Corporation receives an incomplete claim certification, the Corporation shall return the claim certification with notice that a claim certification which complies with the requirements of paragraph (a) of this section must be submitted to the Corporation before the Corporation will consider effecting an offset.

(2) The Corporation may rely on the information contained in the claim certification provided by a requesting creditor agency. The Corporation is not authorized to review a creditor agency's determination of indebtedness.

(c) Only the creditor agency may agree to enter into an agreement with the debtor for the repayment of the claim. Only the creditor agency may agree to compromise, suspend, or terminate collection of the claim.

(d) The Corporation may decline, for good cause, a request by another agency to effect an offset. Good cause includes that the offset might disrupt, directly or indirectly, essential Corporation operations. The refusal and the reasons shall be sent in writing to the creditor agency.

§ 1408.26 Stay of offset.

(a)(1) When a creditor agency receives a debtor's request for inspection of agency records, the offset is stayed for 10 calendar days beyond the date set for the record inspection.

(2) When a creditor agency receives a debtor's offer to enter into a repayment agreement, the offset is stayed until the debtor is notified as to whether the proposed agreement is acceptable.

(3) When a review is conducted, the offset is stayed until the creditor agency issues a final written decision.

(b) When offset is stayed, the amount of the debt and the amount of any accrued interest or other charges will be withheld from payments to the debtor. The withheld amounts shall not be applied against the debt until the stay expires. If withheld funds are later determined not to be subject to offset, they will be promptly refunded to the debtor.

(c) If the Corporation is the creditor agency and the offset is stayed, the Corporation will immediately notify an offsetting agency to withhold the payment pending termination of the stay.

§ 1408.27 Offset against amounts payable from Civil Service Retirement and Disability Fund.

The Corporation may request that monies payable to a debtor from the Civil Service Retirement and Disability Fund be administratively offset to collect debts owed to the Corporation by the debtor. The Corporation must certify that the debtor owes the debt, the amount of the debt, and that the Corporation has complied with the requirements set forth in this part, 4 CFR 102.3, and the Office of Personnel Management regulations. The request shall be submitted to the official designated in the Office of Personnel Management regulations to receive the request.

Subpart C—Offset Against Salary

§ 1408.35 Purpose.

The purpose of this subpart is to implement section 5 of the Debt Collection Act of 1982 (Pub. L. 97–365 (5 U.S.C. 5514)), which authorizes the collection of debts owed by Federal employees to the Federal Government by means of salary offsets. These regulations provide procedures for the collection of a debt owed to the Government by the imposition of a salary offset against amounts payable to a Federal employee as salary. These regulations are consistent with the regulations on salary offset published by the Office of Personnel Management, codified in 5 CFR part 550, subpart K. Since salary offset is a type of administrative offset, the requirements of subpart B also apply to salary offsets.

§ 1408.36 Applicability of regulations.

(a) These regulations apply to the following cases:

(1) Where the Corporation is owed a debt by an individual currently employed by another agency;

(2) Where the Corporation is owed a debt by an individual who is currently employed by the Corporation; or

(3) Where the Corporation currently employs an individual who owes a debt to another Federal agency. Upon receipt of proper certification from the creditor agency, the Corporation will offset the debtor-employee's salary in accordance with these regulations.

(b) These regulations do not apply to the following: (1) Debts or claims arising under the Internal Revenue Code of 1986, as amended (26 U.S.C. 1 *et seq.*); the Social Security Act (42 U.S.C. 301 *et seq.*); the tariff laws of the United States; or to any case where collection of a debt by salary offset is explicitly provided for or prohibited by another statute (e.g., travel advances in 5 U.S.C. 5705 and employee training expenses in 5 U.S.C. 4108).

(2) Any adjustment to pay arising from an employee's election of coverage or a change in coverage under a Federal benefits program requiring periodic deductions from pay if the amount to be recovered was accumulated over four pay periods or less.

(3) A claim which has been outstanding for more than 10 years after the creditor agency's right to collect the debt first accrued, unless facts material to the Government's right to collect were not known and could not reasonably have been known by the official or officials charged with the responsibility for discovery and collection of such debts.

§ 1408.37 Definitions.

In this subpart, the following definitions shall apply:

(a) *Agency* means:

(1) An executive agency as defined by 5 U.S.C. 105, including the United States Postal Service and the United States Postal Rate Commission;

(2) A military department as defined in 5 U.S.C. 102;

(3) An agency or court of the judicial branch, including a court as defined in 28 U.S.C. 610, the District Court for the Northern Mariana Islands, and the Judicial Panel on Multi-district Litigation;

(4) An agency of the legislative branch, including the United States Senate and the United States House of Representatives; or

(5) Other independent establishments that are entities of the Federal Government.

(b) *Disposable pay* means, for an officially established pay interval, that part of current basic pay, special pay, incentive pay, retired pay, retainer pay, or, in the case of an employee not entitled to basic pay, other authorized pay remaining after the deduction of any amount required by law to be withheld. The Corporation shall allow the deductions described in 5 CFR 581.105 (b) through (f).

(c) *Employee* means a current employee of the Corporation or other agency, including a current member of the Armed Forces or Reserve of the Armed Forces of the United States.

(d) *Waiver* means the cancellation, remission, forgiveness, or nonrecovery of a debt allegedly owed by an employee to the Corporation or another agency as permitted or required by 5 U.S.C. 5584 or 8346(b), 10 U.S.C. 2774, 32 U.S.C. 716, or any other law.

§ 1408.38 Waiver requests and claims to the General Accounting Office.

(a) The regulations contained in this subpart do not preclude an employee from requesting a waiver of an overpayment under 5 U.S.C. 5584 or 8346(b), 10 U.S.C. 2774, 32 U.S.C. 716, or in any way questioning the amount or validity of a debt by submitting a subsequent claim to the General Accounting Office in accordance with the procedures prescribed by the General Accounting Office.

(b) These regulations also do not preclude an employee from requesting a waiver pursuant to other statutory provisions pertaining to the particular debts being collected.

§ 1408.39 Procedures for salary offset.

(a) The Chairman, or designee of the Chairman, shall determine the amount of an employee's disposable pay and the amount to be deducted from the employee's disposable pay at regular pay intervals.

(b) Deductions shall begin within three official pay periods following the date of mailing or delivery of the Notice of Intent to Collect by Salary Offset.

(c)(1) If the amount of the debt is equal to or is less than 15 percent of the employee's disposable pay, such debt should be collected in one lump-sum deduction.

(2) If the amount of the debt is not collected in one lump-sum deduction, the debt shall be collected in installment deductions over a period of time not greater than the anticipated period

of employment. The size and frequency of installment deductions will bear a reasonable relation to the size of the debt and the employee's ability to pay. However, the amount deducted from any pay period will not exceed 15 percent of the employee's disposable pay for that period, unless the employee has agreed in writing to the deduction of a greater amount.

(3) A deduction exceeding the 15-percent disposable pay limitation may be made from any final salary payment pursuant to 31 U.S.C. 3716 in order to liquidate the debt, whether the employee is being separated voluntarily or involuntarily.

(4) Whenever an employee subject to salary offset is separated from the Corporation and the balance of the debt cannot be liquidated by offset of the final salary check pursuant to 31 U.S.C. 3716, the Corporation may offset any later payments of any kind against the balance of the debt.

(d) In instances where two or more creditor agencies are seeking salary offsets against current employees of the Corporation or where two or more debts are owed to a single creditor agency, the Corporation, at its discretion, may determine whether one or more debts should be offset simultaneously within the 15-percent limitation. Debts owed to the Corporation should generally take precedence over debts owed to other agencies.

§ 1408.40 Refunds.

(a) In instances where the Corporation is the creditor agency, it shall promptly refund any amounts deducted under the authority of 5 U.S.C. 5514 when:

(1) The debt is waived or otherwise found not to be owed to the United States (unless expressly prohibited by statute or regulations); or

(2) An administrative or judicial order directs the Corporation to make a refund.

(b) Unless required or permitted by law or contract, refunds under this section shall not bear interest.

§ 1408.41 Requesting current paying agency to offset salary.

(a) To request a paying agency to impose a salary offset against amounts owed to the debtor, the Corporation shall provide the paying agency with a claim certification which meets the requirements set forth in § 1408.25(a) of this part. The Corporation shall also provide the paying agency with a repayment schedule determined under the provisions of § 1408.39 or in accordance with a repayment agreement entered into with the debtor.

(b) If the employee separates from the paying agency before the debt is paid in full, the paying agency shall certify the total amount collected on the debt. A copy of this certification shall be sent to the employee and a copy shall be sent to the Corporation. If the paying agency is aware that the employee is entitled to payments from the Civil Service Retirement and Disability Fund, or other similar payments, it must provide written notification to the agency responsible for making such payments that the debtor owes a debt (including the amount) and that the provisions of this section have been fully complied with. However, the Corporation must submit a properly certified claim to the agency responsible for making such payments before the collection can be made.

(c) When an employee transfers to another paying agency, the Corporation is not required to repeat the due process procedures set forth in 5 U.S.C. 5514 and this part to resume the collection. The Corporation shall, however, review the debt upon receiving the former paying agency's notice of the employee's transfer to make sure the collection is resumed by the new paying agency.

(d) If a special review is conducted pursuant to § 1408.11 and results in a revised offset or repayment schedule, the Corporation shall provide a new claim certification to the paying agency.

§ 1408.42 Responsibility of the Corporation as the paying agency.

(a) When the Corporation receives a claim certification from a creditor agency, deductions should be scheduled to begin at the next officially established pay interval. The Corporation shall send the debtor written notice which provides:

(1) That the Corporation has received a valid claim certification from the creditor agency;

(2) The date on which salary offset will begin;

(3) The amount of the debt; and

(4) The amount of such deductions.

(b) If, after the creditor agency has submitted the claim certification to the Corporation, the employee transfers to a different agency before the debt is collected in full, the Corporation must certify the total amount collected on the debt. The Corporation shall send a copy of this certification to the creditor agency and a copy to the employee. If the Corporation is aware that the employee is entitled to payments from the Civil Service Retirement Fund and Disability Fund, or other similar payments, it shall provide written notification to the agency responsible for making such payments that the debtor owes a debt (including the amount).

§ 1408.43 Nonwaiver of rights by payments.

An employee's involuntary payment of all or any portion of a debt being collected under this subpart shall not be construed as a waiver of any rights the employee may have under 5 U.S.C. 5514 or any other provisions of a written contract or law unless there are statutory or contractual provisions to the contrary.

PART 1410—PREMIUMS

Sec.

AUTHORITY: Secs. 12 U.S.C. 2020, 2277a–4, 2277a–5, 2277a–7.

SOURCE: 56 FR 3201, Jan. 29, 1991, unless otherwise noted.

§ 1410.1 Purpose and scope.

This part sets forth the rules for:

(a) The calculation of premiums;

(b) The time for payment of the premium required by sections 5.55 and 5.56 of the Farm Credit Act of 1971, as amended;

(c) Interest charges on delinquent payments;

(d) The form and content of certified statements; and,

(e) Documentation supporting certified statements.

§ 1410.2 Definitions.

(a) *Act* means the Farm Credit Act of 1971, as amended.

(b) *Average principal outstanding* means the average annual principal outstanding on a daily basis using balances as of the close of each day. In computing the average annual principal outstanding in this manner, the closing balance of the most recent past business day shall be the closing balance for days when an institution is closed.

(c) *Direct lending association* means any production credit association or any other association making direct loans under authority provided under section 7.6 of the Act, including, without limitation, agricultural credit associations and Federal land credit associations.

(d) *Government-guaranteed loans or investments* means loans or credits or investments, or portions of loans or credits or investments, that are guaranteed:

(1) By the full faith and credit of the United States Government or any State government; or,

(2) By an agency or other entity of the United States Government whose obligations are explicitly guaranteed by the United States Government; or,

(3) By an agency or other entity of a State government whose obligations are explicitly guaranteed by such State government.

(e) *Insured bank* means any Farm Credit bank whose participation in notes, bonds, debentures, and other obligations issued under subsection (c) or (d) of section 4.2 of the Act is insured under part E of title V of the Act, including, without limitation, banks that are in or are placed in receivership or conservatorship to the extent that those banks' participation in such obligations is insured.

(f) *Loan* means any extension of credit or lease resulting from direct negotiations between a lender and a borrowing entity that is recorded as an asset of an insured bank, a direct lending association, or an other financing institution. The term "loan" includes loans, contracts of sale, notes receivable, and other similar obligations and lease financings. The term "loan" includes loans originated through direct negotiations between the insured bank, direct lending association, or other financing institution and a borrowing entity and loans or interests in loans purchased from another lender. Loans purchased subject to recourse shall be considered loans of the seller to the extent of the recourse.

(g)(1) *Nonaccrual loan* means any loan where—

(i) Any amount of outstanding principal and all past and future interest accruals, considered over the full term of the asset, are determined to be uncollectible for any reason; or,

(ii) It has been classified "loss" as a result of a periodic credit evaluation and has not been charged off; or,

(iii) The loan is severely past due and is not adequately secured, in process of collection, and fully collectible with respect to all principal and interest.

(2) For the purposes of determining whether a loan is considered as accrual or nonaccrual under this part, all loans on which a borrowing entity, or a component of a borrowing entity, is primarily obligated to the institution shall be considered as one loan unless a review of all pertinent facts supports a reasonable determination that a particular loan constitutes an independent credit risk and such determination is adequately documented in the loan file.

(h) *Other financing institution* means any bank, company, institution, corporation, union, or association described in section 1.7(b)(1)(B) of the Act.

[56 FR 3201, Jan. 29, 1991; 56 FR 10302, Mar. 11, 1991; 74 FR 17373, Apr. 15, 2009]

§ 1410.3 Calculation and reporting of premiums due.

(a) *Reporting.* For purposes of computing premiums, each insured bank shall, without limitation, report all information concerning the insured bank; each direct lending association that is receiving (or has received) funds provided through the insured bank; and each other financing institution that is receiving (or has received) funds provided through the insured bank; that the Corporation determines is necessary in order to compute the premiums due under the Act.

(b) *Calculating the premium payment for periods from July 1, 2008 through December 31, 2008.* (1) The premium payment for the 3rd Quarter 2008 (defined for purposes of this section as the period from July 1, 2008 through September 30, 2008) and the premium payment for the 4th Quarter 2008 (defined for purposes of this section as the period October 1, 2008, through December 31, 2008) shall be equal to 25 percent of the amount computed by applying the premium calculation formulas contained in sections 5.55 and 5.56 of the Act (unless reduced by the Corporation acting under section 5.55(a)(3) of the Act or under paragraph (d) of this section) to the insured bank during the 3rd Quarter 2008 or 4th Quarter 2008, respectively.

(2) In accord with paragraph (b)(1) of this section, the premium payment for the 3rd Quarter 2008 (having been reduced by the Corporation acting under section 5.55(a)(3) of the Act) shall be equal to 25 percent of the following amount:

(i) The average outstanding insured obligations issued by the bank for the period, after deducting from the obligations the percentages of the guaranteed portions of loans and investments described in section 5.55(a)(2) of the Act, multiplied by 0.0015; and

(ii) The product obtained by multiplying—

(A) The sum of—

(*1*) The average principal outstanding for the period on loans made by the bank (computed in accord with section 5.55 of the Act) that are in nonaccrual status; and

(*2*) The average amount outstanding for the period of other-than-temporarily impaired investments made by the bank (computed in accord with section 5.55 of the Act);

(B) By 0.0010.

(3) In accord with paragraph (b)(1) of this section, the premium payment for the 4th Quarter 2008 (having been reduced by the Corporation acting under section 5.55(a)(3) of the Act) shall be equal to 25 percent of the following amount:

(i) The average outstanding insured obligations issued by the bank for the period, after deducting from the obligations the percentages of the guaranteed portions of loans and investments described in section 5.55(a)(2) of the Act, multiplied by 0.0018; and

(ii) The product obtained by multiplying—

(A) The sum of—

(*1*) The average principal outstanding for the period on loans made by the bank (computed in accord with section 5.55 of the Act) that are in nonaccrual status; and

(*2*) The average amount outstanding for the period of other-than-temporarily impaired investments made by the bank (computed in accord with section 5.55 of the Act);

(B) By 0.0010.

(c) *Calculating the premium payment for periods in 2009 and subsequent years.* (1) The premium payment for periods in calendar year 2009 and subsequent years shall be equal to the amount computed by applying the premium calculation formulas contained in sections 5.55 and 5.56 of the Act (unless reduced by the Corporation acting under section 5.55(a)(3) of the Act or under paragraph (d) of this section) to the insured bank during the period.

(2) In accord with paragraph (c)(1) of this section, the premium payment for the period shall (unless reduced by the Corporation acting under section 5.55(a)(3) of the Act or under paragraph (d) of this section) be equal to:

(i) The average outstanding insured obligations issued by the bank for the period, after deducting from the obligations the percentages of the guaranteed portions of loans and investments described in section 5.55(a)(2), multiplied by 0.0020; and

(ii) The product obtained by multiplying—

(A) The sum of—

(*1*) The average principal outstanding for the period on loans made by the bank (computed in accord with section 5.55 of the Act) that are in nonaccrual status; and

(*2*) The average amount outstanding for the period of other than temporarily impaired investments made by the bank (computed in accord with section 5.55 of the Act);

(B) By 0.0010.

(d) *Secure base amount.* In addition to the Corporation's authority to reduce premiums under section 5.55(a)(3) of the Act, upon reaching the secure base amount determined by the Corporation in accordance with section 5.55 of the Act, the annual premium to be paid by each insured bank, computed in accordance with paragraphs (b) and (c) of this section, shall be reduced by a percentage determined by the Corporation so that the aggregate of the premiums payable by all of the Farm Credit banks for the following calendar year is sufficient to ensure that the Insurance Fund balance is maintained at not less than the secure base amount. The Corporation shall announce any such percentage no later than December 31 of the year prior to the January in which such premiums are to be paid.

[74 FR 17373, Apr. 15, 2009]

§ 1410.4 Payment of premiums.

(a) *Payments.* Each insured bank shall pay to the Corporation the amount of the premium due to the Corporation computed in accordance with sections 5.55 and 5.56 of the Act, and § 1410.3 of this part, and shown on its certified statement, at the time the statement is filed. Certified statements shall be considered to have been filed and payments made in a timely manner if they are received on or before January 31 following the end of the calendar year on which the certified statement is based.

(b) *Premiums as obligations of insured banks.* Premiums required to be paid by § 1410.3 are obligations of the insured banks, and are to be paid at the times required by this section, regardless of whether the insured bank has assessed and collected any assessments under section 1.12 of the Act.

[56 FR 3201, Jan. 29, 1991; 56 FR 10302, Mar. 11, 1991; 74 FR 17374, Apr. 15, 2009]

§ 1410.5 Delinquent premium payments and premium overpayments.

(a) *Delinquent payments.* Each insured bank shall pay to the Corporation interest on delinquent premium payments. All premiums will be considered delinquent if they are received after the time for payment specified in § 1410.4 of this part, including late payments caused by bank errors in the certified statement. The interest rate will be the United States Treasury Department's current value of funds rate, which is issued under the Treasury Fiscal Requirements Manual (TFRM rate) and published quarterly in the FEDERAL REGISTER. The interest rate will be determined as follows:

(1) *Current year.* (i) For delinquent days occurring on or prior to March 31, the rate will be the TFRM rate that is published in the preceding December.

(ii) For delinquent days occurring from April 1 to June 30, the rate will be the TFRM rate that is published in March for the second quarter of the year.

(iii) For delinquent days occurring from July 1 to September 30, the rate will be the TFRM rate that is published in June for the third quarter.

(iv) For delinquent days occurring from October 1 to December 31, the rate will be the TFRM rate that is published in September for the fourth quarter.

(2) *Prior years.* The interest will be calculated quarterly and compounded annually at the rates applicable for each quarter as issued under the TFRM. For the initial year, the rate will be applied to the gross amount of the delinquent payment. For each additional year or portion thereof the rate will be applied to the net amount of the delinquent payment after it has been reduced by any premium credit under paragraph (c) of this section.

(b) *Other rights and remedies.* Payment of the interest specified in paragraph (a) of this section does not affect any other rights and remedies available to the Corporation.

(c) *Overpayments.* To the extent that any payment by a bank exceeds the required amount:

(1) The excess shall be credited against future premium payments by the bank which overpaid; or,

(2)(i) Upon written request to the Corporation by the bank which overpaid, the excess shall be refunded to the bank within 30 days of receipt of the written request; and

(ii) If the Corporation fails to make a refund within such 30-day period, and the Corporation determines that a refund is in order, the Corporation shall pay to the bank interest on the amount of the overpayment, from the end of such 30-day period through the date the refund is issued.

§ 1410.6 Certified statements.

(a) *Forms.* The certified statements required to be filed by insured banks under the provisions of section 5.56 of the Act shall be filed with the Corporation. The certified statement forms will be furnished to all insured banks by, or may be obtained from, the Corporation.

(b) *Amendments to certified statements.* In the event of an amendment or correction of a previously submitted certified statement, the amending insured bank shall resubmit to the Corporation the appropriate certified statement along with a letter of explanation regarding the amendment or correction.

[56 FR 3201, Jan. 29, 1991, as amended at 56 FR 57233, Nov. 8, 1991; 74 FR 17374, Apr. 15, 2009]

§ 1410.7 Documentation.

Each insured bank shall:

(a) Prepare and maintain accurate and complete records as necessary to prepare certified statements, including, but not limited to, records relating to the loans of each direct lending association and other financing institution that are able to make such loans because they are receiving, or have received, funding from the insured bank.

(b) Prepare and maintain on its premises books and records in such a manner as to facilitate reconciliation with certified statements prepared from them.

(c) Maintain in its books and records documentation supporting its certified statement for a period no less than 5 years following the date of each certified statement, unless the bank shall have requested in writing, and the Corporation shall have granted to the bank, written permission to dispose of such documentation prior to the expiration of 5 years.

(d) Make all records and any supporting documentation available, without limitation, to Corporation officials upon request.

PART 1411—RULES OF PRACTICE AND PROCEDURE

AUTHORITY: Secs. 5.58(10), 5.65(c) and (d) of the Farm Credit Act; 12 U.S.C. 2277a–7(10), 2277a–14(c) and (d)); 28 U.S.C. 2461 note.

Subpart A—Rules and Procedures for Assessment and Collection of Civil Money Penalties

§ 1411.1 Inflation adjustment of civil money penalties for failure to file a certified statement, pay any premium required or obtain approval before employment of persons convicted of criminal offenses.

In accordance with the Federal Civil Money Penalties Inflation Adjustment Act of 1990, as amended by the Debt Collection Improvement Act of 1996, a civil money penalty imposed pursuant to section 5.65(c) or (d) of the Act for a violation occurring on or after October 23, 1996 shall not exceed $117 per day for each day the violation continues.

[66 FR 44027, Aug. 22, 2001]

PART 1412—GOLDEN PARACHUTE AND INDEMNIFICATION PAYMENTS

AUTHORITY: 12 U.S.C. 2277a–10b.

SOURCE: 71 FR 7405, Feb. 13, 2006, unless otherwise noted.

§ 1412.1 Scope.

(a) This part limits and/or prohibits, in certain circumstances, the ability of Farm Credit System (System) institutions, their service corporations, subsidiaries and affiliates from making golden parachute and indemnification payments to institution-related parties (IRPs).

(b) This part applies to System institutions in a troubled condition that seek to make golden parachute payments to their IRPs.

(c) The limitations on indemnification payments apply to all System institutions, their service corporations, subsidiaries and affiliates regardless of their financial health.

§ 1412.2 Definitions.

(a) *Act* or *Farm Credit Act* means Farm Credit Act of 1971 (12 U.S.C. 2002(a)), as amended by the Farm Credit System Reform Act of 1996, amending 12 U.S.C. 2277a–10.

(b) *Farm Credit System institution* or *System institution* means any "institution" enumerated in section 1.2 of the Act including, but not limited to, associations, banks, service corporations, the Federal Farm Credit Banks Funding Corporation, the Farm Credit Leasing Services Corporation and their subsidiaries and affiliates, as well as, the Federal Agricultural Mortgage Corporation and its subsidiaries and affiliates, as described in 12 U.S.C. 2279aa–1(a).

(c) *Benefit plan* means any plan, contract, agreement or other arrangement which is an "employee welfare benefit plan" as that term is defined in section 3(1) of the Employee Retirement Income Security Act of 1974, as amended (29 U.S.C. 1002(1)), or other usual and customary plans such as dependent care, tuition reimbursement, group legal services or other benefits provided under a cafeteria plan sponsored by the System institution; provided however, that such term shall not include any plan intended to be subject to paragraph (f)(2)(iii), (vii) and (viii) of this section.

(d) *Bona fide deferred compensation plan or arrangement* means any plan, contract, agreement or other arrangement whereby:

(1) An IRP voluntarily elects to defer all or a portion of the reasonable compensation, wages or fees paid for services rendered which otherwise would

have been paid to such party at the time the services were rendered (including a plan that provides for the crediting of a reasonable investment return on such elective deferrals) and the System institution either:

(i) Recognizes compensation expense and accrues a liability for the benefit payments according to generally accepted accounting principles (GAAP); or

(ii) Segregates or otherwise sets aside assets in a trust which may only be used to pay plan and other benefits, except that the assets of such trust may be available to satisfy claims of the System institution's creditors in the case of insolvency; or

(2) The System institution establishes a nonqualified deferred compensation or supplemental retirement plan, other than an elective deferral plan described in paragraph (d)(1) of this section:

(i) Primarily for the purpose of providing benefits for certain IRPs in excess of the limitations on contributions and benefits imposed by sections 415, 401(a)(17), 402(g) or any other applicable provision of the Internal Revenue Code of 1986 (26 U.S.C. 415, 401(a)(17), 402(g)); or

(ii) Primarily for the purpose of providing supplemental retirement benefits or other deferred compensation for a select group of directors, management or highly compensated employees (excluding severance payments described in paragraph (f)(2)(v) of this section and permissible golden parachute payments described in §1412.5); and

(3) In the case of any nonqualified deferred compensation or supplemental retirement plans as described in paragraphs (d)(1) and (2) of this section, the following requirements shall apply:

(i) The plan was in effect at least 1 year prior to any of the events described in paragraph (f)(1)(ii) of this section;

(ii) Any payment made pursuant to such plan is made in accordance with the terms of the plan as in effect no later than 1 year prior to any of the events described in paragraph (f)(1)(ii) of this section and in accordance with any amendments to such plan during such 1 year period that do not increase the benefits payable thereunder;

(iii) The IRP has a vested right, as defined under the applicable plan document, at the time of termination of employment to payments under such plan;

(iv) Benefits under such plan are accrued each period only for current or prior service rendered to the employer (except that an allowance may be made for service with a predecessor employer);

(v) Any payment made pursuant to such plan is not based on any discretionary acceleration of vesting or accrual of benefits which occurs at any time later than 1 year prior to any of the events described in paragraph (f)(1)(ii) of this section;

(vi) The System institution has previously recognized compensation expense and accrued a liability for the benefit payments according to GAAP or segregated or otherwise set aside assets in a trust which may only be used to pay plan benefits, except that the assets of such trust may be available to satisfy claims of the System institution's creditors in the case of insolvency; and

(vii) Payments pursuant to such plans shall not be in excess of the accrued liability computed in accordance with GAAP.

(e) *Corporation or FCSIC* mean the Farm Credit System Insurance Corporation, in its corporate capacity.

(f) *Golden parachute payment.* (1) The term "golden parachute payment" means any payment (or any agreement to make any payment) in the nature of compensation by any System institution for the benefit of any current or former IRP pursuant to an obligation of such System institution that:

(i) Is contingent on the termination of such party's primary employment or relationship with the System institution; and

(ii) Is received on or after, or is made in contemplation of, any of the following events:

(A) The insolvency (or similar event) of the System institution which is making the payment or bankruptcy or insolvency (or similar event) of the service corporation, subsidiary or affiliate which is making the payment; or

(B) The System institution is assigned a composite rating of 4 or 5 by the FCA; or

(C) The appointment of any conservator or receiver for such System institution; or

(D) A determination by the Corporation, that the System institution is in a troubled condition, as defined in paragraph (m) of this section; and

(iii) Is payable to an IRP whose employment by or relationship with a System institution is terminated at a time when the System institution by which the IRP is employed or related satisfies any of the conditions enumerated in paragraphs (f)(1)(ii)(A) through (D) of this section, or in contemplation of any of these conditions.

(2) *Exceptions.* The term "golden parachute payment" shall not include:

(i) Any payment made pursuant to a pension or retirement plan which is qualified (or is intended within a reasonable period of time to be qualified) under section 401 of the Internal Revenue Code of 1986 (26 U.S.C. 401); or

(ii) Any payment made pursuant to a benefit plan as that term is defined in paragraph (c) of this section; or

(iii) Any payment made pursuant to a "bona fide" deferred compensation plan or arrangement as defined in paragraph (d) of this section; or

(iv) Any payment made by reason of death or by reason of termination caused by the disability of IRP; or

(v) Any severance or similar payment which is required to be made pursuant to a state statute or foreign law which is applicable to all employers within the appropriate jurisdiction (with the exception of employers that may be exempt due to their small number of employees or other similar criteria); or

(vi) Any other payment which the Corporation determines to be permissible in accordance with §1412.6, on permissible indemnification payments; or

(vii) Any payment made pursuant to a nondiscriminatory severance pay plan or arrangement that provides for payment of severance benefits to all eligible employees upon involuntary termination other than for cause, voluntary resignation, or early retirement. Furthermore, such severance pay plan or arrangement shall not have been adopted or modified to increase the amount or scope of severance benefits at a time when the System institution was in a condition specified in paragraph (f)(1)(ii) of this section or in contemplation of such a condition without the prior written consent of the FCA; or in lieu of a payment made pursuant to this paragraph;

(viii) Any payment made pursuant to a severance pay plan or arrangement that provides severance benefits upon involuntary termination other than for cause, voluntary resignation, or early retirement. No employee shall receive any payment under this subpart which exceeds the base compensation paid to such employee during the 12 months (or longer period or greater benefit as the Corporation shall consent to) immediately proceeding termination of employment. Furthermore, such severance pay plan or arrangement shall not have been adopted or modified to increase the amount or the scope of the severance benefits at a time when the System institution was in a condition specified in paragraph (f)(1)(ii) of this section or in contemplation of such a condition without the written approval of the FCA.

(g) The *FCA* means the Farm Credit Administration.

(h) *Institution-related party (IRP)* means:

(1) Any director, officer, employee, or controlling stockholder (other than another Farm Credit System institution) of, or agent for a System institution;

(2) Any stockholder (other than another Farm Credit System institution), consultant, joint venture partner, and any other person as determined by the FCA (by regulation or case-by-case) who participates in the conduct of the affairs of a System institution; and

(3) Any independent contractor (including any attorney, appraiser, or accountant) who knowingly or recklessly participates in any violation of any law or regulation, any breach of fiduciary duty, or any unsafe or unsound practice, which caused or is likely to cause more than a minimal financial loss to, or a significant adverse effect on, the System institution.

(i) *Liability or legal expense* means:

(1) Any legal or other professional fees and expenses incurred in connection with any claim, proceeding, or action;

(2) The amount of, and any cost incurred in connection with, any settlement of any claim, proceeding, or actions; and

(3) The amount of, any cost incurred in connection with, any judgment or penalty imposed with respect to any claim, processing, or action.

(j) *Nondiscriminatory* means that the plan, contract or arrangement in question applies to all employees of a System institution who meet reasonable and customary eligibility requirements applicable to all employees, such as minimum length of service requirements. A nondiscriminatory plan, contract or arrangement may provide different benefits based only on objective criteria such as salary, total compensation, length of service, job grade or classification, which are applied on a proportionate basis, with a modest disparity in severance benefits relating to any one criterion of 20 percent.

(k) *Payment* means:

(1) Any direct or indirect transfer of any funds or any asset;

(2) Any forgiveness of any debt or other obligation;

(3) The conferring of benefits in the nature of compensation, including but not limited to stock options and stock appreciation rights; or

(4) Any segregation of any funds or assets, the establishment or funding of any trust or the purchase of or arrangement for any letter of credit or other instrument, for the purpose of making, or pursuant to any agreement to make, any payment on or after the date on which such funds or assets are segregated, or at the time of or after such trust is established or letter of credit or other instrument is made available, without regard to whether the obligation to make such payment is contingent on:

(i) The determination, after such date, of the liability for the payment of such amount; or

(ii) The liquidation, after such date, of the amount of such payment.

(l) *Prohibited indemnification payment.* (1) The term "prohibited indemnification payment" means any payment (or any agreement or arrangement to make any payment) by any System institution for the benefit of any person who is or was an IRP of such System institution, to pay or reimburse such person for any civil money penalty or judgment resulting from any administrative or civil action instituted by the FCA, or any other liability or legal expense with regard to any administrative proceeding or civil action instituted by the FCA which results in a final order or settlement pursuant to which such person:

(i) Is assessed a civil money penalty;

(ii) Is removed from office or prohibited from participating in the conduct of the affairs of the institution; or

(iii) Is required to cease and desist from or take any affirmative action with respect to such institution.

(2) *Exceptions.* (i) The term "prohibited indemnification" payment shall not include any reasonable payment by a System institution which is used to purchase any commercial insurance policy or fidelity bond, provided that such insurance policy or bond shall not be used to pay or reimburse an IRP for the cost of any judgment or civil money penalty assessed against such person in an administrative proceeding or civil action commenced by the FCA, but may pay any legal or professional expenses incurred in connection with such proceeding or action or the amount of any restitution to the System institution or receiver.

(ii) The term "prohibited indemnification payment" shall not include any reasonable payment by a System institution that represents partial indemnification for legal or professional expenses specifically attributable to particular charges for which there has been a formal and final adjudication or finding in connection with a settlement that the IRP has not violated certain FCA laws or regulations or has not engaged in certain unsafe or unsound practices or breaches of fiduciary duty, unless the administrative action or civil proceedings has resulted in a final prohibition order against the IRP.

(m) *Troubled condition* means a System institution that:

(1) Is subject to a cease-and-desist order or written agreement issued by

the FCA that requires action to improve the financial condition of the System institution or is subject to a proceeding initiated by the FCA which contemplates the issuance of an order that requires action to improve the financial condition of the institution, unless otherwise informed in writing by the FCA; or

(2) Is unable to make a timely payment of principal or interest on any insured obligation (as defined in section 5.51(3) of the Farm Credit Act; 12 U.S.C. 2277a(3)); or

(3) Is receiving assistance as described in section 5.61 of the Farm Credit Act, 12 U.S.C. 2277a–10; or

(4) Is unable to make timely payment of principal or interest on debt obligations issued under the authority of section 8.6(e)(2) of the Farm Credit Act; 12 U.S.C. 2279aa–6(e)(2) or is unable to fulfill the guarantee obligations provided under section 8.6 of the Farm Credit Act; 12 U.S.C. 2279aa–6; or

(5) Is informed in writing by the Corporation that it is in a "troubled condition" for purposes of the requirements of this subpart on the basis of the System institution's most recent report of condition or report of examination or other information available to the Corporation.

§ 1412.3 Golden parachute payments prohibited.

No System institution shall make or agree to make any golden parachute payment, except as provided in this part.

§ 1412.4 Prohibited indemnification payments.

No System institution shall make or agree to make any prohibited indemnification payment, except as provided in this part.

§ 1412.5 Permissible golden parachute payments.

(a) A System institution may agree to make or may make a golden parachute payment if and to the extent that:

(1) The FCA, with the written concurrence of the Corporation, determines that such a payment or agreement is permissible; or

(2) Such an agreement is made in order to hire a person to become an IRP either at a time when the System institution satisfies or in an effort to prevent it from imminently satisfying any of the criteria set forth in § 1412.2(f)(1)(ii), and the FCA and the Corporation consent in writing to the amount and terms of the golden parachute payment. Such consent by the Corporation and the FCA shall not improve the IRP's position in the event of the insolvency of the institution since such consent can neither bind a receiver nor affect the provability of receivership claims. In the event that the institution is placed into receivership or conservatorship, the Corporation and/or the FCA shall not be obligated to pay the promised golden parachute and the IRP shall not be accorded preferential treatment on the basis of such prior approval; or

(3) Such a payment is made pursuant to an agreement which provides for a reasonable severance payment, not to exceed 18-months' salary, to an IRP in the event of a change in control of the System institution; *provided, however*, that the System institution shall obtain the consent of the FCA prior to making such a payment and this paragraph (a)(3) shall not apply to any change in control of System institution which results from an assisted transaction as described in section 5.61 of the Farm Credit Act; 12 U.S.C. 2277a–10 or the System institution being placed into conservatorship or receivership; and

(4) A System institution or IRP making a request pursuant to paragraphs (a)(1) through (3) of this section shall demonstrate that it is not aware of any information, evidence, documents or other materials which would indicate that there is a reasonable basis to believe, at the time such payment is proposed to be made, that:

(i) The IRP has committed any fraudulent act or omission, breach of trust or fiduciary duty, or insider abuse with regard to the System institution that has had or is likely to have a material adverse effect on the institution;

(ii) The IRP is substantially responsible for the insolvency of, the appointment of a conservator or receiver for, or the troubled condition, as defined by applicable regulations concerning the System institution;

(iii) The IRP has materially violated any applicable Federal or state law or regulation that has had or is likely to have a material effect on the System institution; and

(iv) The IRP has violated or conspired to violate section 215, 657, 1006, 1014, or 1344 of title 18 of the United States Code or section 1341 or 1343 of such title affecting a Farm Credit System institution.

(b) In making a determination under paragraphs (a)(1) through (3) of this section the FCA and the Corporation may consider:

(1) Whether, and to what degree, the IRP was in a position of managerial or fiduciary responsibility;

(2) The length of time the IRP was affiliated with the System institution, and the degree to which the proposed payment represents reasonable compensation earned over the period of employment and reasonable payment for services rendered; and

(3) Any other factors or circumstances which would indicate that the proposed payment would be contrary to the intent of the Act or this part.

§ 1412.6 Permissible indemnification payments.

(a) A System institution may make or agree to make reasonable indemnification payments to an IRP with respect to an administrative proceeding or civil action initiated by the FCA if:

(1) The System institution's board of directors, in good faith, determines in writing after due investigation and consideration that the IRP acted in good faith and in a manner he/she believed to be in the best interests of the institution;

(2) The System institution's board of directors, in good faith, determines in writing after due investigation and consideration that the payment of such expenses will not materially adversely affect the institution's safety and soundness;

(3) The indemnification payments do not constitute prohibited indemnification payments as that term is defined in § 1412.2(l); and

(4) The IRP agrees in writing to reimburse the System institution, to the extent not covered by payments from insurance or bonds purchased pursuant to § 1412.2(l)(2), for that portion of the advanced indemnification payments which subsequently become prohibited indemnification payments, as defined herein.

(b) An IRP requesting indemnification payments shall not participate in any way in the board's discussion and approval of such payments; *provided, however*, that such IRP may present his/her request to the board and respond to any inquiries from the board concerning his/her involvement in the circumstances giving rise to the administrative proceeding or civil action.

(c) In the event that a majority of the members of the board of directors are named as respondents in an administrative proceeding or civil action and request indemnification, the remaining members of the board may authorize independent legal counsel to review the indemnification request and provide the remaining members of the board with a written opinion of counsel as to whether the conditions delineated in paragraph (a) of this section have been met. If independent legal counsel opines that said conditions have been met, the remaining members of the board of directors may rely on such opinion in authorizing the requested indemnification.

(d) In the event that all of the members of the board of directors are named as respondents in an administrative proceeding or civil action and request indemnification, the board shall authorize independent legal counsel to review the indemnification request and provide the board with a written opinion of counsel as to whether the conditions delineated in paragraph (a) of this section have been met. If independent legal counsel opines that said conditions have been met, the board of directors may rely on such opinion in authorizing the requested indemnification.

§ 1412.7 Filing instructions.

Requests to make excess nondiscriminatory severance plan payments and permitted golden parachute payments shall be submitted in writing to the

FCA and the Corporation. The request shall be in letter form and shall contain all relevant factual information as well as the reasons why such approval should be granted.

§ 1412.8 Application in the event of receivership.

The provisions of this part or any consent or approval granted under the provisions of this part by the Corporation (in its corporate capacity), shall not in any way bind any receiver of a failed System institution. Any consent or approval granted under the provisions of this part by the Corporation or the FCA shall not in any way obligate such agency or receiver to pay any claim or obligation pursuant to any golden parachute, severance, indemnification or other agreement. Claims for employee welfare benefits or other benefits which are contingent, even if otherwise vested, when the Corporation is appointed as receiver for any System institution, including any contingency for termination of employment, are not provable claims or actual, direct compensatory damage claims against such receiver. Nothing in this part may be construed to permit the payment of salary or any liability or legal expense of any IRP contrary to 12 U.S.C. 2277a–10b(d).

CHAPTER XV—DEPARTMENT OF THE TREASURY

SUBCHAPTER A—GENERAL PROVISIONS

SUBCHAPTER B—RESOLUTION FUNDING CORPORATION

SUBCHAPTER A—GENERAL PROVISIONS

PART 1500—MERCHANT BANKING INVESTMENTS

Sec.

AUTHORITY: 12 U.S.C. 1843(k).

SOURCE: Reg. Y, 66 FR 8489, Jan. 31, 2001, unless otherwise noted.

§ 1500.1 What type of investments are permitted by this part, and under what conditions may they be made?

(a) *What types of investments are permitted by this part?* Section 4(k)(4)(H) of the Bank Holding Company Act (12 U.S.C. 1843(k)(4)(H)) and this part authorize a financial holding company, directly or indirectly and as principal or on behalf of one or more persons, to acquire or control any amount of shares, assets or ownership interests of a company or other entity that is engaged in any activity not otherwise authorized for the financial holding company under section 4 of the Bank Holding Company Act. For purposes of this part, shares, assets or ownership interests acquired or controlled under section 4(k)(4)(H) and this part are referred to as "merchant banking investments." A financial holding company may not directly or indirectly acquire or control any merchant banking investment except in compliance with the requirements of this part.

(b) *Must the investment be a bona fide merchant banking investment?* The acquisition or control of shares, assets or ownership interests under this part is not permitted unless it is part of a bona fide underwriting or merchant or investment banking activity.

(c) *What types of ownership interests may be acquired?* Shares, assets or ownership interests of a company or other entity include any debt or equity security, warrant, option, partnership interest, trust certificate or other instrument representing an ownership interest in the company or entity, whether voting or nonvoting.

(d) *Where in a financial holding company may merchant banking investments be made?* A financial holding company and any subsidiary (other than a depository institution or subsidiary of a depository institution) may acquire or control merchant banking investments. A financial holding company and its subsidiaries may not acquire or control merchant banking investments on behalf of a depository institution or subsidiary of a depository institution.

(e) *May assets other than shares be held directly?* A financial holding company may not under this part acquire or control assets, other than debt or equity securities or other ownership interests in a company, unless:

(1) The assets are held by or promptly transferred to a portfolio company;

(2) The portfolio company maintains policies, books and records, accounts, and other indicia of corporate, partnership or limited liability organization and operation that are separate from the financial holding company and limit the legal liability of the financial holding company for obligations of the portfolio company; and

(3) The portfolio company has management that is separate from the financial holding company to the extent required by § 1500.2.

(f) *What type of affiliate is required for a financial holding company to make merchant banking investments?* A financial holding company may not acquire or control merchant banking investments under this part unless the financial holding company qualifies under at least one of the following paragraphs:

(1) *Securities affiliate.* The financial holding company is or has an affiliate that is registered under the Securities Exchange Act of 1934 (15 U.S.C. 78c, 78o, 78o–4) as:

(i) A broker or dealer; or

(ii) A municipal securities dealer, including a separately identifiable department or division of a bank that is registered as a municipal securities dealer.

(2) *Insurance affiliate with an investment adviser affiliate.* The financial holding company controls:

(i) An insurance company that is predominantly engaged in underwriting life, accident and health, or property and casualty insurance (other than credit-related insurance), or providing and issuing annuities; and

(ii) A company that:

(A) Is registered with the Securities and Exchange Commission as an investment adviser under the Investment Advisers Act of 1940 (15 U.S.C. 80b–1 *et seq.*); and

(B) Provides investment advice to an insurance company.

§ 1500.2 What are the limitations on managing or operating a portfolio company held as a merchant banking investment?

(a) *May a financial holding company routinely manage or operate a portfolio company?* Except as permitted in paragraph (e) of this section, a financial holding company may not routinely manage or operate any portfolio company.

(b) *When does a financial holding company routinely manage or operate a company?*—(1) *Examples of routine management or operation*—(i) *Executive officer interlocks at the portfolio company.* A financial holding company routinely manages or operates a portfolio company if any director, officer or employee of the financial holding company serves as or has the responsibilities of an executive officer of the portfolio company.

(ii) *Interlocks by executive officers of the financial holding company*—(A) *Prohibition.* A financial holding company routinely manages or operates a portfolio company if any executive officer of the financial holding company serves as or has the responsibilities of an officer or employee of the portfolio company.

(B) *Definition.* For purposes of paragraph (b)(1)(ii)(A) of this section, the term "financial holding company" includes the financial holding company and only the following subsidiaries of the financial holding company:

(*1*) A securities broker or dealer registered under the Securities Exchange Act of 1934;

(*2*) A depository institution;

(*3*) An affiliate that engages in merchant banking activities under this part or insurance company investment activities under section 4(k)(4)(I) of the Bank Holding Company Act (12 U.S.C. 1843(k)(4)(I));

(*4*) A small business investment company (as defined in section 302(b) of the Small Business Investment Act of 1958 (15 U.S.C. 682(b)) controlled by the financial holding company or by any depository institution controlled by the financial holding company; and

(*5*) Any other affiliate that engages in significant equity investment activities that are subject to a special capital charge under the capital adequacy rules or guidelines of the Board.

(iii) *Covenants regarding ordinary course of business.* A financial holding company routinely manages or operates a portfolio company if any covenant or other contractual arrangement exists between the financial holding company and the portfolio company that would restrict the portfolio company's ability to make routine business decisions, such as entering into transactions in the ordinary course of business or hiring officers or employees other than executive officers.

(2) *Presumptions of routine management or operation.* A financial holding company is presumed to routinely manage or operate a portfolio company if:

(i) Any director, officer, or employee of the financial holding company serves as or has the responsibilities of an officer (other than an executive officer) or employee of the portfolio company; or

(ii) Any officer or employee of the portfolio company is supervised by any director, officer, or employee of the financial holding company (other than in that individual's capacity as a director of the portfolio company).

(c) *How may a financial holding company rebut a presumption that it is routinely managing or operating a portfolio company?* A financial holding company may rebut a presumption that it is routinely managing or operating a portfolio company under paragraph (b)(2) of this section by presenting information to the Board demonstrating to the Board's satisfaction that the financial holding company is not routinely managing or operating the portfolio company.

(d) *What arrangements do not involve routinely managing or operating a portfolio company?*—(1) *Director representation at portfolio companies.* A financial holding company may select any or all of the directors of a portfolio company or have one or more of its directors, officers, or employees serve as directors of a portfolio company if:

(i) The portfolio company employs officers and employees responsible for routinely managing and operating the company; and

(ii) The financial holding company does not routinely manage or operate the portfolio company, except as permitted in paragraph (e) of this section.

(2) *Covenants or other provisions regarding extraordinary events.* A financial holding company may, by virtue of covenants or other written agreements with a portfolio company, restrict the ability of the portfolio company, or require the portfolio company to consult with or obtain the approval of the financial holding company, to take actions outside of the ordinary course of the business of the portfolio company. Examples of the types of actions that may be subject to these types of covenants or agreements include, but are not limited to, the following:

(i) The acquisition of significant assets or control of another company by the portfolio company or any of its subsidiaries;

(ii) Removal or selection of an independent accountant or auditor or investment banker by the portfolio company;

(iii) Significant changes to the business plan or accounting methods or policies of the portfolio company;

(iv) Removal or replacement of any or all of the executive officers of the portfolio company;

(v) The redemption, authorization or issuance of any equity or debt securities (including options, warrants or convertible shares) of the portfolio company or any borrowing by the portfolio company outside of the ordinary course of business;

(vi) The amendment of the articles of incorporation or by-laws (or similar governing documents) of the portfolio company; and

(vii) The sale, merger, consolidation, spin-off, recapitalization, liquidation, dissolution or sale of substantially all of the assets of the portfolio company or any of its significant subsidiaries.

(3) *Providing advisory and underwriting services to, and having consultations with, a portfolio company.* A financial holding company may:

(i) Provide financial, investment and management consulting advice to a portfolio company in a manner consistent with and subject to any restrictions on such activities contained in §§ 225.28(b)(6) or 225.86(b)(1) of the Board's Regulation Y (12 CFR 225.28(b)(6) and 225.86(b)(1));

(ii) Provide assistance to a portfolio company in connection with the underwriting or private placement of its securities, including acting as the underwriter or placement agent for such securities; and

(iii) Meet with the officers or employees of a portfolio company to monitor or provide advice with respect to the portfolio company's performance or activities.

(e) *When may a financial holding company routinely manage or operate a portfolio company?*—(1) *Special circumstances required.* A financial holding company may routinely manage or operate a portfolio company only when intervention by the financial holding company is necessary or required to obtain a reasonable return on the financial holding company's investment in the portfolio company upon resale or other disposition of the investment, such as to avoid or address a significant operating loss or in connection with a loss of senior management at the portfolio company.

(2) *Duration Limited.* A financial holding company may routinely manage or operate a portfolio company only for the period of time as may be necessary to address the cause of the financial holding company's involvement, to obtain suitable alternative management arrangements, to dispose of the investment, or to otherwise obtain a reasonable return upon the resale or disposition of the investment.

(3) *Notice required for extended involvement.* A financial holding company may not routinely manage or operate a portfolio company for a period greater than nine months without prior written notice to the Board.

(4) *Documentation required.* A financial holding company must maintain and make available to the Board upon request a written record describing its involvement in routinely managing or operating a portfolio company.

(f) *May a depository institution or its subsidiary routinely manage or operate a portfolio company?*—(1) *In general.* A depository institution and a subsidiary of a depository institution may not routinely manage or operate a portfolio company in which an affiliated company owns or controls an interest under this part.

(2) *Definition applying provisions governing routine management or operation.* For purposes of this section other than paragraph (e) and for purposes of § 1500.4(d), a financial holding company includes a depository institution controlled by the financial holding company and a subsidiary of such a depository institution.

(3) *Exception for certain subsidiaries of depository institutions.* For purposes of paragraph (e) of this section, a financial holding company includes a financial subsidiary held in accordance with section 5136A of the Revised Statutes (12 U.S.C. 24a) or section 46 of the Federal Deposit Insurance Act (12 U.S.C. 1831w), and a subsidiary that is a small business investment company and that is held in accordance with the Small Business Investment Act (15 U.S.C. 661 *et seq.*), and such a subsidiary may, in accordance with the limitations set forth in this section, routinely manage or operate a portfolio company in which an affiliated company owns or controls an interest under this part.

§ 1500.3 What are the holding periods permitted for merchant banking investments?

(a) *Must investments be made for resale?* A financial holding company may own or control shares, assets and ownership interests pursuant to this part only for a period of time to enable the sale or disposition thereof on a reasonable basis consistent with the financial viability of the financial holding company's merchant banking investment activities.

(b) *What period of time is generally permitted for holding merchant banking investments?*—(1) *In general.* Except as provided in this section or § 1500.4, a financial holding company may not, directly or indirectly, own, control or hold any share, asset or ownership interest pursuant to this part for a period that exceeds 10 years.

(2) *Ownership interests acquired from or transferred to companies held under this part.* For purposes of paragraph (b)(1) of this section, shares, assets or ownership interests—

(i) Acquired by a financial holding company from a company in which the financial holding company held an interest under this part will be considered to have been acquired by the financial holding company on the date that the share, asset or ownership interest was acquired by the company; and

(ii) Acquired by a company from a financial holding company will be considered to have been acquired by the company on the date that the share, asset or ownership interest was acquired by the financial holding company if—

(A) The financial holding company held the share, asset, or ownership interest under this part; and

(B) The financial holding company holds an interest in the acquiring company under this part.

(3) *Interests previously held by a financial holding company under limited authority.* For purposes of paragraph (b)(1) of this section, any shares, assets, or ownership interests previously owned or controlled, directly or indirectly, by a financial holding company under any other provision of the Federal banking laws that imposes a limited holding period will if acquired under this part be

considered to have been acquired by the financial holding company under this part on the date the financial holding company first acquired ownership or control of the shares, assets or ownership interests under such other provision of law. For purposes of this paragraph (b)(3), a financial holding company includes a depository institution controlled by the financial holding company and any subsidiary of such a depository institution.

(4) *Approval required to hold interests held in excess of time limit.* A financial holding company may seek Board approval to own, control or hold shares, assets or ownership interests of a company under this part for a period that exceeds the period specified in paragraph (b)(1) of this section. A request for approval must:

(i) Be submitted to the Board at least 90 days prior to the expiration of the applicable time period;

(ii) Provide the reasons for the request, including information that addresses the factors in paragraph (b)(5) of this section; and

(iii) Explain the financial holding company's plan for divesting the shares, assets or ownership interests.

(5) *Factors governing Board determinations.* In reviewing any proposal under paragraph (b)(4) of this section, the Board may consider all the facts and circumstances related to the investment, including:

(i) The cost to the financial holding company of disposing of the investment within the applicable period;

(ii) The total exposure of the financial holding company to the company and the risks that disposing of the investment may pose to the financial holding company;

(iii) Market conditions;

(iv) The nature of the portfolio company's business;

(v) The extent and history of involvement by the financial holding company in the management and operations of the company; and

(vi) The average holding period of the financial holding company's merchant banking investments.

(6) *Restrictions applicable to investments held beyond time period.* A financial holding company that directly or indirectly owns, controls or holds any share, asset or ownership interest of a company under this part for a total period that exceeds the period specified in paragraph (b)(1) of this section must—

(i) For purposes of determining the financial holding company's regulatory capital, apply to the financial holding company's adjusted carrying value of such shares, assets, or ownership interests a capital charge determined by the Board that must be:

(A) Higher than the maximum marginal Tier 1 capital charge applicable under the Board's capital adequacy rules or guidelines (*see* 12 CFR 225 appendix A) to merchant banking investments held by that financial holding company; and

(B) In no event less than 25 percent of the adjusted carrying value of the investment; and

(ii) Abide by any other restrictions that the Board may impose in connection with granting approval under paragraph (b)(4) of this section.

§ 1500.4 How are investments in private equity funds treated under this part?

(a) *What is a private equity fund?* For purposes of this part, a "private equity fund" is any company that:

(1) Is formed for the purpose of and is engaged exclusively in the business of investing in shares, assets, and ownership interests of financial and nonfinancial companies for resale or other disposition;

(2) Is not an operating company;

(3) No more than 25 percent of the total equity of which is held, owned or controlled, directly or indirectly, by the financial holding company and its directors, officers, employees and principal shareholders;

(4) Has a maximum term of not more than 15 years; and

(5) Is not formed or operated for the purpose of making investments inconsistent with the authority granted under section 4(k)(4)(H) of the Bank Holding Company Act (12 U.S.C. 1843(k)(4)(H)) or evading the limitations governing merchant banking investments contained in this part.

(b) *What form may a private equity fund take?* A private equity fund may be a corporation, partnership, limited liability company or other type of company that issues ownership interests in any form.

(c) *What is the holding period permitted for interests in private equity funds?*—(1) *In general.* A financial holding company may own, control or hold any interest in a private equity fund under this part and any interest in a portfolio company that is owned or controlled by a private equity fund in which the financial holding company owns or controls any interest under this part for the duration of the fund, up to a maximum of 15 years.

(2) *Request to hold interest for longer period.* A financial holding company may seek Board approval to own, control or hold an interest in or held through a private equity fund for a period longer than the duration of the fund in accordance with § 1500.3(b) of this part.

(3) *Application of rules.* The rules described in § 1500.3(b)(2) and (3) governing holding periods of interests acquired, transferred or previously held by a financial holding company apply to interests in, held through, or acquired from a private equity fund.

(d) *How do the restrictions on routine management and operation apply to private equity funds and investments held through a private equity fund?—(1) Portfolio companies held through a private equity fund.* A financial holding company may not routinely manage or operate a portfolio company that is owned or controlled by a private equity fund in which the financial holding company owns or controls any interest under this part, except as permitted under § 1500.2(e).

(2) *Private equity funds controlled by a financial holding company.* A private equity fund that is controlled by a financial holding company may not routinely manage or operate a portfolio company, except as permitted under § 1500.2(e).

(3) *Private equity funds that are not controlled by a financial holding company.* A private equity fund may routinely manage or operate a portfolio company so long as no financial holding company controls the private equity fund or as permitted under § 1500.2(e).

(4) *When does a financial holding company control a private equity fund?* A financial holding company controls a private equity fund for purposes of this part if the financial holding company, including any director, officer, employee or principal shareholder of the financial holding company:

(i) Serves as a general partner, managing member, or trustee of the private equity fund (or serves in a similar role with respect to the private equity fund);

(ii) Owns or controls 25 percent or more of any class of voting shares or similar interests in the private equity fund;

(iii) In any manner selects, controls or constitutes a majority of the directors, trustees or management of the private equity fund; or

(iv) Owns or controls more than 5 percent of any class of voting shares or similar interests in the private equity fund and is the investment adviser to the fund.

§ 1500.5 What aggregate thresholds apply to merchant banking investments?

(a) *In general.* A financial holding company may not, without Board approval, directly or indirectly acquire any additional shares, assets or ownership interests under this part or make any additional capital contribution to any company the shares, assets or ownership interests of which are held by the financial holding company under this part if the aggregate carrying value of all merchant banking investments held by the financial holding company under this part exceeds:

(1) 30 percent of the Tier 1 capital of the financial holding company; or

(2) After excluding interests in private equity funds, 20 percent of the Tier 1 capital of the financial holding company

(b) *How do these thresholds apply to a private equity fund?* Paragraph (a) of this section applies to the interest acquired or controlled by the financial holding company under this part in a private equity fund. Paragraph (a) of this section does not apply to any interest in a company held by a private equity fund or to any interest held by a person that is not affiliated with the financial holding company.

(c) *How long do these thresholds remain in effect?* This § 1500.5 shall cease to be effective on the date that a final rule issued by the Board that specifically addresses the appropriate regulatory capital treatment of merchant banking investments becomes effective.

§ 1500.6 What risk management, record keeping and reporting policies are required to make merchant banking investments?

(a) *What internal controls and records are necessary?*—(1) *General.* A financial holding company, including a private equity fund controlled by a financial holding company, that makes investments under this part must establish and maintain policies, procedures, records and systems reasonably designed to conduct, monitor and manage such investment activities and the risks associated with such investment activities in a safe and sound manner, including policies, procedures, records and systems reasonably designed to:

(i) Monitor and assess the carrying value, market value and performance of each investment and the aggregate portfolio;

(ii) Identify and manage the market, credit, concentration and other risks associated with such investments;

(iii) Identify, monitor and assess the terms, amounts and risks arising from transactions and relationships (including contingent fees or contingent interests) with each company in which the financial holding company holds an interest under this part;

(iv) Ensure the maintenance of corporate separateness between the financial holding company and each company in which the financial holding company holds an interest under this part and protect the financial holding company and its depository institution subsidiaries from legal liability for the operations conducted and financial obligations of each such company; and

(v) Ensure compliance with this part.

(2) *Availability of records.* A financial holding company must make the policies, procedures and records required by paragraph (a)(1) of this section available to the Board or the appropriate Reserve Bank upon request.

(b) Certain additional recordkeeping and reporting requirements for merchant banking investments are set forth in the Board's Regulation Y, 12 CFR 225.175.

§ 1500.7 How do the statutory cross marketing and sections 23A and B limitations apply to merchant banking investments?

Certain cross-marketing limitations and limitations under sections 23A and 23B of the Federal Reserve Act (12 U.S.C. 371c, 371c-1) applicable to merchant banking investments are set forth in the Board's Regulation Y, 12 CFR 225.176.

§ 1500.8 Definitions.

(a) *What do references to a financial holding company include?*—(1) Except as otherwise expressly provided, the term "financial holding company" as used in this part means the financial holding company and all of its subsidiaries, including a private equity fund or other fund controlled by the financial holding company.

(2) Except as otherwise expressly provided, the term "financial holding company" does not include a depository institution or subsidiary of a depository institution or any portfolio company controlled directly or indirectly by the financial holding company.

(b) *What do references to a depository institution include?* For purposes of this part, the term "depository institution" includes a U.S. branch or agency of a foreign bank.

(c) *What is a portfolio company?* A portfolio company is any company or entity:

(1) That is engaged in any activity not authorized for the financial holding company under section 4 of the Bank Holding Company Act (12 U.S.C. 1843); and

(2) Any shares, assets or ownership interests of which are held, owned or controlled directly or indirectly by the financial holding company pursuant to this part, including through a private equity fund that the financial holding company controls.

(d) *Who are the executive officers of a company?*—(1) An executive officer of a company is any person who participates or has the authority to participate (other than in the capacity as a director) in major policymaking functions of the company, whether or not the officer has an official title, the title designates the officer as an assistant, or the officer serves without salary or other compensation.

(2) The term "executive officer" does not include—

(i) Any person, including a person with an official title, who may exercise a certain measure of discretion in the performance of his duties, including the discretion to make decisions in the ordinary course of the company's business, but who does not participate in the determination of major policies of the company and whose decisions are limited by policy standards fixed by senior management of the company; or

(ii) Any person who is excluded from participating (other than in the capacity of a director) in major policymaking functions of the company by resolution of the board of directors or by the bylaws of the company and who does not in fact participate in such policymaking functions.

(e) *What is the Board?* The Board means the Board of Governors of the Federal Reserve System.

(f) *How are other terms that are used in this part defined?* Unless otherwise defined in this part, all terms used have the meanings given such terms in the Board's Regulation Y (12 CFR Part 225).

PART 1501—FINANCIAL SUBSIDIARIES

Sec.

AUTHORITY: Section 5136A of the Revised Statutes of the United States (12 U.S.C. 24a).

SOURCE: 65 FR 14821, Mar. 20, 2000, unless otherwise noted.

§ 1501.1 How do you request the Secretary to determine that an activity is financial in nature or incidental to a financial activity?

(a) *Requests regarding activities that may be financial in nature or incidental to a financial activity.* A national bank or other interested party may request the Secretary to determine that an activity not defined to be financial in nature or incidental to a financial activity in Section 4(k)(4) of the Bank Holding Company Act (12 U.S.C. 1843(k)(4)), is financial in nature or incidental to a financial activity.

(b) *What information must the request contain?* A request submitted under this section must be in writing and must:

(1) Identify and define the activity for which the determination is sought, specifically describing what the activity would involve and how the activity would be conducted;

(2) Explain in detail why the activity should be considered financial in nature or incidental to a financial activity; and

(3) Provide information supporting the requested determination and any other information required by the Secretary concerning the proposed activity.

(c) *What factors will the Secretary take into account in making his determination?* (1) Section 121 of the Gramm-Leach-Bliley Act (GLBA) (Public Law 106–102, 113 Stat. 1373) requires the Secretary to take into account the following factors in making his determination:

(i) The purposes of section 5136A of the Revised Statutes (12 U.S.C. 24a) and the GLBA;

(ii) Changes or reasonably expected changes in the marketplace in which banks compete;

(iii) Changes or reasonably expected changes in the technology for delivering financial services; and

(iv) Whether the activity is necessary or appropriate to allow a bank and the subsidiaries of a bank to—

(A) Compete effectively with any company seeking to provide financial services in the United States;

(B) Efficiently deliver information and services that are financial in nature through the use of technological means, including any application necessary to protect the security or efficacy of systems for the transmission of data or financial transactions; and

(C) Offer customers any available or emerging technological means for using financial services or for the document imaging of data.

(2) Because the Secretary is required to consider the factors in paragraph (c)(1) of this section in making his determination, any request should address the factors in paragraph (c)(1) of this section. The Secretary may also consider other relevant factors.

(d) *What action will the Secretary take after receiving a request?*—(1) *Consultation with the Board of Governors of the Federal Reserve System (Board).* Upon receiving the request, the Secretary will send a copy to the Board and consult with the Board in accordance with section 5136A(b)(1)(B)(i) of the Revised Statutes (12 U.S.C. 5136A(b)(1)(B)(i)).

(2) *Public notice.* The Secretary may, as appropriate and after consultation with the Board, publish a description of the proposal in the FEDERAL REGISTER with a request for public comment.

(e) *How and when will the Secretary act on a request?* In the case of each request, the Secretary:

(1) Will inform the requester of the Secretary's final determination regarding the requested activity; and

(2) Will endeavor to inform the requester of the Secretary's final determination within 60 days of completion of both the consultative process described in paragraph (d)(1) of this section and the public comment period, if any.

(f) *What must a national bank do in order for a financial subsidiary to engage in activities that the Secretary has determined are financial in nature or incidental to financial activities?* Once the Secretary determines that an activity is financial in nature or incidental to a financial activity (either in accordance with this section or after evaluation of a proposal raised by the Board under section 5136A(b)(1)(B)(ii) of the Revised Statutes), a financial subsidiary may engage in the activity subject to the requirements of 12 CFR part 5 and in accordance with any terms or conditions established by the Secretary in connection with authorizing the activity.

§ 1501.2 What activities has the Secretary determined to be financial in nature or incidental to a financial activity?

(a) *Activities permitted under section 5136A(b)(3) of the Revised Statutes (12 U.S.C. 24a(b)(3)).* (1) The following types of activities are financial in nature or incidental to a financial activity when conducted pursuant to a determination by the Secretary under paragraph (a)(2) of this section:

(i) Lending, exchanging, transferring, investing for others, or safeguarding financial assets other than money or securities;

(ii) Providing any device or other instrumentality for transferring money or other financial assets; and

(iii) Arranging, effecting, or facilitating financial transactions for the account of third parties.

(2) *Review of specific activities.* (i) *Is a specific request required?* A financial subsidiary that wishes to engage on the basis of paragraph (a)(1) of this section in an activity that is not otherwise permissible for a financial subsidiary must obtain a determination from the Secretary that the activity is permitted under paragraph (a)(1).

(ii) *Consultation with the Board of Governors of the Federal Reserve System.* After receiving a request under this section, the Secretary will provide the Board of Governors of the Federal Reserve System (Board) with a copy of the request and consult with the Board in accordance with section 5136A(b)(1)(B)(i) of the Revised Statutes (12 U.S.C. 24a(b)(1)(B)(i)).

(iii) *Secretary action on requests.* After consultation with the Board, the Secretary will promptly make a written determination regarding whether the specific activity described in the request is included in an activity category listed in paragraph (a)(1) of this section and is therefore either financial in nature or incidental to a financial activity.

(3) *What factors will the Secretary consider?* In evaluating a request made under this section, the Secretary will take into account the factors listed in

section 5136A(b)(2) of the Revised Statutes (12 U.S.C. 24a(b)(2)) that the Secretary must consider when determining whether an activity is financial in nature or incidental to a financial activity.

(4) *What information must the request contain?* Any request by financial subsidiary under this section must be in writing and must:

(i) Identify and define the activity for which the determination is sought, specifically describing what the activity would involve and how the activity would be conducted; and

(ii) Provide information supporting the requested determination, including information regarding how the proposed activity falls into one of the categories listed in paragraph (a)(1) of this section, and any other information required by the Secretary concerning the proposed activity.

(b) [Reserved]

[66 FR 260, Jan. 3, 2001]

§ 1501.3 Comparable ratings requirement for national banks among the second 50 largest insured banks.

(a) *Scope and purpose.* Section 5136A of the Revised Statutes permits a national bank that is within the second 50 largest insured banks to own or control a financial subsidiary only if, among other requirements, the bank satisfies the eligible debt requirement set forth in section 5136A or an alternative criteria jointly established by the Secretary of the Treasury and the Board of Governors of the Federal Reserve System. This section establishes the alternative criteria that a national bank among the second 50 largest insured banks may meet, which criteria is comparable to and consistent with the purposes of the eligible debt requirement established by section 5136A.

(b) *Alternative criteria.* A national bank satisfies the alternative criteria referenced in Section 5136A(a)(2)(E) of the Revised Statutes (12 U.S.C. 24a) and 12 CFR 5.39(g)(3) if the bank has a current long-term issuer credit rating from at least one nationally recognized statistical rating organization that is within the three highest investment grade rating categories used by the organization.

(c) *Definition of long-term issuer credit rating.* A "long-term issuer credit rating" is a written opinion issued by a nationally recognized statistical rating organization of the bank's overall capacity and willingness to pay on a timely basis its unsecured, dollar-denominated financial obligations maturing in not less than one year.

[66 FR 8750, Feb. 2, 2001]

PARTS 1502–1503 [RESERVED]

PARTS 1505–1507 [RESERVED]

SUBCHAPTER B—RESOLUTION FUNDING CORPORATION

PART 1510—RESOLUTION FUNDING CORPORATION OPERATIONS

AUTHORITY: 12 U.S.C. 1441b; Sec. 14(d), Pub. L. 105–216, 112 Stat. 910.

SOURCE: 65 FR 12069, Mar. 8, 2000, unless otherwise noted.

§ 1510.1 Authority, purpose, and scope.

(a) *Authority.* This part is issued under the authority of section 14(d) of the Homeowners Protection Act of 1998 (Public Law 105–216, 112 Stat. 910) and section 21B(l) of the Federal Home Loan Bank Act (12 U.S.C. 1441b(l)).

(b) *Purpose and scope.* The purpose of this part is to provide direction to the Funding Corporation in carrying out its statutory mandate to make interest payments on its outstanding debt obligations. This part also provides direction to the Funding Corporation regarding funding the administrative costs of its operations. This part does not provide direction to the Funding Corporation, however, on activities that the Funding Corporation is authorized to carry out under the Act, but that it previously has completed or is not likely to undertake in the future, such as raising capital and issuing obligations. Although the Funding Corporation continues to have statutory authority to undertake these activities, the circumstances under which it would do so are limited. If such circumstances were to arise, the Secretary has the authority to provide any necessary direction to the Funding Corporation.

(c) *Authority of the Funding Corporation.* The Funding Corporation may exercise all authority granted to it by the Act in accordance with its bylaws, whether or not specifically implemented by regulation, subject to the requirements of this part and such other regulations, orders and directions as the Secretary may prescribe.

§ 1510.2 Definitions.

The following definitions apply to terms used in this part unless the context requires otherwise:

Act means the Federal Home Loan Bank Act (12 U.S.C. 1421 *et seq.*).

Administrative expenses means costs incurred as necessary to carry out the functions of the Funding Corporation, including custodian fees, but does not include any interest on obligations.

Bank means a Federal Home Loan Bank established under the authority of the Act.

Custodian fee means any fee incurred by the Funding Corporation in connection with the transfer of any security to, or the maintenance of any security in, the Funding Corporation Principal Fund and any other expense incurred in connection with the establishment or maintenance of the Funding Corporation Principal Fund.

Directorate means the Directorate of the Funding Corporation established pursuant to section 21B(c) of the Act (12 U.S.C. 1421b(c)).

FDIC means the Federal Deposit Insurance Corporation established pursuant to section 1 of the Federal Deposit Insurance Act (12 U.S.C. 1811, *et seq.*).

Finance Board means the Federal Housing Finance Board established pursuant to section 2A(a)(1) of the Act.

FSLIC Resolution Fund means the Federal Savings and Loan Insurance Corporation Resolution Fund established pursuant to section 11A(a)(1) of the Federal Deposit Insurance Act (12 U.S.C. 1811, *et seq.*).

Funding Corporation means the Resolution Funding Corporation established pursuant to section 21B(b) of the Act.

Funding Corporation Principal Fund means the separate account established under section 21B(g)(2) of the Act.

Interest payment due date means the date on which the next quarterly interest payments on obligations are due.

Net earnings means net earnings after deducting expenses relating to section 10(j) of the Act (Affordable Housing Program) and operating expenses, but without reduction for chargeoffs and payments to fund interest payments on obligations.

Obligations means bonds issued by the Funding Corporation under section 21B(f) of the Act.

RTC means the Resolution Trust Corporation established pursuant to section 21A(b)(1)(A) of the Act and which terminated on December 31, 1995, pursuant to section 21A(m) of the Act.

Secretary means the Secretary of the Treasury or the designee of the Secretary of the Treasury.

§ 1510.3 How does the Funding Corporation pay administrative expenses?

(a) *The Directorate proposes a budget.* By November 15 of each year, the Directorate must approve and submit to the Secretary a proposed budget for the administrative expenses of the Funding Corporation for the following year.

(b) *The Secretary approves the budget.* The Funding Corporation's budget is subject to the Secretary's prior approval. The proposed budget submitted by the Directorate shall be deemed to be approved by the Secretary unless the Secretary disapproves it within 45 days of the date submitted. The Funding Corporation must transmit a copy of the approved budget to each Bank.

(c) *Budget changes must be approved by the Secretary.* If the Funding Corporation projects or anticipates incurring expenses exceeding its approved budget, the Directorate must submit an amended budget to the Secretary for approval.

(d) *The Funding Corporation collects funds from the Banks to pay its administrative expenses.* At least semiannually, the Funding Corporation must request that each Bank submit within 10 business days of the request payment for a portion of the administrative expenses in the Funding Corporation's budget for the current calendar year. The amount of each Bank's payment must be pro rated according to the percentage of the total outstanding Funding Corporation capital stock owned by the Bank. The Funding Corporation must adjust the amount of each Bank's payment as necessary to reflect differences between aggregate projected and actual administrative expenses incurred during the calendar year and to reflect any changes in estimated aggregate administrative expenses for the coming period. The Funding Corporation must not request payments from the Banks that, in the aggregate, exceed the administrative expenses in the Funding Corporation's approved budget.

§ 1510.4 Who may act as the depositary and fiscal agent for the Funding Corporation?

(a) *In general, the Federal Reserve Banks.* The Funding Corporation must use one or more Federal Reserve Banks as depositaries for or fiscal agents or custodians of the Funding Corporation.

(b) *For administrative accounts, insured depository institutions.* Subject to approval by the Secretary, the Funding Corporation may establish demand deposit accounts at one or more federally insured depository institutions for the management of funds used to pay administrative expenses.

§ 1510.5 How does the Funding Corporation make interest payments on its obligations?

(a) *The Funding Corporation must obtain funds from up to four sources.* The Funding Corporation must pay the interest due on its obligations with funds it obtains from the following sources and in the following order:

(1) Earnings on assets of the Funding Corporation not invested in the Funding Corporation Principal Fund.

(2) To the extent funds identified in paragraph (a)(1) of this section are insufficient, the Funding Corporation must obtain from each Bank in each calendar year payments totaling 20 percent of the net earnings of the Bank. The Funding Corporation must not obtain funds from a Bank under this paragraph after the date upon which the term of the Bank's payment obligation has ended, as determined by the Finance Board pursuant to section 21B(f)(2)(C)(iii) of the Act.

(3) To the extent funds identified in paragraphs (a)(1) and (2) of this section are insufficient, the Funding Corporation must obtain from the FSLIC Resolution Fund amounts available from any net proceeds from the sale of assets received from the RTC by the FSLIC Resolution Fund.

(4) To the extent that funds from the sources identified in paragraphs (a)(1) through (3) of this section are insufficient, the Funding Corporation must obtain from the Secretary the additional amount due.

(b) *The Funding Corporation must obtain projections of funds availability from the Banks and the FSLIC Resolution Fund.* Not later than March 15, June 15, September 15, and December 15 of each year:

(1) The Funding Corporation must obtain from each Bank a statement signed by an officer of such Bank containing sufficient information on the Banks net earnings to enable the Funding Corporation to make quarterly projections of funds available from the Bank for the current quarter and the next three quarters; and

(2) The Funding Corporation must obtain from an authorized representative of the FSLIC Resolution Fund projections of the amount of funds available in the current quarter and the next three quarters from the net proceeds from the sale of received from the RTC.

(c) *The Funding Corporation must report funding projections to the Secretary.* Not later than March 20, June 20, September 20, and December 20 of each year, the Funding Corporation must submit to the Secretary a report containing:

(1) The aggregate amounts of each of the next four quarterly interest payments due on obligations; and

(2) The amounts projected to be available to fund such payments from:

(i) Earnings on assets of the Funding Corporation not invested in the Funding Corporation Principal Fund;

(ii) Payments from the Banks; and

(iii) Funds transferred from the FSLIC Resolution Fund.

(d) *The Funding Corporation must request funds from the Banks, the FSLIC Resolution Fund, and the Secretary*—(1) *Requests to the Banks.* Not less than four business days prior to the interest payment due date, the Funding Corporation must obtain from each Bank a report of its actual net earnings for the prior quarter and notify each Bank in writing of the interest payment due date and the amount of the payment due from the Bank. To the extent funds identified in paragraph (a)(1) of this section are insufficient to pay the interest due, the amount of each Bank's payment must be 20 percent of the Bank's actual quarterly net earnings, taking into account any adjustment to the Bank's earnings for any previous quarters. The Funding Corporation must request the Bank to provide payment through wiring immediately available and finally collected funds to the Funding Corporation no later than the interest payment due date.

(2) *Request to the FSLIC Resolution Fund.* On the day the Funding Corporation notifies the Banks of the payments due from them under paragraph (d)(1) of this section, the Funding Corporation must:

(i) Notify the FSLIC Resolution Fund in writing of:

(A) The interest payment due date;

(B) The aggregate amount of the quarterly interest payment due on that date; and

(C) The amount of the quarterly interest payment that will be funded by earnings on assets of the Funding Corporation not invested in the Funding Corporation Principal Fund and payments due from the Banks; and

(ii) Request that the FSLIC Resolution Fund transfer to the Funding Corporation by noon on the third business day prior to the interest payment due date any funds available from the net proceeds from the sale of assets received from the RTC, to the extent funds identified in paragraphs (a)(1) and (2) of this section are insufficient to pay the interest due.

(3) *Request to the Secretary.* No less than three business days prior to the interest payment due date, the Funding Corporation must request payment from the Secretary by providing a certification, in a form satisfactory to the Secretary, stating the total amounts of the quarterly interest payment to be paid by the Funding Corporation from sources other than the Secretary and

the amounts necessary to make up the deficiency. Any amount paid by the Secretary becomes a liability of the Funding Corporation to be repaid to the Secretary upon the dissolution of the Funding Corporation, to the extent of its remaining assets.

[65 FR 12069, Mar. 8, 2000, as amended at 66 FR 47071, Sept. 11, 2001]

§ 1510.6 What must the Funding Corporation do with surplus funds?

If the Funding Corporation has funds that are not needed for current interest payments on obligations, it must invest the funds in obligations of the United States issued by the Secretary, in accordance with an investment policy approved by the Secretary.

§ 1510.7 What are the Funding Corporation's reporting requirements?

In addition to the budget submission required by § 1510.3 and the funding projection reports required by § 1510.5, the Funding Corporation must prepare such reports as the Secretary may require, including reports necessary to assist the Secretary in making the annual report to Congress and the President on the Funding Corporation under section 21B(i) of the Act.

§ 1510.8 What are the audit requirements for the Funding Corporation?

The Funding Corporation must obtain an audit of its books and records by an independent external auditor at least annually.

PART 1511—BOOK-ENTRY PROCEDURE

Sec.

AUTHORITY: 12 U.S.C. 1441b.

SOURCE: 61 FR 66875, Dec. 19, 1996, unless otherwise noted.

§ 1511.0 Applicability.

The regulations in this part apply to Book-entry Funding Corporation Securities.

§ 1511.1 Definitions of terms.

In this part, unless the context indicates otherwise:

Act means the Federal Home Loan Bank Act as amended (12 U.S.C. 1421 *et seq.*).

Adverse Claim means a claim that a claimant has a property interest in a Book-entry Funding Corporation Security and that it is a violation of the rights of the claimant for another Person to hold, transfer, or deal with the Book-entry Funding Corporation Security.

Book-entry Funding Corporation Security means a Funding Corporation Security in book-entry form that is issued or maintained in the Book-entry System. Solely for the purposes of this Part, it also means the separate interest and principal components of a Book-entry Funding Corporation Security if such security has been divided into such components as authorized by the Securities Documentation and the components are maintained separately on the books of one or more Federal Reserve Banks.

Book-entry System means the automated book-entry system operated by the Federal Reserve Banks acting as the fiscal agent for the Funding Corporation, on which Book-entry Funding Corporation Securities are issued, recorded, transferred and maintained in book-entry form.

Entitlement Holder means a Person to whose account an interest in a Book-entry Funding Corporation Security is credited on the records of a Securities Intermediary.

Federal Reserve Bank or Reserve Bank means a Federal Reserve Bank or Branch.

Federal Reserve Bank Operating Circular means the publication issued by each Federal Reserve Bank that sets forth the terms and conditions under which the Reserve Bank maintains book-entry Securities accounts (including Book-entry Funding Corporation Securities) and transfers book-entry Securities (including Book-entry Funding Corporation Securities).

Funding Corporation means the Resolution Funding Corporation established pursuant to section 21B(b) of the Act.

Funding Corporation Security or *Security* means a Funding Corporation bond, note, debenture and similar obligations issued under section 21B of the Act.

Funds Account means a reserve and/or clearing account at a Federal Reserve Bank to which debits or credits are posted for transfers against payment, book-entry securities transaction fees, or principal and interest payments.

Participant means a Person that maintains a Participant's Securities Account with a Federal Reserve Bank.

Participant's Securities Account means an account in the name of a Participant at a Federal Reserve Bank to which Book-entry Funding Corporation Securities held for a Participant are or may be credited.

Person means and includes an individual, corporation, company, governmental entity, association, firm, partnership, trust, estate, representative, and any other similar organization, but does not mean or include the United States, the Funding Corporation, or a Federal Reserve Bank.

Revised Article 8 means Uniform Commercial Code, Revised Article 8, Investment Securities (with Conforming and Miscellaneous Amendments to Articles 1, 3, 4, 5, 9, and 10) 1994 Official Text. Revised Article 8 of the Uniform Commercial Code is incorporated by reference in this Part pursuant to 5 U.S.C. 552(a) and 1 CFR Part 51. Article 8 was adopted by the American Law Institute and the National Conference of Commissioners on Uniform State laws and approved by the American Bar Association on February 14, 1995. Copies of this publication are available from the Executive Office of the American Law Institute, 4025 Chestnut Street, Philadelphia, PA 19104, and the National Conference of Commissioners on Uniform State Laws, 676 North St. Clair Street, Suite 1700, Chicago, IL 60611. Copies are also available for public inspection at the Department of the Treasury Library, Room 5030, main Treasury Building, 1500 Pennsylvania Avenue, NW., Washington DC 20220, or at the National Archives and Records Administration (NARA). For information on the availability of this material at NARA, call 202–741–6030, or go to: *http://www.archives.gov/federal_register/code_of_federal_regulations/ibr_locations.html.*

Securities Documentation means the applicable offering circular, supplement, or other documents establishing the terms of a Book-entry Funding Corporation Security.

Securities Intermediary means:

(1) A Person that is registered as a "clearing agency" under the Federal securities laws; a Federal Reserve Bank; any other Person that provides clearance or settlement services with respect to a Book-entry Funding Corporation Security that would require it to register as a clearing agency under the Federal securities laws but for an exclusion or exemption from the registration requirement, if its activities as a clearing corporation, including promulgation of rules, are subject to regulation by a Federal or State governmental authority; or

(2) A Person (other than an individual, unless such individual is registered as a broker or dealer under the federal securities laws) including a bank or broker, that in the ordinary course of its business maintains securities accounts for others and is acting in that capacity.

Security Entitlement means the rights and property interest of an Entitlement Holder with respect to a Book-entry Funding Corporation Security.

State means any State of the United States, the District of Columbia, Puerto Rico, the Virgin Islands, or any other territory or possession of the United States.

Transfer message means an instruction of a Participant to a Federal Reserve Bank to effect a transfer of a Book-entry Funding Corporation Security, as set forth in Federal Reserve Bank Operating Circulars.

[61 FR 66875, Dec. 19, 1996, as amended at 69 FR 18803, Apr. 9, 2004]

§ 1511.2 Law governing rights and obligations of the Funding Corporation and Federal Reserve Banks; rights of any Person against the Funding Corporation and the Federal Reserve Banks.

(a) Except as provided in paragraph (b) of this section, the following are governed solely by the regulations contained in this part 1511, the Securities Documentation and Federal Reserve Bank Operating Circulars:

(1) The rights and obligations of the Funding Corporation and the Federal Reserve Banks with respect to:

(i) A Book-entry Funding Corporation Security or Security Entitlement; and

(ii) The operation of the Book-entry System as it applies to Funding Corporation Securities; and

(2) The rights of any Person, including a Participant, against the Funding Corporation and the Federal Reserve Banks with respect to:

(i) A Book-entry Funding Corporation Security or Security Entitlement; and

(ii) The operation of the Book-entry System as it applies to Funding Corporation Securities.

(b) A security interest in a Security Entitlement that is in favor of a Federal Reserve Bank from a Participant and that is not recorded on the books of a Federal Reserve Bank pursuant to § 1511.4(c)(1), is governed by the law (not including the conflict-of-law rules) of the jurisdiction where the head office of the Federal Reserve Bank maintaining the Participant's Securities Account is located. A security interest in a Security Entitlement that is in favor of a Federal Reserve Bank from a Person that is not a Participant, and that is not recorded on the books of a Federal Reserve Bank pursuant to § 1511.4(c)(1), is governed by the law determined in the manner specified in § 1511.3.

(c) If the jurisdiction specified in the first sentence of paragraph (b) of this section is a State that has not adopted Revised Article 8 (incorporated by reference, see § 1511.1), then the law specified in paragraph (b) shall be the law of that State as though Revised Article 8 had been adopted by that State.

§ 1511.3 Law governing other interests.

(a) To the extent not inconsistent with the regulations in this part, the law (not including the conflict-of-law rules) of a Securities Intermediary's jurisdiction governs:

(1) The acquisition of a Security Entitlement from the Securities Intermediary;

(2) The rights and duties of the Securities Intermediary and Entitlement Holder arising out of a Security Entitlement;

(3) Whether the Securities Intermediary owes any duties to an adverse claimant to a Security Entitlement;

(4) Whether an Adverse Claim can be asserted against a Person who acquires a Security Entitlement from the Securities Intermediary or a Person who purchases a Security Entitlement or interest therein from an Entitlement Holder; and

(5) Except as otherwise provided in paragraph (c) of this section, the perfection, effect of perfection or non-perfection and priority of a security interest in a Security Entitlement.

(b) The following rules determine a "Securities Intermediary's jurisdiction" for purposes of this section:

(1) If an agreement between the Securities Intermediary and its Entitlement Holder specifies that it is governed by the law of a particular jurisdiction, that jurisdiction is the Securities Intermediary's jurisdiction.

(2) If an agreement between the Securities Intermediary and its Entitlement Holder does not specify the governing law as provided in paragraph (b)(1) of this section, but expressly specifies that the securities account is maintained at an office in a particular jurisdiction, that jurisdiction is the Securities Intermediary's jurisdiction.

(3) If an agreement between the Securities Intermediary and its Entitlement Holder does not specify a jurisdiction as provided in paragraph (b)(1) or (b)(2) of this section, the Securities Intermediary's jurisdiction is the jurisdiction in which is located the office identified in an account statement as the office serving the Entitlement Holder's account.

(4) If an agreement between the Securities Intermediary and its Entitlement Holder does not specify a jurisdiction as provided in paragraph (b)(1) or (b)(2) of this section and an account statement does not identify an office serving the Entitlement Holder's account as provided in paragraph (b)(3) of this section, the Securities Intermediary's jurisdiction is the jurisdiction in which is located the chief executive office of the Securities Intermediary.

(c) Notwithstanding the general rule in paragraph (a)(5) of this section, the law (but not the conflict-of-law rules) of the jurisdiction in which the Person creating a security interest is located governs whether and how the security interest may be perfected automatically or by filing a financing statement.

(d) If the jurisdiction specified in paragraph (b) of this section is a State that has not adopted Revised Article 8 (incorporated by reference, see § 1511.1), then the law for the matters specified in paragraph (a) of this section shall be the law of that State as though Revised Article 8 had been adopted by that State. For purposes of the application of the matters specified in paragraph (a) of this section, the Federal Reserve Bank maintaining the Securities Account is a clearing corporation, and the Participant's interest in a Book-entry Funding Corporation Security is a Security Entitlement.

§ 1511.4 Creation of Participant's Security Entitlement; security interests.

(a) A Participant's Security Entitlement is created when a Federal Reserve Bank indicates by book-entry that a Book-entry Funding Corporation Security has been credited to a Participant's Securities Account.

(b) A security interest in a Security Entitlement of a Participant in favor of the United States to secure deposits of public money, including without limitation deposits to the Treasury tax and loan accounts, or other security interest in favor of the United States that is required by Federal statute, regulation, or agreement, and that is marked on the books of a Federal Reserve Bank is thereby effected and perfected, and has priority over any other interest in the securities. Where a security interest in favor of the United States in a Security Entitlement of a Participant is marked on the books of a Federal Reserve Bank, such Reserve Bank may rely, and is protected in relying, exclusively on the order of an authorized representative of the United States directing the transfer of the security. For purposes of this paragraph, an "authorized representative of the United States" is the official designated in the applicable regulations or agreement to which a Federal Reserve Bank is a party, governing the security interest.

(c)(1) The Funding Corporation and the Federal Reserve Banks have no obligation to agree to act on behalf of any Person or to recognize the interest of any transferee of a security interest or other limited interest in favor of any Person except to the extent of any specific requirement of Federal law or regulation or to the extent set forth in any specific agreement with the Federal Reserve Bank on whose books the interest of the Participant is recorded. To the extent required by such law or regulation or set forth in an agreement with a Federal Reserve Bank, or the Federal Reserve Bank Operating Circular, a security interest in a Security Entitlement that is in favor of a Federal Reserve Bank, the Funding Corporation, or a Person may be created and perfected by a Federal Reserve Bank marking its books to record the security interest. Except as provided in paragraph (b) of this section, a security interest in a Security Entitlement marked on the books of a Federal Reserve Bank shall have priority over any other interest in the securities.

(2) In addition to the method provided in paragraph (c)(1) of this section, a security interest in a Security Entitlement, including a security interest in favor of a Federal Reserve Bank, may be perfected by any method by which a security interest may be perfected under applicable law as described in § 1511.2(b) or § 1511.3. The perfection, effect of perfection or non-perfection and priority of a security interest are governed by such applicable law. A security interest in favor of a Federal Reserve Bank shall be treated as a security interest in favor of a

clearing corporation in all respects under such law, including with respect to the effect of perfection and priority of such security interest. A Federal Reserve Bank Operating Circular shall be treated as a rule adopted by a clearing corporation for such purposes.

§ 1511.5 Obligations of Funding Corporation; no adverse claims.

(a) Except in the case of a security interest in favor of the United States or a Federal Reserve Bank or otherwise as provided in § 1511.4(c)(1), for the purposes of this part 1511, the Funding Corporation and the Federal Reserve Banks shall treat the Participant to whose Securities Account an interest in a Book-entry Funding Corporation Security has been credited as the Person exclusively entitled to issue a Transfer Message, to receive interest and other payments with respect thereof and otherwise to exercise all the rights and powers with respect to such Security, notwithstanding any information or notice to the contrary. Neither the Federal Reserve Banks nor the Funding Corporation is liable to a Person asserting or having an Adverse Claim to a Security Entitlement or to a Book-entry Funding Corporation Security in a Participant's Securities Account, including any such claim arising as a result of the transfer or disposition of a Book-entry Funding Corporation Security by a Federal Reserve Bank pursuant to a Transfer Message that the Federal Reserve Bank reasonably believes to be genuine.

(b) The obligation of the Funding Corporation to make payments of interest and principal with respect to Book-entry Funding Corporation Securities is discharged at the time payment in the appropriate amount is made as follows:

(1) Interest on Book-entry Funding Corporation Securities is either credited by a Federal Reserve Bank to a Funds Account maintained at such Bank or otherwise paid as directed by the Participant.

(2) Book-entry Funding Corporation Securities are redeemed in accordance with their terms by a Federal Reserve Bank withdrawing the securities from the Participant's Securities Account in which they are maintained and by either crediting the amount of the redemption proceeds, including both principal and interest where applicable, to a Funds Account at such Bank or otherwise paying such principal and interest, as directed by the Participant. The principal of such Securities shall be paid using the proceeds of the noninterest bearing instruments maintained by the Funding Corporation for such purpose.

§ 1511.6 Authority of Federal Reserve Banks.

(a) Each Federal Reserve Bank is hereby authorized as fiscal agent of the Funding Corporation to perform functions with respect to the issuance of Book-entry Funding Corporation Securities offered and sold by the Funding Corporation, in accordance with the Securities Documentation, and Federal Reserve Bank Operating Circulars; to service and maintain Book-entry Funding Corporation Securities in accounts established for such purposes; to make payments of principal and interest with respect to such Book-entry Funding Corporation Securities as directed by the Funding Corporation; to effect transfer of Book-entry Funding Corporation Securities between Participants' Securities Accounts as directed by the Participants; and to perform such other duties as fiscal agent as may be requested by the Funding Corporation.

(b) Each Federal Reserve Bank may issue Operating Circulars not inconsistent with this Part, governing the details of its handling of Book-entry Funding Corporation Securities, Security Entitlements, and the operation of the Book-Entry System under this Part.

§ 1511.7 Liability of the Funding Corporation and Federal Reserve Banks.

The Funding Corporation and the Federal Reserve Banks may rely on the information provided in a Transfer Message, or other documentation, and are not required to verify the information. The Funding Corporation and the Federal Reserve Banks shall not be liable for any action taken in accordance with the information set out in a

Transfer Message, other documentation, or evidence submitted in support thereof.

§ 1511.8 Notice of attachment.

The interest of a debtor in a Security Entitlement may be reached by a creditor only by legal process upon the Securities Intermediary with whom the debtor's securities account is maintained, except where a Security Entitlement is maintained in the name of a secured party, in which case the debtor's interest may be reached by legal process upon the secured party. The regulations in this part do not purport to establish whether a Federal Reserve Bank is required to honor an order or other notice of attachment in any particular case or class of cases.

CHAPTER XVI—OFFICE OF FINANCIAL RESEARCH, DEPARTMENT OF THE TREASURY

PART 1600—ORGANIZATION AND FUNCTIONS OF THE OFFICE OF FINANCIAL RESEARCH

AUTHORITY: 5 U.S.C. 301, 7301, 31 U.S.C. 321, the Dodd-Frank Wall Street Reform and Consumer Protection Act (Dodd-Frank) (Pub. L. 111–203); E.O. 12674, 3 CFR, 1989 Comp., p. 215, as modified by E.O. 12731, 3 CFR, 1990 Comp., p. 306.

SOURCE: 76 FR 60708, Sept. 30, 2011, unless otherwise noted.

§ 1600.1 Standards of ethical conduct.

This section applies to the employees of the Office of Financial Research and is in addition to 5 CFR 3101.101–104, and 31 CFR part 0:

(a) *Definitions*—For purposes of this subpart:

(1) "Business confidential information" shall include trade secret or other formula, practice, process, design, instrument, pattern, or compilation of information which is not generally known or reasonably ascertainable, by which a business can obtain an economic advantage over competitors or customers. This shall include nonpublic position and transaction data, as well as data provided to supervisors or regulators that is unpublished.

(2) "Position data" is defined as:

(i) Data on financial assets or liabilities held on the balance sheet of a financial company, where positions are created or changed by the execution of a financial transaction; and

(ii) Includes information that identifies counterparties, the valuation by the financial company of the position, and information that makes possible an independent valuation of the position.

(3) "Transaction data" is defined as the structure and legal description of a financial contract, with sufficient detail to describe the rights and obligations between counterparties and make possible an independent valuation.

(4) "Micro-level data" is defined as information specific to an individual transaction or position.

(5) "Masked data" is defined as data that has been altered to prevent attribution to a particular financial company.

(6) "Financial company" has the same meaning given to such term in title II of the Dodd-Frank Wall Street Reform and Consumer Protection Act, 12 U.S.C. 5301 *et seq.* (2010), and includes an insured depository institution and an insurance company.

(b) *One-year post-employment restriction.* (1) A current or former employee of the Office of Financial Research who has had access to the transaction or position data or business confidential information maintained by the Data Center about financial entities required to report to the Office may not, within one year after last having had access in the course of official duties to such transaction or position data or business confidential information, be employed by or provide advice or consulting services to a financial company, regardless of whether that financial company is required to report to the Office.

(2) A current or former employee of the Office of Financial Research who has had limited access to the transaction or position data or business confidential information maintained by the Data Center about financial entities required to report to the Office may request a written waiver pursuant to paragraph (c) of this section from the Designated Agency Ethics Official to be employed by or provide advice or consulting services to a financial company, provided that the issuance of the waiver would not compromise any data or business confidential information.

(c) *Waivers*—The post-employment restrictions set forth in section 152(g) of the Dodd-Frank Wall Street Reform and Consumer Protection Act may be waived in whole or in part for an employee with limited access to the transaction or position data or business confidential information maintained by the Data Center if—

(1) The Designated Agency Ethics Official, in consultation with the Director of the Office of Financial Research or the Department's General Counsel in instances where consultation with the Director poses a conflict or the Director's position is vacant, determines in writing that such waiver is unlikely to compromise any financial company's business confidential information, unfairly advantage or disadvantage any financial company, or affect

the integrity or effectiveness of the Office of Financial Research.

(2) Relevant factors to be considered by the Designated Agency Ethics Official and the Director or General Counsel include—

(i) The nature and importance of the employee's position and the degree to which the employee had access to nonpublic or business confidential data for the purpose of analysis, standardization, or performing applied research or essential long-term research;

(ii) Whether the information to which the employee had access revealed positions or transactions of an individual financial company;

(iii) Whether the data, especially position data, remains sensitive considering changing circumstances or the passage of time;

(iv) Whether the employee had access to micro-level data, as compared to aggregated information;

(v) If the employee had access to micro-level data, whether it was sufficiently masked or coded to protect the identity of the provider or the subject financial company;

(vi) Whether the information to which the employee had access would provide a financial company employer with a competitive commercial advantage;

(vii) Whether the financial company employer has made a satisfactory representation that it has adopted screening measures which will effectively prevent a potential employee from sharing any transaction or position data or business confidential information acquired at the Office of Financial Research one year prior to accepting employment with the company;

(viii) Whether granting the waiver would affect the willingness of a financial company to continue to provide transaction or position data or business confidential information to the Office; and

(ix) Whether the proposed employment would create an appearance of impropriety or would otherwise adversely affect the interests of the government or compromise the integrity of the office.

(d) The following examples are illustrative of how the OFR post-employment prohibitions would apply under certain circumstances:

(1) *Example 1.* (i) Fact pattern: OFR employs a business data manager and such employee has no access to the transaction or position data maintained by the Data Center or other business confidential information about financial entities required to report to OFR.

(ii) Designated Agency Ethics Official's Determination: Upon termination of their employment by OFR, such employee would not be prohibited from being employed by or providing advice or consulting services to a financial company, regardless of whether that financial company is required to report to the Office.

(2) *Example 2.* (i) Fact pattern: OFR employs a data analyst and such employee has access to transaction or position data across all sectors maintained by the Data Center or other business confidential information about specific financial entities required to report to OFR.

(ii) Designated Agency Ethics Official's Determination: Upon termination of their employment by OFR, such employee would be prohibited, for a period of one year immediately after leaving OFR, from being employed by or providing advice or consulting services to a financial company, regardless of whether that financial company is required to report to the Office.

(3) *Example 3.* (i) Fact pattern: OFR employs a data analyst and such employee has access to transaction or position data across all sectors maintained by the Data Center or other business confidential information about specific financial entities required to report to OFR. Employee last had access to such data six months before termination of her employment at OFR.

(ii) Designated Agency Ethics Official's Determination: Upon termination of employment by OFR, such employee would be prohibited, for a period of six months immediately after leaving OFR, from being employed by or providing advice or consulting services to a financial company, regardless of whether that financial company is required to report to the Office.

(4) *Example 4.* (i) Fact pattern: OFR employs a researcher and such employee has access only to "aggregated" or "masked" transaction or position data maintained by the Data Center or other business confidential information about financial entities required to report to OFR.

(ii) Designated Agency Ethics Official's Determination: Upon termination of their employment by OFR, such employee would not be prohibited from being employed by or providing advice or consulting services to a financial company, regardless of whether that financial company is required to report to the Office.

(5) *Example 5.* (i) Fact pattern: OFR employs a data analyst and such employee has access to transaction or position data maintained by the Data Center or other business confidential information *relating to a particular sector (i.e. banking).*

(ii) Designated Agency Ethics Official's Determination: Upon termination of employment by OFR, such employee would be prohibited, for a period of one year immediately after leaving OFR, from being employed by or providing advice or consulting services to a financial company *in that particular sector (i.e. banking)* where such employment or services involves employment or advice or consulting services, regardless of whether that financial company is required to report to the Office. Such employee would be granted a waiver to work in other designated sectors immediately after leaving OFR.

(6) *Example 6.* (i) Fact pattern: OFR employs a data analyst and such employee has access to business confidential information in an area where data, such as equity mutual fund holdings, changes frequently. Employee last had access to such data six months before termination of her employment at OFR and, because of portfolio turnover, there is no risk of compromising business confidential information.

(ii) Designated Agency Ethics Official's Determination: Upon termination of their employment by OFR, such employee would not be prohibited from being employed by or providing advice or consulting services to a financial company, regardless of whether that financial company is required to report to the Office.

(7) *Example 7.* (i) Fact pattern: OFR employs an information technology specialist and such employee has access only to "masked" transaction or position data maintained by the Data Center or other "masked" business confidential information about specific financial entities required to report to OFR.

(ii) Designated Agency Ethics Official's Determination: Upon termination of their employment by OFR, such employee would not be prohibited from being employed by or providing advice or consulting services to a financial company, regardless of whether that financial company is required to report to the Office.

CHAPTER XVII—OFFICE OF FEDERAL HOUSING ENTERPRISE OVERSIGHT, DEPARTMENT OF HOUSING AND URBAN DEVELOPMENT

SUBCHAPTER A—OFHEO ORGANIZATION AND FUNCTIONS

PART 1700—ORGANIZATION AND FUNCTIONS

AUTHORITY: 5 U.S.C. 552; 12 U.S.C 4513, 4526.

SOURCE: 59 FR 62304, Dec. 5, 1994, unless otherwise noted.

§ 1700.1 Office of Federal Housing Enterprise Oversight.

(a) *Scope and authority.* The Office of Federal Housing Enterprise Oversight (referred to as OFHEO) is an independent office within the Department of Housing and Urban Development. OFHEO was created by the Federal Housing Enterprises Financial Safety and Soundness Act of 1992 (Act), Title XIII of the Housing and Community Development Act of 1992 (Pub. L. 102–550, October 28, 1992; 106 Stat. 3943; 12 U.S.C. 4501, *et seq.*). OFHEO is responsible for the examination and financial regulation of the Federal National Mortgage Association (Fannie Mae) and the Federal Home Loan Mortgage Corporation (Freddie Mac) (collectively, the Enterprises). OFHEO is charged with ensuring that the Enterprises are adequately capitalized and operating in a safe and sound manner. OFHEO's costs and expenses are funded by annual assessments paid by the Enterprises. OFHEO is headed by a Director, who is appointed by the President and confirmed by the Senate for a five-year term.

(b) *Location.* OFHEO is located at 1700 G Street NW., 4th Floor, Washington, DC 20552. OFHEO's hours of business are 8:30 a.m.–5:00 p.m. (eastern standard time), Monday through Friday, excluding Federal holidays.

§ 1700.2 Organization of the Office of Federal Housing Enterprise Oversight.

(a) *Director.* The Director has exclusive authority under the Act with respect to the management of OFHEO, and is responsible for directing the development, implementation, and review of all OFHEO programs and functions. The Director appoints such personnel as may be necessary to carry out the functions of OFHEO. The Director may delegate to OFHEO officers and employees any of the functions, powers, and duties of the Director, as the Director considers appropriate. The Director may establish and fix the responsibilities of the offices within OFHEO as the Director deems necessary for the efficient functioning of OFHEO.

(b) *Deputy Director.* The Deputy Director of OFHEO is appointed by the Director in accordance with the Act. In the event of the absence, sickness, death or resignation of the Director, the Deputy Director serves as acting Director until the Director's return or the confirmation of a successor. The Deputy Director performs such functions, powers and duties as the Director determines are necessary with respect to OFHEO's management and the development and implementation of OFHEO's programs and functions.

(c) *Executive Director and Chief of Staff.* The Executive Director and Chief of Staff of OFHEO heads the Office of Executive Director. The Executive Director and Chief of Staff reports to the Director and the Deputy Director. The Executive Director and Chief of Staff is the chief administrative officer of OFHEO, serves as a legal advisor on administrative matters, and coordinates communication and cooperation on administrative issues with the Office of General Counsel.

(d) *Offices and functions.* (1) Office of Executive Director. The Office of Executive Director consists of the Office of Budget and Financial Management, the Office of Human Resources Management, the Office of Technology and Information Management, and the Office of Strategic Planning and Management. The Office of Executive Director is responsible for OFHEO-wide management and oversight of all administrative matters.

(2) *Office of Examination.* The Office of Examination plans and conducts examinations of the Enterprises, as required by the Act, prepares and issues reports of examination summarizing the financial condition and management practices of each Enterprise, and seeks preventative and corrective actions as appropriate. The Office complements its on-site examination activities with off-site financial safety and soundness monitoring.

(3) *Office of Capital Supervision.* The Office of Capital Supervision ensures the comprehensive evaluation and classification of the capital adequacy of the Enterprises, the assessment of risks that impact capital and the development of tools to measure such risks. The Office ensures the integrity of capital classifications by effectively producing results under the minimum and risk based capital models and systems and by implementing appropriate enhancements to those measures. The Office assesses new GSE activities under the capital regime and addresses changes in accounting standards. The Office supports its responsibilities as well as other OFHEO offices through research on alternative models and measurements of risk and capital adequacy.

(4) *Office of General Counsel.* The Office of General Counsel advises the Director and OFHEO staff on all legal matters concerning the functions, activities, and operations of OFHEO and of the Enterprises under the Act. The Office is responsible for interpreting the Act and other applicable law, including financial institutions regulatory issues, securities and corporate law principles, and administrative and general legal matters. This Office also coordinates the preparation of legislation and agency regulations and works with other counsels in the government.

(5) *Office of External Relations.* The Office of External Relations is responsible for coordinating and communicating on behalf of OFHEO with the Congress, for monitoring relevant legislative developments, and for analyzing and assisting the Director in developing legislative proposals. The Office also is responsible for directing and coordinating communication with the news media and the public as well as participating in planning programs for OFHEO.

(6) *Office of Policy Analysis and Research.* The Office of Policy Analysis and Research conducts policy analysis and research to assess the short- and long-term impact on the regulatory and supervisory functions of OFHEO of trends and developments in Enterprise activities, housing finance and financial regulation. The Office also prepares data series, reports and research papers; works with other OFHEO offices to develop policy options; and, makes recommendations to the Director on a broad range of policy issues.

(7) *Office of Compliance.* The Office of Compliance assists the Director in ensuring that the Enterprises operate in compliance with applicable laws, regulations and safety and soundness standards. The Office conducts special review and examinations on focused issues that may arise at the enterprises or that are of concern to OFHEO, often in coordination with other OFHEO offices, to assess compliance and obtain information. The Office also assists in providing information for enforcement actions and other activities as requested by the Director.

(8) *Office of Chief Accountant.* The Office of Chief Accountant advises the Director and OFHEO staff on all accounting matters related to the Enterprises. The Office develops policies regarding accounting and financial reporting and monitors accounting standards that affect the Enterprises, working with the Enterprises at a policy level on emerging issues. The Office supports and coordinates accounting resources within the agency to assure the best and most efficient use of those resources. The Office supports other offices in providing consistent accounting policy interpretation across OFHEO and works with external constituencies on accounting issues.

(e) *Additional information.* Current information on the organization of OFHEO may be obtained by mail from the Office of External Affairs, 1700 G Street NW, 4th Floor, Washington, DC 20552. Such information, as well as other OFHEO information, also may be obtained electronically by accessing

OFHEO's website located at *www.OFHEO.gov.*

[59 FR 62304, Dec. 5, 1994, as amended at 65 FR 39787, June 28, 2000; 69 FR 18809, Apr. 9, 2004; 70 FR 59629, Oct. 13, 2005]

§ 1700.3 Official logo and seal.

The section describes and displays the logo adopted by the Director as the official symbol representing the Office of Federal Housing Enterprise Oversight. It is displayed on correspondence, selected documents, and signage. The logo serves as the official seal to authenticate official documents of the Agency.

(a) *Description.* The logo is a disc consisting of two concentric circles enclosing the words "Office of Federal Housing Enterprise Oversight" and the inaugural year, 1993. In the center of the disc is a stylized image of a structure consisting of a solid two-tiered pedestal base topped by a solid triangular shape, which represents the roof of the structure. Placed between the base and the top are the letters "OFHEO." These letters spell out the acronym of the Office of Federal Housing Enterprise Oversight and act as a visual link between the top and bottom of the structure.

(b) *Display.* The Office of Federal Housing Enterprise Oversight's official logo and seal appears below:

[68 FR 32629, June 2, 2003]

PART 1703—RELEASE OF INFORMATION

AUTHORITY: 5 U.S.C. 301, 552; 12 U.S.C. 4513, 4522, 4526, 4639; E.O. 12600, 3 CFR, 1987 Comp., p. 235.

SOURCE: 63 FR 71005, Dec. 23, 1998, unless otherwise noted. Redesignated at 65 FR 81327, Dec. 26, 2000.

Subparts A–D [Reserved]

Subpart E—Testimony and Production of Documents in Legal Proceedings in Which OFHEO Is Not a Named Party

§ 1703.31 General purposes.

The purposes of this subpart are to maintain the confidentiality of official documents and information of OFHEO, conserve the time of employees for their official duties, maintain the impartial position of OFHEO in litigation in which OFHEO is not a named party, and enable the Director to determine when to authorize testimony and to produce documents in legal proceedings in which OFHEO is not a named party. This subpart sets forth the procedures to be followed with respect to testimony concerning official matters and production of official documents of OFHEO in legal proceedings in which OFHEO is not a named party. This subpart in no way affects the rights and procedures governing public access to official documents pursuant to the FOIA or the Privacy Act.

§ 1703.32 Definitions.

For the purpose of this subpart:

(a) *Court* means any entity conducting a legal proceeding.

(b) *Demand* means any order, subpoena, or other legal process for testimony or documents.

(c) *Legal proceeding* means any administrative, civil, or criminal proceeding, including a discovery proceeding therein, before a court of law, administrative board or commission, hearing officer, or other body in which OFHEO is not a named party or in which OFHEO has not instituted the administrative investigation or administrative hearing.

(d) *OFHEO Counsel* means the General Counsel or his or her designee, a Department of Justice attorney, or counsel authorized by OFHEO to act on behalf of OFHEO or an employee.

§ 1703.33 General policy.

It is the policy of OFHEO that in any legal proceeding in which OFHEO is not a named party, no employee shall, in response to a demand, produce any documents contained in the files of OFHEO, or disclose any information relating to, or based upon, documents contained in the files of OFHEO, or disclose or produce any documents acquired as part of the performance of that employee's official duties or because of that employee's official status. Under appropriate circumstances, the Director may grant exceptions in writing to this policy when the Director determines that the testimony of employees or disclosure of official documents would be in the best interest of OFHEO or in the public interest. Prior to any authorized testimony or release of official documents, the requesting party shall obtain a protective order from the court before which the action is pending to preserve the confidentiality of the testimony or documents subsequently produced. The protective order shall be in a form satisfactory to OFHEO.

§ 1703.34 Request for testimony or production of documents.

(a) No employee shall give testimony concerning official matters or produce any official documents in any legal proceeding to which OFHEO is not a named party without the prior written authorization of the Director.

(b) If testimony by an employee concerning official matters or the production of official documents is desired, the requesting party, or his or her attorney, shall submit a letter to the Director setting forth the title of the case, the forum, the requesting party's interest in the case, a summary of the issues in the litigation, the reasons for the request, and a showing that the desired testimony, documents, or information are not reasonably available from any other source. If an appearance or testimony is requested, the letter shall also set forth the intended use of the testimony, a general summary of the scope of the testimony requested, and a showing that no document could be provided and used in lieu of the testimony or other appearance requested.

(c) The General Counsel is authorized to consult with the requesting party or his or her attorney to refine and limit the request so that compliance is less burdensome, or obtain information necessary to make the determination described in § 1703.33 of this subpart. Failure of the requesting party, or his or her attorney, to cooperate in good faith with the General Counsel to enable the Director to make an informed determination under this subpart may serve as the basis for a determination not to comply with the request.

[63 FR 71005, Dec. 23, 1998. Redesignated and amended at 65 FR 81327, Dec. 26, 2000]

§ 1703.35 Scope of permissible testimony.

(a) The scope of permissible testimony by an employee is limited to that set forth in the written authorization granted that employee by the Director.

(b) Employees are not authorized to give opinion testimony, except as authorized by the Director. OFHEO, as the regulatory agency charged with the responsibility of examining, supervising, and regulating the financial safety and soundness and capital adequacy of the Enterprises under the

Federal Housing Enterprises Financial Safety and Soundness Act of 1992, 12 U.S.C. 4501 *et seq.*, relies on the ability of its employees to gather full and complete information in order to carry out its statutory responsibilities. The use of employees to give opinion testimony would hamper OFHEO's ability to carry out its statutory responsibilities and would cause a serious administrative burden on OFHEO's staff.

§ 1703.36 Manner in which testimony is given.

(a) Authorized testimony of employees ordinarily will be made available only through depositions or written interrogatories.

(b) Where, in response to a request, the Director determines that circumstances warrant authorizing testimony by an employee, the requesting party shall cause a subpoena to be served on the employee in accordance with applicable Federal or State rules of procedure, with a copy of the subpoena sent by registered or certified mail to the General Counsel.

(c) Normally, authorized depositions will be taken at OFHEO's office, at a time arranged with the employee that is reasonably fixed to avoid substantial interference with the performance of the employee's duties.

(d) Upon completion of the deposition of an employee, a copy of the transcript of the testimony shall be furnished, at the expense of the party requesting the deposition, to the General Counsel for OFHEO's files.

§ 1703.37 Manner in which documents will be produced.

(a) An employee's authorization to produce official documents is limited to the authority granted that employee by the Director.

(b) Certified or authenticated copies of official OFHEO documents authorized by the Director to be released under this subpart will be provided upon request.

§ 1703.38 Fees.

Unless waived or reduced, the following fees shall be charged for documents produced by OFHEO in connection with requests subject to this subpart:

(a) *Searches for documents.* OFHEO will charge for the actual search time of the employee performing the work, billed in 15-minute segments, as described in § 1703.22(b)(1)(i).

(b) *Copying of documents.* The standard copying charge for documents in paper copy is $.15 per page. When responsive information is provided in a format other than paper copy, such as in the form of computer tapes and disks, OFHEO will assess the direct costs of the tape, disk, or whatever medium is used to produce the information, as well as any related reproduction costs. Normally, only one copy will be provided. Additional copies will be provided only upon a showing of demonstrated need.

(c) *Certification or authentication of documents.* OFHEO will charge $3.00 for each certification or authentication of documents.

(d) *Computer searches.* Services of personnel in the nature of a computer search shall be charged at rates prescribed in paragraph (a) of this section. A charge shall be made for the computer time involved, based upon the prevailing level of costs to OFHEO and upon the particular types of computer and associated equipment and the amount of time that such equipment is utilized. A charge shall also be made for any substantial amount of special supplies or documents used to contain, present, or make available the output of computers, based upon prevailing levels of costs to OFHEO and upon the type and amount of such supplies or documents that are used.

(e) *Other costs.* When other services and documents not specifically identified in this section are requested and provided, their actual cost to OFHEO shall be charged.

(f) *Payments of fees.* A bill will be forwarded to the requesting party upon completion of the production. Payment shall be made by check or money order payable to the Office of Federal Housing Enterprise Oversight.

[63 FR 71005, Dec. 23, 1998, as amended at 65 FR 55175, Sept. 13, 2000. Redesignated and amended at 65 FR 81327, Dec. 26, 2000]

§ 1703.39 Responses to demands served on employees.

(a) *Advice by employee served.* Any employee who is served with a demand in a legal proceeding requiring his or her personal attendance as a witness or requiring the production of documents or information in any proceeding, shall immediately notify the General Counsel of such service, of the testimony and documents described in the demand, and of all relevant facts which may be of assistance to the General Counsel in determining whether the individual in question should be authorized to testify or the documents requested should be made available.

(b) When authorization to testify or to produce documents has not been granted by the Director, OFHEO Counsel shall provide the party issuing the demand or the court with a copy of the regulations contained in this subpart and shall inform the party issuing the demand or the court that the employee upon whom the demand has been made is prohibited from testifying or producing documents without the prior approval of the Director.

(c) *Appearance by employee served.* Unless OFHEO has authorized disclosure of the information requested, any employee who has OFHEO information that may not be disclosed and who is required to respond to a subpoena or other legal process, shall attend at the time and place required and respectfully decline to disclose or to give any testimony with respect to the information, basing such refusal upon the provisions of this subpart. If the court nevertheless orders the disclosure of the information or the giving of testimony irrespective of instructions from the Director not to produce the documents or disclose the information sought, the employee upon whom the demand has been made shall continue to decline respectfully to disclose the information and shall report promptly the facts to OFHEO for such action as OFHEO may deem appropriate.

(d) A determination under this subpart to comply or not to comply with any demand shall not constitute an assertion or waiver of privilege, lack of relevance, technical deficiencies, or any other ground for noncompliance. OFHEO reserves the right to oppose any demand on any legal ground independent of its determination under this subpart.

§ 1703.40 Responses to demands served on nonemployees.

(a) OFHEO reports of examinations, or any documents related thereto, are the property of OFHEO and are not to be disclosed to any person without the Director's prior written consent.

(b) If any person who has possession of an OFHEO report of examination, or any documents related thereto, is served with a demand in a legal proceeding directing that person to produce such OFHEO documents or to testify with respect thereto, such person shall immediately notify the General Counsel of such service, of the testimony and described documents in the demand, and of all relevant facts. Such person shall also object to the production of such documents or information contained therein on the basis that the documents are the property of OFHEO and cannot be released without OFHEO's consent and that their production must be sought from OFHEO following the procedures set forth in § 1703.33, paragraphs (b) and (c) of § 1703.34, and paragraph (b) of § 1703.37 of this subpart.

[63 FR 71005, Dec. 23, 1998. Redesignated and amended at 65 FR 81328, Dec. 26, 2000]

Subpart F—Rules and Procedures for Service Upon OFHEO

§ 1703.51 Service of process.

(a) Except as otherwise provided by OFHEO regulations, the Federal Rules of Civil Procedure, or order of a court with jurisdiction over OFHEO, any legal process upon OFHEO, including a legal process served on OFHEO demanding access to its records under the FOIA, shall be duly issued and served upon the General Counsel and any OFHEO personnel named in the caption of the documents.

(b) Service of process upon the General Counsel may be effected by personally delivering a copy of the documents to the General Counsel or by sending a copy of the documents to the General Counsel by registered or certified mail, postage prepaid, to the Office of Federal Housing Enterprise Oversight, 1700 G Street, NW., Fourth Floor, Washington, DC 20552.

SUBCHAPTER B [RESERVED]

SUBCHAPTER C—SAFETY AND SOUNDNESS

PART 1710—CORPORATE GOVERNANCE

Subpart A—General

Subpart B—Corporate Practices and Procedures

Subpart C—Indemnification

Subpart D—Modification of Certain Provisions

AUTHORITY: 12 U.S.C. 4513(a) and 4513(b)(1).

SOURCE: 67 FR 38370, June 4, 2002, unless otherwise noted.

Subpart A—General

§ 1710.1 Purpose.

OFHEO is responsible under the Federal Housing Enterprises Financial Safety and Soundness Act of 1992, 12 U.S.C. 4501 *et seq.*, for ensuring the safety and soundness of the Enterprises. In furtherance of that responsibility, this part sets forth minimum standards with respect to the corporate governance practices and procedures of the Enterprises.

§ 1710.2 Definitions.

For purposes of this part, the term:

(a) *Act* means the Federal Housing Enterprises Financial Safety and Soundness Act of 1992, Title XIII of the Housing and Community Development Act of 1992, Pub. L. 102–550, section 1301, Oct. 28, 1992, 106 Stat. 3672, 3941 through 4012 (1993) (12 U.S.C. 4501 *et seq.*).

(b) *Board member* means a member of the board of directors.

(c) *Board of directors* means the board of directors of an Enterprise.

(d) *Chartering acts* mean the Federal National Mortgage Association Charter Act and the Federal Home Loan Mortgage Corporation Act, which are codified at 12 U.S.C. 1716 through 1723i and 12 U.S.C. 1451 through 1459, respectively.

(e) *Compensation* means any payment of money or the provision of any other thing of current or potential value in connection with employment. The term "compensation" includes all direct and indirect payments of benefits, both cash and non-cash, including, but not limited to, payments and benefits derived from compensation or benefit agreements, fee arrangements, perquisites, stock option plans, post employment benefits, or other compensatory arrangements.

(f) *Director* means the Director of OFHEO or his or her designee.

(g) *Employee* means a salaried individual, other than an executive officer, who works part-time, full-time, or temporarily for an Enterprise.

(h) *Enterprise* means the Federal National Mortgage Association or the Federal Home Loan Mortgage Corporation; and the term "Enterprises" means, collectively, the Federal National Mortgage Association and the Federal Home Loan Mortgage Corporation.

(i) *Executive officer* means any senior executive officer and any senior vice president of an Enterprise and any individual with similar responsibilities, without regard to title, who is in charge of a principal business unit, division, or function of an Enterprise, or who reports directly to the chairperson, vice chairperson, chief operating officer, or president of an Enterprise.

(j) *NYSE* means the New York Stock Exchange.

(k) *OFHEO* means the Office of Federal Housing Enterprise Oversight.

(l) *Senior executive officer* means the chairperson of the board of directors, chief executive officer, chief financial officer, chief operating officer, president, vice chairperson, any executive vice president of an Enterprise, and any individual, without regard to title, who has similar responsibilities.

§§ 1710.3–1710.9 [Reserved]

Subpart B—Corporate Practices and Procedures

§ 1710.10 Law applicable to corporate governance.

(a) *General.* The corporate governance practices and procedures of each Enterprise shall comply with applicable chartering acts and other Federal law, rules, and regulations, and shall be consistent with the safe and sound operations of the Enterprise.

(b) *Election and designation of body of law.* (1) To the extent not inconsistent with paragraph (a) of this section, each Enterprise shall follow the corporate governance practices and procedures of the law of the jurisdiction in which the principal office of the Enterprise is located, as amended; Delaware General Corporation Law, Del. Code Ann. tit. 8, as amended; or the Revised Model Business Corporation Act, as amended.

(2) Each Enterprise shall designate in its bylaws the body of law elected for its corporate governance practices and procedures pursuant to this paragraph within 90 calendar days from August 5, 2002.

§ 1710.11 Board of directors.

(a) *Membership*—(1) *Limits on service of board members*—(i) *General requirement.* No board member of an Enterprise may serve on the board of directors for more than 10 years or past the age of 72, whichever comes first; provided, however, a board member may serve his or her full term if he or she has served less than 10 years or is 72 years on the date of his or her election or appointment to the board.

(ii) *Waiver.* Upon written request of an Enterprise, the Director may waive, in his or her sole discretion and for good cause, the limits on the service of a board member under paragraph (a)(1)(i) of this section.

(2) *Independence of board members.* A majority of seated members of the board of directors of an Enterprise shall be independent board members, as defined under rules set forth by the NYSE, as amended from time to time.

(b) *Meetings, quorum and proxies, information, and annual review*—(1) *Frequency of meetings.* The board of directors of an Enterprise shall meet at least eight times a year and no less than once a calendar quarter to carry out its obligations and duties under applicable laws, rules, regulations, and guidelines.

(2) *Non-management board member meetings.* Non-management directors of an Enterprise shall meet at regularly scheduled executive sessions without management participation.

(3) *Quorum of board of directors; proxies not permissible.* For the transaction of business, a quorum of the board of directors of an Enterprise is at least a majority of the seated board of directors and a board member may not vote by proxy.

(4) *Information.* Management of an Enterprise shall provide a board member of the Enterprise with such adequate and appropriate information that a reasonable board member would find important to the fulfillment of his or her fiduciary duties and obligations.

(5) *Annual review.* At least annually, the board of directors of an Enterprise shall review, with appropriate professional assistance, the requirements of laws, rules, regulations, and guidelines that are applicable to its activities and duties.

[70 FR 17310, Apr. 6, 2005]

§ 1710.12 Committees of board of directors.

(a) *General.* The board of directors may rely, in directing the Enterprise, on reports from committees of the board of directors, provided, however, that no committee of the board of directors shall have the authority of the board of directors to amend the bylaws and no committee shall operate to relieve the board of directors or any board member of a responsibility imposed by applicable law, rule, or regulation.

(b) *Frequency of meetings.* A committee of the board of directors of an Enterprise shall meet with sufficient frequency to carry out its obligations and duties under applicable laws, rules, regulations, and guidelines.

(c) *Required committees.* An Enterprise shall provide for the establishment of, however styled, the following committees of the board of directors, which committees shall be in compliance with the charter, independence, composition, expertise, duties, responsibilities, and other requirements set forth under section 301 of the Sarbanes-Oxley Act of 2002, Pub. L. 107–204 (Jul. 30, 2002) (SOA), as amended from time to time, with respect to the audit committee, and under rules issued by the NYSE, as amended from time to time—

(1) Audit committee;

(2) Compensation committee; and

(3) Nominating/corporate governance committee.

[67 FR 38370, June 4, 2002. Redesignated and amended at 70 FR 17310, 17311, Apr. 6, 2005]

§ 1710.13 Compensation of board members, executive officers, and employees.

(a) *General.* Compensation of board members, executive officers, and employees of an Enterprise shall not be in excess of that which is reasonable and appropriate, shall be commensurate with the duties and responsibilities of such persons, shall be consistent with the long-term goals of the Enterprise, shall not focus solely on earnings performance, but shall take into account risk management, operational stability and legal and regulatory compliance as well, and shall be undertaken in a manner that complies with applicable laws, rules, and regulations.

(b) *Reimbursement.* If an Enterprise is required to prepare an accounting restatement due to the material noncompliance of the Enterprise, as a result of misconduct, with any financial reporting requirement under the securities laws, the chief executive officer and chief financial officer of the Enterprise shall reimburse the Enterprise as provided under section 304 of the SOA, as amended from time to time. This provision does not otherwise limit the authority of OFHEO to employ remedies available to it under its enforcement authorities.

[67 FR 38370, June 4, 2002. Redesignated and amended at 70 FR 17310, 17311, Apr. 6, 2005]

§ 1710.14 Code of conduct and ethics.

(a) *General.* An Enterprise shall establish and administer a written code of conduct and ethics that is reasonably designed to assure the ability of board members, executive officers, and employees of the Enterprise to discharge their duties and responsibilities, on behalf of the Enterprise, in an objective and impartial manner, and that includes standards required under section 406 of the SOA, as amended from time to time, and other applicable laws, rules, and regulations.

(b) *Review.* Not less than once every three years, an Enterprise shall review the adequacy of its code of conduct and ethics for consistency with practices appropriate to the Enterprise and make any appropriate revisions to such code.

[70 FR 17311, Apr. 6, 2005]

§ 1710.15 Conduct and responsibilities of board of directors.

(a) *Purpose.* The purpose of this section, and of this subpart, is to set forth minimum standards of the conduct and responsibilities of the board of directors in furtherance of the safe and sound operations of each Enterprise. The provisions of this section neither provide shareholders of an Enterprise with additional rights nor impose liability on any board member under State law.

(b) *Conduct and responsibilities.* The board of directors of an Enterprise is responsible for directing the conduct and affairs of the Enterprise in furtherance of the safe and sound operation of the Enterprise and shall remain reasonably informed of the condition, activities, and operations of the Enterprise. The responsibilities of the board of directors include having in place adequate policies and procedures to assure its oversight of, among other matters, the following:

(1) Corporate strategy, major plans of action, risk policy, programs for legal and regulatory compliance and corporate performance, including but not limited to prudent plans for growth and allocation of adequate resources to manage operations risk;

(2) Hiring and retention of qualified senior executive officers and succession planning for such senior executive officers;

(3) Compensation programs of the Enterprise;

(4) Integrity of accounting and financial reporting systems of the Enterprise, including independent audits and systems of internal control;

(5) Process and adequacy of reporting, disclosures, and communications to shareholders, investors, and potential investors;

(6) Extensions of credit to board members and executive officers; and

(7) Responsiveness of executive officers in providing accurate and timely reports to Federal regulators and in addressing the supervisory concerns of Federal regulators in a timely and appropriate manner.

(c) *Guidance.* The board of directors should refer to the body of law elected under § 1710.10 and to publications and other pronouncements of OFHEO for additional guidance on conduct and responsibilities of the board of directors.

[67 FR 38370, June 4, 2002, as amended at 70 FR 17311, Apr. 6, 2005]

§ 1710.16 Prohibition of extensions of credit to board members and executive officers.

An Enterprise may not directly or indirectly, including through any subsidiary, extend or maintain credit, arrange for the extension of credit, or renew an extension of credit, in the form of a personal loan to or for any board member or executive officer of the Enterprise as provided by section 402 of the SOA, as amended from time to time.

[70 FR 17311, Apr. 6, 2005]

§ 1710.17 Certification of disclosures by chief executive officer and chief financial officer.

The chief executive officer and the chief financial officer of an Enterprise shall review each quarterly report and annual report issued by the Enterprise and such reports shall include certifications by such officers as required by section 302 of the SOA, as amended from time to time.

[70 FR 17311, Apr. 6, 2005]

§ 1710.18 Change of audit partner.

An Enterprise may not accept audit services from an external auditing firm if the lead or coordinating audit partner who has primary responsibility for the external audit of the Enterprise, or the external audit partner who has responsibility for reviewing the external audit has performed audit services for the Enterprise in each of the five previous fiscal years.

[70 FR 17312, Apr. 6, 2005]

§ 1710.19 Compliance and risk management programs; compliance with other laws.

(a) *Compliance program.* (1) An Enterprise shall establish and maintain a compliance program that is reasonably designed to assure that the Enterprise complies with applicable laws, rules, regulations, and internal controls.

(2) The compliance program shall be headed by a compliance officer, however styled, who reports directly to the chief executive officer of the Enterprise. The compliance officer shall report regularly to the board of directors or an appropriate committee of the board of directors on compliance with and the adequacy of current compliance policies and procedures of the Enterprise, and shall recommend any adjustments to such policies and procedures that he or she considers necessary and appropriate.

(b) *Risk management program.* (1) An Enterprise shall establish and maintain a risk management program that is reasonably designed to manage the risks of the operations of the Enterprise.

(2) The risk management program shall be headed by a risk management

officer, however styled, who reports directly to the chief executive officer of the Enterprise. The risk management officer shall report regularly to the board of directors or an appropriate committee of the board of directors on compliance with and the adequacy of current risk management policies and procedures of the Enterprise, and shall recommend any adjustments to such policies and procedures that he or she considers necessary and appropriate.

(c) *Compliance with other laws.* (1) If an Enterprise deregisters or has not registered its common stock with the U.S. Securities and Exchange Commission (Commission) under the Securities Exchange Act of 1934, the Enterprise shall comply or continue to comply with sections 301, 302, 304, 402, and 406 of the SOA, as amended from time to time, subject to such requirements as provided by § 1710.30 of this part.

(2) An Enterprise that has its common stock registered with the Commission shall maintain such registered status, unless it provides 60 days prior written notice to the Director stating its intent to deregister and its understanding that it will remain subject to the requirements of sections 301, 302, 304, 402, and 406 of the SOA, as amended from time to time, subject to such requirements as provided by § 1710.30 of this part.

[70 FR 17312, Apr. 6, 2005]

Subpart C—Indemnification

§ 1710.20 Indemnification.

(a) *Safety and soundness authority.* OFHEO has the authority, under the Act, to prohibit or restrict reimbursement or indemnification of any current or former board member or any current or former executive officer by an Enterprise or by any affiliate of an Enterprise in furtherance of the safe and sound operations of the Enterprise.

(b) *Policies and procedures.* Each Enterprise shall have in place policies and procedures consistent with this part for indemnification, including the approval or denial by the board of directors of indemnification of current and former board members and current or former executive officers. Such policies and procedures should address, among other matters, standards relating to indemnification, investigation by the board of directors, and review by independent counsel.

Subpart D—Modification of Certain Provisions

§ 1710.30 Modification of certain provisions.

In connection with standards of Federal or state law (including the Revised Model Corporation Act) or NYSE rules that are made applicable to an Enterprise by §§ 1710.10, 1710.11, 1710.12, 1710.17, and 1710.19 of this part, the Director, in his or her sole discretion, may modify the standards contained in this part in accordance with 5 U.S.C. 553 and upon written notice to the Enterprise.

[70 FR 17312, Apr. 6, 2005]

PART 1720—SAFETY AND SOUNDNESS

AUTHORITY: 12 U.S.C. 4513(a), 4513(b)(1), 4513(b)(5), 4517(a), 4521(a)(2) through (3), 4631, 4632, and 4636.

SOURCE: 67 FR 55693, Aug. 30, 2002, unless otherwise noted.

§ 1720.1 Authority.

(a) *Authority.* This part is issued by the Office of Federal Housing Enterprise Oversight (OFHEO) pursuant to sections 1313(a), 1313(b)(1), and 1313(b)(5) of the Federal Housing Enterprise Financial Safety and Soundness Act (Act) (12 U.S.C. 4513(a), 4513(b)(1), and 4513(b)(5)). These provisions of the Act authorize OFHEO to take any action deemed appropriate by the Director of OFHEO to ensure that the Federal National Mortgage Association and the Federal Home Loan Mortgage Corporation (the Enterprises) are operated in a safe and sound manner, including by adopting supervisory policies and standards by regulation, guidance, or other process.

(b) *Preservation of existing authority.* No action by OFHEO undertaken with reference to a policy guidance or this regulation will in any way limit the authority of the Director otherwise to address unsafe or unsound conditions or practices, or other violations of law, rule or regulation. Action with reference to a policy guidance or this regulation may be taken separate from, in conjunction with, or in addition to any other supervisory response, enforcement action, or agency-imposed requirements deemed appropriate by OFHEO. Nothing in this regulation or any guidance issued by OFHEO limits the authority of the Director pursuant to section 1313 of the Act (12 U.S.C. 4513) or any other provision of law, rule or regulation applicable to the Enterprises.

§ 1720.2 Safety and soundness standards.

Policy guidances as may be adopted from time to time by OFHEO, addressing safety and soundness standards, shall apply to the Enterprises. If OFHEO determines that an Enterprise does not meet a requirement set out in such policy guidance, it may require corrective or remedial actions by the Enterprise, and take such enforcement action as the Director deems to be appropriate.

Appendix A to Part 1720—Policy Guidance; Minimum Safety and Soundness Requirements

A—Background and Introduction

I. Background. The Federal Housing Enterprises Safety and Soundness Act of 1992, Title XIII of Pub. L. No. 102–550 (the Act) empowers OFHEO to take any such action as the Director determines to be appropriate to ensure that the federally sponsored housing enterprises, Fannie Mae and Freddie Mac, are, among other things, adequately capitalized and operating safely, including by adopting supervisory policies and standards by regulation or other guidance or process.

i. OFHEO herein sets forth the minimum supervisory requirements used by the agency in reviewing the ensuring, the adequacy of policies and procedures of the Enterprises in the areas of: (1) Asset underwriting and credit quality; (2) balance sheet growth; (3) market risks; (4) information technology; (5) internal controls; (6) audits; (7) information reporting and documentation; and (8) board and management responsibilities and functions. If the agency finds that an Enterprise fails to meet any requirement or standard set forth in this pronouncement, the Director may, among other things, require the Enterprise to submit to the agency and implement an adequate plan to achieve timely compliance with the requirement or standard. If the Enterprise fails to submit such an adequate plan within the time specified by the agency or fails in any material respect to implement the plan, the agency may take additional supervisory action. The Director may at any time prescribe such supervisory actions as deemed appropriate to correct conditions resulting from an unsafe or unsound practice or condition or deficiency in complying with regulatory requirements or standards including, but not limited to, issuance of a notice of charges or order, imposition of civil money penalties, or other remedial actions or sanctions as determined by the Director.

ii. The minimum supervisory requirements and standards identify key safety and soundness concerns regarding operation and management of an Enterprise, and ensure that action is taken to avoid the emergence of problems that might entail serious risks to an Enterprise. The minimum supervisory requirements of the Policy Guidance also reflect the need for internal policies and procedures in particular areas that, if not appropriately addressed by the Enterprises, may warrant action by OFHEO in order to reduce risks of loss and possible capital impairment. The proposed minimum requirements set forth herein are intended to effect these purposes without dictating how the Enterprises must be operated and managed; moreover, the Policy Guidance does not set out detailed operational and managerial procedures that an Enterprise must have in place. The Policy Guidance is intended to identify the ends that proper operational and management policies and procedures are to achieve, while leaving the means to be devised by each Enterprise as it designs and implements its own policies and procedures. Where OFHEO does specify particular requirements, each Enterprise's management is left with substantial flexibility to fashion and implement them.

iii. The Policy Guidance is not intended to effect a change in OFHEO's policies; the announced minimum requirements reflect the basic underlying criteria OFHEO uses to assess the operations and managerial quality of an Enterprise. OFHEO will determine compliance with the requirements and related standards through examinations of the Enterprises, as well as off-site surveillance means and other interchanges with each Enterprise.

iv. OFHEO routinely undertakes to evaluate an Enterprise's overall policies, in order to determine whether such policies are safe and sound in principle and in practice. OFHEO also evaluates whether procedures are in place to ensure that an Enterprise's overall policies as adopted by the Enterprise's board of directors and management are, in fact, applied in the normal course of business. As reflected in the Policy Guidance, the Enterprises are, at a minimum, expected to adopt appropriate policies and internal guidelines, and to put in place procedures to ensure they are followed as a matter of routine.

v. Nothing in the Policy Guidance in any way limits the authority of OFHEO to otherwise address unsafe or unsound conditions or practices, or violations of applicable law, regulation or supervisory order. Action referencing the Policy Guidance may be taken separate from, in conjunction with or in addition to any other enforcement action available to OFHEO. Compliance with the Policy Guidance in general would not preclude a finding by the agency that an Enterprise is otherwise engaged in a specific unsafe or unsound practice or is in an unsafe or unsound condition, or requiring corrective or remedial action with regard to such practice or condition. That is, supervisory action is not precluded against an Enterprise that has not been cited for a deficiency under the Policy Guidance. Conversely, an Enterprise's failure to comply with one of the supervisory requirements set forth in the Policy Guidance may not warrant a formal supervisory response from OFHEO, if the agency determines the matter may be otherwise addressed in a satisfactory manner. For example, OFHEO may require timely submission of a plan to achieve compliance with the particular requirement or standard without taking any other enforcement action.

II. Introduction. i. *Authority, purpose, and scope.*

a. Authority. This Policy Guidance is issued by the Office of Federal Housing Enterprise Oversight (OFHEO) pursuant to sections 1313(a), 1313(b)(1), 1313(b)(5) and 1371 of the Federal Housing Enterprise Safety and Soundness Act (Act) (12 U.S.C. 4513(a), 4513(b)(1), 4513(b)(5) and 4631). These provisions of the Act authorize OFHEO to take any action deemed appropriate by the Director of OFHEO to ensure that the Federal National Mortgage Association and the Federal Home Loan Mortgage Corporation (the Enterprises) are operated in a safe and sound manner, including by adopting supervisory policies and standards by regulation, guidance, or other process.

b. Purpose and scope. This Policy Guidance sets out certain minimum safety and soundness requirements for the business and operations of the Enterprises, and reiterates agency policies requiring the Enterprises to establish and implement policies and procedures that are sufficient to effectuate compliance with supervisory standards. If OFHEO determines that an Enterprise does not meet the requirements set forth herein, the Director may require the Enterprise to submit and carry out a plan to achieve compliance, or may take other corrective and remedial actions. The requirements enumerated herein are supervisory minimums. In order to satisfy an Enterprise's overarching obligation under the Act to conduct is operations in a safe and sound manner, it may be necessary and appropriate for an Enterprise to take additional measures in these or other areas, as directed by OFHEO through regulation, guidance, order or otherwise as part of the supervisory process.

ii. *Preservation of existing authority.* Neither this Policy Guidance nor any action by OFHEO to enforce compliance of an Enterprise therewith in any way limits the authority of the Director otherwise to address unsafe or unsound conditions or practices, or other violations of law or other regulation. Action under this Policy Guidance may be taken separate from, in conjunction with, or in addition to any other enforcement action deemed appropriate by OFHEO. Nothing in this Policy Guidance or related guidances limits the authority of the Director pursuant to section 1313 of the Act (12 U.S.C. 4513) or any other provision of law, rule or regulation applicable to the Enterprises.

iii. *Definitions.* For purposes of this Policy Guidance, except as modified therein or unless the context otherwise requires, the terms used have the same meaning as set forth in section 1303 of the Act (12 U.S.C. 4502).

B—OPERATIONAL AND MANAGERIAL REQUIREMENTS

I. Asset underwriting and credit quality. An Enterprise should establish and implement policies and procedures to adequately assess credit risks before they are assumed, and monitor such risks subsequently to ensure that they conform to the Enterprise's credit risk standards on an individual and an aggregate basis. The Enterprise should:

i. For loans purchased and loans collateralizing securities guaranteed by the Enterprise, adopt and implement prudent underwriting standards and procedures commensurate with the type of loan or loans and the markets in which the loan or loans were made that include consideration of the borrower's and any guarantor's financial condition and ability to repay as well as the type and value of any collateral or credit enhancement;

ii. To the extent the Enterprise's assets are serviced or administered by other entities or are covered by mortgage insurance or other credit enhancements or arrangements, the Enterprise's policies and procedures should recognize the consequences and implications of such contractual arrangements for the Enterprise's credit risk;

iii. Establish and implement policies and procedures to address declining credit quality and to require appropriate corrective action; to establish sufficient reserves; and to deal with defaulted assets so as to minimize losses;

iv. Establish and implement policies and procedures to select and price credit risk to ensure that the Enterprise is appropriately compensated commensurate with the credit risk it assumes and its statutory obligations;

v. Establish and implement policies and procedures that address the prudential selection, management and handling of counterparty credit exposure that arises from engaging in hedging activities and the use derivative instruments; and

vi. Establish and implement policies and procedures to identify, monitor and evaluate its credit exposures on an aggregate basis so as to assess the implications and consequences of matters such as concentration exposure (including geographic as well as product concentrations), to identify and evaluate credit risk trends effectively, and to maintain and revise appropriately its systems and procedures for underwriting, servicing, and monitoring of such exposures and changes to those exposures.

II. Balance sheet growth and management. An Enterprise's balance sheet growth should be prudent and consider:

i. The source, volatility, and use of funds that support balance sheet growth;

ii. Any changes in credit risk or interest rate risk resulting from balance sheet growth;

iii. The effect of balance sheet growth on the Enterprise's capital adequacy; and

iv. The appropriate policies and procedures needed to manage changes in risk that may occur as a result of balance sheet growth.

III. Market risk. An Enterprise should establish and implement policies and procedures that allow for the effective identification, measurement, monitoring, and management of market risk. The Enterprise should:

i. Establish and implement policies and procedures sufficient to quantify and monitor the interest rate risk of the Enterprise effectively and to model the effect of differing interest rate scenarios on the Enterprise's financial condition and operations;

ii. Develop risk management strategies that respond appropriately to changes in interest rates;

iii. Establish and implement policies and procedures sufficient to quantify and monitor the Enterprise's liquidity effectively, and to identify and anticipate various market environments and their effects on the Enterprises' liquidity; and

iv. Establish and maintain an effective contingency plan for liquidity under varying scenarios.

IV. Information technology. An Enterprise should establish and implement policies and procedures to ensure that its computing resources, proprietary and nonpublic information and data are:

i. Protected from access by unauthorized users, and otherwise protected by appropriate security measures;

ii. Reliable, accurate and available at all times as needed for its business operations, including an ability to effect timely recovery and resume operations after a reasonably foreseeable adverse event; and

iii. Designed to ensure adequate support of business operations.

V. Internal controls. An Enterprise should maintain and implement internal controls appropriate to the nature, scope and risk of its business activities that, at a minimum, provide for:

i. An organizational structure and assignment of responsibility for management, employees, consultants and contractors, that provide for accountability and controls, including adherence to policies and procedures;

ii. A control framework commensurate with the Enterprise's risks;

iii. Policies and procedures adequate to safeguard and to manage assets; and

iv. Compliance with applicable laws, regulations and policies.

VI. Audits. An Enterprise should establish and implement internal and external audit programs appropriate to the nature and scope of its business activities that, at minimum, provide for:

i. Adequate monitoring of internal controls through an audit function appropriate to the

Enterprise's size, structure and scope of operations;

ii. Independence of the audit function;

iii. Qualified professionals and management for the conduct and review of audit functions;

iv. Adequate testing and review of audited areas together with adequate documentation of findings and of any recommendations and corrective actions; and

v. Verification and review of measures and actions undertaken to address identified material weaknesses.

VII. Information reporting and documentation. An Enterprise should establish and implement policies and procedures for generating and retaining reports and documents that:

i. Enable the Enterprise's board of directors (including appropriate committees) to make informed decisions and to exercise its oversight function, by providing all such relevant information of an appropriate level of detail as necessary;

ii. Enable the Enterprise's managers to make informed business decisions and to assess risks for all aspects of the Enterprise's business on an ongoing basis, by providing sufficient relevant information of an appropriate level of detail as necessary;

iii. Ensure decision-makers have appropriate and necessary information about particular transactions and business operations;

iv. Enable the Enterprise to administer and supervise all assets, liabilities, commitments and other financial obligations appropriately;

v. Enable the Enterprise to enforce legal claims against borrowers, counterparties and other obligors; and

vi. Ensure timely and complete submissions of reports of financial condition and operations, as well as annual and other periodic reports and special reports to OFHEO whenever requested or required by OFHEO.

VIII. Board and management responsibilities and function. An Enterprise's board of directors shall ensure that the board (including appropriate committees) works with executive management to establish the Enterprise's strategies and goals in an informed manner, and that the Enterprise's executive managers and other managers, as appropriate, implement such strategies, by ensuring at a minimum that:

i. The board (including appropriate committees) oversees the development of the Enterprise's strategies in key areas and exercises oversight necessary to ensure that management sets policies and controls to implement such strategies effectively;

ii. The board (including appropriate committees) hires qualified executive management, and exercises oversight to hold management accountable for meeting the Enterprise's goals and objectives;

iii. The board (including appropriate committees) is provided with accurate information about the operations and financial condition of the Enterprise in a timely fashion, and sufficient to enable the board to effect its oversight duties and responsibilities;

iv. Management of the Enterprise sets policies and controls to ensure the Enterprise's strategies are implemented effectively, and that the Enterprise's organization structure and assignment of responsibilities provide clear accountability and controls; and

v. Management of the Enterprise establishes and maintains an effective risk management framework, including review of such framework to monitor its effectiveness and taking appropriate action to correct any weaknesses.

IX. Format of policies and procedures. i. Generally, the policies of an Enterprise contemplated by this Policy Guidance should be in writing and in such form and detail as appropriate in light of their intended purpose, nature, and potential consequences for the operations and financial condition of the Enterprise, and approved by the board of directors (including appropriate committees) or such responsible officer or officers as designated by the board.

ii. The policies and procedures of an Enterprise contemplated by this Policy Guidance should be provided to OFHEO at such time and in such format as OFHEO directs.

C—COMPLIANCE PLANS

I. Notice; submission and review of compliance plans. i. *Determination.* The Director of OFHEO may, based upon a report of examination, or other supervisory information however acquired, determine that an Enterprise has failed or is likely to fail to satisfy the minimum supervisory requirements or standards set forth in part B of this appendix.

ii. *Request for compliance plan.* If the Director determines pursuant to paragraph C.I.i of this appendix that an Enterprise has failed or is likely to fail to satisfy a supervisory requirement or standard, OFHEO may require the submission of a written compliance plan.

iii. *Schedule for filing compliance plan.* An Enterprise may be required to file a written compliance plan with OFHEO within thirty days of receiving a written request for a compliance plan pursuant to paragraph C.I.ii of this appendix.

iv. *Contents of plan.* A required compliance plan should include, subject to additional direction by OFHEO, a detailed description of the steps the Enterprise will take to correct a deficiency and any condition resulting therefrom and the time within which such steps will be undertaken and fully implemented.

v. *Review of compliance plans.* If the compliance plan submitted under this section is deemed to be inadequate or incomplete,

OFHEO may provide written notice of such inadequacy or deficiencies thereof to the Enterprise OFHEO or seek additional information from the Enterprise regarding the plan.

vi. *Amendment of compliance plan.* An Enterprise that has filed a required compliance plan to which no objection has been raised by OFHEO may, after prior written notice to and approval by the Director, amend the plan to reflect changes in circumstance, policies and procedures.

II. Failure to submit acceptable plan or to comply with plan. If an Enterprise does not submit an adequate and complete plan as required by the agency within the time specified by OFHEO or does not implement such an adequate and complete plan, the Director may require the Enterprise to correct any deficiency and may require additional corrective or remedial actions by the Enterprise as deemed to be appropriate pursuant to the Act, including sections 1371 (12 U.S.C. 4631), 1372 (12 U.S.C. 4632), and 1376 (12 U.S.C. 4636).

APPENDIX B TO PART 1720—POLICY GUIDANCE; NON-MORTGAGE LIQUIDITY INVESTMENTS

A—Purpose
B—Activities Covered
C—Standards for Non-mortgage Liquidity Investment Activities
D—Disclosure of Non-mortgage Liquidity Investment Activities
E—Summary

A—PURPOSE

1. Fannie Mae and Freddie Mac (the Enterprises) were chartered by Congress as government-sponsored enterprises with public missions. They perform an important role in the United States mortgage market by gathering funds and purchasing mortgages from mortgage originators and guaranteeing mortgage-backed securities. In chartering the Enterprises, Congress charged the Enterprises with: (1) providing stability to mortgage markets; (2) responding to the changing capital markets; (3) assisting the secondary markets including the support of these markets for affordable housing; and (4) promoting access to credit throughout the country by increasing liquidity and improving distribution of investment capital for residential mortgage finance. These functions require the Enterprises, as principals in the secondary mortgage market, to serve as bedrock in providing liquidity to the U.S. housing finance system.

2. For the Enterprises effectively to perform their public purposes, they must be financially sound and liquid. As the Enterprises' financial safety and soundness regulator, OFHEO conducts its regulatory programs to ensure these companies adhere to safety and soundness standards. In addition, OFHEO interprets this to include heightening the positive effect of market discipline on the Enterprises by encouraging quality disclosures, appropriate accounting standards, and state-of-the-art risk management further strengthens their safety and soundness. More specifically, OFHEO conducts comprehensive safety and soundness examinations and requires the Enterprises to adhere to regulatory capital requirements. In conducting its regulatory programs, OFHEO applies a series of safety and soundness standards to assess the Enterprises' liquidity management, including their investments in non-mortgage liquidity assets. It is appropriate to issue initial guidance that addresses the safety and soundness standards OFHEO uses to evaluate Enterprise investment activities in non-mortgage liquidity assets.

3. Further, it should be noted that the Secretary of HUD, who has general regulatory power over the Enterprises and who is required to make such rules and regulations as necessary to ensure that the purposes of the GSE's respective Charter Acts are accomplished, has issued an Advanced Notice of Proposed Rulemaking on possible substantive and/or procedural rules governing the GSEs' non-mortgage investment activities. Accordingly, the GSEs may be subject to regulations in this area through future HUD actions, in addition to this initial guidance.

B—ACTIVITIES COVERED

1. The Enterprises must maintain sufficient liquidity to meet both known and unexpected payment demands on borrowings and mortgage securities, for operations and to purchase mortgage assets. Liquidity management is the process by which the Enterprises manage the use and availability of various funding sources to meet current and future needs. Liquidity must be closely managed on a daily basis.

2. The Enterprises manage liquidity through three primary channels: securitizations, issuance of debt and conversion of liquid assets into cash. It is through careful management within and among the three channels, that the Enterprises can effectively meet demands and remain safe and sound under all market conditions. This Guidance specifically addresses "non-mortgage liquidity investments" which are conducted within the liquidity channel whereby the Enterprises are able to convert their own assets into cash.

3. There are various types of investments that may be appropriate for non-mortgage liquidity holdings. Appropriate non-mortgage liquidity investments are characterized by both creditworthiness and low price volatility. Even though an investment may be creditworthy, if the holding is subject to undue price volatility (e.g. common stock), the investment is inappropriate for inclusion

in the non-mortgage liquidity portfolio since the investment may not be readily converted into cash without substantial loss.

4. For the purposes of this Guidance, the types of assets listed below are generally considered to be appropriate non-mortgage liquidity investments. This list is subject to revision over time as new asset types are introduced and/or market activities change. The presence of an asset on the list does not mean that OFHEO will necessarily consider any and all Enterprise investments in these assets to be safe and sound, especially if they fail to meet appropriate credit quality, maturity and diversification objectives:

a. Debt issued by the United States Treasury,

b. Debt issued by U.S. Government Agencies,

c. General obligation debt issued by states and municipal authorities,

d. Revenue obligations issued by states and municipal authorities,

e. Corporate debt instruments,

f. Money market instruments,

g. Non-mortgage asset-backed securities, and

h. Reverse repurchase agreements.

5. This Guidance does not address investments in mortgage-backed securities, mortgage revenue bonds, or other investments secured by housing (including commercial mortgage-backed securities with a significant housing component) since these assets are not principally held for liquidity purposes. Also, upon implementation of FAS 133, this Guidance is not intended to address the use of derivative instruments. For activities not covered in this Guidance on non-mortgage liquidity investments, there should be no inferences drawn about OFHEO's views.

C—Standards for Non-Mortgage Liquidity Investment Activities

To ensure there are sufficient funds available to the mortgage market, the Enterprise must actively manage liquidity across all three channels. OFHEO assesses the safety and soundness of non-mortgage liquidity investment activities against five criteria. The five criteria and details about each of the criteria are:

- Prudent investment policies and procedures that guide the Enterprise's process;
- Quality management information that ensures timely performance measures and governance data;
- Safe & sound investment holdings and investment culture;
- Quality controls and personnel administering and governing the process; and
- Independent testing of the process to assure compliance.

1. Prudent Investment Policies and Procedures That Guide the Enterprise's Process

a. The Enterprise must have a comprehensive written investment policy that clearly expresses the goals for the non-mortgage liquidity investment activities. The Board of Directors and management must evaluate the effectiveness of non-mortgage liquidity investments in meeting the goals set out in the policy; and management must evaluate activities against the procedures and limitations in the policy. At a minimum, the policy should cover:

i. The purpose of the non-mortgage liquidity investment holdings;

ii. The institutional goal(s) for the non-mortgage liquidity investment holdings;

iii. The authorized instruments and activities;

iv. The internal control standards;

v. The limits structure;

vi. The performance standards and measures; and

vii. The reporting requirements.

b. The policy should clearly document the purpose for non-mortgage liquidity investment holdings. Management should install a series of procedures and controls that produce behaviors and performance that are consistent with the defined purpose for the non-mortgage liquidity investment activities.

c. The policy should establish the primary goals for the non-mortgage liquidity investment activities. For an Enterprise, some primary goals should be to augment liquidity and to generate a rate of return that is reasonable in light of the purpose of such investments. The emphasis placed on individual goals may vary based upon institutional differences. However, non-mortgage liquidity investments made with a goal of maximizing earnings or maximizing arbitrage opportunities would be inconsistent with this Guidance for the maintenance of an Enterprise's liquidity portfolio.

d. The policy should clearly define the authorized investment vehicles and establish guidelines for the introduction of new types of investment vehicles.

e. The Enterprise's procedures should include a framework of controls that provide an appropriate separation of duties and responsibilities. There should be responsibility assigned for an independent review of non-mortgage liquidity investments by a designated unit, such as audit or an independent risk oversight group.

f. The Enterprise should adopt a limit structure to promote diversification in the non-mortgage liquidity investment portfolio and emphasizes strategies for risk mitigation. Additionally, there should be limits for the aggregate size of the non-mortgage liquidity investment portfolio.

g. The Enterprise should adopt measures to evaluate performance against the policy and its objectives.

h. The Enterprise should adopt internal reporting requirements that quantify performance, document exceptions, and serve as a basis for communicating information about activities involving non-mortgage liquidity assets.

i. The Enterprise should periodically evaluate the adequacy and content of its public disclosure for non-mortgage investment liquidity activities.

2. Quality Management Information That Ensures Timely Performance Measures and Governance Data

a. The Enterprise must maintain systems that adequately identify, measure and report the nature and level of exposure associated with their non-mortgage liquidity investments. Management must remain appropriately informed about the activity in non-mortgage liquidity investments. Also, the Board of Directors should periodically be provided a summary of non-mortgage liquidity investment activities. At a minimum, management's reports to the Board should:

i. Summarize non-mortgage investment activity since the last report;

ii. Identify and explain any material changes or trends in the non-mortgage liquidity investment portfolio risk and returns; and

iii. Report and explain exceptions to the policy or risk guidelines for liquidity investments.

b. Meaningful changes in portfolio volume and spreads from period to period should be identified and explained to the Board in terms of why they occurred (*e.g.*, changes in portfolio composition, changes in funding costs, etc.). In overseeing the day-to-day management of non-mortgage liquidity investment activities, management should consider the discrete risks associated with the non-mortgage liquidity investment portfolio as well as the exposure of this portfolio within the context of risks across the entire Enterprise. This includes assessing the non-mortgage liquidity investment portfolio's sensitivity to changes in interest rates, expressed in terms of net interest income sensitivity and portfolio value sensitivity.

3. Safe and Sound Investment Holdings and Investment Culture

a. The Enterprise should implement and enforce policies and/or procedures for non-mortgage liquidity investments. Management should establish limits and procedures in a manner that is consistent with the Board's sanctioned goals and risk appetite. Certain risk-limits for non-mortgage liquidity investments may be expressed in terms of how they affect the Enterprise's overall risk-profile, such as those pertaining to interest-rate sensitivity. Other risk limits may be more appropriately expressed in terms of individual portfolios and instruments. In addition, limits restricting the size-range and scope of the non-mortgage liquidity investment activities should be established.

b. The limits and procedures should delineate the acceptable investment instruments, acceptable markets, acceptable counterparties, along with unacceptable investment or portfolio activities. The Enterprise should maintain sufficient documentation to demonstrate due diligence in adhering to policies, procedures, limits and guidelines.

c. At a minimum, limits should be established and reviewed annually, for:

i. Credit threshold guidelines: Credit quality is a compelling factor for liquidity investments. Since liquidity investments should be able to be readily converted into cash without substantial exposure to losses, investments should be insulated from price vulnerabilities that are associated with creditworthiness. The most effective means of insulating against price exposure from credit quality concerns is to invest in high-quality instruments and the debt obligations of high-quality issuers. The Enterprise should establish thresholds identifying the minimum credit standards of any security eligible for purchase. Where these standards involve credit ratings, the ratings should come from a nationally recognized rating organization. Procedures should be included that determine the steps to be taken by management if an instrument's credit rating falls below the minimum threshold before maturity.

ii. Maturity guidelines: Because the maturity of an investment significantly affects its exposure to credit risk and price volatility, longer maturity instruments have limited suitability as liquidity investments. The Enterprise should establish the maximum maturity allowable for non-mortgage liquidity investments. It would be appropriate to have different maturity limits for certain types of instruments. For example, management may wish to establish shorter maturity limits for fixed-coupon instruments than for adjustable-rate securities. Management may have different maturity limits for bullet securities and amortizing structures. It would be appropriate to establish a maturity matrix based upon an instrument's credit rating at the time of purchase.

iii. Diversification and concentration guidelines: Credit concentrations can increase credit risk. Accordingly, the Enterprise should establish guidelines that limit investments in the securities of any single issuer. Such limits may be established as a percentage limit (*e.g.*, as a percentage of capital) or as an absolute dollar amount. To enhance portfolio liquidity, there should also be a limit on the percentage of any particular issue held by the Enterprise.

4. Quality Controls and Personnel Administering and Governing the Process

a. The Enterprise should maintain a comprehensive set of controls to enforce the appropriate separation of duties and responsibilities. These controls should translate into clear procedures for routine operations. At a minimum, the internal control program for non-mortgage liquidity investment activities should include procedures for the following: portfolio valuation, personnel, settlement, physical control and documentation, conflict of interest, and accounting.

i. Portfolio valuation procedures. Portfolio valuation procedures should require pricing that is independent of the investment portfolio managers. Pricing securities provides an indication of the market depth and liquidity for individual instruments, and is an important process for providing data to the risk management function, particularly within a framework of estimating market value sensitivity. Pricing is particularly important for securities that are classified as "available-for-sale" for accounting purposes.

ii. Personnel guidelines. Personnel guidelines should require competent and experienced staff be responsible for conducting transactions and managing the non-mortgage investment portfolio. There should be clear guidance regarding the roles and responsibilities of individuals involved with the non-mortgage liquidity portfolio.

iii. Settlement practices. Procedures should cover standard settlement practices for the various types of non-mortgage liquidity investments in the Enterprise's portfolio. Inadequate understanding of standard settlement practices, coupled with poor internal controls, could result in unnecessary costs or losses.

iv. Control and documentation. Procedures covering control and documentation should be comprehensive and consistent with the evolving better practices in the marketplace. The procedures should include, for example, standards for: processing and controlling purchased instruments, safeguarding investment documentation and reviewing trade tickets and confirmations.

v. Conflict of interest. Conflict of interest guidelines should govern all Enterprise personnel authorized to purchase or sell non-mortgage liquidity investments. These guidelines should ensure that all directors, officers and employees act in the Enterprise's best interest. Conflict of interest guidelines should address employee relationships with authorized broker/dealers. Guidelines should also address personnel accepting gifts and travel expenses from broker/dealers.

vi. Accounting. Accounting practices should be evaluated to determine the level of compliance with GAAP standards.

5. Independent Testing and Review of the Process To Assure Compliance

a. An independent review of non-mortgage liquidity investment activities should be conducted periodically to ensure:

i. The accuracy and integrity of information provided to the Board, management and other oversight bodies;

ii. The adherence to policy, procedures, limits and guidelines;

iii. The timeliness, accuracy and usefulness of non-mortgage investment reports;

iv. The adequacy of personnel resources and capabilities; and

v. The non-mortgage liquidity investment activities remain appropriate in the context of the marketplace and the external environment.

b. This review may be conducted by a risk oversight unit or internal audit department, or any party that is independent of the routine risk-taking decisions and should be commensurate with the level of review of other primary Enterprise activities. Independent review findings for non-mortgage liquidity investments should be reported to the Board directly or through one of its committees. The Board should consider the independent review when reaffirming policies, and should address any issues raised.

D—Disclosure of Non-Mortgage Liquidity Investment Activities

1. Sound risk management practices include thorough disclosures about the Enterprise's risks and further regulators' efforts to increase financial transparency for regulated financial companies. Quality disclosures about risks and risk management can be an effective deterrent to excessive risk-taking. Three essential elements needed to promote market discipline for non-mortgage liquidity investments are (1) type of issuer and security, (2) maturity, and (3) credit quality or rating. Accordingly, quality disclosure for a portfolio of non-mortgage liquidity investments should include a detailed categorization of the portfolio with respect to each of these elements and cross-categorization, so that (for example) the quantity of any longer-maturity, lower-credit-quality assets is clearly identified. Information about fair values; yields; and narrative discussions of objectives, risk management policies, and controls can also promote transparency of risk and should be included. Such disclosures should be made quarterly, and they should be made using average balances so that average risks can be assessed—not just the risks on a given date.

2. Over the next few quarters, OFHEO will discuss more specifically with the Enterprise

how these disclosures will meet the expectations expressed in this guidance. An example of a disclosure format that may be used by the Enterprise is available on the OFHEO Web site at *http://www.ofheo.gov*. However, the Enterprise may disclose the risks in its non-mortgage liquidity investment activities, consistent with the expectations expressed in this guidance, using a format of its choice.

E—SUMMARY

This Guidance sets forth OFHEO's process for evaluating the safety and soundness of liquidity non-mortgage investment activities. OFHEO remains committed to ensuring the Enterprises remain financially sound, have appropriate control environments, and engage only in financially sound business and investment activities. OFHEO's examiners have been instructed to incorporate this evaluation process into their ongoing safety and soundness examinations. Examiners will evaluate and test the Enterprise's non-mortgage liquidity investment processes and activities to ensure they are in compliance with this guidance.

APPENDIX C TO PART 1720—POLICY GUIDANCE; SAFETY AND SOUNDNESS STANDARDS FOR INFORMATION

A—INTRODUCTION

1. Scope.
2. Preservation of Existing Authority.
3. Definitions.

B—SAFETY AND SOUNDNESS STANDARDS FOR INFORMATION

1. Information Security Program.
2. Objectives.

C—DEVELOPMENT AND IMPLEMENTATION OF INFORMATION SECURITY PROGRAM

1. Involve the Board of Directors.
2. Assess Risk.
3. Manage and Control Risk.
4. Oversee Service Provider Arrangements.
5. Adjust the Program.
6. Report to the Board.
7. Implementation.

A—INTRODUCTION

The Policy Guidance on Safety and Soundness Standards for Information sets forth standards pursuant to section 1313 of the Federal Housing Enterprise Safety and Soundness Act (12 U.S.C. 4513). The Guidance addresses standards for developing and implementing administrative, technical, and physical safeguards to protect the security, confidentiality, and integrity of information.

1. Scope. The Guidance applies to information maintained by or on behalf of the Federal National Mortgage Association (Fannie Mae) and the Federal Home Loan Mortgage Corporation (Freddie Mac) (collectively, the Enterprises).

2. Preservation of Existing Authority. Nothing in the Guidance in any way limits the authority of OFHEO to otherwise address unsafe or unsound conditions or practices or violations of applicable law, regulation or supervisory order. Action referencing the Policy Guidance may be taken separate from, in conjunction with or in addition to any other enforcement action available to OFHEO. Compliance with the Policy Guidance in general would not preclude a finding by the agency that an Enterprise is otherwise engaged in a specific unsafe or unsound practice or is in an unsafe or unsound condition, or requiring corrective or remedial action with regard to such practice or condition. That is, supervisory action is not precluded against an Enterprise that has not been cited for a deficiency under the Policy Guidance. Conversely, an Enterprise's failure to comply with one of the supervisory requirements set forth in the Policy Guidance may not warrant a formal supervisory response from OFHEO, if the agency determines the matter may be otherwise addressed in a satisfactory manner. For example, OFHEO may require the submission of a plan to achieve compliance with the particular requirement or standard without taking any other enforcement action.

3. Definitions. For purposes of the Guidance, the following definitions apply:

a. *Information* means any record of an Enterprise, whether in paper, electronic, or other form, that is handled or maintained by or on behalf of an Enterprise;

b. *Information security program* means the administrative, technical, or physical safeguards used by an Enterprise to access, collect, process, store, use, transmit, dispose of, or otherwise handle information;

c. *Information systems* means any methods used to access, collect, store, use, transmit, protect, or dispose of information;

d. *Service provider* means any person or entity, including any third party vendor, that maintains, processes or otherwise is permitted access to information through its provision of services directly or indirectly to an Enterprise.

B—SAFETY AND SOUNDNESS STANDARDS FOR INFORMATION

1. Information Security Program. Each Enterprise shall implement a comprehensive written information security program that includes administrative, technical, and physical safeguards appropriate to the nature and scope of its activities. While all parts of the Enterprise are not required to implement a uniform set of policies, all elements of the information security program must be coordinated.

2. *Objectives.* An Enterprise's information security program shall be designed to:

a. Ensure the security and confidentiality of information;

b. Protect against any anticipated threats or hazards to the security or integrity of such information; and

c. Protect against unauthorized access to or use of such information.

C—DEVELOPMENT AND IMPLEMENTATION OF INFORMATION SECURITY PROGRAM

1. *Involve the Board of Directors.* The board of directors or an appropriate committee of the board of each Enterprise shall:

a. Approve the Enterprise's written information security program; and

b. Oversee the development, implementation, and maintenance of the Enterprise's information security program, including assigning specific responsibility for its implementation and reviewing reports from management.

2. *Assess Risk.* Each Enterprise shall:

a. Identify reasonably foreseeable internal and external threats that could result in unauthorized disclosure, misuse, alteration, or destruction of information or information systems;

b. Assess the likelihood and potential damage of these threats, taking into consideration the sensitivity of nonpublic information; and

c. Assess the sufficiency of policies, procedures, information systems, and other arrangements in place to control risks.

3. *Manage and Control Risk.* Each Enterprise shall:

a. Design its information security program to manage and control the identified risks, commensurate with the sensitivity of the information as well as the complexity and scope of the Enterprise's activities. Each Enterprise should consider whether the following security measures are appropriate for the Enterprise and, if so, adopt those measures the Enterprise concludes are appropriate:

i. Access controls over information systems, including controls to authenticate and permit access only to authorized individuals and controls to prevent employees from providing information to unauthorized individuals who may seek to obtain this information through fraudulent means;

ii. Access restrictions at physical locations containing information, such as buildings, computer facilities, and records storage facilities to permit access only to authorized individuals;

iii. Encryption of electronic information, including while in transit or in storage on networks or systems to which unauthorized individuals may have access;

iv. Procedures designed to ensure that information system modifications are consistent with the Enterprise's information security program;

v. Dual control procedures, segregation of duties, and employee background checks for employees with responsibilities for or access to information;

vi. Monitoring systems and procedures to detect actual and attempted attacks on or intrusion into information systems;

vii. Response programs that specify actions to be taken when the Enterprise suspects or detects that unauthorized individuals have gained access to information systems, including appropriate reports to regulatory and law enforcement agencies; and

viii. Measures to protect against destruction, loss or damage of information due to potential environmental hazards, such as fire and water damage or technological failures.

b. Train staff to implement the Enterprise's information security program; and

c. Regularly test the key controls, systems and procedures of the information security program. The frequency and nature of such tests should be determined by the Enterprise's risk assessment. Tests should be conducted or reviewed by independent third parties or staff that are independent of those that develop or maintain the security programs.

4. *Oversee Service Provider Arrangements.* Each Enterprise shall:

a. Exercise appropriate due diligence in selecting its service providers;

b. Require its service providers by contract to implement appropriate measures designed to meet the objectives of the Guidance; and

c. Where indicated by the Enterprise's risk assessment, monitor its service providers to confirm that they have satisfied their obligations as required by section 9(b). As part of this monitoring, an Enterprise should review audits, summaries of test results, or other equivalent evaluations of its service providers.

5. *Adjust the Program.* Each Enterprise shall monitor, evaluate, and adjust, as appropriate, the information security program in light of any relevant changes in technology, the sensitivity of its information, internal or external threats to information, and the Enterprise's own changing business arrangements, such as acquisitions, alliances and joint ventures, outsourcing arrangements, and changes to information systems.

6. *Report to the Board.* Each Enterprise shall report to its board or an appropriate committee of the board at least annually. This report should describe the overall status of the information security program and the Enterprise's compliance with the Guidance. The reports should discuss material matters related to its program, addressing issues such as: risk assessment; risk management and control decisions; service provider arrangements; results of testing; security

breaches or violations and management's responses; and recommendations for changes in the information security program.

7. *Implementation.* a. Each Enterprise should implement an information security program pursuant to the Guidance.

b. Until January 1, 2004, a contract that an Enterprise has entered into with a service provider to perform services for it or functions on its behalf satisfies the provisions of section 9, even if the contract does not include a requirement that the servicer maintain the security and confidentiality of information, as long as the Enterprise entered into the contract on or before the effective date.

PART 1730—DISCLOSURE OF FINANCIAL AND OTHER INFORMATION

Sec.

AUTHORITY: 12 U.S.C. 4513; 12 U.S.C. 4514; 12 U.S.C. 4631; and, 12 U.S.C. 4632.

SOURCE: 68 FR 16718, Apr. 7, 2003, unless otherwise noted.

§ 1730.1 Purpose.

(a) The purpose of this part is to require the Enterprises to prepare and submit financial and other disclosures as specified by OFHEO.

(b) This part does not limit or restrict the authority of OFHEO to act under its safety and soundness mandate to regulate the Enterprises, including conducting examinations, requiring reports and disclosures, and enforcing compliance with applicable laws, rules and regulations.

§ 1730.2 Definitions.

For purposes of this part, the term:

(a) *Commission* means the Securities and Exchange Commission (or SEC).

(b) *Disclosure or disclosures* means any report[s], form[s], or other information submitted by the Enterprises pursuant to this part and may be used interchangeably with the terms "report[s]" or "form[s]."

(c) *Enterprise* means the Federal National Mortgage Association or the Federal Home Loan Mortgage Corporation; and the term "Enterprises" means, collectively, the Federal National Mortgage Association and the Federal Home Loan Mortgage Corporation.

(d) *Exchange Act* means the Securities Exchange Act of 1934.

(e) *OFHEO* means the Office of Federal Housing Enterprise Oversight (or the office).

§ 1730.3 Periodic disclosures.

(a) Each Enterprise shall prepare disclosures relating to its financial condition, results of operation, business developments, and management's expectations that include supporting financial information and certifications.

(b) The requirement of paragraph (a) of this section for disclosures will be satisfied if:

(1) In the case of an Enterprise having a class of securities registered pursuant to Section 12 of the Exchange Act, the Enterprise prepares and makes public an annual report, quarterly report and current reports and such other materials that may be required under the rules and regulations of the Commission, including interpretations of the Commission and its staff and rules governing audited financial statements;

(2) The Enterprise files with the Commission all reports, statements, and forms required pursuant to Sections 14(a) and (c) of the Exchange Act and by rules and regulations adopted by the Commission under those sections that would be required to be filed by the Enterprises if the Enterprises has a class of equity securities registered under Section 12(g) of the Exchange Act that were not exempted securities under the Exchange Act; and,

(3) The officers and directors of the Enterprise file with the Commission all reports and forms relating to the common stock of the Enterprise that would be required to be filed by the officers and directors pursuant to Section 16 of the Exchange Act and by rules and regulations adopted by the Commission under that section if the Enterprises had a class of equity securities registered under Section 12(g) of the Exchange Act that were not exempted securities under the Exchange Act.

§ 1730.4 Submission of disclosures.

Unless otherwise required by OFHEO, the Enterprises shall provide to OFHEO on a concurrent basis copies of all disclosures filed with the SEC pursuant to § 1730.3.

PART 1750—CAPITAL

Subpart A—Minimum Capital

AUTHORITY: 12 U.S.C. 4513, 4514, 4611, 4612, 4614, 4615, 4618.

Subpart A—Minimum Capital

§ 1750.1 General.

The regulation contained in this subpart A sets forth the methodology for computing the minimum capital requirement for each Enterprise. The board of directors of each Enterprise is responsible for ensuring that the Enterprise maintains capital at a level that is sufficient to ensure the continued financial viability of the Enterprise and that equals or exceeds the minimum capital requirement contained in this subpart A.

§ 1750.2 Definitions.

For purposes of this subpart A, the following definitions shall apply:

Affiliate means any entity that controls, is controlled by, or is under common control with, an Enterprise, except as otherwise provided by the Director.

Commitment means any contractual, legally binding agreement that obligates an Enterprise to purchase or to securitize mortgages.

Core Capital—(1) Means the sum of (as determined in accordance with generally accepted accounting principles)—

(i) The par or stated value of outstanding common stock;

(ii) The par or stated value of outstanding perpetual, noncumulative preferred stock;

(iii) Paid-in capital; and

(iv) Retained earnings; and

(2) Does not include debt instruments or any amounts the Enterprise could be required to pay at the option of an investor to retire capital instruments.

Director means the Director of OFHEO.

Enterprise means the Federal National Mortgage Association and any affiliate thereof or the Federal Home Loan Mortgage Corporation and any affiliate thereof.

Foreign exchange rate contracts—

(1) Means cross-currency interest rate swaps, forward foreign exchange contracts, currency options purchased (including currency options purchased over-the-counter), and any other instrument that gives rise to similar credit risks; and

(2) Does not mean foreign exchange rate contracts with an original maturity of 14 calendar days or less and foreign exchange rate contracts traded on exchanges that require daily payment of variation margins.

Interest rate contracts—

(1) Means single currency interest rate swaps, basis swaps, forward rate agreements, interest rate options purchased (including caps, collars, and floors purchased), over-the-counter options purchased, and any other instrument that gives rise to similar credit risks (including when-issued securities and forward deposits accepted); and

(2) Does not mean such instruments traded on exchanges that require daily payment of variation margins.

Mortgage-backed security means a security, investment, or substantially equivalent instrument that represents an interest in a pool of loans secured by mortgages or deeds of trust where the principal or interest payments to the investor in the security or substantially equivalent instrument are guaranteed or effectively guaranteed by an Enterprise.

Multifamily credit enhancement means any guarantee, pledge, purchase arrangement, or other obligation or commitment provided or entered into by an Enterprise with respect to multifamily mortgages to provide credit enhancement, liquidity, interest rate support, and other guarantees and enhancements for revenue bonds issued by a state or local governmental unit (including a housing finance agency) or other bond issuer.

1992 Act means the Federal Housing Enterprises Financial Safety and Soundness Act of 1992, found at Title XIII of the Housing and Community Development Act of 1992, Pub. L. 102–550, 12 U.S.C. 4501 *et seq.*

Notional amount means the face value of the underlying financial instrument(s) on which an interest rate or foreign exchange rate contract is based.

Off-balance sheet obligation means a binding agreement, contract, or similar arrangement that requires or may require future payment(s) in money or kind by another party to an Enterprise, or that effectively guarantees all or part of such payment(s) to third parties (including commitments), where such agreement or contract is a source of credit risk that is not included on its balance sheet.

OFHEO means the Office of Federal Housing Enterprise Oversight.

Other off-balance sheet obligations means all off-balance sheet obligations of an Enterprise that are not mortgage-backed securities or substantially equivalent instruments and that are not resecuritized mortgage-backed securities, such as real estate mortgage investment conduits or similar resecuritized instruments.

Perpetual, noncumulative preferred stock means preferred stock that—

(1) Does not have a maturity date;

(2) Provides the issuer the ability and the legal right to eliminate dividends and does not permit the accruing or payment of impaired dividends;

(3) Cannot be redeemed at the option of the holder; and

(4) Has no other provisions that will require future redemption of the issue, in whole or in part, or that will reset the dividend periodically based, in whole or in part, on the Enterprise's current credit standing, such as auction rate, money market, or remarketable preferred stock, or that may cause the dividend to increase to a level that could create an incentive for the issuer to redeem the instrument, such as exploding rate stock.

Qualifying collateral means cash on deposit; securities issued or guaranteed by the central governments of the OECD-based group of countries,[1] United States Government agencies, or United States Government-sponsored agencies; and securities issued by multilateral lending institutions or regional development banks.

§ 1750.3 Procedure and timing.

(a) Each Enterprise shall file with the Director a minimum capital report each quarter or at such other times as the Director requires, in his or her sole discretion. The report shall contain the information that responds to all of the items required by OFHEO in written

[1] The OECD-based group of countries comprises full members of the Organization for Economic Cooperation and Development (OECD) regardless of entry date, as well as countries that have concluded special lending arrangements with the International Monetary Fund (IMF) associated with the IMF's General Arrangements to Borrow, but excludes any country that has rescheduled its external sovereign debt within the previous 5 years. A rescheduling of external sovereign debt generally would include any renegotiation of terms arising from a country's mobility or unwillingness to meet its external debt service obligations, but generally not include any renegotiation to allow the borrower to take advantage of a decline in interest rate or other change in market conditions. As of November 1995, the OECD countries included the following countries: Australia, Austria, Belgium, Canada, Denmark, Finland, France, Germany, Greece, Iceland, Ireland, Italy, Japan, Luxembourg, Mexico, the Netherlands, New Zealand, Norway, Portugal, Spain, Sweden, Switzerland, Turkey, the United Kingdom, and the United States; and Saudi Arabia has concluded special lending arrangements with the IMF associated with the IMF's General Arrangements to Borrow.

instructions to the Enterprise, including, but not limited to:

(1) Estimate of the minimum capital requirement;

(2) Estimate of core capital overage or shortfall relative to the estimated minimum capital requirement;

(3) Such other information as may be required by the Director.

(b) The quarterly minimum capital report shall be submitted not later than April 30, July 30, October 30, and January 30 of each year.

(c) Each minimum capital report shall be submitted in writing and in such other format as may be required by the Director.

(d) In the event an Enterprise makes an adjustment to its financial statements for a quarter or a date for which the information was requested, which would cause an adjustment to a minimum capital report, the Enterprise shall file with the Director an amended minimum capital report not later than 3 business days after the date of such adjustment.

(e) Each minimum capital report or any amended minimum capital report shall contain a declaration by an officer authorized by the board of directors of the Enterprise to make such a declaration, including, but not limited to a president, vice president, or treasurer, that the report is true and correct to the best of such officer's knowledge and belief.

§ 1750.4 Minimum capital requirement computation.

(a) The minimum capital requirement for each Enterprise shall be computed by adding the following amounts:

(1) 2.50 percent times the aggregate on-balance sheet assets of the Enterprise;

(2) 0.45 percent times the unpaid principal balance of mortgage-backed securities and substantially equivalent instruments that were issued or guaranteed by the Enterprise;

(3) 0.45 percent of 50 percent of the average dollar amount of commitments outstanding each quarter over the preceding four quarters;

(4) 0.45 percent of the outstanding principal amount of bonds with multifamily credit enhancements;

(5) 0.45 percent of the dollar amount of sold portfolio remittances pending;

(6)(i) 3.00 percent of the credit equivalent amount of interest rate contracts and foreign exchange rate contracts, except to the extent of the current market value of posted qualifying collateral, computed in accordance with appendix A to this subpart;

(ii) 1.50 percent of the market value of qualifying collateral posted to secure interest rate and foreign exchange rate contracts, not to exceed the credit equivalent amount of such contracts, computed in accordance with appendix A to this subpart; and

(7) 0.45 percent of the outstanding amount, credit equivalent amount, or other measure determined appropriate by the Director, of other off-balance sheet obligations (excluding commitments, multifamily credit enhancements, sold portfolio remittances pending, and interest rate contracts and foreign exchange rate contracts), except as adjusted by the Director to reflect differences in the credit risk of such obligations in relation to mortgage-backed securities.

(b) Any asset or financial obligation that is properly classifiable in more than one of the categories enumerated in paragraphs (a) (1) through (7) of this section shall be classified in the category that yields the highest minimum capital requirement.

(c) As used in this section, the term "preceding four quarters" means the last day of the quarter just ended (or the date for which the minimum capital report is filed, if different), and the three preceding quarter-ends.

Appendix A to Subpart A of Part 1750—Minimum Capital Components for Interest Rate and Foreign Exchange Rate Contracts

1. The minimum capital components for interest rate and foreign exchange rate contracts are computed on the basis of the credit equivalent amounts of such contracts. Credit equivalent amounts are computed for each of the following off-balance sheet interest rate and foreign exchange rate contracts:

a. Interest Rate Contracts

i. Single currency interest rate swaps.
ii. Basis swaps.
iii. Forward rate agreements.

iv. Interest rate options purchased (including caps, collars, and floors purchased).

v. Any other instrument that gives rise to similar credit risks (including when-issued securities and forward deposits accepted).

b. Foreign Exchange Rate Contracts

i. Cross-currency interest rate swaps.

ii. Forward foreign exchange rate contracts.

iii. Currency options purchased.

iv. Any other instrument that gives rise to similar credit risks.

2. Foreign exchange rate contracts with an original maturity of 14 calendar days or less and foreign exchange rate contracts traded on exchanges that require daily payment of variation margins are excluded from the minimum capital requirement computation. Over-the-counter options purchased, however, are included and treated in the same way as the other interest rate and foreign exchange rate contracts.

3. Calculation of Credit Equivalent Amounts

a. The minimum capital components for interest rate and foreign exchange rate contracts are computed on the basis of the credit equivalent amounts of such contracts. The credit equivalent amount of an off-balance sheet interest rate and foreign exchange rate contract that is not subject to a qualifying bilateral netting contract in accordance with this appendix A is equal to the sum of the current exposure (sometimes referred to as the replacement cost) of the contract and an estimate of the potential future credit exposure over the remaining life of the contract.

b. The current exposure is determined by the mark-to-market value of the contract. If the mark-to-market value is positive, then the current exposure is the mark-to-market value. If the mark-to-market value is zero or negative, then the current exposure is zero. Mark-to-market values are measured in United States dollars, regardless of the currency or currencies specified in the contract, and should reflect changes in the relevant rates, as well as counterparty credit quality.

c. The potential future credit exposure of a contract, including a contract with a negative mark-to-market value, is estimated by multiplying the notional principal amount of the contract by a credit conversion factor. The effective rather than the apparent or stated notional amount must be used in this calculation. The credit conversion factors are:

Remaining maturity	Interest rate contracts (percent)	Foreign exchange rate contracts (percent)
1 year or less	0.0	1.0
Over 1 year	0.5	5.0

d. Because foreign exchange rate contracts involve an exchange of principal upon maturity, and foreign exchange rates are generally more volatile than interest rates, higher conversion factors have been established for foreign exchange rate contracts than for interest rate contracts.

e. No potential future credit exposure is calculated for single currency interest rate swaps in which payments are made based upon two floating rate indexes, so-called floating/floating or basis swaps. The credit exposure on these contracts is evaluated solely on the basis of their mark-to-market values.

4. Avoidance of Double Counting

In certain cases, credit exposures arising from the interest rate and foreign exchange instruments covered by this appendix A may already be reflected, in part, on the balance sheet. To avoid double counting such exposures in the assessment of capital adequacy, counterparty credit exposures arising from the types of instruments covered by this appendix A may need to be excluded from balance sheet assets in calculating the minimum capital requirement.

5. Collateral

a. The sufficiency of collateral for off-balance sheet items is determined by the market value of the collateral in relation to the credit equivalent amount. Collateral held against a netting contract is not recognized for minimum capital standard purposes unless it is legally available to support the single legal obligation created by the netting contract. Excess collateral held against one contract or a group of contracts for which a recognized netting agreement exists may not be considered.

b. The only forms of collateral that are formally recognized by the minimum capital standard framework are cash on deposit; securities issued or guaranteed by the central governments of the OECD-based group of countries, United States Government agencies, or United States Government-sponsored agencies; and securities issued by multilateral lending institutions or regional development banks.

6. Netting

a. For purposes of this appendix A, netting refers to the offsetting of positive and negative mark-to-market values in the determination of a current exposure to be used in the calculation of a credit equivalent amount. Any legally enforceable form of bilateral netting (that is, netting with a single counterparty) of interest rate and foreign exchange rate contracts is recognized for purposes of calculating the credit equivalent amount provided that the following criteria are met:

i. Netting must be accomplished under a written netting contract that creates a single legal obligation, covering all included individual contracts, with the effect that the Enterprise would have a claim to receive, or obligation to pay, only the net amount of the sum of the positive and negative mark-to-market values on included individual contracts in the event that a counterparty, or a counterparty to whom the contract has been validly assigned, fails to perform due to default, insolvency, liquidation, or similar circumstances.

ii. The Enterprise must obtain a written and reasoned legal opinion(s) representing that in the event of a legal challenge—including one resulting from default, insolvency, liquidation, or similar circumstances—the relevant court and administrative authorities would find the Enterprise's exposure to be such a net amount under—

A. The law of the jurisdiction in which the counterparty is chartered or the equivalent location in the case of noncorporate entities, and if a branch of the counterparty is involved, then also under the law of the jurisdiction in which the branch is located;

B. The law that governs the individual contracts covered by the netting contract; and

C. The law that governs the netting contract.

iii. The Enterprise must establish and maintain procedures to ensure that the legal characteristics of netting contracts are kept under review in the event of possible changes in relevant law.

iv. The Enterprise must maintain in its files documentation adequate to support the netting of rate contracts, including a copy of the bilateral netting contract and necessary legal opinions.

b. A contract containing a walkaway clause is not eligible for netting for purposes of calculating the credit equivalent amount.[1]

c. By netting individual contracts for the purpose of calculating its credit equivalent amount, the Enterprise represents that it has met the requirements of this appendix A and all the appropriate documents are in the Enterprise's files and available for inspection by OFHEO. OFHEO may determine that an Enterprise's files are inadequate or that a netting contract, or any of its underlying individual contracts, may not be legally enforceable under any one of the bodies of law described in this appendix A. If such a determination is made, the netting contract may be disqualified from recognition for minimum capital standard purposes or underlying individual contracts may be treated as though they are not subject to the netting contract.

d. The credit equivalent amount of interest rate and foreign exchange rate contracts that are subject to a qualifying bilateral netting contract is calculated by adding the current exposure of the netting contract and the sum of the estimates of the potential future credit exposures on all individual contracts subject to the netting contract, estimated in accordance with paragraph 3 of this appendix A. Offsetting contracts in the same currency maturing on the same date will have lower potential future exposure as well as lower current exposure. Therefore, for purposes of calculating potential future credit exposure to a netting counterparty for foreign exchange rate contracts and other similar contracts in which notional principal is equivalent to cash flows, total notional principal is defined as the net receipts falling due on each value date in each currency.

e. The current exposure of the netting contract is determined by summing all positive and negative mark-to-market values of the individual contracts included in the netting contract. If the net sum of the mark-to-market values is positive, then the current exposure of the netting contract is equal to that sum. If the net sum of the mark-to-market values is zero or negative, then the current exposure of the netting contract is zero. OFHEO may determine that a netting contract qualifies for minimum capital standard netting treatment even though certain individual contracts may not qualify. In such instances, the nonqualifying contracts should be treated as individual contracts that are not subject to the netting contract.

f. In the event a netting contract covers contracts that are normally excluded from the minimum capital requirement computation—for example, foreign exchange rate contracts with an original maturity of 14 calendar days or less, or instruments traded on exchanges that require daily payment of variation margin—an Enterprise may elect consistently either to include or exclude all mark-to-market values of such contracts when determining net current exposure.

[1] A walkaway clause is a provision in a netting contract that permits a non-defaulting counterparty to make lower payments than it would make otherwise under the contract, or no payment at all, to a defaulter or to the estate of a defaulter, even if the defaulter or the estate of the defaulter is a net creditor under the contract.

Subpart B—Risk-Based Capital

SOURCE: 66 FR 47806, Sept. 13, 2001, unless otherwise noted.

§ 1750.10 General.

The regulation contained in this subpart B establishes the methodology for computing the risk-based capital level for each Enterprise. The board of directors of each Enterprise is responsible for ensuring that the Enterprise maintains total capital at a level that is sufficient to ensure the continued financial viability of the Enterprise and is equal to or exceeds the risk-based capital level computed pursuant to this subpart B.

§ 1750.11 Definitions.

Except where a term is explicitly defined differently in this subpart, all terms defined at § 1750.2 of subpart A of this part shall have the same meanings for purposes of this subpart. For purposes of subpart B of this part, the following definitions shall apply:

(a) *Benchmark loss experience* means the rates of default and severity for mortgage loans that—

(1) Were originated during a period of two or more consecutive calendar years in contiguous areas that together contain at least five percent of the population of the United States, and

(2) Experienced the highest loss rate for any period of such duration in comparison with the loans originated in any other contiguous areas that together contain at least five percent of the population of the United States.

(b) *Constant maturity Treasury yield* means the constant maturity Treasury yield, published by the Board of Governors of the Federal Reserve System.

(c) *Contiguous areas* means all the areas within a state or a group of two or more states sharing common borders. "Sharing common borders" does not mean meeting at a single point. Colorado, for example, is contiguous with New Mexico, but not with Arizona.

(d) *Credit risk* means the risk of financial loss to an Enterprise from nonperformance by borrowers or other obligors on instruments in which an Enterprise has a financial interest, or as to which the Enterprise has a financial obligation.

(e) *Default rate* of a given group of loans means the ratio of the aggregate original principal balance of the defaulted loans in the group to the aggregate original principal balance of all loans in the group.

(f) *Defaulted loan* means a loan that, within ten years following its origination:

(1) Resulted in pre-foreclosure sale,

(2) Completed foreclosure,

(3) Resulted in the acquisition of real estate collateral, or

(4) Otherwise resulted in a credit loss to an Enterprise.

(g) *Financing costs* of property acquired through foreclosure means the product of:

(1) The number of years (including fractions) of the period from the completion of foreclosure through disposition of the property,

(2) The average of the Enterprises' short-term funding rates, and

(3) The unpaid principal balance at the time of foreclosure.

(h) *Interest rate risk* means the risk of financial loss due to the sensitivity of earnings and net worth of an Enterprise to changes in interest rates.

(i) *Loss* on a defaulted loan means:

(1) With respect to a loan in category 1, 2, or 3 of the definition of defaulted loan the difference between:

(i) The sum of the principal and interest owed when the borrower lost title to the property securing the mortgage; financing costs through the date of property disposition; and cash expenses incurred during the foreclosure process, the holding period for real estate collateral acquired as a result of default, and the property liquidation process; and

(ii) The sum of the property sales price and any other liquidation proceeds (except those resulting from private mortgage insurance proceeds or other third-party credit enhancements).

(2) With respect to defaulted loans not in categories 1, 2, or 3, the amount of the financial loss to the Enterprise.

(j) *Mortgage* means any loan secured by such classes of liens as are commonly given or are legally effective to secure advances on, or the unpaid purchase price of, real estate under the laws of the State in which the real estate is located; or a manufactured house that is personal property under the laws of the State in which the manufactured house is located, together with the credit instruments, if any, secured thereby, and includes interests in mortgages.

(k) *Seasoning* means the change over time in the ratio of the unpaid principal balance of a mortgage to the value of the property by which such mortgage loan is secured.

(l) *Severity rate* for any group of defaulted loans means the aggregate losses on all loans in that group divided by the aggregate original principal balances of those loans.

(m) *Stress period* means a hypothetical ten-year period immediately following the day for which capital is being measured, which is a period marked by the severely adverse economic circumstances defined in 12 CFR 1750.13 and Appendix A to this subpart.

(n) *Total capital* means, with respect to an Enterprise, the sum of the following:

(1) The core capital of the Enterprise;

(2) A general allowance for foreclosure losses, which—

(i) Shall include an allowance for portfolio mortgage losses, an allowance for non-reimbursable foreclosure costs on government claims, and an allowance for liabilities reflected on the balance sheet for the Enterprise for estimated foreclosure losses on mortgage-backed securities; and

(ii) Shall not include any reserves of the Enterprise made or held against specific assets.

(3) Any other amounts from sources of funds available to absorb losses incurred by the Enterprise, that the Director by regulation determines are appropriate to include in determining total capital.

(o) *Type of mortgage product* means a classification of one or more mortgage products, as established by the Director, that have similar characteristics from each set of characteristics under the paragraphs (o)(1) through (o)(7) of this section:

(1) The property securing the mortgage is—

(i) A residential property consisting of 1 to 4 dwelling units; or

(ii) A residential property consisting of more than 4 dwelling units.

(2) The interest rate on the mortgage is—

(i) Fixed; or

(ii) Adjustable.

(3) The priority of the lien securing the mortgage is—

(i) First; or

(ii) Second or other.

(4) The term of the mortgage is—

(i) 1 to 15 years;

(ii) 16–30 years; or

(iii) More than 30 years.

(5) The owner of the property is—

(i) An owner-occupant; or

(ii) An investor.

(6) The unpaid principal balance of the mortgage—

(i) Will amortize completely over the term of the mortgage, and will not increase significantly at any time during the term of the mortgage;

(ii) Will not amortize completely over the term of the mortgage, and will not increase significantly at any time during the term of the mortgage; or

(iii) May increase significantly at some time during the term of the mortgage.

(7) Any other characteristics of the mortgage, as specified in appendix A to this subpart.

§ 1750.12 Procedures and timing.

(a) Each Enterprise shall file with the Director a Risk-Based Capital Report each quarter, and at such other times as the Director may require, in his or her discretion. The report shall contain the information required by the Director in the instructions to the Risk-Based Capital Report in the format or media specified therein and such other information as may be required by the Director.

(b) The quarterly Risk-Based Capital Report shall contain information for the last day of the quarter and shall be submitted not later than 30 days after the end of the quarter. Reports required by the Director other than quarterly reports shall be submitted within such time period as the Director shall specify.

(c) When an Enterprise contemplates entering a new activity, as the term is defined in section 3.11 of appendix A to this subpart, the Enterprise shall notify the Director as soon as possible while the transaction or activity is under consideration, but in no event later than 5 calendar days after settlement or closing. The Enterprises shall provide to the Director such information regarding the activity as the Director may require to determine a stress test treatment. OFHEO will inform the Enterprise as soon as possible thereafter of the proposed stress test treatment of the new activity. In addition, the notice of proposed capital classification required by § 1777.21 of this chapter will inform the Enterprise of the capital treatment of such new activity used in the determination of the risk-based capital requirement.

(d) If an Enterprise discovers that a Risk-Based Capital Report previously filed with OFHEO contains any errors or omissions, the Enterprise shall notify OFHEO immediately of such discovery and file an amended Risk-Based Capital Report not later than three days thereafter.

(e) Each capital classification shall be determined by OFHEO on the basis of the Risk-Based Capital Report filed by the Enterprise under paragraph (a) of this section; provided that, in the event an amended Risk-Based Capital Report is filed prior to the issuance of the final notice of capital classification, the Director has the discretion to determine the Enterprise's capital classification on the basis of the amended report.

(f) Each Risk-Based Capital Report or any amended Risk-Based Capital Report shall contain a declaration by the officer who has been designated by the Board as responsible for overseeing the capital adequacy of the Enterprise that the report is true and correct to the best of such officer's knowledge and belief.

[66 FR 47806, Sept. 13, 2001, as amended at 67 FR 19322, Apr. 19, 2002]

§ 1750.13 Risk-based capital level computation.

(a) *Risk-Based Capital Test*—OFHEO shall compute a risk-based capital level for each Enterprise at least quarterly by applying the risk-based capital test described in appendix A to this subpart to determine the amount of total capital required for each Enterprise to maintain positive capital during the stress period. In making this determination, the Director shall take into account any appropriate distinctions among types of mortgage products, differences in seasoning of mortgages, and other factors determined appropriate by the Director in accordance with the methodology specified in appendix A to this subpart. The stress period has the following characteristics:

(1) *Credit risk*—With respect to mortgages owned or guaranteed by the Enterprise and other obligations of the Enterprise, losses occur throughout the United States at a rate of default and severity reasonably related, in accordance with appendix A to this subpart, to the benchmark loss experience.

(2) *Interest rate risk*—(i) *In general.* Interest rates decrease as described in paragraph (a)(2)(ii) of this section or increase as described in paragraph (a)(2)(iii) of this section, whichever would require more capital in the stress test for the Enterprise. Appendix A to this subpart contains a description of the methodology applied to implement the interest rate scenarios described in paragraphs (a)(2)(ii) and (iii) of this section.

(ii) *Decreases.* The 10-year constant maturity Treasury yield decreases during the first year of the stress period and remains at the new level for the remainder of the stress period. The yield decreases to the lesser of—

(A) 600 basis points below the average yield during the 9 months immediately preceding the stress period, or

(B) 60 percent of the average yield during the 3 years immediately preceding the stress period, but in no case to a yield less than 50 percent of the average yield during the 9 months immediately preceding the stress period.

(iii) *Increases.* The 10-year constant maturity Treasury yield increases during the first year of the stress period and will remain at the new level for the remainder of the stress period. The yield increases to the greater of—

(A) 600 basis points above the average yield during the 9 months immediately preceding the stress period, or

(B) 160 percent of the average yield during the 3 years immediately preceding the stress period, but in no case to a yield greater than 175 percent of the average yield during the 9 months immediately preceding the stress period.

(iv) *Different terms to maturity.* Yields of Treasury instruments with terms to maturity other than 10 years will change relative to the 10-year constant maturity Treasury yield in patterns and for durations that are reasonably related to historical experience and are judged reasonable by the Director. The methodology used by the Director to adjust the yields of those other instruments is specified in appendix A to this subpart.

(v) *Large increases in yields.* If the 10-year constant maturity Treasury yield is assumed to increase by more than 50 percent over the average yield during the 9 months immediately preceding the stress period, the Director shall adjust the losses resulting from the conditions specified in paragraph (a)(2)(iii) of this section to reflect a correspondingly higher rate of general price inflation. The method of such adjustment by the Director is specified in appendix A to this subpart.

(3) *New business.* Any contractual commitments of the Enterprise to purchase mortgages or issue securities will be fulfilled. The characteristics of resulting mortgages purchased, securities issued, and other financing will be consistent with the contractual terms of such commitments, recent experience, and the economic characteristics of the stress period, as more fully specified in appendix A to this subpart. No other purchases of mortgages shall be assumed.

(4) *Other activities.* Losses or gains on other activities, including interest rate and foreign exchange hedging activities, shall be determined by the Director, in accordance with appendix A to this subpart and on the basis of available information, to be consistent with the stress period.

(5) *Consistency.* Characteristics of the stress period other than those specifically set forth in paragraph (a) of this section, such as prepayment experience and dividend policies, will be determined by the Director, in accordance with appendix A to this subpart, on the basis of available information, to be most consistent with the stress period.

(b) *Risk-Based Capital Level.* The risk-based capital level of an Enterprise, to be used in determining the appropriate capital classification of each Enterprise, as required by section 1364 of the Federal Housing Enterprises Financial Safety and Soundness Act of 1992 (12 U.S.C. 4614), shall be equal to the sum of the following amounts:

(1) *Credit and Interest Rate Risk.* The amount of total capital determined by applying the risk-based capital test under paragraph (a) of this section to the Enterprise.

(2) *Management and Operations Risk.* To provide for management and operations risk, 30 percent of the amount of total capital determined by applying the risk-based capital test under paragraph (a) of this section to the Enterprise.

APPENDIX A TO SUBPART B OF PART 1750—RISK-BASED CAPITAL TEST METHODOLOGY AND SPECIFICATIONS

1.0 IDENTIFICATION OF THE BENCHMARK LOSS EXPERIENCE

OFHEO will use the definitions, data, and methodology described below to identify the Benchmark Loss Experience.

1.1 Definitions

The terms defined in the Glossary to this appendix shall apply for this appendix.

1.2 Data

[a] OFHEO identifies the Benchmark Loss Experience (BLE) using historical loan-level data required to be submitted by each of the two Enterprises. OFHEO's analysis is based entirely on the data available through 1995 on conventional, 30-year, fixed-rate loans secured by first liens on single-unit, owner-occupied, detached properties. For this purpose, detached properties are defined as single family properties excluding condominiums, planned urban developments, and cooperatives. The data includes only loans that were purchased by an Enterprise within 12 months after loan origination and loans for

which the Enterprise has no recourse to the lender.

[b] OFHEO organizes the data from each Enterprise to create two substantially consistent data sets. OFHEO separately analyzes default and severity data from each Enterprise. Default rates are calculated from loan records meeting the criteria specified above. Severity rates are calculated from the subset of defaulted loans for which loss data are available.

1.3 Procedures

[a] Cumulative ten-year default rates for each combination of states and origination years (state/year combination) that OFHEO examines are calculated for each Enterprise by grouping all of the Enterprise's loans originated in that combination of states and years. For origination years with less than ten-years of loss experience, cumulative-to-date default rates are used. The two Enterprise default rates are averaged, yielding an "average default rate" for that state/year combination.

[b] An "average severity rate" for each state/year combination is determined in the same manner as the average default rate. For each Enterprise, the aggregate severity rate is calculated for all loans in the relevant state/year combination and the two Enterprise severity rates are averaged.

[c] The "loss rate" for any state/year combination examined is calculated by multiplying the average default rate for that state/year combination by the average severity rate for that combination.

[d] The rates of default and Loss Severity of loans in the state/year combination containing at least two consecutive origination years and contiguous areas with a total population equal to or greater than five percent of the population of the United States with the highest loss rate constitutes the Benchmark Loss Experience.

2.0 IDENTIFICATION OF A NEW BENCHMARK LOSS EXPERIENCE

OFHEO will periodically monitor available data and reevaluate the Benchmark Loss Experience using the methodology set forth in this appendix. Using this methodology, OFHEO may identify a new Benchmark Loss Experience that has a higher rate of loss than the Benchmark Loss Experience identified at the time of the issuance of this regulation. In the event such a Benchmark Loss Experience is identified, OFHEO may incorporate the resulting higher loss rates in the Stress Test.

3.0 COMPUTATION OF THE RISK-BASED CAPITAL REQUIREMENT

3.1 Data

3.1.1 Introduction

[a] The Stress Test requires data on all of an Enterprise's assets, liabilities, stockholders equity, accounting entries, operations and off-balance sheet obligations, as well as economic factors that affect them: interest rates, house prices, rent growth rates, and vacancy rates. The Enterprises are responsible for compiling and aggregating data on at least a quarterly basis into a standard format called the Risk-Based Capital Report (RBC Report). Each Enterprise is required to certify that the RBC Report submission is complete and accurate. Data on economic factors, such as interest rates, are compiled from public sources. The Stress Test uses proprietary and public data directly, and also uses values derived from such data in the form of constants or default values. (See Table 3–1, Sources of Stress Test Input Data.) Data fields from each of these sources for Stress Test computations are described in the following tables and in each section of this appendix.

[b] The RBC Report includes information for all the loans owned or guaranteed by an Enterprise, as well as securities and derivative contracts, the dollar balances of these instruments and obligations, as well as all characteristics that bear on their behavior under stress conditions. As detailed in the RBC Report, data are required for all the following categories of instruments and obligations:

- Mortgages owned by or underlying mortgage-backed securities (MBS) issued by the Enterprises (whole loans)
- Mortgage-related securities
- Nonmortgage related securities, whether issued by an Enterprise, (e.g., debt) or held as investments
- Derivative contracts
- Other off-balance sheet guarantees (e.g., guarantees of private-issue securities).

TABLE 3–1—SOURCES OF STRESS TEST INPUT DATA

Section of this Appendix	Table	Data Source(s) R = RBC Report P = Public Data F = Fixed Values			
		R	P	F	Intermediate Outputs
3.1.3, Public Data	3–19, Stress Test Single Family Quarterly House Price Growth Rates			F	
	3–20, Multifamily Monthly Rent Growth and Vacancy Rates			F	
3.2.2, Commitments Inputs	Characteristics of securitized single family loans originated and delivered within 6 months prior to the Start of the Stress Test	R			3.3.4, Interest Rates Outputs
3.2.3, Commitments Procedures	3–25, Monthly Deliveries as a Percentage of Commitments Outstanding (MDP)			F	
3.3.2, Interest Rates Inputs	3–18, Interest Rate and Index Inputs		P		
3.3.3, Interest Rates Procedures	3–26, CMT Ratios to the Ten-Year CMT			F	
3.4.2, Property Valuation Inputs	3–28, Property Valuation Inputs				3.1.3, Public Data 3.3.4, Interest Rates Outputs
3.5.3, Counterparty Defaults Procedures	3–30, Rating Agencies Mappings to OFHEO Ratings Categories		P		
	3–31, Stress Test Maximum Haircut by Ratings Classification			F	
3.6.3.3.2, Mortgage Amortization Schedule Inputs	3–32, Loan Group Inputs for Mortgage Amortization Calculation				3.3.4, Interest Rates Outputs
3.6.3.4.2, Single Family Default and Prepayment Inputs	3–34, Single Family Default and Prepayment Inputs	R		F	3.6.3.3.4, Mortgage Amortization Schedule Outputs
3.6.3.4.3.3, Prepayment and Default Rates and Performance Fractions	3–35, Coefficients for Single Family Default and Prepayment Explanatory Variables			F	
3.6.3.5.2, Multifamily Default and Prepayment Inputs	3–38, Loan Group Inputs for Multifamily Default and Prepayment Calculations	R		F	
3.6.3.5.3.3, Default and Prepayment Rates and Performance Fractions	3–39, Explanatory Variable Coefficients for Multifamily Default			F	3.6.3.3.4, Mortgage Amortization Schedule Outputs

TABLE 3–1—SOURCES OF STRESS TEST INPUT DATA—Continued

Section of this Appendix	Table	Data Source(s) R = RBC Report P = Public Data F = Fixed Values			
		R	P	F	Intermediate Outputs
3.6.3.6.2.6, Single Family Gross Loss Severity Inputs	3–42, Loan Group inputs for Gross Loss Severity			F	3.3.4, Interest Rates Outputs 3.6.3.3.4, Mortgage Amortization Schedule Outputs 3.6.3.4.4, Single Family Default and Prepayment Outputs
3.6.3.6.3.6, Multifamily Gross Loss Severity Inputs	3–44, Loan Group Inputs for Multifamily Gross Loss Severity			F	3.3.4, Interest Rates Outputs 3.6.3.3.4, Mortgage Amortization Schedule Outputs
3.6.3.6.4.8, Mortgage Credit Enhancement Inputs	3–46, CE Inputs for each Loan Group	R			3.6.3.3.4, Mortgage Amortization Schedule Outputs 3.6.3.4.4, Single Family Default and Prepayment Outputs 3.6.3.5.4, Multifamily Default and Prepayment Outputs 3.6.3.6.2.3, Single Family Gross Loss Severity Outputs 3.6.3.6.3.3, Multifamily Gross Loss Severity Outputs
	3–47, Inputs for each Distinct CE Combination (DCC)	R			
3.6.3.7.2, Stress Test Whole Loan Cash Flow Inputs	3–51, Inputs for Final Calculation of Stress Test Whole Loan Cash Flows	R			3.3.4, Interest Rates Outputs 3.6.3.3.4, Mortgage Amortization Schedule Outputs 3.6.3.4.4, Single Family Default and Prepayment Outputs 3.6.3.5.4, Multifamily Default and Prepayment Outputs 3.6.3.6.5.6, Single Family and Multifamily Net Loss Severity Outputs
3.6.3.8.2, Whole Loan Accounting Flows Inputs	3–54, Inputs for Whole Loan Accounting Flows	R			3.6.3.7.4, Stress Test Whole Loan Cash Flow Outputs
3.7.2, Mortgage-Related Securities Inputs	3–56, RBC Report Inputs for Single Class MBS Cash Flows	R			
	3–57, RBC Report Inputs for Multi-Class and Derivative MBS Cash Flows	R			
	3–58, RBC Report Inputs for MRBs and Derivative MBS Cash Flows	R			
3.8.2, Nonmortgage Instrument Inputs	3–66, Input Variables for Nonmortgage Instrument Cash flows	R			

TABLE 3–1—SOURCES OF STRESS TEST INPUT DATA—Continued

Section of this Appendix	Table	Data Source(s) R = RBC Report P = Public Data F = Fixed Values			
		R	P	F	Intermediate Outputs
3.9.2, Alternative Modeling Treatments Inputs	3–70, Alternative Modeling Treatment Inputs	R			
3.10.2, Operations, Taxes, and Accounting Inputs	3–71, Operations, Taxes, and Accounting Inputs	R			3.3.4, Interest Rates Outputs 3.6.3.7.4, Stress Test Whole Loan Cash Flow Outputs 3.7.4, Mortgage-Related Securities Outputs 3.8.4, Nonmortgage Instrument Outputs
3.12.2, Risk-Based Capital Requirement Inputs		R			3.3.4, Interest Rates Outputs 3.9.4, Alternative Modeling Treatments Outputs 3.10.4, Operations, Taxes, and Accounting Outputs

3.1.2 Risk-Based Capital Report

The Risk-Based Capital Report is comprised of information on whole loans, mortgage-related securities, nonmortgage instruments (including liabilities and derivatives), and accounting items (including off-balance sheet guarantees). In addition to their reported data, the Enterprises may report scale factors in order to reconcile this reported data with their published financials (*see* section 3.10.2[b] of this appendix). If so, specific data items, as indicated, are adjusted by appropriate scale factors before any calculations occur.

3.1.2.1 Whole Loan Inputs

[a] Whole loans are individual single family or multifamily mortgage loans. The Stress Test distinguishes between whole loans that the Enterprises hold in their investment portfolios (retained loans) and those that underlie mortgage-backed securities (sold loans). Consistent with Table 3–2, Whole Loan Classification Variables, each Enterprise aggregates the data for loans with similar portfolio (retained or sold), risk, and product characteristics. The characteristics of these loan groups determine rates of mortgage Default, Prepayment and Loss Severity and cash flows.

[b] The characteristics that are the basis for loan groups are called "classification variables" and reflect categories, e.g., fixed interest rate versus floating interest rate, or identify a value range, e.g., original loan-to-value (LTV) ratio greater than 80 percent and less than or equal to 90 percent.

[c] All loans with the same values for each of the relevant classification variables included in 3–2 (and where applicable 3–3 and 3–4) comprise a single loan group. For example, one loan group includes all loans with the following characteristics:

- Single family
- Sold portfolio
- 30-year fixed rate conventional loan
- Mortgage age greater than or equal to 36 months and less than 48 months
- Original LTV greater than 75 percent and less than or equal to 80 percent
- Current mortgage interest rate class greater than or equal to six percent and less than seven percent
- Secured by property located in the East North Central Census Division
- Relative loan size greater than or equal to 75 percent and less than 100 percent of the average for its state and origination year.

TABLE 3–2—WHOLE LOAN CLASSIFICATION VARIABLES

Variable	Description	Range
Reporting Date	The last day of the quarter for the loan group activity that is being reported to OFHEO	YYYY0331 YYYY0630 YYYY0930 YYYY1231
Enterprise	Enterprise submitting the loan group data	Fannie Mae Freddie Mac
Business Type	Single family or multifamily	Single family Multifamily
Portfolio Type	Retained portfolio or Sold portfolio	Retained Portfolio Sold Portfolio
Government Flag	Conventional or Government insured loan	Conventional Government
Original LTV	Assigned LTV classes based on the ratio, in percent, between the original loan amount and the lesser of the purchase price or appraised value	LTV<=60 60<LTV<=70 70<LTV<=75 75<LTV<=80 80<LTV<=90 90<LTV<=95 95<LTV<=100 100<LTV
Interest-only Flag	Indicates if the loan is currently paying interest-only. Loans that started as I/Os and are currently amortizing should be flagged as 'N'	Yes No
Current Mortgage Interest Rate	Assigned classes for the current mortgage interest rate	0.0<=Rate<4.0 4.0<=Rate<5.0 5.0<=Rate<6.0 6.0<=Rate<7.0 7.0<=Rate<8.0 8.0<=Rate<9.0 9.0<=Rate<10.0 10.0<=Rate<11.0 11.0<=Rate<12.0 12.0<=Rate<13.0 13.0<=Rate<14.0 14.0<=Rate<15.0 15.0<=Rate<16.0 Rate=>16.0
Original Mortgage Interest Rate	Assigned classes for the original mortgage interest rate	0.0<=Rate<4.0 4.0<=Rate<5.0 5.0<=Rate<6.0 6.0<=Rate<7.0 7.0<=Rate<8.0 8.0<=Rate<9.0 9.0<=Rate<10.0 10.0<=Rate<11.0 11.0<=Rate<12.0 12.0<=Rate<13.0 13.0<=Rate<14.0 14.0<=Rate<15.0 15.0<=Rate<16.0 Rate=>16.0

TABLE 3–2—WHOLE LOAN CLASSIFICATION VARIABLES—Continued

Variable	Description	Range
Mortgage Age	Assigned classes for the age of the loan	0<=Age<=12 12<Age<=24 24<Age<=36 36<Age<=48 48<Age<=60 60<Age<=72 72<Age<=84 84<Age<=96 96<Age<=108 108<Age<=120 120<Age<=132 132<Age<=144 144<Age<=156 156<Age<=168 168<Age<=180 Age>180
Rate Reset Period	Assigned classes for the number of months between rate adjustments	Period=1 1<Period<=4 4<Period<=9 9<Period<=15 15<Period<=60 60<Period<999 Period=999 (not applicable)
Payment Reset Period	Assigned classes for the number of months between payment adjustments after the duration of the teaser rate	Period<=9 9<Period<=15 15<Period<999 Period=999 (not applicable)
ARM Index	Specifies the type of index used to determine the interest rate at each adjustment	FHLB 11th District Cost of Funds. 1 Month Federal Agency Cost of Funds. 3 Month Federal Agency Cost of Funds. 6 Month Federal Agency Cost of Funds. 12 Month Federal Agency Cost of Funds. 24 Month Federal Agency Cost of Funds. 36 Month Federal Agency Cost of Funds. 60 Month Federal Agency Cost of Funds. 120 Month Federal Agency Cost of Funds. 360 Month Federal Agency Cost of Funds. Overnight Federal Funds (Effective). 1 Week Federal Funds 6 Month Federal Funds 1 month LIBOR 3 Month LIBOR 6 Month LIBOR 12 Month LIBOR Conventional Mortgage Rate 15 Year Fixed Mortgage Rate 7 Year Balloon Mortgage Rate Prime Rate 1 Month Treasury Bill 3 Month CMT

TABLE 3–2—WHOLE LOAN CLASSIFICATION VARIABLES—Continued

Variable	Description	Range
		6 Month CMT 12 Month CMT 24 Month CMT 36 Month CMT 60 Month CMT 120 Month CMT 240 Month CMT 360 Month CMT
Cap Type Flag	Indicates if a loan group is rate-capped, payment-capped or uncapped	Payment Capped Rate Capped No periodic rate cap
OFHEO Ledger Code	OFHEO-specific General Ledger account number used in the Stress Test	Appropriate OFHEO Ledger Code based on the chart of accounts.

TABLE 3–3—ADDITIONAL SINGLE FAMILY LOAN CLASSIFICATION VARIABLES

Variable	Description	Range
Single Family Product Code	Identifies the mortgage product types for single family loans	Fixed Rate 30YR Fixed Rate 20YR Fixed Rate 15YR 5 Year Fixed Rate Balloon 7 Year Fixed Rate Balloon 10 Year Fixed Rate Balloon 15 Year Fixed Rate Balloon Adjustable Rate Step Rate ARMs Second Lien Other
Census Division	The Census Division in which the property resides. This variable is populated based on the property's state code	East North Central East South Central Middle Atlantic Mountain New England Pacific South Atlantic West North Central West South Central
Relative Loan Size	Assigned classes for the loan amount at origination divided by the simple average of the loan amount for the origination year and for the State in which the property is located. Average loan size for the appropriate quarter is provided by OFHEO based upon data from both Enterprises. It is expressed as a decimal	0<=Size<=.4 .4<Size<=.6 .6<Size<=.75 .75<Size<=1.0 1.0<Size<=1.25 1.25<Size<=1.5 Size>1.5

TABLE 3–4—ADDITIONAL MULTIFAMILY LOAN CLASSIFICATION VARIABLES

Variable	Description	Range
Multifamily Product Code	Identifies the mortgage product types for multifamily loans	Fixed Rate Fully Amortizing Adjustable Rate Fully Amortizing 5 Year Fixed Rate Balloon 7 Year Fixed Rate Balloon

TABLE 3–4—ADDITIONAL MULTIFAMILY LOAN CLASSIFICATION VARIABLES—Continued

Variable	Description	Range
		10 Year Fixed Rate Balloon 15 Year Fixed Rate Balloon Balloon ARM Other
New Book Flag	"New Book" is applied to Fannie Mae loans acquired beginning in 1988 and Freddie Mac loans acquired beginning in 1993, except for loans that were refinanced to avoid a default on a loan originated or acquired earlier	New Book Old Book
Ratio Update Flag	Indicates if the LTV and DCR were updated at origination or at Enterprise acquisition	Yes No
Current DCR	Assigned classes for the Debt Service Coverage Ratio based on the most recent annual operating statement	DCR<1.00 1.00<=DCR<1.10 1.10<=DCR<1.20 1.20<=DCR<1.30 1.30<=DCR<1.40 1.40<=DCR<1.50 1.50<=DCR<1.60 1.60<=DCR<1.70 1.70<=DCR<1.80 1.80<=DCR<1.90 1.90<=DCR<2.00 2.00<=DCR<2.50 2.50<=DCR<4.00 DCR>=4.00
Prepayment Penalty Flag	Indicates if prepayment of the loan is subject to active prepayment penalties or yield maintenance provisions	Yes No

3.1.2.1.1 Loan Group Inputs

TABLE 3–5—MORTGAGE AMORTIZATION CALCULATION INPUTS

Variable	Description
	Rate Type (Fixed or Adjustable)
	Product Type (30/20/15-Year FRM, ARM, Balloon, Government, etc.)
UPB_{ORIG}	Unpaid Principal Balance at Origination (aggregate for Loan Group)
UPB_0	Unpaid Principal Balance at start of Stress Test (aggregate for Loan Group), adjusted by UPB scale factor.
MIR_0	Mortgage Interest Rate for the Mortgage Payment prior to the start of the Stress Test, or Initial Mortgage Interest Rate for new loans (weighted average for Loan Group) (expressed as a decimal per annum)
PMT_0	Amount of the Mortgage Payment (Principal and Interest) prior to the start of the Stress Test, or first Payment for new loans (aggregate for Loan Group), adjusted by UPB scale factor.

TABLE 3–5—MORTGAGE AMORTIZATION CALCULATION INPUTS—Continued

Variable	Description
AT	Original loan Amortizing Term in months (weighted average for Loan Group)
RM	Remaining term to Maturity in months (i.e., number of contractual payments due between the start of the Stress Test and the contractual maturity date of the loan) (weighted average for Loan Group)
A_0	Age of the loan at the start of Stress Test, in months (weighted average for Loan Group)
IRP	Initial Rate Period, in months
	Interest-only Flag
RIOP	Remaining Interest-only period, in months (weighted average for loan group)
UPB Scale Factor	Factor determined by reconciling reported UPB to published financials.
Additional Interest Rate Inputs	
GFR	Guarantee Fee Rate (weighted average for Loan Group) (decimal per annum)
SFR	Servicing Fee Rate (weighted average for Loan Group) (decimal per annum)
Additional Inputs for ARMs (weighted averages for Loan Group, except for Index)	
$INDEX_m$	Monthly values of the contractual Interest Rate Index
LB	Look-Back period, in months
MARGIN	Loan Margin (over index), decimal per annum
RRP	Rate Reset Period, in months
	Rate Reset Limit (up and down), decimal per annum
	Maximum Rate (life cap), decimal per annum
	Minimum Rate (life floor), decimal per annum
NAC	Negative Amortization Cap, decimal fraction of UPB_{ORIG}
	Unlimited Payment Reset Period, in months
PRP	Payment Reset Period, in months
	Payment Reset Limit, as decimal fraction of prior payment

TABLE 3–6—ADDITIONAL INPUTS FOR SINGLE FAMILY DEFAULT AND PREPAYMENT

Variable	Description
PROD	Mortgage Product Type
A_0	Age *immediately prior to* start of Stress Test, in months (weighted average for Loan Group)
LTV_{ORIG}	Loan-to-Value ratio at Origination (weighted average for Loan Group)

TABLE 3–6—ADDITIONAL INPUTS FOR SINGLE FAMILY DEFAULT AND PREPAYMENT—Continued

Variable	Description
UPB_{ORIG}	UPB at Origination (aggregate for Loan Group), adjusted by UPB scale factor.
MIR_{ORIG}	Mortgage Interest Rate at origination ("Initial Rate" for ARMs), decimal per annum (weighted average for loan group)
UPB_0	Unpaid Principal Balance immediately prior to start of Stress Test (aggregate for Loan Group),
IF	Fraction (by UPB, in decimal form) of Loan Group backed by Investor-owned properties
RLS_{ORIG}	Weighted average Relative Loan Size at Origination (Original UPB as a fraction of average UPB for the state and Origination Year of loan origination)
$CHPGF_0^{LG}$	Cumulative House Price Growth Factor since Loan Origination (weighted average for Loan Group)

TABLE 3–7—ADDITIONAL INPUTS FOR MULTIFAMILY DEFAULT AND PREPAYMENT

Variable	Description
	Mortgage Product Type
A_0	Age *immediately prior to* start of Stress Test, in months (weighted average for Loan Group)
NBF	New Book Flag
RUF	Ratio Update Flag
LTV_{ORIG}	Loan-to-Value ratio at loan origination
DCR_0	Debt Service Coverage Ratio at the start of the Stress Test
PMT_0	Amount of the mortgage payment (principal and interest) prior to the start of the Stress Test, or first payment for new loans (aggregate for Loan Group)
PPEM	Prepayment Penalty End Month number in the Stress Test (weighted average for Loan Group)
RM	Remaining term to Maturity in months (i.e., number of contractual payments due between the start of the Stress Test and the contractual maturity date of the loan) (weighted average for Loan Group)

TABLE 3–8—MISCELLANEOUS WHOLE LOAN CASH AND ACCOUNTING FLOW INPUTS

Variable	Description
GF	Guarantee Fee rate (weighted average for Loan Group) (decimal per annum)
FDS	Float Days for Scheduled Principal and Interest (weighted average for Loan Group)
FDP	Float Days for Prepaid Principal (weighted average for Loan Group)
FREP	Fraction Repurchased (weighted average for Loan Group) (decimal)

TABLE 3–8—MISCELLANEOUS WHOLE LOAN CASH AND ACCOUNTING FLOW INPUTS—Continued

Variable	Description
RM	Remaining Term to Maturity in months
UPD_0	Sum of all unamortized discounts, premiums, fees, commissions, etc. for the loan group, such that the unamortized balance equals the book value minus the face value for the loan group at the start of the Stress Test, adjusted by the Unamortized Balance Scale Factor
Unamortized Balance Scale Factor	Factor determined by reconciling reported Unamortized Balance to published financials

TABLE 3–9—ADDITIONAL INPUTS FOR REPURCHASED MBS

Variable	Description
Wtd Ave Percent Repurchased	For sold loan groups, the percent of the loan group UPB that gives the actual dollar amount of loans that collateralize single class MBSs that the Enterprise holds in its own portfolio
$SUPD_0$	The aggregate sum of all unamortized discounts, premiums, fees, commissions, etc. associated with the securities modeled using the Wtd Ave Percent Repurchased, such that the unamortized balance equals the book value minus the face value for the relevant securities at the start of the Stress Test, adjusted by the percent repurchased and the Security Unamortized Balance Scale Factor
Security Unamortized Balances Scale Factor	Factor determined by reconciling reported Security Unamortized Balances to published financials

3.1.2.1.2 Credit Enhancement Inputs

To calculate reductions in mortgage credit losses due to credit enhancements, the following data are required for any credit-enhanced loans in a loan group. For this purpose, a Loan Group is divided into Distinct Credit Enhancement Combinations, as further described in section 3.6.3.6.4, Mortgage Credit Enhancement, of this appendix.

TABLE 3–10—CE INPUTS FOR EACH LOAN GROUP

Variable	Description
UPB_{ORIG}^{LG}	Origination UPB.
LTV_{ORIG}^{LG}	Original LTV.

TABLE 3–11—INPUTS FOR EACH DISTINCT CE COMBINATION (DCC)

Variable	Description
P^{DCC}	Percent of Initial Loan Group UPB represented by individual loan(s) in a DCC
$R^{MI,DCC}$ or $R^{LSA,DCC}$	Credit rating of Loan Limit CE (MI or LSA) Counterparty
$C^{MI,DCC}$ or $C^{LSA,DCC}$	Weighted Average Coverage Percentage for MI or LSA Coverage (weighted by Initial UPB)
$AB_0^{DCC,C1}$	DCC Available First Priority CE Balance immediately prior to start of the Stress Test
$AB_0^{DCC,C2}$	DCC Available Second Priority CE Balance immediately prior to start of the Stress Test

TABLE 3–11—INPUTS FOR EACH DISTINCT CE COMBINATION (DCC)—Continued

Variable	Description
$R^{DCC,C1}$	DCC Credit Rating of First Priority CE Provider or Counterparty; or Cash/ Cash Equivalent (which is not Haircutted)
$R^{DCC,C2}$	DCC Credit Rating of Second Priority CE Provider or Counterparty; or Cash/Cash Equivalent (which is not Haircutted)
$C^{DCC,C1}$	DCC Loan-Level Coverage Limit of First Priority Contract (If Subtype is MPI; otherwise = 1)
$C^{DCC,C2}$	DCC Loan-Limit Coverage Limit of Second Priority Contract (if Subtype is MPI; otherwise = 1)
$ExpMo^{DCC,C1}$	Month in the Stress Test (1...120 or after) in which the DCC First Priority Contract expires
$ExpMo^{DCC,C2}$	Month in the Stress Test (1...120 or after) in which the DCC Second Priority Contract expires
$ELPF^{DCC,C1}$	DCC Enterprise Loss Position Flag for First Priority Contract (Y or N)
$ELPF^{DCC,C2}$	DCC Enterprise Loss Position Flag for Second Priority Contract (Y or N)

3.1.2.1.3 Commitments Inputs

[a] The Enterprises report Commitment Loan Group categories based on specific product type characteristics of securitized single family loans originated and delivered during the six months prior to the start of the Stress Test (*see* section 3.2, Commitments, of this appendix). For each category, the Enterprises report the same information as for Whole Loan Groups with the following exceptions:

1. Amortization term and remaining term are set to those appropriate for newly originated loans;
2. Unamortized balances are set to zero;
3. The House Price Growth Factor is set to one;
4. Age is set to zero;
5. Any credit enhancement coverage other than mortgage insurance is not reported.

3.1.2.2 Mortgage Related Securities Inputs

[a] The Enterprises hold mortgage-related securities, including single class and Derivative Mortgage-Backed Securities (certain multi-class and strip securities) issued by Fannie Mae, Freddie Mac, and Ginnie Mae; mortgage revenue bonds issued by State and local governments and their instrumentalities; and single class and Derivative Mortgage-Backed Securities issued by private entities. The Stress Test models the cash flows of these securities individually. Table 3–12, Inputs for Single Class MBS Cash Flows sets forth the data elements that the Enterprises must compile in the RBC Report regarding each MBS held in their portfolios. This information is necessary for determining associated cash flows in the Stress Test.

TABLE 3–12—INPUTS FOR SINGLE CLASS MBS CASH FLOWS

Variable	Description
Pool Number	A unique number identifying each mortgage pool
CUSIP Number	A unique number assigned to publicly traded securities by the Committee on Uniform Securities Identification Procedures
Issuer	Issuer of the mortgage pool
Government Flag	Indicates Government insured collateral
Original UPB Amount	Original pool balance adjusted by UPB scale factor and multiplied by the Enterprise's percentage ownership

TABLE 3–12—INPUTS FOR SINGLE CLASS MBS CASH FLOWS—Continued

Variable	Description
Current UPB Amount	Initial Pool balance (at the start of the Stress Test), adjusted by UPB scale factor and multiplied by the Enterprise's percentage ownership
Product Code	Mortgage product type for the pool
Security Rate Index	If the rate on the security adjusts over time, the index that the adjustment is based on
Unamortized Balance	The sum of all unamortized discounts, premiums, fees, commissions, etc., such that the unamortized balance equals book value minus face value, adjusted by Unamortized Balance Scale Factor
Wt Avg Original Amortization Term	Original amortization term of the underlying loans, in months (weighted average for underlying loans)
Wt Avg Remaining Term of Maturity	Remaining maturity of the underlying loans at the start of the Stress Test (weighted average for underlying loans)
Wt Avg Age	Age of the underlying loans at the start of the Stress Test (weighted average for underlying loans)
Wt Avg Current Mortgage Interest Rate	Mortgage Interest Rate of the underlying loans at the start of the Stress Test (weighted average for underlying loans)
Wt Avg Pass-Through Rate	Pass-Through Rate of the underlying loans at the start of the Stress Test (Sold loans only) (weighted average for underlying loans)
Wtg Avg Original Mortgage Interest Rate	The current UPB weighted average mortgage interest rate in effect at origination for the loans in the pool
Security Rating	The most current rating issued by any Nationally Recognized Statistical Rating Organization (NRSRO) for this security, as of the reporting date
Wt Avg Gross Margin	Gross margin for the underlying loans (ARM MBS only) (weighted average for underlying loans)
Wt Avg Net Margin	Net margin (used to determine the security rate for ARM MBS) (weighted average for underlying loans)
Wt Avg Rate Reset Period	Rate reset period in months (ARM MBS only) (weighted average for underlying loans)
Wt Avg Rate Reset Limit	Rate reset limit up/down (ARM MBS only) (weighted average for underlying loans)
Wt Avg Life Interest Rate Ceiling	Maximum rate (lifetime cap) (ARM MBS only) (weighted average for underlying loans)
Wt Avg Life Interest Rate Floor	Minimum rate (lifetime floor) (ARM MBS only) (weighted average for underlying loans)
Wt Avg Payment Reset Period	Payment reset period in months (ARM MBS only) (weighted average for underlying loans)
Wt Avg Payment Reset Limit	Payment reset limit up/down (ARM MBS only) (weighted average for underlying loans)
Wt Avg Lockback Period	The number of months to look back from the interest rate change date to find the index value that will be used to determine the next interest rate (weighted average for underlying loans)

TABLE 3–12—INPUTS FOR SINGLE CLASS MBS CASH FLOWS—Continued

Variable	Description
Wt Avg Negative Amortization Cap	The maximum amount to which the balance can increase before the payment is recast to a fully amortizing amount. It is expressed as a fraction of the original UPB (weighted average for underlying loans)
Wt Avg Original Mortgage Interest Rate	The current UPB weighted average original mortgage interest rate for the loans in the pool
Wt Avg Initial Interest Rate Period	Number of months between the loan origination date and the first rate adjustment date (weighted average for underlying loans)
Wt Avg Unlimited Payment Reset Period	Number of months between unlimited payment resets i.e., not limited by payment caps, starting with origination date (weighted average for underlying loans)
Notional Flag	Indicates if the amounts reported in Original Security Balance and Current Security Balance are notional
UPB Scale Factor	Factor determined by reconciling reported UPB to published financials
Unamortized Balance Scale Factor	Factor determined by reconciling reported Unamortized Balance to published financials
Whole Loan Modeling Flag	Indicates that the Current UPB Amount and Unamortized Balance associated with this repurchased MBS are included in the Wtg Avg Percent Repurchased and Security Unamortized Balance fields
FAS 115 Classification	The financial instrument's classification according to FAS 115
$HPGR_K$	Vector of House Price Growth Rates for quarters q=1. . .40 of the Stress Period

[b] Table 3–13, Information for Multi-Class and Derivative MBS Cash Flows Inputs sets forth the data elements that the Enterprises must compile regarding multi-class and Derivative MBS (e.g., REMICs and Strips). This information is necessary for determining associated cash flows in the Stress Test.

TABLE 3–13—INFORMATION FOR MULTI-CLASS AND DERIVATIVE MBS CASH FLOWS INPUTS

Variable	Description
CUSIP Number	A unique number assigned to publicly traded securities by the Committee on Uniform Securities Identification Procedures
Issuer	Issuer of the security: FNMA, FHLMC, GNMA or other
Original Security Balance	Original principal balance of the security (notional amount for interest-only securities) at the time of issuance, adjusted by UPB scale factor, multiplied by the Enterprise's percentage ownership
Current Security Balance	Initial principal balance, or notional amount, at the start of the Stress Period, adjusted by UPB scale factor, multiplied by the Enterprise's percentage ownership
Current Security Percentage Owned	The percentage of a security's total current balance owned by the Enterprise
Notional Flag	Indicates if the amounts reported in Original Security Balance and Current Security Balance are notional
Unamortized Balance	The sum of all unamortized discounts, premiums, fees, commissions, etc., such that the unamortized balance equals book value minus face value, adjusted by the Unamortized Balance Scale Factor
Unamortized Balance Scale Factor	Factor determined by reconciling reported Unamortized Balance to published financials

TABLE 3–13—INFORMATION FOR MULTI-CLASS AND DERIVATIVE MBS CASH FLOWS INPUTS—Continued

Variable	Description
UPB Scale Factor	Factor determined by reconciling the reported current security balance to published financials
Security Rating	The most current rating issued by any Nationally Recognized Statistical Rating Organization (NRSRO) for this security, as of the reporting date

[c] Table 3–14, Inputs for MRBs and Derivative MBS Cash Flows Inputs sets forth the data elements that the Enterprises must compile in the RBC Report regarding mortgage revenue bonds and private issue mortgage related securities (MRS). The data in this table is supplemented with public securities disclosure data. This information is necessary for determining associated cash flows in the Stress Test.

TABLE 3–14—INPUTS FOR MRBS AND DERIVATIVE MBS CASH FLOWS INPUTS

Variable	Description
CUSIP Number	A unique number assigned to publicly traded securities by the Committee on Uniform Securities Identification Procedures
Original Security Balance	Original principal balance, adjusted by UPB scale factor and multiplied by the Enterprise's percentage ownership
Current Security Balance	Initial Principal balance (at start of Stress Period), adjusted by UPB scale factor and multiplied by the Enterprise's percentage ownership
Unamortized Balance	The sum of all unamortized discounts, premiums, fees, commissions, etc., such that the unamortized balance equals book value minus face value, adjusted by Unamortized Balance scale factor
Unamortized Balance Scale Factor	Factor determined by reconciling reported Unamortized Balance to published financials
UPB Scale Factor	Factor determined by reconciling the reported current security balance to published financials
Floating Rate Flag	Indicates the instrument pays interest at a floating rate
Issue Date	The issue date of the security
Maturity Date	The stated maturity date of the security
Security Interest Rate	The rate at which the security earns interest, as of the reporting date
Principal Payment Window Starting Date, Down-Rate Scenario	The month in the Stress Test that principal payment is expected to start for the security under the statutory "down" interest rate scenario, according to Enterprise projections
Principal Payment Window Ending Date, Down-Rate Scenario	The month in the Stress Test that principal payment is expected to end for the security under the statutory "down" interest rate scenario, according to Enterprise projections
Principal Payment Window Starting Date, Up-Rate Scenario	The month in the Stress Test that principal payment is expected to start for the security under the statutory "up" interest rate scenario, according to Enterprise projections
Principal Payment Window Ending Date, Up-Rate Scenario	The month in the Stress Test that principal payment is expected to end for the security under the statutory "up" interest rate scenario, according to Enterprise projections
Notional Flag	Indicates if the amounts reported in Original Security Balance and Current Security Balance are notional

TABLE 3–14—INPUTS FOR MRBS AND DERIVATIVE MBS CASH FLOWS INPUTS—Continued

Variable	Description
Security Rating	The most current rating issued by any Nationally Recognized Statistical Rating Organization (NRSRO) for this security, as of the reporting date
Security Rate Index	If the rate on the security adjusts over time, the index on which the adjustment is based
Security Rate Index Coefficient	If the rate on the security adjusts over time, the coefficient is the number used to multiply by the value of the index
Security Rate Index Spread	If the rate on the security adjusts over time, the spread is added to the value of the index multiplied by the coefficient to determine the new rate
Security Rate Adjustment Frequency	The number of months between rate adjustments
Security Interest Rate Ceiling	The maximum rate (lifetime cap) on the security
Security Interest Rate Floor	The minimum rate (lifetime floor) on the security
Life Ceiling Interest Rate	The maximum interest rate allowed throughout the life of the security
Life Floor Interest Rate	The minimum interest rate allowed throughout the life of security

3.1.2.3 Nonmortgage Instrument Cash Flows Inputs

Table 3–15, Input Variables for Nonmortgage Instrument Cash flows sets forth the data elements that the Enterprises must compile in the RBC Report to identify individual securities (other than Mortgage Related Securities) that are held by the Enterprises in their portfolios. These include debt securities, preferred stock, and derivative contracts (interest rate swaps, caps, and floors). All data are instrument specific. The data in this table are supplemented by public securities disclosure data. For instruments with complex or non-standard features, the Enterprises may be required to provide additional information such as amortization schedules, interest rate coupon reset formulas, and the terms of the call options.

TABLE 3–15—INPUT VARIABLES FOR NONMORTGAGE INSTRUMENT CASH FLOWS

Data Elements	Description
Amortization Methodology Code	Enterprise method of amortizing deferred balances (e.g., straight line)
Asset ID	CUSIP or Reference Pool Number identifying the asset underlying a derivative position
Asset Type Code	Code that identifies asset type used in the commercial information service (e.g. ABS, Fannie Mae pool, Freddie Mac pool)
Associated Instrument ID	Instrument ID of an instrument linked to another instrument
Coefficient	Indicates the extent to which the coupon is leveraged or de-leveraged
Compound Indicator	Indicates if interest is compounded
Compounding Frequency	Indicates how often interest is compounded
Counterparty Credit Rating	NRSRO's rating for the counterparty
Counterparty Credit Rating Type	An indicator identifying the counterparty's credit rating as short-term ('S') or long-term ('L')
Counterparty ID	Enterprise counterparty tracking ID

TABLE 3–15—INPUT VARIABLES FOR NONMORTGAGE INSTRUMENT CASH FLOWS—Continued

Data Elements	Description
Country Code	Standard country codes in compliance with Federal Information Processing Standards Publication 10–4
Credit Agency Code	Identifies NRSRO (e.g., Moody's)
Current Asset Face Amount	Current face amount of the asset underlying a swap adjusted by UPB scale factor
Current Coupon	Current coupon or dividend rate of the instrument
Current Unamortized Discount	Current unamortized premium or unaccreted discount of the instrument adjusted by Unamortized Balance Scale Factor. If the proceeds from the issuance of debt or derivatives or the amount paid for an asset were greater than par, the value should be positive. If the proceeds or the amounts paid were less than par, the value should be negative
Current Unamortized Fees	Current unamortized fees associated with the instrument adjusted by Unamortized Balance Scale Factor. Generally fees associated with the issuance of debt or derivatives should be negative numbers. Fees associated with the purchase of an asset should generally be reported as positive numbers
Current Unamortized Hedge	Current unamortized hedging gains (positive) or losses (negative) associated with the instrument adjusted by the Unamortized Balance Scale Factor
Current Unamortized Other	Any other unamortized items originally associated with the instrument adjusted by Unamortized Balance Scale Factor. If the proceeds from the issuance of debt or derivatives or the amount paid for an asset were greater than par, the value should be positive. If the proceeds or the amounts paid were less than par, the value should be negative
CUSIP_ISIN	CUSIP or ISIN Number identifying the instrument
Day Count	Day count convention (e.g. 30/360)
End Date	The last index repricing date
EOP Principal Balance	End of Period face, principal or notional, amount of the instrument adjusted by UPB scale factor
Exact Representation	Indicates that an instrument is modeled according to its contractual terms
Exercise Convention	Indicates option exercise convention (e.g., American Option)
Exercise Price	Par = 1.0; Options
First Coupon Date	Date first coupon is received or paid
Index Cap	Indicates maximum index rate
Index Floor	Indicates minimum index rate
Index Reset Frequency	Indicates how often the interest rate index resets on floating-rate instruments
Index Code	Indicates the interest rate index to which floating-rate instruments are tied (e.g., LIBOR)
Index Term	Point on yield curve, expressed in months, upon which the index is based
Instrument Credit Rating	NRSRO credit rating for the instrument

TABLE 3–15—INPUT VARIABLES FOR NONMORTGAGE INSTRUMENT CASH FLOWS—Continued

Data Elements	Description
Instrument Credit Rating Type	An indicator identifying the instruments credit rating as short-term ('S') or long-term ('L')
Instrument ID	An integer used internally by the Enterprise that uniquely identifies the instrument
Interest Currency Code	Indicates currency in which interest payments are paid or received
Interest Type Code	Indicates the method of interest rate payments (e.g., fixed, floating, step, discount)
Issue Date	Indicates the date that the instrument was issued
Life Cap Rate	The maximum interest rate for the instrument throughout its life
Life Floor Rate	The minimum interest rate for the instrument throughout its life
Look-Back Period	Period from the index reset date, expressed in months, that the index value is derived
Maturity Date	Date that the instrument contractually matures
Notional Indicator	Identifies whether the face amount is notional
Instrument Type Code	Indicates the type of instrument to be modeled (e.g., ABS, Cap, Swap)
Option Indicator	Indicates if instrument contains an option
Option Type	Indicates option type (e.g., Call option)
Original Asset Face Amount	Original face amount of the asset underlying a swap adjusted by UPB scale factor
Original Discount	Original premium or discount associated with the purchase or sale of the instrument adjusted by Unamortized Balance Scale Factor. If the proceeds from the issuance of debt or derivatives or the amount paid for an asset were greater than par, the value should be positive. If the proceeds or the amounts paid were less than par, the value should be negative
Original Face	Original face, principal or notional, amount of the instrument adjusted by UPB scale factor
Original Fees	Fees or commissions paid at the time of purchase or sale adjusted by the Unamortized Balance Scale Factor. Generally fees associated with the issuance of debt or derivatives should be negative numbers. Fees associated with the purchase of an asset should generally be reported as positive numbers
Original Hedge	Gains (positive) or losses (negative) from closing out a hedge associated with the instrument at settlement, adjusted by the Unamortized Balance Scale Factor
Original Other	Any other items originally associated with the instrument to be amortized or accreted adjusted by the Unamortized Balance Scale Factor. If the proceeds from the issuance of debt or derivatives or the amount paid for an asset were greater than par, the value should be positive. If the proceeds of the amounts paid were less than par, the value should be negative
Parent Entity ID	Enterprise internal tracking ID for parent entity
Payment Amount	Interest payment amount associated with the instrument (reserved for complex instruments where interest payments are not modeled) adjusted by UPB scale factor

TABLE 3–15—INPUT VARIABLES FOR NONMORTGAGE INSTRUMENT CASH FLOWS—Continued

Data Elements	Description
Payment Frequency	Indicates how often interest payments are made or received
Performance Date	"As of" date on which the data is submitted
Periodic Adjustment	The maximum amount that the interest rate for the instrument can change per reset
Position Code	Indicates whether the Enterprise pays or receives interest on the instrument
Principal Currency Code	Indicates currency in which principal payments are paid or received
Principal Factor Amount	EOP Principal Balance expressed as a percentage of Original Face
Principal Payment Date	A valid date identifying the date that principal is paid
Settlement Date	A valid date identifying the date the settlement occurred
Spread	An amount added to an index to determine an instrument's interest rate
Start Date	The date, spot or forward, when some feature of a financial contract becomes effective (e.g., Call Date), or when interest payments or receipts begin to be calculated
Strike Rate	The price or rate at which an option begins to have a settlement value at expiration, or, for interest-rate caps and floors, the rate that triggers interest payments
Submitting Entity	Indicates which Enterprise is submitting information
Trade ID	Unique code identifying the trade of an instrument
Transaction Code	Indicates the transaction that an Enterprise is initiating with the instrument (e.g. buy, issue reopen)
Transaction Date	A valid date identifying the date the transaction occurred
UPB Scale Factor	Factor determined by reconciling reported UPB to published financials
Unamortized Balances Scale Factor	Factor determined by reconciling reported Unamortized Balances to published financials

3.1.2.4 Inputs for Alternative Modeling Treatment Items

TABLE 3–16—INPUTS FOR ALTERNATIVE MODELING TREATMENT ITEMS

Variable	Description
TYPE	Type of item (asset, liability or off-balance sheet item)
BOOK	Book Value of item (amount outstanding adjusted for deferred items)
FACE	Face Value or notional balance of item for off-balance sheet items
REMATUR	Remaining Contractual Maturity of item in whole months. Any fraction of a month equals one whole month
RATE	Interest Rate
INDEX	Index used to calculate Interest Rate

TABLE 3–16—INPUTS FOR ALTERNATIVE MODELING TREATMENT ITEMS—Continued

Variable	Description
FAS115	Designation that the item is recorded at fair value, according to FAS 115
RATING	Instrument or counterparty rating
FHA	In the case of off-balance sheet guarantees, a designation indicating 100% of collateral is guaranteed by FHA
MARGIN	Margin over an Index

3.1.2.5 Operations, Taxes, and Accounting Inputs

[a] Table 3–17, Operations, Taxes, and Accounting Inputs sets forth the data the Enterprises must compile in the RBC Report to permit the calculation of taxes, operating expenses, and dividends. These data include:

- Average monthly Operating Expenses (i.e., administrative expenses, salaries and benefits, professional services, property costs, equipment costs) for the quarter prior to the beginning of the Stress Test;
- Income for the current year-to-date, one year, and two years prior to the beginning of the stress test, before taxes and provision for income taxes;
- Dividend payout ratio for the four quarters prior to the beginning of the Stress Period;
- Minimum capital requirement as of the beginning of the Stress Period.

TABLE 3–17—OPERATIONS, TAXES, AND ACCOUNTING INPUTS

Input	Description
FAS 115 and 125 fair value adjustment on retained mortgage portfolio	
FAS 133 fair value adjustment on retained mortgage portfolio	
Reserve for losses on retained mortgage portfolio	
FAS 115 and 125 fair value adjustments on non-mortgage investments	
FAS 133 fair value adjustments on non-mortgage investments	
Total cash	
Accrued interest receivable on mortgages	
Accrued interest receivable on non-mortgage investment securities	
Accrued interest receivable on non-mortgage investment securities denominated in foreign currency—hedged	
Accrued interest receivable on non-mortgage investment securities denominated in foreign currency—unhedged	
Accrued interest receivable on mortgage-linked derivatives, gross	
Accrued interest receivable on investment-linked derivatives, gross	

TABLE 3–17—OPERATIONS, TAXES, AND ACCOUNTING INPUTS—Continued

Input	Description
Accrued interest receivable on debt-linked derivatives, gross	
Other accrued interest receivable	
Accrued interest receivable on hedged debt-linked foreign currency swaps	Underlying instrument is GSE issued debt
Accrued interest receivable on unhedged debt-linked foreign currency swaps	
Accrued interest receivable on hedged asset-linked foreign currency swaps	Underlying instrument is an asset
Accrued interest receivable on unhedged asset-linked foreign currency swaps	
Currency transaction adjustments—hedged assets	Cumulative gain or loss due to changes in foreign exchange rates relative to on-balance sheet assets originally denominated in foreign currency
Currency transaction adjustments—unhedged assets	Cumulative gain or loss due to changes in foreign exchange rates relative to unhedged assets and off-balance sheet items originally denominated in foreign currency
Federal income tax refundable	
Accounts receivable	
Fees receivable	
Low income housing tax credit investments	
Fixed assets, net	
Clearing accounts	Net book value of all clearing accounts
Other assets	
Foreclosed property, net	Real estate owned including property acquired through foreclosure proceedings
FAS 133 fair value adjustment on debt securities	
Accrued interest payable on existing fixed-rate debt securities	
Accrued interest payable on existing floating-rate debt securities	
Accrued interest payable on existing debt issued in foreign currency—hedged	
Accrued interest payable on existing debt issued in foreign currency—unhedged	
Accrued interest payable on mortgage-linked derivatives, gross	
Accrued interest payable on investment-linked derivatives, gross	

TABLE 3–17—OPERATIONS, TAXES, AND ACCOUNTING INPUTS—Continued

Input	Description
Accrued interest payable on debt-linked derivatives, gross	
Other accrued interest payable	
Accrued interest payable debt-linked foreign currency swaps—hedged	
Accrued interest payable debt-linked foreign currency swaps—unhedged	
Accrued interest payable asset-linked foreign currency swaps—hedged	
Accrued interest payable asset-linked foreign currency swaps—unhedged	
Principal and interest due to mortgage security investors	Cash received on sold mortgages for onward submission to mortgage security investors
Currency transaction adjustments—hedged debt	Cumulative gain or loss due to changes in foreign exchange rates relative to on-balance sheet debt originally denominated in foreign currency
Currency transaction adjustments—unhedged debt	Cumulative gain or loss due to changes in foreign exchange rates relative to unhedged liabilities and off-balance sheet items originally denominated in foreign currency
Escrow deposits	Cash balances held in relation to servicing of multifamily loans
Federal income taxes payable	
Preferred dividends payable	
Accounts payable	
Other liabilities	
Common dividends payable	
Reserve for losses on sold mortgages	
Common stock	
Preferred stock, non-cumulative	
Additional paid-in capital	
Retained earnings	
Treasury stock	
Unrealized gains and losses on available-for-sale securities, net of tax, in accordance with FAS 115 and 125	
Unrealized gains and losses due to mark to market adjustments, FAS 115 and 125	
Unrealized gains and losses due to deferred balances related to pre-FAS 115 and 125 adjustments	

TABLE 3–17—OPERATIONS, TAXES, AND ACCOUNTING INPUTS—Continued

Input	Description
Unrealized gains and losses due to other realized gains, FAS 115	
Other comprehensive income, net of tax, in accordance with FAS 133	
OCI due to mark to market adjustments, FAS 133	
OCI due to deferred balances related to pre-FAS 133 adjustments	
OCI due to other realized gains, FAS 133	
Operating expenses	Average of prior three months
Common dividend payout ratio (average of prior 4 quarters)	Sum dollar amount of common dividends paid over prior 4 quarters and divided by the sum of total of after tax income less preferred dividends paid over prior 4 quarters
Common dividends per share paid 1 quarter prior to the beginning of the stress period	
Common shares outstanding	
Common Share Market Price	
Dividends paid on common stock 1 quarter prior to the beginning of the stress period	
Share Repurchases (average of prior 4 quarters)	Sum dollar amount of repurchased shares, net of newly issued shares, over prior 4 quarters and divided by 4
Off-balance-sheet Guarantees	Guaranteed instruments not reported on the balance sheet, such as whole loan REMICs and multifamily credit enhancements, and not 100% guaranteed by the FHA
Other Off-Balance Sheet Guarantees	All other off-balance sheet guaranteed instruments not included in another category, and not 100% guaranteed by the FHA
YTD provision for income taxes	Provision for income taxes for the period beginning January 1 and ending as of the report date
Tax loss carryforward	Net losses available to write off against future years' net income
Tax liability for the year prior to the beginning of the Stress Test	
Tax liability for the year 2 years prior to the beginning of the Stress Test (net of carrybacks)	
Taxable income for the year prior to the beginning of the Stress Test	
Taxable income for the year 2 years prior to the beginning of the Stress Test (net of carrybacks)	
Net after tax income for the quarter preceding the start of the stress test	

TABLE 3–17—OPERATIONS, TAXES, AND ACCOUNTING INPUTS—Continued

Input	Description
YTD taxable income	Total amount of taxable income for the period beginning January 1 and ending as of the report date
Minimum capital requirement at the beginning of the Stress Period	
Specific allowance for loan losses	Loss allowances calculated in accordance with FAS 114
Zero coupon swap receivable	
Unamortized discount on zero coupon swap receivable	

3.1.3 Public Data

3.1.3.1 Interest Rates

[a] The Interest Rates component of the Stress Test projects Treasury yields as well as other interest rate indexes that are needed to calculate cash flows, to simulate the performance of mortgages and other financial instruments, and to calculate capital for each of the 120 months in the Stress Period. Table 3–18, Interest Rate and Index Inputs, sets forth the interest rate indexes used in the Stress Test

[b] The starting values for all of the Interest Rates are the monthly average of daily rates for the month preceding the start of the stress test.

[c] For the 10-year CMT, monthly values are required for the three years prior to the start of the Stress Test (m = −35, −34...0). For all other indexes, monthly values for the prior two years are required (m = −23, −22...0).

TABLE 3–18—INTEREST RATE AND INDEX INPUTS

Interest Rate Index	Description	Source
1 MO Treasury Bill	One-month Treasury bill yield, monthly simple average of daily rate, quoted as actual/360	Bloomberg Generic 1 Month. U.S. Treasury bill. Ticker: GB1M (index).
3 MO CMT	Three-month constant maturity Treasury yield, monthly simple average of daily rate, quoted as bond equivalent yield	Federal Reserve H.15 Release.
6 MO CMT	Six-month constant maturity Treasury yield, monthly simple average of daily rate, quoted as bond equivalent yield	Federal Reserve H.15 Release.
1 YR CMT	One-year constant maturity Treasury yield, monthly simple average of daily rate, quoted as bond equivalent yield	Federal Reserve H.15 Release.
2 YR CMT	Two-year constant maturity Treasury yield, monthly simple average of daily rate, quoted as bond equivalent yield	Federal Reserve H.15 Release.
3 YR CMT	Three-year constant maturity Treasury yield, monthly simple average of daily rate, quoted as bond equivalent yield	Federal Reserve H.15 Release.
5 YR CMT	Five-year constant maturity Treasury yield, monthly simple average of daily rate, quoted as bond equivalent yield	Federal Reserve H.15 Release.

TABLE 3–18—INTEREST RATE AND INDEX INPUTS—Continued

Interest Rate Index	Description	Source
10 YR CMT	Ten-year constant maturity Treasury yield, monthly simple average of daily rate, quoted as bond equivalent yield	Federal Reserve H.15 Release.
20 YR CMT	Twenty-year constant maturity Treasury yield, monthly simple average of daily rate, quoted as bond equivalent yield	Federal Reserve H.15 Release.
30 YR CMT	Thirty-year constant maturity Treasury yield, monthly simple average of daily rate, quoted as bond equivalent yield; after February 15, 2002, estimated according to the Department of Treasury methodology using long-term average rates and extrapolation factors as referenced in OFHEO guideline 402	Federal Reserve H.15 Release, Extrapolation Factors used for estimation, U.S. Dept. of Treasury.
12-mo Moving Treasury Average (MTA)	12-month Federal Reserve cumulative average 1 year CMT, monthly simple average of daily rate	Bloomberg Ticker: 12MTA (Index).
Overnight Fed Funds (Effective)	Overnight effective Federal Funds rate, monthly simple average of daily rate	Federal Reserve H.15 Release.
Certificate of Deposits Index (CODI)	12-month average of monthly published yields on 3-month certificates of deposit, based on the Federal Reserve Board statistical release, H–15	Bloomberg Ticker: COF CODI (index).
1 Week Federal Funds	1 week Federal Funds rate, monthly simple average of daily rates	Bloomberg Term Fed Funds U.S. Domestic Ticker: GFED01W (index).
6 Month Fed Funds	6 month Federal Funds rate, monthly simple average of daily rates	Bloomberg Term Fed Funds U.S. Domestic Ticker: GFED06M (index).
Conventional Mortgage Rate	FHLMC (Freddie Mac) contract interest rates for 30 YR fixed-rate mortgage commitments, monthly average of weekly rates	Federal Reserve H.15 Release.
Constant Maturity Mortgage (CMM) Index	Bond equivalent yield on TBA mortgage-backed security which prices at the par price	TradeWeb.
1-mo Freddie Mac Reference Bill	1-month Freddie Mac Reference Bill, actual price and yield by auction date	Freddiemac.com website: *http://www.freddiemac.com/debt/data/cgi-bin/refbillaucres.cgi?order=AD.*
FHLB 11th District COF	11th District (San Francisco) weighted average cost of funds for savings and loans, monthly	Bloomberg Cost of Funds for the 11th District Ticker: COF11 (index).
1 MO LIBOR	One-month London Interbank Offered Rate, average of bid and asked, monthly simple average of daily rates, quoted as actual/360	British Bankers Association Bloomberg Ticker: US0001M (index).

TABLE 3–18—INTEREST RATE AND INDEX INPUTS—Continued

Interest Rate Index	Description	Source
3 MO LIBOR	Three-month London Interbank Offered Rate, average of bid and asked, monthly simple average of daily rates, quoted as actual/360	British Bankers Association Bloomberg Ticker: US0003M (index).
6 MO LIBOR	Six-month London Interbank Offered Rate, average of bid and asked, monthly simple average of daily rates, quoted as actual/360	British Bankers Association Bloomberg Ticker: US0006M (index).
12 MO LIBOR	One-year London Interbank Offered Rate, average of bid and asked, monthly simple average of daily rates, quoted as actual/360	British Bankers Association Bloomberg Ticker: US0012M (index).
Prime Rate	Prevailing rate as quoted, monthly average of daily rates	Federal Reserve H.15 Release.
1 MO Federal Agency COF	One-month Federal Agency Cost of Funds, monthly simple average of daily rates, quoted as actual/360	Bloomberg Generic 1 Month Agency Discount Note Yield Ticker: AGDN030Y (index).
3 MO Federal Agency COF	Three-month Federal Agency Cost of Funds, monthly simple average of daily rates, quoted as actual/360	Bloomberg Generic 3 Month Agency Discount Note Yield Ticker: AGDN090Y (index).
6 MO Federal Agency COF	Six-month Federal Agency Cost of Funds, monthly simple average of daily rates, quoted as actual/360	Bloomberg Generic 6 Month Agency Discount Note Yield Ticker: AGDN180Y (index).
1 YR Federal Agency COF	One-year Federal Agency Cost of Funds, monthly simple average of daily rates, quoted as actual/360	Bloomberg Generic 12 Month Agency Discount Note Yield. Ticker: AGDN360Y (index).
2 YR Federal Agency COF	Two-year Federal Agency Fair Market Yield, monthly simple average of daily rates	Bloomberg Generic 2 Year Agency Fair Market Yield. Ticker: CO842Y (index).
3 YR Federal Agency COF	Three-year Federal Agency Fair Market Yield, monthly simple average of daily rates	Bloomberg Generic 3 Year Agency Fair Market Yield. Ticker: CO843Y (index).
5 YR Federal Agency COF	Five-year Federal Agency Fair Market Yield, monthly simple average of daily rates	Bloomberg Generic 5 Year Agency Fair Market Yield. Ticker: CO845Y (index).
10 YR Federal Agency COF	Ten-year Federal Agency Fair Market Yield, monthly simple average of daily rates	Bloomberg Generic 10 Year Agency Fair Market Yield. Ticker: CO8410Y (index).
30 YR Federal Agency COF	Thirty-year Federal Agency Fair Market Yield, monthly simple average of daily rates	Bloomberg Generic 30 Year Agency Fair Market Yield. Ticker: CO8430Y (index).
15 YR fixed-rate mortgage	FHLMC (Freddie Mac) contract interest rates for 15 YR fixed-rate mortgage commitments, monthly average of FHLMC (Freddie Mac) contract interest rates for 15 YR	Bloomberg FHLMC 15 YR, 10 day commitment rate Ticker: FHCR1510 (index).

TABLE 3–18—INTEREST RATE AND INDEX INPUTS—Continued

Interest Rate Index	Description	Source
7-year balloon mortgage rate	Seven-year balloon mortgage, equal to the Conventional Mortgage Rate less 50 basis points	Computed.
2-yr Swap	2-yr U.S. Dollar Swap Rate, quoted as semi-annually fixed rate vs. 3-mo U.S. dollar	Bloomberg Ticker: USSWAP2 (index).
3-yr Swap	3-yr U.S. Dollar Swap Rate, quoted as semi-annually fixed rate vs. 3-mo U.S. dollar LIBOR	Bloomberg Ticker: USSWAP3 (Index).
5-yr Swap	5-yr U.S. Dollar Swap Rate, quoted as semi-annually fixed rate vs. 3-mo U.S. dollar LIBOR	Bloomberg Ticker: USSWAP5 (Index).
10-yr Swap	10-yr U.S. Dollar Swap Rate, quoted as semi-annually fixed rate vs. 3-mo U.S. dollar LIBOR	Bloomberg Ticker: USSWAP10 (Index).
30-yr Swap	30-yr U.S. Dollar Swap Rate, quoted as semi-annually fixed rate vs. 3-mo U.S. dollar LIBOR	Bloomberg Ticker: USSWAP30 (Index).

3.1.3.2 Property Valuation Inputs

Table 3–19, Stress Test Single Family Quarterly House Price Growth Rates and Table 3–21, HPI Dispersion Parameters, set forth inputs which are used to project single family mortgage performance. Table 3–20, Multifamily Monthly Rent Growth and Vacancy Rates, sets forth inputs which are used to project multifamily mortgage performance.

TABLE 3–19—STRESS TEST SINGLE FAMILY QUARTERLY HOUSE PRICE GROWTH RATES [1]

Stress Test Months	Historical Months	House Price Growth Rate	Stress Test Months	Historical Months	House Price Growth Rate
1–3	Jan-Mar 1984	−0.005048	61–63	Jan-Mar 1989	0.006292
4–6	Apr-Jun 1984	0.001146	64–66	Apr-Jun 1989	0.010523
7–9	Jul-Sep 1984	0.001708	67–69	Jul-Sep 1989	0.017893
10–12	Oct-Dec 1984	−0.007835	70–72	Oct-Dec 1989	−0.004881
13–15	Jan-Mar 1985	−0.006975	73–75	Jan-Mar 1990	−0.000227
16–18	Apr-Jun 1985	0.004178	76–78	Apr-Jun 1990	0.008804
19–21	Jul-Sep 1985	−0.005937	79–81	Jul-Sep 1990	0.003441
22–24	Oct-Dec 1985	−0.019422	82–84	Oct-Dec 1990	−0.003777
25–27	Jan-Mar 1986	0.026231	85–87	Jan-Mar 1991	0.009952
28–30	Apr-Jun 1986	0.022851	88–90	Apr-Jun 1991	0.012616
31–33	Jul-Sep 1986	−0.021402	91–93	Jul-Sep 1991	0.002267
34–36	Oct-Dec 1986	−0.018507	94–96	Oct-Dec 1991	0.012522

TABLE 3–19—STRESS TEST SINGLE FAMILY QUARTERLY HOUSE PRICE GROWTH RATES [1]—Continued

Stress Test Months	Historical Months	House Price Growth Rate	Stress Test Months	Historical Months	House Price Growth Rate
37–39	Jan-Mar 1987	0.004558	97–99	Jan-Mar 1992	0.013378
40–42	Apr-Jun 1987	−0.039306	100–102	Apr-Jun 1992	−0.000519
43–45	Jul-Sep 1987	−0.024382	103–105	Jul-Sep 1992	0.016035
46–48	Oct-Dec 1987	−0.026761	106–108	Oct-Dec 1992	0.005691
49–51	Jan-Mar 1988	−0.003182	109–111	Jan-Mar 1993	0.005723
52–54	Apr-Jun 1988	0.011854	112–114	Apr-Jun 1993	0.010614
55–57	Jul-Sep 1988	−0.020488	115–117	Jul-Sep 1993	0.013919
58–60	Oct-Dec 1988	−0.007260	118–120	Oct-Dec 1993	0.011267

[1] Source: OFHEO House Price Report, 1996:3.

TABLE 3–20—MULTIFAMILY MONTHLY RENT GROWTH [1] AND VACANCY RATES [2]

Stress Test Month	Historical Month	Rent Growth Rate	Va-cancy Rate	Stress Test Month	Historical Month	Rent Growth Rate	Va-cancy Rate
1	Jan 1984	0.001367	0.136	61	Jan 1989	0.000052	0.135
2	Feb 1984	0.001186	0.136	62	Feb 1989	0.000284	0.135
3	Mar 1984	0.001422	0.136	63	Mar 1989	0.000404	0.135
4	Apr 1984	0.001723	0.136	64	Apr 1989	0.000150	0.135
5	May 1984	0.001537	0.136	65	May 1989	0.000331	0.135
6	Jun 1984	0.001354	0.136	66	Jun 1989	0.001483	0.135
7	Jul 1984	0.000961	0.136	67	Jul 1989	0.000759	0.135
8	Aug 1984	0.000601	0.136	68	Aug 1989	0.001502	0.135
9	Sep 1984	0.001106	0.136	69	Sep 1989	0.002254	0.135
10	Oct 1984	0.001623	0.136	70	Oct 1989	0.002768	0.135
11	Nov 1984	0.001395	0.136	71	Nov 1989	0.002220	0.135
12	Dec 1984	0.001170	0.136	72	Dec 1989	0.002040	0.135
13	Jan 1985	0.001014	0.150	73	Jan 1990	0.002180	0.120
14	Feb 1985	0.000857	0.150	74	Feb 1990	0.002772	0.120
15	Mar 1985	0.000315	0.150	75	Mar 1990	0.002867	0.120
16	Apr 1985	–0.000225	0.150	76	Apr 1990	0.003243	0.120
17	May 1985	0.000154	0.150	77	May 1990	0.002963	0.120
18	Jun 1985	0.000534	0.150	78	Jun 1990	0.003588	0.120
19	Jul 1985	0.001115	0.150	79	Jul 1990	0.004885	0.120

TABLE 3-20—MULTIFAMILY MONTHLY RENT GROWTH [1] AND VACANCY RATES [2]—Continued

Stress Test Month	Historical Month	Rent Growth Rate	Vacancy Rate	Stress Test Month	Historical Month	Rent Growth Rate	Vacancy Rate
20	Aug 1985	0.001702	0.150	80	Aug 1990	0.004564	0.120
21	Sep 1985	0.001576	0.150	81	Sep 1990	0.005491	0.120
22	Oct 1985	0.001450	0.150	82	Oct 1990	0.005475	0.120
23	Nov 1985	0.001357	0.150	83	Nov 1990	0.005763	0.120
24	Dec 1985	0.001266	0.150	84	Dec 1990	0.005817	0.120
25	Jan 1986	0.001823	0.168	85	Jan 1991	0.005261	0.108
26	Feb 1986	0.002392	0.168	86	Feb 1991	0.005456	0.108
27	Mar 1986	0.002665	0.168	87	Mar 1991	0.005637	0.108
28	Apr 1986	0.002942	0.168	88	Apr 1991	0.005843	0.108
29	May 1986	0.002517	0.168	89	May 1991	0.005970	0.108
30	Jun 1986	0.002105	0.168	90	Jun 1991	0.005719	0.108
31	Jul 1986	0.001372	0.168	91	Jul 1991	0.005533	0.108
32	Aug 1986	0.000652	0.168	92	Aug 1991	0.004512	0.108
33	Sep 1986	0.000110	0.168	93	Sep 1991	0.003916	0.108
34	Oct 1986	−0.000431	0.168	94	Oct 1991	0.003779	0.108
35	Nov 1986	−0.000201	0.168	95	Nov 1991	0.004226	0.108
36	Dec 1986	0.000030	0.168	96	Dec 1991	0.004791	0.108
37	Jan 1987	−0.001448	0.175	97	Jan 1992	0.005361	0.098
38	Feb 1987	−0.002162	0.175	98	Feb 1992	0.004085	0.098
39	Mar 1987	−0.001202	0.175	99	Mar 1992	0.003885	0.098
40	Apr 1987	−0.001136	0.175	100	Apr 1992	0.002992	0.098
41	May 1987	−0.001466	0.175	101	May 1992	0.002941	0.098
42	Jun 1987	−0.002809	0.175	102	Jun 1992	0.002851	0.098
43	Jul 1987	−0.002069	0.175	103	Jul 1992	0.002346	0.098
44	Aug 1987	−0.002530	0.175	104	Aug 1992	0.003850	0.098
45	Sep 1987	−0.001033	0.175	105	Sep 1992	0.003245	0.098
46	Oct 1987	−0.001148	0.175	106	Oct 1992	0.003194	0.098
47	Nov 1987	−0.001617	0.175	107	Nov 1992	0.001931	0.098
48	Dec 1987	−0.002064	0.175	108	Dec 1992	0.001494	0.098
49	Jan 1988	−0.001372	0.158	109	Jan 1993	0.001527	0.104
50	Feb 1988	−0.001524	0.158	110	Feb 1993	0.002317	0.104

TABLE 3–20—MULTIFAMILY MONTHLY RENT GROWTH [1] AND VACANCY RATES [2]—Continued

Stress Test Month	Historical Month	Rent Growth Rate	Vacancy Rate	Stress Test Month	Historical Month	Rent Growth Rate	Vacancy Rate
51	Mar 1988	−0.001972	0.158	111	Mar 1993	0.001904	0.104
52	Apr 1988	−0.001363	0.158	112	Apr 1993	0.002545	0.104
53	May 1988	−0.001143	0.158	113	May 1993	0.002570	0.104
54	Jun 1988	−0.001194	0.158	114	Jun 1993	0.002449	0.104
55	Jul 1988	−0.001429	0.158	115	Jul 1993	0.002161	0.104
56	Aug 1988	−0.001315	0.158	116	Aug 1993	0.001857	0.104
57	Sep 1988	−0.002581	0.158	117	Sep 1993	0.001664	0.104
58	Oct 1988	−0.002337	0.158	118	Oct 1993	0.002184	0.104
59	Nov 1988	−0.001218	0.158	119	Nov 1993	0.002932	0.104
60	Dec 1988	−0.000203	0.158	120	Dec 1993	0.002776	0.104

[1] Source: U.S. Department of Labor, Bureau of Labor Statistics, Rent of Primary Residence component of the Consumer Price Index—All Urban Consumers.
[2] Source: U.S. Census Bureau, Housing Vacancy Survey—Annual 1999.

TABLE 3–21—HPI DISPERSION PARAMETERS [1]

	Linear (α)	Quadratic (β)
Dispersion Parameter	0.002977	−0.000024322

[1] Source: OFHEO House Price Report, 1996:3.

3.1.4 Constant Values

Certain values are numerical constants that are parameters of the cash flow simulation. These values are established by OFHEO on the basis of analysis of Benchmark and other historical data.

3.1.4.1 Single Family Loan Performance

TABLE 3–22—LOAN GROUP INPUTS FOR SINGLE FAMILY GROSS LOSS SEVERITY

Variable	Description	Value	Source
MQ	Months Delinquent: time during which Enterprise pays delinquent loan interest to MBS holders	4 for sold loans 0 otherwise	
MF	Months to Foreclosure: number of missed payments through completion of foreclosure	13 months	Average value of BLE data
MR	Months in REO	7 months	Average value of BLE data
F	Foreclosure Costs as a decimal fraction of Defaulted UPB	0.037	Average of historical data from Enterprise loans, 1979–1999

TABLE 3–22—LOAN GROUP INPUTS FOR SINGLE FAMILY GROSS LOSS SEVERITY—Continued

Variable	Description	Value	Source
R	REO Expenses as a decimal fraction of Defaulted UPB	0.163	Average of historical data from Enterprise loans, 1979–1999
RR	Recovery Rate for Defaulted loans in the BLE, as a percent of predicted house price using HPI (decimal)	0.61	Average value of BLE data

See also Table 3–35, Coefficients for Single Family Default and Prepayment Explanatory Variables.

3.1.4.2 Multifamily Loan Performance

TABLE 3–23—LOAN GROUP INPUTS FOR MULTIFAMILY DEFAULT AND PREPAYMENT

Variable	Description	Value	Source
OE	Operating expenses as a share of gross potential rents	0.472	Average ratio of operating expenses to gross rents, 1970–1992 Institute for Real Estate Management annual surveys of apartments.
RVR_o	Initial rental vacancy rate	0.0623	National average vacancy rate, 1970–1995, from census surveys.

TABLE 3–24—LOAN GROUP INPUTS FOR MULTIFAMILY GROSS LOSS SEVERITY

Variable	Description	Value	Source
MQ	Time during which delinquent loan interest is passed-through to MBS holders	4 for sold loans 0 otherwise	
RHC	Net REO holding costs as a decimal fraction of Defaulted UPB	0.1333	UPB-weighted average, Freddie Mac "old book" REO through 1995.
MF	Time from Default to completion of foreclosure (REO acquisition)	18 months	UPB-weighted average, Freddie Mac "old book" REO through 1995.
MR	Months from REO acquisition to REO disposition	13 months	UPB-weighted average, Freddie Mac "old book" REO through 1995.
RP	REO proceeds as a decimal fraction of Defaulted UPB	0.5888	UPB-weighted average, Freddie Mac "old book" REO through 1995.

See also Table 3–39, Explanatory Variable Coefficients for Multifamily Default.

3.2 Commitments

3.2.1 Commitments Overview

The Enterprises make contractual commitments to purchase or securitize mortgages. The Stress Test provides for deliveries of mortgages into the commitments that exist at the start of the Stress Period. These mortgages are grouped into "Commitment Loan Groups" that reflect the characteristics of the mortgages that were originated in the six months preceding the start of the Stress Period and securitized by the Enterprise, except that they are assigned coupon rates consistent with the projected delivery month in each interest rate scenario. These Commitment Loan Groups are added to the Enterprise's sold portfolio and the Stress Test projects their performance during the Stress Period. In the down-rate scenario, the Stress Test provides that 100 percent of the mortgages specified in the commitments are delivered within the first three months. In the up-rate scenario, 75 percent are delivered within the first six months.

3.2.2 Commitments Inputs

The Stress Test uses two sources of data to determine the characteristics of the mortgages delivered under commitments:

- Information from the Enterprises on the characteristics of loans originated and delivered to the Enterprises in the six months preceding the start of the Stress Period, broken out into four categories, scaled by the dollar value of commitments outstanding at the start of the Stress Period;
- Interest Rate series generated by the Interest Rates component of the Stress Test.

3.2.2.1 Loan Data

[a] The Enterprises report Commitment Loan Group categories based on the following product type characteristics of securitized single family loans originated and delivered during the six months prior to the start of the Stress Test:

- 30-year fixed-rate
- 15-year fixed-rate
- One-year CMT ARM
- Seven-year balloon

[b] For each Commitment Loan Group category, the Enterprises report the same information as in section 3.6 for Whole Loan groups with the following exceptions:

- Amortization term and remaining term are set to those appropriate for newly originated loans
- Unamortized balances are set to zero
- The House Price Growth Factor is set to one
- Age is set to zero
- Any credit enhancement coverage other than mortgage insurance is not reported.

[c] For each Commitment Loan Group category, the Enterprises report the Starting UPB defined as follows:

$$\text{Starting UPB} = \begin{bmatrix}\text{Total dollar amount}\\ \text{of Commitments}\\ \text{Outstanding}\end{bmatrix} \times \begin{bmatrix}\dfrac{\begin{array}{c}\text{Starting UPB for the}\\ \text{Commitment Loan Group Category}\end{array}}{\begin{array}{c}\text{Total Starting UPB for all}\\ \text{Commitment Loan Group}\\ \text{Categories}\end{array}}\end{bmatrix}$$

3.2.2.2 Interest Rate Data

The Stress Test uses the following Interest Rate series, generated from section 3.3, Interest Rates, of this appendix, for the first 12 months of the Stress Period:

- One-year Constant Maturity Treasury yield (CMT)
- Conventional mortgage rate (30-year fixed rate)
- 15-year fixed-rate mortgage rate
- Seven-year balloon mortgage rate.

3.2.3 Commitments Procedures

[a] Determine Commitment Loan Groups from the Commitment Loan Group categories as follows:

1. Divide each category into one subcategory for each delivery month. Three subcategories are created in the down-rate scenario and six in the up-rate scenario.
2. Calculate the total starting UPB for each subcategory as follows:

$$\text{Subcategory Starting UPB} = \begin{bmatrix}\text{Starting UPB for}\\ \text{Commitment Loan}\\ \text{Group Category}\end{bmatrix} \times \text{MDP}$$

Where: MDP is taken from Table 3–25.

TABLE 3–25—MONTHLY DELIVERIES AS A PERCENTAGE OF COMMITMENTS OUTSTANDING (MDP)

Delivery Month (DM)	Up-Rate Scenario MDP	Down-Rate Scenario MDP
1	18.75%	62.50%
2	18.75%	25.00%
3	12.50%	12.50%

TABLE 3-25—MONTHLY DELIVERIES AS A PERCENTAGE OF COMMITMENTS OUTSTANDING (MDP)—Continued

Delivery Month (DM)	Up-Rate Scenario MDP	Down-Rate Scenario MDP
4	12.50%	0.00%
5	6.25%	0.00%
6	6.25%	0.00%
Total	75%	100%

3. Set the Initial Mortgage Interest Rate for each subcategory using the interest rate series consistent with the commitment product type. For fixed rate loans, this rate = $INDEX_{DM}$. For ARM loans, the Initial Mortgage Interest Rate and the Mortgage Interest Rate at Origination are equal and set to $INDEX_{DM-LB-1}$+MARGIN, where LB (Lookback Period) and MARGIN for ARM commitment loan groups come from the RBC Report. Calculate the mortgage payment amount consistent with the Initial rate and amortizing term.

[b] Cash flows for the commitment loan groups, broken down by subcategory corresponding to assumed month of delivery to the Enterprises, are to be generated using the same procedures as contained in section 3.6, Whole Loan Cash Flows, of this appendix, except as follows:

1. For purposes of generating cash flows, treat each commitment loan subcategory as if the loans were newly originated and delivered just prior to the start of the Stress Test (that is, treat them as if mortgage age at time zero, A_0, were zero).
2. Wherever section 3.6, Whole Loan Cash Flows, of this appendix, refers to interest rate or discount rate adjustments, add Delivery Month (DM) to the Interest Rate or discount rate monthly counter, where constant DM $\in$ [1,2,3,4,5,6] refers to the number of months into the Stress Test that the commitment subcategory is assumed to be delivered to the Enterprise. For example,

a. Section 3.6.3.3.3[a]1.b.3) of this appendix, if m is a rate reset month, then:

$$MIR_m = INDEX_{m-1-LB+DM} + MARGIN$$

b. Section 3.6.3.4.3.1[a]3.a., of this appendix,

$$B_q = 1 \text{ if } MCON_{m+DM} + 0.02 \le MIR_m$$

c. Section 3.6.3.4.3.1[a]4., of this appendix,

$$RS_q = avg\left(\frac{MIR_{ORIG} - MCON_{m+DM}}{MIR_{ORIG}}\right)$$

d. Section 3.6.3.4.3.1[a]5., of this appendix,

$$YCS_q = avg\left(\frac{T120Y_{m+DM}}{T12Y_{m+DM}}\right)$$

e. Section 3.6.3.6.5.1, of this appendix. Throughout this section replace DR_m with DR_{m+DM} wherever it appears.

f. Section 3.6.3.7.3[a]9.b., of this appendix. The formula for float income received should replace FER_m with FER_{m+DM}

3. For purpose of computing LTV_q as defined in section 3.6.3.4.3.1[a]2.a., of this appendix, adjust the quarterly index for the vector of house price growth rates by adding DQ=2 if the loans are delivered in the Stress Test month 6, DQ = 1 if the loans are delivered in Stress Test months 3, 4 or 5, and 0 otherwise. That is, in the LTV_q formula:

$$Exp\left(\sum_{k=1}^{q} HPGR_{k+DQ}\right)$$

Where:

$$DQ = int\left(\frac{DM}{3}\right)$$

4. The note at the end of section 3.6.3.4.3.2[a]5., of this appendix, should be adjusted to read: for m > 120−DM, use MPR_{120-DM} and MDR_{120-DM}.
5. Adjust the final outputs for each commitment subcategory by adding DM to each monthly counter, m. That is, the outputs in Table 3-52 and 3-55 should be revised to replace each value's monthly counter of m with the new counter of m + DM, which will modify the description of each to read "in month m = 1 + DM, ... RM+DM". (Note that for one variable, $PUPB_m$, the revised counter will range from DM to RM + DM). The revised monthly counters will now correspond to the months of the Stress Test. For values of m under the revised description which are less than or equal to DM, each variable (except Performing UPB) in these two tables should equal zero. For Performing UPB in month DM, the variable will equal the Original UPB for month DM and will equal zero for months less than DM.

3.2.4 Commitments Outputs

[a] The outputs of the Commitment component of the Stress Test include Commitment Loan Groups specified in the same way as

loan groups in the RBC Report (*See* section 3.6, Whole Loan Cash Flows, of this appendix) with two exceptions: mortgage insurance is the only available credit enhancement coverage; and delivery month is added to indicate the month in which these loan groups are added to the sold portfolio. The data for these loan groups allow the Stress Test to project the Default, Prepayment and loss rates and cash flows for loans purchased under commitments for the ten-year Stress Period.

[b] The Commitment outputs also include cash flows analagous to those specified for Whole Loans in section 3.6.4, Final Whole Loan Cash Flow Outputs, of this appendix, which are produced for each Commitment Loan Group.

3.3 *Interest Rates*

3.3.1 Interest Rates Overview

[a] The Interest Rates component of the Stress Test projects Constant Maturity Treasury yields as well as other interest rates and indexes (collectively, "Interest Rates") that are needed to project mortgage performance and calculate cash flows for mortgages and other financial instruments for each of the 120 months in the Stress Period.

[b] The process for determining Interest Rates is as follows: first, identify the values for the necessary Interest Rates at time zero; second, project the ten-year CMT for each month of the Stress Period as specified in the 1992 Act; third, project the 1-month Treasury yield, the 3-month, 6-month, 1-, 2-, 3-, 5-, 20-year, and 30-year CMTs; fourth, project non-treasury Interest Rates, including the Federal Agency Cost of Funds Index; and fifth, project the Enterprises Cost of Funds Index, which provides borrowing rates for the Enterprises during the Stress Period, by increasing the Agency Cost of Funds Index by 10 basis points for the last 108 months of the Stress Test. Guidance in determining interest rates is available under OFHEO Guideline No. 402, "Risk Based Capital Process for Capturing and Utilizing Interest Rates Files," which is available on OFHEO's Web site, *http://www.OFHEO.Gov*.

[c] In cases where the Stress Test would require interest rates for maturities other than those specifically projected in Table 3–18 of section 3.1.3, Public Data, of this appendix, the Interest Rates component performs a monthly linear interpolation. In cases where the Stress Test would require an Interest Rate for a maturity greater than the longest maturity specifically projected for that index, the Stress Test would use the longest maturity for that index.

3.3.2 Interest Rates Inputs

The Interest Rates that are input to the Stress Test are set forth in Table 3–18 of section 3.1.3, Public Data, of this appendix. Inputs for the 30-year CMT yield after February 15, 2002 are estimated according to the Department of Treasury methodology using long-term average rates and extrapolation factors.

3.3.3 Interest Rates Procedures

[a] Produce Interest Rates for use in the Stress Test using the following three steps:

1. Project the Ten-Year CMT as specified in the 1992 Act:
   a. *Down-Rate Scenario*. In the Stress Test, the ten-year CMT changes from its starting level to its new level in equal increments over the first twelve months of the Stress Period, and remains constant at the new level for the remaining 108 months of the Stress Period. The new level of the ten-year CMT in the last 108 months of the down-rate scenario equals the lesser of:
      1) The average of the ten-year CMT for the nine months prior to the start of the Stress Test, minus 600 basis points; or
      2) The average yield of the ten-year CMT for the 36 months prior to the start of the Stress Test, multiplied by 60 percent;

   but in no case less than 50 percent of the average for the nine months preceding the start of the Stress Period.
   b. *Up-Rate Scenario*. In the Stress Test, the ten-year CMT changes from its starting level to its new level in equal increments over the first twelve months of the Stress Period, and remains at the new level for the remaining 108 months of the Stress Period. The new level of the ten-year CMT in the last 108 months of the up-rate scenario is the greater of:
      1) The average of the ten-year CMT for the nine months prior to the start of the Stress Test, plus 600 basis points; or
      2) The average of the ten-year CMT for the 36 months prior to the start of the Stress Test, multiplied by 160 percent;

   but in no case greater than 175 percent of the average of the ten-year CMT for the nine months preceding the start of the Stress Period.
2. Project the 1-month Treasury and other CMT yields:
   a. *Down-Rate Scenario*. For the down-rate scenario, the new value of each of the other Treasury and CMT yields for the last 108 months of the Stress Test is calculated by multiplying the ten-year CMT by the appropriate ratio from Table 3–26. For the first 12 months of the Stress Period, the other rates are computed in the same way as the ten-year CMT, i.e. from their time zero levels. Each of the other CMTs changes in equal steps in each of the first twelve months of the Stress Period until it reaches the new level for the remaining 108 months of the Stress Test.

TABLE 3–26—CMT RATIOS TO THE TEN-YEAR CMT [1]

1 MO / 10 YR	0.68271
3 MO / 10 YR	0.73700
6 MO / 10 YR	0.76697
1 YR / 10 YR	0.79995
2 YR / 10 YR	0.86591
3 YR / 10 YR	0.89856
5 YR / 10 YR	0.94646
20 YR / 10 YR	1.06246
30 YR / 10 YR	1.03432

[1] Source: calculated over the period from May, 1986, through April, 1995.

b. *Up-Rate Scenario*. In the up-rate scenario, all other Treasury and CMT yields are equal to the ten-year CMT in the last 108 months of the Stress Test. Each of the other yields changes in equal increments over the first twelve months of the Stress Test until it equals the ten-year CMT.

3. Project Non-Treasury Interest Rates:

a. *Non-Treasury Rates*. For each of the non-Treasury interest rates with the exception of mortgage rates, rates during the Stress Test are computed as a proportional spread to the nearest maturity Treasury yield as given in Table 3–27. The proportional spread is the average over the two years prior to the start of the Stress Test, of the difference between the non-Treasury rate and the comparable maturity Treasury yield divided by that Treasury yield. For example, the three month LIBOR proportional spread would be calculated as the two year average of the ratio:

$$\frac{\begin{pmatrix}\text{3-month LIBOR minus} \\ \text{3-month Treasury}\end{pmatrix}}{\text{3-month Treasury}}$$

During the Stress Test, the 3-month LIBOR rate is projected by multiplying the 3-month Treasury yield by 1 plus this average proportional spread.

b. *Mortgage Rates*. Mortgage interest rates are projected as described in this section for other non-Treasury interest rates, except that an average of the additive, not proportional, spread to the appropriate Treasury interest rate is used. For example, the 30-year Conventional Mortgage Rate spread is projected as the average, over the two years preceding the start of the Stress Test, of: (Conventional Mortgage Rate minus the ten-year CMT). This spread is then added to the ten-year CMT for the 120 months of the Stress Test to obtain the projected Conventional Mortgage Rate.

TABLE 3–27—NON-TREASURY INTEREST RATES

Mortgage Rates	Spread Based on
15-year Fixed-rate Mortgage Rate	10-year CMT
30-year Conventional Mortgage Rate	10-year CMT
7-year Balloon Mortgage Rate	(computed from Conventional Mortgage Rate)
Constant Maturity Mortgage Index	10-year CMT
Other Non-Treasury Interest Rates	
Overnight Fed Funds	1-month Treasury Yield
7-day Fed Funds	1-month Treasury Yield
1-month LIBOR	1-month Treasury Yield
1-month Federal Agency Cost of Funds	1-month Treasury Yield
1-mo Freddie Mac Reference Bill	1-month Treasury Yield
3-month LIBOR	3-month CMT
3-month Federal Agency Cost of Funds	3-month CMT
PRIME	3-month CMT

TABLE 3–27—NON-TREASURY INTEREST RATES—Continued

Mortgage Rates	Spread Based on
6-month LIBOR	6-month CMT
6-month Federal Agency Cost of Funds	6-month CMT
6-month Fed Funds	6-month CMT
FHLB 11th District Cost of Funds	1-year CMT
12-month LIBOR	1-year CMT
12-mo Moving Treasury Average	1-year CMT
Certificate of Deposits Index	1-year CMT
1-year Federal Agency Cost of Funds	1-year CMT
2-year Federal Agency Cost of Funds	2-year CMT
3-year Federal Agency Cost of Funds	3-year CMT
5-year Federal Agency Cost of Funds	5-year CMT
10-year Federal Agency Cost of Funds	10-year CMT
30-year Federal Agency Cost of Funds	30-year CMT
2-yr Swap	2-year CMT
3-yr Swap	3-year CMT
5-yr Swap	5-year CMT
10-yr Swap	10-year CMT
30-yr Swap	30-year CMT

c. *Enterprise Borrowing Rates.* In the Stress Test, the Federal Agency Cost of Funds Index is the same as the Enterprise Cost of Funds Index during the Stress Period, except that the Stress Test adds a 10 basis-point credit spread to the Federal Agency Cost of Funds rates to project Enterprise Cost of Funds rates for the last 108 months of the Stress Period.

3.3.4 Interest Rates Outputs

Interest Rate outputs are monthly values for: the projected ten points on the Treasury yield curve (1-month, 3-month, 6-month, 1-year, 2-year, 3-year, 5-year, 10-year, 20-year and 30-year); the 21 non-Treasury rates contained in Table 3–27; and the nine points on the Enterprise Cost of Funds curve.

3.4 Property Valuation

3.4.1 Property Valuation Overview

[a] The Property Valuation component applies inflation adjustments to the single family house price growth rates and multifamily rent growth rates that are used to determine single family property values and multifamily current debt-service coverage ratios during the up-rate scenario, as required by the 1992 Act.

[b] Single family house price growth rates during the 120 months of the Stress Test are calculated from the HPI series for the West South Central Census Division for the years 1984–1993, as derived from OFHEO's Third Quarter, 1996 HPI Report. The West South Central Census Division includes Texas and all of the Benchmark states except Mississippi. This series is applied to single family loans nationwide during the Stress Test because the 1992 Act applies a regional loss experience (the BLE) to the entire nation. In contrast, house prices are brought forward to the start of the Stress Test based on local Census Division HPI values available at the start of the Stress Test.

[c] Multifamily rent growth rates during the 120 months of the Stress Test are computed using a population-weighted average of the monthly growth of the Rent of Primary

Residence component of the Consumer Price Index-Urban, which is generated by the U.S. Department of Labor Bureau of Labor Statistics. The metropolitan areas used for this computation are the Dallas/Ft. Worth CMSA, the Houston/Galveston/Brazoria CMSA, and the New Orleans MSA.

[d] Multifamily rental vacancy rates during the 120 months of the Stress Test are computed using a population-weighted average of annual rental vacancy rates from the U.S. Department of Commerce, Bureau of the Census' Housing Vacancy Survey. The metropolitan areas used for this computation are the Dallas, Houston and Fort Worth PMSAs and the San Antonio, New Orleans and Oklahoma City MSAs.

[e] *Inflation adjustment.* In the up-rate scenario, if the ten-year CMT rises more than 50 percent above the average yield during the nine months preceding the Stress Period, rent and house price growth rates are adjusted to account for inflation as required by the 1992 Act. The single family House Price Growth Rates and the multifamily Rent Growth Rates are increased by the amount by which the ten-year CMT exceeds 50 percent of its annualized monthly yield averaged over the nine months preceding the Stress Test. The inflation adjustment is applied only in the last 60 months of the Stress Period.

3.4.2 Property Valuation Inputs

The inputs required for the Property Valuation component are set forth in Table 3–28.

TABLE 3–28—PROPERTY VALUATION INPUTS

Variable	Description	Source
$CMT10_m$	10-year CMT yield for months m = 1...120 of the Stress Test	section 3.3, Interest Rates
$ACMT_o$	Unweighted nine-month average of the ten-year CMT yield for the nine months immediately preceding the Stress Test. (Monthly rates are unweighted monthly averages of daily rates, bond equivalent yield)	section 3.3, Interest Rates
$HHPGR_q^{HSP}$	Quarterly single family historical house price growth rates computed from the HPI series for the Benchmark region and time period, unadjusted for inflation. The specific series is the West South Central Census Division for the years 1984–1993, as reported in OFHEO's Third Quarter, 1996 HPI Report	Table 3–19 of section 3.1.3, Public Data
RG_m^{HSP}	Multifamily Rent Growth Rates for months m = 1...120 of the Benchmark region and time period, unadjusted for inflation	Table 3–20 of section 3.1.3, Public Data
RVR_m^{HSP}	Multifamily Rental Vacancy Rates for months m = 1...120 of the Benchmark region and time period	Table 3–20 of section 3.1.3, Public Data

3.4.3 Property Valuation Procedures for Inflation Adjustment

[a] Calculate inflation-adjusted House Price Growth Rates and Rent Growth Rates using the following six steps:

1. Calculate the Inflation-Adjustment (IA) for the up-rate stress test, as follows:

$$IA = max\begin{bmatrix} CMT10^{MAX} \\ -(1.50 \times ACMT_0), 0 \end{bmatrix}$$

Where:

$CMT10^{MAX}$ is the value of the ten-year CMT during the last 108 months of the up-rate Stress Test.

2. The Inflation Adjustment (IA) is compounded annually over 9 years and 2 months (110 months) to obtain the Cumulative Inflation Adjustment (CIA) according to the following equation:

$$CIA = (1 + IA)^{\frac{110}{12}}$$

3. For single family house prices, convert the CIA to continuously compounded quarterly factors, the Quarterly House Price Growth Adjustments ($QHGA_q$), which take on positive values only in the last twenty quarters of the Stress Test, using:

$$QHGA_q = \frac{ln(CIA)}{20} \text{ for } q = 21...40$$

in the up-rate Stress Test

$$QHGA_q = 0, \text{ otherwise}$$

4. For Multifamily rent growth, the CIA is converted to discrete monthly factors or Monthly Rent Growth Adjustments ($MRGA_m$), and is applied only in the last 60 months of the Stress Test in the up-rate scenario, as follows:

$$MRGA_m = \left[(CIA)^{\frac{1}{60}} - 1 \right] \text{ for } m = 61...120$$

in the up-rate Stress Test

$$MRGA_m = 0, \text{ otherwise}$$

5. Calculate the inflation-adjusted House Price Growth Rates ($HPGR_q$), used in updating single family house prices during the Stress Test:

$$HPGR_q = HHPGR_q^{HSP} + QHGA_q$$

6. Calculate inflation-adjusted Rent Growth Rates (RGR_m), used in updating Multifamily debt-service coverage ratios during the Stress Test:

$$RGR_m = RG_m^{HSP} + MRGA_m$$

3.4.4 Property Valuation Outputs

[a] The outputs of the Property Valuation component of the Stress Test are set forth in Table 3–29.

TABLE 3–29—PROPERTY VALUATION OUTPUTS

Variable	Description
$HPGR_q$	House price growth rates for quarters 1...40 of the Stress Test, adjusted for inflation, if applicable.
RGR_m	Multifamily Rent Growth Rates for months m = 1...120 of the Stress Test, adjusted for inflation, if applicable.
RVR_m	Multifamily Rental Vacancy Rates for months m = 1...120 of the Stress Test.

[b] Inflation-adjusted House Price Growth Rates ($HPGR_q$) are inputs to the Single Family Default and Prepayment component of the Stress Test (*see* section 3.6.3.4, of this appendix). Inflation-adjusted Rent Growth Rates (RGR_m) and Rental Vacancy Rates (RVR_m) are inputs to the Multifamily Default and Prepayment component (*see* section 3.6.3.5, of this appendix).

3.5 Counterparty Defaults

3.5.1 Counterparty Defaults Overview

The Counterparty Defaults component of the Stress Test accounts for the risk of default by credit enhancement and derivative contract counterparties, corporate securities, municipal securities, and mortgage-related securities. The Stress Test recognizes five rating categories (“AAA”, “AA”, “A”, “BBB”, and “Below BBB and Unrated”) and establishes appropriate credit loss factors that are applied during the Stress Period. Securities rated below BBB are treated as unrated securities, unless OFHEO determines to specify a different treatment upon a showing by an Enterprise that a different treatment is warranted.

3.5.2 Counterparty Defaults Input

For counterparties and securities, information on counterparty type and the lowest public rating of the counterparty is required. The Stress Test uses credit ratings issued by Nationally Recognized Statistical Rating Organizations (“NRSROs”) to assign rating categories to counterparties and securities. If a counterparty or security has different ratings from different rating agencies, i.e., a “split rating,” or has a long-term rating and a short-term rating, then the lower rating is used.

3.5.3 Counterparty Defaults Procedures

[a] Apply the following three steps to determine maximum haircuts:

1. *Identifying Counterparties.* The Stress Test divides all sources of credit risk other than mortgage default into two categories—(1) derivative contract counterparties and (2) non-derivative contract

counterparties and instruments. Non-derivative contract counterparties and instruments include mortgage insurance (MI) counterparties, seller-servicers, mortgage-related securities such as mortgage revenue bonds (MRBs) and private label REMICS, and nonmortgage investments such as corporate and municipal bonds and asset-backed securities (ABSs).

2. *Classify Rating Categories.*

a. Stress Test rating categories are defined as set forth in Table 3–30. Organizations frequently apply modifiers (numerical, plus, minus) to the generic rating classifications. In order to determine the correct mapping, ignore these modifiers except as noted in Table 3–30.

TABLE 3–30—RATING AGENCIES MAPPINGS TO OFHEO RATINGS CATEGORIES

OFHEO Ratings Category	AAA	AA	A	BBB	Below BBB and Unrated
Standard & Poor's Long-Term	AAA	AA	A	BBB	Below BBB and Unrated
Fitch Long-Term	AAA	AA	A	BBB	Below BBB and Unrated
Moody's Long-Term	Aaa	Aa	A	Baa	Below Baa and Unrated
Standard & Poor's Short-Term	A–1+ SP–1+	A–1 SP–1	A–2 SP–2	A–3	SP–3, B or Below and Unrated
Fitch Short-Term	F–1+	F–1	F–2	F–3	B and Below and Unrated
Moody's [1]	Prime-1 MIG1 VMIG1	Prime-1 MIG1 VMIG1	Prime-2 MIG2 VMIG2	Prime-3 MIG3 VMIG3	Not Prime, SG and Unrated
Fitch Bank Individual Ratings	A	B A/B	C B/C	D C/D	E D/E
Moody's Bank Financial Strength Rating	A	B	C	D	E

[1] Any rating that appears in more than one OFHEO category column is assigned the lower OFHEO rating category.

b. The Stress Test also includes a ratings classification called cash. This includes cash equivalents as defined in FAS 95, Government securities, and securities of the reporting Enterprise.

c. Unrated, unsubordinated obligations issued by Government Sponsored Enterprises other than the reporting Enterprise are treated as AAA. Unrated seller-servicers are treated as BBB.

d. The Stress Test will permit a higher rating to be used for an unrated seller-servicer who participates in a multifamily delegated underwriting and servicing program that requires a loss-sharing agreement when: (1) The loss sharing agreement is collateralized by a fully funded reserve account pledged to the Enterprise; and (2) the reserve account is in an amount that is equal to or exceeds the amount that OFHEO has determined to be adequate to support the seller-servicer's loss-sharing obligation under the program. Determinations of the reserve requirement and of the rating that will be permitted will be made on a program-by-program and Enterprise-by-Enterprise basis by the Director.

3. *Determine Maximum Haircuts.* The Stress Test specifies the Maximum Haircut (i.e., the maximum reduction applied to cash flows during the Stress Test to reflect the risk of loss due to counterparty (including security) default) by rating category and counterparty type as shown in Table 3–31.

a. The Maximum Haircut for a rating category is the product of its default rate and its loss severity rate. For all counterparties, the default rates are 5 percent for AAA, 12.5 percent for AA, 20 percent for A, 40 percent for BBB and 100 percent for Below BBB and Unrated. For non-derivative counterparties, the loss severity rate is 70 percent; for derivative counterparties, it is 10 percent. For all Below BBB and Unrated counterparties, the loss severity rate is 100 percent.

b. For periods prior to the implementation of netting, a separate set of Maximum Haircuts (set forth in Table 3–31) will be applied to derivative contract cash flows to approximate the impact of the net exposures to derivative contract counterparties (see section 3.8.3, Nonmortgage Instrument Procedures). After the implementation of netting, exposures will be netted as described in section 3.8.3 before the haircut is applied.

c. With the exception of haircuts for the Below BBB and Unrated category, haircuts for all counterparty categories are phased-in linearly over the 120 months of the Stress Period. The Maximum Haircut is applied in month 120 of the Stress Period. Haircuts for the Below BBB and Unrated category are applied fully starting in the first month of the Stress Test.

TABLE 3–31—STRESS TEST MAXIMUM HAIRCUT BY RATINGS CLASSIFICATION

Ratings Classification	Derivative Contract Counterparties prior to Implementation of Netting	Derivative Contract Counterparties after Implementation of Netting	Non-Derivative Contract Counterparties or Instruments	Number of Phase-in Months
Cash	0%	0%	0%	N/A
AAA	0.3%	0.5%	3.5%	120
AA	0.75%	1.25%	8.75%	120
A	1.2%	2%	14%	120
BBB	2.4%	4%	28%	120
Below BBB and Unrated	100%	100%	100%	1

3.5.4 Counterparty Defaults Outputs

The Maximum Haircut for a given Counterparty Type and Rating Classification is used in section 3.6, Whole Loan Cash Flows, section 3.7, Mortgage-Related Securities Cash Flows, and section 3.8, Nonmortgage Instrument Cash Flows, of this appendix.

3.6 Whole Loan Cash Flows

3.6.1 Whole Loan Cash Flows Overview

[a] *Loan Aggregation.* In the Stress Test calculations (except as described in section 3.6.3.6.4, Mortgage Credit Enhancement, of this appendix), individual loans having similar characteristics are aggregated into Loan Groups as described in section 3.1.2.1, Whole Loan Inputs, of this appendix (RBC Report). All individual loans within a Loan Group are considered to be identical for computational purposes. In the discussions in this section, quantities described as "loan level" will actually be computed at the Loan Group level.

[b] *Loan Participations.* In some cases, an Enterprise may hold only a *pari passu* fractional ownership interest in a loan. This interest is referred to as a participation, and is specified by the ownership percentage held by the Enterprise (the participation percentage). In such cases, the Unpaid Principal Balance (UPB) and Mortgage Payment reported in the RBC Report will be only the Enterprise's participation percentage of the loan's actual UPB and Mortgage Payment. The actual UPB is not explicitly used in the calculations described in this section 3.6 but it is used in the creation of the RBC Report.

[c] *Retained Loans vs. Sold Loans.* The Stress Test models cash flows from single family and multifamily mortgage loans that are held in portfolio (Retained Loans) and loans that are pooled into Mortgage-Backed Securities (MBSs) that are sold to investors and guaranteed by the Enterprises (Sold Loans). Together, Retained Loans and Sold Loans are referred to as "Whole Loans." The treatment of cash flows for loans not guaranteed by the Enterprises, e.g., loans backing GNMA Certificates and private label MBSs and REMICs, is discussed in section 3.7, Mortgage-Related Securities Cash Flows, of this appendix.

[d] *Repurchased MBSs.* From time to time an Enterprise may repurchase all or part of one of its own previously issued single-class MBSs for its own securities portfolio. At an Enterprise's option, these "Repurchased MBSs" may be reported with the underlying Whole Loans for computation in this section 3.6 rather than in section 3.7, Mortgage-Related Securities Cash Flows, of this appendix. In such cases, the Enterprise will report the underlying Whole Loans as sold loans, along with the appropriate Fraction Repurchased and any security unamortized balances associated with the purchase of the MBS (not with the original sale of the underlying loans, which unamortized balances are reported separately).

[e] *Sources of Enterprise Whole Loan Cash Flows.* For Retained Loans, the Enterprises receive all principal and interest payments on the loans, except for a portion of the interest payment retained by the servicer as compensation (the Servicing Fee). For Sold Loans, the Enterprises receive Guarantee Fees and Float Income. Float Income is the earnings on the investment of loan principal and interest payments (net of the Servicing Fee and Guarantee Fee) from the time these payments are received from the servicer until they are remitted to security holders. The length of this period depends on the security payment cycle (the remittance cycle). For both retained and sold loans, the Enterprises retain 100 percent of their credit losses

and experience amortization of discounts as income and amortization of premiums as expense. For Repurchased MBSs, the Enterprise receives the Fraction Repurchased of the cash flows it remits to investors, and retains 100 percent of the Credit Losses and the Guarantee Fee. *See* section 3.6.3.7, Stress Test Whole Loan Cash Flows and section 3.6.3.8, Whole Loan Accounting Flows, of this appendix.

[f] *Required Inputs.* The calculation of Whole Loan cash flows requires mortgage Amortization Schedules, mortgage Prepayment, Default and Loss Severity rates, and Credit Enhancement information. The four mortgage performance components of the Stress Test are single family Default and Prepayment, single family Loss Severity, multifamily Default and Prepayment, and multifamily Loss Severity. Mortgage Amortization Schedules are computed from input data in the RBC Report. (For ARMs, selected interest rate indexes from section 3.3, Interest Rates, of this appendix, are also used.) Prepayment and Default Rates are computed by combining explanatory variables and weighting coefficients according to a set of logistic equations. The explanatory variables are computed from the mortgage Amortization Schedule and external economic variables such as Interest Rates (section 3.3, Interest Rates, of this appendix), historical house-price indexes (HPIs) or rental-price indexes (RPIs), and Stress Period HPI growth rate, RPI and Vacancy Rate (RVR) series from section 3.4, Property Valuation, of this appendix. The weighting coefficients determine the relative importance of the different explanatory variables, and are estimated from a statistical analysis of data from the Benchmark Loss region and time period as described in section 1, Identification of the Benchmark Loss Experience, of this appendix. Mortgage Amortization information is also combined with HPI, RPI and VR series to determine Gross Loss Severity rates, which are offset by Credit Enhancements. Finally, the Amortization Schedules, Default and Prepayment rates and Net Loss Severity rates are combined to produce Stress Test Whole Loan Cash Flows to the Enterprises for each Loan Group, as well as amortization of any discounts, premiums and fees.

[g] *Specification of Mortgage Prepayment.* Mortgages are assumed to prepay in full. The model makes no specific provision for partial Prepayments of principal (curtailments).

[h] *Specification of Mortgage Default and Loss.* Mortgage Defaults are modeled as follows: Defaulting loans enter foreclosure after a number of missed payments (MQ, Months in Delinquency), and are foreclosed upon several months later. Months in Foreclosure (MF) is the total number of missed payments through foreclosure. Upon completion of foreclosure, the loan as such ceases to exist and the property becomes Real Estate Owned by the lender (REO). Foreclosure expenses are paid and MI proceeds received when foreclosure is completed. After several more months (MR, Months in REO), the property is sold, REO expenses are paid, and sales proceeds and other credit enhancements are received. These timing differences are not modeled explicitly in the cash flows, but their economic effect is taken into account by calculating the present value of the Default-related cash flows back to the initial month of Default.

[i] *Combining Cash Flows from Scheduled Payments, Prepayments and Defaults.* Aggregate Whole Loan Cash Flows, adjusted for the effects of mortgage performance, are based on the following conceptual equation, which is made more explicit in the calculations in the sections specified in section 3.6.2 of this appendix:

$$\begin{bmatrix} \text{Aggregate Cash Flows from} \\ \text{Whole Loans that Default} \\ \text{and Prepay at Rates that} \\ \text{vary in each month m} \end{bmatrix} = \begin{bmatrix} \begin{pmatrix} \text{scheduled Mortgage} \\ \text{Payment} \end{pmatrix} \times \begin{pmatrix} \text{fraction of loans that remain} \\ \text{on original schedule} \end{pmatrix} \\ \text{plus} \\ \begin{pmatrix} \text{entire loan UPB plus} \\ \text{final interest payment} \end{pmatrix} \times \begin{pmatrix} \text{fraction of loans that} \\ \text{Prepay in month m} \end{pmatrix} \\ \text{plus} \\ \begin{pmatrix} \text{present value of Default-related} \\ \text{receipts minus expenses} \end{pmatrix} \times \begin{pmatrix} \text{fraction of loans that} \\ \text{Default in month m} \end{pmatrix} \end{bmatrix}$$

3.6.2 Whole Loan Cash Flows Inputs

Inputs for each stage of the Whole Loan Cash Flows calculation are found in the following sections:

- Section 3.6.3.3.2, Mortgage Amortization Schedule Inputs
- Section 3.6.3.4.2, Single Family Default and Prepayment Inputs

- Section 3.6.3.5.2, Multifamily Default and Prepayment Inputs
- Section 3.6.3.6.2.2, Single Family Gross Loss Severity Inputs
- Section 3.6.3.6.3.2, Multifamily Gross Loss Severity Inputs
- Section 3.6.3.6.4.2, Mortgage Credit Enhancement Inputs
- Section 3.6.3.7.2, Stress Test Whole Loan Cash Flow Inputs
- Section 3.6.3.8.2, Whole Loan Accounting Flows Inputs, of this appendix

3.6.3 Whole Loan Cash Flows Procedures

3.6.3.1 Timing Conventions

[a] *Calculations are monthly.* The Stress Test operates monthly, with all events of a given type assumed to take place on the same day of the month. For mortgages, unless otherwise specified, all payments and other mortgage-related cash flows that are due on the first day of the month are received on the fifteenth. Biweekly loans are mapped into their closest term-equivalent monthly counterpart.

[b] *"Time Zero" for Calculations.* Time Zero refers to the beginning of the Stress Test. For example, if the 2Q2000 Stress Test uses Enterprise Data as of June 30, "month zero" represents conditions as of June 30, the Stress Period begins July 1, and July 2000 is month one of the Stress Test. In this document, UPB_0 is the Unpaid Principal Balance of a loan immediately prior to (as of) the start of the Stress Test, i.e. as reported by the Enterprise in the RBC Report. Origination refers to the beginning of the life of the loan, which will be prior to the start of the Stress Test for all loans except those delivered later under Commitments, for which Origination refers to the delivery month (*See* section 3.2, Commitments, of this appendix).

[c] *Definition of Mortgage Age.* The Mortgage Age at a given time is the number of scheduled mortgage payment dates that have occurred prior to that time, whether or not the borrower has actually made the payments. Prior to the first payment date, the Mortgage Age would be zero. From the first payment date until (but not including) the second loan payment date, the Mortgage Age would be one. The Mortgage Age at Time Zero (A_0) is thus the number of scheduled loan payment dates that have occurred prior to the start of the Stress Test. The scheduled payment date for all loans is assumed to be the first day of each month; therefore, the Mortgage Age will be A_1 on the first day of the Stress Test (except for Commitments that are delivered after the start of the Stress Test).

[d] *Interest Rate Setting Procedure.* Mortgage interest is due in arrears, i.e., on the first day following the month in which it is accrued. Thus, a payment due on the first day of month m is for interest accrued during the *prior* month. For example, for Adjustable Rate Mortgages (ARMs) the Mortgage Interest Rate (MIR_m) applicable to the July reset is set on the first day of June, and is generally based on the May or April value of the underlying Index, as specified in the loan terms. This Lookback Period (LB) is specified in the Stress Test as a period of one or two months, respectively. Thus, PMT_m will be based on MIR_m, which is based on $INDEX_{m-1-LB}$.

[e] *Prepayment Interest Shortfall.* In some remittance cycles, the period between an Enterprise's receipt of Prepayments and transmittal to investors exceeds a full month. In those cases, the Enterprise must remit an additional month's interest (at the Pass-Through Rate) to MBS investors. *See* section 3.6.3.7.3, Stress Test Whole Loan Cash Flow Procedures, of this appendix.

[f] *Certain Calculations Extend Beyond the End of the Stress Test.* Even though the Stress Test calculates capital only through the ten year Stress Period, certain calculations (for example, the level yield amortization of discounts, premiums and fees, as described in section 3.10, Operations, Taxes, and Accounting, of this appendix) require cash flows throughout the life of the instrument. For such calculations in the Stress Test, the conditions of month 120 are held constant throughout the remaining life of the instrument: specifically, Interest Rates (which are already held constant for months 13 through 120), Prepayment and Default rates for months m > 120 are taken to be equal to their respective values in month 120.

3.6.3.2 Payment Allocation Conventions

3.6.3.2.1 Allocation of Mortgage Interest

[a] *Components of Mortgage Interest.* The interest portion of the Mortgage Payment is allocated among several components. For all Whole Loans, a Servicing Fee is retained by the servicer. For Sold Loans, the Enterprise retains a Guarantee Fee. An additional amount of interest (Spread)[1] may be deposited into a Spread Account to reimburse potential future credit losses on loans covered by this form of Credit Enhancement, as described further in section 3.6.3.6.4, Mortgage Credit Enhancement, of this appendix. The remaining interest amount is either retained by the Enterprise (Net Yield on Retained Loans) or passed through to MBS investors (Pass-Through Interest on Sold Loans).

[b] *Effect of Negative Amortization.* If the Mortgage Payment is contractually limited to an amount less than the full amount accrued (as may be the case with loans that permit Negative Amortization), then the Servicing Fee, the Guarantee Fee and the

[1] The spread may or may not be embedded in the recorded Servicing Fee.

spread are paid in full, and the shortfall is borne entirely by the recipient of the Net Yield or Pass-Through Interest.

[c] *Effect of Variable Rates.* For ARMs, the Servicing Fee, Guarantee Fee and Spread rates are taken to be constant over time, as they are for Fixed Rate Loans. Thus in the Stress Test the Mortgage Interest Rate and the Net Yield or Pass-through Rate will change simultaneously by equal amounts. All other details of the rate and payment reset mechanisms are modeled in accordance with the contractual terms using the inputs specified in section 3.6.3.3.2, Mortgage Amortization Schedule Inputs, of this appendix.

3.6.3.2.2 Allocation of Mortgage Principal

[a] Scheduled Principal is that amount of the mortgage payment that amortizes principal. For calculational purposes, when a loan prepays in full the amount specified in the Amortization Schedule is counted as Scheduled Principal, and the rest is Prepayment Principal. For a Balloon Loan, the final Balloon Payment includes the remaining UPB, all of which is counted as Scheduled Principal.

[b] Mortgages that prepay are assumed to prepay in full. Partial Prepayments (curtailments) are not modeled.

[c] Any loan that does not prepay or Default remains on its original Amortization Schedule.

3.6.3.3 Mortgage Amortization Schedule

3.6.3.3.1 Mortgage Amortization Schedule Overview

[a] The Stress Test requires an Amortization Schedule for each Loan Group. A mortgage is paid down, or amortized over time, to the extent that the contractual mortgage payment exceeds the amount required to cover interest due.

[b] *Definitions.*

1. *Fully Amortizing Loans.* The Amortization Schedule for a mortgage with age A_0 at the beginning of the Stress Test is generated using the starting UPB (UPB_0), the Remaining Term to Maturity (RM), the remaining Amortization Term ($AT-A_0$), the remaining Mortgage Payments (PMT_m for m = 1...RM) and Mortgage Interest Rates (MIR_m for m = 1...RM). The Amortization Schedule is generated by repeating the following three steps iteratively until the UPB is zero:
   a. Interest Due = UPB × Mortgage Interest Rate
   b. Principal Amortization = Payment − Interest Due
   c. Next period's UPB = UPB − Principal Amortization
2. *Balloon Loans.* A Balloon Loan matures prior to its Amortizing Term, i.e. before the UPB is fully amortized to zero. Computationally, $AT-A_0 > RM$, usually by at least 180 months. In order that $UPB_{RM} = 0$, the principal component of the resulting lump sum final payment (the Balloon Payment, equal to UPB_{RM-1}) is counted as Scheduled Principal, not as a Prepayment.

[c] *Special Cases.* In general the UPB of a mortgage decreases monotonically over time, i.e. $UPB_m > UPB_{m+1}$, reaching zero at maturity except for Balloon Loans as described in [b]2. in this section. However, in practice certain exceptions must be handled.

1. *Interest-Only Loans.* Certain loans are interest-only for all or part of their term. The monthly payment covers only the interest due, and the UPB stays constant until maturity (in some cases), in which case a Balloon Payment is due or a changeover date (in other cases) at which time the payment is recast so that the loan begins to amortize over its remaining term. If the loan does not amortize fully over its remaining term, a Balloon Payment will be due at maturity.
2. *Negative Amortization.* For some loans, the UPB may increase for a period of time if the mortgage payment is contractually limited to an amount that is less than the amount of interest due, and the remainder is added to the UPB. At some point, however, the payment must exceed the interest due or else the loan balance will never be reduced to zero. In the calculation, this is permitted to occur only for payment-capped ARMs that contractually specify negative amortization. Certain types of FRMs, notably Graduated Payment Mortgages (GPMs) and Tiered Payment Mortgages (TPMs), also have variable payment schedules that result in negative amortization, but in the Stress Test all such loans are assumed to have passed their negative amortization periods.
3. *Early Amortization.*
   a. If a borrower has made additional principal payments (curtailments or partial prepayments) on a FRM prior to the start of the Stress Test, the contractual mortgage payment will amortize the loan prior to its final maturity, i.e. $UPB_m = 0$ for some $m < RM$. *This is an acceptable outcome in the Stress Test. Note:* for ARMs, the mortgage payment is recalculated, and thus the amortization schedule is recast to end exactly at m = RM, on each rate or payment reset date.
   b. When this calculation is performed for a fully amortizing FRM using weighted average values to represent a Loan Group, the final scheduled payment may exceed the amount required to reduce the UPB to zero, or the UPB may reach zero prior to month RM. This is because the mortgage payment calculation is nonlinear, and as a result the average mortgage

payment is not mathematically guaranteed to amortize the average UPB using the average MIR. This is an acceptable outcome in the Stress Test.

4. *Late Amortization*. According to its contractual terms, the UPB of a mortgage loan must reach zero at its scheduled maturity. The borrower receives a disclosure schedule that explicitly sets forth such an Amortization Schedule. If the characteristics of a mortgage loan representing a Loan Group in the RBC Report do not result in $UPB_{RM} = 0$, it must be for one of three reasons: a data error, an averaging artifact, or an extension of the Amortization Schedule related to a delinquency prior to the start of the Stress Test. In any such case, the Stress Test does not recognize cash flows beyond the scheduled maturity date and models the performing portion of UPB_{RM} in month RM as a credit loss.
5. *Biweekly Loans*. Biweekly loans are mapped into the FRM category that most closely approximates their final maturity.
6. *Step-Rate (or "Two-Step") Loans*. Certain loans have an initial interest rate for an extended period of time (typically several years) and then "step" to a final fixed rate for the remaining life of the loan. This final fixed rate may be either a predetermined number or a margin over an index. Such loans can be exactly represented as ARMs with the appropriate Initial Mortgage Interest Rate and Initial Rate Period, Index and Margin (if applicable). If the final rate is a predetermined rate (e.g., 8 percent per annum) then the ARM's Maximum and Minimum Rate should be set to that number. The Rate and Payment Reset Periods should be set equal to the final rate period after the step.
7. *Reverse Mortgages*. In a reverse mortgage, a borrower receives one or more payments from the lender and the lender is repaid with a lump sum when the borrower dies, sells the property or moves out of the home permanently. The stress test models reverse mortgages as a ladder of zero-coupon securities:
   a. 11 proxy securities for each reverse mortgage program are created.
   b. A 10% conditional payment rate is used to create the zero-coupon securities that will mature in every year of the stress test. The zero-coupon securities are a laddered series of floating-rate coupon-bearing accreting bonds with a first payment date at maturity.
   c. The 11th zero-coupon security will mature three months after the stress test to reflect the 35% of UPB not paid down during the stress period.
   d. An OFHEO credit rating equivalent to AAA for the FHA insured programs and AA for other reverse mortgage programs is assigned.
8. *Split-Rate ARM Loans*. In split-rate ARM loans, the principal portion of the payment is based on a fixed-rate amortization schedule while the interest portion is based on a floating rate index. These multifamily loans are available as fully amortizing product or with a balloon feature. The stress test model does not provide treatment for split-rate ARM loans. Split-rate loans shall be treated as ARMs when they are issued without a balloon payment feature or as Balloon ARMs when the loans contain a balloon payment feature.

3.6.3.3.2 Mortgage Amortization Schedule Inputs

The inputs needed to calculate the amortization schedule are set forth in Table 3–32:

TABLE 3–32—LOAN GROUP INPUTS FOR MORTGAGE AMORTIZATION CALCULATION

Variable*	Description	Source
	Rate Type (Fixed or Adjustable)	RBC Report
	Product Type (30/20/15-Year FRM, ARM, Balloon, Government, etc.)	RBC Report
UPB_{ORIG}	Unpaid Principal Balance at Origination (aggregate for Loan Group)	RBC Report
UPB_0	Unpaid Principal Balance at start of Stress Test (aggregate for Loan Group)	RBC Report
MIR_0	Mortgage Interest Rate for the Mortgage Payment prior to the start of the Stress Test, or Initial Mortgage Interest Rate for new loans (weighted average for Loan Group) (expressed as a decimal per annum)	RBC Report

TABLE 3–32—LOAN GROUP INPUTS FOR MORTGAGE AMORTIZATION CALCULATION—Continued

Variable*	Description	Source
PMT_0	Amount of the Mortgage Payment (Principal and Interest) prior to the start of the Stress Test, or first payment for new loans (aggregate for Loan Group)	RBC Report
AT	Original loan Amortizing Term in months (weighted average for Loan Group)	RBC Report
RM	Remaining term to Maturity in months (i.e., number of contractual payments due between the start of the Stress Test and the contractual maturity date of the loan) (weighted average for Loan Group)	RBC Report
A_0	Age immediately prior to the start of the Stress Test, in months (weighted average for Loan Group)	RBC Report
	Interest-only Flag	RBC Report
RIOP	Remaining Interest-only period, in months (weighted average for loan group)	RBC Report
Additional Interest Rate Inputs		
GFR	Guarantee Fee Rate (weighted average for Loan Group) (decimal per annum)	RBC Report
SFR	Servicing Fee Rate (weighted average for Loan Group) (decimal per annum)	RBC Report
Additional Inputs for ARMs (weighted averages for Loan Group, except for Index)		
$INDEX_m$	Monthly values of the contractual Interest Rate Index	section 3.3, Interest Rates
LB	Look-Back period, in months	RBC Report
MARGIN	Loan Margin (over index), decimal per annum	RBC Report
RRP	Rate Reset Period, in months	RBC Report
	Rate Reset Limit (up and down), decimal per annum	RBC Report
	Maximum Rate (life cap), decimal per annum	RBC Report
	Minimum Rate (life floor), decimal per annum	RBC Report
NAC	Negative Amortization Cap, decimal fraction of UPB_{ORIG}	RBC Report
	Unlimited Payment Reset Period, in months	RBC Report
PRP	Payment Reset Period, in months	RBC Report
	Payment Reset Limit, as decimal fraction of prior payment	RBC Report
IRP	Initial Rate Period, in months	RBC Report

* Variable name is given when used in an equation

3.6.3.3.3 Mortgage Amortization Schedule Procedures

[a] For each Loan Group, calculate a mortgage Amortization Schedule using the inputs in Table 3–32 and the following ten steps. *Note:* Do not round dollar amounts to the nearest penny.)

For months m = 1...RM, calculate quantities for month m based on values from month m−1 as follows:

1. Calculate current month's Mortgage Interest Rate (MIR_m).
   a. For FRMs: $MIR_m = MIR_0$ for all m = 1 to RM
   b. For ARMs, use the following procedure:
   1) If RRP = PRP then month m is a rate reset month if:

$$\left[A_0 + m - (IRP + 1)\right] \, mod \, RRP = 0$$

$$\text{and} \quad A_0 + m - 1 \geq IRP$$

   2) If RRP ≠ PRP then month m is a rate reset month if either:
   a) A_0 + m − (IRP + 1) = 0, or
   b) [A_0 + m − 1] *mod* RRP = 0 and A_0 + m − 1 ≥ IRP
   3) If m is a rate reset month, then:

$$MIR_m = INDEX_{m-1-LB} + MARGIN,$$

but not greater than MIR_{m-1} + Rate Reset Limit
nor less than MIR_{m-1} − Rate Reset Limit
and in no case greater than Maximum Rate
and in no case less than Minimum Rate

   4) If month m is not a rate reset month, then $MIR_m = MIR_{m-1}$.
   c. In all cases, $MIR_m = MIR_{120}$ for m > 120, and MIR_m = 0 for m > RM.

2. Calculate current month's Payment (PMT_m).
   a. For FRMs:
   1) For Interest-Only Loans, if m = RIOP + 1 then month m is a reset month; recompute PMT_m as described for ARMs in step b.4)b), of this section without applying any payment limit.
   2) $PMT_m = PMT_0$ for all m = 1 to RM
   b. For ARMs, use the following procedure:
   1) For Interest Only Loans, if m = RIOP + 1 then month m is a payment reset month.
   2) If PRP = RRP, then month m is a payment reset month if m is also a rate reset month.
   3) If PRP ≠ RRP then month m is a payment reset month if:

$$\left[A_0 + m - 1\right] \, mod \, PRP = 0$$

   4) If month m is a payment reset month, then:
   a) For loans in an Interest-only Period,

$$PMT_m = UPB_{m-1} \times \frac{MIR_m}{12}$$

   b) Otherwise, PMT_m = the amount that will fully amortize the Loan over its remaining Amortizing Term (i.e. AT−A_o−m+1 months) with a *fixed* Mortgage Interest Rate equal to MIR_m as determined in Step 1 of this section
   but not greater than PMT_{m-1} × (1 + Payment Reset Limit Up)
   nor less than PMT_{m-1} × (1−Payment Reset Limit Down)
   unless month m is the month following the end of an Unlimited Payment Reset Period, in which case PMT_m is not subject to any reset limitations.
   5) If month m is not a payment reset month, then $PMT_m = PMT_{m-1}$
   6) If, in any month,

$$UPB_{m-1} \times \left(1 + \frac{MIR_m}{12}\right) - PMT_m$$

$$> UPB_{ORIG} \times NAC,$$

then recalculate PMT_m without applying any Payment Reset Limit.
   c. For Balloon Loans, or for loans that have RIOP = RM, if m = RM then:

$$PMT_m = UPB_{m-1} \times \left(1 + \frac{MIR_m}{12}\right)$$

   d. In all cases, PMT_m should amortize the loan within the Remaining Maturity:

$$PMT_m = 0 \text{ for } m > RM \text{ or after } UPB_m = 0$$

3. Determine Net Yield Rate (NYR_m) and, for sold loans, Pass-Through Rate (PTR_m) applicable to the mth payment:

$$NYR_m = MIR_m - SFR$$

$$PTR_m = NYR_m - GFR$$

4. Calculate Scheduled Interest Accrued (during month m−1) on account of the mth payment (SIA_m)

$$SIA_m = UPB_{m-1} \times \frac{MIR_m}{12}$$

5. Calculate the Scheduled Interest component of the mth payment (SI_m)

$$SI_m = min\left(SIA_m, \; PMT_m\right)$$

6. Calculate Scheduled Principal for the mth payment (SP_m):

$$SP_m = min\left(PMT_m - SIA_m, \; UPB_{m-1}\right)$$

NOTE: Scheduled Principal should not be greater than the remaining UPB. SPM can be negative if the Scheduled Payment is less than Scheduled Interest Accrued.

7. Calculate Loan Unpaid Principal Balance after taking into account the mth monthly payment (UPB_m):

$$UPB_m = max\left(UPB_{m-1} - SP_m, \; 0\right)$$

8. In the month when UPB_m is reduced to zero, reset

$$PMT_m = UPB_{m-1} \times \left(1 + \frac{MIR_m}{12}\right)$$

9. Repeat all steps for m = 1...RM or until $UPB_m = 0$.

NOTE: If UPB_{RM} is greater than zero, the performing portion is included in Credit Losses (section 3.6.3.7.3, Stress Test Whole Loan Cash Flow Procedures, of this appendix).

10. Determine Net Yield Rate (NYR_o) and, for sold loans, Pass-Through Rate (PTR_o) for month 0:

$$NYR_0 = MIR_0 - SFR$$

$$PTR_0 = NYR_0 - GFR$$

3.6.3.3.4 Mortgage Amortization Schedule Outputs

The Mortgage Amortization Schedule Outputs set forth in Table 3–33 are used in section 3.6.3.4, Single Family Default and Prepayment Rates, section 3.6.3.5, Multifamily Default and Prepayment Rates, section 3.6.3.6, Calculation of Single Family and Multifamily Mortgage Losses, section 3.6.3.7, Stress Test Whole Loan Cash Flows, and section 3.6.3.8, Whole Loan Accounting Flows, of this appendix.

TABLE 3–33—MORTGAGE AMORTIZATION SCHEDULE OUTPUTS

Variable	Description
UPB_m	Unpaid Principal Balance for months m=1...RM
MIR_m	Mortgage Interest Rate for months m=1...RM
NYR_m	Net Yield Rate for months m=1...RM
PTR_m	Passthrough Rate for months m=1...RM
SP_m	Scheduled Principal (Amortization) for months m=1...RM
SI_m	Scheduled Interest for months m=1...RM
PMT_m	Scheduled Mortgage Payment for months m=1...RM

3.6.3.4 Single Family Default and Prepayment Rates

3.6.3.4.1 Single Family Default and Prepayment Overview

[a] The Stress Test projects conditional Default and Prepayment rates for each single family Loan Group for each month of the Stress Period. The conditional rate is the percentage (by principal balance) of the remaining loans in a Loan Group that defaults or prepays during a given period of time. Computing Default and Prepayment rates for a Loan Group requires information on the Loan Group characteristics at the beginning of the Stress Test, historical and projected interest rates from section 3.3, Interest Rates, and house price growth rates and volatility measures from section 3.4, Property Valuation, of this appendix.

[b] *Explanatory Variables.* Several explanatory variables are used in the equations to determine Default and Prepayment rates for single family loans: Mortgage Age, Original Loan-to-Value (LTV) ratio, Probability of Negative Equity, Burnout, the percentage of Investor-owned Loans, Relative Interest Rate Spread, Payment Shock (for ARMs only), Initial Rate Effect (for ARMs only), Yield Curve Slope, Relative Loan Size, and Mortgage Product Type. Regression coefficients (weights) are associated with each variable. All of this information is used to compute conditional quarterly Default and Prepayment rates throughout the Stress Test. The quarterly rates are then converted to monthly conditional Default and Prepayment rates, which are used to calculate Stress Test Whole Loan cash flows and Default losses. *See* section 3.6.3.7, Stress Test Whole Loan Cash Flows, of this appendix.

[c] The regression coefficients for each Loan Group will come from one of three models. The choice of model will be determined by the values of the single family product code and Government Flag in the RBC Report. *See* section 3.6.3.4.3.2, Prepayment and Default Rates and Performance Fractions, of this appendix.

[d] *Special Provision for Accounting Calculations.* For accounting calculations that require cash flows over the entire remaining life of the instrument, Default and Prepayment rates for months beyond the end of the Stress Test are held constant at their values for month 120.

3.6.3.4.2 Single Family Default and Prepayment Inputs

The information in Table 3–34 is required for each single family Loan Group:

TABLE 3–34—SINGLE FAMILY DEFAULT AND PREPAYMENT INPUTS

Variable	Description	Source
PROD	Mortgage Product Type	RBC Report
A_0	Age *immediately prior to* start of Stress Test, in months (weighted average for Loan Group)	RBC Report
LTV_{ORIG}	Loan-to-Value ratio at Origination (weighted average for Loan Group)	RBC Report
UPB_{ORIG}	UPB at Origination (aggregate for Loan Group)	RBC Report
MIR_{ORIG}	Mortgage Interest Rate at Origination ("Initial Rate" for ARMs), decimal per annum (weighted average for loan group)	RBC Report
UPB_0	Unpaid Principal Balance immediately prior to start of Stress Test (aggregate for Loan Group)	RBC Report
UPB_m	Unpaid Principal Balance in months m = 1...RM	section 3.6.3.3.4, Mortgage Amortization Schedule Outputs
MIR_m	Mortgage Interest Rate in months m = 1...RM (weighted average for Loan Group)	section 3.6.3.3.4, Mortgage Amortization Schedule Outputs
$MCON_m$	Conventional (30 Year Fixed-Rate) Mortgage Rate series projected for months 1...RM and for the 24 months prior to the start of the Stress Test	section 3.3.2, Interest Rates Inputs, and section 3.3.4, Interest Rates Outputs
$T12Y_m$	1-year CMT series projected for months 1...120 of the Benchmark region and time period	section 3.3.4, Interest Rates Outputs
$T120Y_m$	10-year CMT series projected for months 1...120 of the Benchmark region and time period	section 3.3.4, Interest Rates Outputs
$HPGR_q$	Vector of House Price Growth Rates for quarters q = 1...40 of the Stress Period	section 3.4.4, Property Valuation Outputs
$CHPGF_0^{LG}$	Cumulative House Price Growth Factor since Loan Origination (weighted average for Loan Group)	RBC Report
α, β	HPI Dispersion Parameters for the Stress Period (Benchmark Census Division, currently West South Central Census Division, as published in the OFHEO House Price Report for 1996:3)	$\alpha = 0.002977$ $\beta = -0.000024322$
IF	Fraction (by UPB, in decimal form) of Loan Group backed by Investor-owned properties	RBC Report
RLS_{ORIG}	Weighted average Relative Loan Size at Origination (Original UPB as a fraction of average UPB for the state and Origination Year of loan origination)	RBC Report

3.6.3.4.3 Single Family Default and Prepayment Procedures

3.6.3.4.3.1 Single Family Default and Prepayment Explanatory Variables

[a] Compute the explanatory variables for single family Default and Prepayment in the seven steps as follows:

1. Calculate A_q, the loan Age in quarters, for quarter q:

$$A_q = int\left(\frac{A_0}{3}\right) + q,$$

Where:

int means to round to the lower integer if the argument is not an integer.

2. Calculate $PNEQ_q$, the Probability of Negative Equity in quarter q:

$$PNEQ_q = N\left(\frac{ln LTV_q}{\sigma_q}\right),$$

where:

N designates the cumulative normal distribution function.

a. LTV_q is evaluated for a quarter q as:

$$LTV_{ORIG} \times \frac{\left(\begin{array}{l}\text{Ratio of current}\\ \text{Loan Group UPB}\\ \text{to Original UPB}\end{array}\right)}{\left(\begin{array}{l}\text{Ratio of current property}\\ \text{value (based on HPI in}\\ \text{quarter q) to original}\\ \text{property value (based on}\\ \text{HPI at Origination)}\end{array}\right)}$$

The HPI at Origination is updated to the beginning of the Stress Test using actual historical experience as measured by the OFHEO HPI; and then updated within the Stress Test using House Price Growth Factors from the Benchmark region and time period:

$$LTV_q = LTV_{ORIG} \times \frac{\left(\frac{UPB_{m=3_q-3}}{UPB_{ORIG}}\right)}{\left[CHPGF_0^{LG} \times exp\left(\sum_{k=1}^{q} HPGR_k\right)\right]}$$

Where:

$UPB_{m=3q-3}$ = UPB for the month at the end of the quarter prior to quarter q

$CHPGF_o^{LG}$ = 1.0 if the loan was originated in the same quarter as or after the most recently available HPI as of the reporting date

3. Calculate B_q, the Burnout factor in quarter q. A loan's Prepayment incentive is "burned out" (i.e., reduced) if, during at least two of the previous eight full quarters, the borrower had, but did not take advantage of, an opportunity to reduce his or her mortgage interest rate by at least two percentage points. For this purpose, the mortgage interest rate is compared with values of the Conventional Mortgage Rate (MCON) Index.

a. Compare mortgage rates for each quarter of the Stress Test and for the eight quarters prior to the start of the stress test (q = −7, −6,...0, 1,...40):

$$\begin{aligned} b_q &= 1 \text{ if } MCON_m + 0.02 \le MIR_m \\ &\quad \text{for all three months in quarter q} \\ &\quad \text{(i.e., m} = 3q-2,\ 3q-1,\ 3q), \\ b_q &= 0 \text{ otherwise} \end{aligned}$$

Note: For this purpose, $MCON_m$ is required for the 24 months (eight quarters) prior to the start of the Stress Test. Also, MIR_m = MIR_0 for $m < 0$.

b. Determine whether the loan is "burned out" in quarter q (Burnout Flag, B_q^f):

$$\begin{aligned} B_q^f &= 1 \text{ if } b_{q'} = 1 \text{ for two or more} \\ &\quad \text{quarters q}' \text{ between q-8 and q-1} \\ &\quad \text{inclusive, or since Origination if} \\ &\quad 2 < A_q < 8 \text{ (Note: by definition,} \\ &\quad B_q = 0 \text{ if } A_q < 3); \\ B_q^f &= 0 \text{ otherwise} \end{aligned}$$

Where:

q′ = index variable for prior 8 quarters

c. Adjust for recently originated loans as follows:

$$\begin{aligned} B_q &= 0.25 \times B_q^f \text{ if } A_q = 3 \text{ or } 4 \\ &= 0.50 \times B_q^f \text{ if } A_q = 5 \text{ or } 6 \\ &= 0.75 \times B_q^f \text{ if } A_q = 7 \text{ or } 8 \\ &= B_q^f \text{ otherwise} \end{aligned}$$

4. Calculate RS_q, the Relative Spread in quarter q, as the average value of the monthly Relative Spread of the Original

mortgage interest rate to the Conventional (30-Year Fixed Rate) Mortgage Rate series for the three months in the quarter.

NOTE: Use the Current MIR for Fixed Rate Loans and the Original MIR for Adjustable Rate Loans.

$$RS_q = avg\left(\frac{MIR - MCON_m}{MIR}\right)$$

$$\text{over all three months m in quarter q}$$

If MIR = 0, then RS_q = −0.20 for all q.

5. Calculate YCS_q, the Yield Curve Slope in quarter q, as the average of the monthly ratio of the 10-Year CMT to the One-Year CMT for the three months in the quarter:

$$YCS_q = avg\left(\frac{T120Y_m}{T12Y_m}\right)$$

$$\text{for all three months in quarter q}$$

6. Evaluate the Payment Shock Indicator (PS_q) for ARMs only:

$$PS_q = RS_q \text{ if } PROD = ARM$$

7. Evaluate the Initial Rate Effect Flag ($IREF_q$) for ARMS only:

$$IREF_q = 1 \text{ if } A_q \le 12 \text{ and } PROD = ARM$$
$$= 0 \text{ otherwise}$$

3.6.3.4.3.2 Prepayment and Default Rates and Performance Fractions

[a] Calculate Prepayment and Default Rates and Performance Fractions using the following five steps:

1. Compute the logits for Default and Prepayment using the formulas for simultaneous processes using inputs from Table 3–34 and explanatory variable coefficients in Table 3–35.

NOTE: $\beta_{BCal_{LTV}}$ is the LTV-specific constant used to calibrate the Default rates to the BLE.

$$X\beta_q = \beta_{A_q} + \beta_{LTV_{ORIG}} + \beta_{PNEQ_q} + \beta_{B_q}B_q + \beta_{IF}IF + \beta_{PS_q} + \beta_{IREF} \times IREF_q + \beta_{Prod} + \beta_{BCal_{LTV}} + \beta_0$$

$$X\gamma_q = \gamma_{A_q} + \gamma_{LTV_{ORIG}} + \gamma_{PNEQ_q} + \gamma_{B_q}B_q + \gamma_{IF}IF + \gamma_{RS_q} + \gamma_{PS_q} + \gamma_{YCS_q} + \gamma_{IREF} \times IREF_q + \gamma_{RLS_{ORIG}} + \gamma_{Prod} + \gamma_0$$

TABLE 3–35—COEFFICIENTS FOR SINGLE FAMILY DEFAULT AND PREPAYMENT EXPLANATORY VARIABLE

Explanatory Variable (V)	30-Year Fixed-Rate Loans		Adjustable-Rate Loans (ARMs)		Other Fixed-Rate Loans	
	Default Weight (β_v)	Prepayment Weight (γ_v)	Default Weight (β_v)	Prepayment Weight (γ_v)	Default Weight (β_v)	Prepayment Weight (γ_v)
A_q $0 \le A_q \le 4$	−0.6276	−0.6122	−0.7046	−0.5033	−0.7721	−0.6400
$5 \le A_q \le 8$	−0.1676	0.1972	−0.2259	0.1798	−0.2738	0.1721
$9 \le A_q \le 12$	−0.05872	0.2668	0.01504	0.2744	−0.09809	0.2317
$13 \le A_q \le 16$	0.07447	0.2151	0.2253	0.2473	0.1311	0.1884
$17 \le A_q \le 20$	0.2395	0.1723	0.3522	0.1421	0.3229	0.1900
$21 \le A_q \le 24$	0.2773	0.2340	0.4369	0.1276	0.3203	0.2356
$25 \le A_q \le 36$	0.2740	0.1646	0.2954	0.1098	0.3005	0.1493
$37 \le A_q \le 48$	0.1908	−0.2318	0.06902	−0.1462	0.2306	−0.2357

TABLE 3–35—COEFFICIENTS FOR SINGLE FAMILY DEFAULT AND PREPAYMENT EXPLANATORY VARIABLE—Continued

Explanatory Variable (V)	30-Year Fixed-Rate Loans		Adjustable-Rate Loans (ARMs)		Other Fixed-Rate Loans	
	Default Weight (β_v)	Prepayment Weight (γ_v)	Default Weight (β_v)	Prepayment Weight (γ_v)	Default Weight (β_v)	Prepayment Weight (γ_v)
$49 \le A_q$	−0.2022	−0.4059	−0.4634	−0.4314	−0.1614	−0.2914
LTV_{ORIG} $LTV_{ORIG} \le 60$	−1.150	0.04787	−1.303	0.08871	−1.280	0.02309
$60<LTV_{ORIG} \le 70$	−0.1035	−0.03131	−0.1275	−0.005619	−0.06929	−0.02668
$70<LTV_{ORIG} \le 75$	0.5969	−0.09885	0.4853	−0.09852	0.6013	−0.05446
$75<LTV_{ORIG} \le 80$	0.2237	−0.04071	0.1343	−0.03099	0.2375	−0.03835
$80<LTV_{ORIG} \le 90$	0.2000	−0.004698	0.2576	0.004226	0.2421	−0.01433
$90< LTV_{ORIG}$	0.2329	0.1277	0.5528	0.04220	0.2680	0.1107
$PNEQ_q$ $0< PNEQ_q \le 0.05$	−1.603	0.5910	−1.1961	0.4607	−1.620	0.5483
$0.05< PNEQ_q \le 0.1$	−0.5241	0.3696	−0.3816	0.2325	−0.5055	0.3515
$0.1< PNEQ_q \le 0.15$	−0.1805	0.2286	−0.1431	0.1276	−0.1249	0.2178
$0.15< PNEQ_q \le 0.2$	0.07961	−0.02000	−0.04819	0.03003	0.07964	−0.02137
$0.2< PNEQ_q \le 0.25$	0.2553	−0.1658	0.2320	−0.1037	0.2851	−0.1540
$0.25< PNEQ_q \le 0.3$	0.5154	−0.2459	0.2630	−0.1829	0.4953	−0.2723
$0.3< PNEQ_q \le 0.35$	0.6518	−0.2938	0.5372	−0.2075	0.5979	−0.2714
$0.35< PNEQ_q$	0.8058	−0.4636	0.7368	−0.3567	0.7923	−0.3986
B_q	1.303	−0.3331	0.8835	−0.2083	1.253	−0.3244
RLS $0<RLS_{ORIG} \le 0.4$	....	−0.5130	....	−0.4765	....	−0.4344
$0.4<RLS_{ORIG} \le 0.6$	....	−0.3264	....	−0.2970	....	−0.2852
$0.6<RLS_{ORIG} \le 0.75$	....	−0.1378	....	−0.1216	....	−0.1348
$0.75<RLS_{ORIG} \le 1.0$	....	0.03495	....	0.04045	....	0.01686
$1.0<RLS_{ORIG} \le 1.25$	....	0.1888	....	0.1742	....	0.1597
$1.25<RLS_{ORIG} \le 1.5$	....	0.3136	....	0.2755	....	0.2733
$1.5<RLS_{ORIG}$	....	0.4399	....	0.4049	....	0.4045
IF	0.4133	−0.3084	0.6419	−0.3261	0.4259	−0.3035
RS_q $RS_q \le -0.20$	....	−1.368	....	−0.5463	....	−1.195
$-0.20 <RS_q \le -0.10$	....	−1.023	....	−0.4560	....	−0.9741
$-0.10 < RS_q \le 0$	....	−0.8078	....	−0.4566	....	−0.7679

TABLE 3–35—COEFFICIENTS FOR SINGLE FAMILY DEFAULT AND PREPAYMENT EXPLANATORY VARIABLE—Continued

Explanatory Variable (V)	30-Year Fixed-Rate Loans		Adjustable-Rate Loans (ARMs)		Other Fixed-Rate Loans	
	Default Weight (β_v)	Prepayment Weight (γ_v)	Default Weight (β_v)	Prepayment Weight (γ_v)	Default Weight (β_v)	Prepayment Weight (γ_v)
$0< RS_q \le 0.10$	....	−0.3296	....	−0.3024	....	−0.2783
$0.10 < RS_q \le 0.20$	....	0.8045	....	0.3631	....	0.7270
$0.20 < RS_q \le 0.30$	....	1.346	....	0.7158	....	1.229
$0.30 < RS_q$	....	1.377	....	0.6824	....	1.259
PS_q $PS_q \le -0.20$	....	....	0.08490	0.6613	....	....
$-0.20 < PS_q \le -0.10$	....	....	0.3736	0.4370	....	....
$-0.10 < PS_q \le 0$	....	....	0.2816	0.2476	....	....
$0< PS_q \le 0.10$	....	....	0.1381	0.1073	....	....
$0.10 < PS_q \le 0.20$	....	....	−0.1433	−0.3516	....	....
$0.20 < PS_q \le 0.30$	....	....	−0.2869	−0.5649	....	....
$0.30 < PS_q$	....	....	−0.4481	−0.5366	....	....
YCS_q $YCS_q < 1.0$	....	−0.2582	....	−0.2947	....	−0.2917
$1.0 \le YCS_q < 1.2$	....	−0.02735	....	−0.1996	....	−0.01395
$1.2 \le YCS_q < 1.5$	....	−0.04099	....	0.03356	....	−0.03796
$1.5 \le YCS_q$	....	0.3265	....	0.4608	....	0.3436
$IREF_q$	....	....	0.1084	−0.01382	....	....
PROD ARMs	....	....	0.8151	0.2453	....	....
Balloon Loans	....	....	....	....	1.253	0.9483
15−Year FRMs	....	....	....	....	−1.104	0.07990
20−Year FRMs	....	....	....	....	−0.5834	0.06780
Government Loans	....	....	....	....	0.9125	−0.5660
$BCal_{LTV}$ $LTV_{ORIG} \le 60$	2.045	....	2.045	....	2.045	....
$60<LTV_{ORIG} \le 70$	0.3051	....	0.3051	....	0.3051	....
$70<LTV_{ORIG} \le 75$	−0.07900	....	−0.07900	....	−0.07900	....
$75<LTV_{ORIG} \le 80$	−0.05519	....	−0.05519	....	−0.05519	....
$80<LTV_{ORIG} \le 90$	−0.1838	....	−0.1838	....	−0.1838	....
$90< LTV_{ORIG}$	0.2913	....	0.2913	....	0.2913	....

TABLE 3–35—COEFFICIENTS FOR SINGLE FAMILY DEFAULT AND PREPAYMENT EXPLANATORY VARIABLE—Continued

Explanatory Variable (V)	30-Year Fixed-Rate Loans		Adjustable-Rate Loans (ARMs)		Other Fixed-Rate Loans	
	Default Weight (β_v)	Prepayment Weight (γ_v)	Default Weight (β_v)	Prepayment Weight (γ_v)	Default Weight (β_v)	Prepayment Weight (γ_v)
Intercept (β_0, γ_0)	−6.516	−4.033	−6.602	−3.965	−6.513	−3.949

2. The choice of coefficients from Table 3–35 will be governed by the single family product code and Government Flag, according to Table 3–36.

TABLE 3–36—SINGLE FAMILY PRODUCT CODE COEFFICIENT MAPPING

Single Family Product Code	Model Coefficient Applied
Non-Government Loans	
Fixed Rate 30YR	30-Year FRMs
Fixed Rate 20YR	20-Year FRMs
Fixed Rate 15YR	15-Year FRMs
5-Year Fixed Rate Balloon	Balloon Loans
7-Year Fixed Rate Balloon	Balloon Loans
10-Year Fixed Rate Balloon	Balloon Loans
15-Year Fixed Rate Balloon	Balloon Loans
Adjustable Rate	ARMs
Second Lien	Balloon Loans
Other	Balloon Loans
Government Loans	
Government Flag	Model Coefficient Applied
All government loans except for ARMs	Government Loans
Government ARMs	ARMs

3. Compute Quarterly Prepayment and Default Rates (QPR, QDR) from the logistic expressions as follows:

$$QDR_q = \frac{exp\left\{X\beta_q\right\}}{1+exp\left\{X\beta_q\right\}+exp\left\{X\gamma_q\right\}}$$

$$QPR_q = \frac{exp\left\{X\gamma_q\right\}}{1+exp\left\{X\beta_q\right\}+exp\left\{X\gamma_q\right\}}$$

4. Convert quarterly rates to monthly rates using the following formulas for simultaneous processes. The quarterly rate for q = 1 gives the monthly rate for months m = 1,2,3, and so on through q = 40:

$$MDR_m = \frac{QDR_q}{QDR_q + QPR_q} \times \left[1 - \left(1 - QDR_q - QPR_q\right)^{\frac{1}{3}}\right]$$

$$MPR_m = \frac{QPR_q}{QDR_q + QPR_q} \times \left[1 - \left(1 - QDR_q - QPR_q\right)^{\frac{1}{3}}\right]$$

5. Calculate Defaulting Fraction (DEF), Prepaying Fraction (PRE), and Performing Fraction (PERF) of the Initial Loan Group. Initially (at the beginning of the Stress Test), all loans are assumed to be performing, i.e. $PERF_0 = 1.0$. For each month m = 1...RM, calculate the following quantities. *Note:* For m > 120, use MPR_{120} and MDR_{120}:

$$PRE_m = PERF_{m-1} \times MPR_m$$
$$DEF_m = PERF_{m-1} \times MDR_m$$
$$PERF_m = PERF_{m-1} - PRE_m - DEF_m$$

3.6.3.4.4 Single Family Default and Prepayment Outputs

Single family Default and Prepayment outputs are set forth in Table 3–37. Prepayment, Default and Performing Fractions for single family loans for months m = 1...RM are used in section 3.6.3.6, Calculation of Single Family and Multifamily Mortgage Losses; and section 3.6.3.7, Stress Test Whole Loan Cash Flows, of this appendix. Quarterly LTV ratios are used in section 3.6.3.6.2.3, Single Family Gross Loss Severity Procedures, of this appendix.

TABLE 3–37—SINGLE FAMILY DEFAULT AND PREPAYMENT OUTPUTS

Variable	Description
LTV_q	Current Loan-to-Value ratio in quarter q = 1...40
PRE_m^{SF}	Prepaying Fraction of Initial Loan Group in month m = 1...RM (single family Loans)
DEF_m^{SF}	Defaulting Fraction of Initial Loan Group in month m = 1...RM (single family Loans)
$PERF_m^{SF}$	Performing Fraction of Initial original Loan Group in month m = 1...RM (single family loans)

3.6.3.5 Multifamily Default and Prepayment Rates

3.6.3.5.1 Multifamily Default and Prepayment Rates Overview

[a] The Stress Test projects conditional Default and Prepayment rates for each multifamily Loan Group for each month of the Stress Period. Computing Default rates for a Loan Group requires information on the Loan Group characteristics at the beginning of the Stress Test and the economic conditions of the Stress Period—interest rates (section 3.3 of this appendix), vacancy rates and rent growth rates (section 3.4 of this appendix). These input data are used to create values for the explanatory variables in the Multifamily Default component.

[b] *Explanatory Variables for Default Rates.* Eight explanatory variables are used as specified in the equations in section 3.6.3.5.3.1, of this appendix, to determine Default rates for multifamily loans: Mortgage Age, Mortgage Age Squared, New Book indicator, Not Ratio-updated ARM indicator, current Debt-Service Coverage Ratio, Underwater Current Debt-Service Coverage indicator, Loan-To-Value Ratio at origination/acquisition, and a Balloon Maturity indicator. Regression coefficients (weights) are associated with each variable. All of this information is used to compute conditional annual Default rates throughout the Stress Test. The annualized Default rates are converted to monthly conditional Default rates and are used together with monthly conditional Prepayment rates to calculate Stress Test Whole Loan Cash Flows. (*See* section 3.6.3.7, Stress Test Whole Loan Cash Flows, of this appendix).

[c] *Specification of Multifamily Prepayment Rates.* Multifamily Prepayment rates are not generated by a statistical model but follow a set of Prepayment rules that capture the effect of yield maintenance, Prepayment penalties and other mechanisms that effectively curtail or eliminate multifamily Prepayments for a specified period of time.

[d] *Special Provision for Accounting Calculations.* For accounting calculations, which require cash flows over the entire remaining life of the instrument, Default and Prepayment rates for months beyond the end of the

Stress Test are held constant at their values for month 120.

3.6.3.5.2 Multifamily Default and Prepayment Inputs

The information in Table 3–38 is required for each multifamily Loan Group:

TABLE 3–38—LOAN GROUP INPUTS FOR MULTIFAMILY DEFAULT AND PREPAYMENT CALCULATIONS

Variable	Description	Source
	Mortgage Product Type	RBC Report
A_o	Age immediately prior to start of Stress Test, in months (weighted average for Loan Group)	RBC Report
NBF	New Book Flag	RBC Report
RUF	Ratio Update Flag	RBC Report
LTV_{ORIG}	Loan-to-Value ratio at loan Origination	RBC Report
DCR_o	Debt Service Coverage Ratio at the start of the Stress Test	RBC Report
PMT_o	Amount of the mortgage Payment (principal and interest) prior to the start of the Stress Test, or first Payment for new loans (aggregate for Loan Group)	RBC Report
PPEM	Prepayment Penalty End Month number in the Stress Test (weighted average for Loan Group)	RBC Report
RM	Remaining term to Maturity in months (i.e., number of contractual payments due between the start of the Stress Test and the contractual maturity date of the loan) (weighted average for Loan Group)	RBC Report
RGR_m	Benchmark Rent Growth for months m = 1...120 of the Stress Test	section 3.4.4, Property Valuation Outputs
RVR_m	Benchmark Vacancy Rates for months m = 1...120 of the Stress Test	section 3.4.4, Property Valuation Outputs
PMT_m	Scheduled Payment for months m = 1... RM	section 3.6.3.3.4, Mortgage Amortization Schedule Outputs
OE	Operating expenses as a share of gross potential rents (0.472)	fixed decimal from Benchmark region and time period
RVR_o	Initial rental vacancy rate	0.10

3.6.3.5.3 Multifamily Default and Prepayment Procedures

3.6.3.5.3.1 Explanatory Variables

[a] Compute the explanatory variables for multifamily Default and Prepayment in five steps as follows:

1. Calculate Loan Age in Years for months m = 0...120 of the Stress Test (AY_m):

$$AY_m = \frac{A_0 + m}{12}$$

Where:

A_0 + m is Loan Age in months at the beginning of month m of the Stress Test.

NOTE: AY_m is calculated for each month m, whereas the corresponding Age variable for single family Loans A_q is calculated only quarterly.

2. Assign product and ratio update flags (NBF, NRAF). *Note:* these values do not change over time for a given Loan Group.

a. New Book Flag (NBF):

NBF = 1 for Fannie Mae loans acquired after 1987 and Freddie Mac loans acquired after 1992, *except* for loans that were refinanced to avoid a Default on a loan originated or acquired earlier.

NBF = 0 otherwise.

b. Not Ratio-updated Arm Flag (NRAF):

NRAF = 1 if both ARMF = 1 and RUF = 0,

NRAF = 0 otherwise.

Where:

ARMF = 1 for ARMs (including Balloon ARMs)

ARMF = 0 otherwise, and

RUF = 1 if the LTV and DCR were calculated or delegated to have been calculated at origination or recalculated or delegated to have been recalculated at Enterprise acquisition according to current Enterprise standards.

RUF = 0 otherwise

3. Calculate Debt Service Coverage Ratio in month m (DCR_m):

The standard definition of Debt Service Coverage Ratio is current net operating income divided by current mortgage payment. However, for the Stress Test, update DCR_m each month from the prior month's value using Rent Growth Rates (RGR_m) and Rental Vacancy Rates (RVR_m) starting with DCR_m from Table 3-38, as follows:

$$DCR_m = DCR_{m-1} \times \left[\frac{(1+RGR_m)\left(\frac{1-OE-RVR_m}{1-OE-RVR_{m-1}} \right)}{\frac{PMT_m}{PMT_{m-1}}} \right]$$

4. Assign Underwater Debt-Service Coverage Flag ($UWDCRF_m$):

$UWDCRF_m = 1$ if $DCR_m < 0.98$ in month m

$UWDCRF_m = 0$ otherwise.

5. Assign Balloon Maturity Flag (BMF_m) for any Balloon Loan that is within twelve months of its maturity date:

$$BMF_m = 1 \text{ if } RM - m < 12$$

$$BMF_m = 0 \text{ otherwise.}$$

3.6.3.5.3.2 Default and Prepayment Rates and Performance Fractions

[a] Compute Default and Prepayment Rates and Performance Fractions for multifamily loans in the following four steps:

1. Compute the logits for multifamily Default using inputs from Table 3-38 and coefficients from Table 3-39. For indexing purposes, the Default rate for a period m is the likelihood of missing the m_{th} payment; calculate its corresponding logit ($X\delta_m$) based on Loan Group characteristics as of the period *prior* to m, i.e. *prior* to making the mth payment.

$$\begin{aligned} X\delta_m &= \delta_{AY}AY_{m-1} + \delta_{AY^2}AY_{m-1}^2 \\ &+ \delta_{NBF}NBF + \delta_{NRAF}NRAF \\ &+ \delta_{DCR}\, ln\left(DCR_{m-1}\right) \\ &+ \delta_{UWDCRF}UWDCRF_{m-1} \\ &+ \delta_{LTV}\, ln\left(LTV_{ORIG}\right) \\ &+ \delta_{BMF}BMF_{m-1} + \delta_0 \end{aligned}$$

TABLE 3–39—EXPLANATORY VARIABLE COEFFICIENTS FOR MULTIFAMILY DEFAULT

Explanatory Variable (V)	Default Weight (δ_v)
AY	0.5256
AY²	0.0284
NBF	−1.219
NRAF	0.4193
DCR	−2.368
UWDCRF	1.220
LTV	0.8165
BMF	1.518
Intercept (δ_0)	−4.553

2. Compute Annual Prepayment Rate (APR) and Annual Default Rate (ADR) as follows:

$$ADR_m = \frac{exp\{X\delta_m\} \times (1-APR_m)}{1+exp\{X\delta_m\}}$$

APR_m is a constant, determined as follows:

a. For the up-rate scenario, $APR_m = 0$ for all months m

b. For the down-rate scenario,

APR_m = 0 percent during the Prepayment penalty period (i.e., when $m \leq PPEM$)

APR_m = 25 percent after the Prepayment penalty period (i.e., when $m > PPEM$)

3. Convert annual Prepayment and Default rates to monthly rates (MPR and MDR) using the following formulas for simultaneous processes:

$$MPR_m = \frac{APR_m}{ADR_m + APR_m} \times \left[1 - \left(1 - ADR_m - APR_m\right)^{\frac{1}{12}} \right]$$

If both ARMF = 0 and RUF = 0, then

$$MDR_m = \left[\frac{ADR_m}{ADR_m + APR_m} \times \left[1-(1-ADR_m - APR_m)^{\frac{1}{12}}\right]\right] \times 1.2$$

otherwise,

$$MDR_m = \frac{ADR_m}{ADR_m + APR_m} \times \left[1-(1-ADR_m - APR_m)^{\frac{1}{12}}\right]$$

4. Calculate Defaulting Fraction (DEF_m), Prepaying Fraction (PRE_m), and Performing Fraction ($PERF_m$) of the Initial Loan Group for each month m = 1...RM. Initially (immediately prior to the beginning of the Stress Test), all loans are assumed to be performing, i.e. $PERF_0$ = 1.0. *Note:* For m> 120, use MPR_{120} and MDR_{120}.

$$PRE_m = PERF_{m-1} \times MPR_m$$

$$DEF_m = PERF_{m-1} \times MDR_m$$

$$PERF_m = PERF_{m-1} - PRE_m - DEF_m$$

3.6.3.5.4 Multifamily Default and Prepayment Outputs

[a] Multifamily Default and Prepayment Outputs are set forth in Table 3–40.

TABLE 3–40—MULTIFAMILY DEFAULT AND PREPAYMENT OUTPUTS

Variable	Description
PRE_m^{MF}	Prepaying Fraction of initial Loan Group in month m=1...RM (multifamily Loans)
DEF_m^{MF}	Defaulting Fraction of initial Loan Group in month m=1...RM (multifamily Loans)
$PERF_m^{MF}$	Performing Fraction of initial Loan Group in month m=1...RM (multifamily Loans)

[b] Multifamily monthly Prepayment Fractions ($PERF_m^{MF}$) and monthly Default Fractions (DEF_m^{MF}) for months m=1...RM are used in section 3.6.3.6, Calculation of Single Family and Multifamily Mortgage Losses; section 3.6.3.7, Stress Test Whole Loan Cash Flows, and section 3.6.3.8, Whole Loan Accounting Flows, of this appendix.

3.6.3.6 Calculation of Single Family and Multifamily Mortgage Losses

3.6.3.6.1 Calculation of Single Family and Multifamily Mortgage Losses Overview

[a] *Definition.* Loss Severity is the net cost to an Enterprise of a loan Default. Though losses may be associated with delinquency, loan restructuring and/or modification and other loss mitigation efforts, foreclosures are the only loss events modeled during the Stress Test.

[b] *Calculation.* The Loss Severity rate is expressed as a fraction of the Unpaid Principal Balance (UPB) at the time of Default. The Stress Test calculates Loss Severity rates for each Loan Group for each month of the Stress Period. Funding costs (and offsetting revenues) of defaulted loans are captured by discounting the Loss Severity elements using a cost-of-funds interest rate that varies during the Stress Period. Table 3-41 specifies the Stress Test Loss Severity timeline. Loss Severity rates also depend upon the application of Credit Enhancements and the credit ratings of enhancement providers.

TABLE 3–41—LOSS SEVERITY EVENT TIMING

Month	Event
1	First missed payment
4 (= MQ)	Loan is repurchased from securitized pool and UPB is passed through to MBS investors (Sold Loans only)
13 (= MF^{SF})	Single family foreclosure
18 (= MF^{MF})	Multifamily foreclosure
20 (= MF^{SF}+ MR^{SF})	Single family property disposition
31 (= MF^{MF}+MR^{MF})	Multifamily property disposition

[c] *Timing of the Default Process.* Mortgage Defaults are modeled as follows: defaulting loans enter foreclosure after a number of months (MQ, Months in Delinquency) and are foreclosed upon several months later. MF (Months in Foreclosure) is the total number of missed payments. Upon completion of foreclosure, the loan as such ceases to exist and the property becomes Real Estate Owned by the lender (REO). After several more months (MR, Months in REO), the property

is sold. Foreclosure expenses are paid and MI proceeds (and, for multifamily loans, loss sharing proceeds) are received when foreclosure is completed. REO expenses are paid, and sales proceeds and other Credit Enhancements are received, when the property is sold. These timing differences are not modeled explicitly in the cash flows, but their economic effect is taken into account by present-valuing the default-related cash flows to the month of Default.

[d] *Gross Loss Severity, Credit Enhancement, and Net Loss Severity.* The calculation of mortgage losses is divided into three parts. First, Gross Loss Severity is determined by expressing the principal loss plus unpaid interest plus expenses as a percentage of the loan UPB at the time of Default (section 3.6.3.6.2, Single Family Gross Loss Severity, and section 3.6.3.6.3, Multifamily Gross Loss Severity, of this appendix). Second, Credit Enhancements (CEs) are applied according to their terms to offset losses on loans that are covered by one or more CE arrangements (section 3.6.3.6.4, Mortgage Credit Enhancement, of this appendix). Finally, to account for the timing of these different cash flows, net losses are discounted back to the month in which the Default initially occurred (section 3.6.3.6.5, Single Family and Multifamily Net Loss Severity, of this appendix).

3.6.3.6.2 Single Family Gross Loss Severity

3.6.3.6.2.1 Single Family Gross Loss Severity Overview

The Loss Severity calculation adds the discounted present value of various costs and offsetting revenues associated with the foreclosure of single family properties, expressed as a fraction of UPB on the date of Default. The loss elements are:

[a] *Unpaid Principal Balance.* Because all Loss Severity elements are expressed as a fraction of Default date UPB, the outstanding loan balance is represented as 1.

[b] *Unpaid Interest.* Unpaid interest at the Mortgage Interest Rate is included in the MI claim amount. Unpaid interest at the Pass-Through Rate must be paid to MBS holders until the Defaulted loan is repurchased from the MBS pool.

[c] *Foreclosure Expenses and REO Expenses.* Foreclosure expenses are reimbursed by MI. REO expenses are incurred in connection with the maintenance and sale of a property after foreclosure is completed. Stress Test values for these quantities are derived from historical Enterprise REO experience.

[d] *Net Recovery Proceeds from REO sale (RP).* This amount is less than the sale price for ordinary properties as predicted by the HPI, because of the distressed nature of the sale.

3.6.3.6.2.2 Single Family Gross Loss Severity Inputs

The inputs in Table 3–42 are used to compute Gross Loss Severity for single family loans:

TABLE 3–42—LOAN GROUP INPUTS FOR GROSS LOSS SEVERITY

Variable	Description	Definition or Source
	Government Flag	RBC Report
MQ	Months Delinquent: time during which Enterprise pays delinquent loan interest to MBS holders	4 for sold loans 0 otherwise
MF	Months to Foreclosure: number of missed payments through completion of foreclosure	13 months
MR	Months from REO acquisition to REO disposition	7 months
F	Foreclosure Costs as a decimal fraction of Defaulted UPB	0.037
R	REO Expenses as a decimal fraction of Defaulted UPB	0.163
DR_m	Discount Rate in month m (decimal per annum)	6-month Enterprise Cost of Funds from section 3.3, Interest Rates
LTV_q	Current LTV in quarter q = 1...40	section 3.6.3.4.4, Single Family Default and Prepayment Outputs

TABLE 3–42—LOAN GROUP INPUTS FOR GROSS LOSS SEVERITY—Continued

Variable	Description	Definition or Source
MIR_m	Mortgage Interest Rate in month m (decimal per annum)	section 3.6.3.3.4, Mortgage Amortization Schedule Outputs
PTR_m	Pass-Through Rate applicable to payment due in month m (decimal per annum)	section 3.6.3.3.4, Mortgage Amortization Schedule Outputs
RR	Recovery Rate for Defaulted loans in the BLE, as a percent of predicted house price using HPI (decimal)	0.61

3.6.3.6.2.3 Single Family Gross Loss Severity Procedures

[a] Calculate single family gross Loss Severity using the following three steps:

1. Compute REO Proceeds in month m (RP_m) as a fraction of Defaulted UPB:

$$RP_m = \frac{RR}{LTV_q}$$

2. Compute MI Claim Amount on loans that Defaulted in month m (CLM_m^{MI}) as a fraction of Defaulted UPB:

$$CLM_m^{MI} = 1 + \left(\frac{MF}{12} \times MIR_m\right) + F$$

for all loans other than Government Loans

$$= 1 + \left(0.75 \times \frac{MF}{12} \times MIR_m\right) + (0.67 \times F) \text{ for Government Loans}$$

Where:

0.67 = FHA reimbursement rate on foreclosure-related expenses

0.75 = adjustment to reflect that FHA reimbursement on unpaid interest is at a government debenture rate, not MIR.

3. Compute Gross Loss Severity of loans that Defaulted in month m (GL_m) as a fraction of Defaulted UPB:

$$GLS_m = 1 + \left(\frac{MQ}{12} \times PTR_m\right) + F + R - RP_m \text{ but not} < 0$$

3.6.3.6.2.4 Single Family Gross Loss Severity Outputs

The single family Gross Loss Severity outputs in Table 3–43 are used in the Credit Enhancement calculations in section 3.6.3.6.4 of this appendix.

TABLE 3–43—SINGLE FAMILY GROSS LOSS SEVERITY OUTPUTS

Variable	Description
GLS_m	Gross Loss Severity for loans that defaulted in month m = 1...120
CLM_m^{MI}	MI claim on account of loans that defaulted in month m = 1...120
RP_m	REO Proceeds on account of loans that defaulted in month m = 1...120

3.6.3.6.3 Multifamily Gross Loss Severity

3.6.3.6.3.1 Multifamily Gross Loss Severity Overview

The multifamily Loss Severity calculation adds the discounted present value of various costs and offsetting revenues associated with the foreclosure of multifamily properties, expressed as a fraction of Defaulted UPB. The loss elements are:

[a] *Unpaid Principal Balance (UPB).* Because all Loss Severity elements are expressed as a fraction of Default date UPB, the outstanding loan balance is represented as 1.

[b] *Unpaid Interest.* Unpaid interest at the Net Yield Rate is included in the Loss Sharing Claim amount. Unpaid interest at the Pass-Through Rate must be paid to MBS holders until the defaulted loan is repurchased from the MBS pool.

[c] *Net REO Holding Costs (RHC).* Foreclosure costs, including attorneys fees and other liquidation expenses are incurred between the date of Default and the date of foreclosure completion (REO acquisition). Operating and capitalized expenses are incurred and rental and other income are received between REO acquisition and REO disposition. As a result, half of the Net REO Holding Costs (RHC) are expensed at REO acquisition and the remainder are expensed at REO disposition.

[d] *Net Proceeds from REO sale (RP).* The gross sale price of the REO less all costs associated with the disposition of the REO asset are discounted from the date of REO sale.

3.6.3.6.3.2 Multifamily Gross Loss Severity Inputs

The inputs in Table 3–44 are used to compute Gross Loss Severity for multifamily Loans:

TABLE 3–44—LOAN GROUP INPUTS FOR MULTIFAMILY GROSS LOSS SEVERITY

Variable	Description	Value or Source
	Government Flag	RBC Report
DR_m	Discount Rate in month m (decimal per annum)	6-month Enterprise Cost of Funds from Section 3.3, Interest Rates
MQ	Time during which delinquent loan interest is passed-through to MBS holders	4 for sold loans 0 otherwise
PTR_m	Pass Through Rate applicable to payment due in month m (decimal per annum)	section 3.6.3.3.4, Mortgage Amortization Schedule Outputs
NYR_m	Net Yield Rate applicable to payment due in month m (decimal per annum)	section 3.6.3.3.4, Mortgage Amortization Schedule Outputs
RHC	Net REO holding costs as a decimal fraction of Defaulted UPB	0.07
MF	Time from Default to completion of foreclosure (REO acquisition)	9 months
MR	Months from REO acquisition to REO disposition	15 months
RP	REO proceeds as a decimal fraction of Defaulted UPB	0.63

3.6.3.6.3.3 Multifamily Gross Loss Severity Procedures

[a] Calculate multifamily gross loss severity in the following two steps:

1. For Conventional Loans, compute the Loss Sharing Claim Amount (CLM_m^{LSA}) and Gross Loss (GLS_m) on loans that Defaulted in month m, as a fraction of Defaulted UPB:

$$CLM_m^{LSA} = 1.75 + \left(\frac{MF}{12} \times NYR_m\right) + RHC - RP$$

$$GLS_m = 1 + \frac{MQ}{12} \times PTR_m + RHC - RP$$

2. For FHA-insured (i.e., government) multifamily Loans, separate Gross Loss Severity and Credit Enhancement calculations are not necessary. Net Loss Severity is determined explicitly in section 3.6.3.6.5, Single Family and Multifamily Net Loss Severity, of this appendix).

3.6.3.6.3.4 Multifamily Gross Loss Severity Outputs

Multifamily Gross Loss Severity Outputs in Table 3–45 are used in the Credit Enhancements Calculations section 3.6.3.6.4, of this appendix.

TABLE 3–45—MULTIFAMILY GROSS LOSS SEVERITY OUTPUTS FOR USE IN CREDIT ENHANCEMENT CALCULATIONS

Variable	Description
GLS_m	Gross Loss Severity for loans that Defaulted in month m = 1...120
CLM_m^{LSA}	Loss Sharing Claim on account of loans that Defaulted in month m = 1...120

3.6.3.6.4 Mortgage Credit Enhancement

3.6.3.6.4.1 Mortgage Credit Enhancement Overview

[a] *Types of Mortgage Credit Enhancements.* Credit Enhancements (CE) reimburse losses on individual loans. The CE most often utilized by the Enterprises at the present time is primary Mortgage Insurance (MI) including both private and government MI or loan guarantees (e.g. FHA, VA), which pays claims up to a given limit on each loan. Most other types of CE do not limit the amount payable on each loan individually, but do limit the aggregate amount available under a given CE arrangement or Contract. These two types of CE must be computed differently. To denote this distinction, this appendix will refer to "Loan Limit" and "Aggregate Limit" CE types. Loan Limit CE includes Mortgage Insurance for single family loans and Loss-Sharing Arrangements (LSA) for multifamily loans. Aggregate Limit CE includes Pool Insurance, Spread Accounts, Letters of Credit, Cash or Collateral Accounts, and Subordination Agreements. For operational convenience in the Stress Test, the Aggregate Limit classification also includes Unlimited Recourse, which has neither loan-level nor aggregate-level coverage limits, and Modified Pool Insurance, Limited Recourse, Limited Indemnification and FHA risk-sharing, which may have both loan-level and aggregate-level coverage limits.

[b] *Loan Limit Credit Enhancements.* Loan Limit Credit Enhancements are applied to every covered loan individually, without regard to how much has been paid on any other covered loan. For example, an MI policy covers losses on an individual loan up to a specified limit. If every loan with MI were to Default, every claim would be payable regardless of the total outlay on the part of the MI provider. Loss Sharing Arrangements on multifamily loans operate the same way.

[c] *Aggregate Limit Credit Enhancements.* Aggregate Limit Credit Enhancements cover a group of loans on an aggregate basis. In most such arrangements, the coverage for any individual loan is unlimited, except that the total outlay by the provider cannot exceed a certain aggregate limit. Thus, the amount of Aggregate Limit coverage available to an individual loan depends, in practice, on how much has been paid on all previous claims under the specified Contract.

[d] *Credit Enhancement Counterparty Defaults.* CE payments from a rated counterparty are subject to Haircuts to simulate counterparty failures during the Stress Test. These Haircuts are based on the rating of the counterparty or guarantor immediately prior to the Stress Test, and are applied each month as described in section 3.5, Counterparty Defaults, of this appendix.

[e] *Stress Test Application of Credit Enhancement.* The Stress Test calculates mortgage cash flows for aggregated Loan Groups, within which individual loans are assumed to have identical characteristics, and therefore are not differentiated in the computations. However, a single Loan Group may include loans with Loan Limit CE and/or one or more types of Aggregate Limit CE. Additionally, this coverage may come from a rated provider or from cash or cash-equivalent collateral. Therefore, for computational purposes it is necessary to distinguish among the different possible CE combinations that each loan or subset of loans in a Loan Group may have. In the Stress Test, this is accomplished by creating Distinct Credit Enhancement Combinations (DCCs).

1. *Distinct Credit Enhancement Combinations.* When aggregating individual loans into Loan Groups for the RBC Report, the applicable CE arrangements will have been identified for each loan:

a. Loan Group (LG) Number
b. Initial UPB of individual loan
c. Rating of MI or LSA Counterparty

d. Loan-Limit Coverage Percentage for MI or LSA
e. Contract Number for Aggregate Limit CE, First Priority
f. Contract Number for Aggregate Limit CE, Second Priority
g. Contract Number for Aggregate Limit CE, Third Priority
h. Contract Number for Aggregate Limit CE, Fourth Priority

2. Individual loans for which all of the entries in step 1) of this section (except UPB and Loan-Limit Coverage Percent) are identical, are aggregated into a DCCs. For example, all loans in a given Loan Group with MI from a AAA-rated provider and no other CE would comprise one DCC whose balance is the aggregate of the included loans and whose MI Coverage Percent is the weighted average of that of the included loans. In each month, within each Loan Group, for each DCC, each applicable form of CE is applied in priority order to reduce Gross Loss Severity as much as possible to zero. The total CE payment for each DCC, as a percentage of Defaulted UPB is converted to a total CE payment for each Loan Group and then factored into the calculation of Net Loss Severity in section 3.6.3.6.5, Single Family and Multifamily Net Loss Severity, of this appendix.

3. *DCC First and Second Priority Available Aggregate CE Balance.* In the Stress Test, First and Second Priority Available Aggregate CE Balances are allocated to the DCCs that are parties to each Contract on a pro-rata basis. Third and Fourth Priority Aggregate Limit Contracts are not modeled because they are extremely rare. In each month of the Stress Test these CE Balances, adjusted by appropriate Haircuts, are reduced by the losses incurred by each DCC that is a party to each Contract. Spread Account deposits, if applicable, are included in the First and Second Priority DCC Available Aggregate CE Balances.

a. Spread Accounts may take one of two forms: Balance-Limited, or Deposit-Limited. A Balance-Limited Spread Account receives monthly spread payments based on the UPB of the covered loans until a required balance is achieved and maintained. Any amounts paid to cover losses must be replenished by future spread payments from the covered loans that are still performing. Thus, there is no known limit to the amount of spread deposits that may be made over the life of the covered loans. In contrast, for a Deposit-Limited Spread Account the limit is similar to a customary coverage limit. The total amount of spread deposits made into the account is limited to a maximum amount specified in the Contract.

b. In the Stress Test, the Available Contract Balance of a Spread Account is adjusted prior to the calculation of the DCC Available Balance as reported in the RBC Report. For each Spread Account contract, the Enterprises report the Remaining Limit Amount, which represents the maximum dollar amount of additional spread deposits that could be required under the Contract. For Deposit-Limited Spread Accounts, this amount is the maximum remaining dollar amount of spread deposits required under the Contract. For Balance-Limited Spread Accounts, this amount is defined as one-twelfth of the annualized spread rate times the UPB of the covered loans at the start of the Stress Test times the weighted average Remaining term to Maturity of those loans. However, the maximum amount of spread deposits that could be received will generally be higher than the amount reasonably expected to be received during the Stress Test, because the UPB of the covered loans, which is the basis for determining the amounts of future spread deposits, declines over the term of the Contract due to Amortization, Defaults, and Prepayments. Therefore, the Enterprises report an adjusted Available Contract Balance for both types of Spread Accounts before reporting the DCC Available Balance by adding the lesser of the Remaining Limit Amount or one-twelfth of the spread rate times the UPB of the covered loans at the start of the stress test times 60 months.

c. Modified Pool Insurance, Limited Recourse, Limited Indemnification and FHA risk-sharing contracts may have both loan-level and aggregate-level coverage limits. To account for this aspect of these types of Aggregate Limit CE, the Enterprises report a DCC Loan Level Coverage Limit Amount, which represents the share of each loss after deductibles (such as MI or First Priority Contract payments) covered by a given MPI Contract. (The Loan Level Coverage Limit Amount takes the value of one if the Contract is not of this type, representing that 100 percent of losses are covered by other types of Contracts).

d. In practice, Unlimited Recourse Contracts have neither loan-level nor aggregate-level coverage limits. However, the Enterprises report the Available Aggregate CE Balance of Unlimited Recourse Contracts as the summation of the Original UPB of all covered loans.

e. The Available Aggregate CE Balances of Collateral Account Contracts funded with anything other than Cash or Cash-equivalents are discounted by thirty percent to account for market risk in securities that are not cash equivalents.

f. Enterprise Loss Positions are treated as Aggregate Limit CE in terms of reducing remaining losses eligible to be covered by a next-priority Contract. However, since Enterprise Loss Positions are typically a deductible for other forms of supplementary coverage, payments from such accounts do not reduce loss severity.

[f] *Multiple Layers of Credit Enhancement.* For loans with more than one type of Credit Enhancement, MI or Loss Sharing is applied first, and then other types of CE (if available) are applied in priority order to the remaining losses. MI and Loss Sharing claims are payable regardless of whether (and to what extent) a loan is also covered by other forms of CE. MI is unique in that the MI payment is based on a percentage of a Claim Amount equal to the entire Defaulted UPB plus expenses, not the actual loss incurred upon liquidation. Therefore, an Enterprise can receive MI payments on a defaulted loan in excess of the actual realized loss on that loan. However, it is frequently the case that MI payments are insufficient to cover the entire loss amount. In such cases, one or more types of Aggregate Limit CE may be available to make up the deficiency. Unlike MI claims, however, the Claim Amounts for Loss Sharing and for all Aggregate Limit CE types do depend on the actual losses incurred; and unlike Loss Sharing and MI, Claim Amounts payable under other forms of CE are net of payments received on account of other forms of CE. When a single loan is covered by multiple forms of CE, the order in which they are to be applied (First Priority, Second Priority, etc.) must be specified. To avoid double-counting, a higher-numbered priority CE only covers losses that were not covered by a lower-numbered priority CE.

3.6.3.6.4.2 Mortgage Credit Enhancement Inputs

[a] For each Loan Group, the inputs in Table 3–46 are required:

TABLE 3–46—CE INPUTS FOR EACH LOAN GROUP

Variable	Description	Source
UPB_{ORIG}^{LG}	Origination UPB	RBC Report
UPB_0^{LG} and UPB_m^{LG}	Initial UPB and UPB in month m = 0,1...120	section 3.6.3.3.4, Mortgage Amortization Schedule Outputs
LTV_{ORIG}^{LG}	Original LTV	RBC Report
DEF_m^{LG} and $PERF_m^{LG}$	Defaulting and Performing Fractions of Initial Loan Group UPB in month m = 1...120	section 3.6.3.4.4, Single Family Default and Prepayment Outputs and section 3.6.3.5.4, Multifamily Default and Prepayment Outputs
$CLM_m^{MI,LG}$ $CLM_m^{LSA,LG}$	MI Claim Amount and LSA Claim Amount	section 3.6.3.6.2, Single Family Gross Loss Severity and section 3.6.3.6.3, Multifamily Gross Loss Severity
GLS_m^{LG}	Gross Loss Severity	section 3.6.3.6.2, Single Family Gross Loss Severity and section 3.6.3.6.3, Multifamily Gross Loss Severity

[b] For each DCC covering loans in the Loan Group, the inputs in Table 3–47 are required:

TABLE 3–47—INPUTS FOR EACH DISTINCT CE COMBINATION (DCC)

Variable	Description	Source
P^{DCC}	Percent of Initial Loan Group UPB represented by individual loan(s) in a DCC	RBC Report
$R^{MI,DCC}$ or $R^{LSA,DCC}$	Credit rating of Loan Limit CE (MI or LSA) Counterparty	RBC Report

TABLE 3–47—INPUTS FOR EACH DISTINCT CE COMBINATION (DCC)—Continued

Variable	Description	Source
$C^{MI,DCC}$ or $C^{LSA,DCC}$	Weighted Average Coverage Percentage for MI or LSA Coverage (weighted by Initial UPB)	RBC Report
$AB_0^{DCC,C1}$	DCC Available First Priority CE Balance immediately prior to start of the Stress Test	RBC Report
$AB_0^{DCC,C2}$	DCC Available Second Priority CE Balance immediately prior to start of the Stress Test	RBC Report
$R^{DCC,C1}$	DCC Credit Rating of First Priority CE Provider or Counterparty; or Cash/Cash Equivalent (which is not Haircutted)	RBC Report
$R^{DCC,C2}$	DCC Credit Rating of Second Priority CE Provider or Counterparty; or Cash/Cash Equivalent (which is not Haircutted)	RBC Report
$C^{DCC,C1}$	DCC Loan-Level Coverage Limit of First Priority Contract (If Subtype is MPI; otherwise = 1)	RBC Report
$C^{DCC,C2}$	DCC Loan-Limit Coverage Limit of Second Priority Contract (if Subtype is MPI; otherwise = 1)	RBC Report
$ExpMo^{DCC,C1}$	Month in the Stress Test (1...120 or after) in which the DCC First Priority Contract expires	RBC Report
$ExpMo^{DCC,C2}$	Month in the Stress Test (1...120 or after) in which the DCC Second Priority Contract expires	RBC Report
$ELPF^{DCC,C1}$	DCC Enterprise Loss Position Flag for First Priority Contract (Y or N)	RBC Report
$ELPF^{DCC,C2}$	DCC Enterprise Loss Position Flag for Second Priority Contract (Y or N)	RBC Report

[c] In the RBC Report, Aggregate Limit CE Subtypes are grouped as illustrated in Table 3–48.

TABLE 3–48—AGGREGATE LIMIT CE SUBTYPE GROUPING

Symbol	Subtype	Also Includes
REC	Unlimited Recourse	Unlimited Indemnification
PI	Pool Insurance	Pool Insurance
		Letter of Credit
		Subordination Arrangements
MPI	Modified Pool Insurance	Modified Pool Insurance
		Limited Recourse
		Limited Indemnification
		FHA Risk-sharing Agreements
CASH	Cash Account	Cash Account

TABLE 3–48—AGGREGATE LIMIT CE SUBTYPE GROUPING—Continued

Symbol	Subtype	Also Includes
COLL	Collateral Account	Collateral
ELP	Enterprise Loss Position	GSE Loss Position (ledger item)
SA	Spread Account	Spread Account

3.6.3.6.4.3 Mortgage Credit Enhancement Procedures

[a] For each month m of the Stress Test, for each Loan Group (LG), carry out the following six steps [a] 1–6 for each DCC.

NOTE: Process the Loan Groups and DCCs using the numerical order assigned to them in the RBC Report.

1. Determine Mortgage Insurance Payment (MI_m) for single family loans in the DCC, or Loss Sharing Payment (LSA_m) for multifamily loans in the DCC, as a percentage of Defaulted UPB, applying appropriate counterparty Haircuts from section 3.5., of this appendix:

$$MI_m^{DCC} = \left(1 - MIExp_m^{LG}\right) \times C^{MI,DCC} \times CLM_m^{MI,LG} \times \left[1 - \frac{m'}{120} \times MaxHct\left(R^{MI,DCC}\right)\right]$$

$$LSA_m^{DCC} = C^{LSA,DCC} \times CLM_m^{LSA,LG} \times \left[1 - \frac{m'}{120} \times MaxHct\left(R^{LSA,DCC}\right)\right]$$

Where:

m′ = m, except for counterparties rated below BBB, where m′ = 120

$$MIExp_m^{LG} = 1\ if \left(\left(LTV_{ORIG} \times \frac{UPB_m^{LG}}{UPB_{ORIG}^{LG}}\right) < 0.78\right) \text{ and the loan group comprises conventional loans}$$

$MIExp_m^{LG} = 0$ otherwise

0.78 (78%) = the LTV at which MI is cancelled if payments are current

2. Determine Remaining Loss in Dollars (RLD) after application of MI or LSA and prior to application of other Aggregate Limit CE:

$$RLD_m^{DCC,(MI-LSA)} = max\left[\left(GLS_m^{LG} - MI_m^{DCC}\right), 0\right] \times P^{DCC} \times UPB_{m-1}^{LG} \times DEF_m^{LG}$$

3. Determine the contractual CE Payment in Dollars under the First Priority Contract C1. Determine Payment after Haircut. Update Remaining Loss Dollars and DCC Available Balance.

a. Determine CE Payment as the minimum of the Remaining Loss Dollars after MI or LSA (if applicable) times the DCC Loan-Level Coverage Limit (=1 if not MPI Contract) or the previous month's ending DCC Available Balance:

$$PD_m^{DCC,C1} = min\left(RLD_m^{DCC,(MI-LSA)} \times C^{DCC,C1}, AB_{m-1}^{DCC,C1}\right)$$

b. Determine CE Payment in Dollars after application of Haircuts:

$$PD_m^{DCC,C1,H} = PD_m^{DCC,C1} \times \left[1 - \frac{m'}{120} \times MaxHct\left(R^{DCC,C1}\right)\right]$$

Where:

m′ = m, except for counterparties rated below BBB, where m′ = 120

c. Update DCC Remaining Loss Dollars and DCC Available Balance under the First Priority Contract C1:

$$RLD_m^{DCC,C1} = max\left(RLD_m^{DCC,(MI-LSA)} - PD_m^{DCC,C1,H}, 0\right)$$

$$AB_m^{DCC,C1} = max\left(\left[AB_{m-1}^{DCC,C1} - PD_m^{DCC,C1}\right] \times \left(1 - Exp_m^{DCC,C1}\right), 0\right)$$

Where:

Exp_m^C = 1 if the Contract has expired, i.e. if the calendar month corresponding to the mth month of the Stress Test is on or after the expiration month ($ExpMo^C$)

Exp_m^C = 0 otherwise

4. Determine the contractual CE Payment in Dollars under the Second Priority Contract C2. Determine Payment after Haircut. Update Remaining Loss Dollars and DCC Available Balance.

a. Determine CE Payment as the minimum of the Remaining Loss Dollars after C1 Payment (if applicable) times a DCC Loan-Level Coverage Limit (=1 if not MPI Contract) or the previous month's ending DCC Available Balance:

$$PD_m^{DCC,C2} = min\left(RLD_m^{DCC,C1} \times C^{DCC,C2}, AB_{m-1}^{DCC,C2}\right)$$

b. Determine CE Payment in Dollars after application of Haircuts:

$$PD_m^{DCC,C2,H} = PD_m^{DCC,C2} \times \left[1 - \frac{m'}{120} \times MaxHct\left(R^{DCC,C2}\right)\right]$$

Where:

m′ = m, except for counterparties rated below BBB, where m′ = 120

c. Update DCC Remaining Loss Dollars and DCC Available Balance under the Second Priority Contract C2:

$$RLD_{m}^{DCC,C2} = max\left(RLD_{m}^{DCC,C1} - PD_{m}^{DCC,C2,H}, 0\right)$$

$$AB_{m}^{DCC,C2} = max\left(\left[AB_{m-1}^{DCC,C2} - PD_{m}^{DCC,C2}\right] \times \left(1 - Exp_{m}^{DCC,C2}\right), 0\right)$$

Where:

Exp_m^C = 1 if the Contract has expired, i.e. if the calendar month corresponding to the mth month of the Stress Test is on or after the expiration month ($ExpMo^C$)

Exp_m^C = 0 otherwise

5. Convert Aggregate Limit First and Second Priority Contract receipts in Dollars for each DCC in month m to a percentage of DCC Defaulted UPB:

$$\text{If } DEF_m = 0, \text{ then } ALPD_m^{DCC} = 0$$

$$ALPD_{m}^{DCC} = \frac{\left(PD_{m}^{DCC,C1,H} \times ELPI^{DCC,C1}\right) + \left(PD_{m}^{DCC,C2,H} \times ELPI^{DCC,C2}\right)}{DEF_m \times UPB_{m-1}^{LG} \times P^{DCC}}$$

Where:

$ELPI^{DCC,C}$ = 0 if $ELPF^{DCC,C}$ = Y (Yes, indicating that Contract C is an Enterprise Loss Position)

$ELPI^{DCC,C}$ = 1 otherwise

6. Add the Loan Limit CE (MI and LSA) and Aggregate Limit CE (ALPD), each expressed as a share of DCC Defaulted UPB, separately for each DCC to increment the respective Loan Group totals:

$$MI_{m}^{LG} = MI_{m}^{LG} + \left(P^{DCC} \times MI_{m}^{DCC}\right) \text{ for single family Loans; or}$$

$$LSA_{m}^{LG} = LSA_{m}^{LG} + \left(P^{DCC} \times LSA_{m}^{DCC}\right) \text{ for multifamily Loans; and}$$

$$ALCE_{m}^{LG} = ALCE_{m}^{LG} + \left(P^{DCC} \times ALPD_{m}^{DCC}\right) \text{ for both single family and multifamily Loans}$$

3.6.3.6.4.4 Mortgage Credit Enhancement Outputs

[a] Mortgage Credit Enhancement Outputs are set forth in Table 3–49.

TABLE 3–49—SINGLE FAMILY AND MULTIFAMILY CREDIT ENHANCEMENT OUTPUTS

Variable	Description
MI_m	MI payments applied to reduce single family Gross Loss Severity in month m of the Stress Test (as a fraction of Defaulted UPB in month m)
LSA_m	LSA payments applied to reduce multifamily Gross Loss Severity in month m of the Street Test (as a fraction of Defaulted UPB in month m)
$ALCE_m$	Aggregate receipts from all forms of Aggregate Limit Limit Credit Enhancement applied to reduce single- and multifamily Gross Loss Severity in month m of the Stress Test (as a fraction of Defaulted UPB in month m)

[b] MI_m^{LG} or LSA_m^{LG} and $ALCE_m^{LG}$ for months m = 1...120 of the Stress Test are used in section 3.6.3.6.5, Single Family and Multifamily Net Loss Severity, of this appendix.

3.6.3.6.5 Single Family and Multifamily Net Loss Severity

3.6.3.6.5.1 Single Family and Multifamily Net Loss Severity Procedures

Combine inputs and outputs from Gross Loss Severity and Credit Enhancements (Table 3–42 through Table 3–49) in the following formulas for each Loan Group in month m:

[a] For Conventional single family Loan Groups:

$$MIExp_m^{LG} = 1 \; if \left(\left(LTV_{ORIG} \times \frac{UPB_m^{LG}}{UPB_{ORIG}^{LG}} \right) < 0.78 \right) \text{and the loan group comprises conventional loans}$$

$$MIExp_m^{LG} = 0 \text{ otherwise}$$

0.78 (78%) = the LTV at which MI is cancelled if payments are current

[b] For Government single family Loan Groups, complete the following three steps:

1. Compute a Loss Severity value for FHA-insured loans using the Conventional formula for all government loans. FHA reimbursement rates will be reflected in the value of MI_m, as computed in section 3.6.3.6.4.3, Mortgage Credit Enhancement Procedures, of this appendix.
2. Compute a Loss Severity value for VA-insured loans as follows for all government loans:

$$LS_m^{VA} = \max \left[\frac{1 + F + \left(\frac{MQ}{12} \times PTR_m \right) + (R - RP_m) - 0.30}{\left(1 + \frac{DR_m}{2}\right)^{\frac{MF}{6}}}, 0 \right]$$

Where:

0.30 is a fixed percentage representing the VA guarantee coverage percentage. (The VA coverage rate is a function of the initial loan size.)

3. Compute Net Loss Severity by combining FHA-insured and VA-insured Loss Severity values as follows:

$$LS_m^{SF,GVT} = \left(\frac{2}{3} \times LS_m^{SF} \right) + \left(\frac{1}{3} \times LS_m^{VA} \right)$$

[c] For multifamily Loan Groups other than FHA-Insured:

$$LS_m^{MF} = \frac{1 + \left(\frac{MQ}{12} \times PTR_m \right)}{\left(1 + \frac{DR_m}{2}\right)^{\frac{MQ}{6}}} + \frac{\frac{RHC}{2} - LSA_m}{\left(1 + \frac{DR_m}{2}\right)^{\frac{MF}{6}}} + \frac{\frac{RHC}{2} - RP - ALCE_m}{\left(1 + \frac{DR_m}{2}\right)^{\frac{MF+MR}{6}}}$$

[d] For FHA-Insured multifamily Loan Groups:

$$LS_m^{MF} = 0.03 \text{ (3 percent) for all months}$$

3.6.3.6.5.2 Single Family and Multifamily Net Loss Severity Outputs

Net Loss Severity outputs are set forth in Table 3–50:

TABLE 3–50—SINGLE FAMILY AND MULTIFAMILY LOSS SEVERITY OUTPUTS

Variable	Description
LS_m^{SF}	Loss Severity (as a fraction of Defaulted UPB) for single family loans in month m
LS_m^{MF}	Loss Severity (as a fraction of Defaulted UPB) for multifamily loans in month m

Single family and multifamily Loss Severities for months 1...120 of the Stress Test are used in section 3.6.3.7, Stress Test Whole Loan Cash Flows, of this appendix.

3.6.3.7 Stress Test Whole Loan Cash Flows

3.6.3.7.1 Stress Test Whole Loan Cash Flow Overview

This section combines the mortgage Amortization Schedules with Default, Prepayment and Net Loss Severity Rates to produce performance-adjusted cash flows for Enterprise Whole Loans in the Stress Test.

3.6.3.7.2 Stress Test Whole Loan Cash Flow Inputs

The inputs required to compute Stress Test Whole Loan Cash Flows for each Loan Group are listed in Table 3–51.

TABLE 3–51—INPUTS FOR FINAL CALCULATION OF STRESS TEST WHOLE LOAN CASH FLOWS

Variable	Description	Source
UPB_m	Aggregate Unpaid Principal Balance in month m = 0 ... RM	section 3.6.3.3.4, Mortgage Amortization Schedule Outputs
NYR_m	Net Yield Rate in month m = 1 ... RM	section 3.6.3.3.4, Mortgage Amortization Schedule Outputs
GF	Guarantee Fee rate (weighted average for Loan Group) (decimal per annum)	RBC Report
PTR_m	Pass-Through Rate in month m = 1 ... RM	section 3.6.3.3.4, Mortgage Amortization Schedule Outputs
SP_m	Aggregate Scheduled Principal (Amortization) in month m = 1 ... RM	section 3.6.3.3.4, Mortgage Amortization Schedule Outputs
PRE_m^{SF} PRE_m^{MF}	Prepaying Fraction of original Loan Group in month m = 1 ... RM	section 3.6.3.4.4, Single Family Default and Prepayment Outputs and, section 3.6.3.5.4, Multifamily Default and Prepayment Outputs
DEF_m^{SF} DEF_m^{MF}	Defaulting Fraction of original Loan Group in month m = 1 ... RM	section 3.6.3.4.4, Single Family Default and Prepayment Outputs and, section 3.6.3.5.4, Multifamily Default and Prepayment Outputs

TABLE 3–51—INPUTS FOR FINAL CALCULATION OF STRESS TEST WHOLE LOAN CASH FLOWS—Continued

Variable	Description	Source
$PERF_m^{SF}$ $PERF_m^{MF}$	Performing Fraction of original Loan Group in month m = 1 ... RM	section 3.6.3.4.4, Single Family Default and Prepayment Outputs and, section 3.6.3.5.4, Multifamily Default and Prepayment Outputs
FDS	Float Days for Scheduled Principal and Interest (weighted average for Loan Group)	RBC Report
FDP	Float Days for Prepaid Principal (weighted average for Loan Group)	RBC Report
FER_m	Float Earnings Rate in month m = 1 ... RM	1 week Fed Funds Rate; section 3.3, Interest Rates
LS_m^{SF}	Loss Severity Rate in month m = 1 ... RM	section 3.6.3.6.5.2, Single Family and Multifamily Net Loss Severity Outputs
FREP	Fraction Repurchased (weighted average for Loan Group) (decimal)	RBC Report

3.6.3.7.3 Stress Test Whole Loan Cash Flow Procedures

[a] Calculate Stress Test whole loan cash flows using the following nine steps:

1. Calculate Scheduled Principal Received (SPR) in month m:

$$SPR_m = max\left(SP_m, 0\right) \times \left(PERF_m + PRE_m\right)$$

NOTE: Scheduled Principal Received is zero, not negative, when amortization is negative.

2. Calculate Net Interest Received (NIR) in month m. Any interest shortfall due to Negative Amortization reduces Net Yield directly. *Note:* NIR includes loans that default in month m, because lost interest is included in Credit Losses in step 6) of this section. (*See* section 3.6.3.6, Calculation of Single Family and Multifamily Mortgage Losses, of this appendix.)

$$NIR_m = \left[\left(UPB_{m-1} \times \frac{NYR_m}{12}\right) + min\left(SP_m, 0\right)\right] \times PERF_{m-1}$$

3. Calculate Prepaid Principal Received (PPR) in month m:

$$PPR_m = UPB_m \times PRE_m$$

4. Calculate newly Defaulted Principal (DP) in month m:

$$DP_m = UPB_{m-1} \times DEF_m$$

5. Calculate Recovery Principal Received (RPR) on account of loans that Defaulted in month m:

$$RPR_m = UPB_{m-1} \times DEF_m \times \left(1 - LS_m\right)$$

6. Calculate Credit Losses (CL) on account of loans that Defaulted in month m:

$$CL_m = UPB_{m-1} \times DEF_m \times LS_m$$

In addition, if m = RM and $UPB_{RM} > 0$ then,

$$CL_{RM} = \left(UPB_{RM} \times PERF_{RM}\right) + \left(UPB_{RM-1} \times DEF_{RM} \times LS_{RM}\right),$$

and

$$PUPB_{RM} = 0$$

7. Calculate Performing Loan Group UPB in month m ($PUPB_m$), including $PUPB_0$.

NOTE: All loans are assumed to be performing in month 0; therefore $PUPB_0 = UPB_0$.

$$PUPB_m = UPB_m \times PERF_m$$

8. Calculate Total Principal Received (TPR) and Total Interest Received (TIR) in month m:

$$TPR_m = SPR_m + PPR_m + RPR_m$$

$$TIR_m = NIR_m$$

9. For Sold Loans, calculate the following cash flow components:

a. Guarantee Fee (GF) received in month m:

$$GF_m = UPB_{m-1} \times \frac{GFR}{12} \times (PERF_m + PRE_m)$$

b. Float Income (FI) received in month m

$$FI_m = \left(\left[\left(\left[(SPR_m + NIR_m - GF_m) \times \frac{FDS}{365}\right] + \left[PPR_m \times \frac{FDP}{365}\right]\right) \times FER_m\right] - PIS_m\right) \times (1 - FREP)$$

where: Prepayment Interest Shortfall (PIS) in month m is:

$$PIS_m = UPB_{m-1} \times PRE_m \times \frac{PTR_m}{12} \quad \text{if } FDP \geq 30$$

$$PIS_m = UPB_{m-1} \times PRE_m \times \frac{PTR_m}{24} \quad \text{if } 15 \leq FDP < 30$$

3.6.3.7.4 Stress Test Whole Loan Cash Flow Outputs

The Whole Loan Cash Flows in Table 3–52 are used to prepare pro forma balance sheets and income statements for each month of the Stress Period (*see* section 3.10 Operations, Taxes and Accounting, of this appendix). For Retained Loan groups, cash flows consist of Scheduled Principal, Prepaid Principal, Defaulted Principal, Credit Losses, and Interest. For Sold Loan groups, cash flow consists of Credit Losses, Guarantee Fees and Float Income. For Repurchased MBSs, cash flows are allocated according to the Fraction Repurchased. Table 3–52 covers all cases; for Retained Loans FREP = 1.0.

TABLE 3–52—OUTPUTS FOR WHOLE LOAN CASH FLOWS

Variable	Description
SPR_m	Scheduled Principal Received in month m = 1...RM
PPR_m	Prepaid Principal Received in month m = 1...RM
DP_m	Defaulted Principal in month m = 1...RM
CL_m	Credit Losses in month m = 1...RM
$PUPB_m$	Performing Loan Group UPB in month m = 0...RM
TPR_m	Total Principal Received in month m = 1...RM
TIR_m	Total Interest Received in month m = 1...RM
GF_m	Guarantee Fees received in month m = 1...RM
FI_m	Float Income received in month m = 1...RM

TABLE 3–53—ADDITIONAL OUTPUTS FOR REPURCHASED MBSS

Variable	Quantity	Description
$STPR_m$	FREP × (SPR_m + PPR_m+ DP_m)	Enterprise's portion of Total Principal Received in months m = 1...RM, reflecting its fractional ownership of the MBS

TABLE 3–53—ADDITIONAL OUTPUTS FOR REPURCHASED MBSS—Continued

Variable	Quantity	Description
$STIR_m$	FREP × (TIR_m − GF_m)	Enterprise's portion of Total Interest Received (at the Pass-Through Rate) in months m = 1...RM, reflecting its fractional ownership of the MBS
$SPUPB_m$	FREP × $PUPB_m$	Enterprise's portion of the Performing UPB of the repurchased MBS in months m = 0...RM, reflecting its fractional ownership of the MBS

3.6.3.8 Whole Loan Accounting Flows

3.6.3.8.1 Whole Loan Accounting Flows Overview

[a] For accounting purposes, cash flows are adjusted to reflect (1) the value over time of discounts, premiums and fees paid or received (Deferred Balances) when an asset was acquired; and (2) the fact that mortgage interest is paid in arrears, i.e. it is received in the month after it is earned. In the Stress Test calculations, payments are indexed by the month in which they are received. Therefore, interest received in month m was earned in month m−1. However, principal is accounted for in the month received.

[b] Deferred Balances are amortized over the remaining life of the asset. Therefore, these calculations go beyond the end of the Stress Test if the Remaining Maturity (RM) is greater than the 120 months of the Stress Test. The projection of cash flows beyond the end of the Stress Test is discussed in the individual sections where the cash flows are first calculated. In general, for interest rate indexes, monthly Prepayment rates and monthly Default rates, the value for m = 120 is used for all months 120 < m ≤ RM, but LS = 0 for m > 120.

3.6.3.8.2 Whole Loan Accounting Flows Inputs

The inputs in Table 3–54 are required to compute Accounting Flows:

TABLE 3–54—INPUTS FOR WHOLE LOAN ACCOUNTING FLOWS

Variable	Description	Source
RM	Remaining Term to Maturity in months	RBC Report
UPD_0	Sum of all unamortized discounts, premiums, fees, commissions, etc. for the loan group, such that the unamortized balance equals the book value minus the face value for the loan group at the start of the Stress Test, adjusted by the Unamortized Balance Scale Factor	RBC Report
NYR_0	Net Yield Rate at time zero	section 3.6.3.3.4, Mortgage Amortization Schedule Outputs
$PUPB_m$	Performing Loan Group UPB in months m = 0 ... RM	section 3.6.3.7.4, Stress Test Whole Loan Cash Flow Outputs
PTR_0	Pass-Through Rate at time zero	section 3.6.3.3.4, Mortgage Amortization Schedule Outputs
$SPUPB_m$	Security Performing UPB in months m = 0 ... RM	section 3.6.3.7.4, Stress Test Whole Loan Cash Flow Outputs

TABLE 3–54—INPUTS FOR WHOLE LOAN ACCOUNTING FLOWS—Continued

Variable	Description	Source
$SUPD_0$	The sum of all unamortized discounts, premiums, fees, commissions, etc. associated with the securities modeled using the Wtd Ave Percent Repurchased, such that the unamortized balance equals the book value minus the face value for the relevant securities at the start of the Stress Test, adjusted by the percent repurchased and the Security Unamortized Balance Scale Factor	RBC Report

3.6.3.8.3 Whole Loan Accounting Flows Procedures

3.6.3.8.3.1 Accounting for Retained and Sold Whole Loans

[a] Complete the following three steps to account for Retained and Sold loans:

1. Compute Allocated Interest in month m (AI^m) as follows:

$$AI_m = PUPB_{m-1} \times \frac{NYR_0}{12}$$

NOTE: Allocated Interest is used only to determine the allocation of Amortization Expense over time, not to generate actual cash flows)

2. Calculate the monthly Internal Rate of Return (IRR) that equates the adjusted cash flows (actual principal plus Allocated Interest) to the Initial Book Value (BV_0) of the Loan Group. A single IRR is used for all months m. Solve for IRR such that:

$$BV_0 = \sum_{m=1}^{RM} \frac{ACF_m}{(1+IRR)^m}$$

Where:

$$BV_0 = PUPB_0 + UPD_0$$

$$ACF_m = AI_m - PUPB_m + PUPB_{m-1}$$

3. Calculate the monthly Amortization Expense for each month m:

a. If $BV_0 < 0$, or if $12 \times IRR > 1.0$ (100%), or if

$$BV_0 > \sum_{m=1}^{RM} ACF_m$$

then the full amount of UPD_0 is realized in the first month ($AE_1 = -UPD_0$)

b. Otherwise:

$$AE_m = (BV_{m-1} \times IRR) - AI_m$$
$$\text{if } PUPB_m > 0$$

$$AE_m = -UPD_{m-1} \text{ if } PUPB_m = 0$$

$$UPD_m = UPD_{m-1} + AE_m$$

$$BV_m = PUPB_m + UPD_m$$

3.6.3.8.3.2 Additional Accounting for Repurchased MBSs

[a] Complete the following three steps to account for Repurchased MBSs:

1. Compute Security Allocated Interest in month m (SAI_m) as follows:

$$SAI_m = SPUPB_{m-1} \times \frac{PTR_0}{12}$$

Note: Security Allocated Interest is used only to determine the allocation of Security Amortization Expense over time, not to generate actual cash flows.

2. Calculate the monthly Internal Rate of Return (IRR) that equates the adjusted cash flows (actual principal plus Allocated Interest) to the Initial Book Value (SBV_0) of the Loan Group. A single IRR is used for all months m. Solve for IRR such that:

$$SBV_0 = \sum_{m=1}^{RM} \frac{SACF_m}{(1+IRR)^m}$$

Where:

$SBV_0 = SPUPB_0 + SUPD_0$

$SACF_m = SAI_m - SPUPB_m + SPUPB_{m-1}$

3. Calculate the monthly Security Amortization Expense for each month m:

a. If $SBV_0 < 0$, or if $12 \times IRR > 1.0$ (100%), or if

$$SBV_0 > \sum_{m=1}^{RM} SACF_m$$

then the full amount of $SUPD_0$ is realized in the first month ($SAE_1 = -SUPD_0$).

b. Otherwise:

$$SAE_m = (SBV_{m-1} \times IRR) - SAI_m \quad \text{if } SPUPB_m > 0$$

$$SAE_m = -SUPD_{m-1} \text{ if } SPUPB_m = 0$$

$$SUPD_m = SUPD_{m-1} + SAE_m$$

$$SBV_m = SPUPB_m + SUPD_m$$

3.6.3.8.4 Whole Loan Accounting Flows Outputs

Whole loan accounting flows outputs are set forth in Table 3–55. Amortization Expense for months m = 1...RM are used in section 3.10, Operations, Taxes, and Accounting, of this appendix.

TABLE 3–55—OUTPUTS FOR WHOLE LOAN ACCOUNTING FLOWS

Variable	Description
AE_m	Amortization Expense for months m = 1...RM
SAE_m	Security Amortization Expense for months m = 1...RM

3.6.4 Final Whole Loan Cash Flow Outputs

The final outputs for section 3.6, Whole Loan Cash Flows, of this appendix are as specified in Table 3–52, and Table 3–55.

3.7 Mortgage-Related Securities Cash Flows

3.7.1 Mortgage-Related Securities Overview

[a] Mortgage-Related Securities (MRSs) include Single Class MBSs, Multi-class MBSs (REMICs or Collateralized Mortgage Obligations (CMOs)), Mortgage Revenue Bonds (MRBs), and Derivative Mortgage Securities such as Interest-Only and Principal-Only Stripped MBSs. MBSs and Derivative Mortgage Securities are issued by the Enterprises, Ginnie Mae and private issuers. MRBs are issued by State and local governments or their instrumentalities. For computational purposes, certain Asset-Backed Securities (ABS) backed by mortgages (Mortgage ABSs backed by manufactured housing loans, second mortgages or home equity loans) are treated as REMICs in the Stress Test.

[b] Cash flows from Single Class MBSs represent the pass-through of all principal and interest payments, net of servicing and guarantee fees, on the underlying pools of mortgages. Cash flows from Multi-Class MBSs and Derivative Mortgage Securities represent a specified portion of the cash flows produced by an underlying pool of mortgages and/or Mortgage-Related Securities, determined according to rules set forth in offering documents for the securities. MRBs may have specific maturity schedules and call provisions, whereas MBSs have only expected maturities and, in most cases, no issuer call provision (other than "cleanup calls" if the pool balance becomes quite small). However, the timing of principal payments for MRBs is still closely related to that of their underlying mortgage collateral. The Stress Test treats most MRBs in a manner similar to single class MBSs. Finally, a small number of Enterprise and private label REMIC securities for which modeling information is not readily available and which are not modeled by a commercial information service (referred to as "miscellaneous MRS") are treated separately.

[c] In addition to reflecting the defaults of mortgage borrowers during the Stress Period, the Stress Test considers the possibility of issuer Default on Mortgage-Related Securities. Credit impairments throughout the Stress Period are based on the rating of these securities, and are modeled by reducing contractual interest payments and "writing down" principal. No Credit Losses are assumed for the Enterprise's own securities and Ginnie Mae securities (*see* section 3.5.3, Counterparty Defaults Procedures, of this appendix).

[d] The calculation of cash flows for Mortgage-Related Securities requires information from the Enterprises identifying their holdings, publicly available information characterizing the securities, and information on the interest rate, mortgage performance and credit rating (for rated securities).

[e] Cash and accounting flows—monthly principal and interest payments and amortization expense—are produced for each month of the Stress Period for each security. (Principal- and interest-only securities pay principal or interest respectively.) These cash flows are input to the Operations, Taxes, and Accounting component of the Stress Test.

3.7.2 Mortgage-Related Securities Inputs

3.7.2.1 Inputs Specifying Individual Securities

3.7.2.1.1 Single Class MBSs

The information in Table 3–56 is required for single class MBSs held by an Enterprise at the start of the Stress Test. This information identifies the Enterprise's holdings and describes the MBS and the underlying mortgage loans.

TABLE 3–56—RBC REPORT INPUTS FOR SINGLE CLASS MBS CASH FLOWS

Variable	Description
Pool Number	A unique number identifying each mortgage pool
CUSIP Number	A unique number assigned to publicly traded securities by the Committee on Uniform Securities Identification Procedures
Issuer	Issuer of the mortgage pool
Original UPB Amount	Original pool balance multiplied by the Enterprise's percentage ownership
Current UPB Amount	Initial Pool balance (at the start of the Stress Test), multiplied by the Enterprise's percentage ownership
Product Code	Mortgage product type for the pool
Security Rate Index	If the rate on the security adjusts over time, the index that the adjustment is based on
Unamortized Balance	The sum of all unamortized discounts, premiums, fees, commissions, etc., such that the unamortized balance equals book value minus face value, adjusted by the Unamortized Balance Scale Factor
Wt Avg Original Amortization Term	Original amortization term of the underlying loans, in months (weighted average for underlying loans)
Wt Avg Remaining Term of Maturity	Remaining Maturity of the underlying loans at the start of the Stress Test (weighted average for underlying loans)
Wt Avg Age	Age of the underlying loans at the start of the Stress Test (weighted average for underlying loans)
Wt Avg Current Mortgage Interest rate	Mortgage Interest Rate of the underlying loans at the start of the Stress Test (weighted average for underlying loans)
Wt Avg Pass-Through Rate	Pass-Through Rate of the underlying loans at the start of the Stress Test (weighted average for underlying loans)
Wtg Avg Original Mortgage Interest Rate	The current UPB weighted average Mortgage Interest Rate in effect at Origination for the loans in the pool
Security Rating	The most current rating issued by any Nationally Recognized Statistical Rating Organization (NRSRO) for this security, as of the reporting date. In the case of a "split" rating, the lowest rating should be given
Wt Avg Gross Margin	Gross margin for the underlying loans (ARM MBS only) (weighted average for underlying loans)
Wt Avg Net Margin	Net margin (used to determine the security rate for ARM MBS) (weighted average for underlying loans)
Wt Avg Rate Reset Period	Rate reset period in months (ARM MBS only) (weighted average for underlying loans)
Wt Avg Rate Reset Limit	Rate reset limit up/down (ARM MBS only) (weighted average for underlying loans)
Wt Avg Life Interest Rate Ceiling	Maximum rate (lifetime cap) (ARM MBS only) (weighted average for underlying loans)
Wt Avg Life Interest Rate Floor	Minimum rate (lifetime floor) (ARM MBS only) (weighted average for underlying loans)

TABLE 3–56—RBC REPORT INPUTS FOR SINGLE CLASS MBS CASH FLOWS—Continued

Variable	Description
Wt Avg Payment Reset Period	Payment reset period in months (ARM MBS only) (weighted average for underlying loans)
Wt Avg Payment Reset Limit	Payment reset limit up/down (ARM MBS only) (weighted average for underlying loans)
Wt Avg Lookback Period	The number of months to look back from the interest rate change date to find the index value that will be used to determine the next interest rate (ARM MBS only) (weighted average for underlying loans)
Wt Avg Negative Amortization Cap	The maximum amount to which the balance can increase before the payment is recast to a fully amortizing amount. It is expressed as a fraction of the original UPB. (ARM MBS only) (weighted average for underlying loans)
Wt Avg Initial Interest Rate Period	Number of months between the loan origination date and the first rate adjustment date (ARM MBS only) (weighted average for underlying loans)
Wt Avg Unlimited Payment Reset Period	Number of months between unlimited payment resets, *i.e.*, not limited by payment caps, starting with Origination date (ARM MBS only) (weighted average for underlying loans)
Notional Flag	Indicates that amounts reported in Original UPB Amount and Current UPB Amount are notional
UPB Scale Factor	Factor applied to the current UPB that offsets any timing adjustments between the security level data and the Enterprise's published financials
Whole Loan Modeling Flag	Indicates that the Current UPB Amount and Unamortized Balance associated with this Repurchased MBS are included in the Wtg Avg Percent Repurchased and Security Unamortized Balance fields
FAS 115 Classification	The financial instrument's classification according to FAS 115
$HPGR_K$	Vector of House Price Growth Rates for quarters q=1...40 of the Stress Period

3.7.2.1.2 Multi-Class MBSs and Derivative Mortgage Securities

[a] The information in Table 3–57 is required for Multi-Class MBSs and Derivative Mortgage Securities held by an Enterprise at the start of the Stress Test. This information identifies the MBS and an Enterprise's holdings.

TABLE 3–57—RBC REPORT INPUTS FOR MULTI-CLASS AND DERIVATIVE MBS CASH FLOWS

Variable	Description
CUSIP Number	A unique number assigned to publicly traded securities by the Committee on Uniform Securities Identification Procedures
Issuer	Issuer of the security: FNMA, FHLMC, GNMA or other
Original Security Balance	Original principal balance of the security (notional amount for Interest-Only securities) at the time of issuance, multiplied by the Enterprise's percentage ownership
Current Security Balance	Initial principal balance, or notional amount, at the start of the Stress Period multiplied by the Enterprise's percentage ownership
Current Security Percentage Owned	The percentage of a security's total current balance owned by the Enterprise

TABLE 3–57—RBC REPORT INPUTS FOR MULTI-CLASS AND DERIVATIVE MBS CASH FLOWS—Continued

Variable	Description
Unamortized Balance	The sum of all unamortized discounts, premiums, fees, commissions, etc., such that the unamortized balance equals book value minus face value, adjusted by the Unamortized Balance Scale Factor.

[b] The Stress Test requires sufficient information about the cash flow allocation rules among the different classes of a Multi-Class MBS to determine the cash flows for the individual class(es) owned by an Enterprise, including descriptions of the component classes of the security, the underlying collateral, and the rules directing cash flows to the component classes. This information is obtained from offering documents or securities data services. In the Stress Test, this information is used either as an input to a commercial modeling service or, for securities that are not so modeled, to derive an approximate modeling treatment as described more fully in this section.

[c] If a Derivative Mortgage Security is itself backed by one or more underlying securities, sufficient information is required for each underlying security as described in the preceding paragraph.

3.7.2.1.3 Mortgage Revenue Bonds and Miscellaneous MRSs

[a] The Stress Test requires two types of information for Mortgage Revenue Bonds and miscellaneous MRS held by an Enterprise at the start of the Stress Test: information identifying the Enterprise's holdings and the contractual terms of the securities. The inputs required for these instruments are set forth in Table 3–58.

TABLE 3–58—RBC REPORT INPUTS FOR MRBS AND DERIVATIVE MBS CASH FLOWS

Variable	Description
CUSIP Number	A unique number assigned to publicly traded securities by the Committee on Uniform Securities Identification Procedures
Original Security Balance	Original principal balance, multiplied by the Enterprise's percentage ownership
Current Security Balance	Initial principal balance (at start of Stress Period), multiplied by the Enterprise's percentage ownership
Unamortized Balance	The sum of all unamortized discounts, premiums, fees, commissions, etc., such that the unamortized balance equals book value minus face value, adjusted by the Unamortized Balance Scale Factor
Issue Date	The Issue Date of the security
Maturity Date	The stated Maturity Date of the security
Security Interest Rate	The rate at which the security earns interest, as of the reporting date
Principal Payment Window Starting Date, Down-Rate Scenario	The month in the Stress Test that principal payment is expected to start for the security under the statutory "down" interest rate scenario, according to Enterprise projections
Principal Payment Window Ending Date, Down-Rate Scenario	The month in the Stress Test that principal payment is expected to end for the security under the statutory "down" interest rate scenario, according to Enterprise projections
Principal Payment Window Starting Date, Up-Rate Scenario	The month in the Stress Test that principal payment is expected to start for the security under the statutory "up" interest rate scenario, according to Enterprise projections
Principal Payment Window Ending Date, Up-Rate Scenario	The month in the Stress Test that principal payment is expected to end for the security under the statutory "up" interest rate scenario, according to Enterprise projections

TABLE 3–58—RBC REPORT INPUTS FOR MRBS AND DERIVATIVE MBS CASH FLOWS—Continued

Variable	Description
Security Rating	The most current rating issued by any Nationally Recognized Statistical Rating Organization (NRSRO) for this security, as of the reporting date. In the case of a "split" rating, the lowest rating should be given.
Security Rate Index	If the rate on the security adjusts over time, the index on which the adjustment is based
Security Rate Index Coefficient	If the rate on the security adjusts over time, the coefficient is the number used to multiply by the value of the index
Security Rate Index Spread	If the rate on the security adjusts over time, the spread is added to the value of the index multiplied by the coefficient to determine the new rate
Security Rate Adjustment Frequency	The number of months between rate adjustments
Security Interest Rate Ceiling	The maximum rate (lifetime cap) on the security
Security Interest Rate Floor	The minimum rate (lifetime floor) on the security

[b] The Payment Window Starting and Ending Dates are projected by the Enterprise on the basis of prospectus information or simulations from a dealer in the securities or other qualified source, such as the structured finance division of an accounting firm, for the two statutory scenarios.

3.7.2.2 Interest Rate Inputs

Interest rates projected for each month of the Stress Period are used to calculate principal amortization and interest payments for ARM MBSs and MRBs, and for Derivative Mortgage Securities with indexed coupon rates. This information is produced in section 3.3, Interest Rates, of this appendix.

3.7.2.3 Mortgage Performance Inputs

Default and Prepayment rates for the loans underlying a single- or multiclass MBS are computed according to the characteristics of the loans as specified in this section 3.7.2, Mortgage-Related Securities Inputs. LTV and Census Region are not uniquely specified for the loans underlying a given security; instead, the Prepayment and Default rates are averaged over all LTV categories, weighted according to the distribution of LTVs given in Table 3–59. (This weighting applies to Time Zero, i.e., the start of the Stress Test; the weightings will change over time as individual LTV groups pay down at different rates. *See* section 3.7.3, Mortgage-Related Securities Procedures, of this appendix.) Instead of Census Division, the national average HPI is used for all calculations in this section.

TABLE 3–59—AGGREGATE ENTERPRISE AMORTIZED ORIGINAL LTV ($AOLTV_0$) DISTRIBUTION [1]

Original LTV	UPB Distribution	Wt Avg AOLTV for Range
00<LTV<=60		
60<LTV<=70		
70<LTV<=75		
75<LTV<=80		
80<LTV<=90		
90<LTV<=95		
95<LTV<=100		
100<LTV		

[1] SOURCE: RBC Report, combined Enterprises single-family sold loan portfolio. Table 3–59 is updated as necessary with combined Enterprises single-family sold loan group data from the RBC Report in accordance with OFHEO guideline #404. The contents of the table appear at *http://www.OFHEO.gov.*

NOTE: Amortized Original LTV (also known as the "current-loan-to-original-value" ratio) is the Original LTV adjusted for the change in UPB but not for changes in property value.

3.7.2.4 Third-Party Credit Inputs

For securities not issued by the Enterprise or Ginnie Mae, issuer Default risk is reflected by haircutting the instrument cash flows based on the rating of the security, as described in section 3.5, Counterparty Defaults, of this appendix.

3.7.3 Mortgage-Related Securities Procedures

The following sections describe the calculations for (1) single class MBSs, (2) Multi-Class MBSs and derivative mortgage securities, and (3) MRBs and miscellaneous MRS.

3.7.3.1 Single Class MBSs

[a] The calculation of cash flows for single class MBSs is based on the procedures outlined earlier in section 3.6, Whole Loan Cash Flows, of this appendix. The collateral (i.e., the mortgage pool) underlying each MBS is treated as one single family Loan Group with characteristics equal to the weighted average characteristics of the underlying loans.

[b] For each MBS, compute the scheduled cash flows specified in Table 3–33, as directed in section 3.6.3.3.3, Mortgage Amortization Schedule Procedures of this appendix, with the following exceptions and clarifications:

1. The Net Yield Rate (NYR) is not used in the MBS calculation. Instead, the Pass-Through Rate (for Fixed-Rate MBSs) and INDEX + Net Margin (for Adjustable-Rate MBSs) are used.
2. PMT is not a direct input for MBSs. (That is, it is not specified in the RBC Report.) Instead, compute PMT from UPB, MIR and remaining amortizing term $AT-A_0$, using the standard mortgage payment formula (and update it as appropriate for ARMs, as described in the Whole Loan calculation).
3. For ARM MBS, interest rate and monthly payment adjustments for the underlying loans are calculated in the same manner as they are for ARM Loan Groups.
4. MBSs backed by Biweekly mortgages, GPMs, TPMs, GEMs, and Step mortgages are mapped into mortgage types as described in section 3.6, Whole Loan Cash Flows, of this appendix.

[c] Use the Loan Group characteristics to generate Default and Prepayment rates as described in section 3.6.3.4.3, Single Family Default and Prepayment Procedures, of this appendix. For the following explanatory variables that are not specified for MBSs, proceed as follows:

1. For fixed rate Ginnie Mae certificates and the small number of multifamily MBS held by the Enterprises, use the model coefficients for Government Loans. For loans underlying Ginnie Mae ARM certificates, use the conventional ARM model coefficients.
2. Set Investor Fraction (IF) = 7.56%
3. Set Relative Loan Size (RLS) = 1.0. For Ginnie Mae certificates, use RLS = 0.75.
4. For LTV_{ORIG} of the underlying loans: Divide the MBS's single weighted average Loan Group into several otherwise identical Loan Groups ("LTV subgroups"), one for each Original LTV range specified in Table 3–59. UPB_0 for each of these LTV subgroups is the specified percentage of the aggregate UPB_0. $AOLTV_0$ for each subgroup is also specified in Table 3–59. For Ginnie Mae certificates, use only the 95 < LTV ≤ 100 LTV category and its associated weighted average LTV.
5. For each LTV subgroup, compute LTV_0 as follows:

$$LTV_0 = AOLTV_0 \times \left(\frac{HPI_{ORIG}}{HPI_{AQ'_0}} \right)^{\frac{AQ_0}{AQ'_0}}$$

Where:

HPI = the national average HPI figures in Table 3–60 (updated as necessary from subsequent releases of the OFHEO HPI).

A_0 = weighted average age in months of the underlying loans immediately prior to the start of the Stress Test.

AQ_0 = weighted average age in quarters of the underlying loans immediately prior to the start of the Stress Test. $AQ_0 = int(A_0/3)$.

AQ'_0 = AQ_0 minus the number of whole quarters between the most recently available HPI at the start of the Stress Test and time zero.

If $AQ'_0 \leq 0$, then $LTV_0 = AOLTV_0$.

TABLE 3–60—HISTORICAL NATIONAL AVERAGE HPI [1]

Quarter [2]	HPI	Quarter	HPI	Quarter	HPI
1975Q1	62.45	1983Q4	116.63	1992Q3	177.94
1975Q2	63.50	1984Q1	118.31	1992Q4	178.71
1975Q3	62.85	1984Q2	120.40	1993Q1	178.48
1975Q4	63.92	1984Q3	121.68	1993Q2	179.89
1976Q1	65.45	1984Q4	122.94	1993Q3	180.98
1976Q2	66.73	1985Q1	124.81	1993Q4	182.38

TABLE 3–60—HISTORICAL NATIONAL AVERAGE HPI [1]—Continued

Quarter [2]	HPI	Quarter	HPI	Quarter	HPI
1976Q3	67.73	1985Q2	126.91	1994Q1	183.35
1976Q4	68.75	1985Q3	129.38	1994Q2	183.95
1977Q1	70.70	1985Q4	131.20	1994Q3	184.43
1977Q2	73.34	1986Q1	133.77	1994Q4	184.08
1977Q3	75.35	1986Q2	136.72	1995Q1	184.85
1977Q4	77.71	1986Q3	139.37	1995Q2	187.98
1978Q1	79.96	1986Q4	141.99	1995Q3	190.81
1978Q2	82.75	1987Q1	145.07	1995Q4	192.42
1978Q3	85.39	1987Q2	147.88	1996Q1	194.80
1978Q4	87.88	1987Q3	150.21	1996Q2	195.00
1979Q1	91.65	1987Q4	151.57	1996Q3	195.78
1979Q2	94.26	1988Q1	154.26	1996Q4	197.48
1979Q3	96.24	1988Q2	157.60	1997Q1	199.39
1979Q4	98.20	1988Q3	159.25	1997Q2	201.00
1980Q1	100.00	1988Q4	160.96	1997Q3	203.94
1980Q2	100.86	1989Q1	163.10	1997Q4	206.97
1980Q3	104.27	1989Q2	165.33	1998Q1	210.09
1980Q4	104.90	1989Q3	169.09	1998Q2	212.37
1981Q1	105.69	1989Q4	170.74	1998Q3	215.53
1981Q2	107.85	1990Q1	171.42	1998Q4	218.09
1981Q3	109.21	1990Q2	171.31	1999Q1	220.80
1981Q4	109.38	1990Q3	171.85	1999Q2	224.32
1982Q1	111.02	1990Q4	171.03	1999Q3	228.46
1982Q2	111.45	1991Q1	172.41	1999Q4	232.41
1982Q3	110.91	1991Q2	173.14	2000Q1	235.91
1982Q4	111.96	1991Q3	173.14	2000Q2	240.81
1983Q1	114.12	1991Q4	175.46	2000Q3	245.15
1983Q2	115.33	1992Q1	176.62		
1983Q3	116.15	1992Q2	176.26		

[1] These numbers are updated as necessary from subsequent releases of the HPI after 2000Q3.
[2] *Note:* If the underlying loans were originated before 1975, use the HPI from 1975Q1 as HPI_{ORIG}.

6. For each quarter q of the Stress Test, use UPB_q and the house price growth rates from the Benchmark regional time period:

$$LTV_q = LTV_0 \times \frac{\left(\frac{UPB_{m=3q-3}}{UPB_0}\right)}{exp\sum_{k=1}^{q} HPGR_K}$$

7. Generate Default, Prepayment and Performance vectors PRE_m, DEF_m and $PERF_m$ for each LTV subgroup. When LTV_{ORIG} is used as a categorical variable, use the corresponding range defined for each LTV subgroup in Table 3–59. For LTV subgroup 95 < LTV < 100, use 90 < LTV_{ORIG} in Table 3–35.

[d] For each LTV subgroup, do not compute any Loss Severity or Credit Enhancement amounts. MBS investors receive the full UPB of defaulted loans.

[e] Compute Total Principal Received (TPR), Total Interest Received (TIR), and Amortization Expense (AE) for each LTV subgroup as directed in section 3.6.3.7.3, Stress Test Whole Loan Cash Flow Procedures and section 3.6.3.8.3, Whole Loan Accounting Flows Procedures, of this appendix, with the following exception:

1. For Net Interest Received (NIR), do not use the Net Yield Rate (NYR_m). Instead, use the Pass-Through Rate (PTR_m) for Fixed Rate Loans, and $INDEX_{m-1-LB}$ + Wt Avg Net Margin, subject to rate resets as described in section 3.6.3.3.3, Mortgage Amortization Schedule Procedures, [a]1.b.3) of this appendix, for ARMs.

2. Calculate Recovery Principal Received using a Loss Severity rate of zero (LS = 0).

[f] Sum over the LTV subgroups to obtain the original MBS's TPR, TIR and AE for m = 1...RM.

[g] Apply counterparty Haircuts in each month m as follows:

1. Compute:

$$HctFac_m = \frac{m'}{120} \times MaxHct\,(R)$$

Where:

m' = m, except for MBS credit rating below BBB where m'=120

R = MBS credit rating

2. Compute:

$$HctAmt_m = (TPR_m + TIR_m) \times HctFac_m$$

[h] The resulting values, for each MBS, of TPR, TIR, AE, and HctAmt for months m = 1...RM are used in the section 3.10, Operations, Taxes, and Accounting, of this appendix.

3.7.3.2 REMICs and Strips

[a] Cash flows for REMICs and Strips are generated according to standard securities industry procedures, as follows:

1. From the CUSIP number of the security, identify the characteristics of the underlying collateral. This is facilitated by using a securities data service.
2. Calculate the cash flows for the underlying collateral in the manner described for whole loans and MBS, based on Stress Test interest, Default, and Prepayment rates appropriate for the collateral.
3. Calculate cash flows for the Multiclass MBS using the allocation rules specified in the offering materials.
4. Determine the cash flows attributable to the specific securities held by an Enterprise, applying the Enterprise's ownership percentage.
5. For securities not issued by the Enterprise or Ginnie Mae, reduce cash flows by applying the Haircuts specified in section 3.5, Counterparty Defaults, of this appendix, as appropriate.

[b] If a commercial information service is used for steps [a] 1 through 4 of this section, the information service may model mortgage product types beyond those described for Whole Loans in section 3.6, Whole Loan Cash Flows, and ARM indexes in addition to those listed in section 3.3, Interest Rates, of this appendix. In such cases, the cash flows used are generated from the actual data used by the information service for the underlying security.

3.7.3.3 Mortgage Revenue Bonds and Miscellaneous MRS

[a] Cash flows for mortgage revenue bonds and miscellaneous MRS are computed as follows:

1. From the start of the Stress Test until the first principal payment date at the start of the Principal Payment Window, the security pays coupon interest at the Security Interest Rate, adjusted as necessary according to the Security Rate Index and Adjustment information in Table 3–58, but pays no principal.
2. During the Principal Payment Window, the security pays principal and interest equal to the aggregate cash flow from a level pay mortgage whose term is equal to the length of the Principal Payment Window and whose interest rate is the Security Interest Rate. If the Security Interest Rate is zero (as in the case of zero-coupon MRBs), then the security pays principal only in level monthly payment amounts equal to the Current Security Balance divided by the length of the Principal Payment Window.
3. For securities not issued by the Enterprise or Ginnie Mae, reduce cash flows by applying the Haircuts specified in section 3.5, Counterparty Defaults, of this appendix, as appropriate.

3.7.3.4 Accounting

Deferred balances are amortized as described in section 3.6.3.8, Whole Loan Accounting Flows, of this appendix, using the Pass-Through Rate (or Security Interest Rate for MRBs) rather than the Net Yield Rate. For principal-only strips and zero-coupon MRBs, assume Allocated Interest is zero. If the conditions in section 3.6.3.8.3.1[a]3.a. of this appendix, apply, do not realize the full amount in the first month. Instead, amortize the deferred balances using a straight line method over a period from the start of the Stress Test through the latest month with a non-zero cash flow.

3.7.4 Mortgage-Related Securities Outputs

[a] The outputs for MBS and MRS Cash Flows, found in Table 3–61, are analogous to those specified for Whole Loans in section 3.6.4, Final Whole Loan Cash Flow Outputs, of this appendix, which are produced for each security for each month.

TABLE 3–61—OUTPUTS FOR MORTGAGE-RELATED SECURITIES

Variable	Description
TPR_m	Total Principal Received in month m = 1...RM
TIR_m	Total Interest Received in month m = 1...RM
$HctAmt_m$	Total Haircut amount in month m = 1...RM
AE_m	Amortization Expense for months m = 1...RM

[b] These outputs are used as inputs to the Operations, Taxes, and Accounting component of the Stress Test, which prepares pro forma financial statements. *See* section 3.10, Operations, Taxes, and Accounting, of this appendix.

3.8 Nonmortgage Instrument Cash Flows

3.8.1 Nonmortgage Instrument Overview

[a] The Nonmortgage Instrument Cash Flows component of the Stress Test produces instrument level cash flows and accounting flows (accruals and amortization) for the 120 months of the Stress Test for:

1. Debt
2. Nonmortgage investments
3. Guaranteed Investment Contracts (GICs)
4. Preferred stock
5. Derivative contracts
   a. Debt-linked derivative contracts
   b. Investment-linked derivative contracts
   c. Mortgage-linked derivative contracts
   d. Derivative contracts that hedge forecasted transactions
   e. Non-linked derivative contracts

[b] Although mortgage-linked derivative contracts are usually linked to mortgage assets rather than nonmortgage instruments, they are treated similarly to debt-linked and investment-linked derivative contracts and, therefore, are covered in this section.

[c] Debt, nonmortgage investments, and preferred stock cash flows include interest (or dividends for preferred stock) and principal payments or receipts, while debt-linked, investment-linked, and mortgage-linked derivative contract cash flows are composed of interest payments and receipts only. Debt, nonmortgage investments, and preferred stock are categorized in one of six classes[2] as shown in Table 3–62.

TABLE 3–62—DEBT, NON-MORTGAGE INVESTMENTS, AND PREFERRED STOCK CLASSIFICATIONS

Classification	Description
Fixed-Rate Bonds or Preferred Stock	Fixed-rate securities that pay periodic interest or dividends
Floating-Rate Bonds or Preferred Stock	Floating-rate securities that pay periodic interest or dividends
Fixed-Rate Asset-Backed Securities	Fixed-rate securities collateralized by nonmortgage assets
Floating-Rate Asset-Backed Securities	Floating-rate securities collateralized by nonmortgage assets
Short-Term Instruments	Fixed-rate, short-term securities that are not issued at a discount and which pay principal and interest only at maturity
Discount Instruments	Securities issued below face value that pay a contractually fixed amount at maturity

[d] Derivative contracts consist of interest rate caps, floors, and swaps. The primary difference between financial instruments and derivative contracts, in terms of calculating cash flows, is that interest payments on financial instruments are based on principal amounts that are eventually repaid to creditors, whereas interest payments on derivative contracts are based on notional amounts

[2] In addition to the items listed here, there are instruments that do not fit into these categories. Additional input information and calculation methodologies may be required for these instruments.

that never change hands. Debt- and investment-linked derivative contracts are categorized in one of seven classes[3] as shown in Table 3–63:

TABLE 3–63—DEBT- AND INVESTMENT-LINKED DERIVATIVE CONTRACT CLASSIFICATION

Classification	Description of Contract
Basis Swap	Floating-rate interest payments are exchanged based on different interest rate indexes
Fixed-Pay Swap	Enterprise pays a fixed interest rate and receives a floating interest rate
Floating-Pay Swap	Enterprise pays a floating interest rate and receives a fixed interest rate
Long Cap	Enterprise receives a floating interest rate when the interest rate to which it is indexed exceeds a specified level (strike rate)
Short Cap	Enterprise pays a floating interest rate when the interest rate to which it is indexed exceeds the strike rate
Long Floor	Enterprise receives a floating interest rate when the interest rate to which it is indexed falls below the strike rate
Short Floor	Enterprise pays a floating interest rate when the interest rate to which it is indexed falls below the strike rate

[e] Mortgage-linked swaps are similar to debt-linked swaps except that the notional amount of a mortgage-linked swap amortizes based on the performance of certain MBS pools. Mortgage-linked derivative contracts are divided into two classes[4] as shown in Table 3–64:

TABLE 3–64—MORTGAGE-LINKED DERIVATIVE CONTRACT CLASSIFICATION

Classification	Description of Contract
Fixed-Pay Amortizing Swaps	Enterprise pays a fixed interest rate and receives a floating interest rate, both of which are based on a declining notional balance
Floating-Pay Amortizing Swaps	Enterprise pays a floating interest rate and receives a fixed interest rate, both of which are based on a declining notional balance

[f] In a currency swap, the Enterprise receives payments that are denominated in a foreign currency and it makes payments in U.S. dollars. The main difference between currency swaps and the type of swaps discussed above is that in a currency swap principal amounts are actually exchanged between the two counterparties. Currency swaps are divided into two classes, as shown in Table 3–65.[5]

TABLE 3–65—CURRENCY SWAP CONTRACT CLASSIFICATION

Classification	Description of Contract
Fixed-for-Fixed Currency Swap	Enterprise receives fixed interest payments denominated in a foreign currency and makes fixed, US dollar-denominated payments
Fixed-for Floating Currency Swap	Enterprise receives fixed interest payments denominated in a foreign currency and makes payments in US dollar based on a floating interest rate

3.8.2 Nonmortgage Instrument Inputs

[a] The Nonmortgage Instrument Cash Flows component of the Stress Test requires numerous inputs. Instrument level inputs provided by the Enterprises in the RBC Report are listed in Table 3–66. Many instrument classes require simulated Interest Rates because their interest payments adjust periodically based on rates tied to various indexes. These rates are generated as described in section 3.3, Interest Rates, of this appendix.

[3] *Ibid.*
[4] *Ibid.*
[5] *Ibid.*

TABLE 3-66—INPUT VARIABLES FOR NONMORTGAGE INSTRUMENT CASH FLOWS

Data Elements	Description
Amortization Methodology Code	Enterprise method of amortizing deferred balances (e.g., straight line)
Asset ID	CUSIP or Reference Pool Number identifying the asset underlying a derivative position
Asset Type Code	Code that identifies asset type used in the commercial information service (e.g., ABS, Fannie Mae pool, Freddie Mac pool)
Associated Instrument ID	Instrument ID of an instrument linked to another instrument
Coefficient	Indicates the extent to which the coupon is leveraged or de-leveraged
Compound Indicator	Indicates if interest is compounded
Compounding Frequency	Indicates how often interest is compounded
Counterparty Credit Rating	NRSRO's rating for the counterparty
Counterparty Credit Rating Type	An indicator identifying the counterparty's credit rating as short-term ('S') or long-term ('L')
Counterparty ID	Enterprise counterparty tracking ID
Country Code	Standard country codes in compliance with Federal Information Processing Standards Publication 10-4
Credit Agency Code	Identifies NRSRO (e.g., Moody's)
Current Asset Face Amount	Current face amount of the asset underlying a swap
Current Coupon	Current coupon or dividend rate of the instrument

TABLE 3-66—INPUT VARIABLES FOR NONMORTGAGE INSTRUMENT CASH FLOWS—Continued

Data Elements	Description
Current Unamortized Discount	Current unamortized premium or unaccreted discount of the instrument adjusted by the Unamortized Balance Scale Factor. If the proceeds from the issuance of debt or derivatives or the amount paid for an asset were greater than par, the value should be positive. If the proceeds or the amounts paid were less than par, the value should be negative
Current Unamortized Fees	Current unamortized fees associated with the instrument adjusted by the Unamortized Balance Scale Factor. Generally fees associated with the issuance of debt or derivatives should be negative numbers. Fees associated with the purchase of an asset should generally be reported as positive numbers
Current Unamortized Hedge	Current unamortized hedging gains (positive) or losses (negative) associated with the instrument adjusted by the Unamortized Balance Scale Factor
Current Unamortized Other	Any other unamortized items originally associated with the instrument adjusted by the Unamortized Balance Scale Factor. If the proceeds from the issuance of debt or derivatives or the amount paid for an asset was greater than par, the value should be positive. If the proceeds or the amounts paid were less than par, the value should be negative
CUSIP_ISIN	CUSIP or ISIN Number identifying the instrument
Day Count	Day count convention (e.g., 30/360)
End Date	The last index repricing date
EOP Principal Balance	End of Period face, principal or notional, amount of the instrument
Exact Representation	Indicates that an instrument is modeled according to its contractual terms

TABLE 3–66—INPUT VARIABLES FOR NONMORTGAGE INSTRUMENT CASH FLOWS—Continued

Data Elements	Description
Exercise Convention	Indicates option exercise convention (e.g., American Option)
Exercise Price	Par = 1.0; Options
First Coupon Date	Date first coupon is received or paid
Index Cap	Indicates maximum index rate
Index Floor	Indicates minimum index rate
Index Reset Frequency	Indicates how often the interest rate index resets on floating-rate instruments
Index Code	Indicates the interest rate index to which floating-rate instruments are tied (e.g., LIBOR)
Index Term	Point on yield curve, expressed in months, upon which the index is based
Instrument Credit Rating	NRSRO credit rating for the instrument
Instrument Credit Rating Type	An indicator identifying the instruments credit rating as short-term ('S') or long-term ('L')
Instrument ID	An integer used internally by the Enterprise that uniquely identifies the instrument
Interest Currency Code	Indicates currency in which interest payments are paid or received
Interest Type Code	Indicates the method of interest rate payments (e.g., fixed, floating, step, discount)
Issue Date	Indicates the date that the instrument was issued
Life Cap Rate	The maximum interest rate for the instrument throughout its life
Life Floor Rate	The minimum interest rate for the instrument throughout its life
Look-Back Period	Period from the index reset date, expressed in months, that the index value is derived
Maturity Date	Date that the instrument contractually matures
Notional Indicator	Identifies whether the face amount is notional
Instrument Type Code	Indicates the type of instrument to be modeled (e.g., ABS, Cap, Swap)
Option Indicator	Indicates if instrument contains an option
Option Type	Indicates option type (e.g., Call option)
Original Asset Face Amount	Original face amount of the asset underlying a swap
Original Discount	Original premium or discount associated with the purchase or sale of the instrument adjusted by the Unamortized Balance Scale Factor. If the proceeds from the issuance of debt or derivatives or the amount paid for an asset were greater than par, the value should be positive. If the proceeds or the amounts paid were less than par, the value should be negative
Original Face	Original face, principal or notional, amount of the instrument
Original Fees	Fees or commissions paid at the time of purchase or sale adjusted by the Unamortized Balance Scale Factor. Generally fees associated with the issuance of debt or derivatives should be negative numbers. Fees associated with the purchase of an asset should generally be reported as positive numbers
Original Hedge	Gains (positive) or losses (negative) from closing out a hedge associated with the instrument at settlement, adjusted by the Unamortized Balance Scale Factor

TABLE 3–66—INPUT VARIABLES FOR NONMORTGAGE INSTRUMENT CASH FLOWS—Continued

Data Elements	Description
Original Other	Any other amounts originally associated with the instrument to be amortized or accreted adjusted by the Unamortized Balance Scale Factor. If the proceeds from the issuance of debt or derivatives or the amount paid for an asset were greater than par, the value should be positive. If the proceeds or the amounts paid were less than par, the value should be negative
Parent Entity ID	Enterprise internal tracking ID for parent entity
Payment Amount	Interest payment amount associated with the instrument (reserved for complex instruments where interest payments are not modeled)
Payment Frequency	Indicates how often interest payments are made or received
Performance Date	"As of" date on which the data is submitted
Periodic Adjustment	The maximum amount that the interest rate for the instrument can change per reset
Position Code	Indicates whether the Enterprise pays or receives interest on the instrument
Principal Currency Code	Indicates currency in which principal payments are paid or received
Principal Factor Amount	EOP Principal Balance expressed as a percentage of Original Face
Principal Payment Date	A valid date identifying the date that principal is paid
Settlement Date	A valid date identifying the date the settlement occurred
Spread	An amount added to an index to determine an instrument's interest rate
Start Date	The date, spot or forward, when some feature of a financial contract becomes effective (e.g., Call Date), or when interest payments or receipts begin to be calculated
Strike Rate	The price or rate at which an option begins to have a settlement value at expiration, or, for interest-rate caps and floors, the rate that triggers interest payments
Submitting Entity	Indicates which Enterprise is submitting information
Trade ID	Unique code identifying the trade of an instrument
Transaction Code	Indicates the transaction that an Enterprise is initiating with the instrument (e.g., buy, issue reopen)
Transaction Date	A valid date identifying the date the transaction occurred
UPB Scale Factor	Factor applied to UPB to adjust for timing differences
Unamortized Balances Scale Factor	Factor applied to Unamortized Balances to adjust for timing differences

[b] In addition to the inputs in Table 3–66, other inputs may be required depending on the characteristics of the instrument modeled. For example, the mortgage-linked derivative contract cash flows require inputs describing the performance of the mortgage assets to which they are linked, including Single Family Default and Prepayment rates (*See* section 3.6.3.4, Single Family Default and Prepayment Rates, of this appendix). Mortgage-linked derivative contract identification numbers (Asset IDs) are used to link the derivative contract to the required pool information that will be used to calculate the cash flows of the corresponding swap.

3.8.3 Nonmortgage Instrument Procedures

In general, non mortgage instruments are modeled according to their terms. The general methodology for calculating cash flows for principal and interest payments is described in this section and is not intended to serve as definitive text for calculating all possible present and future complex instruments. As mentioned in section 3.8.2, Nonmortgage Instrument Inputs, of this appendix, there are some instruments that may require additional input information and calculation methodologies. Simplifying assumptions are made for some instrument terms until they can be modeled more precisely.

3.8.3.1 Apply Specific Calculation Simplifications

[a] In order to produce cash flows, accruals, or amortization of deferred balances, the following simplifications are used for all instruments to which they apply. Should the language in any other portion of section 3.8, Nonmortgage Instrument Cash Flows, of this appendix, seem to conflict with a statement in this section, the language in section 3.8.3.1 takes precedence.

1. For day count methodology, use one of three methodologies 30/360, Actual/360, and Actual/365. All special day counts (i.e. Actual/366 B, Actual/366 S, Actual/366 E, and Actual/Actual) are treated as Actual/365.
2. Set the first index reset date to the First Coupon Date. If the Issue Date is later than the start of the Stress Test, use the Current Coupon Rate to determine the interest paid from Issue Date to First Coupon Date. When a calculation requires a rate that occurs before the start of the Stress Test, use the Current Coupon Rate. This applies to interest accrued but not paid for the start of the Stress test and to rate indexes where applying a Look Back Period requires data prior to the start of the Stress Test.
   a. If periodic caps are zero, change them to 999.99; If periodic floors are greater than 1, change them to zero.
   b. For instruments which have principal balance changes other than those caused by compounding interest, perform calculations as if the principal changes occur only on coupon dates (coupon dates on the fixed-rate leg for swaps) on or later than the first principal change date.
   c. When using a rate index for a specified term in an option exercise rule or as an index, assume that rate is appropriate for the calculation. Do not convert from bond equivalent yield to another yield form for a discount, monthly pay, quarterly pay, semi-annual pay or annual pay instrument.
3. When applying the option exercise rule:
   a. For zero coupon and discount securities, instruments with European options, and zero coupon swaps, evaluate option exercise only on dates listed in the instrument's option exercise schedule. For Bermudan options, evaluate option exercise on the first option date in the instrument's option exercise schedule and subsequent coupon dates (coupon dates on the fixed-rate leg for swaps). For American options, evaluate option exercise on the first option date in the instrument's option exercise schedule and subsequent monthly anniversaries of the instrument's first coupon date.
   b. Assume all call/put premiums/discounts are zero except for zero coupon instruments (including zero coupon swaps and discount notes). For these exceptions, when calculating a rate to compare with the Enterprise Cost of Funds, use the yield to maturity calculated by equating the face or notional amount plus the unamortized discount at the start of the Stress Test to the present value of the face or notional amount at maturity.
   c. Assume basis swaps and floating rate securities have no cancel, put, or call options.
   d. If the remaining maturity is greater than 360 months, use the equivalent-maturity Enterprise Cost of Funds as if the remaining maturity is 360 months.
   e. In the Stress Test, no preferred stock issued by the Enterprise will be called.

3.8.3.2 Determine the Timing of Cash Flows

Project payment dates from the payment date immediately prior to the start of the stress test according to the Payment Frequency, First Coupon Date, and Maturity Date.

3.8.3.3 Obtain the Principal Factor Amount at Each Payment Date

[a] Where there is no amortization or prepayment of principal, the Principal Factor Amount is 1.0 for each payment date until the stated Maturity Date, when it becomes zero.

[b] For debt and debt-linked derivative contracts that amortize, either a principal or a notional amortization schedule must be provided. If amortization information is unavailable, then the Principal Factor Amount is 1.0 for each payment date until the stated Maturity Date, when it becomes zero.

[c] Monthly prepayment rates are 3.5 percent for fixed-rate and 2.0 percent for floating-rate asset-backed securities. Furthermore, asset-backed securities are modeled through a commercial information service where possible. Instruments that cannot be modeled through the commercial information service are treated in accordance with section 3.9, Alternative Modeling Treatments, of this appendix.

[d] In the case of mortgage-linked derivative contracts, notional amounts are amortized based on the characteristics of the underlying pool in the manner described for principal balances of mortgage-backed securities held by an Enterprise in section 3.7, Mortgage-Related Securities Cash Flows, of this appendix.

3.8.3.4 Calculate the Coupon Factor

The Coupon Factor applicable to a given period, which applies to dividends also, depends on day count conventions used to calculate the interest payments for the instrument. For example, the Coupon Factor for a bond that pays interest quarterly based on a non-compounded 30/360 convention would be 3 (representing the number of months in a quarter) times 30 days divided by 360 days, or 0.25. Table 3–67 lists the most common day count conventions.

TABLE 3–67—DAY COUNT CONVENTIONS

Convention	Coupon Factor Calculation
30/360	Number of days between two payment dates assuming 30 days per month/360
Actual/360	Number of days between two payment dates/360
Actual/365	Number of days between two payment dates/365
Actual/Actual	Number of days between two payment dates/Number of days in the year

3.8.3.5 Project Principal Cash Flows or Changes in the Notional Amount

For all financial instruments, principal outstanding for the current period is determined by multiplying the Original Face by the Principal Factor Amount for the current period. The principal payment equals the amount of principal outstanding at the end of the previous period less the principal outstanding at the end of the current period, or zero if the instrument has a notional amount.

3.8.3.6 Project Interest and Dividend Cash Flows

3.8.3.6.1 Non-Complex Financial Instruments

[a] *Fixed-Rate Instruments.* The current period principal outstanding is multiplied by the product of the Current Coupon and current period Coupon Factor and rounded to even 100ths of a dollar.

[b] *Zero-Coupon Bonds.* Interest payments equal zero.

[c] *Discount Notes.* Interest payments equal zero.

[d] *Floating-Rate Instruments.* Interest payments are calculated as principal outstanding multiplied by the coupon for the current period. The current period coupon is calculated by adding a spread to the appropriate interest rate index and multiplying by the Coupon Factor. The coupon for the current period is set to this amount as long as the rate lies between the periodic and lifetime maximum and minimum rates. Otherwise the coupon is set to the maximum or minimum rate.

[e] *Interest Rate Caps and Floors.* These derivative instruments pay or receive interest only if the underlying index is above a Strike Rate (for caps) or below it (for floors). Interest payments are based on notional amounts instead of principal amounts.

1. The interest payment on a long cap is the Original Face multiplied by the amount, if any, by which the index exceeds the Strike Rate, as defined by the equation in Table 3–68. The interest payment on a long floor is the Original Face multiplied by the amount, if any, by which the index is below the Strike Rate. Otherwise interest payments are zero for caps and floors. Interest payments are either paid or received depending on whether the Enterprise is in a long or short position in a cap or a floor.
2. Monthly cash flows for long caps and floors are calculated as illustrated in Table 3–68:

TABLE 3–68—CALCULATION OF MONTHLY CASH FLOWS FOR LONG CAPS AND FLOORS

Instrument	Cash Flows
Cap	$(I-K) \times N \times D$ if $I > K$; 0 if $I \leq K$
Floor	$(K-I) \times N \times D$ if $I < K$; 0 if $I \geq K$

Where:

N = Original Face
K = Strike Rate
I = interest rate index
D = Coupon Factor

[f] *Swaps.* A derivative contract in which counterparties exchange periodic interest payments. Each swap leg (pay side or receive side) is modeled as a separate instrument, with interest payments based on the same notional amount but different interest rates.

1. For debt- and investment-linked swaps, each leg's interest payment is determined in the same manner as payments for fixed-rate, floating-rate or zero coupon instruments as described in paragraph [a], [b] and [d] of this section.
2. For mortgage-linked swaps, calculate the reduction in the notional amount due to scheduled monthly principal payments (taking into account both lifetime and reset period caps and floors), Prepayments, and Defaults of the reference MBS or index pool. Reduce the notional amount of the swap for the previous period by this amount to determine the notional amount for the current period. Calculate interest payments or receipts

for a given period as the product of the notional amount of the swap in that period, the coupon, and the Coupon Factor applicable for that period.

3.8.3.6.2 Complex Financial Instruments

[a] Some instruments have more complex or non-standard features than those described in section 3.8.3.6.1, Non-Complex Financial Instruments, of this appendix. These complexities can include more sophisticated variants of characteristics such as principal or notional amortization schedules, interest accrual methodologies, coupon reset formulas, and option features. In these instances, additional information may be required to completely specify the contractual cash flows or a proxy treatment for these instruments.

[b] An example of an instrument with complex features is an indexed amortizing swap. This instrument is non-standard because its notional amount declines in a way that is related to the level of interest rates. Its amortization table contains a notional amount reduction factor for a given range of interest rates. To compute cash flows for this instrument, reduce the notional amount on each payment date as specified in the amortization table. (The notional amount at the beginning of the Stress Period is given as an input to the calculation.)

[c] Special treatment is also required for foreign-currency-linked notes, the redemption value of which is tied to a specific foreign exchange rate. These require special treatment because the Stress Test does not forecast foreign currency rates. If these instruments are currency-hedged, then the note plus the hedge comprise a synthetic debt instrument for which only the pay side of the swap is modeled. If these instruments are not currency-hedged, the following treatment applies:

1. In the up-rate scenario, the U.S. dollar per unit of foreign currency ratio is increased in proportion to the increase in the ten-year CMT; therefore, the amount of an interest or principal payment is increased accordingly. For example, if the ten-year CMT shifts up by 50 percent, then the U.S. dollar per unit of foreign currency ratio shifts up by 50 percent. In the Stress Test, the payment would be multiplied by 1.5.
2. In the down-rate scenario, the foreign currency per U.S. dollar ratio is decreased in proportion to the decrease in the ten-year CMT.

[d] Futures and Options on Futures also require special treatment:

1. Settle positions on their expiration dates. Exercise only in-the-money options (settlement value greater than zero).
2. Settle all contracts for cash
3. Calculate the cash settlement amount—the change in price of a contract from the contract trade date to its expiration date. Calculate the price on the expiration date based on stress test interest rates (or, as necessary, forward rates extrapolated from these rates).
4. Amortize amounts received or paid at the expiration date into income or expense on a straight-line basis over the life of the underlying instrument (in the case of an option on a futures contract, the life of the instrument underlying the futures contract).
5. Amortize an option premium on a straight-line basis over the life of the option. (Amortize any remaining balances upon option exercise.)

[e] Swaptions also require special treatment:

1. Assume swap settlement (i.e., initiation of the underlying swap) when a swap option is exercised.
2. Calculate a "normalized" fixed-pay coupon by subtracting the spread over the index, if any, from the coupon on the fixed-rate swap leg.
3. For all exercise types (American, Bermudan, and European), consistent with RBC Rule section 3.8.3.7, assume exercise by the party holding the swap option if the equivalent maturity Enterprise Cost of Funds is more than
   a. 50 basis points above the normalized fixed-pay coupon, for a pay-fixed swaption (a call or 'payor' swaption), or
   b. 50 basis points below the normalized fixed pay coupon for a receive-fixed swaption (a put or 'receiver' swaption).
4. Amortize option premiums on a straight-line basis over the option term. (Amortize any remaining balances upon option exercise).

[f] CPI-Linked Instruments also require special treatment. The stress test lacks the ability to accommodate floating-rate instruments that reset in response to changes in the consumer price index (CPI) as published by the Bureau of Labor Statistics. Enterprise issuance of CPI-linked instruments is tied to swap market transactions intended to create desired synthetic debt structure and terms. In such cases, the true economic position nets to the payment terms of the related derivative contract. Accordingly, in order to accommodate and address the existence of CPI-linked instruments in the Enterprises' portfolios, the net synthetic position shall be evaluated in the stress test. That is, for CPI-linked instruments tied to swap transactions that are formally linked in a hedge accounting relationship, the Enterprise should substitute the CPI-linked instrument's coupon payment terms with those of the related swap contract.

[g] Pre-refunded municipal bonds also require special treatments. Pre-refunded municipal bonds are collateralized by securities that are structured to fund all the cash flows

of the refunded municipal bonds until the bonds are callable. Since the call date for the bonds, also referred to as the pre-refunded date, is a more accurate representation of the payoff date than the contractual maturity date of the bonds, the stress test models the bonds to mature on the call date.

[h] If a financial instrument's inputs are described in section 3.1, Data, of this appendix, then model the instrument according to its terms; however, the Director reserves the authority to determine a more appropriate treatment if modeling the instrument according to its terms does not capture the instrument's impact on Enterprise risk. If the financial instrument's inputs are not described in section 3.1, then treat it as described in section 3.9, Alternative Modeling Treatments, of this appendix.

3.8.3.7 Apply Call, Put, or Cancellation Features, if Applicable

[a] In some cases, principal and interest cash flows may be altered due to options imbedded in individual financial instruments. Securities can be called or put and contracts can be cancelled at the option of the Enterprise or the counterparty. The Option Type, Exercise Convention Type, and the Start Date determine when an option may be exercised. There are three standard Exercise Convention Types, all of which are accommodated in the Stress Test:

- American—Exercise can occur at any time after the Start Date of the option.
- European—Exercise can occur only on the Start Date of the option.
- Bermudan—Exercise can occur only on specified dates, usually on coupon payment dates between the Start Date of the option and maturity.

[b] The options are treated in the following manner for each date on which the option can be exercised:

1. Project cash flows for the instrument with the imbedded option assuming that the option is not exercised. If the instrument is tied to an index, assume that the index remains constant at its value on that date.
2. Determine the discount rate that equates the outstanding balance of the security plus option premium and accrued interest to the sum of the discounted values of the projected cash flows. This discount rate is called the yield-to-maturity.
3. Convert the yield-to-maturity to a bond-equivalent yield and compare the bond-equivalent yield with the projected Enterprise Cost of Funds for debt with an equivalent maturity. Interpolate linearly if the maturity is not equal to one of the maturities specified in section 3.3, Interest Rates, of this appendix.
4. If the equivalent-maturity Enterprise Cost of Funds is lower (higher) than 50 basis points below (above) the bond-equivalent yield of the callable (putable) instrument, then the option is exercised. Otherwise, the option is not exercised, and it is evaluated at the next period when the option can be exercised.

[c] Some swap derivative contracts have cancellation features that allow either counterparty to terminate the contracts on certain dates. The cancellation feature is evaluated by comparing the fixed-rate leg of the swap to the Enterprise Cost of Funds. If either leg of the swap is cancelled, then the other leg is cancelled concurrently. Cancellable swaps are treated in the following manner:

1. For each period when an option can be exercised, compare the swap's fixed-leg coupon rate to the Enterprise Cost of Funds with a maturity equivalent to the maturity date of the swap.
2. If the option is a Call, it is deemed to be exercisable at the discretion of the Enterprise. If the option is a Put, it is deemed to be exercisable at the discretion of the Counterparty. If the option is a PutCall, it is deemed to be exercisable at the discretion of either party to the swap. Exercise the option when the swap is out of the money for the party who holds the option. A swap is considered out of the money when the rate on its fixed leg is at least 50 basis point higher or lower, depending upon whether the fixed rate is paid or received, than the like-maturity Enterprise Cost of Funds. For zero coupon swaps in all option exercise periods, use the yield to maturity calculated by equating the notional amount plus the unamortized discount at the start of the Stress Test to the present value of the notional amount at maturity.
   a. For example, if the Enterprise holds a call option for a fixed-pay swap and the coupon rate on the fixed-pay leg is at least 50 basis points above the Enterprise cost of funds for a maturity equivalent to that of the swap, then cancel the swap. Otherwise, the swap is not cancelled and it is evaluated the next time that the swap can be cancelled.

3.8.3.8 Calculate Monthly Interest Accruals for the Life of the Instrument

[a] Monthly interest accruals are calculated by prorating the interest cash flows on an actual-day basis. In this section, the term "from" means from and including, "to" means up to and not including, and "through" means up to and including. As an example, from the first to the third of a month is two days from the first through the third is three days. This convention is used to facilitate the day count and does not imply on which day's payments or accruals are actually made. Use one of the three following methodologies with the exception

that interest cash flow dates occurring on or after the 30th of a month are considered as occurring on the last day of the month:

1. If the final interest cash flow occurs within the month, the interest accrual for that month is calculated by multiplying the final interest cash flow amount (as calculated in section 3.8.3.6 of this appendix) times the number of days from the beginning of the month through the final maturity date divided by the number of days from the previous interest cash flow date to the maturity date.
2. If an interest cash flow other than the final interest cash flow occurs within a month, the interest accrual for that month is determined by multiplying the interest cash flow amount for the current month times the number of days from the beginning of the month through the interest cash flow date, divided by the number of days from the previous interest cash flow date (or issue date) to this interest cash flow date. To this add the interest cash flow amount for the next interest cash flow date times the number of days from the current month's interest cash flow date to the end of the month, divided by the number of days from the current month's interest cash flow date to the following next interest cash flow date.
3. If no interest cash flows occur during a month other than the issue month, the monthly interest accrual is calculated by multiplying the next interest cash flow amount times the number of days in the month divided by the number of days from the previous interest cash flow date to the next interest cash flow date.
4. If the issue month occurs after the start of the Stress Test, the monthly interest accrual is calculated by multiplying the next interest cash flow amount by the number of days in the month minus the day of issue, divided by the number of days from the issue date to the next interest cash flow date.

3.8.3.9 Calculate Monthly Amortization (Accretion) of Premiums (Discounts) and Fees

[a] Adjust monthly interest accruals (*see* section 3.10.3.6.1[a]3., of this appendix) to reflect the value over time of discounts, premiums, fees and hedging gains and losses incurred (Deferred Balances). Amortize Deferred Balances that exist at the beginning of the Stress Test until the instrument's Maturity Date. If there are any put, call, or cancel options that are executed, amortize any remaining Deferred Balances in the execution month.

TABLE 3–69—INPUTS FOR NONMORTGAGE INSTRUMENT ACCOUNTING FLOWS

Variable	Description	Source
MD	Maturity Date	Table 3–66, Input Variables for Nonmortgage Instrument Cash Flows
UDB_0	The sum of Current Unamortized Discount, Current Unamortized Hedge, and Current Unamortized Other (Deferred Balances) for the instrument at the start of the Stress Test	Table 3–66, Input Variables for Nonmortgage Instrument Cash Flows
$MACRU_m$	Monthly Interest Accruals	section 3.8.3.8, Calculate Monthly Interest Accruals for the Life of the Instrument
$EOMPBAO_m$	Principal Balance at the end of the month for months m = 0...RM after modeling all options execution	section 3.8.3.6, Project Interest and Dividend Cash Flows
$EOMPB_m$	Principal Balance at the end of the month for months m = 0...RM before modeling any options execution	section 3.8.3.6, Project Interest and Dividend Cash Flows

1. Compute Remaining Term (RM) as follows:

$$RM = 12 \times (\text{year}(MD) - \text{year}(STDT)) + \text{month}(MD) - \text{month}(STDT) + 1$$

Where:

STDT is the Starting Date of the Stress Test

2. For nonmortgage instruments with notional principal, calculate the monthly Amortization Amount (AA_m) for each month m = 1...RM:

$$AA_m = -\frac{UDB_0}{RM} \text{ if } EOMPBAO_m > 0$$

$$AA_m = -UDB_{m-1} \text{ if } EOMPBAO_m = 0$$

$$UDB_m = UDB_{m-1} + AA_m$$

3. For nonmortgage instruments with principal and interest payments,
   a. Compute Allocated Interest for all months m (AI_m) as follows:

$$AI_m = \left[\frac{EOMPB_{m-1}}{\sum_{k=0}^{RM} EOMPB_k}\right] \times \sum_{k=1}^{RM} MACRU_k$$

   b. Calculate the monthly Internal Rate of Return (IRR) that equates the adjusted cash flows (actual principal plus allocated interest) to the Initial Book Value (BV_0) of the instrument. Solve for IRR such that:

$$BV_0 = \sum_{m=1}^{RM} \frac{ACF_m}{(1+IRR)^m}$$

Where:

$BV_0 = EOMPB_0 + UPD_0$

$ACF_m = EOMPB_{m-1} - EOMPB_m + AI_m$

   c. Calculate the monthly Amortization Amount (AA_m) for each month m = 1...RM:

$$AA_m = (BV_{m-1} \times IRR) - AI_m \text{ if } EOMPBAO_m > 0$$

$$AA_m = -UDB_{m-1} \text{ if } EOMPBAO_m = 0$$

$$UDB_m = UDB_{m-1} + AA_m$$

$$BV_m = EOMPBAO_m + UDB_m$$

4. For discount notes,
   a. Calculate Remaining Maturity in Actual Days (RMD):

$$RMD = MD - STDT + 1$$

   b. Calculate the month Amortization Amount (AA_m) for each month m = 1...RM:

$$AA_m = -UDB_0 \times \frac{ADAYS_m}{RDM} \text{ if } EOMPBAO_m > 0$$

$$AA_m = -UDB_{m-1} \text{ if } EOMPBAO_m = 0$$

$$UDB_m = UDB_{m-1} + AA_m$$

Where:

$ADAYS_m$ = actual number of days in month m (days from the first of the month through maturity in month RM)

5. For zero coupon bonds,
   a. Calculate Remaining Maturity in Actual Days (RMD):

$$RMD = MD - STDT + 1$$

   b. Calculate Yield Factor (YF):

$$YF = \left(\frac{EOMPB_0}{EOMPB_0 + UDB_0}\right)^{\frac{1}{RMD}}$$

   c. Calculate the monthly Amortization Factor (AF_m) for each month m = 1...RM:

$$AF_m = 1 \text{ if } m = 0$$

$$AF_m = AF_{m-1} \times YF^{ADAYS_m}$$

Where:

$ADAYS_m$ = actual number of days in month m (days from the first of the month through maturity in month RM):

   d. Calculate the monthly Amortization Amount (AA_m) for each month m = 1...RM

$$AA_m = (EOMPB_0 + UDB_0) \times (AF_m - AF_{m-1}) \text{ if } EOMPBAO_m > 0$$

$$AA_m = -UDB_{m-1} \text{ if } EOMPBAO_m = 0$$

$$UDB_m = UDB_{m-1} + AA_m$$

3.8.3.10 Apply Counterparty Haircuts

[a] Finally, the interest and principal cash flows received by the Enterprises for nonmortgage instruments other than swaps and foreign currency-related instruments are

Haircut (i.e., reduced) by a percentage to account for the risk of counterparty insolvency, if a counterparty obligation exists. The amount of the Haircut is calculated based on the public rating of the counterparty and time during the stress period in which the cash flow occurs, as specified in section 3.5, Counterparty Defaults, of this appendix.

[b] An Enterprise may issue debt denominated in, or indexed to, foreign currencies, and eliminate the resulting foreign currency exposure by entering into currency swap agreements. The combination of the debt and the swap creates synthetic debt with principal and interest payments denominated in U.S. dollars. The Haircuts for currency swaps are applied to the pay (dollar-denominated) side of the currency swaps, or to the cash outflows of the synthetic debt instrument. Therefore, the payments made by the Enterprise on a foreign currency contract are increased by the haircut amount. The Haircuts and the Phase-in periods for currency swaps are detailed in Table 3–31, under Derivative Contracts.

[c] Haircuts for swaps that are not foreign currency related are applied to the Monthly Interest Accruals (as calculated in section 3.8.3.8, of this appendix) on the receive leg minus the Monthly Interest Accruals on the pay leg when this difference is positive. Use the maximum haircut from Table 3–31 for periods before and after the implementation of netting, as appropriate. After the implementation of netting, net the swap proceeds for each counterparty before applying the haircuts. The following example applies to an Enterprise having two swaps with the same counterparty. On the first swap, the Enterprise pays fixed and receives floating and on the second swap it pays floating and receives fixed. If the counterparty is a net payer to the Enterprise, the haircuts will be applied to the sum of the two receive legs net of the sum of the two pay legs.

3.8.4 Nonmortgage Instrument Outputs

[a] Outputs consist of cash flows and accounting information for debt, nonmortgage investments, preferred stock, and derivative contracts. Cash flows and accounting information outputs are inputs to section 3.10, Operations, Taxes, and Accounting, of this appendix.

[b] Cash flows include the following monthly amounts:

1. Interest and principal payments for debt and nonmortgage investments,
2. Dividends and redemptions for preferred stock, and
3. Interest payments for debt-linked, investment-linked, and mortgage-linked derivative contracts.

[c] Accounting information includes the following monthly amounts:

1. Accrued interest and
2. Amortization of discounts, premiums, fees and other deferred items.

3.9 Alternative Modeling Treatments

3.9.1 Alternative Modeling Treatments Overview

[a] This section provides treatment for items that cannot be modeled in one of the ways specified in paragraph [b] of this section, but must be included in order to run the Stress Test. Because the rule provides treatments for a wide variety of instruments and activities that can be applied to accommodate unusual instruments, OFHEO expects few items to fall into this category.

[b] An Alternative Modeling Treatment (AMT) applies to any on- or off-balance-sheet item that is missing data elements required to calculate appropriate cash flows, or any instrument with unusual features for which this appendix does *not*:

1. Provide an explicit computational procedure and set of inputs (i.e., the appendix specifies exact data inputs and procedures for a class of instruments to which the item belongs); or,
2. Provide an implicit procedure (used for a general class of instruments), and explicit inputs that allow the item to be fully characterized for computational purposes (i.e., the appendix specifies procedures and data inputs for a class of instruments to which the item does not belong that can be applied to the item to accurately compute its cash flows); or
3. Provide an implicit procedure by exact substitution, i.e., by representing the item as a computationally equivalent combination of other items that are specified in paragraphs (1) or (2) in this section (i.e., the appendix specifies treatments for two or more instruments, which, in combination, exactly produce the item's cash flows); or
4. Permit the approximation of one or more computational characteristics by other similar values that are explicitly specified in this appendix, or in the RBC Report instructions (i.e., the appendix specifies a treatment, or combination of treatments, that can be used as a reasonable proxy for the computational characteristics of the item). Such proxy treatments must be approved by OFHEO. OFHEO may, in its discretion, approve a proposed proxy treatment, adopt a different proxy treatment, or treat items for which a proxy treatment has been proposed by the Enterprises according to the remaining provisions of section 3.9, Alternative Modeling Treatments, of this appendix.

[c] For a given on- or off-balance sheet item, the appropriate AMT is determined according to the categories specified in section

3.9.3, Alternative Modeling Treatments Procedures, of this appendix, based on the information available for that item. The output for each such item is a set of cash and accounting flows, or specific amounts to be applied in section 3.12, Calculation of the Risk-Based Capital Requirement, of this appendix.

3.9.2 Alternative Modeling Treatments Inputs

Table 3–70 identifies the minimal inputs that are used to determine an AMT. (*See also* section 3.1, Data, of this appendix)

TABLE 3–70—ALTERNATIVE MODELING TREATMENT INPUTS

Variable	Description
TYPE	Type of item (asset, liability or off-balance sheet item)
BOOK	Book Value of item (amount outstanding adjusted for deferred items)
FACE	Face Value or notional balance of item for off-balance sheet items
REMATUR	Remaining Contractual Maturity of item in whole months. Any fraction of a month equals one whole month.
RATE	Interest Rate
INDEX	Index used to calculate Interest Rate
FAS115	Designation that the item is recorded at fair value, according to FAS 115
RATING	Instrument or counterparty rating
FHA	In the case of off-balance sheet guarantees, a designation indicating 100% of collateral is guaranteed by FHA
MARGIN	Margin over an Index

3.9.3 Alternative Modeling Treatments Procedures

For each item, one of the following alternatives will be applied:

3.9.3.1 Off-Balance Sheet Items

[a] If the item is a guarantee of a tax-exempt multifamily housing bond, or a single family or multifamily whole-loan REMIC class rated triple-A, or other similar transaction guaranteed by the Enterprises, multiply the face value of the guaranteed instruments by 0.45 percent. This amount is added to the amount of capital required to maintain positive total capital throughout the ten-year Stress Period. Any instruments or obligations with 100 percent of collateral guaranteed by the Federal Housing Administration (FHA) are excluded from this calculation.

[b] Otherwise, add to the amount of capital required to maintain positive total capital throughout the ten-year Stress Period an amount equal to the face or notional value of the item at the beginning of the Stress Period times three percent.

3.9.3.2 Reconciling Items

Reconciling items falling into this category will be treated according to the specifications in section 3.10, Operations, Taxes, and Accounting, of this appendix.

3.9.3.3 Balance Sheet Items

[a] If the item is a trading security recorded at fair value according to FAS 115, then the book value (the face value adjusted for deferred balances) will be converted to cash in the first month of the Stress Test.

[b] Otherwise, if the item is an earning asset, then it is treated as a held-to-maturity asset, based on book value, as follows:

1. In the up-rate scenario, it will be treated as a held-to-maturity bond paying compound interest on a 30/360 basis at maturity, with the item's contractual maturity and rate. The item will be Haircut according to its rating. If no maturity is provided, maturity will be set at 120 months. If no rate is provided, a rate will be assigned at the Initial Enterprise Cost of Funds whose term is equal to the remaining maturity, less 200 basis points (but not less than zero). If no rating is provided, the asset will be classified as unrated.
2. In the down-rate scenario, it will be treated as a held-to-maturity bond paying compound interest on a 30/360 basis at maturity, with the item's contractual

maturity and rate. The item will be Haircut according to its rating. If no maturity is provided, maturity will be set at 120 months. If no rate is provided, a rate will be assigned at the floating one-month Enterprise Cost of Funds less 200 basis points (but not less than zero). If no rating is provided, the asset will be classified as unrated.

[c] If the item is a non-earning asset it will remain on the books and earn no interest throughout the Stress Period.

[d] Otherwise, if the item is a liability, then it is treated as follows, based on book value:

1. In the up-rate scenario, it will be treated as non-callable and monthly coupon-paying to maturity on a 30/360 basis. If the coupon rate is not specified, the liability will be given a floating rate at the one-month Enterprise Cost of Funds plus 200 basis points. If no maturity is provided, maturity will be set at 120 months.
2. In the down-rate scenario, it will be treated as non-callable and monthly coupon paying to maturity. If no coupon is provided, the liability will be given a fixed rate at the Initial Enterprise Cost of Funds plus 200 basis points. If no maturity is provided, maturity will be set at ten years.

[e] Unamortized Balances should be amortized on a straight-line basis over the designated remaining maturity of the instrument.

[f] All items in this section are treated as if they had no options or cancellation features. The face value will be held constant until maturity. If an item has an adjustable rate, it is assumed that the interest rate will adjust monthly with no caps and a lifetime floor of zero percent.

3.9.4 Alternative Modeling Treatments Outputs

For each AMT item, the output is a set of cash and accounting flows appropriate to its respective treatment as specified in section 3.9.3, Alternative Modeling Treatments Procedures, or specific amounts to be applied in section 3.12, Calculation of the Risk-Based Capital Requirement, of this appendix.

3.10 Operations, Taxes, and Accounting

3.10.1 Operations, Taxes, and Accounting Overview

This section describes the procedures for determining new debt issuance and investments, computing capital distributions, calculating operating expenses and taxes, and creating pro forma balance sheets and income statements. Input data include an Enterprise's balance sheet at the beginning of the Stress Period, interest rates from the Interest Rates component of the Stress Test, and the outputs from cash flow components of the Stress Test. The outputs of the procedures discussed in this section—monthly pro forma balance sheets, cash flow and income statements for each month of the Stress Test—are the basis for the capital calculation described in section 3.12, Calculation of the Risk-Based Capital Requirement, of this appendix.

3.10.2 Operations, Taxes, and Accounting Inputs

[a] Data described in section 3.1, Data, section 3.3.4, Interest Rates Outputs, section 3.6.4, Final Whole Loan Cash Flow Outputs, section 3.7.4, Mortgage-Related Securities Outputs, and section 3.8.4, Nonmortgage Instrument Outputs, of this appendix, is used to produce monthly pro forma balance sheets and income statements for the Enterprises. In addition to the starting position data, described in the cash flow components, the Enterprises provide the starting position dollar values for the items in Table 3–71.

TABLE 3–71—OPERATIONS, TAXES, AND ACCOUNTING INPUTS

Input	Description
FAS 115 and 125 fair value adjustment on retained mortgage portfolio	
FAS 133 fair value adjustment on retained mortgage portfolio	
Reserve for losses on retained mortgage portfolio	
FAS 115 and 125 fair value adjustments on non-mortgage investments	
FAS 133 fair value adjustments on non-mortgage investments	

TABLE 3–71—OPERATIONS, TAXES, AND ACCOUNTING INPUTS—Continued

Input	Description
Total cash	
Accrued interest receivable on mortgages	
Accrued interest receivable on non-mortgage investment securities	
Accrued interest receivable on non-mortgage investment securities denominated in foreign currency—hedged	
Accrued interest receivable on non-mortgage investment securities denominated in foreign currency—unhedged	
Accrued interest receivable on mortgage-linked derivatives, gross	
Accrued interest receivable on investment-linked derivatives, gross	
Accrued interest receivable on debt-linked derivatives, gross	
Other accrued interest receivable	
Accrued interest receivable on hedged debt-linked foreign currency swaps	Underlying instrument is GSE issued debt
Accrued interest receivable on unhedged debt-linked foreign currency swaps	
Accrued interest receivable on hedged asset-linked foreign currency swaps	Underlying instrument is an asset
Accrued interest receivable on unhedged asset-linked foreign currency swaps	
Currency transaction adjustments—hedged assets	Cumulative gain or loss due to changes in foreign exchange rates relative to on-balance sheet assets originally denominated in foreign currency
Currency transaction adjustments—unhedged assets	Cumulative gain or loss due to changes in foreign exchange rates relative to unhedged assets and off-balance sheet items originally denominated in foreign currency
Federal income tax refundable	
Accounts receivable	
Fees receivable	
Low income housing tax credit investments	
Fixed assets, net	
Clearing accounts	Net book value of all clearing accounts
Other assets	
Foreclosed property, net	Real estate owned including property acquired through foreclosure proceedings

TABLE 3–71—OPERATIONS, TAXES, AND ACCOUNTING INPUTS—Continued

Input	Description
FAS 133 fair value adjustment on debt securities	
Accrued interest payable on existing fixed-rate debt securities	
Accrued interest payable on existing floating-rate debt securities	
Accrued interest payable on existing debt issued in foreign currency—hedged	
Accrued interest payable on existing debt issued in foreign currency—unhedged	
Accrued interest payable on mortgage-linked derivatives, gross	
Accrued interest payable on investment-linked derivatives, gross	
Accrued interest payable on debt-linked derivatives, gross	
Other accrued interest payable	
Accrued interest payable debt-linked foreign currency swaps—hedged	
Accrued interest payable debt-linked foreign currency swaps—unhedged	
Accrued interest payable asset-linked foreign currency swaps—hedged	
Accrued interest payable asset-linked foreign currency swaps—unhedged	
Principal and interest due to mortgage security investors	Cash received on sold mortgages for onward submission to mortgage security investors
Currency transaction adjustments—hedged debt	Cumulative gain or loss due to changes in foreign exchange rates relative to on-balance sheet debt originally denominated in foreign currency
Currency transaction adjustments—unhedged debt	Cumulative gain or loss due to changes in foreign exchange rates relative to unhedged liabilities and off-balance sheet items originally denominated in foreign currency
Escrow deposits	Cash balances held in relation to servicing of multifamily loans
Federal income taxes payable	
Preferred dividends payable	
Accounts payable	
Other liabilities	
Common dividends payable	
Reserve for losses on sold mortgages	

TABLE 3–71—OPERATIONS, TAXES, AND ACCOUNTING INPUTS—Continued

Input	Description
Common stock	
Preferred stock, non-cumulative	
Additional paid-in capital	
Retained earnings	
Treasury stock	
Unrealized gains and losses on available-for-sale securities, net of tax, in accordance with FAS 115 and 125	
Unrealized gains and losses due to mark to market adjustments, FAS 115 and 125	
Unrealized gains and losses due to deferred balances related to pre-FAS 115 and 125 adjustments	
Unrealized gains and losses due to other realized gains, FAS 115	
Other comprehensive income, net of tax, in accordance with FAS 133	
OCI due to mark to market adjustments, FAS 133	
OCI due to deferred balances related to pre-FAS 133 adjustments	
OCI due to other realized gains, FAS 133	
Operating expenses	Average of prior three months
Common dividend payout ratio (average of prior 4 quarters)	Sum dollar amount of common dividends paid over prior 4 quarters and divided by the sum of total of after tax income less preferred dividends paid over prior 4 quarters
Common dividends per share paid 1 quarter prior to the beginning of the stress period	
Common shares outstanding	
Common Share Market Price	
Dividends paid on common stock 1 quarter prior to the beginning of the stress period	
Share Repurchases (average of prior 4 quarters)	Sum dollar amount of repurchased shares, net of newly issued shares, over prior 4 quarters and divided by 4
Off-balance-sheet Guarantees	Guaranteed instruments not reported on the balance sheet, such as whole loan REMICs and multifamily credit enhancements, and not 100% guaranteed by the FHA
Other Off-Balance Sheet Guarantees	All other off-balance sheet guaranteed instruments not included in another category, and not 100% guaranteed by the FHA

TABLE 3–71—OPERATIONS, TAXES, AND ACCOUNTING INPUTS—Continued

Input	Description
YTD provision for income taxes	Provision for income taxes for the period beginning January 1 and ending as of the report date
Tax loss carryforward	Net losses available to write off against future years' net income
Tax liability for the year prior to the beginning of the Stress Test	
Tax liability for the year 2 years prior to the beginning of the Stress Test (net of carrybacks)	
Taxable income for the year prior to the beginning of the Stress Test	
Taxable income for the year 2 years prior to the beginning of the Stress Test (net of carrybacks)	
Net after tax income for the quarter preceding the start of the stress test	
YTD taxable income	Total amount of taxable income for the period beginning January 1 and ending as of the report date
Minimum capital requirement at the beginning of the Stress Period	
Specific allowance for loan losses	Loss allowances calculated in accordance with FAS 114
Zero coupon swap receivable	
Unamortized discount on zero coupon receivable	

[b] Amounts required to reconcile starting position balances from cash flow components of the Stress Test with an Enterprise's balance sheet will be reported in the RBC Report with the related instrument. The corresponding balance for the related instrument will be adjusted accordingly.

3.10.3 Operations, Taxes, and Accounting Procedures

The Stress Test calculates new debt and investments, dividends, allowances for loan losses, operating expenses, and income taxes. These calculations are determined by, and also affect, the pro forma balance sheets and income statements during the Stress Period.

3.10.3.1 New Debt and Investments

[a] For each month of the Stress Test, cash deficits and surpluses are eliminated by issuing new debt or purchasing new investments. The Stress Test calculates cash received and cash disbursed each month in order to determine the net availability of cash. Depending on the calculated net cash position at month end, new short term investments are purchased at mid-month or a mix of long and short term debt is issued at mid-month so that the recalculated net cash position at month end is zero.

[b] For each month of the Stress Test, the following calculations are performed to determine the amount and type of new debt and investments. The short-term investments and appropriate mix of long-term and short-term debt are reflected in the pro forma balance sheets. Interest income or interest expense for the new investments or debt are reflected in the pro forma income statements.

1. In any month in which the cash position is positive at the end of the month, the Stress Test invests the Enterprise's excess cash on the 15th day of that month in one-month Treasury bills that yield the six-month Treasury rate for that month as specified in section 3.3, Interest Rates, of this appendix.
2. In any month in which the cash position is negative at the end of the month, the Stress Test issues a mix of new short-term and long-term debt on the 15th day of that month. New short-term debt issued is six-month discount notes with a

discount rate at the six-month Enterprise Cost of Funds as specified in section 3.3, Interest Rates, of this appendix, with interest accruing on a 30/360 basis. New long-term debt issued is five-year bonds not callable for the first year ("five-year-no call-one") with an American call at par after the end of the first year, semiannual coupons on a 30/360 basis with principal paid at maturity or call, and a coupon rate set at the five year Enterprise Cost of Funds as specified in section 3.3, Interest Rates, of this appendix, plus a 50 basis point premium for the call option. During the Stress Test, the call option for new long-term debt issued is not executed in the up-rate scenario and in the down-rate scenario follows the same call exercise rule as other debt. An issuance cost of 2.5 basis points is assessed on new short-term debt at issue and an issuance cost of 20 basis points is assessed on new long-term debt at issue. New long-term debt is issued to target a total debt mix of short- to long-term debt that is the same as the short- to long-term debt mix at the beginning of the Stress Test. Issuance fees for new debt are amortized on a straight line basis to the maturity of the appropriate instrument.

3. Given the Net Cash Deficit (NCD_m) in month m, use the following constants and method to calculate the amount of short-term and long-term debt to issue in month m:

a. Set the Issuance Cost on new short-term debt at issue (ISCOST):
ISCOST = 0.00025

b. Set the Issuance Cost on new long-term debt at issue (ILCOST):
ILCOST = 0.002

c. Calculate Net Short-term Debt Outstanding ($NSDO_0$) and Total Debt Outstanding (TDO_0) at the start of the Stress Test (m = 0) using the following methodology:

1) For each month m and each debt and swap instrument i (each swap leg is considered a separate instrument), determine the Month of Next Repricing (MNR_m) defined as the first month greater than m in which the instrument matures or repricing can occur whether or not the coupon rate actually changes. Set the Principal Balance (PB_m) to be:

a) The principal (or notional principal) outstanding if the instrument cash flows are paid by the Enterprise,

b) Minus the principal (or notional principal) outstanding if the instrument cash flows are received by the Enterprise.

c) Zero if m is less than or equal to the issue month or the month in which an option exercised during the stress test would begin accruing cash flows to or from the Enterprise.

d) Zero if m is greater than or equal to the maturity month or the month in which an option exercised during the stress test would cease further cash flows to or from the Enterprise.

2) Calculate $NSDO_m$ by summing $PB_{m,i}$ for all instruments where $MNR_{m,i}$ is less than or equal to m plus 12.

3) Calculate TDO_m by summing $PB_{m,i}$ for instruments where $MNR_{m,i}$, is greater than m.

d. Set the Maximum Proportion of Total Debt (MPD):

$$MPD = \frac{TDO_0 - NSDO_0}{TDO_0}$$

e. Calculate Discount Rate Factor (DRF_m):

$$DRF_m = \left(1 + \frac{CF_m}{12}\right)^6$$

Where: CF_m = six month Enterprise Cost of Funds for month m

f. Calculate the Adjustment Factor for Short-Term Debt Issuance Fees ($AFSIF_m$):

$$AFSIF_m = \frac{DRF_m}{1 - ISCOST \times DRF_m}$$

g. Calculate the Adjustment Factor for Long-Term Debt Issuance Fees ($AFLIF_m$):

$$AFLIF_m = \frac{1}{1 - ILCOST}$$

h. Calculate the Maximum Long-Term Issuance ($MLTI_m$):

$$MLTI_m = NCD_m \times AFLIF_m$$

i. Calculate Net Short-Term Debt Outstanding ($NSDO_m$) and Total Debt Outstanding (TDO_m) for month m using the methodology described in paragraph 3.10.3.1.[b]3.c. of this appendix. *Note:* This calculation must reflect all new issuances, option exercises, and maturities between the beginning of the Stress Test and month m.

j. Calculate Interim Face Amount of Long-Term Debt to be issued this month ($IFALD_m$):

$$IFALD_m = \frac{((MPD-1)\times TDO_m) + NSDO_m + (MPD \times AFSIF_m \times NCD_m)}{1 - MPD + \left(AFSIF_m \times \frac{MPD}{AFLIF_m}\right)}$$

k. Calculate Face Amount of Long-Term Debt to be issued ($FALD_m$):

$$FALD_m = min(MLTI_m, max(0, IFALD_m))$$

l. Calculate Face Amount of Short-Term Debt to be issued ($FASD_m$):

$$FASD_m = AFSIF_m \times max\left(0, NCD_m - \frac{FALD_m}{AFLIF_m}\right)$$

3.10.3.2 Dividends and Share Repurchases

[a] The Stress Test determines quarterly whether to pay dividends and make share repurchases. Dividends are decided upon and paid during the first month after the end of the quarter for which they are declared. If any dividends are paid, the dividend payout cannot exceed an amount equal to core capital less the estimated minimum capital requirement at the end of the quarter. Share repurchases are made during the middle month of the quarter.

1. *Preferred Stock.* An Enterprise will pay dividends on preferred stock as long as that Enterprise meets the estimated minimum capital requirement before and after the payment of these dividends. Preferred stock dividends are based on the coupon rates of the issues outstanding. The coupon rates for any issues of variable rate preferred stock are calculated using projections of the appropriate index rate. Preferred stock dividends may not exceed core capital less the estimated minimum capital requirement at the end of the preceding quarter.
2. *Common Stock.* In the first year of the Stress Test, dividends are paid on common stock in each of the four quarters after preferred dividends, if any, are paid unless the Enterprise's capital is, or after the payment, would be, below the estimated minimum capital requirement.

a. *First Quarter.* In the first quarter, the dividend is the dividend per share ratio for common stock from the quarter preceding the Stress Test times the current number of shares of common stock outstanding.

b. *Subsequent Quarters.*

1) In the three subsequent quarters, if the preceding quarter's after tax income is greater than after tax income in the quarter preceding the Stress Test, (adjusted by the ratio of the Enterprise's retained earnings and retained earnings after adjustments are made that revert investment securities and derivatives to amortized cost), pay the larger of (1) the dividend per share ratio for common stock from the quarter preceding the Stress Test times the current number of shares of common stock outstanding or (2) the average dividend payout ratio for common stock for the four quarters preceding the start of the Stress Test times the preceding quarter's after tax income (adjusted by the reciprocal of the ratio of the Enterprise's retained earnings and retained earnings after adjustments are made that revert investment securities and derivatives to amortized cost) less preferred dividends paid in the current quarter. In no case may the dividend payment exceed an amount equal to core capital less the estimated minimum capital requirement at the end of the preceding quarter.

(2) If the previous quarter's after tax income is less than or equal to after tax income in the quarter preceding the Stress Test (adjusted by the ratio of the Enterprise's retained earnings and retained earnings after adjustments are made that revert investment securities and derivatives to amortized cost), pay the lesser of (1) the dividend per share ratio for common stock for the quarter preceding the Stress Test times the current number of shares of common stock outstanding or (2) an amount equal to core capital less the estimated minimum capital requirement at the end of the preceding quarter, but not less than zero.

3. *Share Repurchases.* In the first two quarters of the Stress Test, the capital of the Enterprises will be reduced to reflect the

repurchase of shares. The amount of the capital reduction in each of those two quarters will be equal to the average net stock repurchases by the Enterprise during the four quarters preceding the start of the Stress Period. Net stock repurchases equal repurchases less receipts from new stock issued, but not less than zero. Repurchases in each of the first two quarters may occur only up to the point that the amount of core capital exceeds the estimated minimum capital requirement at the end of the first month of the quarter.

4. *Minimum Capital Requirements*. For the purposes of the Stress Test, the Enterprise's minimum capital requirement is computed by applying leverage ratios to all assets (2.50 percent) and off-balance sheet obligations (0.45 percent), and summing the results. Repurchases of an Enterprise's own previously-issued MBSs are excluded from the minimum capital calculation used in section 3.10.3.2, Dividends and Share Repurchases, of this appendix.

3.10.3.3 Allowances for Loan Losses and Other Charge-Offs

[a] The Stress Test calculates a tentative allowance for loan losses monthly by multiplying current-month Credit Losses (CL in Table 3–52) by twelve, thus annualizing current month Credit Losses. This is a proxy for a loss contingency where it is probable that a loss has been incurred and the amount can be reasonably estimated. For both the retained and sold portfolios, these credit losses include lost principal (net of recoveries from credit enhancements and disposition of the real estate collateral), and foreclosure, holding, and disposition costs. If the tentative allowance for loan losses for the current period is greater than the balance from the prior month less charge-offs (i.e., credit losses) for the current month, a provision (i.e., expense) is recorded. Otherwise, no provision is made and the allowance for loan losses is equal to the prior period amount less current month charge-offs.

[b] Other charge-offs result from Haircuts related to mortgage revenue bonds, private-issue MBS, and non mortgage investments, described in their respective cash flow components.

1. In the case of Enterprise investments in securities, these Haircuts result in the receipt of less principal and interest than is contractually due. Lost principal is recorded as Other Losses when due and not received, while lost interest is recorded as a reduction of Interest Income.
2. In the case of interest rate derivative instruments, these Haircuts result in the receipt of less net interest than is contractually due from, or the payment of more interest than is contractually due to, an Enterprise counterparty. For those swaps that are linked to Enterprise investments, the increase or decrease of net swap interest due is recorded as an adjustment of Interest Income. For those swaps that are linked to Enterprise debt obligations, the increase or decrease of net swap interest due is recorded as an adjustment of Interest Expense.

3.10.3.4 Operating Expenses

[a] The Stress Test calculates operating expenses, which include non-interest costs such as those related to an Enterprise's salaries and benefits, professional services, property, equipment and office space. Over the Stress Period, operating expenses are equal to the sum of two components. The first component in each month is equal to one-third (⅓) of the average monthly operating expenses of the Enterprise in the quarter immediately preceding the start of the Stress Test. The second component changes in proportion to the change in the size of the Enterprise's mortgage portfolio (i.e., the sum of outstanding principal balances of its retained and sold mortgage portfolios). The Stress Test calculates the Enterprise's mortgage portfolio at the end of each month of the Stress Period as a percentage of the portfolio at the start of the Stress Test, and then multiplies the percentage of assets remaining by two-thirds (⅔) of the average monthly operating expenses of the Enterprise in the quarter immediately preceding the start of the Stress Test.

[b] The sum of the two components in paragraph [a], of this section, is multiplied by a factor which equals

$$\left(1-\frac{m}{36}\right)$$

for the first 12 months of the Stress Test and then equals two-thirds for months 13 and beyond. This product is the Enterprise's operating expense for a given month in the Stress Period.

3.10.3.5 Income Taxes

[a] Both Enterprises are subject to Federal income taxes, but neither is subject to state or local income taxes.

[b] The Stress Test applies an effective Federal income tax rate of 30 percent when calculating the monthly provision for income taxes (e.g., income tax expense). OFHEO may change the 30 percent income tax rate if there are significant changes in Enterprise experience or changes in the statutory income tax.

[c] The Stress Test sets income tax expense for tax purposes equal to the provision for income taxes. The effects of timing differences between taxable income and Generally Accepted Accounting Principles

(GAAP) income before income taxes are ignored. Income before taxes is adjusted by the ratio of Enterprise retained earnings and retained earnings after adjustments are made that revert investment securities and derivatives to amortized cost. Therefore, Net Operating Loss (NOL) occurs only when the net income, before the provision for income taxes, is negative.

[d] Payments for estimated income taxes are made quarterly, in the month after the end of the quarter. At the end of each year, the annual estimated tax amount is compared to the annual actual tax amount. In March of the next year, a payment of remaining taxes is made or a refund for overpayment of income taxes is received.

[e] The NOL for the current year is "carried back" to offset taxes in any or all of the preceding two calendar years. (The Enterprises' tax year is the same as the calendar year.) This offset of the prior years' taxes results in a negative provision for income taxes (e.g., income) for the current year. Use of a carry back reduces available carry backs in subsequent years. Any NOL remaining after carry backs are exhausted becomes a carry forward.

[f] Carry forwards represent NOLs that cannot be carried back to offset previous years' taxes, but can be used to offset taxes in any or all of the subsequent 20 years. Carry forwards accumulate until used, or until they expire 20 years after they are generated.

[g] A valuation adjustment is used to eliminate any deferred tax asset.

3.10.3.6 Accounting

[a] The 1992 Act specifies that total capital includes core capital and a general allowance for foreclosure losses. For the Enterprises, this general allowance is represented by general allowances for loan losses on their retained and sold mortgage portfolios. As defined at 12 CFR 1750.2, core capital includes the sum of the following components of equity:

1. The par or stated value of outstanding common stock,
2. The par or stated value of outstanding perpetual, noncumulative preferred stock,
3. Paid-in capital, and
4. Retained earnings.

[b] In order to determine the amount of total capital an Enterprise must hold to maintain positive total capital throughout the ten-year Stress Period, the Stress Test projects the four components of equity listed in paragraph [a] of this section plus general loss allowances as part of the monthly pro forma balance sheets.

[c] Details of an Enterprise's actual balance sheet at the beginning of the Stress Test are recorded from a combination of starting position balances for all instruments for which other components of the Stress Test calculate cash flows and other starting position balances for assets, liabilities, and equity accounts needed to complete an Enterprise's balance sheet.

[d] After recording an Enterprise's balance sheet at the beginning of the Stress Period, the Stress Test creates monthly pro forma balance sheets and income statements by recording output from the cash flow components of the Stress Test; recording new debt and investments (and related interest), dividends, loss allowances, operating expenses, and taxes; and applying accounting rules pertaining to pro forma balance sheets and income statements.

3.10.3.6.1 Accounting for Cash Flows and Accounting Flows

[a] Balances at the beginning of the Stress Test are obtained from the RBC Report. Subsequent changes to related pro forma balance sheet and income statement accounts are obtained from data generated by cash flow components of the Stress Test as follows:

1. *Retained Loans.* For Retained Loans, interest cash flows in the first month of the Stress Period reduce accrued interest receivable at the beginning of the Stress Test. Subsequent months interest cash flows are recorded as accrued interest receivable and interest income in the month prior to receipt. When the interest cash flows are received, accrued interest receivable is reduced. Monthly principal cash flows (including Prepayments and defaulted principal) are recorded as reductions in the outstanding balance of the loan group. Net losses on Defaults are charged off against the allowance for loan losses. Amortization of deferred discounts increases interest income; amortization of deferred premiums decreases interest income.
2. *Mortgage Revenue Bonds.* For mortgage revenue bonds, interest cash flows in the first month of the Stress Period reduce accrued interest receivable at the beginning of the Stress Test. Subsequent months' interest cash flows are recorded as accrued interest receivable and interest income in the month prior to receipt. When the interest cash flows are received, accrued interest receivable is reduced. Monthly principal cash flows (including Prepayments) are recorded in the month received as a reduction in the outstanding balance of mortgage assets. Defaulted principal is charged off when due and is not received. Amortization of deferred discounts increases interest income; amortization of deferred premiums decreases interest income.
3. *Nonmortgage Instruments.* Principal repayments of nonmortgage instruments reduce the nonmortgage instrument and

increases or decreases cash. When the interest cash flows are received or paid, accrued interest receivable or payable is reduced. Accrued interest includes both amounts at the beginning of the Stress Period and subsequent monthly accruals (also recorded as interest income or interest expense). Amortization of deferred discounts and premiums increases or decreases interest income or interest expense. Defaulted principal is charged off when due and not received.

4. *Sold Portfolio.* Sold portfolio cash flows include monthly guarantee fees, float, and principal and interest due MBS investors. Guarantee fees are recorded as income in the month received. Principal and interest due mortgage security investors does not affect the balance sheet; however, interest earned on these amounts (float) is recorded as income in the month the underlying principal and interest payments are received. Principal payments received and defaulted loan balances reduce the outstanding balance of the sold portfolio. Losses (net of recoveries) are charged off against the allowance for losses on the sold portfolio (a liability on the pro forma balance sheets) and reduce cash. Amortization of deferred premiums and discounts increases or decreases guarantee fees.

3.10.3.6.2 Accounting for Non-Cash Items

[a] Changes in the pro forma balances for other parts of the Enterprise's balance sheet not resulting from cash flows are recorded as described in the following nine steps:

1. *Unrealized Gains and Losses.*

a. The valuation impact of any Applicable Fair Value Standards (AFVS), cumulative from their time of implementation, will be reversed out of the starting position data, by debiting any accumulated credits, and crediting any accumulated debits.

(1) AFVS are defined as GAAP pronouncements that require or allow fair value measurements, e.g., EITF 99–20, FAS 65, FAS 87, FAS 115, FAS 133, FAS 140, FAS 149 and FIN 45. Valuation impacts of AVFS pertain only to amounts that are measured at fair value and not to other amounts that are included in AFVS but are not measured at fair value.

(2) The GAAP pronouncements covered by this treatment are subject to OFHEO review. The Enterprises will submit a list of standards and pronouncements that are being reversed in their RBC Reports.

b. After reversing the valuation impact of AFVS, any affected items are presented as follows:

(1) If absent the adoption of the AFVS, the affected transactions measured at fair value would have been accounted for on an amortized cost basis, they are presented as if they had always been accounted for on an amortized cost basis. Amounts not measured at fair value are represented as specified by GAAP and are presented using current GAAP rules.

(2) To the extent that transactions would not have been accounted for on an amortized cost basis, they are accounted for as if they were income and expense items.

2. *Low Income Housing Tax Credit Investments.* Low income housing tax credit investments at the beginning of the Stress Test are converted to cash on a straight line basis over the first six months of the Stress Period.

3. *Other Assets.* The following other assets at the beginning of the Stress Test are converted to cash as follows:

a. Clearing accounts and other miscellaneous receivables (e.g., fees receivable, accounts receivable, and other miscellaneous assets) in the first month of the Stress Test.

b. Earning assets (*see* section 3.9, Alternative Modeling Treatments, of this appendix)

c. Items not covered by a. and b. of this section on a straight-line basis over the first five-years of the Stress Test.

4. *Real Estate Owned (REO).* Real estate owned at the beginning of the Stress Test is converted to cash on a straight-line basis over the first six months of the Stress Test.

5. *Fixed Assets.* 25 percent of fixed assets (net of accumulated depreciation) as of the beginning of the Stress Test remain constant over the Stress Test. The remaining 75 percent is converted to cash on a straight line basis over the ten-year Stress Period. Depreciation is included in the base on which operating expenses are calculated for each month during the Stress Period.

6. *Principal and Interest Payable.* Principal and interest payable to an Enterprise's mortgage security investors at the beginning of the Stress Test are paid during the first two months of the Stress Test (one-half in month one and one-half in month two).

7. *Other Liabilities.* The following liabilities at the beginning of the Stress Test are paid in the first month of the Stress Test, reducing cash:

a. Escrow deposits

b. Other miscellaneous liabilities

8. *Commitments.* No gains or losses are recorded when commitments are added to the Enterprise's sold portfolio. *See* section 3.2.1, of this appendix.

9. *Fully-Hedged Foreign Currency-Denominated Liabilities.* Amounts that relate to currency swaps and foreign currency-denominated liabilities will be treated as follows:

a. Recorded balances that correspond to converted foreign currency-denominated liabilities will be amortized in a manner that is consistent with scheduled pay leg exchanges of notional amounts as set forth in corresponding currency swaps. The unamortized premiums, discounts and/or fees that are associated with these liabilities will be amortized as described in section 3.8, of this appendix, as if they were associated with the pay legs of the corresponding currency swap. Any differences will be reflected as an increase or decrease in Retained Earnings.
b. Interest payable amounts associated with currency swaps will be settled in a manner that is consistent with the contractual terms for these instruments.
c. Receivable amounts associated with currency swaps and interest payable amounts associated with foreign currency-denominated debt will be reversed against Retained Earnings.
d. The adjustments in a., b. and c., of this section, will take place at the start of the Stress Test. These treatments are not applied to instruments that are modeled under AMT (*see* section 3.9, Alternative Modeling Treatments, of this appendix) or foreign currency-denominated instruments that are not fully hedged.

3.10.3.6.3 Other Accounting Principles

The following additional accounting principles apply to the pro forma balance sheets and income statements:

1. All investment securities are treated as held to maturity. As such, they are recorded as assets at amortized cost, not at fair value.
2. All non-securitized mortgage loans will be classified as "held-to-maturity" and will be accounted for on an amortized cost basis.
3. Effective control over the collateral for collateral financings is with the party that originally delivered such collateral.
4. Enterprise Real Estate Investment Trust (REIT) subsidiaries are consolidated. Specifically, REIT assets are treated as Enterprise assets. Preferred stock of the REIT is reflected as Enterprise debt. Dividends paid on the preferred stock are reported as interest expense.
5. Treasury stock is reflected as a reduction in retained earnings.

3.10.4 Operations, Taxes, and Accounting Outputs

For each month of the Stress Period, the Stress Test produces a pro forma balance sheet and income statement. The Operations, Taxes and Accounting component outputs 121 monthly and 11 annual balance sheets, 120 monthly and 10 annual income statements, and 120 monthly and 10 annual cash flow statements, including part-year statements for the first and last calendar years of the Stress Test when necessary. These pro forma financial statements are the inputs for calculation of the risk-based capital requirement (*see* section 3.12, Calculation of the Risk-Based Capital Requirement, of this appendix).

3.11 Treatment of New Enterprise Activities

3.11.1 New Enterprise Activities Overview

[a] Given rapid innovation in the financial services industry, OFHEO anticipates the Enterprises will become involved with new mortgage products, investments, debt and derivative instruments, and business activities, which must be accommodated in the Stress Test in order to capture all of the risk in the Enterprises' businesses. New accounting entries resulting from these innovations and changes in accounting must also be accommodated. The regulation is sufficiently flexible and complete to address new Enterprise activities as they emerge, using the procedures outlined in this section. However, OFHEO will monitor the Enterprises' activities and, when appropriate, propose amendments to this regulation addressing the treatment of new instruments, activities, or accounting treatments.

[b] For the purpose of this section of the appendix, the term New Activity means any type of asset, liability, off-balance-sheet item, accounting entry, or activity to which a Stress Test treatment has not previously been applied. In addition, the Director has the discretion to treat as a New Activity: (1) any activity or instrument with characteristics or unusual features that create risks or hedges for the Enterprise that are not reflected adequately in the specified treatments for similar activities or instruments; and (2) any activity or instrument for which the specified treatment no longer adequately reflects the risk/benefit to the Enterprise, either because of increased volume or because new information concerning those risks/hedges has become available.

3.11.2 New Enterprise Activities Inputs

[a] Complete data and full explanations of the operation of the New Activity sufficient to understand the risk profile of the New Activity must be provided by the Enterprise. The Enterprises are required to notify OFHEO, pursuant to § 1750.12(c), of proposals related to New Activities as soon as possible, but in any event no later than five calendar days after the date on which the transaction closes or is settled. The Enterprises are encouraged to suggest an appropriate capital treatment that will fully capture the credit and interest rate risk in the New Activity. Information on New Activities must also be

submitted and appropriately identified as such in the RBC Report.

[b] The Stress Test will not give an Enterprise the capital benefit associated with a New Activity where OFHEO determines that the impact of that activity on the risk-based capital level of the Enterprise is not commensurate with the economic benefit to the Enterprise.

3.11.3 New Enterprise Activities Procedures

[a] OFHEO will analyze the risk characteristics and determine whether an existing approach specified in the appendix appropriately captures the risk of the New Activity or whether some combination or adaptation of existing approaches specified in the appendix is appropriate. For example, the Stress Test might employ its mortgage performance components and adapt its cash flow components to simulate accurately the loss mitigating effects and counterparty credit risk of credit derivatives.

[b] Where there is no reasonable approach using existing combinations or adaptations of treatments specified in this appendix that could be applied within the timeframe for computing a quarterly capital calculation, the Stress Test will employ an appropriately conservative treatment, consistent with OFHEO's role as a safety and soundness regulator. Such treatment may include an alternative modeling treatment specified in section 3.9, Alternative Modeling Treatments, of this appendix, or some other conservative treatment that OFHEO deems more appropriate.

[c] OFHEO will provide the Enterprise with its estimate of the capital treatment as soon as possible after receiving notice of the New Activity. In any event, the Enterprise will be notified of the capital treatment in accordance with the notice of proposed capital classification provided for in § 1777.21 of this chapter.

[d] After a treatment has been incorporated into a final capital classification, OFHEO will provide notice of such treatment to the public, including the other Enterprise. OFHEO will consider any comments it receives from the public regarding the treatment during subsequent quarters. OFHEO may change the treatment as a result of such input or otherwise, if OFHEO determines that the risks of the New Activity are not appropriately reflected in a treatment previously adopted.

3.11.4 New Enterprise Activities Outputs

The Stress Test will generate a set of cash and/or accounting flows reflecting the treatment applied to the New Activity.

3.12 Calculation of the Risk-Based Capital Requirement

3.12.1 Risk-Based Capital Requirement Overview

The risk-based capital requirement is the sum of (1) the minimum amount of total capital that an Enterprise must hold at the start of the Stress Test in order to maintain positive total capital throughout the ten-year Stress Period, for all financial instruments explicitly modeled in the Stress Test (Stress Test capital subtotal) and (2) certain additional amounts relating to off-balance-sheet items addressed in section 3.9, Alternative Modeling Treatments, of this appendix, and (3) 30 percent of that sum for management and operations risk. The Stress Test capital subtotal is determined based on monthly total capital figures from the pro forma financial statements, the additional amounts related to off-balance-sheet items, and Enterprise short term borrowing and investment rates.

3.12.2 Risk-Based Capital Requirement Inputs

[a] Inputs to the capital calculation are outputs from section 3.3, Interest Rates, section 3.9, Alternative Modeling Treatments, and section 3.10, Operations, Taxes, and Accounting, of this appendix.

[b] For each month of the Stress Test, the following inputs are from, or used in the creation of, pro forma financial statements projected in section 3.10, Operations, Taxes, and Accounting, of this appendix:

1. Total capital
   a. The par or stated value of outstanding common stock,
   b. The par or stated value of outstanding perpetual, noncumulative preferred stock,
   c. Paid-in capital,
   d. retained earnings, and
   e. allowance for losses on retained and sold mortgages less specific losses calculated in accordance with FAS 114,
2. Provision for income taxes (income tax expense),
3. Valuation adjustment that reduces benefits recorded from net operating losses when no net operating loss tax carrybacks are available, and
4. An Enterprise's cash position prior to the decision to issue new debt or purchase new investments to balance the balance sheet (*see* section 3.10.3.1, New Debt and Investments, of this appendix).

[c] For present-value calculations, the Stress Test uses the six-month Enterprise Cost of Funds or the six-month CMT yield as described in section 3.3, Interest Rates, of this appendix.

[d] The amount for off-balance-sheet items that are not explicitly modeled is obtained

from section 3.9.3.1, Off-Balance Sheet Items, of this appendix.

3.12.3 Risk-Based Capital Requirement Procedures

[a] The following eight steps are used to determine the Stress Test capital subtotal and the risk-based capital requirement for an Enterprise:

1. Determine the effective tax rate in each month. If the provision for income taxes is positive (reflecting taxes owed) or negative (reflecting tax refunds to be received), then the effective tax rate is 30 percent. If the provision for income taxes is zero after applying any valuation adjustments (*see* section 3.10.3.6, Accounting, of this appendix), then the effective tax rate applied in step 3. of this section is zero.
2. Determine whether an Enterprise is an investor or a borrower in each month of the Stress Period. In months where an Enterprise has outstanding six-month discount notes that were issued during the stress test, then the Enterprise is a borrower. Otherwise, the Enterprise is an investor.
3. Determine the appropriate monthly discount factor for each month of the Stress Period:
   a. In months where an Enterprise is an investor, the monthly discount factor is based on the yield of short-term assets:

$$\text{Monthly Discount Factor} = \left[1 + \frac{(1 - \text{Effective Tax Rate}) \times \text{6-month CMT yield}}{2}\right]^{1/6}$$

   b. In months where an Enterprise is a borrower, the monthly discount factor is based on the cost of the Enterprise's short-term debt:

$$\text{Monthly Discount Factor} = \left[\frac{1 + \left[(1 - \text{Effective Tax Rate}) \times \left(\frac{\text{6-month Enterprise Cost of Funds}}{2}\right)\right]}{1 - \left[(1 - \text{Effective Tax Rate}) \times 0.00025\right]}\right]^{1/6}$$

Where:

0.00025 is the factor that incorporates the issuance and administrative costs for an Enterprise's new discount notes.

4. Compute the appropriate cumulative discount for each month of the Stress Period. The cumulative discount factor for a given month is the monthly discount factor for that month multiplied by the cumulative discount factor for the preceding month. (The cumulative discount factor for the first month of the Stress Period is the monthly discount factor for that month.) Thus, the cumulative discount factor for any month incorporates all of the previous monthly discount factors.
5. Discount total capital for each month of the Stress Period to the start of the Stress Period for both interest rate scenarios. Divide the total capital for a given month by the cumulative discount factor for that month.
6. Identify the Stress Test capital subtotal, which is the lowest discounted total capital amount from among the 240 monthly discounted total capital amounts.
7. From the Stress Test capital subtotal, subtract the capital required for off-balance sheet items not explicitly modeled in the Stress Test, as calculated in section 3.9.3.1, Off-Balance Sheet Items, of this appendix. Then subtract the resulting difference from the Enterprise's total capital at the start of the Stress Period. The resulting number is the amount of total capital that an Enterprise must hold at the start of the Stress Test in order to maintain positive total capital throughout the ten-year Stress Period.
8. Multiply the minimum total capital amount by 1.3 for management and operations risk.
9. Subtract the net increase (or add the net decrease) in Retained Earnings related to Fair Value Hedges at the start of the stress test made in accordance with section 3.10.3.6.2[a]1.b. of this appendix.

3.12.4 Risk-Based Capital Requirement Output

The output of the calculations in this section is the risk-based capital requirement for an Enterprise at the start date of the Stress Test.

4.0 GLOSSARY

This glossary is intended to define terms in the Regulatory appendix that are used in a computationally specific sense that require a precise quantitative definition.

A

Accounting Flows: one or more series of numbers tracking various components of the accounting computations over time, analogous to "Cash Flows."

Age: of a Mortgage Loan, for computational purpose: the number of scheduled payment dates that have occurred prior to the time at which the Age is determined. The Age of a newly originated Mortgage is zero prior to its first payment date.

Amortization Expense: used in the accounting sense of the monthly allocation of a one-time amount (positive or negative) over time, not to describe amortization of principal in a mortgage.

Amortization Schedule: for a Mortgage Loan, a series of numbers specifying the (1) principal and (2) interest components of each Mortgage Payment, and (3) the Unpaid Principal Balance after each such payment is made.

Allocated Interest: in certain accounting calculations, the amount of interest deemed to be received on a certain date according to an allocation formula, whether or not equal to the amount actually received on that date (*see*, e.g., section 3.6.3.8.3, Whole Loan Accounting Flows Procedures, of this appendix).

Aggregate Limit: see section 3.6.3.6.4.1, Mortgage Credit Enhancement Overview, of this appendix.

B

Balance Limit: see section 3.6.3.6.4.1, Mortgage Credit Enhancement Overview, of this appendix.

Balloon Payment: the final payment of a Balloon Loan, the principal component of which is the entire Unpaid Principal Balance of said loan at the time the Balloon Payment is contractually due.

Balloon Loan: a Mortgage Loan that matures before the Unpaid Principal Balance is fully amortized to zero, thus requiring a large final Balloon Payment.

Balloon Date: the maturity date of a Balloon Loan.

Benchmark: used as an adjective to refer to the economic environment (including interest rates, house prices, and vacancy and rental rates) that prevailed in the region and time period of the Benchmark Loss Experience.

Benchmark Census Division: the Census Division, designated by OFHEO, that is used to determine house prices and vacancy and rental rates of the Stress Period.

Benchmark Loss Experience (BLE): the rates of default and loss severity of loans in the state/year combination (containing at least two consecutive origination years and contiguous areas with a total population equal to or greater than five percent of the population of the United States) with the highest loss rate.

Burnout: in describing Mortgage Prepayments, the reduced rates of Prepayment observed with Mortgage Loans that were not prepaid during earlier periods when it would have been advantageous to do so.

C

Cash Flow Hedges: cash flow hedges as defined by FAS 133.

Census Division: any one of the nine geographic areas of the United States so designated by the Bureau of the Census. The OFHEO House Price Index determined at the Census Division level is used in the Stress Test.

Claim Amount: the amount of Credit Enhancement that an Enterprise is eligible to receive as a reimbursement on mortgage loan losses, which is often but not always equal to the total amount of the loss.

Commitment Loan Groups: hypothetical groups of Mortgage Loans assumed to be originated during the months immediately after the start of the Stress Test pursuant to Commitments made but not yet fulfilled by the Enterprises prior to the start of the Stress Test to purchase or securitize loans.

Contract: a Mortgage Credit Enhancement contract covering a distinct set of loans with a distinct set of contractual terms.

Constant Maturity Treasury (CMT) Rate: see table 3–18, Interest Rate and Index Inputs.

Counterparty Type: classification used to specify the appropriate Haircut level in section 3.5, Counterparty Defaults, of this appendix.

Credit Enhancement: for the GSEs, agreements with lenders or third-parties put in place to reduce or limit mortgage credit (default) losses for an individual loan. *See* section 3.1.2.1.1, Loan Group Inputs, of this appendix.

D

Debt Service Coverage Ratio: see section 3.6.3.5.3.1, Explanatory Variables, of this appendix.

Default: for purposes of computing rates of mortgage default and losses, *see* the specific process specified in section 3.6.1, Whole Loan Cash Flows Overview, of this appendix.

Defaulting Fraction: in any month, for any group of loans, the proportion of loans newly defaulted in that month expressed as a fraction of the *initial* loans (by number or by balance, depending on how Prepayment and Default Rates are measured) in the loan group; *see*, e.g., section 3.6.3.4.3.2, Prepayment and

Default Rates and Performance Fractions, of this appendix.

Defaulted UPB: the Unpaid Principal Balance (UPB) of a loan in the month that it Defaults.

Deferred Balances: see section 3.6.3.8.1, Whole Loan Accounting Flows Overview, of this appendix.

Derivative Mortgage Security: generally refers to securities that receive cash flow with significantly different characteristics than the aggregate cash flow from the underlying mortgage loans, such as Interest-Only or Principal-Only Stripped MBSs or REMIC Residual Interests. *See* section 3.7.1, Mortgage-Related Securities Overview, of this appendix.

Deposit Limit: see section 3.6.3.6.4.1, Mortgage Credit Enhancement Overview, of this appendix.

Distinct Credit Combination (DCC): see section 3.6.3.6.4.1, Mortgage Credit Enhancement Overview, of this appendix.

E

Enterprise Cost of Funds: Cost of funds used in computing the cost of new debt for the Enterprises during the Stress Test, as specified in section 3.3.3.[a]3.c., of this appendix.

Enterprise Loss Position: see section 3.6.3.6.4.1, Mortgage Credit Enhancement Overview, of this appendix.

F

Fair Value Hedges: fair value hedges as described in FAS 133.

Float Income: the earnings on the investment of loan principal and interest payments (net of the Servicing Fee and Guarantee Fee) from the time these payments are received from the servicer until they are remitted to security holders. *See* section 3.6.1, Whole Loan Cash Flows Overview, of this appendix.

G

Gross Loss Severity: Loss Severity including the excess, if any, of Defaulted UPB over gross sale price of an REO property, fees, expenses and certain unpaid interest amounts, before giving effect to Credit Enhancement or any other amounts received on account of a defaulted loan (all such amounts expressed as a fraction of Defaulted UPB); *see* section 3.6.3.6.2, Single Family Gross Loss Severity, and section 3.6.3.6.3, Multifamily Gross Loss Severity, of this appendix.

Guarantee Fee: the amount received by an Enterprise as payment for guaranteeing a mortgage loan; *see,* e.g., section 3.6.3.2, Payment Allocation Conventions, of this appendix.

H

Haircut: the amount by which payments from a counterparty are reduced to account for a given probability of counterparty failure.

I

Initial: used as an adjective to specify conditions at the start of the Stress Test, except in defined terms; *see also* Time Zero.

Initial Rate Period: for an Adjustable Rate Mortgage, the number of months before the mortgage interest rate changes for the first time. Also known as "teaser period."

Interest-only Period: for interest-only loans, the period of time for which the monthly payment covers only the interest due. (During the interest-only period, the UPB of the loan stays constant until maturity or a changeover date. For loans that mature, a Balloon Payment in the amount of the UPB is due at maturity. In other cases, the loan payment is recast at the changeover date and the loan begins to amortize over its remaining term.) *See* section 3.6.3.3.1, Mortgage Amortization Schedule Overview, of this appendix.

Interest Rates: the Constant Maturity Treasury yields and other interest rates and indexes used in the Stress Test.

Investor-owned: a property that is not owner-occupied.

L

Loan Limit: used to describe a type of Credit Enhancement; *see* section 3.6.3.6.4.1, Mortgage Credit Enhancement Overview, of this appendix.

Loan Group: a group of one or more mortgage loans with similar characteristics, that are treated identically for computational purposes in the Risk-Based Capital calculations.

Loss Severity: the amount of a mortgage loss divided by the Defaulted UPB.

Loss Sharing Arrangements (LSA): see section 3.6.3.6.4.1, Mortgage Credit Enhancement Overview, of this appendix.

M

Maximum Haircut: as defined in section 3.5, Counterparty Defaults, of this appendix.

Modified Pool Insurance: a form of Single Family Mortgage Credit Enhancement described in section 3.6.3.6.4.1, Mortgage Credit Enhancement Overview, of this appendix.

Mortgage Insurance (Primary Mortgage Insurance): a type of credit enhancement that pays claims up to a given limit on each loan. *See* section 3.6.3.6.4.1, Mortgage Credit Enhancement Overview, of this appendix.

Mortgage Related Security: a collective reference for (1) securities directly backed by mortgage loans, such as Single Class MBSs, Multi-Class MBSs (REMICs or Collaterilized Mortgage Obligations (CMOs)); (2) Derivative Mortgage-Backed Securities (certain multi-class and strip securities) issued by Fannie

Mae, Freddie Mac, and Ginnie Mae; (3) Mortgage Revenue Bonds issued by State and local governments and their instrumentalities; or (4) single class and Derivative Mortgage-Backed Securities issued by private entities. *See* section 3.1.2.2, Mortgage-Related Securities Inputs, of this appendix.

N

Negative Amortization: as defined in section 3.6.3.2.1, Allocation of Mortgage Interest, of this appendix.

Net Loss Severity: Gross Loss Severity reduced by Credit Enhancements and any other amounts received on account of a defaulted loan (all such amounts expressed as a fraction of Defaulted UPB).

Net Yield Rate: the Mortgage Interest Rate minus the Servicing Fee Rate.

New Activity: as defined in section 3.11, Treatment of New Enterprise Activities, of this appendix.

Notional Amount: the amount analogous to a principal balance which is used to calculate interest payments in certain swap transactions or derivative securities.

O

Original: used as an adjective to specify values in effect at Loan Origination.

Origination: for a Mortgage Loan with monthly payments, the date one month prior to the first contractual payment date.

Owner-Occupied: a property, or a Mortgage Loan backed by a property, that is a single family residence which is the primary residence of the owner.

P

Pass-Through Rate: the Mortgage Interest Rate minus the Servicing Fee and the Guarantee Fee.

Performing Fraction: in any month, for any group of loans, the proportion of loans that have not either prepaid or defaulted in that month or any prior month, expressed as a fraction of the loans at the start of the Stress Test (by number or by balance, depending on how Prepayment and Default rates are measured) in a loan group; *see* e.g., section 3.6.3.4.3.2, Prepayment and Default Rates and Performance Fractions, of this appendix.

Prepaying Fraction: in any month, for any group of loans, the proportion of loans that prepay in full in that month expressed as a fraction of the loans at the start of the Stress Test (by number or by balance, depending on how Prepayment and Default rates are measured) in the loan group; *see* e.g., section 3.6.3.4.3.2, Prepayment and Default Rates and Performance Fractions, of this appendix.

Prepayment: the prepayment in full of a loan before its contractual maturity date

Prepayment Interest Shortfall: as defined in section 3.6.3.1, Timing Conventions, of this appendix.

R

Risk-Based Capital (RBC) Report: The form in which Enterprise data is to be submitted for purposes of calculating the risk-based capital requirement, as described in section 3.1, Data, of this appendix.

Relative Spread: as defined in section 3.6.3.4.3.1, Single Family Default and Prepayment Explanatory Variables, of this appendix.

Retained Loans: as described in section 3.6.1, Whole Loan Cash Flows Overview, of this appendix.

S

Scheduled Principal: the amount of principal reduction that occurs in a given month according to the Amortization Schedule of a mortgage loan; *see* section 3.6.3.3, Mortgage Amortization Schedule, of this appendix.

Servicing Fee: portion of mortgage interest payment retained by servicer.

Sold Loans: as described in section 3.6.1, Whole Loan Cash Flows Overview, of this appendix.

Spread Accounts: a form of Credit Enhancement; section 3.6.3.6.4, Mortgage Credit Enhancement, of this appendix.

Stress Period: the 10-year period covered by the Stress Test simulation.

Stress Test: the calculation, which applies specified economic assumptions to Enterprise portfolios, described in this appendix.

Strike Rate: the interest rate above/below which interest is received for caps/floors.

Subordination Agreements: a form of Credit Enhancement in which the cash flows allocable to a portion of a mortgage pool are used to cover losses on loans allocable to another portion of the mortgage pool; *see* section 3.6.3.6.4, Mortgage Credit Enhancement, of this appendix.

T

Time Zero: used to designate the conditions in effect at the start of the Stress Test, as defined in section 3.6.3.1, Timing Conventions, of this appendix.

U

Unpaid Principal Balance (UPB): the Unpaid Principal Balance of a loan or loan group based solely on its Amortization Schedule, without giving effect to any missed or otherwise unscheduled payments.

W

Whole Loan: a mortgage loan.

[66 FR 47806, Sept. 13, 2001, as amended at 67 FR 11861, Mar. 15, 2002; 67 FR 66535, Nov. 1, 2002; 68 FR 7312, Feb. 13, 2003; 71 FR 75087, Dec. 14, 2006; 73 FR 35895, June 25, 2008]

APPENDIX B TO SUBPART B OF PART 1750 [RESERVED]

PART 1770—EXECUTIVE COMPENSATION

AUTHORITY: 12 U.S.C. 1452(h)(2), 1723a(d)(3)(B), 4501(6), 4502(3), 4502(7), 4513, 4514, 4517, 4518(a), 4631, 4632, 4636, 4641.

SOURCE: 66 FR 47554, Sept. 12, 2001, unless otherwise noted.

§ 1770.1 Authority and scope.

(a) *Authority.* Title XIII of the Housing and Community Development Act of 1992, Pub. L. No. 102–550, entitled the Federal Housing Enterprises Financial Safety and Soundness Act of 1992 ("the Act") (12 U.S.C. 4501 *et seq.*), established the Office of Federal Housing Enterprise Oversight ("OFHEO") as an independent office within the Department of Housing and Urban Development. In general, OFHEO is the safety and soundness regulator of two housing-related government sponsored enterprises: the Federal National Mortgage Association ("Fannie Mae") and the Federal Home Loan Mortgage Corporation ("Freddie Mac") (collectively, "the Enterprises"). The supervisory responsibilities of the Director of OFHEO (the "Director") include oversight of compensation provided by the Enterprises to their executive officers.

(b) *Scope.* The procedures set forth in this part apply to OFHEO's oversight of executive compensation under the following two statutory mandates:

(1) *Prohibition of excessive compensation.* The Act requires the Director to prohibit an Enterprise from providing compensation to any executive officer that is not reasonable and comparable with that paid by other similar businesses to executives doing similar work, *i.e.*, having similar duties and responsibilities. Businesses used for comparison purposes include publicly held financial institutions or major financial services companies. (12 U.S.C. 4518(a)). To effectuate this compensation oversight responsibility, the Act provides that the Director has full authority to take such actions as the Director determines are necessary. (12 U.S.C. 4513(8)). However, the Director may not prescribe or set a specific level or range of compensation for executive officers of the Enterprises. (12 U.S.C. 4518(b)).

(2) *Prior approval of termination benefits.* The Enterprises' enabling statutes ("charter acts") similarly provide that an Enterprise may not enter into any agreement or contract to provide any payment of money or other thing of current or potential value in connection with the termination of employment of an executive officer unless the agreement or contract is approved in advance by the Director. The Director may only approve termination benefits that are comparable to benefits provided by other public or private entities involved in financial services and housing interests to executives with comparable duties and responsibilities. Agreements or contracts that provide for termination payments to executives that were entered into before October 28, 1992 are not retroactively subject to approval or disapproval by the Director. However, a renegotiation, amendment or change to such an agreement or contract entered into on or before October 28, 1992 shall be considered as entering into an agreement or contract that is subject to approval by the Director. (Section 309(d)(3)(B); 12 U.S.C. 1723a(d)(3)(B) of Fannie Mae's Charter Act; Section 303(h)(2); 12 U.S.C. 1452(h)(2) of Freddie Mac's Corporation Act)

§ 1770.2 Purpose.

In exercising responsibilities related to executive compensation, the Director has established a structured process for the submission of relevant information by each Enterprise. This part codifies those procedures and clarifies the terms used therein in order to facilitate and enhance the efficiency of OFHEO's oversight.

§ 1770.3 Definitions.

The following definitions apply to the terms used in this part:

(a) *The Act* is Title XIII of the Housing and Community Development Act of 1992, Pub. L. No. 102–550, Oct. 28, 1992, 106 Stat. 3672, 3941 through 4012 (1993), 12 U.S.C. 4501 *et seq.*, separately entitled the "Federal Housing Enterprises Financial Safety and Soundness Act of 1992."

(b) *Affiliate* means, except as provided by the Director, any entity that controls, is controlled by, or is under common control with, an Enterprise.

(c) *Charter acts* mean the Federal National Mortgage Association Charter Act and the Federal Home Loan Mortgage Corporation Act, which are codified at 12 U.S.C. 1716 through 1723i and 12 U.S.C. 1451 through 1459, respectively.

(d) *Compensation* means any payment of money or the provision of any other thing of current or potential value in connection with employment. Compensation includes all direct and indirect payments of benefits, both cash and non-cash, granted to or for the benefit of any executive officer, including, but not limited to, payments and benefits derived from an employment contract compensation or benefit agreement, fee arrangement, perquisite, stock option plan, post employment benefit or other compensatory arrangement.

(e) *Director* means the Director of OFHEO or his or her designee.

(f) *Enterprise* means the Federal National Mortgage Association and the Federal Home Loan Mortgage Corporation and, except as provided by the Director, any affiliate thereof.

(g)(1) *Executive officer* means, with respect to an Enterprise:

(i) The chairman of the board of directors, chief executive officer, chief financial officer, chief operating officer, president, vice chairman, any executive vice president, and any individual who performs functions similar to such positions whether or not the individual has an official title; and

(ii) Any senior vice president (SVP) or other individual with similar responsibilities, without regard to title:

(A) Who is in charge of a principal business unit, division or function, or

(B) Who reports directly to the Enterprise's chairman of the board of directors, vice chairman, president or chief operating officer.

(2) The Director shall inform the Enterprises of those officers covered by this definition.

(h) *OFHEO* means the Office of Federal Housing Enterprise Oversight.

§ 1770.4 Submission requirements.

(a) *Submission of information to OFHEO.* All information required to be filed for purposes of this part is to be provided in a timely fashion by each Enterprise to OFHEO's Associate Director of the Office of Policy Analysis and Research, as specified in this section, or as designated by the Director.

(b) *Categories of information relating to prohibition of excessive compensation.* The following materials, unless otherwise specified, shall be provided by each Enterprise to OFHEO for review within one week after the specified action or event:

(1) Resolutions, including supporting materials and related reports, from meetings of the Enterprise's committee responsible for compensation when the committee takes any action regarding a compensation matter that under the committee's authority is effective without further action by the committee or the board of directors;

(2) Resolutions, including supporting materials and related reports (not otherwise provided to OFHEO under paragraph (b)(1) of this section), from meetings of the board of directors relating to executive compensation when the board of directors takes any action regarding a compensation matter that is effective without any further action by the board of directors;

(3) Minutes, including supporting materials and related reports, when adopted by the committee responsible for compensation and those portions of minutes of the board of directors, including supporting materials and related reports, related to compensation matters (except for materials previously provided under paragraphs (b)(1) or (2) of this section);

(4) General benefit plans applicable to executive officers when adopted or amended;

(5) Any study conducted by or on behalf of an Enterprise with respect to compensation of executive officers;

(6) The Enterprise's annual compensation report to Congress when submitted;

(7) A current organizational chart when changes occur affecting the status of executive officers under this part;

(8) Proxy statements when issued; and,

(9) Such other information as deemed appropriate by the Director, except that submissions required under this paragraph shall not include materials related to the performance of specific individuals.

(c) *Timing of submissions related to prior approval of termination benefits.* All relevant information, except as provided under § 1770.5(a), should be provided to OFHEO, unless already provided under paragraph (b) of this section:

(1) Before an Enterprise enters into any agreement or contract with a new or existing executive officer that includes termination benefits;

(2) Before an Enterprise makes any extension or other amendment to such an agreement or contract;

(3) Before an Enterprise takes any other action to provide termination benefits to a specific executive officer, regardless of how effected; or

(4) When an Enterprise makes any changes to the termination provisions of any compensation or benefit program affecting multiple executive officers.

(d) *Specific information required for calculation of termination benefits.* For submissions under paragraph (c) of this section, an Enterprise shall submit to OFHEO the following materials:

(1) The details of the agreement or program change, e.g., employment agreements, termination agreements, severance agreements, and portions of minutes of the board of directors relating to executive compensation and minutes and supporting materials of the compensation Committee of the board of directors;

(2) All information, data, assumptions and calculations for the potential total dollar value or range of values of the benefits provided, such as but not limited to salary, bonus opportunity, short-term incentives, long-term incentives, special incentives and pension provisions or related contract or benefit terms; and

(3) Such other information deemed appropriate by the Director, except that information required to be submitted under paragraph (c) of this section or under this paragraph shall not include information on benefit plans of general applicability.

§ 1770.5 Compliance.

(a) An employment agreement or contract subject to the Director's prior approval, as set forth in § 1770.1(b)(2), may be entered into prior to that approval, *provided that* such agreement or contract specifically provides that termination benefits under the agreement or contract shall not be effective and no payments shall be made thereunder unless and until approved by OFHEO. Such notice should make clear that alteration of benefit plans subsequent to OFHEO approval under this section, that affect final termination benefits of an executive officer, requires review at the time of the individual's termination from the Enterprise and prior to the payment of any benefits.

(b) Failure by an Enterprise to comply with the requirements this regulation may warrant remedial action by OFHEO. Such action may be taken in the form determined appropriate by the Director and may be taken separately from, in conjunction with, or in addition to any other corrective or remedial action, including an enforcement action to require an individual to make restitution to or reimbursement to the Enterprise of excessive compensation or inappropriately paid termination benefits.

PART 1777—PROMPT CORRECTIVE ACTION

Subpart B—Capital Classifications and Orders Under Section 1366 of the 1992 Act

AUTHORITY: 12 U.S.C. 1452(b)(2), 1456(c), 1718(c)(2), 1723a(k), 4513(a), 4513(b), 4514, 4517, 4611–4619, 4622, 4623, 4631, 4635.

SOURCE: 67 FR 3598, Jan. 25, 2002, unless otherwise noted.

§ 1777.1 Authority, purpose, scope, and implementation dates.

(a) *Authority*. This part is issued by the Office of Federal Housing Enterprise Oversight (OFHEO) pursuant to sections 1313, 1371, 1372, and 1376 of the Federal Housing Enterprises Financial Safety and Soundness Act (1992 Act) (12 U.S.C. 4513, 4631, 4632, and 4636). These provisions broadly authorize OFHEO to take such actions as are deemed appropriate by the Director of OFHEO to ensure that the Federal National Mortgage Association and the Federal Home Loan Mortgage Corporation (collectively, the Enterprises) maintain adequate capital and operate in a safe and sound manner.

(b) *Authority, purpose and scope of subpart A*. In addition to the authority set forth in paragraph (a) of this section, subpart A of this part is also issued pursuant to section 1314 of the 1992 Act (12 U.S.C. 4514), section 307(c) of the Federal Home Loan Mortgage Corporation Act (12 U.S.C. 1456(c)), and section 309(k) of the Federal National Mortgage Association Charter Act (12 U.S.C. 1723a(k)), requiring each Enterprise to submit such reports to OFHEO as the Director of OFHEO determines, in his or her judgment, are necessary to carry out the purposes of the 1992 Act. Subpart A of this part is also issued in reliance on section 1317 of the 1992 Act (12 U.S.C. 4517) authorizing OFHEO to conduct examinations of the Enterprises. The purpose of subpart A of this part is to set forth a framework of early intervention supervisory measures, other than formal enforcement actions, that OFHEO may take to address emerging developments that merit supervisory review to ensure they do not pose a current or future threat to the safety and soundness of an Enterprise. OFHEO's initiation of procedures under subpart A does not necessarily indicate that any unsound condition exists. The supervisory responses enumerated in § 1777.11 do not constitute orders under the 1992 Act for purposes of sections 1371 and 1376 thereof (12 U.S.C. 4631 and 4636).

(c) *Authority, purpose, and scope of subpart B*. In addition to the authority set forth in paragraph (a) of this section, subpart B of this part is also issued pursuant to subtitle B of the 1992 Act (12 U.S.C. 4611 through 4623), section 303(b)(2) of the Federal Home Loan Mortgage Corporation Act (12 U.S.C. 1452(b)(2)), and section 303(c)(2) of the Federal National Mortgage Association Charter Act (12 U.S.C. 1718(c)(2)). These provisions authorize OFHEO to administer certain capital requirements for the Enterprises, to classify the capital of the Enterprises based on capital levels specified in the 1992 Act, and, in appropriate circumstances, to exercise discretion to reclassify an Enterprise into a lower capital category. Under these provisions, there are also automatic consequences for an Enterprise that is not classified as adequately capitalized, as well as discretionary authority for OFHEO to require an Enterprise to take remedial actions. Subpart B implements the provisions of sections 1364 through 1368, 1369(b) through (e), 1369C, and 1369D of the 1992 Act as they apply to the Enterprises (12 U.S.C. 4614 through 4618, 4619(b) through (e), 4622 and 4623). The principal purposes of subpart B are to identify the capital measures and capital levels that OFHEO uses in determining the capital classification of an Enterprise; to set out the procedures OFHEO uses in determining such capital classifications; to establish procedures for submission and review of capital restoration plans of an Enterprise that is not classified as adequately capitalized; and to establish procedures under which OFHEO issues orders pursuant to section 1366(b)(1) through (4) of the 1992 Act (12 U.S.C. 4616(b)(1) through (4)).

(d) *Effective dates of capital classifications.* Section 1364 of the 1992 Act (12 U.S.C. 4614(d)) directs OFHEO to determine capital classifications for the Enterprises by reference to two capital standards, consisting of the minimum or critical capital level on the one hand, and the risk-based capital level on the other. Section 1364(d) of the 1992 Act (12 U.S.C. 4614(d)) excludes consideration of whether the Enterprises meet the risk-based capital level in determining capital classifications or reclassifications under 1364, until one year after the effective date of OFHEO's regulation implementing OFHEO's risk-based capital test (issued under section 1361(e) of the 1992 Act (12 U.S.C. 4611(e)), until such time, section 1364(d) provides that an Enterprise is to be classified as adequately capitalized so long as it meets the minimum capital level. Subpart B contains a currently effective set of capital classifications omitting consideration of the risk-based capital level, as well as another set of capital classifications which will take effect, and displace the current set of capital classifications, on September 13, 2002 that is, one year after the effective date of OFHEO's risk-based capital rule published at 66 FR 47730, September 13, 2001.

§ 1777.2 Preservation of other authority.

(a) *Supervisory standards.* Notwithstanding the existence of procedures in § 1777.10 for the Director of OFHEO to designate certain developments for supervisory response under subpart A of this part, nothing in this part in any way limits the authority of OFHEO otherwise to take such actions with respect to any issue as is deemed appropriate by the Director of OFHEO to ensure that the Enterprises maintain adequate capital, operate in a safe and sound manner, and comply with the 1992 Act and regulations, orders, and agreements thereunder.

(b) *Capital floor.* Classification of an Enterprise as adequately capitalized in accordance with subtitle B of the 1992 Act and subpart B of this part indicates that the Enterprise meets the capital levels under sections 1361 and 1362 of the 1992 Act (12 U.S.C. 4611 and 4612) and regulations promulgated thereunder as of the times specified in the classification determination. Nothing in subpart B of this part or subtitle B of the 1992 Act limits OFHEO's authority otherwise to address circumstances that would require additional capital through regulations, orders, notices, guidance, or other actions.

(c) *Form of supervisory action or response.* In addition to the supervisory responses contemplated under subpart A of this part, and the authority to classify and reclassify the Enterprises, to issue orders, and to appoint conservators under subpart B of this part, the 1992 Act grants OFHEO broad discretion to take such other supervisory actions as may be deemed by OFHEO to be appropriate, including issuing temporary and permanent cease and desist orders, imposing civil money penalties, appointing a conservator under section 1369(a)(1) through (2) of the 1992 Act (12 U.S.C. 4619(a)(1) through (2)), entering into a written agreement the violation of which is actionable through enforcement proceedings, or entering into any other formal or informal agreement with an Enterprise. Neither the 1992 Act nor this part in any way limit OFHEO's discretion over the selection of the type of these actions, and the selection of one type of action under this part or under these other statutory authorities, or a combination thereof, does not foreclose OFHEO from pursuing any other action.

§ 1777.3 Definitions.

For purposes of this part, the following definitions will apply:

1992 Act means the Federal Housing Enterprises Financial Safety and Soundness Act, 12 U.S.C. 4501 *et seq.*

Affiliate means an entity that controls an Enterprise, is controlled by an Enterprise, or is under common control with an Enterprise.

Capital distribution means:

(1) Any dividend or other distribution in cash or in kind made with respect to

any shares of, or other ownership interest in, an Enterprise, except a dividend consisting only of shares of the Enterprise; and

(2) Any payment made by an Enterprise to repurchase, redeem, retire, or otherwise acquire any of its shares or other ownership interests, including any extension of credit made to finance an acquisition by the Enterprise of such shares or other ownership interests, except to the extent the Enterprise makes a payment to repurchase its shares for the purpose of fulfilling an obligation of the Enterprise under an employee stock ownership plan that is qualified under section 401 of the Internal Revenue Code of 1986 (26 U.S.C. 401 *et seq.*) or any substantially equivalent plan as determined by the Director of OFHEO in writing in advance.

Core capital has the same meaning as provided in 12 CFR 1750.2.

Critical capital level means the amount of core capital that is equal to the sum of one half of the amount determined under 12 CFR 1750.4(a)(1) and five-ninths of the amounts determined under 12 CFR 1750.4(a)(2) through 1750.4(a)(7).

Enterprise means the Federal National Mortgage Association and any affiliate thereof, and the Federal Home Loan Mortgage Corporation and any affiliate thereof.

Minimum capital level means the minimum amount of core capital specified for an Enterprise pursuant to section 1362 of the 1992 Act (12 U.S.C. 4612), as determined under 12 CFR 1750.4.

OFHEO means the Office of Federal Housing Enterprise Oversight.

Risk-based capital level means the amount of total capital specified for an Enterprise pursuant to section 1361 of the 1992 Act (12 U.S.C. 4611), as determined under OFHEO's regulations implementing section 1361.

Total capital has the same meaning as provided at 12 CFR 1750.11(n).

Subpart A—Prompt Supervisory Response

§ 1777.10 Developments prompting supervisory response.

In the event of any of the following developments, OFHEO shall undertake one of the supervisory responses enumerated in § 1777.11, or a combination thereof:

(a) OFHEO's national House Price Index (HPI) for the most recent quarter is more than two percent less than the national HPI four quarters previously, or for any Census Division or Divisions in which are located properties securing more than 25 percent of single-family mortgages owned or securing securities guaranteed by an enterprise, the HPI for the most recent quarter for such Division or Divisions is more than five percent less than the HPI for that Division or Divisions four quarters previously;

(b) An Enterprise's publicly reported net income for the most recent calendar quarter is less than one-half of its average quarterly net income for any four-quarter period during the prior eight quarters;

(c) An Enterprise's publicly reported net interest margin (NIM) for the most recent quarter is less than one-half of its average NIM for any four-quarter period during the prior eight quarters;

(d) For single-family mortgage loans owned or securities by an Enterprise that are delinquent ninety days or more or in foreclosure, the proportion of such loans in the most recent quarter has increased more than one percentage point compared to the lowest proportion of such loans in any of the prior four quarters; or

(e) Any other development, including conduct of an activity by an Enterprise, that OFHEO determines in its discretion presents a risk to the safety and soundness of the Enterprise or a possible violation of applicable law, regulation, or order.

§ 1777.11 Supervisory response.

(a) *Level I supervisory response*—(1) *Supervisory letter.* Not later than five business days after OFHEO determines that a development enumerated in § 1777.10 has transpired, OFHEO shall deliver a supervisory letter alerting the chief executive officer or the board of directors of the Enterprise to OFHEO's determination.

(2) *Contents of supervisory letter.* The supervisory letter shall notify the Enterprise that, pursuant to this subpart, OFHEO is commencing review of a potentially adverse development. As is

appropriate under the particular circumstances and the nature of the potentially adverse development, the letter may direct the Enterprise to undertake one or more of the following actions, as of such time as OFHEO directs:

(i) Provide OFHEO with any relevant information known to the Enterprise about the potentially adverse development, in such format as OFHEO directs;

(ii) Respond to specific questions and concerns that OFHEO poses about the potentially adverse development; and

(iii) Take appropriate action.

(3) *Review; further action.* Based on the Enterprise's response to the supervisory letter and consideration of other relevant factors, OFHEO shall promptly determine whether the Level I supervisory response is adequate to resolve any supervisory issues implicated by the potentially adverse development, or whether additional supervisory response under this section is warranted.

(4) *Sequence of supervisory responses.* The Level II through Level IV supervisory responses in paragraphs (b) through (d) of this section may be carried out in any sequence, including simultaneous performance of two or more such responses. OFHEO may also carry out one or more such responses simultaneously with a Level I supervisory response pursuant to this paragraph (a).

(b) *Level II supervisory response*—(1) *Special review.* In addition to any other supervisory response described in this section, OFHEO may conduct a special review of an Enterprise in order to assess the impact of the potentially adverse development on the Enterprise.

(2) *Review; further action.* Based on the results of the special review and consideration of other factors deemed by OFHEO to be relevant, OFHEO shall promptly determine whether additional supervisory response under this section is warranted.

(c) *Level III supervisory response*—(1) *Action plan.* In addition to any other supervisory response described in this section, OFHEO may direct the Enterprise to prepare and submit an action plan to OFHEO, in such format and at such time as OFHEO directs.

(2) *Contents of action plan.* Such action plan shall include, subject to additional direction by OFHEO, the following:

(i) In the case of any potentially adverse development arising from conditions or practices internal to the Enterprise, any relevant information known to the Enterprise about the circumstances that led to the potentially adverse development;

(ii) An assessment of likely consequences that the potentially adverse development may have for the Enterprise; and

(iii) The proposed course of action the Enterprise will undertake in response to the potentially adverse development, including an explanation as to why such approach is preferred to any other alternative actions by the Enterprise and how such approach will address the concerns of OFHEO.

(3) *Review; further action.* If OFHEO in its discretion determines that the information, assessment, or proposed course of action contained in the action plan is incomplete or inadequate, OFHEO shall promptly direct the Enterprise to correct such deficiencies to the extent OFHEO determines such corrections will aid in resolving supervisory issues implicated by the potentially adverse development, and will promptly determine whether additional supervisory response under this section is warranted.

(d) *Level IV supervisory response*—(1) *Notice to show cause.* In addition to any other supervisory response described in this section, OFHEO may issue written notice to the chief executive officer or the board of directors of the Enterprise directing the Enterprise to show cause, on or before the date specified in the notice, why OFHEO should not issue one or more of the following:

(i) A notice of charges to the Enterprise under section 1371 of the 1992 Act (12 U.S.C. 4631) and the procedures in 12 CFR part 1780 commencing an action to order the Enterprise to cease and desist conduct, conditions, or violations specified in the notice to show cause;

(ii) A temporary order to the Enterprise under section 1372 of the 1992 Act (12 U.S.C. 4632) and the procedures in 12 CFR part 1780 to cease and desist from, and take affirmative actions to prevent or remedy harm from, conduct, conditions, or violations specified in the notice to show cause;

(iii) A notice of charges under section 1376 of the 1992 Act (12 U.S.C. 4636) and the procedures in 12 CFR part 1780 commencing imposition of a civil money penalty against the Enterprise; or

(iv) A notice of discretionary reclassification of the Enterprise's capital classification under section 1364(b) of the 1992 Act (12 U.S.C. 4614(b)) and subpart B of this part.

(2) *Review; further action.* Based on the Enterprise's response to the notice to show cause and consideration of other relevant factors, OFHEO shall promptly determine whether to commence the actions described in the notice, and whether additional supervisory response under this section is warranted.

§ 1777.12 Other supervisory action.

Notwithstanding the pendency or completion of one or more supervisory responses described in § 1777.11, OFHEO may at any time undertake additional supervisory steps and actions in the form of any informal or formal supervisory tool available to OFHEO under the 1992 Act, including, but not limited to, issuing guidance or directives under section 1313 (12 U.S.C. 4513), requiring reports under section 1314 (12 U.S.C. 4514), conducting other examinations under section 1317 (12 U.S.C. 4517), issuing discretionary reclassification under section 1364 (12 U.S.C. 4614), initiating discretionary action under section 1366(b) (12 U.S.C. 4616(b)), appointing a conservator under section 1369(a) (12 U.S.C. 4619(a)), or initiating administrative enforcement action under sections 1371, 1372, and 1376 (12 U.S.C. 4631, 4632 and 4636). In addition, OFHEO may take any such steps or actions with respect to an Enterprise that fails to make a submission or comply with a directive as required by § 1777.11, or to address an Enterprise's failure to implement an appropriate action in response to a supervisory letter or under an action plan under § 1777.11.

Subpart B—Capital Classifications and Orders Under Section 1366 of the 1992 Act

§ 1777.20 Capital classifications.

(a) *Capital classifications after the effective date of section 1365 of the 1992 Act.* The capital classification of an Enterprise for purposes of subpart B of this part is as follows:

(1) *Adequately capitalized.* Except as otherwise provided under paragraph (a)(5) of this section, an Enterprise will be classified as adequately capitalized if the Enterprise:

(i) As of the date specified in the notice of proposed capital classification, holds total capital equaling or exceeding the risk-based capital level; and

(ii) As of the date specified in the notice of proposed capital classification, holds core capital equaling or exceeding the minimum capital level.

(2) *Undercapitalized.* Except as otherwise provided under paragraph (a)(5) of this section or § 1777.23(c) or § 1777.23(h), an Enterprise will be classified as undercapitalized if the Enterprise:

(i) As of the date specified in the notice of proposed capital classification, holds total capital less than the risk-based capital level; and

(ii) As of the date specified in the notice of proposed capital classification, holds core capital equaling or exceeding the minimum capital level.

(3) *Significantly undercapitalized.* Except as otherwise provided under paragraph (a)(5) of this section or § 1777.23(c) or § 1777.23(h), an Enterprise will be classified as significantly undercapitalized if the Enterprise:

(i) As of the date specified in the notice of proposed capital classification, holds core capital less than the minimum capital level; and

(ii) As of the date specified in the notice of proposed capital classification, holds core capital equaling or exceeding the critical capital level.

(4) *Critically undercapitalized.* An Enterprise will be classified as critically undercapitalized if, as of the date specified in the notice of proposed capital classification, the Enterprise holds core capital less than the critical capital level.

(5) *Discretionary reclassification—determination to reclassify.* If OFHEO determines in writing that an Enterprise is engaging in action or inaction (including a failure to respond appropriately to changes in circumstances or unforeseen events) that could result in a rapid depletion of core capital, or that the value of property subject to mortgages held or securitized by the Enterprise has decreased significantly, or that reclassification is otherwise deemed necessary to ensure that the Enterprise holds adequate capital and operates safely, OFHEO may reclassify the Enterprise as:

(i) Undercapitalized if the Enterprise is otherwise classified as adequately capitalized;

(ii) Significantly undercapitalized if the Enterprise is otherwise classified as undercapitalized; or

(iii) Critically undercapitalized if the Enterprise is otherwise classified as significantly undercapitalized.

(b) *Duration of reclassification; successive reclassifications.* (1) A reclassification of an Enterprise based on action, inaction, or conditions under paragraph (a)(5) or (c)(5) of this section shall be considered in the determination of each subsequent capital classification of the Enterprise, and shall only cease being considered in the determination of the Enterprise's capital classification after OFHEO determines that the action, inaction or condition upon which the reclassification was based has ceased or been eliminated and remedied to OFHEO's satisfaction.

(2) If the action, inaction, or condition upon which a reclassification was based under paragraph (a)(5) or (c)(5) of this section has not ceased or been eliminated and remedied to OFHEO's satisfaction within such reasonable time as is determined by OFHEO to be appropriate, OFHEO may consider such failure to be the basis for additional reclassification under such paragraph (a)(5) or (c)(5) of this section into a lower capital classification.

(c) *Capital classifications before the effective date of section 1365 of the 1992 Act.* Notwithstanding paragraph (a) of this section, until September 13, 2002, the capital classification of an Enterprise for purposes of subpart B of this part is as follows:

(1) *Adequately capitalized.* Except as otherwise provided in paragraph (c)(5) of this section, an Enterprise will be classified as adequately capitalized if the Enterprise, as of the date specified in the notice of proposed capital classification, holds core capital equaling or exceeding the minimum capital level.

(2) *Undercapitalized.* An Enterprise will be classified as undercapitalized if the Enterprise:

(i) As of the date specified in the notice of proposed capital classification, holds core capital equaling or exceeding the minimum capital level; and

(ii) Is reclassified as undercapitalized by OFHEO under paragraph (c)(5) of this section.

(3) *Significantly undercapitalized.* Except as otherwise provided under paragraph (c)(5) of this section or § 1777.23(c) or § 1777.23(h), an Enterprise will be classified as significantly undercapitalized if the Enterprise:

(i) As of the date specified in the notice of proposed capital classification, held core capital less than the minimum capital level; and

(ii) As of the date specified in the notice of proposed capital classification, held core capital equaling or exceeding the critical capital level.

(4) *Critically undercapitalized.* An Enterprise will be classified as critically undercapitalized if, as of the date specified in the notice of proposed capital classification, the Enterprise held core capital less than the critical capital level.

(5) *Discretionary reclassification.* If OFHEO determines in writing that an Enterprise is engaging in action or inaction (including a failure to respond appropriately to changes in circumstances or unforeseen events) that could result a rapid depletion of core capital, or that the value of the property subject to mortgages held or securitized by the Enterprise has decreased significantly or that reclassification is deemed necessary to ensure that the Enterprise holds adequate capital and operates safely, OFHEO may reclassify the Enterprise as:

(i) Undercapitalized if the Enterprise is otherwise classified as adequately capitalized:

(ii) Significantly undercapitalized if the Enterprise is otherwise classified as undercapitalized; or

(iii) Critically undercapitalized if the Enterprise is otherwise classified as significantly undercapitalized.

(d) *Prior approvals.* In making a determination to reclassify an Enterprise under paragraph (a)(5) or (c)(5) of this section, OFHEO will not base its decision to reclassify solely on action or inaction that previously was given specific approval by the Director of OFHEO in connection with the Director's approval of the Enterprise's capital restoration plan under section 1369C of the 1992 Act (12 U.S.C. 4622), or of a written agreement with the Enterprise that is enforceable in accordance with section 1371 of the 1992 Act.

§ 1777.21 Notice of capital category, and adjustments.

(a) *Notice of capital classification.* OFHEO will classify each Enterprise according to the capital classifications in § 1777.20(a) or § 1777.20(c) on at least a quarterly basis. OFHEO may classify an Enterprise according to the capital classifications in § 1777.20(a) or § 1777.20(c), or reclassify an Enterprise as set out in § 1777.20(a)(5), § 1777.20(c)(5), § 1777.23(c), or § 1777.23(h), at such other times as OFHEO deems appropriate.

(1) *Notice of proposed capital classification.* (i) Before OFHEO classifies or reclassifies an Enterprise, OFHEO will provide the Enterprise with written notice containing the proposed capital classification, the information upon which the proposed classification is based, and the reason for the proposed classification.

(ii) Notices proposing to classify or reclassify an Enterprise as undercapitalized or significantly undercapitalized may be combined with a notice that OFHEO may further reclassify the Enterprise under § 1777.23(c), without additional notice.

(iii) Notices proposing to classify or reclassify an Enterprise as significantly undercapitalized or critically undercapitalized may be combined with a notice under § 1777.24 that OFHEO intends to issue an order under section 1366 of the 1992 Act (12 U.S.C. 4616).

(iv) Notices proposing to classify an Enterprise as undercapitalized or significantly undercapitalized may be combined with a notice proposing to simultaneously reclassify the Enterprise under § 1777.20(a)(5) or § 1777.20(c)(5).

(2) *Response by the Enterprise.* The Enterprise may submit a response to OFHEO containing information for OFHEO's consideration in classifying or reclassifying the Enterprise.

(i) The Enterprise may, within thirty calendar days from receipt of a notice of proposed capital classification, submit a response to OFHEO, unless OFHEO determines the condition of the Enterprise requires a shorter period or the Enterprise consents to a shorter period.

(ii) The Enterprise's response period may be extended for up to an additional thirty calendar days if OFHEO determines there is good cause for such extension.

(iii) The Enterprise's failure to submit a response during the response period (as extended or shortened, if applicable) shall waive any right of the Enterprise to comment on or object to the proposed capital classification.

(3) *Classification determination and written notice of capital classification.* After the Enterprise has submitted its response under paragraph (a)(2) of this section or the response period (as extended or shortened, if applicable) has expired, whichever occurs first, OFHEO will make its determination of the Enterprise's capital classification, taking into consideration such relevant information as is provided by the Enterprise in its response, if any, under paragraph (a)(2) of this section. OFHEO will provide the Enterprise with a written notice of capital classification, which shall include a description of the basis for OFHEO's determination.

(4) *Timing.* OFHEO may, in its discretion, issue a notice of proposed capital classification to an Enterprise at any time. If a notice of proposed classification is pending (under the process set out in paragraphs (a)(1) through (3) of this section) at that time, OFHEO may, in its discretion, specify whether the subsequent notice of proposed capital classification supersedes the pending notice.

(b) *Developments warranting possible change to capital classification*—(1) *Notice to OFHEO.* An Enterprise shall promptly provide OFHEO with written notice of any material development that would result in the Enterprise's core or total capital to fall to a point causing the Enterprise to be placed in a lower capital classification than the capital classification assigned to the Enterprise in its most recent notice of capital classification from OFHEO, or than is proposed to be assigned in the Enterprise's most recent notice of proposed capital classification from OFHEO. The Enterprise shall deliver such notice to OFHEO no later than ten calendar days after the Enterprise becomes aware of such development.

(2) OFHEO, in its discretion, will determine whether to issue a new notice of proposed capital classification under paragraph (a) of this section, based on OFHEO's review of the notice under paragraph (b)(1) of this section from the Enterprise and any other information deemed relevant by OFHEO.

§ 1777.22 Limitation on capital distributions.

(a) *Capital distributions in general.* An Enterprise shall make no capital distribution that would decrease the total capital of the Enterprise to an amount less than the risk-based capital level or the core capital of the Enterprise to an amount less than the minimum capital level without the prior written approval of OFHEO.

(b) *Capital distributions by an Enterprise that is not adequately capitalized*—(1) *Prohibited distributions.* An Enterprise that is not classified as adequately capitalized shall make no capital distribution that would result in the Enterprise being classified into a lower capital classification than the one to which it is classified at the time of such distribution.

(2) *Restricted distributions.* An Enterprise classified as significantly or critically undercapitalized shall make no capital distribution without the prior written approval of OFHEO. OFHEO may grant a request for such a capital distribution only if OFHEO determines, in its discretion, that the distribution:

(i) Will enhance the ability of the Enterprise to meet the risk-based capital level and the minimum capital level promptly;

(ii) Will contribute to the long-term financial safety and soundness of the Enterprise; or

(iii) Is otherwise in the public interest.

§ 1777.23 Capital restoration plans.

(a) *Schedule for filing plans*—(1) *In general.* An Enterprise shall file a capital restoration plan in writing with OFHEO within ten days of receiving a notice of capital classification under § 1777.21(a)(3) stating that the Enterprise is classified as undercapitalized, significantly undercapitalized, or critically undercapitalized, unless OFHEO in its discretion determines an extension of the ten-day period is necessary and provides the Enterprise with written notice of the date the plan is due.

(2) *Successive capital classifications.* Notwithstanding paragraph (a)(1) of this section, an Enterprise that has already submitted and is operating under a capital restoration plan approved by OFHEO under this part is not required to submit an additional capital restoration plan based on a subsequent notice of capital classification, unless OFHEO notifies the Enterprise that it must submit a new or amended capital restoration plan. An Enterprise that receives such a notice to submit a new or amended capital restoration plan shall file in writing with OFHEO a complete plan that is responsive to the terms of and within the deadline specified in such notice.

(b) *Contents of capital restoration plan.* (1) The capital restoration plan submitted under paragraph (a)(1) or (2) of this section shall:

(i) Specify the level of capital the Enterprise will achieve and maintain;

(ii) Describe the actions that the Enterprise will take to become classified as adequately capitalized;

(iii) Establish a schedule for completing the actions set forth in the plan;

(iv) Specify the types and levels of activities (including existing and new programs) in which the Enterprise will engage during the term of the plan;

(v) Describe the actions that the Enterprise will take to comply with any mandatory or discretionary requirements to be imposed under Subtitle B of the 1992 Act (12 U.S.C. 4611 through 4623) or subpart B of this part;

(vi) To the extent the Enterprise is required to submit or revise a capital restoration plan as the result of a reclassification of the Enterprise under § 1777.20(a)(5) or § 1777.20(c)(5), describe the steps the Enterprise will take to cease or eliminate and remedy the action, inaction, or conditions that caused the reclassification; and

(vii) Provide any other information or discuss any other issues as instructed by OFHEO.

(2) The plan shall include a declaration by the chief executive officer, treasurer, or other officer designated by the Board of Directors of the Enterprise to make such declaration, that the material contained in the plan is true and correct to the best of such officer's knowledge and belief.

(c) *Failure to submit*—(1) *Failure to submit; submission of unacceptable plan.* If, upon the expiration of the period provided in paragraph (a)(1) or (2) of this section for an Enterprise to submit a capital restoration plan, an Enterprise fails to comply with the requirement to file a complete capital restoration plan, or if the capital restoration plan is disapproved after review under paragraph (d) of this section, OFHEO may, in accordance with § 1777.21(a)(1)(ii) without additional notice, reclassify the Enterprise:

(i) As significantly undercapitalized if it is otherwise classified as undercapitalized; or

(ii) As critically undercapitalized if it is otherwise classified as significantly undercapitalized.

(2) *Duration of reclassification.* An Enterprise's failure to submit an approved capital restoration plan as described in paragraph (c)(1) of this section shall continue to be grounds for reclassification at each subsequent capital classification of the Enterprise, and shall only cease being considered grounds for reclassification after the Enterprise files a capital restoration plan that receives OFHEO's approval under paragraph (d) of this section.

(3) *Successive reclassifications.* If an Enterprise has not remedied its failure to file a complete capital restoration plan or an acceptable capital restoration plan within such period as is determined by OFHEO to be appropriate, OFHEO may consider such failure to be the basis for additional reclassification under paragraph (c)(1) of this section into a lower capital classification. Such reclassification may be made without additional notice in accordance with § 1777.21(a)(1)(ii).

(d) *Order approving or disapproving plan.* Not later than thirty calendar days after receipt of the Enterprise's complete or amended capital restoration plan under this section (subject to extension upon written notice to the Enterprise for an additional thirty calendar days as OFHEO deems necessary), OFHEO shall issue an order to the Enterprise approving or disapproving the plan. An order disapproving a plan shall include the reasons therefore.

(e) *Resubmission.* An Enterprise that receives an order disapproving its capital restoration plan shall submit an amended capital plan acceptable to OFHEO within thirty calendar days of the date of such order, or a longer period if OFHEO determines an extension is in the public interest.

(f) *Amendment.* An Enterprise that has received an order approving its capital restoration plan may amend the capital restoration plan only after written notice to OFHEO and OFHEO's written approval of the modification. Pending OFHEO's review and approval of the amendment in OFHEO's discretion, the Enterprise shall continue to implement the capital restoration plan under the original approval order.

(g) *Termination*—(1) *Termination under the terms of the plan.* An Enterprise that has received an order approving its capital restoration plan remains bound by each of its obligations under the plan until each such obligation terminates under express terms of the plan itself identifying a date, event, or condition upon which such obligation shall terminate.

(2) *Termination orders.* To the extent the plan does not include such express terms for any obligation thereunder, the Enterprise's obligation continues until OFHEO issues an order terminating such obligation under the plan.

The Enterprise may also submit a written request to OFHEO seeking termination of such obligations. OFHEO will approve termination of such obligation to the extent that OFHEO determines, in its discretion, that the obligation's purpose under the plan has been fulfilled and that termination of the obligation is consistent with the overall safety and soundness of the Enterprise.

(h) *Implementation*—(1) An Enterprise that has received an order approving its capital restoration plan is required to implement the plan.

(i) If OFHEO determines, in its discretion, that an Enterprise has failed to make, in good faith, reasonable efforts necessary to comply with the capital restoration plan and fulfill the schedule thereunder, OFHEO may reclassify the Enterprise:

(A) As significantly undercapitalized if it is otherwise classified as undercapitalized; or

(B) As critically undercapitalized if it is otherwise classified as significantly undercapitalized.

(ii) *Duration of reclassification.* An Enterprise's failure to implement an approved capital restoration plan as described in paragraph (h)(1)(i) of this section shall continue to be grounds for reclassification at each subsequent capital classification of the Enterprise, and shall only cease being considered grounds for reclassification after OFHEO determines, in its discretion, that the Enterprise is making such efforts as are reasonably necessary to comply with the capital restoration plan and fulfill the schedule thereunder.

(iii) *Successive reclassifications.* If an Enterprise has not remedied its failure to implement an approved capital restoration plan within such period as is determined by OFHEO to be appropriate, OFHEO may consider such failure to be the basis for additional reclassification under paragraph (h)(1)(i) of this section into a lower capital classification.

(2) *Administrative enforcement action.* A capital plan that has received an approval order from OFHEO under this section shall constitute an order under the 1992 Act. An Enterprise, regardless of its capital classification, as well as its executive officers, and directors may be subject to action by OFHEO under sections 1371, 1372, and 1376 of the 1992 Act (12 U.S.C. 4631, 4632, and 4636) and 12 CFR part 1780 for failure to comply with such plan.

§ 1777.24 Notice of intent to issue an order.

(a) *Orders under section 1366 of the 1992 Act (12 U.S.C. 4616).* In addition to any other action taken under this part, part 1780 of this chapter, or any other applicable authority, OFHEO may, in its discretion, issue an order to an Enterprise that is classified as significantly undercapitalized or critically undercapitalized, or is in conservatorship, directing the Enterprise to take one or more of the following actions:

(1) Limit any increase in, or reduce, any obligations of the Enterprise, including off-balance sheet obligations;

(2) Limit or eliminate growth of the Enterprise's assets or reduce the amount of the Enterprise's assets;

(3) Acquire new capital, in such form and amount as determined by OFHEO; or

(4) Terminate, reduce, or modify any activity of the Enterprise that OFHEO determines creates excessive risk to the Enterprise.

(b) *Notice of intent to issue an order.* Before OFHEO issues an order to an Enterprise pursuant to section 1366 of the 1992 Act (12 U.S.C. 4616), OFHEO will provide the Enterprise with written notice containing the proposed order.

(c) *Contents of notice.* A notice of intent to issue an order under this subpart shall include:

(1) A statement of the Enterprise's capital classification and its minimum capital level or critical capital level, and its risk-based capital level;

(2) A description of the restrictions, prohibitions, or affirmative actions that OFHEO proposes to impose or require; and

(3) The proposed date when such restrictions or prohibitions would become effective or the proposed date for the commencement and/or completion of the affirmative actions.

§ 1777.25 Response to notice.

(a) *Content of response.* The Enterprise may submit a response to OFHEO containing information for OFHEO's consideration in connection with the proposed order. The response should include, but is in no way limited to, the following:

(1) Any relevant information, mitigating circumstances, documentation, or other information the Enterprise wishes OFHEO to consider in support of the Enterprise's position regarding the proposed order; and

(2) Any recommended modification to the proposed order, and justification thereof.

(b) *Time to respond.* The Enterprise may, within thirty calendar days after receipt of the notice of proposed order, submit a response to OFHEO, unless OFHEO determines a shorter period to be appropriate or the Enterprise consents to a shorter period. OFHEO may extend the Enterprise's response period for up to an additional thirty calendar days if OFHEO determines, in its discretion, that there is good cause for such extension.

(c) *Waiver and consent.* The Enterprise's failure to submit a response during the response period (as extended or shortened, if applicable) shall waive any right of the Enterprise to comment on or object to the proposed order.

§ 1777.26 Final notice of order.

(a) *Determination and notice.* After the Enterprise has submitted its response under § 1777.25 or the response period (as extended or shortened, if applicable) has expired, whichever occurs first, OFHEO will determine, in its discretion, whether to take into consideration such relevant information as is provided by the Enterprise in its response, if any, under § 1777.25. OFHEO will provide the Enterprise with a written final notice of any order issued by OFHEO under this subpart, which is to include a description of the basis for OFHEO's determination.

(b) *Termination or modification.* An Enterprise that has received an order under paragraph (a) of this section remains subject to each provision of the order until each such provision terminates under the express terms of the order. The Enterprise may submit a written request to OFHEO seeking modification or termination of one or more provisions of the order. Pending OFHEO's review and approval, in OFHEO's discretion of the Enterprise's request, the Enterprise shall remain subject to the provisions of the order.

(c) *Enforcement of order*—(1) *Judicial enforcement.* An order issued under paragraph (a) of this section is an order for purposes of section 1375 of the 1992 Act (12 U.S.C. 4635). An Enterprise in any capital classification may be subject to enforcement of such order in the United States District Court for the District of Columbia pursuant to such section.

(2) *Administrative enforcement.* An order issued under paragraph (a) of this section constitutes an order under the 1992 Act. An Enterprise, regardless of its capital classification, as well as its executive officers and directors may be subject to action by OFHEO under sections 1371, 1372, and 1376 of the 1992 Act (12 U.S.C. 4631, 4632, and 4636) and 12 CFR part 1780 for failure to comply with such order.

§ 1777.27 Exhaustion and review.

(a) *Judicial review*—(1) *Review of certain actions.* An Enterprise that is not classified as critically undercapitalized may seek judicial review of a final notice of capital classification issued pursuant to § 1777.21(a)(3) or a final notice of order issued pursuant to § 1777.26(a) in accordance with section 1369D of the 1992 Act (12 U.S.C. 4623)

(2) *Other review barred.* Except as set out in paragraph (a)(1) of this section, or review of conservatorship appointments to the limited extent provided in section 1369(b) of the 1992 Act (12 U.S.C. 4619(b)) and § 1777.28(c), no court shall have jurisdiction to affect, by injunction or otherwise, the issuance or effectiveness of a capital classification or any other action of OFHEO pursuant to this subpart B, as provided in section 1369D of the 1992 Act (12 U.S.C. 4623).

(b) *Exhaustion of administrative remedies.* In connection with any issue for which an Enterprise seeks judicial review in connection with an action described in paragraph (a)(1) of this section, the Enterprise must have first exhausted its administrative remedies, by presenting all its objections, arguments, and information relating to such issue for OFHEO's consideration pursuant to § 1777.21(a)(2), as part of the

Enterprise's response to OFHEO's notice of capital classification, or pursuant to §1777.25, as part of the Enterprise's response to OFHEO's notice of intent to issue an order.

(c) *No stay pending review.* The commencement of proceedings for judicial review of a final capital classification or order as described in paragraph (a)(1) of this section shall not operate as a stay thereof.

§ 1777.28 Appointment of conservator for a significantly undercapitalized or critically undercapitalized Enterprise.

(a) *Significantly undercapitalized Enterprise.* At any time after an Enterprise is classified as significantly undercapitalized, OFHEO may issue an order appointing a conservator for the Enterprise upon determining that:

(1) The amount of core capital of the Enterprise is less than the minimum capital level; and

(2) The alternative remedies available to OFHEO under the 1992 Act are not satisfactory.

(b) *Critically undercapitalized Enterprise*—(1) *Appointment upon classification.* Not later than thirty days after issuing a final notice of capital classification pursuant to §1777.21(a)(3) classifying an Enterprise as significantly undercapitalized, OFHEO shall issue an order appointing a conservator for the Enterprise.

(2) *Exception.* Notwithstanding paragraph (b)(1) of this section, OFHEO may determine not to appoint a conservator if OFHEO makes a written finding, with the written concurrence of the Secretary of the Treasury, that:

(i) The appointment of a conservator would have serious adverse effects on economic conditions of national financial markets or on the financial stability of the housing finance market; and

(ii) The public interest would be better served by taking some other enforcement action authorized under this title.

(c) *Judicial review.* An Enterprise for which a conservator has been appointed pursuant to paragraph (a) or (b) of this section may seek judicial review of the appointment in accordance with section 1369(b) of the 1992 Act (12 U.S.C. 4619(b)). Except as provided therein, no court may take any action regarding the removal of a conservator or otherwise restrain or affect the exercise of the powers or functions of a conservator.

(d) *Termination*—(1) *Upon reaching the minimum capital level.* OFHEO will issue an order terminating a conservatorship appointment under paragraph (a) or (b) of this section upon a determination that the Enterprise has maintained an amount of core capital that is equal to or exceeds the minimum capital level.

(2) *In OFHEO's discretion.* OFHEO may, in its discretion, issue an order terminating a conservatorship appointment under paragraph (a) or (b) of this section upon a determination that such termination order is in the public interest and may safely be accomplished.

SUBCHAPTER D—RULES OF PRACTICE AND PROCEDURE

EFFECTIVE DATE NOTE: At 76 FR 74649, Dec. 1, 2011, subchapter D was removed, effective January 3, 2012.

PARTS 1780–1799 [RESERVED]

CHAPTER XVIII—COMMUNITY DEVELOPMENT FINANCIAL INSTITUTIONS FUND, DEPARTMENT OF THE TREASURY

PART 1805—COMMUNITY DEVELOPMENT FINANCIAL INSTITUTIONS PROGRAM

AUTHORITY: 12 U.S.C. 4703, 4703 note, 4710, 4717; and 31 U.S.C. 321.

SOURCE: 70 FR 73888, Dec. 13, 2005, unless otherwise noted.

Subpart A—General Provisions

§ 1805.100 Purpose.

The purpose of the Community Development Financial Institutions Program is to promote economic revitalization and community development through investment in and assistance to Community Development Financial Institutions.

§ 1805.101 Summary.

Under the Community Development Financial Institutions Program, the Fund will provide financial and technical assistance to Applicants selected by the Fund in order to enhance their ability to make loans and investments and provide services. An Awardee must serve an Investment Area(s), Targeted Population(s), or both. The Fund will select Awardees to receive financial and technical assistance through a merit-based qualitative application process. Each Awardee will enter into an Assistance Agreement which will require it to achieve performance goals negotiated between the Fund and the Awardee and abide by other terms and conditions pertinent to any assistance received under this part.

§ 1805.102 Relationship to other Fund programs.

(a) *Bank Enterprise Award Program.* (1) No Community Development Financial Institution may receive a Bank Enterprise Award under the Bank Enterprise Award (BEA) Program (part 1806 of this chapter) if it has:

(i) An application pending for assistance under the Community Development Financial Institutions Program;

(ii) Directly received assistance in the form of a disbursement under the Community Development Financial Institutions Program within the preceding 12-month period prior to the date the Fund selected the CDFI to receive a Bank Enterprise Award (meaning, the date of the Fund's BEA Program notice of award); or

(iii) Ever directly received assistance under the Community Development Financial Institutions Program for the same activities for which it is seeking a Bank Enterprise Award.

(2) An equity investment (as defined in part 1806 of this chapter) in, or a loan to, a Community Development Financial Institution, or deposits in an Insured Community Development Financial Institution, made by a BEA Program Awardee may be used to meet the matching funds requirements described in subpart E of this part. Receipt of such equity investment, loan, or deposit does not disqualify a Community Development Financial Institution from receiving assistance under this part.

(b) *Liquidity enhancement program.* No entity that receives assistance through the liquidity enhancement program authorized under section 113 (12 U.S.C. 4712) of the Act may receive assistance under the Community Development Financial Institutions Program.

§ 1805.103 Awardee not instrumentality.

No Awardee (or its Community Partner) shall be deemed to be an agency, department, or instrumentality of the United States.

§ 1805.104 Definitions.

For the purpose of this part:

(a) *Act* means the Community Development Banking and Financial Institutions Act of 1994, as amended (12 U.S.C. 4701 *et seq.*);

(b) *Affiliate* means any company or entity that Controls, is Controlled by, or is under common Control with another company;

(c) *Applicant* means any entity submitting an application for CDFI Program assistance or funding under this part;

(d) *Appropriate Federal Banking Agency* has the same meaning as in section 3 of the Federal Deposit Insurance Act (12 U.S.C. 1813(q)), and includes, with respect to Insured Credit Unions, the National Credit Union Administration;

(e) *Appropriate State Agency* means an agency or instrumentality of a State that regulates and/or insures the member accounts of a State-Insured Credit Union;

(f) *Assistance Agreement* means a formal agreement between the Fund and an Awardee which specifies the terms and conditions of assistance under this part;

(g) *Awardee* means an Applicant selected by the Fund to receive assistance pursuant to this part;

(h) *Community Development Financial Institution* (or *CDFI*) means an entity currently meeting the eligibility requirements described in § 1805.200;

(i) *Community Development Financial Institution Intermediary* (or *CDFI Intermediary*) means an entity that meets the CDFI Program eligibility requirements described in § 1805.200 and whose primary business activity is the provision of Financial Products to CDFIs and/or emerging CDFIs;

(j) *Community Development Financial Institutions Program* (or *CDFI Program*) means the program authorized by sections 105–108 of the Act (12 U.S.C. 4704–4707) and implemented under this part;

(k) *Community Facility* means a facility where health care, childcare, educational, cultural, or social services are provided;

(l) *Community-Governed* means an entity in which the residents of an Investment Area(s) or members of a Targeted Population(s) represent greater than 50 percent of the governing body;

(m) *Community-Owned* means an entity in which the residents of an Investment Area(s) or members of a Targeted Population(s) have an ownership interest of greater than 50 percent;

(n) *Community Partner* means a person (other than an individual) that provides loans, Equity Investments, or Development Services and enters into a Community Partnership with an Applicant. A Community Partner may include a Depository Institution Holding Company, an Insured Depository Institution, an Insured Credit Union, a State-Insured Credit Union, a not-for-profit or for-profit organization, a State or local government entity, a quasi-government entity, or an investment company authorized pursuant to the Small Business Investment Act of 1958 (15 U.S.C. 661 *et seq.*);

(o) *Community Partnership* means an agreement between an Applicant and a Community Partner to collaboratively provide Financial Products or Development Services to an Investment Area(s) or a Targeted Population(s);

(p) *Comprehensive Business Plan* means a document covering not less than the next five years which meets the requirements described in an applicable Notice of Funds Availability (NOTICE OF FUNDS AVAILABILITY);

(q) *Control* means: (1) Ownership, control, or power to vote 25 percent or more of the outstanding shares of any class of Voting Securities of any company, directly or indirectly or acting through one or more other persons; (2) Control in any manner over the election of a majority of the directors, trustees, or general partners (or individuals exercising similar functions) of any company; or (3) The power to exercise, directly or indirectly, a controlling influence over the management, credit or investment decisions, or policies of any company.

(r) *Depository Institution Holding Company* means a bank holding company or a savings and loan holding company as defined in section 3 of the Federal Deposit Insurance Act (12 U.S.C. 1813(w)(1));

(s) *Development Services* means activities that promote community development and are integral to the Applicant's provision of Financial Products and Financial Services. Such services shall prepare or assist current or potential borrowers or investees to utilize the Financial Products or Financial Services of the Applicant. Such services include, for example: financial or credit counseling to individuals for the purpose of facilitating home ownership, promoting self-employment, or enhancing consumer financial management skills; or technical assistance to borrowers or investees for the purpose of enhancing business planning, marketing, management, and financial management skills;

(t) *Equity Investment* means an investment made by an Applicant that, in the judgment of the Fund, supports or enhances activities that serve an Investment Area(s) or a Targeted Population(s). Such investments must be made through an arms-length transaction with a third party that does not have a relationship with the Applicant as an Affiliate. Equity Investments may comprise a stock purchase, a purchase of a partnership interest, a purchase of a limited liability company membership interest, a loan made on such terms that it has sufficient characteristics of equity (and is considered as such by the Fund), a purchase of secondary capital, or any other investment deemed to be an Equity Investment by the Fund;

(u) *Financial Products* means: Loans, Equity Investments and similar financing activities (as determined by the Fund) including the purchase of loans originated by certified CDFIs and the provision of loan guarantees; in the case of CDFI Intermediaries, grants to CDFIs and/or emerging CDFIs and deposits in Insured Credit Union CDFIs, emerging Insured Credit Union CDFIs, and/or State-Insured Credit Union CDFIs.

(v) *Financial Services* means checking, savings accounts, check cashing, money orders, certified checks, automated teller machines, deposit taking, safe deposit box services, and other similar services;

(w) *Fund* means the Community Development Financial Institutions Fund established under section 104(a) (12 U.S.C. 4703(a)) of the Act;

(x) *Indian Reservation* means any geographic area that meets the requirements of section 4(10) of the Indian Child Welfare Act of 1978 (25 U.S.C. 1903(10)), and shall include land held by incorporated Native groups, regional corporations, and village corporations, as defined in and pursuant to the Alaska Native Claims Settlement Act (43 U.S.C. 1602), public domain Indian allotments, and former Indian reservations in the State of Oklahoma;

(y) *Indian Tribe* means any Indian Tribe, band, pueblo, nation, or other organized group or community, including any Alaska Native village or regional or village corporation, as defined in or established pursuant to the Alaska Native Claims Settlement Act (43 U.S.C. 1601 et seq.), which is recognized as eligible for special programs and services provided by the United

States to Indians because of their status as Indians;

(z) *Insider* means any director, officer, employee, principal shareholder (owning, individually or in combination with family members, five percent or more of any class of stock), or agent (or any family member or business partner of any of the above) of any Applicant, Affiliate or Community Partner;

(aa) *Insured CDFI* means a CDFI that is an Insured Depository Institution or an Insured Credit Union;

(bb) *Insured Credit Union* means any credit union, the member accounts of which are insured by the National Credit Union Share Insurance Fund;

(cc) *Insured Depository Institution* means any bank or thrift, the deposits of which are insured by the Federal Deposit Insurance Corporation;

(dd) *Investment Area* means a geographic area meeting the requirements of § 1805.201(b)(3);

(ee) *Low-Income* means an income, adjusted for family size, of not more than:

(1) For Metropolitan Areas, 80 percent of the area median family income; and

(2) For non-Metropolitan Areas, the greater of:

(i) 80 percent of the area median family income; or

(ii) 80 percent of the statewide non-Metropolitan Area median family income;

(ff) *Metropolitan Area* means an area designated as such by the Office of Management and Budget pursuant to 44 U.S.C. 3504(e) and 31 U.S.C. 1104(d) and Executive Order 10253 (3 CFR, 1949–1953 Comp., p. 758), as amended;

(gg) *Non-Regulated CDFI* means any entity meeting the eligibility requirements described in § 1805.200 which is not a Depository Institution Holding Company, Insured Depository Institution, Insured Credit Union, or State-Insured Credit Union;

(hh) *State* means any State of the United States, the District of Columbia or any territory of the United States, Puerto Rico, Guam, American Samoa, the Virgin Islands, and the Northern Mariana Islands;

(ii) *State-Insured Credit Union* means any credit union that is regulated by, and/or the member accounts of which are insured by, a State agency or instrumentality;

(jj) *Subsidiary* means any company which is owned or Controlled directly or indirectly by another company and includes any service corporation owned in whole or part by an Insured Depository Institution or any Subsidiary of such a service corporation, except as provided in § 1805.200(b)(4);

(kk) *Targeted Population* means individuals or an identifiable group of individuals meeting the requirements of § 1805.201(b)(3); and

(ll) *Target Market* means an Investment Area(s) and/or a Targeted Population(s).

(mm)(1) *Voting Securities* means shares of common or preferred stock, general or limited partnership shares or interests, or similar interests if the shares or interest, by statute, charter, or in any manner, entitle the holder:

(i) To vote for or select directors, trustees, or partners (or persons exercising similar functions of the issuing company); or

(ii) To vote on or to direct the conduct of the operations or other significant policies of the issuing company.

(2) *Nonvoting shares.* Preferred shares, limited partnership shares or interests, or similar interests are not Voting Securities if:

(i) Any voting rights associated with the shares or interest are limited solely to the type customarily provided by statute with regard to matters that would significantly and adversely affect the rights or preference of the security or other interest, such as the issuance of additional amounts or classes of senior securities, the modification of the terms of the security or interest, the dissolution of the issuing company, or the payment of dividends by the issuing company when preferred dividends are in arrears;

(ii) The shares or interest represent an essentially passive investment or financing device and do not otherwise provide the holder with control over the issuing company; and

(iii) The shares or interest do not entitle the holder, by statute, charter, or in any manner, to select or to vote for the selection of directors, trustees, or partners (or persons exercising similar functions) of the issuing company.

§ 1805.105 Waiver authority.

The Fund may waive any requirement of this part that is not required by law upon a determination of good cause. Each such waiver shall be in writing and supported by a statement of the facts and the grounds forming the basis of the waiver. For a waiver in an individual case, the Fund must determine that application of the requirement to be waived would adversely affect the achievement of the purposes of the Act. For waivers of general applicability, the Fund will publish notification of granted waivers in the FEDERAL REGISTER.

§ 1805.106 OMB control number.

The collection of information requirements in this part have been approved by the Office of Management and Budget and assigned OMB control numbers 1559–0006, 1559–0021 and 1559–0022.

Subpart B—Eligibility

§ 1805.200 Applicant eligibility.

(a) *General requirements.* (1) An entity that meets the requirements described in § 1805.201(b) and paragraph (b) of this section will be considered a CDFI and, subject to paragraph (a)(4) of this section, will be eligible to apply for assistance under this part.

(2) An entity that proposes to become a CDFI is eligible to apply for assistance under this part if the Fund:

(i) Receives a complete application for certification from the entity within the time period set forth in an applicable Notice of Funds Availability; and

(ii) Determines that such entity's application materials provide a realistic course of action to ensure that it will meet the requirements described in § 1805.201(b) and paragraph (b) of this section within the period set forth in an applicable Notice of Funds Availability.

(3) The Fund will not, however, disburse any financial assistance to such an entity before it meets the requirements described in this section. Moreover, notwithstanding paragraphs (a)(1) and (a)(2)(ii) of this section, the Fund reserves the right to require an entity to have been certified as described in § 1805.201(a) prior to its submission of an application for assistance, as set forth in an applicable Notice of Funds Availability.

(4) The Fund shall require an entity to meet any additional eligibility requirements that the Fund deems appropriate.

(5) The Fund, in its sole discretion, shall determine whether an Applicant fulfills the requirements set forth in this section and § 1805.201(b).

(b) *Provisions applicable to Depository Institution Holding Companies and Insured Depository Institutions.* (1) A Depository Institution Holding Company may qualify as a CDFI only if it and its Affiliates collectively satisfy the requirements described in this section.

(2) No Affiliate of a Depository Institution Holding Company may qualify as a CDFI unless the holding company and all of its Affiliates collectively meet the requirements described in this section.

(3) No Subsidiary of an Insured Depository Institution may qualify as a CDFI if the Insured Depository Institution and its Subsidiaries do not collectively meet the requirements described in this section.

(4) For the purposes of paragraphs (b)(1), (2) and (3) of this section, an Applicant will be considered to be a Subsidiary of any Insured Depository Institution or Depository Institution Holding Company that controls 25 percent or more of any class of the Applicant's voting shares, or otherwise controls, in any manner, the election of a majority of directors of the Applicant.

§ 1805.201 Certification as a Community Development Financial Institution.

(a) *General.* An entity may apply to the Fund for certification that it meets the CDFI eligibility requirements regardless of whether it is seeking financial or technical assistance from the Fund. Entities seeking such certification shall provide the information set forth in the application for certification. Certification by the Fund will verify that the entity meets the CDFI eligibility requirements. However, such certification shall not constitute an opinion by the Fund as to the financial viability of the CDFI or that the CDFI will be selected to receive an award from the Fund. The Fund, in its sole discretion, shall have the right to decertify a certified entity after a determination that the eligibility requirements of paragraph (b) of this section, § 1805.200(b) or (a)(4) (if applicable) are no longer met.

(b) *Eligibility verification.* An Applicant shall demonstrate whether it meets the eligibility requirements described in this paragraph (b) of this section and § 1805.200 by providing the information described in the application for certification demonstrating that the Applicant meets the eligibility requirements described in paragraphs (b)(1) through (b)(6) of this section. The Fund, in its sole discretion, shall determine whether an Applicant has satisfied the requirements of this paragraph (b) and § 1805.200.

(1) *Primary mission.* A CDFI shall have a primary mission of promoting community development. In determining whether an Applicant has such a primary mission, the Fund will consider whether the activities of the Applicant are purposefully directed toward improving the social and/or economic conditions of underserved people (which may include Low-Income persons and persons who lack adequate access to capital and/or Financial Services) and/or residents of economically distressed communities (which may include Investment Areas).

(2) *Financing entity.* A CDFI shall be an entity whose predominant business activity is the provision, in armslength transactions, of Financial Products, Development Services, and/or other similar financing. An Applicant may demonstrate that it is such an entity if it is a(n):

(i) Depository Institution Holding Company;

(ii) Insured Depository Institution, Insured Credit Union, or State-Insured Credit Union; or

(iii) Organization that is deemed by the Fund to have such a predominant business activity as a result of analysis of its financial statements, organizing documents, and any other information required to be submitted as part of its application. In conducting such analysis, the Fund may take into consideration an Applicant's total assets and its use of personnel.

(3) *Target Market.* (i) *General.* An Applicant may be found to serve a Target Market by virtue of serving one or more Investment Areas and/or Targeted Populations. An Investment Area shall meet specific geographic and other criteria described in paragraph (b)(3)(ii) of this section, and a Targeted Population shall meet the criteria described in paragraph (b)(3)(iii) in this section.

(ii) *Investment Area.* (A) *General.* A geographic area will be considered eligible for designation as an Investment Area if it:

(*1*) Is entirely located within the geographic boundaries of the United States (which shall encompass any State of the United States, the District of Columbia or any territory of the United States, Puerto Rico, Guam, American Samoa, the Virgin Islands, and the Northern Mariana Islands); and either

(*2*) Meets at least one of the objective criteria of economic distress as set forth in paragraph (b)(3)(ii)(D) of this section and has significant unmet needs for loans, Equity Investments, or Financial Services as described in paragraph (b)(3)(ii)(E) of this section; or

(*3*) Encompasses (i.e. wholly consists of) or is wholly located within an Empowerment Zone or Enterprise Community designated under section 1391 of the Internal Revenue Code of 1986 (26 U.S.C. 1391).

(B) *Geographic units.* Subject to the remainder of this paragraph (B), an Investment Area shall consist of a geographic unit(s) that is a county (or equivalent area), minor civil division that is a unit of local government, incorporated place, census tract, block numbering area, block group, or American Indian or Alaska Native area (as such units are defined or reported by the U.S. Bureau of the Census). However, geographic units in Metropolitan Areas that are used to comprise an Investment Area shall be limited to census tracts, block groups and American

Indian or Alaskan Native areas. An Applicant may designate one or more Investment Areas as part of a single application.

(C) *Designation.* An Applicant may designate an Investment Area by selecting:

(*1*) A geographic unit(s) which individually meets one of the criteria in paragraph (b)(3)(ii)(D) of this section; or

(*2*) A group of contiguous geographic units which together meet one of the criteria in paragraph (b)(3)(ii)(D) of this section, provided that the combined population residing within individual geographic units not meeting any such criteria does not exceed 15 percent of the total population of the entire Investment Area.

(D) *Distress criteria.* An Investment Area (or the units that comprise an area) must meet at least one of the following objective criteria of economic distress (as reported in the most recently completed decennial census published by the U.S. Bureau of the Census):

(*1*) The percentage of the population living in poverty is at least 20 percent;

(*2*) In the case of an Investment Area located:

(*i*) Within a Metropolitan Area, the median family income shall be at or below 80 percent of the Metropolitan Area median family income or the national Metropolitan Area median family income, whichever is greater; or

(*ii*) Outside of a Metropolitan Area, the median family income shall be at or below 80 percent of the statewide non-Metropolitan Area median family income or the national non-Metropolitan Area median family income, whichever is greater;

(*3*) The unemployment rate is at least 1.5 times the national average;

(*4*) In counties located outside of a Metropolitan Area, the county population loss during the period between the most recent decennial census and the previous decennial census is at least 10 percent; or

(*5*) In counties located outside of a Metropolitan Area, the county net migration loss during the five-year period preceding the most recent decennial census is at least five percent.

(E) *Unmet needs.* An Investment Area will be deemed to have significant unmet needs for loans or Equity Investments if a narrative analysis provided by the Applicant adequately demonstrate a pattern of unmet needs for Financial Products or Financial Services within such area(s).

(F) *Serving Investment Areas.* An Applicant may serve an Investment Area directly or through borrowers or investees that serve the Investment Area or provide significant benefits to its residents.

(iii) *Targeted Population.* (A) *General.* Targeted Population shall mean individuals, or an identifiable group of individuals, who are Low-Income persons or lack adequate access to Financial Products or Financial Services in the Applicant's service area. The members of a Targeted Population shall reside within the boundaries of the United States (which shall encompass any State of the United States, the District of Columbia or any territory of the United States, Puerto Rico, Guam, American Samoa, the Virgin Islands, and the Northern Mariana Islands).

(B) *Serving A Targeted Population.* An Applicant may serve the members of a Targeted Population directly or indirectly or through borrowers or investees that directly serve or provide significant benefits to such members.

(4) *Development Services.* A CDFI directly, through an Affiliate, or through a contract with another provider, shall provide Development Services in conjunction with its Financial Products.

(5) *Accountability.* A CDFI must maintain accountability to residents of its Investment Area(s) or Targeted Population(s) through representation on its governing board or otherwise.

(6) *Non-government.* A CDFI shall not be an agency or instrumentality of the United States, or any State or political subdivision thereof. An entity that is created by, or that receives substantial assistance from, one or more government entities may be a CDFI provided it is not controlled by such entities and maintains independent decision-making power over its activities.

Subpart C—Use of Funds/Eligible Activities

§ 1805.300 Purposes of financial assistance.

The Fund may provide financial assistance through investment instruments described under subpart D of this part. Such financial assistance is intended to strengthen the capital position and enhance the ability of an Awardee to provide Financial Products and Financial Services.

§ 1805.301 Eligible activities.

Financial assistance provided under this part may be used by an Awardee to serve Investment Area(s) or Targeted Population(s) by developing or supporting, through lending, investing, enhancing liquidity, or other means of finance:

(a) Commercial facilities that promote revitalization, community stability or job creation or retention;

(b) Businesses that:

(1) Provide jobs for Low-Income persons;

(2) Are owned by Low-Income persons; or

(3) Enhance the availability of products and services to Low-Income persons;

(c) Community Facilities;

(d) The provision of Financial Services;

(e) Housing that is principally affordable to Low-Income persons, except that assistance used to facilitate home ownership shall only be used for services and lending products that serve Low-Income persons and that:

(1) Are not provided by other lenders in the area; or

(2) Complement the services and lending products provided by other lenders that serve the Investment Area(s) or Targeted Population(s);

(f) The provision of consumer loans (a loan to one or more individuals for household, family, or other personal expenditures); or

(g) Other businesses or activities as requested by the Applicant and deemed appropriate by the Fund.

§ 1805.302 Restrictions on use of assistance.

(a) An Awardee shall use assistance provided by the Fund and its corresponding matching funds only for the eligible activities approved by the Fund and described in the Assistance Agreement.

(b) An Awardee may not distribute assistance to an Affiliate without the Fund's consent.

(c) Assistance provided upon approval of an application involving a Community Partnership shall only be distributed to the Awardee and shall not be used to fund any activities carried out by a Community Partner or an Affiliate of a Community Partner.

§ 1805.303 Technical assistance.

(a) The Fund may provide technical assistance to build the capacity of a CDFI or an entity that proposes to become a CDFI. Such technical assistance may include training for management and other personnel; development of programs, products and services; improving financial management and internal operations; enhancing a CDFI's community impact; or other activities deemed appropriate by the Fund. The Fund, in its sole discretion, may provide technical assistance in amounts, or under terms and conditions that are different from those requested by an Applicant. The Fund may not provide any technical assistance to an Applicant for the purpose of assisting in the preparation of an application. The Fund may provide technical assistance to a CDFI directly, through grants, or by contracting with organizations that possess the appropriate expertise.

(b) The Fund may provide technical assistance regardless of whether the recipient also receives financial assistance under this part. Technical assistance provided pursuant to this part is subject to the assistance limits described in § 1805.402.

(c) An Applicant seeking technical assistance must meet the eligibility requirements described in § 1805.200 and submit an application as described in § 1805.600.

(d) Applicants for technical assistance pursuant to this part will be evaluated pursuant to the merit-based qualitative review criteria in subpart G of this part, except as otherwise may be provided in the applicable Notice of Funds Availability. In addition, the requirements for matching funds are not applicable to technical assistance requests.

Subpart D—Investment Instruments

§ 1805.400 Investment instruments—general.

The Fund will provide financial assistance to an Awardee through one or more of the investment instruments described in § 1805.401, and under such terms and conditions as described in this subpart D. The Fund, in its sole discretion, may provide financial assistance in amounts, through investment instruments, or under rates, terms and conditions that are different from those requested by an Applicant.

§ 1805.401 Forms of investment instruments.

(a) *Equity.* The Fund may make nonvoting equity investments in an Awardee, including, without limitation, the purchase of nonvoting stock. Such stock shall be transferable and, in the discretion of the Fund, may provide for convertibility to voting stock upon transfer. The Fund shall not own more than 50 percent of the equity of an Awardee and shall not control its operations.

(b) *Grants.* The Fund may award grants.

(c) *Loans.* The Fund may make loans, if permitted by applicable law.

(d) *Deposits and credit union shares.* The Fund may make deposits (which shall include credit union shares) in Insured CDFIs and State-Insured Credit Unions. Deposits in an Insured CDFI or a State-Insured Credit Union shall not be subject to any requirement for collateral or security.

§ 1805.402 Assistance limits.

(a) Except as provided in paragraph (b) of this section, the Fund may not provide, pursuant to this part, more than $5 million, in the aggregate, in financial and technical assistance to an Awardee and its Affiliates during any three-year period.

(b) If an Awardee proposes to establish a new Affiliate to serve an Investment Area(s) or Targeted Population(s) outside of any State, and outside of any Metropolitan Area, currently served by the Awardee or its Affiliates, the Awardee may receive additional assistance pursuant to this part up to a maximum of $3.75 million during the same three-year period. Such additional assistance:

(1) Shall be used only to finance activities in the new or expanded Investment Area(s) or Targeted Population(s); and

(2) Must be distributed to a new Affiliate that meets the eligibility requirements described in § 1805.200 and is selected for assistance pursuant to subpart G of this part.

(c) An Awardee may receive the assistance described in paragraph (b) of this section only if no other application to serve substantially the same Investment Area(s) or Targeted Population(s) that meets the requirements of § 1805.701(a) was submitted to the Fund prior to the receipt of the application of said Awardee and within the current funding round.

§ 1805.403 Authority to sell.

The Fund may, at any time, sell its equity investments and loans, provided the Fund shall retain the authority to enforce the provisions of the Assistance Agreement until the performance goals specified therein have been met.

Subpart E—Matching Funds Requirements

§ 1805.500 Matching funds—general.

All financial assistance awarded under this part shall be matched with funds from sources other than the Federal government. Except as provided in § 1805.502, such matching funds shall be provided on the basis of not less than one dollar for each dollar provided by the Fund. Funds that have been used to satisfy a legal requirement for obtaining funds under either the CDFI Program or another Federal grant or award program may not be used to satisfy the matching requirements described in this section. Community Development Block Grant Program and other funds provided pursuant to the

Housing and Community Development Act of 1974, as amended (42 U.S.C. 5301 *et seq.*), shall be considered Federal government funds and shall not be used to meet the matching requirements. Matching funds shall be used as provided in the Assistance Agreement. Funds that are used prior to the execution of the Assistance Agreement may nevertheless qualify as matching funds provided the Fund determines in its reasonable discretion that such use promoted the purpose of the Comprehensive Business Plan that the Fund is supporting through its assistance.

§ 1805.501 Comparability of form and value.

(a) Matching funds shall be at least comparable in form (*e.g.*, equity investments, deposits, credit union shares, loans and grants) and value to financial assistance provided by the Fund (except as provided in § 1805.502). The Fund shall have the discretion to determine whether matching funds pledged are comparable in form and value to the financial assistance requested.

(b) In the case of an Awardee that raises matching funds from more than one source, through different investment instruments, or under varying terms and conditions, the Fund may provide financial assistance in a manner that represents the combined characteristics of such instruments.

(c) An Awardee may meet all or part of its matching requirements by committing available earnings retained from its operations.

§ 1805.502 Severe constraints waiver.

(a) In the case of an Applicant with severe constraints on available sources of matching funds, the Fund, in its sole discretion, may permit such Applicant to comply with the matching requirements by:

(1) Reducing such requirements by up to 50 percent; or

(2) Permitting an Applicant to provide matching funds in a form to be determined at the discretion of the Fund, if such an Applicant:

(i) Has total assets of less than $100,000;

(ii) Serves an area that is not a Metropolitan Area; and

(iii) Is not requesting more than $25,000 in assistance.

(b) Not more than 25 percent of the total funds available for obligation under this part in any fiscal year may be matched as described in paragraph (a) of this section. Additionally, not more than 25 percent of the total funds disbursed under this part in any fiscal year may be matched as described in paragraph (a) of this section.

(c) An Applicant may request a "severe constraints waiver" as part of its application for assistance. An Applicant shall provide a narrative justification for its request, indicating:

(1) The cause and extent of the constraints on raising matching funds;

(2) Efforts to date, results, and projections for raising matching funds;

(3) A description of the matching funds expected to be raised; and

(4) Any additional information requested by the Fund.

(d) The Fund will grant a "severe constraints waiver" only in exceptional circumstances when it has been demonstrated, to the satisfaction of the Fund, that an Investment Area(s) or Targeted Population(s) would not be adequately served without the waiver.

§ 1805.503 Time frame for raising match.

Applicants shall satisfy matching funds requirements within the period set forth in the applicable Notice of Funds Availability.

§ 1805.504 Retained earnings.

(a) An Applicant may use its retained earnings to match a request for a financial assistance grant from the Fund. An Applicant that proposes to meet all or a portion of its matching funds requirements by committing available earnings retained from its operations shall be subject to the restrictions described in this section. Retained earnings shall be calculated as directed by the Fund in the applicable Notice of Funds Availability, the financial assistance application and/or related guidance materials. Retained earnings accumulated after the end of the Applicant's most recent fiscal year ending prior to the appropriate application deadline may not be used as matching funds.

(b) In the case of an Applicant that is not an Insured Credit Union or a State-Insured Credit Union, retained earnings that may be used for matching funds purposes shall consist of:

(1) The increase in retained earnings (meaning, for purposes of §1805.504(b), operating income minus operating expenses less any dividend payments) that has occurred over the Applicant's most recent fiscal year (*e.g.*, retained earnings at the end of fiscal year 2003 less retained earnings at the end of fiscal year 2002); or

(2) The annual average of such increases that has occurred over the Applicant's three most recent fiscal years.

(c)(1) In the case of an Applicant that is an Insured Credit Union or a State-Insured Credit Union, retained earnings that may be used for matching funds purposes shall consist of:

(i) The increase in retained earnings that has occurred over the Applicant's most recent fiscal year;

(ii) The annual average of such increases that has occurred over the Applicant's three most recent fiscal years; or

(iii) The entire retained earnings that have been accumulated since the inception of the Applicant, provided that the Assistance Agreement shall require that:

(A) The Awardee shall increase its member shares, non-member shares, outstanding loans and/or other measurable activity as defined in and by an amount that is set forth in an applicable Notice of Funds Availability; and

(B) Such increase must be achieved by a date certain set forth in the applicable Notice of Funds Availability;

(C) The Applicant's Comprehensive Business Plan shall discuss its strategy for achieving the increases described in (c)(1)(iii)(A) of this section and the activities associated therewith;

(D) The level from which the achievement of said increases will be measured will be as of July 31 of the calendar year in which the applicable application deadline falls (or such other date as set forth in the applicable Notice of Funds Availability); and

(E) Financial assistance shall be disbursed by the Fund only as the amount of increases described in paragraph (c)(1)(iii)(A) of this section is achieved.

(2) The Fund will allow an Applicant to utilize the option described in paragraph (c)(1)(iii) of this section for matching funds only if it determines, in its sole discretion, that the Applicant will have a high probability of success in achieving said increases to the specified amounts.

Subpart F—Applications for Assistance

§ 1805.600 Notice of Funds Availability.

Each Applicant shall submit an application for financial or technical assistance under this part in accordance with the applicable Notice of Funds Availability published in the FEDERAL REGISTER. The Notice of Funds Availability will advise potential Applicants on how to obtain an application packet and will establish deadlines and other requirements. The Notice of Funds Availability may specify any limitations, special rules, procedures, and restrictions for a particular funding round. After receipt of an application, the Fund may request clarifying or technical information on the materials submitted as part of such application.

Subpart G—Evaluation and Selection of Applications

§ 1805.700 Evaluation and selection—general.

Applicants will be evaluated and selected, at the sole discretion of the Fund, to receive assistance based on a review process, that could include an interview(s) and/or site visit(s), that is intended to:

(a) Ensure that Applicants are evaluated on a merit basis and in a fair and consistent manner;

(b) Take into consideration the unique characteristics of Applicants that vary by institution type, total asset size, stage of organizational development, markets served, products and services provided, and location;

(c) Ensure that each Awardee can successfully meet the goals of its Comprehensive Business Plan and achieve community development impact;

(d) Ensure that Awardees represent a geographically diverse group of Applicants serving Metropolitan Areas, non-Metropolitan Areas, and Indian Reservations from different regions of the United States; and

(e) Take into consideration other factors as described in the applicable Notice of Funds Availability.

§ 1805.701 Evaluation of applications.

(a) *Eligibility and completeness.* An Applicant will not be eligible to receive assistance pursuant to this part if it fails to meet the eligibility requirements described in § 1805.200 or if it has not submitted complete application materials. For the purposes of this paragraph (a), the Fund reserves the right to request additional information from the Applicant, if the Fund deems it appropriate.

(b) *Substantive review.* In evaluating and selecting applications to receive assistance, the Fund will evaluate the Applicant's likelihood of success in meeting the goals of the Comprehensive Business Plan and achieving community development impact, by considering factors such as:

(1) Community development track record (e.g., in the case of an Applicant with a prior history of serving a Target Market, the extent of success in serving such Target Market);

(2) Operational capacity and risk mitigation strategies;

(3) Financial track record and strength;

(4) Capacity, skills and experience of the management team;

(5) Understanding of its market context, including its analysis of current and prospective customers, the extent of economic distress within the designated Investment Area(s) or the extent of need within the designated Targeted Population(s), as those factors are measured by objective criteria, the extent of need for Equity Investments, loans, Development Services, and Financial Services within the designated Target Market, and the extent of demand within the Target Market for the Applicant's products and services;

(6) Program design and implementation plan, including an assessment of its products and services, marketing and outreach efforts, delivery strategy, and coordination with other institutions and/or a Community Partner, or participation in a secondary market for purposes of increasing the Applicant's resources. In the case of an Applicant submitting an application with a Community Partner, the Fund will evaluate the extent to which the Community Partner will participate in carrying out the activities of the Community Partnership; the extent to which the Community Partner will enhance the likelihood of success of the Comprehensive Business Plan; and the extent to which service to the designated Target Market will be better performed by a Community Partnership than by the Applicant alone;

(7) Projections for financial performance, capitalization and raising needed external resources, including the amount of firm commitments and matching funds in hand to meet or exceed the matching funds requirements and, if applicable, the likely success of the plan for raising the balance of the matching funds in a timely manner, the extent to which the matching funds are, or will be, derived from private sources, and whether an Applicant is, or will become, an Insured CDFI or a State-Insured Credit Union;

(8) Projections for community development impact, including the extent to which an Applicant will concentrate its activities on serving its Target Market(s), the extent of support from the designated Target Market, the extent to which an Applicant is, or will be, Community-Owned or Community-Governed, and the extent to which the activities proposed in the Comprehensive Business Plan will expand economic opportunities or promote community development within the designated Target Market;

(9) The extent of need for the Fund's assistance, as demonstrated by the extent of economic distress in the Applicant's Target Market and the extent to which the Applicant needs the Fund's assistance to carry out its Comprehensive Business Plan;

(10) In the case of an Applicant that has previously received assistance

under the CDFI Program, the Fund also will consider the Applicant's level of success in meeting its performance goals, financial soundness covenants (if applicable), and other requirements contained in the previously negotiated and executed Assistance Agreement(s) with the Fund, the undisbursed balance of assistance, and whether the Applicant will, with additional assistance from the Fund, expand its operations into a new Target Market, offer more products or services, and/or increase the volume of its activities; and

(11) The Fund may consider any other factors, as it deems appropriate, in reviewing an application as set forth in an applicable Notice of Funds Availability.

(c) *Consultation with Appropriate Federal Banking Agencies.* The Fund will consult with, and consider the views of, the Appropriate Federal Banking Agency prior to providing assistance to:

(1) An Insured CDFI;

(2) A CDFI that is examined by or subject to the reporting requirements of an Appropriate Federal Banking Agency; or

(3) A CDFI that has as its Community Partner an institution that is examined by, or subject to, the reporting requirements of an Appropriate Federal Banking Agency.

(d) *Consultation with Appropriate State Agencies.* Prior to providing assistance to a State-Insured Credit Union, the Fund may consult with, and consider the views of, the Appropriate State Agency.

(e) *Awardee selection.* The Fund will select Awardees based on the criteria described in paragraph (b) of this section and any other criteria set forth in this part or the applicable Notice of Funds Availability.

Subpart H—Terms and Conditions of Assistance

§1805.800 Safety and soundness.

(a) *Regulated institutions.* Nothing in this part, or in an Assistance Agreement, shall affect any authority of an Appropriate Federal Banking Agency or Appropriate State Agency to supervise and regulate any institution or company.

(b) *Non-Regulated CDFIs.* The Fund will, to the maximum extent practicable, ensure that Awardees that are Non-Regulated CDFIs are financially and managerially sound and maintain appropriate internal controls.

§1805.801 Notice of Award.

(a) The Fund will generally signify its selection of an Applicant as an Awardee by delivering a signed notice of award to the Applicant. The notice of award will contain the general terms and conditions underlying the Fund's provision of assistance to an Awardee including, but not limited to, the requirement that an Awardee and the Fund enter into an Assistance Agreement.

(b) To become an Awardee under paragraph (a) of this section, an Applicant shall execute the notice of award and return it to the Fund.

(c) By executing a notice of award, an Awardee agrees that, if prior to entering into an Assistance Agreement with the Fund, information comes to the attention of the Fund that either adversely affects the Awardee's eligibility for funding, or adversely affects the Fund's evaluation of the Awardee's application, or indicates fraud or mismanagement on the part of the Awardee, the Fund may, in its discretion and without advance notice to the Awardee, terminate the notice of award or take such other actions as it deems appropriate. Moreover, by executing a notice of award, an Awardee also agrees that, if prior to entering into an Assistance Agreement with the Fund, the Fund determines that the Awardee is not in compliance with the terms of any previous Assistance Agreement entered into with the Fund, the Fund may, in its discretion and without advance notice to the Awardee, either terminate the notice of award or take such other actions as it deems appropriate. An Awardee shall notify the Fund of information that an Awardee may reasonably believe may affect its eligibility or ability to achieve the objectives of its Comprehensive Business Plan as submitted to the Fund (such as changes in management).

(d) The Fund will notify an Awardee of either the Fund's termination of a notice of award or such other action(s) taken by the Fund under paragraph (c) of this section.

§ 1805.802 Assistance Agreement; sanctions.

(a) Prior to providing any assistance, the Fund and an Awardee shall execute an Assistance Agreement that requires an Awardee to comply with performance goals and abide by other terms and conditions of assistance. Such performance goals may be modified at any time by mutual consent of the Fund and an Awardee or as provided in paragraph (c) of this section. If a Community Partner or an Affiliate is part of an application that is selected for assistance, such partner must be a party to the Assistance Agreement, if deemed appropriate by the Fund.

(b) An Awardee shall comply with performance goals that have been negotiated with the Fund and which are based upon the Comprehensive Business Plan submitted as part of the Awardee's application. Such performance goals may include measures that require an Awardee to:

(1) Be financially sound;

(2) Be managerially sound;

(3) Maintain appropriate internal controls; and/or

(4) Achieve specific lending, investment, and development service objectives. Performance goals for Insured CDFIs shall be determined in consultation with the Appropriate Federal Banking Agency, as applicable. Such goals shall be incorporated in, and enforced under, the Awardee's Assistance Agreement. Performance goals for State-Insured Credit Unions may be determined in consultation with the Appropriate State Agency, if deemed appropriate by the Fund.

(c) The Assistance Agreement shall provide that, in the event of fraud, mismanagement, noncompliance with the Act and the Fund's regulations, or noncompliance with the terms and conditions of the Assistance Agreement on the part of the Awardee (or the Community Partner, if applicable), the Fund, in its discretion, may:

(1) Require changes in the performance goals set forth in the Assistance Agreement;

(2) Require changes in the Awardee's Comprehensive Business Plan;

(3) Revoke approval of the Awardee's application;

(4) Reduce or terminate the Awardee's assistance;

(5) Require repayment of any assistance that has been distributed to the Awardee;

(6) Bar the Awardee (and the Community Partner, if applicable) from reapplying for any assistance from the Fund; or

(7) Take such other actions as the Fund deems appropriate.

(d) In the case of an Insured CDFI, the Assistance Agreement shall provide that the provisions of the Act, this part, and the Assistance Agreement shall be enforceable under 12 U.S.C. 1818 of the Federal Deposit Insurance Act by the Appropriate Federal Banking Agency, as applicable, and that any violation of such provisions shall be treated as a violation of the Federal Deposit Insurance Act. Nothing in this paragraph (d) precludes the Fund from directly enforcing the Assistance Agreement as provided for under the terms of the Act.

(e) The Fund shall notify the Appropriate Federal Banking Agency before imposing any sanctions on an Insured CDFI or other institution that is examined by or subject to the reporting requirements of that agency. The Fund shall not impose a sanction described in paragraph (c) of this section if the Appropriate Federal Banking Agency, in writing, not later than 30 calendar days after receiving notice from the Fund:

(1) Objects to the proposed sanction;

(2) Determines that the sanction would:

(i) Have a material adverse effect on the safety and soundness of the institution; or

(ii) Impede or interfere with an enforcement action against that institution by that agency;

(3) Proposes a comparable alternative action; and

(4) Specifically explains:

(i) The basis for the determination under paragraph (e)(2) of this section and, if appropriate, provides documentation to support the determination; and

(ii) How the alternative action suggested pursuant to paragraph (e)(3) of this section would be as effective as the sanction proposed by the Fund in securing compliance and deterring future noncompliance.

(f) In reviewing the performance of an Awardee in which its Investment Area(s) includes an Indian Reservation or Targeted Population(s) includes an Indian Tribe, the Fund shall consult with, and seek input from, the appropriate tribal government.

(g) Prior to imposing any sanctions pursuant to this section or an Assistance Agreement, the Fund shall, to the maximum extent practicable, provide the Awardee (or the Community Partner, if applicable) with written notice of the proposed sanction and an opportunity to comment. Nothing in this section, however, shall provide an Awardee or Community Partner with the right to any formal or informal hearing or comparable proceeding not otherwise required by law.

§ 1805.803 Disbursement of funds.

Assistance provided pursuant to this part may be provided in a lump sum or over a period of time, as determined appropriate by the Fund. The Fund shall not provide any assistance (other than technical assistance) under this part until an Awardee has satisfied any conditions set forth in its Assistance Agreement and has secured in-hand and/or firm commitments for the matching funds required for such assistance pursuant to the applicable Notice of Funds Availability. At a minimum, a firm commitment must consist of a written agreement between an Awardee and the source of the matching funds that is conditioned only upon the availability of the Fund's assistance and such other conditions as the Fund, in its sole discretion, may deem appropriate. Such agreement must provide for disbursal of the matching funds to an Awardee prior to, or simultaneously with, receipt by an Awardee of the Federal funds.

§ 1805.804 Data collection and reporting.

(a) *Data—General.* An Awardee (and a Community Partner, if appropriate) shall maintain such records as may be prescribed by the Fund that are necessary to:

(1) Disclose the manner in which Fund assistance is used;

(2) Demonstrate compliance with the requirements of this part and an Assistance Agreement; and

(3) Evaluate the impact of the CDFI Program.

(b) *Customer profiles.* An Awardee (and a Community Partner, if appropriate) shall compile such data on the gender, race, ethnicity, national origin, or other information on individuals that utilize its products and services as the Fund shall prescribe in an Assistance Agreement. Such data will be used to determine whether residents of Investment Area(s) or members of Targeted Population(s) are adequately served and to evaluate the impact of the CDFI Program.

(c) *Access to records.* An Awardee (and a Community Partner, if appropriate) must submit such financial and activity reports, records, statements, and documents at such times, in such forms, and accompanied by such reporting data, as required by the Fund or the U.S. Department of Treasury to ensure compliance with the requirements of this part and to evaluate the impact of the CDFI Program. The United States Government, including the U.S. Department of Treasury, the Comptroller General, and their duly authorized representatives, shall have full and free access to the Awardee's offices and facilities and all books, documents, records, and financial statements relating to use of Federal funds and may copy such documents as they deem appropriate. The Fund, if it deems appropriate, may prescribe access to record requirements for entities that are borrowers of, or that receive investments from, an Awardee.

(d) *Retention of records.* An Awardee shall comply with all record retention requirements as set forth in OMB Circular A–110 (as applicable).

(e) *Data collection and reporting.* Each Awardee shall submit to the Fund, at least annually and within 180 days after the end of the Awardee's fiscal year, such information and documentation that will permit the Fund to review the Awardee's progress (and the progress of its Affiliates, Subsidiaries, and/or Community Partners, if appropriate) in implementing its Comprehensive Business Plan and satisfying the terms and conditions of its Assistance Agreement. The information and documentation shall include, but not be limited to, an Annual Report, which shall comprise the following components:

(1) *Financial Report:*

(i) All non-profit organizations (excluding Insured CDFIs and State-Insured Credit Unions) must submit to the Fund financial statements that have been reviewed by an independent certified public accountant in accordance with *Statements on Standards for Accounting and Review Services*, issued by the American Institute of Certified Public Accountants, no later than 180 days after the end of the Awardee's fiscal year (audited financial statements can be provided by the due date in lieu of reviewed statements, if available). Non-profit organizations (excluding Insured CDFIs and State-Insured Credit Unions) that are required to have their financial statements audited pursuant to OMB Circular A–133 *Audits of States, Local Governments and Non-Profit Organizations*, must also submit their A–133 audited financial statements to the Fund no later than 270 days after the end of the Awardee's fiscal year. Non-profit organizations (excluding Insured CDFIs and State-Insured Credit Unions) that are not required to have financial statements audited pursuant to OMB Circular A–133, *Audits of States, Local Governments and Non-Profit Organizations*, must submit to the Fund a statement signed by the Awardee's Authorized Representative or certified public accountant, asserting that the Awardee is not required to have a single audit pursuant OMB Circular A–133.

(ii) For-profit organizations (excluding Insured CDFIs and State-Insured Credit Unions) must submit to the Fund financial statements audited in conformity with generally accepted auditing standards as promulgated by the American Institute of Certified Public Accountants, no later than 180 days after the end of the Awardee's fiscal year.

(iii) Insured CDFIs are not required to submit financial statements to the Fund. The Fund will obtain the necessary information from publicly available sources. State-Insured Credit Unions must submit to the Fund copies of the financial statements that they submit to the Appropriate State Agency.

(iv) If multiple organizations sign the Assistance Agreement: The Awardee may submit combined financial statements and footnotes for the Awardee and other entities that signed the Assistance Agreement as long as the financial statements of each signatory are shown separately (for example, in combining financial statements).

(v) If the Assistance is in the form of a loan or a deposit: The Awardee must provide the Fund with financial statements annually throughout the term of the loan or deposit.

(vi) If the Assistance is in the form of an equity investment (common or preferred stock, secondary capital, certificate of deposit, partnership interest, or debentures): The Awardee must provide the Fund with financial statements annually for each year in which the Fund holds the equity investment.

(2) *Performance Goals Report/Annual Survey:* Performance Goals include performance goals and measures that are specific to the Awardee's application for funding.

(i) *Performance Goals Report:* The Awardee will submit to the Fund information through the Annual Survey that will inform the Fund of its compliance toward meeting the Performance Goals set forth in the Performance Goals Report.

(ii) *Annual Survey:* The Fund will use the Annual Survey to collect data by which to assess the Awardee's compliance toward meeting its Performance Goals and the impact of the CDFI Program and the CDFI industry. The Annual Survey is comprised of two components, the Institution-Level Report and the Transaction-Level Report.

(A) *Institution-Level Report.* The Institution-Level Report includes, but is not limited to, organizational, financial, portfolio and community development impact information and any other information that the Fund deems appropriate.

(B) *Transaction-Level Report.* The Transaction-Level Report includes, but is not limited to, specific data elements on each of the Awardee's loans and investments including, but not limited to, borrower location, loan/investment type, loan/investment amount, and terms. The Awardee must submit the Transaction-Level Report to the Fund at least annually but no more frequently than quarterly. If the Fund requires the Awardee to submit the Transaction-Level Report on a semi-annual or quarterly basis, the Fund will notify the Awardee of the due date for the submission of said report at least 60 days prior to the due date. Only Awardees that receive financial assistance awards are required to submit Transaction-Level Reports.

(3) *Financial Status Report:* The Financial Status Report is applicable only to Awardees that receive technical assistance awards and must be signed by the Awardee's authorized representative, and submitted to the Fund with the Annual Report. This form is only applicable to the technical assistance portion of the award.

(4) *Uses of Financial Assistance and Matching Funds Report:* This report describes the Awardee's use of its financial assistance award and its matching funds during its preceding fiscal year.

(5) *Explanation of Noncompliance:* Any Awardee that fails to meet a performance goal in its Performance Goals Report must submit to the Fund a narrative explanation.

(6) Awardees are responsible for the timely and complete submission of the Annual Report, even if all or a portion of the documents actually are completed by another entity or signatory to the Assistance Agreement. If such other entities or signatories are required to provide Annual Surveys or Financial Reports, or other documentation that the Fund may require, the Awardee is responsible for ensuring that the information is submitted timely and complete. The Fund reserves the right to contact such additional signatories to the Assistance Agreement and require that additional information and documentation be provided.

(7) The Fund's review of the progress of an Insured CDFI, a Depository Institution Holding Company or a State-Insured Credit Union in implementing its Comprehensive Business Plan and satisfying the terms and conditions of its Assistance Agreement may also include information from the Appropriate Federal Banking Agency or Appropriate State Agency, as the case may be.

(8) The Fund shall make reports described in this section available for public inspection after deleting any materials necessary to protect privacy or proprietary interests.

(f) *Exchange of information with Appropriate Federal Banking Agencies and Appropriate State Agencies.* (1) Except as provided in paragraph (f)(4) of this section, prior to directly requesting information from or imposing reporting or record keeping requirements on an Insured CDFI or other institution that is examined by or subject to the reporting requirements of an Appropriate Federal Banking Agency, the Fund shall consult with the Appropriate Federal Banking Agency to determine if the information requested is available from or may be obtained by such agency in the form, format, and detail required by the Fund.

(2) If the information, reports, or records requested by the Fund pursuant to paragraph (f)(1) of this section are not provided by the Appropriate Federal Banking Agency within 15 calendar days after the date on which the material is requested, the Fund may request the information from or impose the record keeping or reporting requirements directly on such institutions with notice to the Appropriate Federal Banking Agency.

(3) The Fund shall use any information provided by an Appropriate Federal Banking Agency or Appropriate State Agency under this section to the extent practicable to eliminate duplicative requests for information and reports from, and record keeping by, an Insured CDFI, State-Insured Credit Union or other institution that is examined by or subject to the reporting requirements of an Appropriate Federal Banking Agency or Appropriate State Agency.

(4) Notwithstanding paragraphs (f)(1) and (2) of this section, the Fund may require an Insured CDFI, State-Insured Credit Union, or other institution that

is examined by or subject to the reporting requirements of an Appropriate Federal Banking Agency or Appropriate State Agency to provide information with respect to the institution's implementation of its Comprehensive Business Plan or compliance with the terms of its Assistance Agreement, after providing notice to the Appropriate Federal Banking Agency or Appropriate State Agency, as the case may be.

(5) Nothing in this part shall be construed to permit the Fund to require an Insured CDFI, State-Insured Credit Union, or other institution that is examined by or subject to the reporting requirements of an Appropriate Federal Banking Agency or Appropriate State Agency to obtain, maintain, or furnish an examination report of any Appropriate Federal Banking Agency or Appropriate State Agency, or records contained in or related to such report.

(6) The Fund and the Appropriate Federal Banking Agency shall promptly notify each other of material concerns about an Awardee that is an Insured CDFI or that is examined by or subject to the reporting requirements of an Appropriate Federal Banking Agency, and share appropriate information relating to such concerns.

(7) Neither the Fund nor the Appropriate Federal Banking Agency (or Appropriate State Agency, as the case may be) shall disclose confidential information obtained pursuant to this section from any party without the written consent of that party.

(8) The Fund, the Appropriate Federal Banking Agency (or Appropriate State Agency, as the case may be), and any other party providing information under this paragraph (f) shall not be deemed to have waived any privilege applicable to the any information or data, or any portion thereof, by providing such information or data to the other party or by permitting such data or information, or any copies or portions thereof, to be used by the other party.

(g) *Availability of referenced publications.* The publications referenced in this section are available as follows:

(1) OMB Circulars may be obtained from the Office of Administration, Publications Office, 725 17th Street, NW., Room 2200, New Executive Office Building, Washington, DC 20503 or on the Internet (*http://www.whitehouse.gov/OMB/grants/index.html*); and

(2) General Accounting Office materials may be obtained from GAO Distribution, 700 4th Street, NW., Suite 1100, Washington, DC 20548.

§ 1805.805 Information.

The Fund and each Appropriate Federal Banking Agency shall cooperate and respond to requests from each other and from other Appropriate Federal Banking Agencies in a manner that ensures the safety and soundness of Insured CDFIs or other institution that is examined by or subject to the reporting requirements of an Appropriate Federal Banking Agency.

§ 1805.806 Compliance with government requirements.

In carrying out its responsibilities pursuant to an Assistance Agreement, the Awardee shall comply with all applicable Federal, State, and local laws, regulations, and ordinances, OMB Circulars, and Executive Orders.

§ 1805.807 Conflict of interest requirements.

(a) *Provision of credit to Insiders.* (1) An Awardee that is a Non-Regulated CDFI may not use any monies provided to it by the Fund to make any credit (including loans and Equity Investments) available to an Insider unless it meets the following restrictions:

(i) The credit must be provided pursuant to standard underwriting procedures, terms and conditions;

(ii) The Insider receiving the credit, and any family member or business partner thereof, shall not participate in any way in the decision making regarding such credit;

(iii) The board of directors or other governing body of the Awardee shall approve the extension of the credit; and

(iv) The credit must be provided in accordance with a policy regarding credit to Insiders that has been approved in advance by the Fund.

(2) An Awardee that is an Insured CDFI, a Depository Institution Holding Company or a State-Insured Credit

Union shall comply with the restrictions on Insider activities and any comparable restrictions established by its Appropriate Federal Banking Agency or Appropriate State Agency, as applicable.

(b) *Awardee standards of conduct.* An Awardee that is a Non-Regulated CDFI shall maintain a code or standards of conduct acceptable to the Fund that shall govern the performance of its Insiders engaged in the awarding and administration of any credit (including loans and Equity Investments) and contracts using monies from the Fund. No Insider of an Awardee shall solicit or accept gratuities, favors or anything of monetary value from any actual or potential borrowers, owners or contractors for such credit or contracts. Such policies shall provide for disciplinary actions to be applied for violation of the standards by the Awardee's Insiders.

§ 1805.808 Lobbying restrictions.

No assistance made available under this part may be expended by an Awardee to pay any person to influence or attempt to influence any agency, elected official, officer or employee of a State or local government in connection with the making, award, extension, continuation, renewal, amendment, or modification of any State or local government contract, grant, loan or cooperative agreement as such terms are defined in 31 U.S.C. 1352.

§ 1805.809 Criminal provisions.

The criminal provisions of 18 U.S.C. 657 regarding embezzlement or misappropriation of funds is applicable to all Awardees and Insiders.

§ 1805.810 Fund deemed not to control.

The Fund shall not be deemed to control an Awardee by reason of any assistance provided under the Act for the purpose of any applicable law.

§ 1805.811 Limitation on liability.

The liability of the Fund and the United States Government arising out of any assistance to a CDFI in accordance with this part shall be limited to the amount of the investment in the CDFI. The Fund shall be exempt from any assessments and other liabilities that may be imposed on controlling or principal shareholders by any Federal law or the law of any State. Nothing in this section shall affect the application of any Federal tax law.

§ 1805.812 Fraud, waste and abuse.

Any person who becomes aware of the existence or apparent existence of fraud, waste or abuse of assistance provided under this part should report such incidences to the Office of Inspector General of the U.S. Department of the Treasury.

PART 1806—BANK ENTERPRISE AWARD PROGRAM

Sec.

AUTHORITY: 12 U.S.C. 1834a, 4703, 4703 note, 4713, 4717; 31 U.S.C. 321.

SOURCE: 74 FR 5791, Jan. 30, 2009, unless otherwise noted.

Subpart A—General Provisions

§ 1806.100 Purpose.

The purpose of the Bank Enterprise Award Program is to provide financial assistance to Community Development Financial Institutions, and provide an incentive for insured depository institutions to increase their activities in Distressed Communities.

§ 1806.101 Summary.

(a) Under the Bank Enterprise Award Program, the Fund makes awards to selected Applicants that:

(1) Increase their investments in or other support of Community Development Financial Institutions;

(2) Increase lending and investment activities within Distressed Communities; or

(3) Increase the provision of certain services and assistance.

(b) Distressed Communities must meet minimum geographic, poverty and unemployment criteria.

(c) Applicants are selected to participate in the program through a competitive application process. Awards are based on increases in Qualified Activities that are carried out by the Applicant during an Assessment Period. Bank Enterprise Awards are distributed after successful completion of projected Qualified Activities and must be used for BEA Qualified Activities. All awards shall be made subject to the availability of funding.

§ 1806.102 Relationship to other Community Development Financial Institutions Programs.

Prohibition against double funding. A BEA Applicant may not submit as Qualified Activities any transactions funded with award proceeds from another Fund program.

§ 1806.103 Definitions.

For purposes of this part the following terms shall have the following definitions:

(a) *Act* means the Community Development Banking and Financial Institutions Act of 1994, as amended (12 U.S.C. 4701 *et seq.*);

(b) *Affordable Housing Development Loan* means origination of a loan to finance the acquisition, construction, and/or development of single- or multifamily residential real property, where at least sixty percent of the units in such property are affordable, as may be defined in the applicable NOFA, to Low- and Moderate-Income Eligible Residents.

(c) *Affordable Housing Loan* means origination of a loan to finance the purchase or improvement of the borrower's primary residence, and that is secured by such property, where such borrower is a Low- and Moderate-Income Eligible Resident. Affordable Housing Loan may also refer to second (or otherwise subordinated) liens or "soft second" mortgages, and other similar types of down payment assistance loans but may not necessarily be secured by such property originated for the purpose of facilitating the purchase or improvement of the borrower's primary residence, where such borrower is a Low- and Moderate-Income Eligible Resident.

(d) *Applicant* means any insured depository institution (as defined in section 3(c)(2) of the Federal Deposit Insurance Act (12 U.S.C. 1813)) that is applying for a Bank Enterprise Award;

(e) *Appropriate Federal Banking Agency* has the same meaning as in section 3 of the Federal Deposit Insurance Act (12 U.S.C. 1813);

(f) *Assessment Period* means an annual or semi-annual period specified in the applicable Notice of Funds Availability in which an Applicant will carry out, or has carried out, Qualified Activities;

(g) *Award Agreement* means a formal agreement between the Fund and an Awardee pursuant to § 1806.300;

(h) *Awardee* means an Applicant selected by the Fund to receive a Bank Enterprise Award;

(i) *Bank Enterprise Award (or BEA Program Award)* means an award made to an Applicant pursuant to this part;

(j) *Bank Enterprise Award (or BEA) Program* means the program authorized by section 114 of the Act and implemented under this part;

(k) *Baseline Period* means an annual or semi-annual period specified in the applicable NOFA in which an Applicant has previously carried out Qualified Activities;

(l) *Commercial Real Estate Loan* means an origination of a loan (other than an

Affordable Housing Development Loan or Affordable Housing Loan) that is secured by real estate and used to finance the acquisition or rehabilitation of a building in a Distressed Community, or the acquisition, construction and/or development of property in a Distressed Community, used for commercial purposes;

(m) *Community Development Entity (or CDE)* means any Qualified Community Development Entity that meets the requirements set forth at Internal Revenue Code (IRC) § 45D(c) and that has been certified as such by the Fund;

(n) *Community Development Financial Institution (or CDFI)* means an entity that has been certified as a CDFI by the CDFI Fund as of the date specified in the applicable NOFA.

(o) *Community Services* means the following forms of assistance provided by officers, employees or agents (contractual or otherwise) of the Applicant:

(1) Provision of technical assistance and financial education to Eligible Residents regarding managing their personal finances;

(2) Provision of technical assistance and consulting services to newly formed small businesses and nonprofit organizations located in the Distressed Community;

(3) Provision of technical assistance and financial education to, or servicing the loans of, Low- or Moderate-Income homeowners and homeowners that are Eligible Residents; and

(4) Other services provided to Low- and Moderate-Income Eligible Residents or enterprises Integrally Involved in a Distressed Community, as deemed appropriate by the Fund;

(p) *CDFI Partner* means a CDFI that has been provided assistance in the form of CDFI Related Activities by an Applicant;

(q) *CDFI Related Activities* means Equity Investments, Equity-Like Loans and CDFI Support Activities;

(r) *CDFI Support Activity* means assistance provided by an Applicant or its Subsidiary to a CDFI that meets criteria set forth by the Fund in the applicable NOFA, that is Integrally Involved in a Distressed Community, in the form of the origination of a loan, technical assistance, or deposits if such deposits are:

(1) Uninsured and committed for a term of at least three years; or

(2) Insured, committed for a term of at least three years, and provided at an interest rate that is materially (in the determination of the Fund) below market rates;

(s) *Deposit Liabilities* means time or savings deposits or demand deposits, accepted from Eligible Residents at offices of the Applicant, or a Subsidiary of the Applicant, located within the Distressed Community. Depository Liabilities may only include deposits held by individuals in transaction accounts (*i.e.*, demand deposits, NOW accounts, automated transfer service accounts and telephone or preauthorized transfer accounts) or non-transaction accounts (*i.e.*, money market deposit accounts, other savings deposits and all time deposits), as defined by the Appropriate Federal Banking Agency;

(t) *Distressed Community* means a geographic community which meets the minimum area eligibility requirements specified in § 1806.200, and such additional criteria as may be set forth in the applicable NOFA;

(u) *Distressed Community Financing Activities* means Affordable Housing Loans, Affordable Housing Development Loans and related Project Investments; Education Loans; Commercial Real Estate Loans and related Project Investments; Home Improvement Loans; and Small Business Loans and related Project Investments;

(v) *Education Loan* means an advance of funds to a student, who is an Eligible Resident, for the purpose of financing a college or vocational education.

(w) *Electronic Transfer Account (or ETA)* means an account meeting the requirements, and with respect to which the Applicant has satisfied the requirements, set forth in the FEDERAL REGISTER on July 16, 1999 at 64 FR 38510, as such requirements may be amended from time to time;

(x) *Eligible Resident* means an individual that resides in a Distressed Community;

(y) *Equity Investment* means financial assistance provided by an Applicant or its Subsidiary to a CDFI, which CDFI meets such criteria as set forth in the applicable NOFA, in the form of a grant, a stock purchase, a purchase of a partnership interest, a purchase of a limited liability company membership interest, or any other investment deemed to be an Equity Investment by the Fund;

(z) *Equity-Like Loan* means a loan provided by an Applicant or its Subsidiary to a CDFI, and made on such terms that it has characteristics of an Equity Investment which meets such criteria as set forth in the applicable NOFA;

(aa) *Financial Services* means check-cashing, providing money orders and certified checks, automated teller machines, safe deposit boxes, new branches, and other comparable services as may be specified by the Fund in the applicable NOFA, that are provided by the Applicant to Low- and Moderate-Income Eligible Residents or enterprises Integrally Involved in the Distressed Community;

(bb) *Fund* means the Community Development Financial Institutions Fund, established under section 104(a) of the Act (12 U.S.C. 4703(a));

(cc) *Geographic Units* means counties (or equivalent areas), incorporated places, minor civil divisions that are units of local government, census tracts, block numbering areas, block groups, and American Indian or Alaska Native areas (as each is defined by the U.S. Bureau of the Census) or other areas deemed appropriate by the Fund;

(dd) *Home Improvement Loan* means an advance of funds, either unsecured or secured by a one-to-four family residential property, the proceeds of which are used to improve the borrower's primary residence;

(ee) *Indian Reservation* means a geographic area that meets the requirements of section 4(10) of the Indian Child Welfare Act of 1978 (25 U.S.C. 1903(10)), and shall include land held by incorporated Native groups, regional corporations, and village corporations, as defined in and pursuant to the Alaska Native Claims Settlement Act (43 U.S.C. 1601 *et seq*), public domain Indian allotments, and former Indian Reservations in the State of Oklahoma;

(ff) *Individual Development Account (or IDA)* means an account that meets the requirements, and with respect to the provision of which Applicant has satisfied the requirements, set forth in the U.S. Department of Health and Human Services Program Announcement OCS–2000–04, published on December 14, 1999 in the FEDERAL REGISTER at 64 FR 69824, as such requirements may be amended from time to time;

(gg) *Integrally Involved* means:

(i) For a CDFI Partner, having provided or transacted the percentage of financial transactions or dollars (*e.g.*, loans or equity investments as defined in 12 CFR 1805.104(s)), or Development Service activities, in the Distressed Community identified by the Applicant or the CDFI Partner, as applicable, or having attained the percentage of market share for a particular product in a Distressed Community, set forth in the applicable NOFA; or

(ii) For a non-CDFI, having directed the percentage of its business activities (*e.g.*, investments, revenues, expenses, or other appropriate measures) to serving the Distressed Community identified by the Applicant, or having provided the percentage of its business activities in said Distressed Community, set forth in the applicable NOFA.

(hh) *Low- and Moderate-Income* means income that does not exceed 80 percent of the median income of the area involved, as determined by the Secretary of Housing and Urban Development, with adjustments for smaller and larger families pursuant to section 102(a)(20) of the Housing and Community Development Act of 1974 (42 U.S.C. 5302(a)(20));

(ii) *Metropolitan Area* means an area designated as such (as of the date of the application) by the Office of Management and Budget pursuant to 44 U.S.C. 3504(d)(3), 31 U.S.C. 1104(d), and Executive Order 10253 (3 CFR, 1949–1953 Comp., p. 758), as amended;

(jj) *Notice of Funds Availability (or NOFA)* means the public notice, published by the Fund in the FEDERAL REGISTER, that announces the availability of BEA Program funds for a particular funding round and that advises Applicants with respect to obtaining application materials, establishes application submission deadlines, and establishes other requirements or restrictions applicable for the particular funding round;

(kk) *Priority Factor* means a numeric value assigned to each type of activity within each category of Qualified Activity, as may be established by the Fund in the applicable NOFA. A priority factor represents the Fund's assessment of the degree of difficulty, the extent of innovation, and the extent of benefits accruing to the Distressed Community for each type of activity;

(ll) *Project Investment* means providing financial assistance in the form of a purchase of stock, limited partnership interest, other ownership instrument, or a grant to an entity that is Integrally Involved in a Distressed Community and formed for the sole purpose of engaging in a project or activity, approved by the Fund, including Affordable Housing Development Loans, Affordable Housing Loans, Commercial Real Estate Loans, and Small Business Loans;

(mm) *Qualified Activities* means CDFI Related Activities, Distressed Community Financing Activities, and Service Activities;

(nn) *Service Activities* means the following activities: Deposit Liabilities; Financial Services; Community Services; Targeted Financial Services; and Targeted Retail Savings/Investment Products;

(oo) *Small Business Loan* means an origination of a loan used for commercial or industrial activities (other than an Affordable Housing Loan, Affordable Housing Development Loan, Commercial Real Estate Loan, Home Improvement Loan) to a business or farm that meets the size eligibility standards of the Small Business Administration's Development Company or Small Business Investment Company programs (13 CFR 121.301) and is located in a Distressed Community;

(pp) *Subsidiary* has the same meaning as in section 3 of the Federal Deposit Insurance Act, except that a CDFI shall not be considered a subsidiary of any insured depository institution or any depository institution holding company that controls less than 25 percent of any class of the voting shares of such corporation and does not otherwise control, in any manner, the election of a majority of directors of the corporation;

(qq) *Targeted Financial Services* means ETAs, IDAs, and such other similar banking products as maybe specified by the Fund in the applicable NOFA;

(rr) *Targeted Retail Savings/Investment Products* means certificates of deposit, mutual funds, life insurance and other similar savings or investment vehicles targeted to Low- and Moderate-Income Eligible Residents, as may be specified by the Fund in the applicable NOFA; and

(ss) *Unit of General Local Government* means any city, county town, township, parish, village or other general-purpose political subdivision of a State or Commonwealth of the United States, or general-purpose subdivision thereof, and the District of Columbia.

§ 1806.104 Waiver authority.

The Fund may waive any requirement of this part that is not required by law, upon a determination of good cause. Each such waiver will be in writing and supported by a statement of the facts and grounds forming the basis of the waiver. For a waiver in any individual case, the Fund must determine that application of the requirement to be waived would adversely affect the achievement of the purposes of the Act. For waivers of general applicability, the Fund will publish notification of granted waivers in the FEDERAL REGISTER.

§ 1806.105 OMB control number.

The collection of information requirements in this part have been approved by the Office of Management and Budget and assigned OMB control number 1559–0005.

Subpart B—Awards

§ 1806.200 Community eligibility and designation.

(a) *General.* If an Applicant proposes to carry out Service Activities or Distressed Community Financing Activities, the Applicant shall designate one or more Distressed Communities in which it proposes to carry out those activities. The Applicant may designate different Distressed Communities for each category of activity. If an Applicant proposes to carry out CDFI Support Activities, the Applicant shall provide evidence that the CDFI it is proposing to support is Integrally Involved in a Distressed Community as specified in the applicable NOFA.

(b) *Minimum area and eligibility requirements.* A Distressed Community must meet the following minimum area and eligibility requirements:

(1) Minimum area requirements. A Distressed Community:

(i) Must be an area that is located within the jurisdiction of one (1) Unit of General Local Government;

(ii) The boundaries the area must be contiguous; and

(iii) The area must:

(A) Have a population, as determined by the most recent census data available, of not less than 4,000 if any portion of the area is located within a Metropolitan Area with a population of 50,000 or greater; or

(B) Have a population, as determined by the most recent census data available, of not less than 1,000 in any other case; or

(C) Be located entirely within an Indian Reservation.

(2) Eligibility requirements. A Distressed Community must be a geographic area where:

(i) At least 30 percent of the Eligible Residents have incomes that are less than the national poverty level, as published by the U.S. Bureau of the Census in the most recent decennial census for which data is available;

(ii) The unemployment rate is at least 1.5 times greater than the national average, as determined by the U.S. Bureau of Labor Statistics' most recent data, including estimates of unemployment developed using the U.S. Bureau of Labor Statistics' Census Share calculation method; and

(iii) Such additional requirements as may be specified by the Fund in the applicable NOFA.

(c) *Area designation.* An Applicant shall designate an area as a Distressed Community by:

(1) Selecting Geographic Units which individually meet the minimum area eligibility requirements set forth in paragraph (b) of this section; or

(2) Selecting two or more Geographic Units which, in the aggregate, meet the minimum area eligibility requirements set forth in paragraph (b) of this section, provided that no Geographic Unit selected by the Applicant within the area has a poverty rate of less than 20 percent.

(d) *Designation and notification process.* The Fund will provide a prospective Applicant with data and other information to help it identify areas eligible to be designated as a Distressed Community. Applicants shall submit designation materials as instructed in the applicable NOFA.

§ 1806.201 Measuring and reporting Qualified Activities.

(a) *General.* An Applicant may receive a Bank Enterprise Award for engaging in any of the following categories of Qualified Activities during an Assessment Period: CDFI Related Activities, Distressed Community Financing Activities, or Service Activities. The Fund may further qualify such Qualified Activities in the applicable NOFA, including such additional geographic and transaction size limitations as the Fund deems appropriate.

(b) *Reporting Qualified Activities.* An Applicant should report only its Qualified Activities for the category in which it is seeking a Bank Enterprise Award. For example, if an Applicant is seeking a Bank Enterprise Award for Distressed Community Financing Activities only, it should report only its activities for the Distressed Community Financing Activities category.

(1) If an Applicant elects to apply for an award in either the CDFI Related Activities category or the Distressed Community Financing Activities category, it must report on all types of activity within that category unless the Applicant can provide a reasonable explanation acceptable to the Fund, in its sole discretion, as to why it cannot report on all activities in such category.

(2) If an Applicant elects to apply for an award in the Service Activities category, it may elect not to report each type of activity within the Service Activities category.

(c) *Area served.* CDFI Related Activities must be provided to a CDFI Partner Integrally Involved in a Distressed Community. Service Activities and

Distressed Community Financing Activities must serve a Distressed Community. An activity is considered to serve a Distressed Community if it is:

(1) Undertaken in the Distressed Community; or

(2) Provided to Low- and Moderate-Income Eligible Residents or enterprises Integrally Involved in the Distressed Community.

(d) *Certain Limitations on Qualified Activities*—Activities funded with the proceeds of Federal funding or tax credit programs may be ineligible for purposes of calculating or receiving a Bank Enterprise Awards. Please see the applicable BEA NOFA for current limitations on Qualified Activities.

(e) *Measuring the Value of Qualified Activities.* Subject to such additional or alternative valuations as the Fund may specify in the applicable NOFA, the Fund will assess the value of:

(1) Equity Investments, Equity-Like Loans, loans, grants and certificates of deposits, at the original amount of such Equity Investments, Equity-Like Loans, loans, grants or certificates of deposits. Where a certificate of deposit matures and is then rolled over during the Baseline Period or the Assessment Period, as applicable, the Fund will assess the value of the full amount of the rolled over deposit. Where an existing loan is refinanced (a new loan is originated to pay off an existing loan, whether or not there is a change in the applicable loan terms), the Fund will only assess the value of any increase in the principal amount of the refinanced loan;

(2) Project Investments at the original amount of the purchase of stock, limited partnership interest, other ownership interest, or grant;

(3) Deposit Liabilities at the dollar amount deposited as measured by comparing the net change in the amount of applicable funds on deposit at the Applicant during the Baseline Period with the net change in the amount of applicable funds on deposit at the Applicant during the Assessment Period, as described below:

(i) The Applicant shall calculate the net change in deposits during the Baseline Period, by comparing the amount of applicable funds on deposit at the close of business the day before the beginning of the Baseline Period and at the close of business on the last day of the Baseline Period; and

(ii) The Applicant shall calculate the net change in such deposits during the Assessment Period, by comparing the amount of applicable funds on deposit at the close of business the day before the beginning of the Assessment Period and at the close of business on the last day of the Assessment Period;

(4) Financial Services and Targeted Financial Services based on the predetermined amounts as may be set forth by the Fund in the applicable NOFA; and

(5) Financial Services (other than those for which the Fund has established a predetermined value), Community Services, and CDFI Support Activities consisting of technical assistance based on the administrative costs of providing such services.

(f) *Closed Transactions.* A transaction shall be considered to have been carried out during the Baseline Period or the Assessment Period if the documentation evidencing the transaction:

(1) Is executed on a date within the applicable Baseline Period or Assessment Period, respectively; and

(2) Constitutes a legally binding agreement between the Applicant and a borrower or investee which specifies the final terms and conditions of the transaction, except that any contingencies included in the final agreement must be typical of such transaction and acceptable (both in the judgment of the Fund); and

(3) An initial cash disbursement of loan or investment proceeds has occurred in a manner that is consistent with customary business practices and is reasonable given the nature of the transaction (as determined by the Fund) unless it is normal business practice to make no initial disbursement at closing and the Applicant demonstrates that the borrower has access to the proceeds, subject to reasonable conditions as may be determined by the Fund.

(g) *Reporting Period.* An Applicant may only measure the amount of a Qualified Activity that it reasonably expects to disburse to an investee, borrower, or other recipient within one year of the end of the applicable Assessment Period, or such other period as may be set forth by the Fund in the applicable NOFA.

§ 1806.202 Estimated award amounts.

(a) *General.* An Applicant shall calculate and submit to the Fund an estimated award amount as part of the Bank Enterprise Award application.

(b) *Award Percentages.* The Fund will establish the award percentage for each category of Qualified Activities in the applicable NOFA. Applicable award percentages for activities undertaken by Applicants that are CDFIs will be equal to three times the award percentages for activities undertaken by Applicants that are not CDFIs.

(c) *Calculating the estimated award amount.* The estimated award amount for each category of Qualified Activities will be equal to the applicable award percentage of the increase in the weighted value of such Qualified Activities between the Baseline Period and Assessment Period. The weighted value of the applicable Qualified Activities shall be calculated by:

(1) Subtracting the Baseline Period value of such Qualified Activity from the Assessment Period value of such Qualified Activity to yield a remainder; and

(2) Multiplying the remainder by the applicable Priority Factor (as set forth in the applicable NOFA).

(d) *Estimated Award Eligibility Review.* The Fund will determine the eligibility of each transaction for which an Applicant has applied for a Bank Enterprise Award. Based upon this review, the Fund will calculate the actual award amount for which such Applicant is eligible.

§ 1806.203 Selection Process, actual award amounts.

(a) *Sufficient Funds Available to Cover Estimated Awards.* All Bank Enterprise Awards are subject to the availability of funds. If the amount of funds available during a funding round is sufficient to cover all estimated award amounts for which Applicants are eligible, in the Fund's determination, and an Applicant meets all of the program requirements specified in this part, then such Applicant shall receive an actual award amount that is calculated by the Fund in the manner specified in § 1806.202.

(b) *Insufficient Funds Available to Cover Estimated Awards.* If the amount of funds available during a funding round is insufficient to cover all estimated award amounts for which Applicants are eligible, in the Fund's determination, then the Fund will select Awardees and determine actual award amounts based on the process described in this section.

(c) *Priority of Awards.* The Fund will rank Applicants in each category of Qualified Activity according to the priorities described in this paragraph (c). Selections within each priority category will be based on the Applicants' relative rankings within each such category, subject to the availability of funds.

(1) First priority. If the amount of funds available during a funding round is insufficient for all estimated award amounts, first priority will be given to Applicants that propose to engage in CDFI Related Activities, ranked in the order set forth in the applicable NOFA.

(2) Second priority. If the amount of funds available during a funding round is sufficient for all Applicants that propose to engage in CDFI Related Activities but insufficient for all remaining estimated award amounts, second priority will be given to Applicants that propose to engage in Distressed Community Financing Activities, ranked in the order set forth in the applicable NOFA.

(3) Third Priority. If the amount of funds available during a funding round is sufficient for all Applicants that propose to engage in CDFI Related Activities and Distressed Community Financing Activities, but insufficient for all remaining estimated award amounts, third priority will be given to Applicants that propose to engage in Service Activities, ranked in the order set forth in the applicable NOFA.

(d) *Calculating actual award amounts.* The Fund will determine actual award amounts based upon the availability of funds, increases in Qualified Activities from the Baseline to the Assessment Period, and an Applicant's priority ranking. If an Applicant receives an award for more than one priority category described in this section, the Fund will combine the award amounts into a single Bank Enterprise Award.

(e) *Unobligated or deobligated funds.* The Fund, in its sole discretion, may use any deobligated funds or funds not obligated during a funding round:

(1) To select Applicants not previously selected, using the calculation and selection process contained in this part;

(2) To make additional monies available for a subsequent funding round; or

(3) As otherwise authorized by the Act.

(f) *Limitation.* The Fund, in its sole discretion, may deny or limit the amount of an award for any reason.

§ 1806.204 Applications for Bank Enterprise Awards.

(a) *Notice of Funds Availability; Applications.* Applicants shall submit applications for Bank Enterprise Awards in accordance with this section and the applicable NOFA. After receipt of an application, the Fund may request clarifying or technical information related to materials submitted as part of such application or to verify that Qualified Activities were carried out in the manner prescribed in this part.

(b) *Application contents.* An application for a Bank Enterprise Award shall contain:

(1) A completed worksheet that reports the increases in Qualified Activities actually carried out during the Baseline and Assessment Period. If an Applicant has merged with another institution during the Assessment Period, it shall submit a separate Baseline Period worksheet for each subject institution and one Assessment Period worksheet that reports the activities of the merged institutions. If such a merger is unexpectedly delayed beyond the Assessment Period, the Fund reserves the right to withhold distribution of an award until the merger has been completed;

(2) A report of Qualified Activities that were closed during the Assessment Period. Such report shall describe the original amount, census tract served, and the dates of execution, initial disbursement, and final disbursement of the instrument;

(3) With respect to all CDFI Related Activities and Distressed Community Financing Activities where the amount of the Qualified Activity is $250,000 or greater, documentation that meets the conditions described in § 1806.201(f);

(4) Information necessary for the Fund to complete its environmental review requirements pursuant to part 1815 of this chapter;

(5) Certifications, as described in the applicable NOFA and Bank Enterprise Award application, that the information provided to the Fund is true and accurate and that the Applicant will comply with all relevant provisions of this chapter and all applicable Federal, State, and local laws, ordinances, regulations, policies, guidelines, and requirements;

(6) In the case of an Applicant proposing to engage in Service Activities, or Distressed Community Financing Activities, an Applicant must submit a Distressed Community map and other documentation as described in the applicable NOFA and Bank Enterprise Award application;

(7) Information that indicates that each CDFI to which an Applicant has provided CDFI Support Activities is Integrally Involved in a Distressed Community as described in the applicable NOFA and Bank Enterprise Award application; and

(8) Any other information requested by the Fund, or specified by the Fund in the applicable NOFA or the Bank Enterprise Award application, in order to document or otherwise assess the validity of information provided by the Applicant to the Fund.

Subpart C—Terms and Conditions of Assistance

§ 1806.300 Award Agreement; sanctions.

(a) *General.* After the Fund selects an Awardee, the Fund and the Awardee will enter into an Award Agreement. The Award Agreement shall provide that an Awardee shall:

(1) Carry out its Qualified Activities in accordance with applicable law, the approved application, and all other applicable requirements;

(2) Comply with such other terms and conditions (including record keeping

and reporting requirements) that the Fund may establish; and

(3) Not receive any monies until the Fund has determined that the Awardee has fulfilled all applicable requirements.

(4) Comply with performance goals that have been established by the Fund. Such performance goals will include measures that require an Awardee to use its BEA Program Award funds for Qualified Activities.

(b) *Sanctions.* In the event of any fraud, misrepresentation, or noncompliance with the terms of the Award Agreement by the Awardee, the Fund may terminate, reduce, or recapture the award, bar the Awardee and/or its Affiliates from applying for an award from the Fund for a period to be decided by the Fund in its sole discretion, and pursue any other available legal remedies.

(c) *Compliance with Other CDFI Fund Awards.* In the event that an Awardee or its Subsidiary or Affiliate is not in compliance, as determined by the Fund, with the terms and conditions of any other award under the Bank Enterprise Award Program or any component of the Community Development Financial Institutions Program, the Fund may, in its sole discretion, reject an application for or withhold disbursement (either initial or subsequent) on a Bank Enterprise Award.

(d) *Notice.* Prior to imposing any sanctions pursuant to this section or an Award Agreement, the Fund will provide the Awardee with written notice of the proposed sanction and an opportunity to respond. Nothing in this section, however, will provide an Awardee with the right to any formal or informal hearing or comparable proceeding not otherwise required by law.

§ 1806.302 Compliance with government requirements.

In carrying out its responsibilities pursuant to an Award Agreement, the Awardee shall comply with all applicable Federal, State, and local laws, regulations and ordinances, OMB Circulars, and Executive Orders.

§ 1806.303 Fraud, waste and abuse.

Any person who becomes aware of the existence or apparent existence of fraud, waste, or abuse of assistance provided under this part should report such incidences to the Office of Inspector General of the U.S. Department of the Treasury.

§ 1806.304 Books of account, records and government access.

An Awardee shall submit such financial and activity reports, records, statements, and documents at such times, in such forms, and accompanied by such supporting data, as required by the Fund and the U.S. Department of the Treasury to ensure compliance with the requirements of this part. The United States Government, including the U.S. Department of the Treasury, the Comptroller General, and its duly authorized representatives, shall have full and free access to the Awardee's offices and facilities, and all books, documents, records, and financial statements relevant to the award of the Federal funds and may copy such documents as they deem appropriate.

§ 1806.305 Retention of records.

An Awardee shall comply with all record retention requirements as set forth in OMB Circular A–110 (as applicable). This circular may be obtained from Office of Administration, Publications Office, 725 17th Street, NW., Room 2200, New Executive Office Building, Washington, DC 20503.

PART 1807—CAPITAL MAGNET FUND

Subpart A—General Provisions

Subpart B—Eligibility

Subpart C—Use of Funds/Eligible Activities

AUTHORITY: Housing and Economic Recovery Act of 2008, Pub. L. No.110–289, section 1131

SOURCE: 75 FR 75380, Dec. 3, 2010, unless otherwise noted.

Subpart A—General Provisions

§ 1807.100 Purpose.

The purpose of the Capital Magnet Fund (CMF) is to attract private capital for and increase investment in Affordable Housing Activities and related Economic Development Activities and Community Service Facilities.

§ 1807.101 Summary.

(a) Through the CMF, the CDFI Fund will competitively award grants to CDFIs and qualified Nonprofit Organizations to leverage dollars for:

(1) The Development, Preservation, Rehabilitation or Purchase of Affordable Housing primarily for Low-Income Families; and

(2) Financing Economic Development Activities or Community Service Facilities.

(b) The CDFI Fund will select Awardees to receive financial assistance grants through a merit-based, competitive application process. Financial assistance grants that are awarded through the CMF may only be used for eligible uses set forth in subpart C of this part. Each Awardee will enter into an Assistance Agreement which will require it to leverage the CMF grant amount and abide by other terms and conditions pertinent to any assistance received under this part.

§ 1807.102 Relationship to other CDFI Fund programs.

A Certified CDFI will automatically be deemed to meet the eligible entity requirements, provided that it has been in business as an operating entity for a period of at least three years prior to the application deadline.

§ 1807.103 Awardee not instrumentality.

No Awardee shall be deemed to be an agency, department, or instrumentality of the United States.

§ 1807.104 Definitions.

For the purpose of this part:

(a) *Act* means the Housing and Economic Recovery Act of 2008, as amended, Public Law 110–289, section 1131;

(b) *Affiliate* means any entity that Controls, is Controlled by, or is under common Control with, an entity;

(c) *Affordable Housing* means rental or for-sale single-family or multi-family housing that meets the requirements set forth in subpart D of this part;

(d) *Affordable Housing Activities* means the Development, Preservation, Rehabilitation, or Purchase of Affordable Housing;

(e) *Affordable Housing Fund* means a loan, grant or investment fund, managed by the Awardee, whose capital is used to finance Affordable Housing Activities;

(f) *Appropriate Federal Banking Agency* has the same meaning as in section

3 of the Federal Deposit Insurance Act, 12 U.S.C. 1813(q), and includes, with respect to Insured Credit Unions, the National Credit Union Administration;

(g) *Applicant* means any entity submitting an application for assistance under this part;

(h) *Appropriate State Agency* means an agency or instrumentality of a State that regulates and/or insures the member accounts of a State-Insured Credit Union;

(i) *Assistance Agreement* means a formal, written agreement between the CDFI Fund and an Awardee which specifies the terms and conditions of assistance under this part;

(j) *Awardee* means an Applicant selected by the CDFI Fund to receive assistance pursuant to this part;

(k) *Capital Magnet Fund (or CMF)* means the program authorized by section 1131 of the Act, Public Law 110–289, and implemented under this part;

(l) *Certified Community Development Financial Institution (or Certified CDFI)* means an entity that has been determined by the CDFI Fund to meet the eligibility requirements set forth in 12 CFR 1805.201;

(m) *Committed* means that the Awardee is able to demonstrate, in written form and substance that is acceptable to the CDFI Fund, a commitment for use pursuant to § 1807.501;

(n) *Community Development Financial Institutions Fund (or CDFI Fund)* means the Community Development Financial Institutions Fund, an office of the U.S. Department of Treasury, established under the Community Development Banking and Financial Institutions Act of 1994, as amended, 12 U.S.C. 4701 *et seq.;*

(o) *Community Service Facility* means the physical structure in which service programs for residents or service programs for the broader community (including, but not limited to, health care, childcare, educational programs including literacy and after school programs, job training, food and nutrition services, cultural, and/or social services) operate which, In Conjunction With Affordable Housing Activities, implements a Concerted Strategy to stabilize or revitalize a Low-Income Area or Underserved Rural Area;

(p) *Concerted Strategy* means a formal planning document that evidences the connection between Affordable Housing Activities and Economic Development Activities or Community Service Facilities. Such documents include, but are not limited to, a comprehensive, consolidated, or redevelopment plan, or some other local or regional planning document adopted or approved by the jurisdiction;

(q) *Control* means:

(1) Ownership, control, or power to vote 25 percent or more of the outstanding shares of any class of Voting Securities of any company, directly or indirectly or acting through one or more other persons;

(2) Control in any manner over the election of a majority of the directors, trustees, or general partners (or individuals exercising similar functions) of any company; or

(3) The power to exercise, directly or indirectly, a controlling influence over the management, credit or investment decisions, or policies of any company;

(r) *Depository Institution Holding Company* means a bank holding company or a savings and loan holding company as defined in section 3 of the Federal Deposit Insurance Act, 12 U.S.C. 1813(w)(1);

(s) *Development* means land acquisition, demolition of existing facilities, and construction of new facilities, which may include site improvement, utilities development and rehabilitation of utilities, necessary infrastructure, utility services, conversion, and other related activities;

(t) *Economic Development Activity* means the development, preservation, rehabilitation, or purchase of Community Service Facilities and/or other physical structures in which neighborhood-based businesses operate which, In Conjunction With Affordable Housing Activities, implements a Concerted Strategy to stabilize or revitalize a Low-Income Area or Underserved Rural Area;

(u) *Eligible-Income* means:

(1) In the case of owner-occupied housing units, income not in excess of 120 percent of the area median income; and

(2) In the case of rental housing units, income not in excess of 120 percent of the area median income, with adjustments for smaller and larger families, as determined by HUD;

(v) *Eligible Project Costs* means Leverage Costs plus those costs funded directly by a CMF award, exclusive of Operations;

(w) *Extremely Low-Income* means:

(1) In the case of owner-occupied housing units, income not in excess of 30 percent of the area median income; and

(2) In the case of rental housing units, income not in excess of 30 percent of the area median income, with adjustments for smaller and larger families, as determined by HUD;

(x) *Families* means households that reside within the boundaries of the United Sates (which shall encompass any State of the United States, the District of Columbia or any territory of the United States, Puerto Rico, Guam, American Samoa, the Virgin Islands, and the Northern Mariana Islands) and that meet the criteria set forth in §1807.104(u), (w), (jj) or (fff);

(y) *HOME Program* means the HOME Investment Partnership Program set forth in the HOME Investment Partnerships Act under title II of the Cranston-Gonzalez National Affordable Housing Act, as amended, 42 U.S.C. 12701 *et seq.*;

(z) *Homeownership* means ownership in fee simple title or a 99-year leasehold interest in a one- to four-unit dwelling or in a condominium unit, or equivalent form of ownership (which shall include cooperative housing and mutual housing project). For purposes of housing located on trust or restricted Indian lands, homeownership includes leases of 50 years. The ownership interest may be subject only to the following:

(1) Restrictions on resale permitted under the Assistance Agreement;

(2) Mortgages, deeds of trust, or other liens or instruments securing debt on the property; or

(3) Any other restrictions or encumbrances that do not impair the good and marketable nature of title to the ownership interest;

(aa) *Housing* means single- and multifamily residential units, including, but not limited to, manufactured housing and manufactured housing lots, permanent housing for disabled and/or homeless persons, transitional housing, single-room occupancy housing, and group homes. Housing also includes elder cottage housing opportunity (ECHO), as described in 24 CFR 92.258;

(bb) *HUD* means the Department of Housing and Urban Development established under the Department of Housing and Urban Development Act of 1965, 42 U.S.C. 3532–3537;

(cc) *In Conjunction With* means physically proximate to Affordable Housing and reasonably available to residents of Affordable Housing. For a Metropolitan Area, In Conjunction With means located within the same census tract or within 2 miles of the Affordable Housing. For a Non-Metropolitan Area, In Conjunction With means located within the same county, township, or village, or within 20 miles of the Affordable Housing;

(dd) *Insured CDFI* means a Certified CDFI that is an Insured Depository Institution or an Insured Credit Union;

(ee) *Insured Credit Union* means any credit union, the member accounts of which are insured by the National Credit Union Share Insurance Fund by the National Credit Union Administration pursuant to authority granted in 12 U.S.C. 1783 *et seq.*;

(ff) *Insured Depository Institution* means any bank or thrift, the deposits of which are insured by the Federal Deposit Insurance Corporation as determined in 12 U.S.C. 1813(c)(2);

(gg) *Leveraged Costs* means those costs as described in 12 CFR 1807.500;

(hh) *Loan Guarantee* means an agreement to indemnify the holder of a loan all or a portion of the unpaid principal balance in case of default by the borrower;

(ii) *Loan Loss Reserves* means funds that the Applicant or Awardee will set aside in the form of cash reserves, or through accounting-based accrual reserves, to cover losses on loans, accounts, and notes receivable, or for related purposes that the CDFI Fund deems appropriate;

(jj) *Low-Income* means:

(1) In the case of owner-occupied housing units, income not in excess of 80 percent of area median income; and

(2) In the case of rental housing units, income not in excess of 80 percent of area median income, with adjustments for smaller and larger families, as determined by HUD;

(kk) *Low-Income Area (LIA)* means a census tract or block numbering area in which the median income does not exceed 80 percent of the median income for the area in which such census tract or block numbering area is located. With respect to a census tract or block numbering area located within a Metropolitan Area, the median family income shall be at or below 80 percent of the Metropolitan Area median family income or the national Metropolitan Area median family income, whichever is greater. In the case of a census tract or block numbering area located outside of a Metropolitan Area, the median family income shall be at or below 80 percent of the statewide Non-Metropolitan Area median family income or the national Non-Metropolitan Area median family income, whichever is greater;

(ll) *Low Income Housing Tax Credit Program or LIHTC Program* means the program as set forth under Title I of the U.S. Housing Act of 1937, as amended, 42 U.S.C. 1437 *et seq.;*

(mm) *Metropolitan Area* means an area designated as such by the Office of Management and Budget pursuant to 44 U.S.C. 3504(e) and 31 U.S.C. 1104(d) and Executive Order 10253 (3 CFR, 1949–1953 Comp., p. 758), as amended;

(nn) *Multi-family housing* means residential properties consisting of five or more dwelling units, such as a condominium unit, cooperative unit, apartment or townhouse;

(oo) *Non-Metropolitan Area* means an area set forth in the Assistance Agreement;

(pp) *Nonprofit Organization* means any corporation, trust, association, cooperative, or other organization that is:

(1) Designated as a nonprofit or not-for-profit entity under the laws of the organization's State of formation; and

(2) Exempt from Federal income taxation pursuant to the Internal Revenue Code of 1986;

(qq) *Non-Regulated CDFI* means any entity meeting the eligibility requirements described in 12 CFR 1805.200 which is not a Depository Institution Holding Company, Insured Depository Institution, or Insured Credit Union;

(rr) *Operations* means all allowable expenses as defined by Office of Management and Budget (OMB) Circular A–122, "Cost Principles For Non-Profit Organizations," and OMB Circular A–87, "Cost Principles for State, Local, and Indian Tribal Governments," incurred by the Awardee in the administration, operation, and implementation of a CMF award;

(ss) *Participating Jurisdiction* means a jurisdiction designated by HUD, as a participating jurisdiction under the HOME Program in accordance with the requirements of 24 CFR 92.105;

(tt) *Preservation* means:

(1) Activities to refinance, with or without Rehabilitation, single-family or multi-family rental property mortgages that, at the time of refinancing, are subject to affordability and use restrictions under State or Federal affordable housing programs, including but not limited to, the HOME Program, the LIHTC Program, the Section 8 Tenant-Based Assistance and the Section 8 Rental Voucher programs (24 CFR part 982), or the Section 515 Rural Rental Housing program (7 CFR part 3560), hereinafter referred to as "similar State or Federal affordable housing programs," where such refinancing has the effect of extending the term of any affordability and use restrictions on the properties;

(2) Activities to refinance and acquire single-family or multi-family properties that, at the time of refinancing or acquisition, were subject to affordability and use restrictions under similar State or Federal affordable housing programs, by the former tenants of such properties, where such refinancing has the effect of extending the term of any affordability and use restrictions on the properties;

(3) Activities to refinance the mortgages of single-family, owner-occupied housing that at the time of refinancing are subject to affordability and use restrictions under similar State or Federal affordable housing programs, where such refinancing has the effect of extending the term of any affordability and use restrictions on the properties;

(4) Activities to acquire Single-family or Multi-family housing, with or without rehabilitation, with the commitment to subject the properties to the affordability qualifications set forth in subpart D of this part; or

(5) Activities to refinance, with or without Rehabilitation, single-family or multi-family rental property mortgages, with the commitment to subject the properties to the affordability qualifications set forth in subpart D of this part;

(uu) *Project Completion* means that all of the requirements set forth at §1807.503 for a project supported by a CMF award have been met;

(vv) *Purchase* means to provide direct financing to a homeowner to acquire Homeownership through an exchange of money;

(ww) *Rehabilitation* means any repairs and/or capital improvements that contribute to the long-term preservation, current building code compliance, habitability, sustainability, or energy efficiency of Affordable Housing.

(xx) *Revolving Loan Fund* means a pool of funds managed by the Applicant or Awardee wherein repayments on Affordable Housing Activities loans, Economic Development Activities loans and/or Community Services Facilities loans are used to finance additional loans;

(yy) *Risk-Sharing Loan* means loans for Affordable Housing Activities and/ or Economic Development Activities in which the risk of borrower default is shared by the Applicant or Awardee with other lenders (*e.g.*, participation loans);

(zz) *Service Area* means the geographic area in which the Applicant proposes to use CMF funding, and the geographic area approved by the CDFI Fund in which the Awardee shall use CMF funding as set forth in its Assistance Agreement;

(aaa) *Single-family housing* means a one- to four-family residence, condominium unit, cooperative unit, combination of manufactured housing and lot, or manufactured housing lot;

(bbb) *State* means the States of the United States, the District of Columbia, the Commonwealth of Puerto Rico, the Commonwealth of the Northern Mariana Island, Guam, the Virgin Islands, American Samoa, the Trust Territory of the Pacific Islands, and any other territory of the United States;

(ccc) *State-Insured Credit Union* means any credit union that is regulated by, and/or the member accounts of which are insured by, a State agency or instrumentality;

(ddd) *Subsidiary* means any company which is owned or Controlled directly or indirectly by another company;

(eee) *Underserved Rural Area* means a Non-Metropolitan Area that:

(1) Qualifies as a Low-Income Area;

(2) Is experiencing housing stress evidenced by 30 percent or more of resident households with one or more of these four housing conditions in the last decennial census:

(i) Lacked complete plumbing,

(ii) Lacked complete kitchen,

(iii) Paid 30 percent or more of income for owner costs or rent, or

(iv) Had more than 1 person per room; or

(3) Is remote-rural county consisting of a Non-Metropolitan Area that is also not adjacent to a Metropolitan Area;

(fff) *Very Low-Income* means:

(1) In the case of owner-occupied housing units, income not greater than 50 percent of the area median income; and

(2) In the case of rental housing units, income not greater than 50 percent of the area median income, with adjustments for smaller and larger families, as determined by HUD.

§ 1807.105 Waiver authority.

The CDFI Fund may waive any requirement of this part that is not required by law upon a determination of good cause. Each such waiver shall be in writing and supported by a statement of the facts and the grounds forming the basis of the waiver. For a waiver in an individual case, the CDFI Fund must determine that application of the requirement to be waived would adversely affect the achievement of the purposes of the Act. For waivers of general applicability, the CDFI Fund will publish notification of granted waivers in the FEDERAL REGISTER.

§ 1807.106 OMB control number.

The collection of information requirements in this part have been approved by the Office of Management and Budget and assigned OMB control number 1559–0036.

Subpart B—Eligibility

§ 1807.200 Applicant eligibility.

(a) *General requirements.* An Applicant will be deemed eligible for a CMF award if it is:

(1) A Certified or certifiable CDFI. An entity may meet the requirements described in this paragraph (a)(1) if it is:

(i) A Certified CDFI, as set forth in 12 CFR 1805.201, that has been in existence as a legally formed entity as set forth in the Notice of Funds Availability (NOFA) for the applicable funding round; or

(ii) A certifiable CDFI that has been in existence as a legally formed entity as set forth in the NOFA for the applicable round and, although not yet certified as a CDFI, has submitted a complete CDFI certification application as of the date set forth in the applicable NOFA; or

(2) A Nonprofit Organization having as one of its principal purposes the development or management of affordable housing. An entity may meet the requirements described in this paragraph (a)(2) if it:

(i) Has been in existence as a legally formed entity as set forth in the applicable NOFA;

(ii) Demonstrates, through articles of incorporation, by-laws, or other board-approved documents, that the development or management of affordable housing are among its principal purposes; and

(iii) Can demonstrate that at least one-third of the Applicant's resources (either as a portion of total staffing or as a portion of total assets) are dedicated to the development or management of affordable housing.

(b) *Eligibility verification.* An Applicant shall demonstrate that it meets the eligibility requirements described in § 1807.200(a)(2) of this section by providing information described in the application, NOFA, and/or supplemental information, as may be requested by the CDFI Fund. For an Applicant seeking eligibility under § 1807.200(a)(1), the CDFI Fund will verify that the Applicant is a Certified CDFI during the application eligibility review. For an Applicant seeking eligibility under § 1807.200(a)(2), the CDFI Fund, in its sole discretion, shall determine whether the Applicant has satisfied said requirements.

Subpart C—Use of Funds/Eligible Activities

§ 1807.300 Purposes of grants.

The CDFI Fund may provide financial assistance grants to organizations described under subpart B of this part for the purpose of attracting private capital for and increase investment in: (a) The Development, Preservation, Rehabilitation, or Purchase of Affordable Housing for primarily Extremely Low-Income, Very Low-Income, and Low-Income families; and

(b) Economic Development Activities or Community Services Facilities. With respect to an Economic Development Activity or Community Service Facility funded with a CMF grant, the Affordable Housing that it is In Conjunction With may be financed by sources other than the CMF grant.

§ 1807.301 Eligible activities.

Grants awarded under this part shall be used by an Awardee to support Affordable Housing Activities, Economic Development Activities or Community Service Facilities, including the following eligible uses:

(a) To provide Loan Loss Reserves;

(b) To capitalize a Revolving Loan Fund;

(c) To capitalize an Affordable Housing Fund;

(d) To capitalize a fund to support Economic Development Activities or Community Service Facilities;

(e) For Risk-Sharing Loans;

(f) For Loan Guarantees; and

(g) For the Awardee's Operations.

§ 1807.302 Restrictions on use of assistance.

(a) An Awardee's activities under § 1807.301 shall not include the use of CMF for the following:

(1) Political activities;

(2) Advocacy;

(3) Lobbying, whether directly or through other parties;

(4) Counseling services (including homebuyer or financial counseling);

(5) Travel expenses;

(6) Preparing or providing advice on tax returns;

(7) Emergency shelters (including shelters for disaster victims);

(8) Nursing homes;

(9) Convalescent homes;

(10) Residential treatment facilities;

(11) Correctional facilities; or

(12) Student dormitories.

(b) An Awardee may use up to a percentage of CMF award for Operations as specified in the applicable NOFA.

(c) An Awardee shall not use CMF award to support projects that:

(1) Consist of the operation of any private or commercial golf course, country club, massage parlor, hot tub facility, suntan facility, racetrack or other facility used for gambling, or any store the principal business of which is the sale of alcoholic beverages for consumption off premises;

(2) Consist of farming (within the meaning of I.R.C. section 2032A(e)(5)(A) or (B)) if, as of the close of the taxable year of the taxpayer conducting such trade or business, the sum of the aggregate unadjusted bases (or, if greater, the fair market value) of the assets owned by the taxpayer that are used in such a trade or business, and the aggregate value of the assets leased by the taxpayer that are used in such a trade or business, exceeds $500,000.

(d) In any given funding round, no more than 30 percent of an Awardee's CMF award may be used for purposes described in § 1807.300(b).

Subpart D—Qualification as Affordable Housing

§ 1807.400 Affordable housing—general.

Each Awardee that uses CMF funding to support Affordable Housing Activities shall ensure that 100 percent of Eligible Project Costs are attributable to housing units that meet the affordability qualifications set forth below for Eligible-Income Families. In addition, greater than 50 percent of the Eligible Project Costs must be attributable to housing units that meet the affordability qualifications set forth below for either Low-Income, Very Low-Income, or Extremely Low-Income Families.

§ 1807.401 Affordable housing—rental housing.

To qualify as Affordable Housing, a rental Multi-family housing project financed with a CMF award must have at least 20 percent of the housing units occupied by Low-Income, Very Low-Income, or Extremely Low-Income Families and must comply with the rent limits set forth herein.

(a) *Rent limitation.* The maximum rent is a rent that does not exceed:

(1) For an Eligible-Income Family, 30 percent of the annual income of a family whose annual income equals 120 percent of the area median income, with adjustments for smaller and larger families, as determined by HUD;

(2) For a Low-Income Family, 30 percent of the annual income of a family whose annual income equals 80 percent of the area median income, with adjustments for smaller and larger families, as determined by HUD;

(3) For a Very Low-Income Family, 30 percent of the annual income of a family whose annual income equals 50 percent of the area median income, with adjustments for smaller and larger families, as determined by HUD; or

(4) For an Extremely Low-Income Family, 30 percent of the annual income of a family whose annual income equals 30 percent of the area median income, with adjustments for smaller and larger families, as determined by HUD.

(b) *Nondiscrimination against rental assistance subsidy holders.* The Awardee shall require that the owner of a rental unit cannot refuse to lease the unit to a Section 8 Program certificate or voucher holder (24 CFR Part 982, Section 8 Tenant-Based Assistance: Unified Rule for Tenant-Based Assistance under the Section 8 Rental Certificate Program and the Section 8 Rental Voucher Program) or to the holder of a comparable document evidencing participation in a HOME tenant-based rental assistance program because of the status of the prospective tenant as a holder of such certificate, voucher, or comparable HOME tenant-based assistance document.

(c) *Initial rent schedule and utility allowances.* The Awardee shall ensure that the housing adheres to the applicable Participating Jurisdiction's maximum monthly allowances for utilities and services (excluding telephone). If the Participating Jurisdiction's allowances have not been determined or are otherwise unavailable, the Awardee shall rely upon the utility and services allowances established by the applicable city, county or State public housing authority.

(d) *Periods of Affordability.* Housing under §1807.401 must meet the affordability requirements for not less than 10 years, beginning after Project Completion and at initial occupancy. The affordability requirements apply without regard to the term of any loan or mortgage or the transfer of ownership and must be imposed by deed restrictions, covenants running with the land, or other recordable mechanisms, except that the affordability restrictions may terminate upon foreclosure or transfer in lieu of foreclosure. Other recordable mechanisms must be approved in writing and in advance by the CDFI Fund. The affordability restrictions shall be revived according to the original terms if, during the original affordability period, the owner of record before the foreclosure, or deed in lieu of foreclosure, or any entity that includes the former owner or those with whom the former owner has or had family or business ties, obtains an ownership interest in the project or property.

(e) *Subsequent rents during the affordability period.* Any increase in rent for a CMF-funded unit requires that tenants of those units be given at least 30 days prior written notice before the implementation of the rent increase.

(f) *Tenant income determination.*

(1) Each year during the period of affordability the tenant's income shall be re-examined; tenant income examination is the responsibility of the Awardee. Annual income shall include income from all household members.

(2) One of the following three definitions of "annual income" must be used to determine whether a family is income eligible:

(i) Annual income as reported under the Census long-form for the most recent available decennial Census. This definition includes:

(A) Wages, salaries, tips, commissions, *etc.;*

(B) Self-employment income from owned non-farm business, including proprietorships and partnerships;

(C) Farm self-employment income;

(D) Interest, dividends, net rental income, or income from estates or trusts;

(E) Social Security or railroad retirement;

(F) Supplemental Security Income, Aid to Families with Dependent Children, or other public assistance or public welfare programs;

(G) Retirement, survivor, or disability pensions;

(H) Any other sources of income received regularly, including Veterans' (VA) payments, unemployment compensation, and alimony; and

(I) Any other sources of income the CDFI Fund may deem appropriate;

(ii) Adjusted gross income as defined for purposes of reporting under Internal Revenue Service (IRS) Form 1040 series for individual Federal annual income tax purposes; or

(iii) "Annual Income" as defined at 24 CFR 5.609 (except that when determining the income of a homeowner for an owner-occupied rehabilitation project, the value of the homeowner's principal residence may be excluded from the calculation of net family assets).

(3) Although any of the above three definitions of "annual income" are permitted, in order to calculate adjusted income, exclusions from income set forth at 24 CFR 5.611 shall be applied.

(4) The CDFI Fund reserves the right to deem certain government programs, under which a Low-Income family is a recipient, as income eligible for purposes of meeting the tenant income requirements under this subsection.

(g) *Over-income tenants.* (1) CMF-funded units continue to qualify as Affordable Housing despite a temporary noncompliance caused by increases in the incomes of existing tenants if actions satisfactory to the CDFI Fund are being taken to ensure that all vacancies are filled in accordance with this section until the noncompliance is corrected.

(2) Tenants whose incomes no longer qualify must pay rent no greater than the lesser of the amount payable by the tenant under State or local law or 30 percent of the family's annual income, except that tenants of units that have been allocated low-income housing tax credits by a housing credit agency pursuant to section 42 of the Internal Revenue Code of 1986, I.R.C. section 42, must pay rent governed by section 42. Tenants who no longer qualify as Eligible-Income are not required to pay as rent an amount that exceeds the market rent for comparable, unassisted units in the neighborhood.

(3) If the income of a tenant of a CMF-funded unit no longer qualifies, the Awardee may designate another unit, in the CMF-funded project, as a replacement unit that meets the affordability qualifications for Eligible-Income, Low-Income, Very Low-Income, or Extremely Low-Income Families and as set forth in the Awardee's Assistance Agreement. If there is not an available replacement unit, the Awardee must fill the first available vacancy with a tenant that meets the affordability qualifications for Eligible-Income, Low-Income, Very Low-Income, or Extremely Low-Income Families as necessary to maintain compliance with the CMF requirements and the Assistance Agreement.

§ 1807.402 Affordable housing—homeownership.

(a) *Acquisition with or without rehabilitation.* Housing that is for Homeownership purchase must meet the affordability requirements of this subsection.

(1) The housing must be Single-family housing.

(2) The housing price does not exceed 95 percent of the median purchase price for the area as used in the HOME Program and as determined by the applicable Participating Jurisdiction.

(3) The housing must be purchased by a qualifying family as set forth in § 1807.400. The housing must be the principal residence of the family throughout the period described in paragraph (a)(4) of this section.

(4) *Periods of Affordability.* Housing under this subsection must meet the affordability requirements for at least 10 years at the time of purchase by the homeowner.

(5) *Resale.* To ensure that CMF awards are being used for qualifying families for the entire 10-year affordability period, recoupment and redeployment or resale strategies must be imposed by the Awardee. A recoupment strategy must ensure that, in the event the qualifying homeowner sells the housing before the end of the 10-year affordability period and the new homeowner does not meet the affordability qualifications set forth in § 1807.400, the portion of the CMF award used to finance the Affordable Housing Activity is recouped and redeployed to a qualifying family for affordable housing homeownership in the manner set forth in § 1807.402, except that the housing must meet the affordability requirements only for the remaining affordability period. The Awardee may design and implement its own recoupment strategy. Deed restrictions, covenants running with the land, or other similar mechanisms may be used as the mechanism to impose the resale strategy. The Awardee shall report to the CDFI Fund the event of resale, recoupment and redeployment of the CMF award in the manner described in the Assistance Agreement. The affordability restrictions may terminate upon occurrence of any of the following termination events: Foreclosure, transfer in lieu of foreclosure or assignment of an FHA-insured mortgage to HUD. The Awardee may use purchase options, rights of first refusal or other preemptive rights to purchase the housing before foreclosure to preserve affordability. The affordability restrictions shall be revived according to the original terms if, during the original affordability period, the owner of record before the termination event, obtains an ownership interest in the housing.

(b) *Rehabilitation not involving acquisition.* Housing that is currently owned by a qualifying family, as set forth in § 1807.400, qualifies as Affordable Housing if it meets the requirements of this subsection.

(1) The estimated value of the housing, after Rehabilitation, does not exceed 95 percent of the median purchase

price for the area, as used in the HOME Program and as determined by the applicable Participating Jurisdiction; or

(2) The housing is the principal residence of a qualifying family as set forth in § 1807.400, at the time that CMF funding is Committed to the housing.

(3) Housing under this subsection must meet the affordability requirements for at least 10 years after Rehabilitation is completed or meet the resale provisions of § 1807.402(a)(5).

(c) *Ownership interest.* The ownership in the housing assisted under this section must meet the definition of "Homeownership" as defined in § 1807.104(z).

(d) *New construction without acquisition.* Newly constructed housing that is built on property currently owned by a family which will occupy the housing upon completion, qualifies as Affordable Housing if it meets the requirements under paragraph (a) of this section.

(e) *Converting rental units to Homeownership units for existing tenants.* CMF-funded rental units may be converted to Homeownership units by selling, donating, or otherwise conveying the units to the existing tenants to enable the tenants to become homeowners in accordance with the requirements of § 1807.402. The Homeownership units are subject to a minimum period of affordability equal to the remaining affordability period.

Subpart E—Leveraging and Commitment Requirement

§ 1807.500 Leveraged costs—general.

(a) Each CMF grant is expected to result in Eligible Project Costs that total at least 10 times the grant amount. Such costs may be for activities that include Affordable Housing Activities, Economic Development Activities, or Community Service Facilities. Thus, an Awardee shall demonstrate that it leveraged, over its CMF funded portfolio, its CMF award at least 10 times the CMF grant amount or some other standard established by the CDFI Fund in the Awardee's Assistance Agreement. Leveraged Costs are costs that exceed the dollar amount of the Awardee's CMF contribution to each CMF-funded activity. However, the applicable NOFA may set forth a required percentage of Leveraged Costs that must be attributable to non-governmental sources. An Awardee may report to the CDFI Fund all Leveraged Costs, with the following limitations:

(1) No costs attributable to Operations may be reported as Leveraged Costs.

(2) No costs attributable to prohibited uses as identified in § 1807.302(a) and (c) may be reported as Leveraged Costs.

(3) All costs attributable to Affordable Housing Activities reported as Leveraged Costs must be for housing units that qualify as Affordable Housing under § 1807.401 or § 1807.402 for Eligible-Income Families.

(b) Awardees shall self-report leveraging information through forms or electronic systems developed by the CDFI Fund, subject to audit requirements set forth herein. Consequently, Awardees shall maintain appropriate documentation, such as audited financial statements, wire transfers documents, pro-formas, and other relevant records, to support its reports.

§ 1807.501 Commitment for use.

(a) CMF awards shall be Committed for use by the date designated in the Awardee's Assistance Agreement. An Awardee shall demonstrate that its CMF award is Committed by having executed a written, legally binding agreement under which CMF assistance will be provided to the developer or project sponsor for an identifiable project under which:

(1) Construction can reasonably be expected to start within 12 months of the agreement date; or

(2) Property title will be transferred within six months of the agreement date.

(b) An Awardee shall make an initial disbursement of its CMF award for Affordable Housing Activities, Economic Development Activities or Community Service Facilities by the date designated in its Assistance Agreement.

§ 1807.502 Assistance limits.

An eligible Applicant and its Subsidiaries and Affiliates may not be awarded more than 15 percent of the aggregate funds available for CMF grants during any funding year.

§ 1807.503 Project completion.

Once a CMF-funded project has been completed, it must be placed into service by the date designated in the Awardee's Assistance Agreement. Project Completion occurs, as determined by the CDFI Fund, when:

(a) All necessary title transfer requirements and construction work have been performed;

(b) The project complies with the requirements of this part, including the following property standards (these property standards must be complied with at the time of Project Completion and maintained for a period of at least 10 years thereafter):

(1) Housing that is constructed or rehabilitated with CMF funding must meet all applicable local codes, rehabilitation standards, ordinances, and zoning ordinances at the time of project completion. In the absence of a local code for new construction or rehabilitation, such housing must meet, as applicable: One of three model codes (Uniform Building Code (ICBO), National Building Code (BOCA), Standard (Southern) Building Code (SBCCI)); or the Council of American Building Officials (CABO) one or two family code; or the Minimum Property Standards (MPS) in 24 CFR 200.925 or 200.926. Newly constructed housing must meet the current edition of the Model Energy Code published by the Council of American Building Officials.

(2) The housing must meet the accessibility requirements at 24 CFR part 8, which implements section 504 of the Rehabilitation Act of 1973 (29 U.S.C. 794) and covered multifamily dwellings, as defined at 24 CFR 100.201, must also meet the design and construction requirements at 24 CFR 100.205, which implements the Fair Housing Act (42 U.S.C. 3601–3619).

(3) Construction of all manufactured housing must meet the Manufactured Home Construction and Safety Standards established in 24 CFR part 3280. These standards pre-empt State and local codes covering the same aspects of performance for such housing. The installation of all manufactured housing units must comply with applicable State and local laws or codes. In the absence of such laws or codes, the installation must comply with the manufacturer's written instructions for installation of manufactured housing units. Manufactured housing that is rehabilitated using CMF funds must meet the requirements set out in paragraph (b)(1) of this section; and

(c) The final drawdown has been disbursed for the project.

Subpart F—Tracking Requirements

§ 1807.600 Tracking funds—general.

An Awardee receiving a CMF award shall develop and maintain a system to ensure that its CMF award is used in accordance with this part, the Act, its Assistance Agreement, and any requirements or conditions under which such amounts were awarded. Thus, an Awardee may create a separate account or accounting code for CMF activities.

§ 1807.601 Nature of funds.

A CMF award shall be considered Federal financial assistance in regards to applying Federal civil rights laws.

Subpart G—Applications for Assistance

§ 1807.700 Notice of funds availability.

Each Applicant shall submit an application for funding under this part in accordance with the regulations in this subpart. The applicable NOFA will advise potential Applicants on how to obtain and complete an application and will establish deadlines and other requirements. The NOFA will specify any limitations, special rules, procedures, and restrictions for a particular funding round. After receipt of an application, the CDFI Fund may request clarifying or technical information on the materials submitted as part of such application.

Subpart H—Evaluation and Selection of Applications

§ 1807.800 Evaluation and selection—general.

Applicants will be evaluated and selected, at the sole discretion of the CDFI Fund, to receive assistance based on a review process that may include an interview(s) and/or site visit(s) intended to:

(a) Ensure that Applicants are evaluated on a merit basis and in a fair and consistent manner;

(b) Ensure that each Awardee can successfully meet its leveraging goals and achieve Affordable Housing Activity, Community Service Facility and/or Economic Development Activity impacts;

(c) Ensure that Awardees represent a geographically diverse group of Applicants serving Metropolitan Areas and Underserved Rural Areas across the United States that meet criteria of economic distress, which may include:

(1) The percentage of Low-Income Families or the extent of poverty;

(2) The rate of unemployment or underemployment;

(3) The extent of blight and disinvestment;

(4) Economic Development Activities or Community Service Facilities that target Extremely Low-Income, Very Low-Income, and Low-Income families within the Awardee's Service Area; or

(5) Any other criteria the CDFI Fund shall set forth in the applicable NOFA; and

(d) Take into consideration other factors as described in the applicable NOFA.

§ 1807.801 Evaluation of applications.

(a) *Eligibility and completeness.* An Applicant will not be eligible to receive a CMF award if it fails to meet the eligibility requirements described in Part 1807.200 and in the applicable NOFA, or if the Applicant has not submitted complete application materials. For the purposes of this paragraph (a), the CDFI Fund reserves the right to request additional information from the Applicant, if the CDFI Fund deems it appropriate.

(b) *Substantive review.* In evaluating and selecting applications to receive assistance, the CDFI Fund will evaluate the Applicant's likelihood of success in meeting the factors set forth in the applicable NOFA, including but not limited to:

(1) The Applicant's ability to use CMF funding to generate additional investments;

(2) The need for affordable housing in the Applicant's market; and

(3) The ability of the Applicant to obligate amounts and undertake activities in a timely manner. In the case of an Applicant that has previously received assistance under any CDFI Fund program, the CDFI Fund will also consider the Applicant's level of success in meeting its performance goals, reporting requirements, and other requirements contained in the previously negotiated and executed assistance, allocation or award agreement(s) with the CDFI Fund, any undisbursed balance of assistance, and compliance with applicable Federal laws. The CDFI Fund may consider any other factors, as it deems appropriate, in reviewing an application, as set forth in the applicable NOFA.

(c) *Consultation with appropriate regulatory agencies.* In the case of an Applicant that is a federally-regulated financial institution, the CDFI Fund may consult with the Appropriate Federal Banking Agency or Appropriate State Agency prior to making a final award decision and prior to entering into an Assistance Agreement.

(d) *Awardee selection.* The CDFI Fund will select CMF Awardees based on the criteria described in paragraph (b) of this section and any other criteria set forth in this part or the applicable NOFA.

Subpart I—Terms and Conditions of Assistance

§ 1807.900 Assistance agreement.

(a) Each Applicant that is selected to receive a CMF award must enter into an Assistance Agreement with the CDFI Fund. The Assistance Agreement will set forth certain required terms and conditions of the Assistance Agreement which may include, but are not limited to, the following:

(1) The amount of the award;

(2) The approved uses of the award;

(3) The approved Service Area in which the award may be used;

(4) The time period by which the award proceeds must be Committed;

(5) The required documentation to evidence Project Completion; and

(6) Performance goals that have been established by the CDFI Fund based upon the Awardee's application.

(b) The Assistance Agreement shall provide that in the event of fraud, mismanagement, noncompliance with the Act or the CDFI Fund's regulations; or noncompliance with the terms and conditions of the Assistance Agreement on the part of the Awardee; the CDFI Fund, in its discretion, may:

(1) Require changes in the performance goals set forth in the Assistance Agreement;

(2) Revoke approval of the Awardee's Application;

(3) Reduce or terminate the Awardee's assistance;

(4) Require repayment of any assistance that has been distributed to the Awardee;

(5) Bar the Awardee from reapplying for any assistance from the CDFI Fund; or

(6) Take such other actions as the CDFI Fund deems appropriate or as set forth in the Assistance Agreement.

(c) Prior to imposing any sanctions pursuant to this section or an Assistance Agreement, the CDFI Fund shall, to the maximum extent practicable, provide the Awardee with written notice of the proposed sanction and an opportunity to comment. Nothing in this section, however, shall provide an Awardee the right to any formal or informal hearing or comparable proceeding not otherwise required by law.

§ 1807.901 Disbursement of funds.

Assistance provided pursuant to this part may be provided in a lump sum or in some other manner, as determined appropriate by the CDFI Fund. The CDFI Fund shall not provide any assistance under this part until an Awardee has satisfied all conditions set forth in the applicable NOFA and Assistance Agreement.

§ 1807.902 Data collection and reporting.

(a) *Data—General.* An Awardee shall maintain such records as may be prescribed by the CDFI Fund that are necessary to:

(1) Disclose the manner in which CMF funding is used, including providing documentation to demonstrate Project Completion;

(2) Demonstrate compliance with the requirements of this part and the Assistance Agreement; and

(3) Evaluate the impact of CMF funding.

(b) *Customer profiles.* An Awardee shall compile such data on the gender, race, ethnicity, national origin, or other information on individuals that utilize its products and services as the CDFI Fund shall prescribe in an Assistance Agreement. Such data will be used to determine whether residents of the Awardee's Service Area are adequately served and to evaluate the impact of CMF funding.

(c) *Access to records.* An Awardee must submit such financial and activity reports, records, statements, and documents at such times, in such forms, and accompanied by such reporting data, as required by the CDFI Fund or the U.S. Department of Treasury to ensure compliance with the requirements of this part and to evaluate the impact of CMF funding. The United States Government, including the U.S. Department of Treasury, the Comptroller General, and their duly authorized representatives, shall have full and free access to the Awardee's offices and facilities and all books, documents, records, and financial statements relating to use of Federal funds and may copy such documents as they deem appropriate and audit or provide for an audit at least annually. The CDFI Fund, if it deems appropriate, may prescribe access to record requirements for entities that are borrowers of, or that receive investments from, an Awardee.

(d) *Retention of records.* An Awardee shall comply with all record retention requirements as set forth in OMB Circular A–110 (as applicable).

(e) *Data collection and reporting.*

(1) Financial Reporting: (i) All Non-Profit Awardees (excluding Insured

CDFIs and State-Insured Credit Unions) must submit to the CDFI Fund financial statements that have been reviewed by an independent certified public accountant in accordance with *Statements on Standards for Accounting and Review Services*, issued by the American Institute of Certified Public Accountants by a time set forth in the applicable Notice of Funding Availability or Assistance Agreement (audited financial statements can be provided by the due date in lieu of reviewed statements, if available). Non-Profit Awardees (excluding Insured CDFIs and State-Insured Credit Unions) that are required to have their financial statements audited pursuant to OMB Circular A–133 *Audits of States, Local Governments and Non-Profit Organizations*, must also submit their A–133 audited financial statements by a time set forth in the applicable NOFA or Assistance Agreement. Non-Profit Awardees (excluding Insured CDFIs and State-Insured Credit Unions) that are not required to have financial statements audited pursuant to OMB Circular A–133, *Audits of States, Local Governments and Non-Profit Organizations*, must submit to the CDFI Fund a statement signed by the Awardee's authorized representative or certified public accountant, asserting that the Awardee is not required to have a single audit pursuant OMB Circular A–133.

(ii) For-profit Awardees (excluding Insured CDFIs and State-Insured Credit Unions) must submit to the CDFI Fund financial statements audited in conformity with generally accepted auditing standards as promulgated by the American Institute of Certified Public by a time set forth in the applicable NOFA or Assistance Agreement.

(iii) Insured CDFIs are not required to submit financial statements to the CDFI Fund. The CDFI Fund will obtain the necessary information from publicly available sources. State-Insured Credit Unions must submit to the CDFI Fund copies of the financial statements that they submit to the Appropriate State Agency.

(2) Performance Goal Reporting: Performance goals and measures that are specific to the Awardee's application for funding shall be met as set forth in its Assistance Agreement. Awardees shall submit data and information to the CDFI Fund regarding achievement of these Performance Goals as described in the Assistance Agreement.

(f) *Availability of referenced publications.* The publications referenced in this section are available as follows:

(1) OMB Circulars may be obtained from the Office of Administration, Publications Office, 725 17th Street, NW., Room 2200, New Executive Office Building, Washington, DC 20503 or on the Internet (*http://www.whitehouse.gov/omb/grants_circulars/*); and

(2) General Accounting Office materials may be obtained from GAO Distribution, 700 4th Street, NW., Suite 1100, Washington, DC 20548.

§ 1807.903 Compliance with government requirements.

In carrying out its responsibilities pursuant to an Assistance Agreement, the Awardee shall comply with all applicable Federal, State, and local laws, regulations, and ordinances, OMB Circulars, and Executive Orders.

§ 1807.904 Lobbying restrictions.

No assistance made available under this part may be expended by an Awardee to pay any person to influence or attempt to influence any agency, elected official, officer or employee of a State or local government in connection with the making, award, extension, continuation, renewal, amendment, or modification of any State or local government contract, grant, loan or cooperative agreement as such terms are defined in 31 U.S.C. 1352.

§ 1807.905 Criminal provisions.

The criminal provisions of 18 U.S.C. 657 regarding embezzlement or misappropriation of funds is applicable to all Awardees and insiders.

§ 1807.906 CDFI Fund deemed not to control.

The CDFI Fund shall not be deemed to control an Awardee by reason of any assistance provided under the Act for the purpose of any applicable law.

§ 1807.907 Limitation on liability.

The liability of the CDFI Fund and the United States Government arising out of any assistance to an Awardee in accordance with this part shall be limited to the amount of the investment in the Awardee. The CDFI Fund shall be exempt from any assessments and other liabilities that may be imposed on controlling or principal shareholders by any Federal law or the law of any State. Nothing in this section shall affect the application of any Federal tax law.

§1807.908 Fraud, waste and abuse.

Any person who becomes aware of the existence or apparent existence of fraud, waste or abuse of assistance provided under this part should report such incidences to the Office of Inspector General of the U.S. Department of the Treasury.

PART 1815—ENVIRONMENTAL QUALITY

Sec.

AUTHORITY: 12 U.S.C. 4703, 4717; 42 U.S.C. 4332; Chapter X, Pub L. 104–19, 109 Stat. 237 (12 U.S.C. 4703 note).

SOURCE: 60 FR 54130, Oct. 19, 1995, unless otherwise noted.

§1815.100 Policy.

The Community Development Financial Institution Fund's policy is to ensure that environmental factors and concerns are given appropriate consideration in decisions and actions by the Fund and to reduce any possible adverse effects of Fund decisions and actions upon the quality of the human environment.

§1815.101 Purpose.

This part supplements Council on Environmental Quality regulations for implementing the procedural provisions of the National Environmental Policy Act of 1969, as amended, and describe how the Community Development Financial Institutions Fund intends to consider environmental factors and concerns in the Fund's decisionmaking process. This part applies only to the Fund and not to any other bureau, office or organization within the Department of the Treasury.

§1815.102 Definitions.

(a) For the purpose of this part:

(1) *Act* means the Community Development Banking and Financial Institutions Act (12 U.S.C. 4701 et seq.);

(2) *Application* means a request for assistance from the Fund submitted pursuant to parts 1805 or 1806 of this chapter;

(3) *CEQ regulations* means the regulations for implementing the procedural provisions of the National Environmental Policy Act of 1969 as promulgated by the Council on Environmental Quality, Executive Office of the President, appearing at 40 CFR parts 1500–1508 and to which this part is a supplement;

(4) *Comprehensive Business Plan* means a document submitted as part of an Application pursuant to part 1805 of this chapter which describes an organization's proposed process for offering products or services to a particular market, including organizational requirements needed to serve that market effectively;

(5) *Consumer Loans* means loans to one or more individuals for household, family or other personal expenditures;

(6) *Decisionmaker* means the Director of the Fund, unless an appropriate delegation of authority has been made;

(7) *EIS* means an environmental impact statement as defined in 40 CFR 1508.11 of the CEQ regulations;

(8) *Fund* means the Community Development Financial Institutions Fund, established under section 104(a) of the Act (12 U.S.C. 4703(a));

(9) *NEPA* means the National Environmental Policy Act, as amended, 42 U.S.C. 4321–4335; and

(10) *Project* means all closely related actions relating to a specific site.

(b) Other terms used in this part are defined in 40 CFR part 1508 of the CEQ regulations.

§ 1815.103 Designation of responsible Fund official.

The Director of the Fund is the designated Fund official responsible for implementation and operation of the Fund's policies and procedures on environmental quality and control.

§ 1815.104 Specific responsibilities of the designated Fund official.

The designated Fund official shall:

(a) Coordinate the formulation and revision of Fund policies and procedures on matters pertaining to environmental quality and control;

(b) Establish and maintain working relationships with relevant government agencies (including Federal, state and local) concerned with environmental matters;

(c) Develop procedures within the Fund's planning and decisionmaking processes to ensure that environmental factors are properly considered in all proposals and decisions in accordance with this part;

(d) Develop, monitor, and review the Fund's implementation of standards, procedures, and working relationships for protection and enhancement of environmental quality and compliance with applicable laws and regulations;

(e) Monitor processes to ensure that the Fund's procedures regarding consideration of environmental quality are achieving their intended purposes;

(f) Advise the officers and employees of the Fund of technical and management requirements of environmental analysis, of appropriate expertise available, and, with the assistance of the Department of the Treasury's Office of the General Counsel, of relevant legal developments;

(g) Monitor the consideration and documentation of the environmental aspects of Fund planning and decisionmaking processes by appropriate officers and employees of the Fund;

(h) Ensure that all environmental assessments and, where required, all EISs are prepared in accordance with the appropriate regulations adopted by the Council on Environmental Quality and the Fund;

(i) Ensure that, as required, a legislative EIS is submitted with all proposed legislation;

(j) Consolidate and transmit to appropriate parties the Fund's comments on EISs and other environmental reports prepared by other agencies;

(k) Acquire information and prepare appropriate reports on environmental matters required of the Fund; and

(l) Coordinate the Fund's efforts to make available to other parties information and advice on the Fund's policies for protecting and enhancing the quality of the environment.

§ 1815.105 Major decision points.

(a) The possible environmental effects of an Application, including any Comprehensive Business Plan, must be considered along with technical, economic, and other factors throughout the decisionmaking process. For most Fund actions there are two distinct stages in the decisionmaking process:

(1) Preliminary approval stage, at which point applications are selected for funding; and

(2) Final approval and funding stage.

(b) Environmental review shall be integrated into the decisionmaking process of the Fund as follows:

(1) During the preliminary approval stage, the designated Fund official shall determine whether the Application proposes actions which are categorically excluded, or normally require an environmental assessment or an EIS;

(2) If the designated Fund official determines that the Application proposes actions which normally require an environmental assessment or an EIS, the applicant shall be informed that the final approval and funding, in addition to any other conditions, is contingent upon:

(i) The applicant supplying to the Fund all information necessary for the Fund to perform or have performed any environmental review required by this part;

(ii) The applicant not using any Fund financial assistance to perform any of such proposed actions in the Application that affect the physical environment until Fund approval is received; and

(iii) The outcome of the environmental review required by this part;

(3) The Fund will perform or have performed the environmental reviews required by this part;

(4) A preliminary approval of an Application may be withdrawn or further conditions may be imposed based upon the outcome of an environmental review required by this part; and

(5) If the designated Fund official determines that the Application proposes actions that require an environmental assessment or an EIS, the environmental assessment and/or EIS must be completed and circulated prior to the use of Federal funds for any activity that triggers the need for an environmental assessment and/or EIS.

§ 1815.106 Supplemental environmental review.

(a) The designated Fund official shall determine whether the proposed actions in the Application are sufficiently definite to perform a meaningful environmental review during the preliminary approval stage.

(b) If the designated Fund official determines that the Application is sufficiently definite to perform a meaningful environmental review during the preliminary approval stage, no conditions for supplemental environmental review shall be imposed.

(c) If the designated Fund official determines that the Application, or any part of the Application, is not sufficiently definite to complete a meaningful environmental review during the preliminary approval stage, the Fund shall require a supplemental environmental review prior to the taking of any action directly using Fund financial assistance that is not categorically excluded from environmental review or for which an environmental assessment or EIS has not been approved by the Fund. The applicant shall notify the designated Fund official when proposing any action requiring a supplemental environmental review and shall supply to the Fund all information necessary for the Fund to perform the supplemental environmental review. The Fund shall perform or have performed such a supplemental environmental review. The applicant shall not use any Fund financial assistance to perform any of the proposed actions requiring a supplemental environmental review that affect the physical environment until Fund approval for such action is received.

§ 1815.107 Determination of review requirement.

In deciding whether to prepare an EIS, the designated Fund official shall determine whether the proposal is one that normally:

(a) Requires an EIS;

(b) Requires an environmental assessment, but not necessarily an EIS; or

(c) Does not require either an EIS or an environmental assessment (categorical exclusion).

§ 1815.108 Actions that normally require an EIS.

(a) If necessary, the Fund shall perform or have performed an environmental assessment to determine if an Application, or any portion of an Application, requires an EIS. However, it may be readily apparent that a proposed action in an Application will have a significant impact on the environment; in such cases, an environmental assessment is not required and the Fund shall immediately begin to prepare, or have prepared, an EIS.

(b) An EIS normally is required where an Application proposes to directly use financial assistance from the Fund for any Project that would:

(1) Remove, demolish, convert, or substantially rehabilitate 2,500 or more existing housing units, or would result in the construction or installation of 2,500 or more new housing units, or which would provide sites for 2,500 or more new housing units; or

(2) Remove, demolish, convert, or substantially rehabilitate 1,500,000 square feet or more of commercial space, or would result in the construction or installation of 1,500,000 square feet or more of new commercial space, or which would provide sites for 1,500,000 square feet or more of new commercial space.

§ 1815.109 Preparation of an EIS.

(a) If the Fund determines that an EIS should be prepared, it shall publish a notice of intent in the FEDERAL REGISTER in accordance with 40 CFR 1501.7 and 1508.22 of the CEQ regulations. After publishing the notice of intent, the Fund shall begin to prepare or have prepared the EIS. Procedures for preparing the EIS are set forth in 40 CFR part 1502 of the CEQ regulations.

(b) The Fund may supplement a draft or final EIS at any time. The Fund shall prepare or have prepared a supplement to either the draft or final EIS when:

(1) Substantial changes are proposed to an action contained in the draft or final EIS that are relevant to environmental concerns or there are significant new circumstances or information relevant to environmental concerns and bearing on the proposed action or its impacts; or

(2) Actions are proposed which relate or are similar to other action(s) taken or proposed and that together have a cumulatively significant impact on the environment.

§ 1815.110 Categorical exclusion.

The CEQ regulations provide for the categorical exclusion of actions that do not individually or cumulatively have a significant effect on the human environment (40 CFR 1508.4). Therefore, neither an environmental assessment nor an EIS is required for such actions. An action which falls into one of the categories below may still require the preparation of an EIS or environmental assessment if the designated Fund official determines it meets the criteria stated in § 1815.109 or involves extraordinary circumstances that may have a significant environmental effect. The Fund has determined the following categorical exclusions:

(a) Actions directly related to the administration or operation of the Fund (e.g. personnel actions, including, but not limited to, staff recruitment and training; purchase of goods and services for the Fund, including, but not limited to, furnishings, equipment, supplies and services; space acquisition; property management; and security);

(b) Actions directly related to and implementing proposals for which an environmental assessment or an environmental assessment and EIS have been prepared;

(c) Actions directly related to the granting or receipt of Bank Enterprise Act awards pursuant to part 1806 of this chapter;

(d) Actions directly related to training and/or technical assistance;

(e) Projects for the acquisition, disposition, rehabilitation and/or modernization of 500 existing housing units or less when all the following conditions are met:

(1) Unit density is not increased more than 20 percent;

(2) The Project does not involve changes in land use from nonresidential to residential;

(3) The estimated cost of rehabilitation is less than 75 percent of the total estimated cost of replacement after rehabilitation; and

(4) The Project does not involve the demolition of one or more buildings containing the primary use served by the project that, together, have more than 20 percent of the square footage of the Project;

(f) Projects for the construction of 200 housing units or less when all the following conditions are met:

(1) The Project does not involve changes in existing land use from nonresidential to residential; and

(2) The Project does not involve the demolition of one or more buildings containing the primary use served by the project that, together, have more than 20 percent of the square footage of the Project;

(g) Projects for the acquisition, disposition, rehabilitation and/or modernization of 200,000 square feet or less of existing commercial space when all the following conditions are met:

(1) The Project does not involve changes in existing land use from residential to nonresidential;

(2) The estimated cost of rehabilitation is less than 75 percent of the total estimated cost of replacement after rehabilitation; and

(3) The Project does not involve the demolition of more than 10,000 square feet of commercial space containing the primary use served by the Project;

(h) Projects for the construction of 100,000 square feet or less of commercial space when all the following conditions are met:

(1) The Project does not involve changes in existing land use from residential to nonresidential: and

(2) The Project does not involve the demolition of more than 10,000 square feet of commercial space containing the primary use served by the Project;

(i) Projects for the acquisition of an existing structure, provided that the property to be acquired is in place and will be retained in the same use;

(j) Projects involving Fund financial assistance of $1,000,000 or less;

(k) Actions directly related to the provision of residential tenant-based rental assistance, Consumer Loans, health care, child care, educational, cultural and/or social services;

(l) Actions involving Fund financial assistance that is used to increase the permanent capital and/or liquidity of an applicant;

(m) Actions where no use of Federal funds is involved in the activity or Project; and

(n) Actions directly related to the provision of working capital, the acquisition of machinery and equipment or the purchase of inventory, raw materials or supplies.

§1815.111 Actions that require an environmental assessment.

If a Project or action is not one that normally requires an EIS and does not qualify for categorical exclusion, the Fund shall prepare, or have prepared, an environmental assessment.

§1815.112 Preparation of an environmental assessment.

(a) The Fund shall begin the preparation of an environmental assessment as early as possible after the designated Fund official has determined that it is required. The Fund may prepare an environmental assessment at any time to assist planning and decisionmaking.

(b) An environmental assessment is a concise public document used to determine whether to prepare an EIS. An environmental assessment aids in complying with the NEPA when no EIS is necessary, and it facilitates the preparation of an EIS, if one is necessary. The environmental assessment shall contain brief discussions of the following topics:

(1) Purpose and need for the proposed action;

(2) Description of the proposed action;

(3) Alternatives considered, including the no action alternative;

(4) Environmental effects of the proposed action and alternative actions; and

(5) Listing of agencies, organizations or persons consulted.

(c) The most important or significant environmental consequences and effects on the areas listed below should be addressed in the environmental assessment. Only those areas which are specifically relevant to the particular proposal should be addressed. Those areas should be addressed in as much detail as is necessary to allow an analysis of the alternatives and the proposal. The areas to be considered are the following:

(1) Natural/ecological features (such as floodplain, wetlands, coastal zones, wildlife refuges, and endangered species);

(2) Air quality;

(3) Sound levels;

(4) Water supply, wastewater treatment and water runoff;

(5) Energy requirements and conservation;

(6) Solid waste;

(7) Transportation;

(8) Community facilities and services;

(9) Social and economic;

(10) Historic and aesthetic; and

(11) Other relevant factors.

(d) If the Fund completes an environmental assessment and determines that an EIS is not required, then the Fund shall prepare a finding of no significant impact. The finding of no significant impact shall be made available to the public by the Fund as specified in 40 CFR 1506.6 of the CEQ regulations.

§1815.113 Public involvement.

All information collected by the Fund pursuant to this part shall be available to the public consistent with the CEQ regulations. Interested persons may obtain information concerning any pending EIS or any other element of the environmental review process of the Fund by contacting the Community Development Financial Institutions Fund, Department of the Treasury, 1500 Pennsylvania Avenue NW., room 5116, Washington, DC 20220, or such other contact entity designated by the Fund.

§ 1815.114 Fund decisionmaking procedures.

To ensure that at major decisionmaking points all relevant environmental concerns are considered by the Decisionmaker, the following procedures are established:

(a) An environmental document, i.e., the EIS, environmental assessment, finding of no significant impact, or notice of intent, in addition to being prepared at the earliest point in the decisionmaking process, shall accompany the relevant proposal or action through the Fund's decisionmaking process to ensure adequate consideration of environmental factors;

(b) The Decisionmaker shall consider in its decisionmaking process only those alternatives discussed in the relevant environmental documents. Also, where an EIS has been prepared, the decisionmaker shall consider all comments received during any comment process and all alternatives described in the EIS. A written record of the consideration of alternatives during the decisionmaking process shall be maintained; and

(c) Any environmental document prepared for a proposal or action shall be made part of the record of any formal rulemaking by the Fund.

§ 1815.115 OMB control number.

The collection of information requirements in this part have been approved by the Office of Management and Budget and assigned OMB control number 1505–0153 (expires September 30, 1998).

FINDING AIDS

A list of CFR titles, subtitles, chapters, subchapters and parts and an alphabetical list of agencies publishing in the CFR are included in the CFR Index and Finding Aids volume to the Code of Federal Regulations which is published separately and revised annually.

Table of CFR Titles and Chapters

(Revised as of January 1, 2012)

Title 1—General Provisions

I	Administrative Committee of the Federal Register (Parts 1—49)
II	Office of the Federal Register (Parts 50—299)
III	Administrative Conference of the United States (Parts 300—399)
IV	Miscellaneous Agencies (Parts 400—500)

Title 2—Grants and Agreements

	SUBTITLE A—OFFICE OF MANAGEMENT AND BUDGET GUIDANCE FOR GRANTS AND AGREEMENTS
I	Office of Management and Budget Governmentwide Guidance for Grants and Agreements (Parts 2—199)
II	Office of Management and Budget Circulars and Guidance (200—299)
	SUBTITLE B—FEDERAL AGENCY REGULATIONS FOR GRANTS AND AGREEMENTS
III	Department of Health and Human Services (Parts 300— 399)
IV	Department of Agriculture (Parts 400—499)
VI	Department of State (Parts 600—699)
VII	Agency for International Development (Parts 700—799)
VIII	Department of Veterans Affairs (Parts 800—899)
IX	Department of Energy (Parts 900—999)
XI	Department of Defense (Parts 1100—1199)
XII	Department of Transportation (Parts 1200—1299)
XIII	Department of Commerce (Parts 1300—1399)
XIV	Department of the Interior (Parts 1400—1499)
XV	Environmental Protection Agency (Parts 1500—1599)
XVIII	National Aeronautics and Space Administration (Parts 1800—1899)
XX	United States Nuclear Regulatory Commission (Parts 2000—2099)
XXII	Corporation for National and Community Service (Parts 2200—2299)
XXIII	Social Security Administration (Parts 2300—2399)
XXIV	Housing and Urban Development (Parts 2400—2499)
XXV	National Science Foundation (Parts 2500—2599)
XXVI	National Archives and Records Administration (Parts 2600—2699)
XXVII	Small Business Administration (Parts 2700—2799)
XXVIII	Department of Justice (Parts 2800—2899)

Title 2—Grants and Agreements—Continued

Chap.	
XXX	Department of Homeland Security (Parts 3000—3099)
XXXI	Institute of Museum and Library Services (Parts 3100—3199)
XXXII	National Endowment for the Arts (Parts 3200—3299)
XXXIII	National Endowment for the Humanities (Parts 3300—3399)
XXXV	Export-Import Bank of the United States (Parts 3500—3599)
XXXVII	Peace Corps (Parts 3700—3799)
LVIII	Election Assistance Commission (Parts 5800—5899)

Title 3—The President

I	Executive Office of the President (Parts 100—199)

Title 4—Accounts

I	Government Accountability Office (Parts 1—99)
II	Recovery Accountability and Transparency Board (Parts 200—299)

Title 5—Administrative Personnel

I	Office of Personnel Management (Parts 1—1199)
II	Merit Systems Protection Board (Parts 1200—1299)
III	Office of Management and Budget (Parts 1300—1399)
V	The International Organizations Employees Loyalty Board (Parts 1500—1599)
VI	Federal Retirement Thrift Investment Board (Parts 1600—1699)
VIII	Office of Special Counsel (Parts 1800—1899)
IX	Appalachian Regional Commission (Parts 1900—1999)
XI	Armed Forces Retirement Home (Parts 2100—2199)
XIV	Federal Labor Relations Authority, General Counsel of the Federal Labor Relations Authority and Federal Service Impasses Panel (Parts 2400—2499)
XV	Office of Administration, Executive Office of the President (Parts 2500—2599)
XVI	Office of Government Ethics (Parts 2600—2699)
XXI	Department of the Treasury (Parts 3100—3199)
XXII	Federal Deposit Insurance Corporation (Parts 3200—3299)
XXIII	Department of Energy (Parts 3300—3399)
XXIV	Federal Energy Regulatory Commission (Parts 3400—3499)
XXV	Department of the Interior (Parts 3500—3599)
XXVI	Department of Defense (Parts 3600— 3699)
XXVIII	Department of Justice (Parts 3800—3899)
XXIX	Federal Communications Commission (Parts 3900—3999)
XXX	Farm Credit System Insurance Corporation (Parts 4000—4099)
XXXI	Farm Credit Administration (Parts 4100—4199)
XXXIII	Overseas Private Investment Corporation (Parts 4300—4399)

Chap.

XCVII Department of Homeland Security Human Resources Management System (Department of Homeland Security—Office of Personnel Management) (Parts 9700—9799)

Title 6—Domestic Security

I Department of Homeland Security, Office of the Secretary (Parts 1—99)

Title 7—Agriculture

SUBTITLE A—OFFICE OF THE SECRETARY OF AGRICULTURE (PARTS 0—26)

SUBTITLE B—REGULATIONS OF THE DEPARTMENT OF AGRICULTURE

I Agricultural Marketing Service (Standards, Inspections, Marketing Practices), Department of Agriculture (Parts 27—209)

II Food and Nutrition Service, Department of Agriculture (Parts 210—299)

III Animal and Plant Health Inspection Service, Department of Agriculture (Parts 300—399)

IV Federal Crop Insurance Corporation, Department of Agriculture (Parts 400—499)

V Agricultural Research Service, Department of Agriculture (Parts 500—599)

VI Natural Resources Conservation Service, Department of Agriculture (Parts 600—699)

VII Farm Service Agency, Department of Agriculture (Parts 700—799)

VIII Grain Inspection, Packers and Stockyards Administration (Federal Grain Inspection Service), Department of Agriculture (Parts 800—899)

IX Agricultural Marketing Service (Marketing Agreements and Orders; Fruits, Vegetables, Nuts), Department of Agriculture (Parts 900—999)

X Agricultural Marketing Service (Marketing Agreements and Orders; Milk), Department of Agriculture (Parts 1000—1199)

XI Agricultural Marketing Service (Marketing Agreements and Orders; Miscellaneous Commodities), Department of Agriculture (Parts 1200—1299)

XIV Commodity Credit Corporation, Department of Agriculture (Parts 1400—1499)

XV Foreign Agricultural Service, Department of Agriculture (Parts 1500—1599)

XVI Rural Telephone Bank, Department of Agriculture (Parts 1600—1699)

XVII Rural Utilities Service, Department of Agriculture (Parts 1700—1799)

XVIII Rural Housing Service, Rural Business-Cooperative Service, Rural Utilities Service, and Farm Service Agency, Department of Agriculture (Parts 1800—2099)

XX Local Television Loan Guarantee Board (Parts 2200—2299)

Title 7—Agriculture—Continued

Chap.

Chap.	
XXV	Office of Advocacy and Outreach, Department of Agriculture (Parts 2500—2599)
XXVI	Office of Inspector General, Department of Agriculture (Parts 2600—2699)
XXVII	Office of Information Resources Management, Department of Agriculture (Parts 2700—2799)
XXVIII	Office of Operations, Department of Agriculture (Parts 2800—2899)
XXIX	Office of Energy Policy and New Uses, Department of Agriculture (Parts 2900—2999)
XXX	Office of the Chief Financial Officer, Department of Agriculture (Parts 3000—3099)
XXXI	Office of Environmental Quality, Department of Agriculture (Parts 3100—3199)
XXXII	Office of Procurement and Property Management, Department of Agriculture (Parts 3200—3299)
XXXIII	Office of Transportation, Department of Agriculture (Parts 3300—3399)
XXXIV	National Institute of Food and Agriculture (Parts 3400—3499)
XXXV	Rural Housing Service, Department of Agriculture (Parts 3500—3599)
XXXVI	National Agricultural Statistics Service, Department of Agriculture (Parts 3600—3699)
XXXVII	Economic Research Service, Department of Agriculture (Parts 3700—3799)
XXXVIII	World Agricultural Outlook Board, Department of Agriculture (Parts 3800—3899)
XLI	[Reserved]
XLII	Rural Business-Cooperative Service and Rural Utilities Service, Department of Agriculture (Parts 4200—4299)

Title 8—Aliens and Nationality

I	Department of Homeland Security (Immigration and Naturalization) (Parts 1—499)
V	Executive Office for Immigration Review, Department of Justice (Parts 1000—1399)

Title 9—Animals and Animal Products

I	Animal and Plant Health Inspection Service, Department of Agriculture (Parts 1—199)
II	Grain Inspection, Packers and Stockyards Administration (Packers and Stockyards Programs), Department of Agriculture (Parts 200—299)
III	Food Safety and Inspection Service, Department of Agriculture (Parts 300—599)

Title 10—Energy

Chap.

I Nuclear Regulatory Commission (Parts 0—199)

II Department of Energy (Parts 200—699)

III Department of Energy (Parts 700—999)

X Department of Energy (General Provisions) (Parts 1000—1099)

XIII Nuclear Waste Technical Review Board (Parts 1300—1399)

XVII Defense Nuclear Facilities Safety Board (Parts 1700—1799)

XVIII Northeast Interstate Low-Level Radioactive Waste Commission (Parts 1800—1899)

Title 11—Federal Elections

I Federal Election Commission (Parts 1—9099)

II Election Assistance Commission (Parts 9400—9499)

Title 12—Banks and Banking

I Comptroller of the Currency, Department of the Treasury (Parts 1—199)

II Federal Reserve System (Parts 200—299)

III Federal Deposit Insurance Corporation (Parts 300—399)

IV Export-Import Bank of the United States (Parts 400—499)

V Office of Thrift Supervision, Department of the Treasury (Parts 500—599)

VI Farm Credit Administration (Parts 600—699)

VII National Credit Union Administration (Parts 700—799)

VIII Federal Financing Bank (Parts 800—899)

IX Federal Housing Finance Board (Parts 900—999)

X Bureau of Consumer Financial Protection (Parts 1000—1099)

XI Federal Financial Institutions Examination Council (Parts 1100—1199)

XII Federal Housing Finance Agency (Parts 1200—1299)

XIII Financial Stability Oversight Council (Parts 1300—1399)

XIV Farm Credit System Insurance Corporation (Parts 1400—1499)

XV Department of the Treasury (Parts 1500—1599)

XVI Office of Financial Research (Parts 1600—1699)

XVII Office of Federal Housing Enterprise Oversight, Department of Housing and Urban Development (Parts 1700—1799)

XVIII Community Development Financial Institutions Fund, Department of the Treasury (Parts 1800—1899)

Title 13—Business Credit and Assistance

I Small Business Administration (Parts 1—199)

III Economic Development Administration, Department of Commerce (Parts 300—399)

IV Emergency Steel Guarantee Loan Board (Parts 400—499)

V Emergency Oil and Gas Guaranteed Loan Board (Parts 500—599)

Title 14—Aeronautics and Space

Chap.

I Federal Aviation Administration, Department of Transportation (Parts 1—199)

II Office of the Secretary, Department of Transportation (Aviation Proceedings) (Parts 200—399)

III Commercial Space Transportation, Federal Aviation Administration, Department of Transportation (Parts 400—1199)

V National Aeronautics and Space Administration (Parts 1200—1299)

VI Air Transportation System Stabilization (Parts 1300—1399)

Title 15—Commerce and Foreign Trade

SUBTITLE A—OFFICE OF THE SECRETARY OF COMMERCE (PARTS 0—29)

SUBTITLE B—REGULATIONS RELATING TO COMMERCE AND FOREIGN TRADE

I Bureau of the Census, Department of Commerce (Parts 30—199)

II National Institute of Standards and Technology, Department of Commerce (Parts 200—299)

III International Trade Administration, Department of Commerce (Parts 300—399)

IV Foreign-Trade Zones Board, Department of Commerce (Parts 400—499)

VII Bureau of Industry and Security, Department of Commerce (Parts 700—799)

VIII Bureau of Economic Analysis, Department of Commerce (Parts 800—899)

IX National Oceanic and Atmospheric Administration, Department of Commerce (Parts 900—999)

XI Technology Administration, Department of Commerce (Parts 1100—1199)

XIII East-West Foreign Trade Board (Parts 1300—1399)

XIV Minority Business Development Agency (Parts 1400—1499)

SUBTITLE C—REGULATIONS RELATING TO FOREIGN TRADE AGREEMENTS

XX Office of the United States Trade Representative (Parts 2000—2099)

SUBTITLE D—REGULATIONS RELATING TO TELECOMMUNICATIONS AND INFORMATION

XXIII National Telecommunications and Information Administration, Department of Commerce (Parts 2300—2399)

Title 16—Commercial Practices

I Federal Trade Commission (Parts 0—999)

II Consumer Product Safety Commission (Parts 1000—1799)

Title 17—Commodity and Securities Exchanges

Chap.

I Commodity Futures Trading Commission (Parts 1—199)

II Securities and Exchange Commission (Parts 200—399)

IV Department of the Treasury (Parts 400—499)

Title 18—Conservation of Power and Water Resources

I Federal Energy Regulatory Commission, Department of Energy (Parts 1—399)

III Delaware River Basin Commission (Parts 400—499)

VI Water Resources Council (Parts 700—799)

VIII Susquehanna River Basin Commission (Parts 800—899)

XIII Tennessee Valley Authority (Parts 1300—1399)

Title 19—Customs Duties

I U.S. Customs and Border Protection, Department of Homeland Security; Department of the Treasury (Parts 0—199)

II United States International Trade Commission (Parts 200—299)

III International Trade Administration, Department of Commerce (Parts 300—399)

IV U.S. Immigration and Customs Enforcement, Department of Homeland Security (Parts 400—599)

Title 20—Employees' Benefits

I Office of Workers' Compensation Programs, Department of Labor (Parts 1—199)

II Railroad Retirement Board (Parts 200—399)

III Social Security Administration (Parts 400—499)

IV Employees' Compensation Appeals Board, Department of Labor (Parts 500—599)

V Employment and Training Administration, Department of Labor (Parts 600—699)

VI Office of Workers' Compensation Programs, Department of Labor (Parts 700—799)

VII Benefits Review Board, Department of Labor (Parts 800—899)

VIII Joint Board for the Enrollment of Actuaries (Parts 900—999)

IX Office of the Assistant Secretary for Veterans' Employment and Training Service, Department of Labor (Parts 1000—1099)

Title 21—Food and Drugs

I Food and Drug Administration, Department of Health and Human Services (Parts 1—1299)

II Drug Enforcement Administration, Department of Justice (Parts 1300—1399)

III Office of National Drug Control Policy (Parts 1400—1499)

Title 22—Foreign Relations

Chap.

Chap.	
I	Department of State (Parts 1—199)
II	Agency for International Development (Parts 200—299)
III	Peace Corps (Parts 300—399)
IV	International Joint Commission, United States and Canada (Parts 400—499)
V	Broadcasting Board of Governors (Parts 500—599)
VII	Overseas Private Investment Corporation (Parts 700—799)
IX	Foreign Service Grievance Board (Parts 900—999)
X	Inter-American Foundation (Parts 1000—1099)
XI	International Boundary and Water Commission, United States and Mexico, United States Section (Parts 1100—1199)
XII	United States International Development Cooperation Agency (Parts 1200—1299)
XIII	Millennium Challenge Corporation (Parts 1300—1399)
XIV	Foreign Service Labor Relations Board; Federal Labor Relations Authority; General Counsel of the Federal Labor Relations Authority; and the Foreign Service Impasse Disputes Panel (Parts 1400—1499)
XV	African Development Foundation (Parts 1500—1599)
XVI	Japan-United States Friendship Commission (Parts 1600—1699)
XVII	United States Institute of Peace (Parts 1700—1799)

Title 23—Highways

I	Federal Highway Administration, Department of Transportation (Parts 1—999)
II	National Highway Traffic Safety Administration and Federal Highway Administration, Department of Transportation (Parts 1200—1299)
III	National Highway Traffic Safety Administration, Department of Transportation (Parts 1300—1399)

Title 24—Housing and Urban Development

SUBTITLE A—OFFICE OF THE SECRETARY, DEPARTMENT OF HOUSING AND URBAN DEVELOPMENT (PARTS 0—99)

SUBTITLE B—REGULATIONS RELATING TO HOUSING AND URBAN DEVELOPMENT

I	Office of Assistant Secretary for Equal Opportunity, Department of Housing and Urban Development (Parts 100—199)
II	Office of Assistant Secretary for Housing-Federal Housing Commissioner, Department of Housing and Urban Development (Parts 200—299)
III	Government National Mortgage Association, Department of Housing and Urban Development (Parts 300—399)
IV	Office of Housing and Office of Multifamily Housing Assistance Restructuring, Department of Housing and Urban Development (Parts 400—499)

Chap.

- V Office of Assistant Secretary for Community Planning and Development, Department of Housing and Urban Development (Parts 500—599)
- VI Office of Assistant Secretary for Community Planning and Development, Department of Housing and Urban Development (Parts 600—699) [Reserved]
- VII Office of the Secretary, Department of Housing and Urban Development (Housing Assistance Programs and Public and Indian Housing Programs) (Parts 700—799)
- VIII Office of the Assistant Secretary for Housing—Federal Housing Commissioner, Department of Housing and Urban Development (Section 8 Housing Assistance Programs, Section 202 Direct Loan Program, Section 202 Supportive Housing for the Elderly Program and Section 811 Supportive Housing for Persons With Disabilities Program) (Parts 800—899)
- IX Office of Assistant Secretary for Public and Indian Housing, Department of Housing and Urban Development (Parts 900—1699)
- X Office of Assistant Secretary for Housing—Federal Housing Commissioner, Department of Housing and Urban Development (Interstate Land Sales Registration Program) (Parts 1700—1799)
- XII Office of Inspector General, Department of Housing and Urban Development (Parts 2000—2099)
- XV Emergency Mortgage Insurance and Loan Programs, Department of Housing and Urban Development (Parts 2700—2799)
- XX Office of Assistant Secretary for Housing—Federal Housing Commissioner, Department of Housing and Urban Development (Parts 3200—3899)
- XXIV Board of Directors of the HOPE for Homeowners Program (Parts 4000—4099)
- XXV Neighborhood Reinvestment Corporation (Parts 4100—4199)

Title 25—Indians

- I Bureau of Indian Affairs, Department of the Interior (Parts 1—299)
- II Indian Arts and Crafts Board, Department of the Interior (Parts 300—399)
- III National Indian Gaming Commission, Department of the Interior (Parts 500—599)
- IV Office of Navajo and Hopi Indian Relocation (Parts 700—799)
- V Bureau of Indian Affairs, Department of the Interior, and Indian Health Service, Department of Health and Human Services (Part 900)
- VI Office of the Assistant Secretary-Indian Affairs, Department of the Interior (Parts 1000—1199)
- VII Office of the Special Trustee for American Indians, Department of the Interior (Parts 1200—1299)

Title 26—Internal Revenue

Chap.

I Internal Revenue Service, Department of the Treasury (Parts 1—End)

Title 27—Alcohol, Tobacco Products and Firearms

I Alcohol and Tobacco Tax and Trade Bureau, Department of the Treasury (Parts 1—399)

II Bureau of Alcohol, Tobacco, Firearms, and Explosives, Department of Justice (Parts 400—699)

Title 28—Judicial Administration

I Department of Justice (Parts 0—299)

III Federal Prison Industries, Inc., Department of Justice (Parts 300—399)

V Bureau of Prisons, Department of Justice (Parts 500—599)

VI Offices of Independent Counsel, Department of Justice (Parts 600—699)

VII Office of Independent Counsel (Parts 700—799)

VIII Court Services and Offender Supervision Agency for the District of Columbia (Parts 800—899)

IX National Crime Prevention and Privacy Compact Council (Parts 900—999)

XI Department of Justice and Department of State (Parts 1100—1199)

Title 29—Labor

SUBTITLE A—OFFICE OF THE SECRETARY OF LABOR (PARTS 0—99)

SUBTITLE B—REGULATIONS RELATING TO LABOR

I National Labor Relations Board (Parts 100—199)

II Office of Labor-Management Standards, Department of Labor (Parts 200—299)

III National Railroad Adjustment Board (Parts 300—399)

IV Office of Labor-Management Standards, Department of Labor (Parts 400—499)

V Wage and Hour Division, Department of Labor (Parts 500—899)

IX Construction Industry Collective Bargaining Commission (Parts 900—999)

X National Mediation Board (Parts 1200—1299)

XII Federal Mediation and Conciliation Service (Parts 1400—1499)

XIV Equal Employment Opportunity Commission (Parts 1600—1699)

XVII Occupational Safety and Health Administration, Department of Labor (Parts 1900—1999)

XX Occupational Safety and Health Review Commission (Parts 2200—2499)

XXV Employee Benefits Security Administration, Department of Labor (Parts 2500—2599)

Title 29—Labor—Continued

Chap.	
XXVII	Federal Mine Safety and Health Review Commission (Parts 2700—2799)
XL	Pension Benefit Guaranty Corporation (Parts 4000—4999)

Title 30—Mineral Resources

I	Mine Safety and Health Administration, Department of Labor (Parts 1—199)
II	Bureau of Safety and Environmental Enforcement, Department of the Interior (Parts 200—299)
IV	Geological Survey, Department of the Interior (Parts 400—499)
V	Bureau of Ocean Energy Management, Department of the Interior (Parts 500—599)
VII	Office of Surface Mining Reclamation and Enforcement, Department of the Interior (Parts 700—999)
XII	Office of Natural Resources Revenue, Department of the Interior (Parts 1200—1299)

Title 31—Money and Finance: Treasury

	SUBTITLE A—OFFICE OF THE SECRETARY OF THE TREASURY (PARTS 0—50)
	SUBTITLE B—REGULATIONS RELATING TO MONEY AND FINANCE
I	Monetary Offices, Department of the Treasury (Parts 51—199)
II	Fiscal Service, Department of the Treasury (Parts 200—399)
IV	Secret Service, Department of the Treasury (Parts 400—499)
V	Office of Foreign Assets Control, Department of the Treasury (Parts 500—599)
VI	Bureau of Engraving and Printing, Department of the Treasury (Parts 600—699)
VII	Federal Law Enforcement Training Center, Department of the Treasury (Parts 700—799)
VIII	Office of International Investment, Department of the Treasury (Parts 800—899)
IX	Federal Claims Collection Standards (Department of the Treasury—Department of Justice) (Parts 900—999)
X	Financial Crimes Enforcement Network, Department of the Treasury (Parts 1000—1099)

Title 32—National Defense

	SUBTITLE A—DEPARTMENT OF DEFENSE
I	Office of the Secretary of Defense (Parts 1—399)
V	Department of the Army (Parts 400—699)
VI	Department of the Navy (Parts 700—799)
VII	Department of the Air Force (Parts 800—1099)
	SUBTITLE B—OTHER REGULATIONS RELATING TO NATIONAL DEFENSE

Title 32—National Defense—Continued

Chap.

XII Defense Logistics Agency (Parts 1200—1299)

XVI Selective Service System (Parts 1600—1699)

XVII Office of the Director of National Intelligence (Parts 1700—1799)

XVIII National Counterintelligence Center (Parts 1800—1899)

XIX Central Intelligence Agency (Parts 1900—1999)

XX Information Security Oversight Office, National Archives and Records Administration (Parts 2000—2099)

XXI National Security Council (Parts 2100—2199)

XXIV Office of Science and Technology Policy (Parts 2400—2499)

XXVII Office for Micronesian Status Negotiations (Parts 2700—2799)

XXVIII Office of the Vice President of the United States (Parts 2800—2899)

Title 33—Navigation and Navigable Waters

I Coast Guard, Department of Homeland Security (Parts 1—199)

II Corps of Engineers, Department of the Army (Parts 200—399)

IV Saint Lawrence Seaway Development Corporation, Department of Transportation (Parts 400—499)

Title 34—Education

SUBTITLE A—OFFICE OF THE SECRETARY, DEPARTMENT OF EDUCATION (PARTS 1—99)

SUBTITLE B—REGULATIONS OF THE OFFICES OF THE DEPARTMENT OF EDUCATION

I Office for Civil Rights, Department of Education (Parts 100—199)

II Office of Elementary and Secondary Education, Department of Education (Parts 200—299)

III Office of Special Education and Rehabilitative Services, Department of Education (Parts 300—399)

IV Office of Vocational and Adult Education, Department of Education (Parts 400—499)

V Office of Bilingual Education and Minority Languages Affairs, Department of Education (Parts 500—599)

VI Office of Postsecondary Education, Department of Education (Parts 600—699)

VII Office of Educational Research and Improvement, Department of Education [Reserved]

XI National Institute for Literacy (Parts 1100—1199)

SUBTITLE C—REGULATIONS RELATING TO EDUCATION

XII National Council on Disability (Parts 1200—1299)

Title 35 [Reserved]

Title 36—Parks, Forests, and Public Property

I National Park Service, Department of the Interior (Parts 1—199)

Title 36—Parks, Forests, and Public Property—Continued

Chap.

II Forest Service, Department of Agriculture (Parts 200—299)

III Corps of Engineers, Department of the Army (Parts 300—399)

IV American Battle Monuments Commission (Parts 400—499)

V Smithsonian Institution (Parts 500—599)

VI [Reserved]

VII Library of Congress (Parts 700—799)

VIII Advisory Council on Historic Preservation (Parts 800—899)

IX Pennsylvania Avenue Development Corporation (Parts 900—999)

X Presidio Trust (Parts 1000—1099)

XI Architectural and Transportation Barriers Compliance Board (Parts 1100—1199)

XII National Archives and Records Administration (Parts 1200—1299)

XV Oklahoma City National Memorial Trust (Parts 1500—1599)

XVI Morris K. Udall Scholarship and Excellence in National Environmental Policy Foundation (Parts 1600—1699)

Title 37—Patents, Trademarks, and Copyrights

I United States Patent and Trademark Office, Department of Commerce (Parts 1—199)

II Copyright Office, Library of Congress (Parts 200—299)

III Copyright Royalty Board, Library of Congress (Parts 300—399)

IV Assistant Secretary for Technology Policy, Department of Commerce (Parts 400—499)

V Under Secretary for Technology, Department of Commerce (Parts 500—599)

Title 38—Pensions, Bonuses, and Veterans' Relief

I Department of Veterans Affairs (Parts 0—99)

II Armed Forces Retirement Home (Parts 200—299)

Title 39—Postal Service

I United States Postal Service (Parts 1—999)

III Postal Regulatory Commission (Parts 3000—3099)

Title 40—Protection of Environment

I Environmental Protection Agency (Parts 1—1099)

IV Environmental Protection Agency and Department of Justice (Parts 1400—1499)

V Council on Environmental Quality (Parts 1500—1599)

VI Chemical Safety and Hazard Investigation Board (Parts 1600—1699)

VII Environmental Protection Agency and Department of Defense; Uniform National Discharge Standards for Vessels of the Armed Forces (Parts 1700—1799)

Title 41—Public Contracts and Property Management

Title 42—Public Health

Title 43—Public Lands: Interior

Chap.

SUBTITLE A—OFFICE OF THE SECRETARY OF THE INTERIOR (PARTS 1—199)

SUBTITLE B—REGULATIONS RELATING TO PUBLIC LANDS

I Bureau of Reclamation, Department of the Interior (Parts 200—599)

II Bureau of Land Management, Department of the Interior (Parts 1000—9999)

III Utah Reclamation Mitigation and Conservation Commission (Parts 10000—10099)

Title 44—Emergency Management and Assistance

I Federal Emergency Management Agency, Department of Homeland Security (Parts 0—399)

IV Department of Commerce and Department of Transportation (Parts 400—499)

Title 45—Public Welfare

SUBTITLE A—DEPARTMENT OF HEALTH AND HUMAN SERVICES (PARTS 1—199)

SUBTITLE B—REGULATIONS RELATING TO PUBLIC WELFARE

II Office of Family Assistance (Assistance Programs), Administration for Children and Families, Department of Health and Human Services (Parts 200—299)

III Office of Child Support Enforcement (Child Support Enforcement Program), Administration for Children and Families, Department of Health and Human Services (Parts 300—399)

IV Office of Refugee Resettlement, Administration for Children and Families, Department of Health and Human Services (Parts 400—499)

V Foreign Claims Settlement Commission of the United States, Department of Justice (Parts 500—599)

VI National Science Foundation (Parts 600—699)

VII Commission on Civil Rights (Parts 700—799)

VIII Office of Personnel Management (Parts 800—899) [Reserved]

X Office of Community Services, Administration for Children and Families, Department of Health and Human Services (Parts 1000—1099)

XI National Foundation on the Arts and the Humanities (Parts 1100—1199)

XII Corporation for National and Community Service (Parts 1200—1299)

XIII Office of Human Development Services, Department of Health and Human Services (Parts 1300—1399)

XVI Legal Services Corporation (Parts 1600—1699)

XVII National Commission on Libraries and Information Science (Parts 1700—1799)

XVIII Harry S. Truman Scholarship Foundation (Parts 1800—1899)

XXI Commission on Fine Arts (Parts 2100—2199)

Chap.	
XXIII	Arctic Research Commission (Part 2301)
XXIV	James Madison Memorial Fellowship Foundation (Parts 2400—2499)
XXV	Corporation for National and Community Service (Parts 2500—2599)

Title 46—Shipping

I	Coast Guard, Department of Homeland Security (Parts 1—199)
II	Maritime Administration, Department of Transportation (Parts 200—399)
III	Coast Guard (Great Lakes Pilotage), Department of Homeland Security (Parts 400—499)
IV	Federal Maritime Commission (Parts 500—599)

Title 47—Telecommunication

I	Federal Communications Commission (Parts 0—199)
II	Office of Science and Technology Policy and National Security Council (Parts 200—299)
III	National Telecommunications and Information Administration, Department of Commerce (Parts 300—399)
IV	National Telecommunications and Information Administration, Department of Commerce, and National Highway Traffic Safety Administration, Department of Transportation (Parts 400—499)

Title 48—Federal Acquisition Regulations System

1	Federal Acquisition Regulation (Parts 1—99)
2	Defense Acquisition Regulations System, Department of Defense (Parts 200—299)
3	Health and Human Services (Parts 300—399)
4	Department of Agriculture (Parts 400—499)
5	General Services Administration (Parts 500—599)
6	Department of State (Parts 600—699)
7	Agency for International Development (Parts 700—799)
8	Department of Veterans Affairs (Parts 800—899)
9	Department of Energy (Parts 900—999)
10	Department of the Treasury (Parts 1000—1099)
12	Department of Transportation (Parts 1200—1299)
13	Department of Commerce (Parts 1300—1399)
14	Department of the Interior (Parts 1400—1499)
15	Environmental Protection Agency (Parts 1500—1599)
16	Office of Personnel Management, Federal Employees Health Benefits Acquisition Regulation (Parts 1600—1699)
17	Office of Personnel Management (Parts 1700—1799)

Chap.

18 National Aeronautics and Space Administration (Parts 1800—1899)

19 Broadcasting Board of Governors (Parts 1900—1999)

20 Nuclear Regulatory Commission (Parts 2000—2099)

21 Office of Personnel Management, Federal Employees Group Life Insurance Federal Acquisition Regulation (Parts 2100—2199)

23 Social Security Administration (Parts 2300—2399)

24 Department of Housing and Urban Development (Parts 2400—2499)

25 National Science Foundation (Parts 2500—2599)

28 Department of Justice (Parts 2800—2899)

29 Department of Labor (Parts 2900—2999)

30 Department of Homeland Security, Homeland Security Acquisition Regulation (HSAR) (Parts 3000—3099)

34 Department of Education Acquisition Regulation (Parts 3400—3499)

51 Department of the Army Acquisition Regulations (Parts 5100—5199)

52 Department of the Navy Acquisition Regulations (Parts 5200—5299)

53 Department of the Air Force Federal Acquisition Regulation Supplement [Reserved]

54 Defense Logistics Agency, Department of Defense (Parts 5400—5499)

57 African Development Foundation (Parts 5700—5799)

61 Civilian Board of Contract Appeals, General Services Administration (Parts 6100—6199)

63 Department of Transportation Board of Contract Appeals (Parts 6300—6399)

99 Cost Accounting Standards Board, Office of Federal Procurement Policy, Office of Management and Budget (Parts 9900—9999)

Title 49—Transportation

SUBTITLE A—OFFICE OF THE SECRETARY OF TRANSPORTATION (PARTS 1—99)

SUBTITLE B—OTHER REGULATIONS RELATING TO TRANSPORTATION

I Pipeline and Hazardous Materials Safety Administration, Department of Transportation (Parts 100—199)

II Federal Railroad Administration, Department of Transportation (Parts 200—299)

III Federal Motor Carrier Safety Administration, Department of Transportation (Parts 300—399)

IV Coast Guard, Department of Homeland Security (Parts 400—499)

V National Highway Traffic Safety Administration, Department of Transportation (Parts 500—599)

VI Federal Transit Administration, Department of Transportation (Parts 600—699)

Title 49—Transportation—Continued

Chap.

VII National Railroad Passenger Corporation (AMTRAK) (Parts 700—799)

VIII National Transportation Safety Board (Parts 800—999)

X Surface Transportation Board, Department of Transportation (Parts 1000—1399)

XI Research and Innovative Technology Administration, Department of Transportation [Reserved]

XII Transportation Security Administration, Department of Homeland Security (Parts 1500—1699)

Title 50—Wildlife and Fisheries

I United States Fish and Wildlife Service, Department of the Interior (Parts 1—199)

II National Marine Fisheries Service, National Oceanic and Atmospheric Administration, Department of Commerce (Parts 200—299)

III International Fishing and Related Activities (Parts 300—399)

IV Joint Regulations (United States Fish and Wildlife Service, Department of the Interior and National Marine Fisheries Service, National Oceanic and Atmospheric Administration, Department of Commerce); Endangered Species Committee Regulations (Parts 400—499)

V Marine Mammal Commission (Parts 500—599)

VI Fishery Conservation and Management, National Oceanic and Atmospheric Administration, Department of Commerce (Parts 600—699)

CFR Index and Finding Aids

Subject/Agency Index

List of Agency Prepared Indexes

Parallel Tables of Statutory Authorities and Rules

List of CFR Titles, Chapters, Subchapters, and Parts

Alphabetical List of Agencies Appearing in the CFR

Alphabetical List of Agencies Appearing in the CFR

(Revised as of January 1, 2012)

Agency	CFR Title, Subtitle or Chapter
Administrative Committee of the Federal Register	1, I
Administrative Conference of the United States	1, III
Advisory Council on Historic Preservation	36, VIII
Advocacy and Outreach, Office of	7, XXV
African Development Foundation	22, XV
Federal Acquisition Regulation	48, 57
Agency for International Development	2, VII; 22, II
Federal Acquisition Regulation	48, 7
Agricultural Marketing Service	7, I, IX, X, XI
Agricultural Research Service	7, V
Agriculture Department	2, IV; 5, LXXIII
Advocacy and Outreach, Office of	7, XXV
Agricultural Marketing Service	7, I, IX, X, XI
Agricultural Research Service	7, V
Animal and Plant Health Inspection Service	7, III; 9, I
Chief Financial Officer, Office of	7, XXX
Commodity Credit Corporation	7, XIV
Economic Research Service	7, XXXVII
Energy Policy and New Uses, Office of	2, IX; 7, XXIX
Environmental Quality, Office of	7, XXXI
Farm Service Agency	7, VII, XVIII
Federal Acquisition Regulation	48, 4
Federal Crop Insurance Corporation	7, IV
Food and Nutrition Service	7, II
Food Safety and Inspection Service	9, III
Foreign Agricultural Service	7, XV
Forest Service	36, II
Grain Inspection, Packers and Stockyards Administration	7, VIII; 9, II
Information Resources Management, Office of	7, XXVII
Inspector General, Office of	7, XXVI
National Agricultural Library	7, XLI
National Agricultural Statistics Service	7, XXXVI
National Institute of Food and Agriculture	7, XXXIV
Natural Resources Conservation Service	7, VI
Operations, Office of	7, XXVIII
Procurement and Property Management, Office of	7, XXXII
Rural Business-Cooperative Service	7, XVIII, XLII, L
Rural Development Administration	7, XLII
Rural Housing Service	7, XVIII, XXXV, L
Rural Telephone Bank	7, XVI
Rural Utilities Service	7, XVII, XVIII, XLII, L
Secretary of Agriculture, Office of	7, Subtitle A
Transportation, Office of	7, XXXIII
World Agricultural Outlook Board	7, XXXVIII
Air Force Department	32, VII
Federal Acquisition Regulation Supplement	48, 53
Air Transportation Stabilization Board	14, VI
Alcohol and Tobacco Tax and Trade Bureau	27, I
Alcohol, Tobacco, Firearms, and Explosives, Bureau of	27, II
AMTRAK	49, VII
American Battle Monuments Commission	36, IV
American Indians, Office of the Special Trustee	25, VII
Animal and Plant Health Inspection Service	7, III; 9, I

Agency	CFR Title, Subtitle or Chapter
Appalachian Regional Commission	5, IX
Architectural and Transportation Barriers Compliance Board	36, XI
Arctic Research Commission	45, XXIII
Armed Forces Retirement Home	5, XI
Army Department	32, V
Engineers, Corps of	33, II; 36, III
Federal Acquisition Regulation	48, 51
Bilingual Education and Minority Languages Affairs, Office of	34, V
Blind or Severely Disabled, Committee for Purchase from People Who Are	41, 51
Broadcasting Board of Governors	22, V
Federal Acquisition Regulation	48, 19
Bureau of Ocean Energy Management, Regulation, and Enforcement	30, II
Census Bureau	15, I
Centers for Medicare & Medicaid Services	42, IV
Central Intelligence Agency	32, XIX
Chemical Safety and Hazardous Investigation Board	40, VI
Chief Financial Officer, Office of	7, XXX
Child Support Enforcement, Office of	45, III
Children and Families, Administration for	45, II, III, IV, X
Civil Rights, Commission on	5, LXVIII; 45, VII
Civil Rights, Office for	34, I
Court Services and Offender Supervision Agency for the District of Columbia	5, LXX
Coast Guard	33, I; 46, I; 49, IV
Coast Guard (Great Lakes Pilotage)	46, III
Commerce Department	2, XIII; 44, IV; 50, VI
Census Bureau	15, I
Economic Affairs, Under Secretary	37, V
Economic Analysis, Bureau of	15, VIII
Economic Development Administration	13, III
Emergency Management and Assistance	44, IV
Federal Acquisition Regulation	48, 13
Foreign-Trade Zones Board	15, IV
Industry and Security, Bureau of	15, VII
International Trade Administration	15, III; 19, III
National Institute of Standards and Technology	15, II
National Marine Fisheries Service	50, II, IV
National Oceanic and Atmospheric Administration	15, IX; 50, II, III, IV, VI
National Telecommunications and Information Administration	15, XXIII; 47, III, IV
National Weather Service	15, IX
Patent and Trademark Office, United States	37, I
Productivity, Technology and Innovation, Assistant Secretary for	37, IV
Secretary of Commerce, Office of	15, Subtitle A
Technology, Under Secretary for	37, V
Technology Administration	15, XI
Technology Policy, Assistant Secretary for	37, IV
Commercial Space Transportation	14, III
Commodity Credit Corporation	7, XIV
Commodity Futures Trading Commission	5, XLI; 17, I
Community Planning and Development, Office of Assistant Secretary for	24, V, VI
Community Services, Office of	45, X
Comptroller of the Currency	12, I
Construction Industry Collective Bargaining Commission	29, IX
Consumer Financial Protection Bureau	12, X
Consumer Product Safety Commission	5, LXXI; 16, II
Copyright Office	37, II
Copyright Royalty Board	37, III
Corporation for National and Community Service	2, XXII; 45, XII, XXV
Cost Accounting Standards Board	48, 99
Council on Environmental Quality	40, V
Court Services and Offender Supervision Agency for the District of Columbia	5, LXX; 28, VIII

Agency	CFR Title, Subtitle or Chapter
Customs and Border Protection	19, I
Defense Contract Audit Agency	32, I
Defense Department	2, XI; 5, XXVI; 32, Subtitle A; 40, VII
Advanced Research Projects Agency	32, I
Air Force Department	32, VII
Army Department	32, V; 33, II; 36, III, 48, 51
Defense Acquisition Regulations System	48, 2
Defense Intelligence Agency	32, I
Defense Logistics Agency	32, I, XII; 48, 54
Engineers, Corps of	33, II; 36, III
National Imagery and Mapping Agency	32, I
Navy Department	32, VI; 48, 52
Secretary of Defense, Office of	2, XI; 32, I
Defense Contract Audit Agency	32, I
Defense Intelligence Agency	32, I
Defense Logistics Agency	32, XII; 48, 54
Defense Nuclear Facilities Safety Board	10, XVII
Delaware River Basin Commission	18, III
District of Columbia, Court Services and Offender Supervision Agency for the	5, LXX; 28, VIII
Drug Enforcement Administration	21, II
East-West Foreign Trade Board	15, XIII
Economic Affairs, Under Secretary	37, V
Economic Analysis, Bureau of	15, VIII
Economic Development Administration	13, III
Economic Research Service	7, XXXVII
Education, Department of	5, LIII
Bilingual Education and Minority Languages Affairs, Office of	34, V
Civil Rights, Office for	34, I
Educational Research and Improvement, Office of	34, VII
Elementary and Secondary Education, Office of	34, II
Federal Acquisition Regulation	48, 34
Postsecondary Education, Office of	34, VI
Secretary of Education, Office of	34, Subtitle A
Special Education and Rehabilitative Services, Office of	34, III
Vocational and Adult Education, Office of	34, IV
Educational Research and Improvement, Office of	34, VII
Election Assistance Commission	2, LVIII; 11, II
Elementary and Secondary Education, Office of	34, II
Emergency Oil and Gas Guaranteed Loan Board	13, V
Emergency Steel Guarantee Loan Board	13, IV
Employee Benefits Security Administration	29, XXV
Employees' Compensation Appeals Board	20, IV
Employees Loyalty Board	5, V
Employment and Training Administration	20, V
Employment Standards Administration	20, VI
Endangered Species Committee	50, IV
Energy, Department of	2, IX; 5, XXIII; 10, II, III, X
Federal Acquisition Regulation	48, 9
Federal Energy Regulatory Commission	5, XXIV; 18, I
Property Management Regulations	41, 109
Energy, Office of	7, XXIX
Engineers, Corps of	33, II; 36, III
Engraving and Printing, Bureau of	31, VI
Environmental Protection Agency	2, XV; 5, LIV; 40, I, IV, VII
Federal Acquisition Regulation	48, 15
Property Management Regulations	41, 115
Environmental Quality, Office of	7, XXXI
Equal Employment Opportunity Commission	5, LXII; 29, XIV
Equal Opportunity, Office of Assistant Secretary for	24, I
Executive Office of the President	3, I
Administration, Office of	5, XV

Agency	CFR Title, Subtitle or Chapter
Environmental Quality, Council on	40, V
Management and Budget, Office of	2, Subtitle A; 5, III, LXXVII; 14, VI; 48, 99
National Drug Control Policy, Office of	21, III
National Security Council	32, XXI; 47, 2
Presidential Documents	3
Science and Technology Policy, Office of	32, XXIV; 47, II
Trade Representative, Office of the United States	15, XX
Export-Import Bank of the United States	2, XXXV; 5, LII; 12, IV
Family Assistance, Office of	45, II
Farm Credit Administration	5, XXXI; 12, VI
Farm Credit System Insurance Corporation	5, XXX; 12, XIV
Farm Service Agency	7, VII, XVIII
Federal Acquisition Regulation	48, 1
Federal Aviation Administration	14, I
Commercial Space Transportation	14, III
Federal Claims Collection Standards	31, IX
Federal Communications Commission	5, XXIX; 47, I
Federal Contract Compliance Programs, Office of	41, 60
Federal Crop Insurance Corporation	7, IV
Federal Deposit Insurance Corporation	5, XXII; 12, III
Federal Election Commission	5, XXXVII; 11, I
Federal Emergency Management Agency	44, I
Federal Employees Group Life Insurance Federal Acquisition Regulation	48, 21
Federal Employees Health Benefits Acquisition Regulation	48, 16
Federal Energy Regulatory Commission	5, XXIV; 18, I
Federal Financial Institutions Examination Council	12, XI
Federal Financing Bank	12, VIII
Federal Highway Administration	23, I, II
Federal Home Loan Mortgage Corporation	1, IV
Federal Housing Enterprise Oversight Office	12, XVII
Federal Housing Finance Agency	5, LXXX; 12, XII
Federal Housing Finance Board	12, IX
Federal Labor Relations Authority	5, XIV, XLIX; 22, XIV
Federal Law Enforcement Training Center	31, VII
Federal Management Regulation	41, 102
Federal Maritime Commission	46, IV
Federal Mediation and Conciliation Service	29, XII
Federal Mine Safety and Health Review Commission	5, LXXIV; 29, XXVII
Federal Motor Carrier Safety Administration	49, III
Federal Prison Industries, Inc.	28, III
Federal Procurement Policy Office	48, 99
Federal Property Management Regulations	41, 101
Federal Railroad Administration	49, II
Federal Register, Administrative Committee of	1, I
Federal Register, Office of	1, II
Federal Reserve System	12, II
Board of Governors	5, LVIII
Federal Retirement Thrift Investment Board	5, VI, LXXVI
Federal Service Impasses Panel	5, XIV
Federal Trade Commission	5, XLVII; 16, I
Federal Transit Administration	49, VI
Federal Travel Regulation System	41, Subtitle F
Financial Crimes Enforcement Network	31, X
Financial Research Office	12, XVI
Financial Stability Oversight Council	12, XIII
Fine Arts, Commission on	45, XXI
Fiscal Service	31, II
Fish and Wildlife Service, United States	50, I, IV
Food and Drug Administration	21, I
Food and Nutrition Service	7, II
Food Safety and Inspection Service	9, III
Foreign Agricultural Service	7, XV
Foreign Assets Control, Office of	31, V
Foreign Claims Settlement Commission of the United States	45, V
Foreign Service Grievance Board	22, IX

Agency	CFR Title, Subtitle or Chapter
Foreign Service Impasse Disputes Panel	22, XIV
Foreign Service Labor Relations Board	22, XIV
Foreign-Trade Zones Board	15, IV
Forest Service	36, II
General Services Administration	5, LVII; 41, 105
Contract Appeals, Board of	48, 61
Federal Acquisition Regulation	48, 5
Federal Management Regulation	41, 102
Federal Property Management Regulations	41, 101
Federal Travel Regulation System	41, Subtitle F
General	41, 300
Payment From a Non-Federal Source for Travel Expenses	41, 304
Payment of Expenses Connected With the Death of Certain Employees	41, 303
Relocation Allowances	41, 302
Temporary Duty (TDY) Travel Allowances	41, 301
Geological Survey	30, IV
Government Accountability Office	4, I
Government Ethics, Office of	5, XVI
Government National Mortgage Association	24, III
Grain Inspection, Packers and Stockyards Administration	7, VIII; 9, II
Harry S. Truman Scholarship Foundation	45, XVIII
Health and Human Services, Department of	2, III; 5, XLV; 45, Subtitle A,
Centers for Medicare & Medicaid Services	42, IV
Child Support Enforcement, Office of	45, III
Children and Families, Administration for	45, II, III, IV, X
Community Services, Office of	45, X
Family Assistance, Office of	45, II
Federal Acquisition Regulation	48, 3
Food and Drug Administration	21, I
Human Development Services, Office of	45, XIII
Indian Health Service	25, V
Inspector General (Health Care), Office of	42, V
Public Health Service	42, I
Refugee Resettlement, Office of	45, IV
Homeland Security, Department of	2, XXX; 6, I
Coast Guard	33, I; 46, I; 49, IV
Coast Guard (Great Lakes Pilotage)	46, III
Customs and Border Protection	19, I
Federal Emergency Management Agency	44, I
Human Resources Management and Labor Relations Systems	5, XCVII
Immigration and Customs Enforcement Bureau	19, IV
Immigration and Naturalization	8, I
Transportation Security Administration	49, XII
HOPE for Homeowners Program, Board of Directors of	24, XXIV
Housing and Urban Development, Department of	2, XXIV; 5, LXV; 24, Subtitle B
Community Planning and Development, Office of Assistant Secretary for	24, V, VI
Equal Opportunity, Office of Assistant Secretary for	24, I
Federal Acquisition Regulation	48, 24
Federal Housing Enterprise Oversight, Office of	12, XVII
Government National Mortgage Association	24, III
Housing—Federal Housing Commissioner, Office of Assistant Secretary for	24, II, VIII, X, XX
Housing, Office of, and Multifamily Housing Assistance Restructuring, Office of	24, IV
Inspector General, Office of	24, XII
Public and Indian Housing, Office of Assistant Secretary for	24, IX
Secretary, Office of	24, Subtitle A, VII
Housing—Federal Housing Commissioner, Office of Assistant Secretary for	24, II, VIII, X, XX
Housing, Office of, and Multifamily Housing Assistance Restructuring, Office of	24, IV
Human Development Services, Office of	45, XIII

Agency	CFR Title, Subtitle or Chapter
Immigration and Customs Enforcement Bureau	19, IV
Immigration and Naturalization	8, I
Immigration Review, Executive Office for	8, V
Independent Counsel, Office of	28, VII
Indian Affairs, Bureau of	25, I, V
Indian Affairs, Office of the Assistant Secretary	25, VI
Indian Arts and Crafts Board	25, II
Indian Health Service	25, V
Industry and Security, Bureau of	15, VII
Information Resources Management, Office of	7, XXVII
Information Security Oversight Office, National Archives and Records Administration	32, XX
Inspector General	
Agriculture Department	7, XXVI
Health and Human Services Department	42, V
Housing and Urban Development Department	24, XII, XV
Institute of Peace, United States	22, XVII
Inter-American Foundation	5, LXIII; 22, X
Interior Department	2, XIV
American Indians, Office of the Special Trustee	25, VII
Bureau of Ocean Energy Management, Regulation, and Enforcement	30, II
Endangered Species Committee	50, IV
Federal Acquisition Regulation	48, 14
Federal Property Management Regulations System	41, 114
Fish and Wildlife Service, United States	50, I, IV
Geological Survey	30, IV
Indian Affairs, Bureau of	25, I, V
Indian Affairs, Office of the Assistant Secretary	25, VI
Indian Arts and Crafts Board	25, II
Land Management, Bureau of	43, II
National Indian Gaming Commission	25, III
National Park Service	36, I
Natural Resource Revenue, Office of	30, XII
Ocean Energy Management, Bureau of	30, V
Reclamation, Bureau of	43, I
Secretary of the Interior, Office of	2, XIV; 43, Subtitle A
Surface Mining Reclamation and Enforcement, Office of	30, VII
Internal Revenue Service	26, I
International Boundary and Water Commission, United States and Mexico, United States Section	22, XI
International Development, United States Agency for	22, II
Federal Acquisition Regulation	48, 7
International Development Cooperation Agency, United States	22, XII
International Joint Commission, United States and Canada	22, IV
International Organizations Employees Loyalty Board	5, V
International Trade Administration	15, III; 19, III
International Trade Commission, United States	19, II
Interstate Commerce Commission	5, XL
Investment Security, Office of	31, VIII
James Madison Memorial Fellowship Foundation	45, XXIV
Japan–United States Friendship Commission	22, XVI
Joint Board for the Enrollment of Actuaries	20, VIII
Justice Department	2, XXVIII; 5, XXVIII; 28, I, XI; 40, IV
Alcohol, Tobacco, Firearms, and Explosives, Bureau of	27, II
Drug Enforcement Administration	21, II
Federal Acquisition Regulation	48, 28
Federal Claims Collection Standards	31, IX
Federal Prison Industries, Inc.	28, III
Foreign Claims Settlement Commission of the United States	45, V
Immigration Review, Executive Office for	8, V
Offices of Independent Counsel	28, VI
Prisons, Bureau of	28, V
Property Management Regulations	41, 128

Agency	CFR Title, Subtitle or Chapter
National Mediation Board	29, X
National Oceanic and Atmospheric Administration	15, IX; 50, II, III, IV, VI
National Park Service	36, I
National Railroad Adjustment Board	29, III
National Railroad Passenger Corporation (AMTRAK)	49, VII
National Science Foundation	2, XXV; 5, XLIII; 45, VI
Federal Acquisition Regulation	48, 25
National Security Council	32, XXI
National Security Council and Office of Science and Technology Policy	47, II
National Telecommunications and Information Administration	15, XXIII; 47, III, IV
National Transportation Safety Board	49, VIII
Natural Resources Conservation Service	7, VI
Natural Resource Revenue, Office of	30, XII
Navajo and Hopi Indian Relocation, Office of	25, IV
Navy Department	32, VI
Federal Acquisition Regulation	48, 52
Neighborhood Reinvestment Corporation	24, XXV
Northeast Interstate Low-Level Radioactive Waste Commission	10, XVIII
Nuclear Regulatory Commission	2, XX; 5, XLVIII; 10, I
Federal Acquisition Regulation	48, 20
Occupational Safety and Health Administration	29, XVII
Occupational Safety and Health Review Commission	29, XX
Ocean Energy Management, Bureau of	30, V
Offices of Independent Counsel	28, VI
Office of Workers' Compensation Programs	20, VII
Oklahoma City National Memorial Trust	36, XV
Operations Office	7, XXVIII
Overseas Private Investment Corporation	5, XXXIII; 22, VII
Patent and Trademark Office, United States	37, I
Payment From a Non-Federal Source for Travel Expenses	41, 304
Payment of Expenses Connected With the Death of Certain Employees	41, 303
Peace Corps	2, XXXVII; 22, III
Pennsylvania Avenue Development Corporation	36, IX
Pension Benefit Guaranty Corporation	29, XL
Personnel Management, Office of	5, I, XXXV; 45, VIII
Human Resources Management and Labor Relations Systems, Department of Homeland Security	5, XCVII
Federal Acquisition Regulation	48, 17
Federal Employees Group Life Insurance Federal Acquisition Regulation	48, 21
Federal Employees Health Benefits Acquisition Regulation	48, 16
Pipeline and Hazardous Materials Safety Administration	49, I
Postal Regulatory Commission	5, XLVI; 39, III
Postal Service, United States	5, LX; 39, I
Postsecondary Education, Office of	34, VI
President's Commission on White House Fellowships	1, IV
Presidential Documents	3
Presidio Trust	36, X
Prisons, Bureau of	28, V
Procurement and Property Management, Office of	7, XXXII
Productivity, Technology and Innovation, Assistant Secretary	37, IV
Public Contracts, Department of Labor	41, 50
Public and Indian Housing, Office of Assistant Secretary for	24, IX
Public Health Service	42, I
Railroad Retirement Board	20, II
Reclamation, Bureau of	43, I
Recovery Accountability and Transparency Board	4, II
Refugee Resettlement, Office of	45, IV
Relocation Allowances	41, 302
Research and Innovative Technology Administration	49, XI
Rural Business-Cooperative Service	7, XVIII, XLII, L
Rural Development Administration	7, XLII

Agency	CFR Title, Subtitle or Chapter
Rural Housing Service	7, XVIII, XXXV, L
Rural Telephone Bank	7, XVI
Rural Utilities Service	7, XVII, XVIII, XLII, L
Saint Lawrence Seaway Development Corporation	33, IV
Science and Technology Policy, Office of	32, XXIV
Science and Technology Policy, Office of, and National Security Council	47, II
Secret Service	31, IV
Securities and Exchange Commission	5, XXXIV; 17, II
Selective Service System	32, XVI
Small Business Administration	2, XXVII; 13, I
Smithsonian Institution	36, V
Social Security Administration	2, XXIII; 20, III; 48, 23
Soldiers' and Airmen's Home, United States	5, XI
Special Counsel, Office of	5, VIII
Special Education and Rehabilitative Services, Office of	34, III
Special Inspector General for Iraq Reconstruction	5, LXXXVII
State Department	2, VI; 22, I; 28, XI
Federal Acquisition Regulation	48, 6
Surface Mining Reclamation and Enforcement, Office of	30, VII
Surface Transportation Board	49, X
Susquehanna River Basin Commission	18, VIII
Technology Administration	15, XI
Technology Policy, Assistant Secretary for	37, IV
Technology, Under Secretary for	37, V
Tennessee Valley Authority	5, LXIX; 18, XIII
Thrift Supervision Office, Department of the Treasury	12, V
Trade Representative, United States, Office of	15, XX
Transportation, Department of	2, XII; 5, L
Commercial Space Transportation	14, III
Contract Appeals, Board of	48, 63
Emergency Management and Assistance	44, IV
Federal Acquisition Regulation	48, 12
Federal Aviation Administration	14, I
Federal Highway Administration	23, I, II
Federal Motor Carrier Safety Administration	49, III
Federal Railroad Administration	49, II
Federal Transit Administration	49, VI
Maritime Administration	46, II
National Highway Traffic Safety Administration	23, II, III; 47, IV; 49, V
Pipeline and Hazardous Materials Safety Administration	49, I
Saint Lawrence Seaway Development Corporation	33, IV
Secretary of Transportation, Office of	14, II; 49, Subtitle A
Surface Transportation Board	49, X
Transportation Statistics Bureau	49, XI
Transportation, Office of	7, XXXIII
Transportation Security Administration	49, XII
Transportation Statistics Bureau	49, XI
Travel Allowances, Temporary Duty (TDY)	41, 301
Treasury Department	5, XXI; 12, XV; 17, IV; 31, IX
Alcohol and Tobacco Tax and Trade Bureau	27, I
Community Development Financial Institutions Fund	12, XVIII
Comptroller of the Currency	12, I
Customs and Border Protection	19, I
Engraving and Printing, Bureau of	31, VI
Federal Acquisition Regulation	48, 10
Federal Claims Collection Standards	31, IX
Federal Law Enforcement Training Center	31, VII
Financial Crimes Enforcement Network	31, X
Fiscal Service	31, II
Foreign Assets Control, Office of	31, V
Internal Revenue Service	26, I
Investment Security, Office of	31, VIII
Monetary Offices	31, I
Secret Service	31, IV
Secretary of the Treasury, Office of	31, Subtitle A

Agency	CFR Title, Subtitle or Chapter
Thrift Supervision, Office of	12, V
Truman, Harry S. Scholarship Foundation	45, XVIII
United States and Canada, International Joint Commission	22, IV
United States and Mexico, International Boundary and Water Commission, United States Section	22, XI
Utah Reclamation Mitigation and Conservation Commission	43, III
Veterans Affairs Department	2, VIII; 38, I
Federal Acquisition Regulation	48, 8
Veterans' Employment and Training Service, Office of the Assistant Secretary for	41, 61; 20, IX
Vice President of the United States, Office of	32, XXVIII
Vocational and Adult Education, Office of	34, IV
Wage and Hour Division	29, V
Water Resources Council	18, VI
Workers' Compensation Programs, Office of	20, I
World Agricultural Outlook Board	7, XXXVIII

List of CFR Sections Affected

All changes in this volume of the Code of Federal Regulations that were made by documents published in the FEDERAL REGISTER since January 1, 2001, are enumerated in the following list. Entries indicate the nature of the changes effected. Page numbers refer to FEDERAL REGISTER pages. The user should consult the entries for chapters and parts as well as sections for revisions.

For the period before January 1, 2001, see the "List of CFR Sections Affected, 1949–1963, 1964–1972, 1973–1985, and 1986–2000" published in 11 separate volumes.

2001

12 CFR

66 FR Page

Chapter XIV

1411 Authority citation revised....................44027

1411.1 Revised....................44027

Chapter XV

1500 Revised....................8489

1501.2 Redesignated as 1501.3; new 1501.2 added; interim....................260

1501.3 Redesignated from 1501.2; interim....................260

Revised....................8750

1510 Regulation at 65 FR 12069 confirmed....................47070

1510.5 (c) introductory text amended; (d) revised; interim....................47071

Chapter XVII

1701 Added....................18039

1750 Authority citation revised....................47806

1750.10—1750.13 (Subpart B) Added....................47806

1770 Added....................47554

1773 Added....................65101

1780 Authority citation revised....................711, 18043

1780.1 Revised....................18043

1780.80—1780.81 (Subpart E) Revised....................711

2002

12 CFR

67 FR Page

Chapter XVII

1705.10—1705.19 (Subpart B) Appendix A amended....................66535

1710 Added....................38370

1720 Added....................55693

1750.5 Removed....................19322

1750.12 (c) revised....................19322

1750.10—1750.13 (Subpart B) Appendix A amended....................11861, 66535

1777 Added....................3598

2003

12 CFR

68 FR Page

Chapter XVII

1700.3 Revised....................32629

1700.4 Removed....................32629

1730 Added....................16718

1750.10–175.13 (Subpart B) Appendix A amended....................7312

Chapter XVIII

1805 Revised; interim....................5707

1806 Revised; interim....................5720

2004

12 CFR

69 FR Page

Chapter XI

1102 Nomenclature change....................2501

1102.306 (a)(1)(i) amended....................2501

Chapter XVII

1700.2 (b) and (c) revised....................18809

12 CFR—Continued

69 FR Page

Chapter XVIII

1805 Revised; interim 26262

2005

12 CFR

70 FR Page

Chapter XVII

1700.2 (c)(3), (7) and (8) removed; (c) and (d) redesignated as (d) and (e); new (d)(1), (2), (9) and (10) redesignated as (d)(2), (3), (7) and (8); new (c) and (d)(1) added 59629

1710.11 Redesignated as 1710.12; new 1710.11 added 17310

1710.12 Redesignated as 1710.13; new 1710.12 redesignated from 1710.11 17310

1710.12 (b) revised; (c) added 17311

1710.13 Removed; new 1710.13 redesignated from 1710.12 17310

New (a) revised; (b) added 17311

1710.14 Heading and new (a) revised; (b) added 17311

1710.15 (b) revised 17311

1710.16 Added 17311

1710.17 Added 17311

1710.18 Added 17311

1710.19 Added 17311

1710.30 (Subpart D) Added 17311

1731 Added 43627

1780 Authority citation revised 51243

1780.30—1780.81 (Subpart E) Revised 51243

Chapter XVIII

1805 Revised; interim 73888

2006

12 CFR

71 FR Page

Chapter XIV

1412 Added 7405

Regulation at 71 FR 7405 confirmed 25743

Chapter XVII

1700—1799 (Chapter XVII) Response to comments 19985

1732 Added 62884

1750.10—1750.13 (Subpart B) Appendix A amended 75087

2007

12 CFR

72 FR Page

(No regulations published)

2008

12 CFR

73 FR Page

Chapter XII

Chapter XII Established; interim 53357

1206 (Subchapter A) Added 56713

Subchapter B Added; interim 55715

1231 Added; interim 53357

Transferred to Subchapter B; interim 55715

1231.1 Correctly revised 54673

1231.3 Correctly removed; interim 54309

1231.4 Correctly removed; interim 54309

1231.5 Introductory text and (f) correctly revised 54673

Subchapter D Added; interim 55715

1261 Added; interim 55715

1280—1299 (Subchapter E) Added; interim 61664

1291 Redesignated from Part 951; heading revised; nomenclature change; interim 61664

1291.1 Amended; interim 61664

1291.2 (b)(2)(i) amended; interim 61664

1291.3 (a)(1) through (8) amended; interim 61664

1291.5 (c)(9)(i), (ii), (10)(ii), (iii), (13)(iii)(A), (B), (14)(iii), (16)(i)(A), (g)(6), (h)(1)(i) and (ii) amended; interim 61664

1291.6 (c)(2)(iii) and (5) amended; interim 61664

(f) added; interim 61665

1291.7 (a)(1)(i)(C)(*4*), (5), (b)(1)(i), (ii) and (2)(i) amended; interim 61664

(b)(1)(ii) and (2)(i) amended; interim 61665

1291.8 (c)(2) and (i) amended; interim 61664

1291.9 (a)(4)(i), (ii)(A), (B), (5)(i), (ii), (7)(iii)(A), (B), (9) and (b) amended; interim 61664

1291.11 (a) amended; interim 61664

Amended; interim 61665

1291.12 (a) and (b) amended; interim 61664

12 CFR—Continued

73 FR Page

Chapter XVII

1701 Removed 56715

1750 Technical correction 40656

1750.10—1750.13 (Subpart A) Appendix A amended 35895

2009

12 CFR

74 FR Page

Chapter XII

1202 Added 2342

1202.3 (c) revised 18624

1204 Added 33908

1212 Added 51075

1229—1231 (Subchapter B) Heading revised 5102

1229 Added; interim 5604

Technical correction 13083

1229.6 (a)(5) revised 38513

1229.8 (e) and (f) amended; (g) and (h) added 38513

1229.10 (d) revised 38513

1229.11 (a) and (b) revised 38513

1231 Heading revised 5102

1231.5 (f) revised 5102

1250 (Subchapter C) Added 2350

1250 Correctly added 7304

1252 (Subchapter C) Added; interim 5618

1253 Added; interim 31605

Subchapter D Regulation at 73 FR 55715 confirmed 51459

1261 Regulation at 73 FR 55715 confirmed 51459

Authority citation and heading revised 51459

1261.1—1261.16 Designated as Subpart A; heading added 51459

1261.1 Amended 51460

1261.2 (a), (b) and (c) revised 51460

1261.3 Revised 51460

1261.4 (b), (c) and (d) redesignated as (c), (d) and (e); new (b) added; (a)(2), new (d)(2) and new (e) revised 51461

1261.5 (b) revised 51461

1261.6 (a)(5), (c), (d)(1), (2), (e) and (f) revised 51461

1261.7 (a) introductory text, (1)(ii), (v), (c), (f), (g) and (h) revised 51462

1261.9 Heading, (b) and (c) revised 51463

1261.10 (a) and (b) revised 51463

12 CFR—Continued

74 FR Page

Chapter XII—Continued

1261.11 Heading, (a) introductory text, (4), (5), (6) and (d) revised 51463

1261.12 Revised 51463

1261.13 Revised 51464

1261.14 Revised 51464

1261.16 Removed 51464

Subpart B Added 51459

1282 Added 39889

1291.1 Amended; interim 38521

1291.2 (b)(2)(i) and (3) revised; interim 38521

1291.5 (d)(5)(vii) revised; interim 38522

1291.6 (f) revised; interim 38522

Chapter XIV

1410.2 (b) revised; (d) heading, introductory text and (e) amended 17373

Regulation at 74 FR 17373 confirmed 28156

1410.3 Revised 17373

Regulation at 74 FR 17373 confirmed 28156

1410.4 (a) removed; (b) and (c) redesignated as new (a) and (b); new (a) amended 17374

Regulation at 74 FR 17374 confirmed 28156

1410.6 (a) introductory text amended; (a)(1) and (2) removed 17374

Regulation at 74 FR 17374 confirmed 28156

Chapter XVII

1702 Removed 33911

1703.1—1703.2 (Subpart A) Removed 18624

1703.6—1703.9 (Subpart B) Removed 18624

1703.11—1703.18 (Subpart C) Removed 18624

1703.21—1703.25 (Subpart D) Removed 18624

1773 Removed 2350

Chapter XVIII

1806 Revised; interim 5791

2010

12 CFR

75 FR Page

Chapter XI

1101.3 (e) revised 71014

12 CFR—Continued

75 FR Page

Chapter XI—Continued

1101.4 (a), (b) heading, (1) introductory text, (i), (v), (vii), (viii), (2), (3), (4), (5)(i)(C), (D), (E), (G), (H), (ii)(C)(*2*), (F), (H), (iii)(A), (iv), (vii)(B), (C) and (6) revised 71014
1102.100—1102.110 (Subpart C) Authority citation revised 36270
1102.102 (a) introductory text and (2) amended 36270
1102.105 (a) amended.......................36270
1102.107 (a)(2) and (b)(1) amended 36270

Chapter XII

1203 Added.....................................65219
1207 Added; eff. 1–27–11 81402
1208 Added; interim 68958
1233 Added 4258
1249 Added.....................................55928
1252 Regulation at 74 FR 5618 confirmed 81409
1261.1—1261.16 (Subpart A) Redesignated as 1261.2—1261.16 (Subpart B)..17039
1261.1 (Subpart A) Added...............17039
1261.2—1261.16 (Subpart B) Redesignated from 1261.1—1261.16 (Subpart A); nomenclature change...17039
1261.2 Redesignated as 1261.3; new 1261.2 redesignated from 1261.1; amended...................................17039
1261.2 Amended............................17040
1261.3 Redesignated as 1261.4; new 1261.3 redesignated from 1261.2 17039
1261.4 Redesignated as 1261.5; new 1261.4 redesignated from 1261.3; (a)(2) and (b) amended 17039
1261.4 (d) revised; (e) added 17040
1261.5 Redesignated as 1261.6; new 1261.5 redesignated from 1261.4; (b) and (e)(1) amended 17039
1261.5 (e) revised 17040
1261.6 Redesignated as 1261.7; new 1261.6 redesignated from 1261.5; (b) amended 17039
1261.7 Redesignated as 1261.8; new 1261.7 redesignated from 1261.6; (a)(4) amended 17039
1261.8 Redesignated from 1261.7; (a), (iii), (b), (d) introductory text and (g)(2) amended 17039
(a) amended 17040
1261.9 (a) amended.........................17039
1261.14 (b) amended 17040

12 CFR—Continued

75 FR Page

Chapter XII—Continued

1261.20—1261.24 (Subpart C) Added.......................................17040
1263 Transferred from Chapter IX; redesignated from 925 and revised 690
1264 Transferred from Chapter IX, Subpart D; redesignated from Part 926; authority citation revised; nomenclature change 8240
1264.1 Amended 8240
1264.2 Amended 8240
1264.3 (a) introductory text and (b) amended................................8240
(b) amended; eff. 1–10–11................76622
1264.4 (a), (b) introductory text, (c)(1), (d) and (e) amended 8240
1264.5 (b) amended 8240
1264.6 (a) revised; (b) amended.........8240
1265 Transferred from Chapter IX, Subchapter F; redesignated from Part 940 8240
1265 Authority citation revised 8241
1265.1 Revised 8241
1266 Redesignated from Part 950; authority citation revised; nomenclature change; eff. 1–10–11...76622
1266.1 Amended; eff. 1–10–11 76622
1266.2 (e) added; eff. 1–10–11 76623
1266.3 Revised; eff. 1–10–11 76623
1266.4 (g)(2)(i) and (ii) amended; eff. 1–10–11...................................76622
1266.5 (b)(2)(ii) amended; eff. 1–10–11...76622
1266.6 (a) amended; eff. 1–10–11 76622
1266.7 (b)(1) revised; eff. 1–10–11......76623
1266.9 (a)(1) amended; eff. 1–10–11...76622
1266.10 (a) amended; eff. 1–10–11...76622
1266.11 Revised; eff. 1–10–11............76623
1266.16 Amended; eff. 1–10–11..........76622
1266.17 (a), (b)(2)(i) introductory text, (A), (B), (C), (c)(2)(i), (ii), (e)(2) and (3) amended; eff. 1–10–11...76622
1269 Transferred from Chapter IX, Subchapter G; redesignated from Part 960; authority citation revised..........................8241
1269.1 Amended 8241
Amended; eff. 1–10–11....................76623
1269.2 (b) and (c)(1) amended 8241
(c) amended; eff. 1–10–11 76623

12 CFR—Continued

75 FR Page

Chapter XII—Continued

1269.3 (a) introductory text and (b) amended....8241
(a) introductory text and (b) amended; eff. 1-10-11....76623
1269.4 (a)(1) and (c) amended....8241
(a)(1) and (c) amended; eff. 1-10-11....76623
1269.5 (b)(1) and (2) amended....8241
(b)(1) and (2) amended; eff. 1-10-11....76623
1272 Redesignated from Part 980; eff. 1-10-11....76622
Authority citation revised....76623
Nomenclature change; eff. 1-10-11....76624
1272.1 Amended; eff. 1-10-11....76623, 76624
1272.3 Introductory text, (b) introductory text, (2) and (3) amended; eff. 1-10-11....76624
1272.4 (a), (b) and (c) amended; eff. 1-10-11....76624
1272.5 (a) introductory text, (4), (5) and (b) amended; eff. 1-10-11....76624
1281 Added; eff. 1-26-11....81105
1273 Added....23161
1274 Added....23166
1282 Revised....55930
1290 Transferred from Chapter IX; redesignated from 944 and revised....701
1291.2 (b)(2)(i) amended....29883
1291.6 (f)(3), (5) and (6) revised....29883

Chapter XVII

1704 Removed; interim....68969
1705 Removed....65222
1731 Removed....4259

12 CFR—Continued

75 FR Page

Chapter XVIII

1807 Added; interim....75380

2011

12 CFR

76 FR Page

Chapter XII

1202 Revised; interim....29634
1204 Revised; interim....51871
1208 Regulation at 75 FR 68958 confirmed....17332
1209 Added....53607
1213 Added....7481
1225 Added....11674
1229.13 (Subpart B) Added....35733
1235 Added....33127
1237 Added....35733
1267 Added....29151
1270 Added....18369
1278 Added....72833
1281.21 (c) revised; (d) removed; (e) redesignated as new (d); eff. 1-20-12....79051

Chapter XIII

Chapter XIII Established....44773
1320 Added....44773

Chapter XVI

Chapter XVI Established....60708
1600 Added....60708

Chapter XVII

1704 Regulation at 75 FR 68969 confirmed....17332
1732 Removed....33128
1780—1799 (Subchapter D) Removed; eff. 1-3-12....74649
1780 Removed....53629

○